A resident scholar and Direct[...]
Enterprise Institute, Leon Aron [...]
grated to the United States at t[...]
PhD from Columbia University [...]
Dr Aron is the author of numero[...]
and foreign policy and is a frequ[...]
newspapers, television and radio, including the *TLS*, the *Washington Post*, the *Sunday Times*, CNN and the BBC.

He lives in Manassas, Virginia, with his wife, Dr Carol Schiavone, and their daughters, Andrea and Daniella.

...ed as professor of Russian Studies at the American
... was born in Moscow in 1954 and emi-
... the age of twenty-three. He received his
... and taught at Georgetown University.
... his scholarly articles on Russian domestic
... frequent commentator on Russian affairs for

BORIS YELTSIN

A Revolutionary Life

Leon Aron

BORIS YELTSIN
A Revolutionary Life

Leon Aron

HarperCollins*Publishers*

HarperCollins*Publishers*
77–85 Fulham Palace Road,
Hammersmith, London W6 8JB

www.fireandwater.com

This paperback edition 2001
1 3 5 7 9 8 6 4 2

First published in Great Britain by
HarperCollins*Publishers* 2000

ISBN 0 00 653041 9

Set in Sabon by
Rowland Phototypesetting Ltd,
Bury St Edmunds, Suffolk

Printed and bound in Great Britain by
Clays Ltd, St Ives plc

For Carol, Andrea, Daniella and Alexandra

The reigning Error of his Life was that he himself the Love for the

on ne fait rien de grand sans de grands hommes.

Charles de Gaulle, *Le Fil de l'épée*

Блажен, кто посетил сей мир
В его минуты роковые!
Его призвали всеблагие
Как собеседника на пир.

And blessed is he who visited this world
In time to see its fate decided,
Whom, like an equal, gods invited
To their feast before 'tis cold.

Fedor Tyutchev, 'Tsitseron' ('Cicero')
[translated by Leon Aron]

Всё перепуталось, и некому сказать,
Что, постепенно холодея,
Всё перепуталось, и сладко повторять:
Россия, Лета, Лорелея.

Everything's in disarray, and no one's there
To say, as cold sets in, that disarray
Is everywhere, and how sweet becomes the prayer:
Rossia, Lethe, Lorelei.

Osip Mandel'shtam, 'Dekabrist' ('The Decembrist') (1917)
[translated by Leon Aron]

The reigning Error of his Life was that he mistook the Love for the practice of Virtue, and was indeed not so much a good Man as the friend of Goodness.

Dr Samuel Johnson, *Life of Richard Savage*

STATES ON THE TERRITORY OF THE FORMER USSR, AND THEIR NEIGHBOURS

Scale 1:20, 700.00
Lambert Conformal Conic Projection,
standard parallels 47°N and 62° N

300 Kilometers

300 Miles

RUSSIA

• Pechora

Ob'

• Krasnoyarsk

Irtysh

Yenisey

• Kemerovo

• Novosibirsk

• Novokuznetsk

Barnaul

Biya

• Yekaterinburg

• Omsk

Katun'

• Chelyabinsk

Petropavl

Pavlodar

Oskemen

• Ufa

Eртиs

Semey

• Qostanay

Astana
(Akmola)

• Aral

• Qaraghandy

KAZAKHSTAN

Balqash

Lake Balkhash

Saryshaghan

Taldyqorghan •

Aral
Sea

• Aral

• Qyzylorda

Almaty

Taraz

Bishkek

Nukus

Shymkent

KYRGYZSTAN

Dashhowuz

Tashkent

Andijon

Kashi

CHINA

UZBEKISTAN

Khujand •

Osh

Samarqand

• Bukhoro

Dushanbe

TAJIKISTAN

India
claim

TURKMENISTAN

Chärjew

Line of control

Chinese line
of control

• Ashgabat

• Mary

Indus

Mashhad

Kabul •

Islämäbäd •

INDIA

AFGHANISTAN

• Herät

PAKISTAN

CONTENTS

ACKNOWLEDGMENTS

One has no idea, until one does it, to what extent producing a big book, which incorporates years of research, is a collective effort. In the past seven years I have depended on the kindness of so many people for help and good cheer that I am anxious lest I now not remember everyone.

I am grateful, most of all, to the President of the American Enterprise Institute, Chris DeMuth, and Executive Vice President David Gerson. Their passion for excellence was an inspiration. One cannot ask for more in life than a chance to do one's best, and AEI gives one that chance. Cita and Irwin Stelzer gave me the ultimate gift of a literary friendship: an unsolicited, disinterested and absolutely vital assistance in clearing some of the taller obstacles faced by the author of a bulky book on a rather esoteric subject. Their inexhaustible interest, warmth and encouragement helped me through some tense and uncertain times.

Professor Jeane Kirkpatrick's abiding interest in Russia and Yeltsin and her kind words about my work cheered me on. So did, over the last four years, monthly phone conversations with Roy Lennox about the book, Yeltsin, capitalism and democracy – and the GKOs. Roy's insatiable curiosity about Russian politics and culture, first revealed to me during our long walks in the mountains around Beaver Creek, has developed into a personal friendship and a generous association with AEI's Russian Studies programme.

Several colleagues read and critiqued hundreds of pages of the manuscript, much improving it. For their careful and uncompromising reading and for many conversations about Yeltsin and Russia over the years, I am indebted to Professor Harley Balzer, Director of Central European and Russian Area Studies, Georgetown University; Professor George Breslauer, Chairman of the Department of Political Science, University of California, Berkeley; Professor Michael Mandelbaum of Johns Hopkins University; Blair Ruble, Director of the Kennan Institute for Advanced Russian Studies; S. Frederick Starr, Director of the Central Asian Institute of Johns Hopkins University. Deputy Secretary of State Strobe Talbott took time from a well-deserved August respite to go over the manuscript with the eye of a Russian expert, writer and veteran *Time* reporter. Over the past five years, Ambassador Charles Lichenstein read most of the book. I am grateful for Chuck's excellent editorial suggestions and the equally unfailing choices of wines and restaurants where we had our many delightful lunches.

I could not have written the book without the men and women who shared so generously their time and their memories of Yeltsin: Stanislav Alekseev, Dwayne Andreas, Anders Åslund, Vadim Bakatin, Boris Balantsev, Felicity Barringer, Gennadiy Ivanovich Belyankin, Lev Petrovich Belyanskiy, Klavdia Ivanovna Bersenyova, Vladimir Bokser, Gennadiy Burbulis, Ivan Mikhaylovich Dyagilev, Artur Klavdievich Ezhov, Egor Gaidar, Anne Garside, Andrey Goryun, Vasiliy Vasilievich Gudkov, Stephen Hayes, Paul Hendrickson, Aleksandr Il'yin, Vladimir Kadochnikov, Yuriy Karabasov, Sergey Khrushchev, Lidiya Aleksandrovna Khudyakova, Igor Klyamkin, Leonid Borisovich Kogan, Professor Robert Legvold, Aleksandr Livshitz, Valentin Petrovich Lukyanin, Claudia McBride, Gerald Martineau, Ambassador Jack Matlock, Larisa Mishustina, Professor Stephen Muller, Vladimir Nadein, Darren Narayana, Nikolay Grigorievich Nikonov, Aleksandr Novikov, Sergey Ivanovich Peretrutov, Ambassador Vladimir Petrovskiy, Ludmila Pikhoya, Viktor Vasilievich Popov, Provost Condoleezza Rice, Lotti Ross, Yakov Petrovich Ryabov, General Brent Scowcroft, Mira Leontievna Shvartz, the late Galya Starovoytova, Vladimir Volkov, Sergey Borisovich Vozdvizhenskiy and Vittorio Zucconi.

For their invaluable assistance with the research of Yeltsin's Sverdlovsk years, my thanks to the Director of the Sverdlovsk Museum of Youth Movements, Vladimir Bykodorov and his staff who showed me thirty hours of the Yeltsin video archive, contacted respondents and arranged half a dozen interviews; to the Director of the Center for the Support of Deputy Yeltsin, Alya Ivanovna Tanachyova; and to the editor of *Doverie*, Lyudmila Piskareva, who supplied me with nine years' worth of Yeltsin's speeches culled from *Ural'skiy Rabochiy*. Most of all, I am forever indebted to Dr Aleksandr Urmanov, who guided me to people and materials in Sverdlovsk/Ekaterinburg and Moscow, and who, as a manager of Yeltsin's earlier campaigns and his occasional speechwriter, supplied me with invaluable facts and insights.

CBS's longest-serving Moscow correspondent Jonathan Sanders provided me with rare footage (including Yeltsin's 1987 interview with Diane Sawyer). He and his wife, Mary, treated me to some of the best dinners of my life in the Savoy on Rorzhdestvenka. The Special Assistant to the Librarian of Congress for Russian projects, Irene Steckler, handled my queries with enviable equanimity and wonderful expertise. I am especially grateful for her guiding me to the Russian television collection, which added so much to my understanding of the October 1993 drama.

Professor Stephen Cohen, now of New York University, John Hardt of the Congressional Research Service, Professor Rajan Menon of Columbia University, Professor Ellen Mickiewicz of Duke University, Professor Kathleen Parthé of the University of Rochester, Professor Robert Sharlet of Union College, Professor Richard Wartman of Columbia University, and Marc Zlotnik shared with me their thoughts, sources and work, both published and unpublished. I have profited greatly from Matt London's excellent Master's Thesis on Jewish youth organizations in Moscow.

I am grateful to the Smith-Richardson Foundation whose 1992 grant allowed me to devote half a year exclusively to the research for this book. The staff of the Russian Service of Radio Liberty in Munich, under Paul Goble's leadership, gave me access to pre-1990 Yeltsin files from their invaluable 'Red Archive'. Conversations with Tom Friedman were as enjoyable as they were stimulating. Jim Lehrer's incisive questioning on the air and polite but insistent needling before and after the *News Hour* television shows on the subject of the publication date helped propel the project forward.

I found much encouragement in the interest in Russia and my work from my AEI colleagues Karlyn Bowman, Jack Calfee, Isabel Ferguson, Marvin Kosters Michael Ledeen, Allan Meltzer, Herb Stein and the late Allen Wallis. Jim Bowman and his colleagues at the *Times Literary Supplement* opened to me the pages of their magnificent journal, and some of the key theses of the book were born out of the essays I wrote for the *TLS*. I thank Stuart Proffitt, who, as the Publisher of Harper-Collins, UK, acquired the manuscript and was my first editor. Our faxed trans-Atlantic conversations on the book's 'philosophy', its format and our favourite authors made the final product much stronger. Peter James's copy-editing was performed with unfailing diligence and taste and extended far beyond the call of duty. Phyllis Richardson, my in-house editor, resolutely adminstered painful but necessary pruning, shepherded the manuscript through the numerous deadlines and directed the endless stream of e-mail and courier traffic across the ocean with grace and firmness. Taking over from Phyllis, Kate Morris quickly and cheerfully managed to find her way in the mountains of drafts and editorial correspondence, to take care of innumerable details and anxieties, and to see the book to publication.

I am grateful also to Robert Bork, Jim Billington, Tom Friedman and Jim Lehrer for recommending their literary agents to me, to Virginia Bryant for her valiant effort to find a home for *Yeltsin*, and to my lawyer–agent Jay Lefkowitz.

Viktor Ginzburg, a professor of Moscow Conservatory and brilliant pianist, provided the warmth and companionship of a classic Moscow friendship. In addition to other samples of Russian post-communist cinema, Vitya recorded for me some of the most biting, hilarious episodes of the *Kukly* show, without which the politics of the late Yeltsin years are simply impossible to understand.

Misha and Ulita Reznikov generously opened their home to me and made it a refuge from my Moscow chores. Misha's gift of a cache of glasnost artefacts (including the priceless 1988 and 1989 volumes of *Moskovksie Novosti*) made those remarkable years so much more immediate to me and easier to recreate. A close friend and a fellow Muscovite Dr Dmitriy Sviridov recalled for me Yeltsin's 1986–7 Moscow rule and answered many questions about the topography of my native city, parts of which, after twenty years, began, sadly, to fade from memory. Mikhail and Ol'ga Bezrukov advised me on Moscow political trivia and once spent half a day driving me to and around Nikolina Gora, the scene of one of Yeltsin's more mysterious accidents.

Barbara Tiplady saved the day several times by volunteering to deliver, on her way home, manuscripts and disks from Washington to Manassas. I owe a great deal to my excellent research assistants: Laura Libanati, Melissa Preston, Amanda Schnetzer, Lisa Bustin and Rebecca Graeves. Rebecca's watch coincided with the especially intense last two years of the project and she bore up admirably under increasingly brutal deadlines. Interns from half-a-dozen nations performed myriad chores for the project: David Dana, Shoshana Buchholz, Zerxes Spencer, Jennifer Otterbein, Soren Johnson, Celine Hwang, Anatoly Pinksy, Yulia Makarova, Nuria Bolotbaeva, Noémi Tòth, Yaroslava Babych, Aleksandra Markovic and Paul Spivak.

I am grateful to my mother, Ella, and my father, Aron, for almost forty-five years of unwavering support and confidence in my abilities. My wonderful in-laws, Cellerina and Andrew Schiavone, helped us cope with so many crises and chores, and always brought relief and delight to our household's four permanent occupants. From the day they were born my daughters Andrea and Daniella shared their father's time and attention, which was by right theirs, with that mysterious Russian man whose name they still cannot pronounce. I will never be able to repay their marvellous patience and, more precious still, their luminous presence which put everything in its right place.

In all such precarious enterprises, a spouse's contribution is the foundation which supports the edifice made with the assistance of all others whom custom requires to acknowledge first. Carol was the daily adviser, editor and indefatigable proofreader, the creator and keeper of domestic tranquillity and joy amid the usual heroism of full-time motherhood: nursing, healing, consoling, entertaining and educating our two daughters. I can think of no words adequate to describe the immensity of the gift, the hugeness of debt or the intensity of affection.

PREFACE

This book has been written because the material offered a rare and opportune concurrence of subjects: a fascinating and complicated man, who in his prime could touch, sway and lead millions; and a great nation at one of the most fateful moments of its history. This was a chance to write history while telling a tale – a history of the Fourth Russian Revolution* and a tale of one of its leaders. And what a tale it turned out to be: of bitter dramas and exhilarating triumphs; of political death and resurrection; of human strength and frailty; of solidarity and treachery; of the unconquerable appeal of freedom and the dark attraction of servitude; of a yearning for the new and the soothing, numbing, comforting embrace of the old.

Those who lead revolutions give them their faces. They are the epitome of a revolution, its essence and its symbol. By studying these faces one can tell a great deal about a revolution: its achievements, its limitations and, perhaps most importantly, its future. Alongside Mikhail Gorbachev's, Yeltsin's face is etched on the Russian Revolution. Much in the present and future behaviour of the world's youngest nuclear superpower, post-communist Russia, may be divined from the story of its founding father and first President.

This was, also, an invitation to write about a new Russia in a new way – discarding, after the decades of totalitarianism and Cold War, the arcane ways of 'Kremlinology', with its obsession with the minutiae of the Kremlin court and tortured deconstruction of official statements. Perestroika ('renewal') and glasnost ('openness') made the people a political actor and newspapers chroniclers of the country's mood. For this book I have taken advantage of both developments: the archive, the newspaper, the videotape, the interview and the occasional public opinion survey are its major sources. Elected and re-elected by voters, Yeltsin was Russia's first modern leader and a book about him had to be constructed with the tools of modern historiography. For decades, Soviet and Russian modern political history has been badly distorted by the secrecy of Soviet totalitarianism and the Cold War, which made it safe for pontification, ill-informed editorializing and sensationalism. By way of atoning for the sins of some of my predecessors, I saw my main task not in commenting on or interpreting but, as Richard Holmes puts it in his magnificent book on Johnson and Savage, in 'giving the

* The preceding revolutions occurred in 1905–7, February 1917 and October 1917.

evidence as I have found it', letting the material tell the story and allowing readers to judge for themselves. I very much wanted this book to be one in which the authorial presence was subtle, rather than overwhelming. As part of this strategy, wherever possible or practical, the actors – be they Yeltsin, Gorbachev, Gennadiy Zyuganov, the August 1991 putschists or the communists and nationalists of 1993 or 1996 – speak to the reader in their own words.

In deciding what to include in the narrative, I followed Wittgenstein's rule: 'Of that of which nothing is known nothing can be said'. The 'known' was evidence from interviews, archives, video collections and Soviet and Russian periodicals, as well as from a host of publications around the world.

Separating fact from gossip was one of the most difficult chores. For Yeltsin was by far the most open of all Russian rulers. Never before had we learned so much and so fast about the occupant of the Kremlin *while he was still alive and in power*. The freedom of speech, press and entrepreneurship which Yeltsin established, engendered dozens of articles and memoirs by close and distant associates, some of whom publicized the minutest details of his work and some of the most private moments of his life.

As in the cases of other modern politicians, this plethora of facts presents a narrator with two temptations. One is to tell a story of personal weaknesses and failures, forged by crawling underfoot, sifting and burrowing through mole-hills of dirt, revelling in and savouring pieces of refuse. The other is to track the movement of a caravan on the vast plain of a country's history, ignoring the clay and manure stuck to the wheels. While each extreme is to be avoided, a good political biographer must be at once the worm and the eagle. Still, the subject of the book being one of the pivotal moments of the twentieth century, whenever the constraints of space forced me to choose between the two modes, I felt strongly that the eagle must prevail.

Few protagonists are better suited for the man-and-his-times genre of history than Boris Yeltsin. A great Russian poet Marina Tsvetayeva used to say that her dear friend Boris Pasternak looked at once like an Arab thoroughbred and its Arab rider, the driven and the driver. Yeltsin was both a bellwether of the gathering Russian storm and part of the storm itself. There was this connection between Yeltsin and the Russian democratic renaissance: Russian public opinion was awakened, in large measure, by Yeltsin's 1987 'rebellion', and, as the people began to matter in Soviet politics, so did he. The more the people mattered, the higher

Yeltsin rose. For a short but critical period, the Russian democratic revolution and Yeltsin became inseparable: one was wind, the other sail. Together, they began to turn Russia around.

For students of Soviet history, the record of Yeltsin's reign in Sverdlovsk, the Soviet Union's third largest industrial region, is a window on a world gone for ever: Russian communist civilization shortly before it became extinct. The demise was touched off, imperceptibly at first, when Gorbachev appointed Yeltsin to be ruler of Moscow, where the first battles of perestroika and glasnost were fought. Yeltsin's Moscow reign at the very beginning of Gorbachev's reforms in 1986 and 1987 is especially revealing because of the Soviet capital's central place in national life. Turned by Yeltsin into a laboratory of reform, Moscow first encountered all that would later haunt and, eventually, subvert Gorbachev's attempt to reform the Soviet system without breaking it.

The insight offered by this story is enhanced many times over by the new language of Party discourse that Yeltsin introduced. Throughout the Soviet Union, no official communication by a high Party functionary was as candid as Yeltsin's Moscow speeches between 1986 and 1987. Insofar as what later became known as glasnost was practised then at all, it was practised in one place, Moscow, by one man, Boris Yeltsin.

As the pace of the Revolution quickened, Boris Yeltsin's personal story became more tightly entwined with his country's history, occasionally blending with it. The impeccable timing of a born politician, courage and sheer luck thrust him to the very heart of the Revolution and made him indispensable to its history as he marked and eventually shaped its key phases: the end of the party-state in August 1991, the dissolution of the Soviet Union and the launching of an economic revolution four months later, and the establishment of democratic institutions and a market economy.

If done properly, a narrative that weaves together these strands cannot but be at once a biography of a great man and a history of this century's last great revolution. It is my hope that this book does just that.

LIST OF ILLUSTRATIONS

Russian pop art: 'Hammer-and-sickle' and 'Socialism with a human face' (*Ogonyok* 17–24 November 1990).

'The country is tired of waiting.' (*Moskovskie Novosti*, 18 November 1990).

A Democratic Russia leaflet (author's archive).

Congratulations from Gorbachev © Novosti (London).

Tanks enter Moscow on the morning of the coup © AP Photo, Boris Yurchenko.

Yeltsin's Decree No. 59 (author's archive).

Delivery of the decree © AP Photo.

Yeltsin at a victory rally outside the White House (left) © Roberto Koch/Saba (right) © Roberto Koch/Contrasto/Saba.

The Russian tri-colour in Red Square © Shepard Sherbell/Saba.

'Dictatorship has not succeeded!' (*Vechernyaya Moskva*, 22 August 1991).

In a Moscow store, autumn 1991 (*Izvestia*, 28 August 1998).

A bread line, Moscow, November 1991 © S. Sherbell/Saba.

Communist demonstrators breaking through police cordons © AP Photo/Alexander Zemlianichenko.

The attack on Ostankino television centre © Reuters/Sean Ramsay/Archive Photos.

A group of defenders leaves the White House © AP Photo/Alexander Shogin.

The Duma campaign, December 1993 (author's archive).

On the election night at Russia's Choice headquarters (photo by the author).

After the Chechen war had begun: a new Yeltsin behind the mask (*Novoye Vremya*, February 1995).

Campaign – 1996: 'Dmitry Donskoy against Boris Yeltsin' (*Zavtra*, 12 March 1996).

Campaign – 1996: a pro-Zyuganov placard-leaflet (*Sovetskaya Rossia*, 7 May 1996).

Campaign – 1996: Yeltsin: 'I will not let go!' ('Izbiratel' ('The voter'), leaflet-insert in *Sovetskaya Rossia*, 6 June 1996).

Campaign – 1996: A drunken Yeltsin sold Russian television to the Jews (*Sovetskaya Rossia*, 29 February 1996).

Campaign – 1996: With Jews directing the show, Yeltsin is selling Russia to the West ('Izbiratel' ('The voter'), leaflet-insert in *Sovetskaya Rossia*, 5 May 1996.

Campaign – 1996: 'The battle banner of the Motherland' (*Zavtra*, 18 May 1996).

The author is grateful to Mr Lloyd Hill, the owner of The Photo Shop in Manassas, for a masterful job of turning almost 100 photos and documents from the author's archive into usable transparencies.

PART I

A Man from Sverdlovsk

CHAPTER 1

To Survive, to Dare, to Succeed!

F OR AS LONG AS ANYONE could remember, the two families lived
in the two neighbouring villages of the Talitza *uezd*, or district,
about 250 kilometres east of Ekaterinburg: the Yeltsins in Butka
and the Starygins in Basmanovo, or Basmanovskoye. In 1926 Nikolay
Yeltsin, a son of Butka's pre-eminent blacksmith and a church elder,
Ignat, married the eighteen-year-old Klavdia Starygina. They were a
good-looking couple: Nikolay, tall, strong, and with a voice famous in
the village (he sang in a church choir); and the pretty blue-eyed Klavdia,
whose thick, dark-brown braid reached below her waist. She was a
master embroiderer and had taught herself to read and write.[1]

In the one-room wooden house, *izba*, where Ignat Yeltsin and his
wife lived with their four sons – Nikolay, Ivan, Dmitriy and Andrian –
there was only one bed, for the parents. The sons slept on the floor: on
straw mattresses in the summer, and on sheepskin coats (*tulup*s) in the
winter. When Nikolay's young bride moved in, the parents vacated the
bed for her.[2] In that bed, on 1 February 1931 Klavdia gave birth to
their first child, a boy.

To baptize and name the baby, the parents took him to a church in
a nearby village. In the fourteenth year of the Bolshevik state, the local
priest (the *batushka*) was allowed to baptize only once a month, so the
church was full of parents, relatives and spectators. Waiting their turn,
Klavdia and Nikolay watched screaming babies immersed completely
into a tub of holy water, given names and entered into the church record.
At the end of the brief ceremony, grateful parents offered the priest a
glass of moonshine.[3]

By the time the Yeltsin boy was brought forward to be accepted into
the Russian Orthodox Church, the *batushka* was quite tipsy. Having
dropped the infant into the tub, he became absorbed in conversation
and forgot to retrieve the new Christian. After a few seconds, Klavdia
shrieked, rushed past the priest to the tub and pulled out the child, who
was already floating near the bottom. He was still alive. Not the least
perturbed, the *batushka* announced that a boy so strong and victorious
in adversity should be named Boris.[4] In old Russian *boris* meant 'warrior'. In the form of *boris*' (with a soft 's') the word survived as the
second person imperative of the verb *borot'sia*, 'to struggle'. Six decades
later, Yeltsin's supporters would demonstrate with placards exhorting
'Boris, boris'!' 'Boris, fight on!'

The story about the choice of name was related to Yeltsin by his
mother. Either the priest was even more intoxicated than Klavdia Vasilievna recalled, or Yeltsin endowed the story with useful teleology. Most
likely, Russia's first President was named after Prince Boris, a son of

4

Kievan Prince Vladimir Monomakh. Boris was killed in 1015 by the henchmen of his half-brother, Svyatopolk. A first-generation Christian, Boris refused to fight violence with violence and did not defend himself against the assassins. Along with his brother Gleb, also killed on Svyatopolk's orders, Boris was canonized in 1072, becoming the first Russian saint. Instead of resilience and strength, the priest's choice of a name for the nearly drowned baby boy most likely was informed by the memory of another innocent *muchenik* (martyr) Boris.

A few weeks later, Butka was swept up in the war the Soviet Union had been waging against its peasants for over a year. Known as 'collectivization', the campaign was designed by Stalin to eliminate private farmers – the last obstacle in the way of the complete political and economic subjugation of society by the Soviet socialist state. Although officially directed against the rich farmers, the kulaks (a derogatory term meaning, literally, tight fist), who as 'spontaneous, petty-bourgeois regenerators of capitalism' were declared a 'class enemy' to be eliminated by exile and starvation, collectivization deprived all the peasants of their land and equipment by forcing them to join the nominally self-governing 'collective farms' (kolkhozes) or fully state-owned 'soviet farms' (sovkhozes). Ignat Yeltsin, eighty years old and almost blind, was declared a kulak, stripped of all his possessions and, together with his wife, shipped in a box car to a forced-labour settlement in the northernmost corner of the province, near the town of Serov. Along with Boris's grandparents, ten other families from Butka were exiled. Several months later Ignat Yeltsin died.[5]

In the autumn of that year, Yeltsin's mother recalls, the entire harvest collected by the recently 'collectivized' Butka peasants was taken away by the state 'to the last little grain'.[6] In 1932, Nikolay decided to leave the village for ever and took his family and the youngest of his brothers, Andrian, as far away as he could: to a construction site in the city of Kazan on the Volga, more than 1,100 kilometres from Butka. The brothers worked as carpenters for two years until both were arrested as 'de-kulakized kulaks' who had 'conducted anti-Soviet propagaganda' and were sentenced to three years in a hard-labour camp.[7*]

* The Yeltsins never breathed a word about Nikolay's arrest to anyone outside the family. Even at the time of glasnost, even after the Soviet Union had disappeared, Klavdia Vasilievna kept the secret from interviewers. Boris Yeltsin first acknowledged the fact in 1994, when he was sixty-three years old and had been President of Russia for three years.

In 1935 Nikolay's brother Ivan, a blacksmith like his father, failed to deliver to the kolkhoz his grain quota. He was arrested as a 'saboteur' and 'wrecker' and exiled to Berezniki, a town in the Perm region, 400 kilometres north-west of Sverdlovsk, as Ekaterinburg was by that time called.[8] Berezniki was the site of one of the giants of Stalin's 'industrialization', a campaign to make the Soviet Union a major industrial and military power within ten to fifteen years. The Berezniki Potassium-Processing Plant was the 'shock' (*udarniy*) or pre-eminent construction project of the second Five-Year Plan. When he returned from the camp after serving two years, Nikolay took Klavdia and Boris to join his brother in Berezniki.[9]

The Yeltsins were given a room in a *barak*, an enormously long, one-storey hut made of thin wooden boards. The most common variety of communal lodgings in urban Russia at the time, *barak*s were a veritable institution that shaped two generations of Russians. As much a fixture of 'socialist industrialization' as the gulag, these structures became an indelible part of Soviet popular culture. Like hundreds of thousands of other *barak*s throughout Russia, Yeltsin's consisted of a long corridor, into which opened twenty rooms – one per family. Behind the *barak* were a wooden privy and the well from which the tenants drew water for washing and cooking.[10]

Shortly after their arrival in Berezniki, Yeltsin's brother Mikhail was born, in August 1937. The Yeltsins bought a she-goat to secure milk for the children. All five of them – four humans and the goat – 'slept together on the floor, pressed close to one another'.[11] The goat was 'warm, like a stove', and the boys curled up next to her in the winter, when there was no protection against the piercing cold:[12] the *barak* was 'draughty through and through'.[13] Boris was one year old when the Yeltsins moved into their first *barak* in Kazan. He was fourteen when they were given the keys to an apartment of their own. Forty years later, he still hated the memory of the *barak* years.[14]

When Nikolay was promoted to construction supervisor in the late 1930s, the Yeltsins began to have enough to eat. The hunger returned, however, a few years later, in the winter of 1941–2, the first winter of the Great Patriotic War, when the Soviet Union battled against the invading Germans. In Berezniki the workers received 800 grams of bread a day, their dependants 400 grams. There was very little of anything else to eat. Klavdia sewed for the neighbours and occasionally was given bread as payment. The goat helped the Yeltsin children to survive: although 'less than a litre a day, the milk was rich in fat'.[15] Still, it was not enough. The ten-year-old Boris would come home from school, sit down in the corner and moan incessantly: 'I am hu-u-u-ungry, I am hu-u-u-ungry.'[16] Hearing him broke Klavdia's heart, but there was nothing she could do: there was 'not a stale crust in the house'.[17]

By that time, young Boris had plenty of adult responsibilities: carrying water from the well, babysitting for Mikhail (and later for his sister Valentina, born in July 1944), boiling potatoes for dinner, washing dishes, sweeping floors. In the summer, when school was out, Boris and his mother contracted with the nearby collective farms to make hay. They scythed grass off several hectares of meadows and ricked it. There was no pay but they could keep half of the hay. The Yeltsins sold it to the peasants and bought bread.

'And this is how my childhood passed,' Yeltsin wrote fifty years later. 'Rather joyless. Sweets or delicacies of any sort – these were out of the question. Only to survive, to survive and to survive.'[18]

Outside the *barak* room, Boris's universe was the poverty-stricken world of the Soviet 'workers' settlement': dirty, hungry and ridden with drunkenness, wife-beating, petty thievery and obscenities. It was a place where 'physical strength was the foremost factor in a person's self-affirmation, where there was no room for compassion, and where every physical defect, every handicap was a subject of general derision'.[19] To be left alone, to escape beating or molestation by those who were older, stronger or acted in concert, one had to project a determination to retaliate mercilessly for any insult or physical assault.

In this world, two qualities were indispensable for anyone determined to be a leader among the children, as young Boris certainly appeared to be. One was physical courage: the seemingly casual, nonchalant courtship of danger, injury, mutilation, maiming, even death. The other was the nerve to sustain a constant brinksmanship with the adult world, taunting adult authority in school, on the street, at home.

Boris was invariably to be found among the most active and most resourceful participants in all manner of dangerous fun, much of which he himself designed, staged and led his troops to execute. One such operation nearly cost him life. During the Great Patriotic War, several boys conceived the idea of disassembling a hand grenade to 'see what was inside'. Boris volunteered to steal a grenade from an ammunition depot. At night he crawled under the three rows of barbed wire and, when the sentry was on the other side of the building, sawed through the bar on the window. He jumped in, stole two grenades and returned, all the way expecting to be shot in the back. The next day, in the forest, Boris began the disassembling, while the other boys prudently stood a hundred metres away. After a few hammer blows, the fuse detonated.

In the hospital, a surgeon removed what was left of the thumb and index finger of Boris's left hand.[20]

In the merciless world of his playmates Boris became *urod*, *kaleka*, a 'freak', a 'cripple'. (Decades later, in public Yeltsin hid his left hand under the table or covered it with his tie.) But the handicap seemed only to spur him to new feats. He was always, for instance, in the front row of the periodic team fights among local youngsters. One of the most popular pastimes in Russian provinces, such fights pit a row of youths from one village or district against fist-fighters from another (hence the name of the contest: *stenka-na-stenku*, or 'wall-on-wall'). In Berezniki in the 1940s, the combat might involve as many as a hundred participants. 'There were no deaths, although we fought with a great deal of zest,' recalls Yeltsin. 'Still, there were some limits we respected. It was more like a sport but with pretty ruthless rules.'[21] During one of the fights, Boris Yeltsin was struck in the face with a wooden shaft and fell to the ground. Friends carried him home unconscious. The memento of that fight, a broken nose, forever marked Yeltsin's face.

Another of young Yeltsin's favourite pursuits was crossing the nearby river, the Zyryanka, over floating logs. Every spring, the rather inconspicuous Zyryanka swelled with melting snow and was used, as were dozens of rivers in the Urals and Siberia, to transport timber. Usually, the logs floated pretty close to one another and, 'if one calculated everything correctly, one had a chance of crossing' by jumping quickly from log to log. The most elaborate calculations were of no use, however, when a treacherous wet log slipped or rolled under the foot. 'The next moment you are in the icy water with timber over your head,' Yeltsin recalled. 'By the time you manage to squeeze through and breathe in the air, you cannot believe you are still alive.'[22]

In school, meanwhile, Boris was always among the best students – and among the most undisciplined. In the fifth grade, when Boris was eleven years old, he led the class in jumping out of the window (fortunately, the room was on the first floor) and hiding in a storage hut while their unpopular teacher rushed around the building searching for the pupils.[23] Another plot involved studding the teacher's chair with tiny gramophone needles. There followed a scream, the apprehension of the plotters and, of course, the summons for Yeltsin's parents.

At home, Boris's pranks were regularly rewarded by serious beltings. Nikolay Yeltsin was a silent type: upon hearing of a misdemeanour, he would reach for a belt, 'without saying a word'. Klavdia would weep, beg for mercy and try to shield her son. She was usually shoved out of the room, and the door locked. 'Lie down!' Nikolay would say. Boris would lie on his stomach. 'The trousers went down, the shirt up,'[24] and the father struck him methodically. Boris, teeth clenched, would not cry. 'This, of course, angered him even more.' Usually the punishment ended when Klavdia rushed into the room, grabbed the belt, pushed the father aside and stood between father and son. 'She was my eternal protectress [*zashitnitza*],' wrote Yeltsin.[25]

At the end of what at the time was the Soviet equivalent of junior high school (*semiletka*), Boris raised the brinkmanship to a new level, and very nearly precipitated a disaster. During the graduation ceremony, the fourteen-year-old Yeltsin suddenly asked to speak. This was 1945, and the past fifteen years of Stalin's rule had made spontaneous public speaking very rare indeed. Yet Boris was allowed to proceed: perhaps each of the officials responsible for the ceremony assumed that the boy had been coached and cleared by somebody else. He was, after all, an *otlichnik*, an 'A' student, and it was reasonable for the adults to expect yet another expression of gratitude for 'our golden childhood' to the 'dear' Communist Party and, of course, the 'best friend of children', Comrade Iosif Vissarionovich Stalin.

Boris, indeed, thanked everyone briefly. He then said that one of the teachers had no right to be one because she 'mentally tortured' her students. She was a nightmarish teacher, he added, who hit children with a heavy ruler, humiliated them and ordered them to look for food scraps for her pig.[26] The ceremony was hastily brought to an end.

The next day, Nikolay Yeltsin was summoned by the school's Principal and told that his son's *semiletka* diploma had been annulled and, with it, the right to enter secondary school. Boris refused to accept the verdict and went to seek justice from educational and governmental authorities. (It was then that Yeltsin first learned of the existence of the Gorkom, the all-powerful city Party committee.) Eventually, a commission was created to investigate the Yeltsin affair. The offending teacher was suspended, and the boy's certificate was returned. Still, among the grades '5' ('excellent') in all subjects, there was a '2' ('unsatisfactory') for 'discipline'.[27]

In secondary school Boris's daring assumed less dangerous and less violent forms – but hardly less strenuous ones. He became the school's sports star, excelling in skiing, gymnastics, track-and-field, boxing, wrestling and the decathlon. He 'wanted to embrace everything, to be able to do absolutely everything'.[28]

But most of all Boris loved to play volleyball. 'I liked to see the ball obey me, I liked being able to get, by the most unimaginable jump, a hopeless ball.'[29] Because he was without a thumb and index finger on the left hand, he invented an unusual ('non-classic', he called it) way to receive the ball. Every night, he fell asleep with his hand on the volleyball. When he woke up, he began training right away: spinning the ball on a finger and bouncing it off the floor and the wall.[30] In his second year of high school he was drafted into the city's all-star high school team.

Each summer Boris organized backpack expeditions in the taiga, then still a dense, virgin forest of fir trees that surrounded Berezniki. These forays into the wilderness often lasted for weeks. When the contents of the backpacks ran out, the young hikers lived on nuts, berries and mushrooms. In the summer between ninth and tenth grades, the fifteen-year-old Boris led an expedition to discover the source of a local river. The source was found (it turned out to be a sulphuric spring), but the hikers lost their way while returning to the river where they had moored their flat-boat. They were in a young forest, surrounded by swamps, and their usual food was hard to find. Still worse was the absence of fresh water. The boys soaked moss in the swamp, squeezed the water out, using their shirts as filters, and drank the dark brown liquid. By the time they stumbled upon the river and their boat, all of the boys had typhoid fever. One by one, they began to lose consciousness. For a while, Boris steered the boat downstream alone. Then, sensing that he, too, was about to collapse, he tied up the boat under a railway bridge, hoping that there they would be noticed. They were. It was already the end of September and search parties had been looking for them for weeks.[31]

The boys remained in hospital for three months. By the time they were out, half of the school year had passed. Yeltsin's companions decided to start the tenth grade anew the next autumn. Boris, studying day and night on his own, was determined to graduate. When he came to take the secondary-school graduation exams, he was told that he would not be admitted because it was against the rules to graduate without attending classes. As he had three years before, Boris demanded justice from his teachers' bosses: the Ispolkom, the city Soviet's executive committee, and the Gorkom. He won again: he was allowed to take the exams. In the fourteen subjects he received eight 5s and six 4s. The grades on his secondary-school diploma, issued on 1 July 1949, show a greater propensity for natural sciences than for the humanities.

As a teenager, Boris, who had never seen the sea, wanted to be a shipbuilder. He even began reading engineering tomes seeking to understand how to build ships.[32] Towards the end of secondary school, he changed his mind and decided to become a civil engineer. (By that time his father headed a construction site.) Boris passed entrance examinations to the department of civil engineering at the Ural Polytechnic Institute, or UPI, with two 5s and two 4s.

But good grades were not all that was required to enter university in the Soviet Union in 1949, and on 19 August that year Boris Yeltsin filled in his first official questionnaire, a 'personal sheet for the registration of cadres'. He stated his place of birth (for some unknown reason putting Basmanovo rather than Butka), his nationality (Russian), his social origin (peasant) and party affiliation (member of the Komsomol). Boris did not have scholarly degrees or inventions to his name, had not served in the Red Army nor participated in the revolutionary or partisan movements or in the Civil War. But neither had he had 'vacillations with respect to the implementation of the Party line', 'participated in the oppositions', been abroad or lived on territory temporarily occupied by the Nazis in the last war. All in all, young Boris looked quite reliable. He was admitted to the UPI and the next month moved to a hostel in Sverdlovsk to begin his first university term.

Thus, at the age of eighteen, the life and fate of Boris Yeltsin were touched by one of Russia's most interesting cities: Ekaterinburg/Sverdlovsk, situated on the River Iset in the eastern foothills of the Urals, the mountain range that separates Europe from Asia. It was here on the edge of the West Siberian Plain that Yeltsin was to live for the next thirty-six years, where he started a family and made his career. It is the city without which Yeltsin is impossible to understand. As he confessed when he became Russia's pre-eminent leader, 'My heart is in Sverdlovsk.'[33]

Founded in 1723 by Peter the Great, who needed copper for his cannons, Ekaterinburg soon became Russia's principal industrial centre. Throughout the eighteenth and nineteenth centuries, its steelmakers and mining engineers were the best in the nation. The town's coat of arms, approved by the Russian Senate in 1783, portrays a mine and a smeltery. In 1745 the Old Believers, who had been exiled for their rejection of Patriarch Nikon's 1654 liturgical reforms, found the first Russian gold in the vicinity of Ekaterinburg.[34]

The wealth of semi-precious stones (especially malachite) discovered in the Ural Mountains brought forth generations of celebrated stonecutters, who had no equals in all of Russia. Their statuettes, chalices and necklaces, made of malachite, rhodonite and jasper, were shipped directly to the tsarist court in St Petersburg. The Russian pavilion at the

1900 World Exhibition in Paris contained a map of France made in Ekaterinburg from semi-precious stones and weighing around 500 kilograms.[35]

Begun as a fort 'on the edge of the inhabited Russian land'[36] (its first builders were the soldiers of the Tobolsk Regiment),[37] Ekaterinburg became Russia's 'window to Asia',[38] a gateway to Siberia, Russia's equivalent of the American West and the home of Russian pioneers: iconoclasts and exiles. Peasant settlers from Central Russia were attracted to the Urals by the virtual absence of serfdom, larger plots of land and greater economic independence.[39] Two centuries later, assessing the region's peculiar history, the descendants of the Ural pioneers would note that mining and metallurgy 'made the people disciplined, respectful of scientific and technological progress, thirsty for knowledge and accustomed to city living'; the daily battle with the stern climate and the taiga instilled them with courage; the mixture of races, languages and religions produced religious and ethnic tolerance; the relatively free life of mines and settlements strengthened the 'love of liberty' and the 'habit of solving problems themselves'; and the steady inflow of settlers 'made the culture of the Urals and the mentality of its citizens open and dynamic'.[40]

Among the best educated in Russia (there are sixteen colleges in the city today, including the oldest in Russia, its school of mining engineering), Ekaterinburg's industrialists and merchants became well known for their wealth, curiosity and civic-mindedness. They were indefatigable travellers, collectors of nature's curiosities and connoisseurs of the arts. They founded museums, theatres and libraries. The world-famous ballet impresario Sergey Dyagilev was born in the Ekaterinburg province (in the village of Dyagilevo, the Baikalovo district), 200 kilometres northeast of the city.

Anton Chekhov left a characteristically ageless snapshot of the city's inhabitants. This most delicate of Russian writers was terrified by the sheer size and the raw vitality of Yeltsin's ancestors. 'People here instil a visitor with something close to terror,' Chekhov reported from Ekaterinburg to his sister Maria in 1890. 'With prominent cheekbones, large foreheads, broad shoulders, small eyes and huge fists . . . [they must be] born right inside the foundries and present at their birth is not a midwife but a mechanic.'[41] Chekhov was still more alarmed by the sight of a distant relative who paid him a visit in the hotel: 'Gloomy, [his] head nearly touching the ceiling, the huge shoulders. This one, I thought to myself, would kill me for sure.'[42] It turned out, however, that Chekhov's visitor was quite civilized: a deputy to the county council (*zemstvo*), he edited a local newspaper and managed a mill run by electricity. He told Chekhov that there was no time for boredom and advised him to visit museums and factories.[43]

During the Soviet era, in 1924, the city was renamed Sverdlovsk, after Lenin's comrade-in-arms Yakov Sverdlov (it reverted to its original name in 1991). Sverdlovsk grew rapidly, especially in the 1930s when it became one of the key centres of Stalin's industrialization. Between 1926 and 1939 the urban population of the Sverdlovsk region increased almost three-fold to a million and a half. Over the next twenty years, it doubled again to three million, making the Sverdlovsk province the fourth most urbanized in the Soviet Union, after Moscow, Leningrad and Donetsk.[44]

In the Second World War, like the rest of the Ural region, Sverdlovsk became a home for evacuees from Central Russia: 163,000 from Moscow and Leningrad alone.[45] Moscow State University spent the war in Sverdlovsk. The intellectual potential of the city, unusually high for a Russian province, was further increased by its peculiar status as a place of 'soft' exile for those banished as politically unreliable from Central Russia but allowed to live, work and even advance in Sverdlovsk. Twice in peacetime, the stream of newcomers swelled to tens of thousands: in 1934–5, in the aftermath of the murder of Leningrad's Party boss, Sergey Kirov (the so-called 'Kirov stream'), and in 1949–50 as part of the campaign against the Jewish 'cosmopolitans', mostly from Moscow. These were the cream of Russia's intelligentsia: engineers and mathematicians, artists and lawyers, doctors and actors, writers and musicians. Perhaps the most famous of Stalin's Sverdlovsk exiles was the hero of the battles for Moscow and Stalingrad, the vanquisher of the Nazis, Marshal Konstantin Zhukov. He was sent to Sverdlovsk in 1948 to command the Ural Military District and remained there until Stalin's death in 1953.

Combined with its distance from Moscow (more than 1,600 kilometres), Ekaterinburg's two centuries of solid education, culture and brilliant craftsmanship endowed the local character with dignity, self-confidence, independence and strong, albeit quiet, patriotism. It is hard to find another Russian city whose inhabitants were as free from the inferiority complex vis-à-vis Moscow which Chekhov immortalized in the 'To Moscow! To Moscow!' battle cry in *Three Sisters*. The denizens of Ekaterinburg and its environs are talented but modest and direct; cultured but not pretentious or chatty; dignified and sure of themselves but not arrogant; opinionated but willing to listen and change their views. The nine generations of stonecutters, smelters and jewellers created a local character which combines creativity and grace with tenacity and physical strength.

In the last thirty years of the Soviet regime Sverdlovsk earned a reputation for less than sterling political reliability. In July 1959, for example, throngs greeted Vice President Richard Nixon with what an American reporter described as 'uninhibited enthusiasm'.[46] By contrast, three years later, the Soviet leader Nikita Khrushchev was given a very different reception. Sverdlovsk folklore cherishes the story of Khrushchev's visit to one of the largest Soviet enterprises, the Ural Heavy Machine Building Plant (known throughout the Soviet Union as the Uralmash), during which he was pelted with rotten tomatoes by workers protesting against the abominable food supply. Sverdlovsk, however, provided Khrushchev with one of the last triumphs of his waning rule: the downing by a Soviet missile of an American high-altitude U-2 spyplane over Sverdlovsk in May 1960.

Ekaterinburg's unique history, demography and industry contributed to the emergence of what might be called the Ural school of the Communist Party leadership. As a rule, the Ural Party bosses were competent, tough, independent, strong, seemingly incorruptible, even austere, and direct. By contrast, the members of the Southern school, which included both Leonid Brezhnev and Mikhail Gorbachev, tended to be more pragmatic, flexible in both ends and means, and bent on good living. (In his eighteen years as General Secretary, Brezhnev never visited Sverdlovsk.)

Among the members of the Ural school were the two men who ruled the Sverdlovsk region in the 1960s and 1970s – First Secretaries of the Sverdlovsk Regional Party Committee, Konstantin Nikolaev (1962–71) and Yakov Ryabov (1971–6) – and a former director of the Uralmash, Yeltsin's friend and Mikhail Gorbachev's first Prime Minister, Nikolay Ryzhkov. Like Yeltsin, all three were engineers. Ryabov and Ryzhkov graduated from the UPI.

Like his 5,000 fellow students at the UPI, Boris received free education, a bed in a tiny dormitory with five roommates, and in his first year a niggardly stipend of 290 rubles a month (increased steadily to 790 rubles in his fifth year).[47] This was a very inconsiderable sum at the time when a kilo of meat cost forty rubles, a kilo of butter twenty-five rubles and bread three rubles a loaf.[48] His parents could only contribute another 250 rubles a month.[49] When they ran out of money, Boris and his classmates unloaded railway trucks: the last of the legal resorts for hundreds of thousands of impoverished Soviet students. The extra income was certainly not enough to diversify Boris's wardrobe: throughout his six years in college, he wore the same outfit: a corduroy jacket, trousers of coarse fabric and black tarpaulin boots.

This sartorial deficiency did not prevent young Yeltsin from occupying his accustomed place as ringleader. From his first to his last year in the UPI he was responsible in the Komsomol Committee for organizing sports events for the entire college. (Komsomol was a contraction of Kommunisticheskiy Soyuz Molodezhi, the Communist Union of Youth. By Yeltsin's time membership was routine from the age of fourteen to twenty-eight.) When students decided to ask for more time to prepare for a particularly difficult exam, Yeltsin led the delegation that presented the demand to the professor teaching the course. This professor, Boris Speranskiy, retaliated by giving Yeltsin one of the handful of 4s he received in college. 'I should have given him a 5,' Speranskiy admitted thirty-five years later. 'He was my favourite student but he disappointed me.'[50] Boris was the 'soul' at the weddings of many of his classmates, who, like most Soviet college students, married in their senior years. These occasions, which usually took place in the school cafeteria, made up in enthusiasm, camaraderie and good cheer for the very limited assortment of refreshments and the drabness of attire. Boris arranged the day's innumerable skits, mock odes, costumes, surprise home-made presents, noisy chorus singing, posters and toasts.

He is also reported to have been incessantly on the lookout for practical jokes, be they whipping a chair from under someone he had just invited to sit down, or balancing a pail of water over the door and manipulating it by a string to douse an unsuspecting entrant.[51] Three and a half decades later, responding to a common observation that he smiles rarely, Yeltsin would write that 'although deep inside [he was] an optimist', he must have 'laughed [himself] out' during his student days.[52]

Never having seen the country outside Berezniki and Sverdlovsk, Boris resolved to see as much of the Soviet Union as he could in one long trip during the summer after his first year at the UPI. With very little money, he planned to stow away and hitchhike the entire journey. He departed Sverdlovsk in a straw hat, tracksuit trousers, a shirt and tennis shoes. His luggage consisted of a tiny imitation-leather suitcase containing an extra shirt. A classmate whom Boris had talked into accompanying him returned home after the first day.[53]

Most of the distance was covered on the roofs and platforms of railway carriages. The schedule was established as follows: travelling by night to famous cities, sightseeing during the day, and sleeping on park benches or in railway terminals until the next suitable train. He was, of course, picked up by police several times and questioned about his destination. His response never varied: he was a poor teenager travelling to his grandmother who lived in whatever city was the closest. When the police demanded the grandmother's address, Boris without hesitation named Lenin Street, which he knew could be found in every Soviet town. He was always released. In this manner he crisscrossed Russia from Leningrad in the north to Batumi in the south and as far to the west as Minsk: twenty cities altogether.[54]

During one unforgettable journey on the roof of a railway carriage, Boris found himself in the company of 'criminals' just released from jail. Forced to play cards and stake the clothes on his back, he initially lost all and was stripped to his undershorts. 'We will now play for your life,' he was told. 'You lose, and we throw you off the roof.' Then his luck turned, and a much relieved Boris gradually won back the trousers, the shoes, even the hat.[55]

He worked for food. In the Ukrainian city of Zaparozhie, the home of one of the largest steel mills in the Soviet Union, Boris ran into a Soviet Army colonel who was to take entrance exams to a military academy in a week's time but was afraid of failing the maths. Would Boris, an 'A' student, tutor him? He would, with success guaranteed, but on two conditions: first, the tutor should be given as much food as he could eat; second, they should study twenty hours a day for the entire week. The colonel passed, and, for the first time since he left Sverdlovsk, Boris had put on weight.[56]

When the victorious traveller returned to Sverdlovsk, the soles of his shoes were gone and he continued wearing them 'just for show'. The hat, which had developed a hole in the crown, had been discarded along the way. And the tracksuit trousers were 'quite transparent in the seat'.[57]

And, of course, there was volleyball. At first, the coaches of the Institute's volleyball team were reluctant to draft Yeltsin because of his mutilated left hand. After they relented, he rapidly became the captain.[58] Soon, Yeltsin remembers, he was playing for the city of Sverdlovsk in the top national league among the twelve best teams in the Soviet Union.[59] They never became champions, he recalls, but were consistently placed sixth or seventh in the country and, most important for Yeltsin, 'were taken seriously'.[60] (According to the coach of the UPI volleyball team, Ekaterina Nikolaevna Chernous, however, Yeltsin played for the Institute only, not for the city.) Boris also coached the Institute's women's and men's (second) teams. A college friend recalled that 'the girls came to volleyball games especially to "look at Yeltsin"'.[61]

Counting practice, games and coaching, Yeltsin spent no fewer than six hours on the court every day. He studied at night. It was during his six years at the UPI that he acquired the habit of sleeping no more than four hours a night. Twice a year, during the examination sessions, when he had to make up for the weeks on the road with the team, he hardly slept at all. In this tough engineering school, where students sat at least half-a-dozen oral and written exams every six months, his grades were very good: out of a total of fifty-five exams, he was found 'excellent' (the highest grade) in forty and 'good' in the rest.[62]

During the winter examination session of his third year in 1952, Yeltsin fell sick with quinsy but continued to play and to take exams, striving, as usual, to get only 5s. With a sore throat and high fever Boris went to a volleyball game and fainted. He was taken to the hospital, his heart-rate at 150, and ordered to stay in bed for four months – or risk permanent heart damage.[63]

He ran away from the hospital after a few days – as soon as he could walk (friends arranged an escape during which Boris climbed down a wall on a rope made of several sheets tied together). At his parents' house in Berezniki, Boris began his own programme of physical therapy. Unsteady on his feet, with his heart 'pounding', he made his way to the gym. At first, he could do no more than hit the ball a couple of times before collapsing ('the guys would drag me to the bench and I would just lie there'). But Yeltsin persisted and, little by little, he started playing again – at first no longer than a minute, then two, then five. In a month he could stay on the court for an entire game.[64] His recovery confirmed for Boris the veracity of an old Russian proverb, which he had made his motto and which later would define his political style: *Klin klinom vyshibayut*[65] – literally 'To drive out a wedge, hit it with another', but better translated as 'Fight adversity with adversity!' or 'When attacked, attack!'

Nonetheless, by 'UPI Order Number 358' of 27 March 1952 he was 'dismissed' from the Institute 'because of illness'.[66] Five months later, on 30 August, Boris Yeltsin submitted a written application to the Director of the UPI: 'I request that I be admitted to the third year in the Department of Civil Engineering.'[67] Two weeks later, the Director endorsed Boris's application with the words: 'Restore to the student body of the Department, with [space in] the hostel.'[68]

After six years in college, instead of the usual five, Yeltsin graduated in June 1955. His diploma project was 'A path inside a coal mine and the organization of work for its construction'.[69] He received an 'excellent' for it. Indulging his propensity for exaggeration and embellishment

– a problem which a biographer must constantly guard against by checking Yeltsin's words against documents and the testimony of others – Yeltsin claimed for his diploma project a more glamorous topic: 'A Television Tower'. 'I still do not know how I managed [to write the thesis, Yeltsin recorded]. The amount of mental and physical effort was unimaginable. And I could not count on anyone's help: this was a novel subject, no one knew anything about it. So I had to do everything myself: drafting, calculations – everything from beginning to end.'[70]

It appears that only once in his college days was young Boris Yeltsin uncharacteristically hesitant. The dormitory, which he shared with five male students, was next to a room that housed six young women studying in the same Department of Civil Engineering. Very soon the two sets of roommates became fast friends. Boris, despite the time consumed by his scholarly and athletic feats, is reported to have been 'by no means a hermit'.[71] (Once, on a cold autumn night, he jumped into the river with his clothes on to impress a date.)[72] Even forty years later, several of his female classmates distinctly remembered having 'noticed' him.[73]

One of the six young women was Naya (short for Anastasia, but soon changed to Naina) Girina from Orenburg, an old Russian city 650 kilometres south-west of Sverdlovsk. For a while Boris and Naya did not pay much attention to one another, dating each other's friends. If they kissed at all during their first year, recalls Yeltsin, it was only 'on the cheek'.[74] By the second year, Yeltsin realized that he had 'fallen in love, fallen deeply, and there was nothing [he] could do [about it]'. He describes the young Naya as friendly, modest, gentle and kind – the attributes young Boris felt 'went very well' with his 'rather troublesome character'.[75] One night, as they stood by a pillar on the balcony over the Main Hall of the Institute, Boris confessed his feelings. This time they kissed 'for real'.[76]

There was no talk of marriage, however. The job assignment which awaited every Soviet college graduate at the end of his or her studies took Naya to her native Orenburg, while Boris's orders, which he received when he dropped in at the Institute on his way to yet another out-of-town volleyball game, were to stay in Sverdlovsk. They decided to 'test [their] love', to see 'how strong and how deep it was', and meet exactly a year later on neutral territory, in the city of Kuybyshev on the Volga.[77]

CHAPTER 2

The Builder

O N 6 SEPTEMBER 1955, BACK in Sverdlovsk from the volleyball tournament in Riga, Boris Yeltsin reported for his first job, at the Sverdlovsk branch of the giant building *trest*, or 'construction organization', Yuzhgorstroy (a typical Soviet bureaucratic acronym – the name is deciphered as 'Southern City Construction'). Like every novice civil engineer in his country, he was to become a *master*: a rather ill-defined, jack-of-all-trades junior supervisory position at a construction site, just above the blue-collar construction crew leader, the *brigadir*.

Yeltsin refused to take the job. He explained to the *prorab* ('site supervisor') that the Ural Polytechnic, although a 'strong' engineering school, had not prepared him well enough for the real life of a construction site. He requested that he be given a year to study *in vivo* the major building trades. He wanted to 'feel them with [his] own hands'.[1] More than a thirst for learning and experience was behind this decision: he 'knew for certain that [without direct knowledge of the construction operations] any *brigadir* would wrap [Yeltsin] around his finger'.[2] This was a strange request, which puzzled the *trest*'s officials. Here was a college graduate, an engineer, a budding Soviet *nachal'nik* or 'boss', who wanted to descend the very steep Soviet social ladder and to tread, if only temporarily, on the other side of the never acknowledged but real gulf that separated the Soviet professional class from the blue-collar workers. Still, the petition was granted, marking the first of many instances of what was to become Yeltsin's *métier*: proving that in the post-Stalin Soviet Union one could do fairly unconventional things – if only one dared ask for them.

During the next year Yeltsin learned to be bricklayer, concrete-maker, truck-driver, carpenter, joiner, glass-cutter, plasterer, house-painter and crane-operator. He worked one and a half, often two shifts a day. The workers chuckled at his enthusiasm but helped the 'young specialist' learn the ropes.[3]

Along the way, the Soviet construction site of the 1950s – a truly hazardous place for a novice – brought back to Yeltsin the thrill of physical danger that had filled his childhood. When he worked as a concrete-maker, he had to 'run along very high and narrow scaffolding' pushing a wheelbarrow filled to the brim with concrete. This was a 'very complicated' task, and on several occasions both apprentice and wheelbarrow fell three metres down to the boards on the lower level of the scaffolds.[4] During his truck-driving month, his decrepit ZIS, with some 500,000 kilometres on the clock and a heavy load of cement in its hold, died suddenly at a railway crossing. With a train approaching,

Yeltsin managed to start the truck by a series of jerks produced by turning the ignition on and off.[5]

As a crane-operator, he forgot, on leaving the site one evening, to fasten the monstrous contraption to its rails by special hooks. Awakened later that night by a powerful storm, Boris remembered what he had not done, looked out of the window (he lived in a hostel next to the site) and saw the crane rolling slowly towards the end of the rails. Yeltsin jumped out of bed, ran to the machine in his underwear, climbed the narrow ladder to the cabin at the top, and put the crane's gears in reverse – a few seconds before the crane would have rolled off the rails and collapsed. For a long time afterwards, he had a recurring nightmare of climbing the cold, wet, black ladder and crashing down with the crane.[6]

A year later, the engineer Yeltsin reported to his *prorab* that he now was ready to work as a *master*. His first *ob'ekt* ('site') was a miserable, on-again, off-again job. Its entire workforce, including Yeltsin, consisted of eleven people. The garb of the young *master* went well with the pitiful site: a long grey cotton jacket, high tarpaulin boots and a steelmaker's helmet. Tall and still thin, Yeltsin looked like a 'veritable scarecrow'.[7]

One morning, shortly after he took over the site, Yeltsin found the entire crew and all the machinery gone. He discovered that they had been dispatched by the *prorab* to build a garage for one of the *trest*'s bosses. Periodic siphoning off of labour and materials for private projects of the higher-ups was a common practice in Soviet construction, and the workers were startled when a furious Yeltsin arrived at the site of the future garage and ordered them back to their official workplace. The *prorab* lodged with the *trest* a complaint of insubordination – the first of many that would dot Yeltsin's construction career.[8]

A few months later, at a meeting of the *trest*'s employees in the House of Builders in downtown Sverdlovsk, Yeltsin voiced a complaint of his own. As he had done ten years before at the junior high school graduation, he gave no warning to the meeting organizers before getting up to address the hall. Why, he asked, after sixteen years of schooling, had he, a UPI *cum laude* graduate, been assigned to a fourth-rate site? Was that a good utilization of the state's resources when a qualified engineer, eager to work hard, was sent to a half-dead *ob'ekt*?[9] To everyone's surprise, the *trest*'s leadership agreed with the young *master*. Within two weeks, he was given his first 'real' site: a five-storey, eighty-flat apartment building on Griboedova Street in Sverdlovsk.

Boris Yeltsin's first substantial project was a typical Soviet civilian construction *ob'ekt*: mired in mud and plagued by waste, absenteeism, alcoholism, mindless vandalism and unceasing, almost instinctive thievery. An irregular supply of construction materials and a lackadaisical pace of work resulted in days, often weeks, during which no more than a few hours of actual construction were completed. The site was months behind schedule.

The twenty-five-year-old engineer confronted the 'depressing technological illiteracy' of his workers and the near total absence of motivation: 'the people were utterly indifferent to, even contemptuous of, their labour'.[10] Cement, for instance, was unloaded from trucks directly on to the ground, where half of it was lost instantly and the rest became unfit for bricklaying after a few hours. Window panes were routinely broken, doors damaged and appliances stolen, especially toilet bowls and taps. (At the time, the most common decorative material for the outside panels of apartment buildings in Sverdlovsk was faience of broken toilet bowls.)[11] In the chaos and dirt of the site, the workers barely noticed the arrival of the new *master*.

They noticed him a day later, however, when Yeltsin ordered the perimeter of the foundation pit cleared of mud and debris and covered with asphalt. The site's unanimous opinion was that this island of extravagance would soon be consumed by the sea of mud churned up by the tyres of delivery trucks. The site was wrong: Yeltsin assigned a special team to hose down after each truck. 'I am building as I was taught,' Yeltsin told a fellow *master*.[12]

A month later, he took on the most sacred cow of Soviet construction: fraudulent work-pay sheets, called *naryady*. These were traditionally distorted, or 'padded', to exaggerate the volume and quality of work performed so as to secure higher salaries for the workers. At the time, the practice was known as *pripiska*, literally 'added writing'. Every night, tape in hand, Yeltsin measured and counted the brick walls erected, the asphalt laid and the appliances installed.[13] He began to impose fines – up to half a month's salary – for damaged construction materials, theft and absenteeism. Every month, each worker was handed a sheet of paper on which Yeltsin had detailed the work actually performed and calculated the earnings.[14]

Another of Yeltsin's innovations was to invite future tenants to inspect the apartment buildings before the official 'accepting commission' pronounced them fit for habitation. The prospect of facing angry families, who had waited ten, fifteen or twenty years to move from communal apartments or *barak*s into one-bedroom flats, proved sufficiently menacing for the construction workers to pay for repairs out of their own pockets. On one occasion they replaced the entire plumbing system, which had been decimated by theft and wrecked by incorrect installation.[15]

The workers bitterly resented these deviations from the norm. Most, in the Soviet manner, sulked silently, occasionally cursing the *master* under their breath.[16] In the case of prisoner-workers, common at Soviet construction sites, the protest was quite explicit: one of them marched into the *master*'s cabin on the site with an axe and demanded that the *naryady* be filled in 'as before'.[17]

No less irritating to the site was the persona of the new *master* himself. He was at work by seven every morning, two hours before the official workday began, and rarely left before ten at night.[18] He did not drink on the job, not even at lunch or to celebrate the end of the day. But, strangest of all, the young engineer seemed immune to two habits that were among the essential rites of passage to Russian manhood: he did not smoke and, even more startlingly, did not use *mat*, the Russian tongue's vast, rich and powerful collection of foul words. During his college days, friends would bet Yeltsin that, sooner or later, he would use a least one 'bad' word. They always lost.

Yet, as more working hours were spent working, deadlines began to be met, salaries grew (the workers on the site began to earn more, on average, than anywhere else in the *trest*, which employed nearly 5,000 people), and the site's assessment of the young *master* began to change. And at meetings in the *trest*'s headquarters the twenty-six-year-old Yeltsin, by now promoted to *prorab*, was touted as an example for other supervisors to emulate.[19]

Every successful manager is, of course, part politician, manipulating his subordinates into performing adequately. Yet for an ambitious Soviet manager – unable in most cases to rely even on a rudimentary work ethic, devoid of meaningful material incentives in a country of permanent shortages and substandard goods, and deterred from getting rid of the laggard by lengthy, cumbersome and often nerve-racking procedures – to be a success was virtually synonymous with being a skilled purveyor of symbolic, rather than material, carrots and sticks. To an extent far exceeding that of his colleagues in the West, he (almost always he) had to inspire and command personal, rather than institutional, loyalty and translate it into passable work attitudes. Young engineer Yeltsin appeared to have mastered this art with uncommon ease and speed, and with very impressive results.

In the weeks preceding the deadline for the official handing over of a building to the accepting commission, when the site worked around the clock, the young *prorab* never went home without first calling on the *brigada*s ('crews') of plasterers, painters and wallpaperers, who worked the night shift. (At Soviet construction sites, these finishing jobs were the lowest paid, and were almost always performed by female workers.) He would chat with the young women, kiss them jokingly on the cheek, work alongside them for half an hour, praise the best and hand them small presents, often bought with his own money: fabric for a dress, lipstick, perfume, an apron. 'All the girls were in love with him,' a witness reports.[20]

Once, on the eve of the accepting commission's appearance at the site, Yeltsin discovered that the hinges on all outside doors had been fitted upside down. The doors and the floors had just been painted, the better to impress the commission, and a fine 'filigree' job was required to refit the hinges and hang the doors. Yeltsin asked the best carpenter at the site to work through the night. The following morning, at six, Yeltsin entered the building with his own transistor radio: a luxury and a status symbol in the Soviet Union of the late 1950s. The carpenter, Vasiliy Mikhaylishin, was finishing the last entrance door. Without saying a word, the *prorab* handed the radio to the man and embraced him.[21] After this, Yeltsin insisted, 'how could [the carpenter] have been upset for being left to work alone all night?'[22] He intended this as a rhetorical question – and he was probably right.

Before the year Boris and Naya had given themselves as a test was over, Yeltsin found himself on the way to Kuybyshev for one of the last volleyball tournaments of his semi-professional career. He called Naya (who had by now officially changed her name from Anastasia to Naina) to remind her of their agreement to meet in Kuybyshev. She was so nervous on the telephone, he could barely recognize her voice.[23] They met in the evening in the central square of Kuybyshev, and all night long 'walked and talked about everything'.[24] They returned to Sverdlovsk together.

Boris and Naina went straight to the Zags* to be married, returned to Yeltsin's hostel, and announced their marriage to a cheering crowd of roommates and neighbours.[25] The wedding was celebrated in the

---

* Perhaps the most ubiquitous of Soviet civil institutions, Zags was the place where every Soviet citizen had to register a change in his or her civil status: marriage, birth of children, divorce and death. Every such event was duly marked by an entry in one's domestic passport. Each district (*rayon*), rural or urban, had its own Zags. The word is an acronym for Zapis' Aktov Grazhdanskogo Sostoyaniya, or 'Recording of the Acts of Civil Status'.

House of the Peasant, a two-storey building in downtown Sverdlovsk designated by local authorities for all sorts of mass gatherings: from movies to weddings to lying-in-state. One hundred and fifty friends attended, many arriving from distant corners of the Soviet Union, where their work assignments had taken them. Engineered by Boris's UPI classmates in the same spirit of unbridled merriment that had marked many a wedding scripted and stage-managed by Yeltsin himself in his college days, this was a loud and boisterous affair. Another wedding, this time for Yeltsin's relatives, soon followed, and then another, in Orenburg, for Naina's 'traditional, old, really peasant' family.[26]

Naina soon found a job at a scientific research institute, which designed waterways and canals. She was to stay there for the next twenty-nine years, rising to be Chief Project Engineer and Group Leader. A soft-spoken, gentle and conscientious colleague, she was universally liked. 'Somehow,' her husband notes wistfully, 'it seems to me that she had an easier time at work than I did.'[27]

This was certainly true of the next two years. While the Griboedova building (and, after it, a block of eight apartment houses, called 'multi-storey' because they had nine floors, a rarity in the Russian provinces in the 1950s)[28] made the *trest*'s bosses take note of the *prorab* Yeltsin, it was the Textile Kombinat ('factory') that, in 1957, launched his career into celestial orbit.

By the time Yeltsin was put in charge of the site, the Kombinat had been under construction for ten years.[29] Now, following a recent decision of the Party's Central Committee, which emphasized the development of light industry, the Kombinat was to be completed in eighteen months.[30] In the parlance of Russian builders, the Kombinat was a *dolgostroy*, a 'long-to-be-built'.[31] In large measure this state of affairs was due to the Kombinat's civilian status: it did not entitle the workers to the benefits available at defence-related heavy-industry *ob'ekt*s: the hardship bonus (the so-called 'Ural coefficient'), which increased salaries by 15 per cent for all the workers on the site, and the addition of several months of 'labour service' credits for each year spent on the work, which made retirement and pension possible at an earlier date. Hence, by the time Yeltsin arrived, the Kombinat's workforce was 'largely bums': workers and engineers eased out of previous jobs for absenteeism and alcoholism.[32]

A seven-storey rusting metal skeleton[33] was Yeltsin's introduction to the site. At his feet, in the dirt, lay the remnants of equipment reduced by theft and vandalism. The pile of debris reached as high as the third storey. Steel beams and concrete reinforcement rods protruded from the heaps of refuse.[34]

Yeltsin looked around the site for a few days. Then he composed a timetable for the Kombinat's completion and reported to his superiors: 'Here is what I need – labour, machinery and materials – and here is how long it will take me to finish the job.'[35] He needed a lot. So much, in fact, that even the *nachal'nik* of Yeltsin's Construction Upravlenie ('Administration') Number 13 (SU-13), a division of Yuzhgorstroy, could not deliver it all. But the young *prorab* exuded confidence, promising to drive a stake through the heart of the interminable site, and the *nachal'nik* went 'upstairs' to the head of the Glavk, the regional construction administration.

There Yeltsin's timetables and calculations were carefully examined and found plausible, so the author was called in to 'defend' his project. As a result of that interview, the bosses of various *upravlenie*s of the Glavk were assembled at the headquarters to be introduced to the twenty-seven-year-old engineer, whose rank was instantly raised to senior *prorab* to correspond to the job at hand. To dispel whatever scepticism the *prorab*'s youth and lack of experience might have engendered in the seasoned construction *nachal'nik*s – a notoriously hard lot to impress – the head of the Glavk concluded the meeting by saying: 'Here is the man, here is his timetable. Anyone falling behind in supplies will be fired on the spot.'[36]

It took Yeltsin a month just to clear the site and dig up the materials buried in the debris.[37] For the next seventeen months he built in a rhythm that was to become his trademark. He left the hostel at six, walked twelve kilometres and was at work by eight.[38] Sometimes he stayed at the site for days on end. He did not come home, for instance, when, in the deadly cold of a Ural winter, the Kombinat's watertower was being built, with the cement warmed continuously on a huge bonfire.[39] Now that the construction was a 'shock project', destined to produce six million metres of fabric annually, Yeltsin's command swelled to around a thousand workers.

On the day before the completed Kombinat was to be shown to the accepting commission, Yeltsin discovered that an underground passageway, which in the original project was to lead from one of the Kombinat's buildings to the other, had never been dug. Apparently, there had once existed a separate blueprint for the passageway, but it had been lost.[40] The day was saved by the sort of inspired crisis management that would make Yeltsin famous. By six o'clock the next morning, three hours before the commission's arrival, the 'cursed passageway'[41] had been finished and the Sverdlovsk Textile Kombinat was ready for operation.

The construction of the passageway was, first and foremost, a professional triumph. But, reading Yeltsin's description of the operation – almost poetical in its intensity, rhythm and economy – it is difficult not to conclude that for him the pride stemmed not just from a job well done, but rather from enacting what he thought was a generally superior and aesthetically enjoyable approach to life's crises:

> Immediately, the best intellect of the site gathers and decides how to organize the work quickly and precisely, and spends on all the discussions less than half an hour. Everything is calculated by the minute: ground works from this time to this time, concrete work, finishing work, one brigade is thrown here, another there. One excavator begins to dig the trench, another follows, then another. I am at my place, not leaving even for a minute. Everybody is responsible for his segment of work. There is no fuss, everything is organized with optimal precision . . .[42]

*

After Yeltsin handed over the Kombinat, 'they began to talk about him throughout the city'.[43] Half a year later, he was promoted to Chief Engineer of SU-13, becoming second in command of the same Construction Administration (Stroitelnoye Upravlenie) where only four years before he had begun his building career. He was twenty-nine years old.

From his first day as Chief Engineer, Yeltsin promulgated the strategy that had paid off so handsomely for him: each constuction site's *nachal'nik* was to bear full responsibility for his site and was to have maximum flexibility and autonomy in allocating resources and motivating the workers. Yeltsin 'educated' his constuction-site chiefs to be not 'just clock punchers but true masters of their sites'.[44]

He assembled the managers and told them to prepare a detailed account of the financial affairs on their site for the next week's conference. They were ordered to go through the books, find out exactly what funds they had available, what salaries they paid and what their expenses were for machinery, materials, electricity and services. The *nachal'nik*s were annoyed by the order – they were builders, not 'office rats'! – but they did dive into the maze of 'socialist accounting' and interviewed their subordinates, the *master*s and the *prorab*s. At the conference, each *nachal'nik* reported in full and then endured energetic questioning by the Chief Engineer. It immediately became apparent that he had been conducting a thorough investigation of his own.[45]

The review conference contributed to what was to become a pattern at every new job: at first, Yeltsin was intensely disliked by his subordinates. 'We were', one of them recalls, 'like enemies.'[46] The managers of SU-13 nicknamed him 'Stalin': he was 'strict' and 'did not forgive'.[47] One day, a college friend of Yeltsin's, a fellow civil engineer who was in charge of ground work for a new building, overlooked a telephone cable, which was damaged as a result. Yeltsin ordered him to restore the cable overnight and the next morning signed an order firing the man. Never easily intimidated by his superiors, Yeltsin now flaunted his self-confidence. With others in his office, he would put the receiver on the desk when a boss whose professionalism he held in low esteem was on the telephone.[48]

Walking to work in the morning from the bus stop, Yeltsin pretended not to notice the SU-13 workers around him. His subordinates began to grumble. 'Who is this new jerk?' they would complain to Yeltsin's friend and colleague Sergey Peretrutov. '[He has his] nose up in the sky and refuses to say hello to us!' Peretrutov advised the offended men to hold fast and not greet Yeltsin first. After a few weeks, Yeltsin confided to Peretrutov: 'Listen, Sergey Ivanovich,* am I doing something wrong? You know, the people are turning away from me. Really, they are turning away . . .' Peretrutov suggested that Yeltsin look at himself. Yeltsin seemed genuinely surprised. 'But I . . . I was just following the rules of etiquette, the rules of subordination,' he said. Starting the following morning, however, Yeltsin began to say hello first, and the whole affair was soon forgotten.[49]

More difficult to repair was Yeltsin's relationship with his own boss, Nikolay Sitnikov, the *nachal'nik* of SU-13. The two had had a very inauspicious start, when four years before Sitnikov ended Yeltsin's volleyball career by forbidding him to take time off from work for competitions. 'You must choose,' he said, 'sport or work.' Another early sign of incompatibility was Sitnikov's habits of speech: like most Russian builders he was foul-mouthed, 'a terrible *matershinnik*'[50] – a trait which Yeltsin could tolerate only with great difficulty. One morning, after Sitnikov had loosed at his Chief Engineer a mighty volley over the telephone, Yeltsin replied: 'If you do that again, I will not speak to you.' Sitnikov responded with a still stronger torrent. Yeltsin hung up. When

---

* Ivanovich means 'son of Ivan'. Patronymics are always used in official documents and in polite address to adults.

Sitnikov called again, Yeltsin said: 'You, Nikolay Ivanovich, are a hooligan. I will not talk to you.' And he banged down the receiver.[51]

Often, chastising Yeltsin in his office, Sitnikov would pick up a chair for emphasis and make a step or two towards his obstreperous subordinate. Yeltsin would respond by seizing the chair closest to him. He would then move towards his boss and announce: 'I hope you are aware that if you make the slightest move, I will hit you first: my reaction is faster than yours.'[52] At least once a chair was actually used, albeit purely for demonstration. Driven to distraction by Sitnikov's harangues, Yeltsin lifted a chair and slammed it to the floor. The chair was smashed to pieces.[53]

The two frequently continued their debates while riding in Sitnikov's car. After a time, the furious Sitnikov would order the driver to stop the car and tell Yeltsin to get out. Yeltsin would refuse, demanding to be driven to the nearest tram stop. Sitnikov would repeat the order. Pushing out the younger, stronger and much taller Yeltsin was out of the question. For half an hour the car would stand motionless, as the amused driver observed the warring *nachal'nik*s. Eventually, Yeltsin would win and would be duly delivered to the nearest public transportation route.[54]

Sitnikov, of course, tried to have Yeltsin fired. He served his Chief Engineer with eighteen 'written reprimands'.[55] Ordinarily, half that amount would have sufficed for a dismissal. But the young engineer already had the best protector possible: the Sverdlovsk Gorkom ('City Committee') and, inside it, the Second Secretary, Fedor Morshakov. It may very well have been Morshakov who, in 1960, suggested to Yeltsin a strategic manoeuvre that would not only render him considerably less vulnerable to the Sitnikovs of the world but, more importantly, enable him to continue his spectacular career climb. Yeltsin was 'invited' to join the Communist Party.

The offer was hardly unexpected. It was, in a sense, a correction of an obvious oversight. The chief engineer of a large Construction Administration had to be a Party member. But, apparently, so impressed were the construction officials in the aftermath of the Kombinat triumph, so eager were they to have Yeltsin the wonderboy take over SU-13, that the Gorkom, the highest Party organ in the city, in whose nomenklatura* Yeltsin's new position was listed, chose to overlook the membership requirement.

Yeltsin's entrance into the Party was smooth. In his membership

---

* The term describes both the list of positions for which candidates must be vetted by a given Party body and the occupants of those positions.

request, submitted to the Party cell of the Yuzhgorstroy *trest*, the young Chief Engineer wrote: 'I request that you consider my application and admit me a candidate member of the CPSU, because I want to be active in the building of communism.'[56] Yeltsin prepared for the examining interview with customary diligence: he studied the Party rules, the Ustav, and the Programme of the Communist Party, and re-read Lenin, Marx and Engels.[57]

In their recommendations Yeltsin's colleagues noted that he was a 'qualified, knowledgeable and conscientious' engineer, who 'pays a lot of attention to new technologies and to the questions of implementation of progressive construction'.[58] The Buro or 'executive body' of the Chkalovskiy District Committee of Komsomol stated that he was 'disciplined, politically literate, morally sturdy' and a 'propagandist of a Komsomol cell' to boot.[59]

The only hurdle during the candidate's examination was thrown up by the *trest*'s Chief Accountant. He asked Yeltsin for the number of the page in *Das Kapital* on which Marx 'talked about commodity–money relations' under capitalism. Quite sure that his questioner had 'never held *Das Kapital* in his hands' Yeltsin bluffed instantly: 'Volume Two, page 387.' For a moment, the Chief Accountant affected pensiveness, then he said: 'Well done. You know Marx well.'[60]

On 17 March 1961, at the end of the mandatory year-long probation period, a closed meeting of the Party cell of Yuzhgorstroy convened to make a final decision. One of the speakers stated that during the past year Yeltsin had 'systematically raised his political education' and had taken courses at the evening University of Marxism–Leninism.[61] Another stressed the Chief Engineer's abilities as 'a good organizer' who 'had the respect of the collective'.[62] The only cautionary note was sounded by the cell's Secretary, A. Vinogradov, who said that 'Comrade Yeltsin was sometimes rude to the workers' and that he 'should make a note of this and not allow this to happen ever again'.[63] At the end, however, the meeting moved to 'admit Yeltsin, Boris Nikolaevich to membership of the CPSU'.

Boris Yeltsin thus became a member of the Communist Party of the Soviet Union. He was thirty: a rather late demonstration of loyalty for a career Party apparatchik, as his enemies would remind him twenty-six years later. Yet, for a successful construction manager, Yeltsin was not, apparently, late – at least as far as the Sverdlovsk Gorkom was concerned. And the Gorkom was all that mattered. The next year he was appointed the *nachal'nik* of SU-13.

*　　*　　*

It was during his year at the head of SU-13 that Yeltsin's work habits crystallized into a style of management easily recognizable at every job that followed. It was a style different from, indeed in many instances opposite to, that of a big Russian *nachal'nik*.

The new boss was never tardy either with his superiors or with his subordinates, 'not for a minute'.[64] Whatever their reason, engineers and construction supervisors who were as little as ten minutes late for a meeting were not admitted to the boss's office.[65] (He was just as strict with Naina. A fellow *nachal'nik*, who shared a hospital room with Yeltsin when the latter was recuperating from tonsilectomy, remembers that even when Naina was 'as much as one minute' late, Yeltsin 'would be sour through the entire visit'.)[66]

He abhorred *boltovnia*, 'empty talk'. One of his managers recalls the 'three key rules' for speakers at Yeltsin's staff meetings (*operativki*): 'to the point, briefly, and fast. Not ready? Say so! Do not get up to speak.'[67] When Yeltsin conducted *operativki*, one 'could hear a mosquito flying, so quiet was the room'.[68]

> My style of management has been called tough [Yeltsin wrote twenty-five years later]. And this is true. I demanded strict discipline and fulfilment of promises ... My main arguments have been my own total devotion to the work, exactingness, control over perform- ance ... He who works better, lives better and is better valued [by me]. Good, professional, quality work will not go unnoticed – and neither will substandard performance and slovenliness. If you have given your word, don't go back on it; if you do – you must be held responsible.[69]

Yeltsin never censured his subordinates in front of their superiors: 'he never said [that] somebody is to blame, [it was] always "I am to blame." '[70] But, with the bosses out of sight, Yeltsin 'demanded the world' of his staff.[71] He did not 'need *mat*' for emphasis: he was 'merci- lessly frank'.[72] Yet, quite uncommon for a Soviet *nachal'nik*, he also respected his subordinates' privacy, and never called anyone at home. 'Once he let a man go home, that was the end of it.'[73]

Yeltsin introduced 'directorates': picnics to celebrate the fulfilment of a plan. At these outings 'everything was allowed': talking about the past year's mistakes, arguing one's point of view, criticizing everyone, regardless of rank, including the boss. And, of course, they drank vodka, and Yeltsin drank like everyone else, and sang in a strong but pleasant baritone. But, a colleague insists, 'in all the fourteen years that we worked together I never saw him drunk'.[74]

In his year at SU-13, Yeltsin found a large and appreciative audience for a trait that was to become legendary: his memory. It was rare, a witness claims, even 'extraordinary'.[75] The boss knew almost every worker by first name and patronymic. Three or four palm-size pages from a notebook, with a few bullet points scribbled on them, was all that he needed even for a major business presentation.[76] These small white leaves, with improvised speeches jotted on them, would later feature at some of the most dramatic moments of his, and Russia's, history.

As Yeltsin was preparing to leave SU-13 in 1963, he worked late into the night, compiling for his successor a detailed report on the current projects. The report was then distributed at a meeting of the Buro of the Chkalovskiy Raikom of Sverdlovsk, where Yeltsin was invited to take his farewell. Suddenly, Lidiya Khudyakova, the Raikom's First Secretary, asked Yeltsin to make a presentation. Yeltsin protested: the members of the Buro had the written report in front of them. No, said Khudyakova, we want to hear from you. And, with 'just a bare desk surface in front of him', Yeltsin described the nature of the work, the scope of the operations, and the deadlines, with 'not a single number off'.[77]

At about that time, a clerk at the headquarters of the *trest* Yuzhgorstroy filled in the last lines in Yeltsin's personnel card. It stated that Yeltsin, Boris Nikolaevich, Russian by nationality, was born in the town of Butka (misspelled as Budka) and was a member of the official trade union. He lived on Eighth of March Street, No. 179(v), flat 10. His domestic passport number (566156) was registered in the militia headquarters No. 8, to be renewed in 1965. As did every Soviet college graduate, Yeltsin had a military rank (second lieutenant) and was in the 'active category' of the 'commanding corps'.

Page Two listed promotions: 5 January 1960 to Chief Engineer, and 12 February 1962 to *nachal'nik*. His salary in 1960 was listed as 2,400 rubles a year, or 200 rubles a month, a formidable sum in the Soviet Union at the time. Holidays were always taken in July. The 'State Awards' section was still empty, but, in an unintended pun, the clerk mistakenly listed there his wife Anastasia (born in 1932) and daughters Elena (1958) and Tat'yana (1960).

Indeed, engineer Yeltsin was now *paterfamilias*. 'Of course,' he later admitted, he had wanted a boy.[78] When, after Lena's birth, Naina was again pregnant, he 'followed all the traditions' to secure the wanted gender, including putting an axe and a cap under the pillow. Still, contrary to the assurances of the 'experts' that 'this time it would definitely be a boy', Tat'yana arrived.[79]*

The change in family status had little effect on Yeltsin's work routine. Even before the girls were born, 'to be the wife of Yeltsin was a feat in and of itself', remembers Naina's sister Galina. 'He worked like a man possessed. Many nights, Naina fell asleep waiting for her husband over a cold dinner.'[80] To drag Yeltsin to see the last showing at the cinema, Naina and her sister had to pick him up at work.[81]

After the girls were born, Naina was 'torn between the office and home'.[82] In her travails, she could not depend on the traditional backbone of Russian families, the grandmother: Klavdia Vasilievna had moved back to Butka and Naina's parents lived in Orenburg. (When the girls were still very young, Naina's parents died in a freak accident in Orenburg, crushed to death by a drunken motorcyclist.) Often, rushing to work in the morning, Naina would ask her neighbour, Katerina Dyagileva, to see that the girls had breakfast before they left for school, and check on them when they came back home to 'please make sure they are not hungry'.[83]

Later Yeltsin could not remember when and how the girls had begun to walk or talk.[84] In their ten school years, not once did he attend parents' meetings with the teachers.[85] His participation in his daughters' upbringing was limited largely to raising expectations and distributing tasks. When the girls began school, their father told them that the grade 4, or 'good', 'must not exist' for them – only 5, 'excellent'.[86] At night, Yeltsin wrote out for each of the girls, by then soundly asleep, 'what was to be done' the next day.[87] Once, waiting for her father to come home, one of the girls told Dyagileva: 'Auntie Katia, I have not fulfilled two points [on her father's list]. Papa will haul me over the coals.'[88]

During the week, Yeltsin rarely saw his daughters awake for more than a few minutes. But on some Sunday afternoons he took the family to the Great Ural restaurant for lunch. (For the girls, the much awaited culmination of the outing was ice-cream.)[89] A day after one of these Sunday trips, some old women who spent a great deal of time gossiping on the bench in front of the Yeltsins' apartment building said to Naina:

---

* Many years hence, Yeltsin's longing for a male offspring was finally answered with the arrival of Tat'yana's son, Boris. After Tat'yana divorced Boris's father and remarried, it was decided that the boy would keep the Yeltsin name. Of Yeltsin's three grandchildren, Boris junior is clearly his grandfather's favourite. From the age of seven, at Yeltsin's urging, the boy took up tennis and wrestling.

'Sweetie, we are so glad that you have finally got married, and you have such a good husband. How he was smiling at your daughters!' Naina looked at them bewildered: 'What husband? What daughters? This is their papa!' The women had thought Naina was a single mother.[90]

Lengthier rendezvous with the family had to wait until annual holidays. For Yeltsin, these were exclusively a family affair. Only once did he find himself – in a sanatorium in Kislovodsk in the Caucasus – without Naina. After five days he sent her a telegram: 'Join me immediately. Cannot stand [being without you].'[91] The girls were too young to travel. Naina had to leave them with friends and hurried to her husband.

The two 'most memorable holidays' of Yeltsin's life were those spent with Naina and the daughters in a tent at a lakeside in northern Russia and on the Black Sea coast. 'The laughter never stopped. All day long we joked, played tricks on one another and thought up all sorts of funny quizzes.'[92] That was, Yeltsin wrote, 'a real rest, psychological and moral relaxation'.[93] Later, those interludes of family tranquillity would become impossible to recreate: Yeltsin would remember them as the last ones during which he did not 'think of work from the first to the last day'.[94]

On those increasingly rare occasions when Yeltsin found time for friends, the old Boris reappeared: an inexhaustible fount of merriment, exuberance and hospitality. Once, on a December evening in the late 1950s, he presented a female college friend with a basket of flowers for her birthday. The cost of the present, which must have equalled a greater part of his monthly salary as starting engineer, amazed his friends less than finding flowers in Sverdlovsk in the winter: 'they were impossible to get in principle!'[95]

For all his friendliness, the young engineer well knew his worth. He made no secret of the stringent selection criteria for those whom he admitted into his circle. 'Too early; [he] must grow to measure up,' was Yeltsin's frequent response to a suggestion that a new person be invited to a party.[96] It was not an official post that determined acceptance: most of Yeltsin's closest friends never reached the higher managerial spheres. Instead, recalls a friend, 'it was important [for Yeltsin] that a person had proved, by deed, his professional competence and his moral fastidiousness – the two qualities Yeltsin valued most in people'.[97]

Those judged worthy of his friendship were generously treated to the Yeltsin camaraderie: a strong blend of undying loyalty, trust and boundless enthusiasm for companionship. When, after graduation from the UPI, he and his friends decided to holiday together every five years, Yeltsin was elected chairman of the 'organizing committee', a post he retained for the next fifteen years until his friends decided to relieve him of this duty because of his workload. Not once during the next thirty-five years was the tradition broken. The choices of the organizing committee were never state rest homes or sanatoriums. Instead, the group – with the arrival of the children, it eventually grew to eighty-seven people – hiked in the Ural Mountains, camped on the shore of the Black Sea and travelled on board an excursion ship down the Volga river and up the Enisey to the Arctic Ocean.[98] The children in the group were tasked by Yeltsin with taking turns to keep a detailed travel journal, noting which ports they stopped at, which islands were passed, which rivers crossed and what plants and animals seen. At the end of the trip, the children presented the journal to the parents.[99]

The choice of the holiday format clearly reflected the preferences of the chairman of the organizing committee. For him, there was only active leisure. Fishing, a Russian national male pastime, left him cold: only once did his colleagues at SU-13 prevail upon him to join them.[100] On Sunday evenings he played volleyball. In the winter, there was cross-country skiing.[101]

The only sedentary pastime Yeltsin appeared to permit himself was watching, together with the entire Russian male population, the pride of Soviet sports: the unbeatable national hockey team. The world and European championships were held in Western Europe (Vienna, Prague or Helsinki) and, because of the time difference, Soviet television broadcasts of these matches lasted well into the night. This rare violation of the rules (at the time, Soviet television closed down for the night between eleven and midnight) afforded Yeltsin an unusual opportunity to watch TV after work. Long after Naina and the girls had gone to bed, he would cross the landing to watch hockey with his neighbour, Ivan Dyagilev. Yeltsin would bring a bottle of Armenian brandy, Ararat, and Dyagilev would supply another delicacy, instant coffee. Yeltsin, Dyagilev recalls, 'never drank more than a shot, never more'.

In April 1963 Boris Yeltsin was appointed Chief Engineer of the newly created Homebuilding Kombinat (Domostroitel'niy Kombinat, or DSK), a *trest*-like giant organization which employed 1,854 workers,[102] had its own concrete-making plant and consisted of eight constituent *upravlenie*s, each the size of the SU-13 he had just headed.[103]

At his first *operativka*, Boris met his subordinates: grey-haired, veteran builders, most with the highest government decorations, some even members of the Buro of the Obkom, or Party Regional Committee. The youngest was fifteen years older than Yeltsin.[104] Yet the Chief Engineer saw no need for any change in his style of management. He was every bit as confident and businesslike at his first *operativka* at the Kombinat as he had been at SU-13. Of course, a witness reports, the *nachal'nik*s 'smirked' at the thirty-two-year-old boss: 'molodoy da ranniy', as the Russian saying goes, 'young but early', or 'too big for your breeches'.[105] There were no smirks at the second *operativka*, before which Yeltsin had been seen visiting the sites at six, sometimes even at five in the morning. This time, the *nachal'nik*s 'listened carefully': Yeltsin knew their sites as well as, if not better than, they did.[106]

Those who hoped for a quiet life were quickly disabused. 'He was always searching for something – something better, something new,' recalls one of the Kombinat's managers. 'He would torture everyone with this search.'[107] 'Yeltsin always approached each task with a view to finding a solution which might not be the simplest but was always the most spectacular,' said a former DSK engineer. 'It was important for him to turn a routine work task into an event.'[108] He ordered, for instance, the preparation of a 'model' apartment building – to serve as the quality standard. These models were ready for tenants immediately at the end of construction – not after months of repairs and repeated visits by the accepting commission. He himself checked the buildings and approved their 'move-in' condition by issuing special certificates (*pasport*s).[109]

At the time, the fad in Soviet construction was the 'complex' (multi-operation) *brigada*, which began and finished a building on its own, performing all the construction jobs: from the digging of the foundation pit to the installation of the last tap. As with other such 'movements' which periodically swept Soviet industry, the 'movement of complex brigades' was accompanied by a deafening propaganda campaign.

Shortly after his arrival at the DSK, Yeltsin assembled his own 'complex' brigade. It was staffed with fifty of his best workers and received all the necessary materials without delay. The brigade was 'noticed'. It became known 'all over the Soviet Union', and was awarded a medal at the All-Union Exhibition of People's Economy.[110] For its creator, the yield of the 'noticeable' brigade was unexpectedly large and swift.

Less than two years after Yeltsin became Chief Engineer, at a meeting of the Glavk, Yeltsin's boss, the *nachal'nik* of the DSK, Arkadiy Mikunis, proceeded to extol the exploits of the famous *brigada*. The head of the Glavk, Nikolay Girenko, interrupted Mikunis and demanded to know if the *nachal'nik* himself had met the members of the brigade face to face. A man in his mid-sixties, a much decorated builder and construction boss for many years, Mikunis had to admit that he had not. Embarrassed, he sat down without finishing his presentation.

Girenko then pushed one of the half-dozen coloured buttons on his telephone and said, 'Get me Yeltsin!'

Yeltsin, as usual, was away on a site. He was tracked down and, an hour later, brought to the august gathering. 'Tell us, Boris Nikolaevich, how are things at the Kombinat?' Girenko asked. Yeltsin protested: 'My boss is here, I do not feel it is appropriate for me to report.' 'Let me decide whom to ask! I want to hear your opinion,' Girenko replied. And, 'snatched' off the building site as he was, with 'no paper or anything in front of him', Yeltsin described in minute detail the many projects of the Kombinat. When the celebrated *brigada* came up for discussion, each member was identified by name and patronymic, and his or her tasks explained in detail. Turning to the pale Mikunis, Girenko said: 'Here is how you should report!'[111] The same day, Mikunis had a heart attack and was soon pensioned off. Three weeks later, Yeltsin reached the pinnacle of his building career: the *nachal'nik* of the huge DSK. He was thirty-four.

Now a full-fledged member of the Soviet industrial nomenklatura, Yeltsin was as insistent on moulding the position to his specifications as he had been when he was a novice *master*. He began with the customary quest for self-sufficiency. A practitioner–builder, he knew very little about large-scale accounting. In his first week on the job as the *nachal'nik* of the DSK, he ordered the chief accountant to get him the textbooks on accounting. He studied at night and in the morning asked the accountant to explain to him things he did not understand.[112]

Another breach of protocol concerned the business presentations, the *doklad*s. They had long been written by the heads of the DSK divisions, who were Yeltsin's deputies, but the *nachal'nik* decided to write them himself. He 'never used somebody else's writing', a witness reports.[113] Instead, he called those concerned into his office, asked them questions and, in the evening, sat down, opened the familiar small pad, wrote a few lines on a page, and tore the page out to serve as his prepared text. He always spoke briefly 'with no superfluous words'.[114] As before, he was helped by an excellent memory, which allowed him to 'keep all the numbers in his head'.[115] All the staff meetings began on time. 'We checked our watches by him,' said Yeltsin's manager. 'He was never a minute late. He taught us to be punctual and he began with himself.'[116]

Soon after taking over the DSK, Yeltsin began making adjustments to institutional traditions. One of those changed was the leadership picnic held to celebrate the Glavk's approval of the annual report. When the time came, Yeltsin notified the managers that, instead of being funded out of the 'state's pocket', the money for the picnic would, from that point on, have to come from the picnickers themselves. As was his wont, he began with himself by putting on the Chief Accountant's desk a twenty-five-ruble bill for transportation and food.

This break with custom proved too sudden for the managers. Instead of following Yeltsin's order, they quietly deducted the necessary sum from the employees' salaries. Soon after the picnic, rumours about this ploy began to reach Yeltsin. He ordered the errant managers into his office, where he demanded and received a confession of guilt. The managers were then told to reimburse each of the employees involved out of their own salaries, 'everything to the last kopeck'. 'Remember,' Yeltsin said as he finished his admonition, 'embezzlement of state funds will not be condoned here any longer.'[117]

At the DSK Yeltsin continued his SU-13 routine: coming to work at seven in the morning and rarely leaving before nine at night. The official car, which Yeltsin now had at his disposal, was used only for visits to construction sites during the working day. Yeltsin's chauffeur, Volodya, came in at nine and was let go at six. To and from work Yeltsin travelled by public transport.[118]

He felt restless in his office and went into the 'field' at every opportunity. Every Monday of every week he 'worked with the *brigada*s': visiting as many as he physically could to see 'who worked and how they worked'. Do they have enough supplies? Are they given enough work? What do they need?[119] Both the City Party Committee and the City Soviet* were told not to call Yeltsin on Mondays. These excursions, of course, were necessary for keeping in good repair an essential ingredient of Yeltsin's style of management: 'to know the subject at least as well as the subordinates; if possible, better'.[120] In the evening he would call the sites' *nachal'nik*s and inquire, casually, about the goings-on. 'You knew that he had visited at least one site that day, but you did not know which,' remembers one of them. 'It could very well have been yours. And so you could not lie to him: the risk was too great.'[121]

Every now and then, the yield of these expeditions was quite dramatic. Once, late at night, an entire brigade of fitters became drunk at one of the Kombinat's sites and stopped all work on the night shift. Still in the office when the news arrived, Yeltsin went to investigate, at two in the

---

* Although nominally independent and 'elected' in keeping with the myth of 'Soviet power', the City Soviet was, in fact, subordinate to the City Party Committee, which supervised its work, cleared candidates for 'elections' and effectively appointed the Chairman. Of course, all candidates in such elections were those pre-approved by the City Party Committee.

morning and on foot, since the buses were no longer running. By the time the inspection was over, it was too late to go home. He went straight back to his office and ordered the brigade to come see him right away. One by one, the still groggy fitters were called into the office for a session with the boss. For a long time after that early-morning lecture the fitters 'forgot how vodka flowed from the bottle's neck'.[122]

The young *nachal'nik* was just as stern with the headquarters staff. He is remembered as 'unusually strict' and 'exacting' towards himself and others. It was not easy to deal with Yeltsin at the office:[123] he made his subordinates 'self-conscious' and 'a bit fearful'.[124] He was 'deliberately formal, rather cold and distant' and 'he accepted no excuses'.[125] He was never 'soft' or 'nice': when he had to, he 'twisted arms' and 'wrung necks'.[126] Yet, when he wanted to, 'he could find ways to charm people and have them do what he wanted'. At those moments, it was 'hard to believe' that he was the same stiff-necked taskmaster.[127]

As at SU-13, Yeltsin at first had difficulty calibrating the social format of his newly acquired power. When he walked up the stairs to his office in the morning – usually taking two steps at a time – he again failed to greet his subordinates. The rumbling reached the supreme enforcer of office mores: the secretary of the Kombinat's Party organization. At the end of a business meeting, he told Yeltsin that there had been 'signals' that 'Boris Nikolaevich was not saying hello to the workers'. 'Who told you? Name the names!' thundered Yeltsin. The secretary wisely refused. Yeltsin paused for a moment and then said: 'I apologize to everyone. This will never happen again.' He kept his word.[128]

As the DSK began to exceed its planned quota ('and not just annually, but each quarter') and to win the all-Union 'socialist competition' among the construction organizations of its size, salaries rose, bonuses 'flowed' and the new boss began to be liked despite his continuing *strogiy* (tough and exacting) style.[129] The *nachal'nik*'s popularity further improved when he introduced another novelty: a uniform for the DSK workers. These were not the shapeless, grey, one-size-fits-all jackets (*robas*) of Soviet construction sites, but spiffy blue cotton overalls with the DSK emblem on the front. These were sewn individually for each worker – a rare luxury in the Soviet Union.

By that time, Yeltsin appeared to have found the right tenor in his relationship with his subordinates. When he attended office parties around the New Year, May Day and 7 November (the anniversary of the 1917 Bolshevik Revolution), he was 'absolutely different' from the unsparing overseer at the office. He sang in his strong baritone and proved to be a formidable practitioner of the Russian folk art of 'spoon playing': tucking several aluminium spoons from the office cafeteria between the fingers of one hand and striking them against the palm of the other.[130]

And, of course, he continued to experiment. ' "How can this be done better?" This was the question he seemed to struggle with at all times,' said a former DSK manager. 'He was charged with it, it was in his genes.'[131] One of Yeltsin's innovations at the DSK was 'fully completed' housing, 'as in the West'.[132] Each floor was 'stuffed' with amenities (windows, plumbing, doors, toilets, bathtubs) right away rather than after the entire building had been completed, as was usual. Vandalism and thievery at Soviet construction sites made this a risky strategy. Yet Yeltsin calculated that, even with some appliances stolen, some window panes and doors broken, it was still faster and cheaper to 'complete each floor fully' right away than to 'go back to it' later, as was the traditional Soviet practice.[133]

Another novel exercise was erecting five-storey apartment buildings in five days of round-the-clock frenzy[134] – instead of the usual months of the traditional Soviet effort. 'Everything was scheduled to the minute': which *brigada* did what, when it entered the building, how fast it pro- ceeded from floor to floor. Three cranes worked night and day. Con- struction panels were pre-positioned throughout the site next to a network of rails, saving a great deal of time. Of course, there was no shortage of hard-to-get materials during this experiment.[135]

This industrial equivalent of street theatre, this labour *Sturm und Drang*, was utterly irrelevant to the chaotic and lackadaisical routine of the Soviet construction site, plagued by shortages and truancy. But it was, most certainly, 'noticeable'. And, unlike in his salad days, Yeltsin no longer relied on word of mouth to procure publicity. For instance, he showcased his innovations at an all-Union conference on 'modern methods of construction', which he organized in Sverdlovsk.[136] On another occasion, a DSK manager overheard the boss considering out loud whom he should invite for the show: the Obkom or a building administration of the next rung. 'Who cares, Boris Nikolaevich! What's the difference?' the manager, Artur Ezhov, said to Yeltsin at the time. 'Come now, Artur,' replied Yeltsin. 'I see that you are not a politician. What do you mean, "no difference"? There is a big difference!'[137] In this case, the wisely chosen audience was the Obkom.

Most likely, the word went directly to Yakov Ryabov, the Second Secretary of the Sverdlovsk Regional Party Committee. A UPI graduate, like Yeltsin, he headed the Sverdlovsk Gorkom until 1966 and had 'recommended'[138] Yeltsin for the DSK directorship. By that time,

Ryabov had come to depend on Yeltsin for an important service. The Sverdlovsk province was a favourite playground for the immensely rich Soviet military–industrial complex and defence-related 'heavy' industry. Never short of cash, the generals ordered more and more plants to be built, and Ryabov, who was a mechanical engineer by training, chose the young, energetic and already renowned builder as his unofficial adviser on construction matters.[139] In this capacity, Yeltsin travelled to the most important sites, assessed progress and then briefed the Party boss. Accompanying 'high guests' from Moscow to the more important construction sites, Ryabov dazzled them with his expertise.[140]

In 1966, a year after he took over the DSK, Yeltsin received his first government award: the Order Znak Pochyota, 'Sign of Esteem'. According to Ryabov, who had recommended the young director for the distinction, Yeltsin would have received the highest award, the Order of Lenin, but, around that time, one of the 'experimental' large-panel buildings collapsed.[141] Two years later, when 'a need arose to strengthen the Construction Department of the Regional Party Committee',[142] Ryabov recommended Yeltsin to head the Department (or *odtel*). Only seven years into his Party membership Yeltsin found himself on the middle rung of a very tall ladder reaching to the Kremlin heaven. Before the decision became final, Ryabov told Yeltsin of complaints about his toughness towards subordinates. 'I am doing this for the good of the cause!' Yeltsin answered. 'I know, I know,' said Ryabov, 'but still . . .'[143]

Summing up his career as construction manager, Yeltsin noted proudly that he had been 'fortunate' to be an absolute sovereign of smaller domains rather than deputy king of larger ones: 'I have never been anyone's deputy. I was the *nachal'nik* of a site – and not deputy *nachal'nik* of an *upravlenie*; the *nachal'nik* of an *upravlenie* but not deputy chief of a *trest*.'[144]

When he was leaving the Kombinat for the Obkom, Yeltsin was surprised to see tears in the eyes of his staff.[145] Twenty-one years later, in 1989, many DSK offices looked 'like a Yeltsin museum' – so many photographs of him were kept on the walls by his former subordinates.[146]

Although Boris Yeltsin had become a mid-level provincial Party official, he remained what he had been all his life: a builder. Only now he worked as a regional construction manager of the Party-run corporation called the Soviet economy. 'The Party work was less than half of our duties,' recalls Yeltsin's subordinate, a staffer (*instruktor*) of the Construction Department.[147] The days were filled with maintaining working order both on the 'front line', the construction sites of the province, and in the 'rear', production and maintenance of machinery, bricks, concrete, paints, wood, metal fittings.[148] Unable, despite incessant propaganda campaigns, to increase productivity and eliminate waste, the Party was prosecuting the daily 'labour battle' the only way it knew how: by throwing into the fray the ever increasing supplies of labour and resources embodied in newer and larger factories and plants.

The Obkom was the centre of gravity of economic life in the province and the ultimate arbiter of frequent disputes between local *nachal'nik*s of all ranks. It was there that the industrial nomenklatura reported, fought for its priorities and received orders.[149] Like other Obkom departments (industry, agriculture, health, education) Yeltsin's *otdel* prepared background and recommendations for Obkom decisions on construction matters. It was up to the head (*zaveduushiy*, or *zav*) of the Construction Department, as Yeltsin now was, to decide on local building priorities and to recommend where millions of rubles and as many work-hours were to be spent.

Once *ob'ekt*s were approved and tasks assigned, the Department oversaw the implementation. The *otdel* often assisted in linking the builders with the suppliers of construction materials and machines – no mean feat in the institutional labyrinths of the Soviet economy. As the deadline for an important *ob'ekt* approached, the Department of Construction developed a final schedule and then made it official either through Obkom 'resolutions' or through the decisions of lower Party organizations, subordinated to the Obkom.[150]

As a rule, the routine taskmastering was done by the Department's *instruktor*s. But in cases of especially pernicious institutional recalcitrance, negligence or fierce competition for resources a case was taken to the *zav*. On rare occasions, Yeltsin had to go to enforcers at a higher level, the Obkom Secretaries. They, in turn, if need be, would call the Party Olympus: the Central Committee in Moscow. 'Most of our time was spent organizing production and work at the large projects,'[151] recalls one of Yeltsin's *instruktor*s. That meant renovation of ageing enterprises of heavy industry, and the construction of new ones, such as the giant steel mill in Nizhniy Tagil. Along the way, Yeltsin dealt with projects ranging from the water-purification facilities for the city of Sverdlovsk to the construction of a mechanized poultry farm, which helped alleviate the perennial meat shortages in the province. Twenty-five years later, the farm still supplied Sverdlovsk with chickens.[152]

Most of the Party work of the Construction Department was 'work with the cadres', selecting and vetting construction managers for positions that fell within the nomenklatura range of the Obkom. That included all the top jobs in the construction field: the *nachal'nik*s of building administrations, directors of cement and armature plants and factories, chief engineers of construction enterprises, even the editor of the construction section of the regional newspaper *Ural'skiy Rabochiy*.

The *instruktor*s would drop by a candidate's workplace, and chat with his co-workers, fishing for rumours of political infirmities or moral rot. The visit inevitably ended with a closed-door session with the head of the enterprise's Party committee. If the net came up empty of signs of social or political unreliability, the *instruktor* invited the candidate to the Obkom for a chat. If the impression remained favourable, the *instruktor* reported to the *zav* and began preparations for a presentation of his charge to the final arbiter, the Buro of the Obkom.[153]

When Yeltsin moved to the Obkom, he suddenly disappeared from the daily circuit of business meetings. His former colleagues began to suspect that 'Boris was lost, stuck in the bureaucratic swamp.'[154] He would not have been the first – or the last. Instead, as it turned out, Yeltsin was exploring his bailiwick: the hundreds of construction sites of the huge province.[155] This temporary absence would become a prelude to every new job that Yeltsin took: a long initial solitary pause devoted to an intense, often round-the-clock study of a new field of responsibilities. Yeltsin liked to emerge grandly, like Athena out of Zeus' head: fully armed and ready for battle.

After a few weeks, the new *zav* of the Construction Department, having mastered the detail, started to mould the job with his customary drive. As before, 'seeing for himself' was the pivot around which the daily routine revolved. With his tenacious mind and memory, a walk through the *ob'ekt* invariably yielded 'problems with management and labour organization' at the construction site, which were duly presented to those in charge.[156]

Gradually, the new boss began to gain the respect of the professionals he was appointed by the Party to lead. First, the builders of the Sverdlovsk province established to their satisfaction that 'in civil engineering he was a professional of the highest order'.[157] The directors of *upravlenie*s and *nachal'nik*s of the *trest*s were impressed by his ability to get to the heart of the matter and to structure and present his impressions and suggestions in an effective and constructive way.[158] Those who now took orders from him soon saw that he was a 'deciding man'.[159] Perspective and strategic planning were Yeltsin's hobby, recalls a former *instruktor*.[160]

In 1970, Yeltsin ordered a repeat performance of the DSK construction theatre: a five-storey building in five days. This time, however, the audience was not just the Obkom but an all-Union conference on the Scientific Organization of Labour (known by the acronym NOT) – at the time, another temporary rage of the Party's industrial policy.[161] Yeltsin was the 'soul' of the conference,[162] which, although its organizer was only the head of the Construction Department of an Obkom, had the imprimatur of the Central Committee.[163] Three years later he organized another all-Union affair: a seminar on the renovation of industrial enterprises.[164]

The new *zav* ruled the Construction Department's permanent staff of six with a familiar combination of distance, exactitude, attention to detail and abhorrence of wasted time. The official workday began at nine, and Yeltsin arrived no later than eight. Every morning he conducted a staff meeting at which the staff reported on current projects. Yeltsin listened and asked questions, always precise and clear, to which he demanded precise and clear answers. His time and that of his interlocutors was precious: 'he could speak to a person and convey what he needed without a single superfluous minute'. The meeting never lasted longer than half an hour.[165]

It was not easy to see the boss afterwards: his 'every day was planned to the minute'. The *instruktor*s could have an appointment but only on substantive matters, several questions at a time, and for no longer than fifteen minutes. Sometimes he called an *instruktor* in, but never more often than once a day. 'Working with him was not easy,' recalls an *instruktor*. 'He never allowed us to waste time on second-rate issues. [We were to bring up] only what was important.'[166]

The new *zav* was not overly familiar with his staff, and did not flirt with the women. He never raised his voice either, and never used the *mat*. 'I think he simply did not know those [foul] words,' said a former *instruktor*, who worked under Yeltsin for five years.[167] Still, without the traditional cursing and yelling of a Soviet bureaucrat, Yeltsin managed to convey to his subordinates that, if he tasked a person, the boss would see that it was done.[168] 'We were', a former staffer reports, 'somewhat afraid' of the boss.[169]

For the first time in Yeltsin's career his job involved public speaking, though only on special occasions, and the results were quite auspicious. One day, for example, he addressed the mourners at the funeral of one of the *nachal'nik*s of a giant *trest*, a much decorated Hero of Socialist Labour, the Soviet Union's highest civilian honour. Yeltsin spoke briefly and without official clichés. 'We were amazed at Yeltsin's ability to find the right, very personal words at this largely official ceremony,' recalled a former *instruktor*. Although he had long forgotten the exact words,

Viktor Popov remembered 'for the rest of [his] life' the feeling that Yeltsin's address conveyed.

Two years after he had joined the Regional Party Committee, Yeltsin received a medal 'For Distinguished Labour'. Four years later, in 1974, he was decorated with his first serious order, the Red Banner of Labour, for supervising the construction of the steel mill at the Nizhniy Tagil Metalworks Kombinat. In 1975 he was given another medal: 'Thirtieth Anniversary of the Victory in the Great Patriotic War 1941–1945'. The medal was intended for veterans, and Yeltsin was fourteen when the war ended. But his nomenklatura rank entitled him to the award and he duly received it.

It was at this time that Yeltsin began to be directly affected by a key arrangement of the Soviet political system: the non-monetary remuneration of the Soviet political elite. Yeltsin's reaction was not so much a conscious protest as a strange lack of curiosity about the daily rituals of the initiated, an indifference to the key status symbol of the Soviet state. This attitude first surfaced when Yeltsin was still the *nachal'nik* of the DSK. One Saturday afternoon, the head of one of the Kombinat's divisions knocked on the door of Yeltsin's apartment. Under his arm he had a tightly wrapped parcel. Yeltsin opened the door: 'Here, Boris Nikolaevich, look at this present I have for you.' Yeltsin understood right away: 'Evgeniy Ivanovich, take it back where it came from.' And he shut the door.

Saddened and confused, the nomenklatura present-bearer rang the bell of the flat of his, and Yeltsin's, colleague Ivan Dyagilev, who lived opposite the Yeltsins on the same landing. Evgeniy did not know what to do with the parcel. Would Dyagilev take it? Of course Dyagilev would. The parcel was 'first class', Dyagilev remembers, full of delicacies every Russian dreamed of: caviar, hard salami, sturgeon.[170] It was well worth the 147 rubles Dyagilev promptly paid for it. He then gave his friend Evgeniy a shot of vodka and saw him to the door. Next morning, Dyagilev's wife Katerina began baking a pie with the sturgeon. Just as she was finishing, Naina Yeltsina dropped by, hungrily sniffed the air, and asked how they had obtained the sturgeon. The Dyagilevs told her of their sudden windfall. Naina showed the family no hard feelings.[171]

A week after Yeltsin became the *zav* of the Construction Department, he was visited by the Obkom's 'nurse administrator' (*sestra-khozyayka*). A venerable Soviet institution, the 'nurse' was a kind of nomenklatura den mother, whose duty was to procure maximum comfort for the labouring leaders. She asked Yeltsin about his food request (*zakaz*) for the next two weeks. The *zakaz* was to be delivered from a special food depot. Oh the magic word, *zakaz*! The most tangible of the proofs of belonging to the rulers of the land, a tasty reminder of one's elevation above the crazed, sweaty, cursing queues of hapless compatriots battling each other for scrawny, hairy chickens, sausage with bits of paper and entrails in it, or frozen fish.

Yeltsin was puzzled and embarrassed. No, he did not think he would need anything. They were fine. He had a wife, thank God, she bought everything. And sometimes he himself shopped. Thanks, we have everything. When the amazed *sestra-khozyayka* shared this strange story with the rest of the Obkom, 'they thought he was crazy'.[172]

He seemed equally cool towards another Soviet status symbol: a large apartment. Until the nomenklatura rules forced him to move into a special apartment building for the provincial leadership, Yeltsin was perfectly happy with the dream of the Soviet *hoi polloi*: a one-bedroom apartment for a family of four in a regular housing project. While always clean and orderly, the apartment contained nothing but 'proletarian furniture'.[173] The only exception was that embodiment of Soviet provincial chic: a suite of Bulgarian bedroom furniture. Even when Yeltsin was the *nachal'nik* of the Kombinat, his refrigerator was old and smaller than that of his neighbour.[174]

The one thing the Yeltsins' apartment contained in unusual quantity was books. The shelves had been made by the owner himself, although, comments a witness, he 'could easily have ordered' them made by one of countless *brigada*s in his command: that would have been 'normal, even traditional'.[175] But the owner liked to do things himself. When Yeltsin was the Secretary for Construction, he proudly displayed to a friend a home-made contraption which sprayed whitewash on the walls using a vacuum-cleaner exhaust.[176]

Still, Yeltsin's entrance into the ruling class was accompanied by the most cherished of rewards the Soviet system bestowed on the deserving: the ability to travel abroad. In 1964 and 1966 he holidayed in Bulgaria and Rumania.[177] After he joined the Obkom, his vacation destination was upgraded to Sweden and Finland (1971). Business trips took him to France (1966, in a delegation from Gosstroy, the Soviet Union's chief building authority), Cuba (1970, in a Central Committee delegation) and France again (1974). In 1975 he led the regional Party delegation to Czechoslovakia.

There was only one nomenklatura privilege that Yeltsin avidly availed himself of: tickets for first-night performances in Sverdlovsk's three theatres. Naina on his arm, he went to them all: opera and ballet, musical comedy and drama.[178] When Russia's best repertory theatre company, Moscow Art Academic Theatre, established by Konstantin Stanislavskiy and known throughout the Soviet Union by the acronym MKhAT, came to Sverdlovsk in 1975, Yakov Ryabov (by now First Secretary) had a picture of the leading actors taken on Labour Square in front of the Obkom. There were only three members of the Obkom on hand: Ryabov, the proud host; Lidiya Khudyakova, the *zav* of the Culture Department, which covered theatres; and the Secretary for Construction, Boris Yeltsin. (He was promoted in April 1975.) In the photograph he stands next to the celebrated actor Oleg Tabakov.

This was not an obligatory, official function: otherwise, accompanying the 'First', Ryabov, there would have been at least a dozen Party functionaries. Yeltsin did not have to be there at all: his bailiwick could not have been further from the subject matter. He was there because he wanted to be: on the square, with the actors.

CHAPTER 3

The Pervyi

FOR OFFICEHOLDERS OF YELTSIN'S RANK, there had never been in the Soviet Union anything approaching established rules of advancement. Party etiquette prohibited even admitting to knowing of a pending promotion, much less lobbying for it. The myth of the omniscient, arbitrary and omnipotent Centre, what George Orwell called the 'mystique of the Party',[1] was upheld by the feigned surprise of the chosen at their sudden good fortune. In affecting, even a decade later, complete ignorance of his coming elevation to the next step of the nomenklatura ladder, Yeltsin followed the ritual charade.[2]

True, after his meteoric career in construction, Yeltsin's advancement within the Obkom hierarchy had been somewhat slow. It took him seven long years, from 1968 to 1975, to graduate from being the head of an Obkom department to becoming a Secretary. Yeltsin was deeply offended and hurt by the delay in promotion. 'Those seven years were not the best for him,' remembered a former Obkom colleague. 'He took it very hard when he did not play the leading role.'[3] He was temperamentally unsuited, as a former high Sverdlovsk official put it, 'to stay put for more than five years without growing restless, moody, sour'.[4] Yakov Ryabov called this Yeltsin's 'obsessive ambition'.[5]

To the trained eyes and noses of the Obkom staffers, the portents of Yeltsin's promotion were unmistakable. Of the three Obkom Secretaries, Yeltsin was manifestly the best liked by Ryabov and the closest to him. Ryabov said later that the only reason he had not made Yeltsin the Second Secretary, in effect his deputy, was to enable Yeltsin to 'acquire broad experience' within the Obkom apparatus.[6] Meanwhile, to facilitate the Yeltsin succession, Ryabov appointed as Second Secretary Evgeniy Korovin, whom he judged much inferior to Yeltsin in 'organizational ability, forcefulness and even health'.[7] The final portent materialized in October 1976 when Yeltsin was sent to attend a course for 'the retraining of leading cadres' at the Central Committee's Academy of Social Sciences in Moscow. The Academy was the road station where virtually all rising Party stars made a stop on their way up. Ryabov himself had been among its students before he took over the province.

Thus, when Ryabov was promoted to Secretary of the Central Committee (to oversee the Soviet defence industry) and was ordered to Moscow within days of Yeltsin's departure for the Academy, the identity of his successor was quite obvious – and most certainly so to the protégé himself. With characteristic directness, Ryabov stated a decade and a half later: 'Yeltsin writes in his book that he did not know [of his coming promotion]. Of course he knew everything. I told him!'[8]

Still, appearances were kept up, with all the surprise and suspense required by the ritual. One morning, interrupting a lecture, the Dean of the Academy himself climbed on to the podium to announce that Yeltsin had been 'invited' to the Central Committee two hours later.[9]

The headquarters of the Soviet empire and world communism on Staraya Square was quiet, clean and businesslike. The pink carpet in the middle of the glistening parquet led visitors past the oak doors with their uniform nameplates stating just the initials and last name, whether for the lowliest aide or for a Politburo member – a tradition preserved, somehow, from the earliest days of Party rule. Along the walls, low thin-legged tables bore neatly arranged crystal siphon bottles and glasses.[10]

Yeltsin was first ushered into the office of Ivan Kapitonov, the Central Committee Secretary and the head of the Organizational Party Work Department. Small talk ensued. How are your studies at the Academy? What are relations like inside the Buro of the Obkom? Not a word, so far, about the reasons for the invitation.[11] The next stop was the office of Andrey Kirilenko, the Third Secretary in charge of the entire Party cadre. Again, the conversation was general, and nothing was said about the purpose of it all.[12] The final examiner in the Central Committee was Mikhail Suslov, the second most powerful man in the Soviet Union, the party's Ideologist-in-Chief. Here, Yeltsin noticed quickly, the conversation became 'more cunning'. Does Yeltsin have 'enough strength'? How well does he know the Sverdlovsk Party organization?[13] Still nothing definite.

But, as an experienced apparatchik, Yeltsin could hardly have expected more. The Pope personally appoints his Cardinals, and the General Secretary of the CPSU his local potentates. At the close of the Suslov interview, Yeltsin was told that he was invited to see Leonid Brezhnev, in the Kremlin.[14]

Accompanied, as tradition demanded, by the one who had recommended and the one who had cleared, Yakov Ryabov and Ivan Kapitonov, Yeltsin was promptly admitted into the General Secretary's office. Brezhnev got up from a vast desk, and they shook hands. 'So', he said, 'is this the one who is about to seize power in the Sverdlovsk province?'[15] Kapitonov replied hurriedly that Yeltsin knew nothing. 'What do you mean, "does not know"?' persisted a jovial Brezhnev. 'How could he not know if he has already decided to seize power?'[16] Then, back to the script at last, Brezhnev announced that the Politburo had sat and had decided to 'recommend' Yeltsin for First Secretary (Pervyi) of the Sverdlovsk Obkom.

'And so?' asked Brezhnev, this time seriously. Yeltsin responded with ritual platitudes: total surprise . . . the huge Party organization . . . great responsibility . . . would do his best to justify the trust . . . As they got up to part, Brezhnev, almost apologetically, mentioned that Yeltsin was not a member of the Central Committee nor a Deputy of the Supreme Soviet of the USSR[17] – the usual *ex officio* titles of the First Secretary of such an important province. Not 'yet', Brezhnev said pointedly. Presiding over the most predictable of all Soviet regimes, in which 'respect for cadres' was elevated to the cardinal rule, the General Secretary knew what *his* obligations to Party cardinals were. The 'yet' held the firm promise of delivery. 'And don't dawdle convening a Plenum,' were the General Secretary's parting words.

There was no dawdling. A Plenum of the Sverdlovsk Obkom took place a few days later. The Politburo's 'recommendation', personally delivered by the deputy head of the Organizational Party Work Department, Evgeniy Razumov, carried the day. On 2 November 1976 Boris Yeltsin became First Secretary of the Sverdlovsk Regional Committee of the Communist Party of the Soviet Union.[18]

Obkom First Secretaries have been compared, rather ingeniously, to French *préfets*.[19] This is a very strained parallel. Although, like the original *préfets*, invented by Napoleon, the Pervyis were unelected officials responsible for the maintenance of law and order in their provinces and enjoying control over all officials and bureaucracies there, the degree of their mastery over the provinces, the concentration of power delegated to them by the totalitarian state and the virtually limitless scope of its application were unprecedented in modern Western European history.

Having stood Marx on his head by subjugating the economy to politics, the Party granted its local representatives mastery over local industries. In the Soviet Union, the market's 'invisible hand' acquired colour, flesh, substantial weight and a very definite provenance: the Obkom. Unlike the *préfet*, the First Secretary was not just a political commissar but a regional manager of USSR Inc., which owned everything and employed everyone: the arbiter-in-chief, the distributor-in-chief, the taskmaster-in-chief. 'The power of the Pervyi was practically unlimited,' Yeltsin wrote later. 'In those days, the Obkom Secretary was God and tsar . . . the master of the province. On any issue, the opinion of the First Secretary was the final one.'[20]

Even by Russian standards, the size of Yeltsin's 'prefecture' was notable: 194,800 square kilometres, equivalent to more than four-fifths of Great Britain. Over four-and-a-half million people lived in Yeltsin's fief,[21] making the Sverdlovsk province the fourth most populous *oblast* in the USSR – after Moscow, Donetsk and Krasnodar.[22] It was also the fourth most urbanized in the country: 86 per cent of its population lived in cities and towns.[23] Only Moscow, Leningrad and Donetsk provinces had larger shares of urban population.[24] The provincial Party organization had a membership of over 252,000.[25]

With a population of 1,269,000 on 1 January 1983, the capital of the province, Sverdlovsk, was the tenth largest city in the Soviet Union.[26] Among its denizens were 93,000 students enrolled in fifteen colleges and the Ural State University, and 22,000 scholars and researchers working in the institutes of the Ural division of the Academy of Sciences and enterprise laboratories.[27] In 1980, Yeltsin's *alma mater*, the Ural Polytechnic Institute, won the competition for the best technical college in the Russian Federation.[28] Two years later, competing against the other universities of Russia, the Ural University took second place, after the University of Leningrad.[29]

With 740 plants and factories within its borders,[30] the concentration of industrial enterprises in the Sverdlovsk province was 4.6 times Russia's average.[31] As it had done for the preceding two-and-a-half centuries, the Middle Ural produced the best steel in the country, millions of tonnes of it. Mechanical engineering was its other claim to fame. Forty per cent of freight railway trucks and 20 per cent of all steel pipes produced in the USSR were made in Sverdlovsk.[32]

But, in the late 1970s, the province's weightiest distinction was the third largest – after Moscow and Leningrad – concentration of defence-related enterprises. These made not just thousands of tanks, aircraft and cannons, produced since 1941, when the Nazi invasion forced the evacuation of armament plants from Central and Southern Russia, but the deadliest stuff as well. Among 200 enterprises in the city of Sverdlovsk, dozens made nuclear and biological weapons* and deployed them

---

* In the second and third weeks of April 1979, sixty-four people in Sverdlovsk died, most within forty-eight hours, from a mysterious disease whose symptoms were similar to those of advanced pneumonia. At the time, the authorities claimed poisoning from tainted meat. However, studies of the victims, conducted at the time of the epidemic and declassified in 1992, showed that all lived, worked or walked by the 'Military

in warheads. The province had its own nuclear power plant.* These industries were responsible for Sverdlovsk's status as a 'closed city', which no foreigner, other than a member of an official delegation from a 'fraternal socialist country', was allowed to visit.

As he was taking over this enormity, Yeltsin did not seem in the least perturbed by the official myth of Soviet power, in which 'all power' belonged to local councils, the Soviets. He quickly pensioned off the head of the Regional Soviet, replacing him with a man very much to his liking: an engineer, the Director of a huge plant, with a PhD to boot.[33] A slew of lesser 'elected' officials followed, among them the Chairmen of the City Soviets of Pervouralsk and Alapaevsk.[34] The hapless Obkom Second Secretary Evgeniy Korovin was offered the chairmanship of the Regional Trade Union Council. The defeated contender promptly accepted.[35]

Whereas some pretence of formal deference had to be maintained

---

Settlement No. 19', a top-secret military research installation engaged in the development of a vaccine against anthrax, one of the biological-warfare weapons in the Soviet arsenal.

Interviewed twelve years later, the pathologist who performed the autopsies dismissed food poisoning as the cause of death, insisting that all the symptoms pointed to the spread of disease via inhalation. The brains of the deceased, extracted at the time and preserved, were reddish at the top, a characteristic of anthrax poisoning (Video archive, Museum of Youth Movements). Only one hospital in Sverdlovsk, the City Clinic No. 40, was allowed to admit the patients. The bodies were not released to families for burial, and the relatives of the deceased were warned not to talk to anyone about the accident, or face criminal charges (*ibid.*).

Thirteen years later, Yeltsin admitted that he had been privately notified by the KGB that 'our military development was the cause' of the deaths. He claimed to have spoken with KGB Chairman Yuriy Andropov, who shortly thereafter ordered the facility moved out of Sverdlovsk. (*Washington Post*, 6 June 1992. For further details, see also Natal'ya Zenova, 'Taynoye Stalo Yavnym', *Literaturnaya Gazeta*, 24 March 1993, p. 2; Philip J. Hilts, 'US and Russian Researchers Tie Anthrax Death to Soviets', *New York Times*, 15 March 1993; and Zenova, 'Voyennaya tayna', *Literaturnaya Gazeta*, 22 August 1990, p. 12.)

* In the first crisis of the Yeltsin administration this plant in Beloyarsk, only forty kilometres from Sverdlovsk, nearly became a precursor of Chernobyl. On the night of 31 December 1978, when the temperature dropped to −57°C, a supporting metal construction in the reactor hall cracked, fell, struck a spark on impact and began a fire, which very nearly engulfed the reactor. As hundreds of buses were standing by for possible evacuation of Beloyarsk, the fire fighters prevailed after a few hours. (Yeltsin, *Ispoved'*, p. 60.)

The Flow of Power in the Soviet Union during Yeltsin's Sverdlovsk Years

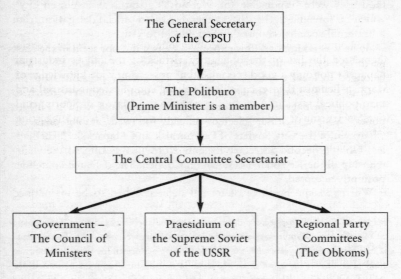

vis-à-vis the local Soviets, no equivocation was allowed in affirming the Party's grip on the twin levers of real power: the Army and the KGB. Like his predecessors, Yeltsin was an *ex officio* member of the Military Council of the Ural District. He even had a military rank, Colonel, awarded after he took over the province. The head of the Regional KGB, General Yuriy Kornilov, was a candidate member of the Obkom Buro[36] and thus Yeltsin's subordinate in the Party hierarchy.

Whatever unlikely ambiguity there might have been regarding the disposition of power in the province between the Party and the KGB was dispelled one day by a visiting KGB bigwig. During a conversation in Yeltsin's office, General Kornilov said that he worked 'with' the Obkom. 'Don't you ever forget, General,' bellowed the Moscow visitor, 'you don't work "with" the Party organs, you work *under* their guidance!'[37] Kornilov did not seem to mind the lecture. His only perennial complaint to Yeltsin was that not a single spy had been caught by his vigilant department. 'Such a huge province,' he used to sigh. 'And not one spy!'[38]

The executive purge visited by the new Pervyi on his fiefdom did not pass over the industrial leadership. In the first four years of his rule, Yeltsin replaced Directors of such huge enterprises as the Nizhniy Tagil Metalworks, the Vysokogorskyi Mechanical Plant, and the

Tagilspetsstroy Trest.[39] Yeltsin saw no need to hide the obvious. 'Of course,' he told the main Party newspaper at the time, 'the Obkom controls the management of the enterprises.'[40]

Along the way, with customary bluntness, the Pervyi made known his personnel predilections. Describing one of his favourites, Yeltsin augmented the list of the obligatory virtues of the Soviet industrial manager ('not only a good specialist, but possessing wide knowledge of Marxist–Leninist theory, capable of solving complicated industrial and socio-political tasks'): 'And, by the way, he is a Master of Sports* and loves poetry, music and painting . . . Of course, I am far from suggesting that every manager must be an athlete, a poet or a painter. But, as far as his abilities allow, he should be interested in sports records and the affairs of the factory's poets, painters and champions.'[41]

Contrary to the official myth, in which the regional Party organization exerted influence strictly through 'ideological guidance' and 'politico-educational upbringing of the masses',[42] the Obkom conducted a minute, day-to-day supervision of the local economy. The Obkom 'made the wheels of the economic mechanism revolve faster', as Yeltsin put it.[43] Through its local potentates, the Party strove ceaselessly to untangle the monstrously irrational, wasteful and unwieldy maze it had itself created. A correspondent of the national Party newspaper, *Pravda*, supplied this vignette of the Sverdlovsk Obkom routine:

> Here [an enterprise] did not receive metal, there a railway failed to transport the finished output. Of course, they ought to have phoned or sent a telegram to a [relevant] Ministry. They have but . . . no one can help them there. Moreover, the heads of the Ministries themselves send requests to the Obkom: straighten things out at our enterprise. For instance, a slew of telegrams were sent to the Obkom by the Deputy Minister of the Automobile Industry who demanded that the Irbit Motorcycle Plant be supplied with mazut [fuel and coarse lubricant].[44]

One day Yeltsin's former subordinate from the DSK found himself in a similar predicament: an allotment of cement which he had foolishly 'loaned' to a military site had never been returned by the brass. After countless telegrams and telephone calls to the local and Moscow

---

* A title conferred by the State Committee for Sports for very serious athletic achievements. Most of the Masters of Sports in the Soviet Union were *de facto* professional athletes.

*nachal'nik*s, he went to the Obkom and left a note for Yeltsin describing his travails. The next morning Yeltsin called: 'Your problem has been solved. Go to work.'[45]

Although heavy industry was Yeltsin's primary responsibility, hardly anything was outside his bailiwick, which ranged from 'persistent attention [to] literature, arts, culture and sports' to 'better results from militia, the Office of Public Prosecutor, Soviets of People's Deputies and the courts'[46] and to the availability of scallions and fresh cucumbers.[47] The city's soccer team, Uralmash (named after the most famous of Sverdlovsk's heavy-industry giants), was also within the Obkom's purview. Asked to exert Party influence on the team, whose play at the time left much to be desired, Yeltsin revealed that the manager and the senior coach had been removed and that the Obkom hoped the team would make it into the top league.[48]

Saddled with the Herculean task of procuring food for the giant smokestack province, the First Secretary found himself expatiating on the 'wintering' of cows. On that occasion, Yeltsin rebuked certain kolkhozes for 'inefficient use of feed': 160 kilos of feed to produce only 100 kilos of milk. He recommended pine branches, hydroponic greenery and a 'wide use of food refuse' as a means of seeing the herds through the winter.[49]

Boris Yeltsin's reign in Sverdlovsk commenced most propitiously: with a record harvest. Never before had so much grain (1,647,000 tonnes) been gathered in the province.[50] In addition to grain, the province exceeded the 1976 state delivery quota in two other critical areas, 'fully satisfying the needs of the population of the province in potatoes and vegetables'.[51]

A cause for celebration under any circumstances, the record harvest was engineered by Yeltsin's guardian angel to occur at the best of all times: the first year of the Tenth Pyatiletka (Five-Year Plan) and a year after the disastrous 1975 harvest, the worst crop failure in recent Soviet history. Olympus responded with personal congratulations from Leonid Brezhnev to the agricultural labourers of the Sverdlovsk province. The General Secretary 'expressed hope that the labourers of the province would make permanent and multiply the achieved results'.[52]

The record harvest was followed by an equally weighty crop of medals: 1,700 were disbursed in one day.[53] The disbursement of the awards had to be divided among the local leaders. Yeltsin bestowed the Party's recognition in the Cinema–Concert Hall Kosmos; the Chairman of the Executive Committee of the Sverdlovsk Oblast Soviet, Aleksandr

Borisov, in the Grand Hall of the Soviets; Yeltsin's deputy, Second Secretary Leonid Bobykin, in the Obkom; another Obkom Secretary, Leonid Ponomarev, discharged the pleasant duty in the building of the Provincial Council of Trade Unions; and the Deputy Chairman of the *oblast* executive Soviet, Fedor Morshakov, in the Dzerzhinskiy Club.[54] Of course, the disposition of the Soviet Union's highest civilian awards – the Gold Star of the Hero of Socialist Labour and the Order of Lenin – was left to the First Secretary. He pinned them on the Chief Agronomist of the Chapaev kolkhoz of the Alapaevsk district, Evgeniy Rostetskiy, and on the Director of the Borodulinskiy sovkhoz, Petr Zuev.[55]

A Soviet joke gave four reasons for the poor performance of Soviet agriculture: winter, spring, summer and autumn. Amazingly, given such odds, Yeltsin's luck held for another year, his first full one on the job. In 1977 another record harvest allowed the Sverdlovsk *oblast* to 'over-fulfil' the state plan for the first two years of the Tenth Pyatiletka, prompting the new Pervyi to declare that 'the grain production of the *oblast* is getting on the road of stable development' and that, for the second year running, the 'needs of the towns and workers' settlements of the province in potatoes and vegetables have been fully met'.[56] More-over, the Sverdlovsk province was even able to export to other areas of the country 90,000 tonnes of potatoes and 30,000 tonnes of vegetables. Again, the timing could not have been better: the sixtieth anniversary of the 1917 Revolution. Another 'personal greeting' from the General Secretary duly followed.[57]

Although undoubtedly encouraged by so auspicious a start, Yeltsin was too experienced a functionary to leave the husbandry of his career to the whims of nature. Some of the tools he used were standard issue – employed, day in and day out, by dozens of other disciplined, eager and ambitious Party bosses throughout the Soviet Union. The Sverdlovsk Pervyi marked various festivals of the Soviet political calendar punctu-ally and with ardour. The consolidation of power in the hands of Leonid Brezhnev, who had himself 'elected' Chairman of the Supreme Soviet in 1977, was immediately hailed by Yeltsin as 'enthusiastically approved not only by all the Soviet people but by millions of people abroad'.[58] The same year, the 'elections' to local Soviets moved the Sverdlovsk Pervyi to declare them:

a giant success in the development of socialist democracy, which demonstrated with a renewed vigour the indestructibility of the bloc of communists and non-Party members, the unity of the Party and the people . . . In the Soviet land there exists the law of the free development of the man, scrupulously guarded by the Constitution. Contrary to the lying foreign propaganda, which harps on the allegedly 'constrained', 'shackled' mode of life of the Soviet man, the abilities of each worker are richly and comprehensively developed in a socialist society. And, as a result, the labour and political initiative of the masses increases.[59]

Half a year later, the adoption of a new constitution was greeted by the Sverdlovsk Pervyi with the avowal that 'in the conditions of Soviet reality, in the society of developed socialism, the liberties and rights of man are truly realized'.[60]

Boris Yeltsin was a loyal and vocal courtier, especially zealous in the first several years of his Secretaryship. In his maiden speech to the Obkom *aktiv* (a gathering of leading members of the provincial nomenklatura) ten days after his appointment, he mentioned Leonid Brezhnev six times.[61] The leader's speech at the October 1976 Plenum of the Central Committee was called 'brilliant and deep', its key points to be studied 'thoroughly'.[62] An excellent opportunity to affirm his devotion to the General Secretary conveniently presented itself at the very beginning of Yeltsin's reign, and he took full advantage of it. On the occasion of Brezhnev's seventieth birthday, Yeltsin sent the General Secretary a congratulatory missive in which he extolled the supreme leader's 'wisdom, giant talent for organization, human charm and bubbling energy'.[63] Brezhnev's entire life, Yeltsin insisted, was 'remarkable and inspiring', and:

we who live in the Urals thank you ardently and from the bottom of our soul, Leonid Ilyich, for the constant care you take of the strengthening of the economic and military might of our Motherland, for the raising of the material and cultural level of the people's lives, for your titanic activity on behalf of the establishment of solid peace in the whole world.[64]

The same year, in a short article, Yeltsin's first for a major Soviet daily,[65] the General Secretary was referred to thrice, a number greater than what seemed at the time the norm for Party functionaries of Yeltsin's rank. A few months later in a Party magazine, Yeltsin extolled the General Secretary ten times in seven pages.[66] The next year, in a speech to an Obkom Plenum, Comrade Brezhnev was evoked five times.[67]

Yeltsin's reaction to the Centre's* 'initiatives' was always swift and conspicuous. An accomplished athlete, he was always ready to receive and return a ball served by the Central Committee, and he played political volleyball with the same gusto and lightning reaction that had made him famous on the court. For instance, the 1977 'appeal' of the Central Committee 'To Work Today Better than Yesterday, and Tomorrow Better than Today!' immediately 'found a genuine response in the hearts of the working people of the Sverdlovsk province':[68] ten construction brigades in Sverdlovsk 'stepped forward' with a patriotic initiative of their own, 'To Fulfil the Five-Year Plan with a Smaller Work Force!' Yeltsin's zeal was duly noted and received the highest blessing at the December 1977 Plenum of the Central Committee.[69] The Sverdlovsk First Secretary was given a great deal of space in *Pravda* to expound his views on the subject.[70]

A year later, immediately after the *postanovlenie* ('resolution') of the Central Committee and the Council of Ministers 'On the Further Perfection of the Economic Mechanism', the Sverdlovsk Obkom 'called a meeting of chief economists of the enterprises and scholars, seminars with the top staffers of district and city committees of the CPSU, leaders of the propaganda and agitation groups' as well as a meeting of the regional Party *aktiv* and the Plenum of the Obkom.[71] Striving to kill a second bird with the same stone, Yeltsin told *Pravda* that, in 'explaining' the *postanovlenie* to the 'masses', the Obkom was guided by another recent Party encyclical, 'On Further Betterment of Ideological, Political and Educational Work'.[72]

When, for the first and last time, his cloudless relations with Moscow were marred by a mild reprimand, Yeltsin's *mea culpa* was prompt and heartfelt. On that sad occasion for the Sverdlovsk Obkom, *Pravda* stated that the Obkom's 'branch' departments, while doing quite well in supervising local industry, had neglected the 'educational' work necessary to create a proper 'moral and political climate' in working collectives.[73] The following month, the Party's main organ carried Yeltsin's response. The First Secretary readily conceded that 'the level of the work of the branch departments of the Obkom was not up to the standards set by the Central Committee's Resolution "On Further Betterment of Ideological, Political and Educational Work"'.[74] He further reported that the Buro

---

* At once grave and elastic, the word connoted Moscow, government, highest authority. Its concrete, narrow meaning depended on the speaker. To a plant manager it meant the branch Ministry to which he reported; to a military officer, the General Staff; to a local party official, like Yeltsin, the Centre was the Central Committee.

had discussed the issue and 'demanded' that the departments 'raise the responsibility of the [local Party] leadership for the educational impact of economic activity, inspiring the desire and ability to unite collectives, to conduct educational work with people, to raise the level of their social and labour initiative'.[75]

The perimeter of the permissible in intra-Party dialogue was set by the Centre. The disposition of the borders was not negotiable, and their crossing lethal for the career of an ambitious apparatchik. Yet in the late Brezhnev era, more relaxed than any of the preceding Soviet regimes, the boundaries were somewhat flexible. A local leader was allowed, indeed expected, to structure the region's priorities by choosing from the long menu of Central Committee initiatives those that were more consonant with local needs and his own proclivities. In the complex Party oratorio to which the Obkom First Secretaries daily lent their voices, the timing and the theme of the propaganda choir were largely outside the local soloists' control (these were the provinces of the Central Committee's Propaganda Department), yet the exact wording, pitch and emphases were left to the Pervyis.

Boris Yeltsin wasted no time in declaring himself. He began ten days after his 'election' with his maiden address to the *aktiv*. The structure of this acceptance speech would become Yeltsin's trademark: a lengthy and unusually frank recitation of problems skilfully wrapped in protestations of loyalty to the current Party leadership. The criticism-to-paeans ratio was decidedly skewed in the direction of the former: only the first fifth of the speech contained the customary recitation of successes.[76]

The gripes of the new Pervyi ranged from the insufficient development of local deposits of iron ore (it had to be imported from 'faraway areas of the country') to the slow growth of electricity for popular consumption, and especially the supply of heat to the towns of the province. Also condemned were the low levels of production of 'sophisticated metal products', such as high-quality steel; the unsatisfactory growth of popular consumption goods (ten towns and districts of the province had not fulfilled their planned quotas); and the low level of mechanization of lumber cutting and processing.[77] The final sentence of the speech assured Moscow that the 'labourers of the Middle Ural are full of determination to bring to life the decisions of the Twenty-Fifth Party Congress, the October Plenum of the CC of the Party, and directions of Comrade L. I. Brezhnev, which are contained in his speech at the Plenum'.[78]

Two months later, Yeltsin delivered to the *aktiv* a considerably better-prepared, longer and more substantial address, a kind of 'inaugural' speech. It replicated the unusual mode of the acceptance speech by stressing the unfinished tasks. Entitled 'Work Better, Raise the Effectiveness and Quality!', the speech filled almost an entire page of the Obkom's newspaper, *Ural'skiy Rabochiy*. Only the first seven paragraphs listed achievements.[79] Sixty-four enterprises in the province had not fulfilled planned quotas, Yeltsin thundered. The province was behind the plan in steel pipes, superphosphate, logging and woodworking. One of the largest plants, the Nizhniy Tagil Metalworks, was 14,000 tonnes of pig-iron short of the plan. Electricity was wasted profligately: in 1976 its consumption grew twice as fast as the volume of industrial production.[80]

Both the acceptance speech and the inaugural address clearly marked the parts of Yeltsin's political garden that he intended to cultivate with especial assiduity. And Yeltsin was consistent: in the eight-and-a-half years of his reign in Sverdlovsk, the concerns voiced in the first three months would form the refrain of his public utterances, belying the fickle Party fashion.

His first concern was the steadily decreasing effectiveness of investments in industry and agriculture. Long before it became a safe and fashionable commonplace, Yeltsin identified this key symptom of the grave illness that was enveloping the Soviet economy. The 'return on investment in industry has been falling every year', he told the *aktiv*.[81] He would disclose later that in the previous ten years 'only half of the newly built industrial facilities have produced the planned volume of output'.[82] During the same period, in the rural areas of the province, investment had grown 2.7 times while the per-capita output of agricultural production increased by only 40 per cent.[83]

Another major problem was the intolerably large share of manual labour in the plants and factories of the province. Thirty-five per cent of all industrial workers performed 'unmechanized' labour.[84] Later, when either his information was more accurate or, more likely, he could afford to be even more honest, Yeltsin expanded his estimate to 'over half' of the entire workforce, noting that the number of those performing manual labour decreased (with painful slowness) by three-tenths of 1 per cent a year.[85]

Yeltsin's third worry was the catastrophic shortage of housing. As with manual labour, his childhood memories undoubtedly lent this shortcoming a large and disturbing dose of reality. In the inaugural address he stated that 'the liquidation of the *barak*s and basement dwellings is proceeding very slowly' and that a number of towns in the province lagged behind in the building of 'living space'.[86] Four years later, he would declare 'the fulfilment of the planned volume of housing in every enterprise, every district and every city the most important task, the subject of special attention'.[87]

The meagre production and inefficient distribution of consumer goods were his fourth preoccupation. Yeltsin suggested that all city and district Party committees should examine the state of affairs at each enterprise of the province.[88]

There existed, of course, the old and much honoured Soviet and Russian political tradition in which sudden and spectacular revelation of past failures coincided with the arrival of a new *nachal'nik*. This could well have explained both the volume and the stridency of Yeltsin's complaints had it not been for the fact that he persisted in the critical mode throughout the term of his Secretaryship. He affirmed this stance in a *Pravda* article written five years after his 'election'. Ostensibly critiquing resolutions (*postanovlenia*) of the Gorkom of the industrial town of Irbit in the Sverdlovsk province, Yeltsin took on the culture of self-congratulation that dominated the Party's public discourse:

> The resolutions are marked by neither depth nor exactitude of analysis. But in every *postanovlenie*, there is a recitation of successes, no matter how small. 'This is customary,' one usually hears, when such recitations are justified. But for what reason 'customary'? So as not to offend those who bungled their task, those who carry out their duties badly? Recitation of successes and their analysis are needed where they are relevant to a progressive experience, which deserves wide dissemination.[89]

Yeltsin would not bend his rules even for occasions that Party tradition designated as festive, mellow, glowing. One such happening was a provincial Party Conference, a quinquennial affair held before the Party Congress, to which the Conference elected delegates. It was, moreover, the first Conference over which Yeltsin presided as Pervyi. No matter. Deliberately confusing Party genres, Yeltsin turned a celebratory 'state of the province' address into the kind of speech Obkom First Secretaries would confine to strictly off-the-record meetings of the Obkom's *aktiv*. The obligatory laudation was confined to a short introduction, after which he plunged into a recitation of defects and losses. He spoke of the failure to organize the timely delivery of coal to the steel mills.[90] Every year this reduced steel production by 343,000 tonnes. 'Very serious' were deficiencies in the supply of goods for popular consumption. The shortage of doctors and nurses was 'most urgent'.

Perhaps most startling in this 1981 speech was an admission of a trend in the Soviet economy that, five years later, would prompt a new leadership to begin reforms. The growth of industrial output in the province had been decreasing steadily in the last fifteen years: from 33 per cent in the Eighth Pyatiletka to 24 per cent in the Ninth, and to 11 per cent in the one just completed, the Tenth. The corresponding figures for the growth in labour productivity were 30, 26 and 9 per cent.[91] The economy of the province was inexorably slowing down.

After twenty years 'in the field', Yeltsin must have felt familiar enough with the state of industrial affairs in his fiefdom to discuss them at length even in his largely impromptu acceptance speech. Yet his customary conscientiousness stopped the new Pervyi from expounding on the province's agriculture for almost two years. At the time, Yeltsin's wife Naina complained to a friend that her husband 'stayed up night after night studying crops and milk yields per cow'.[92]

When he finally did speak, at a Plenum of the Sverdlovsk Obkom in July 1978, the critical bent was no different from that of his industrial soliloquies. This usual introduction extolled the 'present-day agrarian policy of the Party' as having had 'an exceptionally salutary impact on the development of agriculture in the province', praised the latest ('comprehensive' and 'deeply scientific') speech of Comrade L. I. Brezhnev and listed the successes of the past two years.[93] What followed was anything but glowing. The cities and 'industrial centres' of the province were not sufficiently provisioned with meat, milk and eggs. In 'many' kolkhozes and sovkhozes, the 'provision of forage' for farm animals, mostly cows and pigs, was 'primitive' and 'insufficient'. Every year, 50,000 to 60,000 cows of weight below the accepted minimum of 450 kilos were delivered to the slaughterhouses. Fifty-seven sovkhozes had not fulfilled plans for the state procurement of potatoes.[94]

Storage space for potatoes and fertilizer was desperately short. In 1977, some 80,000 tonnes of precious mineral fertilizers were lost in transportation and storage. There were not enough grain elevators.[95] Many barns were in an 'inadequate or even dangerous' condition. Of the twenty-four new large mechanized barns planned, only seven had actually been built, their construction having taken twice the amount of time allocated.[96] Of the planned 790 kilometres of paved roads, only 154 had been completed.[97]

As was his wont, Yeltsin ended the speech by squaring the circle. He assured the audience that 'the authority of the Party in the countryside is growing' and that a 'new phase of the struggle for the uplifting of agriculture must be reflected in a higher level of Party leadership of the masses'.[98]

Among Yeltsin's economic campaigns, two were prosecuted with a passion and single-mindedness that exceeded even his habitual zeal. One was 'intensification' of local industrial production; the other, support for 'complex brigades'.

At the root of Yeltsin's near-obsession with 'intensification' was a systemic tension built into the role of the First Secretary, the strain between the two functions he was to perform simultaneously: that of the local facilitator of relentless industrial expansion, forced upon the provinces by Moscow, and that of the keeper of social peace in his domain.

Difficult for any Obkom, in Sverdlovsk the two tasks were especially hard to combine. The immensely rich heavy-industry Ministries in Moscow, all in one way or another connected with the military–industrial complex, insisted on building more and larger plants, adding tens of thousands of workers to the Obkom's already overlong list of those in need of food, kindergartens, hospitals, schools and, most desperately, apartments. By the time Yeltsin took over the province, it was among Russia's most industrially developed: out of every 1,000 inhabitants of the Sverdlovsk province, 225 worked in plants and factories, as compared with an all-Russian average of 155.[99] If new construction were not somehow slowed, the 'social infrastructure' of the Sverdlovsk province, meagre and badly worn out, could degenerate to breaking point. The results were not difficult to predict: further erosion of motivation among the dispirited workers, still lower productivity and, perhaps, even strikes. And he, Yeltsin, would be held responsible – not some anonymous ministry! 'Intensification' was an attempt to lengthen the fuse of this time bomb by combining a continuing increase in industrial output, as demanded by Moscow, with a slower rate of industrial expansion.

In the ongoing duel with the Ministries, Yeltsin stressed the staggering waste that inevitably accompanied Soviet construction. The Pervyi, who had spent a decade on construction sites, knew what he was talking about: in 1981, over 5,000 construction sites were operating simultaneously in the province, each requiring, on average, 'no fewer than six years to complete'.[100] Many buildings had been under construction for ten years and more. The unfinished projects in the province were valued at over two billion rubles.[101]

Yeltsin's other case against industrial expansion drew on the steadily shrinking workforce – a countrywide trend which surfaced first in heavily industrialized regions like Sverdlovsk. He cited an example of a recently constructed large shop (*tsekh*), which had cost 2.7 million rubles. It had been built 'in vain': there were not enough workers to service it. 'We should instead', wrote Yeltsin, 'have constructed a [far more modest] division [*uchastok*] in the already existing shop, and devoted the money and workforce to the construction of housing, so badly needed by the enterprise.'[102]

This was the key to Yeltsin's 'intensification' scheme: modernization ('reconstruction') of the existing enterprises. Throughout his tenure, he would argue that, instead of investing in new enterprises – which would require increased consumption of energy, raw materials and, most importantly, 'social infrastructure' for additional workers – 'the main and prevailing' means of increasing production in the Middle Ural 'must be reconstruction and technical modernization of the already functioning enterprises'.[103] He called modernization the 'most critical task',[104] and insisted that 'reconstruction of enterprises with minimal expenditure is one of the shortest routes to raising productivity of labour'.[105]

The battle had not begun with Yeltsin. The 'General Plan of the Development of Sverdlovsk', adopted in 1972, was to 'remove the disproportion' between the quality of life in the city and its 'industrial might', and to bolster the 'defence of the air and water from pollution'.[106] The new First Secretary went to the very top of Soviet industrial planning, the Gosplan of the USSR. Promising the same rate of industrial growth, Yeltsin begged the Moscow planners to reduce investments in new industrial construction in the Sverdlovsk province by one billion rubles, an astronomic sum in those days.[107]

The new Pervyi's effort was not without success. The Obkom staved off the construction of a giant clay-cement complex, advocated by the Ministry of Non-Ferrous Metallurgy, which would have required finding several thousand new workers.[108] Even more impressive was a concession the Obkom wrenched from Moscow: in the Tenth Pyatiletka, from 1976 to 1981, one-third of capital investments in the Sverdlovsk province went into reconstruction of already existing enterprises.[109] Yeltsin was encouraged enough to declare that 'reconstruction and technological modernization' would become the 'the main mode of development of non-ferrous metallurgy in the Middle Ural' region.[110]

In the autumn of 1980, four months before the Twenty-Sixth Party Congress was to adopt a new five-year plan, Yeltsin used a *Pravda* article to launch a frontal assault on new industrial construction:

Most super-plants are now planning to construct new shops, even new blocks, which will inevitably entail an increase in the workforce.

But is there a real need to do so? Could they not expand production using the industrial space and equipment they already have? How does their new construction fit the general plan of city development? Some [managers] do not ask themselves these questions ... New construction is planned on the initiative or with the active support of the Ministries and administrations. At the same time, the Ministries, for instance, of Heavy Machine Building, Energy Machine Building, Ferrous Metallurgy and some others are little concerned about the needs of the cities, in which their enterprises are situated. Sometimes, they do not take into account the shortage of labour, which becomes more and more acute.[111]

Still, although it had won a few battles, Sverdlovsk was losing the war. The Moloch of industrial expansion, cranked up by Stalin in the 1930s, kept grinding on. 'Some leaders of the central administrations,' Yeltsin complained, 'not recognizing the value of reconstruction, again demand the building of new, expensive sites,' and 'often succeed in bypassing the local organs'.[112] The disproportion between industrial expansion and social infrastructure 'not only had not been removed but, in fact, was growing'.[113] For the leadership of 'big enterprises' the needs of the city were the 'lowest priority'.[114] The reconstruction began to slow down: 120 million rubles less were spent on it compared with the previous Pyatiletka. As Yeltsin had warned, down went productivity: the 'effective use of the most precious commodity today – human labour'.[115]

Known also as 'complex-finalizing' and 'brigade contract', the 'complex brigade' (CB), which appeared in the late 1960s was the closest approximation to entrepreneurial initiative the official Soviet economy ever tolerated. Unlike normal Soviet industrial and agricultural production, where there was little individual responsibility for the final result and where salaries were unrelated to the work actually accomplished, the CB would contract to carry out a particular operation or even an entire project (such as construction of a building, or the seeding and harvesting of a kolkhoz field) and was rewarded according to the final result of the members' efforts.

There are good reasons to trace this fondness for CBs to Yeltsin's pre-Obkom past. He had spent years on construction sites: the area of the Soviet economy where the lack of collective, let alone personal, responsibility for the results was among the most visible and most disconcerting. The sloppy, wasteful and interminable work which he had seen every day might well have convinced him that, as he put it in an article, only 'the brigade form of organization ... creates conditions for the maximum efficiency of labour for all workers without exception'.[116] And, of course, it was precisely such a brigade, sponsored by him ten years before, that had helped him perform the last leap of his 'civilian' career: to the directorship of the DSK.

Yeltsin's touting of CBs also seemed to have a great deal to do with the peculiar, tough populism of the Ural school of the Party leadership, with its stress on fairness, personal responsibility and discipline. For the CB was an arrangement in which both authority and social control were, to a considerable degree, shifted from the Party, government or plant administration down to the 'work collective', that is, a group of people sharing a workplace (whether teachers, plumbers, doctors, coalminers or ballet dancers) – an entity central to the myth of the Soviet 'workers' state' and glorified by official propaganda. The CB was to become the epitome of a work collective – a self-regulating and self-policing entity, which punished the tardy and the lazy and which replaced with collective responsibility the fear of sanctions from above.

Yeltsin called the arrangement 'collective material and moral responsibility for the condition of work discipline'.[117] His favourite example of the arrangement, which he cited repeatedly, was the Severskiy Pipe Plant, where an entire CB would refuse a bonus because of the occasional 'violation of discipline' by a few members.[118] (The arrangement, Yeltsin admitted, had been criticized in the 'central press' and by the 'jurists' as 'contradicting the labour law',[119] but the Obkom refused to veto it.) He insisted that the CB was 'precisely the cell in which questions of production and of the upbringing of the working man came together in an organic whole'.[120]

Like most of Yeltsin's choices from the Party menu, the CB campaign was signalled in his acceptance speech in January 1977. He praised the spread of CBs, and cited the Uralmash plant, where the introduction of complex brigades into some shops had allegedly increased productivity by 13 to 20 per cent. At the time, Yeltsin complained that 'other branches of the people's economy' had not responded properly to the initiative.[121]

The CB advocacy continued in the main Party journal, *Partiynaya Zhizn'*[122] and in the pages of the Soviet Union's most popular government daily, *Izvestia*. 'We believe', Yeltsin told the latter, 'that the *kompleksnaya brigada* is the prime production and political cell; it effectively assists the professional and moral growth of the working man, developing in him the features of the statesman and creator of all material values.'[123]

By 1978, the Sverdlovsk Pervyi had more or less become the designated Party spokesman on the subject of complex brigades.[124] And when the resolution of the Central Committee and the Council of Ministers of the USSR on 'Further Perfection of the Economic Mechanism' identified the 'brigade form of labour organization' as the 'main' one for the Eleventh Pyatiletka, Yeltsin was rewarded with a long interview on the subject in *Pravda*. He assured its readers that the labourers of the Sverdlovsk province had reacted to the *postanovlenie* with 'sincere approval' and 'businesslike inspiration'.[125] Naturally, as a result of the Party's approbation, the number of applications to organize CBs in Sverdlovsk and Nizhniy Tagil had 'increased twofold, and, at some enterprises, three times'.[126] A year later, Yeltsin instigated the expansion of the CB movement throughout the Mid-Ural region.[127]

The particularity of Yeltsin's style – his frequent carping and zealous crusading – could easily have earned him a reputation as a crank or, worse yet, a gadfly. Neither category of Party functionaries had fared especially well in Soviet history. Under Brezhnev, the Centre's response to such transgressions, while no longer lethal for the mavericks themselves, was still fatal for their careers.

The opposite was true of Yeltsin. His stock in Moscow rose steadily. He was duly elected to the Central Committee, then to the Supreme Soviet, then to the Praesidium of the Supreme Soviet, the only Russian Obkom Pervyi so honoured. In 1984 he was even entrusted with leading a Central Committee delegation to such an important 'capitalist' country as the Federal Republic of Germany. These achievements were due to Yeltsin's uncanny ability to manoeuvre at close political quarters. His occasional heterodoxies were skilfully packaged in the accepted formats of intra-Party communications. No matter how dramatic the content, the form was familiar and non-threatening.

One such format was the *pochin*: a political or industrial propaganda campaign, ostensibly initiated by the 'masses from below'. Invented by Stalin during the industrialization of the 1930s and implemented innumerable times since, the *pochin* was much more than a mere propaganda exercise. It was a kind of sign language by which the Centre signalled new policies to the local chieftains, as well as to the country at large. To the more attentive and ambitious, a *pochin* promised rewards and promotions; to those slow to adjust to yet another turn in the Party's course, it was a spur.

For an ambitious provincial Party boss willing to gamble, the key to a successful *pochin* was the timing. Out of a myriad of potentially winning initiatives he had to stake considerable political capital on the one whose stock, in his estimate, would fit best into the strategy-of-the-day and, therefore, was likely to rise. Once launched, the success of the *pochin* was defined by the manner in which the province–Centre–province circle was closed. The reaction could range from a telephone call from the Central Committee's *instruktor* in charge of the province to a report in *Pravda*, to a favourable mention in a *Pravda* editorial, to – the dream of all functionaries! – a recommendation by the Central Committee to all other Party organizations, the so-called 'all-Union' *pochin*. This was the perfect closing of the *pochin* circle: an 'initiative from below' met with regal approval in Moscow and, stamped with the highest imprimatur, returned to the 'masses' for implementation.

Compared with the 1930s, or even the early 1960s under the mercurial Nikita Khrushchev, the stolid, even lackadaisical Brezhnev regime was decidedly less generous with *pochin*s. A provincial Party Secretary was lucky to close the *pochin* circle once or twice in his career. Less than three years into his tenure, Yeltsin already had several *pochin*s under his belt – all related, moreover, to his pet concerns. In March 1979 he proudly listed the '*pochin*s of the Sverdlovsk Obkom approved by the Central Committee': the introduction of 'scientific organization of labour' (Nauchnaya Organizaytsiya Truda – known, as we have seen, by its acronym NOT); an increase in production as a result of reconstruction of existing enterprises; 'socialist competition' in economizing raw materials; and the 'patriotic movement', 'A Brigade's Five-Year Quota – with Fewer Workers!'[128]

Even amid this dazzling display, the closing of the circle of the *pochin* that dealt with 'popular consumption goods' was especially spectacular. Although Yeltsin first bemoaned the sorry state of the production and distribution of consumer goods in his acceptance speech in November 1976, the right moment for the launching of the *pochin* did not arrive until four years later.

As dictated by the ritual, the *pochin* was officially originated in the collectives of the four largest heavy-industry plants in response to the 'decisions of the Twenty-Sixth Party Congress'.[129] In fact, Yeltsin himself admitted, the Obkom had already been promoting light industry in the province through a number of resolutions which called for increased production of 'furniture, children's clothing, haberdashery, toys, china and leather goods'.[130] In this very early variant of 'conversion' of heavy industry to consumer products, which would become so fashionable ten years hence, shops producing 'goods for the people' began operating in such giants of heavy industry as the Uralmash, the Uralkhimmach and the Kalinin Mechanical Engineering Plant. One of the collectives pledged to double the production of 'lamps, children's toys and furniture'.[131]

Moscow's endorsement came in the most exalted of all formats. On 20 June 1981, *Pravda* published a *postanovlenie* of the Central Committee 'On the Initiative of the Collectives of the Forward Enterprises of the City of Moscow and the Sverdlovsk Region Regarding the Increase in the Production of Goods for Popular Consumption'. Three weeks later, the Sverdlovsk Obkom responded with a Plenum devoted solely to the Central Committee's resolution.

In a long speech Yeltsin, a Moscow licence now in hand, pontificated on one of his favourite subjects. He even treated the audience to praise for market research: 'Unfortunately, we do not sufficiently study market demands. Hence, miscalculations that lead to production losses, lower quality, shortages of some goods and overproduction of others. We need a more creative, businesslike, flexible and rapid linkage between trade and production.'[132] He ended, of course, by pledging 'the strengthening of the Party influence on the organization of the production of goods for the people'.[133]

Two weeks later Yeltsin was awarded a lengthy interview in *Izvestia* on the subject of consumer-goods production. Among other things, he revealed that, 'responding' to the Central Committee resolution, the 'masters of knitted goods of Nizhniy Tagil' had revised their previous 'socialist obligations' and pledged to produce 250,000 rubles' worth of 'extra underwear and stockings'.[134] The *pochin* circle was now closed, perfectly.

The Twenty-Sixth Congress of the Communist Party of the Soviet Union came to order in Moscow at exactly 10 a.m. on 23 February 1981. Convened every five years, the Congresses were by far the most important events in the official Soviet Union – grandiose and minutely scripted political happenings.

It was the first Congress to which Yeltsin was 'elected' as a delegate. He was, moreover, asked to speak. This was a professional triumph: only five years into the First Secretaryship, he was among thirty-nine of the 4,994 delegates so honoured, and one of only twelve Obkom First Secretaries out of 165 in the USSR.* After a long twenty-five years 'in the field', Boris Yeltsin had finally been admitted into the antechamber of the Party Olympus.

---

* In addition to the 121 regions (*oblasts*), there were twenty Autonomous Republics, eight Autonomous Regions, six territories (*krais*) and ten Autonomous Areas (*okrugs*), whose Party organizations were equivalent to that of the Obkoms.

Just a month before, at the close of the Tenth Pyatiletka, he had received the Soviet Union's highest civilian award, the Order of Lenin. The *ukaz* ('decree') of the Praesidium of the Supreme Soviet of 30 January 1981 cited 'services rendered to the Communist Party and the Soviet state, and to mark the occasion of [Yeltsin's] fiftieth birthday'.

Yet the celebration turned out to be less perfect than Yeltsin might have expected. The Twenty-Sixth Congress was a strange affair at which the cymbals of victory reverberated through an atmosphere filled with the faint but distinct smell of decay.

Two months before the Congress, the year 1980 had quietly ended. The 1961 Party Programme had designated it the one in which 'the material and technical basis of communism' was to be completed and the 'whole population' was to be 'guaranteed abundant material and cultural benefits'.[135] The Central Committee now settled for a 'developed socialism', and a new Party Programme was said to be in the works. Paradise, in which one was to give 'according to one's talents' and receive 'according to one's needs',[136] was postponed indefinitely.

The crude and wasteful but until then durable economic machine Stalin had forged in the 1930s to devour labour, coal and electricity and spew out giant factories bursting with steel and pig-iron, was shaking and sputtering. The 'extensive' industrial development, whose rapacious gods each year demanded more and bigger sacrifices in people's time and the earth's bounty, was collapsing. The Twenty-Sixth Congress and the economic plan it produced were to become eulogy and farewell to this economic order.

After the Congress, the Central Committee and the Council of Ministers would issue a joint decree that, for the first time in Soviet history, attempted to set the limits for the cost of production by spelling out how much raw materials and labour would be acceptable per ruble of output.[137] This stratagem would fail: ever-increasing 'inputs' was the only mode for which the Soviet economy had been designed and in which it could function.

By 1981 the economy had crossed the line that separated serious trouble from crisis. The oil of Western Siberia, that magic well which for the preceding fifteen years had produced nearly half of all oil extracted in the USSR and had more than doubled the amount of oil the Soviet Union could sell for hard currency abroad,[138] began to dry. The billions of petrodollars generated in Western Siberia had circulated through the clogged and worn-out veins of the Soviet economy like a magic elixir, making the 1970s the most prosperous time the Soviet Union ever knew. They bought both bigger and deadlier 'guns' for the Party and a thin but tangible layer of 'butter' for the starved Soviet consumer, who began to get used to television sets, refrigerators, even cars.

Those halcyon days were coming to a close: the natural depletion had been hastened by rapacious extraction, in which less than half of the oil in the deposits was recovered.[139] And the country, which plunged at least a third of its gross national product into its military–industrial complex, did not have the money to buy expensive specialized machinery abroad or to pay its oilers enough to develop deposits that lay under the permafrost of the north or under the continental shelf in the Far East.

Ten weeks before the Congress, Soviet experts had concluded that the growth in Soviet oil production 'may come to an end within the next year or two'.[140] At the Congress, Leonid Brezhnev told the country that it 'must reduce the share of oil' in overall energy production, replacing it with gas, coal and nuclear energy.[141] Prime Minister Nikolay Tikhonov called on industry to 'save every tonne of oil'.[142] On the same day, the First Deputy Chairman of Gosplan, Nikolay Ryzhkov, felt it necessary to deny publicly that the Soviet Union might become an importer of oil.[143]

The thinning fountain of Siberian oil could not delay the reckoning for much longer. With the growth of GNP officially estimated at the time at no more than a paltry 2 per cent between 1981 and 1985, the country could sustain its habitual increase in military spending of at least 4–5 per cent annually only at the cost of cannibalizing the rest of the economy and impoverishing the consumer. That fateful choice, too, was made at the Twenty-Sixth Congress. It would haunt Russia, and Yeltsin, long after those who had made it were gone and forgotten.

The departure of these Soviet leaders could not have taken much longer, for they were old – older than were the rulers at any other point in Soviet history. The age of the fourteen Politburo members averaged sixty-nine. Of the seven leading oligarchs, Leonid Brezhnev and Andrey Kirilenko were seventy-four, Konstantin Chernenko sixty-nine, Mikhail Suslov seventy-eight, Dmitriy Ustinov seventy-two, Andrey Gromyko seventy-one and Yuriy Andropov sixty-six. Forty years earlier, they, as a group, had been the youngest political elite of the twentieth century. Propelled into national politics by the Great Purge of 1937–9, they had leapfrogged several rungs of the career ladder, over the barely cold bodies of the previous occupants annihilated by Stalin. Still in their fifties when they seized power from Khrushchev in 1964, they – who had spent most of their adult lives waiting for a midnight knock on the door; who, in Czechoslovakia in 1968, exorcised, once and for all, the spectre of 'socialism with a human face'; and who now enjoyed a long-postponed, unhurried meal at the table of power, unafraid either of a mad dictator or of aroused masses – were determined to part with power only in death.

The next generation had been effectively barred from approaching the pinnacle in any significant numbers. This was the first Congress in the almost eighty years of the Party's history at which not a single change – by retirement or promotion – occurred in the Party's highest councils, the Politburo and the Secretariat. In the larger body, the Central Committee, 'elected' by the Congress, those aged fifty and younger made up less than 10 per cent. (One of them, labelled by Western Sovietologists an 'agriculture specialist', was Mikhail Gorbachev, who had been admitted into the Politburo only four months before the Congress.)

Presiding over the gerontocracy was its symbol and its guardian, Leonid Il'ich Brezhnev. Aside from Stalin's, his was the longest rule in Soviet history. A mediocrity even in his prime, after several heart attacks in the previous decade he was now barely competent. He sat as if in a trance through six-and-a-half days of speeches, impassive and distant, seemingly unaware of the Party's greatest festival swirling around him.

According to a long-time aide, Brezhnev's 'entire theoretical background' was drawn from 'studying for exams in the required courses of the most elemental Marxism–Leninism'.[144] In twenty-one years of close observation, the leader of world communism was never spotted reading Lenin, 'let alone Marx or Engels'.[145] It was 'nearly impossible to persuade [him] to read serious fiction'.[146] If he read at all, it was magazines with big colour photographs or cartoons: *Ogonyok* and *Krokodil*.[147] He preferred the circus to any other entertainment.

Yeltsin was, of course, privy to the widespread snickering in the Party. Two years before, his own mentor, Yakov Ryabov, at the time Secretary of the Central Committee, was rumoured to have said at a party hosted by Yeltsin in Sverdlovsk: 'It's about time this fool was pensioned off.'[148] Yeltsin's own impression was hardly more favourable. By 1981 he had had several meetings with Brezhnev (one of them to solicit Brezhnev's approval for the construction of a metro in Sverdlovsk). He concluded that in the last years of his life Brezhnev 'did not understand what he was doing, what he signed, what he said'.[149]

From 1977, the Sverdlovsk Pervyi genuflected less and less before the General Secretary. In the articles published by Yeltsin in the Soviet Union's two main dailies, *Pravda* and *Izvestia*, the number of paeans to Brezhnev had diminished steadily: from three mentions in all 1978 pieces to one in 1979, one in 1980 and none in 1981. In his 1979 article in the *Partiynaya Zhizn'* magazine, he praised the supreme leader only twice.[150] In the very year of the Congress, 1981, at the height of the Brezhnev cult, Yeltsin called the head of the Obkom's Group of Lecturers, Ivan Blinov, into his office and told him: 'You should mention Brezhnev twice: at the beginning of speeches and at the end! Don't stick him in after every other word.'[151] This was an order.

Yet there he was, in Yeltsin's clear view, at the centre of the dais: doddering, sick with emphysema and unable to speak properly (only eleven minutes of his three-hour forty-minute speech was broadcast live on Soviet television) – a prop in a farce, scripted out by the Party nobles who had brought him to power seventeen years before – a farce in which strong and intelligent men, like Yeltsin, were forced to play bit parts.

And play he did, in the usual way: well within the perimeter but by a game-plan distinctly his own. The script demanded shameless encomiums to Brezhnev, and Yeltsin complied. In his fifteen-minute speech, Brezhnev's name surfaced five times. Yeltsin noted the General Secretary's place at the head of the Politburo; acknowledged Brezhnev's 'personal' contribution to the 'difficult and intense' work of the Politburo;[152] and thanked Brezhnev for his 'kind words' about the Sverdlovsk Party organization in his speech to the Congress (Brezhnev praised it for the 'link between science and industry'). Yeltsin also stated that the 'directives of Comrade L. I. Brezhnev' had made practically all ministries and agencies interested in aiding the production of consumer goods.[153] In the inevitable finale, Yeltsin averred that 'the communists, [and] all labourers of the Sverdlovsk province pledge to the delegates of the Congress, the Leninist Central Committee and Leonid Il'ich Brezhnev personally that they will struggle for the beautiful and grandiose future with all of their revolutionary passion and steadfast devotion to the cause of the Communist Party'.[154]

Yet, compared to the speeches of other First Secretaries, his was a decidedly reserved performance both in the number of paeans and in their pitch. Only two other Pervyis were as restrained as Yeltsin: Boris Kachura of Donetsk, and a fellow Siberian, Aleksandr Filatov of Novosibirsk, who mentioned Brezhnev five times each. Another First Secretary, Vasiliy Konotop of the Moscow region, praised the General Secretary seven times. The rest of the twelve Pervyis filled their fifteen minutes with no fewer than eight encomiums each, and some with as many as eleven.

The degree of sycophancy in Yeltsin's speech was far below the average as well. Midkhat Shakirov (Bashkiria) extolled Brezhnev for possessing the 'outstanding qualities of a revolutionary of the Lenin type, giant political and organizational talents and theoretical wisdom'.[155] Grigoriy Romanov (Leningrad) saw in the General Secretary 'the most authoritative political and state leader of our times, the true standard-bearer of peace'.[156] Vladimir Gusev (Saratov) expressed 'the most sincere gratitude' of 'all the working people' of the Saratov province to 'dear Leonid Il'ich' for 'caring for the happiness of the Soviet people, for the indefatigable and fruitful effort aimed at the preservation of peace on earth and the strengthening of friendship between peoples'.[157]

There were subtler but weightier differences as well. Other First Secretaries used up their quota of obligatory self-criticisms and complaints (if they got around to them at all) on nebulous items: the general obsolescence of the industrial equipment, the failure to fulfil the Five-Year Plan by 'a number of indicators', the slowdown in the rate of growth, and the arbitrary, disjointed and wasteful industrial policy practised by the myriad of ministries.

Yeltsin's speech stood out in both scale of vision and explicitness of detail. The required victory cymbals struck a muted, even cautious note: 'the constant care of the Central Committee of the Party for the development of the economy and culture of the Middle Ural Area ... has produced some positive results'.[158] From the lengthy menu of tasks, the Sverdlovsk Pervyi chose to stress the strides his province had made in three by now familiar areas: mechanization of manual labour; rational and economic utilization of fuel, electricity and metal; and – of course, of course – modernization of existing enterprises.

He then launched into an enumeration of sores: 'a certain slowdown in the growth rate of industrial production; ineffective utilization by many enterprises of funds and resources, and the lagging behind in the solution of a number of social problems'.[159] To illustrate the 'extremely complex and ineffective' system of management in a number of branches Yeltsin cited construction and wood processing. Three hundred and eighty-seven building firms in the province belonged to thirty-six different ministries and administrations, and logging was run by twenty-five more. The ministries preferred to have small and technologically backward plants, so long as they could be exclusively 'theirs'. The labour productivity at such enterprises was 'significantly lower' than in the industry as a whole, but 'the number of administrative and auxiliary personnel is one and a half to two times higher'.[160] The small wood-processing factories wasted up to 70 per cent of timber cut.

For those awake in the Hall of Congresses that morning, the true scope of Yeltsin's critique was not difficult to discern. He took aim at the entire nation-wide system of Soviet economic planning, which walled off branch from branch, ministry from ministry. The 'objective opportunities and the need for the integrated utilization of resources of economic districts and provinces' were ignored or, at best, insufficiently utilized.[161] 'Given the immense territory of our country,' Yeltsin continued, 'this leads to the complication of industrial ties, sharpens the problems of transportation, and sometimes leads to machinery and enterprises standing idle for lengthy periods,' which results in 'not just material but serious moral losses as well'.[162] Heady stuff for a provincial Party functionary barely four years in the job!

Unlike his colleagues, Yeltsin ventured a solution that matched the problem in scale. He proposed collecting all local enterprises under one administrative roof and managing them through powerful local 'bases of industry'.[163] This proposal was virtually indistinguishable from Nikita Khrushchev's attempt at local 'Councils of People's Economy', the *sovnarkhoz*es, designed to reduce waste, alleviate neglect of the consumer and weaken bureaucratic impediments to technological progress by assuming control over local industry and agriculture 'liberated' from the Moscow ministries. Along with other transgressions against the central bureaucracies, the *sovnarkhoz*es, scrapped immediately after Khrushchev's fall, had been recalled to the hapless reformer in the long indictment read to him sixteen and a half years before by the successful plotters. The coup leaders now sat on the red dais behind the giant flower-filled urns, pretending to listen to the upstart from Sverdlovsk.

Yeltsin might as well not have bothered. That the thought put into his speech and the potential risks that its delivery entailed were in vain became obvious three days before Yeltsin spoke, when General Secretary Leonid Brezhnev read (or, rather, mindlessly mumbled) the 'Report of the Central Committee to the XXVI Congress'. The futility of Yeltsin's effort was obvious not because the level of candour in his speech was disproportionate to that of the Report. On the contrary, Brezhnev's speech to the Twenty-Sixth Party Congress was by far the frankest in recent Party history. It was as if the oligarchs, sensing their fast-approaching demise,* wished to make up with this Report for the shameless propaganda lies in which they had been drowning the country since 1964.

The litany of problems was endless. After decades of virtually unlimited resources and human labour, the 'socialist economy' was consuming

---

* Of the seven leading Politburo members only Andrey Gromyko would be alive four years later.

more than it was producing. Brezhnev suggested, cautiously, that 'results of production' should 'grow faster than expenses'.[164] The great Five-Year Plan, by which the Soviet economy was ostensibly run, turned out to be fiction: after adoption, production plans were revised downwards 'on a broad scale', 'disorganizing the economy, corrupting the workers and teaching them irresponsibility'.[165] The squandering of metal was such that reducing waste by half would save 10 per cent of all metal produced. Sixty-four years after the Great Socialist Revolution, there were 'palpable shortages in the supplies of foodstuffs, first of all meat and other products of animal husbandry'.[166] 'Year in and year out', the production of many consumer goods did not reach the planned targets. Nor had there been a 'sufficient movement' towards better quality or choice for the consumer. Millions of people were employed in manual and heavy labour, which constituted 'not just an economic but a serious social problem'.[167] 'More than a few' families lived in 'ill-equipped' communal apartments, with newlyweds waiting years for a place of their own. The healthcare system lacked qualified medical personnel, new equipment and drugs.[168]

The hopelessness of the Soviet predicament lay in the contrast between the picture that Brezhnev painted and the remedies he offered. The sadly toothless nostrums consisted mostly of exhortations: 'all-round economy of all resources and betterment of the quality of work', 'thrifty attitude towards public property, the ability to use well what we have',[169] 'further deployment of criticism and self-criticism' and 'improvement of ideological and political education'.[170] Local Soviets, those helpless and penniless appendages of the Party, were told to 'take concrete measures to improve the production and sale of consumer goods and services'. The housing crisis was to be alleviated through 'attention, objectivity and decency' in the distribution of apartments and 'firm control' over it by 'public organizations'.[171] And, of course, new ministries were to be created: one for Chemical Industry, another for Fruit and Vegetables.[172]

To an observer of even mildly independent thinking, the Report suggested the worst. The Soviet Union was in the most precarious position a political regime could find itself in: its crisis widely acknowledged yet its leaders confessing an utter lack of remedies. The looming economic dead-end was especially perilous for a system that had for decades proclaimed the rate of material progress the key to its legitimacy.

When, after a long and arduous climb, Boris Yeltsin finally trod the slopes of the Party Olympus, his first steps met not a firm and fecund soil but a swamp: wobbly, shorn of fresh growth, reeking of impotence, sycophancy and death. His first Party Congress was also the last of the era during which Boris Yeltsin had succeeded so spectacularly. In one of the best poems in the Russian language, Fedor Tyutchev had Cicero complain:

> I rose late – and on the road
> The night of Rome fell on me.[173]

The home stretch of Yeltsin's march to power coincided if not with the night of the Soviet 'Rome' then surely with its twilight.

Meanwhile, almost 10,000 kilometres away, in Washington, a renowned chronicler of Soviet Russia wrote of the grand convocation in the Kremlin: 'We seem to have an older generation of fanatics and a younger one of power-maniacs, both concerned to protect and extend their power and devoted to enmity against any system that offers an alternative.'[174] Almost as an afterthought, he added melancholically: 'Perhaps among the thousands of delegates there is one who is looking around with the same revulsion you or I might feel. Perhaps, but I doubt it.'[175]

On the last day of the Twenty-Sixth Party Congress, 3 March 1981, Boris Nikolaevich Yeltsin, was elected a member of the Central Committee of the Communist Party of the Soviet Union.

If the local political lore is to be believed, the 'populists' of the Ural school of Party leadership had always been somewhat closer to the 'masses' than their stuffier colleagues in Central and especially Southern Russia. In Sverdlovsk the Party-to-'masses' traffic seemed to proceed on straighter routes, over shorter distances and with fewer stop signs.

Yeltsin took the custom a step further by developing, almost from the very beginning, a strange and continuously growing appetite for what the French call *bain de foule*, 'bathing in the crowd'.[176] It was this proclivity, very unusual for a big Soviet *nachal'nik*, that, more than anything else Yeltsin did in his eight-and-a-half years in Sverdlovsk, contributed to the Yeltsin legend there and helped forge a bond between the Party boss and his subjects unprecedented in the Soviet Russia of the 1980s.

Yeltsin first dipped into the *bain* towards the end of his second year at the helm, in the autumn of 1978. Unusually heavy rains threatened to bury a record harvest of wheat and vegetables in a sea of mud. The devastated and depopulated countryside, mired in poverty, alcoholism and near total indifference to the fate of the crop, could not cope without assistance from the city dwellers.

By the late 1970s, the annual deliverance of vegetable crops (first and foremost potatoes, which Russians call 'the other bread') by city brigades had been a national autumnal ritual for decades. Engineers and doctors, students and workers, soldiers and scholars – entire universities, laboratories and factories – were dispatched to the fields. They stayed for a weekend, a week or a month of rainy days and frosty nights, working knee-deep in mud and sleeping in draughty barns or, if lucky, in summer-camp barracks without heat, hot water or indoor toilets.

The most popular of the Soviet underground bards of the 1970s, Vladimir Vysotskiy, even wrote a song about the autumn pilgrimage. The sarcastic lyrics berated 'comrade scientists' who 'suffocated' from their intellectual exertions at the synchrotrons, 'forgetting that potatoes are rotting in the field'.[177] They were invited to visit the 'airy' country-side. The song's refrain sounded like an order:

A bus will take us all the way to Skhodnya.
But after that you'll have to jog – and don't complain!
Back home, you all love the 'tatoes, don't ya?
Especially when salted, when not plain![178]

And that is what the call to the countryside had always been: an order. The command was not communicated by the local Party authorities directly to the reluctant pilgrims. Rather, the autumn summons was relayed by the supervisor, the foreman, the teacher or the professor. This, for as long as anyone could remember, was the mode of annual harvest mobilization. It had worked innumerable times before and would undoubtedly have worked again in Sverdlovsk in 1978. Instead, in what appears to have been the first such address by an Obkom First Secretary anywhere in the Soviet Union, Yeltsin went on local television to appeal for help.

For the first time, the master of the province appeared to his subjects not according to the tediously familiar image: exhibiting stately concern and solemnity on a dais; pinning medals; handing over red banners to the winners of 'socialist competitions'; or bellowing slogans from a podium. He talked to them like a human being requesting aid from fellow citizens. The text of the appeal has not survived, but a witness recalls that Yeltsin 'spoke calmly, unhurriedly, without dramatization but in a way that touched the hearts' of his listeners.[179] According to the Obkom, 30,000 workers, 43,000 students, 12,000 drivers and mechanics from the cities of the province came to work the fields that autumn[180] – 'not', Yeltsin proudly claimed, 'obeying an order but moved by their conscience'.[181]

Although this was, without doubt, a familiar exaggeration, Yeltsin as always was prompt and generous in sharing with his fellow Party leaders the secret of his success: the power of a simple and direct address to the 'masses'. In a book published in 1981 he cited the 'potato address' as evidence that 'microphone and camera allow [one to] crisply and quickly respond to the problems people are concerned about, pre-empt uninformed questions and, sometimes, unnecessary speculation around difficulties and shortcomings'.[182] He contrasted this approach with the Soviet media's 'tendency towards blather, simple repetition of common-places', and reprimanded 'officials of all ranks' for 'availing themselves too little of the possibilities offered by radio and television to inform the populace of important economic and political issues'.[183]

A year after he published this nostrum, Yeltsin stepped in front of the camera again – this time for a longer and more complicated show: a televised question-and-answer session on 18 December 1982. In advance of the broadcast, local radio and television announced that questions, complaints and suggestions should be directed to the Obkom. The province eagerly responded with 906 letters, signed by nearly 4,000 people.[184] For two hours and twenty minutes[185] Yeltsin answered some of them. The rest were responded to in writing by the Obkom or the 'appropriate Party and Soviet organs'.[186]

After the show, Yeltsin chaired a meeting of the Obkom Buro to discuss the lessons of this extraordinary exercise – right there, in the studio of Sverdlovsk television. One of the persistent themes in the questions and comments of the irate subjects was the use of official cars by the wives and children of Obkom functionaries. From now on, Yeltsin announced, the cars were to be used for official business only. With the First Secretary scrupulously adhering to the new rule in the months and years ahead, the new ordinance was to become quite effective.[187]

As was his wont, Yeltsin pressed his subordinates into the service of what he thought was a good cause. After his performance, a new pro-gramme featuring the Party, Soviet and industrial leaders of the province went on the air on Sverdlovsk television. It was called *Leaders Answer People's Letters*.[188] (Later the dangerously 'populist' title was toned down to *The Communist and our Times*.) Among the guests on the show were two of the most powerful men in the region: Chairman of the Regional Soviet Anatoliy Mekhrintsev and First Secretary of the Sverdlovsk Gorkom Vladimir Kadochnikov.

Outside his domain, however, Yeltsin's feat was not promoted quite as unreservedly. The only public record of his television performance was a *Pravda* article, which appeared four months after the event.[189] The eventual publication of the account on the one hand and its paucity and tardiness on the other were a measure of the ambivalence that Moscow must have felt towards one of its brightest and most effective, though also most unconventional, local potentates.

On the face of it, this was a newsworthy event. The First Secretary of one of the most important Obkoms in the country had answered, on television, queries from the 'labourers'. There was even an aura of the by then ancient and quaint, but still officially revered, Leninist tradition of being 'in the thick of the masses'. Yet just as unmistakable was a whiff of heterodoxy about the whole affair, something that smacked of the 'petit-bourgeois populism' that had nearly undermined the socialist state in 'fraternal' Czechoslovakia fourteen years before.

The matter was resolved in an ingenious manner. A medium-size article eventually marked the event but contained not a word about Yeltsin's appearance on television. Noting that 'speaking before the people is becoming a norm for the leadership of the Sverdlovsk region', *Pravda* stated that 'recently' (*sic*) Sverdlovsk television had 'requested' that the four-and-a-half million residents of the Middle Ural should write about 'what worried them' and 'ask questions to which they would like to receive answers'.[190] Of the thousands of questions and comments that the article claimed had been received by the Obkom, *Pravda* chose half a dozen on which Yeltsin had commented,[191] illustrating the 'statesmanlike approach of the letters' authors to our economic and social problems'.[192] The citizens were concerned with such lofty subjects as the 'acceleration of the growth of labour productivity' and 'ideological, politico-educational work'. These noble themes were followed by preoccupations less exalted but undoubtedly far more representative of the Obkom's correspondents: shortage of 'goods for popular consumption'; 'difficulties' in the production of food; and 'dissatisfaction' with housing, public transportation, trade, public catering and telephone lines.[193]

A 'veteran of the Verkh-Isetsk Metalworks Plant' complained that customers were reluctant to buy certain Soviet-made goods: for instance, the shoes made by the Sverdlovsk factory Uralobuv'. Yeltsin's response held out little prospect of speedy improvement: 'I agree . . . the factory is, so far, incapable of satisfying the demand [for fashionable shoes]. To be perfectly honest, the factory would have to undergo a thorough renovation: a third of its equipment is obsolete.'[194] To those who wondered about 'the implementation of the Food Programme in the Sverdlovsk *oblast*', Yeltsin again proffered truth instead of cheer. 'So far our agricultural sector is not doing as well as required today. We must apply all our energy to improving the situation. The Food Programme is the business of all people. Unfortunately not everyone understands that.'[195]

By the time *Pravda* published its paltry rendering of the experiment, Yeltsin was well into a still wider breach of the customary modes of the Party's intercourse with the 'masses': no-holds-barred question-and-answer sessions with live audiences. As in most of what he set out to master, Yeltsin succeeded. 'He did it brilliantly, artistically, and thoroughly enjoyed doing it,' recalled an Obkom colleague.[196] Another said: 'He had a God-given talent: he could talk to people and could make them listen.'[197] 'He had a superb sense of what this particular audience wanted,' remembered an ex-member of Sverdlovsk's cultural nomenklatura, whose job required frequent attendance at the Obkom's functions, 'and he could expertly manage any audience.'[198]

In November 1981, a young professor of Sverdlovsk University attended a conference of teachers of the 'social sciences'. Because the gathering had been organized, as were all such conferences in the Soviet Union, by the local Obkom, the professor expected the usual: 'boring presentations, which had nothing to do with the real problems, an exchange of views borrowed from Party publications, the tedious preaching by the ideology bosses'.[199]

Something quite different happened. There was only one speaker, a 'tall, white-haired man, in an elegant suit which accentuated his athletic figure'.

From the first words we listened with bated breath. Many grabbed their notebooks [trying] to write down every word he uttered. He was telling us such things! . . . It was at that conference that, for the first time, I heard the truth about the USSR. Perhaps not all the truth, perhaps only a small part of it. But what I heard was a genuine revelation.[200]

In the question-and-answer period that followed, Yeltsin 'directly answered all and any questions, no matter how difficult'.[201] 'It did not take more than an hour', continued the witness, 'to realize that here was a man who worked his heart out at his job; a man who sought to master every detail of his business, no matter how small; and a man who felt personally responsible for everything he was saying.'[202]

Just as unexpected to a *Pravda* correspondent was the format of Yeltsin's address to a gathering of journalists from regional, district and city newspapers of the Sverdlovsk province:

It would have been far simpler [for Yeltsin] to begin with a wordy introductory speech. Instead, Boris Nikolaevich asked the audience: 'Do we need a speech, or shall we begin with your questions right away?' 'With questions!' was the response that followed a period of silence caused, most likely, by the unexpected readiness of the First Secretary of an Obkom to scrap the customary order of meetings of this sort . . .[203]

[After the session had been going for] over two hours, interest had not abated. No matter how many questions were put to the First Secretary of the Obkom, and no matter how varied they were, the answers were precise and candid.[204]

Yeltsin's *foules* were not limited to tame audiences such as 'social scientists' or journalists, whose appointments had been cleared by the Obkom's Department of Ideology. He began to engage the common folk and, among them, the hardest of all, blue-collar workers. Unschooled in the allusions of intra-Party communications and with not much to lose, they were sometimes unsparingly direct in their queries and criticisms.

As they are everywhere, miners were the most difficult audience. When Yeltsin came to the Severouralsk bauxite mines, the gathering was 'speechless with tension', and there was 'an explosive mixture of fear and desperation in the air'.[205] The miners had been driven to the edge by the empty food stores, especially the absence of tea and bed-linen, and by scanty meals in the cafeteria.[206] But, a local journalist recalled,

after a vigorous and simply worded address by the man who looked and sounded so much like one of themselves, the miners felt both relieved and excited: 'He'll help us! He welcomes complaints in writing!' The flurry of notes that followed was like a sign of hope that things could be changed.[207]

The notes poured in to the dais and were being sorted out by topics: tea, linen, salaries. Yeltsin announced that he would answer them all and threatened to punish the culprits responsible for the problems that were mentioned (some of whom sat next to him on the dais). Then, sheaves of notes in hand, he 'rushed' to the rostrum and castigated the management of the mine and the Chairman of the local Soviet. Shaking the 'linen' notes above his head, he explained that the country as a whole was 'short of cotton' but, still, something must be done. From now on, Yeltsin declared to a 'deadly hush' in the hall, 'each pillowcase must be justly distributed!' The audience burst into applause. 'No one doubted' that from that time on, each pack of tea, each slice of cheese, each bedsheet would be fairly rationed out.[208]

Yeltsin's most celebrated immersion in the *bain de foule*, the jewel in his 'populist' crown and the event they talked about in Ekaterinburg a decade later, occurred on the evening of 19 May 1981 in the city's largest auditorium, the Palace of Youth. It was a session with the students of Sverdlovsk.

As with most of Yeltsin's ventures, the timing was dictated by the Centre. The Twenty-Sixth Congress had ended two months before, and the local Party committees all over the country were striving mightily to 'carry the Party word to the masses' in a noisy but universally ignored propaganda campaign. The format of Yeltsin's appearance could have been just as predictable: a three-hour speech before the student nomenklatura, known as the 'Party and Komsomol *aktiv*', on the 'tasks of Soviet youth in light of the decisions of the Twenty-Sixth Party Congress' – or some other equally daring topic. 'What could have been simpler', Yeltsin bragged later to the leading Party magazine, 'than to have a traditional meeting with the student *aktiv* complete with the usual speech. But the Obkom decided otherwise.'[209] The coy reference to the 'Obkom's decision' was made solely to conform to the ritual of 'collective leadership': the meeting was entirely Yeltsin's idea.[210] Later, of course, the Propaganda Department of the Obkom 'sat down' with Sverdlovsk television to 'organize' the event.[211]

As with the television show a year and a half later, the session with the students would prove too hot a dish to feed to the Soviet public without cooling it off first. *Pravda* and *Izvestia* passed over the event entirely. *Komsomol'skaya Pravda*, the main newspaper of Communist Youth and at the time the most liberal of the all-Union dailies, waited two-and-a-half months to mention the happening,[212] and another month to supply examples of the questions and the answers.[213] Even then the editors apparently felt they needed to protect their flanks with this quotation from the student newspaper of the Sverdlovsk Polytechnic Institute: 'The session turned out to be very useful, and not only from the point of view of receiving interesting and truthful information. It showed once again that the attitude of our Party towards domestic and international problems is honest, Leninist, very humane.'[214]

Still, even the pasteurized version conveyed the flavour of this most unorthodox dialogue between the Party seigneur and his youthful subjects:

It does not happen too often that college students will sit through six hours of lectures in a row, and if you add the fact that the meeting took place in the evening after the regular courses, you must admit that you are dealing with an extraordinary event . . .

. . . Listening to Boris Nikolaevich was not an effortless exercise. He made no allowances for the age of his audience – he spoke to them in the same way he would have spoken to those at the helm of industry, agriculture, transportation or science of the Ural region.

[Later] the students of the Polytechnic Institute wrote in the student newspaper: 'We very much appreciated . . . the clear and precise answers to the questions, without blunting the sharp edges of the problems.

In the dormitories of UPI those who had been in the audience sat up until late in the evening excitedly repeating what they had heard to their amazed roommates, 'provoking' questions and debates.[215]

A month before the meeting, special mailboxes had been placed 'in the most visible places in all sixteen colleges of the city',[216] and the students were asked to send their 'questions, thoughts, arguments, doubts'[217] to the Obkom. The organizers of the meeting promised that all the letters, without exception, would reach the Obkom leadership. They did: Yeltsin's explicit directive forbade not only hiding 'inconvenient' questions but even 'editing'.[218] Only 'thematic grouping' of the letters was allowed to save the speaker's time.[219]

The students of Sverdlovsk were not about to pass up a miraculous opportunity to speak directly to the master of the province. As Yeltsin later reported, his future audience was 'active'.[220] The Obkom received 930 missives, some of them filling 'entire notebooks'.[221] The recipient of the letters was just as diligent. 'It was the first time in my life', recalls a witness, 'that I saw a man of such rank work with letters so carefully and with such interest . . .'[222]

The complaints were 'immediately forwarded to the appropriate authorities' for response.[223] Among these authorities were the Chief of the Trade Administration of the Executive Committee of the Sverdlovsk Regional Soviet,[224] the Chairman of the Council of College Deans,[225] the Chief of the Public Catering Administration,[226] the Secretary of the Party Committee of the Institute of People's Economy,[227] the Secretary of the Party Committee and Dean of the Institute of Forestry and Wood Processing,[228] and the Dean of the Ural State University.[229] The task must have been a shock to the local mandarins: for the first time in their lives they were composing *spravka*s ('memos') for the consumption of *hoi polloi* – and college kids to boot.

Into some matters, however, Yeltsin looked himself. One such instance was a complaint submitted in advance of the meeting by sixty-nine students of the Institute of People's Economy (IPE):

> Respected Boris Nikolaevich! Requesting your attention are students of the IPE, from the Economic Planning Department. We would like to tell you about the shortcomings in the work of the cafeteria in our Institute. It is very, very dirty; one can often see flies on the products, cockroaches crawl on the tables and on the floor. The quality of food is low, it does not taste good and is unappetizing. There is no choice in the menu. There are constant queues and the service is slow.[230]

After reading the letter, Yeltsin ordered the head of the Public Catering Department of the City Soviet to accompany him on a surprise visit to the cafeteria early the next morning.[231] Yeltsin called late at night to preclude an emergency clean-up of the eatery. But, of course, nothing was too good for the Pervyi: when they entered the cafeteria, it was sparkling clean and the food was of a variety and freshness never seen before. After a brief tour, Yeltsin told the cafeteria's manager that he expected this state of affairs to be renewed every day – or the manager 'could kiss his job goodbye'.[232] (In the *Komsomol'skaya Pravda* version, Yeltsin 'asked the administration never again to lower its standards'.)[233]

While, in the long run, the utility of such raids was rather dubious, their rhetorical efficacy was beyond doubt. At public meetings these pre-emptive strikes proved showstoppers. Yeltsin's favourite routine was to glance at a slip of paper calling for the dismissal of an especially incompetent or corrupt official, and then announce, to loud applause: 'Already fired. Next question.'[234]

Preparing for the session with students, Yeltsin rejected three drafts of his introductory speech because its tone did not seem right to him.[235] ('Just think about it!' said a witness to the effort. 'The First Secretary was worried about the "right tone" in speaking to college kids!')[236] The search continued until his assistant, Viktor Ilyushin, gave him an unpublished transcript of a meeting with Tbilisi students of another Party progressive, the First Secretary of the Communist Party of Georgia, Eduard Shevardnadze. 'That's it,' Yeltsin said.[237] The 'right tone' had been found.

One morning, Yeltsin dropped by the University's Department of Philosophy. The visit was a total surprise not only to the students but to the administration as well. The door of a class room opened and in came the First Secretary. He was alone, without the usual retinue. 'I know I should not have disturbed your studies,' said Yeltsin. 'But, please understand, I cannot adjust my schedule to yours. I would like to talk to you, to hear about your life, your problems.'[238] He sat down at the teacher's desk and began to talk. In this manner, in the spring of 1981, he is believed to have visited all sixteen colleges of Sverdlovsk.[239]

A few days before the meeting in the Palace of Youth, Yeltsin gave an order to favour 'real' students to fill the auditorium.[240] The Pervyi knew the habits of his minions only too well. As soon as the session had been announced, the college nomenklatura began compiling the list of 'delegates' – most of whom were themselves: Party and Komsomol organizers, activists and faculty. To everyone's surprise, the order was enforced, and, in another odd development surrounding the event, many of the functionaries found themselves seated outside the hall, watching the meeting on television monitors.[241]

For most of those who were in the Palace of Youth that night, merely to be in the presence of the First Secretary was a marvel. Yet even those few who had been sufficiently trusted, active and well connected to be in the same hall with the Pervyi before, looked at the stage in disbelief. His subjects expected the Obkom First to be pontificating from a distant podium. But that was not what they were to see on the evening of 19 May. In violation of the ritual, the master of the province was not seated on a dais covered with red velvet, behind the ubiquitous rows of potted plants. Neither was he stern, majestically silent or delivering a three-hour monologue. Instead, armed with a long wooden pointer, a huge map of the province[242] behind him, he stood before the capacity audience of 1,700 ready to answer 'all and any questions, provided that the questioners identify themselves'.[243]

In addition to questions submitted in advance of the session, 144 additional notes were passed to Yeltsin during the meeting.[244] The session lasted for over five hours. The transcript was never published, but an hour and a half was broadcast by local television several days later.[245]

Behind Yeltsin, in the 'room of the Praesidium', a 'travelling brigade' of the Obkom's Propaganda Department was feverishly preparing short memos, *spravka*s, for Yeltsin's replies to the questions from the floor. Since Yeltsin's plunge into larger and far less predictable *bains*, the information brigade's hours had become longer and considerably more hectic: compressed by the weight of years of official silence and lies, the geyser of questions spewed forth jet-like, hot and strong. 'There were more and more notes with questions [*zapiski*] passed to Yeltsin.

A veritable torrent,' recalled a former member of the brigade.[246]

While Yeltsin spoke, all the questions were quickly and neatly typed. If answers required specialized knowledge, the notes were passed to the heads of the Obkom's departments,[247] who usually accompanied Yeltsin on his speaking tours.[248] Not infrequently, problems described in the notes were settled then and there – with a telephone call from a department head to his subordinates. Yeltsin visibly relished such occasions. They were among the main attractions of the show: to watch Yeltsin answering *zapiski* was akin to enjoying 'terrific theatre'.[249]

One day, speaking before the principals of Sverdlovsk secondary schools, Yeltsin received a note in which a principal complained that he could not get from a bank the money appropriated for construction and renovation. Yeltsin read the last sentence, 'The bank manager would not release the funds,' paused and said, 'He is already releasing them. See him after this meeting.'[250] Another principal passed on a *zapiska* about a director of the District Public Catering Administration who refused to open a cafeteria in his school, claiming that it would not be profitable. 'He is no longer refusing,' answered Yeltsin.[251]

But, beyond theatrics, there was a general rule of 'answering each question in as businesslike and precise a manner as possible, and announcing a decision then and there'.[252] According to a close observer of the Obkom routines, it was this habit that 'distinguished Yeltsin from both his predecessors and his successors'.[253] The latter 'refrained' from spontaneous responses, 'drowned the essence of a problem in a sea of empty words',[254] and, at best, promised 'to think more' about an issue raised.[255] For Yeltsin, the question-and-answer segments of his meetings were visibly the most enjoyable. He relished them,[256] and disported himself before his audience.[257]

At times, however, the careful staff work ended up by the wayside. One day, Yeltsin was asked if he knew about the pervasive system of *blat* (use of connections to obtain quality goods and services) and, if he did, how the Obkom was fighting it. Yeltsin cited the number of those he claimed had been punished – twice the figure given in the *spravka* prepared by the Department of Administrative Organs. The improvisation did not end there, however. 'Too few [officials jailed]?' he asked the audience. 'Too few! Too few!' was the loud, enthusiastic, multi-throated response. 'All right: we will throw more in the slammer!' This coda never failed to provoke an ovation.[258]

On 19 May 1981, the largest segment of questions, comments and complaints for the Palace of Youth meeting concerned the familiar travails of daily existence in the big, bulging, sooty and barely solvent Soviet metropolis, with its million-and-a-quarter population, of whom 76,000 were students. There were tram and bus routes to be added or extended to accommodate the urban sprawl;[259] buildings 'drowning' in mud and 'impossible to get to by car because the roads are all rutted and strewn with upturned concrete slabs';[260] the 'barbaric' cutting down of trees to accommodate more construction;[261] the polluted city ponds;[262] the rutted roads; neglected, decaying and impoverished museums;[263] the dearth of telephone lines.[264]

As always, housing was the sorest spot. Students were having an especially rough time of it: virtually all the state apartments were distributed among full-time employees through the workplace, while private housing was in the shortest supply (and extremely expensive). Thus, for the duration of the housing crisis, the sole hope for out-of-town students was dormitories. Yet of these, too, there were not enough. When would there be enough dorms for all students, Yeltsin was asked?[265] Where could married students with children live, since dorms did not have family quarters?[266] How much new housing was planned in Sverdlovsk?[267] Would the housing problem ever be solved?[268] 'When will each family in our city have its own, separate apartment?'[269]

Respected Boris Nikolaevich, we are asking for your help in solving a problem concerning our dorm. Because of the disrepair of the sewage pipes, the ground around the dorm and the basement of the dorm are continuously flooded. We have petitioned all the organizations in one way or another connected with our territory and the sewers, but still the dorm is surrounded by a foul-smelling pond, several lower floors are damp and infested with insects. The building itself is beginning to decay and the asphalt around the building is sinking. Please help to solve this problem as soon as possible.[270]

(In his *spravka*, the Dean of the Institute of People's Economy, whose dorm this was, wrote: 'During the construction of the dorm, the sewage pipes were not installed. Therefore, all efforts directed at the alleviation of the situation have been futile.)[271] 'Is it possible to provide hot water for Dorm Number Four?'[272] 'There are shower rooms in Dorm Number Seven. Yet they do not work. Will they ever work?'[273]

After housing, the paucity of teaching equipment drew the most ire. Good Whatman paper for drawing was impossible to get: what was sold to future engineers and architects was more like 'blotting paper'.[274] The Department of Dentistry of the Sverdlovsk Medical Institute did not have enough textbooks. 'Could you somehow help the students to acquire the textbooks because the quality of their preparations suffers greatly?'[275]

> Comrade Yeltsin! I am a student of the Piano Department of the Conservatory. We have great difficulties in the repairing and tuning of the instruments. Very often we have to practise on the instruments with broken strings, badly tuned and with non-functioning pedals. New instruments have not been delivered to the Conservatory for a long time, while piano-tuners do not have the necessary materials for repairs. As a result the quality of graduates suffers. What do we spend our time on, then, for five years? Could the region help the Conservatory to acquire new instruments?[276]

Even with all the *spravka*s commandeered from the rulers of Sverdlovsk, Yeltsin did not have good, politically correct answers to many questions. So he told them the truth. There was no hope for an apartment for each family until 1990 at the earliest.[277] Food rationing would continue. Students, like everyone else in Sverdlovsk, could hope for one kilo of 'meat products per person on holiday occasions'[278] (that is, twice a year, for May Day and on the anniversary of the Revolution, 7 November). The United States was, indeed, ahead of the USSR in labour productivity: it was twice as high in industry and four times higher in agriculture. Why? 'Capitalist competition is the strongest stimulus for the intensification of labour,' Yeltsin answered. 'The fittest survive . . . In addition, today, the USA produces twice the amount of electricity generated in the Soviet Union.'[279]

Along the way, Yeltsin acknowledged inflation, which had no place in the theory of 'socialist economy' and, therefore, in public discourse. 'The rise in prices of [new] books is connected with the rise in the price of paper, printing equipment and materials.'[280]

He also admitted to substantial belt-tightening in the state budget: the mark of a silent but steep economic downturn which was shrinking the boundaries of the Soviet welfare state. Asked why work on the construction of the Drama Theatre had been halted,[281] Yeltsin cited an unpublished resolution by the Central Committee and the Council of Ministers which 'temporarily terminated' construction of all 'cultural, athletic and administrative buildings and sites' that were less than half finished at the time. This had been done in order to allow for the 'concentration of means and resources at the most important sites of the people's economy'.[282] Yeltsin was blunter still in answering an inquiry about a proposed city swimming pool: 'The building of swimming pools has been forbidden in the Eleventh Pyatiletka by the Council of Ministers' resolution. As yet, comrades, we are not that rich. As they say, "Cut your coat according to your cloth." '[283]

Yeltsin told the students the sorts of things that, if heard by ubiquitous secret police informers in a less exalted setting, would definitely have been classified as 'defamation of the Soviet state' and the 'spreading of bourgeois propaganda', and reported to the local KGB authorities. Alcoholism was sharply on the rise, and the number of intoxicated people picked up on the streets of Sverdlovsk and delivered to the 'sobering-up stations' (*vytrezviteli*) had doubled in the previous four years to reach over 79,000 in 1980.[284] The shortage of paper accounted for the 'impossibility' of finding novels in the city.[285] The 'frequent absence' of meat, milk, cheese and cottage cheese in the stores[286] was explained by the 'patently insufficient' level of production by the local *sovkhoz*es and *kolkhoz*es and the disappearance of the private dairy farmer.[287]

As the evening progressed, candour extended to the person of the First Secretary himself:

Q: Have you decided on the relation between the public and private in your life?

A: I have – and not in favour of the private. I put public activity in the very first place.

Q: Your attitude towards cigarettes?

A: Haven't smoked, do not smoke, and would advise you against smoking.

Q: How do you see the meaning of life?

A: ... To be needed by other people. Because of that I've always had a deeply felt desire to show my worth. When I was a student of the Polytechnic Institute [I wanted] to distinguish myself in my studies. Same in my work in the economy, Party, sports.

Q: What is your attitude towards sports?

A: Loved and continue to love. Still play volleyball. Sport means health. And one needs a lot of it in any job.

Q: What is your understanding of your duty as a communist?

A: To devote whatever energy I have to making better the lives of the people of my native Middle Ural ...[288]

Even during this astonishing performance, on a number of subjects Yeltsin remained well within conventional confines. Some stemmed from the apparently genuine beliefs of a provincial Party boss. Thus, responding to a request for more discotheques, Yeltsin opined that 'in their attempts to achieve the ideological disarmament of Soviet youths, Western ideologues have special hopes for art, especially music. I am telling you frankly: we are worried today about the ideological level of student discos . . . Some of them, to various degrees, have become conduits for bourgeois culture. Such a state of affairs we are not going to tolerate.'[289]

Nor did he dare take on certain administrative taboos. One such was Sverdlovsk's status as a 'closed city', which, although known to everyone in the region, was officially unmentionable. The students wanted to know whether it was true that foreigners were forbidden to visit Sverdlovsk. Why, they asked, 'has our large city never hosted foreign musicians and conductors?' And why were Mongolians the only foreign students at Sverdlovsk University?[290] Yeltsin fudged the truth. Sverdlovsk, he said, was 'continuously visited by foreign delegations', and 'foreign specialists' worked at its 'enterprises'.[291]

On 19 May 1981 Boris Yeltsin deployed and very successfully tested what would later become his key political asset: the ability to project seemingly genuine respect for common men and women. In one witness's words, 'he extended the boundaries of freedom, loosened the corset a bit'.[292] His audience, exhilarated by this newly bestowed dignity, would reciprocate with intense personal loyalty, even devotion. 'After that evening we were ready to do anything for him,' recalled a young history student who was in the audience in the Palace of Youth. 'If Yeltsin had ordered us to storm the Obkom, we would have!'[293]

At the time, however, storming the Obkom could not have been further from Yeltsin's designs. It was the Obkom that did the storming. 'I had been brought up in this system,' Yeltsin wrote a decade later. 'Everything was instilled with the command methods of leadership – and that was how I behaved too. Whether I chaired a conference, conducted a Buro meeting, or spoke at a Plenum – it all was force, onslaught, pressure.'[294]

He was a restlessly peripatetic Pervyi. Early in his reign, Yeltsin resolved to visit each of the sixty-three cities and towns of the province no less than once every two years. Each trip involved meetings with local officials and, increasingly, with 'workers' and 'collective farmers'.[295] Although the First Secretary's preferred mode of transportation was helicopter, a veteran Obkom driver remembered Yeltsin's tenure as 'one of the most hectic times' of his career: he often spent 'as much as ten hours a day at the wheel'.[296]

Yeltsin's forays into his enormous domain did not omit the many military bases of the province. He observed exercises, drove tanks and climbed into cockpits of fighter planes. To impress still further upon the local brass who was in charge, he even attempted to rock, at least a bit, the massive, leaden and already slightly rusting Soviet military boat. The 'unspeakable conditions' in some of the bases ('the Ministry of Defence considered soldiers slaves with no voice of their own') prompted Yeltsin to exhort the soldiers to 'criticize' their superiors 'from below'. He persisted in encouraging this homegrown version of the 'Fire on the headquarters' slogan so famously tried a decade earlier in China, until, gradually, some 'critical remarks directed at the [local] military leadership' began to surface at the soldiers' Party and Komsomol meetings.[297]

When travels took Yeltsin outside his fiefdom, on the way to Sverdlovsk's Koltsovo airport the cavalcade of black Obkom Volgas would pull off the highway into a clearing in the forest. There, perched on tree stumps around Yeltsin, the farewell party would 'knock down' a shot of vodka for the road and get last-minute instructions from the departing boss on how to run the province in his absence.[298] Upon the chief's return, the same clearing was revisited to toast a safe arrival and to brief Yeltsin on what had transpired while he was away – much like the big Russian noblemen who for centuries stopped in their suburban villas before re-entering the intrigue-laden and often murderous courts of Moscow and St Petersburg.

Keeping up with the Pervyi's feverish tempo was not easy. Although Yeltsin did not explicitly order long office hours (and, contrary to custom, never called people at home), everyone in his orbit gradually adjusted to his work habits – although no one ever matched his working hours.[299] 'Some approached [my] rhythm [of work],' Yeltsin recalled, 'others actually attempted to keep pace. Mekhrintsev, for example.'[300]

'Keeping pace' might not have been the best strategy for Anatoliy Mekhrintsev, Yeltsin's hand-picked Chairman of the Sverdlovsk Regional Soviet, who soon became a close friend and neighbour (they lived on the same landing of the apartment building reserved for the Sverdlovsk leadership).* This slight, scholarly and private man had at

---

* The building, No. 2 Eighth of March Street, known in Sverdlovsk as the House of Old Bolsheviks, had been built for the leadership of the province in the 1930s. The Yeltsins moved into flat number 22 in April 1975, after his promotion to Obkom Secretary. Two years later, after he became First Secretary, they moved to a larger flat (number 24) in the same building. Yeltsin broke yet another tradition when in February 1979 he moved out of the Old Bolsheviks and settled at No. 1 Embankment of Working Youth, where he lived until his departure from Sverdlovsk.

first refused outright the Chairmanship of the Soviet offered him by Yeltsin in 1976. Pressed by Yeltsin, he resisted for a while[301] but then submitted to Party discipline. In accordance with the Soviet ritual of governing, in which the Party's role was to 'direct' the Soviets and the government but not to 'supplant' them openly, Mekhrintsev was Yeltsin's official *alter ego*, charged with implementing a great many of the often short-order and invariably urgent schemes that poured forth from Yeltsin's office. When Mekhrintsev died in early 1985, many in Sverdlovsk believed that overwork had contributed to his untimely death. Some discerned guilt, as well as grief, in Yeltsin's demeanour at Mekhrintsev's funeral.[302]

The brutal routine, of which Anatoliy Mekhrintsev was perhaps the most serious and most conspicuous but, almost certainly, not the only casualty, was unavoidable given the long-term plans of the Pervyi. To the extent that Yeltsin (and not commands from Moscow or local crises) shaped the seemingly *ad hoc*, hectic and crowded schedule of the Sverdlovsk Obkom, there was a method to his organizational omnivorousness. 'He was an ambitious man,' remembered a former head of one of the Obkom's departments. 'He was satisfied only when he achieved something serious. He was not interested in the routine. Long-term perspective, strategy were his passions. He always wanted to do what was both truly needed and noticeable.'[303]

There were, of course, exceptions to these criteria. While the 'noticeable' component was invariably present, the 'need' for some of Yeltsin's projects was less than obvious. Like any other ambitious Soviet boss, he built his share of monuments to his own omnipotence. There was, for example, the new Obkom building: a twenty-four-storey glass-and-concrete monster, completed towards the end of Yeltsin's Secretaryship. Sverdlovsk's only skyscraper, it was immediately labelled by local wits, traditionally inclined to bawdy puns, 'a member of the CPSU'.[304]

When the then world chess champion, Anatoliy Karpov, lamented in a 1979 book that so large a province as Sverdlovsk did not have its own chess club, Yeltsin 'freed' an old building, renovated it and invited Karpov to the opening ceremony.[305] After Karpov had cut the ribbon, he was given a poster with the incriminating quotation from his book. He was then asked to 'rip the poster into shreds' and to promise that in the next edition of his book the phrase about the Sverdlovsk province would be omitted. 'To the great delight' of local chess enthusiasts, Karpov obliged on both scores.[306] (The poster, of course, was Yeltsin's idea.)

Perhaps the most publicity was garnered, in 1983, from the 'experimental agricultural settlements': Baltym, seven kilometres north of

Sverdlovsk and near the dachas of the local Party and government nobility;[307] and Patrushi, which was almost exactly the same distance to the south. They were built in record time (two years) and at the cost of slowing down construction in the entire province.[308] Three months before the due date, so much of the construction was still unfinished that the Deputy Chairman of the State Committee for Construction and Architecture, who had come to Sverdlovsk from Moscow to examine the project, harangued the builders gathered in Yeltsin's office. 'You may leave assured that everything shall be done on time and to the highest standards,' Yeltsin assured him.[309]

Meanwhile, the ground had not even been broken for the centrepiece of the 'model settlement': the Cultural-Health Centre, which was to house, among many other facilities, the outpatient clinic and the sports complex.[310] The Centre's planned location was most inauspicious: on a narrow strip of land between a swamp and the already paved road. The Chief Architect of Sverdlvosk, Gennadiy Belyankin, came to Yeltsin: 'Boris Nikolaevich, this cannot be done.' 'What do you mean, "cannot"?' Yeltsin said. 'The opening is in three months! You need help? Just tell me what you need!'[311]

The model settlements, which Yeltsin is said to have shown off to 'all the stars of the Politburo, except for the General Secretary',[312] consisted of sixty-seven detached town houses containing a total of 152 flats, each 'with a full range of modern conveniences'.[313] The key objective of the experiment was 'to choose, through experimentation, from a wide variety, the types of houses most useful for the population of the countryside, the most economical, and to raise the level of amenities and architectural expression'. There was even a convenience store. Understandably dazzled by so sudden a display of the Party's largess amid the squalor and poverty of their habitat, the locals were initially wary of the project. Later, Yeltsin was happy to report, the peasants became curious and then were 'filled with an ardent desire to move to the new flats'. Naturally, he reported, they 'expressed their gratitude to the Party and the government for such care'.[314]

The experiment was certainly 'noticed'. Yeltsin made sure that it would be by timing the completion of the project to coincide[315] with no less an affair than an All-Russian conference-seminar, which gathered in Sverdlovsk to 'study the progressive work method for the construction of and provision of amenities for agricultural settlements of the Russian Federation'.[316] The keynote speaker was the First Deputy Prime Minister of the Russian Federation. The latter, among other useful things he found in the Baltym and Patrushi experiment, recommended that a compound of plaster and concrete, invented at the Sverdlovsk Polytechnic Institute, be adopted 'everywhere in Russia'.[317]

When the conference ended and the hoopla died down, it became clear, of course, that the prohibitive costs of construction[318] and a myriad other practical matters, overlooked in the rush to finish and to impress, rendered Baltym and Patrushi irrelevant for the Russian village in the 1980s. They turned out to be, in the words of a former high Sverdlovsk official, 'Potemkin villages'.[319]

A much more 'needed' legacy of Yeltsin's reign was the Sverdlovsk–Serov highway. Until it was built, there had been no road between Sverdlovsk and the northern part of the province (where fifty years before Yeltsin's grandfather Ignat had been exiled and died), except in winter when frozen ground was firm enough to bear heavy trucks. There were many fatal accidents.[320] Today, the highway remains the only link (apart from an indirect rail route) that connects the centre of the province with its northernmost lands, where bauxite, iron ore, coal and precious metals are extracted and processed.

Contrary to Yeltsin's claim in his memoirs that he set the construction in motion,[321] the project had started before he took the helm of the province. The meeting of the Obkom at which the task was first announced was chaired by Ryabov.[322] In his acceptance speech in November 1976, Yeltsin had called the construction of the Sverdlovsk–Serov highway 'one of the most important tasks of the Tenth Pyatiletka'[323] and had bemoaned the fact that 'in the preceding nine months only half of the planned construction work had been done'.[324]

To spur the project along, Yeltsin convened the Obkom enforcers: Party Secretaries and Chairmen of the Soviets from districts and cities through which the highway would run. After a long discussion the gathering adopted the First Secretary's idea: the Party and Soviet leadership of each city or district would be responsible for a segment of the highway.[325] Of course this typically Yeltsinite heterodox scheme required 'a precise organization of labour, discipline and constant control'. Fortunately, there was never a shortage of these in the Yeltsin Obkom. A 'permanent headquarters'[326] of the project was set up to follow the daily progress of the construction. Yeltsin himself took many helicopter trips to the sites, where 'turners, locksmiths and engineers', on leave from their plants, felled the trees and rooted out stumps along the route.[327]

The road was constructed with Yeltsin's customary assiduousness: 'thoroughly and conscientiously, with multi-layer surfacing, so that it could serve many years'.[328] A full year before the scheduled date of completion, Yeltsin fixed the day and even hour of the maiden ride. A vehicle, too, was designated: a bus filled with the local *nachal'nik*s in charge of the highway's sectors. If any of these sectors were not completely finished, those responsible were to get off the bus – in front of their neighbours and subordinates gathered to celebrate the opening with red flags flapping in the breeze, and bands blaring marches. Soviet maps listed the Sverdlovsk–Serov highway not as 'local' or 'regional' but as of 'republican significance' – the second highest category after 'all-Union'.

Perhaps the truest exemplar of the 'noticeable and the needed', and the one Yeltsin was most proud of, was the razing of *barak*s in Sverdlovsk. This legacy of Stalin's industrialization had been compounded in 1941 by the Second World War evacuation of 437 plants and factories from Central Russia and Ukraine to the Urals. In the desperate rush to start production right away, plants and factories began working 'without foundation, walls or ceiling', while the workers and their families were crammed into 'dug-outs and *barak*s'.[329]

In time, the plants and factories acquired walls and ceilings, but the shanties remained. That is why the Sverdlovsk region had on its territory more *barak*s than almost any other part of Russia.[330] In the late 1970s, the city's pre-eminent plant and the jewel of Soviet heavy industry, Uralmash, was still surrounded by a 'veritable city of *barak*s',[331] where three generations had lived since the 1930s.

Thirty years after his Berezniki childhood, Yeltsin still remembered the 'decrepit, draughty hovels', the 'wooden huts for ten, fifteen, twenty families', and was 'deeply upset' by the memories. Having concluded that 'in the twentieth century people could not live like that', he decided to 'liquidate'[332] the *barak*s almost as soon as he had taken over the province. As with the Sverdlovsk–Serov highway, the idea predated Yeltsin's reign – and, as with the highway, Yeltsin's memoirs conveniently omit the previous work and give the impression that he began from scratch.[333] Yet in June 1976 the provincial Soviet had adopted a resolution to 'liquidate the *barak* housing space' within three years.[334] But, of course, the decision lacked the essential ingredient for implementation: the Obkom imprimatur. The latter came less than five months after Yeltsin's ascent. In March 1977 the Obkom passed a resolution 'On raising the level of responsibility of the leadership for carrying out . . . the [17 June 1976] decision'.[335]

To the cause of 'raising the responsibility' the Obkom enlisted its master's favourite technique: relentless 'systematic control over the implementation'. To ensure that the *barak* dwellers were given priority in new housing, the Obkom ordered that all towns and districts whose territories contained *barak*s should 'co-ordinate the distribution of newly built housing' with the provincial Soviet. The Housing Administration of the Sverdlovsk City Soviet issued month-by-month updates for the Party committees of the cities and districts. The local Party organizations held monthly hearings 'on the process of liquidation of *barak*s' and 'criticized sternly those who lagged behind'.[336]

To spur the campaign along, twice in 1978 the Regional Soviet held hearings and endorsed 'additional measures'. Still the progress was not satisfactory and, in July 1979, Yeltsin convened the Secretariat of the Obkom to assess the situation and adopt 'additional measures'.[337] Of these, the key one was 'freezing all the queues'[338] for apartments at dozens of enterprises and municipal sites, and giving apartments only to those who lived in the *barak*s.

'Freezing the queues' meant denying thousands of 'veterans, invalids, families with many children, young professionals'[339] apartments for which they had been waiting for years, often decades. The Obkom simply took over the 'housing funds' of enterprises – the completed, near-completed and even future apartment buildings for employees – and handed them over to the *barak* dwellers, letting the enterprise directors face the enraged workers, whose dream of a few square metres in a dwelling with running water and an indoor toilet had eluded them yet again. 'People must understand', declared Yeltsin, that 'now we must help those who live worse than anyone else'.[340]

But, of course, people's 'understanding' meant infinitely less than Moscow's. For this was yet another of Yeltsin's initiatives that diverged quite widely from the Centre's designs. 'Various government *postanovlenia* ordered us to build so many industrial sites every year that we could not have built them in five years,' recalled the head of the Obkom's Department of Machine Building. 'No one in the capital even tried to calculate things right. If we had so much as begun doing everything we were ordered to do, we would have had to terminate our social programmes for ever.'[341]

In the Sverdlovsk province, as everywhere in the Soviet Union, housing was provided mainly through the workplace. The myriad Moscow ministries and administrations were masters of the housing funds. The response to Yeltsin's crusade, as reported by the Obkom's Secretary Oleg Lobov, was quite reserved: 'a number of ministries and administrations viewed [it] with understanding'.[342]

To deepen this 'understanding' and protect his flanks, Yeltsin travelled to Moscow, where he spoke with Andrey Kirilenko and Prime Minister

Aleksey Kosygin. He warned both of the coming avalanche of angry complaints from the enterprises whose housing the Obkom was about to embargo. Yeltsin requested that 'all protests' that reached the Central Committee and the Council of Ministers be ignored 'for just a year'.[343] Both Kirilenko and Kosygin agreed. Along the way, Yeltsin managed to collect 4.8 million rubles for new housing from sympathetic Moscow agencies.[344]

Even though they had procured Moscow's benign neglect, the Obkom had to be careful. The immediate target, according to a staffer in the Obkom's Construction Department, was pre-war and wartime *barak*s, 'the worst of the lot: without foundation, without heat or plumbing'.[345] While liquidating 'the most threadbare, most disastrous'[346] shanties, the Obkom left standing two-storey structures which had foundations but were just as short on indoor plumbing and just as crowded. Yeltsin's description of his 'war on the *barak*s'[347] was not concerned with such trifles. It was, instead, bursting with the characteristic self-imagery of a mighty Party Samson advancing on the whining Philistines: 'The directors [of the robbed enterprises] complained and protested . . . but we razed one *barak* after another, advanced on the shanties, demolished, destroyed them.'[348] In keeping with this description of the battle, the victory, as described by Yeltsin, could not have been other than swift and total: 'within a year all former *barak* dwellers moved into new apartments with modern conveniences'.[349] In fact, the campaign took six years, and even then there were still *barak*s in the Sverdlovsk province.

The success was undeniably impressive: between January 1976 and August 1982, the number of *barak*s was reduced from 924 to 25, and thirty-five thousand *barak* dwellers moved into apartments of their own.[350] Nor were the *barak* dwellers the only or even the most numerous beneficiaries of this policy.

Yeltsin proudly claimed that a total of 3,100,000 square metres of housing had been built between 1976 and 1981,[351] and that 'every fourth family had a house-warming party'.[352] Assuming an average of at least six people per family, which often included three generations, there were at least 750,000 families in the 4.5 million population of the Sverdlovsk province. Of these, according to Yeltsin's claim, 187,500 families, or 1,125,000 people, moved. This means that each one of the lucky new tenants ended up with only 2.75 square metres of housing.[353]

Still, amid the disastrous shortage of apartments, for which the word 'crisis' seemed almost a gentle euphemism, a separate family dwelling with indoor plumbing was so precious a boon – it was theirs! it was separate! no matter how many were in the family – that Yeltsin's self-congratulation was justified. 'It was his initiative,' said a former fellow builder, 'his credit, his courage.'[354] A former Obkom department head, generally critical of Yeltsin in most of his reminiscences, conceded that the 'undeniable success [in building housing] in Sverdlovsk and the province would hardly have been possible without Yeltsin'.[355]

There were, however, projects for which local ingenuity and self-sufficiency, so prized and flaunted by Yeltsin, were not enough: they required not only direct assistance from the Central Committee, but the celestial intervention of the Politburo itself. One such endeavour was the metro, which Yeltsin decided Sverdlovsk needed badly. Some time in 1981, he arranged an appointment with Brezhnev.

It was a Thursday afternoon, and the General Secretary, who no longer worked on Fridays, was impatient to leave for his favourite country villa in Zavidovo. There was little time for small talk. Well informed of Brezhnev's 'style of work at the time',[356] Yeltsin already had a memo ready on which the General Secretary could inscribe his decision. 'Tell me what to write,' Brezhnev said. 'For the Politburo: prepare a draft decision on the construction of the metro in Sverdlovsk,' Yeltsin answered. Brezhnev wrote this down exactly as dictated, and signed the paper. But Yeltsin, who 'knew only too well that even documents signed by Brezhnev sometimes disappeared', was not done with the General Secretary yet. He asked that an aide be tasked with 'officially registering' the memo and sending it to the Politburo members. Brezhnev obliged again. They shook hands, and Yeltsin left for Sverdlovsk. Soon there was a Politburo decision authorizing the construction of the metro in Sverdlovsk.[357] The project would take eight years to complete and cost the Soviet Treasury 265 million rubles.[358]

While the Sverdlovsk metro was the most spectacular booty of Yeltsin's Moscow raids, it was neither the most important nor the most expensive. His largest prize was a huge grant for agricultural improvement that he managed to tease out of Moscow between 1976 and 1981. This feat was doubly impressive because Yeltsin succeeded in stretching by over 1,600 kilometres the geographic eligibility of his province: the giant appropriation, a slice of which Yeltsin so deftly diverted to Sverdlovsk, had been explicitly designed as emergency assistance to the catastrophically depopulated villages of Central and North-western Russia, the so-called 'non-black-earth' areas. The result was an injection into the Sverdlovsk countryside of 2.4 billion rubles between 1975 and 1981 – or, as Yeltsin did not fail to underscore publicly, more than had been invested in the province's agriculture in the previous fifteen years.[359]

Spilled on the parched soil of the devastated countryside, golden rain brought no spring to Russian agriculture, and Sverdlovsk province was no exception. The production of milk, for instance, had increased by a meagre 1.3 per cent in the same six years, and there were not enough potatoes to last from harvest to harvest.[360] The collective farms were fifty million rubles in debt. The exodus from the countryside continued unabated: in the previous fifteen years, 30,000 people (almost one person in five) had left the collective farms for the cities of the Sverdlovsk province.[361] In 1981, Yeltsin had to admit that, according to the 'scientifically calculated norms of consumption', only 75 per cent of the needs of the population were satisfied.[362] The same year, he was forced to introduce food rationing in the province: 400 grams of butter and 800 grams of boiled sausage per person per month, plus a kilo of meat twice a year for the main national holidays – May Day and the anniversary of the October Revolution on 7 November. Families with infants could purchase one litre of milk daily.[363]

So, when another effort to resuscitate Russian agriculture was about to get under way, Yeltsin was anxious to procure for his province as big a share as he could get. This time, he targeted the last major economic initiative of the, literally, dying Brezhnev regime: Prodovolstvennaya Programma, the 'Food Programme'. This effort, unprecedented in scale, to fix Soviet agriculture once and for all, was launched in May 1982 at the Central Committee Plenum, which was to be Brezhnev's last. The ailing General Secretary, hardly able to speak, declared the 'uninterrupted supply of food not just an economic but an urgent socio-political task'.[364]

Again, Yeltsin had to contest geography: the bulk of the Programma's money was to go to Central Russia. Yeltsin's domain could qualify only if the criteria were stretched almost to breaking point. The Sverdlovsk province was under snow 200 days a year, with average annual temperature barely above 0°C.[365] Only half of the meat and milk consumed by the Sverdlovsk province was produced locally.[366] Yeltsin was forever dependent on the kindness of the Centre and of the First Secretaries from more benign climes. (One of the latter was the young First Secretary of the Krasnodar Obkom, Mikhail Gorbachev. They first met over the telephone, 'helping each other':[367] Gorbachev facilitated food shipments to Sverdlovsk from his fabulously rich black-earth region, and Yeltsin sent metal and timber south.)

Yeltsin spared no effort to get the money. In describing the Programma to the Regional Committee at a hastily convened Plenum, he uncharacteristically passed on to his audience some of the propaganda gibberish he had just heard in Moscow. 'The adoption of the Food Programme coincided with the completion by the United States of the "new strategy for a protracted nuclear war"';[368] 'all the people of the Urals must understand deeply the international situation in which the Food Programme was being implemented, and show maximum organization, discipline and a sense of responsibility before the Motherland'.[369]

All this grovelling and fanfare, apparently, were worth the prize: 1.8 billion rubles, which the Sverdlovsk province received for 'agricultural development' over the next ten years.[370] After the first instalment, the rationing of milk was abolished, and even sausages began to appear in Sverdlovsk stores 'from time to time . . .'[371]

Just turned fifty and fully confident in his mastery of the province, Boris Yeltsin was now permanently settled into a *modus operandi* shaped by the twenty-five years that had passed since his first job: the never ending crises; the urgency and the self-reliance of the Soviet manager's life; the unquenchable thirst for 'the needed and the noticeable'; the urge for complete command of every detail of the business at hand; the unrelenting devotion to work; and the habit of almost twenty years of giving and enforcing orders. 'He was a commanding man who could, and liked, to take the entire responsibility upon himself,'[372] remembers a former department head and Secretary of the Sverdlovsk Obkom.

The 'tough manner'[373] persisted and became a habit, but he had 'changed very much'[374] after he became the Pervyi: he 'matured', and 'the rudeness and harshness disappeared'.[375] This was, a former Obkom aide recalls, a conscious decision: 'He was very serious about his image.'[376] Both the man and his subordinates were subjected to the 'most exacting standards'.[377] At regular meetings of the Obkom staff, he talked 'mostly about shortcomings and failures, rarely about successes'.[378] Under Yeltsin, it became acceptable to criticize the Obkom: the department heads, the Secretaries and even the Pervyi himself.[379] In a breach of tradition, the high functionaries responsible for mishaps were now mentioned by name.[380] Yet even in the late 1970s when the foul language, *mat*, moved from the street to the highest Party and government offices and, from the Kremlin down, became fashionable, even chic, Yeltsin refused to humiliate his subordinates by using it, even though that made him look 'like a white crow' among other Party bosses.[381]

Yeltsin was merciless towards those who bungled an assignment. 'He accepted no explanations. The culprits became his punch-bags.'[382] His wrath was usually short-lived and he often seemed embarrassed by the outburst afterwards.[383] But 'if Yeltsin did not like somebody, [the feeling] was serious and sustained. Regardless of whether they were above or below him, he would work tirelessly to remove them.'[384]

He was 'no democrat [in running the province] and in many areas no decision could be taken without his explicit approval'.[385] Still, those who proved their ability to work hard and well were treated with unfailing respect and accorded considerable freedom of action. One of the latter was Sergey Vozdvizhenskiy, who, while the head of one of the largest construction concerns in the province, found that his and Yeltsin's positions on 'some key professional issues did not coincide'.[386] Vozdvizhenskiy stuck to his guns and expected to be fired any day. Instead, he was invited by Yeltsin to join the Obkom as Secretary for Construction.[387]

The Chief Architect of Sverdlovsk, Gennadiy Belyankin, who for seven years, every other Saturday, briefed Yeltsin on the problems of construction in Sverdlovsk, could not recall a single occasion where Yeltsin overruled the city builders by fiat.[388] Belyankin's colleagues 'from all over Russia' were amazed and envious of these regular conferences with the Pervyi: 'No other city in Russia had anything like it!' And when Belyankin found himself in a fair amount of trouble with Moscow ministries for raising, in a collection of essays he had edited, 'urgent and sharp' issues of Soviet urban development, including rampant destruction of historic landmarks, Yeltsin came to his assistance. Upon discovering that Belyankin was routinely struck off the list of speakers at local conferences on urban planning and construction, Yeltsin ordered that he be given the floor. 'That's how he was,' Belyankin recalled. 'Always – sometimes against the majority – supporting those who, in his view, did the right thing.'[389]

Yeltsin insisted on 'delving into every detail of a problem' and went to the 'specialists for clarification'[390] only after he had mastered the essence of a subject. Sometimes, the staffers in the Propaganda Department found speeches they prepared for Yeltsin almost completely rewritten. Every figure was checked and rechecked. 'When Yeltsin wrote his speeches,' remembers a member of the Sverdlovsk nomenklatura, 'the entire Obkom staff worked like crazy.'[391] His predecessor, Yakov Ryabov, would recite what was given to him without changing a word.[392]

An occasional observer of the Buro meetings was 'stunned by Yeltsin's toughness and firmness of purpose'.[393] Having obviously studied the matter thoroughly before the meeting, he ended his short remarks in the same way: the Buro must adopt this or that decision. There was not a chance that the decision would be changed in the course of discussion.

He was intolerant of speculation and long speeches. Watching Yeltsin speak to his subordinates, one felt 'a powerful, overwhelming movement towards the well-defined and firmly established objective'.[394] 'He could get what he wanted – by hook or by crook.'[395] 'One could argue with him,' remembers the head of an Obkom department, 'and, occasionally, he accepted the arguments of his opponent. But this happened only when he was convinced of his opponent's greater competence and absolute confidence.'[396]

This was a tall order: Yeltsin 'had all the data at his fingertips. Not on paper but in his head: milk yields, harvests, people.'[397] And Obkom offices were not the only forums where Yeltsin deployed and flaunted this hard-earned knowledge. On his field expeditions he visibly enjoyed impressing 'some lowly milkmaid' by remembering her name and patronymic. On such occasions, the object of the master's generous attention would invariably 'just burst with joy and pride, eyes sparkling'.[398]

Yet even as he developed into a competent, confident and highly successful seigneur enjoying Moscow's trust and considerable autonomy, Yeltsin remained just as incurious about the spoils of the office as he had been when he first joined the Obkom. This was not, it seems, any sort of principled or consistent opposition – he moved into the House of Old Bolsheviks built for the Sverdlovsk leadership; he used and, undoubtedly, very much enjoyed the Obkom dacha in Baltym – but a strange and, to many, inexplicable indifference to amassing, using and studiously expanding the assortment of comforts and pleasures that the Party held out to its field commanders.

A friend of the family recalls running into Naina Yeltsina in the early 1980s at a session of the City Soviet. Naina was about to report on a project of her Water Canal Institute, where she was by then Chief Engineer, and was very much relieved to find somebody she knew. 'Here, would you hold this for me while I am presenting?'[399] She handed the friend an *avos'ka*, a fishnet shopping bag,* which contained a bottle of milk. 'Just bought it in *molochnaya kukhnya* [a special store for milk products] for my granddaughter.' Ten years later the friend was still amazed: 'Here was the wife of the First Secretary of the Regional Party Committee – and she runs to the *molochnaya kukhnya*! She could have had the best of milk delivered to her home daily, hourly!'[400]

---

* A monument to the ever foraging and resourceful Soviet consumer, the *avos'ka* was an essential ingredient of daily existence, a permanent presence in the pockets, briefcases and handbags of Russian men and women – 'in case', *avos'*, something good to eat or wear was spotted for sale.

An extremely private lot, the Yeltsins never warmed to any sort of domestic help, to which they were entitled. The former Chairman of the Sverdlovsk Soviet remembers a clean-up effort after a party in Yeltsin's apartment. The father distributed the tasks: Lena to sweep the floor, Tanya to clear the table. The Obkom's First Secretary, aproned, was doing the dishes.[401]

Never especially fond of the plush and stolid sanatoria for the nomenklatura, Yeltsin liked to spend a few days of rare holiday in Butka. His parents had returned there after forty years in Berezniki to live out their time as they began it: farming a tiny parcel of land, their *ogorod*, a kitchen garden. Their fellow villagers were more than a little surprised to see the master of the province digging in the garden 'with gusto',[402] carrying water from the well and chopping wood, 'just like everybody else'.[403]

Of course, despite the new farmer's efforts, he could not leave his rank outside the village. In the beginning, quite a few people, most of them relatives of various degrees of closeness, approached him with their many problems. Yeltsin asked his mother to put an end to the stream of needful kin: 'I must treat everybody the same way.'[404] A witness overheard him firmly telling a Butka relative, 'I cannot help you.' Yeltsin then turned around and walked away.[405]

Yeltsin did, however, practise personal charity. He sent to orphanages the hefty honoraria received from major newspapers and Party journals.[406] Once, during a visit to a Sverdlovsk plant, he was intercepted by a shabby cleaning lady, who claimed to have been 'left without means because of the callousness of the bureaucrats'.[407] She begged for Yeltsin's intervention. 'Of course, of course, we shall fix it all,' he said.[408] He spoke to the manager right away, but it seemed that 'fixing it' was going to take time. Yeltsin went back to the woman, who was waiting outside the manager's office. 'Here,' he said forcing a stack of rubles into her hand. 'Since I promised you help, I will help you myself until the issue is resolved.'[409] He continued to support the woman and her family for a 'fairly long time'.

Unlike many in the increasingly brazen nomenklatura of the late Brezhnev regime, Yeltsin appeared to seek diversion and refuge from his jealous and unsparing work not in new and multiplying modes of privileged consumption, but in the familiar pleasures of friends, theatre and, of course, volleyball. Despite his efforts, these favourite pastimes, like practically everything else in his life, could not be insulated from the aura of his high office: unbidden, it invaded his leisure as well. A measure of awkwardness, arising out of the growing disparity of status between Yeltsin and his companions, crept into his once easy relations with friends.

In 1982, Sergey Peretrutov, who had worked with Yeltsin in construction for fourteen years, was celebrating his birthday. He came to the Obkom to invite Yeltsin but, as happened more and more frequently, could not get to see him and left word with an aide. The next evening Yeltsin came to the office party for Peretrutov at his old SU-13. The Pervyi was alone, without aides. 'Here I am,' said Yeltsin as he hugged Peretrutov, 'come to wish you a happy birthday.'[410] The construction chiefs, who were milling around near by, saw the First Secretary and, in an instant, surrounded the two friends. Yeltsin was annoyed: 'And what are you doing here? All right, all right, stay . . .' He gave Peretrutov a transistor radio with a silver plaque inscribed with his signature.[411]

They hid from the crowd in Peretrutov's office. 'Well?' said Yeltsin. 'Well what?' asked Peretrutov. 'You have been preparing, haven't you?' Yeltsin answered. 'Well, then, open the fridge.' Indeed, the office refrigerator had been stocked for the occasion with delicacies and two bottles of cognac. They drank a shot each. Yeltsin wandered alone around the offices, where he had worked almost twenty years before, and was visibly touched to find on many a wall pictures of himself with his former colleagues and subordinates. When he came back to Peretrutov's office, Yeltsin said: 'Again, Sergey Ivanovich, happy birthday. But, please forgive me, I cannot come to your home for the party. You fellows will be doing this a lot . . .' Yeltsin raised a hand to his throat, joined the index finger and thumb in a circle and then flicked the index finger against the throat – a Russian gesture to indicate drinking. 'Sorry, cannot come. The position forbids.'[412]

He remained an ardent theatregoer. 'No other Pervyi before or after him went to the theatre as often.'[413] On these 'festive' occasions, Naina was always on his arm.[414] The Yeltsins never missed guest performances by touring companies, especially those from Moscow. Following their leader, other Party functionaries began to make family appearances at Sverdlovsk theatres.[415]

Yeltsin's favourite was the Sverdlovsk Theatre of Musical Comedy, which performed operettas, vaudevilles and musicals. It was the most famous of all Sverdlovsk theatres, and, some thought, the best for operetta in the Soviet Union.[416] One of its many claims to fame was the ideologically suspect *Hello, Dolly*, produced in 1974 by the Theatre's Chief Director, the brilliant Vladimir Akimovich Kurochkin. He was also the first Soviet director to have attempted (and, of course, failed) to obtain permission for staging such exemplars of 'bourgeois art' as *Cabaret* and *Fiddler on the Roof*.[417]

Ekaterinburg theatregoers still proudly recall their Musical Comedy playing to full houses and receiving the ovations of that most snobbish, most difficult of Russian audiences: the Muscovites. *Izvestia* called the theatre's 1983 Moscow tour 'a resounding, brilliant, solid success'.[418] The Musical Comedy became the first operetta theatre in the Soviet Union to receive the title of 'Academic', *Akademicheskiy*,[419] the Soviet Union's most prestigious distinction, awarded by the Ministry of Culture for 'the highest standards of artistic excellence'.[420] (When Yeltsin left for Moscow, he arranged for Kurochkin's transfer there.)

From a votary of the Sverdlovsk muses Yeltsin changed into Maecenas-in-Chief. He 'treated the actors very well' and organized 'very nice' receptions for them.[421] During Yeltsin's time, a circus and the Children's Theatre were built in Sverdlovsk, as well as a college for actors, the Sverdlovsk Theatre Institute. Towards the end of his reign, two other theatres, in addition to the Musical Comedy, were awarded the *academicheskiy* title: the Drama, and the Opera and Ballet.

When the Musical Comedy was awarded the Order of the Red Banner of Labour in October 1983, it was not the head of the Department of Culture, Lidiya Khudyakova, nor even the Secretary for Ideology, Vladimir Zhitinev, who came to pin the Order on the theatre's banner, but the Pervyi himself.[422] Yeltsin cordially congratulated the troupe and called on the actors to 'keep and expand the glorious tradition and mastery of the art'.[423]

The Pervyi's two most valuable offerings to the Sverdlovsk performing arts were a new building for the Drama Theatre and a renovated Opera and Ballet. Both were undertaken entirely on his initiative, in defiance of explicit belt-tightening orders from Moscow. The Drama Theatre was a more difficult case. When, during the May 1981 session with the students, Yeltsin (as we have seen) was asked why the construction of the Drama Theatre had been stopped,[424] he explained that the Theatre's new building had fallen victim to the *postanovlenie* of the Central Committee and the USSR's Council of Ministers, 'temporarily freezing' the construction of 'cultural, sports and administrative buildings' that were less than half completed by 1981.[425] Yeltsin quipped that 'the construction of the Drama Theatre is proceeding rather dramatically'.[426] Still, he promised, 'the Obkom . . . is taking measures to continue'[427] the construction. He kept his word.

The Opera and Ballet was the pride of Sverdlovsk. Built in 1912 for travelling Ekaterinburg opera troupes, which had been known throughout Russia since the middle of the nineteenth century,[428] the magnificent building was now, seventy years later, badly worn out. The reconstruction was to 'restore the glory and expand the space while preserving the cosy interior'.[429] The Obkom mobilized twenty-three construction and production enterprises in the region.[430] One night a week, Yeltsin personally chaired the *operativkas*[431] where the progress of the renovation was reviewed.

The Pervyi wanted the theatre to be done up in a grand style – and there were to be no compromises. A decision by the Council of Ministers was needed to gild the ceilings with gold. Yeltsin personally travelled to Moscow and came back with the authorization.[432] In addition, the 705 chairs, handmade, upholstered in red,[433] cost 393 rubles each[434] – at a time when an experienced medical doctor earned 200 rubles a month.

Renovated in an impossibly short time – a year and three months – the Opera and Ballet was reopened on the last Sunday of 1982, the Pervyi's New Year gift to the city. With an orchestra playing, Yeltsin cut the red ribbon at the entrance.[435] In a brief speech, he 'wholeheartedly' thanked the architects and all others who had participated in the effort, naming the construction organizations that had especially distinguished themselves.[436] He recalled the 'historical value' of the building and expressed confidence that the 'collective of the theatre would achieve notable successes in the new, excellent environment'.[437]

'The theatre is opened!' rhapsodized the city newspaper, which entitled the report 'White Swan in the Centre of Sverdlovsk'.[438] 'But before they entered the hall, sparkling with fresh gilt, the people wandered through the foyer, admiring the new cloakroom, the well-equipped buffets, the staircases, glittering with new marble ... Like a beautiful white bird, the renewed and rejuvenated building soars over the city.'[439]

Yeltsin never lost his passion for volleyball, the game that so precisely mirrored his preferred and most successful mode of operation: careful preparation, a build-up to a lightning climax, maximum exertion over a brief but intense period – and, although not always a win, a guaranteed temporary resolution. A relief. A *result*.

His strength and his pleasure lay not in patient, drawn-out marathons, where one measured and adjusted one's pace to that of the opponent, but in sprints, where there was little time for tactics. More and more, Yeltsin showed a clear preference for composing his life not in long, elaborate blocks but in bursts of short, energetic and bold paragraphs followed by empty spaces.

Before he became First Secretary, Yeltsin was the only department head who came to play volleyball with the staffers and even formed a department team, though his Construction Department was small.[440] He organized a volleyball team of the Obkom's leadership, the Buro, very shortly after he became First Secretary.[441] They played every Tuesday night 'at 7.15 sharp' and every Sunday morning at 11 (even if 'one had just returned from the business trip, one had to be there!')[442] in the House of Physical Culture in downtown Sverdlovsk, in the sports hall of a military base, made available by the Chief of the Air Defence of the Sverdlovsk region and member of the Regional Party Committee, Colonel Yuriy Khandanian,[443] or in the Baltym Cultural-Health Centre next to the dachas of the regional leadership.[444] 'Soon,' Yeltsin noted proudly, 'it was impossible to imagine the life of the Sverdlovsk Obkom without volleyball.'[445]

The Buro was divided into two teams, and, on the rare occasions when the Yeltsin team lost, for the rest of the week until the next game the victors would have to endure the boss's special attention focused on their work: 'Why isn't this right? Why isn't that right? And how about this?'[446] They wished 'it were Tuesday already, so that we could lose to him [on the court] and get him off our backs . . .'[447]

For a while, separated by the chasm of rank, the two volleyball teams in the Obkom – the Buro team with Yeltsin as captain and the staffers' team, headed by Stanislav Alekseev from the Propaganda Department – coexisted without ever meeting on the court. (The Buro members trained by splitting the team into two.) Then, in June 1978, Yeltsin dispatched an aide to watch a few games of the staffers' team: to 'make sure that we were worth playing with', as Alekseev put it. The aide took notes, and reported to the boss. Soon thereafter Yeltsin ordered a match. The staffers prepared for the game by making a pennant, a placard, which read 'Friendship has won', and a commemorative button depicting a volleyball net and a handshake across it.

Yeltsin's team included Second Secretary Leonid Bobykin (he had a fever that day but begging off was, of course, out of the question), Secretaries Yuriy Petrov and Vladimir Zhitinev, the head of the KGB of the Sverdlovsk region, candidate member of the Buro, Colonel Yuriy Kornilov, and Colonel Khandanyan, who, although not in the Buro, was honoured, apparently, on account of his hospitality. Only Yeltsin and Petrov, in Alekseev's estimation, played well. But, he correctly noted, the Buro being the most exclusive club in the province, 'this was all Yeltsin had to work with'.[448]

In the first game of that historic match, the staffers' team completely 'routed' the Buro: 15–2. Yeltsin grew 'very nervous' and 'testy'.[449] Having demolished their bosses, the staffers thought better of it and decided to field a 'second' team for the next game. Yet even that team was better than the Buro's, and the staffers began to win again. Only Yeltsin's desperate efforts helped to 'pull the team together' and fend off defeat: he and Petrov did all the scoring for their side.[450] Alekseev ordered his team to help the Buro save face by losing the second game. 'We'll take the third game,' he promised the teammates. Yet when, after a break, Alekseev ordered, 'First team, on the court!' he heard Yeltsin's voice: 'No, this [second] team stays.' Forgetting himself 'in the heat of the game', Alekseev turned to Yeltsin and said: 'This is an order to lose, isn't it?'[451] Yeltsin did not answer. The Buro won the third game and, with it, the match.

Right away, Yeltsin walked over to Alekseev: 'Enough of playing *poddavki*!'[452] (*Poddavki* is a Russian game of draughts or checkers, in which the player wins who sacrifices his pieces first.) The teams thereupon divided the talent more evenly, with some of Alekseev's men playing with Yeltsin and Petrov, and there followed 'some genuine, good, enjoyable' volleyball. Afterwards, as he was handing Yeltsin the winner's pennant, Alekseev could not resist a barb. Mocking the official slogan, he said: 'Still, Boris Nikolaevich, it was friendship that won.' Yeltsin, red in the face and sweaty, snapped: 'What do you mean, "friendship"? Our team has won!' To Alekseev, this retort was 'like a lash'. In the changing room, Yeltsin's aide came up to him: 'You must not talk to the First Secretary like that!' 'Look,' protested Alekseev, 'we were both in gym shorts, on the court, not in the office . . .' Fifteen years later, Yeltsin's disagreeable reaction was quite fresh for Alekseev. 'But', he adds, 'I think that was all in the heat of competition. Yeltsin hated to lose – in anything, anywhere. He would fight to the end. This was his character.'[453]

Never again did Yeltsin bring out the Buro team against the staffers'.

Moscow's attitude towards its mildly but undeniably heterodox Sverdlovsk potentate was surprisingly lenient. One reason for this forbearance might have been the general weakening of Moscow's control over the daily affairs of the giant country's provinces that was so characteristic of the late Brezhnev period. Having granted the provincial Party bosses tenures of unprecedented length, the old men in the Party headquarters in the Old Square were too distracted by their illnesses, too tired, too preoccupied with imminent successions to watch closely the local mandarins. 'At the time, Brezhnev did not occupy himself with running the country, or, to be more exact, occupied himself less and less,' Yeltsin recalled. 'His example was followed by other Central Committee Secretaries. And so, in practice, we worked quite independently. We did receive directives from the Central Committee, of course, but it was largely *pro forma*, for reports.'[454] Indeed, Yeltsin's predecessor, Yakov Ryabov, during his own tenure, also undertook initiatives 'independent of the Politburo': for instance, production of fertilizers and agricultural machinery, and large-scale irrigation projects.[455]

No doubt Yeltsin was also greatly helped by the 1,600 kilometres that lay between Moscow and Sverdlovsk. Even in the overall sloth that settled on the Party apparatus in the late 1970s and early 1980s, he could not have got away with some of his schemes if his bailiwick had been in Central or Southern Russia. He was lucky, too, with his province's *kurator* in the Central Committee apparatus, one Pavel Simonov. A 'wonderful man', Yeltsin recalled, he adopted a policy of 'non-interference in the business of the [Sverdlovsk] Party organization'.[456] And, 'having noticed a great deal' of the unconventional in Yeltsin's speeches, Simonov regularly 'saved' his mildly iconoclastic charge by not passing the offending passages along to the leadership but, instead, 'quietly storing them away in the archives'.[457]

The roots of Moscow's indulgence might have run deeper. There seemed to have been a kind of tacit understanding between the Centre and the leadership of the Ural (and Siberian) provinces, which guaranteed the latter a measure of independence far greater than was the norm west of the Ural Mountains. This contract preceded Yeltsin. Much as it must have disliked the style of the Ural school, Moscow understood that these big, proud and wilful men ruled over an equally stubborn lot. Unlike their compatriots in Central Russia, these descendants of pioneers and exiles had not been cowed by centuries of serfdom and bureaucracy. Fear and propaganda alone might not have been sufficient to keep order behind the Urals. The hands on the wheel of the Sverdlovsk province had to be reasonably clean as well as firm. The Party's diktat had to be combined with a degree of probity, integrity and trust.

And so long as the leaders of the Ural school kept the fourth most populous Soviet province in reasonable working order, so long as they continued to supply the Party with steel, pipes, tanks, missiles and nuclear warheads, the rulers of Sverdlovsk were granted a measure of independence and allowed by Moscow to indulge, cautiously and within well-defined limits, in 'petit-bourgeois populism'.

There were, however, instances in Sverdlovsk's relations with the Centre when no second-guessing, much less evasion or dilution, was to be tolerated. One such occasion was the order to raze the Ipatiev House, in the basement of which the last Russian Tsar, Nicholas II, his family, his personal physician and three servants were executed on the night of 17 July 1918.

On 26 July 1975, the KGB Chairman Yuriy Andropov sent to the Central Committee a memo that read:

Secret. Copy No. 2 CC CPSU
   On the demolition of the IPATIEV mansion in the city of Sverdlovsk 26 July 1975 No. 2004-A

The anti-Soviet circles in the West periodically generate various propaganda campaigns around the tsar's family of the ROMANOVS, and, in that connection, the former mansion of merchant IPATIEV in the city of Sverdlovsk [crossed out: 'in which the tsar's family was shot'] is not infrequently mentioned.

The IPATIEV house continues to stand in the centre of the city. It is occupied by an educational centre of the regional Administration of Culture. The mansion has no architectural or any other value, and is attractive only to a small segment of the city's population and tourists.

Of late, Sverdlovsk has been visited by some foreign experts. In the future, the circle of foreigners may widen significantly, and the IPATIEV house will become an object of their considerable attention.

In that connection, it is deemed advisable to task the Sverdlovsk Obkom of the CPSU with resolving the issue by demolishing the mansion as part of the planned renovation of the city. [Passage crossed out: 'This has been co-ordinated with the Sverdlovsk Obkom /RYABOV/.']

A draft of the CC CPSU's *postanovlenie* is attached.
   A hearing is requested.
   Chairman of the Committee for State Security ANDROPOV*

Eight days later, the Central Committee adopted the *postanovlenie*, drafted by Andropov:

---

* Never before published, copies of this document and of the one that follows it were given to the author by a friend in Moscow. The most likely provenance of the originals today is the Presidential Archive, which is closed to outside researchers. The translation from Russian is by the author.

Secret
Draft
POSTANOVLENIE CC CPSU
On demolishing the IPATIEV mansion in the city of Sverdlovsk

I. Approve the suggestion of the USSR Council of Ministers' Committee for State Security, as stated in the memorandum No. 2004-A of 26 July 1975.
II. Task the Sverdlovsk Obkom of the CPSU to resolve the issue of the demolition of the IPATIEV mansion as part of the planned renovation of the city.

   Secretary of CC
      Checked with the *Postanovlenie* by me
      Manyakhin 4.08.75
      Correct: Deputy Department Chief Colonel Kotov

The order, which Yeltsin found 'impossible to disobey', arrived from Moscow in a 'secret package' in the autumn of 1977: two months before the celebration of the sixtieth anniversary of the 'Great October Socialist Revolution' and a year before the executions' sixtieth anniversary. A few days later, Yeltsin dispatched bulldozers and steam-rollers into the night. In the morning, only a fresh patch of asphalt marked the spot.[458]

When the man on whose order the Ipatiev House had been demolished came to power with the death of Brezhnev in November 1982, Yeltsin's compliance with the priorities set by the new regime was just as prompt.

Yuriy Andropov's brief rule was a kind of Bolshevik renaissance, in which the expansion of the totalitarian controls and their more vigorous and brutal enforcement were to be combined with a leaner, less corrupt officialdom and more honest public discourse. This was to be the last, forced spasm of the once solid Bolshevik self-confidence and optimism, an attempt to breathe a modicum of creativity and integrity into the thoroughly decayed Party.

Along the way, Andropov undertook to renegotiate the social contract which had evolved in the Brezhnev years. With customary precision, a Soviet underground joke defined its essence as 'They pretend to pay us, we pretend to work.' Andropov's 'new deal' attempted to extract from the state's sullenly resigned subjects more than just passive acquiescence: it aimed at a spirited participation, at rekindling the long-lost enthusiasm in a populace daily tormented by queues and shortages, lied to, insulted and humiliated by the incompetent, cynical and venal bureaucracies.

Reaching for inspiration all the way back to the 1902 Congress of the Russian Social Democratic Workers' Party, from whose members the Bolshevik faction was cobbled by Lenin, the Andropov Central Committee called for the restoration of the 'Leninist style of Party work: a businesslike approach, exactitude, reliance on the masses, intolerance of formalism and bureaucratism'.[459] The 'Leninist style', wrote Andropov in an article with characteristic solemnity entitled 'Karl Marx and Some Problems of Socialist Construction in the USSR', was incompatible with 'bombast, commands, endless talks in lieu of concrete action'.[460]

Like every Party leader before him, Andropov confronted the accursed problem of authoritarian and totalitarian regimes: control over its ruling class. History knows only two consistently effective antidotes to the natural rapacity, corruption and arbitrariness of ruling political elites: fear of the tyrant or openness of democracy. In one of those rare *in vivo* experiments in political science, Brezhnev's rule confirmed that there was no third way: removing terror without introducing democracy had produced, almost across the board, a nomenklatura increasingly ossified, unwieldy – and corrupt, on a massive scale.

The Andropov interlude was another doomed search for a third way between Stalin's perennial purge and Brezhnev's nearly life-long tenures; between paralysing insecurity and just as damaging unaccountability. Having concluded, quite correctly, that either full-fledged democratization or earnest re-Stalinization would be equally fatal for the system, Andropov began by throwing into the stew carefully measured spoonfuls of both. He removed corrupt officials *en masse*, and imprisoned some. He introduced a soupçon of openness, encouraging 'criticism from below' and a limited expansion of permissible criticism in the newspapers. It was under Andropov that brief accounts of Politburo meetings began to be published for the first time.

After almost a decade of modest retraction of the state's tentacles from areas outside immediate political relevance, Andropov renewed the state's assault on society. That state, however, was to be cleaner, more efficient and more responsive to the populace than its predecessor. In addition to special mailboxes for denouncing 'suspicious activity' of neighbours, and police raids on bath houses and cinemas in search of 'parasites' absent from their workplaces, the government called for better healthcare, improved food supply and greater availability of more attractive consumer goods.[461] The wholesale arrests and even executions of corrupt managers and 'speculators' were accompanied by plans for a 'technological and scientific revolution' in industry, greater efficiency

and productivity of labour, bolder innovation in industry, more manoeuvring room for managers, and 'co-operative' housing construction.[462]
Appeals for an 'increased intensity' of ideological warfare, 'intolerance
of ideologically alien' works of art and 'dynamic and effective counter-
propaganda' were interspersed with calls for 'greater openness' in the
leadership, its 'accountability before the people', severe sanctions against
incompetence, and even appeals to the spineless trade unions to stand
up for workers' rights.[463]

There was no more exact embodiment of Andropov's police renaissance
than Egor Kuzmich Ligachev. Despairing of finding probity closer to
Moscow, Andropov reached into Western Siberia and plucked out Ligachev, who had served as First Secretary of the Tomsk province for more
than seventeen years. He was a Siberian communist *par excellence*:
tough, incorruptible, hard-working, decisive and a teetotaller to boot.
His belief in what he described as Andropov's goal of 'perfecting [and]
renewing socialism' while 'maintaining continuity' seemed exuberant
and genuine.[464]

Summoned to Moscow a few months after Andropov's ascent to
supreme power in the Soviet Union, Ligachev was appointed head of
the Department of Organizational Party Work and put in charge of the
vast cadre overhaul so critical to the new General Secretary's design.[465]
He did not disappoint the boss. In less than eight months, Ligachev
replaced one-fifth of all Obkom First Secretaries.[466]

In the third week of January 1984, Ligachev came to Sverdlovsk. He
stayed an unusually long time for a guest of his rank – four full days –
travelling extensively and holding dozens of meetings with Party functionaries and enterprise managers.[467] Using the occasion of the regional
Party conference, which was to 'elect' the local communist leadership,
Ligachev delivered Moscow's message in a long speech.

This was the kind of address Andropov demanded from his lieutenants: toughly worded, short on praise, analytical, businesslike, concrete
in its criticisms – and brimming with 'historic optimism'. Industrial
production was plagued by the tardiness of deliveries, Ligachev told the
conference, and by underfulfilment of orders.[468] Raw materials were
wasted. Foodstuffs were in short supply. Inside the Party, criticism was
often stifled, and Party meetings were not always conducive to a 'frank
exchange of views'. Such 'negative phenomena' as 'padding of production reports, the spawning of dachas, dishonesty in the distribution
of apartments, alcoholism' were harmful to the Party and the state, since
the people 'paid close attention to the behaviour of the communist

leaders' and 'judge the Party as whole' by the way they live and work. Closer to home, in the Sverdlovsk province, every second industrial enterprise was failing to honour delivery contracts. Industrial growth was slower than planned. Urban transportation caused dissatisfaction. Agricultural production was insufficient and uneven.[469]

Still, declared Egor Kuzmich, the past year had demonstrated that the 'measures of economic, organizational and ideological nature, developed by the Central Committee on the initiative and under the leadership of Comrade Yu. V. Andropov, were correct and timely'.[470] Now 'not only our friends but our foes note that, against the background of the crisis in the capitalist countries, the results of the last year were a testimony to the steady development of the Soviet economy and further social progress in the USSR'.[471]

By all indicators, Yeltsin and his province held up rather well under this intense scrutiny. Ligachev endorsed Yeltsin's pet projects: the emphasis on labour productivity to make up for shortages in the work-force; expansion of housing construction; and an increase in the supply of 'popular consumption' goods.[472] The Moscow emissary felt 'convinced' that the regional Party organization had 'understood the essence and tactics of the contemporary tasks set by the Central Committee and persistently searched for ways to carry them out, seeking new channels for the increase of Party influence on the solution of economic and ideological problems'. Furthermore, the atmosphere of the 'labour and political upsurge' that Ligachev had discerned during his tour of the province 'added optimism, confidence' that the Party's plans would be fulfilled.[473]

Not for a moment in those four days did Yeltsin leave the side of the high Moscow emissary. Local observers noted wryly that for four days the two were 'in a veritable embrace'.[474] Yet the harmony between the two rising Party stars was not as perfect as appeared from the outside. First Yeltsin took Ligachev on a tour of the city. Better to impress upon Ligachev the urban improvements with which he had blessed the metropolis, the proud father of the province had the Chief Architect of Sverdlovsk, Gennadiy Ivanovich Belyankin, accompany them inside the black Obkom Volga. Belyankin did his best to point to a new store here, a new cinema there. An apartment building. A theatre. A park.[475]

Ligachev was not impressed. The Central Committee Secretary greeted virtually all sights by grumbling: 'This is nothing. You should see what we have done in Tomsk!' After a while, a much discouraged Belyankin glanced at his boss, who was sitting next to him. Yeltsin was silent, but suddenly Belyankin felt the pressure of the First Secretary's foot. The architect's interpretation, which turned out to be correct, was that he was to ignore the guest's reaction and go on praising Sverdlovsk.[476] And so, as the black limo rolled on, they continued as before: Belyankin chattering away; Ligachev expostulating on the architectural riches of Tomsk; and Yeltsin, jaws clenched, keeping pressure on Belyankin's foot. When they pulled up at the Obkom, their final destination, and Ligachev got out, Yeltsin whispered to Belyankin: 'I guess you'll have to go to Tomsk to see what this jerk [*mudak*] has built there.'[477]

Yeltsin acted on both aspects of the Andropov programme – the repressive and the 'populist' – with customary alacrity. Following the November 1982 Plenum of the Central Committee, at which Andropov had been elected General Secretary, the Sverdlovsk Obkom declared its determination to eradicate the state of affairs in which 'Party organizations exhibited a liberal attitude towards those communists whose behaviour [was] unworthy'.[478] Seventy-nine leading officials of the Sverdlovsk province were expelled from the Party for 'deceiving the state, violating the laws on the protection of socialist property, allowing production of substandard goods and utilizing office for selfish objectives'. The Sverdlovsk Obkom 'aimed' the local Party organizations at 'criticism and self-criticism'. Yeltsin's choice of an obligatory quote from Lenin was portentous: 'Glasnost is a sword that itself heals the wounds it inflicts.'[479]

Now armed, after years of unauthorized 'populism', with the highest imprimatur, Yeltsin could openly indulge his affinity for communing with the 'masses' and for letting the local media know what he saw. He travelled in packed city buses and was horrified by the experience;[480] he visited 'virtually all' the stores of the Chkalov district of Sverdlovsk and found 'unexpected queues for goods that should not be in short supply, rudeness on the part of sales clerks, and thievery';[481] and he called on the local newspapers to 'reveal problems more boldly, get to their roots, to show the true face of the dishonest and the slacking'.[482]

The Sverdlovsk Pervyi was bursting with the official optimism which was at the heart of the Andropov renaissance. To a gathering of construction workers and engineers he declared that 'the Soviet Union, the union of brotherly republics, [was] mighty in the flourishing of its economy and culture, full of optimism and firm confidence in its future'.[483] He elaborated on the new General Secretary's beloved subject of 'ideological warfare':

The class maturity of the Soviet people occurs in the irreconcilable struggle with hostile ideology. The enemies of socialism cannot give up the hope of achieving their objectives through ideological aggression. The special services of imperialism pay increasing attention to ideological sabotage, expand its geographical scope, utilize various channels: broadcasts, cultural and scientific exchange, tourism, religion, smuggling of anti-Soviet literature.[484]

And, straying even further into territory he had very rarely trodden before, the Sverdlovsk Pervyi revealed that:

> critical analysis of works of literature and art, created in the last few years, shows that there have appeared, in their midst, some works without a clearly drawn class position . . . Creative effort is directed at little, uninteresting people, artificially exaggerated shadow sides of reality. Taken together, the small scope of vision and petty everyday details create a broad social background in which hypertrophied negative features, which are presented as social phenomena, prevail.[485]

It was here, in the exotic realm of belle-lettres, that the Sverdlovsk Obkom was to erect its most notorious monument to Yuriy Andropov's short and nasty reign. As the official record of the province's achievements summarized the operation, 'The Party's control over literature in the Sverdlovsk region has acquired concrete forms.'[486]

The 'concrete forms' crashed down on Sverdlovsk's other claim, alongside the Musical Comedy, to national attention: the monthly literary magazine *Ural*. By the early 1980s it had acquired a well-deserved reputation as a purveyor of good, serious literature with a 'left', that is mildly critical, slant. This combination was very much within the peculiarly Russian tradition of 'thick' (*tolstyi*) magazines. Begun in 1836 by the codifier of modern Russian and its greatest poet Aleksandr Pushkin, with the publication of *Sovremennik* ('The Contemporary'), the 'thick' magazines were the first to publish major works by Nikolay Gogol, Leo Tolstoy, Fedor Dostoevsky, Ivan Turgenev. In November 1962, the best of Soviet 'thick' magazines, *Noviy Mir*, heralded the arrival of Aleksandr Solzhenitsyn with the publication of *One Day in the Life of Ivan Denisovich*.

The *Ural* affair began almost exactly twenty years later, with the publication of Konstantin Lagunov's novel *Bronzovyi dog* ('The Bronze Mastiff') in the August, September and October 1982 issues of the magazine. Lagunov's *opus*, although long and populated by a multitude of characters, was not a 'novel' as defined by the canons of classical Russian literature. Lagunov's style, well known to *Ural*'s readers, was

more of a reportage, in which meticulously researched facts and person-
ages copied almost verbatim from real people, including their first names
and patronymics,[487] were woven into a fictionalized narrative. It was
the writer's reputation for verisimilitude that made the storm unleashed
by the publication especially heavy.

Ural's editor-in-chief, Valentin Lukyanin, summarized *Bronzovyi dog*
as a 'portrayal of the true face of the oil barons' of Tumen,[488] the capital
of the West Siberian oil empire. The Tumen region produced 'every
second tonne of oil and every third cubic metre of gas'[489] extracted in
the Soviet Union at that time. To the masters of the city, the 'barons',
Moscow entrusted enormous power, resources and autonomy in the
race for more and more 'black gold' for export. 'Practically uncontrol-
lable',[490] they ruled like 'feudal lords in their fiefdoms'.[491] As Lagunov
put it in his novel, they 'dared and were able to rule other people's fates,
changing and moulding them'.[492]

The transgressions against 'communist morality' recorded by Lagunov
were numerous and were portrayed in compelling and devastating detail.
There was, for example, a state auditor who, upon discovering the
disappearance of two-and-a-half million rubles from a building trust's
budget, was invited by the trust's *nachal'nik* to choose a bribe. She did:
a three-room apartment to be found and refurbished 'inside a week'.[493]
Or an aide to the all-powerful Director of the oilfield who notified the
boss's young wife of a 'customary' delivery to her home of 'meat, fish,
fruit and their derivatives'.[494] 'What about the money?' she asked. 'Don't
worry,' answered the gofer. 'There is plenty. We have socialism here,
don't we?' Or this description of the streets of Tumen, the oldest Siberian
city, 'sitting on' the Trans-Siberian pipeline: 'rusting metal rods, frozen
into the ground, piles of rubbish and broken bricks, packs of wandering
dogs, and unimaginable mud all year round'.[495]

Protests from the Tumen state and Party nobility poured in almost
from the day of publication in letters and telephone calls to the magazine
or directly to Lukyanin, who, as part of the Sverdlovsk nomenklatura,
was well known to the Tumen leadership. *Ural*'s editor was convinced
that the First Secretary of the Tumen Obkom, Georgiy Bogomyakov,
had telephoned Yeltsin and complained – in a 'neighbourly sort of
way'.[496] Yet, along with the criticism, for which they were prepared, the
magazine started to receive letters of praise and support from 'all
corners' of the Soviet Union. 'The whole country was reading *Ural*!'[497]
The magazine's editors were overcome by a matchless sense of triumph
that only those who must deal with censors all their lives can enjoy
to the fullest: the feeling of having taken a risk on a truly important

publication, of having got away with it, and of having the entire country talk about the work. This euphoria and the strange silence of the Obkom made for a heady mix, which moved the magazine's editors, with hardly a breather after *Bronzovyi dog*, to push even further. The January 1983 issue of *Ural* went to press with *Starikova gora* ('The Old Man's Mountain') by Nikolay Nikonov.

This was, in Lukyanin's judgment, a 'considerably more powerful' work than the *Dog*, both in its 'literary qualities' and in the 'depth of its critical penetration'.[498] The *Gora* was a true Russian *povest'*, a literary format somewhere between story and novel, in the tradition of Turgenev, Tolstoy, late Chekhov and, in the 1970s, the incomparable Yuriy Trifonov. Its main character, however, was closest to Solzhenitsyn's Ivan Denisovich: a simple Russian peasant who had gone through hell but had preserved a soul of amazing strength and decency. But, whereas *One Day* was austere, lean and hard-edged, Nikonov's tale was round and supple and filled with the delicate smells and colours of the Ural summer.

Nikonov himself describes the main theme of the *povest'* as the *odichanie* (literally, 'the state of wilderness', but better translated as 'degradation') of the Russian countryside in the early 1980s.[499] The fictional Makarovka was no better or worse than tens of thousands of Russian villages fifty years after collectivization. It was a 'depopulated village of pensioners',[500] where a third of the houses were boarded up; where aspens took over abandoned gardens; where half of the villagers 'had no connection whatsoever with land, working odd jobs in the neighbouring town, or at the nearby timber mill – or with no jobs at all, collecting bottles in commuter trains, and drinking'.[501] There were only three cows left in the entire village, no spade or axe could be found, and the villagers dreamed of 'such an animal that would give milk, meat and wool and lay eggs' without requiring feed or care. Observing this sorry lot – the invalids, the decrepit old women and the long-haired, drunken teenagers on noisy and smelly mopeds – the tale's narrator (a painter who had come to Makarovka to do some work 'for the soul') asks himself: 'Do they look like farmers? Don't they look like someone who does not give a hoot about anything, here today, gone tomorrow, God knows where – with no regrets, no sadness, but perhaps gladly leaving the land where their fathers and grandfathers sowed and tilled?'[502]

'Oh, what a kolkhoz it was – I cannot describe!' writes Nikonov. 'As if gathered in it were its own worst enemies.'[503] The unsupervised cattle drowned in a swamp. Both sowing and harvesting were late, and entire fields, tonnes and tonnes of potatoes and rye, were left to rot unharvested. One such field, of ripe rye, was 'crushed into the ground' by tractors: the kolkhoz chairman knew he could not harvest on time and was afraid of a 'commission from the district centre'.[504] Another field, where barley grew tall and strong, was, for some unknown reason, mowed and left to rot under an open sky. Soon it turned from bright green to dark grey, almost black. 'Why was it sown?' asks the narrator. 'Why brought into this world? Why has Mother-earth fed it, the sun warmed, the sky watered? Only to perish?'[505]

Such was the village to which the main character of the *povest'*, the eponymous Starik, the Old Man, came back thirty years after he was arrested and exiled as a kulak in the early 1930s during Stalin's collectivization. One of a handful of kulaks who made it back, he returned to nothing: his house had been destroyed, the fields that he had worked so hard with his father and brothers had been abandoned and reclaimed by the forest. With no help from anyone, the eighty-year-old Starik built a house, cultivated a garden around it and acquired animals: a cow, two calves, several sheep. Up before dawn every day ('as if he did not sleep at all'),[506] before anyone in the entire kolkhoz, he toiled in his tiny garden, watering and weeding cucumbers, tomatoes and cabbage; scything grass in the forest to feed, 'like a Noah', the inhabitants of his ark, his 'horned children'.[507] In the winter, unable to live without work, he wove strong and pretty baskets.

For this love of land and labour, so utterly strange in the Russian countryside of the 1970s, Starik was hated with a passion by the entire village. No one talked to him. He was never referred to other than as 'greedy bastard' or 'sorcerer'. To annoy him, the long-haired adolescents nightly played their ugly and loud music in front of his wooden hut. The haystack in which he so carefully collected grass scythed at dawn was torched. Somebody burned his cow's udder.

The Old Man's philosophy was simple: 'If only the land could be your own! Even if only a tiny parcel! Then everything will be all right. If [the land is] not your own – nothing works, nothing gives pleasure. No joy in life, no desire to live. One would love this land, if one knew that no one would take it away, ever.'[508] The *povest'* ends with the death of the Old Man. Its last line reads, 'The land was waiting for the owner.'[509]

The theme of collectivization had a special poignancy in the Sverdlovsk province. It was in the village of Gerasimovka, in the easternmost corner of the province, that one of the key propaganda myths of the Soviet Union had been forged: that of the valiant *pioner* Pavlik Morozov, who was allegedly killed by the kulaks for denouncing his own father to the authorities. Once a major Stalinist shrine, complete with the only paved road within hundreds of kilometres, Gerasimovka, like thousands of other Russian villages, was eerily empty by the time Nikonov's *povest'* was published. The Morozov museum, in a large log-house seized from an arrested kulak, had no visitors, and the monument to the brave little Stalinist stood almost completely obscured by overgrown lilac bushes.

Whether the infamous Pavlik was on the mind of *Ural*'s censor, a 'very serious lady by the name of Irina Vasilievna',[510] when the galley proofs of *Starikuva gora* were delivered to her for authorization, was hard to ascertain. But she became 'very agitated'. The censors' power over literary works was absolute and their verdict final. Unless words, lines or entire pages which they had marked in the galleys for excision were taken out by the editors, a work was not to be signed 'for publication'. And without the censor's signature, the printers were forbidden to set the type.[511]

In the case of *Gora*, however, the usually decisive Irina Vasilievna found herself in a quandary. Her experienced nose sniffed something distinctly suspect. In Lukyanin's opinion, 'until then, so frank a word had not been said about the contemporary Russian village' anywhere in the official Soviet media. Yet, try as she might, the *Ural* censor could not find in what was known as the 'Censor's Bible' (the standard handbook which listed things, people and situations forbidden for publication) anything that would explicitly authorize the killing of *Gora*. Unable to dispose of the importunate *opus* herself, the censor carried the galleys to the ultimate arbiter, the Obkom.

Such forays were the last resort, undertaken by Soviet censors only in special circumstances. For, insofar as censorship itself was among the biggest Soviet official 'secrets' (Lukyanin was told to 'tell the authors whatever he wanted about why their works were mangled – but never mention censorship'),[512] the Party's ultimate responsibility for what was or was not allowed to reach the reader was guarded as closely.

The Obkom, in the persona of the Secretary for Ideology Vladimir Zhitinev, agreed with the censor about the generally subversive nature of Nikonov's *povest'*. Still, it wanted to kill the story quietly, 'at the hands of the editor'.[513] Lukyanin refused. Luckily for *Ural* and *Gora*, the nebulous character of the transgressions, and the Obkom's general aversion to issuing direct orders for outright prohibition where the 'creative intelligentsia' were concerned, combined to ensure the work's survival at the cost of what the magazine's editor called a 'shameful compromise' of major deletions. Among the excised segments was the Old Man's arrest after a village meeting, where he had said, 'I have tilled the land all my life. How can Stalin, who has never spent a day in the countryside, tell me what to do?' After innumerable and 'torturing' tussles with the censor 'over every line' of the galleys, the *povest'* was published, with about one-sixth of its original text deleted.[514]

The publication was followed by what Valentin Lukyanin called 'infernal' developments. For the next three months, he felt as if every inch of the ground under the magazine were being worked over by an army of moles: silent, persistent and methodical. Only the briefest of explanations was allowed to surface: Lukyanin was told that a commission had been formed by the Obkom 'to study the work' of the magazine. Oh, but there was nothing to worry about: just a routine sort of thing, one of many periodic and tactful inquiries into the work of the local mass media undertaken by the Obkom's Departments of Culture and Propaganda.

Then whispers from friendly Obkom staffers revealed that each section of the magazine, including 'Humour', was being examined 'under a magnifying glass'.[515] During all this time, no Obkom official spoke to the *Ural* editors. There was a rumour that the Secretary for Ideology would visit the magazine, but he never came. Lukyanin began to feel like a man who, sensing that he was being followed, turned his head but every time saw only fleeting shadows.[516]

Eventually, the shadows took corporeal form, and Lukyanin was invited to attend a special session of the Obkom's Buro to be held on 24 May 1983. There was only one item on the agenda: 'On the work of the editorial staff in the area of raising the ideological and creative level of *Ural* magazine in the light of the demands of the Twenty-Sixth Party Congress and the decree of the CC CPSU "On the creative connection between magazines of belle-lettres and the practice of the building of communism"'.[517]

Not one of the magazine's authors had been 'invited' to the Buro's session, not even the culprits Lagunov and Nikonov. Nor, despite Lukyanin's repeated suggestion, had a single professional literary critic been asked to attend. Only the editor-in-chief and the secretary of the magazine's Party cell, Yuriy Gorbunov, had been summoned. Facing them, in a solid wall of overt, red-faced, unrelenting hostility, were First Secretary Boris Yeltsin, Chairman of the Regional Soviet Anatoliy Mekhrintsev, Obkom Secretaries Oleg Lobov and Vladimir Zhitinev, and the head of the Cultural Department, Lidiya Khudyakova. The presence of Yeltsin and Mekhrintsev raised the affair to the highest level of local politics.

For four-and-a-half hours, the Obkom's *sanctum sanctorum*, the small Buro's meeting room, rang with variations on an endless and increasingly loud diatribe against the magazine. The latter's 'editorial staff [had] allowed serious flaws and shortcomings in defining the thematic direction of the publications; absent were the necessary exactitude in dealing with the [magazine's] authors, aimed at raising the ideological and creative level of the works'.[518] As a result, there had been published in the magazine's pages 'a number of materials without clearly defined ideological positions . . .'[519]

A case in point was 'K. Lagunov's novel', whose characters, 'first and foremost the leadership of a gas pipeline construction project, are portrayed as deeply flawed and morally dissipated money-grubbers and drunkards'.[520] As to 'Nikonov's work', it 'questioned the results of collectivization. The life of the modern village [was] portrayed in colours far from the optimistic spirit [sic], from the constructive tasks carried out by our society.'[521]

Altogether, the 'literary works' published by the magazine had been marked by 'biased, superficial assessments of our times, by concentration on shortcomings, [and] creation of a distorted picture of the real life of our society. At the same time, the magazine lacked sharp, socially significant materials about ideological struggle that would facilitate civil and moral upbringing.'[522] There were dark hints at still more serious, almost treasonous misdeeds. 'In the last three years, thirty-five facts containing state secrets have been excised from the galleys [by the censor], in four cases [the secrets] were of an ideological [sic] nature.'

Yeltsin thundered at Lukyanin: 'Do you know what enormous ideological harm you have done with your publications? Do you know how much we, the soldiers of the ideological front, will have to work to heal these wounds? I am deeply ashamed that such a magazine is published in our city!'[523]

Lukyanin was given seven minutes at the beginning of the session and one minute at the very end.[524] On the latter occasion he was ordered to tell the gathering if he 'accepted the critique' or 'rejected' it. 'Rejection' would have meant Lukyanin's immediate dismissal, a thorough purge of the editorial staff and, most likely, the end of *Ural* as the Russian reading public knew it.[525] Lukyanin 'accepted'.

After the *mea culpa*, Lukyanin was read the Buro's verdict – miraculously ready, even typed. The work of the editorial staff of *Ural* magazine was 'not satisfying the requirements contained in the decisions of the Twenty-Sixth Party Congress and the decree of the CC of the CPSU'.[526] For 'mistakes' and 'flaws' in the work, chief among them 'the publication of a number of ideologically faulty materials', Lukyanin and Gorbunov 'deserved a severe Party reprimand [a very serious form of

Party disciplinary action, just short of expulsion], but, taking into consideration . . . the fact that the editor has admitted his mistakes, [the Buro] found it sufficient to limit itself to a warning'.[527] The Buro 'recommended' cures for the ideologically infirm magazine: the 'creation and publication of works of high quality, deeply national, Party-like, reflecting the theme of labour, examining social phenomena from clearly defined class positions, brightly portraying the socialist way of life, the positive, socially active hero, and the vanguard role of the communists'.[528]

The Obkom also assigned tasks to the local chapter of the Writers' Union. It was ordered to 'pay special attention to creating and publishing works dealing with moral and aesthetic themes, affirming the life goals worthy of the Soviet man, his high moral qualities'; to 'debunk apolitical attitudes and psychology of consumption, sloppiness, to publish more materials aimed at the strengthening of labour and civic discipline, at the successful fulfilment of the objectives of the Eleventh Five-Year Plan'; and to 'educate the people in the spirit of the readiness to defend the revolutionary achievements of the Soviet people'.[529]

The magazine was given five weeks, until 1 July 1983, to 'outline measures for the elimination of the noted problems'.[530] To aid the wayward periodical back on to firm Party ground, the Buro generously volunteered the 'necessary assistance' of the City (Comrade Manyukhin) and District (Comrade Ilyushin) Party Committees.[531]

Assessing Yeltsin's role in the *Ural* affair ten years later, Nikolay Nikonov was surprisingly charitable.* He believed that it was only because of Yeltsin's intervention that *Starikova gora* had been published at all, against the resistance of the censor.[532] There could have been sanctions against the magazine's staff, as well as against Lagunov and Nikonov himself. None followed. The Obkom could have ordered local libraries to destroy all the January 1983 issues, but not a single copy was taken out of circulation. Overall, Nikonov thought, 'Yeltsin managed, somehow, to smooth the whole thing over.'[533] As to the Buro inquisition, 'There must have been an order from very high above,' said Nikonov. 'Under Brezhnev, the order could have been ignored altogether. But at the time everybody was scared [of Andropov]. Everybody was trembling, including me.'[534]

Sverdlovsk belles-lettres were not the only victim of Andropov's

---

* This was not the end of Yeltsin's dealings with *Ural*. Two years later, he received Lukyanin in his Obkom office and told him how much he enjoyed the magazine and how he 'encouraged' his staff to 'develop a taste' for it. In 1990, Yeltsin gave *Ural* the manuscript of his memoirs, *Ispoved' na zadannuyu temu*.

fourteen months in power. A less noted but far more severe blow was struck against politically incorrect music, which had advanced steadily in Sverdlovsk since the 1960s, when the city became famous for its underground jazz, pioneered by the pianist Vladimir Lukichev. In the early 1970s Sverdlovsk established itself as the base of one of the three main 'schools' of Soviet rock, alongside Moscow and Leningrad. Sverdlovsk rock was famous for the 'intellectual' nature of its lyrics. By the mid-1980s, the city became home to some of the leading rock bands in the USSR: Nautilus-Pampilius, Alisa and Nastya. In 1983 the KGB put on trial one of the best-known underground bards, Aleksandr Novikov. Convicted on trumped-up criminal charges (he was accused of stealing parts to make concert amplifiers) he was sentenced to ten years in prison and labour camp. Like Nikonov, however, Novikov did not blame Yeltsin for his ordeal, believing that there was nothing the Obkom could do against the KGB when its erstwhile chief was the General Secretary. He credited Yeltsin with his early release in 1989.[535]

Fortunately for Nikolay Nikonov and millions of his compatriots, the Bolshevik renaissance ended with Yuriy Andropov's death nine months later. As the country shuddered in revulsion and humiliation, the Politburo gerontocrats installed the last of their own: Brezhnev's devoted and colourless aide for thirty years, Konstantin Chernenko. Rumours that swept the country at the time claimed that Chernenko's distinguished services to the Soviet state had included procuring young women for Brezhnev's steam-bath entertainment. He invariably pleased the boss with his choice.

The last leader of the Soviet Union to die in office, Chernenko expired thirteen months later: on Sunday, 10 March 1985, at 7.20 p.m. in the exclusive 'Kremlin Hospital' in the Moscow suburb of Kuntsevo.

An emergency Politburo session was scheduled for the same evening. Aleksandr Yakovlev, at the time Director of the Moscow Institute of World Economy and International Relations, sensed 'something of a gathering storm', 'the impression . . . that the moment was at hand when the people would say: "That's it. We cannot live like this any longer." '[536]

A Central Committee Secretary, the head of its Economic Department and the soon to be Prime Minister, Nikolay Ryzhkov, remembers that:

> the stuffiness in the country had reached its maximum: after that only death . . . Nothing was done with any care . . . [We] stole from ourselves, took and gave bribes, lied in our reports, in newspapers, from high podiums, wallowed in our lies, hung medals on one

another. And all of this – from top to bottom and from bottom to top ... The country was drinking itself into the ground. [People] drank everywhere. Before work. After work. In the Obkoms and in the Raikoms. At the construction sites and on the shop floor. In offices and in the apartments. Everywhere.[537]

Unable yet to say it openly, many of the more intelligent and honest Party functionaries saw, as did Yakovlev, that:

in seventy years a system had been built [that was] *a priori* indifferent to the real, live human being, hostile to him. [This was true] not only with respect to the mass repressions, which had touched millions. [This was true] also of everyday life, in which a human being means nothing, has nothing, and cannot get the most elementary things without humiliation.[538]

In 1982, for the first time since the end of the Second World War, the Soviet Union had posted zero growth in the real income of its population.[539] It was more than a recession. After almost seventy years of unimaginable sacrifice and suffering, this immensely rich and seemingly industrialized nation had developed the economy of a colony. As Ryzhkov put it:

[The Soviet Union] imported everything! From grain and pantyhose to industrial machinery and equipment. Half of the chemical industry worked on imported equipment, 80 per cent of light industry and food production. Of total imports, the share of machinery and equipment was 40 per cent![540]

Those summoned to the Kremlin that Sunday night in March 1985 went directly to the Politburo Conference Hall on the third floor of one of the old buildings, whose floor-to-ceiling windows overlooked the redbrick Kremlin wall.[541] The office of the General Secretary was on the same floor. Between that office and the Conference Hall there was the so-called Walnut Room, with a large round table in the middle. Only the full, that is voting, members of the Politburo were admitted. There the handful of men who ruled the Soviet Union often conferred about 'the most important and the most complicated issues on the agenda'[542] before the official Politburo meetings, which were open to the non-voting (candidate) members and the Central Committee Secretaries.

When Nikolay Ryzhkov arrived, he found the candidate members of the Politburo and the Central Committee Secretaries gathered around a long table in front of the massive door to the Walnut Room.[543] At exactly 10.00 p.m. the door opened and, striding briskly, in came the 'Second Secretary',* Mikhail Gorbachev, followed by the Politburo members. Conforming to the ritual, each of the Politburo members shook hands with each of the lesser Soviet gods – like soccer teams before a match.[544] Everyone sat down, and Gorbachev declared the meeting open. Within an hour, there was agreement on the two points of the agenda: the organization of the state funeral, and a Plenum of the Central Committee to be held the next day.

The Plenum was scheduled for 5.00 p.m. At three o'clock that afternoon, in the same room, the Politburo gathered again to prepare its 'recommendation' to the Plenum. Gorbachev paused, and then said: 'Now we must decide the question of the General Secretary . . .'[545] Suddenly, without formally asking for the floor, Foreign Minister Andrey Gromyko stood up. One did not have to get up to speak at Politburo meetings. One, and only one, subject could warrant this solemnity. 'Allow me to speak,' Gromyko began in his muffled but firm voice. 'I have thought a great deal, and would like to make a motion to consider as a candidate for the post of the General Secretary . . .'[546]

Less than an hour later, the Soviet Union had its supreme leader. Five-and-a-half years of unimaginable change were about to begin. For Boris Yeltsin, that afternoon's yield was a telephone call that would prove to be an invitation to the making of Russia's history.

---

* Although never officially acknowledged – unlike the General Secretary and Central Committee Secretaries – the Second Secretary was, in effect, the deputy and second-in-command.

PART II

The Bellwether

CHAPTER 4

Perestroika, Mark I

THE FATEFUL CALL, TO YELTSIN's limousine, came on 3 April 1985. Central Committee Secretary Vladimir Dolgikh, on behalf of the Politburo, offered Yeltsin the position of head of the Department of Construction of the Central Committee. Yeltsin refused.[1]

A provincial Party boss was expected to be coy on such an occasion. Yeltsin, too, trotted out the ritual excuses: strong 'contacts with the [local] people', 'still unsolved problems', the 'habits' of work.[2] Of course, none of these protestations was given, or taken, seriously. Nor had the refusal been prompted by Yeltsin's resentment of the 'snobbery and haughtiness' with which Muscovites treated the 'provincials'.[3] In answering the all-important summons, which he had worked and hoped for all his adult life, a man of Yeltsin's ambition, scope and will would not have been deterred by such considerations.

No, the reason for Yeltsin's reticence was far more practical: the promotion was not high enough. For the governor of so prominent a province, a man so proud of his 'unique knowledge and experience',[4] the offer of just a department was insultingly paltry. Besides, precedent had been broken here: two of his predecessors, Kirilenko and Ryabov, had gone to Moscow as Central Committee Secretaries – the rank second only to Politburo membership, with which the Secretaryship was often combined. Gorbachev, Yeltsin angrily recalled, had ruled a 'province whose economic potential was significantly below' that of Sverdlovsk's and yet had been given a Secretaryship when called to Moscow seven years before![5]

The next day Yeltsin received a call from Egor Ligachev, the Party's cadres chief and *de facto* Gorbachev's deputy. The deployment of artillery of such calibre signified an end to negotiations. Yeltsin's objection was met with a reminder of 'Party discipline'. A week later he was in Moscow.

The departure of the man who for almost nine years had headed the country's third largest industrial region populated by five million people was marked by as little sentimentality and publicity as his promotion had been. *Ural'skiy Rabochiy* published a terse report on a Plenum of the Regional Party Committee and announced Yeltsin's successor, Yuriy Petrov, a former Second Secretary of the Sverdlovsk Obkom who had been working in the Central Committee in Moscow.[6]

As he sat for a farewell picture in the Obkom, surrounded by the Secretaries and department heads, Yeltsin, although appropriately dignified, looked unmistakably content. Belying his alleged reluctance to leave for Moscow, his was not the face of an unhappy man.

*   *   *

In a career full of lucky breaks, Yeltsin, as previously mentioned, especially treasured the fact that he had never been anyone's deputy – whether on a construction site, in a *trest* or in an Obkom department.[7] In that respect, his first three months in the Central Committee differed from the previous thirty years. Just turned fifty-four, Yeltsin had to learn subordination: his department was part of Dolgikh's portfolio.

This was a painful adjustment. 'For my free and proud character this cold, bureaucratic framework turned out to be a hard test,' he wrote later.[8] As always, work became a refuge: he was in his office from eight in the morning till midnight.[9] In June that year, however, Yeltsin's career reverted to the old pattern: he was promoted from head of the Construction Department to be Central Committee Secretary in charge of construction, still somewhat below the long-serving Dolgikh in the hierarchy but no longer his subordinate. Once again, he was his own boss.

He travelled widely, both as the Soviet Union's builder-in-chief and as a purveyor of the new Party style which Gorbachev was beginning to develop. One such trip took him to Tashkent, the capital of the Uzbek Soviet Socialist Republic. Barely three years hence, Soviet newspapers would portray Uzbekistan as a hopelessly corrupt and clan-based colonial satrapy of Moscow, virtually pre-modern despite the imported industrial veneer. Yeltsin chastised the local Party leaders for constructing 'prestige objects' (a euphemism for offices and various palaces – of culture, sports, political education, science) while neglecting the 'social development of the city'[10] (that is, hospitals, kindergartens, food stores). He called on the communist beys to infuse their work with 'exhaustive truthfulness' and even 'broad glasnost', and their style with 'modesty, honesty, exactitude and attentiveness to the people', whose 'trust and respect' the beys ought to 'treasure'.[11]

On 23 December 1985, Yeltsin was called to a Politburo session and told that he was to head the Moscow City Party organization. With 1,120,000 members, this was the largest and by far the most important local organization in the Soviet Union. Traditionally, the General Secretary picked one of his strongest and most trusted lieutenants for the job. Gorbachev himself came to the emergency Plenum of the Moscow City Committee (the MGK) to recommend Yeltsin – a recommendation that, in a ritual charade, the committee deigned to 'accept'.[12]

Gorbachev's choice of a provincial Party boss for the First Secretary of the Moscow Party Committee was a bold and shrewd gamble. He needed someone, fast, who could take over and thoroughly clean up the city, which for almost two decades had been ruled by Viktor Grishin, the servile 'conservative' rumoured to be Gorbachev's chief competitor for the General Secretaryship eight months earlier. Yeltsin fitted the bill better than anyone in the top echelon. After less than a year in the Centre, this provincial battle-tank was eager, devoted, rough, hardworking and honest – and also not sophisticated enough to realize that he operated in a minefield of incredible sensitivity and power of devastation. The tank's drive and speed would not be constrained.

At the first Plenum of the Central Committee over which he presided as General Secretary, Gorbachev had said: 'The ability to carry out orders is no longer enough. There is a growing need for such qualities as competence, feeling for the new, initiative, courage, the readiness to take upon oneself difficult decisions; the ability to set a task and see it through to fulfilment . . .'[13] A year later Gorbachev would add: 'A great many big and small problems have piled up. We need a large bulldozer to clear the way.'[14] On 24 December 1985, Gorbachev sent his largest bulldozer to tackle the tallest pile.*

Yeltsin plunged in without delay. He tried to see as much of his new domain as he physically could and to deliver, everywhere, a message of renewal and hard work. On his third day on the job, he went to the flagship of Soviet industry, the Likhachev car and truck plant. That excursion set a pattern that would be repeated hundreds of times in the next two years. After examining the plant's motor and press shops, he urged the workers to find 'unused reserves . . . for raising quality and reliability of products', to work to the 'strictest regime of economizing [with raw materials] and reduction of unproductive losses'.[15] The First Secretary then stressed the role of workers themselves in eradicating the 'laggard' attitude to work and in increasing effectiveness of production. He then proceeded to the plant's 'culture club', its gym and its hospital, and pointed to the need for organizing better conditions for leisure, and for improving the work of shops, cafeterias and food deliveries, as well as healthcare.[16]

After the Likhachev, Yeltsin met with the leadership of the city police (the 'organs of internal affairs') and 'underscored the importance of creating conditions for peaceful life, leisure and productive labour

---

* Later Gorbachev would explain Yeltsin's appointment thus: 'When we recommended Comrade Yeltsin [to the post of] First Secretary of the Moscow City Party Committee, we did so because the work in the capital's organization required a serious improvement and the entire situation in Moscow needed cleansing. We needed an experienced, energetic man, who could look at things critically. All these qualities were present in Comrade Yeltsin.' (Speech at the XIX Party Conference, 1 July 1988: *XIX Vsesoyuznaya Konferentsiya Kommunisticheskoy Partii Sovetskogo Soyuza*, vol. II, p. 182.)

among Muscovites'.[17] As his rank required, the new Pervyi of the MGK was accompanied by the Minister of Internal Affairs of the Soviet Union. Later that day, Yeltsin 'familiarized himself' with the conditions at 'outlets of public catering' – eateries (*stolovye*), cafeterias, restaurants – and of public transportation. In the course of the expedition, the First Secretary 'talked to Muscovites, asking their opinion of the measures for improvement in services'.[18]

In January 1986, the pace of field trips continued unabated. In one week, between the 11th and 17th of that month, Yeltsin visited five Moscow districts, holding, in each one, 'tens' of meetings. The choice of sites and topics for conversations was characteristic: a housing complex; a grocery store (Yeltsin was interested in how well 'amenities and services' were provided, how 'quickly and accurately the requests of the population were satisfied'); and a bus and tram depot, where he had a long talk with the drivers about what hindered the 'establishment of on-schedule transportation of passengers'. The tour of the city ended at a food factory, where Yeltsin extolled 'the special importance of those who work in food production' and called on them to 'increase the assortment of produce, and improve quality'.[19]

Even the more esoteric parts of the fiefdom did not evade his attention. In the Lebedev Physics Institute, the First Secretary inquired after the 'projects the scholars worked on' and 'discussed increasing the effectiveness of scholarly labour and its connection with the solution of practical tasks of the people's economy'.[20]

Suddenly, the Buro of the MGK, which had not been heard from for years, became an exemplar of publicity. The first reported session emphasized 'social questions': 'a further improvement in Muscovites' welfare and standard of living'; the quality of housing construction, schools, kindergartens, hospitals' outpatient facilities, the work of cafeterias (before and during the New Year holidays) and the retail trade. The Buro 'sharply criticized' the trade organizations for shortages of eggs and milk products, noted 'glaring inadequacies in the desserts', and deplored the 'low level of the service culture'.[21] An alert Moscow reader would not have missed another novelty: for the first time in anyone's memory the entire city government (the Buro of the MGK and the 'leaders' of the Moscow City Soviet, the Mossovet) 'visited a number of enterprises, organizations, construction sites, health maintenance and educational organizations'.[22]

On 24 January *Moskovskaya Pravda*, the newspaper of the MGK, treated its readers to more exotic fare: poetry on its front page. It was poetry, of course, only under the most charitable of definitions. Old Party rhymester hacks Sergey Smirnov and Lev Oshanin whipped and cajoled the exhausted and stumbling agitprop Pegasus:

> For us, there is no respite.
> We hold our flag sky-high.
> The red Party card we treasure
> With our very lives . . .
>
> The day when the dreams come true
> Is close, but – listen! – the foe's near.
> You must, Communist, prevail
> And win us a glorious future!
>
> I know you can succeed
> In making the earth so happy.
> Yet our hardest task
> May still be around the corner.

The purpose of the exercise (no doubt conceived in the bowels of the Gorkom's Propaganda Department) was to capture in an inspired flight of poesy the official enthusiasm occasioned by the first major event of Yeltsin's regime: a City Party Conference.

Yet, even disfigured by every cliché and pitiful in its mediocrity, the doggerel managed somehow to impart something unseen since Khrushchev's 'thaw' of the early 1960s: a stirring of expectation, a vague and tenuous hope for a better, cleaner and more interesting life – and a recognition of the enormity of the task involved in bringing that life about. An unusually long editorial next to the verses sought to convey the same message of long-awaited renewal, urgency and strenuous effort. Teeming with exclamation marks, the editorial welcomed the 'fresh wind of change! Fresh, healthy, bracing! It blows into our sails! . . . [This wind] will help sweep out of all corners everything that impedes our progress, contradicts the demands of socialism, prevents people from living normally and working hard and creatively. What fast-moving, interesting times we live in, comrades! So much room for testing one's strength, so much room for initiative!'

Previewing the conference, *Moskovskaya Pravda* apprised the reader of unusual features. The gathering would 'provide a deep, objective and sharply critical analysis of all aspects of the Moscow Party organization's work'. The 'giant preparatory work' included a 'broad, direct and frank conversation with the people'. The Party cadres were 'learning to listen attentively to the voice of the people ... and shorten the distance between the word and the deed'. 'Sharp and constructive criticism', exactitude and personal responsibility were 'becoming the norm'. Finally, the 'deepening and widening' of 'socialist democracy' were promised, as well as a search for 'new forms of social activity for ... voluntary associations of citizens'.[23] This, of course, would not have been the first time in communist Moscow that a preview had been far bolder than the show. As it turned out, the advertisement did not do justice to the product.

Following tradition, the Conference was held in one of the prettiest of the pre-revolutionary buildings in Moscow, the former Hall of Noblemen's Conventions, now the Hall of Columns of the House of Unions. The new Soviet nobility gathered there regularly for Party festivals. These were occasions to unwind from the rigours of governing: to sit in comfortable chairs in the airy marble hall, under the high cupola, amid snow-white columns wrapped for the occasion in flowing silk crimson bands; to enjoy a lunch at a buffet stocked with delicacies unavailable even in one's own exclusive canteen; to flirt with a pretty comrade in a red Finnish dress; and to snooze quietly through the afternoon speeches before going to the Bolshoi for a concert of the best dancers and singers just for the delegates.

Yeltsin woke them up. Not since the late 1920s, when Stalin swept the last remnants of candour out of intra-Party dialogue, had the august Hall witnessed anything like it. With the entire Politburo, including Gorbachev, looking on from the dais, the new First Secretary told the 1,015 delegates that 'an atmosphere of ostentatiousness, exaggeration of success and concealment of shortcomings has penetrated the work [of the Moscow City Party organization] and has led to complacency and inertia'.[24]

In the previous five years the return on industrial investment in Moscow had fallen by 18 per cent. Between 30 and 40 per cent of industrial equipment was more than fifteen years old, yet less than 3 per cent of it was modernized annually, and the huge sums allocated for industrial modernization were wasted. Thirty per cent of metal used in Moscow plants was lost either because the final product was substandard or because of 'violation of proper technological processes'. Absenteeism cost Moscow industries two million man-days annually. Thirty-five per cent of the municipal transportation stock was out of commission on any given day. 'Muscovites are not just complaining. They are indignant!'

Thirty-six per cent of Muscovites were doing 'hard menial' work. Yet, instead of raising labour productivity and modernizing the equipment, every year Moscow industries imported between 65,000 and

70,000 workers (the so-called *limitchiki*, from the word 'limit', or 'restriction') from all over the country. After obtaining the Moscow residence permit, most of the *limitchiki* quit the enterprise that had imported them to look for better jobs – and the enterprise imported still more workers the next year. Meanwhile, Moscow was already gripped by a housing crisis, with over one million Muscovites (one in eight) waiting for years, sometimes decades, for an apartment.

Yeltsin's arrows hit the most sensitive spots. Years later a witness still smarted from the tone: 'tough', 'sharp' and 'hurtful'.[25] Yeltsin 'blew to smithereens everything [to which] the people sitting in the hall had devoted their lives'.[26]

The most disturbing nostrum was saved for last. Revealing what would form the leitmotif of his Moscow reign, long before it became the official line, Yeltsin said:

Many Raikoms ['district Party committees'] continue to put up with the unwillingness of . . . cadres to conduct an honest and direct dialogue with the people. Yet it is precisely such sharp, direct dialogue that prompts the leaders to undertake concrete measures. It is precisely such a dialogue that helps knock off the barnacles of indifference, arrogance, the feeling of superiority, and promotes the sense of duty before the people, prompting one to consult one's conscience more often. This [dialogue] is an effective form of mutual development. Contrary to the established habit, it is not just we [the leaders] who educate the working class. No. It [is the working class that] has educated and continues to educate us . . .

We must conduct an open, candid struggle for the clean and honest image of the communist . . . We cannot allow disdain for the basic democratic rules, suppression of glasnost, criticism and self-criticism . . . We must . . . create in each Party organization an atmosphere that would completely exclude partiality and create conditions for an open, honest and principled discussion . . . We need criticism and self-criticism like air to breathe.[27]

After the shock had worn off, most of that audience of Party functionaries – a hardened and cynical lot* – no doubt calmed themselves by

---

* Not everyone was despondent. A Politburo member, who listened to the speech from the Praesidium, remembered the audience 'kindled and stirred' by Yeltsin's enthusiasm, his 'new ideas' and the 'interesting questions' he had raised. (*Izvestiya TsK KPSS*, 1989, no. 2, p. 261.)

repeating a familiar saying, 'The new broom always sweeps clean.' For centuries, Russians had muttered this proverb as their new bosses, from the Kremlin masters down to the meanest local bureaucrat, began their rule with a denunciation of their predecessors and promises of reform.

Yet, either because these were indeed different times or because Yeltsin was a different man, for once the Moscow cynics proved wrong. The new First Secretary continued to storm around the city, raising dust, and annoying the Party bureaucracy. One day in February, for example, he was sighted at a plant in the distant Moscow suburb of Medvedkovo. There he talked with the management about modernization and with the workers on the plant floor about the 'social sphere', especially public transport, which 'complicated arriving at work on time and getting home'.[28] The same day he visited grocery stores in another district and heard the shoppers' complaints about 'interruptions in the supplies of basic products' and 'not too high quality' (sic) of bread.[29] Later still, the First Secretary stopped by a construction site, where he 'expressed serious concern' about protecting the finished apartment buildings from the elements and vandalism while they awaited tenants.[30]

Scarcely a month and a half after he took over Moscow, the rumble of surprise aroused by his words and deeds grew loud enough to reach the gilded ghetto of American journalists in Moscow. 'According to the stories now making the rounds,' reported the *Washington Post* correspondent, 'the tall, broad-shouldered 55-year-old Party leader stood in lines for pastry on Gorki street and tried to buy a cut of good meat from a surly shop clerk at the food counter at the Hotel Minsk. To see how snow removal was going, he is said to have walked the back streets. To find out about the city's cheap but overcrowded transit system, he rode the bus.'[31] Yet the most celebrated event of Yeltsin's first Moscow months was still to come.

The occasion was the Twenty-Seventh Party Congress, which convened on 25 February 1986. Although timed by Gorbachev to coincide, thirty years to the day, with the opening of the Twentieth Congress, at which Nikita Khrushchev had launched deStalinization in his 'secret speech', it was not the General Secretary who delivered the Congress's most daring and instantly famous speech. Elevated to the position of candidate (non-voting) member of the Politburo a week before, Yeltsin must have felt confident enough in terms both of national politics and of his own position in the Party hierarchy to deliver to a national (and international) audience the kind of speech that had become so familiar to the people of Sverdlovsk and that was quickly becoming the staple of his Moscow addresses: of its twenty-six paragraphs, only four (opening and concluding) were celebratory; the rest were critical.

'Why, Congress after Congress, do we deal with the same problems over and over again?' Yeltsin asked. 'Why have we not been able to root out social injustice and abuse of power? Why is it that even now the demand for a radical change is bogged down, as in a swamp, in the inert layer of time-servers carrying the Party card? . . . How many times can we make deities of certain Party leaders?'[32]

Not content with leaving these dangerous questions rhetorical, Yeltsin went on to outline answers that were even more unsettling than the questions. First, courage was needed to tell the truth, no matter how 'bitter', about yourself, about your colleagues, about your superiors. 'We must assess the state of affairs and every leader personally in a principled, sometimes even tough, way . . . We can no longer tolerate the unquestioned authority of rank, the infallibility of the leader, the double moral standards,' one for the bosses and the other for the people. Second, 'we must, at long last, develop a system of periodic public accounts to be given [to the rank and file] by all [Party] leaders at all levels . . . [including] Secretaries of the Central Committee and the members of the Politburo . . .'

Having prescribed it, Yeltsin proceeded to take his own medicine – then and there. The two sentences that followed were to become the most talked-about and best-remembered quotation of the early Gorbachev era. 'The delegates may ask: why did I not say all this when I spoke at the last Congress? I can answer and answer frankly: perhaps I lacked courage and political experience.'[33]

Yet even this, the first and, so far, only *mea culpa* from a candidate member of the Politburo, was not the culmination of the speech. 'I am sure', continued Yeltsin,

that delegates have had to deal in their work with the problems of social justice. These are always discussed very hotly, for they touch upon many of the most vital interests of the people. I feel uncomfortable listening to expressions of indignation directed against instances of injustice – recent or chronic. But it is especially painful to hear people talking directly about special amenities for the leaders . . . My opinion is this: where such amenities are not justified, they must be abolished. This will undoubtedly lead to an increase in people's activity at the workplace and in public life.[34]

Here, Yeltsin had crossed the boundary of the acceptable. Although the literal translation of the term Yeltsin used (*rukoviditel'*) is 'leader', in Soviet Russian the term denoted a considerably more inclusive group: not just high Party and government officials but local Party functionaries, local government bureaucrats and industrial managers as well. Alongside terror, the secret distribution of amenities to the ruling elite (political, cultural, scientific and military) in strict and minute accordance with rank had been the cornerstone of the Soviet system. Rigidly delineated and jealously guarded compartments marked virtually every category of human need: food, goods, services, housing, education, healthcare, pensions, travel, entertainment and information.* (In Moscow alone, 40,000 people had access to different rungs of the state's horn of plenty.)[35]

By now Yeltsin knew first-hand of what he spoke. He was entitled to an enormous official dacha:† two storeys, a cinema hall, a dining-room table ten metres long, marble floors, crystal chandeliers, a mammoth underground refrigerator,[36] three cooks, three waitresses, a maid and a gardener with 'a staff'.[37] At weekends, a mechanic from Moscow would bring a projector and a choice of films.

A 'special' (which in Soviet Russian became a synonym for 'closed' or 'exclusive') section of the State Department Store (GUM) next to Red Square served the 'Kremlin ration': a gargantuan package of the choicest and freshest food. Everything else was 'special' too: hospitals, doctors, repair shops, cafeterias. In a country where millions spent hours (sometimes days and nights) in a queue to buy rare quality goods, Yeltsin's colleagues could order gifts from catalogues. When travelling, a high functionary had a jumbo jet all to himself. 'Special' dachas in the best resorts 'in the South' awaited holidaying leaders. When unoccupied by the 'special' guests, these palaces were empty and their permanent staff idle.[38]

'Social justice', as the subject was euphemistically labelled, was just beginning to surface in the official discourse. In Gorbachev's five-and-a-half-hour opening speech, the phrase had been used only once – in connection with the control over 'unearned incomes' of 'parasites' and 'unlawful payments of salaries and bonuses' at state enterprises. Asked

---

* A very good description of the arrangement is to be found in *Klass*, an undeservedly neglected book by David K. Willis, who reported from Moscow for the *Christian Science Monitor* between 1976 and 1981.

† Although now two ranks higher than when he had come to Moscow, Yeltsin did not bother to move from a hastily chosen two-bedroom apartment in a decidedly 'unprestigious, noisy and dirty' area near the Belorusskiy railway station. He and Naina shared it with Tat'yana's family.

about the elite's privileges at a press conference, Politburo member Gaidar Aliev first denied the existence of special shops, then stated that it was not just the Party workers who enjoyed special privileges. As they worked harder than other categories of 'labourers', Aliev added, Party workers had no time to shop in regular stores.[39] This segment of Aliev's press conference was deleted from the Soviet television broadcast.

Two weeks before the Congress, on 13 February, *Pravda* had published a review of readers' letters. The article, entitled 'Ochishchenie' ('Cleansing'), deplored the 'alien phenomena' of Soviet life, especially the venality of Party and government functionaries. It concluded with an emotional request from a reader that 'the Party be honest and open' with the people. One of the quoted letters read:

> Talking about social justice, one cannot close [one's] eyes to the fact that Party, Soviet, trade union, industrial and even Komsomol leaders sometimes objectively deepen the social inequality by using all sorts of special cafeterias, special stores, special hospitals etc. True, we have socialism, and everyone is supposed to receive in accordance with his labour. So, let's have it this way: a leader will have a higher salary, but there should be no other privileges. Let a *nachal'nik* go to an ordinary store and stand in line there, like everyone else, then perhaps the queues, of which every one is sick and tired, will disappear sooner.

In his speech to the Congress, the Party's second-in-command, Egor Ligachev, who spoke the day after Yeltsin, criticized *Pravda* for publishing the article.

In the mid-1980s, no other indignity of the totalitarian state rankled with millions of ordinary Russians as much or as deeply, generated more pent-up fury or was discussed more frequently in hushed conversations around kitchen tables than the privileges of the elite, and none did more damage to the legitimacy of the Soviet system. The censorship, the secret police, the one-party dictatorship, the inability to travel abroad – these were concerns of the intelligentsia, many of whose members were covered by the nomenklatura distribution system. For the Russian *hoi polloi*, relatively content, thoroughly cowed and seemingly docile, the system's fault line, which divided 'us' and 'them', passed through the unmarked 'distribution points', *raspredeliteli*.

In light of what was to happen in a few years, Yeltsin's choice of 'social justice' as a key theme of his short speech was remarkably prescient and politically brilliant. Still, the most intriguing part of his speech, although it went unnoticed at the time, came near the end: 'We must not be lulled by the permanent political stability in the country. How many times can we make the same mistakes, ignoring the lessons of history?'[40]

Bismarck is said to have remarked that political genius consisted in the ability to hear the 'distant hoofbeat' of the horse of history and then, by a superhuman effort, to 'leap and catch the horseman by the coat-tails'.[41] Not even a contour of the horse was visible then; but perhaps a very faint beating of the hoofs had already begun to shape the rhythm of Yeltsin's thoughts.

In the beginning it looked as if Yeltsin's Moscow reign would unfold very much like his Sverdlovsk tenure: a faithful implementation of the Party line with an emphasis on a few matters of special concern to the Pervyi. No item on Yeltsin's Moscow agenda was outside the perimeter of what was deemed permissible, indeed desirable, by the new leadership. Some of the tasks had been already added by the Kremlin to the Party's core agenda; others were, at the time, only hinted at but would, in Yeltsin's eager hands, acquire substance, detail and sharpness.

To be sure, he intended, and perhaps was expected, to venture, every now and then, close to the radical edge of the acceptable, and he trusted his inner censor, until then flawless, to tell him when and where to step back. The limits of the politically acceptable, while vigorously pushed, were never meant to be broken. And while he would sometimes cause irritation at the very top, in the end his worth would surely be more than redeemed, as it had been in Sverdlovsk, by the social peace, political conformity and industrial output maintained by the tough and hard-working Pervyi in a critically important part of the country. That the Sverdlovsk pattern was not to be repeated in Moscow was due to the confluence of two sets of circumstances which would endow Yeltsin's Moscow rule with a unique and dramatic plot, and with import and impact far beyond the city's realm.

First, Yeltsin's new exalted status – only a step below the Politburo Olympus – presupposed a licence to indulge his predilections to a degree unthinkable for a mere First Secretary of a provincial Obkom. He could now, with studied casualness, tell an awed audience that the Politburo had discussed this or that question 'the other day';[42] or mention that he had dispatched letters to the forty-two Ministers in charge of Moscow-based enterprises, telling them of his plans for Moscow and 'requesting' compliance, adding that thirty ministries had replied promptly and that he was satisfied with 'most' of the replies.[43] In the rendition of the Party symphony Yeltsin could now afford a pitch and abandon that had been impossible in Sverdlovsk, and there was no need to look over his shoulder at the Conductor-in-Chief nearly as often. It was hard to imagine a climate in which Yeltsin's customary boldness, his confidence bordering on cockiness and the single-mindedness and decisiveness of his *modus operandi* would grow taller or bloom in brighter hues.

The other harbinger of things to come was the nature of his new fiefdom and the character of its nobility. The title, 'First Secretary', was the same, yet the Pervyi's relative standing was quite different from the one he had grown used to in Sverdlovsk. Bound, for decades, with each other and the Central Committee by a myriad ties – colleges and Party schools, children's and grandchildren's marriages, exclusive buildings in exclusive parts of the city, 'special' hospitals and rest homes – the Moscow *nachal'nik*s were a powerful, experienced and arrogant crowd, who had grown even more self-confident in the golden decade of the 1970s under Leonid Brezhnev's indulgent 'respect for cadres', which often granted them life-long tenure. Although he was, as in Sverdlovsk the potentate with all the power and responsibility, the Party hierarchy over which he ruled no longer consisted of unquestioningly obedient, awed and mostly speechless underlings. Such was Moscow's political tradition, which Yeltsin took an inordinately long time to discern and which he never – much to his peril – accepted.

To an extent unmatched by most modern capitals, Moscow during Yeltsin's reign boasted a concentration of the country's politics, its economic governance and its culture. Thus the first coherent campaign launched by Yeltsin to locate, sort out and correct the city's problems was emblematic of a larger, country-wide effort by the new regime. Everything that would bedevil and, eventually, subvert this effort was first encountered by Yeltsin in Moscow. In this regard, the collisions that Yeltsin would touch off were much more than local skirmishes, more than a quarrel between an overzealous and wilful *nachal'nik* and his no less proud and haughty subordinates. It was a contest between a determined (if not terribly politic) reformer and the system's core, its beating heart, its collective brain, its habit of living and working.

As he had in Sverdlovsk ten years before, Yeltsin began with a programme contained in his 'inaugural speech'. As in Sverdlovsk, it had taken three months since the appointment to develop; and, now as then, he ordered the speech published. It was delivered on 29 March 1986 to the first Plenum over which he presided and which he had convened to 'evaluate the first practical steps and to outline a programme for near- and long-term tasks'.[44] Throughout his reign Yeltsin did not deviate from the priorities set out in his 'inaugural'.

The programme's opening section was quite traditional: the 'acceleration of socio-economic development in the capital'. Yeltsin faithfully reproduced the line laid down by Gorbachev at the Congress a month before: a mixture of utterly utopian objectives, the discipline of Andropov's police renaissance, an ever so cautious loosening of the rigid control of ministries over enterprises and an emphasis on the 'human factor' – that is, the worker's personal stake in the quality of the final product. 'Unearned' incomes would be eliminated, and 'additional measures' would be taken against 'parasites', that is, those not employed by the state.[45] Yeltsin promised to fight alcoholism and drunkenness. Workers' salaries would depend on the quality of the final product, not on volume. The existing productive capacities should be used more efficiently, partly by means of multi-shift work. Workers' influence over the management of enterprises would be 'widened step by step'. Bureaucrats would have to undergo 'certification'.

In the chorus of Party shamans who, following Gorbachev's example, extolled favourable economic portents and dispensed wild pledges, Yeltsin's voice at the beginning of his Moscow stint was among the loudest. Although at the time the annual increase in Moscow's industrial output was planned at a measly 2.8 per cent, Yeltsin promised that in the next five years it would grow by 'no less than' between 125 and 175 per cent.[46] The breakthrough was to be secured by giant increases in labour productivity (20 per cent annually), modernization of industry,* and a decrease in the numbers of manual labourers employed (20 per cent). The standard practice of increasing output by pouring in more and more raw materials and labour† was to stop.

By promising drastically to reduce the share of manual labour in industry, Yeltsin took on a giant social and economic task. In Moscow, 900,000 people were engaged in hard manual labour,[47] and the *limitchiki*, the 'guest workers', had the worst jobs. Since 1964, when Moscow first began to import labour on a grand scale,[48] more than 700,000 workers had been transferred to the capital. They, Yeltsin later wrote, were:

> the slaves of 'developed socialism', with no rights whatsoever, forever tied to their enterprise by the temporary resident permit [*propiska*],

---

* According to Yeltsin, Moscow enterprises spent almost as much on repairs of the machinery as they did on modernization.

† Yeltsin cited the example of one of Moscow's largest enterprises, the Ball-Bearing Plant: since 1975, investment had grown by 85 per cent while output had increased by only 2 per cent and productivity by only 14 per cent.

by the hostel, and by the dream of permanent *propiska*. [The enter-
prise] could do whatever it wished with them, breaking the law: they
would not complain. And if they did – all right, we lift your Moscow
propiska, and go to hell.[49]

'A teacher was hired as an unskilled labourer,' a newspaper wrote of
the *limitchiki*'s plight,

> a librarian became a cleaning lady, an experienced driver worked as
> a turner of a lowest grade, and an actor as a repairman . . . This was,
> literally, a test of survival . . . The best years of their lives were spent
> in the struggle for the *propiska*. A twenty-five-year-old man would
> be forty before he could, with a sigh of relief, say: 'I am a Muscovite!'[50]

The influx of a cheap and docile workforce, whose Moscow residence
permits were renewed only for as long as they were employed, 'corrupted' enterprise managers.[51] The latter, Yeltsin insisted, felt little need
to modernize and mechanize the labour force. In addition, the *limitchiki*
'weakened workplace discipline, and increased violations of public
order'.[52] They also added to the strain of the already badly overpopulated city: in the previous ten years, Moscow had grown by 900,000[53]
residents. Yeltsin promised first to reduce and then, from 1987 on, stop
completely the import of labour. The Moscow managers would have to
learn to fulfil plans without the *limitchiki* through 'harder work' and
more effective organization.[54]

While the declaration of war on the *limitchiki*, who epitomized the
extensive mode of Soviet economic development sustained by an ever-
expanding supply of raw materials and labour, was expected (and had
been previewed in Yeltsin's Conference speech), the other object of his
crusade for the 'intensification of production' came as a surprise. It lay
at the opposite end of the Soviet labour market, as far away as one
could get from the guest workers' dirty workplaces and squalid dorms.
It was the most comfortable, most sought-after employment the Soviet
Union had to offer: the 'scientific research institutes', known throughout
an envious nation by their Russian initials NII.

Here Yeltsin rudely trod on exclusive ground. For the NIIs were
preserves of well-connected surplus intelligentsia, the trend-setters of
cultural norms and sartorial fashions. These gentle, smart, likeable and
utterly cynical idlers, so brilliantly portrayed by the great Yuriy Trifonov
in his 'intelligentsia novels' of the 1970s, spent days chatting, trading
rumours and anti-Soviet political jokes, reading and passing along the

underground *samizdat* manuscripts, flirting, talking on the telephone, taking hourly smoking breaks, and raiding nearby stores on hot tips about new shipments of Japanese umbrellas, Finnish boots or Turkish leather coats. These were veterans of evasion, grandmasters of bamboozling and windowdressing, aces at avoiding work – much of it, to be fair, senseless and invented by the despised *oni*, 'them', the Party and state bureaucrats, whom these safely and very privately indignant anti-communist radicals, most of them Party members in good standing, hated with a passion.

Repeating Gorbachev's demand for a 'shorter distance between science and production', Yeltsin pledged to 'harness the scientific potential of the capital to solve concrete industrial and social problems'.[55] He vowed to reduce the staff of the Moscow NIIs, which, he noted, had increased by 100,000 in the previous ten years, despite repeated orders from the high Party quarters. 'We get the same answer,' Yeltsin said, 'we are afraid that firing would bring complaints. But of wasting the state's money we are not afraid!'[56] (One NII, called Automatization of Storage Equipment, reported that its labours had resulted in thirty million rubles' worth of profit for the economy in the previous five years. After 'a persistent but futile search' by two commissions, no 'real effect', not even one ruble's worth, was discovered.)[57] Yeltsin insisted that '70 per cent of all the resources go to concrete projects' and that 'the main criterion for evaluation of [institutes'] work must be implementation of their projects'.[58]

The crude firebreather from Sverdlovsk suggested unheard-of and draconian measures. If within five years an institute showed no visible results, it ought to be 'liquidated' or, at least, drastically reduced in funds and staff. He announced that he would 'do a spot-check right now' and close ten to fifteen institutes immediately, as a means of 'activating' others.[59] To those 'scientific workers' who failed a special exam (*attestatsiya*), the monstrous First Secretary would mete out a fate worse than death: a transfer to plants and factories.[60]

Although, as we shall see, almost nothing came of these plans, Yeltsin would never be forgiven by the intelligentsia for the assault on the NIIs. No matter what he said or did later, the blood between him and the Moscow intelligentsia would remain spoiled for ever. The memory of the offence would occasionally recede or lie dormant, but it would never stop dogging him.

Unlike in his Sverdlovsk inaugural, the economy occupied only slightly over a third of the Moscow speech. The rest was devoted to what Yeltsin called 'social urban problems'. Of these (and they were legion), Yeltsin decided to concentrate on four: housing, 'reconstruction and preservation' of the 'historic centre' of the city, public transportation and the retail trade, especially the provision of 'the basic categories of food'. These proved giant tasks.

Public transport was overcrowded and worn out, the equipment aged and increasingly unsafe. The vaunted Moscow Metro was falling desperately behind the times. While the entire length of the Metro was twenty-eight kilometres, sixty kilometres of additional metro routes were necessary just to keep pace with the growth and sprawl of the population.[61] In 1985, there had been 2,000 accidents in the Metro.[62]

There were not enough buses, especially in the so-called 'small districts' (*mikrorayons*) in the outlying areas. A few years before, the City Soviet had resolved that four additional bus depots were needed. Not one had been built.[63] Because of the perennial tardiness and outright cancellations, the schedules posted at bus stops served only to 'mislead' people.[64] During the morning and evening rush hours, the *mikrorayons* were a scene of mayhem as desperate crowds stormed the buses – shoving, screaming and cursing the authorities.

The housing crisis was choking the Soviet capital, while the existing buildings and infrastructure, including those built only a few years before, were crumbling. Of the City's 8.7 million residents, 2.5 million were in line for larger apartments, and, of these, 1 million shared apartments with several other families.[65] In one Moscow district, every fourth building had deteriorated to the point where evacuation of the tenants was required.[66] During the unusually cold winter of 1986–7, some 50 per cent of all water and heating pipes in the downtown districts were found to be in a 'state of near collapse'.[67]

In a typical dorm for workers of a Moscow construction *trest* there were 'huge cracks in the walls and yellow water stains on the ceiling'.[68] Lobbies were 'cold and draughty'. There were two communal kitchens and two sinks on each floor, or one kitchen and one sink for fourteen family rooms. The sinks, the residents complained, had been installed in such a way that the water 'seeped into the adjacent rooms'. The pipes were 'old and corroded', and water often gushed out and covered the floors of the bathrooms.[69] In another tale of housing woes, two lifts, delivered for installation in an apartment block, were left in the yard and lay there, unclaimed, for a year under rain and snow.[70]

Yeltsin pledged a 150 per cent increase in investment in the 'social sphere'.* Over the next fifteen years housing construction was to grow by 170 per cent – the minimum Yeltsin considered necessary to address both the industrial and 'social urban' problems.[71] Even such a gigantic (and, in the current state of the Soviet Treasury, utterly unrealistic) commitment of funds would not provide every Moscow family with an apartment of its own before the year 2000.[72] Still, Yeltsin hoped, by 1993, to reduce to two years the wait for an apartment, which could otherwise take decades – or a lifetime.[73] He also pledged, by 1990, to have telephones installed within a year of request.[74]

In an attempt to do something – anything – to alleviate the housing crisis, Yeltsin brought with him from Sverdlovsk the practice of the Youth Housing Complex. After work and at weekends, young professionals constructed their own apartment buildings. Special courses taught physicians, engineers, teachers and mechanics how to handle armature, fit together concrete panels and mix mortar.[75] This was a characteristic Yeltsin solution: crude and irrational for a 'normal' economy, but somehow effective in bypassing the state and Party bureaucrats and allowing a measure of self-help and individual initiative.

The new First Secretary demanded of the 'construction organizations, ministries and agencies' that 'no less' than 50 per cent of all construction work be of a 'social or cultural nature': housing, kindergartens, schools, cinemas. (He went as far as to call it a 'non-Party' attitude – a very serious charge indeed – 'to build in Moscow and not to build for Muscovites'.)[76] He also promised to double the length of the Metro routes in the next five years and to bring order to the scheduling and routing of buses and trams.

Yeltsin found Moscow's architectural and historic landmarks neglected, polluted, slowly decaying, systematically destroyed or recklessly 'renovated'. It was one of very few European capitals where dozens of harmful smokestack plants, including metallurgical and petrochemical,[77] operated at full capacity. Since 1935 an estimated 2,200 'significant architectural landmarks' had been destroyed.[78] Those that survived were in sorry condition. Most were used as shops, offices, even warehouses.

---

* This included healthcare – another 'sore spot' in the Soviet capital. The Chairman of the Moscow City Soviet bemoaned the neglected state of many hospitals (which needed large-scale repair and reconstruction work), the shortage of doctors, nurses and aides, the 'low level of service' and 'simply disdain for the sick' (*Moskovskaya Pravda*, 6 April 1986). At the time, a Soviet doctor was officially required to spend no more than fifteen minutes with each patient, including examination, diagnosis and prescription of treatment (L. Ivchenko, 'Bednye millionery' ('The poor millionaires'), *Izvestia*, 21 January 1986).

The lovely small church where Russia's greatest poet Aleksandr Pushkin had married (formerly the Church of Resurrection, near Nikitskie Vorota) housed the Moscow branch of the Ministry of Electricity and Electrification. The city's historic centre, including the Old Arbat, was daily corroded by thousands of cars, trucks and buses. 'The historic face of Moscow has been badly disfigured,' Yeltsin concluded in an April 1986 speech.[79] It took this *'muzhik* ["peasant"] from Sverdlovsk', much despised by the Moscow *beau monde*, to launch a forceful campaign to save old Moscow from the wrecking ball and pollution.

Shortly after Yeltsin took over the city, a plan was developed to remove harmful industries from Moscow[80] and to 'forbid construction in Moscow of new plants, factories and administrative buildings'.[81] He vowed not to grant permissions to raze historic landmarks, 'even though such requests continue to be made'.[82] 'Our position is firm,' he told an interviewer, 'maximum preservation and restoration of the invaluable landmarks of history and culture. This is a most serious problem and it is constantly the focus of the Gorkom's attention. We are against filling the city with faceless boxes.'[83] He proudly informed the interviewer that pre-revolutionary names had been returned to several streets (Khamovnichekiy Val, Ostozhenka), and even to a Metro station (Krasnye Vorota).[84]

Under the Gorkom's guidance, the City Soviet designated 'safe' zones in the city centre that were 'to be restored and modernized with maximum tact'.[85] No large-scale ('global', to use Yeltsin's word) new construction would be allowed there.[86] Yeltsin envisaged the restored areas as 'living space for work and leisure, not as a state-owned museum quarter'. One such zone, the Arbat, was designated by Yeltsin (who personally chaired the meetings of the Consultative Committee on Urban Construction)[87] as 'exclusively pedestrian'. The designation is still in force – the most conspicuous legacy of Yeltsin's rule.

Yeltsin also promised to remove 200 government offices from the ground floors of their buildings and replace them with shops and cafés.[88] He began by using his newly acquired Politburo membership to force the Minister of Electricity and Electrification himself to come to the church of Pushkin's marriage and finally agree to vacate the building.[89]

Among Yeltsin's attempts to make good the pledges given in the inaugural speech, no campaign was prosecuted with more persistence, accorded more prominence or accompanied so frequently and mercilessly by his heavy administrative sword than 'improving the provisioning of Muscovites with the basic categories of food'.[90]

Muscovites had long reconciled themselves to the fact that good meat was a luxury. But the increasing difficulties in finding fruit and vegetables were beginning to irk them to an uncommon degree, and it was threatening to become a political problem. And while the new First Secretary endeavoured to make it easier for his charges to obtain the entire range of retail food – from ice-cream and sweet rolls to sausages – it was an improvement in the supply of fruit and vegetables that Yeltsin was particularly determined to bring about.

He needed all the determination he could muster. One New Year's eve, when by tradition Moscow authorities spoiled their citizenry with all manner of suddenly available produce, including such exotic fare as oranges and bananas, a shopper reported that there was an 'at least two-hour, eighty- to ninety-people' queue for potatoes in a vegetable store.[91] A store near by had no potatoes at all, only horseradish and onions. The shopper, determined to procure that staple of the Russian diet, then visited eight other stores in the area. None had potatoes. Cabbage and carrots were missing as well.[92]

The general deterioration of the Soviet food situation in the 1980s, when not only meat but increasingly eggs, butter and milk became hard to obtain, began to be felt even in Moscow, the country's showcase, its 'model communist city', supplied more effectively than any other place in the country. In addition, the stores of the Soviet capital were raided every year by two to three million[93] foraging visitors from all over the Soviet Union, who, enormous sacks in hand, queued up for virtually anything.

Before they reached the eager shoppers, the hundreds of thousands of tonnes of vegetables that arrived in Moscow had to survive the decrepit, dark, unventilated and dirty vegetable depots (bazy). In these smelly warehouses the produce was kept for days, sometimes weeks, before hands and trucks could be found to deliver it to the stores. Entire factories, colleges and NIIs were mobilized to sort out and load the produce at the bazy. Some worked, most picnicked and drank, and left in the evening with bags full of fruit and vegetables. Often depots were empty on the day when the 'volunteers' were dispatched, and were bursting with fast-perishing produce the next day when there was no one to help out. In December 1986, for example, 'scholarly researchers' from the Scientific Institute of Television were sent to a warehouse for a night shift to unload a shipment of cabbage. They waited all night, but the trucks never came.[94]

There was another, still weightier reason for bare shelves at state stores in the Soviet capital: the universal thievery, graft and cheating, and the booming black market in food products. In his inaugural speech

Yeltsin identified what had been known for decades but never officially acknowledged: a 'whole system of bribes and "taxes"' within the food trade. He promised that 'no matter how difficult it is to wage war on this evil, we must uproot it completely'.

A good place to start would have been the Café Iskra, in the Dzerzhin-skiy district. The menu there listed peach and pomegranate juices but the patrons were told that these were not available. Instead, they were 'persistently' offered a 'drink' (which was not on the menu) of water, sugar and syrup. Meanwhile, in a kiosk at a subway entrance, a few blocks away, an employee of the café was doing a brisk trade in the missing juices, liberally diluted with water.[95] This was, of course, a petty racket practised by small-time crooks. Yet, reproduced in myriad forms, hourly and daily, in every corner of the giant metropolis, the 'system', as it came to be known, digested a giant share of retail turnover, siphon-ing off millions of rubles from the state and laying bare kilometres of shelves in state stores.

Only gradually, and never entirely, did the 'system' reveal itself to the new First Secretary – breathtaking in its scope, depth, complexity and durability. One day, in the spring of 1986, as he was leaving a store, Yeltsin was stopped by a young sales-clerk, who looked scared and asked to be received in the Gorkom. At the appointed day and hour she entered Yeltsin's office and for two hours straight talked to him about a most elaborate 'system of taxes' (*pobory*) that permeated the Moscow retail trade from top to bottom. Everyone had a daily quota. Sales-clerks cheated customers and paid the section-chiefs, who passed larger sums to the store manager, who in turn channelled his share up to the district administration. The heads of the storage depots, too, got their cuts at delivery time.[96] The anxious woman was afraid and begged Yeltsin to keep her identity secret. She was later quietly transferred to another store.

Following a discussion within 'a narrow circle' of the MKG, it was decided to replace sales personnel 'not individually but by entire sections, stores and warehouses'.[97] Eight hundred store managers were arrested.[98] 'It is going to be long and difficult work,' Yeltsin said in April 1986, 'but we are determined to scoop all the dirt to the bottom.'[99] Before the end of the year, the public prosecutor's office uncovered 'organized groups of plunderers' and 'bribe-takers' who worked in the retail trade (as well as in public catering, hotels, public healthcare system, transpor-tation, housing and construction).[100] Even so, complained Yeltsin, 'we are scooping and scooping and scooping the mud but still do not see the bottom of this dirty well.'[101]

His frustration was genuine. The near-universal thievery and venality, lack of supplies and bad organization were but a few of the many tails of the giant and silent animal that nestled deeply and comfortably at the heart of the Soviet economy: the artificial and irrational prices and the consequent lack of incentive by the sales-people to sell at those prices in stores which they did not own and from whose operation they in no way profited.

What Yeltsin found in Moscow could be called Adam Smith's revenge. The market's 'invisible hand' – working through thousands of thieving and conniving sales-clerks and trade officials – removed most of the best produce from the shelves of the state stores and distributed them secretly at real prices, paid in bribes, barter or favours. Even Moscow could never keep up with the merciless efficiency of a market bent on restoring balance between dwindling supply and boundless demand.

While the reach of this 'secondary market' was eventually impressed on the new First Secretary, the root economic cause was, of course, entirely incomprehensible to him at the time. He fought the battle the only way he knew how: by personal vigilance, administrative engineering and relentless chopping at the animal's tails but never, even for a moment, endangering the beast itself. He began by visiting Moscow stores, incognito, at least once a week:[102] his face was not yet known to the people. One day, having learned that a store had received a shipment of veal (a rare delicacy), he hastened there and joined the queue in the meat department. In due course, he reached the counter and asked for a 'kilo of veal'. 'We don't have veal,' the saleswoman answered. Yeltsin insisted. He asked to speak to the manager and forced his formidable frame behind the counter. There, through the window of a small storage room, porters were handing out chunks of meat[103] for further distribution to a select clientele.

Yeltsin's other stratagem was the Party's, and his own, all-time favourite: believing that corruption was the cause, rather than a symptom, he set out to replace the thieves with people 'honest and devoted to the Party',[104] with 'uncontaminated youth'.[105] 'Cadres are the most important thing [in trade],' he declared after barely a month on the job. 'If we do not solve the problems of cadres, do not rid trade of dishonest people, do not inject there fresh reliable forces, there is always going to be a shortage of something in the city, and there will always be an artificial shortage, and the militia will constantly be catching criminals.'[106] The district Party committees were instructed to 'take urgent measures to combat mercilessly theft, bribery and cheating [in the stores], and to charge personally those responsible'.[107]

The purge was accompanied by another tried and true gambit: administrative reorganization. The City Party Committee, having examined 'the command structure of the food trade in the city', resolved to 'widen and strengthen' the district 'link' of the city trade organizations.[108] To that end 'district food *trests*' were to be created to take over the city stores from the all-city Trade Administration (the MosTorg).

Finally, in the middle of his first Moscow summer, an angry and impatient First Secretary reached for the ultimate levers. On 24 July, the First Secretary of the Kievskiy district was fired for evincing an 'irresponsible attitude towards providing the populace with fruit, vegetables and potatoes', the 'bad organization of the retail [vegetable] trade' and the 'shirking of responsibility for solving the acute problems with the vegetable trade in the district'.[109] The First Secretary of the Baumanskiy district was 'strictly warned'. The Buro 'warned' First Secretaries of the other districts that the 'slackening of attention to the organization of an uninterrupted supply of fruit and vegetables' was 'unacceptable' and that they would be held 'personally responsible for the timely correction of the defects'.[110]

Two weeks later Yeltsin fired the head of the Main Trade Administration of Moscow for the 'extremely unsatisfactory condition of the trade servicing of the population' and for not finishing the 'work aimed at removing the conditions engendering embezzlement, bribery and other negative phenomena'.[111] Two months passed, and Yeltsin expelled from the Party and fired Moscow's top crime investigator at the Chief Administration of Internal Affairs of the Ispolkom (the City Soviet's Executive Committee), V. V. Anikin, for 'maintaining non-businesslike relations with persons working in the trade and services, some of whom have been indicted or arrested'.[112]

Unlike dismissals and administrative engineering, Yeltsin's other device, deployed at about the same time, was not from the conventional arsenal. Believing that the key impediment was an insufficient number of retail outlets,[113]* he thought of something that would, he believed, in one go take care of the thieving managers, deadly *bazy* and long queues. The miraculous agency was the *yarmarka* ('fair'). By this scheme, which was 'totally' Yeltsin's own,[114] much, if not most, of the 800,000 tonnes of potatoes and 1,000,000 tonnes of other vegetables

---

* Having discovered that 'apartment buildings, even entire blocks', were constructed without a single store, Yeltsin ordered that no apartment building be passed by the accepting commission without a grocery store near by – 'even if this leads to the scuttling of a [construction] plan' (*Moskovskie Novosti*, 24 August 1986).

that arrived in Moscow every year would bypass the warehouses and the stores and be available for sale at dozens of fairs throughout the city. An additional advantage of this plan was the competition with the private markets that these state-run bazaars were eventually to provide.* To underscore the MGK's commitment to the idea, one of its Secretaries, Alla Afanasievna Nizovtzeva, was given full-time responsibility for overseeing the *yarmarki* and vegetable procurement, and each of Moscow's thirty-three districts was ordered to build its own fair 'village', *gorodok*.[115]

On 26 July 1986 the first *yarmarka* was opened with a great fanfare in the Zhdanovskiy district. While customers shopped, 'folk ensembles' belted out Russian tunes from a specially built podium. The plywood kiosks, decorated to look like the brightly coloured huts (*teremki*) of Russian folktales, sold cucumbers, tomatoes, aubergines, cabbages and cauliflowers, as well as clothes, household goods, juices and ice-cream. The ground had been cleared by the workers and engineers of nearby plants: the Automated Lines, the Experimental Plant of Metals and the Mosstroy Building Trust. 'We found a task for everyone,' declared the Deputy Chairman of the Zhdanovskiy Ispolkom; 'some put together the kiosks, others made colourful umbrellas, still others cast a metal fence and paved with asphalt.'[116]

The reach of the campaign expanded rapidly. Two months later, a fair from North Caucasus opened in the Kuybyshevskiy district. The traders wore traditional Cossack garb, complete with shawls and astrakhan-trimmed hats. For entertainment, there was a group of amateur singers and dancers, who regaled the shoppers with 'real festival shows'.[117] Overnight a mock Cossack village was got up: thatched huts, wattle fences and a log-lined well. The props, the singers and the produce – cucumbers, tomatoes, watermelons, walnuts, sausage – sold off trucks which had travelled almost 2,000 kilometres. The entire show had been prepared in just two weeks.[118]

Because of the dearth of refrigerated or even air-conditioned warehouses, the fruit, vegetables and meats were kept for days in the refrigerator trucks, whose motors had to be kept running round the clock.[119] Miraculously, given their overheads, the valiant North Caucasian

---

* After Sverdlovsk, Yeltsin was appalled by Moscow market prices: 'a kilo of meat 8 rubles!' But he had enough common sense to add that 'we cannot simply dictate prices: this has been tried and brought no results'. He proposed instead to 'pressure the market with the [state] trade competition. Near every market there should be a [state] store.' ('Vypiska', p. 3.)

traders still managed to 'dampen the prices' of the bona-fide private merchants in the nearby market.[120] What, in the Soviet Union of 1986, were such pedestrian matters as self-cost, pricing and profit when set against the wishes of a candidate member of the Politburo!

The *yarmarki* rage reached its apogee the week before New Year's Eve 1987. All fourteen Union republics and countless regions had been pressed into participating. In the rush to please the powerful Moscow chief, the Uzbeks sent tomatoes and cucumbers by plane, as did the Armenians, who shipped by air their national flat bread, *lavash*.[121] They certainly stood out among the shivering customers in heavy overcoats and fur hats: a bearded Tajik in a traditional gown and skullcap, or Ukrainian girls in bright red-and-white embroidered dresses.

One of the *yarmarki*, that of Azerbaijan at the Usachevskiy Rynok, was graced by the appearance of the Pervyi himself. Trailed by a retinue of Moscow and Azerbaijan worthies, Yeltsin toured the fair, visibly pleased with the progress of his brainchild.[122] Then, standing in the centre of the market, he proceeded to accost the Azerbaijani traders: 'Aren't you ashamed of yourself – profiting from the Muscovites like this? They send you all sorts of machinery, machine tools, refrigerators. And you? Can't you take a ruble off the fruit, fifty kopecks off the vegetables?'[123] The prices, recalls a witness, dropped immediately. That evening, Moscow kitchens were abuzz with reports of the Pervyi's feat. He 'became a legend'.[124]

All 'revolutions from above' begin as reforms of the ways of governing. Gorbachev's effort and its most visible and most radical forward deployment, perestroika ('renewal') in Moscow, were no exception. While ministering to the ailing city was important to Yeltsin, something else was paramount: a reform of the Party bureaucracy, the apparat. It is in this theatre that perestroika's first major battles were fought. Their outcome, carefully watched by Gorbachev, entered into a complex political calculation that produced a fateful change in the General Secretary's strategy.

The paths to the 'renewal' of the Moscow City Party organization were laid out in the inaugural speech. Able, at long last, to force on the Party's largest and haughtiest regiment the drills and routines developed and practised in the relative obscurity of Sverdlovsk, Yeltsin must have felt even more confident and virtuous than usual. He was, therefore, especially blunt.

First, he announced that henceforth the City Party organization would adopt a different approach: practical, concrete and businesslike, with a minimum of festive speechifying and an end to voluminous reports of glorious victories. 'Utmost attention' was to be given to 'real problems of real people and real improvements.'[125] 'We must', Yeltsin continued, 'totally block any "general" talk, any empty speeches . . . Every speech must be concrete, must contain deep analysis based on real life and must carry weighty, thought-out information about practical experience in solving socio-economic problems.'[126]

Second, the distance between the rulers and the ruled would be greatly reduced. There was to be a 'closer connection with the masses'.[127] 'Conversations with people at places of work or residence . . . allow the leaders to feel the pulse of life, tightly linking their work with the needs of the people, while being guided by their opinions and recommendations.'[128] To force such contacts on the reluctant Moscow Party nobility, Yeltsin, even before his inaugural speech, introduced to Moscow one of his Sverdlovsk routines: the so-called 'general political day' (*edinyi politden*'). Once a month, on a Tuesday,[129] the city political elite repaired to plants and factories: the Secretaries of the MGK and of the district committees, the leaders of the Mossovet and of 'economic administrations'.[130] On Moscow's first *politden*', on 11 February 1986, the First Secretary himself went to the Radioparts Plant.[131]

Finally, there would be no hiding of shortcomings, no window dressing, but a merciless baring of the problems and an equally unforgiving treatment of those who lagged behind in initiating reforms. 'The Buro demands strict retribution for the violators of the norms of the Party life,' Yeltsin warned, 'and insists on evaluating the actions of the leadership from the most exacting and principled position.'[132] From then on, in a startling departure from the Party's tradition of dealing with its black sheep in deep secret, the names of the violators would be made public. To drive the point home, Yeltsin demanded that 'our mass media tell Muscovites' the names of the thirty directors of enterprises that had not fulfilled the plan for the first quarter of 1986. A week later the list was duly published. *Moskovskaya Pravda* even went beyond the original brief: to the names of the directors it added those of the Party Secretaries at the guilty enterprises.

Yeltsin promised to 'begin with ourselves, with the Gorkom, the Gorkom departments'.[133] He kept his word. 'Enough talk. The time [has come] to get things done,' was his initial message to the apparat.[134] 'People are used to working to a slow rhythm,' he told a Party audience. 'We cannot afford this now.'[135] Within weeks of his arrival, the MGK staff no longer worked from 'nine to six' but, following their boss's lead, till 'nine, ten or midnight'.[136] Saturday was the MGK's busiest day.[137] Occasionally, Yeltsin convened the Buro and the Executive Committee of the Moscow Soviet even on Sundays. One such Sunday joint session, on 30 November 1986, was held to 'discuss the tempo of fulfilment of socialist pledges regarding the delivery of new housing'.[138]

The changes in the MGK's routine went beyond heavier workloads and longer hours. Yeltsin aimed at creating a working regime where the Pervyi was first among equals and where no one had 'the monopoly on thought ... on correctness in the final degree'.[139] Overcoming the 'stereotypes' of unlimited personal authority and unquestioning subordination was difficult, Yeltsin admitted, both for himself, 'a person of a mature age', and for the Buro members:[140]

> There was a particular [political] climate, which one was used to and in which one was formed as a leader. And, all of a sudden, [there are] new criteria, new approaches to work. Everything is different. [It is] understandable [that] one loses one's bearing. Yet one has to mobilize one's willpower at the right time, and, day in and day out, keep eyes on the final objective, and move towards that objective ... Am I successful in extricating myself from the past? ... Past mistakes, too, were made with our complicity.[141]

Was he successful? As far as the atmosphere in the MGK was concerned, the answer seems to be yes. 'As he was gathering a [new Buro] team,' recalls a former Secretary of the Moscow Party Committee,

> he created a distinct atmosphere, a distinct style of work. The central characteristics of this team were utmost candour and a totally frank analysis of every step of the Buro. He spared no effort to make sure that all had an opportunity to express their views both as a team and one on one to Yeltsin. He created a degree of trust, a degree of solidarity in which one felt able to share anything ... He could work with a team. Whenever Yeltsin was working on a particular problem, he managed to ask, in person, the opinion of every member of the Buro. And then to discuss with everyone together again. And then ask again.[142]

To Yeltsin's subordinates his adherence to the new rules of work and aversion to unquestioning obedience was demonstrated by, among other things, his behaviour vis-à-vis his own boss. They were struck by the fact that, when interrupted during Wednesday Buro sessions by a call from Gorbachev, Yeltsin 'did not stop in mid-phrase and rush headlong out of the room' to take the call. Instead, he 'calmly finished his remarks and walked out at a normal pace'.[143]

The style of work was changed in more tangible ways as well. In his inaugural speech, he proudly announced that the Party functionaries already 'sit in the offices less, and appear in the city more'. Field trips by Buro members to 'familiarize themselves with the local problems' in order to participate in 'collective decision-making' had become 'common'.[144] 'Common' was an understatement. A call from Yeltsin's office to the MGK Secretaries – 'Drop everything! Let's go! We will confer when we get there' – could come several times a day, and no day, including Sunday, was safe.[145] This was done, Yeltsin explained, 'in order to see real life, not Potemkin villages'.[146]

Yeltsin especially favoured surprise expeditions to the gates of Moscow factories just as the morning shift poured in. One morning, at a plant's entrance, 'no fewer than a hundred' angry workers told him of their woes: 'the unbearable conditions of labour and everyday existence, and the utter indifference' of the management.[147] 'You should have seen how annoyed people were when talking about all of this,' Yeltsin told an MGK Plenum.

One got the impression that until that morning the workers had had no opportunity to talk about their hardships to the management, the Ministry, the Raikom. And that, indeed, was the case! The functionaries had cut themselves off from the cares of the people, from their problems ... Haughtiness, irresponsibility, superficiality – there are no other words to describe this inattention to the people.[148]

Many of Yeltsin's field trips were made by the Metro or bus. These supplied the candidate member of the Politburo with an abundance of novel experiences. 'A person is battling to get to the [Metro] station, squeezes himself into the car and is not quite sure that the train will not get stuck in the tunnel, that the escalator will not stop all of a sudden, or that a ticket collector at the turnstile will not be rude to him ... The passenger comes to work rumpled, irritated and late.'[149] Such observations, related by Yeltsin to the gathering of the Moscow Metro senior management, could not have been obtained second-hand.

These trips by public transport annoyed the Moscow Party establishment more than Yeltsin's other, often more serious, transgressions. Later, they would be cited as key evidence of his 'populism', his 'search for cheap popularity'. Yeltsin was puzzled by the reaction: 'In Sverdlovsk this was a perfectly normal kind of thing; people paid little attention to the fact that the First Secretary of the Obkom was riding a tram . . . Here in Moscow this, for some reason, caused endless rumours.'[150] As for the 'cheap popularity', why, Yeltsin wondered,

> was no one but me eager to acquire it? . . . For some reason, even those who had long forgotten even the meaning of the word 'popularity' had no desire [to gain it]. No, it was, indeed, far more comfortable to ride in the ZIL [limousine]. No one steps on your foot, no one pushes from behind, no one pokes you in the side. Just breeze along, with no stops, the green light all the way, and the cops salute you. Nice, isn't it?[151]

The descents from Olympus both disturbed and energized him. 'Every now and then, there is a thought: something has been done, something is turning out well,' Yeltsin told an interviewer in the spring of 1987. 'But . . . I am cured from conceit by regular visits to enterprises, face-to-face meetings with the people at their workplaces, in the streets, in the stores . . .'[152]

Yeltsin had barely settled when, not yet four months master of the Soviet capital, he introduced Moscow to yet another of his Sverdlovsk habits: a no-holds-barred question-and-answer session (*vstrecha*). On 11 April, Yeltsin met, for several hours, with over a thousand Party functionaries, most of whom were full- or part-time 'propagandists' lecturing at workplaces about the 'current policy of the Party': economic, political, cultural, social or foreign. Never before had so much startling truth emanated from so high and authoritative a source. Unused to such recklessness, a cautious, pompous and sclerotic Moscow was shocked – and dazzled. It was to become, a former Soviet journalist recalled, 'Yeltsin's first Moscow triumph'.[153]

A brief report in *Moskovskaya Pravda* the day after the session was very circumspect and carried no quotations. Yet for a Moscow audience adept at reading between the lines, even this weak and censored echo contained more than enough hints at something quite extraordinary: 'nearly 400 questions'; 'a detailed, sometimes sharp, lively and trusting conversation'; the 'greatest possible level of frankness'; 'issues that deeply interested labour collectives and the populace of the capital'; an 'acute interest shown by those in the hall'.[154] A few pages of notes, jotted down by someone in the hall that night, became the hottest underground reading in Moscow. It was the first time in the history of the Moscow *samizdat* that quotations from a candidate member of the Politburo became a bestseller.[155]

The staging of the event heightened the effect. The opening scene, especially, marked a further refinement in Boris Yeltsin's political theatre. The vast hall of the House of Political Enlightenment was filled with excited murmurs. The stage was bare except for a long table and a row of chairs.[156] Suddenly, there was a noise at the very back of the hall. Everyone fell silent, then turned round to look. With deliberate slowness, shaking hands and responding to greetings, Yeltsin was making his way across the floor to the stage. Still alone, in silence, he mounted the steps and sat down at the table. He waved a hand and instantly, from behind the curtain, appeared the Secretaries and the heads of department, who walked in single file, by rank, towards the table. When they had seated themselves on either side of Yeltsin, the *vstrecha* began.[157]

For several hours Yeltsin showered the audience with jarring opinions and previously classified facts and figures. 'The [previous] city authorities have been building Potemkin villages: everything is fine, we are the best in the world, there is no need to expose the city's problems. Those who continue to think that way should resign.'[158] The portrait of the Soviet capital that he presented was quite the opposite of a Potemkin village. The slogan 'Let us turn Moscow into a model communist city' was sheer 'mockery'. The City Administration, the Mossovet, had become 'the epitome of bureaucratization'. Drug addiction was 'widespread': there were 3,600 officially registered addicts. 'And how many have we still not found?' The fight against alcoholism was 'only beginning' and there could be no 'self-satisfaction'. The drunkenness had been 'pushed from the streets into apartments'. The number of apartment burglaries was up.

In the past few months, 800 leading trade officials had been arrested for theft, bribery and embezzlement. Yet the fight was far from over. Yeltsin quoted from a letter he had received shortly before: 'Khrushchev, too, tried to dress us all in padded jackets [of menial labourers]. He failed and so will you. We have stolen and shall continue to steal.' It was only through 'our mutual effort', Yeltsin commented, that we can 'break this [vicious] circle'.

In the three months before the *vstrecha*, he had visited twenty-nine large Moscow enterprises, and only two paid 'adequate attention' to the 'social sphere' (that is, the conditions of labour, leisure, healthcare, housing and childcare). Meanwhile, at one of the Moscow enterprises

Yeltsin had found four different 'hierarchical' dining rooms, each 'half-a-peg' better than the other. As for the one in which the Director ate, it had 'everything you could possibly want, including a blue toilet bowl'. (Four months later, during another *vstrecha*, Yeltsin told Moscow journalists that, in place of four dining rooms, there was now 'only one – for everyone'.)[159] While he was on the subject of privileges, Yeltsin told the audience that previously the staff of the MGK would have come to meetings like this 'each in his personal car'. Such things had been abolished. Yeltsin pointed to those sitting next to him on the podium: 'See, the Secretaries are smiling. They came today all in one car.'

As always, it was Yeltsin's answers to some of the 300 (anonymous)* questions and comments that the audience, and the speaker, enjoyed the most.

Q: We hear that Yeltsin travels by Metro. But we have not seen him there.

A: What can I say? I have not seen you there either.

Q: Could you help protect products in short supply [*defitsit*] from the visitors?

A: We cannot, like 800 years ago, put a wall around Moscow. [In allocating goods to Moscow stores] we have to realize that we are not 9 million but 11–12. Plus we must widen the sale of *defitsit* at places of work.

Q: What are the main difficulties you encountered after becoming First Secretary?

A: The main difficulty is the lack of knowledge of the cadres.

Q: What do you do in your spare time?

A: To be honest, such time is virtually absent. Mainly reading.

Q: Which [personal] qualities do you like and which hate?

A: I treasure honesty, adherence to principles and character. I hate dishonesty and sycophancy.

Q: Where do you buy shoes?

A: I can tell you a secret: I bought my clothes not in Moscow but in Sverdlovsk. I am wearing shoes made by the Uralobuv' factory; they cost twenty-three rubles. I strongly recommend the brand: very durable, will last you for five years.

---

* Ninety per cent of the questions [are] not signed,' Yeltsin thundered. 'And that is from the propagandists! Haven't we agreed to be honest tonight? All right, I will answer unsigned notes today, but for the last time.'

Q: What is your workday routine?

A: I work from eight to midnight. Sleep four hours. From 5 a.m. to 7 a.m. – self-education and self-improvement.

Q: Are you strong enough to maintain such a rhythm?

A: Please do not worry. I am quite healthy. If the health begins to deteriorate, I shall rest an extra couple of hours. Meanwhile, we simply have to work extremely hard, otherwise we will not achieve a breakthrough.

Visibly revelling in his performance, Yeltsin regaled the audience with humorous asides that would circulate in Moscow for months after the meeting. Discussing the fate of many shoddy five-storey apartment buildings constructed in the 1950s and now falling apart, Yeltsin mentioned the tiny kitchens, 3.5 metres square: 'We have many corpulent women in our country. If such a woman enters such a kitchen, there is no longer room for her husband.' (In another version Yeltsin was said to have added: 'and that leads to family quarrels'.)

As usual, he built up to a dramatic finale. He read a note that said, 'Your plans are Napoleon-like [grandiose]. Aren't you out of your depth? Get the hell back to your Sverdlovsk, before it's too late.' He read another note that reminded him that in a few years he would 'have to account for all the promises' he had given. 'I am ready and intend wholly to devote these years to the struggle.' He ended the meeting with a characteristic admonishment: 'Everyone sitting in this hall today is tasked [by the MGK] with speaking in as many Party cells as possible and with speaking absolutely frankly, without hiding anything about what was said today. Of all our difficulties and shortcomings, and of our intentions, people ought to learn not from gossip and rumours, not from the BBC, but from the mouths of Party propagandists.'

Although resembling the Sverdlovsk prototype, Yeltsin's Moscow *bains de foule* quickly took on a larger role than the original. In the suffocating political climate of the early 1980s, his Sverdlovsk *vstrechi*, albeit just as daring, brimming with bravado and with the intoxicating oxygen of truth, produced only a brief and ephemeral resonance. Instilled with the enormous authority of the Pervyi's new office, and in the slowly but unmistakably changing Soviet Union of 1986, the impact of the *bains* was far greater and more durable. So long as everything remained paralysed by fear, glasnost ('openness'), which began in Yeltsin's Moscow, unfolded as a two-step process: the boss's personal example served as a licence for the wary newspapers, which channelled it, often diluted but still potent, down to the 'masses'.

In the beginning, however, Yeltsin tried a more conventional form of persuasion: exhortation. In his inaugural speech, he castigated the organ of the MGK, *Moskovskaya Pravda*, for publishing little about the 'key problems of the city' and the work of Party organizations and their leadership.[160] Moscow radio and television were condemned for programmes that were not listened to or watched by anyone, save perhaps 'the journalists who made them and small children'.[161] Of the newspapers he demanded 'fewer slogans, especially those that are not based in reality and, sometimes, totally useless. We do not need the artificially rouged face of Moscow. We need the truth. And real deeds.'[162] He urged representatives of the mass media to write and broadcast about the 'sore points' of Moscow 'openly, truthfully, without secrets'.[163]

Yet the exhortations to be daring and leave no 'zone outside criticism' did little good. Few journalists dared look beyond the walls that for decades had marked the boundary of the permissible, much less climb over them. It took the giant battering ram of a candidate member of the Politburo to break some of the taboos* and to persuade the

---

* So strong was the inertia of fear that some subjects continued to remain 'closed' even after they had been mentioned by Yeltsin. Having first broached drug addiction at the meeting with the propagandists, Yeltsin renewed the assault five months later in a speech devoted to Moscow high schools (*Moskovskaya Pravda*, 21 September 1986). He deplored the steady growth in the number of crimes committed by students of Moscow schools, and declared that 'narcomania' was becoming 'a serious problem'. There were, he repeated, 3,700 registered drug addicts in Moscow, and an additional 164 were discovered in the first nine months of 1986. 'For a long time we averted our eyes,' Yeltsin continued, 'were ashamed to talk about it, pursuing an ostrich policy' (*ibid.*). Not until December 1986 did the most 'liberal' of the Soviet newspapers, *Literaturnaya Gazeta*, dare mention drug addiction – by way of acknowledging the official ban on this matter! (Vladimir Treml, 'Gorbachev's Anti-Drinking Campaign: A Noble Experiment or a Costly Exercise in Futility', *RL Supplement* 2/87, *Radio Liberty Research*, 18 March 1987, p. 17.)

In the same speech Yeltsin touched on another subject in terms never before used by a Party functionary of his rank: the stifling bureaucratization and over-regulation of the Soviet school. One 'got lost' in the lists of all sorts of functions that were planned for schoolchildren by 'big uncles and aunts'. 'What sort of initiative [by the children] can we talk about here? And add to that a required report for every function! What are we teaching our children from an early age? Should we then be surprised by red tape and paper-pushing [in society at large]?'

fearful media that it was, indeed, safe to publish truth. Although not by anyone's design, it seemed fitting that Yeltsin, who was in Hamburg leading a Soviet delegation to the Congress of the West German Communist Party, became the first high Soviet official to acknowledge the Chernobyl nuclear accident of May 1986 and even disclose a few details.*

Yeltsin pressed on with free-wheeling sessions for journalists and editors – a year and a half before Mikhail Gorbachev's much celebrated 'meetings with the intelligentsia', the accounts of which would take entire pages of *Pravda* and *Izvestia*. On 23 August 1986, in the same House of Political Education, he held a 'frank, businesslike and engaged discussion with the representatives of the mass media'.[164] It lasted five hours, and its main section was devoted to answers to the 'nearly 200 questions' concerning 'a very diverse group of issues'.[165] During the session, the audience 'not only asked questions but also expressed their own opinions, and made suggestions'.[166] This format and the atmosphere at the meeting 'reflected the current style of the Gorkom based on an open, interested, critical discussion of any problem [and] the widest possible glasnost'.[167] The *Moskovskie Novosti* account of the meeting was published under the heading, 'B. N. Yeltsin: There is neither a ceiling for criticism, nor limits to glasnost'. Its candour extending well beyond anything he had said in Sverdlovsk, the new language of the Party's public discourse invented by Yeltsin would prove his most important innovation and the central and enduring legacy of his Moscow reign.

The reform of the Moscow Party organization was not, of course, limited to changes in what the leaders could tell the led. The leaders themselves were subject to change. From the very beginning, the 'spirit of renewal' was filled with a hefty literal content. Barely a week after taking over, Yeltsin fired Moscow's 'mayor', the Chairman of the City Soviet's Executive Committee, the Ispolkom, Vladimir

---

* In an interview with the weekly *Stern*, Yeltsin said two people had died, twenty to thirty had received dangerously high doses of radiation, and 49,000 people had been evacuated. Having left Moscow on 1 May, Yeltsin may not have known much more than that himself. (The first official press conference on Chernobyl, organized by the Ministry of Foreign Affairs, took place on 7 May. Gorbachev spoke to the nation on television on the 15th.) 'Do you believe me?' Yeltsin asked at the end of the interview. 'Now, look me in the eye.' ('Vielleicht war nur ein Mensch schuld' ('Perhaps only one person was to blame'), interview with Dieter Gütt and Uwe Zimmer, *Stern*, 7 May 1986, p. 245.)

Promyslov.[168]* At his first Plenum of the MGK, Yeltsin pensioned off Grishin's two top aides: Second Secretary Raisa Dementieva and Secretary Leonid Borisov.[169] These heads had been expected to roll. Firing the predecessor's closest associates was well within the Party tradition. The new occupant of an office was allowed to discard, or move, the old furniture. A new broom sweeps clean. What followed, however, had not been anticipated.

First, there was the sheer scale of the purge. Altogether Yeltsin replaced twenty-three of the thirty-three Raikom First Secretaries. Three went up the ladder or were transferred laterally, the rest, 60 per cent,[170] were fired. Later Yeltsin would try to justify the unprecedented ferocity of his assault on Party bureaucracy by pointing to Gorbachev's record: the General Secretary replaced an even higher percentage of Obkom First Secretaries. The comparison was, of course, silly: Gorbachev dealt with the provinces – this was Moscow.

Here in the capital, a Raikom could be far more important and influential than almost any Obkom in the country – and, most certainly, than any Raikom Yeltsin had had under his command in Sverdlovsk. These urban principalities had on their territories the Academy of Sciences and the Ministry of Internal Affairs, the country's best and most prestigious colleges, stores, theatres, book publishers and cinema studios. All these, no matter how powerful or famous, were dependent every day on the Raikom's First Secretary for small and large favours in the impoverished and overpopulated metropolis. Thousands of neighbourly, business and familial ties (what a former Moscow Party functionary called a 'deepest root system')[171] increased a hundred-fold the gravitas of the Moscow Raikom.

Accustomed to treatment befitting their office's informal strength, this contingent of the Party nobility must have found the manner in which Yeltsin carried out the purge even more disturbing than its startling scale. The First Secretary acted indecorously, nay outrageously, and publicly; his comments bordered on derision and contempt, calculated,

---

* Promyslov's replacement, Valeriy Saikin, was of a type clearly favoured by Yeltsin. Like Mekhrintsev in Sverdlovsk, he was not a professional Party functionary but an engineer and the successful Director of a huge industrial plant, the Likhachev Autoworks, the pride of the Soviet automobile industry. The enumeration of Saikin's merits, cited at the time of his appointment, bore an unmistakably Yeltsinite imprint: 'a most qualified specialist . . . an outstanding organizer of production . . . attention to people . . . high capacity for work . . . [and] responsibility for the entrusted tasks' (*Moskovskaya Pravda*, 4 January 1986). Similarly, a new Secretary of the MGK, Oleg Korolev, had been the Director of a large Moscow machine-building plant, the Red Proletarian.

it seemed, to produce maximum humiliation not just of the immediate targets but of the entire Moscow political establishment. The insult was as enormous as the injury.

The decorum was first punctured on 24 April 1986. That morning dozens of leading functionaries opened *Moskovskaya Pravda* looking for the results of the 'socialist competition' between the districts of Moscow in the first quarter of the year, the deadline coinciding with Lenin's 116th birthday. Many offices had eagerly anticipated a citation, which would be followed by orders and promotions. Yet, instead of the traditional glowing report, a tiny dry note informed them that, in view of 'the low tempo of the increase in production of goods for popular consumption' and 'serious shortcomings in the construction and main-tenance of public housing and in the provision of amenities to the popu-lation', the Buro of the MGK had decided not to award the first prize to any of Moscow's thirty-three districts!

When, three months later, the results of the second quarter were announced, the Buro's decision was even more offensive. Only five of the thirty-three districts had managed so much as to remain in the running by satisfying the new criteria for the competition.[172] The per-formance of seven districts – all listed by name – had been found 'abso-lutely unacceptable', because they had failed to meet the planned housing and 'socio-cultural' targets. In language designed to scandalize, not just criticize, many of the 'economic leaders' were accused of having 'demon-strated economic illiteracy'.[173]

Before the establishment could catch its breath, *Moskovskaya Pravda* published the first of what would become almost monthly features: an obituary-like, bottom-of-the-page article that did not just announce the dismissal of a Raikom First Secretary but, contrary to custom, detailed his transgressions. The First Secretary of the Kievskiy Raikom had been 'relieved of his duties for complete failure in organizing work to secure the supply of vegetables for the populace'.[174]

And if the first political 'obituary' was short and still somewhat cryp-tic, the account of the second firing a month later (that of the First Secretary of the Frunzenskiy Raikom) was wholly outside the norms of the Party's public discourse. By the summer of 1986 in Yeltsin's Mos-cow, a seasoned Party bureaucrat might have come to accept 'ineffective usage of production technologies'[175] or even an inadequate supply of vegetables as legitimate reasons for dismissal. But an 'authoritarian style', which had 'disrupted links with the Party rank and file' and 'muzzled the initiative of communists'?[176] A lack of 'real progress' in solving social problems?[177] 'Callousness, inattentiveness to the people's daily needs'?[178] A failure to achieve 'the planned repair of housing and provision of amenities'? The 'unsatisfactory development of trade and provision of daily services to the population'? Or, to top it all, 'violation of social justice'?[179]

Without warning or preparation, Yeltsin for the first time in the Party's history threw open the doors of the Raikoms – the Party's field offices that daily managed the country, its indispensable eyes, ears and arms. What people saw there was not news to most of them. That their daily overseers were found to be uncaring, incompetent and haughty was hardly a surprise. That they were publicly so labelled by their own boss and in their own main newspaper was astounding and exhilarating. Even though no major tremor was felt at the time, the ground floor in the Moscow wing of the house that Stalin had built was showing cracks, which would grow wider and deeper with every day of Yeltsin's rule.

Because of Yeltsin's publicity campaign, the Raikom Secretaries were the most visible casualties of the 'renewal'. Yet the new broom's reach extended further still. What seemed a fairly representative sample of stricken Moscow functionaries surfaced at a session of the Moscow City Soviet, whose 'Deputies' they had been until then. In true Soviet style, the sackings were said to have taken place with the full compliance of those involved. 'Following a personal request [from the culprits] in connection with the loss of the moral right to perform the duties [of Deputies of Mossovet]', the ex-Secretary of the Party Committee of the Ministry of Foreign Affairs, the ex-Director of the 'scientific-practical' *trest* Emergency Medical Assistance, the ex-editor-in-chief of Radio Programmes for Moscow and the ex-Secretary of the Moscow City Trade Unions were expelled.[180] This was turning out to be more than a few cavalry raids on a handful of outposts. This looked like a war on the Moscow ruling class.

This war's most brutal aspect (which surely must hitherto have been barred by some informal intra-Party equivalent of the Geneva Convention) was Yeltsin's relentless attempt to rob the Moscow establishment of its most treasured possession, the mark that separated the lords from the serfs who roamed the city searching for food and clothes, standing in long queues, packing buses and Metro carriages, fighting at the counters and waiting years for an apartment of their own. That birthright which Yeltsin sought to deny was the nomenklatura privileges.

Yeltsin's attempt on the nomenklatura's trove began with the four largest gems: housing, transport, food and education. Already in February 1986, the Second Secretary of the Oktyabr'skiy Raikom, I. V. Danilov, was fired 'for lack of modesty and gross violation of Party ethics'.[181]

Two months later, Yeltsin explained that Comrade Danilov had erected, within a regular apartment building, 'a magnificent place for himself',[182] complete with a private fireplace and private chimney. 'There is no room in the Party for such princes!'[183] Yeltsin declared. Later, a 'special session of the Party Group of the Mossovet', devoted to the housing problem, found and highlighted the 'many facts of flagrant violation of the rules of fair distribution of housing'.[184] The Deputy Chairman of the Ispolkom, whom Yeltsin had put in charge of housing, was warned of his 'personal responsibility for . . . the strictest adherence to . . . the principles of social justice in the resolution of housing problems'.[185]

After four months on the job, Yeltsin noted the 'ubiquitous black Volga saloons' that usually took a child to school, then papa to work and then went back to pick up the wife.[186] He gave warning – 'this ought to stop' – and, to show that he meant business, disclosed his tactic of implementation: 'first observation, then conversation, then administrative action'.[187]

As for all those 'special' buffets and food orders for the elite, Yeltsin called them an 'outrage' (*bezobrazie*).[188] He publicly acknowledged what had been known for decades. In large grocery stores the 'table of orders' (where organizations could order food products in advance, usually for holidays) offered different food packages to different organizations: better ones for ministries, worse for factories and plants.[189] Yeltsin called upon Moscow journalists to 'add heat' if they found 'any manifestations of inequality'.[190] Meanwhile, he shut down the exclusive store inside the MGK. 'I think this is useful,' Yeltsin said. 'The staffers of the MGK will be more sensitive to the shortages [outside] . . .'[191]

By his first summer in Moscow, Yeltsin began to probe in the most sensitive and most tender spot: the ability of the Moscow elite to perpetuate its status, to pass it on to its children, with the access, the connections, the goods. As in other modern societies, a great deal of this was accomplished through elite 'institutions of higher education'.

Of these, one was by far the most exclusive and prestigious: the Moscow State Institute of International Relations, the fabled MGIMO. This was a veritable finishing school for offspring of the communist nobility* and a handful of its best-connected servants. By the 1970s, the low-born (unless part of the small quota of 'workers and peasants' recommended by the local Obkoms) had no chance whatsoever of being accepted into

---

* Like Cambridge and Oxford during Britain's colonial empire, the MGIMO successfully socialized the sons of Moscow's non-Russian potentates in the 'national republics': hence the occasional Georgian, Armenian or Azeri among the sea of ethnic Russians and Russified Ukrainians in the Soviet diplomatic service.

the school. MGIMO trained 'international' journalists, 'international' economists and 'international' historians.

'International' was the operative term. 'The situation was most curious,' Yeltsin later remembered.

> It very accurately reflected the essence of the dual morality and open hypocrisy that permeated the society. From all the podiums, high and low, from propaganda cannons of every calibre we thundered hysterically about 'rotting capitalism', the horrible diseases of 'Western society', the 'horror' of their 'way of life'. Meanwhile, the nomenklatura Papas did everything possible and impossible to push their beloved progeny into the institutions that prepared diplomats or [other] specialists who travelled abroad. They were ready to tell any lie, to spin any fairytale about 'developed socialism' or the 'death convulsions of the West' which was 'living out its last days' so that they could be allowed to go there to rot for a month or for a year.[192]

First, Yeltsin publicly noted a 'complicated situation'[193] in the MGIMO. Three days later, the Mossovet 'terminated the mandate of Deputy N. I. Lebedev, the former dean of the MGIMO', because he had been removed from his post for 'abuse of his official position'.[194] At the same time, the Pervyi hit the Diplomatic Academy of the Ministry of Foreign Affairs, where '70 per cent of the students [were] children of the leading officials, and 40 per cent of the faculty were related to the leading officials'.[195] The new broom had reached the nursery.

Half a year had passed since Yeltsin took over Moscow. It was time to sum up the preliminary results of perestroika's first offensive. For all the stomping, exhortations, threats and backbreaking work,* for all the rocking of the boat, the shock-waves and the whispers he had generated in the high offices and on the street, the yield was startlingly, pitifully and confoundingly puny.

On every major axis of attack, Yeltsin's advance on the 'old ways and practices' had been halted, diluted or repelled outright. On the economic front, the half-century-old tradition of economic growth based on increasing inputs of raw materials and labour proved virtually imper-

---

* Often, when he was driven home late at night ('twelve, one, two'), and the bodyguard opened the limousine's door, Yeltsin was too exhausted to get out, 'too tired even to move an arm'. He simply sat in the car for a few minutes, 'coming to', while Naina waited anxiously at the door (Yeltsin, *Ispoved'*, p. 97).

meable to the slogans of 'intensification' and 'acceleration'. The giant flywheel of the 'plan', which measured progress, and rewarded actors, by money spent rather than money earned, proved exceedingly difficult to slow down, much less to halt. Despite Yeltsin's insistence that, 'if the design is obsolete, if the technology is of yesterday', better stop the construction and installation of equipment, 'better lose a year but resist the temptation for a quick fix, half-measures and, eventually, harm', not a single Moscow enterprise, 'having found the project obsolete, had the courage to stop the implementation'.[196]

In direct violation of the order to achieve an increase in production solely through greater labour productivity, every fourth enterprise in a typical Moscow district projected a larger workforce in its five-year plan, and every third enterprise, Yeltsin discovered to his dismay, even forecast lower output per unit of investment.[197] In the same district, only one of the dozens of enterprises had abandoned the *limit* as a means of expanding the workforce.

The war on the *limitchiki* fared no better in the rest of the city. 'Hardly had the ink dried on the Gorkom resolution' that required a dramatic reduction in the number of the *limitchiki* than managers of top Moscow enterprises began a 'furious' lobbying of the MGK, claiming that 'without *limit*, we would not be able to fulfil the plan'.[198]

Similarly, the 'research institutes' had been barely dented by Yeltsin's tilting. Of the twenty-six randomly checked institutes, only three planned a reduction in staff.[199] When, 'at the suggestion' of the Gorkom, one institute was finally closed, the Ministry in charge transferred its entire staff to other institutes under its command. 'This is simply reshuffling!' Yeltsin thundered. 'This is cheating!'[200] Ignoring the Pervyi's orders, the Moscow 'scientific establishments' were requesting permission to hire an additional 50,000 staffers![201]

Things were no better in food retail. Freight cars with produce were not unloaded for days.[202] 'You can see for yourself what is happening in Moscow as far as potatoes, fruit and vegetables are concerned,' Yeltsin told an MGK Plenum in July. 'This, in the middle of the summer, is a shame!'[203] 'How long are we to watch empty counters and [railway] trucks with rotting produce?'[204] The Buro discussed the 'state of trade servicing the population' and found it to be 'extremely unsatisfactory'.[205] Although a significant number of managers had been subjected to criminal prosecution, the 'work to remove the conditions engendering theft and bribery . . . was not finished'.[206] Perestroika in the retail-trade work collectives was being conducted 'unacceptably sluggishly, and the encrusted faulty methods and style of work were being changed extremely slowly'.[207]

Most disappointing of all, this description also applied to progress in the primary objective of Yeltsin's 'renewal': the Party nomenklatura. By July, only five of thirty-three Raikoms satisfied him by 'conducting their Plenums truly in the spirit of perestroika'.[208] This he found very disturbing: the 'disease must have reached very deep'.[209] First among those who had failed to restructure, Yeltsin announced ruefully, were the Secretaries of the Party committees and industrial leaders.[210]

The immediate and most noticeable part of Yeltsin's response to his first major setback was a characteristically stubborn repetition of the same strategy. The attack was to continue along the same axes. There was to be no halt, no slackening, no regrouping. And so he went on preaching dedication, experimentation and, most of all, initiative. 'We are to undertake a strenuous search,'[211] he told a Plenum of the Zhdanovskiy Raikom. 'The most important thing is not to wait for commands from above. The tasks are known. You must act as real masters, independently, evaluating with maximum exactitude what has been achieved and striving towards what you are capable of, what the people expect.'[212] He exhorted the leaders of the economic nomenklatura to make 'non-standard' decisions. 'There is a great deal of fear of making a mistake when taking a never-before-travelled path. But better risk than passivity.'[213]

There would be no respite from glasnost either. Openness, Yeltsin declared, was vital in order to 'try and cure our long-term illnesses'.[214] To those who were 'hearing our old lullaby "things are not that bad, really"' his response was 'No, they *are* bad ... We cannot and will not allow time to be, again, on the side of those who would like to push us back into the swamp of hibernation and external, false glitter.'[215] To the 'loud voices' that decried the 'allowing of too much criticism', he said, 'No ... the shortcomings must be mercilessly revealed and removed.'[216] '[We must] honestly talk about our failures and problems. The Muscovites will understand and support [this policy]. [We must] liberate people's energy, the energy shackled by bureaucratism, shallowness of views, lack of trust, the harmful force of habit ...'[217] The 'campaign' began to look more and more like a policy.

Nor had his zeal for 'democratization' diminished. In October 1986 Yeltsin called on the MGK's Plenum to 'tangibly deepen perestroika, engaging all spheres and categories, pursuing it more boldly'.[218] He implored them not to be 'afraid [of] greater democratism in all aspects of our work', including the selection of cadres.[219] This last 'inclusion', although introduced in a subordinate clause, was ominous. It hinted at opening doors into the Party's *sanctum sanctorum* – personnel selection, the very foundation of the Party state. Before the year was over, at least one Raikom held 'elections to the Party, Komsomol and Trade Unions committees on the Raikom territory with nominations from the floor' and 'replaced passive people, incapable of working in new ways, with people with initiative and good reputation in work collectives'.[220]

As he continued to harangue and to plead, Yeltsin's rhetoric began to show the first signs of irritation, fatigue and frustration. While attending a Komsomol meeting at the Likhachev Autoworks, Yeltsin abruptly ordered a change in the decades-old routine. First, 'preliminary written requests' would no longer be required before people were allowed to speak. Anyone who wanted the floor should simply raise a hand. Second, no one would be allowed to read a prepared text.[221]

Look what we have come to! Yeltsin roared. 'Every speaker has been selected beforehand, everyone has been well "worked with", so there is no need to worry – he'll say exactly what he is supposed to say. And, of course, he will. But whose thoughts will those be? Whose problems? Whose language? This is the main question.' Perhaps because this was a Komsomol, rather than a Party meeting, and he could, for a moment, lower his guard, the seemingly invincible and imperturbable Pervyi suddenly gave vent to an uncharacteristic outpouring of bitterness and despair: 'I cannot believe that the Komsomol today lives without a heartache for the cause, without anxiety, without ambition, without the desire for a breath of fresh air, for breaking free from the paper prison of bureaucracy, the spider's web of directives! This is not even a swamp, this is a peat compost, which contains no live organisms.'[222]

Yet, in addition to these still jarring but by now quite familiar philippics, designed to clean and repair the Party's internal machinery, something quite novel crept into Yeltsin's speeches in the second half of 1986. Still relatively rare and incoherent – disparate notes rather than a theme – these utterances shifted the entire enterprise of perestroika to a different plane. For they introduced the idea of the Party functionaries' responsibility not to the Party but to the people,* with a deeply seditious

---

* As we shall see, the very same matter – to whom or to what the Party should be accountable and its right to rule – would become one of the key debating points of early glasnost, beginning with the second half of 1988. At the time, one of the more daring analysts of the Soviet structure of power would write of the previous decades during which Party functionaries had been 'brought up convinced that it was not the CPSU that serves the people but the people that serve the CPSU' (S. Yu. Andreev, 'Nashe proshloye, nastoyashchee, budushchee: struktura vlasti i zadachi obshchestva' ('Our past, present, future: the structure of power and the tasks of society'), in F. M. Borodkin et al., eds, Postizhenie, p. 578). Yeltsin was at least two years ahead of his time.

implication that the Party's right to rule was not divinely and permanently ordained, but needed to be earned and justified.

'We should not ask the officials how the work is going,' Yeltsin told the MGK Plenum on 4 October. 'We should ask the people, whom the officials serve, if they [the officials] are capable of doing the job.'[223] Towards the end of the speech he made an appeal to 'all those sitting in the hall today: daily, hourly, not sparing yourself, bridge the gap between word and deed, thus *justifying the trust* of all Muscovites.'[224] Two months later he declared 'timidity, indecisiveness, the wait-and-see attitude incompatible today with the [Party's] *right to lead* . . .'[225] When he urged 'absolutely no delay' in delivering the planned housing, that was 'not only because this will damage our reports. This is a secondary issue. We simply cannot *disappoint the hopes of Muscovites.*'[226]

That same summer Mikhail Gorbachev, while touring the Soviet Far East, took his first widely publicized *bain de foule* in 'spontaneous' exchanges with crowds in Komsomolsk-on-the-Amur and Vladivostok. What he said on these occasions constituted the outer, most radical limit of official perestroika to date, and a comparison with Yeltsin's version is instructive.

The success of perestroika is predicated on people's support. 'We cannot get by without people's support,' said Gorbachev.[227] Thus the people should be heard: every worker had the right to 'make himself heard on subjects of industrial production, daily life, upbringing, discipline, order'.[228] Finally, the Party ought not to 'try to conceal things from the people . . . The people must know everything . . .'[229] The *nachal'nik*s were there to 'serve the people'.[230] And, before an official appointment was made, 'people should be consulted'.[231]

Each of the three themes that formed the leitmotif of the General Secretary's remarks during his Far Eastern tour were, of course, present in Yeltsin's speeches as well. Yet the differences are as telling as the similarities. Gorbachev encourages people to speak out. Yeltsin groans under the enormous load of responsibility before the people. Gorbachev brims with confidence and optimism. (Referring to the latest campaign to raise the quality of industrial output, Gorbachev said to a crowd in Komsomolsk-on-the-Amur: 'It will be difficult in the beginning, we'll struggle for two or three months, but then everything will go swimmingly.')[232] Yeltsin is anxious: 'Perestroika is proceeding slowly and with difficulty . . . We cannot call this perestroika . . . The results . . . are quite modest, in many cases lamentable . . .'[233]

Gorbachev serves notice on the 'unreconstructed' party elite: 'Leaders who will not restructure themselves will have to be asked to find another job.'[234] Yeltsin declares war on them: 'The time for excuses and indulgence is receding into the past . . . There must be only one criterion [for keeping someone in a leadership post]: he who has not understood the [new] requirements, who has not drawn conclusions from the hard lessons of the past, cannot remain in a position of leadership.'[235]

Gorbachev the theorist is kind, mellow, unhurried, gradual, general and Pollyannaish. Yeltsin the practitioner is intense, restless, biting, concrete, sharp and urgent: 'Muscovites will judge the Gorkom by concrete results . . . We can see that the people are impatient. They are waiting for a quick turn [for the better] in reality, quick implementation of the announced plans. And we cannot reproach them for their demand for quick and bold changes . . . The people believe in . . . the new course, acceleration, further democratization, greater social justice and the unity of word and deed. And we have no right to betray their hope, trust, expectations.'[236]

Then suddenly, half a year later, the marshal of perestroika almost caught up with his fastest-moving, most advanced and impatient general.

Although at the time neither actors nor spectators knew it, the border that separated reform from revolution was breached between 28 and 30 January 1987 during the three days of the Central Committee's Plenum.*

The fuse lit by Mikhail Gorbachev's opening and concluding speeches had two strands. First, there was a stream of astounding declarations and policy proposals. The General Secretary identified a 'serious and deep democratization' as the most important theme of the Politburo report that he delivered. 'We need democracy like air,' he declared.[237] To prove to the angry, oppressed and cynical nation that democracy was not 'just a slogan but the essence of perestroika', he hinted at a few changes in Soviet political practice. Several candidacies for the local Party leadership, up to the First Secretaries of the regional committees,

---

* This is not to say, of course, that the importance of the Plenum's decisions was not clear at the time either to Gorbachev or to his opponents. 'We value the Plenum very highly,' Gorbachev said two weeks later (*Pravda*, 14 February 1987). A year later he would tell Moscow literati, 'Let's once again remember the January Plenum with a kind word: it led us to the realization of the necessity of broad democratization of our society' (*Pravda*, 13 January 1988). That the Plenum had been repeatedly postponed, in violation of the Party statutes, is an indication that the conservative opposition in the Politburo was also well aware of the event's scope.

might be allowed, as well as elections by a secret ballot, rather than by a *pro forma* show of hands. The Party's grip on the steering wheel was to loosen somewhat as non-members were now allowed to be promoted to leading positions.[238]

The other component of the fuse was a radically expanded licence for glasnost. In Soviet political tradition, personalities, subjects and entire themes of history and ideology, once 'opened' by the General Secretary in a nationally publicized address, became fair game for the media – until the end of the 'campaign' was signalled from the Staraya Square. In that sense, the menu served up by Gorbachev was unprecedented in both length and richness. Indeed, so sudden and overwhelming was the expansion of the allowable that more than a year would pass before disbelieving Russian literati, starved but wary, dared to partake of the feast the General Secretary had laid for them.

Even for Muscovites, somewhat prepared by Yeltsin's year-long campaign, which had hinted at most of what Gorbachev was now officially blessing, the General Secretary's words must have come as a striking departure from all that had been said before, even during Khrushchev's deStalinization. What set glasnost apart from Khrushchev's 'thaw' was, first, the culprit: it was no longer just the fallen supreme leader but 'the leading organs of the Party and state' as a whole that bore responsibility for the 'mistakes and lapses', 'conservatism' and 'inertia'. Second, there was the nature of the blemishes: they were no longer 'separate drawbacks' but the slowing down of the economy, 'alien phenomena' in 'social and spiritual spheres', 'stagnation' and the penetration of the Party by 'dishonest, pushy, mercenary' people.[239]

'Socialist property' had come to mean nobody's. It was free for the taking and, in many cases, a source of 'unlawful income'. 'Socialist democracy' was plagued by serious shortcomings – as were housing, food production, transportation, healthcare and education. 'Socialist justice' was 'distorted', and had become a 'serious political problem'. Laws were neglected and bribery thrived. Some of the leading functionaries, whose job it was 'to protect the interests of the state', 'misappropriated the power', 'suppressed criticism', 'enriched themselves' and were accessories to (and some even perpetrators of) crime. The 'societal mores' began to deteriorate, as evidenced by the increase in alcoholism, drug addiction and crime.[240]

To prevent the 'dark corners from spawning mildew again', the people should be given 'an opportunity to have their say on any subject of the society's life'. As to control from above, Gorbachev promised that zones where criticism was forbidden were becoming a thing of the past. 'People must know the whole truth . . . As never before, we need the Party and the people to know everything. More light!' Gorbachev declared in his concluding speech.[241]

The road to January 1987 had been paved, as authoritarian liberalizations usually are, with hurried improvisations, forced choices, voluntarily adopted moral constraints, unfounded optimism, misplaced hope and ignorance. A few years later Gorbachev would be criticized by Moscow's amateur political strategists (and some of their Western colleagues) for not trying the 'Chinese option', the 'soft landing' that, by confining radical reform to the economy, rather than allowing it to embrace the political system, would have preserved stability. Apart from the myopia that failed to see the inevitable reckoning on China's political horizon, this reprimand was unjust.

Between April 1985 and January 1987 the new Soviet leadership sought to implement something very much like a Chinese option: effecting economic reform without touching the foundations of the political order. January 1987 marked the forced abandonment of this attempt and the entry into the completely uncharted waters of 'democratization'.

The reasons for the failure to confine reform to the economy are many, complex and interrelated, and a detailed description would take this narrative too far afield. It is possible, nevertheless, to identify a few milestones that marked the progression. From the beginning the new regime's internal deliberations and reform strategies proceeded, almost simultaneously, along two increasingly divergent paths. One of these routes was charted largely by inertia and ignorance, the other by new knowledge and a search for remedies which that knowledge made urgent. The first came to be called 'acceleration' (*uskorenie*), the other 'restructuring' (perestroika).

Inherited from Andropov's police renaissance, 'acceleration', which was implemented first with much enthusiasm, stemmed from the belief that the Soviet economic system was fundamentally sound and required only a vigorous fine-tuning to recover its somewhat tarnished potential. As Gorbachev said upon assuming power, the country had 'achieved big successes in all areas of the societal life', and had 'a powerful, comprehensively developed economy'. All that was needed was to modernize the country's ageing industrial sector[242] and 'the world's highest level of labour productivity' would be within reach. Much of this was due to sheer ignorance. A few years later Gorbachev would admit that even when he had served as a *de facto* Deputy General Secretary to an ailing Yuriy Andropov, the latter would not let him see the 'real' budget figures.*

Andropov's shadow, however, was the longest in the realm of policy prescriptions for an economic turnaround. The new regime initially accepted as an axiom that the by now obvious economic crisis was largely (if not entirely) a problem of management: the unsatisfactory state of labour discipline and the 'weakness in the style and method of the Party and state work'.[243] Both of these defects, were, of course, correctable by a simple, bold and determined administrative effort.

For instance, the 'strengthening of contract discipline' and the 'fight against waste and losses', both among the key declared tasks, were to be enforced by a new agency, 'state product acceptance', or *gospriemka*, which was introduced in May 1986. Deployed at enterprises but not employed by them, the controllers were to inspect the output and reject items that did not meet the standards. Bonuses and even the regular pay of workers and managers could be cut because of low quality. Coming as it had after decades of 'socialist competition' and twenty years of experimentation with 'material incentives' as a means of ensuring quality, the brutal simplicity of *gospriemka* epitomized the Andropov legacy in the new leadership approach to economic reform: a stern overseer, cracking the whip and junking millions of rubles' worth of output.

To the extent that this version of the reform took society into consideration at all, *gospriemka*'s twin pillar was the law-and-order campaign, something that Mikhail Gorbachev shortly after coming to power called the 'resolute struggle against phenomena alien to our socialist way of life, to our communist mores' – in other words the 'strengthening of order and discipline'.[244]

The jewel in the tight iron crown of 'acceleration' was to be the fight against drunkenness. It proved the regime's first major political stumble. The 'anti-alcohol campaign' was adopted by the Politburo only three weeks after Gorbachev acceded to power. The urgency was most cer-

---

* Gorbachev first made this startling admission in a 1990 *Pravda* article ('Krepit' klyuch-evoe zveno ekonomiki' ('To strengthen the key link in the economy'), *Pravda*, 10 December 1990). Five years later, in his memoirs, he described how, after he and Ryzhkov had been tasked by Andropov with thinking through a proposed price increase, they asked for access to the budget figures. Andropov 'laughed that off: "Nothing doing! You are asking too much. The budget is off-limits to you." ' Gorbachev went on to say that 'many secrets of the budget were so well kept that I found out about some of them only on the eve of my stepping down as President.' (Mikhail Gorbachev, *Memoirs*, New York: Doubleday, 1996, pp. 146–7.)

tainly warranted. The Soviet Union annually consumed an estimated eight litres of strong (40 to 80 per cent proof) alcoholic beverages per capita – more than any other country in the world.[245] Between 1958 and 1984, production of vodka doubled. Each year, fifteen million drunks were arrested and put in sobering-up stations (*vytrezviteli*). In the early 1980s premature deaths directly or indirectly caused by alcohol accounted for about one-fifth of all deaths in the USSR. In the late 1970s around fifty thousand people died of 'acute alcohol poisoning' every year: 19.5 deaths per 100,000 as compared with an average of 0.3 for the nineteen countries that compiled and published such data. Between 1964 and the end of the 1970s male life expectancy fell by five years, from sixty-seven to sixty-two years.[246]

When it came to remedies, however, the tin ear and elephant touch traditionally displayed by Russian reformers in dealing with the objects of their cares, the 'people', were on full view. First, a reduction in consumption was to be achieved through higher prices. Yet even the virtually overnight 100 per cent increases, repeated over and over again, did little to reduce what had become a national addiction. Even when the price reached ten rubles for a half-litre bottle, after it had been two rubles and eighty-seven kopecks for the previous twenty years, the popular resolve to drink remained steady, as evidenced by this widely circulated doggerel:

Price her high, or price her low –
We shall never let her go.
You tell Misha, Comrade Kvas:
Even ten's OK by us.

('Misha', a diminutive of Mikhail, refers to Gorbachev, as does the derisive nickname 'Mr Kvas' – *kvas* is a Russian version of non-alcoholic root beer, made from bread. Vodka, in Russian, is feminine, hence 'her'.)

Soon, economic levers were supplemented by the more familiar agents of Soviet social control: cuts in production and restrictions on consumption. Stores were ordered to close liquor departments, drastically cut the sales hours and limit them to one bottle per person. Restaurants were forbidden to serve alcohol in any form. Striving to prove their zeal, local Party functionaries and state bureaucrats competed for Moscow's attention by cutting down some of the best vineyards in Moldova, Georgia and the Crimea.

The biggest immediate effect was a drastic reduction in revenue from what had been by far the most profitable category of goods on the domestic market. Occurring at the time when, to make good on its promises, the Kremlin was raising salaries and expanding budget outlays for the long-neglected 'social sphere' (schools, hospitals, pensions), the tax shortfall led to a skyrocketing budget deficit and, very soon, inflation.

The most damage, however, was done on the street. Witnesses recall 'giant queues, where one had to stand for hours just to buy a bottle of wine', the humiliation of having to show a death certificate to buy a bottle of vodka for the traditional Russian wake (*pominki*), and the thousands of 'broken lives' when overzealous police arrested and threw into jail people coming home from parties.[247] A former Soviet journalist remembers that in 1985 and 1986 the editorial offices of local and central newspapers were 'swamped by tens of thousands of letters' from indignant citizenry describing the 'barbaric methods' of the campaign: the destruction of priceless vineyards and imported equipment, 'crazy' queues and the arbitrariness of arrests. Not a single one of these letters, he asserts, was published at the time.[248]

A flood of moonshine (*samogon*) spread over the country, consuming one million tonnes of sugar annually.[249] For the first time since the Second World War, nation-wide sugar rationing was introduced and continued for six years until, under a new regime, prices were freed in January 1992. One hundred and fifty-eight thousand *samogon* makers were arrested in 1986 alone.[250] People began drinking aftershave lotion and cologne. Stores responded by limiting the sales of these items to two bottles per customer, and police had to be called to quell riots in queues. The most desperate turned to technical fluids. Antifreeze, methanol and brake fluid were drained off cars, trucks and planes. Newspapers reported five people dead from methanol poisoning at a factory, and fifteen from drinking antifreeze.[251]

Both the timing and the execution of the anti-alcohol campaign could not have been worse. The Russians felt subjected to yet another national humiliation – this time by a self-declared 'liberal' regime. The Gorbachev leadership managed to incite anger and contempt at precisely the moment when it most needed respect and trust (it was at this time that Gorbachev received the derisory title of *mineral'niy secretar'* a play on *general'niy sekretar'*, 'General Secretary'). 'By putting us in the humiliating position of alcoholics ready to do anything to get to the glass [of vodka], those in power . . . gravely offended each and every one of us, both drinkers and non-drinkers,' a Russian journalist wrote later. 'The state, in effect, created two hundred million criminals . . . The perestroika rhetoric was discredited. The authorities showed their stupidity and powerlessness. The [people's] belief that the [new] leaders knew what they were doing, and could do it, was undermined.'[252]

Gradually, alongside 'acceleration', the contour of the other path of economic reform began to emerge, that of perestroika. Much of the impetus was generated by wider access to more honest data. 'The problems accumulated in society [were] deeper than we had thought,' Gorbachev told the January 1987 Plenum. 'The deeper into perestroika we get, the clearer becomes its scale, as more and more problems inherited from the past are discovered.'[253]

As the scope and nature of the problems became more vivid, so apparently did the realization that most of them (and, certainly, the key ones) might not be amenable to the cavalry charge of 'acceleration'. The new knowledge prompted a broader front of reform and, most importantly, highlighted the need to secure from workers more than passive acquiescence in prescriptions and proscriptions from above. To make sure that 'everyone labours conscientiously and with maximum effect at his workplace', the Kremlin began to stress the 'human factor'.

This new insight prompted several steps down the path towards the 'Chinese variant'. By September 1986, Prime Minister Nikolay Ryzhkov was already talking about 'overcoming the egalitarian tendency in the compensation for labour' and promoting measures to encourage the '*personal* interest' of workers in raising the quality of their output.[254] These measures were to include bonuses to workers for '*personal* results'[255] and greater salary differentials between skilled and unskilled workers.

Even bolder departures were contemplated in the state's management of the economy. Among these were, first, greater autonomy of enterprises from the 'petty tutelage' of various ministries and administrations[256] and, later, their 'full business accounting', 'self-financing' and even 'independence', as announced in the draft of the Law on State Enterprise, distributed at the January Plenum.[257] After fulfilling the state 'contracts', industrial enterprises could now transact business with one another or even directly with 'customers'. In the interests of 'fuller satisfaction of the needs of the population', unjust restrictions on individual economic activity' were to be removed and co-operatives in various spheres of production and services were to be encouraged.[258] Kremlin economists began contemplating the rudiments of market discipline by raising artificially low wholesale and retail prices (especially for fuel and raw materials) to eliminate giant state subsidies and the notorious waste.

Closer still to the 'Chinese variant' was a plan to allow collective farms to dispose as they saw fit of what was left after the mandated state deliveries – including selling produce at market prices.[259] By the summer of 1987, small co-operatives and family-based agriculture were broached as important components of economic reform.

Insofar as both 'acceleration' and perestroika aimed, on markedly different levels of sophistication, at economic transformation without political change, they had, for all the disparity between them, one thing in common: an extreme difficulty in implementation. The lack of progress and the Gorbachev leadership's interpretation of the reasons behind it led to the abandonment of the narrow 'Chinese' path and the fateful shift of the reform effort from the economy to politics that occurred at the January Plenum.

There were many differences between Gorbachev's Soviet Union in 1987 and China in 1978, when Deng Xiaoping launched his economic reforms, that made the 'Chinese variant' unsuitable for Moscow. Of these, one of the most consequential was the prodigiously populous, apolitical and enterprising – if impoverished – Chinese village. The Chinese economic miracle was jump-started in and by the village, where four-fifths of the Chinese lived. Once liberated from the commune's slavery by Deng, within a few years family-based agriculture fed the country and created a huge market for industrial products. In the Soviet Union, after half a century of collectivized agriculture (thirty years, or almost two generations, longer than that in China), there was no living tradition of family farming, and little respect for peasant labour or love of land. Only one-fifth of the population remained in the degraded and depopulated countryside. Another important difference was the degree of militarization of the economy. In the Soviet Union of the Gorbachev years, no less than one-fifth of GNP, and possibly as much as one-third, was consumed by the military–industrial complex, which employed up to a third of the working population and the most valuable raw materials and machinery.[260]

But the critical difference between the two countries concerned the leadership's ability to impose its designs on the nation's political and economic elites. When Deng took over China, its nomenklatura, still shellshocked and cowed by the purges of the Cultural Revolution and the recent victimization by the 'Gang of Four' radicals, could be ordered to allow, accommodate and, eventually, participate in a limited market.

The Soviet case was exactly the opposite. Excluding the brief Andropov interlude, over two decades of 'respect for cadres' had created the most self-confident, fearless, even brazen ruling class in Soviet history. It had grown too fat and insolent to take notice of orders to depart from the customary ways which had for so long guaranteed it almost unlimited power and, increasingly, riches as well. At least in the short run, a 180-degree turn required a quality almost totally absent from the *Weltanschauung* of the Party and economic bureaucracies: fear of the central authority. In spring 1986, for example, after a new decree on agricultural reform had been adopted by the Kremlin, a young Swedish diplomat went to the Soviet mega-agency, Gosagroprom, to find out what the decree meant. His questions were 'met with laughter from senior agricultural officials. They openly declared that nothing would change, and they could not have cared less about decrees passed by Gorbachev.'[261]

At the most elemental level, that of *gospriemka* ('quality control'), the Moscow example was indicative of the general trend. When, ostensibly after a year of preparation,[262] quality control was introduced at fifty-nine Moscow enterprises in January 1987, every third plant failed to fulfil the planned quota. A month later, only one-fifth of the output was found 'acceptable'.[263] For the first two months after *gospriemka* was introduced at one of the best Moscow enterprises, the machine-tool plant Red Proletarian, not a single 'automatically controlled' lathe could be certified 'acceptable'.[264] As late as October 1987, *gospriemka* still rejected 20 per cent of the output.[265] Of the 732 Moscow enterprises spot-checked for quality control, 451 were found to be in violation of standards.[266] No political authority determined to uphold the present economic system could have sustained such losses for long. By the beginning of 1988, after less than two years, *gospriemka*, which had rejected an average of 15 per cent of goods nation-wide, was quietly phased out, and the same shoddy output was now 'passed' twice as frequently as in 1987.[267]

Perestroika ran into similar, although less quantifiable, opposition. Aleksandr Yakovlev remembered the 'desperate' resistance of the nomenklatura. 'Future historians will, perhaps, be able to extract from the paper mountains left by the apparat', he wrote, 'a refined sequence of orders, instructions, elucidations – all aimed at preserving everything as before in the country, with all the "liberties" declared at high meetings in Moscow evaporating *en route* to those for whom those liberties were intended ... The administrative-command system ... turned out to be far more perfidious than anyone could have expected.'[268]

By October 1986, the Kremlin was forced to admit that:

the course of renewal is being implemented without due dynamism. Although society as a whole is decisively in favour of changes, the process of perestroika is beset with complications ... [and] is met with resistance by those who, guided by their egotistical interests, are trying to preserve obsolescent customs and privileges. The brake on perestroika is formed by bureaucratic distortions in the administrative apparatus ... Important political decisions of the Central Committee and government ... are infrequently hampered by the inertia of ministries and agencies which are in no hurry to transfer rights to enterprises ... [and] continue to produce a multitude of reports, creating a semblance of work and not fulfilling on time the actual tasks.[269]

By 1988, a Russian economist who supplied the best contemporary analysis of the congenital deficiencies and contradictions of the Gorbachev reform concluded that the 'attempts to exit the economic cul-de-sac are no longer confronted with inertia but with a real resistance (which is only camouflaged as inertia). Cumulatively, the processes that hamper perestroika look like well-organized sabotage.' He added, 'There is not a single major decision in this area [of economic reform] that has not been distorted in practice ... Masterful in its knowledge of the system, the administrative apparatus – sometimes delicately, sometimes openly – separates both the people and the government from real policy-making.'[270]

Even the remote possibility that unprofitable enterprises would be shut down made Party and government officials at all levels rise to their defence.[271] According to a student of these matters, Gorbachev was forced to retreat, 'leaving thousands of inefficient, overstuffed, obsolete' plants and factories in place[272] to waste mountains of precious raw materials and years of human labour.

One of the founders of communist China, Chen Yun, who, with Deng Xiaoping, was the author of the 1978 reforms, compared limited market mechanisms within a one-party communist state to a caged bird: 'A bird should be allowed to fly but only within a cage. Without a cage, the bird will fly away.'[273] Gorbachev could expand the cage but he could not make the Soviet nomenklatura fly.

Not all of the nomenklatura's resistance stemmed from the desire to guard the power and material well-being that even a limited but serious and consistent economic reform would have endangered. Even those who were sympathetic to Gorbachev's economic design felt (quite prophetically, it turned out) that he was not capable of dealing with the political consequences of reform. As far as they were concerned, the present order of things was 'less than perfect but it was rambling along, while no one knew what to expect from a new one'.[274]

And herein lies the final difference between Gorbachev's Soviet Union and Deng's China. Deng's bold balancing act was, in the end, predicated upon his will and the ability, of which the Chinese communist bureaucracy was quite confident, to maintain the separation of the 'liberated' economy from the still policed society. When the time came to deploy terror to maintain this division, Deng did not blink. The Tiananmen Square massacre proved his determination and ability to prop up the crumbling wall between politics and the economy.

But then Deng was a revolutionary and a nation-builder. He had been hardened by having both practised terror and been subjected to it. The Chinese political elite trusted him to interfere if and when the experiment got out of hand. Gorbachev & Co. were the pampered fourth generation of Soviet rulers. Unlike the battalions of Lenin and Stalin, they had inherited power, not taken it by force. Unlike the Khrushchev and Brezhnev cohort, they had not been brutalized by Stalinist terror (either as perpetrators or as victims) or by a horrific war in which the regime's existence hung by a thread.

For the 'Chinese variant' to have a chance in Gorbachev's Soviet Union, a credible threat of terror was critical both for persuading the willing but wary segment of the apparat and for scaring along the reluctant and the sceptical. A new, untested Kremlin could not succeed in making such a deployment plausible. A largely unknown quantity, Gorbachev was asking the nomenklatura for a huge political loan secured by the rather flimsy collateral of his credentials. His application was denied.

Faced with the passive but massive and unyielding resistance of the political and economic nomenklatura, by 1987 Gorbachev and a small but determined group of his supporters in the leadership were confronted with two obvious choices. Gorbachev could become another Brezhnev who, having tried a limited economic decentralization (the so-called 'Kosygin reform') in the mid-1960s, sensed the nomenklatura opposition, abandoned the reform and ruled happily for eighteen years. In 1987 the Soviet economy was still growing, by official reckoning, at slightly over 3 per cent a year.[275] Without a doubt, at the same level of repression, the current leadership could have ruled for at least another decade, if not longer, before the creeping economic crisis entered an acute state and the economy began to shrink. A leading Russian scholar of perestroika was certainly right when he claimed that there was no

physical danger to the regime, that it 'was not threatened by revolutionaries', and that 'M. Gorbachev with his comrades did not really have
to undertake any reforms.'[276]

Yet – and this was perestroika's central paradox – while the 'economics' was their banner, Gorbachev and his supporters in the top leadership had set out to fight a mostly moral battle. In the minds of the key
players, ethics – not economy or politics – informed the initial reform
impulse.

As we have seen, when the future 'godfather of glasnost', Aleksandr
Yakovlev, returned to Moscow after ten years in Canada (where he had
been ambassador), he had 'the impression . . . that the moment was at
hand when the people would say "That's it! We cannot live like this
any longer. Everything must be done in a new way. We must reconsider
our concepts, approaches, our views of past and future.'[277] Another
Gorbachev confidant and his future Foreign Minister Eduard Shevardnadze recalled how, as early as 1979, he and Gorbachev 'spoke of the
many absurdities of our life and came to the conclusion that we just
could not go on like this.'[278] Gorbachev's own 'moral position' in 1985
was the same: 'we couldn't go on like that any longer and we had to
change life radically, break away from the past malpractice.'[279] Although
politicians' memories are notoriously faulty and selective, the uniformity
of these recollections lends them credence.

Certainly the disastrous anti-alcohol campaign could not possibly
have been prompted by short-term economic considerations. In 1985
the state's annual income from alcoholic beverages was between 12 and
14 per cent of total budgetary revenues.[280] Between 1985 and 1988, the
anti-alcohol campaign cost the Soviet Treasury sixty-seven billion rubles
in lost revenues.[281] This amount was equal to almost 9 per cent of the
1985 GNP, 17 per cent of that year's state revenues, and nearly four
times the sum spent on healthcare.[282] Later, in an article in *Pravda*,
Gorbachev disclosed that, alongside oil exports, vodka had sustained
the Soviet Union between 1970 and 1985.[283]

Yet when Gorbachev's first Prime Minister Nikolay Ryzhkov, in 1985,
objected in the Central Committee to the anti-alcohol campaign's early
excesses he was overruled by other members of Gorbachev's team
because he was 'concerned about economy instead of morality'.[284] 'The
morals of the nation', he was told, 'must be rescued by any means
available.'[285] It was this normative imperative that made reliving Brezh-
nevism, in any form, moral anathema to the Gorbachev leadership.

Gorbachev's other alternative was to try a version of Khrushchev's
'thaw': limited political liberalization and economic decentralization,

greater openness and turnover in the Party bureaucracy. Yet those who reprised Khrushchev's reform would almost certainly have met with Khrushchev's end at the hands of a coalesced nomenklatura opposition. For Gorbachev's closest advisers, the central lesson of 'Krushchevism' was that it had failed because, in Yakovlev's words, Khrushchev himself had been 'afraid of democracy, afraid of relying on the people'.[286] This conclusion shines through Gorbachev's startling statement at the January Plenum: 'Perestroika is only possible because of democracy and through democracy ... [Democratization] is the lever that would allow to engage into perestroika its decisive force – the people ... If we do not achieve this ... we shall not be able to maintain [the momentum] of perestroika, it will simply fail to materialize.'[287]

Thus, after almost two years of earnest but limited and largely futile reformism, Gorbachev faced the moment of truth. Having found the two obvious choices unacceptable either morally or politically, he opted, instead, for a third way that alone offered hope for the survival of his regime as reformist and reforming. This third road entailed a dramatic expansion of the reform's base beyond the thin layer of reform-minded Party apparatchiks and beyond the Kremlin's walls. As Gorbachev said shortly after the Plenum, 'It was necessary to come up with proposals that would engage the entire society in the work [of perestroika].'[288] Gorbachev's conclusion must have been similar to that of an astute Russian analyst of his policies: 'stagnation and inertia had penetrated so deeply into the cells of the Party organs that a serious shakedown was necessary to change the course of events'.[289] And since the Party was clearly incapable of administering such a shakedown, only an 'outside force could make the Party apparatus work as required'.[290]

It is this conclusion, made public at the January Plenum, that became Gorbachev's first revolutionary act, breaking with the unwritten law of Russian (and Soviet) politics: from the Decembrists to Khrushchev, intra-elite disputes had been settled almost exclusively within the tight boundaries of the political class. For the first time, the Party's leader, speaking at the Plenum of the Central Committee, appealed over the heads of its members for the people's support in exchange for a dramatic expansion of liberties.

The January choice proved both bold and brilliant. In less than two years, the events that were then set in motion made the regime and the political reform invulnerable to the Party 'conservatives'. The unintended consequence was that, having saved the reform, the January choice ultimately killed the very system the reform was supposed to mend.

This result poses a final question for an autopsy of perestroika: why was such an outcome – shocking and, in January 1987, unlikely but by no means impossible – so cavalierly disregarded? Why was caution, very much in evidence at first, thrown to the wind? Why did the mortal perils of 'socialism with a human face', so evident to the mediocrities of the Brezhnev Politburo twenty years before when they suppressed the liberalization of Czechoslovakia, seem so ephemeral to the bright and hardworking group now in the Kremlin? And why did Gorbachev embark on a quest to recover the long-gone romance of the Prague Spring, with its ideal of a dynamic, prosperous and free one-party socialism?

Of a host of reasons that prevent autocratic rulers from relaxing their grip, four seem the most formidable: blind faith in the virtues of the present system; ignorance of the reality both inside and outside the country; personal responsibility for the present state of affairs; and fear for the stability of the regime. While the confluence of all four factors is relatively rare (although characteristic of those who ruled the Soviet Union from 1964 to 1985), any two are probably enough to prevent any serious reform.

In the case of the Gorbachev leadership, each of the four impediments to change was seriously weakened.* Their faith was undermined by Khrushchev's 1956 'secret speech' and the mini-glasnost of 1961–3, known as the 'thaw'. Their ignorance of the world outside the Soviet borders was shattered by travel during the Brezhnev era, especially the 'detente' of 1972–9. Meanwhile, restricted and closely guarded reprints of the major works of Western Sovietologists and native dissidents, which circulated among the top nomenklatura, supplied something of a corrective to their view of the Soviet political and economic system.[291] Third, as youngish newcomers to supreme power, the Gorbachev cohort could plausibly deny personal responsibility for the Soviet Union's sorry state. And, finally, after over two decades of economic growth, domestic stability and military parity with the United States, the Soviet state seemed quite capable of withstanding some well-managed opening and a limited reduction in police control.

The uniqueness of Gorbachev & Co. did not lie in their ability to

---

* The much, and deservedly, maligned Brezhnev regime must be given credit for nurturing the 'captains of perestroika'. In the sterility and stagnation of the 1970s, many a seditious seed germinated quietly and unmolested. The tolerance of loose thought and even loose talk (as long as it was not public), the first officially sanctioned mass emigration since the establishment of the regime, and detente with the United States were some of the policies that bore fruit a decade later.

distinguish right from wrong, nor even in their desire to do right. Many in the Soviet leadership of the post-Stalin era must have been just as capable of seeing the difference and wanting to do good. Khrushchev, certainly, showed some selective but real ability to do so. The key divide that separated the Gorbachev team from their predecessors was their belief that what was morally right was now politically manageable.

And so, self-absolved of responsibility for the past, at least partly rid of ideological blinkers, well informed of the warts of the present, and yet supremely confident of the future, the Kremlin turned, in January 1987, to 'democratization'.

In the months that followed the January Plenum, Yeltsin's hitherto near-flawless sense of the official line appeared faulty – perhaps compromised by commitments too deep and too personal, stakes suddenly too high and pride too closely and intimately engaged for cool calculation.

In the results of the Plenum Yeltsin chose to see only the declared radicalism of 'democratization'. Unnoticed or deliberately ignored by him was the other, just as unmistakably obvious outcome: a stalemate on the issue of intra-Party reform.* The complexity of Gorbachev's multi-layered game was, perhaps, too subtle (or too alien) for Yeltsin: incapable of either coercing or reforming the nomenklatura, yet unwilling to surrender to it, Gorbachev bypassed it for the moment, counting on the pressures from *outside* the Party eventually to effect an intra-Party 'renewal'.

An odd matador, the General Secretary wished not to kill the recalcitrant bull (he was incapable of doing so even if he wanted to) but only to tame and harness it. Having met with little success, he climbed out of the arena, and began to egg on the public. Yeltsin, the lone *banderillero*, did not notice the matador's departure and continued to stick barbs into the bull's neck.

Yeltsin's public interpretation of the Plenum's slogans and the policies he pursued in its wake between January and November 1987 would mark the outermost boundary of his insider reformism. More importantly, the

---

* For instance, whereas Gorbachev's opening speech at the Plenum hinted at secret-ballot election of the local Party leaders up to the First Secretaries of regions and Union Republics, the Plenum's resolution contained only a vague reference to 'improving mechanisms for the formation of elective party organs with the aim of its further democratization' (TASS, 28 January 1988). Similarly, Gorbachev had talked about promoting non-Party personnel to 'leading positions'. The resolution changed this to 'positions of responsibility' (*ibid.*).

positions that began to crystallize at that time would, largely without change, be found not just timely but widely appealing and winning two years later, when the Fourth Russian Revolution began in earnest. They would become central to the Revolution's early agenda and would propel their author to its vanguard.

In Yeltsin's eager rendition, both glasnost and 'democratization' were instilled with purposes far deeper and placed within limits far wider than those intended by the Plenum. Glasnost, he told *Moskovskaya Pravda*, was more than a 'research instrument for a historian', more than 'merely an opportunity to throw a stone in the garden of the past'.[292] No, it was 'a powerful means of moral cleansing and social renewal'.[293] As such, glasnost should not be rationed: 'two half-truths do not make the truth'.[294] Even if it is 'shocking', the truth should not be stopped at 'half-glasnost'.[295]

The 'essence of perestroika is truth',[296] Yeltsin said, and:

> truth cannot be partial. If it is, then it is a lie. Likewise, glasnost cannot be glasnost if it is fitted with blinkers: you can talk about this, but not about that. It is an 'either–or' situation. Either we open widely the windows so that the breeze sweeps up the cobwebs, or again hide the dirt in the dark corners, behind heavy bolts.[297]

Hence, the goal was now to 'move Moscow towards full glasnost, towards complete candour in the discussion of any and all problems'.[298] Abandon 'the old habit of speaking in hushed tones, of criticizing only by command', Yeltsin ordered Moscow journalists, whom he found 'still in the grip of the internal censor'.[299] There ought to be no 'zones beyond criticism', and it was high time journalists looked boldly at certain high offices.[300]

As was his wont, Yeltsin proceeded to take the medicine he prescribed. The 'internal censor' was publicly discarded at the first post-January Plenum of the MGK, three weeks after the Central Committee's gathering. *Moskovskaya Pravda*'s account of the 22 February Plenum began with a note in bold type above the front-page text of Yeltsin's speech: 'Following the decision of the Plenum, the materials are published by this newspaper in full'[301] – that is, without the usual omissions or editing of passages intended solely for the ears of the initiated. The speeches, published verbatim, were a startlingly frank litany of facts, figures and statements. Among other revelations was Yeltsin's disclosure that there had been 'massive' embezzlements in the Moscow administrations for retail trade, public catering (cafeterias and restaurants) and transport, while many in the police were 'up to their necks in corruption' and worked for 'criminals'.[302]

Yeltsin's version of 'full glasnost' included another unprecedented innovation: contacts with foreigners that went beyond official receptions and banquets. In May 1987 he became the first member of the Soviet leadership ever to invite an American television crew into his office, to allow them to follow him around town and to tape a lengthy and spontaneous interview. He talked to Diane Sawyer about the opposition to perestroika and about his own attitude towards criticism ('Of course I don't love it, as one loves a woman. I was brought up during stagnation: I, too, am an accomplice. But I need to learn to live with glasnost, to live with democracy'). 'Don't Russians – alone, in the privacy of their homes – think that, in the end, capitalism does work?' Sawyer asked him. 'Well,' Yeltsin answered after a long pause, 'they probably do.' 'Do you?' 'Of course, I do.' But when Sawyer said, 'Some in America say that glasnost means that socialism failed,' Yeltsin retorted, 'I pity them. They will have to change their mind. I am confident of that.' When his interviewer added, 'Khrushchev said, "We will bury you [the West]." Do you still believe this?' the Pervyi replied, after another lengthy pause, 'Well, we are not saying this any more, are we?'[303]

On 6 October, Yeltsin invited ambassadors accredited to the Soviet capital[304] for a three-hour 'conversation'. This was an event without precedent in the Party's history. But Yeltsin's main transgression was more egregious still: he washed the Party's dirty linen before foreigners. 'We do not subdivide information into that for "home consumption" and that for "foreign use",' Yeltsin said. 'In accordance with glasnost and democratization, we tell all the truth, and not half-truths, to readers at home and abroad.'[305]

According to the official TASS account, Yeltsin told the ambassadors that twenty-three (of the thirty-three) Raikom First Secretaries had been replaced in the past year and a half.[306] TASS neglected to mention that Yeltsin also said that 'perestroika in Moscow is proceeding with great difficulty';[307] that, in addition to the Raikom purge, the Buro membership had been changed 'completely'; and that 40 per cent of the MGK staff had been fired as well.[308] According to one of the diplomats present, Yeltsin also openly discussed drug addiction and prostitution.[309] He broke one of the last taboos by talking about the enormous number of prisoners in the USSR. This was more than a violation of the iron rules. This was a personal affront to all those who still lived by them and guarded them jealously. His offence was duly, but for now silently, registered.

*   *   *

The January Plenum's call for 'democratization' was readily interpreted by Yeltsin as the need to 'mobilize people not by loud commands but by intellect, competence; to lead by reliance not on blind obedience but on the collective intellect and trust'.[310] Neither 'the boss's will' nor 'even that of a simple arithmetical majority' was sufficient any longer.[311] 'What is important, of course,' he explained, 'is not what the First Secretary, the Buro or the Gorkom think, but what Muscovites think.' The Party ought to learn to 'respect the opinion of an opponent' and 'to seek, together, solutions' acceptable not just to the state or the collective, but to the individual as well.[312]

In 'democratization' Yeltsin saw endorsement of his theme of the Party's responsibility before the people, and proceeded to broaden and elaborate on it. It was during this time that he first singled out an aspect of this responsibility which would resurface so fatefully before the year was over: the responsibility for slogans and pledges. 'At this stage of perestroika, a correct assessment of its tempo acquires paramount importance,' for 'the chasm between the word and the deed' was most dangerous.[313] The main threat to perestroika was the loss of people's trust because of the disappointment that would inevitably follow the absence of practical, concrete improvements of their lot.[314] Haste in making promises, Yeltsin warned, was to be avoided.[315]

There could be one and only one criterion of Party work: concrete final results. They, and not vast lists 'of measures to the year 2000', would matter to the people and, therefore, ought to matter to the Party.[316] One could not feed promises to the people, and 'one [could not] sail far on [boats made of] paper programmes'.[317] Hence the 'colossal responsibility of the Party [as a whole] and every Party member' for the practical implementation of perestroika. Again and again Yeltsin called on the Moscow Party organization to 'raise the level of responsibility of everyone for exact and unequivocal fulfilment of promises and to evaluate leaders by the results [of their work]'.[318]

The most passionate and vocal of Yeltsin's 1987 campaigns was also the riskiest, because the official licence for it was so weak. This was the wide-ranging reform aimed at the fundamentals of the apparat's existence: the way it transacted its daily business, made decisions, selected leadership, treated *hoi polloi* and even lived. Shrugging off the ominous vagueness of the Plenum's resolution on the subject of intra-Party 'democratization', Yeltsin opened the campaign in mid-March with salvoes of heavy rhetorical artillery. In past decades, he told the Moscow functionaries, Soviet communists had outdone even the Russian Ortho-dox Church in the rituals and ceremonies which had 'burrowed their way into our very skin, like coal dust', and (which was 'most dangerous of all') had 'become habitual and necessary'.[319]

What rituals did he have in mind? For one, the 'incorrect' understanding of the relationship between the 'collegiality and leadership' in Party practice. 'The leader does not just set the tone, he dictates. And the rest are either silent or nodding. Absent is real collective thinking, comparison of different opinions . . . The damage from such a "unity of thought" is first and foremost to the cause we all serve.'[320] Another ritual was the exaggeration of a leader's 'personal merits'.[321] That, Yeltsin told the troops, was 'simply unacceptable'. Modesty and scrupulousness ought to be the key qualities of a Party leader – and vigilance against the recurrence of the old ways.[322] Yeltsin claimed to be talking only about 'Raikoms, Party committees of ministries, agencies and enterprises'. As we shall see shortly, he had in mind far more elevated offices.

As always, changes in policy followed the declaration without delay. The August 1987 Plenum of the MGK witnessed a novel arrangement: the First Secretary, after setting the general tone, interrupted his speech to incorporate comments from the floor.[323] Yeltsin had a double target here. Such a format, he explained, would allow everyone to participate in truly collective decision-making, and would ensure their personal responsibility for implementation.[324]

At the same time, Yeltsin ordered all Party functionaries, including those working in the Raikoms and the Gorkom, to give account of their work before the work collectives by the end of the year.[325] The industrial nomenklatura was to do the same – leaving it to the workers to decide if the *nachal'nik* 'was worthy of their trust' and could continue to head an enterprise.[326] 'We must', Yeltsin said, 'break the nomenklatura circle' by replacing time-serving functionaries with leaders of a new type.'[327]

Another innovation violated one of the most venerable of the Party's traditions: the injunction against resignations. To those leaders who had proved incapable or had reached their limits, Yeltsin suggested submitting a resignation – be they 'a director, manager, department head or Secretary of a Party committee'.[328] This, he explained, would be the 'honourable thing to do for their colleagues, for the Muscovites'.[329]

And, of course, no Party ritual was in greater danger than the nomenklatura privileges. Yeltsin's assault on the elite's paraphernalia began to acquire unprecedented ferocity and precision. Nothing was sacred any longer. Yeltsin was putting on the chopping block of 'social justice' the 'entire gamut of social benefits',[330] including the admission of the nobility's offspring to 'special' English-language schools, and 'holiday food packages', finely graded by rank. He went so far as to suggest that the

Party give up entirely its second most important mechanism of social control (after terror): distribution of goods and services. 'We must insist on the principle that those who produce goods distribute them.'[331]

In the same breath, he questioned another central feature of the regime: inequality before the law for the rulers and the ruled. 'We cannot allow again [a situation in which] some live under the law and others above it. And that was indeed so! Not only fathers who occupied high positions in the Party, in the Soviets, in trade, were above the law. Their children and grandchildren lived in the shadow of that paternal immunity and did whatever they wanted.'[332]

That spring Yeltsin received an anonymous letter from the wife of a nomenklatura official. It read: 'Don't waste your arrows on us. Isn't it clear that it would be in vain? We are the elite and you will never stop the stratification of society. You'll run out of steam. We'll tear the puny sails of your perestroika and you will never reach the shore.'[333] This was a fair warning, and Yeltsin would have done well to pay attention to it.

Yeltsin said later that his only lasting accomplishment as the ruler of Moscow was a change in the 'spirit' of Moscow.[334] By spring 1987, that new spirit began to engender some wondrous things in the city which only a year and a half before had seemed hopelessly frozen in lies, fear, passivity and cynicism.

In one such instance, occasioned by one of his field trips to a housing project, three of Yeltsin's central campaigns – for leaders closer and more responsible to the people, for newspaper reporting in which reality was recognizable, and for the citizens' right, and duty, to tell the bosses all the truth to their face – combined to achieve a remarkable result: something quite unSoviet, barely distinguishable from a visit by a local politico to the slums as covered by a Western tabloid.

Upon arrival, Yeltsin was instantly surrounded by a tight ring of hundreds of shouting people, while others watched from the balconies.[335] Their voices carried notes of desperation, hope and rage. 'Come down into our basement,' people cried from the balconies. 'We are up to our knees in stinking muck! The sewer pipe has long rusted through! The roofs are leaking and no one gives a damn!' Yeltsin went into the basement. When he emerged, he was told to look at the heaps of rubbish in the yard, where it stayed, uncollected, 'for weeks at a time'.[336] The ring around the First Secretary tightened further. 'Rats are crawling among the refuse and our children play alongside!' people shouted at him. Yeltsin walked around the yard. 'Everywhere [there is] only eye-wash, Potemkin villages, only words about the "human factor",' somebody who stood close to Yeltsin said angrily. 'The cracks in the walls of my apartment are as wide as a finger, and all my begging for repairs is for nothing,' someone else called out. Yeltsin visited some of the apartments.

In the twenty-five years since they had been erected, these apartment buildings had never really been repaired – only touched up for appearances' sake, editorialized *Moskovskaya Pravda*. When the walls cracked, the cracks were covered by wallpaper. When the water-pipes rusted through, they were wrapped with rags. So it was 'not surprising' that the previous winter, when the pipes burst and, at −30°C, there was no hot water, the people should have been 'outraged by the uselessness of the district organs of Soviet power'.[337]

While Gorbachev and his colleagues in the Kremlin charted the route of the perestroika train, Yeltsin's trips took him down to the engine room. He found the pressure in the boiler rising dangerously fast. His anxiety, which they did not share because they did not see what he saw, set him further apart from his Politburo colleagues.

The spring and summer of 1987 bloomed with most extraordinary flowers in Yeltsin's Moscow. In the early evening of 6 May, a milling crowd of 400 people gathered on the Square of the Fiftieth Anniversary of the October Revolution. They carried placards: 'We demand a meeting with M. S. Gorbachev and B. N. Yeltsin', 'Down with the saboteurs of perestroika', 'The memory of the people is sacred'. This was Soviet Moscow's first mass unofficial demonstration* since the 1920s.

The participants belonged to the 'historical–patriotic society' Pamyat' ('Memory'). The label 'nationalist', under which the world media served this overnight sensation, did not quite describe the odd mixture of ideas that inspired this perennially agitated bunch. They were obsessed with Jews, Masons and the 'agents of the CIA' (who, together, were responsible for each and every calamity that befell Soviet Russia), enamoured of Stalin and heartbroken about the destruction of historic monuments and landmarks.[338]

The crowd refused to disperse despite the entreaties of Mayor Valeriy Saikin, who arrived on the scene. Then Yeltsin sent word that he would

---

* If 'demonstrations' are confined to walking, that is. On 31 March 1986, taxi-drivers had gathered in front of the MGK. Petrol had long been rationed in the Soviet Union and coupons were reissued to cab drivers on the last day of every quarter. There were queues at petrol pumps several kilometres long. Many furious drivers drove their cabs to the MGK and honked their horns.

meet with the demonstrators in the building of the Moscow City Soviet.[339] Visibly buoyed by this unprecedented gesture, and still not quite believing their own recklessness and luck, the exhilarated assembly marched to the Mossovet – under pre-revolutionary Russian flags.[340] They were ushered into the large Marble Hall of Meetings. When Yeltsin and Saikin entered, the crowd burst into applause. 'Enough, enough,' said Yeltsin, 'we should unlearn this habit [of applauding when the leaders appear]. You asked me to come. Here I am. To talk to you as your equal. What questions do you have?'[341] The meeting lasted for two hours.

Towards the end, Yeltsin looked at the pile of questions in front of him and said, 'We have talked for two hours but there are still a lot questions. Shall we go on?' 'Enough, enough. The rest is for your home reading,' the audience responded. 'Thanks for meeting with us.' 'Thank you,' Yeltsin replied. 'As they say, "See you again!"'[342] As Moscow's first unsanctioned demonstrators filed out of the Mossovet building, one of them remembered Russia's patron saint: 'Not for nothing is it George the Victorious Day today!'[343]

A summer that begins with a nineteen-year-old German landing a single-engine Cessna on Red Square (Mathias Rust performed this feat on 28 May) is not likely to be a calm one. In late July, two months after the Pamyat' event, more than 300 Crimean Tatars demanding the right to return to their homeland, from which Stalin had expelled them in 1944, held vigil under the Kremlin walls. Cordoned off by several thick rings of police, these demonstrators carried babies, Gorbachev's portraits and suitcases containing their belongings and food. Many were barefoot. The sit-in on Red Square went on for three days and nights.

After the Tatars had finally been dispersed, the US embassy was accused by the official news agency, TASS, of instigating 'Soviet citizens to commit illegal actions'. Very much in the style of the pre-glasnost treatment of dissidents, *Izvestia* portrayed the leaders of the demonstration as cowardly 'extremists' who had lied to their followers.[344] Still, no one was hurt or arrested.

Moscow's extraordinary political summer of 1987 concluded with the first ever officially sanctioned conference of 'informal' (unofficial) groups. Between 20 and 23 August, representatives of forty-seven such organizations met to discuss issues ranging from a monument to the victims of Stalin's purges to industrial self-management, the democratization of the Soviet electoral system, and 'social inequality'.[345] Some of the participants had formerly been regarded as dissidents and had been persecuted by the KGB. The conference had been prepared 'under the auspices' of the Moscow City Party Committee.[346]

In no other line of attack was Yeltsin's advance even close to so spectacular a result. In fact, after twenty months of strenuous exertion, the Moscow perestroika was failing to live up to its engineer's expectations on virtually every front. 'In terms of concrete results, very little has been done,' he admitted in August 1987, at what turned out to be the last MGK Plenum over which he presided.[347]

For all the talk about 'self-sufficiency' and 'business accounting', Moscow enterprises lost 60 million rubles annually because of unusable or low-quality products; another 60 million rubles in fines for broken delivery schedules; and 360 million rubles because of 'technological backwardness'. Every fifth plant or factory failed to achieve its planned profit, and many more produced only a 'very low' profit. Twenty-three industrial and forty-seven construction enterprises and *trest*s operated at a loss.[348]

The ministries, meanwhile, took the easiest route – keeping the enterprises on life support by feeding them state funds. Thus, at the very beginning of the reform, 'we are already deceiving the state', Yeltsin told the Plenum. How, in such conditions, can enterprises 'learn to save money?' What economy, he demanded to know, could sustain such wastefulness? Perhaps the time had come to talk about bankruptcy . . .[349]

Yeltsin's bugbear, the 'scientific research institutes', remained invulnerable. There had been 1,041 of them when he took over Moscow. Seven had, with 'great difficulty', been closed down. Yet in August 1987, there were 1,087! And they were just as 'useless', at best copying foreign technology.[350]

Things were no better in the social sphere, which, for the first time, had been discussed before the economy in Yeltsin's speech and declared the 'key link'. The four critical areas of Yeltsin's inaugural speech – housing, consumer goods, public transport and healthcare – had lost none of their urgency. Moreover, the problems of housing and consumer goods, which had formerly been listed as 'acute', were now for the first time declared by Yeltsin to be 'most acute' – a label of grave political import in the Soviet political vocabulary.

No less meagre were the results of the ferocious administrative battle that Yeltsin had waged to supply Moscow with fresh produce. Even the Pervyi's zeal, persistence and capacity for work had proved no match for the jealous 'invisible hand' of the Soviet market. Gradually and quietly the old balance, upset somewhat by the *yarmarki*, was restored. 'The summer is almost over,' complained Muscovites, 'and we still have not seen vegetables and fruit.'[351] In the main grocery store of the Sevasto-polskiy district, a spot-check produced only 'rotten and cracked water-melons, crushed peaches and green tomatoes'.[352]

As for the *yarmarki*, Yeltsin's proudest achievement, they began to wane the moment he felt it was safe to lessen his personal attention and relieve, somewhat, administrative pressure. Soon the queues there grew to be as long (an hour and forty-five minutes, in one instance, to buy apples in August),[353] the produce as unappealing and the organization as atrocious as they were in regular stores, with the stalls closing for lunch and 'parsley, dill and peppers all sold separately in different kiosks, with a queue of 1.5 to 2 hours each'.[354]

The Moscow trade functionaries behaved in a predictable manner. Rather than increase the delivery of fresh produce to the city, improve its quality and facilitate its distribution through *yarmarki*, which had been intended to supplement the regular grocery stores, the district trade officials sought to curry favour with the Gorkom by switching the same paltry supplies from the stores to the fairs.[355] In many districts stores received no vegetables at all on the 'fair days', Fridays and Saturdays.[356] Tens of thousands of hapless seekers after fruit and vegetables, already brutalized by the queues and the rotten choice in their local store, now had to travel to the nearest *yarmarka* and stand in the same queues to buy the same battered and aged produce.[357]

At the end of August 1987, Moscow's evening newspaper, *Vecher-nyaya Moskva*, taking up the First Secretary on his invitation to tell the whole truth, slapped him in the face with this verdict on his brainchild: 'It seems that the *yarmarki* are not living up to expectations. They do not help improve the supply of fruit and vegetables and do not force the private traders to lower their prices.'[358]

In another year or so, barely a ripple would remain of the waves made by the mighty rocks Yeltsin had hurled into the stagnant and leech-infested pond that was Moscow's food retail trade. The *yarmarki*, writes a witness, soon 'degenerated into a drunken porter selling potatoes'.[359]

The final and perhaps most painful disappointment for the self-appointed Hercules was the results of his efforts at 'cleansing' the Party's house. After all the shovelling, cutting, burning, sweeping and scrubbing, after dozens of firings and as many new appointments, attended with heartbreak and resentment, the Augean stables of the apparat were nearly as impassable as before. Some 'small half-steps' had been taken and some 'pitiful' progress achieved, Yeltsin noted, yet the prevalent mood was to forget about 'everything that had been promised but not done'.[360] Many good decisions remained unimplemented, 'stuck as if in cotton wool'.[361]

Lack of responsibility and low discipline affected many a Party leader, and even entire Party organizations. 'Any decision could be left unimplemented, shifted, postponed, drowned in endless examinations, consultations and clarifications,' delays and half-measures. These, Yeltsin astutely observed, were 'the symptoms of the most dangerous malaise' that had 'killed so many excellent' reforms in the past.[362] Again, that August, the Pervyi sounded a familiar alarm: there was 'a real danger of a chasm between word and deed'.[363] A lot had been promised, 'but the results [were] insignificant'.

The further perestroika proceeded, Yeltsin claimed, the stronger became the resistance.[364] That was not habitual hyperbole, built into the battlefield metaphors common in the language of Russian communism. During the summer of 1987 the apparat's response to Yeltsin's relentless assault moved beyond passive resistance.

While Yeltsin was on holiday, his hand-picked editor-in-chief at *Moskovskaya Pravda*, Mikhail Poltoranin, was called to the Central Committee and 'invited' to sign a statement that the articles on violation of 'social justice' published by the paper had been 'imposed on us by Yeltsin'.[365] Poltoranin refused and told Yeltsin about the request. 'I know,' Yeltsin replied. 'They are digging my grave.'[366]

The subject of Poltoranin's recantation was not, of course, accidental. 'Social justice' and Yeltsin's strikes against the nomenklatura privileges were the largest of the many bones the apparat had to pick with the First Secretary. The grievances, with appropriate exaggerations and dramatizations, were communicated to the Second Secretary in charge of the Party cadres, Egor Ligachev, who, partly because of his position and partly out of personal inclination, acted as the apparat's guardian angel. 'Their [Ligachev's and Yeltsin's] relationship reached crisis point on the question of social justice,' Poltoranin recalled a year later.

In Moscow Yeltsin began to close down the special stores for officials and to abolish other special privileges for the nomenklatura. He tried, for example, to re-establish order in the special schools reserved for the children of high officials . . . Ligachev [said] that this [was] 'social demagoguery'. According to him, one should not touch existing privileges but should improve conditions for those who do not enjoy certain opportunities.[367]

About that time, Yeltsin was apparently forbidden by the Politburo to dismiss any more First Secretaries of the Raikoms: 'when he realized that the decisions were not being implemented, he tried to replace those responsible but was "advised not to"'.[368] 'My hands are tied,' he told Poltoranin.[369] The Politburo injunction had been caused by more than just Ligachev's urging. Following his strategy of letting the apparat be for now, Gorbachev too felt it was necessary to restrain Yeltsin. 'When he [Yeltsin] started a second and a third round of dismissals, this began to worry us,' Gorbachev said a year later. 'I criticized him at a Politburo meeting. In a comradely kind of way, I told Boris Nikolaevich that he had to draw conclusions, and act accordingly.'[370]

In a characteristic response, and in violation of Party etiquette, Yeltsin made public his dispute with Ligachev. At a meeting with the Party *aktiv* that summer he admitted 'differences of view' with Ligachev and 'openly accused [him] of not concerning himself enough with the overall situation, as the Number Two leader should'.[371] Worse still, Yeltsin hinted at these same differences at his meeting with foreign diplomats: 'The rise in social tension is obvious. There is a clear parting of the ways between those who are for perestroika and those who are against it.'[372]

The latter admission was accompanied by a predictable rejoinder: 'It is precisely the kind of situation in which one must work especially hard, in which the responsibility of a leader increases dramatically.'[373] Yet in private, with his guard down, Yeltsin began to sound not quite as confident. 'I have never been as lonely as in Moscow,' he told his college friends on 16 September at the annual reunion of the graduates of the Civil Engineering Department of the UPI. '[In] another year, year and a half, you'll read my obituary in the papers.'[374]

On 12 September, in his Gorkom office, Yeltsin finished writing a letter. He put it in an envelope, sealed it, put it aside and paused for a moment. To send or not to send? Yeltsin called in an aide.[375] The letter was on its way.

The letter was addressed to 'Dear Mikhail Sergeevich' Gorbachev, who was holidaying at the exclusive government resort of Pitsunda on the Black Sea. Yeltsin began by recalling that it was a year and nine months since Gorbachev and the Politburo had entrusted to him the Moscow Party organization.[376] He had known, Yeltsin continued, that it was an 'incredibly hard assignment' and that he would have to learn a great deal to cope with it. Thus far, he had achieved 'very little'. If there were anything to brag about, it was his attempt to work with the new Buro 'selflessly' and 'collegially,' in a 'spirit of comradeship' and 'dedication to principles'. Yeltsin believed that he had also succeeded in 'changing the mood' of Muscovites – although that too, Yelstin hastened to add, was 'due to the change in the country as a whole'.[377]

Despite the difficulties, he had not been discouraged because he felt Gorbachev's support. Of late, however, Yeltsin began to sense 'indifference to the affairs of Moscow' and coolness towards him personally from 'certain leaders of the highest rank'. He was especially aggrieved by the 'style of work favoured' by the Party's second-in-command, Egor Ligachev. That 'style', imitated by the Central Committee's Secretariat, was 'wrong', especially 'these days'. Yeltsin had himself insisted on 'exactitude and strict personal responsibility' but, instead, Ligachev instilled 'fear' in the work of the Party organizations. As a result, Yeltsin insisted,

> Party organizations are lagging behind in all the great movement [of renewal] events. There is practically no perestroika here ...
>
> Perestroika has been designed and formulated in revolutionary terms. Yet, as to the practical implementation, and especially in the Party itself – [there is] the same old approach: time-serving, petty, bureaucratic, loud without substance. It is here that begins a rift between the Party's word and deed ...
>
> As to the attempts to criticize 'from below', this is totally hopeless. It is very disturbing that many think this way but are afraid to speak up. This, I think, is the most dangerous [development] for the Party ...[378]

Yeltsin wrote that he was 'greatly depressed' by the insincerity of the support for Gorbachev and perestroika shown by 'some comrades in the Politburo'.[379] They were 'clever' and 'smooth', but could they be fully trusted in their conversion to perestroika? Most alarming ('forgive me, Mikhail Sergeevich, for saying so') was the apparent 'comfortableness' which characterized Gorbachev's relations with these fair-weather friends of perestroika.

By contrast, Yeltsin admitted, he knew that he was not 'comfortable' to work with, he was not 'smooth'. He had always tried to 'voice my own point of view, even if it did not coincide with the opinion of others'.[380] He felt, increasingly, that his 'style', his 'directness', made him 'unsuitable' for work in the Politburo.

He understood only too well that it was not easy for Gorbachev to 'decide what to do with me'.[381] Yet the longer this conflict was to fester, the greater would be the 'number of problems connected with my persona' and the more they would hamper Gorbachev's work by creating instability in the Party's highest ranks. This,

> with all my heart, I would not want to happen. I would not want this, in part, because, despite your incredible efforts, [instability] will lead to stagnation, which we have already had [under Brezhnev]. And this must not be allowed to happen.[382]

It was these considerations, Yeltsin insisted, and not 'weakness or cowardice', that had prompted him to ask 'to be relieved' both of his position as the First Secretary of the Moscow City Party Committee and of his membership of the Politburo. He asked that his request be considered 'official' and hoped that he would not have to raise it publicly at a Central Committee Plenum.

Gorbachev would say later that he decided 'not to rush, but, instead, to look into the matter with great care'.[383] He told no one about Yeltsin's missive. Instead, on his return from holiday, he called Yeltsin and suggested that they talk 'later'.[384] According to Gorbachev, 'later' meant after the next Plenum and after the October Revolution anniversary holiday.[385] Yeltsin insisted that there was no such understanding. 'Later', he thought, meant in a day or two, at most within a week: it was not every day, after all, that a candidate member of the Politburo asked to be relieved of his post.[386] But a week passed, then another. Nothing was heard from Gorbachev.

In Vasiliy Grossman's *Zhizn' i sud'ba* ('Life and fate'), next to those of Orwell and Solzhenitsyn one of the great novels about totalitarianism, a gulag inmate recites this verse:

> 'What's your shell made of, my dear?'
> Once I asked a turtle. And was told:
> It's of fear. Stored and hardened fear.
> There is nothing stronger in this world.[387]

Yeltsin's resolve to crack his own shell of fear – a very personal and painful decision that would nearly cost him his life – turned out to be much more than one man's liberation. His rendezvous with Russian history was set.

The seventieth anniversary of the October Revolution was to be celebrated with great pomp in less than three weeks. On 21 October, a Plenum of the Central Committee convened to discuss the approaching political holiday. Gorbachev's long report was the sole item on the agenda.

Gorbachev was finishing his speech. In a few minutes, Yeltsin knew, the Plenum would be adjourned. 'To speak? Not to speak?'[388] He, who used to write and rewrite his speeches over and over again, had only a few lines in a notebook for this most important speech of his life. Until the last moment, 'deep in the subconscious' there 'lodged' the possibility of remaining silent, 'a tiny crack for retreat'.[389] After all, he had told no one of his plan: not even the closest of his subordinates in the Moscow City Committee, and, of course, no one in the Politburo.

Gorbachev finished. Here is how the official protocol recorded what followed:

> *Ligachev*, the Chair: Comrades! Thus the report is over. Does anyone have questions? Please, go ahead. If there are no questions, we should decide [whether to declare the Plenum adjourned] . . .
> *Gorbachev*: Comrade Yeltsin has a question.
> *Ligachev*: Then let's decide. Is it necessary to open debates?
> *Voices from the floor*: No.
> *Ligachev*: No.
> *Gorbachev*: Comrade Yeltsin has a statement.
> *Ligachev*: The floor is given to Comrade Yeltsin Boris Nikolaevich, candidate member of the Politburo, First Secretary of the Moscow City Party Committee. Please, Boris Nikolaevich.[390]

Yeltsin's short address (it lasted less than ten minutes) was not his usual performance. 'Yeltsin was not at all like his old self,' remembers a witness.[391] Gone was the usual care, the 'painstaking substantiation of every argument, the deliberateness of every word': he 'jumped from topic to topic, interrupted his train of thought, then suddenly returned to it'.[392] The text of the speech, which would not be made public for two years, confirms the witness's impression. In place of the customary march of hard-hitting facts, figures and detailed recommendations, there was a crowded and rushed stream – as if he expected to be interrupted any moment – of unfinished thoughts and disjointed observations, barely contained by a breathless, twisted syntax.

Perestroika was encountering 'great difficulties', Yeltsin began, and each of those in the hall had 'a great responsibility and a great duty' to move it along. Yet, at a time when the Party 'must take a revolutionary road and act in a revolutionary way', such a 'revolutionary spirit, such a revolutionary thrust', was absent in the work of the Secretariat of

the Central Committee under 'Comrade Ligachev'. We need, Yeltsin
continued,

> to draw lessons from the past, from the 'blank spots' of our history*
> that Mikhail Sergeevich talked about today to draw conclusions for
> today, to draw conclusions for tomorrow. What are we to do? How
> can we correct, how can we prevent from happening that which
> happened before? What happened was that the Leninist norms† of
> our life were discredited. And this led, simply, to the exclusion, for
> the most part, of these norms from the life and behaviour of our
> Party.

Yeltsin found two developments especially disturbing. First, the Party
had created unrealistic expectations. Since early spring of 1986 the people
had been promised a sharp improvement in their lives within two to
three years. Yet most of the time since then had been spent on 'drafting
the plans' while the people had not yet 'received anything tangible'
from perestroika. Repeated over and over again, the pledge of rapid
betterment 'disoriented the people, disoriented the party'. The result
was disillusionment: the 'great' popular 'enthusiasm' that had greeted
perestroika had begun to 'flag' and he was 'very much, very much
concerned about that'. Even if the Party 'revolutionized its work, as it
must, perestroika was 'not a two-year project'. The Party needed to be
more 'cautious' in its proclamations, otherwise it would soon find itself
'with a diminished authority'.

  The other issue was 'not an easy one' to talk about, but this was a
Plenum of the Central Committee, which Yeltsin considered 'the most
trustworthy, most truthful body' before which one 'can, and must,
express everything that is in one's heart'.

> I must say that the lessons of the past seventy years are hard lessons.
> There have been victories, just as Mikhail Sergeevich has said, but
> there have been lessons as well – the lessons of serious, painful set-
> backs. These setbacks came about gradually because of the absence
> of collegiality . . . because the power in the Party was given exclusively
> into one pair of hands, and he, that one man, was absolutely shielded
> from any criticism.

---

* *Belye pyatna*, officially 'closed' parts of Soviet history, such as the crimes of Stalin.
† *Leninskie normy*, in Party parlance, stood for freedom of debate within the Party and
the absence of intra-Party terror unleashed by Stalin.

In that respect, Yeltsin was 'very much troubled' by a certain increase in glorification' of the General Secretary by 'some members of the Politburo.' He found this phenomenon 'especially unacceptable' at the time when the foundation was being laid for 'democratic relations' with the Party, for 'comradely attitudes towards one another'.

To criticize in one's face, directly – yes, that is needed. But not to be carried away by glorification, which gradually, gradually, may again become the 'norm'. We simply cannot let this happen. This must not be allowed. I understand that right now this does not lead to [visible] defects but, nevertheless, the first signs of such an attitude are there, and it would seem to me that this, of course, ought to be stopped in the future.

Yeltsin paused.

And lastly. It seems that I cannot manage to work in the Politburo. For various reasons. It could be [my] experience [that is to blame for this] . . . and a certain lack of support from outside, especially by Comrade Ligachev, I would underscore this. [All this] has led me to the thought of putting to you a question about relieving me from the position, the duties, of a candidate member of the Politburo. I have handed in the appropriate written request. And as far as [the post of] the First Secretary of the City Party Committee is concerned, that question, it seems, will be decided by a Plenum of the City Party Committee.[393]

Yeltsin walked back to his seat and sat down. His 'heart was pounding, ready to jump out of [his] chest'.[394]

Never in seventy years had the Central Committee heard anything like this. No one had ever left the Party Olympus of his own will. No one had ever asked to resign. The demi-gods were fired, jailed, shot, pensioned off, sent abroad as ambassadors. An act of God, such as terminal illness or mental incapacity, was no exception: the afflicted continued to be listed as holding office until their death, as was the senile Andrey Kirilenko. The Party giveth, and only the Party, not anyone or anything else, taketh away.

In the stunned and silent auditorium, Gorbachev was the first to recover. He took over the chair from Ligachev. In a few well-organized sentences, he proceeded to summarize, fairly, Yeltsin's statement. Then, suddenly and without preparation, with a quick motion of the strong and well-trained wrist of a Party propagandist, he made the first deep cut:

> Comrade Yeltsin thinks he cannot any longer work in the Politburo but, at the same time, in his opinion, the question of his job as the First Secretary ought to be decided not by the Central Committee but by the City Committee. Now, here's something new and original. Perhaps, we are talking here about a secession of the Moscow Party organization? Or did Comrade Yeltsin decide to raise at the Plenum the question of his resignation from the Politburo but, at the same time, decide to continue as First Secretary of the MGK? Looks like he wishes to fight the Central Committee. This is how I understand it, although I may be sharpening a bit.[395]

Everyone in the hall that afternoon knew that Yeltsin's request was in full accordance with Party rules: it was up to the Moscow Party Committee (pro forma, of course) to relieve Yeltsin of his position as that Committee's head.

Yeltsin jumped up from his seat to protest his innocence of so monstrous a scheme. 'Sit down, sit down, Boris Nikolaevich,' Gorbachev insisted. 'You have not raised the issue of resigning from the post of First Secretary. You said: "This is up to the Gorkom." '[396] Gorbachev called for comments. He was especially eager to hear those outside the Politburo: he did not want, he explained, to create an impression that the Politburo was defending itself as 'a team'.[397] No one volunteered. Gorbachev gave the floor to Egor Ligachev.

While Gorbachev had been on holiday, Ligachev said, and he, Ligachev, had chaired the Politburo meetings, Yeltsin had been 'largely silent'. Perhaps, Ligachev suggested, Yeltsin had been 'accumulating' his thoughts in secret so as to 'splash them out' here, at the Plenum. Then it was Ligachev's turn with the knife. Yeltsin's statement was 'in principle incorrect politically' because he, Ligachev, 'felt with his very soul that the people [were] supporting' the Party's 'course'.[398]

When Ligachev had finished, Gorbachev again exhorted the Central Committee members who were not in the Politburo: 'Perhaps someone from the Central Committee will finally speak?' This time someone did get up, although, while outside the Politburo, it was still a figure from the central apparat: the Chairman of the Party Control Committee, Sergey Manyakin. He forged the third axis of attack. To Gorbachev's impugning of Yeltsin's motives and Ligachev's repudiation of his key contention, Manyakin added a denunciation of Yeltsin's entire political persona and his record in Moscow. The mode of assault was different as well: added to Gorbachev's deep incision were a thousand cuts and pricks with anything that could draw blood.

Yeltsin had 'flirted' with Muscovites (that is, he had sought cheap popularity), Manyakin said. There was a shortage of fruit and vegetables in Moscow. Yeltsin was 'politically immature', because, among other things, he had joined the Party late (at thirty) and had risen too fast through the ranks. That, on top of other 'bad character traits', made his speech a 'natural and predictable finale'. 'By his speech, Comrade Yeltsin sowed doubt in the cause of perestroika ... In essence, he expressed his disagreement with the Politburo, with the general line of the Party.'[399]

With the tenor now fairly well set, there was no shortage of volunteers: twenty-four members spoke after Manyakin. Gorbachev even had to announce a short break after the first twelve speeches.

In addition to rehashing at least one of the obligatory counts of the indictment established by the first three speeches,* every harangue contained praise for Gorbachev. 'As to the glorification of Mikhail Sergeevich, I, for one, respect him with all my soul both as a man and as a Party leader,' said the First Secretary of the Astrakhan Obkom, Leonid Borodin. 'Why can I not say something nice about him? This is not glorification.'[400] The head of the Soviet Trade Unions, Stepan Shalaev, called upon the audience to 'rejoice that such a man as Mikhail Sergeevich Gorbachev is at the helm of the Central Committee'. Prime Minister Nikolay Ryzhkov 'could not believe Yeltsin could force his tongue' to say such terrible things about the General Secretary. 'To be frank,' Ryzhkov confided to the audience, 'I rejoice in working with [Gorbachev].'[401]†

Protestations of unity and solidarity with the Politburo flowed thickly and exuberantly, as did affirmations of confidence in the future to which the grateful masses were joyfully marching behind the multifarious and omnipotent Party. As the First Secretary of the Poltava Oblast, Fedor Morgun, put it: 'Under the banners that the Party unfurled, we know where our march will end.'[402]

---

* There was only one clear exception: Gennadiy Kolbin, First Secretary of the Kazakh Republic, who had worked under Yeltsin in the Sverdlovsk Obkom. After praising Yeltsin's record in Sverdlovsk, he limited his criticism to stating, simply, that his ex-boss had made a 'mistake'.

† A few years later, in his memoirs, Ryzhkov would portray Gorbachev as incompetent, indecisive, vain and cowardly. The book was titled *Perestroika: The History of Betrayals*.

Naturally, there were variations and improvisations. Without them, after all, one did not look sincere. One speaker saw in Yeltsin's statement 'a clear desire to lead us astray'.[403] Another, the First Secretary of the Moscow Oblast, Valentin Mesyats, recalled, among Yeltsin's other transgressions, a session of the Moscow City Soviet during which, instead of sitting on the dais, like a good Party boss, Yeltsin and the entire Gorkom Buro had sat below in the hall, with the rank-and-file delegates.[404] Ryzhkov now remembered that from the 'very beginning' of his Moscow rule, Yeltsin had begun to develop 'political nihilism'.[405] Yeltsin was a 'man in disagreement with the Party line', said the KGB Chairman, Viktor Chebrikov. In deciding to speak now, before so great an anniversary, Yeltsin had 'forgotten about the country', about the Party, about Moscow and the Muscovites. 'No, you never really liked Muscovites. For, if you really liked Moscow, you would never have allowed yourself to say such things.'[406]

One of the recurring themes of these accusations was Yeltsin's attempt at what might be called 'external' glasnost. The session with the ambassadors, mentioned above, turned out to be especially irritating. One speaker declared himself 'stunned' after he had learned of Yeltsin's claim that 'there were more prisoners in the Soviet Union than in any other country': 'Is this a becoming statement for a candidate member of the Politburo? Couldn't he find another example of democratization which our full life is brimming with?'[407] The same speaker felt 'depressed' by Yeltsin's admission to the diplomats that there were – here he apologized to the handful of women in the hall – 1,100 prostitutes in Moscow and 2,000 drug addicts.[408] 'Imperialism' is scared of perestroika, declared Chebrikov. It was 'already taking concrete steps to hinder perestroika', and Russians should, at this time, 'guard our unity like the apple of one's eye'. Yeltsin, instead, 'engaged in calumny'.[409]

Yeltsin liked the fact that 'various foreign radio "voices"' quoted him, said Ryzhkov. 'All sorts of [foreign] publications' looked for 'what Yeltsin was saying'. Yeltsin 'must have very much liked' this sort of thing, this 'kind of distancing from the entire Politburo'.[410] The Chairman of the Party Control Committee, Mikhail Solomentsev, asked why it was that Yeltsin's speeches and interviews were published 'not in our newspapers' but in the West? Why were they so 'attractive'? Because they 'went contrary to the line of the Party', that was why. And that was 'precisely what the foes needed'. It was a 'real find' for them because it 'came not from some Godforsaken province but from the Secretary of the Moscow Party Committee'.[411] The prisoners surfaced again: 'Did you think it was appropriate to spread these numbers all over the world?

Who needs this? Does our Party need it, do our people? No, it is our ill-wishers who need this, our enemies who need this.'[412]

Some, while they tore into the body, sought to affix plasters to the wounds. Georgiy Arbatov, the Director of the USA and Canada Institute, 'could not deny the courage' of Yeltsin's statement – and then proceeded to accuse him of a lack of 'responsibility' and 'political maturity', which had led to his 'doing a great deal of damage to the cause'.[413] Yeltsin's hand-picked Chairman of the Moscow City Soviet, Valeriy Saikin, talked of 'positive results' in Moscow and suggested that it 'would not, perhaps, be fair' to deny Yeltsin some credit: he 'had worked a great deal, day and night'. But, of course, 'we, the Muscovites, do not agree with his statement today and fully support the current course of the Party and the government'.[414] The Chairman of the Supreme Soviet of the Russian Federation, Vitaliy Vorotnikov, admitted that he had long known Yeltsin as an 'active, responsible, hard-working' man with a great deal of 'initiative'. But, after a while, he, Yeltsin, had succumbed to 'leftist phrases' and began to 'hide behind a mask'.[415]

Yeltsin's accusers were not just petty apparatchiks, grey Party work-horses or well-known Politburo 'conservatives'. Prominent among them were those whom Western diplomats and journalists liked to call the 'liberals'. Only two years later, they would be revealed to the world as the titans of perestroika, the fearless paladins of glasnost and 'new political thinking'. They would shatter the most sacrosanct taboos, cross the hitherto forbidding chasms in giant leaps, and melt the icebergs of the Cold War. Raymond Aron wrote in his memoirs that, in the French Communist Party of the 1930s, the 'supreme crime' was to be 'right at the wrong time'.[416] Fifty years later, in Moscow, the dictum was just as valid.

Aleksandr Yakovlev, soon to be known as 'the godfather of glasnost', called Yeltsin's statement 'immoral'.[417] Yeltsin had 'put his personal ambitions, personal interests, above the interests of the Party'.[418] No, Yeltsin was neither 'courageous' nor 'principled'. Instead, he had become a 'mouthpiece for petit-bourgeois' views. Of course, 'vanity and ambitions' had played a role, but, most of all, it was Yeltsin's 'disagreement' with the 'very essence of perestroika, with its very purpose'.[419] Another prominent 'liberal', Foreign Minister Eduard Shevardnadze, called Yeltsin's speech 'primitive' and 'irresponsible' – irresponsible 'before the Party, the people, his friends, his colleagues, his comrades on the Politburo'.[420] 'This is a betrayal . . . I cannot find another word. I simply cannot understand where [Yeltsin's] mental outlook was formed. No, this was not a simple phenomenon, a simple speech.' And, turning to Yeltsin now, Shevardnadze rose to pathos: 'you will not succeed in sowing hostility between the Central Committee and the Moscow Party organization. No, you will not succeed! ... And you will not succeed in forcing on us a different style of leadership. No, this shall not pass!'[421]

The memory of that afternoon 'stuck' in Yeltsin's heart 'like a rusty nail'.[422] Two years later, when the protocol of the meeting was published, 'the heart still bled', and Yeltsin could not bring himself to read the transcript, could not force himself to 'relive that terrifying condition of injustice, the feeling of being betrayed'.[423]

He had known he would be savaged but had hoped that those whom he thought to be personally close to him, as well as functionaries of a 'large calibre', would abstain from joining the pack.[424] He had been wrong. Fellow Obkom First Secretaries from the neighbouring *oblasts*, Georgiy Bogomyakov from Tumen and Boris Konoplyov from Perm, who had been colleagues and friends for many years, stood up to speak. Listening to his former mentor, Yakov Ryabov, now in semi-retirement as ambassador to France, who confessed and repented the preferment he had arranged for Yeltsin ten years before,[425] Yeltsin thought: 'Why? Why did he do it? To beat a path to a better pension?'[426] Ryzhkov and Yakovlev were the two Politburo members Yeltsin respected the most, and it was 'especially painful' to hear them speak.[427]

Finally, Gorbachev announced the end of the 'debate'. Yeltsin, amazingly, could still summon the will to ask for the floor. Gorbachev obliged.

First, Yeltsin wished to 'correct a few things'. He had never had doubts about perestroika – whether the strategy itself or the Party's political line.[428] As for the 'wave-like' character of popular attitudes towards perestroika, he referred only to the time between January and June 1987: he had been 'in hundreds of work collectives' and knew their mood. Regarding the diminution of popular enthusiasm after the June 1987 Plenum, it was due to the complex nature of the Plenum's economic decisions, which had not been adequately explained to the people. He himself was to blame for it as well.[429] And he had spoken only about his Party organization, Moscow, 'not at all' trying to generalize. All he had meant to say was that they could not count on the people's support going 'always and sharply up', that there might be, perhaps, 'some abatements'.[430]

With respect to Party unity, Yeltsin felt that it would be a 'sacrilege' to try to split the Central Committee. This was something that he categorically denied having had in mind, and he did not accept the accusation.[431] With respect to the 'glorification' of the General Secretary, again he had not tried to 'generalize'. He had in mind only 'two or three comrades' who tended to go overboard with their praise, which, sincere though it might be, was not 'in the interests of the cause'.[432]

Gorbachev, interrupting: Boris Nikolaevich!

Yeltsin: Yes?

Gorbachev: We all know what the cult of personality was. It was a system of certain ideological views, positions, which characterized the regime of implementation of political power, democracy, laws, attitude towards the cadres, people. Are you so illiterate that we have to have a primary school class for you here?

Yeltsin: No, now this is not necessary.

Gorbachev: Nowadays the entire country is gradually moving towards democratization ... The new economic mechanism is connected with the independence of enterprises, with the development of initiative ... And just to think that after all this [you] accuse the Politburo of not drawing conclusions from the past? Hasn't [my] report today touched on this?

Yeltsin: By the way, about the report, I ...

Gorbachev, interrupting: No, not 'by the way'. We even had to postpone the discussion of the report because of your escapade.

Yeltsin: No, I began with the report ...

Voices from the floor, interrupting: He thought only of himself, of his unsatisfied ambitions.

Gorbachev: I think so too. And the Central Committee members understood you that way. Obviously, it is not enough for you that only Moscow is revolving around your persona. What, now you want the Central Committee to be preoccupied with you as well? That we begged you, right? ... It is hard to imagine that one can come to be so vain, so arrogant to put one's personal pride above the interests of the Party, of our cause. And to do such a thing when we are at so critical a stage of perestroika! Just to think that such a discussion has been forced on the Central Committee! ... Now you tell us what is your real attitude to the critique.

Yeltsin: I have already said what my attitude was, politically.

Gorbachev: You tell us, tell us, what is your attitude towards the comments of the comrades from the Central Committee. They have told you a great deal and they must know what you think ...

Yeltsin: Apart from a few expressions, on the whole, I agree with the evaluation. By speaking today I let down the Central Committee and the Moscow Party organization, that was a mistake.

Gorbachev was still not completely satisfied. He asked Yeltsin if he could continue as the Moscow Party chief. (Voices from the floor: 'No, he cannot. We cannot leave him in such a high position.')[433] Yeltsin replied that he would like to repeat his request that he be relieved of his position on the Politburo and within the Moscow Party organization.

Gorbachev concluded with a long soliloquy. At a time when the Party was taking responsibility for the future, Yeltsin 'pushed forward his egotistical questions'. He was in a rush, he was 'missing something', he 'hustles' all the time. 'How irresponsible can one be, how lacking in respect for one's comrades to drag such questions before the Central Committee!'[434] Didn't Comrade Yeltsin know that the Politburo had given pay rises to schoolteachers, doctors and pensioners and found an extra six billion rubles for healthcare? Then how did he come to make such statements? No, his real objective was to thwart what the Party had begun, to find fellow conspirators.[435] Comrade Yeltsin wanted to 'shake' the Party apparatus. That the Central Committee most certainly would not do. He had attempted to 'disorient' the Committee and to 'throw a shadow' over the Politburo and the Secretariat.[436] As for Comrade Ligachev, he was an 'emotional man', a man with a 'fighting character', and he was completely devoted to perestroika. And it was a fiction and 'prattle' concocted by foreign radios to claim that there was no unity in the Politburo. 'They want to set us one against the other, Gorbachev with Ligachev, Yakovlev with Ligachev, and so on.'[437]

Towards the end, the General Secretary suddenly grew mellow. He, for one, would not 'dramatize the situation'.[438] In Lenin's time, there had been debates even sharper than this one, and the Leninist 'spirit' should be 're-created'. He implored the comrades not to 'rush into a decision', but to 'task' the Moscow City Party Committee with examining Comrade Yeltsin's request, 'taking into consideration the exchange of opinions' that had just occurred.[439]

Gorbachev called for a vote. Who is for? All. Against? None. Abstained? None.

It was evening when the Plenum adjourned. But the Party, and Mikhail Sergeevich Gorbachev, were not done with Yeltsin yet.

For the next two weeks, through the October Revolution celebration on 7 November, Yeltsin was the Party's faithful soldier. A walking political corpse, he submitted to the Party discipline and pretended to be alive, so as not to spoil the high Party holiday with any semblance of 'discord'. He attended the receptions. With other Politburo members he mounted the Lenin Mausoleum to review the military parade and the demonstration. He even made a keynote speech at the 'festive meeting' in the Bolshoi – and repeated, defiantly, that although perestroika had achieved 'certain results', the 'main difficulties were still ahead of us'.[440]

Gorbachev's closest aides, Anatoliy Lukyanov and Aleksandr Yakovlev, had been instructed to parry questions from foreign journalists and diplomats about the 'Yeltsin affair'. They were as vague as they could be without looking silly. TASS, reporting Lukyanov's 30 October press conference, 'categorically recommended' to Soviet editors that neither the question that had been asked about Yeltsin nor the answer be published. They were not.[441] With customary skill and speed, the Kremlin was enveloping the 'Yeltsin affair' in the cocoon it used for officially designated non-events: vast, soft, thick and impenetrable.

On 9 November Yeltsin was taken to hospital with 'heart pains' and 'terrible', 'barely manageable' headaches.[442] He was connected to an intravenous machine and 'stuffed' with sedatives. Even his wife was not allowed a visit, so 'bad' did the doctors feel his condition was.[443]

On his third day in the hospital, Gorbachev telephoned. 'Casually, as if he was calling a dacha, not a hospital', he told Yeltsin to 'drop by' his office and then go the Moscow Party Plenum. Yeltsin replied that he could not go anywhere. The doctors would not even let him get out of bed. 'Don't worry,' Gorbachev replied. 'The doctors will help.'[444]

'Pumped' full of tranquillizers, Yeltsin began putting on his clothes. His head was swimming, his legs gave way, his tongue hardly moved. Naina tried to stop him. She 'pleaded, she demanded, she cajoled'.[445] 'How can you do this? You have taken the Hippocratic oath!' she screamed at one of the doctors. 'I have my own Hippocrates,' he answered.[446]

When the Politburo members entered the Gorkom's Hall of Meetings it was filled to capacity. The place was well suited for what was to come: long and narrow, with its starkly bare, whitewashed walls, full of sharp angles, and lit harshly by two massive crystal chandeliers, it looked like a courtroom. On the stage stood an oak-panelled podium and, to the left of it, a long table with three rows of chairs, as if for a jury.[447] It was there that, led by Gorbachev, the Party leaders proceeded in single file by rank, and sat down. Yeltsin was told to sit there too, in the first row.

The audience, Yeltsin recalled, 'stared at the dais scared and obedient, like a rabbit looking at a python'.[448] But, of course, it was he who was the rabbit, facing, for the second time in three weeks, a 'pack ready to tear [him] apart'.[449] Yet this time even the thin veneer of collegial, senatorial civility of the Central Committee was gone. Everything was cruder, smellier, dirtier. To those in the hall that day he was not a wayward colleague but a fallen *nachal'nik*. The slaves had captured the overseer, the inmates had got the warden. This was Gorbachev's equivalent of Ivan the Terrible's favourite punishment, when a nobleman suspected of treason was thrown over the palace wall to the murderous city rabble below.

Still, Gorbachev would not trust sheer bloodlust to accomplish the mission. The eagerness to pull down and tread on yesterday's icon had to be moulded, channelled, sharpened. 'Of course the Plenum had been prepared,' remembered a Gorkom Secretary. 'But the Gorkom Secretaries had nothing to do with the preparation. I did not know the people who prepared the Plenum. They were not from the Gorkom apparat.'[450]

Gorbachev's introductory remarks, too, had been calibrated accordingly. Like the audience before him, they were cruder, angrier and harsher than what he had said three weeks before. Yeltsin's statement had been 'demagogical'.[451] He had attempted to 'subject to doubt' the policy of perestroika and the decisions of the Twenty-Seventh Party Congress. He had tried to 'subvert' the work of the Plenum by using his 'special position'. He had put his personal ambitions above the interests of the Party. It was an 'immoral and irresponsible' act.[452] Yeltsin had furthermore attempted to pass the ruinous consequences of his own errors on to others, first and foremost the Party cadres. The Politburo, of course, had warned Yeltsin not to 'shake' the cadres, but he had not drawn the 'necessary conclusions'.[453] Gorbachev was deliberately dangling raw meat before a hungry tiger. He knew, of course, that most of those who would speak after him were current or former Raikom Secretaries,* whose life Yeltsin had made so difficult, whose positions he had threatened and, in the case of quite a few, taken away.

The first person to speak after Gorbachev had been selected with care. Fedor Kozyrev-Dal had been the First Secretary of the Krasnopresnenskiy Raikom, removed by Yeltsin and appointed to head the Mosagroprom, the agency responsible for bringing fruit and vegetables to the capital's stores. Then, for months, he had been relentlessly castigated by Yeltsin for shoddy food supplies. Yeltsin had 'systematically' rejected

---

* Of the twenty-three speakers, sixteen were Raikom First Secretaries, current (ten) or removed by Yeltsin (six). 'This was a very unusual line-up of speakers,' recalls a former Moscow Party functionary. 'Especially inexplicable, and in violation of all the canons, was the absence of the "representatives of work collectives". Absent was even the obligatory feature of all Plenums: a speech by a "simple worker".' (Oleg Agranyanz, 'Uroki dela El'tsina' ('Lessons of the Yeltsin affair'), *Russkaya Mysl'*, 29 January 1988.)

'sober, correct and truthful' assessments of the situation, Kozyrev-Dal averred. He was a 'political adventurist' with 'elements of Bonapartism'. His speech had not been a 'mistake'. No, it had been a carefully planned 'stab in the back' of the Central Committee calculated for maximum 'political dividend'.[454]

In the ensuing bacchanalia of obloquy, which lasted for over four hours, nothing seemed off-limits. The already established 'stab in the back' became, first, a 'perfidious and treacherous' one, and then an 'enormous crime against the Party'. To work for Yeltsin was 'torture'. His 'comprehensive programmes of development', of which he was so proud, were ill-conceived and useless. He did not like Moscow or Muscovites. His fabled trips around town and visits to stores and factories were nothing but sham, 'flirtation' with the people.[455]

A Secretary of the City Soviet's Executive Committee, Yuriy Prokofiev (a former First Secretary of the Kuybyshevskiy Raikom, fired by Yeltsin), distinguished himself by claiming that Yeltsin had 'surrendered one position after another' during his meeting with Pamyat'. And *Moskovskaya Pravda*, Prokofiev averred, had been replete with 'paeans' to Yeltsin: 'how wonderful he was, how courageous, how sensitive'.[456]

In the bloodthirsty chant, a handful of voices courageously sounded some mildly discordant notes. Those closest to Yeltsin – the Second Secretary Yuriy Belyakov, and Secretaries Yuriy Karabasov and Alla Nizovtseva – mentioned 'the collegiality, open criticism and exchange of views' which Yeltsin had brought to the Buro. The Buro had followed Yeltsin with 'enormous enthusiasm', had admired his 'selfless, hard and creative work', which had had a 'significant' impact on the Moscow Party organization. 'It would be incorrect and dishonest to state', said Nizovtseva, 'that we ever heard from him an incorrect political assessment.'[457]

Witnesses remember Yeltsin looking 'resigned'[458] and 'lost'[459] throughout the *auto-da-fé*. He did not seem 'to react at all' to what was happening around him.[460] Only a few times, when a blow came from someone whom he thought to be especially close to him, Yeltsin lifted his head and looked at the speaker, 'as if in disbelief'.[461]

As the meeting progressed, Gorbachev began to look strangely uncomfortable, even 'embarrassed'.[462] He fidgeted. He grew red in the face. His eyes crisscrossed the hall 'restlessly'.[463] A few times, he shook his head, as if 'struck by the fury and the spite' he had unleashed.[464] By contrast, next to him Egor Ligachev sat with arms crossed on his chest staring 'triumphantly' at the hall below.[465]

The session was coming to an end but could not close just yet.

According to Party ritual, the lesson could not be judged complete and edifying unless it produced something that Yeltsin had stubbornly refused to deliver three weeks before: a *mea culpa*. Now, at long last, the prey's backbone was broken. It could no longer run or resist. The hunt was over.

When Yeltsin finally spoke, it was 'hard' to listen to him.[466] He spoke slowly, with difficulty, in a muffled voice. His lips were bluish.[467] He began with a setpiece used by crushed and contrite Party sinners since the 1920s: he protested loyalty and pleaded guilty.

I only want to tell you, Mikhail Sergeevich, the members of the Politburo, the Central Committee Secretaries, the members of the Gorkom, to all who are here today: I can give you my Party word that I, most certainly, did not have any secret designs and there was no political agenda in my speech. Second, I agree with the critique expressed today.[468]

Yeltsin was 'convinced absolutely of the correctness of the general line of the Party'. Just as 'absolutely' he believed in perestroika. They should have no doubt about it. He said it with 'absolute honesty'. And should any action of his contradict this statement, he should be given the harshest of punishments: expulsion from the Party.

It was 'especially difficult' for him to listen to those Comrades with whom he had worked for two years. Yet they, of course, were right: 'working against me was one of my main traits, ambition [*ambitsiya*], which has been mentioned here today. I have tried to fight it, but without success.'

Like a star defendant of Stalin's show trials in the 1930s, Nikolay Bukharin, Yeltsin attempted to save a shred of dignity amid the abjection of it all. His behaviour was monstrous, yes, he admitted, but there were some mildly mitigating circumstances. Perestroika, for instance, was 'proceeding differently' in various Party organizations and regions of the country. Therefore, nuances in its evaluation were understandable. He blamed 'overwork' for his 'tactical error' and attributed his outburst to desperation: he had begun to 'notice that I was doing not as good a job' as before.[469]

He, furthermore, could not agree that he did not 'like' Moscow, as several of his accusers had argued: 'other things may have gone wrong but, no, I have had time to fall in love with Moscow and have tried to do everything to eliminate somehow the shortcomings' inherited from the previous administration.

The grandparents.

Young Borya at a relative's funeral.

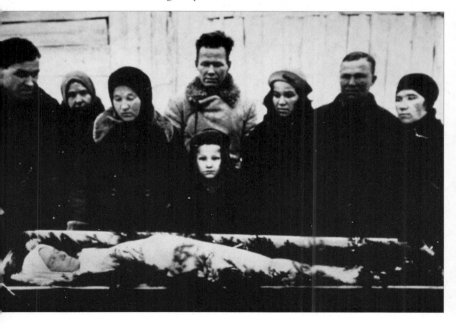

'My eternal protectress': with mother Klavdia Vasilievna Yeltsina.

Klavdia Vasilievna Yeltsina.

The two pillars of love and support: with wife Naina and mother.

The first page of the 'personal sheet for the registration of cadres' filled by Yeltsin on admission to the UPI on 19 August 1949.

Cossack Ermak, the conqueror of Western Siberia (cast pig iron).

Above: The young couple: Boris and Naina.

Below left: After a volleyball game.

Below right: Daughter Tatyana and grandson 'Boris Jr.'

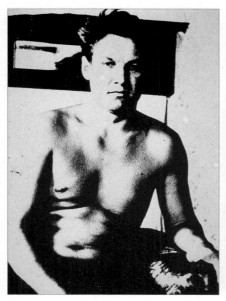

В первичную партийную
организацию треста
Кжгорстрой от
Ельцина Бориса
Николаевича

ЗАЯВЛЕНИЕ

Прошу рассмотреть мое заявление и принять
кандидатом в члены КПСС, т.к. я хочу быть в
активных рядах строителей коммунизма.

I7/2 - 60   Ельцин

/расположении слов в копии соответствует подлиннику/

A copy of Yeltsin's request for admittance to the Communist Party of the Soviet Union, submitted to the Party cell of the Yuzhgorstroy trest, 17 February 1960.

Two of Yeltsin's predecessors in the Sverdlovsk Obkom: (*below left*) Andrey Kirilenko (1955–62) and (*below right*)Yakov Ryabov (1971–6).

The Pervyi speaks:
'Napor, natisk,
davlenie!' (Force,
attack, pressure).

In a lighter moment.

Awarding a medal for excellence in 'socialist labour'.

During Kim Il Sung's visit to Sverdlovsk. To the left of Kim is Anatoliy Mekhrintsev, the Chairman of the Executive Committee of the Sverdlovsk Regional Soviet.

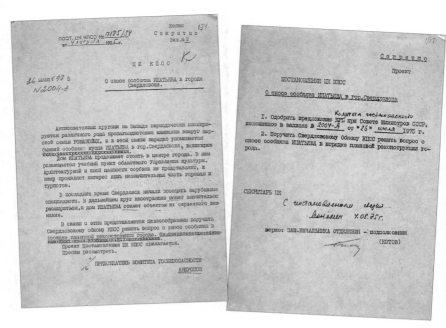

The destruction of the Ipatiev house: Yuriy Andropov's memo of 26 July 1975 and a Central Committee resolution of 4 August 1975.

A farewell photo in the Obkom with all five Secretaries and the heads of all fifteen departments before Yeltsin's departure for Moscow. Sitting, strictly according to rank, are the Secretaries and the heads of the more important of the Obkom's fifteen departments.

But the ending was fully within the canon: reiteration of guilt, re-affirmation of devotion and a call for unity. He had done 'a great deal of damage', and not only to the Moscow Party organization.

I am very guilty before the Moscow Party organization, very guilty before the Gorkom, before the Buro, before all of you and, of course, I am very guilty before Mikhail Sergeevich Gorbachev, whose authority is so high in our country and in the whole world. And, as a communist, I am sure that the Moscow [Party] organization is one with the Central Committee, that it has confidently followed and will follow the Central Committee.[470]

In his concluding speech Gorbachev was mild, generous, almost conciliatory. He said he had been personally upset by Yeltsin's action. He stressed the need for 'criticism, self-criticism and collegiality'. He even 'joined the comrades who mentioned the positive qualities' of Yeltsin's work. But 'you have been badly let down by your vanity, Boris Nikolaevich, very badly'.[471]

Gorbachev chose to end with a kick at Western enemies. 'Our foes call us utopians, they forecast our failure. But they say it because they fear our perestroika . . . After the January (1987) Plenum, after the June Plenum they were seized by panic. And now everything is done to sow doubts among the working class, disbelief among the people, to compromise perestroika. Let them talk! It is their custom to cast aspersions on us. Our road is not easy . . . but we shall stand our ground!'[472]

Everyone stood up and moved towards the exits. Yeltsin sat on the dais, motionless, his head in his hands.[473] The monstrous boulder that he, day and night, had pushed up, up, up the steep slope, through briars, his hands cut and bleeding, his knees in muck, his sides bruised and his heart strained – had finally crushed Sisyphus.

Perestroika, Mark I – which had sought to procure for the people a more comfortable, better-supplied, more decent and freer life through the efforts of a 'cleansed' Party, remade quickly and decisively by enlightened and charismatic leaders with 'human faces' into something more democratic, more responsible, more honest, more open, more attentive and more accessible to the people – was over.

As he was about to leave through the Praesidium door behind the stage, Gorbachev glanced back and saw Yeltsin. He walked back to the table, bent over, put his arm under Yeltsin's, helped him to get up and walked with him to the door.

CHAPTER 5

Antaeus

Y ELTSIN'S EJECTION FROM OLYMPUS WAS timed with a precision that history grants only those for whom it has truly big plans. A year earlier the Soviet Union would have had another comfortably retired 'personal pensioner of all-Union rank' or a new ambassador to Mongolia, Burundi, Nepal or some other nation whose importance to the Soviet Union was less than obvious.* A year later, and the rising din of glasnost, the novelty, the drama, would have muted the breathtaking daring. Most important of all, the nimbus of the martyr would have lost that inimitable, spellbinding shine, which would lighten Yeltsin's path for the next three and a half years.

And, of course, history received a great deal of assistance from the General Secretary himself. For, as 1987 ended and 1988 began, Yeltsin's banishment did not fit Gorbachev's political calendar. By the General Secretary's reckoning, perestroika was about to enter a new, crucial phase. From the 'in-depth investigation' of the social, political and economic legacy of the *ancien régime*; from the 'painstaking development of the concepts'; and from a kind of strategic reconnaissance of 'what should be done and how', it was to move now to the actual implementation of an increasingly radical agenda.[1] And if during the first stage perestroika was largely confined to debates within and directives to the Party, the intelligentsia and the mass media, it was now to 'touch the practical activity of millions of Soviet people'.[2]

There was a great deal of wishful thinking in Gorbachev's solemn declaration of the new era of practical deeds, which was not to materialize for at least another year. His instinct, however, was correct. With the approaching anniversary of the January 1987 proclamation of a political revolution, the decisive moment was nearing when his revolution from above would have to spark the fire below – or risk being put out by its foes in the Party and state bureaucracy. And, for better or worse, by that time Yeltsin had become, for thousands, a weathervane of that revolution. A harsher punishment would have undermined the credibility of the entire design and retarded the arrival of the 'second phase' of perestroika – less than a month before Gorbachev's first visit to the United States.†

* Yeltsin himself repeatedly mentioned Ethiopia as a most likely destination (see, for instance, his interview with *Molodaya Gvardia* (Perm), 4 December, 1988).

† The 'Yeltsin affair' was first mentioned by NBC's anchor Tom Brokaw on 2 December 1987 – and would continue to be brought up in virtually all foreign interviews with Gorbachev for the next year and a half. In an interview before the Washington summit, Brokaw asked Gorbachev if the manner of Yeltsin's dismissal had been an 'echo of Stalinism', 'a mistake'. 'As to what happened with B. N. Yeltsin,' Gorbachev answered,

For the first time in seventy years, quite a few Russians seemed to care about a casualty of the struggle at the top. The shock and anxiety were very much in evidence three days after the Moscow Gorkom Plenum at the headquarters of the radical intelligentsia, the House of Cinema, where the editor of glasnost's flagship, the weekly magazine *Ogonyok*, Vitaliy Korotich, moderated a panel on current affairs. 'Today Yeltsin, tomorrow Gorbachev,' said a playwright, who refused to divulge his last name.[3] 'Comrade Yeltsin was a personality. He fought for glasnost. Why was even Gorbachev afraid of him? Or is 1937 [the height of Stalin's purges] here again?' asked the author of an anonymous note.[4] 'It was Stalin who branded all people who expressed different views enemies,'[5] wrote another nameless member of the audience. Elsewhere, an American reporter spotted tears in the eyes of a woman reading the *Pravda* transcript of the Gorkom session. 'What next?' she asked. 'All his [Yeltsin's] effort for nothing.'[6] 'We're waiting to hear [that he has been] taken out and shot,' said another Muscovite.[7]

A week later, in a demonstration of civic courage unseen since the 1960s, 'several hundred' students of Moscow State University gathered to protest against the ousting of Yeltsin and to demand the publication of his 21 October speech.[8] Several 'informal' groups in Moscow circulated petitions in Yeltsin's defence, in which they asked: 'If Yeltsin cannot say what he thinks, who can?'[9] Soon Gorbachev had to admit that 'the Party's rebuff' to 'ultra-perestroika phraseology' at the October Plenum had been interpreted by 'a segment of the intelligentsia, especially among the young people, as a blow to perestroika'.[10]

Yet, quite apart from the grand strategy of perestroika, Gorbachev's reluctance to deal Yeltsin the *coup de grâce* could have been prompted by purely tactical considerations. To him Yeltsin was what Medusa's head was for Perseus. The General Secretary must have strongly suspected that a time would come when it would be helpful (if not, indeed, necessary) to reach into the bag, produce the firebreathing 'radical' – and scare the Party 'conservatives' into submission: by contrast, Gorbachev would seem moderate, reasonable and worthy of support.

The Medusa tactic dictated that Yeltsin be kept handy in Moscow and in the Central Committee. A week after the *auto-da-fé* in the Gorkom, Yeltsin was appointed 'First Deputy Chairman of the USSR State Construction Committee [Gosstroy] in the rank of a USSR Minister',[11] a post which was created especially for him.[12] When, in a telephone call

---

'listen, it was a normal process for any democracy. I am not going to count to you here how many ministers have been dismissed during Mr Reagan's term ...'

to the hospital, he offered the job to Yeltsin, Gorbachev was blunt about the limits of Yeltsin's new brief. 'I'll never let you into politics again,' he told him.[13]

Gorbachev's decision to keep Yeltsin around had ramifications far beyond the General Secretary's political game. One could, it turned out, openly challenge the Party line – and avoid 'retirement', remain in Moscow and even work as a minister! Until glasnost became rooted in something more formidable, Yeltsin's very ability to go to the office every morning, walk the streets and talk to people was the most dramatic symbol of a new tolerance, a living omen of different times, a bellwether.

Despite the frightful ugliness of his 'civic execution', the unprecedented challenge presented by Yeltsin's physical presence in the capital was a sign of change to many – and a temptation to be braver for some. The latter, from the Party establishment's intellectual and moderately radical wing, apparently decided that, so long as the rebel remained free and unmolested, they too could risk a more sophisticated interpretation of the 'Yeltsin affair' than the one handed down in the Gorkom on 12 November. To be sure, the deviation was cautious, carefully wrapped in a harsh critique of Yeltsin – but it was nevertheless quite real. 'Many . . . think that the former First Secretary of the Moscow Gorkom had no special concept of perestroika,' wrote a Moscow University professor, Gavriil Popov.

> I believe that such a special concept did exist. It was set forth in his speech at the Twenty-Seventh Party Congress. It was implemented by his actions [when he was the First Secretary of the Moscow Party organization] . . . I understand very well that he had to fight the most powerful elite of the braking mechanism . . .* And, this must be stated unequivocally, Yeltsin not only overcame the resistance [of the enemies of perestroika], he dealt them staggering blows, which earned him the support and sympathy of all honest Muscovites.[14]

Characteristically, Sverdlovsk did not bother to measure out and dress up its response with the precision and political acumen of the capital's wily intelligentsia. After they had read the account of the MGK Plenum, the 'most concerned' of Yeltsin's compatriots met in the central square of the city, 'poured out their feelings' and went home.[15] The next day they reconvened and marched to the Obkom, demanding to meet with

---

* 'Braking mechanism' was a fashionable euphemism for the anti-reform forces, those who try to apply the brakes to the process of reform, to slow it down.

the First Secretary, Yeltsin's long-time associate Yuriy Petrov. 'To every-one's surprise', Petrov received the demonstrators, who handed him a protest letter addressed to the Politburo.[16] This was the first mass protest demonstration by ethnic Russians since perestroika began.*

Meanwhile, the *vox populi* busily concocted its own theories of the 'Yeltsin affair'. As many as eight versions of Yeltsin's 'speech' at the October Plenum were soon circulating in Moscow. Some were sold openly for a few rubles, often at Metro entrances.[17] All subsequently proved to be forgeries, but this political folklore reflected the sorest peeves in the Russian popular mind: the war in Afghanistan; Raisa Gorbacheva, whose studied elegance and cheerful omnipresence began to annoy the Russians; and, of course, the glaring disparities between the elite and the people.

'The troops must be withdrawn from Afghanistan,' the 'speech' had Yeltsin saying. 'I think it is precisely this question which [Minister of Foreign Affairs] Comrade Shevardnadze should closely examine. At pre-sent he is dealing with other matters, which I regard as less urgent, and he has been abroad for months.' As regards Mrs Gorbachev, Yeltsin was reported to have said that he was 'forced to ask the Politburo to spare me petty supervision from Raisa Maximovna, her telephone calls, and her almost daily reprimands'.

Not surprisingly, this being the New Year season, the inequities in food supplies were dwelt upon in most infuriating, mouthwatering detail:

It is hard for me to explain to the factory worker why, in the seventieth year of his political power, he is obliged to stand in line for sausages in which there is more starch than meat, while on our table there is sturgeon, caviar and all sorts of delicacies easily acquired from a place which he cannot even approach ... How can I explain that to veterans and to those who fought in the Civil War, the survivors of which can be counted on your fingers? Have you seen the list of foods ordered for the anniversary celebrations? How can I look them in the eye? It was they who laid down their lives to win power and entrusted it to us. Perhaps Comrade Ligachev will whisper the answer to me? I think, comrades, that all these binges, as the people call them, are a legacy from the great period of stagnation. We must put an end to this phenomenon.[18]

---

* Within half a year, Petrov was removed and sent as ambassador to Cuba.

Years later, Yeltsin's former mentor, Yakov Ryabov, would thus define the secret of Yeltsin's political success: 'Yeltsin provided a soundtrack for what people really thought.'[19] It was in the winter of 1987–8 that this 'soundtrack' was first tested – thus far without Yeltsin's participation or even approval.

'A boy being flogged is not so severe as a man having the hiss of the world against him,' Dr Johnson is reported to have said.[20] For Yeltsin, the man in the middle of the mini-storm, the 'hiss' of the world that for many years had been his was deafening.

The banishment from high Party politics felt like 'exile'.[21] He looked around and saw only a 'vacuum'. Those who used to call all the time had suddenly stopped. He was a 'leper':[22] a circle had been drawn around him, and everyone was afraid of crossing the boundary, lest they 'touch him and become infected'.[23] When he ran into them at various meetings and they could not escape, the high functionaries acknowledged his existence by a nod, but he was already a 'political corpse'.[24] 'Everything around was burned, everything inside was burned.'[25] For the next few months, a 'dreadful feeling of doom' never left him.[26]

Yeltsin could not, as before, seek refuge where he had invariably found it in the past: in his work. He did not like his new job: it dealt with 'papers, not people'.[27] Besides, he was somebody's deputy and it was not 'an easy thing for a fifty-seven-year-old . . . to be satisfied with the deputy's role after many years at the helm'.[28] Gone was the heavy shield of overwork, the narcotic exhaustion of power and accomplishment. For the first time in his busy and successful life, Boris Yeltsin was forced to look inward, to take stock. He knew he had to 'climb out',[29] and he began the 'hardest struggle – a struggle with oneself'.[30] He knew that, if he lost this battle, he would lose his life.[31]

In his analysis, Yeltsin remembered and 'sifted through' everything and everybody: his actions, his principles, his every word, his relations with people, 'hundreds' of people – friends, colleagues, neighbours, wife, children and grandchildren.[32] This was a 'constant analysis – day and night, day and night'. He slept three to four hours a night, before the 'thoughts began to stir again'.[33] He was racked by terrible headaches, and at night he barely managed not to scream from pain.[34] His wife and daughters stayed at his bedside. Often his 'nerves gave in', and he would 'take it out on the family'.[35]

Gradually, 'month by month' and with great difficulty,[36] he 'reconquered himself'. Slowly something began to emerge, 'restored', from the charred debris. He regained a measure of trust – but only in 'truly devoted friends': there was no longer room in his soul for 'naive faith'.[37] He began to walk the Moscow streets. He had long forgotten what it felt like to wander around, without bodyguards and aides, like an ordinary Muscovite.[38] The experience proved wonderful and became his 'only joy' during that 'black time'.[39] Strangers' friendly smiles in stores, streets and cinemas 'softened' him. 'Here they are,' he thought, 'ordinary passers-by but with much more nobility than those who used to call themselves friends or those who are in power.'[40] He still slept badly, but the torture of the headaches was gone.

During this and other crises in his life, Yeltsin must have benefited greatly from the support of his wife, Naina. And yet there is no record of her own thoughts and opinions at these times. There are a number of reasons why this should be the case: the natural reserve of the Ural Russians, in contrast with the frequent exuberance of the Muscovites; Naina's taciturn persona; and the political culture censorious of wives' involvement in husbands' business (witness the backlash against Raisa Gorbacheva). Most of all, it seems that (very much unlike Gorbachev) Yeltsin neither sought nor tolerated advice from his wife where his job was concerned. One can only speculate as to her feelings about the enormous pressure on her husband and his response to it. However, her strength and commitment, her graceful acceptance of the daily loneliness and uncertainty created by her husband's relentless drive, are not in question.

In contrast, Yeltsin's behaviour – his letter to Gorbachev and his speech at the October 21 Plenum, as well as his actions immediately prior to the Plenum – speaks to a variety of motives: frustration with Ligachev, whom he had come to view as the main obstacle to intra-Party perestroika; or the obvious (to him) and painful gap between the policies he felt were needed and the ones emanating from the Politburo. Most of all, there was a lack of 'revolutionary change' in society and the economy which he had come to expect, which he loudly promised and of which, willingly, he became a symbol. To Yeltsin, the absence of a marked change for the better in people's daily lives was far more than an unsuccessful policy. It was, quite clearly, a personal defeat: for the first time in his life he could not advance his agenda, for the first time his plan was subverted, for the first time he had failed.

That the forces arrayed against Perestroika Mark I were well beyond his (or any one person's) abilities to overcome was not, to Yeltsin, an excuse or even a consolation. The dread of personal failure tormented him, and his Plenum outburst was the product of the anxiety accumulated month after frustrating month. But it was also a consciously taken last stand: he would not accept defeat quietly, be made a speechless scapegoat and retired 'for reasons of health', like innumerable Party hacks before him. He might have heard the hoofbeat of Bismarck's horse of history, decided to follow his instinct in divining the country's mood – and rolled the dice.

Yeltsin's arrival at his new job in Gosstroy on 8 January 1988 was a grandiose affair: he was still, even if pro forma, a candidate member of the Politburo. For a few minutes, all movement along Pushkinskaya Street was stopped to make way for Yeltsin's black ZIL limousine and the cars of the security detail.[41] Four bodyguards crowded the small reception room in front of Yeltsin's new office.*

Yeltsin entered the room: in an elegant dark-blue suit, starched white shirt and smart tie.[42] After a tour of his new office, he invited his new aide in and asked him to sit down. 'I am used to being frank with my aides,' Yeltsin told Lev Sukhanov, who would be his assistant and gatekeeper for the next three years. 'Sometimes, I have trusted them with things that one does not always tell one's wife about. I am totally sincere with my aides and, therefore, expect the same from them. I do not tolerate flattery, do not like hypocrisy and hate cowardice.'[43] Sukhanov replied that he was quite happy with these 'rules'. Yeltsin said, 'All right, if we are in agreement . . . we shall work together.'[44] Although Sukhanov thought that he and Yeltsin had 'accepted each other', he did not feel much 'at ease' after the interview.[45]

Yeltsin soon left. For the next two months, his doctors allowed him to work only four hours a day.[46] Yet even this regime, laughably light by his normal standards, seemed more demanding than he could handle at the time. Through January and February, Yeltsin would come to work in the morning after sleepless nights looking 'already tired'.[47] (Soon he would be taken to the hospital again with 'heart trouble'. He began working full-time only at the beginning of April.)

The contaminated 'circle' followed Yeltsin the 'leper' to his new job. It was, his aide remembers, an ' "ice age" of alienation'.[48] Even Yeltsin's staff was being avoided by other assistants.[49] Only rarely did this

---

* The next day a department head from the 'Kremlin hospital' arrived accompanied by a dietician. They tasted the fare in the Gosstroy's cafeteria, were not satisfied and made necessary recommendations. Both the desk in Yeltsin's office and the long table for staff meetings were fitted with hidden alarm buttons. (Sukhanov, *Tri goda s El'tsinym* ('Three years with Yeltsin'), pp. 37–8.)

treatment turn into open hostility: for the most part the quarantine around him and his subordinates was enforced by 'psychological nuances and small strokes'.[50] But, of course, Yeltsin, who 'absorbed everything like a sponge', was deeply hurt.[51]

On 18 February, he came to work looking especially 'awful'.[52] That morning, at the Central Committee Plenum, he was 'relieved of the duties of a candidate member of the Politburo'.[53] Following the loss of the Moscow post, the removal from the Politburo was automatic. Still, his assistant recalled, 'how upset he was!'[54] That day Yeltsin went home without bodyguards in an old Chaika, not the shining ZIL with bullet-proof windows.

Although expected, the blow visibly stunned Yeltsin.[55] 'It was as if two Yeltsins lived side by side: one was a high Party functionary used to power and accolades and [who was] lost when all that was gone,' remembered his aide. 'The other Yeltsin was a rebel, rejecting, or rather beginning to reject, the rules of the game forced on him. These two Yeltsins were struggling and it would not be an exaggeration to say that the struggle was cruel and the victory far from quick.'[56]

The shadow of this struggle lay thick on Yeltsin's public persona. Gone was the confidence, the flamboyance, the poise, the studiously cultivated devil-may-care manner with which he had formerly orchestrated his encounters with the press. In his first interview, which was never to reach the Russian reader (*Moskovskie Novosti* could not summon the nerve to publish it in Russian or English, only in German), he was reluctant, cryptic, even furtive.[57] When he heard of the unauthorized versions of his speech circulating in Moscow, he looked 'very much surprised and worried'.[58] He feigned indignation at the 'falsehoods' yet refused to divulge the content of the original: 'The Central Committee decided not to publish the speeches given at the Plenum. As a Central Committee member, I am not permitted to break that rule.'[59] And in general, Yeltsin 'did not want to talk about what I said half a year ago'. 'Maybe I erred in some things,' he added. 'However, I spoke honestly and I said what I was feeling and what I considered the right thing . . .'[60]

He was just as reticent when foreign reporters mobbed him and Naina as they were leaving the official May Day festivities at Red Square. For the first time since 1986, he was seated on the wooden benches – not standing on the Mausoleum with the rest of the Politburo. Asked why his interview in *Moskovskie Novosti* had never made it into the Russian edition, Yeltsin replied impatiently: 'It still hasn't been decided if they will publish in Moscow and in Russian.'[61] When an American reporter quizzed him about alleged disagreements between Gorbachev and Liga-chev, Yeltsin 'laughed a long, deep laugh' and then said, 'Of course, you know this is not for me to say.'[62] To a small group of well-wishers who surrounded him, he said only, 'Thank you, thank you, it is good to see you, very good, happy holiday.' As the Yeltsins turned to leave the square, someone spotted Naina wipe away a tear.[63]

Gradually Yeltsin began to discover that the 'island' on which he thought he had been marooned was, after all, a 'peninsula' with a narrow path leading to the mainland.[64] That path was first blazed by his fellow townsmen. Not knowing Yeltsin's Moscow address, dozens of Sverd-lovsk's citizens still attempted to convey messages of support to their disgraced countryman. Soon all Sverdlovsk post offices displayed a sign declaring that 'Mail for B. N. Yeltsin will not be forwarded.'[65] Yet, somehow, the letters kept coming to Yeltsin's apartment – hundreds of them.[66] Unable to respond to and, later, even to open all the mail when Yeltsin was in and out of the hospital, Naina and the daughters began to store the letters and telegrams in a large wooden crate, which eventu-ally was filled to the brim. The crate became one of the 'most treasured mementoes' of the Yeltsin family.[67]

Letters began to be delivered to his office as well and soon turned into a 'steady stream'.[68] That spring, for the first time, Yeltsin met face to face with a member of his emergent national constituency. Ilya Ivanovich Malashenko, a lawyer and a retired Army lieutenant-colonel, called the office and demanded to 'see Boris Nikolaevich in person'[69] in order to shake his hand. This was the sole objective of his 350-kilometre trip from Bryansk. Their meeting lasted only a few minutes. Malashenko said 'something to this effect: "Boris Nikolaevich, I am completely on your side and there are many people like me in Bryansk. You hold on, and we shall not leave you in the lurch."'[70]

This was Yeltsin's first glimpse of a pattern that would become an indispensable ingredient of all of his triumphs. Given to despondency, self-doubt and despair, he 'received a huge charge of optimism from dealing with people'.[71] A fledgling Antaeus of new Soviet politics, almost crushed to death, was revived by a touch of Mother Earth. Soon, for the first time in almost half a year, he began cautiously talking to his faithful assistant, Lev Sukhanov, about the future.[72]

That future was inseparable from the approaching Nineteenth Party Conference: the second milestone, after January 1987, of Gorbachev's revolution from above. The format itself was symbolic: designed to be discussion fora in between Party Congresses, Conferences were convened frequently in the early years of Soviet power but became very rare from the late 1930s when Stalin stamped out the last vestiges of 'Party democracy'. A Conference was thus another step towards the revival of 'Lenin's norms' in intra-Party dialogue.

During the previous thirteen months, Gorbachev had worked relentlessly to bring about the Conference. The General Secretary's persistence was justified by the urgency of the goals he hoped the gathering would achieve: to bolster his mandate for an increasingly radical transformation of the Soviet state; to appeal to the Party rank and file over the heads of the functionaries; and, most of all, to provide a setting (one of the last, as it turned out, and certainly the last of such scale and grandeur) for a long-awaited breakthrough in the Party's internal democratization. The Conference was to herald the arrival of the 'second stage' of perestroika, the stage of 'practical deeds', and Gorbachev, again, wished to begin with the Party itself.

In those four days in June and July 1988, the General Secretary was to take stock of how much the Party had learned in the eighteen months since the January 1987 Plenum, which had declared an end to the apparat's absolute control over the mass media, public opinion and political activity. As Gorbachev put it in his opening speech, the key question which the Conference was to answer was 'whether or not the Party will be able to play its role of political vanguard at a new stage of the development of Soviet society'.[73]

The answer became clear before long and was less than encouraging. Even before the formal voting and the final wording of the resolutions, the majority in the Kremlin's Palace of Congress displayed little enthusiasm for voluntary democratization or power-sharing. Such was the anticipated resistance that Gorbachev himself had to chair the commission drafting the central 'Resolution on democratization of the Soviet society and reform of the political system'.[74] In the end, as a Russian observer noted at the time, 'even such a tough, principled dialogue as occurred at the Conference was largely drowned in the diluted formulations of its resolutions'.[75]

Opened on 28 June and adjourned, a day later than scheduled, on the evening of 1 July, the Conference confirmed the essential accuracy of the analysis which had informed the January 1987 strategy: left to its own devices the Party was unlikely to undertake any meaningful internal democratization. Its modernization and 'liberalization' (and thus acceptance of reform) could result only from outside pressure. 'We shall not be able to defeat this monster, bureaucratism, if we do not engage the entire society . . .', Gorbachev told the Conference. 'One resolution, another – this is nothing. The entire political system must be remade.'[76]

Hence Gorbachev's renewed and much reinvigorated commitment to his January 1987 strategy: without surrendering either the Party's primacy in the 'historically formed one-party system'[77] or its 'leading role' in perestroika (which was to unfold strictly 'within the boundaries of the socialist choice'), the Party was to be transformed through political competition without the overwhelming advantage of total control over the mass media, the state or the economy. In pursuit of this objective, glasnost was to usher in 'pluralism of opinions', 'free competition of minds'[78] and the 'rejection of spiritual monopoly'.[79] Legal reform was to secure 'a socialist law-abiding state', whose 'key feature [would be] the primacy and dominance of law that reflected the will of the people'.[80] And the elimination of the Party's minute control of the economy would create a 'clear demarcation between Party and state organs'.[81] Finally there would be 'absolutely no diktat' with respect to the trade unions, the Komsomol and other public organizations.[82]

The most remarkable policy proposal that Gorbachev attempted to implement was directly subjecting the Party leadership to trial by public opinion: local Party bosses were to stand for elections for a new post of 'chairman' of a Soviet. Behind the soothing protestations ('lending a hand to the Soviets', 'preserve the guiding role of the Party'),[83] Gorbachev's intent was in line with his grand strategy: to let society do to the Party what the Party refused to do for itself. 'He [a Party Secretary] would be under the control of the people,' Gorbachev explained to the understandably wary audience. 'If a Soviet does not elect him, then his fate as a Party Secretary, too, will be, most likely, sealed. If the delegates of the people would not trust him to be Chairman of a Soviet, he can hardly remain a Party Secretary either. That, you see, means strengthening the people's control over the Party Committee through the mechanism of the Soviets.'[84] The delegates' resistance to this plank caused Gorbachev to issue an unprecedented threat: without the item's adoption, he could not vote for the resolution as a whole. In his final appeal, he even claimed not to be able to understand the delegates' 'bewilderment, suspicion and apprehension'.[85] In the end, the still overwhelming authority of his office prevailed, and the proposal was passed. (The Party clerisy would deal with the setback in its customary way: the measure was implemented only sporadically, never enforced and eventually abandoned.)

In one of the rare successes of the internal Party reform, the Conference agreed to pass an amendment to Party statutes that would limit occupants of Party posts to two consecutive five-year terms. But the opposition to the proposal to elect the Party Secretaries (from district to General) by secret ballot of all delegates at conferences or congresses (and not at closed meetings of the Party committees as was the practice) was insurmountable. Determined not to lose control over the right to select the leadership, the apparat dealt the measure a mortal blow, voting it down: 4,841 to 145.[86]

Exasperated by the Party's inability to lead democratization, Gorbachev took his strategy of bypassing the Party to the riskiest and most fateful turn. Late in the evening, in the final moments of the Conference, after the debate had been formally closed, all resolutions adopted and everyone was about to stand up, clap and sing 'The Internationale', the General Secretary took a small piece of paper out of his pocket and read another resolution, the shortest of all. It called for the 'organization of elections to and the convocation of the Congress of People's Deputies, at which new organs of state power shall be formed'.[87] This was clearly a last-minute improvisation, as neither the mechanism of the election nor the prerogatives of the Congress were mentioned by Gorbachev. He knew he needed to replace the obsequious and toothless Supreme Soviet with a new national parliament that would bit by bit begin to take power away from the conservative party apparatus. He was content that he had found the formula and left the details for later. Tired, overwhelmed and surprised, the delegates unanimously voted 'aye', Gorbachev closed the Conference, and the revolution from above began in earnest.

For both participants and observers, who were too close to the unfolding spectacle to see its true magnitude, it was not the sweep of Gorbachev's stratagems or the cleverness of his tactical manoeuvring that made the Conference an event that for four days and nights held the entire nation spellbound. It was, rather, a spontaneous political debate before the television cameras. Gorbachev was certainly right when, summing up, he declared that the country had seen 'nothing of this kind in six decades'.[88] Almost audible was the cracking of a shell and the sound of fresh air rushing into the dark and ritual-bound chambers of a Byzantine court. In four days, Russia leapfrogged centuries of political time.

The proceedings were televised for two hours every evening and the transcripts published verbatim in the national newspapers. In Moscow, Russia's most politicized city, people formed long queues at kiosks to get a morning newspaper and then read hungrily as they walked away.[89] 'I could hardly believe what I was seeing,' a passer-by told an American reporter. 'Real history.'[90] 'It's a revolution, I guess,' said another, a visitor to Moscow, a man who had spent his life working 'on pig farms and assembly lines'.[91] A delegate to the Conference swore that one day he would tell his grandchildren 'that I was there, that I was part of the revolution'.[92]

The tone was set by Gorbachev's opening oration. The best speech of his entire career, before or after 28 June 1988, this four-hour, impassioned plea for a 'truly humane' and 'democratic' one-party social-ism was delivered with a directness and earnestness that would remain unmatched. In this socialism, there would be 'full-blooded and un-equivocal democracy'; 'glasnost in things big and small'; 'brotherhood and camaraderie in relationships [between people]'; and 'respect for hard work and talent'.[93] Gorbachev insisted on the 'vitality' of Marxism–Leninism, which had supplied a 'scientific basis for the possibility of building a society of social justice, a civilization of free and equal people'.[94]

Since such one-party state 'socialism' had not existed before (and also because it was tactically necessary to instil the entire enterprise with utmost urgency), Gorbachev sought to make this vision of socialism vivid by contrasting it with the present Soviet reality. It is here that the conceptual shift occurred and an official glasnost reached its furthermost limit of candour. For, instead of extolling, as usual, a system somewhat tired, in places seriously worn out and frayed but, on the whole, sound and praiseworthy, the General Secretary offered a blunt and detailed indictment of a giant pathology that had advanced inexorably and grown in malignancy in all but a few of the seventy years of the Soviet state's existence. Never before had the word 'crisis' – economic, social and spiritual – been used to describe the country's condition.

The political regime created by the October Revolution had been 'subjected to serious deformations', which had resulted in the 'total power of Stalin and his group, the wave of repression and lawlessness'.[95] 'Democratic principles' had been proclaimed from the 'podiums', while in fact 'authoritarianism' had reigned. There had been a great deal of 'empty talk' about 'people's power' and 'democratic institutions' but, in reality, there had been 'violation of socialist norms' and alienation of the people from 'socialized property' and governance.[96]

The assessment of the economy was particularly astonishing in its frankness and sophistication. Gone was the snake oil of 'acceleration'. Instead, with precision and clarity, Gorbachev analysed the structural problems of the Soviet economic system and summarized the agenda of radical economic reform. Artificial prices, which did not reflect cost, were the key obstacle to 'normal economic relations',[97] preventing the saturation of the market with food, goods and services. Below-cost prices for raw materials and fuel made an efficient economy simply impossible. The Soviet Union was caught in a vicious circle of 'production for production's sake', with millions of tonnes of steel, cement or coal incapable of satisfying the people's real needs.[98] Artificially low prices for some products and just as 'unjustifiably' high ones for others undermined incentives for production. Huge state subsidies ('tens of billions of rubles') for housing, transportation and food products – especially meat, milk and bread – handicapped production, encouraged waste and were responsible for a growing budget deficit and inflation.

Having introduced the words 'budget deficit' and 'inflation' into the vocabulary of the Soviet leadership's public discourse, Gorbachev went on to announce that for many years state expenditure had surpassed income. Measures to improve financial health were just as necessary as price reform and would have to include balancing the budget and bringing order to the system of credits and banking.

The perspicacity of Gorbachev's economic analysis contrasted dramatically with the toothlessness of the measures adopted at the Conference. The brief segment on the economy in the 'Resolution on the tasks of the deepening of perestroika' reflected none of the gravity of Gorbachev's diagnosis. Price reform, state subsidies and the budget deficit were not mentioned at all. This retreat on the economic front at the Conference was the first of many symptoms of a fundamental and growing asymmetry in the political cost of perestroika's twin components: democratization and glasnost on the one hand, and economic liberalization on the other. Political change had begun to attract the ardent support of millions. Even among the Party aristocracy, totalitarian control and the distribution of amenities according to political loyalty had few committed defenders. Economic reform, on the other hand, advocated by a small number of Moscow and Leningrad intellectuals and fledgling entrepreneurs whose businesses did not depend on stealing from the state, aroused little enthusiasm. It would, after all, have resulted in rising prices and a drastic reduction of state subsidies, with an inevitable drop in living standards. The Conference thus marked another watershed: originally designed as a means to an end, political reform became an end in itself.

Nonetheless, propelled by the radical tone of the General Secretary's address, eager delegates took the Conference beyond even the most *outré* scenario imaginable. Some Politburo members, sitting a few metres from the podium, were told to retire.* Another delegate insisted that the Soviet people knew more about President Ronald Reagan's income or the budget of the British royal family than about the privileges of the Party elite.[99] The Chairman of the State Committee on Environmental Protection told the gathering that in 102 Soviet cities (total population fifty million) concentration of hazardous substances was ten times above the safety level.[100]

'Where is perestroika?' asked a steelworker from the Urals. 'The stores are just as badly supplied with food as before. There was no meat before, and no meat now. Popular consumption goods have disappeared.'[101] Nowhere in the world were there as many Ministers as in the Soviet Union, said the Director of a giant machine-tool plant, but the business was 'awful'.[102] Look, he continued, 'the entire system of production everywhere in our country is on a primitive level, a level of natural economy ... It is considered normal that it takes fifteen or twenty years to build a plant, without anyone committing suicide or going mad.'[103]

And, through it all, a novel, or almost forgotten, sentiment swept Russia: pride in its leader. These four summer days were to become Gorbachev's most glorious hour, unsurpassed before or after. As he guided and cajoled the Conference – reprimanding the intolerant, delivering mini-lectures on the rules of free debate, restraining the hot-headed, interrupting and bantering (albeit awkwardly) with the speakers – the General Secretary was the national hero.

For a luminous instant, the still awesome power of his office blended with genuine moral authority, each strengthening the other. And certain of his traits, which before long would begin to seem anachronistic, ridiculous or annoying – his unshakable optimism, incessant pontification, feeble attempts at humour – either appeared endearing or were overlooked at this intoxicating moment. A benign, liberalizing autocracy was still shrouded in fear and mystery, and these two strongest

---

* 'Those who have actively implemented the policy of stagnation cannot work any longer in the central Party or state organs. One must be responsible for everything, personally responsible,' said Vladimir Melnikov, First Secretary of the Komi Regional Committee. Gorbachev interrupted him: 'Do you have any concrete suggestions? We sit here [in the Praesidium] and don't know if you are talking about me, or him, or what?' Melnikov responded: 'This would apply first of all to Comrade [Politburo member Mikhail] Solomentsev, to Comrades [Chairman of the Supreme Soviet Andrey] Gromyko, [Editor-in-Chief of *Pravda* Viktor] Afanasiev, [Director of the Institute of USA and Canada Georgiy] Arbatov and some others.' (*Pravda*, 1 July 1988.)

ingredients of fascination had not yet been worn thin by familiarity. Still untarnished, the liberator's crown Gorbachev wore shone forth clear and bright: a guarantor of a freer and more decent life.

It was in this advantageous setting that Yeltsin was to execute his scheme.

'But is he lucky?' Napoleon used to ask before promoting a general. Like every successful public figure, Yeltsin was lucky. Magnified by good fortune in the crucial summer of 1988, the courage of his design would yield dividends beyond his most extravagant expectations. His luck, like that of most victorious politicians, stemmed largely from two circumstances: his timing and the vulnerabilities of his opponents. Both were in evidence even before the conference opened.

By the end of May, Yeltsin's confidence and strength were repaired enough to pick up the gauntlet again. In a lengthy interview with Peter Snow of BBC Television, he restated (far more coherently and pointedly than seven months before) the key points of his Plenum speech. It was a deft performance: carefully worded, steering clear of traps* yet deliberately forceful at well-chosen junctures. The Party was 'lagging behind' perestroika in the style and methods of its work.[104] Democratization in the Party was not developing. Gorbachev could have acted more decisively in renewing 'the top rung' of the Party and the government, and speeding up the process of perestroika.[105] The past three years had brought no basic changes in people's lives. Should the next three years be just as futile, people's faith in perestroika would be undermined. The most important task was to improve the food supply, consumer goods and services.[106]

The privileges enjoyed by a certain section of the leadership could not 'help the morale of everyone else'. People were unhappy about them. 'If there was a shortage of anything in our society – and that is the case – then every member of society should experience that shortage to an equal degree.'[107] Egor Ligachev's 'authoritarian' style was 'unacceptable'. Since the internal party machinery was Ligachev's responsibility, he was to blame for the slow democratization of the Party. Yeltsin linked Ligachev with the defence of nomenklatura privileges, claiming that he was 'one of the main opponents of social justice'.[108] This was

---

* *Interviewer*: 'There are reports that at that meeting on 21 October you were critical of Raisa Gorbacheva. Do you think the way that she conducts herself is wholly in line with how you think the First Lady should behave?' *Yeltsin*: 'I think it would not be entirely ethical to answer that question.'

an adroit thrust, which, repeated at every opportunity, would eventually prove fatal to Yeltsin's chief nemesis.

Towards the middle of the interview, Yeltsin detonated another carefully placed mine. When the interviewer asked what he thought was his most awkward question ('Let me be quite blunt with you. Would you like to see Mr Ligachev removed from his position, removed from the centre of power, because he is, in your judgment, opposed to reform?'), Yeltsin answered simply: 'Yes.'[109]

Knowing full well that the interview would be carefully studied at the very top, he showed no repentance. His mistake had lain not in the substance of his October speech but in its timing: 'immediately before the seventieth anniversary of the October Revolution . . . such a critical speech, particularly criticizing the leaders and perestroika and so on – that was not good timing . . .'[110] He was not an 'ultra-reformist, ultra-radical'. He was 'simply in favour of energetic action for perestroika, energetic, fast and effective action which would bring results'. Results he repeated, had so far been 'very, very insignificant'.[111] The 'charges' against him at the Gorkom Plenum had been 'abstract, even demagogic'. And, in any case, those who had spoken at the Gorkom Plenum had been 'in effect selected', the people whose 'toes' he had stepped on.

In the end Yeltsin spoke frankly about his present condition. He had been 'knocked out' but they 'did not manage to count me out'. He was not a 'political corpse'. Still, his condition was 'serious', less in a physical sense than in a psychological one. He was 'not entirely satisfied' with his new job and felt 'a bit pushed aside from active politics'.[112]

Ordinarily, such a public show of defiance would have been the last straw, resulting in expulsion from the Central Committee. At the very least, Yeltsin would have been barred from attending the Conference. Luckily, the leadership's response to yet another of Yeltsin's 'provocations' was constrained by the strategic political calendar, which mattered far more than any contretemps caused by a crushed functionary who stubbornly refused to acknowledge that his career was over. The publicity attracted by another harsh act of retribution would have interfered with Gorbachev's pre-Conference manoeuvring, spoiling the carefully cultivated atmosphere of openness and free discussion. At just that time, the General Secretary was entertaining President Reagan on his first and only visit to Moscow. The Soviet political tradition, in which an improvement in relations with America invariably coincided with a temporary 'liberalization' of Soviet domestic politics, was in evidence again, precluding, at least for the moment, a tougher response to Yeltsin's challenge.

Instead, the Kremlin's reaction was confined to Gorbachev's casual comment in a nationally televised press conference held after the US–Soviet summit. 'We must ask Comrade Yeltsin in the Central Committee', Gorbachev said, 'what he meant and what he is trying to achieve.'[113] There was never a question of Ligachev's resignation, added the General Secretary. It would have been difficult to imagine a better way to remind the country of Yeltsin's existence and to arouse the people's interest.

There was, to be sure, an attempt to keep Yeltsin from attending the Conference. But, in the absence of an unambiguous signal from the top, the effort proved half-hearted and no match for sudden pressure from below.* The best the apparat could do was to humiliate Yeltsin by forcing him to seek, at the last minute, a mandate from the Party organization of the tiny Autonomous Republic of Karelia in the Soviet northwest. Yeltsin travelled to Karelia's capital, Petrozavodsk, was 'warmly' met and was duly elected to the Conference.[114]

Yeltsin worked on his Conference speech throughout June. In the morning he would call in his assistant and 'test' on him yet another handwritten version composed the night before.[115] The aide was shocked by what he heard and 'began to be afraid' for his daring boss.[116] Yeltsin dismissed his suggestions for toning the address down. By the time the Conference opened on 28 June, he had gone through nine drafts.

On the first day of the Conference, he sent a note to the Praesidium requesting the floor. For the next three mornings he was in the office at seven and had the secretary type up more drafts – updated 'to take into consideration the previous day's speeches'.[117]

The last morning of the Conference had come with no word on his request. After a mid-morning break, Gorbachev presented the agenda for the rest of the day: in the two hours left before the lunch break he could give the floor to eight people and, at the most, to four more after lunch. After that the Conference would start voting on the resolutions.[118] Then Gorbachev sketched a list of those who absolutely must be given the floor: four First Secretaries of Union Republics; a 'representative' from the trade unions; a delegate from 'women's councils' and a kolkhoz chairman.[119]

Yeltsin, who was sitting in the top balcony at the back of the hall

---

* The 15,000 Party members at the giant Uralmash plant in Sverdlovsk voted to nominate Yeltsin their delegate to the Conference. The Sverdlovsk Obkom, for the first time in its history, hesitated between pleasing Moscow and accommodating local political protest as the workers threatened to strike. Eventually, the Obkom said no.

with other members of the Karelian delegation, turned to his comrades and asked their permission to go down. 'I must storm the podium!' he told them.[120] He was given leave.

KGB agents guarded the entrance at ground level. Yeltsin asked them to open the door. They did.[121] He took the red mandate of a delegate out of his pocket, raised it above his head and began the long walk to the stage down the thick red carpet, which absorbed the sound of his heavy tread.

When Yeltsin suddenly appeared in the middle of the hall, a witness recalls, 'everyone watched only him, no one listened to whoever was speaking from the podium'.[122] Yeltsin, the card in his outstretched hand, approached the stage and walked up the steps to the Praesidium. Then, looking directly at Gorbachev, he said: 'I demand the floor – or let the Conference decide by a vote.'[123] Visibly irritated, Gorbachev and Mikhail Solomentsev, who was chairing the session, could be heard hushing him in unison: 'Go and sit down! Just wait a minute! Cool it, will you?'[124] Yeltsin perched himself on the edge of a seat in the front row.

As speakers took their turns at the podium, the Praesidium was in the throes of indecision. After the Politburo members had whispered among themselves, Yeltsin saw Gorbachev giving instructions to the head of the Central Committee's General Department. Soon a Central Committee staffer came to Yeltsin's seat. 'Please go to the Room of the Praesidium [behind the stage]. Someone will talk to you.' 'Who?' Yeltsin asked. 'I don't know.' 'In that case,' Yeltsin said, 'I am staying right here.'[125] The Praesidium's envoy disappeared.

A few minutes later, another messenger arrived: 'Someone from the leadership will meet with you [behind the stage].'[126] 'All right,' Yeltsin said, 'I'll be making my way [out of the hall] but I'll be watching to see if anyone from the Praesidium gets up to leave.'

Yeltsin stopped a few metres before the exit and looked back. Every member of the Praesidium was still in his place. 'Boris Nikolaevich, don't leave the hall!' whispered journalists sitting at the very edge of the auditorium.[127] He knew that himself: once he had left, he would not be let back in.

Another ambassador walked up to him. Mikhail Sergeevich, he told Yeltsin, promised to give him the floor but he would have to go back to his delegation, on the balcony. Yeltsin said no, walked back along the first row of seats and sat at the very centre on the aisle, directly opposite Gorbachev.

Meanwhile, the First Secretary of the Rostov Obkom, Boris Volodin, was finishing his speech, in which he had chastised a Soviet magazine for publishing an article by a recent émigré 'who had deserted his Motherland'.[128] There was applause at the end.

Then Solomentsev stood up to announce the next speaker: 'Comrade Yeltsin, member of the Central Committee of the CPSU, First Deputy Chairman of the Gosstroy of the USSR, Minister of the USSR.'

The beginning of the second most important speech of his life had been, in effect, written for Yeltsin by others. The day before, referring to Gorbachev's post-summit press conference, a delegate from Moscow had said:

> You, Mikhail Sergeevich, said that you would be interested to know what Comrade Yeltsin had told foreign journalists. We, rank-and-file members, too, would be interested to know. We are in no way questioning the decision on Yeltsin by the Central Committee, but he is well known in the Party by his whole-hearted support for perestroika. His incoherent statement at the [12 November 1987] Plenum of the Moscow Gorkom did not clarify his position. Why hasn't he given interviews to our newspapers? We would like to hear his explanations at the Conference.[129]

This was Yeltsin's luck again, an ideal opening for a counterstroke, which could be interpreted now not as the expression of a personal grievance that only distracted the delegates from the 'historic' Conference, but as a response to a comrade's inquiry. With the businesslike refrain, 'Otvechayu. All right, here's the answer,' Yeltsin set a tone that from the first moment made the nation catch its breath.

Why had he given interviews to Western television networks and not to the Soviet press? 'All right,' said Yeltsin, 'here is the answer.'[130] He had been interviewed by *Moskovskie Novosti* but nothing was ever published. He had spoken with the magazine *Ogonyok* for two hours. This was a month and a half ago, and the interview still had not been published. According to its editor Comrade Korotich, publication had not been 'allowed'.*

---

* The most daring of Soviet magazines, *Ogonyok* advanced glasnost by breaking taboos in almost every issue. A sceptical Yeltsin agreed to be interviewed only after he had been assured that the magazine did not need clearance from anyone, that Korotich 'took all the responsibility' and would publish the material without showing it to anyone. When the interview was ready for publication, Yeltsin was told that Korotich had gone to the Central Committee, shown it the interview and been prohibited from publishing it. (Yeltsin, *Ispoved'*, p. 159.)

Why had he been 'incoherent' at the Moscow Gorkom Plenum? '*Otvechayu:*' he had been very sick, bed-ridden, incapable of getting up. An hour and a half before the Plenum, the doctors had 'pumped' him full of medications. As a result, he could sit at the Plenum but 'could not feel anything', much less talk coherently.[131]

As to the 'next question', the interviews with Western television had not been his idea. The State Committee on Radio and Television had been arranging pre-Conference interviews of the leadership with foreign journalists and had asked him to respond to some requests. There had been fifteen of these altogether, and Yeltsin had said he had time for no more than three. When he sensed that questions were in any way 'damaging to the prestige of the state, the Party', he had 'rebuffed them resolutely'.

He had been asked by the interviewers if he thought that 'perestroika would progress faster if there were another person in Comrade Ligachev's place'. Yeltsin paused – and the 5,000 in the hall, including Ligachev, and the millions watching on television paused with him. 'I said "Yes."'

After the interviews had been aired, he was ordered to see the Chairman of the Party Control Committee, Comrade Solomentsev, who 'demanded explanations'. Although 'expressing his indignation about the subject' of the investigation, Yeltsin answered all Solomentsev's questions and handed him a tape of the interview. 'The attempt to find me in violation of Party rules has failed. I consider myself entirely innocent.'[132] The entire affair, Yeltsin concluded ominously, reminded one of 'the shadow of the recent Soviet past'.

The introduction was over. He was assured of the attention of a country ravenous for the truth. And now, Yeltsin said, 'for the speech'.

The themes of the speech were largely the same as those of his BBC interview. But to most inside and outside the Palace of Congresses, who did not listen to foreign broadcasts, the point of reference was not the interview but the 21 October 1987 address, known to tens of thousands by rumour and to several hundred in the audience first-hand. The memory of that buried but never forgotten oration heightened the expectations both of Yeltsin's open detractors and of his secret supporters.

Neither was disappointed. The echo of 21 October was unrepentantly loud: the Party was 'falling behind perestroika' in internal democratization and openness; social justice remained among the most painful of the still unsolved problems; and perestroika's strategy and priorities were deeply flawed.[133]

This time the charges were well substantiated and the reasoning was both weightier and sharper than eight months before. The General Secretary had stated firmly that there were no 'zones above criticism'. Not true. There was a 'plank' above which attempts at criticism were met with shouts of 'Don't touch!' As a result, even members of the Central Committee were afraid of expressing their personal opinion, if it differed from the leadership's report. That deformed the Party. And as long as the practice continued of everyone raising their hands in favour, the leadership would remain outside the people's control. Pluralism of opinions ought to be a norm in the Party. Opinions different from that of the majority would only strengthen the Party.[134]

Luxury villas, dachas and sanatoriums were built on 'such a scale that one felt ashamed'. Small wonder, then, that big Party functionaries were up to their necks in corruption, that they had lost 'decency, moral purity, modesty'.[135] The rot, which had enveloped the 'upper layers' during the Brezhnev period, had spread to many regions and went deeper than many suspected. In Moscow, for instance, 'the mafia, most definitely, existed'.[136]

Over the past seventy years the Party had failed to solve the key problems: to feed and clothe the people, and provide services. And in the past three years of perestroika there had been no real results, much less revolutionary transformations. People were simply not interested in what they would get in the year 2000. 'People's faith [in perestroika] could diminish any minute. So long as everyone remains under the spell of words, the situation is saved. But in the future we risk losing hold of the steering wheel and of political stability.'[137]

This time, Yeltsin followed the description of pathologies with a list of treatments, which rendered this speech more radical than its celebrated prototype. 'The Party is for the people,' and the people 'must know everything the Party is doing'. The Politburo and the Secretariat must give periodic accounts of their activity, provide biographical information of the top leaders, tell about their work and its results. The 'moral health' of the Party's leadership ought to be evident to everyone, not remain a 'mystery'.

The key task was to create a mechanism that would serve as a guarantee against the cult of personality. Yeltsin proposed restricting occupants of Party offices to two consecutive terms and establishing an age limit of sixty-five years for officeholders. When the General Secretary left office, most in his Politburo and the Central Committee should leave as well.[138]

Personal responsibility ought to be strictly enforced. Why was stagnation blamed only on Brezhnev? What of others, who had sat in the Politburo for ten, fifteen and twenty years – and continued to sit there? Where were they? Why were they silent? They must be asked why the Party and the country had been driven to the present state – and then expelled from the Politburo![139]

As regards social justice, if there was something in short supply in the country, the shortage 'must be felt by everyone without exception'. Let salaries be the only measure of different contributions to society. The country should, finally, eliminate all those food 'rations' for the 'hungry nomenklatura', eliminate divisions between upper and lower strata of society and banish the word 'special' from its vocabulary. The lack of resolution in this area 'aroused indignation, lowered the Party's prestige and was harmful to the progress of perestroika'.

Why was the Party Control Committee so afraid of holding top leaders of certain Republics and of certain regions responsible for bribe-taking, for 'the millions of rubles' worth of damage to the country'? Why was Comrade Solomentsev, so eager to investigate petty deviations from Party 'norms,' suddenly so timid in dealing with 'millionaire bribe-takers'?

Instead of proclaiming grandiose projects for the next millennium, the Party ought to set concrete goals for two or three years and during that time solve one or two problems to improve the people's well-being. Everything but everything must be concentrated on achieving real improvements in people's welfare: 'material resources, science, people's energy'. Success in this strategy would mean increasing the people's trust, strengthening their conviction that perestroika was irreversible. Once this was achieved, all other problems would be solved more quickly.

Rehearsed so many times, the speech ended just as the buzzer went off, marking the end of his fifteen minutes. Yeltsin paused and looked at the audience. 'Comrades delegates, [there is] a touchy subject.' He stopped for what seemed a very long time. Only when the clamour in the hall became audible did he continue: 'I wish only to address to you the question of my personal political rehabilitation after the October Plenum of the Central Committee. But if you think that the time is up, then this is all.'

He paused again. He pretended to collect his papers and then looked as if he were about to leave. But he was not leaving. The transcript recorded 'noise in the hall'.[140] Then everyone heard Gorbachev's voice: 'Boris Nikolaevich, speak! They are asking you to. [Applause] I think, Comrades, let's take the veil of mystery from the Yeltsin affair. Let Boris

Nikolaevich say what he considers necessary. And if we find that we too need to say something, we, too, will be able to say it later. Boris Nikolaevich, the floor is yours.'[141]

So Yeltsin spoke again:

Comrades delegates! Rehabilitation in fifty years has by now become habitual and has a salutary effect on society.* But I am asking for political rehabilitation while I am still alive. I consider this a question of principle, appropriate in the light of socialist pluralism of opinions, freedom of criticism, tolerance towards the opponent, declared in [Gorbachev's] report and in the speeches.

You know that my speech at the October Plenum was found to be 'politically mistaken'. But the issues brought up in it have [since] been raised by the press, the Party members. And in these days [of the Conference] virtually all these issues have been raised from this very podium, both in the report and in speeches. I think the only mistake I made in that speech was the inopportune timing of it: just before the seventieth anniversary in October.

Apparently, we all need to master the rules of political discussion, to tolerate an opponent's opinion, as did V. I. Lenin, not to rush to affix labels and to consider [opponents] heretics.

Comrades delegates! The speeches at the Conference, and my own speech, fully reflected the issues which I touched on at the October Plenum of the Central Committee. I am acutely unhappy about what happened and ask the Conference to repeal the decision of the Plenum. If you find it possible to repeal the decision, you will rehabilitate [me] in front of the Party members. And this would be not just a personal [favour] but fully in the spirit of perestroika, would be democratic and, it seems to me, would help [perestroika] by adding to people's trust.

Yes, the renewal of society is proceeding with difficulties. But there are positive changes, if only small ones, and life itself makes us follow only this route.

Yeltsin stepped down from the podium and walked back up to his balcony. There was applause. Immediately, Solomentsev announced a lunch break.

* Yeltsin is referring to the defendants in the show trials of 1936–8, including Grigoriy Zinoviev, Lev Kamenev and Nikolay Bukharin, who were exonerated a few months earlier.

Yeltsin's fellow delegates from Karelia tried to show support – some by smiles, others by shaking his hand. 'Excited and tense',[142] Yeltsin rushed outside and was instantly surrounded by journalists and Conference delegates and answered 'a great many' questions.

Having, apparently, learned little from experience, he was confident that the worst was over and that his was the last word.

To assess properly the fateful effect of the speech, it is important to put it in the context of the day. By the fourth day of this extraordinary gathering, what had horrified his audience eight months previously and shocked his aide even a few weeks before had lost a great deal of its subversive novelty. Leaving aside, of course, his plea for rehabilitation (which implied that the Central Committee and the General Secretary had been wrong!), a number of those who had spoken before him had touched on the same themes and, in some cases, had surpassed Yeltsin in both the robustness of their critique and the reformist sweep of their proposals.

As for the Party's democratization, the two-term limitation on the occupancy of Party posts had been included in the 'Theses' of the Central Committee, published before the Conference.[143] During the Conference, a delegate had proposed making public the structure of the Central Committee, including the areas of personal responsibility of individual Politburo members and the Central Committee Secretaries.[144] The latter should give 'periodic accounts' of their work not just to the Central Committee but to the 'primary cells' as well.[145]

And where Yeltsin chose to refer diplomatically to an 'insufficient understanding' of the controversial proposal to combine local Party posts with the Chairmanship of the Soviet, a number of delegates declared their opposition to the measure because of the well-founded fear that it would strengthen the Party's unaccountable rule over society. 'My first thought', said a worker from Siberia, 'was non-acceptance.'[146] An Academician from Moscow concurred, arguing that the arrangement raised serious questions and demanding to know how it could possibly accord with the declared goal of demarcation of functions between the Party and the Soviets.[147]

Similarly, with respect to another sharply debated issue – how to elect the Party leadership – Yeltsin's was far from the most radical position. Whereas one of the delegates pleaded with Gorbachev and the Conference to make sure that the Secretaries, especially the General Secretary, were elected 'only at a Conference, at a Congress' by a secret vote, because 'this was the position in which a man could do either so much good or just as much evil to the people',[148] Yeltsin sided with the conservative majority, which voted to uphold the existing practice of election by the Buros and committees. (He also found it expedient to reject 'a two-party system, suggested by some'.)[149]

The strategy of perestroika, too, had been criticized for 'the absence of determination in their implementation', and the 'desire to solve everything at once', which had led to 'obvious mistakes'.[150] The suggested cure was to set firm priorities and deadlines, identify those responsible and implement 'forcefully'.[151]

The snail's pace of economic reform was deplored in many speeches, including Gorbachev's opening oration. On the opening day of the Conference, the leading economist Leonid Abalkin announced that 'there [had] been no radical breakthrough in the economy and it [had] not emerged from a state of stagnation', with the national income growing more slowly than during the previous Five-Year Plan.[152]

Gorbachev himself underscored the political centrality of a real improvement in people's lives. Raising the ordinary people's standard of living was now the 'ultimate goal' of the reform.[153] To that effect, the economy would be 'socially reorientated' to procure quality food products, popular consumption goods of the required diversity and high quality, housing and healthcare. The day before Yeltsin spoke, a steelworker from the South Ural city of Novotroitsk had argued that, since perestroika 'could not solve all problems at the same time', all efforts should be concentrated on food supplies, so that 'people could see a real result [from perestroika] in the very near future'.[154]

Even the territory long staked out by Yeltsin – social justice – had been intruded on. There should be only one form of reward, the salary, argued a delegate.[155] If everyone 'came to the same counter', that would be an 'additional stimulus' to make sure that the ruble could actually buy things.[156]*

But it is only a weak politician whose sway does not extend beyond the summary of his or her speeches. In the case of Yeltsin's Conference address, the whole proved far greater than the mere sum of its parts. For one thing, there was the density and directness of critical fire unmatched by any other speaker. Taken separately, many of the things

---

* Still more radical were assessments and policy proposals that formed the Conference's intellectual context. In the preceding months, a barrage of no-holds-barred analyses, sweeping condemnations and radical prescriptions had been unloosed by Moscow newspapers and magazines, especially the weeklies *Moskovskie Novosti* and *Literaturnaya Gazeta* and the monthly 'thick' journals *Znamya* and *Noviy Mir*.

Yeltsin said were not terribly new or even very daring, yet no one else combined so many of them in a single oration.

More importantly, in preparing and delivering the speech, Yeltsin discovered a formula which, replicated hundreds of times in the months and years that followed, would become a cornerstone of his phenomenal success. He borrowed ideas from the radical establishment intellectuals and expressed them in the language of the ordinary Russian* with bluntness, vigour and the occasional demagogical sharpening of a populist opposition politician, whose credibility was greatly helped by his supremely Russian appearance and demeanour.

Further spicing the stew (and making it irresistibly enticing) was the typical Yeltsin mix of direct personal confrontation and candour. As he scoured his foes (each named in turn), shared his thoughts and doubts or confessed his errors, he forged that most precious illusion of masterful public speaking: a sense of being taken into his confidence.

The final two ingredients that multiplied the weight of Yeltsin's words were perhaps the most effective. He had gone all the way up, lived and worked behind the still impenetrable fog of the Party Olympus; he was one of the feared, resented, mysterious *them* – and he had given it all up, and suffered for it, and become one of *us* (well, almost).†

The halo of a martyr (*muchenik*) proved especially valuable. It is here

---

* When Yeltsin mispronounced the newly fashionable word 'pluralism', the mistake was found irrelevant, perhaps even endearing, by most Russian television viewers.

The Moscow *beau monde* was, of course, an entirely different matter. Perhaps nowhere in the world does there exist a more snobbish intelligentsia than in Moscow, where a wrong accent or (God forbid) a grammatical *faux pas* is a perfectly valid reason for excommunication. Although Gorbachev spoke better Russian than any Soviet ruler since Lenin – without the heavy Georgian accent of Stalin or the Ukrainian one of Khrushchev and Brezhnev – he, too, did not escape the linguistic trap. His fall from grace would start a year later, during the televised proceedings of the First Congress of People's Deputies, when he repeatedly used the incorrect third personal plural of the verb *klast'* ('to put down'): saying *lozhut*, instead of *kladut*.

Yeltsin's turn would come soon enough, but, for now, his linguistic transgressions were overlooked because the intelligentsia liked so much what he had to say.

† In the months that followed, Yeltsin himself would often and freely acknowledge mystery and martyrdom as key elements of his success. 'If I had been criticized less, or if at least the mass media had not considered me taboo,' he said in an interview, 'and if the people had at least known what I said at the October 1987 Central Committee session, there would not have been such a great fuss surrounding the name of Yeltsin' (Hungarian television, 20 February 1989 (FBIS, 21 February 1989, p. 79)).

that Yeltsin's luck in the opponents he had was especially conspicuous and timely. For, instead of discussing and adopting the resolutions as intended, the Conference began the final afternoon of its work with what Gorbachev called the 'Yeltsin affair'.

As the country watched – disgusted, scared, fascinated – six out of the eleven afternoon speakers castigated Yeltsin with varying degrees of viciousness. The prize, without a doubt, went to the Director of a Moscow plant, who accused Yeltsin of causing the suicide of a fired Raikom First Secretary: 'Let Comrade Yeltsin carry this death in his heart for ever!' he concluded.[157] (In fact, the man had leaped to his death months after he left the Raikom and was by then safely ensconced in the leadership of a ministry.) A young Raikom Secretary from Moscow declared that the objective of Yeltsin's speech at the Conference was to 'drive a wedge' between the 'Party and the working class, between the Party and the intelligentsia', as well as between the Conference and its Praesidium. 'But in this, Comrade Yeltsin, you will not succeed! This shall not pass!'[158]

There was something comical in the speakers' competition to please the Praesidium, as they strained to uncover yet another, still more egregious transgression of the unrepentant sinner. The First Secretary of the Estonian Communist Party, Vayno Vyalyas, recalled that when he had been ambassador to Nicaragua, Yeltsin had arrived there at the head of the delegation of the Supreme Soviet (he had indeed visited Nicaragua in March 1987). He had been fêted, he had been honoured. The head of the Sandinistas, Daniel Ortega, himself drove him around 'from morning till night'. And how did Yeltsin repay this fervent hospitality? Speaking at a Nicaraguan textile factory, Yeltsin (apparently pointing to a child) said: 'What's wrong with you, don't you want to work? Why are you walking around without trousers?' Yeltsin's tactlessness was 'painful', Vyalyas continued. 'Painful because, indeed, there are children in Nicaragua that do not have clothes. No clothes at all.'[159] (While in all likelihood a canard, to those familiar with Yeltsin's gruff and blunt ways the story did ring true.)

The heaviest cannon in this retaliatory bombardment was Egor Ligachev, who delivered a long diatribe which would be remembered mostly for the apocryphal phrase 'Boris, ty ne prav!' ('Boris, you are wrong!').*

Gorbachev himself succumbed to the temptation and devoted over

---

* Judging by several videotapes of Ligachev's speech, he actually said, 'Boris, you have not reached the right conclusions.' Embarrassed by the rudeness of the *ty* ('thou') address, unacceptable in Russian official language, the Central Committee editors replaced *ty*

half of his concluding speech at what he called a 'historic Conference' to censuring Yeltsin – albeit in considerably milder language than his predecessors. Forgetting that most of what Yeltsin had said had been part of many other speeches (including his own), Gorbachev again responded to Yeltsin's contention that perestroika had been launched without sufficient analysis and that no revolutionary changes had been achieved so far. He reviewed Yeltsin's record in Moscow and even read from the still secret protocol of the October Plenum to prove that Yeltsin had not been fired but had resigned of his accord.[160]

It was indicative of the progress made in the previous eight months that this time Yeltsin had a defender who was not afraid to speak out and who was given an opportunity to do so. The unlikely advocate was Vladimir Volkov, an engineer and a Secretary of the Party organization of the Kalinin machine-tool plant in Sverdlovsk. He decided to speak, he said, because his 'heart would have been heavy' if Ligachev's word were to be final.[161] 'Yes, Yeltsin is a very difficult man,' said Volkov. 'He is a tough man, perhaps even cruel.* But, as a leader of the Sverdlovsk Party organization, he has done a lot to [strengthen] the prestige of the Party functionary and the Party. He was a man whose words did not deviate from his deeds. That is why even today he is very highly regarded by the ordinary people . . .'[162]

'We are not familiar with Yeltsin's speech at the October Plenum,' continued Volkov, 'and thus it would be difficult for us to decide on his rehabilitation . . . But, still, it is not right to affix labels. In his speech [at the Conference], Comrade Yeltsin raised most of the same issues

with *on* ('he') in the published version of the speech. No matter! The apocryphal *ty ne prav* made too juicy a target for Yeltsin's supporters and too tempting a marketing logo for fledgling entrepreneurs, who within days flooded Russia with buttons and T-shirts bearing the words *Boris, ty prav!* ('Boris, you are right!'), *Boris, ty prav'!* ('Boris, you rule!'), *Skazhi im, Boris* ('Tell 'em, Boris') and *Egor, ty ne prav!* ('Egor, you are wrong!').
* This 'cruel' puzzled virtually everyone. Asked afterwards to explain Volkov's epithet, Yeltsin was at a loss. 'A worker whom you berated for laziness and irresponsibility could call you "tough" or even "a villain" . . . When I was the Secretary of the Moscow Party organization, I worked from 8 in the morning to midnight. And I demanded total dedication from others. Many could not manage, some began to grumble and accuse me of cruelty. And, in that sense, I can admit to being "tough" or "overly exacting", but not "cruel". For an irresponsible staffer, a perfectly normal insistence on quality work sometimes looks like an extraordinary "cruelty"' (Aleksandr Ol'bik, 'Sotsial'naya spravedlivost' – kompas perestroiki' (Social justice is the guiding star of perestroika), Yeltsin's interview with *Sovetskaya Molodezh* (Riga), 4 August 1988).

that had been discussed by those who spoke before him . . . Yeltsin has done a great deal for the Sverdlovsk region, where even today his prestige is very high.'[163]*

(Lest we overestimate the sense of security in criticism and the implied immunity from prosecution for public dissent in Gorbachev's Soviet Union in July 1988, Volkov's later testimony ought to be remembered: 'Before I raised my hand, I quickly ran down the consequences. I decided: they are not going to arrest me. At worst they'll fire me, but that did not scare me: experienced engineers are needed everywhere . . .')[164]

Volkov's defence only emphasized the unanimity of official disapprobation. Its effect was predictable, given the traditional Russian affinity for the 'insulted and the injured' and the no less strong mistrust of authority. The embarrassment which the Yeltsin affair caused the Kremlin had become that most delicious feast that is enjoyed, usually only for brief moments of political transition: a still forbidden fruit that could be savoured publicly in safe defiance of the authorities. For the second time in less than a year, some dark inner necessity compelled Yeltsin to engage in a painful and seemingly disastrous tangle with his all-powerful opponents – and in both cases short-term defeats turned into strategic victories.

On that day in July 1988, Yeltsin was also true to the bellwether role destined for him by Russian history. In the previous year and a half, Gorbachev had quietly unlocked the gate to the forbidden city of national politics and lowered the bridge over the moat that separated the polity and society. He made it possible not only to point out tactical shortcomings but to engage the Party in public debate over key policies. Yet someone had to walk the shaky plank over the moat, still full of very hungry crocodiles, push open the gate and step over the threshold. In the critical months between June 1988 and spring 1989 no other national figure was more closely identified with this task than Boris Yeltsin. When, in the autumn of 1988, a popular joke suggested measuring glasnost in *yelt*'s, it reflected the people's perception of his mission.

---

* Sverdlovsk's solidarity with its famous son had its limits. Shortly after Volkov finished, Gorbachev read out a note from the head of the Sverdlovsk delegation, the First Secretary of the Sverdlovsk Obkom, Leonid Bobykin: 'The delegation of the Sverdlovsk region wholeheartedly supports the decision on Comrade Yeltsin by the October (1987) Plenum of the Central Committee. Comrade Volkov has not been authorized by anyone to speak for the delegation. His speech has been roundly repudiated by the delegation.' (*XIX Vsesoyuznaya Konferentsiya*, vol. 2, p. 105.)

Yeltsin personified a critical portent in another respect as well. He confronted Gorbachev with a painful choice – to crack down as the General Secretary had done in October and November (and further diminish hopes for democratization of the Party) or to show new tolerance, which would allow a dissenter to take on the Central Committee, attack the Party's second-in-command and remain a minister and a Central Committee member. When the General Secretary chose the latter; when a disgraced but unrepentant functionary was allowed to restate his views; when, instead of letting the majority in the Politburo, the Central Committee and in the audience finish what was started the previous autumn and have Yeltsin's head, Gorbachev engaged in debate with him; when he sought to explain and justify, instead of assert, the correctness of the Central Committee's decision – a precedent was created that soon proved fatal to the rule of a party which was incapable of accommodating 'deviations'.

All of this, of course, became obvious only in retrospect. The victory was far from apparent to Yeltsin at the time. He sat 'motionless'[165] through a third ritual denunciation in eight months. It was 'physical and moral torture'.[166] The Karelians, who only two hours before had seemed so supportive, were 'afraid even to look'[167] at him. He was taken to a first-aid station inside the Palace, where a nurse injected him with a stimulant so that he could last to the end of the Conference.

Yeltsin sank back into despondency. He was in a 'torpor'.[168] 'I thought it was all over,' he remembered a year later. 'The [1 July afternoon] session of the Conference was broadcast to the entire country. I will never be able to wash off the dirt they poured on me. I felt that they were pleased, they knocked me out, they won. I was seized by apathy. I did not want to struggle, to explain – nothing, just to forget it all, to be left alone.'[169]

He told friends that the Conference was the apparat's 'fourth victory' (after the October, November and February Plenums of the Central Committee and the Gorkom).[170] After all, he had asked the Party for his rehabilitation, and the Party had turned him down. And, in July 1988 in the Soviet Union, there seemed to be no politics outside the Party.

Yet, almost immediately, that assumption was challenged by an avalanche of letters and telegrams – not just from Sverdlovsk but 'from all over the country': by the thousand, by the sackful.[171] This was, Yeltsin remembered, a somewhat 'fantastic' show of support, unreal in its scale. He was offered honey, medicinal grasses, jams and massages.[172] He was told 'not to pay attention' to what his opponents said, because 'no one believed them anyway'.[173] There were 'so many kind, warm letters from totally unknown people' that he could not believe his eyes and kept asking himself, 'whence all of this? why? what for?'[174]

Boris Yeltsin, a disgraced apparatchik, suddenly found himself a banner of still unfocused but swelling protest, a national figure, fitted almost overnight with a loose but rapidly growing national constituency. Before the year was out, aided by the post-Conference resonance, he would be given two more chances to remind Russia of himself. He would use both well. For the second time that year, Mother Earth saved Antaeus. 'People sent their luminous letters . . .', Yeltsin wrote, 'they stretched their hands out to me, so that I could lean on them and get up. And I managed to go on.'[175]

The first opportunity presented itself during a post-Conference holiday in Yurmala, on the Latvian coast of the Baltic Sea. As Yeltsin swam, played badminton and watched the Davis Cup teams play tennis[176] (a sport he was about to learn and fall in love with), he was approached by a reporter from the local newspaper, *Yurmala*. A wary Naina was opposed to any interviews: they had enough trouble with the Solomentsev Committee already.[177] Yeltsin interrogated the reporter, was satisfied about the seriousness of his intentions, and agreed to talk. After months of enforced silence, after *Moskovskie Novosti* and *Ogonyok* had failed him, Yeltsin decided to try to break through to his compatriots in this notoriously rebellious province, where glasnost had already gone much further than in the metropole.

Yeltsin emerged from the interview a loyal Party member who had submitted to Party discipline, which prohibited the disclosure of his Plenum speech, who was in thrall to socialism and to Lenin's and Gorbachev's one-party version of perestroika, and who was aware of 'ideological foes'. There had been no change in his prescriptions for perestroika's success: raising the standard of living and enforcing social justice. Yet, reflecting either the radicalization of his views or a change in his sense of the permissible, his barbs were sharper, his thrusts more vigorous and his critique more sweeping. For the first time, he intimated that the very attractiveness of socialism had, of late, 'dimmed'.[178] 'We have oppressed the human spirit,' Yeltsin continued. 'People found themselves pressed down by the weight of fraudulent moral standards, directives that are impossible to argue with, resolutions. We have trained the people to be unanimous in suppressing dissent [*edinoudushenie*], not united in aspirations [*edinodushie*].'[179]

Social justice in the Soviet Union was exemplified by 'a luxury villa for a *nachal'nik* [being built] next to a *barak*'.[180] When delicacies were home-delivered for the leader of Agroprom, the giant super-agency in charge of agriculture, he was not likely to work hard on the Food Programme. 'For him,' Yeltsin added sarcastically, 'the [food] problem has long been solved.'[181]

Yeltsin used the interview to refute the charges levelled against him at the Conference and to put a human face on the caricature painted by his detractors. When he had been in charge of Moscow, the frequency of his 'contacts with the working class' was something to be proud of: he had visited 200 enterprises in two years. Yes, he did travel by public transport. And he did refuse the food rations: his wife stood in queues at regular stores. Towards the end of the interview he declared that 'emotion', even 'passion', with the excess of which he had been charged, did not hinder Party work but was very much needed there. He again cited Lenin as an example.[182]

Within weeks of the interview, copies of the until then obscure *Yurmala* and *Sovetskaya Molodezh* (Riga), in which the interview was published as well, 'spread around the huge empire with the speed of an express train'.[183] In the end, 140 newspapers, large and small, reprinted the interview, which was also reproduced in hundreds of thousands[184] of photocopies. 'The blockade of silence has been broken,' Yeltsin told the man who interviewed him in Yurmala. 'But this is still not a victory . . .'[185]

Victory became closer two months later, when the students of the Highest Komsomol School, the finishing college for future Komsomol leaders, dared do something that no Party organization would at the time: they invited Yeltsin to speak. Despite the vacillation of the Dean, telephone calls from the Central Committee ordering the School 'to do whatever was necessary not to allow Yeltsin to speak',[186] and even a personal plea from the First Secretary of the national Komsomol organization,[187] the students held firm.

The invitation came in a telephone call, which found Yeltsin in his Gosstroy office looking like the sinecured functionary that he was, wearing reading glasses and a grey woollen pullover.[188] The news 'completely transformed' him.[189] There was a sparkle in his eyes, he began pacing the office saying to Sukhanov, 'Well, what do you think, Lev? Can we do it?'[190] This was, of course, a rhetorical question. Buoyed up by the reception of his Yurmala interview, not for the world would he have passed over this chance: his first *bain de foule* in almost a year.

He met with the students on 12 November, a year to the day since the MGK *auto-da-fé*. It was a masterful, even bravura, performance. On his feet at the podium for five hours without a break, before a capacity audience of 1,500, a suddenly revived Yeltsin answered 320 questions[191] – 'each sharper than the one before'.[192] His assistant compared the show to 'playing at the net' in volleyball: question–answer, question–answer, over the net and back.[193] The audience and the speaker were 'so tense, so electrified' that Yeltsin's aide grew 'scared' for his boss's health.[194]

As usual refreshed, charged, even intoxicated by the sight of a crowd hanging on his every word, Yeltsin was more confident, more radical in analysis and recommendations, and more forceful in defence of his Party record than ever before. Soviet socialism was now labelled 'state authoritarian' and 'state bureaucratic'.[195] Of all the objectives of socialism, the Soviet Union had achieved 'only one': socialization of property. Perestroika's motto of 'renewing socialism' was, therefore, incorrect: one can 'renew' only what existed before.[196]

The monopoly on political power belonged to the Party bureaucracy, the apparat, to which the people had been taught to sacrifice both personal comforts and dignity. First, the people had been forced to sacrifice the countryside, he said, referring to the collectivization of 1929–34. Next, they had been deprived of 'mores and culture'. Lastly, they had been denied the opportunity to think for themselves: 'to set for themselves their tasks and then fulfil them themselves'.[197]

'What have we really achieved in seventy years of Soviet power?' Yeltsin asked. Peasants had seen their land and farm animals taken away, and had been driven from their land to the 'furthest corners'.[198] Workers' salaries had been kept consistently low. People had stopped responding to slogans and could no longer be swayed by appeals.[199]

For the first time, borrowing from the more radical of the perestroika economists, Yeltsin's blueprint for reform had coherence and depth beyond the brightly coloured scheme of more food and consumer goods, and better services. In this analysis, 'economic self-regulation', which was to supplant the 'state administrative' direction of the economy, could take root only when the supply of goods and services exceeded the demand.[200]

Chronic shortages, as well as the national debt and the inflation it engendered, were a function of profligate, incessant and mindless industrial expansion. Yeltsin proposed to cut the latter by 40 per cent and remove the fifty to sixty billion rubles thereby saved from circulation altogether.[201] The material and labour resources thus freed were to be channelled into wholesale trade, which enterprises would conduct via direct contracts with one another, bypassing the ministries. Industrial enterprises should be allowed to 'quit' ministries and exist on their own.[202]

His stance on the two issues raised in the Conference speech had evolved in a similarly stern fashion: the existing 'hierarchy of distribution of amenities' (that is, the 'privileges') was now labelled 'immoral'; and, in contrast to the ambiguity of his Conference speech, he felt confident enough now to call the merging of the Party Secretaryships with the Chairmanship of local Soviets a 'most egregious error'.[203]

Still smarting from the epithet 'cruel', he sought to soften the image of Yeltsin the dictator by explaining his Moscow *modus operandi*. Once a month the Buro had met to discuss questions that the members wished to put to one another. The most difficult part had been to 'teach people to disagree openly with the First Secretary', but little by little that too began to 'move along'.[204] Many Raikom First Secretaries, 'being pure apparatchiks, had lost the habit of working with people. My exacting standards they perceived as cruelty.'[205] Perhaps, Yeltsin conceded, he ought to have been a little more flexible.

Answering the often repeated complaint that he had 'bowed out' by resigning from the Politburo, instead of 'fighting for perestroika' there, Yeltsin said: 'It makes sense to fight only when there is a chance of winning. For that reason there are different weight categories in sports. When [fighters are from] two different weight categories, the outcome is preordained.'[206] He did not agree that his request for resignation was 'cowardice'. If he wanted to live quietly, why would he be meeting with them or giving interviews to foreign journalists, instead of 'sitting peacefully in Gosstroy' and 'living to be ninety', like his mother?[207]

There were definite limits to Yeltsin's iconoclasm. He affirmed his allegiance to Gorbachev's concept of perestroika as a means of reviving the system: the rejection of 'bureaucratic' distortions of the socialist idea did not mean the rejection of the idea itself. Freed from their 'humiliating secondary role', the people would serve that idea 'with a still greater success'.[208]

As in Yurmala, Yeltsin refused to divulge his speech at the October Plenum: since the decision had been made not to publish, he could not bring himself to violate Party discipline. He had never considered himself 'in opposition' to Gorbachev. On the contrary, he had always supported Gorbachev's initiatives. 'Frankly, I consider Mikhail Sergeevich the true leader of the Party and a like-minded person.'[209] And he could 'imagine no higher ideal' than Lenin.[210]

This loyalty, however, did not prevent Yeltsin from using the occasion to announce, unambiguously and unapologetically, his political resurrection. When, towards the end, he was served a deceptively gentle and inviting question ('Among the people you are no less popular than

Gorbachev. Could you lead the Party and the state?'), Yeltsin's return was startling in its matter-of-factness: 'When we have multi-candidate elections, I could participate, like anyone else.'[211]

He concluded the long session (only sketched here) on a decidedly belligerent note, which in the next four months would be sounded over and over again in speeches and interviews: 'The people now have a chance to win a struggle for dignity that was taken away from them long ago. We must get rid of indifference and fear, which have oppressed us until now. We must get rid of the inbred wariness of political struggle. This struggle must become a normal fact of life.'[212]

As usual, Yeltsin was supremely lucky in his timing. By the time the transcripts of the session reached hundreds of thousands of eager readers from Kursk to Perm to Dushanbe (mainly via Komsomol newspapers), the Soviet Union was poised for the first competitive election in its history: to the Congress of People's Deputies.

Like perestroika itself – designed as a one-party democracy directed from above – these elections were a strange hybrid: a political centaur, reasonably transparent and democratic above the shoulders, but showing a great deal of Soviet hoof and tail in the nether areas. One-third of the 2,250 People's Deputies were to be appointed by 'social organizations' rather than by general election. Of these, the Party was given the largest bloc of 100 seats.* It was followed by the Komsomol, the Union

---

* When, on 10 January 1989, the Central Committee nominated the candidates for the Party's list, there were exactly 100 names for 100 seats. Each 'candidate' was voted for separately and, as Gorbachev read the names, all the members in the hall raised their hands in unison, one hundred times. 'One minister did not even bother to lower his arm,' a smiling Yeltsin recalled later. 'He just held it aloft all the time.' (Boris Yeltsin, an interview in Sverdlovsk, 30 January 1989. Video Archive of the Museum of Youth Movements.) Yeltsin's was the only dissenting vote: he voted against Ligachev's 'nomination'. Accustomed to unanimity, Gorbachev at first failed to understand Yeltsin's gesture. 'In favour? All,' droned the General Secretary. 'Against? None.' Finally interpreting the meaning of Yeltsin's raised hand, he said: 'Abstained? One.' Yeltsin did not argue. (*Ibid.*)

Having cracked his own shell of fear a year before, Yeltsin looked at once disgusted and amused as he regaled his interviewers with a story of an unnamed Soviet marshal who, after the Plenum, congratulated Yeltsin on his 'against' vote and told him that he too had wanted to vote against Ligachev. 'Then why didn't you?' Yeltsin asked. 'I shut my eyes,' said the Marshal, 'I said to myself, "I am going to raise my arm now!" But I couldn't, no matter how hard I tried.' (*Ibid.*)

'Can you believe this?' Yeltsin asked his interlocutors. 'Here is a man who, during the

of Soviet Women and other giant 'social organizations' beholden to the Party, which were allocated seventy-five seats each. The official 'creative unions' (cinematographers, musicians, architects, painters and so on) as well as the USSR Academy of Sciences, Second World War veterans and so on – all the way down to stamp collectors* – received their share of safe seats.

The rest of the Deputies were to be elected either from the 'territorial districts' (one Deputy per 257,300 constituents) or from the 'national-territorial' ones. In the latter division, each Union Republic was given thirty-two seats, an autonomous Republic eleven seats, an autonomous region five and an autonomous district one.

In theory, anyone could run. In practice the road was rocky indeed. First, a candidate had to be nominated at a 'meeting of work collectives': local enterprises or groups of citizens living in the district. The next, and tallest, hurdle was the so-called nominating 'district meetings', at which the electoral commissions, set up by the authorities, determined the selection of those who would actually be put on the ballot. The deliberations were open and the audience was allowed to influence the choice by a vote, but in most cases those admitted to the meeting had been selected and instructed by the city or district Party committee, which packed the halls with Party activists and 'leading workers'. (Arriving at his nominating meeting, one 'liberal' candidate – the future Mayor of St Petersburg, Anatoliy Sobchak – found a crowd trying to force its way in and 'young bloods', wearing red armbands, who enforced a 'strict regime of admittance' and were 'ready to suppress any excess of civic enthusiasm'.)[213]

The rules were left deliberately ambiguous, and, depending on the district and the voter participation, the ballot could have anywhere from one to ten candidates (the Gagarin district of Moscow had ten). Yeltsin's view of the nominating procedure was quite accurate: 'The Party's bureaucratic apparatus does not want to let this process slip from its hands,' he said in an election campaign interview in February 1989. 'It wants necessarily to control it and strain through its sieve everyone

---

war, not once but hundreds of times was in mortal danger, stood next to Death! But he could not vote against! You see what nails have been driven [into] our heads!' (*Ibid.*)

* Stamp collectors, usually a most docile lot, staged a floor fight before, predictably, nominating their chairman, Cosmonaut V. Gorbatko, who duly took his seat in the Congress of People's Deputies. A group of dissenting philatelic radicals was led by a stamp collector from Kiev, who campaigned on a platform calling for a drastic reduction in new stamps issued by the Soviet post office each year.

who was nominated ... These elections are only half a step towards democratization – if not less. Isn't this done so that, again, we elect bit-players who can only raise their hands [to vote "in favour"]?'[214]

But the apparat proved helpless against the avalanche of popular sentiment fuelled by the publicity of the Conference, the Yurmala interview and the Komsomol School transcripts. Yeltsin was nominated to run in over fifty constituencies.[215] (The Law on the Elections did not require a candidate's residency in the nominating district.) Visibly proud, Yeltsin went down the list of the nominations during a campaign trip to Sverdlovsk. One could have expected nominations from the Sverdlovsk region, from Moscow, from Perm, he said. But, Yeltsin continued, pausing for effect after each new location, 'Sakhalin? Kamchatka? Kiev? Odessa? Yakutia? the Khabarovsk region? the Krasnoyarsk region? the Leningrad region? the city of Murmansk? the Baltic Fleet? the Northern Fleet? the Black Sea Fleet?'[216]

Yeltsin's explanation for such a dazzling multitude of endorsements (unmatched by any of the 1,449 candidates who eventually ran from 'territorial' districts)[217] was realistic, if uncharacteristically modest: 'This is not because of some special appeal [of mine]. No, the awkward views of the anti-perestroika forces, including some in the leadership, who for a whole year made the name "Yeltsin" taboo, who hampered [him] in every possible way, they have engendered powerful pressure in the opposite direction.'[218]

Although he decided to run as early as 13 December,[219] he took his time choosing where to stand for election. Nor did he attend most nominating meetings even in Moscow, sending his campaign organizers ('entrusted persons') to speak on his behalf, as permitted by the Law on the Elections. This was done, Yeltsin explained later, to throw his opponents off the scent. For he was certain that, once the apparat learned where he had decided to run, it 'would do everything it could' to quash his nomination.[220] Meanwhile, one territorial district of Moscow after another nominated him. (In the end, he would be nominated in ten of the capital's twenty-six electoral districts.) The way he was nominated in the Gagarin district was repeated time and again.

Half a dozen policemen guarded the door to the District House of Culture from several hundred people attempting to get in. 'Only those with invitations!' growled a husky doorman.[221] The invitations, needless to say, had been distributed by the District Soviet. Upstairs, the meetings chairman, who introduced himself as a pensioner and the chairman of the local veteran organization, listed the nominating groups: two Party organizations, two residents' committees from two apartment blocks, two veterans' groups and two women's councils. They had all, it turned out, proposed Yeltsin.[222]

Three more candidates were nominated as the meeting progressed. After a brief debate – should the nominees be voted for individually or as a group? – the decision was made to vote on them one by one. Just before the vote, one of the nominees said, 'I see you want Yeltsin. In that case, I withdraw.' Prolonged applause followed.[223] To get into the second round, the 'district electoral meeting', a candidate had to get at least half of the votes of no fewer than 500 locals. When the vote was taken, Yeltsin received 510. Three were against and five abstained.[224] The 'meeting of work collectives', one of thousands taking place all over the enormous nation, was over.

More days and weeks passed. Yeltsin had been nominated in two cities where his election was absolutely assured: Sverdlovsk and Berezniki, where he had spent his childhood and graduated from high school. But, with the elections scheduled for 26 March, Yeltsin still had not chosen the district to stand in.[225]

In one of the districts, Oktyabr'skiy, Yeltsin withdrew his candidacy in favour of Academician Andrey Sakharov. In the summer of 1988 both had been elected to the Public Council of the National 'Memorial' Society, dedicated to preserving the memory of the victims of Stalinism (not to be confused with the nationalist and anti-Semitic Pamyat', or 'Memory' group that demonstrated in Moscow in 1987). Still, Yeltsin the loyal oppositionist was careful in interviews with the foreign press to underline his differences with the leader of the Soviet human rights movement. 'We have decided to take different routes [to reform],' he told a British interviewer. 'And that will continue unless he [Sakharov] takes other decisions. I think that he has gone too far but [in exiling him] we went further.'[226]

Like Yeltsin, Sakharov was nominated for the 'National-Territorial District Number One', which represented the entire capital. When Sakharov decided not to stand for election in any of the electoral districts,[227] his 'entrusted persons' Anatoliy Shabad and Lev Ponomarev attempted to switch to Yeltsin Sakharov's forty-eight votes (four from each of the twelve nominating collectives) in the decisive district meeting.[228] (Eventually, under pressure from the scientists, the Praesidium of the Academy included Sakharov in the twenty seats allocated to the Academy of Sciences.)

On 11 February, less than two weeks before the deadline, Yeltsin attended a district electoral meeting in Berezniki. To cover his tracks he first flew to Leningrad. He was met there by some unidentified 'comrades', taken to a military airbase and flown to Perm in a noisy transport plane, 'side by side either with a cruise missile or an artillery shell'.[229]

He arrived just in time for the opening of the meeting. The Party organizers were 'in shock',[230] and had no time to gather and deploy the loyal contingent of work collectives. After a speech in which, among other things, Yeltsin deplored the 'three-storey' system of elections and called for a 'direct and secret vote' for all offices,[231] his name was put on the ballot.

Having thus secured his name on the ballot (and assured of victory there), Yeltsin, nevertheless, proceeded to seek 'registration' in several Moscow territorial districts. Five days after the Berezniki triumph, he attended the district electoral meeting in Kuntsevo, a quiet suburb, where many high Party functionaries had their homes and where the 'special' Fourth Department of the Ministry of Health had its largest hospital, the only facility in the USSR filled with state-of-the art imported technology.

Hours before Yeltsin's arrival, over 100 demonstrators were waiting in a wet and chilling February wind outside a Kuntsevo cinema. They held signs reading 'Boris Yeltsin – the people's choice' and 'If not Yeltsin, then who?'[232] At precisely 3 p.m., when the meeting was scheduled to begin, a monstrously long black Chaika limousine pulled up to the front entrance and out climbed Yeltsin.

'Tell 'em, Boris Nikolaevich!' shouted the demonstrators. Yeltsin 'waved slightly'. He was not smiling.[233] His entire demeanour exuded self-importance, grave concern and a determination to win the difficult fight ahead. His lips pursed, he strutted slowly into the meeting, grim and regal. He took the podium, towering over it – all six feet, two inches of him – and gripped it 'as if he were to reduce it to splinters'.[234] His voice was 'an angry rumble' ('like thunder', said someone in the audience).[235]

After Yeltsin had recited his programme (national referendums, political competition as a 'norm of life'), the hall exploded with questions and comments. Wasn't it true that he had a spacious apartment and his grandchild attended an exclusive English-language school? And what about his health; he was, after all fifty-seven. ('I am as fit as a fiddle,' Yeltsin parried, 'and I am playing sports all the time. I invite you to try and beat me.' But, he warned, 'I still could find myself "taken ill" or sent [as ambassador] to Ethiopia.')[236] His supporters were just as vocal. 'When you go to work tomorrow, look your comrades in the eye and say with pride, "I voted for Boris Yeltsin, a new kind of leader." '[237]

Nine hours after the meeting began, the final vote was taken. Yeltsin came in first, ahead of seven other nominees. His name would be on the ballot.

Next came Act II of the Gagarin district nominating drama. Although 'programmed' to winnow out most of the ten nominees, the audience at the district electoral meeting was swayed by the excellent speeches of outstanding candidates.* The people began to vacillate and, eventually, demanded that all ten be registered.[238] The tug of war between the audience and the 'electoral commission' in the Praesidium continued until two in the morning and ended with the audience's victory: all nominees were placed on the ballot.

Yeltsin was exhilarated: the 'people had overcome the nearly hypnotic fear of the authorities'![239] It was such moments, he later recalled, that 'fed [him] energy and renewed the belief that we never would, never could live as before. Moral slavery was over.'[240]

Virtually every appearance on the stump testified to his determination to prove that this was indeed so. One evening, on 23 February, he met with intelligentsia in the exclusive House of Actors club. If he was tired and tense, no sign of that was evident: he answered dozens of questions easily and wittily.[241] 'Would you go with Gorbachev scouting behind the enemy lines?' he was asked. 'Yes,' Yeltsin answered. And, in a rejoinder which would be repeated for months with appreciative laughter from Brest to Vladivostok, added: 'Provided that Ligachev is not creeping behind.'[242] For his audience, who until very recently had dared discuss their leaders only by 'whispering jokes in the kitchen', such talk 'had the effect of an exploding grenade'. 'Why, why is he saying such things?' gasped a woman in the audience,[243] worried about the daredevil's safety.

Usually, the rallies began like the one in the Cheryomushkiy district, witnessed by a British journalist: with the 1,200-seat hall in the district's House of Culture filled to capacity and the 'disappointed crowds' outside in the falling snow hoping for a glimpse of the candidate.[244] At 6 p.m. sharp, the 'biggest crowd-puller' of the campaign strode to the stage and the hall erupted into applause.[245] When Yeltsin began to speak, out came notebooks and pencils – for some out of habit, for others because of the suspicion that the press would never give an honest account of

---

* In addition to Yeltsin, some of the most prominent Moscow 'liberals' were nominated in the same district: essayist Yuriy Chernichenko, film director Eldar Ryazanov and military historian Dmitriy Volkogonov.

anything Yeltsin said or did. They were fortunate to get in and it was their duty to report to the thousands who had not.

In a 'powerful peroration', Yeltsin called for control over the Party by the people, for social justice and for a 'revival of the spirit of compassion'.[246] Give the Fourth Department of the Ministry of Health to pensioners, orphans and Afghan veterans. 'Special' shops ought to be closed. 'Let everyone's ruble be worth the same,' he declared. The audience responded with 'thunderous applause'. Yeltsin was warming up fast, peppering his speech with sarcastic asides. There should be a secret ballot and contested, multi-candidate elections at every level – not like the Politburo's selecting 100 'candidates' for 100 slots on the Party list. 'This is not exactly the pluralism which we are supposed to be learning to live with.'[247]

And how about the Politburo member, Vitaliy Vorotnikov, the Chairman of the Supreme Soviet of Russia, who was originally to stand in the National-Territorial District Number One, but was now running unopposed in the provinces? 'Apparently,' Yeltsin suggested amid laughter, 'he felt it more convenient to run elsewhere.'[248] As to the proposal to combine the posts of the local Party Secretaries with Chairmanships of local Soviets, 'Gorbachev has been energetically convincing us to separate the Party from the state, and then he [just as] energetically convinces us to do the opposite.'[249]

The last of the district electoral meetings in Moscow was held on 21 February, the eve of the deadline. It was to select the candidates for the National-Territorial District Number One, which included the entire capital.

As befitted the seat's exalted status, the electoral commission met in the House of Unions. Of the 900 people in the Hall, 200 were from the enterprises and 'social organizations' which nominated the candidates and the rest were 'representatives of work collectives' from all thirty-three administrative districts of Moscow.[250] Their instructions had been to vote for the registration of only two out of ten nominees – the cosmonaut Georgiy Grechko and the Director of the Likhachev automobile plant, Evgeniy Brakov* – and to blackball the other eight.

The meeting lasted for twelve-and-a-half hours, until 2.30 a.m.[251] Outside, Yeltsin's supporters held banners proclaiming, 'Yeltsin, you are perestroika!'[252] Just before the meeting, Grechko had told Yeltsin

---

* One can discern the elephantine political touch of the apparat strategists whose best choice was Director of the plant producing luxury ZIL limousines for the exclusive use of the top leadership.

that he planned to withdraw because he felt that Yeltsin would make a better Deputy and he did not want to compete with him. Yeltsin advised him not to announce his decision until the very end.

Each candidate was given twelve minutes to answer questions from the floor. Yeltsin received over 100 written queries. He chose the most personal, the most damaging and the most unpleasant. As usual, his frankness worked and he felt the audience begin to thaw.[253]

When, just before the final vote at 2 a.m., Grechko announced his decision, the thaw turned into a flood. With the pre-selected candidate out of the running, the instructions did not seem to apply and many in the hall felt that they could vote as they pleased (fortunately, it was a secret ballot). By the agreed rule, only the top two vote-getters would be placed on the ballot. Brakov received 577 votes. Yeltsin came in second with 532.

The next day Yeltsin's office told journalists that he would now have to decide 'quickly' where to stand.[254] Dozens of telegrams went from Gosstroy to constituencies all over the country: Yeltsin thanked the people for their 'trust' and announced his decision to run 'elsewhere'. Where, the telegrams still did not say.[255]

Three hours after the end of the House of Unions meeting, he was on the plane to Sverdlovsk: his most faithful supporters were too important and dear to him to be sent a telegram. Yeltsin felt that what he had to say should be said in person: he would stand in Moscow, the National-Territorial District Number One, the most populous in the country, with 6.7 million voters. 'I hope you'll understand,' he told his countrymen.[256]* 'This is a question of big politics. This is a question of my rehabilitation. Just think: all of Moscow will vote!'[257] And, referring to his critics' refrain during the 12 November 1987 Gorkom Plenum, he added: 'In the not too distant past, someone stated that I did not have Muscovites' trust. The time has come to clarify this issue . . .'[258]

On 13 January, the entire front page of *Pravda* had been devoted to the 'Address of the Central Committee to the Party, and to all Soviet people'. This was the Party's electoral 'platform'.

It opened with a paean to perestroika, to the Party as the 'political vanguard of society' and to 'revolutionary renewal'. There followed the

---

* They did. Just in case, on 26 March the majority of the citizens of Sverdlovsk would vote against all the candidates from the Sverdlovsk national-territorial district. In such cases the law required a new election, in which Yeltsin, should he fail in Moscow, could run and easily win.

by now common recitation of unsolved problems – chief among them food, consumer goods, housing – and a promise to improve it all. No details were given, no dates, means or ways. The grandiose structure was supported only by the usual rhetorical scaffolding: 'the Party has set a goal,' it 'shared the concern', it 'considered it necessary to . . .' and it would do 'all that was necessary to . . .' The Party was confident that the economy would improve because the Party had a 'concrete plan' for its improvement and because it (the Party) had 'scientific theory and policy' in its arsenal, backed by the 'reawakened energy of a great people capable of great deeds'.

Like that of the Party, the electoral platform of Yeltsin's competitor, Evgeniy Brakov, was well meaning and nebulous. He, too, declared that the time had come for 'concrete actions in the interests of people's welfare', and promised to 'strengthen' this and 'pay attention' to that. A more active social policy, for instance, was to be supported by a 'resource manoeuvre' that would free the necessary funds from an unnamed source. His only concrete proposals were a law on referendums and legislative oversight of the armed forces. The last paragraph of Brakov's platform read: 'I consider it a civic duty of anyone who becomes the people's choice to use his powers to implement the programme contained in the Central Committee's "Address".'[259]

The programme of the country's most famous Party dissenter, Boris Yeltsin, differed in ways large and small. In interviews with the 'central' Soviet and, especially, foreign media Yeltsin would prudently insist that, as far as his strategy was concerned, his platform was 'in line' with the CPSU programme.[260] In fact, it was as much 'in line' with the text that appeared in *Pravda* as a strong gale is with a gentle breeze: both are movements of air and, in this case, they moved in the same 'strategic' direction. (This tactical ploy, as we shall see shortly, fooled neither Yeltsin's supporters nor his detractors.)

Although about fifty times shorter than the Party's, Yeltsin's electoral programme more than made up for this by the concreteness of its proposals. It opened with wide-ranging political reform, which effectively stripped the Party of its 'guiding' role. The supreme legislative organ 'must reflect the will of the people'.[261] Power should be transferred to the elected organs. Politics, the economy and culture ought to be decentralized. The government, as well as all political and social organizations 'without exception', had to be accountable to the legislature. That 'included the Party'. Protecting his flank, Yeltsin would later split hairs asserting that he meant 'legal' rather than 'political' accountability.[262] After the election he continued to insist that he wanted to make the Party 'accountable', rather than 'subordinate', to the new legislature.[263]

Threatening another pillar of the one-party regime, Yeltsin declared that the mass media should be 'accountable to society as a whole, and not to groups of people'. A special Law on the Media ought to be adopted to protect the rights of journalists.

In a new Soviet parliament, People's Deputies should be able to demand national referendums on the most important policy issues. The latter, reflecting protests against the war in Afghanistan and revulsion over Chernobyl, included items that had formerly been the exclusive domain of the two dozen men in the Politburo: the use of armed forces and the construction of nuclear power stations.

Reiterating his demand for an increased supply of food, consumer goods, services and housing, Yeltsin proposed to cut defence and space programmes and use the savings to launch a 'strong social policy'. This, Yeltsin promised, would allow the standard of living to rise 'significantly' in two to three years.

Another proposal dealt with 'social and moral justice'. All Soviet citizens, 'from an ordinary worker to the head of state', should have equal opportunities in acquiring food, goods and services, as well as education and healthcare. The last item included putting the Fourth Directorate of the Ministry of Healthcare to the use of the 'least socially protected': poor families, pensioners, women and invalids.

'Special' food allotments and 'special distribution points' for goods were to be 'liquidated'. Only the ruble, that is one's salary, should be the measure of one's work, and the ruble should have the same purchasing value for everyone: as Yeltsin put it in one of his interviews, 'a minister's ruble must not be different from the ruble of a cleaning lady'.[264]

Appropriating the 1917 Bolshevik slogan 'Land to the Peasants!' Yeltsin proposed that land be made available through a long-term lease and the peasants themselves should 'choose the actual forms of working the land' – a transparent hint at decollectivization of agriculture.

The platform also called for a sharp reduction in the number of ministries and agencies and for the right of enterprises to 'exit freely' from state administration and work independently. A 40 per cent cut in industrial investment, first revealed to the students at the Highest Komsomol School, was aimed at reducing internal debt and stabilizing the ruble.

Three brief items completed the platform: nationalities policy, ecology and youth. Only the first was portentous: 'All peoples of the USSR must have real economic, political and cultural autonomy.'

Yeltsin's electoral programme ended on a decisively combative note: 'Perestroika and democratization are designed to bring revolutionary changes and need to be fought for in a revolutionary manner.' (The version that appeared in most leaflets and posters was even more bellicose: 'In voting for B. N. Yeltsin, you vote for people's power, democracy, the fight against corruption, bureaucracy and social injustice.')*

While the planks quoted above formed the core of Yeltsin's programme, the campaign slogans varied considerably depending on the venue. Thus, in interviews with major Soviet newspapers and foreign journalists he was significantly more circumspect than he was with audiences outside Moscow (the further the better) and in interviews with smaller, especially youth and regional, newspapers. In his home town, he used particularly dark hues for a portrait of the Soviet economy and politics. 'We are on the brink, already on the brink [as far as economy and finances are concerned],' he said during his visit to Sverdlovsk in January 1989.[265] 'The situation is as hard as it was after the [Second World] War . . . If some very decisive measures are not taken, regarding both the Party and the country as a whole, we'd better brace ourselves for some very serious trials within a year at the most.'[266]

'The main danger', Yeltsin told a Sverdlovsk audience a month later, 'is a bureaucratic, elitist regime, the self-reproducing cancer of the power of the nomenklatura. The key task is to remove the roots of that cancer, especially the Party apparatus.'[267] 'Political struggle, which used to be equated with the enemies of the people, is a normal phenomenon in a society, which only grows healthier from it,' Yeltsin told an Estonian newspaper.[268] To a Ural audience he recalled that the Bolsheviks, 'if you forgive me for saying this, [had] pushed out' other parties.[269] It was necessary to have some public organizations, such as People's Fronts,

* It is instructive to compare Yeltsin's platform with that of Andrey Sakharov, who offered voters the following items: removal of all limitations on personal income; freedom to choose one's country of residence; abolition of *propiska* ('residence permit') and freedom to live anywhere in the USSR; abolition of domestic passports; trial by jury; access to the archives of the secret police; access to a lawyer from the beginning of detention; abolition of the death penalty; 'convergence of socialist and capitalist systems' ('Chey kandidat Sakharov', *Komsomol'skaya Pravda*, 27 January 1989, p. 2).

As is immediately apparent, the differences were not those of degree. The two 'reformers' were on different planes. Sakharov, perhaps the world's most famous defender of human rights, was advocating a Western-style state: open and respectful of human rights. Yeltsin was calling for a radically 'democratized', cleaner and fairer one-party socialist welfare state with a 'human face' and a somewhat freer economy.

which were becoming so popular in Estonia, Latvia and Lithuania, because they could conduct open discussions with the Party.[270] And if, only two months before, he 'could not think of a higher ideal' than Lenin, now, asked to comment on the 'critique of Lenin and direct attacks on his persona' in the press, Yeltsin found them 'perhaps justified'.[271] After all, had not Lenin been 'idealized and idolized for too long?' Like everybody else, he had made mistakes and changed positions 'depending on the situation'.[272]

Yeltsin was well ahead of the Party establishment on another hotly debated subject, individual land ownership. As he elaborated on his proposal for the long-term lease of land, he was asked by the editors of a Moscow college newspaper to comment on the land reform in Estonia, which had enabled a handful of peasants to receive parcels of land and to pass them on to their heirs. Some observers had called this 'private property' and had sounded the alarm. Whatever you call it, Yeltsin said, the important thing was to give back to the individual (and his children) the 'feeling of being a master on his land'.[273] As to the terminology, Yeltsin explained, 'you see, the stereotypes are too strong in us, and "private property" means a return to capitalism – something [perceived as] totally horrible. I would not use this term. We must take into consideration people's psychology. "Long-term lease", "eternal lease", are therefore more acceptable and not so scary locutions, but the essence is the same.'[274] And, to preclude reversals, the right to own the land should be added to the Constitution.

He also expanded on the brief 'nationalities' plank of his platform. The issue, Yeltsin said, was 'very painful'.[275] For a long time the problem had been considered solved once and for all. This had led to 'neglect', 'haughtiness' and sometimes 'direct insults' to entire peoples. That was simply unacceptable.[276] Asked which was 'primary' and which 'secondary' – the Soviet Union or individual Republics – Yeltsin ventured what at the time was a very risky response: 'The Republics are primary . . . Every [form] of centralization lowers the level of democracy. The opinion of a people is primary and so is that of a Republic which represents this people.'[277]

Only three months before, he had been suspicious of Popular Fronts in the Baltic Republics because of their 'nationalist tinge'.[278] Asked about the Declaration of Sovereignty recently adopted by the Estonian Supreme Soviet, Yeltsin said he was not too worried about it.[279] He disagreed with some things but, all in all, this was the end result of an 'objective process'.[280] What about the People's Front, which was quickly evolving into a powerful challenge to the Party's political primacy? The root problem, Yeltsin answered, was the one-party system, which precluded free political discussions at any level. Any clash of opinions, even if it involved opposition to the Party line, was a 'positive phenomenon'.[281] In general, it might be a good idea to create an all-Union People's Front.

He no longer rejected out of hand a multi-party system, which, even in theory, was quickly becoming the key dividing issue between radical reformers and establishment 'liberals'. Yet he finessed the theme throughout his campaign, implying personal preference for a multi-party democracy yet, for the time being, remaining safely on the establishment side of the divide. Society, Yeltsin claimed, was 'still not ripe' for a multi-party system, but he 'would not exclude' that possibility in the future.[282] 'We have to heed the views of the people as a whole, not just those of Gorbachev or Yeltsin,' he told an interviewer. 'They are not the important ones. But if the whole of society wants [a multi-party system], then that's serious. The multi-party system must not be a forbidden theme. We must talk about it, then we can draw conclusions in a year or two and decide what to do about it.'[283] In the end, interviewed by the campus newspaper of a leading Moscow college, Yeltsin bit the bullet: 'To have free debates, and to avoid the cult of personality [that is, Stalinism], we must have two parties.'[284]

Yet, with his sense of political timing and his instinct for the politically possible acute as ever, Yeltsin tapdanced around the subject of organized political opposition and his role in it. Typical in that regard was an exchange with the BBC's Moscow correspondent Martin Sixsmith:

Sixsmith: I've spoken to a lot of people over the last few days and a lot of people look on you as an alternative, as the founder of a new party, of a new system in the Soviet Union. Is that what your campaign is about?

Yeltsin: I haven't given people grounds to think that. It is quite a different matter that I've a whole series of elements in my [election] programme which are, I would say, really revolutionary, very serious, very fundamental measures . . . But I am not the founder of a new political opposition. I am not the leader of an opposition party.

Sixsmith: But people want that from you.

Yeltsin: . . . Don't say I'm calling for an opposition party. No! The conditions aren't there for that yet.

Sixsmith: Not yet, you mean?

Yeltsin: The people will have to decide that, but we must open the gates for discussion.[285]

Even in the last week of his campaign, Yeltsin was careful to characterize his platform as 'differing only slightly from the position of the official leadership'.[286] He was especially politic where the General Secretary was concerned: distinguishing deftly between Gorbachev and the 'conservatives' in the leadership. Virtually no speech or interview passed without a solemn denial of his alleged 'rivalry with Gorbachev'. He *was* a threat, Yeltsin told an interviewer, but not to Gorbachev and 'not as a rival'. Rather, he threatened the 'quiet, unperturbed existence' of those who wanted to enjoy power without earning it in a political struggle.[287] Asked, during an election meeting in Moscow, if he was 'setting himself up as an alternative to Gorbachev', Yeltsin replied, 'Not at all. I reject that assumption. I fully support Gorbachev . . . [and] his strategy, though on tactics I have my own opinion.'[288]

He was especially adamant with Western interviewers. 'I don't want people to portray me as a rival to Gorbachev, not under any circumstances,' he told the BBC.[289] 'This is a provocation [to suggest that he was a possible future rival to Gorbachev], and no more than that,' Yeltsin said in an interview with Italy's *La Repubblica*. 'I am not, and do not want to be, an alternative to Gorbachev . . . I will never be against Gorbachev.'[290] 'I am not an alternative candidate to Gorbachev,' Yeltsin told *Time*. 'I accept Gorbachev as a leader.'[291]

These protestations of loyalty did not help. Ten days before the elections, a Central Committee Plenum (convened, ostensibly, to ponder the 'agricultural policy of the CPSU in current conditions') somehow erupted in yet another discussion of Yeltsin's 'mistakes'. On the very first day, several speakers 'expressed a number of criticisms' of Yeltsin's electoral 'positions', not least on the role of the Party, the 'idea of making the Party subordinate to the Soviets', and the creation of a 'new organization as a counterbalance to the Komsomol'.[292] A lathe operator and a construction-team leader from Moscow, a metalworker from Leningrad, a vegetable grower from the Leningrad region and a shoemaker from Kishenev – all, apparently, felt that the issue was urgent enough to warrant 'discussion and assessment' of certain statements by Yeltsin that 'contradicted political guidelines set by the Central Committee, Party ethics and the membership rules of the CPSU'.[293] Following this 'suggestion', the Plenum decided to set up a commission to 'study this question in detail' and report to the next Plenum.[294]

Three days later, *Moskovskaya Pravda* published a long letter from the lathe operator, Vladimir Tikhomirov, who now felt it was his 'Party duty' to explain, 'without equivocation', why he believed it necessary to investigate Yeltsin. First on the list of Yeltsin's offences (culled from his 'many utterances at meetings with voters') was the 'need for a broad discussion of a multi-party system'.[295] Then there was Yeltsin's proposal to subordinate the Party to popularly elected bodies. And how about his 'call' to create, in the newly elected Congress of People's Deputies, an 'opposition group of 20–30 per cent of the Deputies'?[296]

Not only was the turner remarkably knowledgeable about the details of Yeltsin's political stance, he was equally well versed in the personal life of his 'political opponent'. What about Yeltsin's daughter's apartment, 100 square metres, by Soviet standards an extravagantly large abode for a family of four? And how about the Chaika limousine and the dacha that came with his new job? And while he himself no longer used the Fourth Department of the Ministry of Health his family members still did.* Tikhomirov even knew that Yeltsin had recently requested a room in one of the Gosstroy's sanatoriums for a two-week holiday. So much for Yeltsin's fight against privileges![297]

Here and there, concluded Tikhomirov, democratization had brought with it 'demagogues' who 'besmirch' the Party and Soviet power, and the more 'dirt' their speeches exuded, the better they felt. 'We, the communists, shall not allow an attempt on the Party's life to succeed!'[298]

What made this eleventh-hour flare-up in the 'stop Yeltsin' campaign notable was not, of course, its content but the response it received. As regards both Yeltsin and Russian public opinion, the reaction to the Plenum's decision and Tikhomirov's letter was the first instance of a pattern that would manifest itself regularly over the next two-and-a-half years.

Yeltsin responded with his signature tactic: *Klin klinom vyshibayut* – 'When attacked, attack!' This time, his reaction went beyond respectful defiance and reiteration of his views as at the Nineteenth Conference. He called his response 'a massive attack'.[299]

As with most of Yeltsin's seemingly reckless operations, this was not a kamikaze attack but a daringly calculated move. He was not oblivious to danger. 'I cannot tell you that I am not afraid,' he confessed to a foreign reporter.[300] But Antaeus felt the earth, and took the risk. 'Too many grassroots [Party] organizations have expressed their dissent,'

---

* In an interview with *Time* Yeltsin acknowledged that, although he had refused 'foodstuffs, access to special stores and various services', he kept his 'official car', a 'small wooden dacha' and 'special health services' (David Aikman, 'One Bear of a Soviet Politician', 20 March 1989, p. 46).

Yeltsin said at the time. 'I do not believe it is possible to pretend that nothing has happened and to ignore them.'[301]

His rebuttal to *Moskovskaya Pravda** was unyielding, accusatory and belligerent – as were dozens of speeches and interviews in the campaign's final week. The Tikhomirov letter was not a 'single, isolated episode', Yeltsin wrote.[302] It was part and parcel of a campaign conducted by the Gorkom, a campaign that intensified after his registration as a candidate for the National-Territorial District Number One. The campaign against him had been 'less than democratic' and included pressure on the nominating work collectives, and the screening of participants for district electoral meetings.[303]

As was his wont, Yeltsin escalated the stakes by deftly linking a personal affront to the fate of the revolution. The country was in crisis. There was no other way out of it but a 'radical democratization of the Party and society', a 'fight against the Party's bureaucratic apparatus', against corruption and for social justice.[304] Instead, the Central Committee wasted time and effort on discrediting candidates it did not like. This was 'not a smart policy'. It would lead, Yeltsin prophesied darkly, to a confrontation between the Party apparatus and the people, and, in the end, to a break between the Party and the people, and the 'loss of the Party's authority'.[305]

The day after the Tikhomirov letter was published, he roused a rally of 7,000 by charging the authorities with a 'conspiracy' to thwart his election.[306] He bristled with anger and derision when he spoke to the workers of the huge Ordzhonikidze machine-tool plant. The 'case' against him was absolutely without precedent in Party history.[307] 'For many years there sat [in the leadership] those who put not one but several million [rubles] in their pockets, yet no one thought of creating any "commissions". But now, all of a sudden, they decide to investigate – just in case I have said something wrong . . .'[308]

He did not try to hide or to deny. The time for equivocation had passed. 'Subversive' ideas which had been soft-pedalled until then were now put forth at stentorian volume. A day after the Plenum, he told

---

* According to the newspaper's deputy editor-in-chief, Yeltsin's response was censored by order of the City Party Committee, 'probably' advised by the Politburo's chief ideologist Vadim Medvedev. It was published in its original form only a day before the elections, after intervention 'from the highest level', most likely Gorbachev himself. *Moskovskaya Pravda* failed, however, to publish any of around 1,000 letters objecting to Tikhomirov's attack on Yeltsin. (Anne Penketh, Agence France-Presse, 21 March 1989 (FBIS, 24 March 1989, p. 47).)

10,000 people in a Moscow suburb that he would indeed try to form a faction in the new legislature in order to 'promote deep reforms' in the Soviet political system.[309] And, yes, the Party ought to be subject to the country's highest legislative organ and to the law.[310]

Taking the battle to his rival's headquarters, the ZIL, he told the 80,000 workers (who listened to the in-house radio at their workplaces) that if a multi-party system, 'widely discussed in society', continued to remain taboo in the official media, the situation would result in an 'explosion'.[311]

Russian public opinion was now galvanized into an open, mass, nation-wide political protest. No longer confined to telegrams and telephone calls, solidarity with Yeltsin was expressed at dozens of meetings. Like the American President who had left the political scene a few weeks before, in March 1989 Yeltsin was suddenly proved to have Teflon in his political armour.

To their grave peril, his detractors in high places failed to see (and would continue to do so until it was too late) that some time in 1988 Yeltsin had become linked to – indeed, personified and symbolized – the gift of perestroika the Russians cherished the most: freedom to say what was on one's mind, and, especially, freedom to berate those at the top, believed by the vast majority to be crooked, inept, insolent and rapacious. From now on, an attack on Yeltsin, regardless of the substantive merits of the charges, was instantly equated with encroachment on that precious right. Instead of hitting the target, such sorties backfired by animating his followers, recruiting new troops for him and, in the end, greatly damaging those who launched them.

Characteristic in this respect was the sentiment that swept the gathering at Yeltsin's *alma mater*, the Ural Polytechnic Institute, the day after Tikhomirov's letter was published. 'As far as I am concerned,' said one speaker, 'the Yeltsin issue is not a problem of one, isolated individual. It is a common and cardinal problem: how to implement the right of everyone to express their views freely. By signing the letter [of protest to be sent to the Central Committee in Moscow], I am proving my own right to say what I think and to expect others to respond to what I say.'[312]

Another protester, a candidate for the Congress of People's Deputies from one of Sverdlovsk's electoral districts, Gennadiy Burbulis, said:

What is happening to Yeltsin today is happening to each of us. The right to have our say, the right to have our own point of view, the right to be responsible for the Motherland – these are our rights as free people. It is the right of every one of us to express our views in our actions. Today's meeting is such an action . . . I hope that Boris Nikolaevich is hearing us, because hundreds of people, hundreds of organizations are joining their voices in his support, including at these kinds of meetings. I hope also that our meeting will register as well with those who still think that our people do not have a voice, do not have their own point of view, and that they can be lorded over as before.[313]

'The creation of a commission to investigate alleged violations of Party ethics and deviation from the Party line is nothing less than a show trial of the progressive forces of our society,' added another participant.

It is an attempt to put pressure on the candidates who are the people's, not the apparat's, choices, and, in this way, to influence the results of the elections. I cannot but be troubled by the personal position of Comrade Gorbachev. Why is he watching silently, over and over again, the attempts to destroy Yeltsin? I would add to our letter [to the Central Committee] our dissatisfaction with the personal position adopted by the General Secretary as regards this matter of principle. I propose to express no confidence in the current Central Committee and the Politburo.[314]

In Moscow, inflamed public opinion endowed Yeltsin's campaign with a degree of support and an intensity unlike anything the Soviet capital had ever seen. An Estonian journalist, sent by her newspaper to see what the 'Yeltsin phenomenon' was all about, found the Soviet capital positively feverish. People walked the streets, she reported, with sandwich-boards bearing Yeltsin posters and with Yeltsin buttons pinned to their hats.[315] Campaign pickets were deployed at the entrances to Metro stations. Hundreds of Muscovites packed buses racing through Moscow's heavy spring mud to some God-forsaken suburb on a rumour that Yeltsin would speak there. Spontaneous 'mini-rallies' sprang up everywhere – in the Metro, in stores, on the streets – with thousands of people listening, from balconies, roofs, wooden crates. At one such gathering a 'seventy-year-old lady, with torn shopping bags', elbowed her way to the microphones and shouted 'Long live Yeltsin! Long live the Fourth Russian Revolution!'[316]

Overnight, leaflets appeared on the walls of the Metro. These were ripped off by the authorities, only to be replaced by new ones. Many of these fliers contained propaganda verses. Here is one such opus, in a translation that sacrifices rhyme, but not the metre, to literalness.

EL'TSIN

Alone, stubborn and high-browed,
Like Peter [the Great] over six feet tall,
He stands before the functionaries' anger,
And, like a sentry, never leaves his post.

To those wearing expensive felt fedoras
His name is like a thorn in their side:
He is the one who's taken on Goliath,
He is the one who spits against the wind!

They hate him for the thoughts that are his own,
And also for the fact that, unlike them,
He, while belonging to the Party,
Could keep his conscience free, non-Party clean.

He is ashamed of privileges shameless
And for that shame the mighty hate him too:
It's like a bone in the throat of the legions
That occupy the ministries these days.

But is he not himself a big *nachal'nik*?
Why should the nation trust him so much?
But then who cares if he is a fallen angel –
Or Satan who is suddenly a saint.

While those sitting in the high and heavy chairs
Are nipping our freedom in the bud,
We say: please, don't give in, remain courageous, El'tsin!
Boris, fight on for justice to the end![317]

Among thousands of pro-Yeltsin leaflets there was one unlike anything printed in support of any other candidate throughout the entire USSR: a plea from the citizens of a city far away from the one in which the candidate stood for election. The 'Appeal of the work collectives of the Sverdlovsk region to the workers, office workers, intelligentsia and student youth of the city of Moscow' called on the Muscovites to support 'our countryman' Yeltsin.[318] A 'courageous, principled man, who is selflessly dedicated to the cause of the Party' and the 'cause of the people', no matter 'what official post he occupied', Yeltsin was said to be devoting his energy to 'improving' people's lives and 'implementing the principles of social justice'. Political opportunism, 'rapaciousness' and 'spinelessness' were 'alien to him'. It was people like him that perestroika needed badly.

Yeltsin, the leaflet continued, would have received a 'unanimous' vote in Sverdlovsk. Instead, he turned down the nomination and ran in Moscow in order to 'achieve the maximum exposure' for the key planks of his platform and to defend his honour in a 'hard struggle with the open and covert' opponents of perestroika, who had done 'everything' to block his return to the political life of the country.

> Muscovites! It would not be an exaggeration to say that the entire country is anxiously awaiting the results of the elections in the First National-Territorial District. We join our voices with those who will vote for Boris Nikolaevich Yeltsin.[319]

*

After Tikhomirov's letter had been published in *Moskovskaya Pravda* on 19 March, three unprecedented demonstrations, each bigger than the one before, rocked Moscow. On the 19th itself, within hours of the newspaper hitting the street, several thousand people gathered in Gorkiy Park, and then marched to the centre of Moscow.* By the time they were stopped on Gorkiy Street near the Mossovet building, they were between 5,000 and 7,000 strong. After a 'tense standoff with the riot police' ten police vans lined up across the thoroughfare, and the demonstrators were given an electric megaphone and permitted to hold a rally. 'Hands off Yeltsin!' they chanted as a 'city official' clambered on to a bus in an attempt to persuade the crowd to disperse.[320]

The pedestal of Russia's most famous equestrian statue, a monument to the founder of the Russian capital, Prince Yuriy Dolgorukiy, was plastered with leaflets and posters, and people were hanging from every extremity of the pig-iron horse and rider.[321] Posters reading 'Yeltsin [is]

---

* The authorities' utter lack of respect for the feelings of Muscovites was behind this first mass protest in Moscow's centre. The organizers had long before secured permission to hold a pro-Yeltsin rally in Gorkiy Park. When the people began to gather, they were told that the meeting had been cancelled by the Mossovet's Executive Committee. Instead, the participants were urged to take part in yet another anti-alcohol function, a Day of Tea, about to begin in the park. The would-be marchers were encouraged to disperse in an orderly fashion and have a cup of tea. The participants decided instead to march on the Mossovet and 'demand an explanation'. (A. Davydov, 'Manifestatsiya i informatsiya' ('Demonstration and information'), *Izvestia*, 20 March 1989.)

People's Deputy' and 'Hands off Yeltsin!' were held aloft. Over the megaphone, the voice intoned: 'The people feel falsehoods and lies . . . For decades we have been told that the Party and the people [were] one . . . Now it is clear that the vanguard of the Party, its Central Committee, has moved against the people . . .'[322]

One woman stood in the crowd holding open her Party card, on which her name was clearly visible, but she did not care and was not afraid even of being photographed. She did it, she explained, so that people should know that 'we were not some sort of anarchists or anti-Soviets, but Party members in good standing' and also to 'prove that we would not be afraid to turn in our Party cards, if Yeltsin was not elected People's Deputy'.[323] Around her, people repeated over and over again, 'It is not Yeltsin who deviates from the Party line, it is the Party that deviates from the people.'[324] A man, 'unhinged by this bacchanalia of freedom', walked aimlessly around, murmuring to himself: 'What are you doing, people? Talking like that about the Party! You shouldn't, people, you shouldn't . . .'[325]

Three days later, a crowd of more than 8,000 gathered outside the Mossovet again, waved their fists and chanted, 'Yeltsin! Don't touch Yeltsin! Yeltsin, yes! Mafia, no!' and 'Shame on the bureaucracy!'[326] Police blocked the square. *Moskovskaya Pravda* reported, cryptically, that while most of the participants were law-abiding and supported perestroika and reform, 'certain speeches were of an antisocial nature', and that there were 'attempts to create a heated atmosphere' and some 'inflammatory statements were made'.[327]

The biggest pro-Yeltsin meeting was held on the last day of the campaign, 25 March, in the Luzhniki stadium arena. Organizers claimed 40,000 people in attendance, foreign reporters' estimates ran from 'more than 10,000' to 20,000.[328] The two-kilometre stretch between the stadium and the Sportivnaya Metro station was packed with Yeltsin supporters streaming to the rally.[329] Lampposts and bus shelters were covered with posters, poems, Yeltsin's electoral platform and his rebuttal, finally published by *Moskovskaya Pravda*. The posters read: 'Boris [is] right! *Boris prav!*' and 'Yeltsin [is a] candidate of the people'.[330] Accompanied by rhythmic clapping and the shaking of fists in the air, people chanted 'Yeltsin! Yeltsin! Yeltsin!'[331]

The morning of 26 March was almost miraculous in its ordinariness. It was, in the words of an *Izvestia* editorial, 'businesslike, even quotidian on the surface but, as no other day before, brimming with excited expectation, a gigantic inner tension'.[332] Now the people could

CHOOSE, CHOOSE, the newspaper rhapsodized, capitalizing that magic word which suddenly became a fact of their lives.[333] The people, continued *Izvestia*, were discovering their 'civic dignity', they were beginning to believe in the 'reality of their personal impact on affairs of state . . .'[334] 'You must understand,' a participant at a Moscow district electoral meeting told a foreign reporter a month before, 'our people have been waiting decades for something like these elections.'[335]

As a huge nation tasted liberty, the ultimate test of the new reality was to take place in its capital, its heart and its most politicized city. The border that separated the new Soviet Union from the 'moral slavery' of the past ran through the National-Territorial District Number One, whose administrative denomination had acquired an immense symbolic weight. It was, indeed, Number One: if the people's choice were to win here, a new era would have arrived. Perhaps at no time before or after was Boris Yeltsin's bellwether destiny more manifest.

The 3,389 polling stations of Moscow were open from seven in the morning until eight in the evening. In many districts over half of those registered had voted by noon: something that the election workers could not recall ever happening before.[336] Characteristically practical and mistrustful, Muscovites were concerned about the tools of voting: pencils had been provided rather than pens.[337]* Wasn't that to make it possible to doctor the ballots, to cross out those they wanted to elect? And why wasn't there an official stamp on the ballots, as had been promised?[338]†

At 8.05 in the evening, in the presence of representatives of work collectives and the general public and the candidates' 'entrusted persons', the seals on the ballot boxes were broken. In the National-Territorial District Number One, 5,722,937 voters (or 89.44 per cent of those registered) came to the polls. Of these, 5,238,206 (91.53 per cent) voted for Yeltsin. Brakov received 393,633 votes, or 6.88 per cent.[339]‡

---

* In the 26 March elections, voters were to cross out all the names on the ballot, except that of the candidate of their choice.

† Yeltsin volunteers were present at every polling station and observed 'every minutest detail'. They were present when the boxes were sealed and when they were opened. They looked inside to make sure every last ballot was out. Yeltsin called it 'top-to-bottom control'. (Interview with the Sverdlovsk documentary film group on 27 March 1989, from the video archive of the Museum of Youth Movements, Ekaterinburg.) 'And if we had not done this?' he added. 'Well, then, you know, we [in the Soviet Union] have a great deal of experience in these matters [of falsifying elections results] . . .' (*ibid.*).

‡ The total number does not add up to 100 per cent because of invalid ballots and the vote against both candidates.

Two weeks after his victory, several Yeltsin advisers went to his apartment on 2nd Tverskaya-Yamskaya to decide what to do next.[340] Although they had worked eighteen-hour days in the final weeks of the campaign, they had never given a thought to what their candidate would do once elected. They had read his programme, of course, but they did not really believe that they would manage the first comeback in Soviet history of a politician condemned by the Central Committee.

After a while, Yeltsin suggested they continue talking outside. It was an early April night in Moscow: starry, cold, clean and crisp. Ice, which covered puddles after sunset, crackled loudly underfoot, but the smell of spring was unmistakably in the air. An agitated Yeltsin talked loudly and excitedly, and was quickly recognized by the usual Moscow contingent of passers-by: dog-walkers, couples back from the theatre, second-shifters on their way home from plants and factories, an occasional drunk. Before long, a small crowd had grown around him.[341] Yeltsin was showered with congratulations and questions about the future – his own and the country's. Soon, in a small Moscow yard, Yeltsin was making his first post-election speech. Russia's first professional democratic politician was born.

CHAPTER 6

The Year of Truth

T HE INTELLIGENTSIA GLOATED. REVENGE, OH SO sweet
revenge, which they thought they would never live to see visited
on those who for decades had censored their books and articles,
mutilated their plays, cut their films, was suddenly real – complete with
names and titles! In the daring Lenkom, one of the trendiest Moscow
theatres, the national heart-throb, actor Oleg Yankovskiy, descended to
the hall during a play and recited in a stirring baritone the names of
regions and cities whose First Secretaries had been defeated on 26
March: Leningrad, Sverdlovsk, Chelyabinsk, Lvov, Volgograd, Cherni-
gov, Gomel, Alma-Ata, Frunze, Kiev, Samarkand . . .[1]* This was sheer
music to the audience, who had come to see the fashionable high-brow
play by the best-known liberal playwright, Mikhail Shatrov. 'So, what
do you think of this?' Yankovskiy asked a female spectator. 'Beautiful!
Just beautiful!' she cried – and the hall burst into prolonged applause.[2]†

Yet with the feverishness of the spring of 1989 now past, one wonders
about the appropriateness of the cymbals. If this were to be a revolution,
or at least the beginning of one, it certainly was most unusual. Among
the many missing elements that separated this revolution from the classic
canon, one vacancy was immediately apparent. One would have
searched the rows of leading Soviet political actors in vain for anything
even approximating to the familiar archetype: a Danton, Marat, Robes-
pierre, Lenin or Trotsky, whose self-conscious and complete rejection
of the *ancien régime* preceded their participation in its demise by years
or even decades.

Mutatis mutandis, the same glaring lacunae pockmarked the faces of
virtually all other post-totalitarian transitions – Albanian, Bulgarian,
Czechoslovakian, East German, Hungarian and Rumanian – as they
would mark future examples in Cuba, China, North Korea and Vietnam.
Among fallen civilizations, communist totalitarianism would stand out

---

* In at least two instances the electoral defeats stemmed from the losers' attitude towards
Yeltsin. The fate of the First Secretary of the Sverdlovsk Obkom, Leonid Bobykin, had
been sealed at the Nineteenth Conference by his condemnation of Yeltsin's speech. In
Moscow, with the Gorkom's First Secretary, Lev Zaykov, outside the voters' reach (he
was 'elected' on the Party list), the Muscovites decimated the post-Yeltsin leadership by
defeating Mayor Valeriy Saikin and the Gorkom's Secretary, Yuriy Prokofiev, who had
been especially vicious at the 12 November 1987 Plenum.

† The exhilaration lost none of its intensity two months later when the poet Evgeniy
Evtushenko repeated to the Congress of People's Deputies that celebrated number,
'Thirty-eight': the thirty-eight First Secretaries, most of them in regions and large cities,
who had failed to get elected (*Pervyi S'ezd*, vol. II, p. 225).

in this respect too: unlike *ancien régimes* of the past, it was brought down by upheavals that began as revolutions without revolutionaries.

It could not, of course, be otherwise. The peculiarities of anti-totalitarian upheavals followed from the uniqueness of the *ancien régime*. The unprecedented thoroughness and longevity of terror designed to extirpate any real or perceived political challenges to the regime precluded the incubation of revolutionaries inside totalitarian societies. In the Soviet case, with the exception of the miraculous survival of Andrey Sakharov, all potential leaders of a self-conscious and determined opposition – those who publicly questioned and sought to replace the fundamentals of the Soviet political system – were destined to spend most of their lives in detention, and either die there after lengthy consecutive terms, like Anatoliy Marchenko, or be expelled from the country like Aleksandr Solzhenitsyn or Vladimir Bukovskiy.

Before they emerge to lead, revolutionaries are nourished and sustained by an increasingly permissive political culture in which they can, without risking their lives, begin to question the legitimacy of the key cultural, and later political and even economic, arrangements of the old order and to communicate their doubts. Thus, the French Revolution, which serves as the prototype, had been preceded by decades of semi-clandestine but persistent and effective advocacy of alternative social and political models. Adopted by broad segments of the ruling class itself, they first created a vocabulary of revolution (derived from the *Encyclopédie* and Rousseau) and, eventually, an ideology of liberation.[3]

Along with neutralizing or ejecting potential revolutionaries, the totalitarian regimes were almost as effective in vitiating another attribute of 'classic' modern revolutions: an effective political counter-culture. The absence of this prelude was as conspicuous in anti-totalitarian revolutions as that of revolutionaries.* Unlike the liberation from eighteenth-century absolutism and twentieth-century authoritarianism, the demise

---

* Poland was the sole exception. The demise of communism there had been antedated by decades of mass resistance, sustained by the Catholic Church's alternative definitions of community, nationhood and morality. In consequence, Poland's break with communism was not only the first in the 'socialist bloc' but also the most decisive.

Alongside the general and spontaneous abhorrence of political terror, the absence of the sharply alternative revolutionary *Weltanschauung* was responsible for another remarkably uniform attribute of the anti-communist revolutions of the 1980s: their unprecedentedly non-violent, 'velvet' nature. There was simply not enough ideological distance between the leaders of the revolutions and the ruling class to supply even minimal justification for violence.

of communist totalitarianism was not preceded by decades of 'cultural revolution'. Yet the lack of an ideological overhaul *prior* to the Soviet cataclysm did not mean that it never occurred. Compressed into a few short years, the spiritual emancipation did not precede the political one but unfolded alongside it.

Much of what it lacked in length the Russian cultural revolution made up in astonishing intensity. A sceptical intelligentsia, slow to rise to Gorbachev's call, initially responded to glasnost with a verse:

A long-awaited glasnost came –
Unequalled in the taste and purity!
When it is gone, the State Security
Will not forget your hapless name.

After throwing the door open in January 1987, Gorbachev for almost two years (to the end of 1988) had to push and prod the Russian *literati* over the threshold. When they finally did cross over, the gentle, warm and nourishing shower intended by Gorbachev's raindance changed quickly to a merciless hurricane.

Over several years, from a kind of recreational therapy granted to the intelligentsia in exchange for much needed support of reform, glasnost developed into a widespread iconoclasm. Journalism and *belle-lettres* were turning from pliant instruments into weapons that would fatally injure a reformed one-party state socialism 'with a human face' well before it could be established. Gorbachev's banner was slashed mercilessly before it was fully unfurled. To this 'cultural revolution' the year 1989 was central. It was then that glasnost evolved into a cognitive explosion which, in a matter of months, would lay waste the entire symbolic universe which the Soviet regime occupied and from which it derived a modicum of legitimacy.

Like any functioning society, Gorbachev's Soviet Union had its share of legitimizing myths: uplifting and ennobling accounts of people, history and the present state of the nation which are unquestionably accepted by the vast majority of the people and form the basis of political, social and economic arrangements. The relentless, methodical destruction of the Soviet legitimizing mythology was central to the Fourth Russian Revolution.*

* In this the Russian Revolution of 1989–91 was akin to the French. For in France too, during the second stage between August 1790 and July 1791, the ending of censorship and prosecution made it possible for political argument to be read by a nation-wide

Two paths of devastation ran parallel. On a higher level, the state itself, through its suddenly accessible and even more unexpectedly truthful Ministers and experts, made public formerly secret truths. The other hurricane sprang from tens of thousands of letters to newspapers. Never before had the Soviet people been bold enough to write and editors brave enough to publish anything like it. With their odd mixture of desperation, anger and strong residual loyalty to the Soviet state, these missives resembled the *cahiers de doléance*: lists of grievances that Louis XVI called on his subjects to draw up in 1789 and address to the 'King–Father' in preparation for the Estates-General. Revolutionary subversion was the last thing on the authors' minds. Yet the sheer volume of raw human misery that poured through the suddenly open floodgates of censorship and the urgency of the cry for help made the nation shudder. In the tightening vice of official confessions and the damning *cahiers*, Soviet mythology soon developed a dense network of deeply embarrassing fissures, cracks and gouges, and then broke apart.

First to fall was the myth of the Soviet welfare state. Omnipotent, multifarious and largely effective, it might, so most believed until then, overlook a few small things here and there, but generally it kept everyone and everything in good trim. It secured a dignified existence for its citizens and, at the very least, shielded them from the 'evils of capitalism': poverty, hunger, inadequate medical care, lack of housing and organized crime.

In four years, between 1986 and 1990, most of these certitudes vanished. It became an accepted truth, for example, that much of the country was desperately poor. With the official poverty level at seventy-five rubles per person per month ($7.50 at the 1989 market rate of exchange), forty-three million (or 17 per cent) of the population earned less than that amount.[4] Another 100 million (or 40 per cent) lived perilously close to penury on less than 100 rubles a month.[5] In per-capita consumption, the Soviet Union was in seventy-seventh place in the world.[6] The fifty-eight million pensioners were especially hard pressed. Every third pensioner in the city and eight out of ten in the village received less than sixty rubles a month.[7] The handicapped were worse off still. An invalid single mother, for example, was reported to be receiving thirty-one rubles a month.[8]

---

audience. Freedom of speech and assembly 'brought forth a political culture in which the liberation of disrespect literally knew no bounds' (Simon Schama, *Citizens*, p. 521). Schama called it 'the most dramatic creation' of the French Revolution – just as glasnost, in the 1989 radicalized version, surely was for the Russians.

'I am fifty-two years old with more than thirty years' service,' one man wrote to *Pravda*. 'I had a stroke and ... became a pensioner. My pension is forty-one rubles and seventy-one kopecks ... How can we survive?' Those in the countryside were entitled to pensions of forty rubles but only after twenty-five years of work on a collective farm. 'My wife and I are both sixty-three years old,' read another letter.

> She has been in poor health since childhood and worked as a farm-hand. Because of my illness I was unable to acquire a total of twenty-five years of work, which has left us without a pension. We turned to the local authorities for a pension of perhaps no more than twenty rubles, for bread only.
>
> Dear comrades! Please understand me correctly: the point is that my wife and I have no children and that our material situation is very difficult. Believe me, if I had anyone with whom to spend my old age, I would never have bothered a newspaper for these twenty rubles.
>
> Unfortunately, our [local] leaders refused to understand. I regularly read *Izvestia* and see the way you help people in all kinds of situations. I hope that you will help us receive some aid to survive.[9]

Contrary to the widespread belief that no one in the Soviet Union was starving, it was now revealed that the consumption of meat and dairy products by the Soviet poor had declined by 30 per cent since 1970.[10]

Perhaps the greatest damage to the state mythology was inflicted by the gradually divulged enormity of the healthcare crisis in a country where free medicine had from the very beginning served as a key legitimizing symbol. In 1988, according to the Minister of Health, 1,200,000 beds (or 35 per cent of the total) were in hospitals with no hot water; every sixth hospital bed was located in facilities where there was no running water at all; 30 per cent of all Soviet hospitals did not have indoor toilets.[11]* A Supreme Soviet commission found 450 basic medications to be in short supply.[12] A leading pharmacologist disclosed that the pharmaceutical industry was practically non-existent in the Soviet Union, that existing plants were obsolete by 'decades', and that

---

* Two years later, the State Statistical Committee disclosed still gloomier data: 19 per cent of hospitals had no central heating, 45 per cent lacked bathrooms or showers, and 49 per cent hot water (Barrie R. Cassileth, Vasily V. Vlasov and Christopher Chapman, 'Health Care, Medical Practice and Medical Ethics in Russia Today', *JAMA*, 273/20 (24–31 May 1995), p. 1570).

the situation was 'catastrophic'.[13] The shortage of necessary equipment was in large measure responsible for a declining life expectancy: 870 heart-bypass surgeries were performed annually in the Soviet Union, as compared with 22,000 such operations in France, a country whose population was five times smaller.[14]

Of the sixty pieces of equipment that Soviet obstetricians and paediatricians considered absolutely necessary for performing their duty, Soviet industry produced six.[15] Soviet obstetricians lacked not only diagnostic equipment ('Not a single Soviet-made ultrasound machine. Not a single one in thirty years! This is the length of the entire Space Age!' cried a leading specialist)[16] but also wrapping cloths and bottle nipples[17] for newborn babies, and gowns and surgical gloves for doctors.[18] 'Do you think it is not painful for us to see how women give birth?' read a letter from the delivery room personnel of Moscow Maternity Clinic No. 5:

> sitting on chairs (and sometimes we are even short of chairs) and for days after giving birth lying on gurneys? But what can we change? Our clinic is designed for twelve births daily, and yesterday we had double that number. Imagine the picture: a midwife washing floors and throwing the mop down, and rushing to check on women in labour. This no longer amazes anyone.[19]

In early 1988, the Soviet Union had a higher rate of infant mortality than forty-nine other nations, behind Barbados and the United Arab Emirates.[20]

The healthcare broadside ricocheted into another constituent myth of this cluster – the 'golden' Soviet childhood. Generations of Soviet children had been required to learn this song:

> Our golden childhood
> Grows brighter by the day.
> Under a lucky star
> We are growing in our Motherland.

But the very same children whom millions of posters all over the country declared to be 'our future' were attending schools half of which had no central heating, running water or indoor toilets.[21] Thousands, some as young as ten, worked twelve-hour days on collective farms harvesting potatoes and cotton.[22] Hundreds of schoolchildren died in labour accidents each year and thousands were crippled.[23] (In 1988 there were 35,000 labour accidents among working children under fourteen.)

While no one living in the Soviet Union at the time could have been unaware of the shortage of housing, the scale and general hopelessness of the problem bared by glasnost were staggering. A full 100,000,000 Soviet citizens (a third of the population) had less living space than was prescribed by the meagre Soviet 'sanitary norm' of nine square metres per person.[24] Millions lived in communal apartments: honeycombs of one room per family with a shared bathroom and kitchen. Fifteen per cent of the population had no permanent living space of their own, occupying hostels, 'huts and half-basements', or renting – often illegally – from others.[25]

In dozens of cities there was no running water whatsoever and more than 300 cities had no sewer pipes.[26] Six million people were estimated to live in 'disastrous' dwellings. There was little hope for them. In the summer of 1989 *Pravda* published a letter from an elderly man whose house had burned down three years before and who now inhabited an abandoned bathhouse. The damp and rotting building, with no heat or light, was 'killing' him. 'All I want is eight [square] metres in a warm little room,' he wrote. 'There is no way, they tell me . . .'[27]

A woman from the Moscow region wrote that her family of seven lived in eighteen square metres with 'no amenities, no running water, no sewer pipe and no gas'. To her repeated requests for better housing the Executive Committee of the local Soviet replied: 'As your family has no grounds to be acknowledged as needing improvement in their housing conditions, your name cannot be put on the housing waiting list.'[28] Such lists comprised, for instance, 344,800 Moscow families (12 per cent of all families in the city); 282,900 in Leningrad (20 per cent) and 208,000 in Kiev (26 per cent).[29]

Organized crime, forever relegated by the Soviet myth to the West (especially the United States), was now declared very much a part of the native landscape – complete with extortion, hired guns and contract killings,[30] street battles between rival gangs, and teenaged prostitutes in apartment bordellos.[31] Lacking, after decades of forced silence, words and expressions in Russian to describe the freshly discovered vices, Russian journalists borrowed the terminology: *kidnaping*, *raket*, *otmyvanie deneg* (money-laundering), *krestniy otetz* (the godfather).

Historians and publicists, meanwhile, were engaged in their own demolition project. Seeking an answer to Russia's perennial and cursed question 'Who is to blame?' the glasnost diagnosticians moved from warts to malignant tumours and, finally, to the chromosomes. By 1989, the cornerstone of Soviet history – the 'Great October Socialist Revolution' – was reduced to a coup by a group of conspirators, whom 'few people took seriously' and who seized power by virtue of their shameless demagoguery and the desperate economic conditions.[32] The Bolsheviks were now seen as 'the people who in principle did not know how to solve the most complicated problems of society and offered, instead, a set of very simple, primitive quasi-solutions'.[33]

In 1988, a magazine of the Union of Soviet Writers reprinted Maxim Gorkiy's *Nesvoevremennye mysli* ('Untimely thoughts'), a collection of articles from 1917–18 that described the horrors of the revolution. Although the passages attacking Lenin directly were censored, there was more than enough charge to explode the myth of the revolution which had had 'thousands, yes, thousands of people – workers and peasants – starving in prison',[34] which had perpetrated 'violence, unworthy of democracy',[35] and for whose leaders 'the notions of honour and dishonour' had been beyond understanding, as they had been busily 'creating a new statehood based on the old foundation of tyranny and violence'.[36] The last vestige of Russian democracy, the Constituent Assembly, crushed by the Bolsheviks in 1918, was now rescued from oblivion and received sympathetic coverage.[37]

As the regime, desperate for heroes, busily rehabilitated the Bolshevik old guard shot by Stalin, the Russian myth-slayers were telling the nation that 'it was precisely the old guard that created the political mechanism, the tool for absolute power which Stalin subsequently used . . .'[38] The old guard was now blamed for 'voluntarily surrendering into Stalin's hands the infinite power created by the revolution', and for 'leftist impatience that urged the country to take the leaps which turned into national tragedy'.[39]

Like Khrushchev before him, Gorbachev discovered his own Lenin: a 'later' Lenin of the New Economic Policy (NEP), who allowed limited private property, criticized bloated state bureaucracies and, occasionally, defended the peasant. Unlike Khrushchev, however, Gorbachev was unable (or unwilling) to prevent a gradually expanding public exploration of alternative images of the founding *vozhd'* ('the supreme leader').

Before long the deadly tide swirled perilously close to Lenin's pedestal, rising higher and higher. The attack on the shrine was commenced by Vasiliy Selyunin's 'Istoki' ('Sources'),[40] a brave, for 1988, essay which began glasnost in Soviet political history. Selyunin fired the first bullet that pierced the Lenin icon by replacing the humane and kind Lenin of the official canon with a creator of concentration camps, a doctrinaire fanatic whose pre-1921 'education' cost millions of lives, who caused untold suffering and famine, and who brought the country to the brink of national catastrophe.

As with other legitimizing myths, the Lenin canon was dealt several fatal blows in 1989. First came Vasiliy Grossman's *Vsyo techyot* ('Forever flowing') – a loosely joined collection of lugubrious life stories and disquisitions on the nature of tyranny, from which Lenin emerged as both an ideologue of totalitarianism and its first practitioner. Grossman's Lenin was 'merciless, imperious, madly vain and dogmatic'.[41] To his lust for power, in the service of which he employed 'all his capabilities, all his will, all his passions', he sacrificed 'the most sacred – liberty'.[42] Lenin was 'a murderer of Russian liberty', says a labour-camp inmate in the book.[43] Lenin 'laid the foundation for a state without freedom', wrote Grossman. 'Stalin built it.'[44] Stalinism was Lenin in power, a victorious Lenin, whose banner Stalin raised over Russia.[45] In the same year the publishing house of the Union of Soviet Writers announced plans to bring out Aleksandr Solzhenitsyn's *Gulag Archipelago*, which, in Chapter One of the second volume, described Lenin's authorship of the hard-labour 'extermination' camps.

In the late spring of 1989, first a Lenkom director Mark Zakharov and then the essayist Yuriy Karyakin suggested removing Lenin's body from the Mausoleum and interring it, as Lenin had apparently requested, next to his mother in the Volkovo cemetery in Leningrad.[46] For the Soviet mythology, the symbolic patricide of the Founding Fathers became the *coup de grâce*. With the first years of the Soviet regime now shown to have been overshadowed by fanaticism; with Stalin's rule of nearly thirty years a subject of gory revelations every day; and with Brezhnev's eighteen years in power dismissed as 'stagnation', mired in repression, corruption and incompetence, precious little remained of the nation's seventy years to celebrate and inspire.*

Already in 1988, the Dean of Moscow's Institute of History and

---

* Deflated, along the way, was one of the most powerful of the legitimizing myths: the Great Patriotic War against Nazi Germany. 'We have managed to create a fantasy of a different war . . . [with which] I, as a veteran, had nothing to do,' wrote a leading Russian writer, Viktor Astafiev ('Istoriya i literatura' ('History and literature'), *Literáturnaya Gazeta*, 18 May 1988). Emerging from this revision was a picture of a heroic, betrayed and martyred people, caught between two savage tyrannies – Hitler's and Stalin's – and, for four long years, ground relentlessly between the two giant bloodstained millstones. 'We did not know how to fight,' Astafiev added. 'We ended the war not knowing how to fight. We drowned the enemy in our blood, we buried him under our corpses' (*ibid.*).

Archives saw Soviet history as a grim procession of 'millions of *zeks*' ('prisoners'); 'enslaved and robbed peasants'; and a 'long-suffering' Soviet people – deceived, humiliated, 'drowned in sixty years of nihilism, spiritual void and decay', and, in the end, given a 'socialism without freedom and without bread and butter'.[47] A year later, he carried this image to its logical conclusion: the Soviet regime had been 'brought into being through bloodshed, with the aid of mass murder and crimes against humanity',* and 'Soviet history as a whole was not fit to serve as a legal basis for Soviet power.'[48]

Remarkable in both brevity and mercilessness, this bonfire of official fables left behind charred remains. 'The past is shameful, the present is monstrous' – such was, in the opinion of a leading Soviet political commentator, the country's dominant mood in 1989.[49]† The mighty

---

With devastating precision the revisionists established the regime's responsibility both for the war itself and for its disastrous prosecution, replete with incompetence and an appalling disdain for Soviet soldiers' lives. Instead of a 'victory for Soviet diplomacy', the Stalin–Hitler non-aggression pact of 1939 was now portrayed as an 'odious document' and 'one of the most tragic and shameful pages in our history' (Mikhail Semiryaga, '23 avgusta, 1939', *Literaturnaya Gazeta*, 5 October 1988, and Vladimir Omlinskiy, 'Ten' ('The shadow'), *Literaturnaya Gazeta*, 7 September 1988). No longer the clever manoeuvre of the official myth, a cynical but necessary exercise in *Realpolitik*, which was to buy time to prepare for war, the pact with Hitler was seen by the Soviet side as a genuine treaty of friendship. The crusading historians made public the turning over to the Gestapo of German communist refugees and cited Stalin's Foreign Minister, Vyacheslav Molotov, who declared that it was 'not only senseless but even criminal to wage a war to "destroy Hitlerism" under the false banner of a struggle for "democracy"' (A. Novikov, 'Na poroge voyny' ('On the threshold of war'), *Komsomol'skaya Pravda*, 24 August 1988).

* On 20 August 1990, announcing on national television a presidential decree 'on the restoration of the rights of all those repressed in the years 1920–30–40–50', Politburo member Aleksandr Yakovlev read a statement which is among perestroika's most remarkable documents. Reminiscent of the Gettysburg Address in its brevity and the solemn austerity of its cadences, it said, in part: 'It is not they [political prisoners] that we forgive, it is ourselves. We are guilty because they lived, for years, oppressed and maligned. It is we who are being rehabilitated, not those who thought differently, had different ideas and different convictions.' And, speaking of the Soviet regime, Yakovlev added: 'History has not known so concentrated a hatred towards the human being.' (Aleksandr Yakovlev, *Muki prochtenia bytia* ('The torments of reading life'), pp. 260–1.)

† While in February 1989 only 7 per cent of Soviet citizens agreed that 'our country is worst of all', 57 per cent did so two years later. In May 1991, 56 per cent of those

castle of the Soviet state, its thick outer walls still bristling with awesome weapons, stood empty. In less than two years, the *cahiers* at the bottom and intellectuals at the top filled the formerly pristine and luminous space occupied by Soviet mythology with thousands of pulsating black dots, each an instance of past or present calamity, injustice or privation. Suddenly, staring, as if from a giant pointillist canvas, there was the face of a nation entirely and shockingly different from that which the people, their parents and grandparents had imagined.

Whatever else they might discern at a greater remove, future historians will have this to say of the demise of the communist civilization: in the end was the Word.

In his brilliant book on the French Revolution, Simon Schama wrote of the 'cultural revolution that had taken place in the heart of the nobility'.[50] As in France exactly 200 years before, it was the Soviet nobility – professional Party functionaries and their support staff, the intelligentsia – that dominated the Fourth Russian Revolution's initial stages. As we have noted, this cultural revolution occurred not well before the upheaval but in the middle of it. Although brief and riddled with gaps, the education of future revolutionaries by glasnost was real and effective. Inspired by the events and ideas swirling around them, the future leaders marched in step with the revolution, mirroring its depth and maturity. 'In revolutions men live fast,' wrote Lord Macaulay. 'The experience of years is crowded into hours: old habits of thought and action are violently broken; novelties, which at first sight inspire dread and disgust, become in a few days familiar, endurable, attractive.'[51] In no case was this truer than in Yeltsin's.

Two months after he turned fifty-eight, Yeltsin suddenly found himself in an entirely new world: for the first time, he was not in the employ of the party-state. In compliance with a new law that prohibited government officials from serving in the Congress of People's Deputies, he submitted his resignation to Prime Minister Nikolay Ryzhkov on the day after the elections – even though he was far from assured of a seat in the smaller permanent parliament, the Supreme Soviet, which the

---

polled agreed that 'communism had brought Russia nothing but poverty, queues and mass repressions'. About the same proportion of respondents thought that 'a chain of crimes and madness' was an apt description of their country's history. (Lev Gudkov and Boris Dubinin, 'Konets kharizmaticheskoy epokhi' ('The end of the charismatic era'), *Svobodnaya Mysl*', June 1993, p. 39.)

Congress was to elect from its members. That spring he took to calling himself 'unemployed'.

Yet, if he was at all apprehensive and hesitant, he publicly showed no wariness as he embraced, even celebrated, his new state. Emboldened by the electoral triumph, he declared that his victory was not over Brakov, but over 'the Party bureaucracy, the apparat'.[52] He seemed fully recovered and reacquainted with his routine: getting up at five in the morning ('This is sacred – no matter when I go to bed');[53] reading fiction and non-fiction 'with public resonance', including Aleksandr Solzhenitsyn and Anatoliy Rybakov, whose anti-Stalinist novel *Children of the Arbat* was the rage among the intelligentsia; doing morning exercises and taking cold showers.[54] He brimmed with plans. In the absence of any official preparation for the Congress, 'we', the group of deputies from Moscow, were 'taking the initiative into our own hands', he told Soviet television.[55] There were urgent laws that must be prepared and passed by the Congress without delay: on elections, pensions, on the 'press and glasnost', and the law that would enable 'all kinds of social organizations, including parties, to exist'.[56]

At a rally of 20,000 in Zelenograd, Moscow's radical suburb whose population was employed at secret defence plants, Yeltsin accused Gorbachev of 'taking one step forward and two steps back'.[57] He again called for the removal of Ligachev and suggested that the Congress should find an alternative to Prime Minister Nikolay Ryzhkov.[58] Five days before the opening of the Congress, 25,000 Moscow democrats held the largest protest rally to date in the parking lot of the Luzhniki stadium. Scouting the enemy's territory, a correspondent of the hard-line *Sovetskaya Rossia* spotted 'only one' red flag and noted a plethora of subversive slogans: 'Transform the Congress of People's Deputies into a Constituent Assembly', 'Civil disobedience against the criminal authorities', and 'Sit down at the table with the authorities and make them back down'.[59]

The crowd's 'clear favourite', along with Andrey Sakharov,[60] Yeltsin presented the legislative programme of the 'Moscow group' of radical Deputies. He charged that preparations for the First Congress had been hijacked by the apparat ('Shame! Shame! Shame!' the crowd chanted) and demanded that Gorbachev give an account of the past four years. When Yeltsin declared that there ought to be not one but several candidates for the office of the Chairman of the Supreme Soviet,* currently

---

* The new Supreme Soviet was to become a permanent part of the Congress, which was to gather twice a year for general sessions. As the parent body, the Congress was superior to the Soviet and could rescind its decisions.

occupied by Gorbachev, the crowd began to chant 'Yeltsin! Yeltsin! Yeltsin!'[61]

The coincidence of Yeltsin's electoral triumph with the erosion of censorship prompted the first attempts by increasingly independent Russian political observers to assess what they called the 'Yeltsin phenomenon'. Remarkably astute and confident given the novelty of the genre, they offered clear analysis of a rapidly evolving subject. In agreement about much of the external paraphernalia of Yeltsin's success, the political technology and the context of his victory, they differed about the matters on which many other experts, native and foreign, would from that time be similarly divided: the man's personal motives and objectives, and the role he had played in the Russian transformation.

The commentary by Andranik Migranyan projected the residual apprehension and mistrust of the Moscow intelligentsia. Yeltsin's appeal was founded on a 'dangerously' neo-Bolshevik call for 'expropriating the expropriators' – returning to the people what had been stolen from them by the Party nomenklatura.[62] In Yeltsin's ability to 'grasp mass attitudes' and 'simplify complicated problems at the mass level'[63] Migranyan saw a potentially disastrous demagoguery that proffered seemingly effective solutions to complex issues and eventually led to a 'dead end'. Like the Bolsheviks, this Yeltsin was capable only of destruction, not creation.[64]

Vitaliy Tretyakov's analysis covered considerably larger territory. Tretyakov traced the beginning of the 'phenomenon' to Yeltsin's February 1986 speech at the Twenty-Sixth Party Congress.[65] Every revolution, Tretyakov wrote, began with the question 'Who is to blame?' When Yeltsin said, 'The delegates may ask: why did I not say all this when I spoke at the last Congress? I can answer and answer frankly: perhaps I lacked courage and political experience,' he became the first of the Party elite to announce, in effect, 'Yes, I am to blame.' The result was a 'powerful moral boost' that Yeltsin received from millions of people who longed for an admission from above of personal, rather than merely collective, responsibility for all that had happened to them and the country.[66] And, since no other Party functionary of Yeltsin's rank followed him in this *mea culpa*, he retained the moral leadership for the next stage of the revolution, the one that was to deal with the fundamental issue of 'What is to be done?'

According to Tretyakov, Yeltsin continued what Gorbachev had started, but he 'sharpened' the issues, explaining them by examples understood by everyone. He urged the solution not of all problems facing the country but of the ones which were 'directly relevant to the ordinary man': food, housing, social justice, availability of goods and services. Yeltsin's power lay in his ability to hit the bull's-eye of the most 'painful' issues.[67] Yeltsin had succeeded in fledgling democratic politics, Tretyakov argued, because he himself, in effect, had made Soviet politics democratic. He was the first to divest himself of the mystery in which those who exercised power in the Soviet Union wrapped themselves. In doing so, he had destroyed the inferiority complex this mystery had for decades engendered in the common folk, together with the belief that those above were a different species whose thinking and actions were beyond the ordinary man's understanding. 'Yeltsin lowered high politics from the Olympian heights and put it on the doorstep of everyman's house.'[68] And the people repaid him by 'supporting the man who raised them to the level at which major policy decisions are made'.[69]

By resigning from the Politburo in 1987, by promising to resign his ministerial post if he was elected to the Congress of People's Deputies (long before the law requiring him to do so was passed), by his speech at the Nineteenth Conference, Yeltsin created at least the impression of fighting not for personal power but 'for his honour and his convictions'.[70] It is alleged, Tretyakov continued, that Yeltsin was after supreme power. If so, were not his resignation in 1987 and the disagreement with his colleagues rather 'illogical' ways of achieving the goal? Perhaps this was a wily political strategy. But, be that as it may, people were starved of politicians who behaved like that in pursuit of power.[71]

The Yeltsin phenomenon, concluded Tretyakov, was inseparable from Gorbachev's perestroika. It had emerged 'because of the Party' – but it existed 'because of the people'. Like Yeltsin, the people supported perestroika in general but were critical of its slow pace. And the worse perestroika coped with its tasks, the more popular Yeltsin would be.[72]

Belying the vigour, coherence and thirst for action he had displayed that spring, Yeltsin's performance at the central political event of the year – the First Congress of People's Deputies, which opened on 25 May – did not live up to the expectations and hopes of his fans, now numbering tens of thousands throughout the Soviet Union. Some responsibility for this baffling limpness, which took virtually everyone by surprise, was undoubtedly borne by the habit of drawing back, mentally and physically, after major successes, often wasting precious momentum and squandering some of the victory's biggest prizes. In the years to come, this psychological and physical condition would become stronger, more obvious and more regular – puzzling, disappointing and eventually exasperating his supporters and allies.

In this case, however, that syndrome was not the main cause of his lacklustre performance. Rather, like everyone else, Yeltsin was unprepared for, dazzled and dwarfed by what was transacted in the Kremlin's Palace of Congresses. Having, until then, performed best when performing solo – on centre stage against the dark-grey background of the apparat's inept opposition – Yeltsin's sharp but still rather narrow vision of a high Party functionary was momentarily overwhelmed by the disorderly brilliance and plain proto-democratic tumult in which some of the nation's best minds, liveliest tongues and largest egos, suddenly liberated, competed for national attention.

Nothing in the four years of perestroika, not even the Nineteenth Conference, foreshadowed the First Congress. In a year full of cognitive breakthroughs, this was by far the most powerful blast of truth. The Congress was also, and perhaps even more significantly, the greatest step towards reconstructing a nation until then dissolved in the all-powerful and jealous state.

More than by any other aspect of the totalitarian technology, so durably designed by Stalin's perverse genius, the stability of the Soviet political system in the post-Stalin era was preserved by the forced muteness and deafness of the people, by their inability to know what their compatriots really thought. 'Thus we live: feeling not our country's [soil] under our feet, our words [are] not heard ten paces away,' wrote a great Russian poet, Osip Mandel'shtam, who perished in a prison camp.[73] 'The prolonged absence of any free exchange of information', noted this century's best chronicler of totalitarianism, Aleksandr Solzhenitsyn, 'opens up a gulf of incomprehension between whole groups of the population, between millions and millions. We simply cease to be a whole people . . .'[74]

Just as the genesis of the sense of self – of one's separateness and individuality – is not possible without a child's direct communication with others,[75] so national conscience could begin to emerge only with the destruction of the wall of silence between people. In a festival of cognitive emancipation, which the First Congress was to become, the country set out on a long and painful journey of self-discovery, self-awareness and separateness from state without which there could be no civil society and, therefore, no democracy.

The thrill of having lived to hear one's fellow citizens' uncensored public words, of witnessing the nation's first honest dialogue with itself, of feeling, at long last, the country 'beneath one's feet', shone through the commentaries of witnesses and participants alike. 'The entire country spoke from the podium of the Congress in full voice, openly and freely,' rhapsodized an editorial in a national newspaper.[76] 'We have risen to a new level of understanding of ourselves,' said Andrey Sakharov.[77]

The Congress 'helped the people – from head of state to peasant – to [get to] know themselves', wrote a member of the *Izvestia* journalistic team covering the event.[78] Television, radio and newspapers gave the nation time and space, 'a chance to speak out', without omissions and editing.[79] 'For the first time,' noted a participant, 'we have produced a political impression, as if in clay, a mirror of our social organism.'[80]

Even before the Congress came to order, the nation gasped in disbelief at the disappearance of the rituals which had been considered inseparable from the Soviet state. The first image broadcast across the USSR's twelve time zones was an empty dais: the Politburo and the government sat in the hall! 'They did not come marching in single file from behind the curtain – the "leaders of the Party and the government", arranged by rank,' an *Izvestia* Congress reporter wrote the next day in a front-page article. 'Neither did the hall resound to the stentorian voices of the official "chanters", or thunder in interminable applause, long after which both one's palms and one's conscience hurt.'[81]*

Fittingly, the wonder-filled Congress was framed by Andrey Sakharov, whose very name had been anathema only two-and-a-half years before. The only one of 2,500 delegates addressed by Gorbachev by name and patronymic, 'Andrey Dmitrievich', rather than as 'Comrade so and so', he delivered the first speech, calling on the Congress to be 'worthy of its great mission' and to issue a decree declaring itself the 'supreme power of the land' – above the Party and above the state.[82] And even though no such decree was adopted – then or at the very end of the Congress, after another appeal by Sakharov – the notion of society's regeneration, first by separation and then by liberation from the Party state, would remain the central unifying theme of the Congress, and its key achievement.

---

* The journalist who wrote these words later learned that the Politburo members had been ready to fill the dais (instead of sitting in the hall with the Deputies), and the 'chanting group' had been deployed in the audience – and that both arrangements were cancelled by Gorbachev personally (interview with Vladimir Nadein). Arranged and staffed by the Central Committee Secretariat, claques had been part of top-level gatherings since the mid-1920s when Stalin used them to silence the members of the various 'oppositions'.

As in every revolution, the parting of ways between society and the regime began with an indictment of the state. Together the Deputies' speeches, which a Russian journalist rightly called 'fearless',[83] amounted to a collective *cahier*, its veracity validated and effect increased immeasurably because it was expressed by the country's most prominent and respected citizens speaking from what was billed as the nation's highest political forum.

Yet it was not just a superior imprimatur that distinguished the Congress *cahiers* from the newspaper originals, but also a higher level of generalization and dramatically expanded area of scrutiny. For the next three weeks, remembered a Deputy, 'the Kremlin's *sanctum sanctorum* rang with the words which only yesterday would have landed one in a labour camp or psychiatric ward'.[84]*

Nowhere was the distance between the old norm and new standard of public discourse greater than in the speech by the man whose name was known to all Soviet children who grew up in the 1960s: Yuriy Vlasov, the national hero, former world champion weightlifter, the 'strongest man on earth' of propaganda fame. 'The richest country in the world in peacetime is struggling with ration coupons,' he thundered. 'We lack the most elementary food. Our ruble is pitiful compared to any other currency. Our great country is humiliated. We cannot sink any lower because, after this, only disintegration [will follow].'[85]

Other addresses rendered the seemingly hyperbolic harshness and urgency of Vlasov's jeremiad utterly rational and warranted. Trapped between the increasingly toothless state plan and the still officially illegal market – abused by authorities and criminals alike – the country's economy was unravelling. The Deputies lamented the 'half-empty shelves', the 'bitter food queues'[86] and the shortages of the 'twenty or thirty most elementary goods',[87] among them soap, salt, laundry detergent, socks and matches.[88] A leading Russian economist reported that 15 per cent of all industrial enterprises were officially listed as loss-making, and another 50 per cent as minimally profitable.[89] With such an economy, he added, even the present bad life was more than the country could realistically afford. The Soviet state was deeply in debt (external and internal), consuming, instead of investing in technological innovations, and beggaring future generations.[90]

---

* The demise of taboos proved too swift even for the editor-in-chief of the leading 'liberal' government newspaper, *Izvestia*, who asked the reporters covering the Congress to be more 'circumspect', and trimmed, among other things, references to Sakharov and Yeltsin (interview with Vladimir Nadein).

In a state which had amassed more nuclear missiles than any other nation on earth, peasants in the Russian north-west were reported by a celebrated writer to mow grass 'exactly as they did in the twelfth century'.[91] At the Congress, the head of the Counting Commission, a world-renowned scholar, was adding up the votes on an abacus.[92] In the penultimate decade of the twentieth century, Russian villages communicated by horse or tractor because the countryside had only one-tenth of the necessary telephones.[93] (For Soviet cities, the corresponding number was 30 per cent.)[94] Altogether, three-quarters of Soviet homes were without a telephone, with the state unable to fulfil 14.9 million requests for installation, including those from one million invalids.[95]

The Deputies bemoaned the fates of a severely disabled adolescent, without any education or job, who received a pension of twenty-six rubles and no other form of assistance; of single mothers 'strangled by penury and helplessness';[96] of elderly women in the countryside, the mothers to the post-war generation of children, the wives of invalids and the widows of the Second World War, who had tilled the 'bitter soil' on harnessed cows and who now received, if lucky, 'beggar's crumbs' of a pension.[97] (After thirty years in a kolkhoz, a woman was getting thirty-six rubles a month – as a widow, not a labour veteran: work in the kolkhoz did not entitle her to a pension.)[98] With a few terrifying numbers, a former Politburo member, Kirill Mazurov, who now served as the Chairman of the all-Union Veterans' Council, summarized the tales of hundreds of *cahiers*: of fifty million pensioners, twenty-two million received sixty rubles or less – less than the meagre official subsistence minimum.[99]

A female surgeon from rural Siberia informed fellow Deputies that in her region 88 per cent of hospitals in the countryside were housed in decrepit buildings without running water or a sewage system, 'let alone hot water'.[100] She was terrified of coming to the operating table because her hospital lacked the most elementary equipment and drugs.[101] Life expectancy in the Soviet Union was estimated by a scholar–Deputy to be four to eight years shorter than that in Western countries.[102]

The last myth of the Soviet state to be discarded at the Congress lay at the heart of the regime and had been taboo until then, even for the most daring *cahiers*: the 'everlasting friendship and brotherhood' between its peoples and the 'unbreakable union' of the Republics. Frozen by terror but never alleviated, much less resolved, ethnic tensions emerged well preserved and exacerbated by the sixty-year pause. With the bloody pogrom of Meskhetian Turks in Uzbekistan in the background, the Congress heard barely civil exchanges between the Deputies from Armenia and Azerbaijan over an Armenian enclave inside Azerbaijan (the Nagorno-Karabakh Autonomous District), and between the representatives of Georgia and Abkhazia, Georgia's Autonomous Republic, which was determined to become independent.[103]

In addition to ancient animosities, the Congress was apprised of another, potentially lethal strain: between the Republics, on the one hand, and the Centre on the other.* It was not just the perennial rebels, Estonia, Latvia and Lithuania, whose delegates agitated for 'economic sovereignty'[104] and persuaded the Congress to set up a commission for 'political and legal evaluation of the Soviet–German non-aggression pact of 1939', on which they blamed their occupation by the Soviet Union. Horrified by the massacre of peaceful demonstrators in Tbilisi two months before, the Georgians, who had been part of Russia for over 150 years, were now determined to secede. Even among the 'brotherly Slavs' of Ukraine, their leading writer–official, Boris Oleynik, decried the dominance of Russian, which made the native languages of the Republics look like 'hunched-over servants in their own house'.[105] Even the generally docile Kalmyks and Moldavians vented their grievances against Moscow.[106] The Russians, too, felt slighted and robbed by the 'administrative–industrial machine' of the Union.[107] Tired of mockery and alleged 'Russophobia', a leading Russian writer suggested, half in jest, that Russia ought to contemplate seceding from the Union.[108]

The Congress differed from the *cahiers* not only in the reach of its iconoclasm, which now extended to the last frontiers, but in the movement from the enumeration of mammoth failures and daily indignities to the assignment of responsibility. In dozens of speeches, the regime's culpability was no longer implied but fixed most explicitly.

The millions of victims of state terror were no longer blamed on the nebulous 'distortion of socialist legality'. In a rousing oration Yuriy Vlasov called for the removal of the KGB from its current headquarters, in whose 'bowels the best, the pride and the flower of our peoples were tortured' and from where 'orders to exterminate or persecute millions of people had come for decades', causing grief and excruciating pain.[109] The heir of the Stalinist 'organs', the KGB continued to be 'a veritable underground empire', which controlled society as a whole and each individual and which was still a threat to democracy.[110]

---

* In the week preceding the opening of the Congress, the Lithuanian Supreme Soviet passed a constitutional amendment granting the Republic the right to veto all-Union laws. On the same day the Supreme Soviet of Estonia (which had passed a similar amendment in November 1988) declared itself in full control of the Republic's economy.

The crisis in the economy was not due to 'someone's ill-will or mistakes', said the Russian Orthodox metropolitan (and the future Patriarch of All Russia) Aleksey of Leningrad and Novgorod. It was a consequence of the 'spiritual impoverishment that struck our society'.[111]* Other Deputies spelled out what the cautious priest in the state's employ had only hinted at. The Soviet regime had brought 'decades of painful spiritual slavery, indentured labour, self-deception and lies', declared the Kirghiz writer Chingiz Aytmatov. But the worst evil was the 'total alienation of everyone from everyone, the state from the people and people from the state'.[112]

'Violence ruled. It was the sole law,' said Yuriy Vlasov. 'Violence, fear, intolerance, cruelty ran through our entire existence like a central nerve, and even now would not let us straighten ourselves up.' To him, perestroika was more than economic reform, it was an effort to overcome a system based 'entirely on suppression of individual rights, lawlessness and . . . lies'.[113]

It was inevitable that the state's failures (and now crimes) would sooner or later cast a shadow on its living, rather than its dead, leaders. It is because of this burden of incumbency, affirmed by the Congress, that Gorbachev's masterful performance, which had more than once saved the gathering from deteriorating into an endless floor fight, could not be called a triumph – a term that in modern politics is as much a measure of popular admiration as of individual accomplishment. From now on, in domestic politics, triumphs would remain forever outside Gorbachev's reach: demystification of power, which Gorbachev had done so much to promote, and the blame it invariably generates had quickly outpaced gratitude. Still by far the brightest on the Soviet political firmament, Gorbachev's star began very slightly to dim.

On the road to spiritual de-etatization, along which the Congress travelled such a remarkable distance, few discoveries were as crucial as the public acknowledgment of a fundamental asymmetry in the relationship between the party-state and the citizen. A strong and proud state was not, it turned out, synonymous with the happiness of its citizens. The Soviet state had freely taken 'people's strength and health' but had reimbursed them in a 'very niggardly' fashion.[114] It strangled them with

---

* It is to this crisis that a leading actor Rolan Bykov attributed the presence of over a million children in Soviet orphanages – more, by his calculation, than had existed after the Great Patriotic War that killed millions of Soviet citizens (*Pervyi S'ezd*, vol. III, p. 231).

shortages, humiliated them with ration coupons for meat and sugar, and restrictions on soap[115] and impoverished them with 'hundred-, fifty- or even thirty-ruble pensions'.[116] 'We ought to reject the view', argued a leading Moscow editor-turned-Deputy, that 'the richer and mightier the state, the richer and more powerful the people, and the better they lived'.[117]

Beyond registering the state's basic deficiency in meeting its obligations to its subjects, the Congress questioned the state's ability, in principle, to manage every aspect of societal existence. The state 'heaved on to its shoulders' tasks that it could not possibly perform and that ought to be taken up by the institutions of civil society: work collectives, family, individual citizens.[118] It was especially inadmissible for the state to 'manage culture, ethics and morality'.[119]

Society's goals, then, were no longer identical with those of the state. 'The Congress helped us recognize a simple truth,' a major Russian newspaper observed in an editorial entitled 'Turning towards the needs of man'. 'There cannot be a prosperous society where man's needs are not met.'[120] The prosperity of abstract 'people' could no longer be divorced from the prosperity of the individual: 'the wealth of people is formed first and foremost from the property of each, and the freedom of all is made up of the freedom of each'.[121]

In the end – having stripped the state of mystery and immunity from blame; having 'undermined the decades-old trepidation before the state power',[122] as an *Izvestia* reporter put it; having exposed it as grossly incompetent in the discharge of its reciprocal responsibilities – the Congress effected what a Deputy called 'an unprecedented breakthrough in establishing normal relations between the state and the people represented by the Deputies'.[123] In this amended (if not yet re-created) political universe, which was to become the Congress's most important legacy, both power and legitimacy began their inexorable drift away from the party-state. The people, an exuberant Deputy declared, were 'above the Party'; the Congress of People's Deputies 'above the Party Congress'; the Supreme Soviet 'above the Central Committee'; and the Constitution 'above the Party Code'.[124]

At the time, this was a mere declaration of intent rather than a statement of fact. Supported by no more than one-sixth of the Deputies, this and other declarations left no trace in the official documents of the Congress, most of whose members were still beholden to the apparat. Yet, despite its absence from resolutions and laws, word became deed in what turned into the world's first live television coverage of a revolution, recorded by nearly 200 directors, producers and cameramen in ninety-five hours of live broadcasts and fifty-six hours of reports in nationally televised news programmes.[125]

Instilled with a sense of their unique mission, the producers of daily broadcasts instituted a complete change of routine. No more 'glorious panoramic shots' of the Praesidium.[126] No more listeners awed by the supreme leader. No more hands raised in unison. And, most of all, no more vistas of red banners, 'in which individual faces were lost'. At all hours, three cameramen walked the hall seeking out 'the detail, the angle', the faces of the Deputies as they listened, spoke from the podium or argued from the floor. The reporters sought not only a complete transcript, but, as one of the producers put it, 'the spirit, the nerve, and the thought' of the gathering.[127]

There must be, at best, only a handful of instances in the history of television that equalled those three weeks in sustained intensity. 'The people, the entire people, without an iota of exaggeration', were drawn daily and hourly to what an *Izvestia* correspondent called the 'thrill aroused by the frankness and daring of the Deputies'.[128] 'No one is working,' a Deputy informed his colleagues, 'everyone is watching television.'[129] The country 'sat before tens of millions of television sets, as a committed witness', *Izvestia* reported.[130] People listened to the proceedings on portable radios, and then compared what they had heard with the newspaper account.[131] Off Smolenskaya Square in downtown Moscow, an American reporter saw a large crowd mesmerized before a half-dozen television sets in the window of an appliance store.[132] On a random afternoon, the Congress was being watched by an estimated 200 million viewers across the Soviet Union's twelve time zones.[133]

Ranked in significance with only a few decisions in Gorbachev's career ('Everyone sees us – the entire country, and the whole world!' he proudly announced on the first day of the Congress),[134] live broadcasts from the Congress created 'a new climate in society as a whole'.[135] Commented a Russian observer, they 'changed our view of life (if not, in fact, our life itself)'.[136] 'Those ten days, during which almost the entire nation continuously watched the hot debates at the Congress,' Yeltsin wrote at the time, 'gave people more politically than the previous seventy years. We were one people on the day the Congress opened, and [became] another on the closing day ... The people, almost all the people, woke up from hibernation.'[137]

Much to almost everyone's surprise, Boris Yeltsin's contribution to this awakening was rather modest. Thrice the spotlight was on him, and each time his performance did not rise to the occasion. Yeltsin's name was mentioned on the first day (or, rather, night) of the Congress, minutes into the debate on the Chairmanship of the Supreme Soviet. 'We shall vote for Gorbachev,' said a representative of the Ukrainian delegation, the writer Vladimir Yavorivskiy, 'but we will keep Yeltsin in the back of our minds.'[138] The next speaker (who also promised to vote for Gorbachev in the end) 'wanted to hear Yeltsin's point of view' on all the key issues facing the Congress.[139] Another Deputy contrasted the General Secretary's 'insufficient' decisiveness with Yeltsin's courage.[140] In the end, two Deputies,* both from the Sverdlovsk region, nominated Yeltsin for the Chairmanship.

Whether, in the long run, it would have been better for Yeltsin to compete with Gorbachev (and lose) or decline was a difficult question. It was not, however, an unexpected one. Yeltsin had known that he would be nominated from the floor, just as he knew that, in the end, almost everyone would vote for Gorbachev (Gorbachev was elected by 95.6 per cent of the vote). For a man who prided himself on calculating most of his moves well in advance, Yeltsin's response was strangely incongruous. He sounded overwhelmed and shaken, like a perennial critic–outsider awed by the prospect, however minimal, of the responsibility that comes with power.† A few hurried, crumpled, disjointed sentences were all he could muster. In the same hall where the Party's supremacy had already been openly questioned, Yeltsin mumbled something about the decision of the most recent Plenum of the Central Committee. 'As a communist', he felt obliged to abide by the Party's choice.[141] The next day a Russian journalist called Yeltsin's speech 'painfully laboured' and predicted, accurately, that it would 'disappoint his many fans'.[142]

His second chance to reclaim national attention came a few days later, after the election of the Supreme Soviet by the Congress. To demonstrate their dedication to freedom of political competition, the Deputies from Moscow nominated fifty-five candidates for the twenty-nine seats allocated to the capital in the Supreme Soviet. The result was predictable: all leading Moscow 'democrats', including Andrey Sakharov, were voted

---

* One, a turner from a metalwork plant in the city of Serov, would never again enter national politics. The other, a teacher of Marxism–Leninism by the name of Gennadiy Burbulis, would become Yeltsin's top aide, the Russian government's most determined anti-communist, and, during the first year of the post-Soviet Russian state, the country's second most powerful man.

† In the next two weeks Yeltsin would decline floor nominations for two elevated but largely ceremonial posts: Chairman of the Committee of People's Control and Deputy Chairman of the Council of Nationalities, one of the two houses of the Supreme Soviet.

down by the conservative majority of the Congress. 'They have thrown the most active people out of the Supreme Soviet, those who made real proposals for changing the present state of affairs,' Yeltsin commented. 'Those who obediently serve the apparatus remain.'[143]

During the Congress's first Sunday recess, protest meetings swept through Moscow. 'Why has Yeltsin not been elected a Deputy to the Supreme Soviet?' was the rallying cry of the 10,000 people gathered in Luzhniki.[144] '900 "no" votes counted for more than the 6 million Muscovites who voted for Yeltsin!' read a banner.[145] Protest petitions were circulated, together with a telegram to the Congress: 'By not choosing Yeltsin the Congress ignored the will of 5.6 million Muscovites.'[146] In Pushkinskaya Square, a speaker urged Party members to hand in their cards 'to show their support for Yeltsin'.[147] In the suburb of Kuntsevo, a crowd chanted, 'Remove Gorbachev!'[148]

When the Congress reconvened on Monday, 29 May, Aleksandr Kazannik, a bearded professor of jurisprudence from the Siberian city of Omsk, announced that he would give up his seat in the Supreme Soviet on condition that the slot was occupied by Yeltsin. 'If I were the First Secretary of an Obkom, I would not have to make this decision,' Deputy Kazannik told the Congress. 'I would have gone back home and separated myself from the voters by a fence of policemen. I, on the other hand, would not be able to look my voters in the eye.'[149]

Gorbachev fully grasped Yeltsin's singular status as the 'barometer of perestroika' in both domestic and world esteem and shrewdly preferred to keep him tied to the regime through his membership of the Supreme Soviet rather than relieve him of any shared responsibility. The Chairman indicated his 'favourable attitude' to a 'positive solution',[150] and the Congress duly voted to allow Yeltsin to take Kazannik's seat. During the entire contretemps Yeltsin did not say a word.

When he finally spoke, his speech, which would have been audacious four days before, fell somewhat short by the new yardstick forged by the Congress. Virtually everything had already been mentioned from the Congress podium, often to considerably greater dramatic effect. His speech lacked, too, the richness, the allusiveness, the stirring rhythm of his radical comrades, the professional lecturers and publicists, who were the stars of the Moscow delegation: Afanasiev, Popov, Shmelyov, Chernichenko. By comparison, Yeltsin seemed stiff and dry. Nonetheless, as at the Party Conference a year before, Yeltsin's speech was marked by the scope and viability of his proposals. It was not a cry of anger or despair but a carefully drafted, wide-ranging and politically feasible programme designed to appeal, at least in part, not just to the radical minority but to the conservative majority as well. In a characteristic performance, Yeltsin was both ahead of the 'masses' and yet close enough to make his agenda comprehensible and practicable.

The speech's rhetorical core comprised several themes. Power was still in the hands of the bureaucratic apparatus, and people were still 'uninvolved' in the real management of state affairs.[151] By failing to 'take power', the Congress had become a hostage to old Soviet laws and decisions.[152] Meanwhile, the state of the nation was 'most troubling'. People lived in worse conditions than before. The number of poor was growing, and economic inequality increasing. Tens of millions existed below the poverty level, while others 'bathed in luxury'. The privileges of the latter should be eliminated and the very term 'nomenklatura' should be erased from the vocabulary.[153]

Corruption, crime and the black market were on the rise, as were inflation and ration coupons for food. Financial collapse loomed. To avert disaster, the Congress should adopt a 'programme of emergency measures that would lead the country out of the crisis', including laws on pensions, poverty and the 'forms of ownership'.[154] To improve the food supply, Yeltsin suggested the transfer of land to the peasants, who should decide for themselves the 'forms and methods' of production. The amount of money in circulation could be reduced by cutting state investment in industry and industrial construction by 30 per cent.[155] (Yeltsin apparently could not quite decide between a 30 and 40 per cent cut, which he had previously advocated. In the next two years the reduction of the budget investment would remain a key plank in his economic agenda fluctuating between 30 and 40 per cent.)

Yeltsin also proposed a 'radical change' in the structure of government. This would include 'decentralization of power', the removal from Party control of the mass media, election of the head of state by direct popular vote, and annual referendums on public confidence in the head of state. Every Union Republic should be endowed with economic and financial independence and 'territorial sovereignty'. He urged the adoption of laws that would codify the role and the place of the Party and define the limits of its influence on society.[156]

Ten days later, the First Congress of People's Deputies adjourned without acting on any of Yeltsin's suggestions. The Moscow version of the Estates-General, convened in Versailles 200 years before to the month, did not turn itself into a National Assembly – a revolutionary parliament, the self-authorized and self-proclaimed embodiment of national will and power.

This was the essence of Yeltsin's cheerless assessment, which grew progressively harsher. True, the live television coverage and the Deputies' desire to be heard was 'a major victory for glasnost'.[157] At the 1987 Plenum, Yeltsin reminded interviewers, he had been the first to criticize the General Secretary. 'Now, however, criticisms have been heard from several Deputies.'[158] Yet the prevalence of 'apparat candidates' among the Deputies had resulted in a scandalously paltry record where 'concrete' laws were concerned.[159] There were, Yeltsin told anyone willing to listen, too many things wrong with the country and its political system, which the Congress had failed to address. It left too much work unfinished. To have been a truly historic event the Congress would have had, for instance, to amend or eliminate Article Six of the Constitution on the 'guiding' role of the Party.[160] In its seventy-two-year monopoly of power, the Party had in many instances 'played a negative role' in the country's history.[161]

Yeltsin's work in the Supreme Soviet proved equally disappointing. Away from the televised sessions, the mesmerizing rhetoric of truth and defiance was followed by an inability to translate the newly found moral authority into effectively organized power. After all the fire and brimstone, the legislature confirmed the entire current government, minus a few Deputy Ministers in some second-rate departments.

Yeltsin was just as unhappy about the part he had been assigned: the Chairmanship of the relatively obscure Committee for Construction. He had envisaged a powerful body which would control the government's ministries and agencies, whose 'suggestions' the Committee would accept or reject.[162] He had hoped for a commanding role in developing a strategy for the entire national construction industry.[163] Instead, at once very busy and inconsequential, like most other newly created committees of the Supreme Soviet, the Committee for Construction did not even have a paid staff.[164] In a small office on the sixth floor of the Moskva Hotel, volunteers answered telephones and helped sort through 14,000 letters received in recent weeks.[165] The committee's authority had never been spelled out and the members, Yeltsin complained, had been 'left hanging'.[166]

Despite these travails, a visitor to Yeltsin's Committee was struck by an office culture very different from the traditional Soviet combination of incompetence and disdain for the supplicant. Hundreds of letters 'from all over the country' were arranged in neat piles, with a brief summary attached to each. The telephone rang incessantly, but the three aides and a typist, who took turns answering it, 'not once let themselves show annoyance, much less rudeness or indifference, which all of us, alas, still encounter in such places'. The style of the office was 'utterly new: dynamic, precise, polite, encouraging [people] to value time.'[167]

Yeltsin was frustrated by his inability to act on his campaign promise to cut investment in new industrial capacities by 30 to 40 per cent and to channel the freed resources into the 'social sphere'.[168] To him this failure was typical of a Congress that dealt in 'half-measures'. 'If we felt that the citizen was at the centre of our concerns, we should have concentrated on his needs,' he told an interviewer.[169] Instead, having recognized that the housing shortage was the most acute of all social problems, the Congress suggested a cut in industrial investment that was only half as large as Yeltsin thought absolutely necessary.[170]

Forever on the lookout for enemy machinations, he began to suspect that the Chairmanship was a plot to divert him from national politics. 'I do not exclude a quite definite hope [on the part of some] to bury Yeltsin as a politician in routine chores,' he told a Russian journalist three weeks after the Supreme Soviet began its work.[171] If such were his foes' designs, he was determined to upset them. 'Of course, it makes it more difficult for me to continue my struggle. But it does not prevent me from doing so. There are my principles, the mandate of the people who voted for me, and the promises that I made . . .'[172] He would not 'step away' from politics and would 'conduct political work' despite the increased workload.[173]

As frequently happened to Yeltsin, his political and personal resurgence was helped by events.

On Monday morning, 10 July, at the Shevyakov mine in the city of Mezhdurechensk, in the heart of the Kuznetsk coal basin in south-western Siberia known throughout the Soviet Union as the 'Kuzbass', eighty miners who had just come up from the pits after the night shift refused to turn in their headlamps and go home. Half an hour later they were joined by 200 miners from the morning shift. Thus began the third, after the 26 March election and the Congress, seminal event of that extraordinary year.

In the theatre of the Fourth Russian Revolution, only the spectacle of the First Congress equalled the Kuzbass strike in the extent and intensity of the public's absorption in a nationally televised drama. No longer mediated by the esteemed but alien Moscow intelligentsia, the country's discovery of itself was much more immediate and credible in this case. The impact of the revelations was enhanced by the privileged position the miners were believed to enjoy. They were among the highest-paid categories of workers. Their much envied benefits included paid holiday for up to thirty-six days a year and retirement at the age of fifty.

The envy disappeared overnight after the country learned of the miners' demands:

> Distribute work clothes in accordance with the regulation timetable. Give each miner a towel and 800 grams of soap a month for after-shift wash-up. Provide miners with carbonated water. Give miners padded cotton jackets, because of high rates of sickness due to a strong stream of cold air on the way down to the pits during the winter season. Improve the content of salads and meat dishes. Organize and control through personal signatures in a special notebook the sale of meat and sausage and give a monthly public account. Establish a firm schedule for the transportation of workers to and from work. Improve the supply of food: meat, fish etc. Designate Sunday a no-work day.[174]

In a petition submitted to (and ignored by) the Supreme Soviet three weeks before the strike, the miners wrote: 'A miner's entire life is adapted to the extraction plan . . . Miners and their children [endure] degradation and the threat of hunger. In this country miners have the most inhuman regime of work and leisure . . . The scheme of life and leisure is wretched: from work to home, from work to a liquor store.* It turns a person into a submissive animal.'[175]

An *Izvestia* correspondent found that even milk for children was hard to find in Mezhdurechensk.[176] When members of the 'food committee', promptly elected by the strikers, arrived at the local food depot, which the scared authorities had been forced to open, they were stunned. 'I am forty-one years old,' the committee's chairman told a Russian journalist. 'Two-thirds of life have passed. But many [food] products that we found there I not only had not seen before, I did not even know they existed.'[177]

In the Kuzbass, 235,000 families were waiting for housing.[178] Half of all miners lived in apartments with less than the Soviet 'health-required' minimum of nine square metres per person; 23 per cent had less than four metres and 17 per cent did not have separate living space.[179] 'Can

---

* In mining towns notorious for rampant alcoholism, the strike committees voted and scrupulously enforced the 'dry law': liquor stores were shut down, and liquor confiscated by the workers' patrols. Occasional drunks were promptly removed to police sobering-up stations by the strikers themselves. During the strike, the number of crimes in the region fell by half.

people really live under such conditions?' a Kuzbass striker asked on national television. 'Imagine a miner coming from work to such a hovel! How can he rest?'[180]

Forty-eight hours after the Shevyakov incident, the number of strikers reached 20,600, and the Minister of the Coal Industry was dispatched from Moscow to begin negotiations. The country watched the Minister gingerly making his way to the podium through the crowd on the central square of Mezhdurechensk, in front of the Gorkom. The miners were standing, sitting and lying in the grass, their tarpaulin jackets unbuttoned in the unusually hot Siberian summer, their torsoes covered with coal dust caked in sweat. Intoxicated by their own daring and the extraordinary sight of Moscow talking to them as equals, the crowd refused to go home. From a makeshift platform illuminated by thousands of miners' lamps, the Minister answered questions until 5 a.m. Several times the miners interrupted the Minister with the chants 'Za-bas-tov-ka! Za-bas-tov-ka!' ('Strike! Strike!') as they punched the air.[181]

Two days later the strike spread to 103 mines and enterprises, which employed 72,700 workers. By now, their demands had expanded far beyond salaries, bonuses for night shifts or carbonated water. In a freshly drafted 'Letter to the Soviet government' they demanded that Siberia and the Far East be provided 'with foodstuffs in accordance with standard health requirements'; that the privileges of all officials be eliminated;[182] and that a new constitution be drafted for nation-wide discussion and adopted no later than 7 November 1990.[183]

On 16 July, representatives of 100,000 workers from nine Kuzbass towns met to elect the Regional Strike Committee. The proceedings of the meeting were broadcast live throughout the region by loudspeakers attached to poles in town squares and in workers' settlements next to the pits. The same day, Gorbachev and Prime Minister Nikolay Ryzhkov appealed to the strikers and promised to send an 'authoritative' commission. The miners found the appeal 'belated'.[184] The number of idle workers reached 140,000.

The next day the commission, led by Politburo member Nikolay Slyunkov, arrived in the region's capital of Kemerovo. Several hours later, in a speech, which was also broadcast live throughout the region, Slyunkov conceded most of the demands, called the strikers 'dear comrades', and appealed to their 'wisdom at this difficult moment'.[185] On 19 July the Slyunkov commission and the strike committee of Kuzbass settled the strike. The protocol they signed read like a disaster-relief contract. The government had agreed to increase the delivery of foodstuffs to Kuzbass by 10,000 tonnes of sugar, 3,000 tonnes of washing powder, 3,000 tonnes of soap, over 6,000 tonnes of meat, 5 million cans of dairy preserves, and 1,000 tonnes of tea.[186] There would be more footwear, clothes, knitwear, television sets, refrigerators and washing machines.[187] On 20 July most mines in Kuzbass began to unload coal.

Through the third week of July a wave of copycat strikes paralysed Donetsk and Pavlograd in Ukraine, Rostov-on-the-Don in Southern Russia, Karaganda in Kazakhstan, and Vorkuta in the Russian Arctic Circle. As in Kuzbass, the government, represented by top officials including Prime Minister Ryzhkov, granted virtually all of the strikers' demands.

Those in the business of daily maintenance of the Soviet state's local affairs immediately sensed the enormous symbolic wound dealt by the strike. At a post-mortem in the Kemerovo Obkom, one of the Secretaries described the 'moral damage' inflicted by the walk-out as 'immeasurable'.[188] And so, indeed, it was. The strike doomed another core legitimizing myth of the Soviet pantheon: that of a 'workers' state'. Who is striking? asked a Russian columnist rhetorically. The workers, the 'most progressive class'?[189] Could they be the same miners who for decades had 'radiated official optimism' from newspaper pages and from posters that declared, 'Remember, worker: you are the owner of the plant'? All those:

> blandishments, so false and unctuous, now rumbled throughout the country, like warning peals of thunder. The miners' strikes are a reckoning not only for long years of arrogant neglect of people's basic needs, but also for the lies which accompanied our 'movement from victory to victory . . .' Owners do not strike.[190]

For local authorities, already shell-shocked and demoralized by the 26 March election, the strike was the second political earthquake in less than four months. It left them naked, defenceless and pitiable for everyone to see. The speed of the collapse of Soviet power in the Kuzbass, where the strike committees came to power overnight, was indicative of the scale of this débâcle. As was his wont, Gorbachev chose an optimistic interpretation. For all the 'drama of the events', he was very much encouraged by workers' taking 'the matter firmly into their own hands'.[191] Following the Kremlin, the mass media blamed local authorities for the lack of sensitivity, red tape, tardiness of response and most of the other mistakes which were held to have provoked the strike. 'The Centre had deliberately and successfully put the local authorities between itself and the workers and is continuing to squeeze them in this vice,' the manager of a Kuzbass mining enterprise noted astutely. 'This tactic is very convenient for the Centre: it is intended to lower the temperature of the steam at the expense of the local authorities.'[192]

Gorbachev's decision to ally the Centre with the 'bottom' against the 'middle' did buy the Kremlin a few more months of peace. But the victory was Pyrrhic. From its inception, the rigidly centralized Soviet state rested on this foundation: the Centre controlled all the resources, leaving none to its local potentates, but it also deployed coercion instantaneously and ruthlessly to protect its prefects. Gorbachev unilaterally upset the balance: while jealously guarding Moscow's exclusive possession of public goods, he withheld the force. The iron spine of the Soviet state, which for seven decades had connected the Kremlin to the provinces, was now broken. In July 1989, the Centre's control over the country began to shrink daily and inexorably.

That was the moment when Boris Yeltsin took a step designed to animate his stalled political agenda and to serve as a vehicle for reclaiming centre-stage: the creation of a united radical faction of Deputies in the Soviet parliament. The idea was neither new nor exclusively Yeltsin's, although he had hinted at it during the final stages of his campaign. At the end of April, in the regular gathering of Moscow Jacobins, the discussion group Moskovskaya Tribuna, Gavriil Popov broached the issue of a 'progressive club' at the coming Congress and even estimated the size of the potential membership at 300.[193] In the month and a half leading up to the Congress, the Moscow delegation met regularly and worked late into the evenings, hammering out common positions and even drafting bills.[194]

On the third day of the Congress, Popov, disgusted by the election of a Supreme Soviet that followed the 'orders of the apparat', proposed to form an 'opposition': an 'inter-regional independent group of Deputies'.[195] Two weeks later, at the Luzhniki rally that marked the adjournment of the First Congress, Yeltsin's announcement that the 'progressive' Deputies would form a common front with its own programme and its own goals became 'the sensation of the evening'.[196] Yet it was not until five weeks later, as the authorities were about to capitulate to the miners, that he mounted the rostrum of the Supreme Soviet to announce the unthinkable: the creation of open and organized political opposition, the Inter-Regional Group of Deputies, which would soon be known throughout the country by its Russian initials MDG (Mezhregional'naya Deputatskaya Gruppa).

The 'extremely difficult situation' in the country, Yeltsin said, made it imperative that 'all alternative points of view and all possible approaches' should be explored. The tasks facing society were so 'hugely diverse' that there was nothing surprising in the formation of diverse viewpoints in the different social strata, both about the essence and the dynamics of these problems and about possible ways of solving them.[197] Yeltsin described the core of the future faction as those Deputies who expressed the views of the 'left-radical strata'* of the public: the people who considered that the process of perestroika should be carried on more decisively and consistently. Accordingly, the Group planned to offer amendments to the USSR Constitution and the law on local elections, and to discuss changes relating to the economy, taxes, poverty, pensions, administrative (that is, ordered by the state) price increases, inflation and corruption.[198]

He ended by announcing the dates of the founding congress of the Group – 29 and 30 July – and invited all Deputies 'who were trying to make more radical and fundamental proposals in the preparation of documents for the Second Congress of People's Deputies'.

If ever there were, in the early stages of the Russian upheaval, any of Lord Macaulay's novelties 'which at first sight inspire dread and disgust' before becoming 'familiar, endurable, attractive',[199] a faction in the Soviet parliament was such a novelty *par excellence*. From kindergarten to graduate school, the incessant repetition of Lenin's 1921 injunction against factions and the memory of thorough and systematic extermination of 'deviationists' by Stalin permeated the Soviet collective mind. Yeltsin spoke from personal experience (and, most likely, conviction as well) when he told an interviewer that 'opposition' was a dirty word in his country, a word that people found difficult to say, a word they were afraid of because of its immediate association with 'enemies of the people'.[200] For months afterwards, he would split hairs, stubbornly denying the 'oppositional' character of the MDG.

Instead, Yeltsin described his efforts on behalf of the Group as having been prompted by objectives considerably less subversive. First, he felt it necessary to uphold the principle of diversity. 'Unity has already inflicted a great deal of damage on our country,' he explained. ' "Unity" stood for thinking exactly the way the supreme leader thought. It is time we got rid of this stereotype. It is in the clash of opinions that

---

* In so designating the Group's political provenance, Yeltsin followed the Soviet tradition, in which the critics of the party-state were called 'left' and the proponents of the Party orthodoxy 'right', even though in political denominations accepted in the West the labels ought to have been transposed.

the best solution develops.'[201] His other goal, he insisted, was largely technical: to organize a parliamentary minority for effective political action. The First Congress had produced a split between the conservative majority and a radical minority. Still, despite their numerical inferiority, the 'democrats' could have shaped the course of the Congress if they had been united behind 'practical suggestions' instead of turning sessions into rallies or showering the Congress with new proposals before they had succeeded in putting the old ones on the agenda. To correct this deficiency, the minority needed to be 'better organized'.[202]

Yet the key impetus for the effort extended well beyond these important but tactical benefits. For Yeltsin and his comrades, the Group was a means to respond to what they now saw as an urgent societal demand for revolutionary politics. Their conviction that this indeed was the case stemmed from Lenin's definition of a 'revolutionary situation', memorized in innumerable high school and college lectures: the 'top' (*verkhi*) could not rule in the old way, and the 'bottom' (*nizy*) did not want to live in the old way.

The first half of the formula had been firmly in place, with the 'top' pursuing a broad agenda of political reform. But, until 10 July, the 'bottom' had been passive. Despite his shrill and persistent prophecies of gloom following the Congress; despite his public protestations of belief that people's patience 'had limits' and that in one – 'maximum' two – years, the revolution from above would turn into 'a grassroots, spontaneous' one,[203] Yeltsin in private could not have considered this turn of events more than a far-fetched hunch. With the miners' strike spreading from Ukraine to Siberia and from Kazakhstan to Yakutia, he was at long last vindicated. Lenin's formula appeared complete. Yeltsin could now cite the master revolutionary with confidence: 'The "top" can no longer rule in the old way and the "bottom" is beginning to understand that they cannot live in the old way.'[204]

Yeltsin eagerly emphasized the political aspect of the strike. To him it was 'evidence that a smouldering economic crisis is threatening to develop into a comprehensive political one'.[205] Desperate living conditions were only one of the many causes of the strike. Others, Yeltsin argued, included dissatisfaction with the results of the First Congress, which had failed to speed up the slow pace of economic and political reform. The strike supplied proof of his diagnosis: by moving slowly and hesitantly, by adopting half-measures, the current agenda of the Supreme Soviet was not corresponding to the 'state of society', which was 'heaving beneath our feet'.[206]

In the aftermath of the strike, the country's leadership had lost the 'people's trust', Yeltsin contended. Local Soviets, the Party apparatus and trade unions had been discredited. The 'authoritarian regime' had been shaken.[207] The striking regions were in a *de facto* diarchy: demoralized local authorities and strike committees as 'kernels of real people's power'. People, Yeltsin told an interviewer at the end of July, were 'no longer the same'.[208]

The founding meeting of the Inter-Regional Group of Deputies opened as scheduled on 29 July in the House of Cinema.* In the spirit of the location, an enthusiastic crowd of well-wishers[209] greeted arriving Deputies like filmstars: applauding, calling out the names of their favourites and handing them flowers.† Gavriil Popov opened the session. Even he, a usually matter-of-fact, rather aloof professor of economics, was overwhelmed by the solemnity of the occasion and ended his introductory speech by quoting from Anna Akhmatova's famous poem, written in 1942:

> We know what lies on the scale
> And what now is being decided.
> The hour of courage is struck by the clock,
> And courage will not abandon us.[210]

Of the 316 People's Deputies present, 269 would eventually decide to join the Group. Another 119 could not attend but asked to be considered members, bringing the total membership to 388,[211] or just over one-sixth of the 2,250 in the Congress. Contrary to the stereotype, the Group was neither Moscow-centric nor elitist: 72 per cent were from outside the Moscow region and 61 per cent were workers.[212]

---

* The Group's repeated requests for space in the Supreme Soviet building in the Kremlin were denied. On the same day, the Supreme Soviet's administration offered Deputies a free boat excursion down the Moskva river.

† Gorbachev's reaction was characteristic: tolerant but cautious, wary of competition and leaving open as many options as possible. Accordingly, his message, delivered by his handpicked Chairman of the upper chamber of the Supreme Soviet, Evgeniy Primakov, was a study in ambiguity: conciliatorily critical or critically conciliatory, depending on the beholder. There was a nod: Primakov acknowledged the value of the Group and even offered an apology of sorts: it might have been possible to conduct the Congress better if more attention had been paid to the proposals of the Moscow group. But to form a separate group, amounting to – Primakov deployed the biggest scarecrow – an 'opposition'! Why complicate the work? Why not all pull the country together? (Radio Moscow, 29 July 1989 (FBIS, 31 July 1989, p. 54).)

Originally, Yeltsin was to be the sole chairman of the Group, but the idea was later rejected in favour of a collective leadership.[213] Yeltsin, too, thought this was the best solution: 'the idea of a supreme leader has eaten deep into our minds in this country and [we] find it difficult to break with it'.[214] So wary were the MDG members of the cult of the leader that they rejected even annual rotation among the co-chairmen (Yeltsin was favoured to become the chairman for the first year),[215] settling, instead, for a vague principle of 'collective work and functional responsibility'.[216] They 'should rally around a platform, not a personality', was the prevailing sentiment in the hall.[217] Of the thirteen people nominated, the top five vote-getters were to become co-chairmen: Yeltsin (144 votes), Yuriy Afanasiev (143), Popov (132), the Estonian scholar Viktor Pal'm (73) and Andrey Sakharov (69).[218]

For the next two critical years, the three men who received the most votes on 29 July would represent, define and shape the revolution's increasingly radical tilt. They complemented each other well and covered most of the 'left' political spectrum. Gavriil Popov, unflappable, cerebral and deliberate, occupied the MDG's moderate and pragmatic niche – despite having the appearance of an operetta villain, with puffy cheeks, thick black moustache and the prominent nose of his Greek ancestors.

There were only two modes of political development for the Soviet Union, Popov told the gathering, 'revolutionary–lawful' and 'revolutionary–spontaneous'.[219] The French Revolution demonstrated the limits and the glaring contradictions of the revolutionary approach. Anarchy and elemental, spontaneous movement always led to one and only one outcome: dictatorship. Regardless of whether dictatorship was revolutionary or reactionary, it was bound to visit 'uncountable woes' on the country. 'May God spare us the sight of a Russian rebellion, senseless and merciless,' declared Popov, quoting Aleksandr Pushkin.[220] Mirabeau-like, Popov saw the Group's main duty, its mission and its 'enormous responsibility' in preventing this revolutionary explosion and in promoting the 'revolutionary–lawful' option.[221]

The radical end of the MDG was dominated by Yuriy Afanasiev. With piercing blue eyes, short straight nose and the closely cropped hair and fringe of a Roman patrician, he was the radicals' best orator, fiery and fearless. He had made a name by breaking, before anyone else, some of the most sacred taboos of the official mythology and by pouring scorn on the official idols: Lenin, the October Revolution, the Soviet political system. Almost daily, Afanasiev scourged the regime and communism in general with sarcasm and disgust, his passion fuelled by the guilt of an apostate expiating past sins.* Two months before, in front of the entire nation, he accused the 'aggressively obedient' majority of the Congress of electing 'a Stalinist–Brezhnevite' Supreme Soviet.[222] In the same nationally televised speech, he rebuked Gorbachev for either manipulating the conservative majority of the Congress or, at the very least, 'listening to it attentively'.[223]

At the House of Cinema that day, Afanasiev received the loudest applause of the thirty-two speakers after he accused Gorbachev of 'lacking the courage' to decide 'with whom he [was] now': the new leaders of perestroika, who had emerged in the past few years, or the nomenklatura. 'The time has passed when he could successfully remain at the same time the leader of perestroika and the leader of the nomenklatura. Today, he must make a decisive choice.'[224]

By political temperament and rhetorical pitch, Yeltsin was in the middle, equidistant from Popov and Afanasiev. He had been chosen to deliver the founding meeting's keynote address, which outlined the provisions of the Group's political platform. As expected, his interpretation of the radical agenda was bolder than Popov's – and more focused, restrained and practical than Afanasiev's.

Yeltsin summarized the key objective of the MDG's activity as seeking 'the broadest possible participation of the people in the workings of the state, as well as guarantees of civil rights, political and civil liberties'.[225] At the heart of the Group's political effort was a 'decree' declaring that all institutions of the political system would exercise power solely through the elected legislatures, the Soviets. The transfer of 'all power' to the freely elected Soviets should take place *before* the second of the Congress's biannual sessions tentatively scheduled for November. A new constitution should be adopted to 'reflect the new conditions of society' and to codify the devolution of power away from the Centre.[226]

Still a Party 'liberal', Yeltsin continued to believe that democratization of the Party was one of the 'most important factors in overcoming the crises', and that an extraordinary congress of the Party should be convened to accomplish the task.[227] Yet, in the same breath, Yeltsin the

---

* Alone among the leading democrats, he was a former professional Party ideologue, having served as head of the Young Pioneer organization, which indoctrinated children from ten to fourteen before they joined the Komsomol. He had later become Dean of the Moscow Historical Archival Institute, a breeding ground for Party propagandists, speech writers, journalists, teachers of social sciences and other 'fighters of the ideological front'.

democrat called for the Party's removal from power – democratized or not – effectively ending the party-state. The Party would become a party: free to conduct its internal affairs as it pleased but prevented by law from confusing its narrow political interests with the interests of society as a whole.[228]

Yeltsin ended his speech with the list of legislative 'priority' bills that the Group planned to introduce in the Congress and sought to include in a new constitution. For the next two years, these items would form the core of the radical agenda – Yeltsin's own and that of his fellow democrats – that amounted to the foundation of a liberal democratic state: elimination of domestic passports and freedom to leave the USSR and to return; freedom of the press and other media protected by laws; public referendums on all laws 'affecting the rights and freedoms of citizens' and on constitutional amendments; an annual vote of confidence in the government. The KGB would be reformed.* The privileges of the leadership would be 'liquidated'.[229] Power would be divided between Moscow and the Republics on the basis of genuine federalism, regional business autonomy and real sovereignty.[230]

Reflecting the authors' ambivalence, the economic section of the MDG's platform was far less concrete and radical than the political one. It called for a 'new, more attractive model of socialism' and carefully avoided the words 'private', 'market' or 'entrepreneur'. The main economic actors were 'enterprises' and 'work collectives', 'self-ruling' and 'fully independent' from the central authorities in a 'demonopolized economy' – a euphemism for a diminution of state ownership.

The next evening, 31 July, in a speech to the Supreme Soviet, Yeltsin announced the establishment of the Inter-Regional Group of Deputies. As one of the five co-chairmen, he outlined the Group's main objective – a convocation of an emergency session of the Congress of People's Deputies in September to amend the articles of the Constitution that dealt with elections, and after that the preparation for the local and

---

* Speaking in the Supreme Soviet two weeks before, Yeltsin had assailed the KGB for its 'illegal activities', especially for running a network of informers who 'cause great moral damage' to society – the first public acknowledgment of this activity. 'In my ten years as the First Secretary of the Sverdlovsk Regional Committee,' Yeltsin said, 'I do not remember a single spy being caught with [the informers'] assistance. But it is a thousands-strong army that constantly passes information on what is happening in this or that collective.' Describing the continued employment of this army as 'intolerable', Yeltsin proposed a Law on State Security and called for a drastic reduction and 'restructuring' of the KGB. (Moscow Television, 14 July 1989 (FBIS, 17 July 1989, p. 47).)

republican elections of Soviets – and invited all Deputies to join in 'constructive and businesslike co-operation'.[231]

Andrey Dmitrievich Sakharov died on 14 December 1989. The Poles had the Pope; the Czechs, Vaclav Havel; the Soviets, Sakharov. Alone among the national public figures at the close of 1989, he was admired by all. No one else was as trusted and respected in the three progressively more distant camps which now divided the formerly united proponents of perestroika: the establishment Party reformers, the radical intelligentsia and striking workers.

If only for the morning of the funeral, they were together again. The black limousines of the Politburo, led by Gorbachev, pulled up at the Academy of Sciences building, where Sakharov lay in state. For a few minutes, the country's leaders stood, bareheaded, under a cold drizzle. The Marxist dissident Roy Medvedev wept on national television and, from exile in Vermont, the anti-communist nationalist Aleksandr Solzhenitsyn sent a basket of white roses. Communist intelligentsia stood side by side with young monarchists under the blue-and-white banners of St Andrew, patron saint of the Russian pre-revolutionary fleet.[232] In Estonia, Latvia and Lithuania, flags flew at half-mast. Buried with Sakharov was the hope of national reconciliation.

The departure of a leader of such calibre in the middle of an upheaval often delimits the stages of a cataclysm. Sakharov's death marked the end of Gorbachev's Glorious Revolution.

By the second half of December, the enthusiasm was gone, and with it the romanticism in which, for a moment, the daily hardships and indignities dissolved as the people witnessed the broken taboos and the liberation from fear and lies, and grew to expect more, and more spectacular, political miracles. Supplanting them, suddenly, were the colder, harder, lonelier and less forgiving politics of weariness,* tension, pent-up anger and growing mistrust of anyone and anything. For the first time since March 1985, Western reporters found the atmosphere in Moscow tense and depressed.[233]

The year 1989 was still on the calendar, but the Year of Truth was already history. The first stage of the Soviet revolution, in which truth alone, so fresh, magic and omnipotent, was expected to heal by touch, to feed the hungry, to shelter the homeless – that stage was gone for ever.

---

* 'Do you feel confidence in tomorrow?' the Soviet people were asked in a national poll that autumn. Fifty-seven per cent answered no and only 19 per cent yes. (Bill Keller, 'Soviet Poll Finds Deep Pessimism', *New York Times*, 5 November 1989, p. 18.)

The most conspicuous casualty of the turn of the revolution's kaleidoscope – in which the brilliance of summer colours was suddenly replaced by shades of leaden grey – was the MDG, whose sessions were the truth's main festivals. Elena Bonner, leading human rights activist and Sakharov's widow, would write later that the MDG was a 'collection of people who just wanted to talk in public', although it was viewed, for a while, as an effective organization.[234]

No more. Smothered by the vastness of the Congress's conservative majority, this magnificent catalyst, the soul of rallies, the tocsin of glasnost, was no closer to influencing government policies than it was in July. By the following spring, the Group's membership would begin, in the words of one of its founders, to 'melt, like an April snow'.[235] Only slightly more than 300 of its nearly 400 charter members attended the critical session on 9 December, at which the Group was to develop a common platform for the coming Second Congress of People's Deputies.[236] Four months later the Group's conference would collect only 216 delegates.[237]

Mikhail Gorbachev, the supreme practitioner of what was known in Moscow at the time as rowing first with the 'left', radical, oar and then with the 'right', conservative, one, had replaced benign neglect with increasingly shrill attacks. The Group's incessant requests for 'special status' (which would entitle it to facilities, staff, a printing press and publication of its resolutions and its members' speeches, and, most importantly, would confer the right to be given the floor for prompt responses to the majority's motions) were uniformly denied.

The MDG was being treated impudently, Yeltsin complained.[238] Gorbachev did not want to recognize the Inter-Regional Group at all,[239] even refusing point-blank to allow the publication of the Group's newsletter.[240] The Group's statements, Yeltsin's litany continued, were not only unpublished, they were not even read at the Supreme Soviet's sessions – 'as if the Group did not exist at all'.[241] Most importantly, none of the legislative items which the MDG attempted to discuss at the Second Session of the Supreme Soviet in December (bills on property, enterprise, land and the abolition of Article Six) was put on the Session's agenda. 'We have not achieved any significant results,' Yeltsin was forced to admit in December.[242]

The setback to the Group contrasted sharply with Yeltsin's personal momentum. Clearly approaching peak fighting trim, he was vigorous, full of energy and ambition, and confident despite occasional contretemps. Indeed, his position was so strong that a major shock which had occurred on 28 September seemed to make no difference to it at all.

Late that night a wet and muddied Yeltsin stumbled into the police station in Moscow's posh dacha suburb of Nilolina Gora. His story, only half-heartedly presented, was that he had got out of his car and was walking alone towards the dachas when he was seized by assailants, put in a car and thrown off the bridge into the river. He then swam downstream and happened on the militia post. When, following the militia report, the Minister of Internal Affairs Vadim Bakatin called him, Yeltsin asked that the affair be kept secret and stated that he did not want an investigation. Two weeks later, with Gorbachev chairing the session, Bakatin reported the incident to the Supreme Soviet.[243]

Yeltsin's version was full of contradictions and ambiguities. For instance, the height of the bridge, which was personally examined by this author, was not five metres or even four, as he claimed, but several times that.[244] To be thrown from such a height and then to swim, walk or indeed stay alive was to be the beneficiary of a miracle. There were other inconsistencies in Yeltsin's account, listed by Bakatin on 16 October in the Supreme Soviet and in an interview for this book. In the theories that filled Moscow at the time, the culprits ranged from the KGB to an irate mistress throwing a bucketful of water over the hapless Siberian, to Gorbachev himself, whose repose at Nikolay Ryzhkov's dacha was rudely interrupted by an unannounced Yeltsin wishing to make peace with the compatriot from Sverdlovsk.[245] Yeltsin labelled the entire affair a 'political farce, played by Gorbachev', and a link in the chain of 'persecution'.

None of this affected his popularity, however. By this time, with his standing as high as ever, his public agenda had become radicalized and hardened. For the first time, he underscored his differences with Gorbachev, instead of downplaying them as tactical, and attacked the General Secretary–Chairman by name. He even suggested that he and his comrades in the Supreme Soviet 'might one day form the beginnings of an opposition party, when we are braver'.[246] 'We are told [by the Supreme Soviet's leadership] that there are no differences between us,' he said at the MDG conference in September. 'No, there *are* differences! On the national question [there exists a] – difference; on political problems – difference; on economic reform – difference; on property – difference.'[247]

In discussing the last item, Yeltsin, again for the first time, used the taboo word 'private' – and took full responsibility for doing so. 'Let me give you my personal view. I differ in this from Gorbachev. I personally believe that there should be a mixed economy: some share of private property – 5, 10, 15 per cent, and then we shall see – must be introduced.'[248] The absence of laws on ownership rights was 'primarily Gorbachev's fault'.[249] Without these laws economic reforms were impossible: the transition to a 'socialist market economy, a mixed economy, or whatever we are to call it'.[250]

Yeltsin continued this theme in a speech at a session of the Second Congress of People's Deputies, which convened on 12 December. Trenchant and tight – easily his best speech of the year – it contained an important conceptual novelty: never before had he linked the continuation of state control over the economy with the preservation of the political regime, just as never before had he rejected a lengthy, drawn-out transition to the market. Responding to the government's proposals, which he characterized as 'a gradual convergence of the administrative-and-command Soviet system with the market', Yeltsin asked:

> Isn't it clear that such a hybrid would be stillborn? Can't we, finally, understand that everything permitting us to feed the country and to create the abundance of goods is acceptable? How can we agree with the government's estimate [of transition to the market]: six years? It means that for six years the economy will not bring about a real amelioration of living conditions . . .
>
> Property owners are not made by an order from above. Land ought to be given to peasants and the peasant himself would decide how to conduct business . . . But the Law on Land is being thwarted because, as everyone understands, it is also a matter of power. We must, finally, understand, that de-ideologization of the economy is the key condition of its revival. The perverse system of [centralized] economic control has engendered its twin in politics. Without concrete measures aimed at the destruction of the bureaucratic apparatus of power, we shall never radically change the totalitarian regime, built on hypocrisy, lies and mistrust.[251]

He called on the Congress to realize that this was a 'dangerous and critical moment'. The year 1990 would 'decide everything', and should therefore be planned for with utmost care, month by month.[252]

Yeltsin's warning went unheeded. Little progress was made at the Second Congress. By refusing to discuss draft laws on property and land, the Congress, in Yeltsin's opinion, put the country into an 'extremely difficult position'.[253] By wasting the previous few months, the Soviet parliament may have wasted 'the whole of the next year for the reform'.[254]

The sluggishness of progress was highlighted by the collapse of the party-states in Poland, Hungary, East Germany, Czechoslovakia and Bulgaria that autumn. In a short time, Sakharov noted ruefully in his last interview, those countries had accomplished much more than the Soviet democrats in the four preceding years. 'This makes the mood of our people heavy,'[255] as he put it.

Yeltsin's mood, by contrast, was hopeful and decisive. He was not going to waste the next year. The revolution from above was 'on its last legs', he declared at an MDG gathering.[256] A revolution from below was 'swelling up', and he welcomed it.[257] Close contact with the Soviet Union's best minds in the MDG had provided him with much needed education in political theory and economics. The experience was invaluable. He had learned and assimilated a great deal, as his Congress speech demonstrated. (Viktor Pal'm called Yeltsin an 'excellent self-teaching machine'.)[258]

Yet in this new political age neither the MDG, with its ultra-democratic but amorphous and unwieldy structure as a discussion group, nor the mammoth all-Union parliament, whose majority was quickly and hopelessly falling behind the times, was the best vehicle or the best arena for satisfying ambition and advancing an agenda. Accustomed to the unity of control and responsibility in pursuit of his goals, Yeltsin was clearly out of his element in the collective leadership of the MDG. In addition, the two Party mandarins among the MDG's leadership, Yeltsin and Afanasiev, never felt comfortable around each other. They always sat at opposite ends of the dais.[259] Soon Yeltsin would stop attending the MDG's meetings.[260]

An astute observer of the political scene and an MDG activist, Yuriy Chernichenko, noted that the Soviet democrats needed 'less romanticism, less glitter, and more hard work in the trenches'. Before the year 1989 was over, Yeltsin began to plan his second election campaign – and the battle for Russia.

CHAPTER 7

America, America . . .

Y ELTSIN'S TRIP TO THE UNITED STATES (9–17 September 1989)
both fits seamlessly into the Year of Truth and stands out far
enough to merit a separate note. In keeping with the tenor of
that remarkable year, these eight days overflowed with startling and
sometimes painful revelations. Even in 1989, little, if anything, could
match for Yeltsin the trip's sense of discovery or the impact it would
have on him in the long run.*

Yeltsin's discovery of America coincided with his taking stock of, and
testing, his own intellectual and political strengths, as well as his physical
and emotional endurance. The American expedition evolved into the
most systematic and comprehensive articulation of his core beliefs and
political programme to date.

The American journey also supplied an opportunity to see Yeltsin
through the eyes of observers whose impressions were not distorted
either by the fierce partisanship of domestic Soviet politics or by the
light and shadows of power that would soon surround him a year
later. These curious, well-informed, sympathetic but by no means
uncritical journalists, academics and businessmen – many of whom
left written records or readily agreed to be interviewed – forged as
objective and comprehensive a first-hand portrait of Boris Yeltsin on
the stump as we are ever likely to get. Never before or after did so
many outsiders see – day in and day out – so much of Yeltsin for so
long.

Invitations from the United States had been pouring in since his election
landslide. He was wanted by universities, the Rockefeller and the Ford
Foundations, US Senators, the Council on Foreign Relations –
altogether, fifteen invitations arrived.[1] In the end, and after much hesitation, Yeltsin, who knew no one in the United States,[2] was persuaded by
the equally unfamiliar Moscow Foundation for Social Inventions
(recently established with the assistance of Raisa Gorbacheva) to entrust
the organization of a trip to the San Francisco-based Soviet–American
Exchange Program of the Esalen Institute – a New Age Californian
outfit which, among other things, promoted Gestalt therapy, encounter

---

* Years later, a leading Russian journalist with extensive knowledge of the Kremlin
would write that 'Yeltsin more than once recalled how much he gained during his first
visit to America. It made him fearless in his struggle with totalitarianism' (Vladimir
Nadein, 'Oglushitel'sniy uspekh s neyasnymi intogami' ('A deafening success with unclear
results'), *Izvestia*, 25 October 1995).

groups and t'ai chi and explored the power of meditation as a means of bringing about world peace.[3]

According to Esalen's plan, the travelling party's* expenses were to be paid for by Yeltsin's lecture fees, which would vary from $5,000 to as much as $25,000 for an appearance. Thirty per cent of what was left was to go to the agency that booked the speaking tour, and the rest was Yeltsin's.[4]

At first, Yeltsin rejected a commercial tour out of hand.[5] The US ambassador to Moscow, Jack F. Matlock, who saw him shortly before the trip, found Yeltsin emphatic in opposing the pecuniary aspect of the trip.[6] 'He was not interested in the money,' Matlock recalled.[7] Yeltsin was persuaded to go along with paid lectures and speeches as the only way to underwrite the trip – but he did so only on condition that his entire share be spent on single-use disposable syringes.[8] 'I plan to buy disposable hypodermic needles for our hospitals,' Yeltsin told Matlock at the time.[9] This gift, designed to prevent the spread of AIDS in the Soviet Union, was set forth at Yeltsin's first press conference in the United States as the 'other' objective of the visit – in addition to getting acquainted with America.[10]†

An agreement signed by Yeltsin and the Esalen Institute stipulated that 'B. N. Yeltsin forgoes the entire profit [from the trip]'; that 'this profit [was] to be used, entirely and exclusively, to help prevent the spread of AIDS in the USSR'; that Esalen's Program on US–Soviet exchanges was to 'use all the profit for the purchase and delivery to the USSR of $100,000 worth of modern medical equipment, including

---

* Travelling with Yeltsin were his assistant Lev Sukhanov, People's Deputy Viktor Yaroshenko, Chairman of the Foundation for Social Inventions Viktor Alferenko, his Foundation colleague, economist and *Komsomol'skaya Pravda* columnist Pavel Voshchanov (who would become Yeltsin's first press secretary), the executive director of the Esalen Institute's Soviet–American Exchange Program Jim Garrison, his assistant and two translators.

† Earlier in the year the Soviet public had been stunned by the story of nine children in Elista, the capital of Kalmykia, who had been infected with AIDS because of faulty sterilization of syringes. When Yeltsin's syringes arrived in Moscow on 24 September, the national television interviewed a doctor in the Children's City Clinical Hospital – one of nine Moscow children's hospitals that received the gift. 'Every day in each hospital children are given about 3,000 injections,' he said. 'Very few are done with disposable syringes. There is a disastrous shortage of disposable syringes. We use disposable syringes mainly for blood donors.' (FBIS, 25 September 1989, p. 110.)

disposable syringes'.[11]* The delegation's last press conference in the United States, conducted after Yeltsin had returned to Moscow, featured crates filled with 100,000 syringes.[12] A few days later Yeltsin was photographed examining the crates at Moscow's Sheremetievo airport.[13]

When these details suddenly became important a week and a half later, it turned out that Yeltsin received a per-diem payment of $100. With one notable exception, related below, he did not set foot in a store and never touched this money.[14] In his last hours in America, Yeltsin's assistants used it to buy a computer for his office in Moscow, two children's calculators for his granddaughters and a plastic toy handgun for Boris junior.[15]

The organizers had drawn up a very tight schedule ('most cruel',[16] Yeltsin would call it), cavalierly unmindful of the eight-hour time-zone difference between Moscow and New York. Between Sunday, 10 September, his first work day in America, and Sunday, 17 September, he would travel nearly 5,000 kilometres and speak in nine cities: New York, Baltimore, Washington DC, Chicago, Philadelphia, Indianapolis, Minneapolis, Dallas and Miami (and visit the Space Center in Houston). Wherever Yeltsin spent more than a few hours, at least two major speeches had been booked. If a visit covered the better part of a day, he spoke morning, noon and night, with half-a-dozen interviews, meetings and short excursions in between.

His first working day in New York epitomized the feverish rhythm of the trip. At 7.15 a.m. he was interviewed by ABC's *Good Morning, America!* Then he went to the Stock Exchange. More meetings and interviews followed, and, at noon, a luncheon lecture at the Council on Foreign Relations. Afterwards, he recorded an interview for the *MacNeil/Lehrer Newshour*, spoke at Columbia University, and went to the River Club for a dinner hosted by David Rockefeller. Shortly before midnight he boarded the plane to Baltimore.

Bombarded with questions, Yeltsin, who under the best of circumstances eats far less than his formidable bulk would suggest,[17]† rarely

---

* Yeltsin disposed of all his future fees and royalties in the same way. The income from his trip to Japan in January 1990 netted another million syringes (Sukhanov, *op. cit.*, p. 188). The royalties from his first autobiography were spent on more syringes and on the treatment abroad of three chronically ill Russian children.

† Public eating was also somewhat slowed for Yeltsin by the embarrassment he still felt about the two missing fingers on his left hand and his efforts to make the handicap as inconspicuous as possible (Sukhanov, *op. cit.*, p. 107).

had a chance to taste food at any of the many breakfasts, lunches or dinners in his honour. With the forced diet and the time difference in mind, he was wise to exercise caution from the very beginning. When a US network interviewed him in a hotel suite provided with food, brandy, vodka and gin, he drank only coffee.[18] Towards the end of a dinner reception on the same day, Yeltsin, who was 'totally sober', asked a Russian émigré journalist where he could find some water to drink.[19] The next night, at the River Club dinner, an American academic who sat next to him ordered a shot of vodka for himself and suggested that Yeltsin do the same. Yeltsin declined, explaining that 'he would collapse from even one sip'.[20] Later during the trip, witnesses in Chicago and Minneapolis found him 'absolutely sober'[21] and drinking only a 'small glass of vodka' all night.[22]

Abstemiousness, excitement and willpower carried him through the first two days. Yeltsin's first (off-the-record) speech in America was delivered to a most exacting and discriminating audience: the leadership of the Council on Foreign Relations. There was 'strong applause'[23] at the end, and the marks were quite good. The Council's ex-Chairman, David Rockefeller, who introduced Yeltsin, called him a 'charming and impressive person who clearly is a highly skilled politician'.[24] The dean of US Sovietologists, George Kennan, praised Yeltsin's 'self-confidence and humour' and suggested that he was 'not to be underestimated'.[25] Former Secretary of State Cyrus Vance, who thought Yeltsin did 'extremely well', was surprised and pleased to find a modern politician who had somehow managed to emerge in the Soviet Union.[26]

Talking to Yeltsin afterwards, a guest at the luncheon learned that the Russian had not 'slept for the past 40 hours' and was tormented by the humidity and the 35°C heat of New York City.[27] 'If I die of exhaustion,' Yeltsin told him, 'please arrange to send my body to Sverdlovsk – packed in dry ice.'[28]

From the moment Yeltsin emerged beaming from the plane and told reporters in JFK Airport's Pan Am terminal that he 'wanted to see the Washington Monument, museums, libraries, cultural treasures – and I also want to see *you*!';[29] from his first morning in America when he gave a lusty thumbs-up sign on seeing, from a helicopter, the Statue of Liberty (as if, a witness observed, the two had a 'special thing going'),[30] he brimmed with an exuberant, boyish curiosity to see, touch, smell as much as he could of the place which his country had admired and hated for so long.

The national obsession with America, which permeated Soviet society from top to bottom for most of the Soviet Union's existence, had, of course, touched Yeltsin as well. It had been his 'dream for a long time' to visit this 'huge, great country'.[31] The trip was 'a lifelong dream come true'.[32] He said he had come to America with an open mind[33] – ready, in fact determined, at fifty-eight to compare with reality that which had been 'pounded into' him by Stalin's obligatory *Short Course of the History of the Communist Party* and by official propaganda during all those years.[34]

Hardly unpacked, he descended upon Manhattan for a day and a half of walking and sightseeing, interrupted only by short spells of sleep and interviews. In the tension of expectation, purposefulness and heightened receptivity that he brought to the task, even the customary and relatively innocuous sights – Fifth Avenue, the top of the Empire State Building, a Chinese restaurant in Manhattan, the Trump Tower, the Metropolitan Museum and Central Park – yielded rather unusual observations.

He would later say that the trip was an 'endless row of collapsed stereotypes and clichés'.[35] First to fall were the staples of the official propaganda. A professional builder, he almost instantly revised (or rather reversed) his opinion of New York. Instead of the 'piles of giant gravestones' and 'slums' he had expected to find, Yeltsin discovered what he called 'architecturally interesting buildings one cannot help but admire':[36] 'beautifully designed, well constructed' and altogether 'extremely impressive'.[37] As for the 'slums', Yeltsin compared a public housing complex along the East River, which he saw from the window of a helicopter,[38] with *khrushchevki* (shabbily constructed three- and five-storey buildings erected during the building boom of the early 1960s) and concluded that 'some slums would pass for decent housing in the Soviet Union'.[39]

On the streets of Manhattan, where he had been taught to expect to be robbed or killed on any corner,[40] he had a late-night dinner at a Chinese restaurant (where he found no queue, and where the food was 'ten times better' and far cheaper in terms of salaries than in a co-operative restaurant in Moscow)[41] and admired a Korean pavement grocery: the low prices, the cleanliness and, most of all, the fact that there was only one person serving all the customers.[42] And, unable to resist the temptation, Yeltsin recalled Egor Ligachev's efforts to revive 'socialist agriculture': pointing at the stand groaning under mounds of fruit and vegetables, he said: 'And Ligachev is still conducting seminars.'[43]

The Statue of Liberty, until then familiar to Yeltsin only as a crude cartoon from the *Krokodil* magazine, was another favourite target of

Soviet satirists. Having circled it in a helicopter, he found the landmark 'first, not a witch but a very attractive lady and, second, an excellent example of human creativity'.[44]

He was most impressed, however, by Americans themselves, who turned out not to be the aggressive, ill-mannered, malicious, nasty and pushy creatures of Soviet propaganda,[45] but 'wonderfully open, sincere and friendly, industrious and intelligent' people who knew 'how to work and how to enjoy life'.[46] He was struck, as well, by their optimism, their 'belief in themselves and in their country'.[47]

Altogether, his image of the United States 'turned around 180 degrees'.[48] When he compared what he had been told all his life with what he saw, he quoted Aleksandr Griboedov's classic verse-play *Gore ot uma* ('Woe from wisdom'): 'the distance of huge dimensions'.[49] Eager for a similar epiphany for all his compatriots, Yeltsin would return from the trip an ardent advocate of US–Soviet exchanges: 'not just by the legislators, ministers, presidents, scholars and generals – but by high-school students, housewives, workers'.[50] This, Yeltsin felt, would 'build bridges that would withstand the coldest and most cruel wind'.[51]

In that respect the visit was conspicuous for his efforts to see and speak to as many ordinary Americans as possible. In New York he insisted on meeting the homeless. In Indianapolis, he wanted to sit 'among the people', and the organizers 'really had to struggle to get him seated at the head table' with the grandees.[52] In Indiana, he visited a pig farm, wanted – but did not have time – to see the homes of farm hands and inquired what their salaries were.[53] (Learning, with characteristic agility, from the momentary embarrassment of his hosts, Yeltsin would later report to a Moscow audience that, contrary to another stereotype, there was 'no more tactless question to ask Americans than how much they earned'.)[54] On the same excursion, he dusted off the expertise of an Obkom First Secretary and duly impressed his hosts with the precision of his questions: 'how many piglets per sow? how much grain did they consume?' He 'knew what he was talking about', the farmer said afterwards.[55] After visiting his host's home office and climbing into a $150,000 combine,[56] Yeltsin was awed by the technological cornucopia of a large and prosperous American farm – especially by the two computers he spotted on the farmer's desk. The astonishment was still undiminished two weeks later, when Yeltsin recalled the sight in a speech in Moscow. Just think of it: with two computers the farmer was able to track pork prices all over the world and decide when to slaughter for a larger profit – 'today, tomorrow or next week!'[57]

Among Yeltsin's unofficial forays, one was particularly important to him. Still in Moscow, he had spoken about his wish to see President Ronald Reagan. 'Where does he live?' Yeltsin asked an American interviewer.[58] So when his schedule took him to Minneapolis, he insisted on making a side trip to St Mary's Hospital in Rochester where Reagan was recuperating from surgery.

A vase of roses in hand,[59] Yeltsin entered Reagan's room, and the two appeared to have had a most enjoyable conversation, which 'went well beyond the bounds of formality'.[60] They talked about life in the Soviet Union and in the United States, the American and Soviet revolutions and the American and Soviet peoples,[61] who, they agreed, had a similar sense of humour.[62] According to Reagan's spokesman, Yeltsin told the former President that he had precipitated 'the very perceptible warming of relations' between the Soviet Union and the United States, had contributed enormously to this process and had gone about it in a 'wise, courageous and tactful way', for which Yeltsin was 'very grateful'.[63] Reagan, in turn, seemed to have been touched by the visit. In a letter that Yeltsin received on his return to Moscow, the former President cordially thanked Yeltsin for 'the beautiful flowers' which had 'lit up the room'.[64]

With Yeltsin's ability to absorb and assimilate new knowledge, his American journey could not but result in intellectual cross-pollination; nearly everything that he saw or heard was rapidly applied to the political and intellectual tasks he was grappling with in Moscow.

Having come 'to learn more about American experience in democracy',[65] he soon discovered (and was not at all shy of publicly acknowledging) 'lots of good things' in the political system of the nation which still was, at least nominally, his country's principal foe. Without exception, these 'good things' were the ones consonant with his current political preoccupations. First, there was the productive coexistence in the US Congress of 'majority' and 'minority', in which the minority and its voice were protected by law, its positions daily publicized by American newspapers, and its legislative action and draft laws accepted for discussion.[66] Second, there was the protection of civil liberties (what Yeltsin called 'law-based defence of the individual'). Third, Yeltsin very much approved of the direct election of the President. And, finally, he lauded the anti-trust laws that, in his view, prevented the 'monopoly of power in the economic and social realms'.[67]

Towards the end of the trip, his observations began to extend to a higher plane of generalization. He found, for instance, that it was 'absolutely necessary' for his country to emulate the common sense at the heart of the American economy and society.[68] In America, Yeltsin told an interviewer back in Moscow, a manager could not be an idiot because this would damage production. And they did not pay the same salary to those who work badly and those who work well, because to do so 'would be stupid'.[69] Nor would a leader of a local branch of the Republican Party tell a farmer, even a Republican farmer, when he was to plant corn and when wheat.[70] The Soviet Union, he added, always put abstract ideas above practice, above reality.[71]

Of the dozens of revelations, large and minute, that attended Yeltsin's American journey, one proved unequalled in its impact. The occasion was a ride back to Houston airport after a short side-trip to the Lyndon B. Johnson Space Center, the setting a Randall's supermarket: the first and last American store Yeltsin visited.

Outside, the Soviet visitors looked for the customary crowd and queue, but found neither.[72] On entering the store, they were dazzled by the 'profusion of light' and a 'kaleidoscope-like', 'spell-binding' multitude of colours.[73] Yeltsin asked a salesperson how many different products they had in a store. Around 30,000, she said. They examined cheeses and hams, began counting varieties of sausages – and 'lost count'.[74] The myriad of sweets and cakes were 'impossible for the eye to assimilate'.[75]

In the fruit and vegetable section the visitors from Moscow were 'literally shaken' by the quality of goods: large horseradishes, sparkling under bright lights and beads of water from the tiny sprinklers; rows of onions, garlic, aubergines, cauliflower, tomatoes, cucumbers, bananas, pineapples.[76] And all this unimaginable splendour to be found in a 'provincial' store, 'not in New York'! Yet, even to an eternally vigilant Soviet mind, the spontaneous nature of the visit excluded any possibility of a 'Potemkin village' created by cunning local authorities to impress an important Soviet visitor.[77]

'For us,' Yeltsin would tell *Ogonyok* a few weeks later,

> used to empty [grocery store] shelves, canned food, awful, dirty, wrinkled vegetables and equally unappealing fruit, this madness of colours, smells, boxes, packs, sausages, cheeses was – impossible to bear. Only in that supermarket it became very clear to me why Stalinism so painstakingly erected the 'iron curtain'. To see all that is simply beyond the pale [of endurance], damaging even to a hardened [Soviet] person.[78]

Yeltsin stopped a customer, apologized and asked her what her family income was and how much they spent on food: $3,600 a month, and

$170 a week, she answered. Yeltsin would later repeat these figures to a stunned Moscow audience: 'Meat three to four dollars a pound! Fruit four, five, six dollars a pound!' (The effect would have been greater still if Yeltsin, who, flaunting his memory, was speaking without notes, had cited the real prices for fruit and vegetables, rather than these fantastically high ones.) The average family spent '200 to 300 dollars a month on food – with salaries between three and four thousand a month!' rhapsodized Yeltsin. And all of this at a time when the average Soviet family expended 59 per cent of its budget on groceries,[79]* which were increasingly hard to find in state-run stores. Yeltsin was in 'shock'.[80] 'For a long time', on the plane to Miami, he sat motionless, his head in his hands.[81] 'What have they done to our poor people?' he said after a long silence.[82]

On his return to Moscow, Yeltsin would confess the pain he had felt after the Houston excursion: the 'pain for all of us, for our country – so rich, so talented and so exhausted by incessant experiments'.[83] 'I think', he continued, 'we have committed a crime against our people by making their standard of living so incomparably lower than that of the Americans.'[84] His faithful aide, Lev Sukhanov, who walked the aisles of Randall's with Yeltsin and sat next to him on the plane to Miami, believed that it was at that moment that 'the last vestige of Bolshevism collapsed inside' his boss.[85]

Still, Yeltsin would claim that he returned from America without 'self-hate, envy or complexes'.[86] The main lesson of his trip was an optimistic one: it was possible, he now knew, to 'organize people's lives in such a way that they would be free and realize their potential in ways that was beneficial to both society and themselves . . .'[87] And so, 'casting

---

* One of the most devastating publications of glasnost was an article by A. S. Zaychenko in which he compared personal consumption in the United States and the Soviet Union ('SShA–SSSR: lichnoye potreblenie' ('USA–USSR: personal consumption'), SShA, December 1988). Among other startling figures, the author calculated that, given salary differences, an average Soviet citizen had to work eighteen to twenty times longer than his or her American counterpart to buy the same quantity of chicken, ten to fifteen times longer for eggs, three times longer for milk, seven times for butter, eighteen to twenty-five times for oranges and bananas, and two to eight times for bread. To match the quantity of food consumption by an average American family, Soviets would have to spend 90 per cent of their budget on food, and to match quality (an a priori fantastic objective) up to 180 per cent. Given its notoriety, the article had almost certainly been read by Yeltsin. Even so, reading about the contrast apparently proved insufficient protection against the jolt of first-hand experience.

our pride aside', they had to learn from Americans: 'learn to work and learn to live'.[88]

No matter how searing or important in the long run, at the time the discoveries made on the trip were secondary to the main mission Yeltsin had set out to accomplish in America. He came to say that Gorbachev's revolution from above, perestroika, was 'in danger' and 'must be saved'. From the interview with CBS's *Face the Nation* on the second day of his trip to an hour before he flew home from Miami, every speech or interview touched on this theme. Nor did he deviate from the core analysis. Thus far, Yeltsin told each and every audience, Gorbachev's key achievements had been glasnost, democratization and the 'recovery of dignity for the ordinary man' – the dignity which for decades had been trampled underfoot.[89] The 'rusty nail of fear was being slowly pulled out' of people's souls.[90]

Yet the time for 'euphoria' was gone for ever. The revolution from above had almost run its course. Gorbachev had missed some important opportunities.[91] He proceeded too slowly. He was a man of 'half-measures', too much given to compromise. Yet it was 'impossible to succeed in perestroika with half-measures. We can't achieve something positive by compromising. Compromises can be temporary but not continue all the time.'[92] The 'rusty nail' must be 'pulled out once and for all', rather than 'little by little', otherwise the 'wound will never be healed and our people will never be free'.[93]

The confluence of deepening crises – economic, political, social, national and financial – left Gorbachev at best a year in which to right things or face the prospect of a bloody 'revolution from below'. And the writing was already on the wall: the miners' strike and the tension between the nationalities. The 'whole of society' was in crisis. The country was teetering 'on the edge of an abyss'. The people's patience was almost exhausted – especially that of the forty-eight million who lived in poverty. Gorbachev's popularity was declining rapidly.[94]

While this description differed little from Yeltsin's standard stump speech at home, the solutions he outlined were considerably and consistently more radical. A number of factors coalesced to effect this evolution. There was, no doubt, a desire to *épater* the American public by outdoing Gorbachev in his own glasnost game and impressing them with the coherence and depth of his propositions. One comment clearly designed to shock was his reference to communism as an 'idea in the clouds that should not be attempted on earth' – at a time when Gorbachev continued, with passion, to affirm his allegiance to the 'socialist ideal'.[95]

Furthermore, the pressures on him imposed by the impossible schedule and the aggressiveness of American reporters left little energy or time for the carefully crafted, nuanced and hedged responses that marked his domestic performance. The distance from home might have settled the relative magnitude of problems, and ordered his political priorities accordingly. Lastly, the enormity and immediacy of the achievements of the world's largest and most prosperous 'bourgeois democracy', which engulfed him at every stop, made gradualism and ambiguity somewhat awkward, even embarrassing. His political agenda acquired urgency, clarity of focus and hardness that surpassed much of what he had previously said back home.

Suddenly, the rhetoric shifted from 'bureaucracy' and 'privileges' to 'decentralization', 'devolution of power' and 'private property'.[96] Political decentralization, he explained, meant the transfer of power from the Party to Soviets. Economic decentralization involved the 'gradual liquidation of ministries' and the right of enterprises to act independently, and to form 'associations and corporations'. And social decentralization was needed to devolve decisions regarding 'all societal concerns' from the top to the local level.[97] This 'devolution of power from the Centre down to all levels of administration'[98] would leave the Centre only some strategic responsibilities and a small apparatus.[99]

Yeltsin took the slogan of economic decentralization to its operational conclusion. It was time to 'privatize at least 10 to 15 per cent of [state-owned] property',[100] he said. Gorbachev was 'making a mistake in refusing to allow even a small amount of the Country's productive capacity to go into private hands'.[101] Land should also be owned privately,[102] and be returned to those who work it.[103] Foreigners, too, ought to be allowed to own land in the Soviet Union.[104]

Radical decentralization was not confined to the economy. 'The feeling of national dignity is continually being crushed in our country,' he told a New York audience.[105] The sole remedy was to give the Republics economic control of their areas, with which would come 'a genuine independence'.[106] Yet, if even these measures cannot satisfy peoples, they should be allowed to leave. In what was the most spectacular conceptual breakthrough of the trip (and the greatest deviation from the official position), Yeltsin declared that 'If a Republic wished to secede from the Union, it should be allowed to do so.'[107] ('Do you think that all Republics must determine their fate themselves – or only the Baltic ones?' he was asked. 'No: all, all, all! It's just that the Baltic [states] first demanded that right.')[108] And, joining for the first time the imperatives of national liberation with the survival of democratic reform, he told Jim Lehrer that 'if we didn't give them independence, then really perestroika would end'.[109]

Breaking another taboo, with which he had lived all his life, Yeltsin publicly repudiated the mainstay of Soviet patriotism – severe restrictions on emigration from the USSR. He declared it the right of every individual to choose where they wanted to live – be they East Germans (thousands of whom at the time were pouring across the newly opened Hungarian–Austrian border on their way to West Germany) or Soviet citizens going to Israel, America or West Germany.[110] And, treading territory he had never entered before, he called for 'full, unconditional freedom of emigration . . . to all who wish to leave the Soviet Union, especially Soviet Jews'.[111] He called Hungary's decision to allow East Germans out 'perfectly reasonable': it was hard to blame anyone wanting to 'move from a lower standard of living to a higher one'.[112] 'There have been a lot of descriptions of you and your own beliefs,' Jim Lehrer said to Yeltsin. 'How would you describe your own beliefs and what you are?' 'How should I be called?' Yeltsin answered. 'It's difficult to say. I am for radical changes.'[113]

From the first, Yeltsin resolved that America could and should 'participate in this rescue operation'[114] to salvage perestroika and play a leading role in the effort. He was determined to carry his SOS message and a plea for American assistance to the White House.

One of his suggestions was 'full, unconditional freedom of emigration to all who wished to leave the Soviet Union, especially for the Soviet Jews', in exchange for the US granting the Soviet Union most-favoured-nation trade status.[115] (He said he would put emigration reform on the agenda of the Supreme Soviet.)[116] Most of his other proposals were at best vague and often unreal, charitably described by US officials as 'more visionary and philosophical than practical'.[117] These included a plan for private US companies to build a million apartments in the Soviet Union; a fifty-year lease of 1,000,000 hectares of land to American companies to grow soybeans in Russia to provide protein for cattle; American instruction in setting up the Soviet service sector; and a joint expedition to Mars.[118]

There is little doubt, however, that his message of alarm and hope was not the sole reason behind Yeltsin's insistence on a White House rendezvous. His two decades in the Party hierarchy, so jealous of prestige and obsessed with protocol, had magnified his perennial hunger for external validation,* which the humiliation of November 1987 had only exacerbated. And, in the Soviet Union of 1989, no single arrangement could do more for such a validation than a visit to the White House. Indeed, before he left for the United States, Yeltsin told Ambassador Matlock that 'the main purpose' of his visit was political: to consult the US leaders. His 'main request' to Matlock was to arrange a meeting with President Bush.[119]

Throughout Soviet history, official propaganda notwithstanding, the leader's domestic popularity and even legitimacy had been invariably bolstered by a summit with the American President. In Yeltsin's case, the already hefty prize was made even more desirable by circumstances. He would be the first Soviet politician ever outside the Politburo-centred policy-making hierarchy to be accorded the honour. He would receive what in the eyes of the Soviet public was by far the most important imprimatur of his position as *the* leader of the 'radical democratic' opposition. Finally, in the never ending competition with Gorbachev, it would be he, Yeltsin, and not the General Secretary, who would be the first to set foot in the Bush White House! 'For Yeltsin,' his aide recalled, 'a meeting with Bush was a matter of principle.'[120]

The road to the White House proved tortuous. Occupied less than a year before by Ronald Reagan, whose serene confidence in his political instinct had sometimes prompted risky choices, the White House was now taken over by an Administration that was skilful but circumspect. Whereas Reagan had accepted Gorbachev's revolution as genuine and vital to the interests of the United States, and had blessed it with a visit to Moscow, the new Administration was wary of getting involved in an untidy and unpredictable remaking of the world. Always a step or two

---

* When Ambassador Matlock came to see Yeltsin shortly before the trip, Yeltsin asked him who would be meeting the delegation in New York. 'Secretary of State Baker will come, won't he?' Yeltsin asked. When Matlock told him that that would be out of the question, Yeltsin said: 'Well, in that case, I am sure Governor Cuomo [of New York State] will be there.' After Matlock, tactfully stressing only technical difficulties (the Governor's residence is in Albany, not New York), had rejected that eventuality as well, Yeltsin persisted, grumbling, 'Albany can't be more than an hour or so by helicopter.' (Matlock, *Autopsy on an Empire*, p. 248.)

A few days later, speaking at Johns Hopkins University, Yeltsin explained how he would alter his message according to the rank of US leaders he expected to see. To the President, he would deliver the entire range of proposals, to the Vice President slightly less, and still less to the Secretary of State. (Audio recording of Yeltsin's speech in Baltimore.)

behind the times, the Administration would, until the collapse of the Soviet empire, cling to familiar certainties that were rapidly becoming obsolete. During the week of Yeltsin's sojourn, Deputy Secretary of State Lawrence S. Eagleburger exemplified this *Weltanschauung* when he declared that the business of the United States and its allies was not to assist Gorbachev but to take care of 'our own interests'[121] – as if, at the time, the success of Gorbachev's reforms was not by far, and most obviously, the greatest of such interests.

In this White House, the most popular leader of the Soviet loyal radical democratic opposition was hardly a welcome guest. First, because the entire business of perestroika was still very uncertain (and therefore suspect). Second, because it was deemed imprudent to annoy Gorbachev while negotiating arms-control agreements,[122] by which the Administration measured progress in US–Soviet relations. (As a White House spokesman would say later, 'We did not want to indicate we were trying to provide a platform for dissent,'[123] and 'did not want to foster conflict that might be associated with this trip'.[124] And even when the audience was granted, just to be on the safe side President Bush reminded Yeltsin of the 'very positive relationship' with Gorbachev enjoyed by his Administration.[125])

Finally, anything fuelled by or purveying strong beliefs, ideas and ideals (what President Bush would later derisively call 'the vision thing'), even those very much in tune with America's, was treated with scepticism. Anyone emerging from the hot and messy kitchen of history instantly looked out of place in the cool *bon ton* of the Bush White House, especially this truculent Siberian giant: thick, boxy and wearing an ill-fitting suit and a drab tie.

In the end, it was decided that Bush would see Yeltsin but under a rather peculiar arrangement: Yeltsin was to be received by the President's National Security Advisor, General Brent Scowcroft, and the President was to 'drop by'.[126] There would be no reporters or photographers, not even an official White House photo. Yeltsin, for whom an invitation to the White House was synonymous with seeing the President of the United States, 'was not supposed to' know[127] of the plan until the last moment.

The charade was steadfastly played to the end, and the effect on its only unwilling participant was easy to predict. Ambassador Matlock, who at that time knew Yeltsin better than any American, would write later that Yeltsin 'was capable of an occasional social *faux pas* particularly when he was tired, ill, or annoyed'. As his limousine approached the basement entrance of the White House West Wing, Yeltsin was all three. A few moments before, he had finally been told the truth by his handlers, who until then had equivocated and tried to look hopeful: the President would not see him. Yeltsin immediately announced that *he* would not see Scowcroft: the 'level' was not 'appropriate'.[128] 'To be in the White House and not to meet the President!'[129] – he would have none of it.

They pulled into the West Wing's parking lot. Yeltsin refused to get out of the car.[130] He was persuaded to get out and was ushered into the West Executive basement lobby. Greeting him there was Dr Condoleezza Rice, Special Assistant to the President for National Security Affairs, who was in charge of Soviet affairs at the National Security Council. 'This isn't the entrance to the White House for those who see the President!' Yeltsin told Rice.[131] She replied that he was not there to see the President. His appointment was with General Scowcroft. The clarification unleashed a torrent of protest: 'I am not used to this kind of treatment! I am an important man in my country! I can see the General Secretary any time I want!' Arms folded, he refused to go any further.[132]

The contretemps in the West Executive basement had lasted for more than five minutes when an exasperated Rice finally told Yeltsin that it was his decision whether to come in or not, but General Scowcroft was a very busy man and could not wait for visitors indefinitely. His back against the wall, Yeltsin submitted but, as symbolic face-saving, demanded that, in addition to the translator, he be accompanied by his assistant Lev Sukhanov. This violated the agreement with his handlers, but Rice wisely consented.* They were all given 'Visitor' tags to wear. 'I am Yeltsin!' Yeltsin grumbled in declining the tag. His aide hurriedly hid the tag in his own pocket, and they started up the stairs to Scowcroft's office.

Whether intended or not, Scowcroft's opening remark, which he recalls as 'Why are you here?',[133] sounded rather rude when translated into Russian: 'Why did you come here? What, exactly, do you want?'[134] (To describe its effect, Yeltsin's aide used a Russian colloquialism: 'like thunder out of a blue sky' – a total, and unpleasant, surprise.)[135] Yeltsin responded that his visit had more of a 'philosophical' than a purely political purpose.[136] He had come, he continued, because he wanted

---

* A year later, having spotted Rice at the end of a receiving line in Moscow, Yeltsin, who forgets little of importance, shook her hand and, with a twinkle in his eye, said, 'We have met before, haven't we? – and perhaps not very happily . . .' (interview with Dr Rice).

to see this 'great country and get acquainted with its hard-working people'.[137]

Then door opened and President Bush came in. True to form, the President exuded good cheer, smiling broadly and shaking hands vigorously. As they stood face to face, Yeltsin, who found Bush to be exactly the same height, said, 'Yes, we are worthy of each other.'[138] According to the witnesses, their brief conversation,* which was never made public, veered from small talk only in two instances. Almost immediately, Bush asked Yeltsin if he liked Gorbachev.[139] He had a great deal of admiration for Gorbachev, Yeltsin answered, but some people around him made it difficult for them to remain friends.[140] And Gorbachev needed to be more decisive and to 'do more'.[141] Bush, who was about to give a nationally televised speech on drug abuse, also asked Yeltsin if the Soviet Union was confronted with a similar problem. Yes, Yeltsin said, it was a 'serious problem' but they were still 'reluctant to talk about it' in the USSR.[142]

The President departed, telling Yeltsin to address all the issues he would like to discuss with him to Scowcroft,[143] and Yeltsin launched into a 'monologue',[144] interrupted only by a brief appearance by Vice President Dan Quayle. Like a provincial actor who had finally been given a reluctant and hurried audition by a renowned Moscow director, Yeltsin crammed his entire repertoire into the remaining forty minutes: private investment in the Soviet economy; the one million apartments; the most-favoured-nation status in exchange for free emigration from the Soviet Union; co-operation in space . . .[145] In the middle of the presentation General Scowcroft was alleged to have fallen – or to have pretended to fall – asleep.[146]

In the days following the visit, unnamed White House sources, said to have 'attended the meeting', put out word that Yeltsin was 'a political lightweight who would soon fade from the scene',[147] a 'wild and crazy man' who made 'too many off the wall predictions about the imminent collapse of the Soviet economy and ouster of . . . Mikhail Gorbachev [by communist hard-liners]'.[148] General Scowcroft was reported to have called Yeltsin a 'two-bit headline-grabber'.[149] Years later he remembered Yeltsin on first acquaintance as a 'peasant'. The President noted that Yeltsin was no '"Mr Smooth" like Gorbachev'.[150]

Secretary of State James A. Baker III, who met with Yeltsin the same day, was disappointed as well: he found that Yeltsin's understanding of

---

* The White House later said the encounter lasted sixteen minutes, and Yeltsin's assistant claimed to have clocked twelve minutes.

the market economy was not up to par. The Secretary lectured him on the necessity for price reform and convertibility of the ruble,[151] and, after Yeltsin left, was reported to have said: 'What a flake! He sure makes Gorbachev look good by comparison. And you've also got to sympathize with Gorbachev if that's what he's got to deal with.'[152]

The strains, the successes and the disappointments of the trip's political agenda aside, it was Yeltsin's first foreign *bain de foule* and he plunged into it with energy and gusto, which even the murderous schedule failed to extinguish. He seemed to fall in love with every audience he spoke to and would continue his question-and-answer sessions until interrupted by his entourage, no matter how late it was. He would be visibly upset when he had to leave.[153]

His first large public engagement in America – a lecture at Columbia University – epitomized Yeltsin's disposition. On that sweltering afternoon, the steps leading to the Low Library's Rotunda, where he was to speak, presented a tableau familiar to anyone who spent time at the university in the 1980s: bookselling Trotskyites, the Students for Soviet Jewry handing out leaflets and collecting signatures, and all manner of intellectual browsers sitting, lying or standing in the expectation of diversion.

Professor Robert Legvold, who had arranged Yeltsin's speech at the university, stood on the lower steps waiting for his guest to arrive and keeping an eye on both ends of the path that cuts across the campus from Broadway to Amsterdam Avenue. Suddenly, Legvold sensed movement above, looked up the steps and saw at the top, towering over the crowd, a shock of white hair, around which the human tide was thickening by the second. Legvold raced up the stairs, made his way to Yeltsin and suggested that they get inside the Rotunda.

'Why can't I speak here, outside, on the steps?' Yeltsin demanded to know.[154] Legvold explained that the invited dignitaries were waiting inside, where the President of the University was to introduce him. Yeltsin balked. By now, the crowd, not understanding Russian but guessing the nature of the dispute, began to 'egg Yeltsin on'. 'Why can't you use your much touted American technology so that these people, too, could hear me?' Yeltsin asked. Legvold, readily acknowledging America's industrial might, conceded that then and there the means were lacking.[155] Yeltsin seemed to understand and to submit. But when Legvold began to lead him away from the crowd and towards the side entrance, his visitor 'pulled away, bounded towards the people lingering in front' and proceeded to bang on the six-metre-high iron doors seeking admission for himself and his rapidly growing coterie of admirers. Convinced soon of the futility of his effort, he finally followed Legvold to the side entrance.

Another delay followed, as Legvold went to look for the University's President to introduce Yeltsin. After a long wait without the benefit of air-conditioning, the public was palpably restless. Suddenly, Yeltsin 'surged' on to the stage – alone, hands joined, boxer-like, above his head to 'the confused delight of his sweaty audience'.[156] He then removed his jacket, and the spectators, annoyed by the absence of air-conditioning, broke into hearty applause.[157] His opening remarks included 'a small complaint at the fact there [was] a large group of students out there who might like to hear the lecture, and no loud-speakers for them'.[158]

In the days that followed, his appearances would be infused with similar, seemingly improvised gestures that instantly forged a bond of mutual affinity and goodwill between Yeltsin and his audiences. Almost 8,000 miles from home, he appeared completely at ease, trusting his natural instinct to tell him what would, and what would not, please his listeners and deploying the same powerful mix of disarming, loquacious, humorous candour and sarcastic toughness that won over thousands of his compatriots. 'By the way,' he said, opening a New York press conference, 'the shirt I am wearing is not mine. It belongs to the host. Mine has been spoiled by make-up during a television interview today.' He paused. 'But the trousers are most certainly mine.'[159] The next day at Columbia, railing against some 'odious' and 'incompetent' members of the Politburo, he said that since they were holding on to their chairs for dear life, the only way to get rid of them was to 'catapult them out', together with their chairs, 'the way it is done with ejection seats in an aircraft'.[160] All that was needed was a person willing to push the button.

For someone who until then had been treated to friendly, even reverential, questions from the floor, Yeltsin's agility in riposte was remarkable. At Columbia he was taken to task for not meeting with striking workers yet meeting with 'capitalists' and wishing to meet George Bush, who was 'attempting to drive the standard of living in the [US] down to Third World levels'. He had supported the demands of Donbass strikers in his own country, Yeltsin replied. As to whom to choose here, in America, strikers or Bush, that was a 'funny question'. 'You elected Bush, not I, and it's *you* who ought to choose.'[161] Asked (at Columbia, of course) about his reaction to Gorbachev's 'negative evaluation' of Trotsky, he said: 'The only thing I have in common with Trotsky is that he also criticized the General Secretary [that is, Stalin] in 1927, and I did it sixty years later.'[162]

In Baltimore, he lauded an admission of 'error' by the Soviet authorities regarding the 1980 invasion of Afghanistan and apparently felt that the audience was not sufficiently enthusiastic about this achievement. According to a newspaper account, Yeltsin then 'allowed a Jack Benny pause, ran his tongue over his lips and asked, "Why aren't you applauding?"' The audience roared with laughter.[163] He was just as quick on lighter occasions. 'Would you like to see pigs?' an Indiana farmer asked him. 'Generally, I prefer to see Americans,' Yeltsin said, 'but, I guess, pigs would do.'[164]

With a born politician's ability to sense which rhetorical devices are most effective for a particular audience, he quickly adopted the peculiarly American habit of self-deprecation, completely alien to the Russian and Soviet tradition. Noting that the US President was famous for his physical fitness and challenging him to a match, Yeltsin added that if Bush lost, the US would have to stop all nuclear testing. After the applause died down, Yeltsin paused and admitted that it was 'still not clear' what he would do if Bush won.[165] And when the Mayor of Baltimore Kurt Schmoke presented Yeltsin with a badge of participation in the city's literacy project, Yeltsin carefully examined the inscription and said the honour was doubly appropriate since he could not read English.[166]

He turned out to be quite good at poking fun at his 'stereotypes', and soon, encouraged by the reception, assembled a battery of stand-bys with which to enliven almost every speech. As his journey drew to a close, Yeltsin often began his speeches by complaining about 'ruthless capitalist exploitation', of which he had been warned for so many years back home: he now worked three shifts a day – and earned tens of thousands of dollars.[167] Confronted with another example of the same 'exploitation' at an Indiana farm, where the farmer, his wife and two teenage children and several farmhands raised 6,000 hogs, he quipped that back home, on a collective farm, there 'would be 150 people, including accountants – and no pigs'.[168]

After he had failed to find crowds of starving homeless picking through garbage on the streets of America, so vividly described by Soviet newspapers, and after he had talked to the homeless and had concluded that US slums would pass for decent housing in the USSR,[169] he mocked both his credulity and the current vogue for US–Soviet 'exchanges' by suggesting that the homeless of America and the Soviet Union be included in exchange programmes between the two countries.[170]

But the biggest crowd-pleaser, which never failed to cause an 'explosion of applause',[171] was minted on his first morning in America on a private helicopter tour of Manhattan and New York harbour after Yeltsin had asked the pilot to circle the Statue of Liberty for a second time.[172] After they had flown over the Statue once, he would announce later, he immediately felt 'much freer'. After the second time, he said, his 'audience rolling with laughter', he felt 'completely free'.[173]

Soon he developed another rhetorical technique entirely out of character for a Soviet politician: tailoring his speeches to the geography of the occasion and paying homage to local patriotism. As a US reporter, who accompanied him on most of the trip, put it, 'his ability to pick up the cultural nuances of each region to win the hearts of his audiences was amazing'.[174] He delighted an Indianapolis audience by comparing the city's cleanliness to that of New York. He told Texans that Russia for the Soviet Union was like Texas for the US: the cornerstone and the linchpin without which both countries would be 'empty'. (He was 'cheered to the rafters' in response.)[175] And he 'clearly thrilled' the Miami crowd by comparing their city to paradise: 'Although I am not religious, I've often had dreams of heaven. When I flew over Miami in a helicopter, I saw something that exceeded any vision of paradise that I ever had.'[176] (They gave him a standing ovation.)

In assessing the reaction of Yeltsin's hosts, it is necessary to keep in mind what might be called 'Dr Johnson's dog theorem': when a dog walks on his hinder legs, 'it is not done well, but we are surprised to find it done at all'.[177] With some notable exceptions, for those who saw and heard Yeltsin he was the first Soviet politician they had seen in person. After almost half a century of Cold War stereotypes, the fact that he could walk, talk, gesticulate and even smile (and criticize his own government and crack jokes into the bargain) was surprising and exhilarating to behold.

Yet while this broad indulgence (from which Gorbachev profited even more conspicuously in his initial foreign forays) indubitably accounted for part of the response that Yeltsin generated, the uniformity of impression and the coincidence of details in witnesses' accounts throughout the 5,000 kilometres of the journey are significant enough to credit the result to something other than sheer wonderment. Virtually every published account and every available witness testifies to Yeltsin's conscious and tireless effort to interest and please a foreign audience and an intuitive ability to adapt and adjust to its tastes.

The audience 'loved' him in Philadelphia,[178] where he was said to have 'played the crowd like a veteran ward politician'.[179] His speeches were rated 'fabulous' in Minneapolis[180] and 'excellent' in New York.[181] In at least four cities – Baltimore, Philadelphia, Chicago and Miami – he was given standing ovations by several thousand people.[182] Some thought the secret of his success lay in a peculiar combination of 'wide-eyed curiosity and Western-style political savvy' that enchanted his listeners.[183] Others noted flair and 'an enormous skill' in handling an audience.[184] His Minneapolis hosts were taken by his candour.[185]*

He was praised as well for his charm,[186] enhanced by kissing women's hands and passing to them the flowers which had been presented to him.[187] Yeltsin's humour, too, was very favourably judged,[188] and his one-liners were said to have had his audience, 'retainers and veteran journalists rolling in the aisles'.[189] 'He would have made a great Rotarian!' suggested a witness.[190]

Yet, despite all the effort to entertain, energize and please his audience, more astute spectators sensed something very hard inside the velvet glove. There was a 'wilfulness' about the man: he 'would do what he wanted to do'.[191] A New York academic, who was active in the Council on Foreign Relations and saw quite a few foreign dignitaries, thought that while other world leaders exhibited a 'mixture of deference and self-confidence', Yeltsin exuded 'self-confidence only'. He behaved like one who 'would not have to adapt to his environment', but, rather, who 'would bend his environment to adapt to him'.[192]

Others observed a combination of great physical energy with stubbornness and 'a kind of in-your-face, here-I-am-deal-with-me attitude'.[193] Another witness was struck by the potent air of leadership and the unmistakable 'personal power' that Yeltsin projected.[194] He seemed to 'take perverse pleasure in confounding conventional wisdom',[195] recalled a *New York Times* reporter. 'Journalists often take pleasure in [doing that], so I really noticed this. It was striking to see how much he was enjoying this: upsetting other people's little plans, especially when they did not include him!'[196]

Only one discordant note sounded in this generally joyful concert, but it was shrill, deep and so enduring in its effect that it warrants a special note. Yeltsin's visit to Johns Hopkins University (a visit which its organizer, the then President of the University Steven Muller, later called 'at

---

* In June 1990 the same group of Minnesota business leaders would welcome Gorbachev. They found the General Secretary, too, 'very much at ease' – but also 'very much an actor'. With Yeltsin, so they agreed, 'what you see is what you get'. (Interview with Darren Narayana.)

best a mitigated disaster')[197] was to begin at 10 p.m. on Tuesday, 12 September. In the next fourteen hours Yeltsin was to speak at a 7.45 a.m. breakfast to which Muller had invited around one hundred Baltimore and University dignitaries; deliver a Huntington Williams lecture at the University's Shriver Hall; and have lunch in Washington with a group of grandees who were Dr Muller's guests.[198]

When Muller arrived to greet Yeltsin at the BWI Airport, he was advised that his visitor would be late in arriving from New York. After the same message was delivered several more times, the Yeltsin party finally landed in David Rockefeller's personal jet at around 1 a.m. After brief formalities (during which Yeltsin passed a bouquet of flowers, handed to him by Muller, to the only female in the greeting party, saying 'Flowers to the beautiful'),[199] Muller got into a limousine with Yeltsin and his interpreter and they departed for the Johns Hopkins campus.

In the car Muller had a chance to assess his guest's condition, and was not at all pleased by what he saw. 'If there was ever a man who was visibly exhausted, Yeltsin was he.'[200] He was 'dead tired'. Muller also learned that Yeltsin was 'starved' because he had not had time to eat at all those functions in New York. Hardly surprisingly, when Muller attempted to reconfirm Yeltsin's first appointment the next morning, the idea of getting up six hours later was 'very unpleasing' to his guest, who was 'very surly at the prospect'.[201] Muller insisted, stressing the expectations of all the people he had invited. In the end, Yeltsin 'did not say no'.[202]

They arrived at Nichols House, where University Presidents used to live and which now served as a guest house for distinguished visitors. A table loaded with cold cuts, vodka and beer was already laid. The starving Russians made straight for the table, and Muller left.

It was a beautiful September night in Baltimore, warm and starry, and the weary travellers, finally at rest in an elegant, old and quiet house, filled with food and drink, were too excited to go to bed.[203] The party did not break up until 'some time around four in the morning'.[204] No sooner had Yeltsin's faithful aide, Lev Sukhanov, fallen asleep than he was roused by another member of the entourage, Viktor Yaroshenko, who told him that their leader was still up. Sukhanov rushed to Yeltsin's room. 'I feel awful,' Yeltsin said. 'Cannot go to sleep.' Sukhanov reminded the boss that he had a busy day ahead, implored him to go to bed and left.[205] Even though Yeltsin was near collapse from exhaustion, as one of his travelling companions told an American acquaintance next day,[206] he could not sleep. Yaroshenko took him for a walk and gave him 'two shots of whiskey' when they came back. Still unable to relax, Yeltsin swallowed two sleeping pills, and 'instantaneously fell into a void'.[207]

Less than two hours later, Muller came to pick him up for breakfast, a private chat and then a meeting with the Baltimore nobility. Yeltsin begged to cancel the functions. Muller was 'insulted'.[208] Yeltsin was told that his hosts 'would not survive' the disappointment.[209] He responded that 'it would be he who would not survive'.[210] 'Apologize,' he pleaded. 'Tell them anything, tell them that I am dead. I simply cannot do it.'[211] Finally, with 'enormous effort', Sukhanov managed to get him up, but as he saw Yeltsin dress he realized that the boss was still asleep.[212]

In the end, supported by the interpreter and Muller, Yeltsin walked the hundred yards from Nichols House to the Hopkins Club. He managed to get through the receiving line in the Club's main dining room, shaking hands 'listlessly'.[213] On at least one occasion, he appeared to be losing his balance and his interpreter 'held him upright'.[214] He then sat down in the chair in the lounge adjacent to the dining room. He was, a witness recalled, 'out of it'.[215] A much disappointed Muller announced to the breakfast gathering that 'Yeltsin was suffering from both jet-lag and a murderous schedule,'[216] and would not be able to speak.

Less than an hour later, however, Yeltsin revived. Helped to his feet by Dr Muller's assistant, who 'sort of propelled him' towards the door,[217] he entered the dining room – and looked completely transformed, as if someone had 'pushed the "on" button'.[218] 'The audience absolutely turned him on.'[219] He made his way to the podium and began to speak. He was completely lucid,[220] showing no sign of debilitation,[221] and had to be interrupted so that he could be taken to Shriver Hall for the lecture.

There Yeltsin completed his recovery from whatever had ailed him only an hour and a half before. Apart from a slight slurring of his words, neither audio nor video records of the lecture or the press conference[222] contain anything out of ordinary. Correspondents for the *Baltimore Sun*[223] and the University's newsletter[224] did not notice any intoxication. 'It never crossed my mind' that Yeltsin was drunk, recalled the *Washington Post* photographer who took pictures that morning.[225] Yeltsin, he added, was 'convincing, engaging, enthusiastic' and answered questions with gusto.[226] Several Russian émigrés in the hall also saw nothing suspicious.[227] General Scowcroft, who saw Yeltsin a few hours later, detected not the 'slightest sign' of inebriation.

Yeltsin was, however, more than usually excited. His croaking voice rang emphatic and ebullient, like that of an agitated bullfrog.[228] He was also rather uncharacteristically playful, 'clowning exuberantly' as a witness put it.[229] In the middle of Muller's introduction, he suddenly got up, snatched the sheet of notes from the University's President, balled it and threw in the corner. Laughing, he told Muller, 'Let's have some equality here. I am speaking without notes and so should you.'[230] ('I sensed', Muller would later say, 'that Yeltsin did not like me. Hell, if someone were putting me through this type of [schedule] I would hate him too.')[231]

A few minutes later, Yeltsin was in complete control of his words, emotions and memory. In response to a question, he said that he still did not know if Bush would receive him. Sensing immediately a tone that betrayed personal annoyance, he quickly corrected himself by shifting to a more elevated plane and delivered a barb in an impeccably diplomatic manner: he said the issue raised the 'question of the foresightedness and vision of President Bush'. (In the inevitably sharpened translation, the phrase became 'a question of how farsighted President Bush really is' – much to the delight of the politically savvy and predominantly Democratic crowd, which broke into cheers and applause.) A few minutes later, answering a question about his relationship with Pamyat', the reactionary nationalist group, he recounted every detail of the meeting two years before – complete with places, names, sequence of events, agendas, proposals and counter-proposals.[232]

In the middle of the question-and-answer session, he received the long-awaited word from the White House. After a lengthy and heartfelt apology – complete with the rhetorical 'I am your guest and I will do as you say. Should I go or should I not?' – and expressing his wish for the 'freedom and democracy we so much miss at home',[233] Yeltsin left for Washington. He did not, however, leave Baltimore behind – and, in a sense, never would.

Paul Hendrickson's article 'Yeltsin's Smashing Day' (subtitled 'Boris's Boozy Bear Hug for the Capitalists') appeared in the 'Style' section of the *Washington Post* the next morning. It was well written, witty, biting and smart-alecky, but not deliberately malicious.

The piece contained a detailed and, for the most part, accurate description of Yeltsin's Baltimore sojourn: the inability to fall asleep, the 4.45 a.m. walk on the campus, the attempt to greet the breakfast crowd, the retreat to the lounge and the wondrous revival ('That he could stand up, let alone be engaging and sound urgent, seemed a little miraculous . . . Something seemed to pick him up. The neurons fired. The adrenalin flowed. A pol refound himself, a natural-born ham smelled the greasepaint.')[234]

Apart from the title, only a dozen short sentences in the 1,500-word article would live on, forging an image for Yeltsin in Washington (and thus in the United States) that no amount of subsequent denials could alter. 'It wasn't just the two hours' sleep he was going on. It was the amount of Tennessee sipping whiskey he had knocked back overnight. Vodka, okay. But Jack Daniel's Black Label in the land of the free. Yes, and a quart-and-a-half of it too. This has been confirmed by those who saw the bottles. They weren't chambermaids, either. They're high officials of Johns Hopkins University.' And, the night before, in New York, when Yeltsin was supposed to appear on Ted Koppel's *Nightline* and was reported by his associates to be 'beat', he was drinking, according to 'an unverified' but 'reputable source', in a Manhattan bar.[235]

Paul Hendrickson, who had never written anything about Russia or Yeltsin, had to write the article fast, against the same day's afternoon deadline. He had been with Muller as the Johns Hopkins President stood in the hallway of Park Terrace Raddison Hotel on Rhode Island Avenue. This was, for Muller, the third affront of a wretched day, during which he had been embarrassed in front of some very important people: first at the breakfast, second when Yeltsin cut short the speech to go to the White House, and now, when the Russian was hopelessly late for a luncheon to which Muller had invited, among others, Senator Barbara Mikulski, former National Security Advisor Zbigniew Brzezinski, Mrs Pamela Harriman, Representative Staney Hoyer and former Senator Charles McC. Mathias.[236] In the end, running over the schedule in the White House and then in Senator Bill Bradley's office on Capitol Hill, Yeltsin never made it to the Park Terrace.

It was during this frustrating wait that Muller, described in Hendrickson's article as 'a tanned, suave, natty man whose aplomb was being tested' by Yeltsin,[237] volunteered that he had gone to Yeltsin's room and found a bottle and a half of Jack Daniel's whiskey. To Hendrickson, the clear implication of this unsolicited piece of information was that 'Yeltsin had drunk it all himself.'[238] Muller, who insisted on anonymity, became the 'high officials [sic] of Johns Hopkins University'.[239]

'It is here that I failed in my journalistic scrupulousness,' Paul Hendrickson said years later. 'I should have asked: well, did you see him drinking it? Did he drink a whole bottle and a half himself? I should have pressed [Muller], pushed him, and I fault myself for not doing this.'[240] Hendrickson had been present at the breakfast gathering in Baltimore, but could not tell if Yeltsin was drunk: 'I did not give him a breathalyser test. I was not close enough to smell anything. In retrospect, it was probably a combination of tiredness, tranquillizers and, yes, some drink.'[241]

A week later, when the story suddenly became notorious, Muller would say to the *Washington Post*, 'It was my assumption that it was consumed by several people, not just Yeltsin . . . He may have awakened with a hangover, but when he gave his speech he was in the kind of shape I would want to be in if I were giving a talk . . . I hate to see a man pilloried this way when the facts aren't warranted.'[242]

As for the 'Manhattan bar', Hendrickson had received a telephone call from a superior on the *Post* who told him of this 'unverified tip' and suggested that Hendrickson 'check this out'. (He also ordered Hendrickson to 'keep him out' of the story.) Racing against his deadline, Hendrickson tried to check it out by calling 'a couple of people', as well as the ABC offices in New York. He could not confirm anything. So he left the tip in the article with what he thought was 'a deliberately waffling line'.[243]

No such waffling was ever part of the writing style of Vittorio Zucconi, the Washington correspondent of the popular Italian newspaper *La Repubblica*, who was to become the third – after Muller and Hendrickson – participant in this strange informational relay.

Zucconi began the morning of 13 September as he always did: by leafing through the *Post* in search of a story. When he saw Hendrickson's piece, he called Rome right away. His foreign editor was very enthusiastic and told him to 'run with it'. But, this being a 'Style' section story, the editor felt it was too soft and advised Zucconi to 'put some muscle on it'.[244] Deadlines were very strict at *La Repubblica*, and Zucconi's was twelve noon, only three hours later. The *Post* journalists, in Zucconi's experience, were difficult to contact in the morning and he did not have time to get in touch with Hendrickson. Instead he called some 'Soviet émigré sources' in New York, whose names, six years later, he still refused to divulge. These 'sources' did not see anything first-hand but had a 'lot from the word-of-mouth in the émigré community'.[245]

With two hours before the deadline, Zucconi decided on the structure of a story. He would take 60 per cent of his article from Hendrickson, add the rest from his New York 'sources' and 'embellish' the result with 'juicy details to lend colour to the story'.[246] 'We [in *La Repubblica*] did not like the man,' he explained, 'and I came down hard on him.'*

---

* The newspaper's editorial line towards Gorbachev's chief critic, Boris Yeltsin, was a function of its attitude towards the Soviet leader. 'They [the Italian left and *La Repubblica*] adored Gorbachev,' Zucconi recalled. 'Worshipped him. He was a godsend: an ideal communist with a human face, the proof that Soviet communism was reformable.' (Interview with Vittorio Zucconi.)

He did indeed. The story's tone was set in the opening paragraph:

Boris Yeltsin, the people's hero of Moscow, Gorbachev's Cassandra,
a critic of glasnost . . . is leaving in his wake prophecies of disaster,
mad spending, interviews and, especially, the smell of the famous
Kentucky whiskey, the Black Label Jack Daniel's. He downs half-litre
bottles in one night, alone in his hotel room in Baltimore . . . A
Professor [of Johns Hopkins University] was stunned when, having
come to collect Yeltsin early in the morning and to take him to the
University conference hall, he was met with a wet drunken kiss and
a half-empty bottle of whiskey. 'Let's drink to freedom,' Yeltsin suggested to him at six-thirty in the morning, brandishing a full glass,
which hotels put in guests' bathrooms for toothbrushes and
toothpaste.*[247]

Zucconi's Yeltsin possessed a 'phenomenal ability to drink and to
spend money'. In the 'five days and five nights' in the United States he
had drunk two bottles of vodka, four bottles of whiskey and an
uncounted number of cocktails. He had bought 'new clothes and shoes,
boxes full of shirts', two VCRs, videotapes – *Rambo*, *ET* and *Star
Wars*. He had 'raided' supermarkets, where, 'flying between the aisles',
he had 'ordered' Eselen's 'accountant Alfred Ross' to 'charge it all'. (The
'accountant' was quoted by Zucconi as saying, 'If he [Yeltsin] continues
to spend like this, he will leave behind only debts. AIDS patients in the
Soviet Union had better not count on this money.') For Yeltsin America
was a bar, '5,000 kilometres long', and now he had 'everything he had
dreamed of: whiskey, dollars, trinkets [and] "Rambo" videotapes'. And
so on.

By Zucconi's own admission, the image of a madly shopping Yeltsin
was an extrapolation of 'how Russians generally behave once they get
to the West'.[248] Why, Zucconi himself, as *Repubblica*'s Moscow correspondent between 1979 and 1982, 'used to go crazy shopping in Vienna
on trips outside the USSR'![249]†

In *Repubblica*'s story, Hendrickson's never confirmed 'tip' about the

---

* What the TASS translator from Italian meant, of course, was that Yeltsin had taken
an empty glass from his bathroom and filled it with whiskey.

† Zucconi would tell the *Post* later that the 'information on the alleged shopping spree'
came from 'the Soviet grapevine, because I know they are a gossipy bunch . . . and
they told me a few marginal details' (Eleanor Randolph, 'Yeltsin's "Spree" Denied',
Washington Post, 19 September 1989).

'Manhattan bar' became a never found 'ABC producer' who tried, without success, to sober Yeltsin up and 'get him in shape' for a show. Another outright invention was Pamela Harriman 'smiling, mother-like', when Yeltsin fell asleep at dinner next to her, with his head on the table.* As for the 'accountant Alfred Ross', no such man existed.[250]

This, and much more, came into public view the following week, occasioned by an event which neither Muller nor Hendrickson nor Zucconi could possibly have foreseen as they moved the baton along. On 18 September, *Pravda* reprinted Zucconi's piece. The relay crossed the finishing line into Soviet national politics.

Preceded by an unusual front-page advertisement the *Repubblica* reprint in the Party's main newspaper immediately became the central political event in the Soviet Union. As in the case of the *Moskovskaya Pravda* affair half a year before, the substance of the charges was instantaneously overshadowed by a suspicion of political foul play. The Western – and therefore far more credible – presence caused a 'mixture of anger, amazement, and bewilderment'.[251] 'The fact that this was written by a foreign journalist, not a Soviet journalist, is important. This is what *Pravda* counted on when they published the article. Some people will believe this,' a Muscovite told an American reporter at the time.[252]

Predictably, among Yeltsin's advocates anger quickly emerged victorious from the mélange of emotions. 'It is a shame, disgrace,' said one of a group of Yeltsin supporters who had gathered in Pushkinskaya Square to discuss the news. 'They should disqualify this Vittorio . . . No Italian could ever have written such a thing himself. The communists must have paid him to write it.'[253]

The next day, copies of *Pravda* were burned in Red Square.[254] Friends were calling on each other in Moscow to come out and help with the ritual,[255] in which hundreds[256] of copies of the Party's main newspaper were destroyed. Rallies in support of Yeltsin were held in Moscow and the radical suburb of Zelenograd, where thousands cheered calls for a boycott of *Pravda*.[257] The newspaper's office was picketed by people with signs reading 'Hands off Yeltsin!'[258] and eager to let *Pravda* know that they were terminating their subscriptions. *La Repubblica*'s Moscow correspondent feared that his office would be set on fire by hostile demonstrators.[259]

---

* 'He was very much not asleep' at the luncheon at the Council on Foreign Affairs, Mrs Harriman said later (Francis X. Clines, 'Yeltsin in U.S.: Pravda's Ugly Profile', *New York Times*, 19 September 1989).

After a rather lacklustre performance at the Congress and rather meagre publicity from the Inter-Regional Group's founding session, a newly victimized Yeltsin reclaimed the national centre-stage through the good offices of his clumsy detractors. His Teflon armour was tested and emerged with barely a scratch. 'Yeltsin is not an angel,' a Muscovite said to a reporter. 'He has his faults. There are people who are cleverer than him and more diplomatic. But for us he is a symbol – a symbol of our struggle against privileges and for greater democracy.'[260]

In their determined search for high-level intrigue, Yeltsin's defenders did not have to go far. A *Pravda* publication of this kind, especially with front-page advertising, could only have been authorized by someone on the Politburo. As a former editor of *Moskovskaya Pravda*, sacked in 1987 shortly after Yeltsin, told a rally in a Moscow suburb, 'I have known [*Pravda*'s editor Viktor] Afanasiev for many years, I have worked with him. Things like that he does not decide by himself.'[261] One of the rumours, relayed to Zucconi by *Repubblica*'s Moscow bureau, was that Gorbachev had seen the TASS report of the Italian story and 'ordered *Pravda* to publish it'.[262] (This rumour was never confirmed, and *Pravda*'s editor was soon fired.)

Unlike the response to *Moskovskaya Pravda*, in the post-Congress era the reaction was not confined to silent resentment or even public outbursts by the enraged protagonist and his supporters. This time, *Pravda* was contradicted almost immediately by *Moskovskie Novosti*. In a sarcastic retort, written by the deputy editor-in-chief, Vitaliy Tretyakov, the flagship of glasnost wrote:

Glasnost, as is well known, has no boundaries ... Pity, though, that this breakthrough has been effected by the Soviet press not by its own effort but with the help of an Italian newspaper. Apparently, the Soviet correspondents in the USA were on vacation ... *Pravda* published the article without cuts but found no room for a single line informing its readers about the credibility of the author ... But ten million readers of our Number One newspaper are not likely to accept these rules of the game ... And I cannot either – as a reader, a voter, a journalist ...[263]

Just back from the United States, Yeltsin readily added seasoning to the pot. Apparently no longer restrained by 'Party ethics', which had ensured a relatively mild letter to *Moskovskaya Pravda*, he called *Pravda*'s publication a 'simple lie', 'slander' and 'revenge for the fact that Americans received us with admiration'.[264] A week later he escalated the attack, labelling the article a 'dirty fabrication'[265] and a 'planned political provocation'.[266]

In another sign of changing times, the Supreme Soviet's Committee on Glasnost and Citizens' Rights and Complaints issued a statement declaring the article 'not only biased but . . . also written in the style of the gutter press, which is not acceptable for a Soviet publication'.[267] The Committee hinted darkly at 'certain forces' which were 'attempting to sow distrust towards People's Deputies' and 'diminish their role in the renewal of the country's political system'.[268]

But the greatest surprise was yet to come. Three days after the misbegotten reprint, buried at the bottom of *Pravda*'s page seven – but eminently visible to the eager millions – were the following two paragraphs:

At the request of the editorial staff, our correspondent in the United States, V. Linnik, met with Vittorio Zucconi, the author of the article in the Italian newspaper *Repubblica*, which was reprinted by *Pravda*. To the question whether he confirms everything he wrote about B. N. Yeltsin, Zucconi answered that in writing the material he relied on two sources: the *Washington Post* 13 September article and evidence from emigrants from the Soviet Union who had heard conversations about Yeltsin's behaviour in Baltimore.

The editorial staff of *Pravda* offer their apologies to B. N. Yeltsin. We think that *Repubblica* would do well to do the same.[269]*

To his list of records, Yeltsin could now add another: the first ever retraction and apology by *Pravda* – a fitting coda to a journey in whose wake so many other certainties lay in ruins.

---

* *La Repubblica* did apologize through its Moscow correspondent (Radio Moscow, 22 September 1989 (FBIS, 25 September 1989, p. 109)). Zucconi, who offered to resign but was forgiven, appeared shocked that his article should be so ill used by the Soviet authorities: 'My story was basically a sympathetic one,' he told the *Washington Post*. 'He [Yeltsin] shows the more human, spontaneous, if you want, wild face of Russia. I forgot who I was dealing with – the Kremlin. This shows how far glasnost has to go' (Randolph, *op. cit.*).

PART III

The Storm

CHAPTER 8

The Year of Choice

ROM ITS FIRST DAYS, THE year 1990 promised to be hard and contentious. The multitude of facts and figures – noted and often publicized in the previous months but submerged in the excitement of national self-discovery and liberation from lies – suddenly monopolized public attention as portents of powerful downward trends that required urgent interception and deflection.

On a random day, only twenty-three of the 211 basic food items were to be found in state stores.[1] Rationing spread to goods freely available since the end of the Second World War. Soap coupons entitled the bearer to 130 grams per person monthly.[2] In the ancient Russian city of Kostroma, purchasing children's soap required showing a stamp in one's domestic passport to prove that one had 'children under the age of three'.[3] Even potatoes were rationed now at four kilos per person per month.[4] 'Will there be enough potatoes this winter?' asked an *Izvestia* headline.[5] A reader from Novosibirsk, Siberia's leading centre of science and industry, informed the editors of a major Moscow newspaper that he now had a 'book' of ration coupons: 'for all family members and for all products'.[6]

A Supreme Soviet Deputy from the Moscow region was predicting 'a very real famine very soon'. In her district the food coupons entitled a person each month to half a kilo of meat, half a kilo of flour and 300 grams of macaroni. 'How are people supposed to live?' she asked.[7] A Deputy from Leningrad found no bread in the city stores on 7 November, the anniversary of the October Revolution. With the memory of the Nazi siege and famine on their minds, Leningraders began to dry bread for rusks to preserve it better.[8]

The government, overwhelmed and dispirited, no longer tried to soothe. The consumer market in the Soviet Union had collapsed, admitted a Deputy Chairman of the State Commission for Economic Reform.[9] Now, 'a basic range of cheap food products' was needed to reduce social tension. He suggested that the armed forces be used to ferry goods around the country.[10]

Writing of France in 1789, Simon Schama noted that anger was joined with hunger, thus making revolution possible. In the Soviet Union of 1990, this lethal combination began to seem a distinct probability. 'The bony fingers of a consumer famine are at the throat of perestroika,' warned a leading economic publicist.[11]

The Soviet economy was sliding into a serious depression. The rate of economic growth, which began to slow dramatically in 1988, now approached zero, and the country's GNP may even have diminished in absolute terms for the first time since the end of the Second World

War.[12] In the first three months of 1990, industrial production declined by 1.6 per cent compared with the first quarter of 1989.[13] Continuing depression of oil prices (the Soviet Union's main export) sharply reduced Soviet hard-currency revenues and, with them, imports – the traditional source of quality goods for the domestic market. An especially troubling effect of the hard-currency shortfall was the threat it posed to grain imports – in a country where every third loaf of bread was made from foreign grain.[14]

Restricted neither by administrative control nor by market competition, enterprise managers raised both salaries and prices for the same shoddy goods. While labour productivity hardly increased, the population's monetary income grew by 13 per cent in 1989,[15] and continued to expand at the same staggering rate during the first two months of 1990.[16] To pay wages and cover the growing budget deficit – now estimated at 10 per cent of GNP[17] – the state printed money at a furious rate. In 1989 the money supply rose by 56 per cent over the previous year.[18] Eighteen billion rubles were pumped into the sick economy,[19] already incapable of digesting the existing mass of 'empty' money for which there was no equivalent in goods or services.

Disregarding the dire warnings of leading economists, in January and February 1990 alone the government increased the amount of money in circulation by 14 per cent.[20] According to a leading US expert on the Soviet economy, in the spring of 1990 Soviet consumers held 165 billion 'empty' rubles, or about six months' worth of national consumer expenditure.[21] Just the money held in saving accounts reached the astronomical amount of 337.7 billion rubles.[22] The term 'heightened demand' was no longer adequate to describe the Soviet Union's buying patterns, wrote the *Izvestia* economics correspondent. He saw 'consumer hysterics': a condition when people would buy anything (even crude wooden stools), to convert their increasingly worthless rubles.[23]

During 1988 and 1989 inflation, described as 'hidden' because of regulated prices, was estimated at between 5 and 10 per cent, while for some consumer goods it was as high as 17–20 per cent.[24] In the winter of 1989–90, a Moscow joke described the value of the national currency as a 'pound of rubles for a pound sterling'.

The precipitous devaluation of the ruble evoked ominous historical parallels in the Russian collective memory. The collapse of the national currency was one of the calamities that doomed Russia's young democracy in 1917. At the time, the Bolsheviks made the most of the popular revulsion over trillions of worthless rubles, derisively called *kerenki*, after Aleksandr Kerenskiy, the head of the short-lived provisional government. With *kerenki* implanted in the people's minds by decades of official historiography as a symbol of the pitiful ineptitude of a despised government, it began to seem that before long the rubles of the 1990s would be called *gorbachevki*.

The government's attempts to hold the line on salaries and pensions became hopeless when the March elections and the First Congress rendered irresistible the political pressure for cash payments to the needy, who numbered tens of millions. Accumulated over many decades, these and other social bills were coming due all at once.

What the regime could not resolve politically, it sought to ameliorate through the money-printing press, wrote a thirty-three-year-old economist by the name of Egor Gaidar. His articles, in the Party's main theoretical journal, *Kommunist* (by now firmly in the hands of Party reformers), provided the best running commentary on the Soviet economy published inside the Soviet Union in 1989 and 1990.[25] He even found a name for this phenomenon in economic literature: 'conflict inflation'.

Adding to the general unravelling was what Russian historians would later call the 'bacchanalia of embezzling'.[26] Store and factory managers stole goods, or bought them at ridiculously low state prices from their own enterprises, and then sold the loot in the 'shadow economy', whose size was estimated to be at least a quarter of the national income.[27]

Yet the most deleterious of the ills stemmed not from the government's mismanagement or even from the depression but from the eroded credibility of political sanctions. For half a century, orders from the Centre and fear of punishment had supplied the glue that held together that unnatural economy. By 1990 that glue no longer held. An economic system that lived by politics was destined to die by it.

With shortages and inflation making the ruble less and less suitable as a medium of exchange and with Moscow leaving local officials to fend for themselves if – or, rather, when – food riots broke out, provinces more and more frequently refused to surrender their produce and goods to the central ministries for national distribution. Instead, they hoarded their possessions and exported them only when direct barter deals with other provinces – my trucks for your grain, or my chickens for your fuel – looked attractive. In February 1990, the Council of Ministers of the Kirghiz Republic prohibited the export of *defitsit* goods to the rest of the Soviet Union. Among these items were shoes, 'school supplies', dishes and knitted clothes.[28] It was no longer correct to talk about a 'national' economy. The Soviet Union was rapidly regressing to a pre-monetary, semi-feudal state of regional autarky, 'moneyless natural exchange'.[29] 'The Soviet economy is disintegrating right before our eyes,' concluded economist Vasiliy Selyunin.[30]

As scarcity deepened, smaller areas joined Republics and regions in refusing to part with anything valuable in exchange for the worthless currency. In many cities one's domestic passport (in which the local residence permit was stamped) had to be shown before one could make a purchase. A prominent democrat, running for office in one of Moscow's districts, promised to prevent Muscovites from other districts from shopping there. This candidate, Ilya Zaslavskiy, was elected Chairman of the Oktyabr'skiy District Soviet on the first ballot.

On 29 December 1989, what began as a protest against the absence of wine and vodka before the New Year's holiday exploded into perestroika's first major food riot. This happened in Sverdlovsk, where citizens received two ration coupons for meat per year: each for one kilo.[31] The First Secretary of the City Party Committee, sacked shortly afterwards, explained to the furious crowd that virtually every supplier from the other Soviet regions had failed to fulfil its quota of deliveries to the city. The meat deliveries to Sverdlovsk from the Autonomous Republic of Tataria, for instance, amounted to only 13 per cent of the contracted amount, and those from Bashkiria to one-third.[32]

Perhaps the most disconcerting consequence of the economic decomposition was the growing obstruction to grain procurement. No longer subject to effective control by local Party officials and free to ignore various agricultural ministries and agencies, producers began to evade state procurement orders. Instead of surrendering grain at nominal prices (often at or below cost), more and more kolkhoz and sovkhoz managers left it on the farms to feed livestock or sell for profit at semi-private 'kolkhoz markets'. Despite good harvests, the amount of grain delivered to state elevators had declined steadily since 1987. In 1989 it was twenty-five million tonnes below the planned amount.[33] Already spending an equivalent of 10 per cent of GNP on subsidizing agricultural products, the state could match the market prices only at the cost of enlarging the budget deficit.

At the beginning of 1990, at the centre of the Soviet political dynamic was a race between two parallel developments: the disintegration of the economy (and the concomitant erosion of state authority and legitimacy); and the emergence of new political structures enjoying a modicum of popular support. If the former outpaced the latter, if the economy and the party-state collapsed before a legitimate central government was in place, the world's other 'superpower' with 12,000 nuclear weapons could plunge into violent political chaos.

*   *   *

The economic dislocation reinforced the other two crises, political and 'national',* which in 1990 would threaten, for the first time, to rend the country asunder. None of the crises was new. But, in 1990, two developments marked their evolution and mutation into a far more dangerous variety.

First, each crisis was quickly reaching a stage where it could not be solved, or even postponed by incremental and consensual reform. Instead, it presented the decision-makers with a brutally stark choice: a radical departure from the status quo and a structural transformation – or retrenchment and reaction, in an attempt to return to the pre-perestroika state of affairs.

Second, in 1990 the three crises were no longer amenable to separate solutions. They had come together in a Gordian knot. The choice made in one area almost automatically forced fateful decisions in the other two. For instance, argued the democrats, there could be no genuine and permanent political freedom without economic liberty because the economic monopoly of the state would inevitably regenerate the political monopoly as well.[34] Thus further democratization required the abandonment of state control over the economy and recognition of private property's right to exist. To be acceptable to the elites and the peoples of the non-Russian Republics, political decentralization would have to be accompanied by economic de-etatization. If the Soviet state retained direct and centralized control over the economy, the 'sovereignty' of the national Republics would be a sham.

If, on the other hand, preservation of a unitary state controlled from Moscow was to be chosen, such an objective inevitably entailed a slowdown, perhaps even cessation, of both democratization and economic decentralization. A consistent and earnest market reform would inevitably lead to the devolution of economic decision-making, with political autonomy to follow. Given the success of populist 'nationalists' in every Republic, further democratization would produce the

---

* With a few notable exceptions, the 'national' movements were fuelled by political and economic considerations: the lust for power of local elites, communist or ex-communist, coincided with the general revolt against the totalitarian state and abysmal economic conditions. The restoration of nationhood, as a popular battle cry, spurred only the three Baltic states and, perhaps, Georgia. Similarly, purely ethnic conflicts affected only a small portion of the Soviet territory and population: the Armenians and the Azeris; the Georgians, on the one hand, and South Ossetians and the Abkhaz, on the other; and the Uzbeks, the Tajiks and the Kirghiz.

same result.* The Centre would have to accept the loss of a unitary, rigidly centralized state as the price of democracy and market.

Radical economic reform, in turn, was impossible without a popular mandate, for such a transformation would require hard, unpopular decisions and was likely to result, among other things, in skyrocketing retail prices and unemployment.[35] 'Can the present government undertake a radical market reform?' asked Selyunin. 'I doubt it.'[36] No, he continued, only a government of national trust, like the one which at that time was managing the transition in Poland, could cope with the political repercussions of economic revolution.[37] The Gorbachev regime could no longer effect economic transition without bringing the political one to its conclusion: a direct, multi-party national election of the executive branch, including the head of state. In the Soviet Union of 1990, the battles for a more representative and inclusive political system, popular control over the executive, market reform and national liberation were bound to unfold simultaneously.

Meanwhile, still entwined with the discredited and shrinking Party,† still fully responsible for the economy that now failed to deliver the most basic items, and still rigidly centralized and Moscow-centric, the Soviet state suddenly looked vulnerable and unsteady. Its key unifying force, the Party, began to splinter. Despite Gorbachev's personal intervention and pleas, the Lithuanian and then Estonian Communist Parties announced a formal break with the CPSU.

In January, following the Sverdlovsk disturbances, rioters came close to lynching local officials in a dozen Soviet cities, prompting Moscow political observers to coin the term 'Rumaniazation' to underscore the similarities with the violent demise of the Ceausescu regime in Rumania a month before. The television footage from Sverdlovsk captured a police officer addressing a crowd through a megaphone, a shop with near-empty shelves, uniformed soldiers in helmets walking through a crowd which was blocking the path of a trolley.[38] There was a growing sense among both the political elite and the people that, unless something drastic was done soon, these melancholy, almost surreal images looked very much the country's near future.

As the two leading actors in the unfolding Russian drama confronted

---

* In both Lithuania and Estonia, the first free multi-party elections in February and March of 1990 would produce parliaments with pro-independence majorities.

† While 136,000 members quit the Party in all of 1989, 82,000 did so in just the first quarter of 1990 (Elizabeth Teague, 'The Twenty-Eighth Party Congress: An Overview', *Report on the USSR*, 20 July 1990, p. 2, n. 1).

the dilemmas of 1990, they would discover that their disagreements were no longer about the 'tactics' – the pace, sequence, priorities of the march – but about its direction and final destination. That year Yeltsin and Gorbachev would make choices which determined their political futures. In Gorbachev's case, the choice he made in 1990 also sealed the fate of the country he headed.

The three Soviet crises – economic, political and 'national' – would form a star-like cluster around which the events of the next two years would revolve. The configuration of this dark triad was fluid and unstable. The size and prominence of one element vis-à-vis the other two changed frequently and fast. In the first five months of 1990, the 'national' crisis, until then considerably behind the other two in size and prominence, claimed centre-stage, propelled by a suddenly plausible threat to the survival of the Soviet Union, the Centre's inability to contain it, and Russia's unexpected place and role in the drama.

Frozen for decades by terror and censorship, national aspirations, frictions and rivalries poured forth with great force. Following the December 1989 decision of the Communist Party of Lithuania to quit the CPSU, Gorbachev travelled to Vilnius a month later in a bid to persuade the Lithuanians to rejoin the fold. Met with huge protest demonstrations on the streets and polite intransigence in the government and Party offices, he returned to Moscow humiliated.* A week later, after mass pro-independence rallies in the capital of Azerbaijan, Baku, a two-day Armenian pogrom left sixty-six people dead. Troops stormed the city to restore order, killing, by the official count, another 125 people.

But the third, central episode of the January segment was played not in Vilnius or Baku, but in the solidly Russian region of Stavropol, where Mikhail Gorbachev was born, made his early career and ruled until his

---

* On 11 March 1990, the Supreme Soviet of Lithuania passed an Act for Restoration of the Independent Lithuanian State. A week later the Communist Party of Estonia voted for separation from the CPSU 'after a six-month transition'. Five days passed, and the Supreme Soviet of Estonia adopted a decree On the State Status of Estonia, in effect declaring independence. Two weeks later Gorbachev and Ryzhkov sent a message to the Lithuanian government, giving Vilnius two days to rescind its independence-related laws and threatening to block deliveries of raw materials to Lithuania. On 17 April Moscow announced sharp reductions in the natural-gas flow to Lithuania, and, on the following day, oil deliveries to the Republic were stopped. On 4 May, the Supreme Soviet of Latvia passed a Declaration on the Restoration of Independence of the Latvian Republic.

transfer to Moscow. Rightly mistrusting non-Russians in quelling the Azerbaijan rebellion,* the Kremlin reached for an instrument that had never failed before: the empire's ultimate enforcer and protector, the ethnic Russians. In the middle of January, the Army began a secret call-up of reservists in the Russian North Caucasus.

This time, however, the response was most unexpected. For two days Stavropol was embroiled in demonstrations led by the mothers of the reservists. The Russian women unleashed a storm of telephone calls and telegrams to local and central authorities, and, when everything else failed, went on to the streets. 'I won't give my son!' shouted a Russian woman on a nationally televised report from Stavropol. 'I won't! I won't give my son for this! We endure and endure and endure. How long will we have to endure?'[39] Another protester cried: 'We don't want the people of those Republics to call us occupiers! We don't need a second Afghanistan!'[40] On 19 January, the mobilization was called off.

Stavropol's was a message of immense importance. The Russian national idea and the Russian imperial idea, thought to be inextricably interwoven for 400 years,† were suddenly distinct and increasingly at odds with each other.‡ The rigidly centralized Soviet Union controlled by Moscow suddenly seemed fatally wounded: ethnic Russians were no longer willing to die for it.

The second election in less than a year, the 1990 campaign for Russia's Congress differed greatly from its all-Union predecessor. In 1989 voting was less about politics in the generally accepted sense of the word than about spiritual emancipation. Its most important (and exhilarating) result was the process: freedom to differ, the ability to speak the truth,

---

* Because of the low birth rate among Russians, Byelorussians and Ukrainians, by 1990 almost four out of ten conscripts in the Soviet Army were from Central Asia, the Caucasus and Azerbaijan.

† The emergence of the modern Russian state under Ivan the Terrible in the middle of sixteenth century coincided – after the conquest of the Kazan and Astrakhan khanates – with the birth of the Russian empire.

‡ A public opinion poll conducted at the time confirmed the lesson of Stavropol. Asked about their attitude towards the 'right of the Soviet Republics to leave the Soviet Union and become independent countries', two out of three (65.6 per cent) respondents in the Russian cities of Moscow, Leningrad, Irkutsk and Gorkiy were 'completely' or 'partially satisfied', 28 per cent were 'completely' or 'partially dissatisfied', and 6 per cent undecided. (FBIS, 21 March 1990, p. 4.)

the liberty to vote against the local Party boss, and the miracle of honest counting.

In 1990, much of the loftiness of the previous year disappeared. Like the country's daily existence, the campaign was coarser, grittier and greyer. Yet, met as it was with voter cynicism and apathy unimaginable a year before, the 1990 poll was also fairer. Although, as before, only officially registered organizations had the right to nominate candidates, the filter of 'electoral commission' meetings had been abolished, as were uncontested seats for 'social organizations'.*

As a result, most of the 7,018 candidates, who vied for the 1,068 seats before 100 million Russian voters, reflected the Russia outside Moscow and Leningrad far more than those who had made it into the USSR Congress. Ever so lightly, in hesitant and broken lines, the contours of Russia's political map were sketched: the 'progressive' areas, consisting of the North, the Centre, the Urals, parts of Siberia and the Far East, on the one hand, and the 'red' regions, comprising the largely agricultural South and South-East, on the other.

The 1990 campaign also left behind a lexicon of Russian politics, which would likewise be used for years to come, and the division of the Russian political class into three blocs. The 'communists' were increasingly critical of Gorbachev's reforms and definitely hostile to the market. The 'national-patriots' comprised both anti-communists and neo-Stalinists, but, on the whole, were better disposed towards communists than towards the 'democrats'.[41]† The latter, an almost equally protean and undifferentiated group, were far more closely united in their opposition to various aspects of the totalitarian party-state than around a positive agenda. In Moscow, for instance, the democratic group Elections-90 included the anti-communists of the Glasnost Club, the reform communists of the Democratic Platform, the 'Memorial' Society,

---

* The absence of uncontested reserved seats was in large measure responsible for the decidedly lower intellectual calibre of the Russian legislature in comparison with its Union counterpart. The latter included some of the leading members of the national scientific and cultural elite, 'elected' to the Congress from 'creative organizations and unions'. These part-time politicians would not sully themselves with competitive politics, especially because the Russian parliament looked at the time like a junior and much weaker counterpart of the Union legislature.

† The quotation marks are necessary to distinguish between the term and its homonym in the Russian political vocabulary. For instance, by no means all communists were 'communists': there were plenty of them among both the 'patriots' and the 'democrats'. Needless to add, most 'democrats' were patriots.

the writers' club Aprel' (April) and even the Confederation of Anarcho-Syndicalists.

On 20 and 21 January, 158 democratic candidates, who had come from eighteen Russian regions, as well as Moscow and Leningrad, held a conference in the Soviet capital. They proclaimed the creation of a political bloc, which, in its later incarnation, would become one of the most popular and powerful Russian movements: Democratic Russia.

The new organization acknowledged Andrey Sakharov and the MDG as its key influences. The political reform which Democratic Russia set out to implement was based on one fundamental principle: 'the state [is] for the people, not the people for the state'.[42] The new bloc's objectives, listed in the declaration, included the end of the Party's political monopoly, a new constitution, freedom of speech guaranteed by law, and restrictions on the activities of the KGB. The market was declared 'the main regulator of the economy'. Different forms of property – state, joint-stock, co-operative and private – should be 'legally equal'. Land was to be given to those who worked it either as an 'eternal lease' or as private property.[43] Democratic Russia further pledged to bring about a new Union treaty (to be 'drawn up and concluded in the shortest possible time'), which would leave the central authorities only with the powers delegated to them by the Republics.[44]

Persuaded that it was 'hardly realistic', as Yeltsin put it, to expect the Union Congress to advance this agenda, in December 1989 the leadership of the MDG discussed a new strategy: to 'compel the Centre to change its policy because of the radicalization of Russia'.[45] Even if, Yeltsin explained in an interview, the eventual split between 'democrats' and 'conservatives' in the Russian Congress was to be fifty–fifty, there would still be hope for 'some sort of breakthrough'.[46] If the ultimate strategic objective of the 'democrats' was, in Yeltsin's words, 'a Russia that would be taking more democratic, more radical steps [and would] push the Centre in the same direction',[47] much, if not most, in the execution of the plan depended on another breakthrough: Yeltsin's election to the Chairmanship of the new Supreme Soviet of Russia.

As far as Yeltsin was concerned, the two goals were inseparable. When one of his future campaign managers from Sverdlovsk approached him during a break in the work of the Second Congress with an invitation to run for the Russian parliament from his home town, Yeltsin agreed rather quickly ('I don't feel like apologizing again,' he said, smiling, as he recalled the 1989 campaign), but only on condition that the Chairmanship be included in the *nakaz*es (requests from nominating organizations).[48]*

During the first week of campaigning in Sverdlovsk, Yeltsin vowed, if elected, to compete for the post of the Chairman of the Russian Supreme Soviet.[49] After that the Chairmanship *nakaz* was mentioned openly and frequently. His voters demanded that he not withdraw, as he had done at the First Congress of the USSR, and he was not going to disappoint them.[50] If elected, he said in February, his first steps would be precisely those that the Centre would not make: 'radicalization of all reforms'.[51]

The Boris Yeltsin of 1990 differed from the man of a year before almost as much as his campaign did. It was no longer a rebellion, a revenge, a desperate quest for personal vindication and for the elusive trust of the fickle Muscovites. These demons had been pacified, if not expunged. A witness who sat through Yeltsin's 1989 campaign speech in Sverdlovsk remembered 'uncertainty, doubt and hesitation' 'breaking to the surface' every now and then.[52] Now, 'flying into the hall filled to capacity, swiftly ascending the podium and straightaway taking over the audience with his booming, powerful voice', Yeltsin looked like a 'strong and confident politician, a decisive and energetic man'.[53]

A Western journalist was 'surprised' by the 'sharp edge and precision with which [Yeltsin] framed his thoughts' during an interview.[54] She also found him 'more controlled' than the press reports of him had led her to believe.[55] 'The argument against Yeltsin is that he is politically naive, that he has set about reshaping the Kremlin like a bull in a china shop,' wrote London *Times* reporters, who interviewed Yeltsin in his small Committee office, filled with the dank and musty smell of the wet fur hats and winter coats of visitors whose boots dripped 'grimy slush' on the floor of the crowded reception area. 'But there is little room to doubt the man's intellect, his honesty and his instinctive grasp of another vital ingredient of politics: street credibility.'[56]

Now one of Russia's most popular politicians, he generously extended his coat-tails, posing with democratic candidates for the photographs in their leaflets and posters.[57] He provided a solid 'political roof' for the unknown, a democratic candidate from Sverdlovsk remembered.[58] In many districts, the leaflets read like 'party lists' – with Yeltsin's name

---

* Nominated in Moscow, Leningrad, Perm, Sverdlovsk, Chelyabinsk and Kamchatka, Yeltsin chose to run in the National-Territorial District Number Seventy-Four, which included Sverdlovsk and Pervouralsk, with a total population of 1,800,000.

on top, followed by those of Democratic Russia's candidates to the Russian parliament and to regional, district and local Soviets.[59]

During the brief campaign between the end of January and the first week of March, Yeltsin spent two weeks in Sverdlovsk, campaigning, as his manager put it, non-stop.[60] The meetings (of which there was a 'horrendous number')[61] were held not just in the halls of various 'palaces of culture' but on the shop floors of the largest plants of Sverdlovsk and Pervouralsk. There, surrounded by workers, he deployed his magnificent memory, recalling in minutest detail the problems and personalities of that particular enterprise, which he remembered from his visits as First Secretary – five, seven, ten years before.[62] All his speeches were written by Yeltsin himself. The participation of his tiny 'team' – Aleksandr Urmanov, Gennadiy Burbulis, Gennadiy Kharin, Ludmila Pikhoya and Aleksandr Il'yin (the latter two became Yeltsin's permanent speech-writers) – was confined to writing down the best of the improvised replies Yeltsin gave in the question-and-answer sessions and making him repeat them, instead of extemporizing every time.

At first, the 'awfully heavy load' of the campaign was made worse by the uncertainty of night rest. Yeltsin categorically refused to live in the Sverdlovsk Oktyabr'skaya hotel: a local branch of a kind of national chain of rest stops for senior nomenklatura, administered by the local Obkom in every regional capital of the Soviet Union. Insisting on staying in the local inn, Ural'skaya, 'like everyone else', he was immediately subjected to the full gamut of inconvenience and distractions common to such places: drunken rows, police visits, dirty water, bad meals and cockroaches. In the end, his aides persuaded him to move to a furnished apartment kept by one of the Sverdlovsk plants for visiting consultants.

He was an ideal candidate, a campaign manager recalled: never capricious or contrary, and always willing 'to do all that needed to be done'. Only sometimes, late at night, after yet another question-and-answer session, when he sat down for the first time in fourteen hours, Yeltsin would complain that his young managers (none older than thirty-five) were 'torturing the old man'.[63]

He had just turned fifty-nine, yet physical strain was not the only, perhaps not even the heaviest, component of that daily load. Unseen when he was at the rostrum but apparent to those few close to him, Yeltsin carried a 'psychological burden'. Every hour, every minute of the campaign he wrestled with the residual wariness of the unforgiving 'system', the fear of its retaliation.

On the eve of a national Day of Protest, organized by Democratic

Russia on the seventy-third anniversary of the 1917 February Revolution,* a war council was held in Burbulis's apartment. Should Yeltsin speak at the rally in Sverdlovsk? The candidate hesitated. His participation in the national protest would break one of his last, tenuous links to the Party establishment. In the end, however, it was decided that as one of Democratic Russia's leaders, he had to take part.[64] On 25 February Yeltsin spoke at a mammoth anti-communist meeting in downtown Sverdlovsk.

The Yeltsin of 1990 combined the increasingly insurgent mood of his core constituency – Moscow, Sverdlovsk and Leningrad – with the knowledge acquired during the half-year in the MDG. Even on the most contentious and riskiest issues, there was now little hesitation or evasion. 'We have had many misfortunes but, in the final analysis, the main one is the Party's monopoly on power,' he said in early January.[65] The country was bound to have a multi-party system, he declared a month later; this was a 'necessity'.[66] He was also in favour of the 'private ownership of the means of production and of land'.[67] The 'isms' were not the crux of the matter, he told an interviewer that winter: be that 'democratic' socialism, 'humane' socialism or 'socialism at all'. The essence was human rights and the 'freedom of choice'.[68]

Yeltsin was candid about his evolution: we all 'restructure' in this 'complicated, contradictory situation', we all become 'smarter'.[69] 'The situation itself forces one to think and act differently. I cannot say that Yeltsin has become different, but a shift has definitely occurred, a shift to the "left". Today I am supporting more radical reforms.'[70] 'Left', of course, meant right. It was in early spring 1990 that Yeltsin began a political drift, the final destination of which proved so crucial for his country. The reformed communist now dared to say that 'in the depth of [his] soul' he was a 'social democrat'.[71]

In Yeltsin's electoral programme, all power in Russia was to be transferred from the Party to the Soviets. A new constitution, adopted by public referendum, would enshrine the 'primacy of law and of the main rights and liberties of citizens': freedom of demonstration, freedom of

---

* On 25 February, over 900,000 people participated in 350 protest rallies throughout Russia, with 300,000 marching in Moscow. Altogether, between January and March, there were over 2,000 pro-democracy rallies, in which 7,500,000 people were estimated to have taken part. (V. Zhuravlev, L. N. Dobrokhtov and V. N. Kolodezhnyi, eds, *Istoriya sorremennoy Rossii, 1985–1994* ('A history of modern Russia, 1985–1994'), pp. 62, 60.)

political organization, and freedom of conscience and religion.[72] A constitutional court would be established for 'oversight of [the state's] compliance with democratic rights and freedoms'. Russia was to become a presidential republic, with multi-candidate, direct, universal, equal and secret presidential elections held every five years. No one could occupy the office for more than two terms. For the duration of his term, the President would be required to suspend his or her membership of all political parties and organizations.

Yeltsin's Russia would be thoroughly 'de-ideologized'. All provisions and instructions that restricted senior government posts to the members of the Communist Party were to be abolished as discriminatory.[73] The Party's influence in the management of the economy would be abolished and the presence of any political organization at enterprises, colleges, research institutes, kolkhozes 'and so on'* would be allowed only when 'authorized by labour collectives' themselves. All privileges of 'state, party and economic leaders' would be revoked.[74]

The platform promised to carry out the transition to a 'competitive market economy based on a plurality of ownership forms: republican, local, collective, private and individual'. The bans on private enterprise would be repealed. A radical reform would transfer land to peasants with the right of inheritance and grant them the 'absolute right' to choose the way they organized their own labour.[75] Loss-making enterprises would gradually be closed down, and their 'buyouts' by workers encouraged. To carry out radical reform of the credit and finance system, the State Bank of Russia was to be separated from the government. 'Conditions' were to be created for the formation of commercial banks.[76]

The 1990 election campaign quickly registered the Stavropol tremor. At loggerheads about virtually everything else, the candidates affiliated with all the major blocs were remarkably unanimous regarding Russia's position vis-à-vis the Soviet Union and the Centre. Far from evincing pride in the Soviet Union and Russia's central role in it, the 'patriots', the 'communists' and the 'democrats' alike articulated hurt and exhaustion, and the need for contraction and retrenchment. Almost everything was now blamed on the Union's 'gigantic appetite'.[77] Russia and the

---

* Yeltsin also envisaged a second stage of 'de-politicization' that would involve the abolition of the Party's 'political organs' in the armed forces, the police and the KGB. 'An obligatory non-affiliation with the Party?' asked a disbelieving interviewer. 'Isn't this a utopia in our country?' 'I don't think this is a utopia,' Yeltsin answered. (Interviewed by R. Amos.) Three weeks later, he repeated that the 'Armed Forces and the KGB must be separated from the Party'. (Interview with *Corriere della Sera*, 9 March 1990.)

Russians were now said to have paid for the Union's strength and glory with tens of millions of tonnes of oil and billions of cubic metres of gas, with rivers and lakes polluted by toxic waste, forests devastated by barbaric lumbering, and millions of hectares of land ruined by inept irrigation.

This selfless donor, so generous to everyone, had been badly short-changed. While Russia was said to produce 60 per cent of Soviet GNP, its standard of living was among the lowest in the USSR.[78] Impoverished and unhappy, mired in shortages of everything and overwhelmed by an overall 'spiritual decline', Russia was suddenly a 'Cinderella',[79] and its patience was at an end. Having refused, in Stavropol, to pay for the empire in blood, Russia now began to quibble about money as well.

Like virtually every candidate in that campaign, Yeltsin promised the 'economic, cultural and national renaissance' of Russia, the 'rebirth of spiritual and cultural traditions',[80] and paid homage to the Cinderella theme. For many decades Russia had helped the other Republics and by now had nearly exhausted its natural and intellectual resources.[81] Why, he asked, were Ukraine and Byelorussia members of the United Nations while Russia was not?[82] His platform included the creation of a Russian Academy of Sciences, a Russian telegraph agency and national television and radio.[83]

In two respects, however, Yeltsin's campaign differed from most of the field. He did not just condone the centrifugal tendencies, or resign himself to them. He was a consistent and forceful advocate of sover-eignty and even independence. 'The Soviet government should accept the full autonomy of the Republics in the Soviet Union.'[84] The blockade of Lithuania was one of Gorbachev's 'gross mistakes'.[85] The Union was voluntary. The Soviet Constitution provided for the Republics' right to self-determination and right to secede from the Union. Therefore, the three Baltic Republics 'may exercise their right of secession based on this provision'.[86] If Lithuania really wanted to leave the USSR and become a sovereign state, 'that was its right, and I acknowledge this right'.[87] And if Moldavia and Georgia wanted to exercise that right too, Yeltsin would accept that as a fact of life as well.[88]

A loose confederation was, in Yeltsin's view, the only way to save the Soviet Union. He was for the maximum independence of the Repub-lics. All that the Centre should be left with was minimal apparatus for a certain amount of strategic planning. Everything else should be decided by the Republics. Once the Republics were granted 'near maximum' independence, the number of those who wanted to secede would dimin-ish and the tensions subside.[89]

Why couldn't they try full sovereignty (for non-Russian Republics) inside the USSR? The 'change [in] the state system' should happen immediately, that March, at the Third Congress of People's Deputies, which ought to grant the Republics more independence, leaving 'just gentle control, not very much control', at the Centre.[90] Perhaps, under these new rules, the peoples of the Republics would want to experiment: remain in the Union for three years and then decide for themselves. If, on the other hand, the promises of independence turned out to be fiction, if the laws did not work and the Centre did not want to delegate power to the Republics, then it was quite possible that they would leave the Union.[91]

The impact of these statements is hard to overestimate. Behind them loomed an unprecedented choice in one of Russia's most tangled and pernicious historical dilemmas: Russia freer versus Russia imperial. The verdict of history was unequivocal: to be free itself, Russia had first to free others.

In 1989 Mikhail Gorbachev heroically chose the freer Soviet Union over the Soviet East European empire. In 1990, Yeltsin made the same choice – but in respect of the domestic imperial domain. This descendant of Siberian pioneers, for whom the glory of Russia as the 'Third Rome'* and its mastery over faraway dominions had been a vague and, perhaps, hollow notion, had chosen a freer Russia over the unitary Soviet Union. 'The concept of a Soviet Union that has to some extent separated into its parts is not a prospect that holds terror for Yeltsin,' concluded two London *Times* reporters who interviewed him in early February. 'He accepts, without apparent regret, that the Soviet Empire is about to go the way of the British Empire.'[92]

Yeltsin cast the divorce of Russia democratic and Russia imperial in terms of immediate emotional appeal. He wanted every Russian of the Soviet Union to know that 'after all, like an Estonian, Latvian, or Lithuanian, he too had a motherland'.[93] A law should be passed that would assure Russians outside Russia that they would be welcomed there, and given jobs, housing and even compensation for the property they left behind in the non-Russian provinces. They should know that 'Russia was ready to take them back'.[94] Yeltsin's electoral platform promised 'a programme for a voluntary, organized return to Russia of the Russian

---

* In the nationalist mythology, the glory of the Roman empire (the 'first Rome') was inherited by the Orthodox Byzantine Empire (the 'Second Rome') and, through it, by Russia.

population currently residing in the ethnic areas of the USSR'.[95] This was, in effect, a call for the ingathering of ethnic Russians from the colonial outposts, a kind of Russian Law of Return. Come home to the Motherland, he was telling millions of his compatriots: your Motherland is no longer the Soviet Union.

Just as critical was another theme of the campaign. A Russian democratic state was possible only as a genuinely federated state. Decentralization of a new Russian federal state would not stop at the non-Russian autonomies, to which Yeltsin proposed to grant political and economic independence.[96] Russian ethnic areas, too, were to be divided into seven areas akin to German *Länder*. The platform suggested the possibility (after a referendum) of six self-governing Russian territories: Centre, North, South, Urals, Siberia and Far East.[97] Like the United States, India, Brazil or China, Russia was too big and too diverse to be simultaneously democratic and rigidly unitary. Between Russian democracy and the Russian *derzhava*, an all-powerful, centralized state, Yeltsin, again, appeared to choose the former.

On 4 February, on the eve of a Central Committee Plenum, between 200,000 and 300,000 supporters of Democratic Russia, groups affiliated with it and protesters of many political hues marched in Moscow from Gorkiy Park through the Garden Ring to Manezhnaya Square, next to the Kremlin. Their placards read, 'Party Bureaucrats: Remember Rumania!'; 'Freedom now!'; 'Soviet Army – Don't shoot at your own people!'; 'Party! Repent before the people!'; 'Down with the CPSU!'; 'Resignation of the Politburo and the Government!'[98] From a flatbed truck, Yeltsin, Popov and Afanasiev spoke to the crowd. 'This . . . is the Party's last chance,' Yeltsin said. The government 'could not carry on like that' any longer. Later, talking to reporters, he added, 'This is also Gorbachev's last chance: either he acts or he loses us'[99] – that is, the democrats.

Gorbachev decided he did not want to 'lose' them then. Strengthened by the demonstrations, he persuaded a rancorous and at times hostile Central Committee to adopt, as he put it, progressive resolutions, which 'beckoned forward, not backwards'.[100] He claimed that with his 'very skin' he felt the need to act decisively in order to move perestroika along.[101] The Central Committee's platform for the Party Congress, to be held in July, was entitled 'Towards a humane, democratic socialism'. Most importantly, the General Secretary succeeded in forcing the Plenum to take a long-awaited decision: an offer to amend Article Six of the Constitution to prove that the Party no longer 'claimed advantages and constitutional affirmation of [the Party's] special position'.[102]*

Seeking to redeploy 'power structures' outside the Party, the General Secretary persuaded the Third Extraordinary Congress of People's Deputies six weeks later to elect him to the newly created office of President. In his inaugural address, he emphasized the need to radicalize perestroika and pledged to 'act decisively to move forward all the perestroika processes on the democratic platform'.[103]

In retrospect, Gorbachev's success at the February Plenum, his election to the Presidency of the Soviet Union and his inaugural address represented the zenith of the Soviet revolution from above. Never again would the Party's progressive wing be able to stay ahead of the revolution and muster a Central Committee majority for expansion – rather than curtailment – of the change it had set in motion.

As inevitably happens in any revolution worthy of the name, the intra-elite, 'aristocratic' phase of perestroika was ending. The revolution's main arena expanded beyond the highest councils of the Party and the editorial offices of Moscow newspapers and magazines. The struggle between the communist reformers and the communist reactionaries was no longer the sole, or even the main battle, which, increasingly, pitted all those who wanted to preserve a one-party state – whether in a 'progressive', reformist, softer or traditional Stalinist version – against the forces of popular radicalism that wanted to scrap the whole system, 'human face' and all.

With the rapid and ruthless polarization of Soviet politics, Gorbachev's favourite political space, the centre, was shrinking fast, flooded by political currents running in opposite directions. Only 59 per cent

---

* The sole 'nay' among 300-odd votes for the final resolution was indicated by Yeltsin's raised hand. He felt that the Plenum did not go far enough. The Party's monopoly on power had 'driven the country to a desperate situation', he said in his speech. Tens of millions lived in poverty. Calling on the Plenum to seize what could be the Party's last chance for radical renewal, Yeltsin offered ten changes in the Party's structure and policies. Among them were the liquidation of the apparat and the introduction of 'democratic self-rule' in the Party; the abolition of 'democratic centralism' in the Party's decision-making and its replacement with 'pluralism', which would guarantee the rights of dissenting minorities and their proportionate representation in the Party leadership; the change from the unitary structure of state and Party to a voluntary union between the Communist Parties of the Republics; and the transfer of control over the Party press from the Central Committee to the Party as a whole. Only one of Yeltsin's suggestions, made in the first hours of the two-day Plenum, was adopted: the Party's own 'legislative initiative' to abolish Article Six. (*Materialy . . .*, pp. 68–9.)

of the People's Deputies had voted to make him President (495 of 1,878 votes cast were against). He was becoming too radical for some and too conservative for others. As Russian historians would later put it, 'society had already split'.[104]

This split became evident on 1 May, when the Moscow Association of Voters, affiliated with Democratic Russia, organized a protest march through Red Square following an official May Day demonstration. It was, again, a mixed crowd: from 'liberal Christians' and 'Democratic Christians' to monarchists and 'anarcho-syndicalists'. Prominent were the white-blue-and-red flags of pre-revolutionary Russia and the red-green-and-yellow ones of pre-1939 Lithuania, a life-size rendition of Christ on the cross, carried by a monk from the Zagorsk monastery, and portraits of Andrey Sakharov. This was, in the words of Russian historians, a 'new Russia': 'unruly and politically multi-coloured', but united in the desire for freedom and for the destruction of the totalitarian state.[105] 'Seventy-Two Years on the Road to Nowhere!', 'Socialism? No Thanks!', 'Down with the Red Fascist Empire!' read the placards. 'Down with the KGB!', 'Down with the Cult of Lenin!', 'Food Is Not a Luxury!', 'Kremlin Ceausescus: From Armchairs to Prison Plank Beds!'[106]

Most importantly, this was the first mass pro-democracy rally that attacked Gorbachev. As they passed under the reviewing stand on top of the Lenin Mausoleum, where the Politburo members stood, awaiting the end of the demonstration, many shook their fists and shouted, 'Shame! Shame! Shame!' An elderly woman carried a placard declaring, 'Gorbachev, the People Don't Trust You Any More – Resign!' Other slogans read, 'Down with the President–Impostor!',* 'A Dictator = President without Election!'[107] The revolution was overtaking the one who had unleashed it.

Outraged, the President–General Secretary led his Politburo colleagues off the Mausoleum. Later, on national television, Gorbachev would call the demonstrators 'rabble'. And above the rabble, he went on, 'fluttered the flags of anarchists and monarchists and portraits of Nicholas II, Stalin and Boris Yeltsin'.[108]

The next day, one of the most astute of the democratic publicists, Vasiliy Selyunin, wrote in a leading liberal weekly:

---

* Ignoring the democrats' advice, Gorbachev chose to be elected President by the legislature, rather than by the 'people' in a national poll. This would prove one of his costliest mistakes.

We are terribly behind in the formation of a government of national trust: tomorrow may already be too late. We have no time to beat around the bush. We are beginning to form a shadow [opposition] government, which would try to catch power when it slips away from [the current regime] and before it plops in the mud and is picked up by the mafia bandits allied with the right.[109]

A 'new' Russia was 'entering into a political struggle with the Kremlin', wrote chroniclers of those days. 'And her leader in the struggle, her banner and her idol was Boris Yeltsin.'[110]

Because of the record number of contenders and the lower than required turnout in quite a few districts, on 4 March only 120 of 7,018 candidates received more than 50 per cent of the cast votes and so were elected on the first ballot. (It would take two run-off elections – on 18 March and 22 April – to fill the 1,068 seats of the Russian Congress.) In National-Territorial District Number Seventy-Four, however, Boris Yeltsin won with 72 per cent of the vote in a field of twelve candidates.

But the main contest was still ahead, and the stake was huge: the Chairmanship of the Supreme Soviet of Russia. 'As we voted for the Chairman,' a Congress Deputy would later recall, 'we were not voting for the man. We were voting for the direction' Russia would take.[111] Every vote counted, and those who would have preferred anyone but Yeltsin at the helm of the Russian legislature began to prepare early.

The battle for Russia had been joined in December 1989, when Yeltsin decided to run and Mikhail Gorbachev consented to the creation of the Russian Buro within the Central Committee (Russia had been the only Republic without its 'own' Communist Party).[112] The General Secretary did so reluctantly. Most of the pro-reform communists of Russia already worked in all-Union bodies: in the Central Committee apparatus, the Union parliament, national newspapers or Gorbachev's personal secretariat. Thousands of 'liberal' Russian communists and even entire local Party organizations were Yeltsin's key supporters and organizers during the campaign.[113] Gorbachev could not but suspect therefore that the leadership of the Russian Communist Party would be less than enthusiastic about the reforms or, for that matter, about the General Secretary himself.*

---

* Gorbachev recalled that the most important question he asked himself at the time was whether 'the newly created Russian Communist Party would become a tool of anti-reform forces, a stronghold of sorts in the battle against the Central Committee, where at least the tone was set by the General Secretary and his allies' (*Memoirs*, p. 352).

Yet it must have been just as apparent to him that, in the struggle for Russia, Gorbachev's favourite political force – the 'centrists' – would not be dominant, or even influential. The race was between the 'radical democrats', led by Yeltsin, and the conservative (and increasingly reactionary) 'communists'. That December Gorbachev made his choice. Throughout the winter and spring, the General Secretary continued to fortify his Russian contingent. In early February 1990, he approved the convocation of the 'Party Conference of the Russian Republic'.* The following month, he invited the popular nationalist writer Valentin Rasputin and the leftist co-Chairman of the United Front of Russian Workers, Veniamin Yarin, to join the newly created (and largely ceremonial) Presidential Council.

In mid-April, a month before the First Congress of People's Deputies of Russia was due to convene, Gorbachev abandoned the proxy battle and, for the first time that year, attacked Yeltsin directly in his hometown. 'Why, in your view, does Comrade Yeltsin enjoy a great deal of popularity in the Urals but not in the government?' Gorbachev was asked in a note during a question-and-answer session with the workers of Uralmash in Sverdlovsk. 'I think Yeltsin's potential as a politician is quite limited,' Gorbachev answered.[114] Yeltsin's electoral programme and his speeches were 'like an old, scratched record', the General Secretary continued, with their claims that the country's leadership was 'exhausted', 'doomed', 'removed from the people'. He, Gorbachev, rejected such 'unfounded accusations'. Yeltsin, moreover, was exploiting the country's difficulties for his own political profit. True, problems did exist, Gorbachev admitted, but one ought to 'draw lessons from them, attempt to turn things around', instead of gaining popularity by demagoguery. All in all, Gorbachev said, Yeltsin had moved too far into a 'destructive' mode and could not alter his course.[115]

By now a powerful new ingredient had bubbled to the surface of the Russian stew. Just as the Cinderella syndrome seemed to permeate the entire Russian body politic, so, no less thoroughly, did the proposed cure. It was called 'sovereignty' – no longer just for Latvia or Estonia, Georgia or Moldavia, but for the backbone of the Soviet Union, Russia.

* On 19 June the Conference proclaimed itself the founding Congress of the Russian Communist Party, whose future First Secretary would be Yeltsin's opponent in the contest for the Chairmanship of the Supreme Soviet. At the Congress, Gorbachev and his key liberal associates, Aleksandr Yakovlev and Eduard Shevardnadze, were mercilessly attacked by the speakers.

As a practical matter, the new remedy was rendered useless by vagueness of meaning and vast differences between the many interpretations, which had little in common beyond getting away from the arrogant Centre and the ungrateful and rapacious Union. But few looked for an operational meaning in a panacea, an elixir, a philosopher's stone. People and politician alike were positively enchanted, expecting the magic device of sovereignty to 'help the citizens of Russia free themselves from the burden of past injuries and humiliations and become again a great . . . nation'.[116]

By May, political sovereignty, which, unlike its economic counterpart, had not been mentioned in Yeltsin's campaign, became his banner as well. Yeltsin's Russia had the right to 'separate' from the Union and if Russia was treated the way it had been treated so far – robbed by the other Republics – it could consider using this right 'the same way that Lithuania did'.[117]

This was, of course, only campaign rhetoric. 'Without a strong [Russia], a strong Soviet Union [was] impossible,' Yeltsin admitted at a cooler moment, and it was 'unthinkable' for Russia to become independent from the Union.[118] He would fight only for 'maximum independence, for complete decentralization of the economy, politics, finance',[119] and for Russia's right to 'negotiate freely with other Republics'.[120]

These were safe and popular slogans with which almost everyone agreed by now. Yet, as the Russian Congress was about to convene, the vast and empty shell of 'sovereignty' and 'spiritual rebirth' quickly began to fill with increasingly different and incompatible contents. Sovereignty for what? was the question. Was it to be a 'socialist Russia', the heart of the unitary and mighty Soviet Union? A Russia of 'the working class, the Church and the Army', as envisaged by the United Front of Russian Workers? Or a post-colonial Russia, a leader in democracy, the champion of market reform and the engine of a radical transformation of the Union into a loose confederation of equal states?

Yeltsin summarized his plans for a sovereign Russia succinctly: 'radicalization of all reforms'.[121] His was what might be called a 'national democratic' vision of Russian rebirth. The 'renewed democratic Russia' of his electoral programme[122] was a federated, multi-national, multi-party, Presidential republic. On 14 April, the Deputies affiliated with Democratic Russia (which wrote Russia's sovereignty into its charter at the founding conference in January) nominated Yeltsin their candidate for the Chairmanship of the Supreme Soviet of Russia. The lines were drawn.

On the eve of the First Congress of People's Deputies of Russia, the political configuration made Yeltsin's victory extremely difficult. Even though Democratic Russia had won fifty-seven of the sixty-five seats from Moscow and its sister organization in Leningrad, Democratic Elections-90, twenty-eight of the thirty-four seats,* the first conference of the Democratic Russia Deputies on 31 March was attended by slightly over 200 of the Russian parliament's 1,068 members-elect. Even by the most optimistic count – 350 – given by a leading Democratic Russia Deputy,[123] Yeltsin could count on less than one-third of the Congress. Meanwhile, for the majority of the 'communists' and left nationalists he was the 'potential grave-digger of Russia' because of his 'shameless kowtowing to the West and eager support for private property'.[124]

From the first, there was little doubt that Russia's sovereignty would be proclaimed at the Congress, which convened on 16 May. In fact, it was the outgoing Chairman, Politburo member Vitaliy Vorotnikov, who surprised everyone by suggesting that the Congress adopt a Declaration of Sovereignty. Vorotnikov's draft, contained in the report of the outgoing Supreme Soviet, became the 'floor': the lowest common denominator on which all of the 1,060 Deputies-elect actually present in the Kremlin Palace of Congress could agree. In Vorotnikov's version, Russia's successful development within the USSR was possible 'only as an independent and sovereign state'.[125] Like any other Union Republic, it needed to be able to dispose of its material and spiritual assets freely in the interest of the people inhabiting it.[126] The concept of Russian sovereignty did not presuppose a weakening of the ties with the Union. The exact nature of such ties was to be determined by a Union Treaty, which would define the areas of jurisdiction that Russia would voluntarily hand over to the Centre.[127]

No sooner had Vorotnikov finished than half-a-dozen Deputies rushed to the microphones on the floor to demand that an alternative declaration, drafted by the Moscow, Sverdlovsk and Leningrad delegations, be delivered by Yeltsin. It was in this brief and energetic speech that Yeltsin for the first time outlined the strategic triad of his future effort: democracy, federalism, property.

The latter was deliberately soft-pedalled: in the First Congress, the open support for private property and a market economy was still quite risky politically. Still, his euphemisms were transparent. 'All forms of property' were declared legal and protected by law. Russia, moreover, had the right to 'introduce or abolish methods of economic activity and

---

* Democratic majorities in the City Soviets soon elected Gavriil Popov and Anatoliy Sobchak the Mayors of Moscow and Leningrad respectively.

conduct cardinal reforms' – even without the consent of the Union government.[128] A future Russian constitution should guarantee 'political pluralism' and a multi-party system, 'within a framework of a parliamentary democracy'.[129] A monopoly on power by 'any' political party would be prohibited. Non-Russian peoples would be guaranteed sovereignty, economic independence and the right to fair and just representation in all federal ruling bodies of the Russian Federation.

Yeltsin's rendition of 'sovereignty' was broader and more assertive than Vorotnikov's. The Centre existed for the Republics, not vice versa. It was for Russia, and other Republics, to decide what kind of Centre they needed. Russia was primary, the Centre secondary. The Union laws should not contravene those of Russia. 'Economic sovereignty' meant Russia's taking sole possession of all natural resources, rivers and forests, as well as of everything produced on its territory.[130] A transfer of Russia's riches to the Union authorities would have to be approved by the Russian parliament – and only in exchange for a fair remuneration.[131] Russia's contributions to the all-Union budget would be made only on a programme-by-programme basis. The Republic would itself conduct its foreign trade, choose partners and set prices. Its State Bank would be separate from the Soviet Union's and could print currency.[132]

In Yeltsin's summary, democracy – economic and political – was the cornerstone of a new Russian federation. 'The most important, primary sovereignty in Russia [ought to be] the sovereignty of the individual,' followed by the sovereignty of enterprises and local Soviets.[133] As far as the Soviet Union was concerned, perhaps the most troubling part of Yeltsin's manifesto was the reaffirmation of the Stavropol message. Listed by Yeltsin among the most urgent tasks of Russia's democratic renewal was the voluntary abandonment of its role as 'guarantor of the old system of governance'. Laws ought to be passed that would prohibit the use of Russia's natural, economic and intellectual resources, as well as of its armed forces and its citizens, for the 'conduct of a policy of diktat and interference in the internal affairs of other people both outside and inside the Soviet Union'.[134]

He concluded by proffering an olive branch to his opponents. The most urgent necessity in this 'difficult and critical' moment for Russia was 'unity of all national and patriotic forces in Russia', a 'national accord'. No matter how different were the views of the Deputies, they were all united in their desire to see Russia possess 'a full-blooded, real state sovereignty'.[135]

The following day, President Gorbachev, who until then had watched the proceedings from the balcony, was 'asked', as he put it, 'to say a few words about sovereignty'. Of course, such a modest and disarmingly general billing (and his speaking during a recess to emphasize his 'non-interference') fooled no one. In the battle for Russia, the Party had deployed its heaviest weapon. Although he was not mentioned by name until the last third of the speech, the entire oration was an eagerly anticipated rebuttal to Yeltsin.

Gorbachev did not disappoint the expectations. The President's assault on Yeltsin's vision of Russia was at once broad and specific. Listen attentively! the President–General Secretary told the Deputies. Behind all the differences of opinion, behind all the 'scathing and flashy' talk, look for one litmus test, one non-negotiable principle: the principle of 'democratic socialism'.[136] And that was precisely what Gorbachev had not found in Yeltsin's speech. In fact, the latter was nothing but an 'attempt to excommunicate Russia from socialism'. In one fell swoop, Comrade Yeltsin had 'invited us to bid farewell to the socialist choice of 1917'. Boris Nikolaevich had not even found 'room for socialism' in the name of the RSFSR (the full official name of Russia in the USSR was 'Russian Soviet Federated Socialist Republic'). He just wanted to call it the 'Russian Republic'.[137]

For the citizens of Russia, Gorbachev continued, the 'socialist choice' and 'Soviet power' were not empty phrases. They were the 'fundamental values, the reference points'. And what was Comrade Yeltsin offering instead? A change in political system? How could the Soviet peoples carry out the critical task of 'giving socialism a second wind along the line of democratization' if Russia 'wandered off in another direction'?[138] Be vigilant, Gorbachev continued. Beware of those who wanted to palm off on everyone the idea that they had 'the skill to accomplish everything at once'; of those who bragged that the country would flourish if only they were in power; beware, in short, of 'political swindlers'. They played on the difficulties while pursuing their own aims.[139]

'If one was to analyse seriously' Yeltsin's definition of federalism, Gorbachev said, it was nothing but 'a call for the break-up of the Union under the pretext of Russian sovereignty'. Yeltsin should therefore say that he rejected the road on which 'we had travelled since 1922'.[140] In an unmistakable, albeit understated, riposte to Yeltsin's denial of Russia's role as a guarantor of the Soviet domestic empire, Gorbachev insisted that Russia's 'special significance' was rooted in the thousand years during which the 'Russian people [had] done a great deal to unite many peoples on our vast expanses into a single family . . .'[141]

What was on Yeltsin's mind when he said that sovereignty belonged to the individual, the enterprise, the local Soviet? This would lead to anarchy, parochialism, confrontation between the peoples of the Russian Federation. Concluding on a decidedly ominous note, Gorbachev invoked one of the darkest fears of the Russian collective psyche: the bloody 'time of troubles' (*smutnoye vremya*), the three decades of endless fratricidal wars and victorious foreign invasions between the death of Ivan the Terrible in 1582 and the ascendance of the Romanov dynasty in 1613. Perhaps, Gorbachev suggested, Boris Nikolaevich was still attached to his old idea of creating several Russian Republics on the territory of Russia.* But that meant a return to 'principalities, internecine strife, confrontation'. True, Yeltsin had not said anything of the kind in his speech the day before, but, in a 'veiled form', the concept was discernible just the same. And that concept, if implemented, would destroy not only the Soviet Union – it would destroy Russia as well.[142]

Sitting next to Yeltsin during Gorbachev's speech, Larisa Mishustina, a democratic Deputy from Sverdlovsk, remembered the expression on Yeltsin's face: frozen, stone-like, as if paralysed by his effort to contain and conceal tension. Knowing of his heart troubles she offered him a popular Russian medication. 'Validol?' she whispered. Yeltsin thanked her and said, 'Don't worry. I am all right.'

The next day, 24 May, the Deputies began nominating candidates for Chairman of the Supreme Soviet of Russia. Of the original twelve, nine withdrew and by the end of the day only three contenders remained: Yeltsin, the communist candidate Ivan Polozkov, First Secretary of the Krasnodar Obkom, and an obscure, self-nominated candidate from Kazan.

On the eve of the vote, 25 May, Yeltsin and Polozkov formally presented their electoral programmes and answered questions from the floor. This time, whether because after Gorbachev's speech he had little to gain by reticence, or because of the government's own lead,† most of

---

* Gorbachev was not quite accurate. What Yeltsin proposed, cautiously, during his 1990 campaign was decentralization of political and economic authority, eventually leading to the creation of six large regions, or 'states' under a single federal administration. Intended as one of the central planks of his electoral platform, the proposal was subsequently downplayed for fear of nationalist criticism. Indeed, the reactionary Pamyat' saw the scheme as an attempt to make Russia look like the Star of David – yet more proof of the 'Zionist conspiracy'. (Interview with Aleksander Urmanov.)

† On the same day, Prime Minister Nikolay Ryzhkov presented to the Supreme Soviet of the Soviet Union a programme of transition to the market 'by 1995'.

Yeltsin's speech was devoted to the ways and means of radical economic reform. 'How to move to a market economy is the main question today,' he told the Deputies. The people of Russia might give a new parliament and a new leadership two to three years precisely because they were new'. But 'no more than that'.[143]

Echoing the opinion of most reform-minded Moscow economists that a transition to the market was made extremely hard by shortages, inflation, the budget deficit and excess cash, Yeltsin outlined, in great detail, emergency measures for a preliminary stabilization. They included a 10–15 per cent reduction in Russia's contribution to the Union's military expenditure; a drastic (30–40 per cent) cut in new industrial investments; and a sell-off of parcels of state-owned land, industrial equipment and unfinished construction projects.[144] In order further to shrink the deficit and reduce the number of 'empty rubles' in circulation, Yeltsin proposed using loans from the West to purchase consumer goods and to build houses and apartments for sale to private owners.[145]

Again he ended on a note of reconciliation, with what was for him an unprecedented pledge of compromise and flexibility:

I understand how ambivalent is the attitude of the Deputies towards me personally. The complexity of the perestroika processes has made me appreciate the importance of political compromise, the ability to take into consideration various points of view, the significance of dialogue with different political forces, dialogue which alone can assure progress towards real agreement . . .

Today, no matter who we are – democrat, apparatchik, centrist, a Party member or not – we are united by one burning concern and one responsibility. And the fate of Russia today, the fate of each of its citizens, depends on the ways in which we unite and earn people's trust, on how principled and how constructive our defence of our Republic's independence will be. I am ready to take all the responsibility and, with all of you, I am ready to begin working.[146]

The same leitmotif ran through Yeltsin's answers to the Deputies' questions following the speech. He promised, for instance, that if he were elected Chairman the candidates for leadership (his Deputy Chairmen and Chairmen of the two Houses of the Supreme Soviet) would be nominated not by him alone, as Gorbachev had done in the Union parliament, but in 'consultation with groups of Deputies'.[147]

He assured them of co-operation with Gorbachev as well. His relationship with the head of the Soviet Union would be businesslike – 'a dialogue, negotiations' – but not 'at the expense' of Russian sovereignty and independence. If there had been anything personal between them, Yeltsin was prepared to 'cast it aside'.[148] As if to prove the strength of his determination, there was not a word of rebuttal of Gorbachev in Yeltsin's speech.

Nor, however, did he retreat from any of the positions which the President and General Secretary had assailed the day before. When asked to respond to Gorbachev's charge that 'the sovereignty of the individual would lead to anarchy', Yeltsin said, 'I don't agree. What is the "sovereignty of the individual"? It is freedom of choice in entering into a contract with society . . . [or] a group of people – not freedom to do absolutely everything one wants. The "sovereignty of the individual" and "anarchy" are two entirely different notions.' What did he think of the notion of Russia's 'special fate', its 'special destiny'? read another note from the hall. 'I see Russia as an equal among equals among the Republics of our country,' Yeltsin replied.[149]*

On the morning of Saturday, 26 May, the First Congress of People's Deputies of Russia voted for the Chairman of the Republic's smaller permanent legislature, the Supreme Soviet. To win the Chairmanship, a contender needed at least 531 votes: half of the 1,060 Deputies present plus one vote. Yeltsin received 497, Polozkov 473, and the third candidate 32.

Outside the Kremlin walls, meanwhile, Yeltsin's supporters were staging a non-stop rally. Red Square, Manezhnaya Square and the Rossiya Hotel, where the Deputies lived, were picketed by hundreds of people, chanting, waving placards and simply shouting at the Deputies. The din was 'awful', Yeltsin's aide recalled.[150] 'The rowdy crowds of your supporters accost us in the morning, at night, and during the breaks in sessions,' a Deputy complained to Yeltsin during the pre-election

---

* On the surface, there was surprisingly little to distinguish the tenor of Ivan Polozkov's programme from that of Yeltsin's. The future head of the soon-to-be-created Communist Party of Russia supported a multi-party system, democracy, federal decentralization and, of course, the 'full' political and economic sovereignty of Russia. But to 'attentive' Deputies, alerted by Gorbachev to code words, Polozkov's agenda was a clear alternative to Yeltsin's. He pledged allegiance to 'socialist choice'. He insisted on the Party's unique 'consolidating' role. His market was to be 'firmly regulated' by the state. And even for such a market he declared the Russian people 'not ready'. ('S'ezd narodnyth deputatov RSFSR' ('The Congress of People's Deputies of the RSFSR), 25 May 1990, *Sovetskaye Rossia*, 27 May 1990.)

hearing.[151] Yeltsin agreed that 'once you [were] beyond the Spasskaya Tower [of the Kremlin] there was simply no place to hide'. He said that he had asked the Moscow Soviet to 'alleviate the situation' and swore that he had nothing to do with the demonstrations.[152] Soon Red Square was cordoned off by a patrol of military officers: ordinary soldiers were deemed unfit to handle so tense a situation.

On the morning of the first vote, two women with a young girl in tow somehow managed to break through the ring of officers around Red Square and ran to St Basil's Cathedral, where Yeltsin's aide and his driver waited next to his tiny saloon, a Moskvich. As the women caught their breath, they noticed an Army colonel standing near by. 'And you, what are doing here, fatface?' the women accosted him. 'We know, all of you are against Yeltsin. What do you want? Polozkov? One Kuzmich is not enough for you, is he?'[153] (This was a reference to the patron saint of Party conservative Egor Ligachev, whose patronymic, like Polozkov's, was Kuzmich.) 'Now, you two, stop demonstrating here right away!' the colonel barked back. 'Go home and make a borscht, leave politics to others!' 'Against the people you are nothing!' the women shouted. 'Just you wait. The people's anger will sweep away the likes of you, fatso . . .'[154]

Several Deputies entered Red Square from a Kremlin gate, and the word spread instantly: Yeltsin had failed to get elected. One of the women began to cry. 'You should be ashamed of yourselves! What are you doing to Yeltsin?' she screamed at the Deputies. 'Get these fishwives the hell out of here!' one of the Deputies told the officers. The women turned on him. 'Oh yeah? It's you who should be getting the hell out of here . . . We know, we know: you don't love Russia, you kiss the Party's arse . . . Bastards . . .'[155]

Towering over other departing legislators, Yeltsin appeared on the scene: a tense, unnatural smile on his face. The women rushed to him and gave him flowers. 'Hold on, Boris Nikolaevich. We shall elect you no matter what.' Yeltsin got into the car. After they had left the crowd behind, he smashed his fist on the dashboard. The aide saw a tear on his cheek.

The second vote was held on the afternoon of the same day. Yeltsin increased his lead over Polozkov from twenty-four to forty-five votes: 503 against 458. Still, he was twenty-eight votes short of winning.

When the Congress reconvened on Monday, 28 May, an *Izvestia* reporter found 'the atmosphere in the hall heated to boiling point'.[156] Even Yeltsin's faithful aide, Lev Sukhanov, did not accompany his boss to the Palace of Congresses: he could no longer 'bear the nightmare' of tension.[157] Suddenly, as if following an order, motions were put forward by communist Deputies to bar both Yeltsin and Polozkov from further rounds: it was pointless to waste any more time on these obviously deadlocked leaders of polar political trends within the parliament.[158]

The motions did not make it to a vote. Both Yeltsin and Polozkov were renominated, along with seven other Deputies. By the end of the day Polozkov withdrew, as did six other contenders. Yeltsin faced the Party's new hope: Aleksandr Vlasov, a lacklustre apparatchik, an ex-Chairman of the Council of Ministers of Russia (until then a position of little power) and a former Minister of Internal Affairs of the USSR. The third candidate was a Valentin Tsoy, the 'chairman of the board' of a Khabarovsk co-operative. The vote was scheduled for the following morning.

Yeltsin spoke again and underwent another intense interrogation from the floor. No, he had 'never advocated' Russia's secession from the Soviet Union, just sovereignty and equal rights for all the Republics.[159] Yes, no matter who won, a 'coalition government of sorts' ought to be formed from the representatives of all major political blocs in the Congress. Was he really prepared to quit the Party – or were these rumours a 'provocation'? That would all depend on whether the Party managed to restructure itself at the Congress in July.[160]

'Don't you think that swimming in rivers near Moscow or appearing in less-than-perfect shape before an American audience makes impossible, from a moral point of view, not only your claims to the post of Chairman but the continuation of [your] political career as well?' ('Hubbub and whistles in the hall.') He had answered 'these questions often enough', Yeltsin said, and saw no need for returning to them again. 'If the Comrade is really very interested in all the details, let him come up to me in the interval and I will tell him everything.' ('Laughter and applause in the hall.')[161]

'How do you assess your main merits and flaws?' He had been called tough (*zhestkiy*), Yeltsin answered. That was in keeping with his previous activity as a Party boss. He had begun to change with perestroika and democratization and had made 'some kind of progress' towards his own democratization. But it was too early to talk about a full victory on this front.[162]

By the evening of 28 May, thousands of telegrams from their constituencies[163] had been delivered to Deputies in the Rossia Hotel. In at least one case (that of a Deputy from the Far East city of Vladivostok), 90 per cent of the messages were in support of Yeltsin.[164] The miners of Donetsk, Vorkuta and Kuzbass threatened to strike if Yeltsin was not elected.[165] Next door, in the Kremlin, only hours before he was to fly to summits in Canada and the United States, Gorbachev summoned 400 communist Deputies and urged them not to vote for Yeltsin.[166] According to a tape-recording of Gorbachev's address, he called Yeltsin a 'risk' to Russia's future, and his supporters in the Congress a 'rabble'.[167]

In the late morning of 29 May, the Congress of People's Deputies of Russia held the third vote for the office of Chairman. The Deputies filed out of the hall to cast their ballots in another chamber. The Congress recessed until 1 p.m. When they returned, the Chairman of the Counting Commission came to the podium to announce the result. Vlasov had received 467 votes, Tsoy 11, Yeltsin 535. All around Yeltsin his supporters jumped from their seats and screamed for joy. Yeltsin did not move. He even tried, and almost succeeded, in suppressing a broad smile. He was a statesman now.

The election marathon revealed the political profile of the Russian legislature. The 'hard' opposition – those who voted for Vlasov, and would have voted for anyone to defeat Yeltsin and Democratic Russia – comprised 44 per cent of the Deputies. Yeltsin's vote, a hair's breadth over 50 per cent, consisted of 'democrats' plus 25 per cent of the Deputies. It was this volatile and unpredictable swing bloc, instantly labelled the 'swamp', that for the next three years would control the balance of power in the Russian legislature. Yeltsin's victory portended a most uncertain ability to steer the parliament. Most of his victories would be just as narrow and difficult, granted only under intense pressure from the outside.

Because of the amorphous nature of the Congress's political factions, which lacked formal leadership or even caucuses, we may never know for certain what swayed the narrow majority. It was clear, however, that to some Deputies, aflame with the idea of sovereignty, Gorbachev's appearance and speech represented the Centre's rude interference in Russian affairs. Yeltsin's two peace offerings and his promise to nominate Deputy Chairmen by agreement with various political factions, giving up his 'constitutional right' to do so himself,[168]* must also have added to the winning tally.

---

* Yeltsin kept his word. Given the composition of 'political forces' in the legislature, he would soon find himself with two communist Deputy Chairmen and two pro-communist Chairmen of the Houses of the Supreme Soviet. Six months hence, he would pay dearly for his unorthodox method of choosing his 'cabinet'.

Other likely inducements included a 'harder' version of autonomy and a skilful projection of confidence, the detailed nature of his proposals, and his willingness to take responsibility. (Yeltsin had presented, for instance, a list of the twelve most urgent laws he intended to pass and even had a deadline ready for Russian Presidential elections: no later than May 1991.) By contrast, Vlasov cut too mediocre a figure. The more progressive and thoughtful among the communists understood that he lacked the minimum of popular trust and legitimacy necessary to implement even those few reforms which they thought unavoidable.[169]

This last consideration appeared to have been more responsible for Yeltsin's victory than any other. In this potential for reform Russian observers saw the larger meaning of Yeltsin's victory and of the hopes that it engendered. 'For millions of our compatriots,' wrote one of the most subtle and objective observers of the Russian political scene, the political philosopher and sociologist Igor Klyamkin, the most important factor was not the details of Yeltsin's programme or his leadership qualities. 'The only thing that mattered to them was whether or not the man they knew as Yeltsin would or would not be at the head of the Russian republic.'[170] So Yeltsin's presence in the Russian leadership determined (and was likely to continue to determine for a while) the people's trust or mistrust of the Russian Congress, and of perestroika as a whole. The people's willingness to sustain the daily hardships, current or future, depended on this presence. In that sense, Klyamkin continued, the fate of perestroika, and even the fate of its initiator, Gorbachev, was contingent, in large measure, on Yeltsin's victory.[171]

Yeltsin was 'necessary' for Gorbachev, Klyamkin went on, because he, Yeltsin, could now shoulder at least part of the crushing responsibility that the President until then had had to bear alone: the responsibility for Russia. And, if the President was at all interested in the reforms, Yeltsin had two advantages that would help him move 'incomparably more decisively' towards a market economy: popular trust and the absence of any ties to the apparat that would slow him down.[172] The victory of 'Yeltsin's democratic bloc' in such a Republic as Russia, Klyamkin argued, meant that the arrow of the Soviet political compass had moved to the 'left': it was no longer in the Baltic Republics but in the very heart of the Soviet Union where the politicians were 'now compelled to listen less to the whispers from the apparat and more to the din from outside the walls of their offices'. This, too, was extremely beneficial to Gorbachev – 'if, of course, he intends to move forward'.[173]

Gorbachev's options, as Klyamkin saw them, were not 'with Yeltsin or against Yeltsin'. His real choice was 'with Yeltsin forwards' – or 'backwards against Yeltsin'. Between radical Yeltsin and conservative Polozkov, the Congress finally made its choice: hesitant, tortured, slow. Gorbachev, on the other hand, was ready to embrace Polozkov. That the President had chosen to do so – risking, in the event of Yeltsin's defeat, a backlash of popular indignation on an enormous scale – was 'sad', concluded Klyamkin.[174]*

For the moment, however, as he made his way to the podium, flowers in hand, amid 'stormy applause',[175] it seemed that goodwill, patience and compromise might be enough to overcome the deep ideological divisions, intransigence and obsession with power that would soon begin to tear the Russian parliament apart. As he began speaking 'in an emotional, shaking voice',[176] Yeltsin, too, seemed to believe in a brighter future. Yes, he confessed the obvious, he did feel 'some' personal 'satisfaction', but:

> at the same time and to a far greater degree, one feels responsibility at this time, crucial for Russia, at the beginning of its road towards national, economic and spiritual revival, the road out of crisis, towards the prosperity of Russia as a sovereign, independent state within the Soviet Union, [the road] which will be successfully travelled because of our work together, because of the selfless labour of all peoples of Russia.[177]

He was, Yeltsin continued, grateful to 'all Deputies' – those who voted for him and those who had not 'agreed with certain points' in his programme or with him 'personally'. He was grateful to them for 'the dynamic and democratic process', which had led to the election of the Chairman – 'albeit on the twelfth day . . .'[178]

He hoped that the Supreme Soviet's committees and commissions (which were still to be elected) would enable the parliament to adopt 'more radical and bolder' laws. Yet the 'most important thing' was that they be adopted according to the 'principles of national concord'. To ensure such an outcome, Yeltsin announced that he would immediately begin consultations with all the political factions of the legislature and

---

* Gorbachev waited for at least a week before he congratulated Yeltsin on his victory (Egor Yakovlev, 'I snova v poiskakh soglasiya' ('Again, in search of accord'), an interview with Boris Yeltsin, *Moskovskie Novosti*, 10 June 1990; Aleksandr Ol'bik, 'Ya veryu v russkoe chudo' ('I believe in the Russian miracle'), an interview with Boris Yeltsin, *Sovetskaya Molodezh*, 3–4 August 1990).

call on them to select representatives for participation in these 'round table' talks. If a 'round table' could not be found, Yeltsin quipped, let's negotiate at a square one – but immediately. It was imperative to 'settle on the candidates for the key positions' through such a dialogue.[179]

> I am not going to take an oath [Yeltsin concluded], only Presidents, I think, do that, but I definitely promise you that, in the name of Russia, in the name of people and peoples that live there, in the name of our unity, I would spare nothing, absolutely nothing – not health, not time, not labour – to overcome the crisis and to lead Russia towards better times. This I, once again, promise.
>
> Once again, thank you for your enormous trust. Thank you.[180]

*

On 29 August, millions of Soviet viewers were treated to a most unusual spectacle, never to be repeated again. Gorbachev and Yeltsin appeared together on television for a joint interview to announce their agreement on the general outline of a 'programme for the stabilization of the Soviet economy and the transition to the market', as Yeltsin put it.[181] The programme – 'a single document' – would be made public within a week, Gorbachev promised.[182] That document would soon be known as the '500-Day Programme'.

The two were visibly uncomfortable. They grimaced, smiled sarcastically at each other's comments and avoided looking at each other. They interrupted each other, especially Gorbachev. Still, emanating from the screen was a powerful sense of renewal, maturity, responsibility, consensus – and hope. The tableau was especially astonishing given the previous summer, during which the two leaders had appeared to drift steadily apart – sometimes, it seemed, out of hearing distance.

On 12 June, Russia's Congress of People's Deputies adopted a declaration 'On the National Sovereignty of the Russian Soviet Federated Socialist Republic': 907 'yeas', 13 'nays' and 9 abstentions. As these numbers were illuminated on the board, the Deputies greeted them with a standing ovation. Even Yeltsin, who had studiously cultivated the image of an impartial and imperturbable 'speaker', was swept up by the jubilation around him and clapped twice – the first and last such transgression of the self-imposed rules of statesmanship.[183] This day was to become Russia's first post-Soviet national holiday, Independence Day.

The Declaration expressed the Congress's 'determination to create a democratic, law-abiding state within a renewed Soviet Union'. The 'repository of sovereignty' and 'the source of state power' in the Republic was the 'multi-national people' of Russia. The main goal of Russian sovereignty was to secure for everyone the inalienable right to a dignified life and free development. All peoples of the RSFSR had the right to use their native language, and to pursue self-determination through freely chosen forms of national statehood and national culture.* All citizens, political parties and public organizations that operated within the law were entitled to participate in the management of state and public affairs. The new Republic was a 'law-abiding' state, in which the separation of legislative, executive and judicial branches of government was the 'most important principle'.[184]

Even a Russian history textbook largely critical of Yeltsin and the 'democrats' admitted that the Declaration 'marked the beginning of a new era in the development of Russian statehood'.[185] Indeed it had. For the first time in almost five centuries, Russian state-building was not accompanied by militarism, imperial expansion, 'Russia as the Third Rome' messianism or the strengthening of authoritarianism, which, separately or in concert, had been part of every consolidation from Ivan the Terrible to Peter the Great, Catherine, Nicholas I, Lenin and Stalin. Yeltsin and his allies snatched the powerful idea of Russian national 'renewal' from Party conservatives and 'national-patriots' and

---

* The Declaration's most controversial item, which had been debated for longer than any other and which would cause the Centre the most consternation, was Article Five, postulating the primacy of Russian laws over the Soviet Union's. In instances where Russian and Soviet laws came into direct conflict, the latter were to be 'suspended on the territory of the RSFSR'.

Ten days later the Congress passed a resolution that Yeltsin considered the session's other most important achievement. In 'demarcating the administrative functions', Russia 'voluntarily delegated' to the Centre only five areas: defence, national security, railway transportation, civil aviation and the merchant marine. That article of the Declaration freed Russia from the control of sixty Union ministries. 'What a bomb! What a blow to the administrative–distributive system!' a delighted Yeltsin told the equally jubilant delegation of Kuzbass miners the next day. ('Boris El'tsin i Soviet rabochikh komitetov Kuzbassa' ('Boris Yeltsin and the Council of Workers' Committees of Kuzbass'), a transcript, *Nasha Gazeta*, 19, (26 June) 1990, as reprinted in *Russkaya Mysl'*, 29 June 1990.)

The symbolic timing of the resolution – on the last day of the First Congress – was not accidental. Yeltsin would later confess that he had not slept the night before, searching for a way to end the Congress on a note that 'would not be forgotten'. ('The conversation of the RSFSR People's Deputies V. Isakov and V. Skrypchenko with B. N. Yeltsin on 22 June 1990', videotape, Museum of Youth Movements, Ekaterinburg.)

pressed it into the service of democratic modernization. The re-emergence of a 'sovereign' Russia, if only largely symbolic, coincided with its conscious striving for democracy, decolonization, demilitariz-ation and the status of 'equal among equals' vis-à-vis its neighbours. Orchestrating, or at least midwifing, this concurrence was one of Yeltsin's weightiest contributions to the foundation of a new Russian state.

Of all the novelties introduced in his short but busy stewardship of the First Congress, Yeltsin appeared to be proudest of giving content to the hitherto abstract terms of parliamentary democracy. That June, for the first time since 1917, the words 'opposition', 'faction' and 'coalition' re-entered the Russian vernacular. When a Russian television reporter asked him about 'taking into account the views of the minority' in choosing the leadership of the Supreme Soviet, Yeltsin said there was a real attempt to create a coalition – 'the first such case in our country in seventy-three years!'[186]

From the outset, the 'democratic' spirit of the new Russian legislature seemed to please Yeltsin more than anything else. 'The Russian parlia-ment has shown that it is democratic ... Democratic. Yes, yes, there are various points of view, which is perfectly natural at this time, especi-ally in a transitional period. But, even so, in its majority it is demo-cratic.'[187]

Thirty factions of Deputies were officially registered in the first days of the Congress: political, territorial, professional or issue-oriented. The only requirement was that they comprise at least fifty members. And all, Yeltsin repeated contentedly, were absolutely 'equal' in status.[188] He met with every one of them in the evenings, after the sessions, for 'two or three hours of frank, no-holds-barred' talks,[189] and soon felt that after these meetings many Deputies began to understand him. An experienced Western observer of the Soviet political scene at the time likewise noticed that support for Yeltsin appeared to have grown because of the aptitude he had shown for reconciling Deputies who held differing views.[190] 'Pol-itical opposition is a reality,' Yeltsin declared at a press conference at the close of the First Congress. 'We have to take it into account; we have to work with it.'[191]

Working with the opposition proved an arduous task for a fledgling democratic consensus-monger. 'It has been incredibly difficult for me to restrain myself,' he confessed after the Congress adjourned. 'Incredibly. I am, it is quite true, a man rather tough on others but especially on myself. Yet it was absolutely necessary to create an atmosphere [at the Congress] that would help the Deputies understand: here they can say anything. They will be listened to patiently, not interrupted in mid-phrase or subjected to [sarcastic] commentary [from the Chair].'[192]*

Even so, the opposition dealt Yeltsin a major setback by defeating the Decree on Power, which, following Yeltsin's election platform, would have ended the Party's control over industrial enterprises, the armed forces, national security and law-enforcement agencies. The watered-down version that eventually passed prohibited only the occupancy of Soviet and Party posts by the same person.†

Yet in the end it all seemed well worth the effort. 'The Russian giant is awakening,' a jubilant Yeltsin said in the speech with which he concluded the First Congress.

> For the first time in the years of perestroika, there has been a forum as representative as our Congress, the rich palette of different political movements, ideological directions, and positions ... Life itself, and not the whim of fashion, has placed us in a situation where it is

* Lighter but definitely taxing was another self-imposed burden: Yeltsin's own hand-picked Ministers – smart, very well educated, brash, Western-oriented, cocky and very young by Soviet standards. Minister of Finance Boris Fedorov and his namesake, Minister of Justice Nikolay Fedorov, were thirty-two; Deputy Prime Minister and Chairman of the RSFSR Economic Reform Committee Grigoriy Yavlinsky, thirty-five; the head of the newly created Ministry of Foreign Economic Relations, Viktor Yaroshenko, who had travelled with Yeltsin to the United States, forty-four. It was not 'very simple' for Yeltsin to get used to a staff who had no reverence for rank and were 'quite independent'. In the Party system it had been very different: whatever he ordered was 'going to get done'. With his own Ministers he now 'had to discuss and argue'. But he liked it when somebody 'argued and did not just follow orders'. One should have people around who 'did not agree'. (Aleksandra Lugovskaya, 'Boris El'tsin: nikto ne smog menya postavit' na koleni' ('Boris Yeltsin: no one has ever made me kneel'), *Soyuz*, 38, September 1990, as reprinted in *Doverie*, January 1991.)

Yavlinsky, whom Yeltsin had offered the job after only a few conversations, was astonished by the absence of bureaucratic formalities. 'He offered me the post of Deputy Prime Minister of Russia without asking where I was born, who my parents were or how old I was,' remembered Yavlinsky, who until then had worked for the USSR government's top economist, Deputy Prime Minister Leonid Abalkin. (Ye. Yakovlev, 'Yavlinsky's Death Ray', *Moscow News*, 6 January 1991.)

† The democrats need not worry 'on this score', Yeltsin said after the First Congress was over. This law that had been forced on them was better than nothing. He was confident that soon, perhaps even at the next Congress, they would adopt a 'genuinely solid document, equal in significance to the Declaration on state sovereignty'. ('Press konferentsiya po itogam ...')

impossible to get by without compromise – a real compromise, achieved by experience, not born somewhere in the belly of the appa-rat ... Our Congress proved that any crises, any impasses can be overcome if we begin to listen to and hear each other, if we meet each other halfway ... It is pluralism that really has been present at the Congress ... I believe that all of us, without exception, are taking the first steps in really civilized politics.[193]

Look around! Yeltsin said at the press conference immediately after the adjournment of the First Congress: the Russian parliament was no longer 'a grey monolith but a bright mosaic of opinions!'*

This was a 'powerful' and 'historic' Congress, Yeltsin told several close associates in a conversation in his office. 'Historic!' he repeated. 'In five years we have not been able to blow up the system. Now we have! We have blown up this administrative machine. Now only for-ward, forward, forward!'[194] And forward (and away from the Centre) he went: challenging the Kremlin, stretching and jealously guarding the boundaries of his largely imaginary country and the prerogatives of his mostly symbolic power.

Impatient to establish horizontal links that would connect the Republics, bypassing the Centre's rigid vertical lines of subordination, the day after

---

* Yeltsin's newly found political ecumenism appeared to extend even to such exotic items as gender inequality. At the same press conference a correspondent of the Soviet Union's only Russian-language women's magazine, *Rabotnitza*, asked why he did not have 'bright female politicians' around him. The audience chuckled in anticipation of a sultry quip from a fifty-nine-year-old man nurtured in what must have been one of the world's most male-chauvinistic cultures. Instead, Yeltsin was all business: 'I do not agree. During the sessions of the Congress a number of women have proven themselves very well. I can clearly see a number of female professional politicians, bright and skilful. We must seek to attract them to work in the Supreme Soviet and the Cabinet of Ministers.' (He had, indeed, proposed three women for one of the Deputy Chairman posts. One of them, communist Svetlana Goryacheva, was eventually elected.)

Yeltsin's effort at what in other, faraway places would have been called 'diversity' included ethnicity as well. He lobbied very hard to give the next, after his own, most important post of First Deputy Chairman to a non-Russian from one of Russia's twenty-one Autonomous Republics. His first slew of nominees included a government official from Bashkiria, the chairman of the Tatar Writer's Union, a Party Secretary from Dages-tan and a linguist from Khakassia. Eventually, the post went to a Moscow Chechen, Ruslan Khazbulatov.

taking over the Chair he announced Russia's intention to 'conclude fourteen treaties with fourteen Republics, if they agree'.[195] A month later, Yeltsin advertised joint working commissions that were preparing Russia's comprehensive treaties with Estonia, Latvia, Moldavia, Ukraine, Byelorussia and Kazakhstan.

That summer, the Chairman of the Russian Supreme Soviet confronted the Kremlin in an especially sensitive area: the Baltics. Continuing to insist that the economic blockade of Lithuania was Gorbachev's 'gross error' (if a people wanted to be independent, force was 'useless': the 'stronger the pressure of the [Central] authorities, the greater the resistance . . .',[196] he pledged that Russia would be 'among the first to conclude treaties' with Estonia, Latvia and Lithuania.[197] In June he met with the Kremlin's bugbear, the leader of the Lithuanian pro-independent Popular Front and Chairman of the rebellious Lithuanian parliament, Vytautas Lansbergis, and agreed to conclude a comprehensive treaty between the two 'countries': 'economic, political, social, cultural'.[198]

The following month, in the Latvian resort town of Jurmala, Yeltsin held consultations with the leaders of all three Baltic Republics – the first inter-Republican summit ever without the participation of the Union government. He found himself in '100 per cent' agreement with his Latvian counterpart, Anatoliy Gorbunovs. Recognition of Latvia's independence, Yeltsin told Gorbunovs, 'must certainly be included' in the political section of a treaty between the two 'countries'.[199] On 3 August, in the Latvian capital, Riga, Yeltsin addressed the Republic's Supreme Soviet. After reiterating his wish to have a treaty between Russia and Latvia concluded within a month and a half,* he said: 'The front line of defence of the three Baltic Republics [had been] fairly weak and the Centre's pressure great. Then Russia stood shoulder to shoulder with [Estonia, Latvia and Lithuania]. And the Centre began to worry. It is now more difficult [for Moscow] to attack this fortified line of defence . . .'[200]

Shadow-boxing with the President continued throughout August, as Yeltsin embarked on a tour of his bailiwick, twice the size of the United States, in three weeks crossing ten time zones, covering more than 10,000 kilometres and visiting twenty-one cities from Moscow to the Bering Sea. Begun in Kazan, the capital of the Tatar Autonomous Republic, the largest

---

* Russia concluded its first treaty as a sovereign country with Latvia on 17 September. There followed treaties with Byelorussia (18 October), Ukraine (20 November) and Kazakhstan (26 November).

of Russia's thirty-one non-Russian ethnic 'autonomies', the journey took Yeltsin to Vorkuta, Sverdlovsk, Novokuznetsk, Vladivostok, Sakhalin and Kamchatka, with 'six to eight' meetings in each city[201] and dozens of side-trips to smaller towns and villages along the way.

In the capital of Bashkiria, Ufa, he visited a mosque and an Orthodox church. In the mining city of Vorkuta, above the Polar Circle, he went down 'the oldest and most neglected pit'[202] and stopped by the local miners' strike committee. Having donned special 'radioactive safety' clothes, he examined the control room of a nuclear submarine at a naval base on the Kamchatka peninsula,[203] and flew in a helicopter to a Sakhalin offshore drilling rig in the Sea of Okhotsk.

Greeted by large and enthusiastic crowds wherever he went, he spoke to Tatar oil drillers in the city of Al'met'evsk, the crews of the 500 ships of the Pacific Ocean fishing fleet (by a radio hook-up from Yuzhnno-Sakhalinsk), shipyard workers in Vladivostok, the native people of Sakhalin, the Nivkhs, and thousands at the construction site of a nuclear power plant in the Bashkir town of Agidel, where he brokered an agreement between the builders and the local 'Green' protesters afraid of another Chernobyl.[204] In the Bashkir city of Sterlimak, Yeltsin was told that the crowd outside would not be able to hear his speech. Leaving behind the invited audience of local worthies, he squeezed through a window and addressed the crowd from the roof[205] – a moment captured by national television and shown on the main nightly news programme.[206] The Chairman's resilience astonished a *New York Times* reporter who travelled with him for a week – and the 'first 3,000 miles'. He 'never saw any signs that his wit or stamina was impaired during workdays that lasted upward of 16 hours'.[207]

In the end, Yeltsin had but one message for everyone – the Tatar peasants, the miners of Novokuznetsk and the local authorities of Sakhalin: independence and self-reliance. Power ought to flow from the bottom to the top. Decide what you want for yourself, have it, and only then delegate the rest 'upstairs'.

When Yeltsin met with the managers of the Vorkuta mines, he was served the traditional plateful of numbing statistics dished out to visiting Moscow dignitaries. For a few minutes, Yeltsin's 'silver pompadour' bobbed over the map of mines spread on the conference table. Then he looked up and 'silenced his hosts with a blue glare'. What if Russia gave them complete independence? he asked. *Complete* independence. There was an 'awkward hush' in the room. Independence? What about the guaranteed supplies? What about state subsidies?

This response was symptomatic of the ambiguities and contradictions inherent in the near universal desire to defy the Centre and challenge its control of the economy. The paradox first surfaced during the Kuzbass strike a year before. On the one hand, the miners demanded the right to sell 30 per cent of their coal to business partners at home and abroad at 'contract prices' (instead of selling it to the state) and, on the other, insisted on increasing state support for their loss-making industry. (In 1988 Moscow spent 5.4 billion rubles to keep the industry afloat.)[208] The miners wanted to have their cake and eat it too. Like almost everyone in the Soviet Union at the time, they thought 'market' meant a combination of generous state subsidies and social services and freedom to set prices and dispose of produce.

Yeltsin cut them short. No, that was not how reform worked. 'As owners of whatever you produce, you will have to decide to whom you sell, at whatever price. All these are your problems. We are not going to feed you any more.' (By the time he left, the managers were excitedly debating how to upgrade a nearby port to export their coal, and what tax rate they 'could live with'.)[209]

He was equally blunt about political decentralization. Russia would accommodate them, he told Tatars who were about to adopt their own 'declaration of sovereignty'. Russia supported other 'autonomies' in their attempts at self-rule. 'I will repeat once again what I said at the Congress of People's Deputies,' Yeltsin told *Sovetskaya Tataria* in Kazan. 'The formation of power must happen from below – from the city to the Republic. We will welcome whatever independence the Tatar ASSR* chooses for itself ... If you want to govern yourselves completely, go ahead.'[210] Several days later in the neighbouring Bashkir Autonomous Republic, Yeltsin uttered a phrase which, instantly heard all over the Soviet Union, would epitomize the unbridgeable gap between his and the Kremlin's concepts of federation. 'We are saying to the Bashkir people,' said the Chairman of the Russian parliament, 'we are saying to the Supreme Soviet and the government of Bashkiria: take as much power as you can swallow!'[211]

The Party's Twenty-Eighth Congress provided the background for yet another rift between the Chairman and the President. The Party came to this Congress burdened with a very heavy load, Yeltsin said in his speech. The heaviest part of the load was its inability in the previous few years to 'neutralize the conservative forces' inside the Party. The constant refrain about all Party members being 'in the same boat' and 'on

---

* ASSR was an acronym for Autonomous Soviet Socialist Republic, an ethnic and administrative region below a Republic.

the same side of the barricades' had demoralized those who supported changes and strengthened the position of the conservatives.[212]

It could be too late already, but there was a way out, Yeltsin continued. The Party must remake itself into a parliamentary party of 'democratic socialism' and join other parties of socialist orientation in a united 'democratic front', which would provide a 'broad social base' for further reforms. The Party must, once and for all, separate itself from the state and 'liquidate' Party cells in the armed forces, state security agencies and all state organs.[213] All of this should be done without delay. 'Events are developing extraordinarily fast,' and any attempt to thwart them would result in the Party's 'historic defeat'. The present Party – the Party of the conservative apparat – not only would be unable to remain in the vanguard of society. It could not hope even to retain much political influence.

The consequences of the historic defeat would be dire. There would be a Union-wide clamour for the 'nationalization' of the Party's enormous wealth: at the very least it would have to reimburse its debt to the people. Beyond this sort of civil retribution, Yeltsin envisaged darker scenarios. 'One can imagine' calls for putting on trial Party leaders of all levels for the damage they had done to the country and the people. They would be called to account for failures in agriculture, ethnic policy, foreign trade and the armed forces. 'The country must know what sort of legacy the CPSU has left it.'[214]

> We no longer live in the old society. [A new country] would no longer march in step wherever it was told to go. The country can no longer be ruled by commands. Nor can it be hypnotized by demagoguery or scared by threats. The people now can send any political party packing, no matter how influential it was in the past. The people will support not that political organization which calls them into the celestial heights of a communist future, but the one that would daily, by its practical deeds, defend the interests of every man and help make him and our entire country advanced, rich and happy . . .

It was no longer for the Party to decide the country's direction, but for the people 'outside these walls' to do so. All that the Party could resolve was the 'question of the Party itself'.[215]

And that question apparently interested him less and less. Five days later, Yeltsin mounted the rostrum again to announce, amid catcalls and jeering, his exit from the Communist Party of the Soviet Union.

Although his move was a political calculation and, therefore, expected, this choice of Yeltsin the politician was not easy for Yeltsin the man. It was a very hard decision, recalled an aide. He was 'in essence, rejecting and leaving behind a great deal of himself'. 'You are killing me! Killing!' Yeltsin shouted at his speechwriters Gennadiy Kharin and Aleksandr Urmanov, after he had read the 'tough' version of his exit speech. '[The Party] has been my entire life.' In the end, he elected to deliver a 'soft', almost technical version, now reduced to six phrases: 'Have been thinking for a long time . . . Chairman of the Supreme Soviet . . . Great responsibility . . . Cannot implement only the decisions of the CPSU. . . The will of the people . . . Resign the membership to increase [my] influence on the work of the Soviets . . .'[216]

Gorbachev, however, chose the Party – a Party increasingly conservative, even reactionary, following the defection of tens of thousands of 'liberals'. Despite the rhetorical beating he and his Politburo had received at the Congress (his most liberal confidant, Aleksandr Yakovlev, failed even to get elected to the Central Committee); despite the slow handclapping with which the majority tried to silence Party reformers; despite the thunderous applause received by Egor Ligachev, who openly denounced the loss of the Party's monopoly of power, the fall of communism in Eastern Europe and the liberal press – the General Secretary reaffirmed his belief that the 'CPSU, as it restructures itself, is capable of living up to the expectations of the people and of regaining its authority and will become a truly vanguard party'.[217]

While both he and 'Comrade Yeltsin' urged the renewal of the Party, Gorbachev called on the Congress to 'reject as utterly unacceptable' the practical steps that Yeltsin had suggested in his speech. 'Yes,' continued Gorbachev, 'we are for renewal . . . but our course of action must be [followed] solely in the interests of the socialist choice. No objective is higher than that.'[218]

By early autumn, the national and political debates of the summer were overshadowed by the looming economic disaster. With another turn of the revolutionary kaleidoscope, the economic segment moved to the centre. After the summer clashes, Yeltsin and Gorbachev discovered that there was still something they could agree on. For the first and last time, the two leaders of the Russian Revolution formally joined forces.

In the race between economic chaos and the political legitimacy necessary to contain it, the former was gaining steadily. Prices set by the state and distribution administered by it required a strong and feared authority for enforcement. A deflated and weakened regime was no longer either. Run by fiat for decades, inter-Republican trade was dying fast.* Food producers and store managers either hoarded food for barter or bought it at ridiculously low official prices and smuggled it abroad (primarily to Poland, with its *de facto* convertible currency), where market prices were several times higher. Almost nightly, Moscow television showed food storage depots or the back rooms of grocery stores where crooked managers hid for resale mountains of meat, sugar, flour, cereals and thousands of cans of beef and fish. Tonnes of food were found spoiled at city dumps. By one estimate, one million tonnes of meat and half of the entire crop of fruits and vegetables were stolen or hoarded in the Soviet Union in 1990.[219]

In an opinion poll, 73 per cent of respondents said that they experienced shortages of necessary food products either 'quite often' or 'constantly'.[220] Forced to shop at the 'collective farm' markets because there was little in state stores, 38 per cent of those polled said they spent more than half of their income on food. Over one-fifth spent 'almost all'.[221] 'Can you get enough meat, fish and poultry?' the respondents were asked. Over three-quarters answered no.[222]

On 11 July, Donbass miners went on a twenty-four-hour 'warning strike' to protest against the government's inability to fulfil its obligations under the 1989 strike settlement. 'In Donetsk we have nothing in the stores,' said a local Party Secretary. 'No vegetables, no meat, no cigarettes, no matches, nothing, and they are making speeches in Moscow that touch on none of these problems. We have a crisis breathing down our necks and they are giving no clear signal of how we are going to get out of it.'[223] Attempting 'depoliticization from below', the miners shut down Party committees at several mines.

On 22 August, in one of Russia's largest industrial cities, Chelyabinsk, hundreds of people queuing at a wine store stormed a district Soviet and blocked a central thoroughfare. Five trolleys and three buses were pelted with stones and demolished. Dozens of people were injured in a fight with police. According to local newspapers, the authorities were trying to 'talk to people at their places of residence', but their 'arguments and calls to reason [were] often rejected by the populace because of the worsening supplies of basic food products'.[224]

In the same month, a wave of 'tobacco riots' swept Russian cities

---

* In September, Latvia and Lithuania did not receive enough grain from Russia and retaliated by stopping the delivery of meat. At the same time, responding to the supply from Russia of less gasoline than had been agreed, Ukraine ceased the export of sugar. ('Sergey Stankevich: vinovniki ostayutsia v teni' ('Sergey Stankevich: the culprits remain in the shadow'), *Megapolis-Express*, 27 September 1990.)

from Moscow to Yaroslavl' to Sverdlovsk. 'Thousands of enraged men and women', protesting against shortages of cigarettes, blocked the streets and ransacked tobacco kiosks.[225] (At that time, a pack of Marlboro cigarettes became a unit of parallel currency in Moscow for an increasingly wide range of services from a taxi ride to car maintenance inspection and hospital admittance.) In September, for the first time in almost thirty years, there were severe shortages of bread.

In the feverish atmosphere of Russia's cities in the summer and autumn of 1990, economic explanations for the crisis looked silly and vulgar, and satisfied few. Following the pattern well known since 1789, hunger and anger were now joined by conspiracy. 'Sabotage' was the culprit. Instead of aristocrats, bakers and millers, the scapegoats of revolutionary Paris, Russians blamed the 'mafia' and the dark 'conservative' forces inside the Party for organizing shortages in order to provoke 'a head-on confrontation with the democrats from the Moscow [City] Council and millions of Muscovites, who quite simply had nothing to buy'.[226] 'MOSCOW BLOCKADED!' screamed the headline in a popular Moscow newspaper.[227] By mid-September, Moscow was rife with rumours of a coup by the reactionary military, aligned with the Party apparat.

On 16 September, Manezhnaya Square and the streets leading to it were the scene of a meeting at which tens of thousands protested the 'intolerable economic situation'[228] and demanded radical market reforms and the resignation of the Ryzhkov government. The demonstrators expected to be attacked at any moment by the 'paratroopers from Ryazan' in bulletproof vests and armed with shovels, who were said to be 'moving towards Moscow'.[229] (In response to angry queries in the Supreme Soviet of the USSR, the Ministry of Defence insisted that the soldiers had been deployed for picking potatoes, as they always had been in the autumn, and for rehearsals for the 7 November parade.)

This was, in short, Yeltsin's favourite political environment: a fast-moving crisis in which much (better yet, most) depended on him. Powerless in a conventional sense, presiding over a 'country' not recognized by a single state, he converted his only assets – popularity and legitimacy – into a steady accretion of authority through sheer determination to have and use it.

In his persistence and skill in playing a weak hand Yeltsin resembled Charles de Gaulle, when he, a powerless exile in London during the Second World War, maintained his political identity by resisting his immeasurably stronger 'partners', Churchill and Roosevelt, who liked him about as much as Gorbachev liked Yeltsin. Like de Gaulle, Yeltsin proved adept at transforming his small political beachhead into a nation-wide following by claiming popular legitimacy instead of waiting for it to be conferred on him by the politicians around him.

Despite the hearty welcome he received at every stop of his Russian tour, Yeltsin confessed to coming back to Moscow 'not with a feeling of euphoria', but seized with 'enormous anxiety'.[230] He had seen poverty and the low standard of living. In the five years since 1985, 'the people's lives have not improved, and the further you [went] from Moscow the harder' life was.[231]

He had found a people 'tired of waiting' and 'at the end of their patience'.[232] Everywhere, in almost every speech of his tour, he asked for 'a credit of trust' (*kredit doveriya*), a grace period: 'two years for stabilization and the third for an improvement in the standard of living of the people'.[233] The response to his plea was, to Yeltsin, the most important result of the trip: 'While the people's level of confidence in the Union government has sunk, they do have confidence in the Russian parliament, the leadership of the [Russian] Supreme Soviet and the new government.'[234]

The trip added urgency to the '500-Day' project, designed by thirteen economists led by Gorbachev's adviser Stanislav Shatalin and Yeltsin's Deputy Prime Minister Grigoriy Yavlinsky. Now, more than ever, Yeltsin thought it a last chance, the ultimate shield against the advancing chaos and a lever that would begin to turn the country around. There was 'simply no room for retreat', he declared on his return. They should begin 'implementing the programme of transition to the market: faster, faster, faster!'[235] He even interrupted his tour of the country, flying from Sverdlovsk to Moscow for a working session with the document's drafters.[236] His first press conference after his return to Moscow was an impassioned plea for adoption and implementation of the Shatalin–Yavlinsky programme – as quickly as possible and with minimum alter-ations. After meeting with Gorbachev for five hours ('I don't think we have spoken [for] that long in the past five years,' Yeltsin observed),[237] Yeltsin believed that they were in agreement on that score – and hinted at a great deal of trouble for Gorbachev if this was not so.

For two years there had been a lot of talk about a 'programme for transition to a market economy', Yeltsin said at a press conference immediately after his long conversation with Gorbachev. In the previous five years (since Gorbachev came to power) the people's condition had not improved: in his travel across Russia he had just seen a 'low standard of living' or outright poverty.[238] The 'credit of trust' which people had extended to the regime and which was the essential element of a successful reform was still there, but diminishing rapidly. The alternative was economic and political chaos. Each day that the Union government spent resisting or postponing the reform was another day by which Gorbachev's hold on power and ability to stay in office were reduced.[239]

The moment must also be seized without delay, Yeltsin continued, because, for the first time, not only were Russia and the Centre in agreement, but all the twelve Republics as well.* Thus the Shatalin plan was more than just an economic document: it was the 'economic foundation' of a new Union, 'a sort of primary network, if you like, that would keep the Union and our state together'. For that reason, too, there could be no alternative programmes. The programme must be adopted by the Supreme Soviet of Russia and the USSR government as soon as possible: a month from now, 1 October must become the first of the Programme's 500 days.[240]

Gorbachev appeared to agree. 'This is a critical moment in the life of the country,' he said during the joint interview, 'and very profound and responsible decisions and resolute actions are needed. There is no longer room for postponing things.'[241]

The President knew of what he spoke, for he had 'postponed things' several times that year. During April and May, he had seemed to be on the verge of unveiling a radical market reform, only to draw back, unsure of the regime's ability to sustain the course in the face of inevitable popular discontent.[242] A vision of the Four Horsemen of the 'shock therapy' – price increases, inflation, unemployment and a drop in the standard of living for millions – paralysed Gorbachev. At the time, the General Secretary's top economic adviser, Nikolay Petrakov, explained the reason for the paralysis. The Polish government, he said, could launch its radical market reform, 'even though it was a bitter medicine', because there was social consensus. 'The situation in our country is completely different.'[243] For a while that spring, the Kremlin even considered holding a national referendum on economic reform. Yet that design, too, soon disappeared without trace.

When, on 24 May, Prime Minister Ryzhkov finally presented to the USSR's Supreme Soviet 'a concept of transition to a regulated market economy', the blueprint was vague, stretched the reform to 1996, and, most importantly, appeared to have only the tenuous support of the

---

* Estonia, Lithuania and Latvia wanted no part in the Soviet Union, no matter how radically reformed.

President.* Instantly labelled 'shock without therapy', it was soundly rejected by the legislature, which asked that a new version be presented by September.

Now, *pod El'tsina* ('with Yeltsin as collateral'), as they were saying in Moscow, Gorbachev could, at long last, begin. He had power. Yeltsin had 'credit of trust'. It seemed an invulnerable deal.

'Humankind has failed to find anything more effective than a market economy,' began the preamble to the '500-Day Programme'. To create an effectively functioning market, some 'prerequisites' were needed and had to be created during the transition period:

> Maximum freedom of economic subject (enterprise, entrepreneur). Full responsibility of economic subject for the results of his efforts ... Legal equality of all kinds of property, including private ... Competition of producers as the most important stimulus of economic activity ... Prices ... set freely by market through supply and demand ... The openness of the economy, its consistent integration into the system of global economic links ... The state [which] facilitates the creation of a benign environment for economic activity [but which] refrains from direct participation in it.[244]

To its authors, the Programme was, first and foremost, a means to make man, not state, the master of the economy and life. *Razgosudarst-vlenie* ('de-etatization') was the cornerstone of the reform and the operational term mentioned most frequently. Begun a year before by the First Congress of People's Deputies, ideological de-etatization culminated now in a call for the expropriation of the state:

* A public relations disaster, reminiscent of the anti-alcohol campaign in its utter disregard for people's concerns and fears, the 'concept' seemed to promise neither market plenty at higher prices nor shortages at low ones, but the worst of both worlds: much higher prices still set by the state. The cost of basic food products was to increase by 200 to 300 per cent, with the price of bread tripling by 1 July. The plan promised to offset the increases by indexation of salaries and lump-sum payments. No one believed it. There were long bread queues. 'A typhoon of panic buying swept the country,' wrote a Russian journalist, '[and] once and for all destroyed the consumer market.' If in January 1990 65 per cent of Soviet citizens polled were 'for' the market, by the end of May the support had dropped to 43 per cent. (S. Razin, 'Chya ruka v moyom karmane?' ('Whose hand is in my pocket?'), *Komsomol'skaya Pravda*, 14 February 1991; and V. Boykov, 'Chto govoryat v narode' ('What the people are saying'), *Izvestia*, 2 July 1990.)

401

For a long time the policy implemented was, in essence, an anti-people [*antinarodnaya*] policy: the rich state coexisted with the poor people ... The Programme's task is to take everything that can be taken from the state and give it to the people ...

The reform gives citizens the right of economic self-determination ... It is precisely the freedom of choice that is the foundation of liberty, the foundation of the creative potential of individuals ... The right to own property is to be realized through de-etatization, the transfer of state property to the people ... Property owned by everyone is a guarantee of social stability ... On the very first day of the Programme's implementation ... the ownership of any kind of property will be declared legal [and] those convicted of entrepreneurial activity will be amnestied.[245]

The Programme made explicit the nexus between economic reform and the economic independence of the Republics. 'Economic reform is impossible to implement with orders from the Centre, no matter how correct they are. People no longer want to tolerate a situation in which key decisions that shape their lives are made without their participation ... The central role in the transformation is given to the governments of the Republics and to local authorities. The power must be closer to the people.'[246]

The Economic Union of Sovereign States, to be adopted by a treaty between the Republics, was the centrepiece of the thick legislative package attached to the Programme. The Republics themselves would 'define the measure of their independence in the economy'.[247] The prerogative of the Centre would consist of the 'sum of the rights' delegated to it by the Republics. The vast Union bureaucracy would be replaced by an Inter-Republican Economic Committee, whose prerogatives would, again, be determined by the Republics. The Republics would be entirely responsible for their economic policies, including taxation and foreign trade. Such all-Union programmes as defence and internal security would be financed through voluntary contributions by the Republics to specifically designated funds.[248]

As for its implementation, the Programme's most original and valuable section was a detailed timetable for several dozen measures. A quick sell-off of state assets (from trucks to unfinished construction), deep cuts in the defence and KGB budgets, and land reform were to start on Day One. (The Programme envisaged turning some 60,000 state and collective farms into privately or co-operatively owned ones, as well as creating 150,000 to 180,000 family farms.) Gradual price liberalization and privatization of 50 per cent of small enterprises would occur between Days 100 and 250. The freeing of prices on 70 to 80 per cent of goods and services and privatization of between 30 and 40 per cent of industry were to happen between Days 250 and 400. Finally, in the last one hundred days, 70 per cent of industry would be privatized, and 80 to 90 per cent of goods and services sold at market prices.[249]

The Programme was far from perfect and easy to fault. Its 220 pages, complete with tables and draft laws, had been compiled in a month. A great deal of economic data the team had requested had been withheld by the jealous Soviet government, despite Gorbachev's order to co-operate. There were plenty of technical errors, inconsistencies and ambiguities.[250] An utter lack of market experience shone through.

Yet for the key ingredient of any such reform – social consensus – the spirit of the document, its pathos, even its terminology were perhaps just as vital as technical proficiency. It represented a final and complete break with the past. The Programme embodied the regime's commitment to change. This was a manifesto of intent imbued with courage and vigour. For this reason, and despite all its faults, the '500-Day Programme' was, in the words of one of the leading Western specialists on the Soviet economy, 'the most plausible strategy for transforming the USSR'.[251] It was an attempt at radical change before economic crisis turned into collapse and political disarray grew into chaos.

On 11 September, the Supreme Soviet of Russia voted to adopt the '500-Day Programme'. Russia was waiting for the Union government to do the same: 1 October was to be Day One.

Gorbachev had two blueprints on his desk. Behind '500 Days' were Yeltsin, Russia, the Republics, the authority of two top economists from his own staff, Nikolay Petrakov and Stanislav Shatalin, and his, Gorbachev's, own commitment. Behind the other, Ryzhkov's 'Union' or 'government' plan, was the Party and state establishment: Ministers, directors of enterprises, collective farm chairmen and the military brass, fearful of budget cuts and the break-up of the armed forces into 'Republican detachments'. Although labelled 'moderately radical' by its authors, the government plan was found by an *Izvestia* economic observer to be 'an option of half-measures and compromises' which, instead of 'leading to the market', would 'only create disarray in the already feeble economy'.[252]

The critical difference between the two blueprints lay in the balance of Centre–Republican power. The Economic Union of the Shatalin–Yavlinsky Programme was a confederation, akin to the European Union.

Ryzhkov wanted to preserve a looser, gentler but still unmistakably recognizable Soviet Union. 'All the mechanisms in the government programme are designed for a unitary state,' commented *Izvestia*, 'which, with the proclamations of sovereignty and with custom posts and restrictions on export', was disintegrating rapidly.[253]

To Yeltsin, the difference between the two plans was obvious:

> You cannot cross a hedgehog with a snake,* similarly, you cannot cross the Shatalin group's programme with the Union programme. They are based on totally different principles. The advantage of the Shatalin group's programme is that, above all, it accounts for the fact that most of the Union Republics have passed declarations or laws concerning their state sovereignty.† Only through these [laws] and through the legislation of these Republics can this programme be implemented. Meanwhile, the Union government programme again envisages centralization, state planning, directives, which, as we have seen ourselves over many decades, do not work but, instead, merely lead to failure.[254]

Gorbachev vacillated. He asked his former economic adviser, Abel Aganbegyan, to 'combine' the two blueprints. Still hesitant three weeks later, Gorbachev attempted to pass the decision on to the Supreme Soviet of the USSR by sending both programmes to the floor on 21 September. The result was predictable: with no guidance from the President, the legislature could not make up its mind either, and postponed the decision yet again, asking for the final version by 15 October.

A day after that deadline, Gorbachev sent the 'President's Programme' to the Union legislature. Its nebulous title, 'The Guidelines for Stabilization of the People's Economy and Transition to a Market Economy', was indicative of the content. Less than a third the size of the '500-Day Programme' (66 pages against 222), Gorbachev's plan was conspicuous for its lack of specifics. Gone were the details which made the Shatalin–

---

* The genitives of 'hedgehog' (*yozh*) and 'snake', (*uzh*) rhyme in Russian: *ezha i uzha*. Yeltsin often used the expression to convey the ludicrousness of something.

† Between 20 June and 25 August, 'state sovereignty' was declared, in chronological order, by Uzbekistan, Moldavia (now called Moldova), Ukraine, Byelorussia, Turkmenistan, Armenia (which declared 'independence') and Tajikstan. Before the end of the year, Kazakhstan and Kyrgyzstan would follow suit, thus bringing the number of 'sovereign states' to fifteen – the total number of the Soviet Republics. (The three Baltic Republics, as well as Georgia, Azerbaijan and Russia, had become 'sovereign' before 20 June.)

Yavlinsky plan so plausible. Gone, most importantly, was the timetable.

Where the Shatalin–Yavlinsky plan mandated a mammoth sell-off of state assets in the first 100 days, Gorbachev's scenario stated only that the operation 'may take a long time'. Only the privatization of small businesses was mentioned. Price liberalization, which under Shatalin was to become the centrepiece of Days 100 to 250, was postponed until 1992. Instead of an inalienable right, the ownership of land by individual farmers was left to the collective farms for decision. Most importantly, and fatally, for the plan's feasibility, 'all (or almost all)' rights that were to be given to the Republics by the '500 Days' remained with the Centre.[255] Among other things, Moscow was to retain control of the Republics' natural resources for at least two years and to levy a special federal tax.

Gorbachev's attempt to combine the two plans was doomed from the outset. 'The presence of a common goal – the changeover to a market – is no guarantee that they can be successfully combined,' the thirteen authors of the '500 Days' wrote two weeks later. 'The logic of the two programmes is different, and common terms conceal differing content. A choice had to be made.'[256]

And so it was – the long-postponed but now unavoidable choice between further democratization and market reform on the one hand and, on the other, the cornerstones of Gorbachev's personal and political universe: the centralized Soviet state and 'socialist choice' in the economy.* On 16 October, the General Secretary–President appeared to have reached the limits of his elasticity, which, until then, had been nothing short of remarkable. Presented with the chance to become a revolutionary, the brilliant and courageous reformer declined.

A few months later, recalling the President's October choice, a Russian journalist would write that, like Lot's wife, Gorbachev 'looked back at the Staraya Square' (where the Central Committee headquarters were) and turned into a pillar of salt. 'Democracy surpassed its erstwhile leader, flowed around him, like a stream around a stone, and he found himself, suddenly aged, in the rearguard of the marching army.'[257]

The price of Gorbachev's choice would prove enormous. 'We lost our last chance to save ourselves from hyper-inflation,' declared a liberal newspaper. 'A sharp drop in the standard of living became inevitable.'[258]

---

* The main difference between the two programmes, Gorbachev would explain later, was not economic: 'it was really about the future model of our society'. Even though he found '500 Days' preferable technically, the government plan 'was based on the retention of the single Union state' and the 'fundamentals of a socialist system'. (*Memoirs*, p. 381.)

The forecast of a leading US expert on the Soviet economy was just as grim: convinced now that the leadership was offering them more of the 'same old policies', the people's hoarding of food and goods would 'intensify and inflation accelerate'.[259] 'The opportunity for the rapid conclusion of an accord on an Economic Union has been lost,' wrote the authors of '500 Days'. 'A single, all-Union market is in jeopardy ... The unresolved state of key [economic] problems is making the country's Republics and regions, cities and individual districts seek their own paths.'[260] Stanislav Shatalin, who resigned from the Presidential Council three months later, would call the economic policy proposed by the President an 'unintended suicide'.[261]

On the afternoon of 16 October, in a speech to the Russian Supreme Soviet, Yeltsin called the President's Programme 'yet another effort to retain the system that the people [had] come to hate', and predicted that it would result in a 'catastrophe'.[262] The 'drama' of the situation in the Soviet Union, said Grigoriy Yavlinsky, was that the country was experiencing 'death and birth' at the same time. 'The old system was dying and its poisons affected all the new that was still in the womb.'[263] On 16 October, the birth was postponed, while the dying would continue apace for another eleven months.

CHAPTER 9

'Rolling up the Sleeves, Raising the Fists'

G ORBACHEV'S 'OCTOBER CHOICE' WAS THE last act of perestroika – a peaceful revolution from above. If, by attempting to
blend two irreconcilable visions of the country's economy, politics and federal structure, the President hoped to bolster his middle-of-
the-road course, he badly miscalculated. The base for this strategy no
longer existed. The political centre had been torn apart by the widening
chasm between 'left' and 'right', the 'democrats' and the 'conservatives'.
By not allying himself with the former, he now found himself with the
latter.

This brutal logic was obvious to some of his earliest, most faithful
and bravest colleagues. For the first time in five years they decided that
they could no longer follow the President–General Secretary. Foreign
Minister Eduard Shevardnadze resigned, warning the Fourth Congress
of People's Deputies of the 'advent of a dictatorship'. Ousted from his
party posts by the conservative majority at the Twenty-Eighth Congress,
Aleksandr Yakovlev was gone as well. Soon Gorbachev was abandoned
by his top economic advisers, Stanislav Shatalin and Nikolay Petrakov.

Between November 1990 and February 1991, the Gorbachev government changed beyond recognition. Hospitalized after a heart attack, the
well-meaning and decent but utterly ineffectual Prime Minister Ryzhkov
was replaced by the Minister of Finance, Valentin Pavlov, who in the
previous year and a half had presided over the injection into the economy
of thirty-four billion 'empty' rubles, moving the country perilously close
to hyperinflation. The liberal Minister of Internal Affairs, Vadim Bakatin, was succeeded by Boris Pugo, a career Party official and a major-
general of the KGB. In the last week of 1990, Gorbachev pushed through
the reluctant Soviet parliament his choice for the newly created post of
Vice President: Gennadiy Yanaev, leader of the communist faction in
the USSR Supreme Soviet and former Chairman of the notoriously
corrupt and KGB-infiltrated Committee for Youth Organizations.

The dissolution of Gorbachev's alliance with Yeltsin did not mollify
the conservatives. Whatever remained of the Kremlin's reform policy
came under increasingly brazen attacks from the 'right', with the generals and defence industry managers supplanting the Party apparatus
as the most aggressive advocates of reactionary policies. During a
mid-November meeting, the military faction of the Congress almost
shouted Gorbachev down. According to a newspaper account, entitled
'Difficult Dialogue between the President and the Army', he was several
times 'interrupted by catcalls [and] noise in the hall'.[1] A few days later
the leader of the hard-line communist Soyuz ('Union') faction in the
USSR Supreme Soviet publicly called for the removal of Gorbachev and

the transfer of power to a Committee of National Salvation, which would preserve (by force, if necessary) the Party's control over a unitary, Moscow-controlled Soviet Union. Two weeks later a repentant Gorbachev told a conference of the Moscow City Party Committee that he felt 'guilty before the working class'.[2]

In the second week of December KGB Chairman Vladimir Kryuchkov warned 'radical political movements' (some of which, he claimed, were 'generously supported from abroad') that his agency would spare no effort in support of 'emergency measures [directed at] restoration of discipline and law'.[3] Before long, Kryuchkov was warning that the country should be ready 'to accept the possibility of bloodshed if we are to bring about order'. A week later, Pugo and Minister of Defence Dmitriy Yazov signed a decree authorizing joint KGB–Army patrols throughout the country. This was a counter-revolutionary regime with an ex-reformer still nominally at its head. In what might be termed Gorbachev-2, the rhetorical banners of the previous three years – the 'widening' and 'deepening' of reforms – had been replaced with 'stabilization', 'law and order' and 'the protection of the Soviet state'.

In the Russian parliament, the re-energized 'Communists of Russia' were spoiling for a fight. The swing vote (the 'swamp'), always attuned to the direction of the political wind, moved 'right'. At the Second Congress of People's Deputies of Russia in December, the communists diluted the land-reform legislation, mobilized the majority for a 'Kremlin' version of the proposed Union Treaty, defeated the motion to establish the post of Russian President elected by a direct national vote, and pushed through a statement censuring Shevardnadze's support of the US-led effort to drive the occupying Iraqi troops from Kuwait.

On 20 December, speaking to the Soviet parliament, Yeltsin summarized the essence of Gorbachev-2 as 'undermining the sovereignty of the Republics and sabotaging radical [economic] reforms'.[4]

There had been a way out – the Yavlinsky programme, which would have united the Republics' economies. It was accepted by the President, among others, and then cast away. The parliaments and the peoples were deceived. Three months have been lost . . .

Now the Centre – the President and the Union government – had nothing 'constructive' to offer, only 'rigid centralization', only 'resuscitation of the vertical chain of command' from top to bottom. This road, Yeltsin insisted, was bound to lead to a dead end.

The 'hardening' of the Kremlin's position vis-á-vis the Republics would only result in a negative reaction by them, Yeltsin continued. The 'stick' was no longer effective, and by deploying (or threatening to deploy) it, The Union had already lost, at minimum, six Republics.[5]*

> The so-called 'revolution-from-above' is over. The Kremlin has stopped being the initiator of the renewal and its conduit. Blocked at the Centre, the process of renewal has shifted to the Republics . . . In some Republics, the Deputies [of the Supreme Soviets] have seriously undermined the totalitarian control [and] . . . the unlimited power of the party-state bureaucracy . . . In a totalitarian system this [shifting of power to the Republics] was the only real opportunity to defend the independence . . . of [both] peoples [and] every individual from the arbitrariness of Union agencies.

Yeltsin called on the Kremlin to change this course, to recognize – in deeds, not words – the sovereignty declared by the Republics, and to undertake 'an honest and fair dialogue' with them. Contrary to the hard-liners' allegations, such a policy would lead 'not to the break-up of the Union but . . . to its salvation'.[6]

In the early morning of 13 January 1991, in Lithuania's capital of Vilnius, riot-control troops of the Ministry of Internal Affairs of the USSR (the 'special-mission police detachments', or OMON) shot their way into the television tower, killing thirteen unarmed defenders and wounding over 160.

Two hours later, Yeltsin was on a plane to Tallinn, the capital of neighbouring Estonia. There, huddled in the building of the Estonian parliament, ringed by barricades and volunteer defenders armed with kitchen knives and hunting guns and expecting an attack by Soviet troops any minute, Yeltsin and the Presidents of Latvia, Lithuania and Estonia† issued a joint statement:

> The recent action of the Soviet leadership with regard to the Baltic states has created a real danger to their sovereignty, and has resulted in the escalation of violence and in deaths.

---

* Armenia, Azerbaijan, Georgia, Estonia, Latvia and Lithuania had refused to participate in the 'discussions' on the draft Union Treaty, which Gorbachev forwarded to the Republics on 24 November.

† Anatoliy Gorbunovs of Latvia, Vytautas Lansbergis of Lithuania and Arnold Ruutel of Estonia.

Expressing the clear wish of the peoples to preserve and strengthen their sovereignty; understanding the magnitude of the danger of the violation of human rights of all citizens of the Baltics, regardless of their nationality; proceeding from the conviction that further development of our states is possible only on the road of radical reforms founded on liberty and democracy, Latvia, Estonia, Lithuania and Russia state that:

first: the signatories recognize each other's sovereignty;

second: all power on the territories of the signatories' countries belongs solely to the lawfully elected bodies;

third: the signatories consider it inadmissible to employ armed forces to resolve internal problems, except at the official request of the legally elected executive bodies;

fourth: the signatories consider it illegal for their citizens to participate in actions that damage the sovereignty of the signatories' nations;

fifth: the signatories pledge to aid each other whenever a threat to their sovereignty arises;

sixth: the signatories consider unlawful and resolutely condemn attempts to provoke national animosity in order to achieve political aims;

seventh: Latvia, Lithuania, Estonia and Russia confirm their determination to continue to develop relations between them based on principles of international law;

eighth: the signatories call upon the states that are part of the Soviet Union and those outside it to condemn resolutely the acts of armed violence against the independence of the Baltic states and their peaceful population – acts that threaten stability and democracy in the USSR and in the entire international community.

This statement is being made available to international organizations, parliaments, governments and foreign states.[7]

The next day, a leader of the Estonian parliament, Mikk Titma, would tell his colleagues: 'If Yeltsin had not supported Estonia, I am not at all sure we would be meeting here today.'[8]

After the signing of the statement, Yeltsin got into a small car with a bodyguard and three aides and drove all night to Leningrad on country roads. His 'allies' in the KGB, Yeltsin explained later, had advised him not to fly.[9]

On 14 January, Yeltsin held a press conference in the building of the Russian Supreme Soviet. In advance of his appearance, aides distributed his 'Appeal to the Russian Soldiers in the Baltics'. Despite (or perhaps because of) the occasional awkwardness and wooden bureaucratisms from Yeltsin's Party past, this was one of the most moving documents of his political life:

Soldiers, sergeants and officers – our compatriots, who have been drafted on the territory of the Russian Federation and who are currently [serving] in the Baltic Republics:

Today, when the country is in economic and political crisis, and when the healthy forces of our society seek ways out of the complicated situation using legal, constitutional forms [of action], you could be given orders to move against legally constituted state bodies, against the peaceful civilian population which is defending its democratic achievements.

You may be told that your help is needed to restore order in society. But can violation of the constitution and law be considered restoration of order? And yet it is precisely in this direction that you are being pushed by those who seek to solve political problems by the force of armed detachments.

Before you storm non-military installations on Baltic soil, remember your own hearth, the present and future of your own Republic, your own people. Violence . . . against the peoples of the Baltics will engender new crises in Russia itself . . .

The aims of the reaction are:

– to undermine the process of democratization in the country and the transition to the economic arrangements that would guarantee the well-being of all the people, and not just of the privileged groups of the ruling class – the nomenklatura.

– to annul the declaration of sovereignty, for which the peoples of the Republics struggled and suffered, and thus wreck the establishment of a new Union of sovereign states.

Could you possibly agree to the role they have assigned you? . . .

We unreservedly reject the view of the Army as a reactionary, anti-people force. We know that the armed forces are first and foremost citizens of our nation, its children who care about its fate no less than all of us. And we are sure that the healthy forces in the army will not allow it to start down the anti-popular road of support for the reaction.

We believe in you, officers and soldiers of Russia, who, like the previous generations of Russia's warriors, espouse the highest values: honour, valour, courage, allegiance to the people and the Motherland.

Let us remember the historic experience which postulates that a wrong step today will tell not only on those who make it but on the generations that will follow us.

I wish you success in your service, happiness to your families.

Boris Yeltsin. 13 January 1991[10]

As happened almost always when he was under extreme pressure, Yeltsin was in his element: alert, confident, even jovial. From the first minute of the conference, the tone of deliberate, almost insouciant defiance was set by his insistence on reading the statement himself: 'It is short, only two pages. May I?' In the audience that morning, this author saw and heard a hoarse, red-eyed, Yeltsin, his face creased by deep lines after two sleepless nights. Yet he moved and spoke with the confidence and authority of a strong leader. As he began answering questions, the words were chosen carefully, even painstakingly, weighty with thought. The people in the hall were anxious, hushed, frightened, and desperate for truth and hope. Giving them both, Yeltsin, in return, commanded more than rapt attention. The feeling was closer to adoration. The lines of expectant, almost festive tension extended from the hall to the podium, enveloped Yeltsin and, reinforced tenfold, ran back to the hall, closing the circuit. His rare smile prompted smiles, his dry humour invariably produced laughter.

Even Soviet reporters, who could easily teach their Western colleagues lessons in cynicism, fell under the spell. That morning, they forgave Yeltsin his Ural accent, occasionally flawed grammar and less than perfect pronunciation of polysyllabic words. They addressed him not by last name or title but by his first name and patronymic, 'Boris Nikolaevich', a Russian way of showing respect and affection. (By contrast, they referred to Gorbachev as 'Gorbatiy', the Hunchback.)

Question: Do you consider President Gorbachev personally responsible for the events in Vilnius?

Yeltsin [after a long pause]: As diplomats say, thank you for a good question [laughter] . . . When I asked the President, 'Why are you moving to the right so sharply?' the answer was: 'Because society is moving to the right.' Where have you obtained this information from? [Yeltsin asked Gorbachev] You, then, simply do not know what is happening in society. Society is by no means slipping to the right. On the contrary, society is consolidating and moving towards democracy. At the same time, I know that the President is subject to very serious pressure from the right.

413

Yeltsin was asked if he was trying to remove Gorbachev. He said no, Gorbachev was 'not the only problem we have in our country'. But, he added, look at the people's attitude, look at Gorbachev's *reyting* (approval 'rating' in the polls). Power meant 'strength of administration but also people's trust. And if the two are not combined, no renewal in our country is possible, no movement forward.'[11] He continued: 'I told the President [Gorbachev]: we are going to be shamed in front of the entire world because this is nothing if not the end of democracy. It is simply impossible not to have foreseen this. But if such elementary things are not foreseen, then one gets depressed at the kind of leadership we have.'

After Vilnius, Yeltsin was deeply pessimistic about the prospects for a new Union Treaty. 'It seems to me that these actions [of the regime] have struck a serious blow against the possibility of concluding a Union Treaty. I doubt that very many would be willing to sign the Treaty with a noose around their neck.' Meanwhile, the Presidents of Kazakhstan, Byelorussia, Russia and Ukraine had decided to conclude a 'quadripartite treaty' to replace the old Soviet Union. 'I can tell you where,' Yeltsin said, smiling. 'In Minsk. But I will not tell you when.'

Asked about his assessment of US policy towards the Soviet Union, Yeltsin responded: 'They only have one political figure in mind [that is, Gorbachev]. And that figure is surrounded by euphoria. And all other events – the increased sovereignty of the Republics, the move of the political centre of gravity from the Centre to the Republics – are being ignored. This is a *strategic* [Yeltsin stressed the word], strategic error committed by the US leaders.'

Rarely does the true significance of a political act seem as widely divorced from its first impression on contemporaries as did Yeltsin's Baltic blitz. Western journalists in Moscow (television and print alike) ignored it completely. But even those close to the scene – leading Russian political commentators and journalists interviewed in Moscow at the time – were uniformly negative. To them Yeltsin's trip was a foolish waste of political capital, 'an act of desperation'. While the intelligentsia applauded the trip (and after Tallinn finally trusted Yeltsin fully), they were convinced that Yeltsin had defied public opinion, which, it was assumed, wanted to see the 'ungrateful Lithuanians' punished.[12]

Yet the 14 January press conference heralded the emergence of an open democratic resistance to the newly reactionary Gorbachev-2. As Yeltsin put it that day, 'I have the impression that [what happened in Vilnius] is the beginning of a vigorous attack on democracy. The Baltic Republics are only the first of many victims . . . We are witnessing the struggle for the survival of democracy.'[13] That day, Boris Yeltsin became the undisputed leader of that struggle, making the Russian parliament the headquarters of the opposition.

The significance of Yeltsin's act went far beyond tactics. Russia's perennial dilemma – free or imperial? – had again been posed starkly. Sooner than anyone expected, history called on Yeltsin to affirm a historically unique approach to Russian state-building that he had preached during his 1990 campaign and his first half-year as Supreme Soviet Chairman. Yeltsin himself made this connection explicit in his 'Open letter to the peoples of the Baltic states': 'There is a real danger that the Baltic countries could become the starting point from which the reaction would spread throughout the entire country . . . Let us be united in our striving for freedom! Dictatorship shall not pass!'[14]

At no time were the fate of the Fourth Russian Revolution and that of Yeltsin entwined as closely as they were in the first three months of 1991 – or as uncertain. With Gorbachev's silent approval, the Pavlov government worked relentlessly to roll back the advances of the previous six years. Private entrepreneurs were reviled and harassed.* Glasnost was kept alive by a few newspapers and magazines, whose editors expected to be closed down any day. After three years of a slow but steady loosening of public discourse, the propaganda blast that accompanied the Vilnius crackdown left people feeling numb, scared and caught in a time-warp, as if the 1968 propaganda guidelines developed by chief Soviet ideologue Mikhail Suslov to accompany the Soviet invasion of Czechoslovakia had been dusted off by the State Committee for Television and Radio.†

At their national congress the Soyuz faction of the All-Union Congress

---

* Gorbachev's decree On the Struggle with Economic Sabotage empowered the KGB and police to search the premises of co-operatives and examine the books. The government advertised its investigations of some of the most prominent Russian entrepreneurs, among whom was the first Moscow millionaire, Artem Tarasov. Unable to find any evidence of criminal wrongdoing, the authorities charged Tarasov, a Russian parliament Deputy, with 'offending the dignity of the President'.

† Only Leningrad television, one of whose channels could be seen in Moscow, somehow managed, on 17 January, to broadcast the horrific footage of the 13 January massacre: the 'black berets' swinging the butts of their rifles at the unarmed defenders of the television centre, shooting at random and ramming their tanks into the crowd. 'I used to trust Gorbachev,' said a Russian Orthodox priest in Vilnius. 'Now I understand: he does not care about the Soviet Union or Russia. He wants only one thing: the preservation of communist power' (Author's transcript).

of People's Deputies demanded extraordinary measures to secure the preservation of the Soviet Union and the 'stabilization of the politico-economic situation'. If President Gorbachev could not bring himself to do what was necessary, Soyuz was ready to take 'full responsibility' for the restoration of order in the country.[15]

The 16 January issue of *Moskovskie Novosti*, the flagship of glasnost and the home of some of the most daring Russian journalists and intellectuals, carried a black border of mourning on its front page, the banner headline 'KROVAVOYE VOSKRESENIE' ('BLOODY SUNDAY')* and a statement signed by the *crème de la crème* of the Russian liberal intelligentsia.

> On the bloody Sunday of 13 January, it was democracy that was shot up. Now that the final hour of the regime is near, it has joined a decisive battle: economic reform is blocked, the censorship of press and television is being revived, and a stream of insolent propaganda demagoguery has been unleashed . . . What is happening in Lithuania can only be described as CRIME: a crime against one's own people which is being pushed towards civil war . . .
>
> After the bloody Sunday in Vilnius, how much is left of what we have heard so often from our President in the last few years: 'human socialism', 'new thinking', 'the common European home'? Almost nothing . . .
>
> The Lithuanian tragedy should not leave us dispirited. In the opposition to the onslaught of totalitarianism and dictatorship our hopes are with the leaders of the [Russian] Republic . . . We are counting on a mass protest against the anti-democratic wave which is moving towards the Baltic states and threatens to engulf the whole country . . .

This last paragraph of hope and defiance was brave rhetoric. In January 1991 the manic–depressive cycle of the Moscow intelligentsia – breathtakingly soaring and even self-sacrificial one day and cynically fatalistic and resigned the next – was close to its nadir. The mood was one of utter despair. They expected months, if not years, of communist reaction. The Fourth Russian Revolution appeared to be heading the way of the democratic revolution of February 1917.

On 16 January, the staff of a leading liberal think-tank, the Institute of the Economy of the World Socialist System, headed by Academician

---

* This is the popular name of the 9 January 1905 massacre of demonstrators in St Petersburg, which precipitated the First Russian Revolution of 1905–7.

Oleg Bogomolov, gathered at a protest meeting. The resolution they adopted read: 'That night [in Vilnius] democracy was shot to death, and our hopes for a bloodless transformation of the regime which has outlived itself were buried. All our illusions about perestroika and its creators have perished. The reforms revealed themselves as false, they have brought upon us only death and universal impoverishment. The Communist Party is not reformable. It cannot defend its principles other than by blood and death.'[16] Even the Institute's star, Igor Klyamkin, although calm and detached as always, delivered a verdict of profound pessimism:

> In Vilnius the [Gorbachev] regime has proved its genetic anti-democratic nature. What we have is a democracy that failed, a defeat of the democratic forces. In six years [since 1985], we have failed to forge an all-Union Democratic Front . . . The main lesson [of Vilnius] is that democracy has lost – lost because of its disunity, lack of organization, and – let's face it – slovenliness. The only positive message of such resolutions as ours is: let's unite somehow in the future, in the aftermath of this lesson.[17]

Moscow intellectuals advised Yeltsin not to antagonize the regime. Lie low, wait for the worst to pass, hunker down, save what can be saved, cut the losses.[18] The Mayor of Moscow, Gavriil Popov, suggested 'an organized retreat of the democratic forces'.[19] Instead, Yeltsin did what he had always done – and would do again – in a grave crisis. Confident of his ability to hear Russia, he took his case directly to the people, over the shaking heads and clucking tongues of the political class. He followed his favourite Russian proverb, his political motto: *Klin klinom vyshibayut*: 'To drive out a wedge, hit it with another' – 'When attacked, attack!' 'I have always told [my children and grand-children],' Yeltsin had said to an interviewer a few months before, 'if someone on the street picks a fight with you and is about to hit you – hit them first, even if only by a second.'[20] In the first three months of 1991, the habit of his hooligan days became his strategy.

Trusting his instinct before conventional wisdom, he confronted and thrust – instead of evading and parrying. Against overwhelmingly stronger foes, against their enormous resources of bureaucratic power and poised troops, Yeltsin aggressively deployed the only weapons in his possession: popularity and steadily escalating rhetoric.

Although in the next two months the emphases and nuances would vary, the core of Yeltsin's message would remain unchanged from the 20

January 'Appeal to the Peoples of Russia'. The Union leadership, he charged, had *de facto* abandoned the policy of reform. Forgotten were the lengthy discussions about freedom, universal human values and a law-abiding state. Economic reform had been blocked, democracy betrayed, glasnost trampled on, and lawlessness and arbitrariness restored. 'Ignoring his oath, the President has chosen the course of stoking ethnic animosity,' of justifying violence against peaceful populations.

> Peoples of Russia! In this critical moment one needs maximum restraint and vigilance. There must be no room for panic and disorientation. It is in our power to stop reaction . . . to stop the slide of the Union leadership towards lawlessness and violence.
>
> We appeal to all the democratic forces, parties and movements, to all those who hold dear the fate of Russia. We appeal to all honest communists of the country! The time of choice has come. The country is waiting for us to define our position, to reaffirm our opposition to the rebirth of the old order. Do not let yourself become a tool of reaction! . . . Use all means available to make your position known.[21]

A month later, in the final three minutes of an hour-long nationally televised interview (granted only after a month of haggling between the Supreme Soviet of Russia and the State Committee for Radio and Television and deliberately restricted to economic matters), Yeltsin made a statement which would, in the words of a leading Soviet political weekly, 'wreak havoc in Soviet politics':[22]

> recently it has become perfectly obvious that, while retaining the motto of 'perestroika', he [Gorbachev] . . . is attempting to preserve centralized power and to deny independence to the Republics, most of all to Russia. This is anti-people policy: currency manipulations, unprecedented price increases,* a sharp turn to the 'right', the use of

---

* The reference is to the 23 January confiscatory monetary 'reform' and the widely expected price increases. In the course of the 'reform', which completely undermined confidence in the ruble, all 50- and 100-ruble bills were to be exchanged – within three weeks – at state banks for smaller denominations. The warning of administrative price increases proved correct five weeks later when, on 2 April, Gorbachev's decree announced higher prices for consumer goods and food, including bread, eggs, milk, meat, butter, tea and salt, 'for the purpose of stabilizing the consumer market, boosting motivation for highly productive work . . . and to fight against profiteering and the shadow economy' (*Pravda*, 20 March 1991).

the armed forces against civilians, the collapse of the economy . . .

I consider it my personal mistake to have been excessively trustful of the President . . . It is obvious now that the Centre is not going to let the Republics act independently . . . I dissociate myself from the positions and policies of the President. I call for his immediate resignation.

I believe in Russia. I appeal to you, my fellow citizens, to believe in Russia. Everyone has to make his choice and define his position. I want you to hear and understand me. I have made my choice. I will not deviate from this path. I need your trust, and I believe in the support of the peoples of Russia, your support, and hope for it.[23]

The barrage of denunciation from the pro-government left media was furious and deafening. 'Just read *Pravda*, *Moskovskaya Pravda*, *Krasnaya Zvezda*, *Sovetskaya Rossia*, *Rabochaya Tribuna* and *Glasnost*,' reported the pro-Yeltsin radio network (Rossii). 'Watch official television programmes and listen to the all-Union radio. The name of the heretic and troublemaker Yeltsin has almost been made a curse word there. He is being blamed for the disintegration of the economy, inter-ethnic conflict, our mistakes in foreign policy, and so on. One is just left to wonder: how could the man who has headed the RSFSR for less than a year manage to bring about all this?'[24]

His allies in the tussle with the Centre – President of Kazakhstan Nursultan Nazarbaev and the Chairman of the Ukrainian Supreme Soviet, Leonid Kravchuk, with whom Yeltsin had been discussing the quadripartite agreement as an alternative to the Union Treaty – abandoned him the very next day.* Even the liberal *Izvestia* thought the interview a 'mistake': the call for Gorbachev's resignation was 'yet another step towards the exacerbation of a political confrontation which is already extremely tense'.[25]

On that same day, after berating Yeltsin for several hours, the Deputies of the Supreme Soviet of the USSR adopted a 'Resolution on the speech delivered by B. N. Yeltsin on Central Television on 19 February 1991'. Yeltsin was accused of contravening the Constitution and 'creat-

---

* 'Mikhail Sergeevich is the architect of perestroika,' said Kravchuk. 'I categorically disagree with [Yeltsin's statement].' 'There is no way I can agree with what Boris Nikolaevich said on television,' Nazarbaev told a press conference. 'I totally dissociate myself from the calls for resignation of the country's President and from his remarks of distrust of M. S. Gorbachev.' (A. Ladin, 'Ne vremya dlya ul'timatumov' ('Not the right time for ultimatums'), *Krasnaya Zvezda*, 21 February 1991.)

ing an emergency situation in the country'. The Supreme Soviet of the Soviet Union asked its colleagues in the Russian parliament to 'determine their attitude to the aforementioned speech'.[26]

A day later, at the opening of a session of the Russian Supreme Soviet, the communist Deputy Chairman, Svetlana Goryacheva, read a statement signed by the entire leadership of the Russian parliament,* save Yeltsin and his First Deputy, Ruslan Khazbulatov. She charged the Chairman with engineering 'ideological confrontation' with the Centre, settling scores with his political opponents and neglecting, even sacrificing, the vital interests of the Russian people. Yeltsin's transgressions included 'dictatorship' in the management of the Supreme Soviet's affairs, neglect of the Constitution and 'inconsistency and contradictions' in economic reform.[27] 'The Six', as the signatories were immediately labelled, demanded the convocation of an extraordinary Congress of People's Deputies. The sole item on its agenda was to be Yeltsin's 'account' of his work.

Yeltsin's supporters and his enemies alike interpreted the statement as a call for Yeltsin's impeachment. The 'authors [of the statement] did not hide the fact that their aim [was] to make Yeltsin resign', wrote a Russian commentator. 'It is for this reason that they [were] also insisting that an extraordinary Congress be convened so urgently.'[28] The required one-fifth of the Soviet's Deputies quickly signed the petition calling for an emergency session of the Congress to be convened on 28 March.

After a decent, week-long interval as became his high office, the President himself joined the chorus. Leaving the cruder body blows to his many defenders and avengers, Gorbachev claimed an elevated plane for his response. Where they peered through a magnifying glass in search of new warts and scratches, the President deployed a telescope by pointing out the fundamental cause of the conflict between himself and the 'democrats' led by Yeltsin.

The reason for the rift was not 'personal likes or dislikes', Gorbachev said. No, at stake were 'political strategies and ultimate goals'. Before, he and the 'democrats' had differed over tactics; today they differed over the 'objectives' of perestroika. To underscore the point, and to

---

* In addition to Goryacheva, the statement was signed by the other Deputy Chairman of the Supreme Soviet, Boris Isaev, both Chairmen of the two Houses of the Supreme Soviet, the Council of Nationalities and the Council of the Republic, and both Deputy Chairmen of the Houses. Of the six, five were communists whom Yeltsin, keeping his promise, had nominated in consultation with the opposition. The sixth was an ex-'democrat', Vladimir Isakov.

deprive Yeltsin of a popular political label, Gorbachev undertook a very useful (albeit ignored at the time) terminological 'clarification'. What right did Yeltsin and the 'democrats' have to call themselves 'left'? 'Left', Gorbachev explained, means 'communists and socialists'. The 'democrats', meanwhile, denied not just a totalitarian model of socialism; they rejected the socialist idea as such and called for the 'capitalization' of society. Wasn't it obvious that they were a 'typical right-wing opposition'? Let's call a spade a spade, concluded Gorbachev.[29]*

Yeltsin responded by raising the rhetorical level to a glass-shattering pitch. 'Democracy is in danger,' he told a gathering of liberal intelligentsia on 9 March. 'This year will be decisive: either democracy will be strangled or it will survive and triumph.' The time had come for a democratic offensive – broad, open and 'unembarrassed'. The time had come to 'declare a war on the country's leadership, which [was] leading [the country] into a quagmire'. The time had come to 'roll up the sleeves and to raise the fists'.[30]

The closer the decisive battle at the Russian Congress drew, the louder and denser was the crossfire. The leader of the Russian communists, Ivan Polozkov, weighed in by stating that the 'left radicals' (whom he, following Gorbachev's lead, unmasked as the 'right flank') were closely linked to the 'shadow economy' and 'foreign circles', while the communists represented the political centre and were the core around which the forces of renewal and 'socialist choice' should unite.[31] A week before the Congress, the political and ideological lines were drawn with utmost clarity. A dozen Union and Russian communist Deputies described Yeltsin as 'openly appealing to anti-communism and anti-Sovietism and advocating so-called "democratic" ideas'. He, their statement continued, had 'embarked on a path of repudiating the USSR as

---

* The correctness of Gorbachev's label would soon be borne out by the treatment accorded Yeltsin in the European Parliament in Strasbourg. On 15 April, Jean-Pierre Cot, the leader of its largest faction, the Socialists, introduced Yeltsin as a 'provocateur' and 'deliberately irresponsible demagogue'. When Yeltsin winced at such an introduction, Cot told him: 'If here, in a democratically elected assembly, you are not ready to listen to unpleasant words, here's the door, you may leave . . .'

The President of the Parliament, Baron Crespo, went out of his way to let everyone know that he had not invited Yeltsin to Strasbourg. For a stunned Yeltsin, who had been convinced he would find support in Europe for his struggle against 'the evil totalitarian system' and who was most conciliatory towards Gorbachev in his remarks there, the reception was an 'ice shower' and a 'hard blow'. (*Le Figaro*, 16 April; *Le Monde*, 17 April; *Russkaya Mysl'*, 19 April 1991; and Yeltsin, *Zapiski*, pp. 40, 41.)

a socialist state and abandoning the existing system and legitimate bodies of authority'.[32]

Two days later, speaking at one of the largest and most renowned Soviet industrial sites – the Kirov machine-building plant in Leningrad – Yeltsin promised that, if elected President of Russia, he would get rid of the Party members in local government posts. 'Today we need to save the country not from the enemy outside but from the enemy within.'[33] He reaffirmed his dissociation from Gorbachev and repeated the call for his resignation. Captured by Leningrad television, the crowd began to chant, 'Resign! Resign! Resign!', and Yeltsin joined in 'in a strong voice'.[34] 'If we find things too hard at the Congress,' Yeltsin said on leaving, 'I am sure we can count on your support.'[35] The workers promised to go on strike if Yeltsin were to be ousted at the coming Congress.[36]

Amid the daily battles, on 1 February Boris Yeltsin turned sixty. As they had done every year, his Sverdlovsk friends came to celebrate with him. While they waited for him at a Supreme Soviet dacha near Moscow, the mood was 'depressed': those were, one of the guests recalled, 'awful times'.[37] As soon as Yeltsin entered the room, one could 'sense a conscious effort' on his part to leave his political cares behind. He was 'relaxed and jovial', and he spoke to everyone at length. As always, Yeltsin's will – this time, to be merry – overwhelmed those around him: suddenly they all felt 'lighter and brighter'.[38] They drank vodka, recited home-made verses and sang.[39]

Few leaders in Russian history could listen to Russia, hear it and give it voice better than Boris Yeltsin in the winter of 1991. Out of the rhetorical battles of the first three months of that year was born a coherent political, economic and ideological credo incompatible with neo-communist restoration. For the first time since perestroika there was now a clear, self-conscious and practical alternative to Gorbachev's policy for the country to choose from. Yeltsin managed to reduce the choice to three simple and awesome dichotomies: Russian sovereignty against the Centre's diktat; democracy against dictatorship; and Yeltsin against Gorbachev.

The choice was facilitated by yet another display of Yeltsin's mastery of a vital political technique – the ability to define oneself by contrast with his opponents. Half blundering and half lured, they fell, yet again, into a familiar trap as Yeltsin manoeuvred them on to a political terrain where he never lost: a populist rebel persecuted by unpopular authorities and defended solely by public support.

In the winter and spring of 1991 Yeltsin denied the regime the option of a creeping, piecemeal restoration, a sliced-salami technique of repression: cutting up glasnost and perestroika slice by slice, arresting someone here, dissolving a rebellious local Soviet and closing down an opposition newspaper there. Big, stubborn, unwieldy and more popular than anyone else on the Soviet political scene, Yeltsin dramatically narrowed the regime's options: either an all-out, bloody 'pacification', an all-Union Tiananmen Square – or a retreat. Arresting Yeltsin would not have done the job: within hours millions of protesters would have been on the streets. The only way to remove him was murder followed by a ruthless crackdown. At once the focus of the resistance and its banner, Yeltsin raised the stakes.

Already by the beginning of March the more astute of Russian political observers began to discern the contours of Yeltsin's stratagem, which only weeks before had seemed doomed. 'What is Yeltsin counting on? In order to take risks, one should keenly feel public sentiments . . . the direct support of the people,' wrote Marina Shakina in *New Times*. The mandate that Yeltsin had received from the people was his 'only chance, the only support that will provide a strong base for him and give him *carte blanche*'.[40] Yeltsin's 19 February television interview had forced the people back to the battlefield, wrote another Russian political editorialist. Tired of politics, they had 'surged back towards the television screens', and 'gave more work to the post and telegraph' with their protest messages. Yeltsin's attempt to galvanize Russia had been a 'stunning success'.[41]

Three times in the next four weeks, following especially loud rhetorical salvoes and coinciding with the opening of the Third Congress, giant pro-Yeltsin demonstrations swept Russian cities: on 24 February, 10 March and 28 March. In Moscow, the first of the rallies was estimated to have been joined by between 100,000 and 400,000 participants, the second by between 100,000 and 'nearly a half-million', and the third by 100,000.[42] Manezhnaya Square proved too small, and the crowds reached all the way to Gorkiy (Tverskaya) Street and the Kalininskiy Prospekt and spilled on to Red Square. (Sixty thousand marched in Leningrad, and tens of thousands in cities across Russia from Petropavlovsk and Novosibirsk to Volgograd and Stavropol.)[43]

Whether in Moscow, Volgograd or Leningrad, the posters, chants and pictures of Yeltsin, the latter cut out of magazines, newspapers and leaflets and pinned to the demonstrators' chests, told the same story: the people had come to defend Yeltsin against 'constant attacks' from the Centre, and to protect democracy and 'sovereign Russia' against the 'partocracy' (that is, the rule of Party bureaucrats), 'dictatorship' and encroachment of the Union government. The chants of 'Yeltsin! Yeltsin!' were followed by '[Gorbachev,] Resign!'[44] Yeltsin, wrote an American reporter after the first Moscow rally, was 'the focus of the crowd's affection'.[45] 'We think Yeltsin is in a dangerous situation right now,' a female demonstrator, wrapped up against the bitter cold and wind, told a Western correspondent on 25 February. 'If we can protect Yeltsin, he will make it.'[46] 'Yeltsin is our hope,' read a poster in Moscow on 10 March.[47]

Alongside the public demonstrations in the cities, the radical Council of Workers' Committees of Kuzbass appealed to 'The citizens of the region, Russia and the country':

A *coup d'état* is being perpetrated by President Gorbachev's team with the consent of the Supreme Soviet of the USSR. We are being deprived of even that freedom and those rights that were wrested from the totalitarian regime during the years of so-called perestroika. The pro-communist Centre is provoking a civil war by creating self-proclaimed 'committees of national salvation' . . .

Now, at the time of a counter-attack by bloody Bolshevism, we need unity of effort and an explanatory campaign in order to prepare our response to dictatorship. This response is a new STRIKE, the only effective weapon in the hands of the people.

We call on President Gorbachev and the Supreme Soviet of the USSR: 'Resign! We demand a trial of those responsible for the invasion of the Baltic countries: Yazov, Kryuchkov, Pugo!'

NEO-BOLSHEVISM SHALL NOT PASS![48]

Although not heeded at the time (end of January) by the majority of the striking miners, the appeal of a political strike grew stronger over the next two months, and by the second week of March the resignation of the Pavlov government and 'support for Boris Yeltsin's policies in his fight for the sovereignty of Russia', replaced higher salaries and better working conditions as the miners' central demands.[49] Soon the political strike expanded to Donetsk and Vorkuta.

Four days before the Russian Congress was due to convene, President Gorbachev ordered his government to 'ensure public order and safety' and removed the Moscow police from the command of the City Council, the Mossovet, which was dominated by the 'democrats'. Two days later, citing the 'threat of violence', the Kremlin banned demonstrations in

Moscow from 26 March to 15 April. Soon the capital was filled with thousands of troops, riot police in battle gear, a bright-red water cannon, two dozen armoured personnel carriers and innumerable military trucks, which lined 'virtually every street' in the centre of the city.[50]

The Moscow City Council challenged the legality of the ban, and Muscovites supported 'their' government. 'Who is this [Prime Minister] Pavlov, anyway?' an angry man asked a small crowd which had gathered on Sovetskaya Square, opposite the rebellious Mossovet, to support the striking miners. 'We have our own government in Russia.'[51] Will there be a rally? someone asked. 'Of course there will be a rally,' answered a teenager who was collecting donations for the miners in a small wooden box under streamers that read 'MINERS DEMAND: GORBACHEV, RESIGN!' and 'MINERS ARE STRIKING NOT FOR A PIECE OF SAUSAGE BUT FOR FREEDOM FOR EVERY-ONE'. 'Pavlov's decree is illegal,' the teenager advised expertly. 'The Mossovet has allowed the strike ... I live in Russia, what right does this stinking fatface [Pavlov] have to order me around?'[52]

On 26 March the co-ordinating council of Democratic Russia announced that a protest rally 'in support of Boris Yeltsin' would take place as scheduled on the opening day of the Congress.[53] 'On Thursday, 28 March, there will be an all-Moscow protest demonstration,' read a leaflet signed by the leadership of Democratic Russia. 'Muscovites! We must stand up for Yeltsin! We must defend democracy and the sovereignty of Russia! On 28 March, there opens a Congress of the People's Deputies of the RSFSR at which the *polozkovs* intend to dismiss Boris Nikolaevich ... Come to the meeting on 28 March: 29 March might already be too late!'[54]

On 28 March, an estimated 100,000 people marched under white-blue-and-red flags along the Garden Ring chanting 'Yeltsin! Yeltsin!' Barred from Manezhnaya Square, they held a protest rally on the other two central squares: Mayakovskogo and Pushkinskaya.[55]

The extraordinary Congress had barely come to order when the 'democrats' called on the gathering to refuse to work 'under the barrels of guns' and 'in a state of siege'. The Congress, they said, had been 'arrested'.[56] After briefly considering a suggestion that the session move to Leningrad, the Deputies by a lopsided vote adopted a resolution that 'suspended' the government's ban on demonstrations, and returned the Moscow police to the City Council. They voted to adjourn until the troops were removed. The following day the troops were withdrawn from the capital.

Yeltsin requested an unusually long time for his opening speech –

one-and-a-half hours – and the first sentences signalled an intent to use every minute as a coda to his three-month dialogue with the authorities and the Russian people. This was to be a loud and unapologetic reaffirmation of the most radical 'democratic' positions. He began by assailing the totalitarian socialist state (and the economy it had spawned) with a ferocity and directness unmatched by anything heard from high rostrums in almost two years since the First Congress of People's Deputies in 1989. The 'main cause of the people's chronic poverty', Yeltsin declared, was a 'misshapen' economy, preserved and maintained by a political system which ignored the individual 'as a matter of principle', and exercised total control over 'all and any' aspects of people's lives.[57] This system had 'destroyed powerful natural stimuli' for work, and had replaced personal interest with 'orders, directives and fear'. The state, with 'mammoth resources' and unlimited power in its possession, had illusions of being able to 'implement the most unthinkable of dreams'.[58]

Separated by the impenetrable wall of 'Marxist–Leninist dogma' from a market economy and a law-governed state – which, in the rest of the world, had made 'scores of nations' prosperous and flourishing – the Soviet Union had accumulated a colossal debt to its own people. That debt was the legacy of a 'system of totalitarian ideology and power which had engendered the most brutal exploitation of the working people and had channelled the country's gigantic resources into supporting excessive military expenditure'.[59] The continuing dominance of 'ideological dogma' over economic rationale had brought the country to its present state: threatened by famine, with shortages of 'everything', hyper-inflation, spiritual poverty, a catastrophic slump in production and a drop in the standard of living.[60]

There were two fundamentally different strategies for dealing with the 'seventy-year legacy of totalitarianism'. Russia and the Russians were at a crossroads and the choice was stark. The first course was the one taken recently by the regime. Having found itself in 'greater and greater isolation', the conservatives had dropped the mask of support for perestroika. Increasingly bold, they were seeking a *revanche* – in essence, a return to the pre-1985 situation. This policy, Yeltsin continued, included the maintenance of the Centre's economic monopoly, modernization of the centralized, unitary state and 'strangulation' of glasnost. The key element of the regime's economic policy – a price increase without market reform and without a radical diminution of budgetary expenditures – would only further diminish the standard of living and bring the country closer to hyperinflation.

The other, 'opposite' strategy included the formation of a broad democratic coalition, an immediate dialogue between the authorities and all political forces, and a government of national accord. A 'real de-Partyization' would prohibit Party membership for those working in the state apparatus, the procuracy,* the police and the KGB, as well as for officers in the armed forces. Simultaneous holding of Party and state posts would be banned for everyone, including the President. A multi-party political system and freedom of speech should be guaranteed by constitutional amendments, and laws that 'violated the people's personal, economic and political' liberties should be annulled.

The only solution to the economic crisis was a return to the '500 Days' – 'the only correct, honest and consistent' programme for the radical transformation of the country's 'economic foundation'. The months that had passed since the Centre's rejection of the Shatalin–Yavlinsky blueprint had been nothing but a waste of time. The economy was steadily collapsing, and people's lives were continuing to deteriorate. Today, Yeltsin declared, the choice was 'absolutely clear: either a return to repression, orders and ephemeral hopes for an economic miracle – or a hard, exhausting, sometimes thankless but concerted effort aimed at a fundamental change to the ruinous economic system'. He listed the first, imperative steps: a 'sharp tightening' of the state budget to preserve the viability of the ruble; de-etatization and privatization of state enterprises; the creation of an independent banking reserve system; land reform; and foreign investment. Most important and most urgent, however, was price liberalization within a 'sufficiently short' time.

Towards the end of his speech, Yeltsin dwelled on the prospects for Russia's rejoining the 'civilized world' and the ways in which it would have to transform itself in order to succeed. Russia had always been and always would be 'great'. This status was determined by its geography, its population, its resources and, most of all, its 'inexhaustible spiritual potential'. Yet its so-called superpower status, based on military force and the 'striving towards political dominance', had exhausted Russia.

A renewed Russia, Yeltsin concluded, would be guided by fundamentally different principles. It would secure its place in the world through 'economic prosperity, moral and spiritual purity'. The principal characteristics of a new Russian state would be non-interference of the state in the affairs of the civil society, except to protect human rights; the

---

* The Russian *prokuratura* both investigated crimes and provided prosecutors (*prokurors*) for trials.

removal of ideology from all institutions of state; and demilitarization: the armed forces should not exceed what was sufficient for the national defence.

Over the next three days the Congress debated Yeltsin's speech. He was denounced harshly and defended just as passionately. Nine times in three days, the 'democrats' failed even to place on the agenda their single most important issue: the Russian Presidential election which the majority of Russians had approved in the 17 March national referendum. Having failed to dislodge Yeltsin by a frontal attack, the communists repeated tactics used in the Yeltsin–Polozkov deadlock a year before: Deputies began to call on the 'Six' *and* Yeltsin to resign. Yeltsin would not hear of it.

The Chairman appeared immovable, the opposition implacable. Neither side seemed to have enough votes for a decisive breakthrough. An exhausted, tense and angry Congress appeared to be deadlocked. The habitually unruly gathering now seemed to be on the verge of a brawl. On the afternoon of 1 April, the fifth day of the Congress, a small crowd of Deputies rushed to the rostrum, the scheduled speaker 'was drowned in the noise', and the resulting impasse was broken only by an emergency recess.[61]

The next day the ever fluid 'swing' vote suddenly began to shift. The Non-Party (Bespartiynyi) faction and the newly created Communists for Democracy, led by a much decorated veteran of the Afghan war, Colonel Aleksandr Rutskoy, threw in their lot with Yeltsin. One after another, the Congress began to discuss, and briskly approve, items of Yeltsin's report for the final resolution. Soon, the leader of the communists, Ivan Polozkov, declared that the situation in Russia was grave and the time was not ripe for a change in the Supreme Soviet's leadership.[62]

Yeltsin's design had carried the day again. By his incessant rhetorical drumbeat and the rejection of compromise, he had manoeuvred the Congressional majority into an uncomfortable corner: support the Chairman or side with a widely unpopular regime, which had committed the robbery of banknote 'exchange', had effectively frozen people's savings accounts and was palpably helpless in the face of economic collapse and looming famine.

Only a minority of diehard communists seemed to be willing to face an exhausted, angry and impatient country without the mediation of Yeltsin's broad back. After endless demonstrations and strikes and the thousands of telegrams, the Congress appeared finally to have heeded the ominous note on which Yeltsin had chosen to end his speech: 'No matter what the twists and turns of the situation are, the last word always belongs to the people. The loss of their trust is the worst punishment for the top leader, an elected body or an ordinary Deputy. It means political death. But the people also can and will provide the most impenetrable protection and the most powerful support . . .'[63]

The last, and the heaviest, instalment of this 'support and protection' came from the mines of Donbass and Vorkuta. Unlike the 1989 action, the strike now threatened to deplete the reserves of coal and put the largest steel-making plants out of action. By the end of March, twenty blast-furnaces in Kuzbass had been left idle by the strike. A week before the Congress opened, the leaders of the strikers had continued to insist on Gorbachev's resignation and his replacement by Yeltsin. They vowed not to return to work until that demand was met – or until Yeltsin asked them to stop the strike.[64] By 30 March, 200 of the Soviet Union's 580 mines were affected.[65]

On 2 April Gorbachev and Pavlov, until then staunchly opposed to direct negotiations with the miners unless they abandoned their political demands, met with 200 representatives of the strikers. Unmoved by an offer of a substantial pay increase, the miners announced on 4 April that they would continue the strike until the Union government resigned.

On the morning of the same day, citing strikes, dislocation, economic collapse and the necessity promptly to respond to the Centre's pressure, Yeltsin surprised everyone by requesting that the Congress grant some of its legislative power to the Supreme Soviet, its Chairman and the Prime Minister of Russia so that they could 'get Russia out of crisis'.[66] Barely alive politically only forty-eight hours before, Yeltsin had moved to turn the enemy's retreat into a rout.

The Congress was stunned. A two-hour break was announced for factions to conduct caucuses. When the Deputies reconvened, the communists attempted to remove the issue from the agenda. The debate grew raucous. There was a scuffle at one of the microphones on the floor as several Deputies attempted to speak at once.[67] The communist motion was defeated. The question of 'redistribution of power for the implementation of anti-crisis measures' was to be debated the following day.

On 5 April, the last day of the Congress, Yeltsin's request for additional power was passed by 607 votes to 228, with 100 Deputies abstaining. Later in the day, the Congress scheduled the first Russian Presidential elections for 12 June. In a career full of wily manoeuvres and dramatic reversals, this was one of Yeltsin's most impressive feats.

Recalling 1991, the most knowledgeable American official in Moscow at the time, Ambassador Jack Matlock, would write in his memoirs: 'While it might be going too far to say that Boris Yeltsin saved democracy in Russia (since democracy was still in an early state of development here), it is no exaggeration to say that his actions during the first eight months of 1991 preserved the possibility of developing democracy in Russia when that cause was under mortal threat.'[68]

The three-month confrontation was over. The efforts of Gorbachev's 'right oar' had been impeded and eventually paralysed by the resistance which had coalesced around Yeltsin.* In the 17 March referendums both protagonists had scored and, by the rules of the zero-sum political game of that spring, both had lost a point: Gorbachev received a majority for the preservation of the Union,† Yeltsin won approval for the Russian Presidency. In Russia each proposition received an almost equal share of the vote: 71 per cent and 70 per cent of those who came to the polls. With the 'right turn' of the state ship thwarted, and with his hard-line allies unable to overpower Yeltsin, Gorbachev took up the 'left', reform oar again.

No longer in danger of negotiating from a position of weakness, Yeltsin was ready to deal. He first proffered the olive branch during his misbegotten visit to the European Parliament. He did not want Gorbachev's chair.[69] At a time when Gorbachev was 'in serious danger', and the forces of the 'right' were about to overwhelm him, Yeltsin promised his co-operation in 'repulsing the chaos'. 'We do not leave our wounded on the battlefield,' Yeltsin declared.[70] For his part, Gorbachev understood that without Yeltsin the Centre was not likely to withstand

---

* The crushing defeat of Iraqi troops, supplied and trained by the Soviet Union, by the US-led coalition contributed to the demoralization of the communist reaction and its April retreat. In the opinion of Russian liberal analysts, the victory of the West had 'vividly and most persuasively demonstrated that the political, economic and humanitarian advantages of liberty over totalitarianism were embodied in its overwhelming military superiority'. Iraq's débâcle in Kuwait was more than the vanquishing of one army by another: it was a 'victory of a civilized, democratic and professional army over a mass, ideologized and totalitarian' one. (A. Sobyanin and D. Yur'ev, *S'ezd narodnykh deputatove RSFSR v zerkale poimennykh golosovaniy* ('The Congress of People's Deputies of the RSFSR in the mirror of name voting'), p. 16.)

† The Union referendum question read, 'Do you think it necessary to preserve the Union of Soviet Socialist Republics as a renewed federation of equal sovereign Republics, in which a full measure of human rights and liberties will be guaranteed to a person of any nationality?' Armenia, Georgia, Moldova and the three Baltic Republics did not participate.

the dual pressure of the communist reaction and the striking workers – both demanding the President's resignation.*

No sooner had Yeltsin returned from Strasbourg than he was invited by Gorbachev to the Union government dacha in Novo-Ogaryovo near Moscow, where Brezhnev had negotiated with Nixon and where Gorbachev had entertained Reagan and Bush. Yeltsin found there the leaders of eight Union Republics. What Gorbachev told them 'surpassed all expectations'.[71]

On 23 April the Kremlin made public a Joint Declaration signed by Gorbachev and the leaders of nine Republics – Russia, Ukraine, Byelorussia, Uzbekistan, Kazakhstan, Azerbaijan, Kyrgyzstan, Tajikistan and Turkmenia. For the first time, the Centre had agreed to define the Republics as 'sovereign states' independent in their policies, and a new Union as a 'Union of sovereign states' voluntarily joined. It was also agreed that a new constitution of the Soviet Union would be adopted at the time of the signing of the Union Treaty, followed by direct national elections to a dramatically transformed executive branch of the Union, including the Presidency.

Yeltsin called the Joint Declaration a 'tremendous victory'.[72] If the Centre and the Republics 'scrupulously adhered' to their obligations, the signing would be the 'beginning of radical reforms'.[73] Gorbachev, now 'leaning on the "left" shoulder', was an ally again.[74] With Russia behind him, Gorbachev could face down the Central Committee.† The Declaration, the General Secretary told the Party bosses two days later, had 'created a political atmosphere for . . . transition to the market . . . and a transformed Union in accordance with the results of national elections'.[75]

In return, Yeltsin had agreed to the preservation of the all-Union Presidency (and Gorbachev's occupancy of the post until the election)

---

* At a meeting with Gorbachev on 8 April, the members of the hard-line communist Soyuz faction of the USSR Supreme Soviet told him that they wanted an 'emergency session' of the USSR Congress of People's Deputies to consider 'emergency action'. One of the faction's leaders threatened a vote of no-confidence in the President. Meanwhile, 300,000 miners again rejected a settlement until Gorbachev and his government resigned. Workers at huge plants in Leningrad and Minsk were threatening a general strike if the miners' demands were not met.

† In preparation for the Plenum, calls for Gorbachev's resignation surfaced at the meetings of the Leningrad and Moscow City Party Committees. 'The conservative forces within the CPSU', Gorbachev recalled, '[had] decided to confront me at the April Plenum' (Gorbachev, *Memoirs*, pp. 598–9).

and a moratorium on strikes – 'concessions' for which he was taken to task by some of his radical allies from Democratic Russia. A week later, following Yeltsin's three-day visit to Kuzbass, the miners agreed to 'suspend' the strike.

Although the vote for the first Russian President was not being held until 12 June, the campaign was over by the beginning of April: the issues had already been debated and the positions contested in February and March. When they rallied to 'defend Yeltsin' on those three bitterly cold winter nights; when, at the referendum on 17 March, 70 per cent voted to institute the Presidency of Russia; when strikes erupted at mines and plants, Russians chose the winner in advance.

In addition to Yeltsin,* five other candidates vied for the Presidency: ex-Prime Minister Nikolay Ryzhkov; Vadim Bakatin, former Minister of Internal Affairs, sacked by Gorbachev during the latter's 'move to the right' in December 1990; the leftist nationalist hard-liner General Albert Makashov, who vowed to 'respond to a creeping counter-revolution with patriotism of the highest degree'; the leader of an obscure Liberal-Democratic Party, Vladimir Zhirinovskiy, who promised to 'defend the rights' of ethnic Russians and cut the price of vodka; and Amangeldy Tuleev, the Chairman of the Kemerovo Regional Soviet, an advocate of local autonomy and a foe of Western horror movies, which he promised to ban if elected.†

Apart from Zhirinovskiy, Yeltsin was the only non-Party candidate. With the memory of what was now known as the 'winter offensive' of the communist reaction still fresh and the Party still strong, this distinction, undoubtedly and significantly, added to Yeltsin's already formidable lead. It was Yeltsin against 'them' – again.

Widely assumed to be the choice of the apparat and the military–

---

* As his Vice President, Yeltsin chose Aleksandr Rutskoy, the leader of the Communists for Democracy faction in the Russian parliament. Yeltsin explained the Rutskoy candidacy as an effort to demonstrate moderation and 'centrism' and appeal to 'honourable' Party members who were searching for renewal but could not bring themselves to break with the Party. (Boris Yeltsin, 'Tsel' – obnovlenie Rossii. B. N. El'tsin otvechaet na voprosy Izvestiy' ('The goal is the renewal of Russia. B. N. Yeltsin answers *Izvestia*'s questions'), interview with V. Lynev, *Izvestia*, 23 May 1991.)

† According to the law passed by the Fourth Congress of People's Deputies of Russia on 24 April, to be placed on the ballot one had to collect 100,000 signatures or be nominated by 20 per cent of the Deputies. (Zhirinovskiy successfully availed himself of the latter option.) The President was to be elected for a maximum of two five-year terms.

industrial complex, Ryzhkov was Yeltsin's most formidable and best-financed competitor. (His campaign was headed by the Deputy Chairman of the State Committee for Machine Building and was housed in the luxurious headquarters of the state concern Telecom.)[76] The other serious candidate, the uniformly respected and well-liked Bakatin, had a reputation as a Party liberal and was rumoured to be Gorbachev's personal preference for the Presidency of Russia. Like Gorbachev, Bakatin was a self-proclaimed 'radical centrist', who wished for a 'delicate combination of the old and the new'.[77] He positioned himself as a 'common-sense' candidate, between Yeltsin on the 'left' and Ryzhkov on the 'right'.[78]

With democracy (understood largely as freedom from a totalitarian state) having been resoundly affirmed in winter and spring, and with the 'strengthening of Russia's state sovereignty' a popular slogan for over a year, the economy, rather than politics, became the main battlefield of the two leading contenders. Ryzhkov's views had changed little since the 'government programme' of the previous October. He was for a 'regulated market economy'.[79] Large-scale privatization, he contended, would result in the disaster of inflation and unemployment. 'Either we go for capitalism,' Ryzhkov repeated during his campaign, 'or we pursue the choice for which our forefathers fought.'[80] And, he added, those who want capitalism ought to avail themselves of the new freedom of emigration.[81] Ryzhkov 'absolutely opposed' private ownership of land, its purchase or sale.[82]

Yeltsin called radical economic reform the 'thrust' of his election programme.[83] Stabilization and then growth could not be achieved other than through a 'new market model' of the economy.[84] He vowed to remove constraints on entrepreneurship and to eliminate all administrative restrictions on wages.[85] 'If we grant people economic freedom and give them support, they will solve their own problems.'[86] For Yeltsin, privatization was the 'most important direction'.[87] Citizens would become owners through privatization of most state enterprises, housing, the retail trade, services and food processing.[88] The food crisis, too, could be solved only on the basis of large-scale land reform.[89] Yeltsin promised, if elected, to parcel out land to individual farmers.[90]

The speed of reform was the key consideration for him. It had to be effected 'within the shortest possible time':[91] partial reforms, 'implemented gradually [would] destroy us'.[92] People would not stand for a long transition.[93] If, in the next two years, no real progress was made, 'there [would] be an explosion, so powerful that it [would] sweep us all away – leftists, rightists and centrists'.[94]

On 11 June, the eve of the election, the editor of a leading Moscow liberal newspaper wrote: 'It is incredible. Russia has finally lived to see the day when the people themselves are choosing the head of state. Perestroika has had many faults. The democrats have not been able to do many things. But they have succeeded in smashing the tradition of the hereditary monarchy and the one-party dictatorship that succeeded it.'[95]

With nearly three out of four eligible voters having come to the polls, 57 per cent of Russians (or 45,552,041) voted for Yeltsin. Ryzhkov received 17 per cent, Zhirinovskiy 8 per cent, Tuleev 7, Makashov 4 and Bakatin 3.

On 10 July, in the Kremlin Palace of Congresses Yeltsin took the oath of office and delivered an inaugural address – the first such oration in Russian history. He used the occasion to outline a new social contract between the Russian people and the Russian state, to underline his commitment to radical economic reform and to announce a new path for Russia in the affairs of the world.

Words cannot convey the feelings I am experiencing at this minute. For the first time in the thousand-year history of Russia, a President is being solemnly sworn in before his fellow citizens . . .

For centuries in our country power and the people have been at opposite poles . . . For centuries the interests of the state have, as a rule, been put above those of the individual, his needs and his aspirations. We have, regrettably, come later than other civilized peoples to the realization that the state's strength lies in the well-being of its citizens. Negation of this sacred principle laid to ruin the greatest empires of the past . . . We have had to pay a colossal, unprecedented price for our experience . . .

The time when the people were silent is becoming a thing of the past, never to return again . . .

[The people] have chosen not only an individual, not only the President, but, above all, the path our Motherland is to follow. This is the path of democracy, the path of reform, the path of revival of human worth. For the first time a new voluntary interdependence is born between the authorities and the people. State authority becomes answerable to the people who elected it, and the people become answerable to the state, which they have placed above themselves . . .

A worthy life does not come as a gift from above . . . One does not attain it by standing in line and blindly obeying orders from above. It can be founded only on the freedom of enterprise. It is the initiative and the spirit of enterprise on the part of citizens that will ensure prosperity for Russian families and provide the source of the country's revival . . . The revival of our state is to be founded on the spiritual emancipation of man, true freedom of conscience and total rejection of ideological diktat. A special place in this process belongs to religion . . .

Imperial ambitions are deeply alien to the political course which the people have chosen. We are returning to the world community with pure intentions of finding friends and not enemies, of establishing honest and civilized relations with the states of the world . . . At the heart of progress lie creativity, human values, freedom, ownership, legality and openness to the world . . .

Great Russia is rising from her knees. We will, without fail, transform her into a prosperous, democratic, peaceful, law-abiding and sovereign state. The task, which entails a great deal of work for us all, has already begun. Having come through so many trials, with a clear idea of our goals, we can be firmly confident: Russia will be reborn![96]

*

What was now referred to in the Soviet media as the 'Novo-Ogaryovo process' continued apace. While Georgia, Armenia, Azerbaijan, Moldova and the three Baltic Republics seemed to be irretrievably lost to any new Union, no matter how renewed, the leaders of the other eight Republics continued to meet in Novo-Ogaryovo. Along with Gorbachev, Yeltsin was the key member of the 'drafting committee for the Union Treaty'.[97]

The Republics seemed to be recovering from the Vilnius shock. A tenuous but real bond of mutual trust began to span Moscow and the periphery. This delicate equilibrium rested on an unstated but well-understood formula: the Union was to be preserved as a confederation, with the Centre responsible for the common defence and the Republics free to pursue their own policies, including radical market and political reforms, without hindrance by the Kremlin. In a necessarily cryptic manner Gorbachev confirmed the essence of the bargain when, in the second week of July, he said that the 'historic sessions in Novo-Ogaryovo' marked a 'renewal of our society', a 'transition to the market', and the abandonment of the 'unitary command system that blocked the flow of oxygen to the Republics'.[98]

Bidding Gorbachev godspeed for the London summit of the leading Western powers, the G-7, Yeltsin was unusually supportive, even effusive. Referring to Gorbachev as the 'President of a huge and mighty nation', he reiterated that the latter was carrying to London 'not just the position of the Centre' but the agreed view of the eight Republics.[99] Yeltsin described this common attitude as 'the path of radical reform, transition to a market economy, diversity of forms of ownership and privatization'.[100] Novo-Ogaryovo, he added, was 'the cradle of a political process dominated by respect for the Republics'.[101] He extolled a 'reasonable compromise in the name of the construction of our renewed state'.[102]

As always, political truce translated into personal rapprochement. After a year-long break, they began to meet in private.[103] Each seemed to be getting what he most wanted from Novo-Ogaryovo: Gorbachev, a senior, albeit largely ceremonial, status for himself and the Union; Yeltsin, independence for Russia.[104] In front of the entire nation and the world, Gorbachev congratulated Yeltsin after the latter had taken his oath of office. Yeltsin, in turn, said he would support Gorbachev's bid for election as the President of a new Union, 'if he continued to respect the sovereignty of the Union's Republics'.[105]

The new alliance was tested on 20 July, when Yeltsin finally fulfilled the promise of his 1990 campaign by banning political parties from 'state bodies, establishments and organizations of the RSFSR'. What he had failed to get through the Russian parliament the previous June, he accomplished thirteen months later by a Presidential decree. After seventy-four years, the Party state was no more.

Gorbachev protested, of course. Yeltsin's *ukaz* 'complicated' the situation and weakened the 'tendency towards consolidation', the General Secretary said at what was to become the last Plenum of the Central Committee on 26 July. No one had 'the right to forbid the Party to work with labour collectives'.[106]

Still, leaving Novo-Ogaryovo late on warm summer nights at the conclusion of a hard day's work on the Treaty – after a friendly dinner with Gorbachev and other leaders, warmed by Gorbachev's favourite brandy, Yubileyniy – Yeltsin was both 'excited and content': a new Treaty would be signed as scheduled on 20 August.[107]

When Yeltsin landed at Vnukovo airport after midnight on 19 August, on a flight from Alma-Ata, he looked at his watch. Yes, the 'grandiose event' was to take place the next day, already tomorrow! He was pleased. On the way to the government dacha in Arkhangelskoye, his 'soul was filled with peace'.[108]

PART IV

In Power

CHAPTER 10

The Revolution

S HORTLY AFTER SIX O'CLOCK IN the morning of 19 August, all radio stations of the Soviet Union broadcast a statement by Vice President Gennadiy Yanaev: 'In connection with the inability for health reasons of Mikhail Sergeevich Gorbachev to perform the duties of the President of the USSR, effective 19 August 1991 I have assumed the duties of the President on the basis of Article 127(7) of the Constitution of the USSR.'[1]

Every hour throughout the day, this statement, together with declarations, appeals and orders, was repeated, without comment, by sombre television and radio announcers amid the suddenly sparse fare of classical music, ballet and sports. A state of emergency, declared in some localities of the USSR from four o'clock that morning, was to remain in force for the next six months. The country was ruled by the State Committee for the State of Emergency (Gosudarstvennyi Komitet po Cherezvychainomu Polozhenyu, or GKChP). The Committee's members were Yanaev, Prime Minister Valentin Pavlov, the KGB Chairman Vladimir Kryuchkov, Ministers of Defence and Minister of Internal Affairs Dmitriy Yazov and Boris Pugo, First Deputy Chairman of the Defence Council of the USSR Oleg Baklanov, Chairman of the Peasants' Union Vasiliy Starodubtsev, and Chairman of the Association of State Enterprises Aleksandr Tizyakov.[2] After he had refused to endorse the transfer of power to Yanaev, Gorbachev had been placed under house arrest in his holiday villa in Cape Foros, south of Yalta in the Crimea, and held incommunicado.

Racing towards the dachas of the Russian government in Arkhangelskoye, the Mayor of St Petersburg,* Anatoliy Sobchak, passed a column of tanks moving towards Moscow and, closer to the dacha, a detachment of paratroopers.[3]

At Yeltsin's dacha he found the entire Russian leadership: Yeltsin, the Prime Minister Ivan Silaev, the newly elected Chairman of the Supreme Soviet, Ruslan Khazbulatov, Gennadiy Burbulis and Yeltsin's faithful bodyguard, Aleksandr Korzhakov. They were guarded by eight men with Kalashnikov submachine guns – the sole military contingent that the Russian government had under its command that morning.[4]

The decision had already been made: the Russian leaders were calling an emergency session of the Congress of People's Deputies of Russia. Yeltsin dictated an 'Appeal to the People of Russia', in which he called on everyone to resist the State Committee for the State of Emergency.

* The city name was changed from Leningrad following a referendum on 12 June 1991 in which 55 per cent of the residents voted to restore the original name.

The group resolved to drive to Moscow, to the White House.[5] As the guards were putting a bulletproof vest on Yeltsin, the room fell silent. Yeltsin's daughter Tat'yana said: 'Hold on, Papa, now everything depends on you.'[6]

All the decisions of the GKChP were to be considered binding and were to be 'implemented rigorously' by authorities and citizens alike on the entire territory of the Soviet Union.[7] From the Union authorities in Moscow down to settlements and villages, all 'bodies of power' were to 'ensure strict observance of the emergency regime'.[8] Meetings, demonstrations and strikes were banned, as were all parties, public organizations and 'mass movements' that 'hindered normalization'. Where needed, curfew might be declared and enforced. 'Spreading of provocative rumours' and disobeying officials were to be 'resolutely nipped in the bud'.[9] Except for nine newspapers,* all other periodicals published in Moscow had been suspended.

The next day, the Committee decreed that all broadcast organizations – from the All-Union Television and Radio Company to *oblast* radio and television stations – should be 'guided in their work' by the Committee's decisions.[10] All previously issued broadcast licences were declared invalid and their holders subject to re-registration.[11] Russian Television Channel, Radio Rossii and the Echo of Moscow radio station were suspended because they were considered not to 'facilitate the process of stabilization'.[12] The Committee members said they had acted because of the desperate economic and political situation in the country: they wanted to arrest a 'slide towards national catastrophe'.[13]

There was very little to dispute in the picture GKChP sketched in its 'Address to the Soviet People'. Unable to deliver on its promises of prosperity, perestroika was at a 'dead end'.[14] The Soviet Union was gripped by a severe and deepening economic crisis. Shortages of food and housing were becoming desperate. The daily existence of millions was threatened by the disintegration of authority from top to bottom, and by an explosion of crime. Centrifugal tensions had torn apart the national economy.[15] Production was in steep decline.[16] The standard of living for the great majority of people was falling sharply, and had been further eroded by inflation.[17] Because of the lack of fuel and spare parts,

---

* Permitted to publish were the communist *Pravda*, *Moskovskaya Pravda*, *Leninskoye Znamya* (the organ of the Moscow *oblast* Party organization), *Rabochaya Tribuna*, *Sel'skaya Zhizn'*, the leftist nationalist *Sovetskaya Rossia*, the armed forces' *Krasnaya Zvezda*, the newspaper of offical trade unions *Trud* and the rather liberal *Izvestia*.

collective farms were on the brink of catastrophe.[18] In the very near future the Soviet people could face famine.[19] The most urgent task was to save the harvest and procure enough food to last through the winter.[20]

The Committee claimed to support 'genuine democratic processes'[21] and was at pains to justify the takeover as a 'forced measure' dictated by the 'vital need to save the economy from ruin and the country from hunger'.[22] Its members promised not to abandon economic reform. They were not opposed to private enterprise but insisted that the transition to the market must not be 'built on declining living standards'.[23] Accordingly, the Committee pledged to 'regulate, freeze and reduce' prices for a number of industrial goods and foodstuffs and to raise salaries, pensions and allowances.[24]

'Even the elementary personal security of people is coming under threat more and more,' the Committee members declared in their Address. 'Crime is growing rapidly, it is becoming organized and politicized. The country is sinking into an abyss of violence and lawlessness.'[25] The Committee promised to 'cleanse the streets' of criminals,[26] to put an end to the 'tyranny of those who plunder people's assets' and to commence a resolute struggle against the 'octopus of crime', 'scandalous immorality',[27] corruption, speculation, embezzlement and the 'shadow economy'.[28]

Above all, the GKChP wanted to save the Soviet Union, which was in mortal danger.[29] Chaos and anarchy had made the country ungovernable,[30] and disintegration appeared imminent.[31] The country was being destroyed. Violent ethnic conflicts were spreading, and for tens of millions of Soviet people life had lost 'its tranquillity and joy'.[32]

The urgency was warranted. The Union Treaty, negotiated in Novo-Ogaryovo, was to be signed on 20 August by Byelorussia, Kazakhstan, Russia, Tajikistan and Uzbekistan (Azerbaijan, Kyrgyzstan, Turkmenia and Ukraine were to sign in September). The Treaty would, indeed, mean the end of the Soviet Union. Republics would thereby become 'sovereign states',[33] whose power over the internal affairs of their nations would be near complete. Except for specified instances, a Republic's laws would take precedence over the Union's.[34] The prerogatives of the Union authorities would be delegated to them by the Republics and limited largely to foreign and security policy.[35] Henceforth, the country would be called the Union of Soviet Sovereign Republics.[36] If signed, the Treaty would *de facto* have recognized the independence of the six Republics that had declared their intent to leave the Union: Armenia, Estonia, Georgia, Latvia, Lithuania and Moldova.

In the previous weeks, the final draft of the Treaty (which GKChP now promised to submit to a national referendum) had been criticized by the Council of Ministers and the Praesidium of the Supreme Soviet for draining the Union authorities of their power. On the day of the coup, TASS released a statement by the Chairman of the Supreme Soviet, Anatoliy Lukyanov, who would soon be identified as one of the coup's masterminds. The drafters of the Treaty, Lukyanov wrote, had not taken into consideration the attitudes of the People's Deputies of the USSR. The latter objected to the Treaty's silence on a number of provisions they considered critical: a 'single economic space', a 'single banking system' and taxes designated exclusively for the Union Treasury.[37]

As the Committee signed orders and issued appeals, troops were pouring into the capital from the Minsk and Mozhaysk highways and from Kutuzovskiy Prospekt: an endless armada of trucks, tanks and armoured personnel carriers, mounted with heavy machine guns and carrying soldiers armed with Kalashnikovs. These were regiments of three of the Soviet Army's elite divisions: Second Guards (Tamanskaya) Motor Rifle, Fourth Guards (Kantemirovskaya) Tank and the Tula-based 106th Guards Airborne (paratroopers). In addition, the Internal Ministry fielded its own troops: the Dzerzhinskiy Division and the 'special designation' anti-riot detachments, the feared OMON in black uniforms and helmets.

Filling the streets with dense blue exhaust fumes, their treads smashing the pavements, the road surfaces and the cobblestones of squares, tanks and BMPs (*boevaya mashina pekhoty* – 'fighting infantry vehicle' or armoured personnel carrier) rumbled down major thoroughfares and took positions along main streets, around squares and outside key government buildings – the State Bank, the City Council (Mossovet), the Ostankino Television Centre, the Ministries of Foreign Affairs and Defence, the General Staff headquarters – and the editorial offices of major newspapers on Pravda Street and on Pushkinskaya Square, the home of *Izvestia* and *Moskovskie Novosti*. The Central Telegraph on Tverskaya was occupied by a squad of the Tamanskaya Division.[38]

The square outside the Bolshoi was filled with BMPs. Tanks and soldiers blocked Manezhnaya Square, the site of the largest rallies under perestroika. In the middle of Red Square, blocked by OMON, stood three tanks, their long barrels pointing at St Basil's Cathedral and Spasskaya Tower.

By the time Yeltsin's black limousine approached the front of the House of Soviets on Krasnopresnenskaya Embankment, the building was surrounded by tanks. Military trucks filled with artillery shells were parked near by.[39] No one, however, prevented the car from pulling into an underground garage.

Done up in white marble and resembling a submarine with its long base and fourteen-storey elevation in the middle, the building had been known in Moscow as the 'White House' since the beginning of the Russian parliament's confrontation with the Centre a year before, its nickname the creation of sardonic Moscow wits forever fascinated by America. Over the next three days and nights, drained of its original self-deprecation, the name would become universally and proudly accepted by millions of Russians.

Almost immediately Yeltsin held a press conference. The Committee's act was a coup, he said. It was illegal, and it was 'madness'.[40] His credentials, Yeltsin continued, came from the people, and no one but the people of Russia could remove him from office.[41] He called for the immediate reinstatement of Gorbachev, with whom he had been trying unsuccessfully to speak over the telephone, and appealed to Muscovites to stage a demonstration 'in defence of democracy'.[42] In the middle of his remarks, Yeltsin was interrupted by an aide urgently whispering something to him. 'At least fifty tanks are on their way to this building,' Yeltsin announced. 'Anybody who wants to save himself can do so. We are continuing to work.'[43]

After the press conference, Yeltsin walked out of the building, climbed atop a tank and shook hands with the astounded crew. Then he said: 'Since they don't let us on television, and they don't let us on the radio, I'll read it.'[44] In a photograph that was to become famous, a young soldier from the tank crew buried his face in his hands as Yeltsin read an appeal to 'The Citizens of Russia':

A legitimately elected President of the country [Mikhail Gorbachev] was removed from power on the night of 18–19 August. No matter what reasons are given to justify the removal, we are dealing here with a right-wing, reactionary, anti-constitutional coup.

With all the difficulties and trials experienced by the people, the democratic process is becoming deeper, wider and irreversible. The arbitrary rule of extra-constitutional bodies, including the Party, has been substantially limited.

Seeking the unity of the Soviet Union, the unity of Russia, the leaders of Russia have taken a firm position regarding the Union Treaty. Our position has made it possible to expedite the preparation of the Treaty, to obtain the consent of the Republics and to determine the date of the signing – 20 August.

Such developments have caused anger among reactionary forces, pushing them to irresponsible, adventurist attempts to solve the most difficult political and economic problems by strong-arm methods.

We have found and continue to find strong-arm methods unacceptable. They compromise the USSR before the entire world, undermine our prestige in the world community, return us to the Cold War era and to the isolation of the Soviet Union from the world community.

All these considerations make us declare the so-called Committee illegal. Accordingly, we declare illegal all the decisions and orders of this so-called Committee . . .

We call on the citizens of Russia to give the organizers of the coup an appropriate response and to demand the return of the country to normal, constitutional development.

It is imperative to allow the President of the country, Gorbachev, to speak to the people. We demand a convocation of an extraordinary Congress of the People's Deputies of the USSR.

We are completely confident that our compatriots will not permit the establishment of arbitrariness and lawlessness propagated by the coup organizers, who have lost shame and conscience. We call on military personnel not to participate in the reactionary coup.

Until our demands are met, we call for a general strike.

We are confident that the world community will evaluate objectively this cynical attempt at a right-wing coup.[45]*

Yeltsin went back to his office and promulgated much of what he had just said by signing the first two of nearly a dozen decrees (*ukaz*es) to be issued from the White House in the next seventy-two hours. One document ruled the coup 'anti-constitutional' and 'nothing but a state

---

* In the case of the United States, an 'objective evaluation' took some time. On the morning of 19 August, President Bush announced that 'gut instinct' discerned in Gennadiy Yanaev a 'certain commitment to reform'. As for protesting against Gorbachev's imprisonment or supporting Yeltsin, this was not the 'time for flamboyance or posturing on the part of any country, certainly not the United States', Bush said. He carefully labelled the coup 'extra-constitutional', rather than 'anti-' or 'un-'. It was not until over twenty-four hours later that Bush finally called Yeltsin. (Press conference of President Bush, *Washington Post*, 20 August 1991, p. 5; Paul Horvitz, 'Bush, Returning to Capital, Moves to Suspend Aid', *International Herald Tribune*, 20 August 1991, p. 1; and Lionel Barber, 'Bush treads carefully in support for Yeltsin', *Financial Times*, 21 August 1991, p. 5.)

crime'. All decisions made in the name of the Committee were to be considered illegal and without force in the territory of Russia. Office-holders implementing such decisions could be prosecuted under the Criminal Code of the Russian Federation.[46] Citing the paralysis of legal power in the USSR, until the convocation of an emergency Congress of People's Deputies of the USSR the second decree placed under the 'direct authority' of the President of Russia all 'organs of executive power' of the Soviet Union located in the territory of the Russian Repub-lic. The 'organs' included the Ministries of Defence and Internal Affairs as well as the KGB.[47] All bodies of power and officeholders were ordered to take urgent measures to prevent the carrying out of the Committee's decisions.[48]

Thus began Boris Yeltsin's public debate with the GKChP – a battle of appeals and decrees to the bitter end. Those of the Committee were printed in the permitted newspapers and read on national radio and television. Yeltsin's were thrown, by the hundred, out of White House windows[49] as the crowd below (which had already reached between 70,000 and 100,000 people)[50] shouted, 'More! More!'[51] Photocopied on thin, grainy paper, or copied by hand, they were pasted on lampposts, at the entrances to the Metro[52] and on the hitherto pristine walls inside,[53] broadcast by an underground radio station and printed in banned news-papers and leaflets, spreading around Moscow 'like wildfire'.[54]

With the Committee's every thrust, Yeltsin's parries grew sharper and were aimed higher. His favourite political tactic of *klin klinom vyshibayut*, meeting challenge with challenge, pressure with pressure, force with force, had never been starker nor deployed for higher stakes. It had never looked more hopeless either.

At 5 p.m. the Committee began a nationally televised press conference in the press centre of the Ministry of Foreign Affairs. At 5.30 Radio Moscow broadcast Yanaev's decree declaring martial law in Moscow, and the appointment of a general as city commandant.[55] Shortly before nine o'clock, the Committee took notice of Yeltsin's 'Appeal', warned the Russian leadership against instigating 'unlawful actions' and hinted darkly that it had the means and determination to implement its decisions.[56]

Yeltsin responded by signing, at 5.20 p.m., an appeal to Russian soldiers and, at seven o'clock, an address to Muscovites, imploring them not to recognize the authority of the Committee, to defend their 'elected power' at the White House and to 'explain' to the soldiers the 'anti-constitutional' nature of their orders. At 10.30 he responded to the Committee's threats with the angriest and most defiant of his decrees.

'Decree No. 63' charged the members of the Committee, listed by name and official title, with committing the 'gravest state crimes' under five articles of the Russian Criminal Code and declared them 'outlaws'.[57] In the name of the 'people who elected' him, Yeltsin promised 'legal and moral defence' for those who refused to follow the Committee's orders.[58]

The next day, Yeltsin declared himself Commander-in-Chief of the Soviet armed forces on Russian territory until 'full restoration of the activity of constitutional organs' and the return of the President of the USSR.[59] He ordered the troops to return to or remain in their bases, and invalidated all commands issued by Yazov.[60] Later, Yeltsin ordered the dismissal of the GKChP-appointed military commandants of Moscow and Leningrad.[61]

In the afternoon of 20 August, Russian Vice President Aleksandr Rutksoy, acting Chairman of the Russian Supreme Soviet Ruslan Khazbulatov and Chairman of the Council of Ministers of Russia Ivan Silaev delivered to Lukyanov a list of 'actions to be taken immediately': the lifting of all restrictions on the mass media, the withdrawal of troops from Moscow, and the disbandment of the GKChP.[62] Of the ten demands, 'stopping the threats against the leadership of Russia' and ensuring their liberty and freedom of movement was the ninth.[63] First, second and third dealt with Gorbachev. Yeltsin demanded that Lukyanov organize a meeting between the Soviet President and the Russian leadership and that Gorbachev be examined by a committee of physicians from the World Health Organization (the Russian government would pay for their travel). If he was pronounced fit, Gorbachev should immediately be returned to office.[64]

When British Prime Minister John Major called Yeltsin on the same day, everyone in the White House believed that an assault was imminent. Yeltsin told Major that tanks were moving towards the building. Yeltsin's first request to him, however, was to press for the 'immediate freeing of President Gorbachev'.[65]

The most powerful of all public pronouncements to be issued from the besieged White House was Yeltsin's appeal to the soldiers. It contained its share of the by now familiar charges against the GKChP: 'state treason', 'trampled laws', 'a group of adventurists'.[66] The document also reprised the motifs used seven months earlier when Yeltsin had entreated Russian troops not to shoot at Estonians, Latvians and Lithuanians: remember your oath, don't turn your guns on your people, on your loved ones; don't stain the 'honour and glory' of Russian arms with the people's blood.[67] Yet in its key segment the message went far beyond the Committee's 'crimes', broken laws or calls to insubordination. At its heart was a new theme that would prove unmatched in its resonance and mobilizing power. That theme was freedom:

> The 'order' promised by these self-proclaimed saviours of the Fatherland will turn into tragedy, into the suppression of dissent, concentration camps, midnight arrests ... One can build a throne of bayonets but one cannot sit on it for long. There will be no return to the past ... The clouds of terror and dictatorship are thickening over Russia. But they will not turn into an endless night ... Our long-suffering people will regain freedom. This time, for ever![68]

*

In the centre of Moscow crowds stopped trolley buses, slashed their tyres[69] and, helped by the passengers, manoeuvred them across major streets and squares: Tverskaya, Kalininskiy Prospekt, the Garden Ring and Manezhnaya Square.[70] Truck drivers parked their vehicles next to the trolleys.

The crews of tanks and armoured vehicles that had reached their destination were immediately surrounded and their machines invaded. The crowds begged soldiers to explain why they were in Moscow, implored them not to shoot, and proffered cigarettes, food, water and ice-cream. Older women emptied the contents of their knitted shopping bags, the ubiquitous *avos'ka*s, and left their gifts (acquired after hours of foraging and queuing) on the tanks, at once feeding and scolding, in the inimitable manner of Russian grandmothers: 'Whom have you come to shoot at? Your mothers? Is that what we have brought you up for?'[71] Some brought glass jars of home-made jam.[72] Chased off in vain by officers, pretty girls were helped on board by crews to deliver flowers.[73]

Those machines that were still on the move by mid-morning of 19 August were to have much tenser encounters. Heavy steel spokes were jammed in their treads[74] and chains of people and trolleys, filled with protesters, stood in their paths.[75] Most of the vehicles stopped. Some, such as those on Manezhnaya Square, turned back, to the triumphant cries of the bystanders.[76] A few attempted to break through, but not even blank cannon shots[77] could disperse crowds in front of them.

The first protest meeting of several hundred people was held at the Mossovet at nine o'clock in the morning of 19 August. Yeltsin's 'Appeal to the Citizens of Russia' was pasted on the wall there.[78] Placards read 'Yeltsin calls for a strike'.[79] Young men were signing up for 'self-defence detachment'.[80] Three blocks down Tverskaya Street, on Manezhnaya

Square, motorists used their own cars, empty buses and a crane to seal the entrances to the square.[81] A trolley filled with people, 'Down with the GKChP' written on the side, was parked across a street leading to the square.[82] Demonstrators waved Russian tricolours and Yeltsin's portraits.[83] Leaflets fluttered down on to the square from the Moskva Hotel, where many Russian Deputies lived.[84] Crowds of hecklers surrounded tanks, 'lecturing [the soldiers] on the nature of democracy'.[85] Tanks roared to within inches of the trolleys filled with protesters,[86] but no one moved, and the tanks stopped.

As that rainy day wore on, the heart of the resistance shifted from the Mossovet and Manezhnaya to the White House. By the early afternoon indignant crowds had gathered on the Kalininskiy Bridge over the Moskva river.[87] In front of a barricade next to the Ukraina Hotel, directly across the water from the White House, stood women holding a long banner: 'Soldiers, do not shoot at your mothers and sisters'.[88] When two military trucks with sixty soldiers inside tried to crash through the Kalininskiy Prospekt barricade, people threw themselves on the vehicles and tried to break their windows. An officer fired in the air. The crowd did not move. The trucks turned back.[89]

If one climbed over the barricade on the Kalininskiy Bridge or over the overturned trucks and benches[90] that blocked the roads leading to the White House, one could see feverish construction activity. A bull-dozer and a crane were heaving concrete slabs and heavy pipes.[91] *Khuntu na khuy* ('Fuck the junta') was written on one such pipe.[92] Trucks were dragging over more concrete plates. Youths were carrying metal railings, overturned park benches and armature from nearby building sites.[93] Middle-aged academics and office workers carried scaffolding poles and boards, which together with the iron railings from the fence around the White House made the barricades look like an 'ancient phalanx of spears'.[94] All the entrances to the building were already blocked by several dozen trucks and buses.[95]

By mid-morning four tanks had gone over to the Supreme Soviet's side and their crews instantly became everyone's favourites.[96] As 'objects of intense popular adulation',[97] the crew members were constantly fed sandwiches and given hot tea.[98] The tanks were adorned with flowers. Long-haired teenagers from the Anarchist Youth Movement (Russian *gavroches*, as the banned Echo of Moscow radio station called them) guarded the crews from curious visitors and brought them tea.[99]

In the evening of 19 August, a Russian television reporter approached a group of men carrying a Russian tricolour:

– I understand you'll be here at night as well?

– Of course we will, no doubt about it.

– Have you brought some bread?

– Never mind, we will get by without bread.

– Yes, we will get by without bread.

– How did you find out you needed to gather here and build the barricades?

– I was working today, I work at the ZIL plant, and my heart simply prompted me to come here. I went to Manezhnaya [Square] and then came here with the crowd. And I will stay overnight.

– Here is where the legitimate authorities that we elected are. So we do have something to defend.[100]

*

On the second and decisive day of the coup, 20 August, rallies were held outside the White House. Yeltsin was to address the crowd from the balcony but, because of concern for snipers, his speech was first cancelled, then delayed until three o'clock in the afternoon.[101] Eventually, he appeared surrounded by bodyguards holding bullet-proof shields. Once during the speech, an armed militiaman suddenly jumped in front of the President and pointed at what he claimed was a sniper on the upper floor of a nearby building.[102]

Yeltsin was very brief. He vowed to remain in the White House 'as long as necessary' to 'block this junta from power and to bring it to justice'.[103] He called for a boycott of all the Committee's orders, and promised that democracy would be victorious and that 'The junta shall not pass.'[104] 'I ask you to remain calm,' Yeltsin concluded, 'and to avoid provoking the Army.'

An endless stream of speakers waited for their turn at the balcony microphones: People's Deputies (both of Russia and of the USSR); former Foreign Minister Eduard Shevardnadze, who had resigned in December 1990 warning of a dictatorship; democratic activists, leading writers, actors, musicians, cinematographers. Poet Evgeniy Evtushenko read his poem '19 August': 'No, Russia will not kneel again for ages to come. / Standing with us are Pushkin, Tolstoy. / Standing with us is the entire awakened [Russian] people. / And the marble [building of the] Russian parliament, like a wounded swan of freedom / Shielded by people, is swimming into eternity.'[105] A popular comedian, Gennadiy Khazanov, impersonated Yanaev, whose shaking hands at the nationally televised Committee's press conference the day before had made him a national joke.[106] Undeterred by incessant drizzle and rumours of imminent assault, the crowd – estimated to number from 'tens of thousands'[107] to between 100,000 and 150,000[108] – erupted in laughter.[109]

For Yeltsin, the most precious visitor was Mstislav Rostropovich. The great cellist, who had come to attend the Congress of Compatriots, which brought to Moscow several thousand prominent émigrés, slipped away from his hotel, came to the White House, said he wanted to join the defenders and asked for a Kalashnikov. His speech was the shortest. 'I love you,' he told the sea of umbrellas below. 'And I am proud of you.'[110]

To the former Party functionary now at war to the finish with his ex-comrades, the presence of Rostropovich was an invaluable gift. 'Rostropovich was a special magic, special face,' Yeltsin later recalled. 'I suddenly understood that I was being blessed by the old Russia, the great Russia. That I was being blessed by the highest art . . .'[111] Until then, every minute of uncertainty, of expectation of mortal danger, physical pain, arrest, death had weighed down on Yeltsin 'like a thousand-kilo barbell'.[112] Rostropovich came – and for a short while 'gone was this oppressive atmosphere', gone was everything inconsequential, and 'everything assumed its proper place and perspective'.[113]

Yet not even Rostropovich's 'magic' could stop the world for long. By the afternoon of 20 August, rumours of an assault had grown more persistent and were soon corroborated by dozens of reports from the streets. Tanks and soldiers were moving towards the White House. When Radio Moscow broadcast the order of the military commandant of Moscow, Colonel-General Nikolay Kalinin, instituting a curfew from eleven o'clock that night till five in the morning, there could be only one interpretation to those in and around the White House: preparing to storm the White House, the GKChP was trying to scare off the defenders who were preparing to camp out all night in front of the building.

Yeltsin's clandestine supporters inside the KGB called the White House to warn of an attack.[114] Gas masks were distributed inside the White House.[115] Through the public-address system women were ordered to leave the building and the square. (Very few complied.) The second White House night, which Yeltsin's bodyguard would call 'the most terrifying' of the three he spent there,[116] was now upon them.

After it was all over, Yeltsin learned of what was to happen that night. Special machines would clear a passage through the barricades.*

---

* Such machines were indeed spotted on Moscow streets and were identified by *Jane's Intelligence Review* (vol. 3, no. 10, October 1991, p. 446) as 'IRM obstacle-clearing machines'.

Three tank companies were to inflict shell-shock on the defenders by blasts from their cannons. OMON units would then hack a corridor through the crowd, and the elite *spetsnaz* commandos from the Alfa* regiment would approach the building, fire grenade launchers to knock out the doors and push their way to Yeltsin's office on the fifth floor. A helicopter gunship squad would support the attack from above.[117]

Anticipating such a scenario (and arrest, injury or death), Yeltsin had already dispatched to Sverdlovsk a group of Russian officials, headed by his Obkom subordinate and now First Deputy Prime Minister of Russia, Oleg Lobov. As described in a decree, issued on 19 August, their task was to manage the Russian economy and 'ensure the effective functioning of the main state structures'.[118] In fact, as Yeltsin later told Russian Deputies, they were there to 'organize democratic resistance in Russia'[119] if the President and the government had been 'seized and removed'.[120]† Yeltsin also sent the Foreign Minister of Russia, Andrey Kozyrev, to Paris to proclaim a government in exile, if necessary.[121]

A reception room in Yeltsin's office was barricaded with safes, chairs and desks. When the President made himself take half-hour naps, a guard with a Kalashnikov was posted in front of the office, while Yeltsin slept elsewhere in some tiny room about which only a few people knew.[122] Yeltsin spent the first night in the room of the Supreme Soviet's physician: its windows overlooked an inner courtyard unoccupied by troops and the danger from a bullet or shell fragment was thus somewhat mitigated.[123]

That night, Russia's Prime Minister, Ivan Silaev, came to see Yeltsin. 'Forgive me, Boris Nikolaevich, but I am going home. I want to be with my family tonight.'[124] Yeltsin thought he read in Silaev's eyes: 'I am an old man.‡ Defeat is inevitable. I want to see my wife and children for the last time.'[125] After Silaev had left, Yeltsin looked out of the window through a crack in the metal blind, installed to protect him from bullets. On the square below he saw people around bonfires, lines of armoured

---

* Crack units originally designed for anti-terrorist operations and riot control, they had been used against the Afghan guerrillas between 1980 and 1989.

† A 'reserve headquarters' was set up seventy kilometres from Sverdlovsk in a forest bunker equipped with teletype and telegraph. On the evening of 21 August, an underground radio station was to begin national broadcasts from there. (S. Razin, 'Sverdlovsk, 20 avgusta: tenevoy kabinet v lesu' ('Sverdlovsk, 20 August: a shadow cabinet in the woods'), *Komsomol'skaya Pravda*, 27 August 1991, p. 1.)

‡ Silaev was sixty-one, only a year older than Yeltsin, who considered his coevals 'old' (especially those in retirement or in retreat), but never himself.

personnel carriers bumper to bumper, and 'tanks, tanks, tanks'. He 'unbearably' wanted to see Naina and the girls.[126]

Pasted on the walls of the Metro stations, handwritten news bulletins announced: 'Yeltsin calls everyone to a vigil at the White House!'[127] In the passageway of the Belorusskaya Metro station, three boys stood holding a piece of paper: 'All to the defence of the White House!' 'Please! Please!' they begged passers-by.[128] In the afternoon, at the Barrikadnaya Metro station, the one nearest to the White House, a man with a megaphone walked up and down the platform announcing that an attack on the parliament was planned for eight o'clock that evening and urging everyone to go there. Huge crowds were pouring out of the station towards the White House. Those trickling in the opposite direction were exhorted by a woman. 'People,' she cried, 'turn round! You are needed to defend the parliament.'[129]

The brightly lit square around the White House was dotted with bonfires and makeshift tents erected to keep out the rain. Young men and women sat around the fires and on the barricades playing guitars and singing.[130] A premonition of real danger was in the air, but so too festive exhilaration. The would-be defenders were at once alert and relaxed: they were among friends.[131]

As the night wore on, rumours of an attack became more persistent and plausible, and the sense of imminent peril stronger. Those who stood for hours, arms locked together,[132] in heavy rain, in thirty-five or forty human rings[133] around the White House, became more 'anxious' and 'agitated'. Every few minutes they were jolted by 'frenetic and contradictory' announcements of attacks contemplated, postponed and renewed.[134] The number of people at the White House on the night of 20 August was estimated at 50,000,[135] 60,000,[136] 'no fewer that 70,000'[137] and 100,000.[138]

One of them was a woman of about sixty. Shy, quiet and sweet-natured, she reminded a Russian journalist of her own mother.[139] She said she had never gone to meetings or demonstrations before. 'But my heart said this: a black moment has come, go and stand there till victory or die with everyone.'[140] She lived outside Moscow and had come in on the train, leaving behind her husband of thirty-two years, her daughter and her grandson.[141]

Late in the evening of 20 August, General Konstantin Kobetz, whom Yeltsin had just appointed Minister of Russia's non-existent Ministry of Defence, told about a hundred Supreme Soviet Deputies huddled round him that an assault was now definitely set for one o'clock in the morning.[142] Around 300 armed militiamen and soldiers who had sided with the defenders and 300 civilian veterans of the Afghan war were prepared to defend Yeltsin.[143]

Shortly after eleven o'clock, forty tanks were reported to be moving towards the first chain of people.[144] Broadcasting from the White House, Radio Rossii reported that the tanks had broken through several barricades.[145] Inside the building, the public-address system announced that fifteen BMPs had crashed through the outer ring of the defences.[146] Shots rang out near by.[147]

In the underpass on Chaikovskogo Street, where the Garden Ring crossed Novyi Arbat next to the US embassy, three armoured vehicles attempted to push through barricades on the way to the White House. They were stopped by the obstructions and bombed with Molotov cocktails. A young man jumped on to one BMP and opened the hatch to talk to the crew.[148] He was shot from inside and fell backwards, his body hanging from the vehicle's roof. Two other youths rushed to drag him off. They, too, were shot to death and run over.[149] When he heard the shots and the cries, the chief of Yeltsin's bodyguards, Aleksandr Korzhakov, assumed that the assault had finally begun and decided he could not wait any longer. His first responsibility was to save Yeltsin's life. The time had come to evacuate the President.

All sorts of escape schemes had been considered by Yeltsin's security detail. In one Yeltsin was to be taken through the elaborate network of tunnels under the building and led out through a manhole somewhere near the Ukraina Hotel. Disguised by a toupée, moustache and beard, borrowed from the fashionable Taganka Theatre, he would then be whisked from Moscow in a car.[150] (Mercifully, they did not tell Yeltsin about this plan at the time.) But the 'embassy plan' was by far the simplest and most reliable.[151] The back entrance to the new US embassy was across the street, about 200 metres from the White House. The Americans had offered Yeltsin asylum if the worst came to the worst.[152] It was there that Korzhakov was now about to take his charge.

Yeltsin had just fallen asleep when Korzhakov came into the 'secret room'. Still groggy with tiredness, Yeltsin went down in a lift to the garage in the basement and got into the limousine next to Korzhakov. Korzhakov ordered the gate open.

'Wait, where are we going?' Yeltsin asked.

'To the American embassy. Two hundred metres, and we are safe.'

'What embassy!' Yeltsin exclaimed.

'Boris Nikolaevich,' Korzhakov said, 'I reported to you yesterday that we only have two options: either the embassy or the White House basement.'

'No embassy. Let's go back!'

'But you yourself agreed to accept the Americans' offer,' pleaded Korzhakov. 'They are waiting for us. The barricade [in front of the garage gate] has already been dismantled!'

'We are going back,' Yeltsin said.[153]

They went back up in the lift. Yeltsin marched into his office. 'Boris Nikolaevich,' begged Korzhakov, 'can you at least go down into the basement? I must save you. I don't know what is going to happen . . . Your life is more important than all ours.'[154] The bodyguard was loudly supported by women from the President's Secretariat who were busily packing documents, computers, typewriters, paper for a long stay underground. Suddenly Yeltsin said: 'Let's go.'

Built, like all top Soviet government installations, to withstand a nuclear strike, the House of Soviets boasted a very substantial basement. Scouted by Korzhakov beforehand, it was deep, dry, spacious and well lit, it contained supplies of food and water and it could be hermetically sealed by a huge gate.[155] Metal stairs led to escape tunnels and hidden exits above ground and in the Metro.

After several hours in the basement, Yeltsin decided to go back upstairs.[156] The White House radio station was appealing for help: 'Fellow countrymen, Muscovites! The Defence Headquarters of the Russian Supreme Soviet requests that you come to the Supreme Soviet building on the Krasnopresnenskaya Embankment to defend Boris Nikolaevich Yeltsin . . . lawfully elected by the people.'[157]

Soon after six in the morning on 21 August, the drizzle which had been falling all night turned into a downpour. Wet to the bone, the people who had spent the night in front of the White House were preparing to go home. Suddenly, those who had been on their way to the Metro were running back shouting: 'Tanki! Tanki!'[158] As they had done so many times in the last ten hours, the people calmly took their places in the rows around the building and linked arms. The bearers of the bad news, those who a minute ago had been on their way to home and safety, joined their comrades.[159]

But the alarming noise did not come from tanks. It was made by two trucks that were bringing bread to the defenders.[160] This was the last of the tank alerts. And even as Radio Rossii was pleading for assistance; even as national radio and television continued to transmit the Committee's decrees and appeals; even as Yeltsin warned that the danger was not yet past; and even as tens of thousands[161] gathered at the White

House again that night fearing an attack by KGB commandos[162] – the putsch was unravelling. On the order of Dmitriy Yazov, troops began to leave Moscow to cheers and applause from the crowds. Shortly after midnight, on 22 August, Gorbachev was brought back to Moscow on a plane sent by the Russian government.

Long before that, on the morning of 21 August, following the tank alarm, a cry spread across the square: 'Get a doctor! Get a doctor! A woman is giving birth!' 'That's good!' a voice said. 'Someone is being born in freedom.'[163]

Although the revolution was only beginning, fates far more important than those of the hapless putschists* were sealed or revealed on 21 and 22 August.

The first casualty was Mikhail Gorbachev. Even under the best of circumstances, short of actual removal from power, nothing damages a political leader more than being saved by someone else. A cartoon in the US weekly *New Republic* that showed a tiny, limp and dripping Gorbachev held up by the scruff of his neck by Yeltsin conveyed that brutal truth. The Soviet President, furthermore, was perceived by those who had saved him as at least partly responsible for the calamity. Every one of the putschists was one of his top Ministers, and six of the eight members of the GKChP had been appointed to office by him personally. He had continued to trust and support them despite their public statements which, in the months leading up to the coup, had grown increasingly brazen in their condemnation of perestroika and Gorbachev personally.† His 'fierce defence' of Yanaev's candidacy for Vice President (after the future coup leader had been voted down by the all-Union Congress of People's Deputies) was recalled over and over again.[164] Everyone knew who Yanaev was: 'a good old Komsomol boy, a heavy

---

* All of the Committee members (with the exception of Boris Pugo, who committed suicide) surrendered and were arrested on 22 August.

† One instance was especially fresh in everyone's mind. On 17 June, Prime Minister Valentin Pavlov had requested that the USSR Congress of People's Deputies enhance his power at the expense of the President's. Yazov, Pugo and Kryuchkov testified in support of Pavlov and assailed the reforms. With what turned out to be the last effective speech of his career, Gorbachev won the day and defeated the 'constitutional *coup d'état*'. Not only did the President not discipline the culprits but he called on the pro-reform Deputies not to get 'hysterical': the conservatives did not 'worry' him. (Dawn Mann, 'An Abortive Constitutional Coup d'Etat?', *Report on the USSR*, 5 July 1991, pp. 1–6.)

Столица!
Твоей перестройке
цена грош,
коль ЕЛЬЦИНА
НЕ ИЗБЕРЕШЬ!

A Yeltsin campaign leaflet: 'The Capital! Your perestroika is worth nothing, if you don't elect Yeltsin!'

The Soviet Union's First Couple entering a polling station, 26 March 1989.

At the First Congress of People's Deputies of the USSR.

Campaigning for a seat in the Congress of People's Deputies of Russia in Sverdlovsk, February 1990.

On a trip across Russia after his election as Chairman of the Supreme Soviet: at the Kamaz auto plant in Tatarstan on 8 August 1990.

Russian pop art, 1990: 'Hammer-and-sickle' at the anniversary of the October revolution demonstration; and 'Socialism with a human face'.

'THE COUNTRY IS TIRED OF WAITING.'

'Muscovites! Protect Yeltsin! Defend democracy!' A Democratic Russia leaflet calling for a demonstration on 28 March 1991.

Congratulations from Gorbachev at the inauguration, 10 July 1991.

Top left: Tanks enter Moscow on the morning of the coup.

Top right: Yeltsin's Decree No. 59 – the decisions of GKChP are 'unlawful and without force on the territory of the RSFSR', 19 August 1991, 12.30 p.m.

Below: Delivery of the decree.

21 August 1991: Yeltsin at a victory rally outside the White House.

The Russian tri-colour in Red Square.

'DICTATORSHIP HAS NOT SUCCEEDED! Citizens of Russia and Muscovites have defended the Fatherland.'

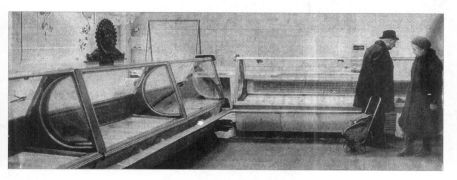

In a Moscow store, autumn 1991.

A bread line, Moscow, November 1991.

Communist demonstrators breaking through police cordons on the way to the White House, 3 October 1993.

The attack on Ostankino television centre, 3 October 1993.

A group of defenders leaves the White House on 4 October.

drinker at government banquets, a henchman of the KGB in the international youth movement'.[165] It was a surprise only to Gorbachev, argued *Izvestia*, that his protégé had 'sold out his credulous protector so quickly'.[166]

Now, those whose dire warnings of 'right-wing' conspiracy and 'conservative opposition' Gorbachev had repeatedly dismissed and mocked; those whom he had mistrusted, kept at arm's length or cast aside – Yakovlev, Shevardnadze, Yeltsin and, with them, pro-reform scholars, columnists and journalists – were at long last vindicated, and furious.

Even before the victory, at a White House rally on 20 August, Shevardnadze went so far as to suggest that, if Gorbachev was found complicit, he ought to be tried with the putschists.[167] Gorbachev had been 'deaf and blind', Shevardnadze wrote later. 'I am convinced', he continued, 'that none other than Gorbachev himself had been spoon-feeding the junta with his indecisiveness, his inclination to back and fill, his fellow-travelling, his poor judgment of people, his indifference towards his true comrades, his distrust of democratic forces and his disbelief in the bulwark whose name is the people . . .'[168] Gorbachev was guilty of 'putting together a team of traitors',[169] said Yakovlev. In front of the Russian Congress of People's Deputies, Russia and the world, Yeltsin, too, gave vent to his ire by forcing Gorbachev to read a protocol of the 19 August USSR Council of Ministers meeting, at which, one after the other, the Ministers had pledged allegiance to the GKChP.[170]

How could he have been so inexplicably, so criminally blind? the democrats wanted to know. Gorbachev had not inherited his aides from Stalin or Brezhnev, *Izvestia* insisted on 23 August. He did not have to contend with what 'God sent' him. He himself had selected them and one would have to try very hard to select a group so uniformly opposed to his course and so readily 'banding together in a group' and uniting against him.[171] These 'dregs' had surrounded Gorbachev for years, 'defiling perestroika with their malodorous aroma of good old communism' – and the President had 'patiently inhaled'.[172]

To the Moscow intelligentsia, the choice between Gorbachev and Yeltsin had never been starker; and, in censuring Gorbachev, they rushed to condemn his Western supporters. 'Human ingratitude is a marvel,' wrote a leading Russian writer Tatyana Tolstaya.

> Yeltsin surrounds himself with democratic forces and people tired of communism. Gorbachev promotes the scoundrels to the highest posts in the land. Yeltsin issues decrees to loosen the deadly grip of the party. Gorbachev issues undemocratic decrees that are simply uncon-

stitutional. The smartest people take Yeltsin's side. Gorbachev's team consists of fools and knaves. Gorbachev falls victim to his own intrigue, casts the country into danger and nearly perishes himself. Yeltsin, in unequal battle with no weapons, wins the day, and saves the life of Gorbachev and his family ... And what is the result, at least in the days immediately following the crisis? The Western media still award laurels to Gorbachev ...[173]

The heavy baggage with which Gorbachev had been burdened even before he flew back to Moscow from Foros was almost instantly compounded by what he said and did – or, rather, did not say and did not do – upon his return. At the denouement of a major political drama, when minutes, let alone hours, were equivalent to days or months of conventional time, he made two of the worst blunders a democratic politician seeking popular redemption after a devastating setback can make: he was slow to thank and he never apologized.

At the White House, tens of thousands of people, who for three days and nights had chanted Gorbachev's name alongside Yeltsin's, were deeply hurt and angered by his unwillingness to come to them immediately after his arrival or even next morning. On that day their mood turned 'quite anti-Gorbachev'.[174] They held a mock election and the majority voted to 'kick Gorbachev out of office as soon as his vacation was over'.[175] In normal politics, Gorbachev's unwillingness to pay homage would have been perfectly correct: this was Yeltsin's territory and Yeltsin's triumph, and Gorbachev did not want to be a bit actor in someone else's victory play. What he failed to see (and what cost him so dearly) was that the laws of normal politics were suspended, that the White House was no longer Yeltsin's territory but Russia's and liberty's, and that the triumph was not Yeltsin's, but the people's.

Usually so agile and artful, Gorbachev seemed to have lost his bearings and his timing. After giving a spirited and, under the circumstances, courageous defence of the Party and of socialism, and after pledging to 'fight to the end for the renewal of the Party',[176] Gorbachev abruptly announced his resignation as Secretary General, called on the Central Committee to dissolve itself and issued a decree ordering the local Soviets to 'take under their protection' the Party's property.[177] He earned the undying hatred of the Russian hard-line left, which felt betrayed, and the disgust of the ascending anti-communist democratic radicals, to whom his conversion appeared belated, reluctant and, ultimately, suspect.

In the end, as with the demise of every truly epochal leader, Gorbachev the politician perished not at men's hands but at history's. The political 'centre' – which had been so vital in securing a gradual and non-violent dismantling of the Soviet totalitarian state and which the General Secretary had so skilfully and stoically defended against both 'left' and 'right' – disappeared. This was a revolution, and in revolutions there is no centre.

The other fatality was the Soviet domestic empire. The main purpose of the coup and the thrust of the GKChP appeal was, without doubt, the preservation of the Soviet Union. The Committee's supporters sensed this immediately. Interviewed on 19 August by one of the permitted newspapers, the Central Committee's *Sel'skaya Zhizn'*, a USSR Supreme Soviet Deputy said of the Committee's goals: 'First and foremost . . . [is] the goal of maintaining a state which was falling apart literally before our eyes . . . Yugoslavia set in its own way a negative example. Reports from that country have shown a state in the process of self-destruction.'[178] A statement by the Central Committee of the Communist Party of Russia decried the 'slide towards a nationwide catastrophe'[179] and insisted that ensuring the 'country's survival' was the main task.[180]

Since the middle of the sixteenth century the Russian state, Russian authoritarianism and the Russian empire had been merged into a trinity as thoroughly fused and inseparable as the original. Empire was incompatible with a liberal Russia. Only a dictatorial Russia could maintain it. In this cursed dilemma, unity and greatness (understood as dominance over other peoples and possession of their lands) were paid for with freedom.

Until then, Russia had invariably opted for the empire. When, on 21 August 1968 Russian tanks crushed the Prague Spring, only the intelligentsia seemed to mourn yet another victory of the empire over liberty. Twenty-three years later to the day, for the first time in their history, hundreds of thousands of Russians chose liberty over the empire. The last, desperate call to save the latter went unheeded. In a resounding confirmation of their response to the January 1990 Baku riots, Russians, in effect, promulgated a nationhood separate from the empire. On 21 August the Soviet Union was finished.

In the long run, perhaps the most momentous consequence of those three days in August was the emergence of an entirely new political phenomenon that would shape the fundamental parameters of Russian politics for years, perhaps decades. It is this new factor that provided the most plausible answer to the question why the GKChP was defeated

– the question which is considerably more interesting than the facile answers (offered at the time and accepted since) suggested.

True, there was a great deal of incompetence in the entire enterprise. ('Fools', Aleksandr Yakovlev famously called the putschists.)[181] The time and the place were also terribly inopportune: August is not the time to launch Russian coups (in December, January or February both popular mood and weather would have cut the number of protesters considerably), and Moscow – along with St Petersburg and Sverdlovsk (Ekaterinburg) – was, and would remain, Russia's most reform-minded, pro-Yeltsin city. Alas, the GKChP had no choice in either matter: the Union Treaty was to be signed on 20 August and in Russia, as in France, he who controls the capital controls the country.

Yet, while contributing to the fiasco, neither timing nor geography may fully account for the extraordinary speed with which the coup collapsed. The ultimate reason, of course, was uniformity and intensity of resistance. What, then, explained such an opposition?

Again, the answer is far from simple. Portrayed at the time as bloodthirsty Stalinists seeking to return the country to its totalitarian past of gulag, Cold War and propaganda lies, the Committee's members were, of course, nothing of the sort. As their words and, most tellingly, their actions testified, the GKChP's goal was not a totalitarian crackdown. And so – when thousands unexpectedly turned out to defend the White House and when the Army, sensing the popular mood, began to hesitate;[182] when, later, the paratroop Commander-in-Chief, General Pavel Grachev, and his deputy, General Aleksandr Lebed (who brought his troops to the White House on 19 August and withdrew them the next day), began to ignore Yazov's orders;[183] and when the Alfa commandos told their commander that they would not storm the White House[184] – not one of the GKChP members proved what Yeltsin called an 'evil genius',[185] who would order the army to kill hundreds, perhaps thousands of defenceless civilians and take full responsibility, as Deng Xiaoping had done two years before.

Nor were they communist fanatics. There was not a word about the Communist Party or even socialism in the plotters' statements. They did, indeed, want to turn the clock back: not to 1937 (the height of Stalin's Great Purge) but to 1988: to glasnost without disorder, crime and 'immorality'; to 'market socialism' before it had been discredited by a spiralling economic crisis and cruel shortages brought about by half-hearted, incompetent and overstretched 'reform'; to privatization without inequality of wealth; and, most importantly, to 'sovereignty' for the Republics without a threat to the Union.

Those might have been fantastic dreams, yet over the next several years tens of millions of Russians would vote in free elections, national and local, for parties that promised much the same: order and security in the chaos of a fledgling democracy; equality and dignity in the ruthless 'primary accumulation' of a first, crude approximation to capitalism; and, some sort of consolation for the dramatic diminution of international prestige, of which the GKChP warned and which, indeed, came to pass with the demise of the Soviet Union.

Although seventy-two hours are hardly long enough for a definitive conclusion, the response to Yeltsin's call for a general strike indicated that Russia's silent majority agreed with at least some items on the Committee's agenda. Except for the traditionally radical miners of Kuzbass and Vorkuta and the just as habitually loyal workers of Sverdlovsk (nearly 500 enterprises and mines in Sverdlovsk and the Sverdlovsk region went on strike on 21 August),[186] very few enterprises went on strike, even in Moscow.

Yet revolutions are never decided by the whole people: sizeable and determined minorities are enough. In Russia they were tens of thousands who stood in front of the White House, 200,000 demonstrators in Palace Square in Leningrad, 100,000 in 1905 Square in Sverdlovsk[187] and several hundred thousand protesters in other Russian cities. What they rejected was not so much the message as the messenger; not the substance, but the form. Politically active Russians in the country's largest cities rejected the indignity of forced choice. 'We had no sausage but at least we had hope and freedom,' a woman was overheard shouting at OMON troops on Manezhnaya Square.[188] 'What do they take us for? They are treating us like swine. They think they can just shut us up again, cut us off from the world and from each other,' was the angry refrain.[189] 'These monsters! They have always thought they could do anything to us!' exclaimed a fifty-five-year-old woman. 'They have thrown out Gorbachev and now they are threatening a government I helped elect.'[190]

Brought to life by a few short years of glasnost, Russian civil society made a first step towards recovering the dignity that had been buried by three-quarters of a century of fear. No longer an angry mob – degraded by censorship, radio jamming and propaganda lies, victimized by terror in the past and fear in the present, humiliated by hours of queuing, hardened by daily battles for a seat on buses, half a kilo of sausage, a pair of tights or rotting fruit – they linked arms, literally, and suddenly became a community of citizens. In the words of one of them, they 'realized themselves as human beings whose point of view can be changed by the power of persuasion, but not by the persuasion of power'.[191]

They, who used to cower before the tantrums of petty bureaucrats and meekly submit to the barked orders and taunts of sales-clerks, suddenly found themselves standing together in the path of moving tanks and staring down paratroopers and black-uniformed OMON. The White House defenders were 'completely indifferent' to their own fate,[192] a witness recalled. When they heard bursts of machine-gun fire from Kalininskiy Prospekt in the early morning of 21 August, there was a pause and then 'thundering' chants of 'Po-zor!' ('Shame!') and 'Ros-si-ya!' ('Russia!').[193] And then many started running in the direction of the shots.[194] They seemed to be instilled with a quiet but desperate determination not to let their self-respect be violated again. 'I am ready to die here, right on this spot,' declared a woman standing in the middle of Kutuzovskiy Prospekt. 'For years nothing but obedience and inertia was pounded into my brain . . . I will ignore the curfew. I'll let a tank roll over me if I have to.'[195]

Out of this resolve was born perhaps the most dramatic non-violent assertion of Russian civil society's sovereignty and power in the nation's history. 'I saw that we were not hopeless, no matter what they do to us,' the Chairwoman of the Sverdlovsk Public Committee for the Defence of the Lawful Authority and Constitution of the RSFSR told those who gathered on the central square of Sverdlovsk in the afternoon of 21 August.[196] 'This was the day I found my "narod" – my people and nation,' remembered a participant in the White House defence. 'For the first time in my life I felt one with those around me and my government [of the Russian Federation]. It was a wholly amazing feeling, completely new and unfamiliar to me, of citizenhood and civic pride.'[197] A triumphant headline in Komsomol'skaya Pravda declared: 'We are alive. We have not perished in queues.'[198] 'We are people, aren't we?' a defender explained to a Russian reporter. 'We are people.'[199] The people's words, overheard on the square in front of the White House, sounded like a poem of 'self-liberation': 'I stood up to them for the first time,' 'Now I can look my grandchildren in the eye,' 'I can finally breathe.'[200]

Foreign witnesses recall a near-magic transformation in those who came to shield the White House with their bodies. The crowd near the White House was unusually polite and considerate, even friendly.[201] Suddenly, they showed one another 'surprising kindness and cordiality',[202] sharing with strangers hot kompot[203] (a sweetish drink of boiled fruit) and the 'last sips' of hot tea.[204] Men warming up near bonfires jumped up to let women take their places.[205] There was a 'feeling of kinship with and constantly re-emphasized mutual respect among the people'.[206] In an endless stream, Muscovites carried to the White House precious food from their meagre rations, acquired in the long queues, and even more precious cigarettes.[207] Russian entrepreneurs set up field kitchens and buffets on the square and would not charge a kopeck.[208]

Amazingly for a Russian crowd of that size, there were no rows, no fights and no drunks. In front of the White House on 20 August, not a single person was reported to be even slightly tipsy.[209] Among the hundreds of thousands of demonstrators he saw in those three days, a Westerner spotted only one drunk.[210] For the first time a frequent American visitor to Moscow felt 'at ease' in a Russian crowd.[211]

Until then, except for brief and violent interludes before another dictatorship consolidated and enslaved them anew, the Russian people's participation in politics had been limited to supplying generously only two categories of actors: victims and executioners. 'Narod bezmolvstvuet' was Pushkin's last line in *Boris Godunov*, 'The people are silent.' After August 1991, they were silent no more. In those three days, a Russian participant wrote, 'the moral foundation of the resistance' to all other such coups was firmly laid.[212]

It is clear now that the scale of the accomplishment was grander: those were moral foundations of a different political order. If not yet democratic, Russia emerged from the coup already post-authoritarian. In the years that followed, no matter how desperate were their circumstances, now matter how angry were they with the powers that be, a majority of Russians would reject, over and over again, programmes, movements and politicians that they identified with political or economic dictatorship.

By instinct, courage and luck Yeltsin again found himself at the centre of the popular revolt against the totalitarian state, and gave it, as he had since 1989, focus and expression. Yet victory was the people's far more than his; it was a victory for liberty far more than for Yeltsin and his agenda. With the perspicuity and political tact which, at his best, he always possessed and displayed, Yeltsin discerned the difference and made sure that people knew that he did.

Never more humble publicly than at this moment of his greatest political triumph, he understood only too well who and what was responsible for the GKChP's failure. 'A malicious attempt was made to smother freedom and democracy,' he told the enormous crowd that gathered for the victory rally at the White House on 22 August.

Your weapon was the enormous will to defend the ideals of freedom, democracy and human worth . . . It has again been shown how great are the powers of the people. The political course of Russia, the honour and virtue of its highest bodies of authority, of its leadership were defended by unarmed, peaceful citizens . . . The forces which organized [the coup] are historically doomed, and first and foremost because the people have already made their choice and do not intend to reject it. The people have already freed themselves from the fear of some years ago.'[213]

When Gorbachev wanted to award him the Soviet Union's highest award, the gold medal of the Hero of the Soviet Union, for his role in the resistance, Yeltsin refused the honour. 'Yeltsin categorically rejected this, believing that victory over the putsch was the victory of the people,' Russian television reported. 'The heroes are those who were on the barricades.'[214]

In those three days the emergent new Russia acquired some of the essential elements of a new polity: heroes (Yeltsin and the White House defenders); symbols (Yeltsin, the White House and the tricolour, which, at the victory rally on 22 August, Yeltsin declared the 'state flag of Russia');[215] and, of course, a glorious victory.

It also now had the martyrs. For the next few days, until the burned and smashed hulls of the trolleys were dragged off the street and blood washed off, the twenty metres of highway under the Garden Ring were a shrine to the three young men – Dmitriy Komar', Ilya Krichevskiy and Vladimir Usov – who died in the early morning of 21 August trying to stop a BMP from breaking through the barricade. The black skeletons of the trolleys were laden with flowers,[216] and the dark-brown patches of blood were framed by offerings: icons, fruits, bread, chocolate, cigarettes.[217] People squatted to scribble a note of thanks or, in Russian tradition, a poem. One such message, torn from a ringed notepad and partly smeared by rain, was written in Chinese but signed in Russian: 'From a participant of Tiananmen, June 1989.'[218]

Three days later at least a million people lined the streets of Moscow or marched from Manezhnaya Square to the White House and then to Vagan'kovskoye Cemetery. In hushed voices parents explained to children that these were 'heroes who had defended the White House and freedom'.[219] Almost certainly for the first time on Soviet television, a rabbi read the Kaddish and a prayer shawl was shown on top of the Russian tricolour on the coffin of Ilya Krichevskiy.[220]

They had come 'to bid farewell to our heroes, our defenders and our rescuers', Yeltsin told the enormous throng of mourners on Manezhnaya Square. 'It was our children who rushed to defend the honour of Russia, its freedom, its independence and its democracy . . . I bow to the mothers and fathers of Dimitriy, Volodya and Ilya, and express my deepest condolences to them and all their relatives and those who were close to them. Forgive me, your President, for not being able to defend, to protect your sons.'[221]

Revolutions differ from large riots not solely in the comprehensiveness of their assault (instead of targeting individuals, building or cities, they engulf entire countries, classes and institutions) but also in the balance, absent from riots, between rage and self-containment, condemnation and dedication, obliteration and generation. A successful revolutionary is always the manager of a hurricane.

The uniqueness of the Russian case in August 1991 was the multiplicity of simultaneous hurricanes that Yeltsin was called to manage. The political revolution destroyed the Soviet party-state and required construction of post-communist institutions and laws. The national-liberation uprising led to the collapse of the Soviet domestic empire and to the emergence of post-communist Russia and of new states around it. The state-owned economy was in the final stages of disintegration, and a new economic order had to be quickly forged.

Clear in retrospect, the boundaries between the three revolutions were blurred in the eyes of the actors. To the defeated putschists, the weakening of the Party's power was inseparable from the demise of the Soviet Union, which they wanted to save. Yeltsin, a year later, would choose the first anniversary of the August Revolution to announce the beginning of the privatization of Russian industry.[222] The 'present situation' meant getting on with '[political] freedom, freedom for entrepreneurship . . . [and] freedom for regions', he told Russian television on 25 August – and the three freedoms were indivisible.[223] Consolidating the power that fell in his lap on 21 August, dismantling the Soviet state, ending the empire and launching radical economic reforms were part and parcel of the same process, which Yeltsin called 'decommunization of all aspects of society's life'.[224]

In interviews and press conferences given in the first few weeks after 21 August, Yeltsin enumerated the components of decommunization – the central, most immediate points of his agenda. They were 'democracy, a market economy, the defence of human rights',[225] private property,[226] and a multi-party political system.[227] Decommunization also meant the end of the 'total sway' of an official ideology,[228] and the establishment of a truly open state, in which all 'hindrances to the free coming and going of Russia's citizens abroad' would be persistently dismantled and in which better opportunities for foreigners to visit Russia would be created.[229]

For Yeltsin a key attraction of decommunization was the promise of Russia's return to the 'civilized world', from which the country had been barred since 1917. 'Climbing up the ladder of civilization',[230] he called it; proceeding 'along the civilized path' of other Western nations.[231] Borrowing a page from Gorbachev's 'new political thinking' of 1987, Yeltsin equated decommunization with the restoration and assertion of universal and common human values.[232] He believed that August had marked a watershed. The people had made their 'main choice' and revealed their true aspirations: 'Russia's future linked [to] . . . democracy and freedom'.[233] It was time to show determination and to 'go the whole way' in implementing this choice.[234]

From this interpretation of the August Revolution stemmed the need for a full and consistent decommunization. As long as 'the communist dogma shackled the individual's activities', Yeltsin explained, as long as it 'defined the style' of national institutions, 'as long as it [was] present in the politics and culture', the country would remain sick, and the people's will would remain unfulfilled.[235] 'We should aim to do whatever we can to restructure ourselves in a fundamental way,' Yeltsin said on 7 September, 'so that we can follow a civilized road.' 'Ourselves', he added, included himself.[236]

Quite unexpectedly, what ought to have been the most painful, complicated and dangerous aspect of decommunization – the political revolution – proved easiest to manage. Hollowed by two years of glasnost, the party-state and its ideological foundations crumbled within days. Devoid of terror or repression of any sort, the Russian 'velvet revolution' was self-restrained even in the realm of symbols.

One of the few exceptions occurred around nine o'clock in the evening of 22 August. Several thousand people gathered on the Marx Prospekt, arranged themselves in a column several hundred metres long and, chanting 'Yeltsin!', 'Down with the KGB!', 'Down with the KPSS!', marched towards the KGB headquarters on Lubyanka Square,[237] in the centre of which stood the giant bronze statue of the founder of the dreaded secret police, the Cheka, Felix Dzerzhinskiy. Its pedestal already bore inscriptions: 'antichrist', 'bloody executioner' and 'shit in a leather coat'.[238] At first by the light of street lamps and soon by searchlights, young men climbed up the monument to attach steel ropes to the statue's neck and the arms. Soon three cranes arrived, met by approving whistles and general 'jubilation'.[239] Against a sky lit by fireworks ordered by the Moscow City Council, Dzerzhinskiy's statue spent its last hours with ropes hanging down its back.[240] Suddenly the spectators held their breath: the 'bronze colossus' canted to one side and then rose in the air.[241] The statue was lowered on to a long flatbed truck, placed face down and taken away.

Two more statues were removed: those of the first Chairmen of the All-Russian Soviet's Central Executive Committee under Lenin, Yakov Sverdlov, and of the Supreme Soviet under Stalin, Mikhail Kalinin. Several large pieces of pink marble were torn from the Karl Marx monument. A simple wooden cross, inserted in the space made by the removed stones, was inscribed 'In memory of those who died in the struggle against the Soviet totalitarian regime from 1917'.

Apart from this most selective and limited iconoclasm, the revolution was remarkable for its self-restraint, even self-doubt. 'Democracy that becomes anarchy' was judged to be 'just as dangerous as dictatorship'.[242] After seven decades of lawlessness and terror, the victors were suspicious, almost fearful, of spontaneity and obsessed with legality and consensus – lest they relapse into 'neo-Bolshevism'. Moscow's liberal newspapers were filled with injunctions against violence and 'vandalism'. The latter, it was said, was a 'manifestation of slavery',[243] which, together with the 'life of lies and humiliation',[244] they had rejected on 19 August. To indulge 'vandalism' (which became a euphemism for violence of any kind) would mean the ultimate moral victory of the putschists, who had 'thought us slaves'.[245] 'There must not be . . . vengefulness,' Yeltsin said on 25 August. 'Otherwise, we would have to stop respecting ourselves as democrats – we would be going from one extreme to the other. The law, and only the law.'[246]

'STOP! DO NOT ALLOW RANSACKING OF THE KGB BUILDING!' Mossovet pleaded in an appeal to 'dear Muscovites' on 23 August.[247] Their 'justified indignation' was acknowledged but it was necessary to 'keep cool heads'.[248] When several thousand people gathered in front of the Central Committee building on Staraya Square on the evening of the 22nd, a leader of the Inter-Regional Group and State Counsellor of Russia Sergey Stankevich and the Chairman of the City Government Yuriy Luzhkov successfully appealed to the people to disperse.[249] Russians should not 'mar the victory of democracy by barbaric and violent actions', Stankevich said at a press conference two days later. 'Those who died defending democracy did not give their lives so that we substitute one kind of lawlessness for another.'[250]

This was a revolution restrained by memory. 'Our people know only too well what revolution is, how great its temptations are and how tragic are the consequences,' Yeltsin was to say on the first anniversary of the attempted coup.[251] He was convinced that a sweeping, unconstrained revolution would have been the 'greatest political error', which would have doomed their country.[252] 'Civil peace' was the most precious thing Russia had.[253]* Decommunization, Yeltsin insisted, did not mean a ban on communist ideology, communist ideas, the works of communist authors or communist newspapers.[254] Most of all, it was not directed against rank-and-file communists.[255]

The dismantling of the triad forming the foundation of the Soviet state – the Party bureaucracy, the secret police and the propaganda machine – was conducted very much in this spirit of caution and wariness of illegality. The few bans were qualified and limited in duration. No organization or party was outlawed – only suspended during investigation and until a court's verdict. On 23 August, Yeltsin 'suspended the activity of organs and organizations' of the Communist Party of the Russian Federation, pending investigation of the Party's 'anticonstitutional activity' during the coup (that is, the Party's support of the GKChP).[256] The Party's final status was to be determined by 'due legal procedure'.[257] The next day, as we have seen, Gorbachev, as the General Secretary, issued a statement calling on the Central Committee of the CPSU to 'make a difficult but honest decision' and dissolve itself.[258] On the same day, as the President of the USSR, Gorbachev decreed that Soviets should take 'under their protection' the property of the Communist Party of the Soviet Union.[259] Despite calls for its removal and burial,[260] Lenin's mummified body continued to lie in the Mausoleum, which retained its employees and continued to receive thousands of visitors every day.

On 29 August, the Congress of People's Deputies of the USSR suspended the CPSU's 'activities' throughout the country. While the Central Committees of both Russia's and the Soviet Union's communist parties obeyed the decrees and disbanded, only a month later several hard-line communist groups – with names like the All-Russian Communist Party of Bolsheviks, Marxist Platform and For the Union of Communists – were openly proclaiming their formation.[261]

---

* 'With one movement of a hand, with one signature', Yeltsin later recalled, he could have turned August 1991 into October 1917 – with pogroms, robbery, anarchy. 'I did not do this,' he wrote. 'And I don't regret [the decision].' To destroy everything, 'Bolshevik-like', was completely outside his plans. (Yeltsin, *Zapiski*, p. 166.)

It took more than two months for Yeltsin to advance from 'suspending' to 'stopping' the activities of the CPSU on Russian territory and of the Communist Party of the Russian Federation, and to order the dissolution of their 'organizational structures' and the transfer of their property to the Russian state.[262] In the same decree, Yeltsin stated that attempts to 'blacken the names of millions of ordinary [CPSU] members' or to subject them to job discrimination were unlawful and ordered local authorities and the procuracies to 'eliminate the possibility' of prosecution of citizens belonging to the CPSU or the Communist Party of the RSFSR.[263]

The following day, the group calling itself the Union of Communists declared its hostility to the 'suppression of political opposition and the establishment of a new dictatorship'.[264] Three weeks later yet another organization, a Communist Workers' Party, held its founding congress in Ekaterinburg and claimed to be the 'formal successor' to the CPSU.[265] At the same time, at a press conference in Moscow, the leader of the Union of Communists said that the country had been on the 'wrong political course since 1987'.[266] The Union's declared objective was to become an umbrella organization of all communist and Marxist groups and to 'restore Soviet power' over the entire territory of the USSR.[267]

After the arrest of the KGB's Vladimir Kryuchkov, the interim head of the service appointed by Gorbachev, he was replaced by Yeltsin's choice, Vadim Bakatin. Several of Kryuchkov's deputies were pensioned off. Yeltsin urged a radical restructuring which would leave intact the intelligence and counter-intelligence operations ('as in other countries') but 'abolish, beyond any shadow of a doubt, the rest of this tale-telling service – surveillance, eavesdropping, informers and so on'.[268] A month later Bakatin shut down the directorate known as the Department for Preservation of the Constitutional Order (formerly the infamous 'Fifth Directorate') that suppressed dissent and spied on Soviet citizens.

The rest of the radical restructuring of the KGB was to await the recommendations of a Supreme Soviet commission, which planned to publish drafts of proposed changes and organize 'round-table discussions' before producing recommendations.[269] The commission, from the outset, declared that it lacked legal authority to punish: that would be left to the courts.[270] The commission even appealed to all Russian citizens not to interpret its formation as the beginning of repression against and prosecution of' KGB employees.[271] 'God save us from repeating 1917!' the commission's chairman said.[272]

Vengeance against the Party propaganda machine was limited to Yeltsin's 22 August decree that temporarily suspended four national communist papers (including *Pravda* and *Sovetskaya Rossia*), and two local ones: *Moskovskaya Pravda* and the newspaper of the Moscow Obkom, *Leninskoye Znamya*.[273] The same decree removed the General Director of the TASS news agency and the Chairman of the Novosti agency. On the 29th, having deplored Yeltsin's decree as 'non-democratic' and 'anti-constitutional', *Pravda*'s journalists re-registered the newspaper with the Ministry of Press and Information: it was no longer the organ of the Central Committee but a private venture of its employees.[274] The paper, which refused to change its name, resumed publication two days later.[275] By the time Yeltsin officially rescinded the suspension on 10 September, all six banned newspapers had already been publishing and selling for days.[276]

Although in seventy-two of the eighty-nine Russian regions the Soviet leadership either openly sided with the putschists or adopted a wait-and-see attitude,[277] Yeltsin retaliated only against twelve Chairmen of Executive Committees of *oblast* Soviets: they were dismissed and their actions were to be 'investigated'.[278]* Not a single local official was arrested.

Finally, the soldiers and officers of the Army and the Ministry of Internal Affairs, whose tanks, machine guns and truncheons were so awesomely deployed by the losing side, were protected against persecution by Yeltsin's 'Statement' of 20 August. In order to 'preclude the escalation of confrontation' and 'avert a civil war', personnel who had been involved in the unlawful activities of the GKChP were not to be held responsible for the coup.[279] The Moscow City Council also appealed to Muscovites to 'show wisdom and composure', to distinguish between the guilty top leadership and their subordinates and to refrain from any provocations against the armed forces.[280]

The seeming ease of the political revolution made the other two crises – imperial and economic – seem far more urgent. To undertake a thorough institutional overhaul at a time of economic collapse would distract from the major task of saving the Russian economy and the Russian state, Yeltsin concluded. At the peak of revolutionary enthusiasm and of his personal popularity, a new legislative election was likely to produce a parliament dominated by his supporters. Still, he rejected

---

* Several times in the next fifteen months, a leader of Democratic Russia, the radical anti-communist and State Councillor Galina Starovoytova urged Yeltsin to dismiss those local leaders who continued to resist his authority and sabotage his decrees. 'No, Galina Vasilievna,' Yeltsin used to reply. 'How will I then be different from the General Secretary?' He believed that, in the end, people would sort things out themselves. (Interview with Galina Starovoytova.)

the dissolution of the Congress of People's Deputies of Russia and early elections urged by radical democrats.[281] He would later call the failure to overhaul the Russian political system his 'greatest missed opportunity'.[282]

He also argued against the election of the 'heads of administrations' (governors), scheduled by the Russian parliament. Gubernatorial election campaigns and conflicts that would inevitably arise between the newly elected governors and the old Soviets would lead to administrative paralysis and would therefore be extremely dangerous at a time of economic crisis.[283] Instead, Yeltsin proposed to hold simultaneous elections of governors and local Soviets in 1992. In the meantime, by the authority granted him by the Congress on 22 August, he would continue to appoint heads of administrations.[284]

The only piece of political engineering Yeltsin adamantly advocated was a new constitution. Adopted within a totalitarian state and designed to 'uphold its horrors', the 1978 Constitution of the RSFSR could not be the foundation of a society whose goal was 'a civilized and democratic society', he declared.[285] No matter how many times amended, such a constitution was an obstacle in the way of radical reforms, Yeltsin told the Congress. An agglomeration of mutually exclusive laws and norms, the current Constitution disoriented people, diminished their trust in the state,[286] and made it more difficult to maintain stability and civil peace 'in a period of fundamental transformations'.[287] 'Dragging out' constitutional reform, in his view, would be a 'great political mistake'.[288] Failing to adopt a new constitution (by a national referendum if necessary) would be tantamount to removing a barrier to 'chaos and disintegration'.[289]

The proposed constitutional reforms Yeltsin chose to emphasize would provide the legal foundation for decommunization. A new Russia, as it emerged from a draft constitution drawn up by the Supreme Soviet's Constitutional Commission and endorsed by Yeltsin, discarded the 'supremacy of ideology' and the notion of violence 'elevated to the rank of a state policy'.[290] The 'de-ideologization' of politics and culture supplied the Constitution's 'anti-doctrinal thrust'.[291] Russia would become 'a modern market economy', in which various forms of ownership would be legal and would enjoy equal protection.[292]

'Legal guarantees against totalitarianism' and barriers against the usurpation and arrogation of power,[293] were to be upheld by separation of powers between the legislative, executive and judicial authorities.[294] Russia would be a Presidential republic, in which the President would have 'a certain independence from the parliament', although under exceptional circumstances the legislature could dismiss the President and other officials.[295]

For Yeltsin, the most remarkable feature of what he called a 'profoundly innovative' constitutional draft was that it placed the people, not the state or a party, at the centre of political and legal institutions.[296] For the first time ever, he declared, Russia was abandoning 'the principle of subordination of a human being to the aims of the state': it was no longer the nation but the human being himself that was most important.[297] The draft Constitution also proclaimed the 'principle of insubordination' of civil society to the 'structures and aims' of the state.[298] Alluding to the cardinal rule of the Soviet state, by which the individual was prohibited everything that was not specifically allowed, Yeltsin extolled another leading principle of the document: a citizen would be permitted everything that had not been banned by law.[299] Human rights would be guaranteed throughout Russia,[300] and observance of human rights was to be the state's main duty.[301]

Yeltsin appealed to the Congress of People's Deputies of Russia to pass any new amendments within the next few months and adopt a final draft of the Constitution. The Congress resolved to 'take notice' of the draft, to send it back to the Constitutional Commission and to task it with bringing forward the text 'for examination' at the next, spring 1992 session of the legislature.[302]

As for the Soviet Union, in the days and weeks following 21 August events seemed to move at several times the normal speed. The cracks in the edifice evident for the past several years suddenly turned into fissures, which widened by the day. Within weeks, consumed by decay, entire segments of the building fell down, one after another, overwhelming Gorbachev's desperate efforts to prop up and to reinforce, until the foundations themselves shook and caved in.

After the putsch had been defeated, the three steel hoops that kept the Union together – the Party, the secret police and the rigidly centralized economy – snapped open. Having in the past few years tasted the power relinquished by the retreating Centre and already accustomed to a great deal of independence, the communist elites in the national Republics saw in the coup a warning that a reactionary regime in Moscow might yet take it all away from them. They hastened to row their boats as far away from the sinking ship as they could, as fast as they could. Declarations of independence followed, prompting some observers to pronounce the Soviet Union dead as early as 30 August.[303] By 10 September, of the former fifteen Republics only three had not yet declared independence: Russia, Kazakhstan and Turkmenia. A month later, only the first two were left.

In his last three months in office, step by desperate step, Gorbachev retreated to positions he thought he could hold but eventually had to give up, settling for progressively smaller and smaller versions of the Centre in an effort to preserve what towards the end became a mostly fictitious Union. In the last demonstration of his famous ability to persuade, with Yeltsin's support (and under the threat of resignation), Gorbachev moved the conservative Congress of People's Deputies of the USSR to adopt, on 5 September, a radically decentralized version of the Union.[304] It was to be a loose confederation, to be called the Union of Sovereign States, although still under one President and with a common parliament. The new country's executive branch would be run by the State Council of the Republics' Presidents. The Congress would disband, and the powerful upper chamber of a new parliament was to consist, like the European Parliament, of delegations from the Republics.

The heads of the Republics and Gorbachev met in Novo-Ogaryovo to agree on the text of a new Union treaty. Yet already the first session was ominous: only ten of the former fifteen Republics were represented, and only four by their heads of state (Yeltsin among them). The rest had sent lesser officials. With every meeting, there were fewer and fewer participants. By the time the signing was agreed for 25 November, only seven of the former Republics remained at the table: Russia, Belarus and the five Central Asian Republics (Kazakhstan, Kyrgyzstan, Uzbekistan, Turkmenistan [formerly Turkmenskaya SSR or Turkmenia] and Tajikistan).* Yet even they, in the end, refused to sign the Treaty, resolving, instead, to subject it to further revisions and discussions in the Republics' Supreme Soviets.

All along, Yeltsin worked relentlessly to stretch the boundaries of Russia's and, by definition, other Republics' competence, and to shrink the Centre's: snatching power where he could, but mostly picking it up as it slipped from the Kremlin, which had been 'stunned into paralysis', as Yeltsin put it.[305] In late October and early November, Russia began a frontal attack, slicing off some Union agencies and assuming the responsibilities of others. About eighty ministries and departments of the Union government were disbanded following Yeltsin's decision to exclude their funding from Russia's contribution to the Union Treasury.[306]

---

* Only these Republics continued to participate in the work of the Union's Supreme Soviet and only they, plus Armenia, signed the Economic Community Treaty on 18 October.

At the end of November, Yeltsin announced that Russia was assuming responsibility for the Union budget for the rest of 1991.[307] The Russian parliament voted to take control of the Soviet State Bank (Gosbank) and the Bank for Foreign Economic Affairs (Vneshekonombank) from 1 January 1992.[308]

Yet Yeltsin's most fateful decision had been made very early in the game, after Estonia and then Latvia – first among the fifteen Union Republics – declared full independence on the night of 20 August and anxiously awaited Russia's response. Of course, Yeltsin's declarations on the Baltic states' independence in 1990 and, especially, in January 1991 seemed to portend to a favourable response. Yet that record, as everyone understood, could be of little use now: Yeltsin's pro-independence rhetoric, no matter how fiery, had been firmly in the realm of fantasy. At the time, the Union seemed destined to exist for years, if not decades. Now that the Union's default had made Russia the guardian of the domestic empire, it was no longer the Centre's but Russia's property that was at stake – not Gorbachev's but, to a larger and larger measure, his, Yeltsin's. This was a true test because it was now in Russia's power to say no. Instead, Yeltsin recognized Estonia and Latvia almost instantaneously – before any other state did. He called on the 'international community', as well as the USSR's President, to recognize Estonia's and Latvia's independence, and within ten days more than forty states did so.[309]

Only several years later could the true dimensions and impact of Yeltsin's act become clear. It was on 24 August, rather than in Belavezh-skaya Pushcha three-and-a-half months later, that Yeltsin sealed the Union's fate. In the words of one of the most sagacious Western observers of Soviet and Russian nationality policies, Yeltsin's decision 'guaranteed that the dissolution of the Soviet Union would be quick', because it 'foreshadowed the notion that the borders of the Union Republics should become the borders of the post-Soviet states'.[310] It meant furthermore that:

> the dissolution process would be peaceful, precisely because independence would result not from struggle or long negotiation but rather from unilateral Russian action . . . In the longer term, Yeltsin's action may have an even greater impact. By righting an historical wrong [the occupation of the Baltic states in 1940], it contributed to the moral renewal of the Russian people, who also suffered under Soviet power. Even more important, it was a significant step in Russia's retreat from empire, which has given many hope that the Russia of

the future may become a country living at peace with its neighbors rather than a cause threatening their existence.[311]

Despite Russia's increasingly aggressive acquisition of the Centre's prerogatives, Yeltsin insisted that he supported a Union of Sovereign States. His only employment of *force majeure* related to Ukraine's membership. 'Until Ukraine signs the [new Union] Treaty, Russia will not sign either,' Yeltsin said before the fateful session of the State Council on 25 November.[312] Yet the probability of Ukraine's joining the Union in any form diminished by the day. Since its declaration of independence on 24 August, Ukraine firmly refused to participate in the 'Novo-Ogaryovo process' and to sign any agreements with the Centre, despite appeals by the State Council initiated by Gorbachev.[313] The Chairman of Ukraine's Supreme Soviet, Leonid Kravchuk, declared again and again that he would 'not take part in ... talks on signing a new Union treaty' and that all suggestions that he intended to join the Treaty were 'nothing but fiction'.[314]

Yeltsin's insistence on Ukraine's centrality was shared by most public figures from Gorbachev to Aleksandr Solzhenitsyn. Yeltsin could not 'conceive' of the Union without Ukraine;[315] the Soviet President could not 'think' of one without Ukraine.[316] 'I cannot imagine it,' Gorbachev said in October.[317] From his exile in Vermont, the author of *Gulag Archipelago* stated that the 'future of the Union would be decided' by the Ukrainian referendum on independence.[318]

On 1 December, 80 per cent of Ukrainian adults went to the polls to respond 'yes' or 'no' to the referendum's question: 'Do you endorse the proclamation of the independence of Ukraine?' By the end of the day, 90 per cent had voted 'yes'. On the same day, Leonid Kravchuk was elected President of Ukraine with 62 per cent of the vote, surpassing the nearest of the other five candidates by almost 40 per cent. On 5 December the Ukrainian parliament, the Rada, voted to nullify the 1922 Union Treaty that had created the USSR.

Gorbachev responded to the Ukrainian vote by issuing an 'appeal to parliamentarians of the Soviet Union', which he read out on Soviet television. Even among the increasingly shrill and desperate personal pleas for help in saving the Union which the Soviet President had authored in the previous three months, this call stood out in its urgency. Begging the remaining Republics not to leave, Gorbachev invoked a 'threat of war' and a 'catastrophe for the world' if the Soviet Union disintegrated.[319]

As it had been with Estonia and Latvia, Russia was the first country to welcome a new Ukrainian state. In a 'Statement' issued on 3 December, Yeltsin 'declared . . . recognition of the independent Ukraine in accordance with the democratic will of its people'.[320] He said he hoped to preserve the traditions of friendship and mutual respect between the two neighbouring nations and called for the 'observance of obligations' in the areas of disarmament, human rights, the rights of national minorities and openness of borders and for the formation of a 'common economic space'.[321] He added that 'the new stage of mutual relations' between Russia and Ukraine necessitated 'a full-scale interstate bilateral treaty' and that 'new possibilities are opening up for . . . forming a genuinely equal community of sovereign states'.[322]

Five days later, in the Belavezhskaya Pushcha hunting resort outside the Belarusian city of Brest, that new community was brought into existence by Yeltsin, Kravchuk and the Chairman of the Supreme Soviet of Belarus Stanislav Shushkevich. The name of the new organization told much of the story: instead of a 'union', as sought by Gorbachev, this was a 'commonwealth'; and instead of 'sovereign', its members were 'independent'. The three states, which together with the Trans-Caucasian Republic (later divided into Armenia, Azerbaijan and Georgia) had been the first members of the Soviet Union in 1922, and which accounted for 80 per cent of the Soviet Union's area, almost three-quarters of its population and the lion's share of its nuclear arsenal,* now declared that the Soviet Union 'was ceasing to exist as a subject of international law and as a geopolitical reality'.[323] Soviet laws were no longer valid on the territory of the Commonwealth.[324]

The Commonwealth of Independent States (Sodruzhestvo Nezavisimykh Gosudarstv, or the SNG) came into being eleven months and one week after the 13 January 1991 press conference in the White House at which Yeltsin had announced that Russia, Ukraine, Byelorussia and Kazakhstan would meet in the capital of Byelorussia, Minsk, to form a new union.[325] Yeltsin did not fail to remind the Supreme Soviet of Russia that 'the main positions and approaches' of the Agreement had been co-ordinated by Belarus, Kazakhstan, Russia and Ukraine a year before when preparations had been made for a four-party agreement.[326]

---

* The only other Soviet Republic with nuclear arms on its territory was Kazakhstan. Invited to Belavezhskaya Pushcha at the last minute, Kazakhstan's cautious President Nursultan Nazarbaev, who was in Moscow at the time, declined to attend, citing his inability to cancel a meeting with Gorbachev.

Although the agreement was not concluded at the time, its 'principles had withstood virtually all the tests of time'.[327]

Signed in Minsk on 8 December,* the two Statements and an Agreement reached in the Pushcha pledged the signatories to respect each other's sovereignty, their inalienable right to self-determination, their territorial integrity and the inviolability of their borders.[328] Belarus, Russia and Ukraine promised to abide by the 'international norms of human and peoples' rights', and to guard the economic, political and cultural rights and liberties of their populations regardless of their ethnicity or citizenship.[329] Their borders were to be open to each other's citizens. The signatories agreed to undertake and to co-ordinate radical economic reforms, to keep the ruble as their currency, to reduce their budget deficits and to control the printing of rubles by their central banks.[330]†

The Commonwealth was to preserve a 'common military–strategic space': the members' nuclear weapons and their armed forces would be under a 'unified military command'. The member states promised to abide by the Soviet Union's international obligations.[331] Membership of the Commonwealth was to be open to 'all state members' of the Soviet Union and could be terminated with a year's notice.[332] Minsk was designated the Commonwealth's capital.

As explained by Yeltsin at the time, Belavezhskaya Pushcha was the Union's last chance to manage disintegration and to salvage anything 'that could be saved'[333] after Ukraine declared its independence. The accords were the only alternative to 'uncontrolled decay'[334] and the only means of preserving stability.[335] Yeltsin emphasized the following aspects as most critical to forestalling a disaster: the permanence and inviolability of existing borders; the placing of nuclear forces under a 'single command' and a 'jointly developed policy on nuclear issues';‡ 'a single

---

* In addition to the three heads of state, the Agreement was signed by Russia's State Secretary Gennadiy Burbulis, Prime Minister of Republic Belarus Vyacheslav Kebich and Prime Minister of Ukraine Vitold Fokin.

† The arrangement proved disastrous for Russia. In large measure, the inflation of 1992 would be brought about by the uncontrolled ruble emission by the central banks of CIS members.

‡ On 10 and 11 December respectively, Gorbachev and Yeltsin had meetings with top military commanders in an effort to secure their support for the Union and the Commonwealth. Yeltsin's case proved more persuasive. (*Facts on File*, vol. 51, no. 2664, 12 December 1991, p. 931; Yeltsin's speech to the Supreme Soviet, 12 December 1991; and his interview with *Trud*, 14 December 1991.)

economic area', the single currency and 'harmonized reforms'; the agreement on nuclear non-proliferation; and open borders between member states.[336] Referring to the brutal internecine conflict between the republics of the former Yugoslavia (a conflict in which some Western and Russian analysts discerned a portent of nuclear war between Russia and Ukraine), Yeltsin was satisfied to note that 'we have avoided the Yugoslav variant'.[337]

Having denounced Belavezhskaya Pushcha as illegitimate, dangerous and likely to 'intensify the chaos and anarchy',[338] Gorbachev added that there were 'positive aspects' to it, especially Ukraine's participation.[339] After the Central Asian Republics had announced their intention to join, Gorbachev declared that the process, which he now found more 'compatible' with the Soviet Constitution, might help to avoid confrontation.[340]

Although, as Yeltsin admitted at the time, he might not have seen the 'entire length of the perspective' before him,[341] beyond the exigencies that had brought the CIS into being there seemed to loom a larger agenda, a deeper purpose and a grander scale. Yeltsin did know, for instance, that by giving up the Soviet domestic empire Russia had 'let go, perhaps for ever', of more than Ukraine and Belarus,[342] more even than the three centuries of imperial conquests. It had renounced a national way of life. By signing the Agreements, Yeltsin wrote, Russia was:

> choosing a different path of development . . . Russia was stepping on a peaceful, democratic, non-imperial path of development. She was choosing a new global strategy. She was rejecting the traditional image as a 'master of half of the world', the armed opposition to the Western civilization, the role of the policeman in the solution of ethnic problems.[343]

Belavezhskaya Pushcha was part of the process of decommunization. When the Russian empire collapsed in 1917, Yeltsin recalled, many of its peoples chose self-determination: in the Caucasus, in Central Asia and, most importantly, Ukraine. 'With iron hand' the Bolsheviks had 'strangled' national liberation, shot the ethnic intelligentsia, outlawed parties.[344] Other empires – British, French, Portuguese – had fallen a long time before, but, sustained by the terror of the party-state, the Soviet one had continued to exist.[345] Of course, an 'empire [was] a powerful thing – fundamental, inspiring trepidation and respect', Yeltsin wrote.[346] But how long could a country maintain an empire? 'The clock of history' was ticking again, Yeltsin concluded, and 'the last hour of the Soviet empire has struck'.[347]

The Soviet Union disappeared in the next three weeks. On 10 December, the Belarusian and Ukrainian parliaments ratified the Belavezhskie Agreements. On the 12th the Supreme Soviet of Russia followed suit: 188 votes in favour, 6 against and 7 abstentions. By a majority the Supreme Soviet also declared null and void the 1922 Treaty that had created the Soviet Union. Nine days later, in the capital of Kazakhstan, Alma-Ata, eight states joined the Commonwealth, which now comprised eleven of the fifteen former Soviet Republics. Apart from the Baltic nations, only Georgia refused to join. At five o'clock in the afternoon of 24 December, the Soviet Union ceased to be a member of the United Nations. Its seat on the Security Council was taken by Russia. In a declaration adopted at its last session on the 26th, the Council of the Republics (the upper chamber of the Soviet Union's Supreme Soviet) pronounced the Soviet Union non-existent. The head of a state that was no more, Mikhail Gorbachev announced his resignation in a brief televised speech on 25 December.

As often happens in history, and as is almost always the case in Russia, the grandeur and solemnity of the drama were marred by the petty passions of the protagonists. The day before Gorbachev's resignation, at what they knew was their last meeting, he and Yeltsin spent hours haggling behind closed doors over the amount of Gorbachev's pension and its indexation for inflation, the size of his apartment, the lifetime use of a state dacha, the number of bodyguards and cars and access to the government communication network.[348] Arguing about rubles and square metres, each spoke, of course, to his own memories of betrayal, humiliation and ingratitude at the hands of the other.*

Yet, although partially obscured by the secondary and the unworthy, the nobility of Gorbachev's last act as Soviet President and Yeltsin's ability to rise, if less than gracefully, to the occasion lent to this parting of the two giants a momentousness that had marked the previous six years of shared effort, bitter conflict and uneasy co-operation: it was a parting that yielded meaning and precedent and changed their country's destiny. For the first time a Russian ruler had resigned. For the first time, by agreement with the victor, his relinquishing of office did not

---

* Gorbachev would later complain of 'impudence and a lack of courtesy' on the part of Yeltsin and blamed Yeltsin's 'feelings of revenge' (Mikhail Gorbachev, *Memoirs*, p. 671).

lead to a loss of honour, or prevent him from earning a (very good) living, travelling and working abroad or participating in his country's politics. In addition to other amenities, Yeltsin gave the private Gorbachev Foundation a large building on Leningradskiy Prospekt, formerly the property of the Academy of Social Sciences.[349] Among other tenants, the building used to house the so-called 'illegals': members of underground communist and leftist parties, groups and movements who came to Moscow to attend the Highest Party School.[350]

'It was important to break a damaging tradition that has long existed in our country,' Yeltsin told the Russian Supreme Soviet on 25 December, when he gave an account of the Alma-Ata summit.

Leaders of the country leave their post and are removed from politics and society, consigned to oblivion and then either reburied after death or vilified ... A decision has been made that will allow Mikhail Sergeevich Gorbachev to continue to play an active role in society after his departure from the post of Union President. A decision on his financial security has also been made by all the members of the Commonwealth.[351]

On the day Gorbachev resigned, Yeltsin was asked by CNN to comment on 'where Gorbachev [had gone] wrong'. Yeltsin mentioned 'the tactics and strategy of perestroika', and then said: 'Today is a difficult day for Mikhail Gorbachev. And because I have a lot of respect for him personally and we were trying to be civilized people and we are trying make [Russia] into a civilized state today, I don't want to focus' on the former General Secretary's mistakes.[352]

On 26 December Yeltsin instructed the Kremlin staff to lower the Soviet Union's red flag and raise the Russian tricolour. He was said to have seen to it personally that the ceremony should be completed on time and be filmed by television cameras.[353] On that occasion, the three revolutions came together again: by the decision of the Russian Supreme Soviet, the words 'Soviet' and 'Socialist' had been taken out of the new country's name. From now on, it was to be called 'Russia' or the 'Russian Federation'.

A week before his resignation Gorbachev mused over the missed opportunity to form a 'strong union' with the 'democrats' against communist hard-liners in the autumn of 1990, instead wasting time and having now to pay dearly for the mistake.[354] If Yeltsin had regrets, he, by contrast, hid them well. Interviewers found him 'feisty' and 'confident'.[355] He was now the elected leader and the most powerful man in the world's youngest superpower: post-Soviet Russia. He had taken Russia away from the Party, away from the Union, and away from Gorbachev. Most of all, from Gorbachev.

At the end of October 1991 the Soviet Union's chief statistical agency, the Goskomstat, had issued a report on the first three quarters of 1991. Even for a nation accustomed to bad economic news, the extent of the crisis that the figures conveyed was shocking. In the previous twelve months the gross domestic product had fallen by 12 per cent and personal consumption by 17 per cent.[356] Retail prices had risen by 203 per cent[357] – that is, they had more than tripled. Production of all four food staples by which Russian households traditionally gauged their well-being had declined precipitously: meat by 12 per cent, milk by 10 per cent, butter by 13 per cent and sugar by 17 per cent.[358] Exports were down by 30 per cent and imports by 45 per cent.[359] Oil exports, the country's largest source of hard-currency revenue, had diminished by half.[360] (On 12 December lack of fuel would make the Soviet state airline Aeroflot cancel most flights throughout the country and close over half of the country's airports.)[361]

In the last three months of 1991 the economy continued to slide towards collapse. Production dropped to 79 per cent of the 1990 level. The budget deficit grew to 30 per cent of gross domestic product. With rubles printed around the clock not only by the USSR State Bank but by the central banks of the other fourteen non-Russian Republics, the currency lost 86 per cent of its value against the dollar.[362] The Soviet state had long ago stolen the bank savings of its citizens and covered the theft by inflating the currency. At the end of October the Vneshekonombank, the sole keeper of the country's hard currency, requested rescheduling of the USSR's external debt and defaulted on hard-currency accounts, totalling $5.4 billion.[363] The country's entire hard-currency reserves were now no more than a minuscule $100 million.[364]

Of course the Russians did not need Goskomstat figures to tell them what their life was like. The diminution of hard-currency exports (and the corresponding decline in imports) was not an abstract figure but a matter of extreme and direct urgency. Even at the best of times, in a country where imports already accounted for more than one-third of all grain for human consumption,[365] such a gap would have been difficult to bridge; with the disastrous shortfall in hard-currency revenues, it could not even be narrowed.

As they had been for the previous two years, the collective farms were reluctant to 'sell' at state-mandated prices denominated in a nearly worthless currency. Now with the harvest 25 per cent lower than the year before (and the worst in fifteen years) and with the near-collapse of authority, the peasants were even slower to bring grain to state elevators. A Russian observer labelled this reluctance an 'unannounced strike of the peasants of all the Republics'.[366] In the week following the failed putsch, deliveries of grain diminished four-fold.[367] By October, of the eighty-five million tonnes necessary for food and animal feed, only thirty-two tonnes had been delivered.[368]

While the Union authorities still could not bring themselves to free food prices by decree, their 'liberation' had in fact occurred by default.[369] Food in state stores was almost twice as expensive as it had been in September 1990. The prices of bread, flower, sugar, meat and sausage had grown between two and a half and three times.[370] A year before, the respondents in a nation-wide survey judged 120 rubles a month their 'subsistence minimum' (and 52 per cent earned less).[371] Now in a new survey the 'minimum' was 328 rubles – and 84 per cent of respondents said they had 'found themselves below the poverty line'.[372]

The perennial saviour of last resort, Russian gold, was almost all gone as well. The Russian government had discovered that between 1989 and 1991 at least 1,000 tonnes of gold had been sold abroad by the Soviet Union, reducing the total gold reserves to an 'unprecedented low' of 290 tonnes.[373] Perhaps for the first time in its history, the Russian state had neither gold nor bread.

Famine was discussed openly and with resignation by experts, decision-makers and ordinary citizens alike.* In November there was a shortage of bread in Moscow for several days[374] – something that had not happened since the end of the Second World War. In the second week of September Gorbachev had sent personal letters to the Chairman of the Group of Seven leading industrial democracies and the heads of state of the European Community asking for up to seven billion dollars to buy over five million tonnes of grain, nearly a million tonnes of meat and sugar, and 350,000 tonnes of butter.[375] A week later the Soviet Union doubled the amount of the loan request for food relief to over fourteen billion dollars.[376]

According to government reports, the following products were sold

---

* Alongside grain, the emptiness of the state Treasury had produced a catastrophic shortage in another essential area: medicine. A year before, Soviet doctors had made do with 70 per cent of the basic drugs, now they had no more than 35 per cent. (See, for example, Eleanor Randolph, 'Soviet Medicine in Dire Straits', *Washington Post*, 18 November 1991, p. A14.)

throughout the country 'mostly' by ration coupons: meat, butter, vegetable oil, macaroni, sugar, salt, matches, tobacco, alcohol and soap.[377] In the Arkhangel'sk region in the north-west, flour was no longer available in retail stores and there were 'interruptions' in the sale of bread.[378] Nizhniy Novgorod in Central Russia was expected by local authorities to run out of grain before the end of the year.[379] In both regions milk was on sale for only one hour a day.[380] In the Perm region west of the Urals, sugar was no longer available even with ration coupons.[381] In Sverdlovsk, arms plants attempted to barter tanks for imported meat, butter and macaroni.[382]

'Stock up on rusks [*sukhari*]!' a popular Moscow daily advised its readers.[383] According to a nation-wide survey, 57 per cent of respondents were stocking up on anything they could find.[384] Of those who were not hoarding, half said they could not get the products and a third did not have the money.[385] A Russian expert estimated that his compatriots spent between forty and sixty-eight hours a month in queues.[386] Even a delivery of pencils caused a riot, in which a policeman attempting to control the crowd was injured.[387] 'The people no longer look for goods,' commented a Moscow television reporter in November. 'They look for queues . . . If you come across a line, join it and count yourself lucky.'[388]

In the autumn of 1991, strategies for surviving winter provided the most common topic of conversation in Moscow. Poets and brain surgeons, nuclear scientists and film directors, ballet dancers and rocket engineers stored sacks of potatoes on the balconies of their apartments. The City Council had allotted plots of land to each resident who wanted to grow potatoes.[389]

A witness left this vignette of Moscow in December 1991: 'Gloomy queues, now even without the usual rows and fights. Virginally empty stores. Women desperately rushing around in search of any food. At the empty Tishinskiy market prices are in dollars. An average monthly salary [is] seven dollars. The universal expectation of catastrophe.'[390]

The decidedly sombre hues of this background distinguished the third component of Yeltsin's decommunization – the economic revolution – from the other two. Unlike the revolt against the party-state and the empire, even at the start there was no jubilation, just quiet and rudderless desperation. Unlike the other two revolutions, this one was launched not into a rising tide, but amid the shallows and fetid waters of the 'command economy', choked with decomposing and toxic debris.

If one could interpret the rejection of the GKChP as a mandate for a post-Party state and a post-imperial Russia, the economic revolution was something on which the August victory had been silent. That revolution thus became a matter of choice – necessitated by a deep crisis, to be sure, yet still a choice to be made by men rather than by events. In the end, after years of debates, recommendations, commissions and resolutions, it was one man's choice that tipped the scales. The economic revolution happened because Yeltsin willed it to happen and managed to persuade those whose support he needed that it should happen.

With the collapse of the putsch, the Centre no longer tied Russia's hands. The political minefield had been cleared, Yeltsin told an interviewer.[391] The time had come, he concluded, to act 'most decisively not just in politics, but in the economy', to proceed vigorously with economic reform.[392] He needed a different government, dynamic, confident and led by an economist with 'his own concept' and 'his own team'.[393]

By the third week of September, Gennadiy Burbulis, State Secretary and, at the time, the second most powerful man in Russia, had gathered a group of economists at a government dacha in Arkhangelskoye.[394] Their task was to develop the strategy and tactics of a Russian economic policy, for the President's 'report on economic issues' to be delivered in October.[395] What they produced was a programme of 'real [economic] liberalism': a radical 'big bang' reform of the kind that Poland had launched twenty months before.[396] The informal leader of the group, which impressed Burbulis by the professional and personal closeness of its members,[397] was the thirty-five-year-old Director of the Institute of Economic Policy, Egor Gaidar, who in the previous few years had published some of the best (and best-written) analytical surveys and forecasts relating to the Soviet economy.[398]

The 'Gaidar team' – who lived and worked at Dacha Number 15 and were all in their twenties and thirties – belonged to a closely knit coterie of Russian scholars with PhDs in economics who had entered the field in the 1970s, when economic research began to offer considerably greater freedom from ideological commissars than the other traditional pursuits of well-connected Russian youth: history, journalism and international relations. In Moscow and Leningrad, a handful of graduate students in the very exclusive economics departments of several leading universities and institutes were allowed to read – but not to copy! – English translations of Friedrich Hayek and books by Milton Friedman (many learned English that way). They wrote doctorates on 'capitalist economies' and 'limited market reforms' (Hungarian or Yugoslav) or, in the case of the thirty-six-year-old Leningrad scholar, Anatoliy Chubais, on ways of improving the 'management of scientific–technical organizations'.

Every now and then the young scholars were asked to submit their heretical proposals 'upstairs', where their papers disappeared without trace – but also with no sanctions against the authors.[399] In the late 1970s and early 1980s these iconoclasts worked under the wing of Dzhermen Gvishiani: the Chairman of the USSR State Committee on Science and Technology, a Georgian bon vivant, pianist, lover of Italy, notorious cynic,[400] and son-in-law of Prime Minister Aleksey Kosygin. Designed to become the Soviet equivalent of the US RAND Corporation – a powerful, multi-disciplinary 'think tank' – Gvishiani's Institute for Systemic Research became a refuge for unorthodox economists.

Almost all of them met for first time in 1986 at a seminar in Zmeinaya Gorka, near Leningrad. At the concluding session, around a campfire, Gaidar offered two scenarios for the future. In one, they became Ministers in a government of radical economic reforms. In the other, he speculated on the length of their prison terms and the size of their labour-camp food rations.[401]

Of all the fateful choices of personnel and agendas that Yeltsin had made and would make, none equalled the choice of Egor Gaidar and his programme in the autumn of 1991: they were to shape Russia's economy, politics and society for years, perhaps decades, to come. Age was a factor, of course: other things being equal, Yeltsin always preferred younger men for government positions.* Himself a fast climber, he was impressed that Gaidar had acquired a doctorate in economics, a directorship at one of the most prestigious institutes and three children – all by 'thirty and bit more' years of age.[402]

Like almost all Russians, Yeltsin knew of Gaidar's family, one of the most famous in the Soviet nobility. Both grandfathers were among the most beloved of children's writers: the Civil War hero Arkadiy Gaidar, with his tales of honesty, courage and kindness, and the only slightly less renowned Pavel Bazhov, the author of Hoffmannesque stories, often dark and sad, of magnificent Ural stonecutters and smelters, their creations animated by superhuman artistic effort. In addition to his scholarly credentials, Yeltsin also trusted Gaidar's 'inherited talent'.[403]

Yeltsin – who became annoyed and sometimes angry when others argued with him and who 'could not stand' it when his mistakes were pointed out to him – more than anything respected independence of

---

* When in the autumn of 1990 Yeltsin considered candidates for Foreign Minister of Russia, both Gorbachev and Eduard Shevardnadze suggested the best career diplomats to him, all in their fifties and sixties: Vorontsov, Adamishin, Petrovskiy. 'I want a Foreign Minister younger than me,' Yeltsin responded. He appointed, instead, Andrey Kozyrev, thirty-nine. (Interview with Ambassador Vladimir Petrovskiy.)

opinion and fearlessness of conviction.[404] He liked aides who were not afraid of him,[405] and might even agree with their 'most unpleasant' arguments.[406] Conversely, he immediately sensed when survival in office at any cost became an official's overriding objective.[407] He might keep such aides on for quite some time (as he did with Foreign Minister Andrey Kozyrev after 1993), but he no longer listened to their opinions and did not hide his contempt.[408] Now that he was about to engineer what he called Russia's 'giant leap into the unknown'[409] and to take full responsibility for the cataclysm, Yeltsin's need for someone who would always tell him the whole truth was especially acute.[410]

In that respect, he could not have chosen better. Behind Egor Gaidar's round face, his quick smile and his indifference to the trappings of power lay an intensity of belief and a confident strength that rendered him unyielding on matters of principle. The young economist, who could be stubborn and tough[411] (the qualities that Yeltsin valued highly),[412] made it clear to the President and to everyone else that he had joined the government to do what he felt was right and necessary for Russia, not to be near the President.[413] He was ready to offer (and, on several occasions in the next fifteen months, did offer) his resignation when he felt the strategy of the reforms was being compromised.

The decisive reason for Gaidar's appointment was the coincidence of his 'scholarly concepts', as Yeltsin put it, with the President's 'resolve' to traverse the roughest, most painful patch of the reforms as quickly as possible: 'the decision has been made – let's go!'[414] Yeltsin wanted 'to make the reforms irreversible',[415] and that was precisely what Gaidar was prepared to do. The heart of Gaidar's programme was a drastic diminution in state ownership of the economy. From a tiny newspaper kiosk to giant machine-building factories, from ice cream to aircraft, the market was to supplant 'the huge hierarchy of functionaries'[416] in allocating resources, in setting prices, in determining the exchange value of the ruble and in regulating imports and exports. To effect this tectonic shift, Gaidar counted on far-reaching liberalization (liberation from state control) through an extensive privatization of the economy, on agrarian reform (which would permit the selling and buying of land), on the opening up of foreign trade and, most of all, on freeing from state control the prices of almost all products, goods and services.[417]

Of the many potential dangers of such a course, the one most often mentioned by critics was freeing prices without first privatizing industry and agriculture and removing monopolies from the heavily concentrated Soviet economy, in which one plant or factory often manufactured a particular product for the entire country or supplied hundreds of factories with one machine part. With shortages and monopolies (which would now be free to charge whatever they wished without improving the quality of their products), price liberalization would fail to bring lower prices or fill stores with food, critics charged, because the programme would fail to produce the central element of capitalism: competition.[418] Instead, free prices would lead to bankruptcy, mass unemployment, economic collapse and the 'poverty of the masses'.[419]

In addition to the absence of privatization and the reign of monopolies, Gaidar himself saw many more institutional and material conditions that hampered and distorted market reform in Russia in the autumn of 1991: the general paralysis of authority, the 'sickly' infrastructure, the absence of a legal foundation.[420] But he felt that the only alternative to an immediate switching on of the market mechanism was chaos and catastrophe.[421] Other vitally necessary structural reforms, the 'details' necessary for the operation of the market, would have to be improvised along the way.[422] Gaidar's equating rapid and deep market reform with the country's survival was the source of the resolve that Yeltsin discerned in Gaidar and found so appealing and reassuring.

If there was one central proviso, the *sine qua non* on which Gaidar predicated the success of the 'shock therapy', it was the implementation of all key elements of the programme simultaneously, as a package. He was especially adamant about what he knew would prove to be most difficult politically: a drastic reduction in the budget deficit and the introduction of a strict monetary policy. The combination of freed prices with an enormous deficit covered by unrestrained printing of rubles would be lethal and result in hyperinflation,[423] Gaidar warned the Supreme Soviet. 'Tough monetary and budgetary policies were the most important thing,' and success (as well as assistance by international financial institutions)* would materialize only 'if we manage to hang on ... if we manage to adhere to tough budgetary guidelines'[424] – that is, to ensure a drastic reduction in the state's spending. (Gaidar began with the military–industrial complex, whose funding he cut a month later by 85 per cent.)[425] Anticipating the key political obstacle that would bedevil the reform, Gaidar said: 'In general, the important thing is that

---

* At the end of November the world's leading industrial democracies agreed to defer payments on the Soviet Union's $70 billion foreign debt (soon to be assumed by Russia) in exchange for the promise of radical economic reform, undertaken in co-operation with and under the guidance of the International Monetary Fund. (See, for instance, Fred Hiatt, 'Soviet Union Wins Reprieve on Debt', *Washington Post*, 22 November 1991, p. A1.)

our policies should be consistent. We must not hesitate, panic or resort once again to administrative methods [of price setting] or to the printing presses.'[426]

To Yeltsin, Gaidar was a physician who proposed to 'rouse our paralysed economy', and to make its vital centres, its resources, indeed the entire body, work.[427] While other doctors argued about the methods of treatment, Gaidar proposed to 'drag the patient off the bed' and force him to walk.[428]

There was a basis for this metaphor in the most recent of Yeltsin's many accidents and injuries: his plane's crash landing in the spring of 1990 in Spain. He had been taken to a hospital in Barcelona with a displaced disc between the third and fourth vertebrae. The pain, Yeltsin recalled, was 'horrible, impossible'.[429] He could not move the lower part of his body. He was told that a flight to Moscow was out of the question: it would be too late then to restore control over his legs. Only an immediate operation could help. Yeltsin agreed.[430]

On the morning after the three-hour operation, he was ordered to get up and walk. Walk? Yeltsin said he 'panicked': in Russia he would have stayed in bed for six months.[431] He looked around for crutches. No crutches, he was told. Get up and walk. Sweating 'from fear and tension', he stood up. Took one step. Then another. Walked to the wall and then back to the bed. After three such attempts he began to walk without fear.[432]

If he could do it, why couldn't Russia?

Yeltsin agreed with the two central premises of Gaidar's plan: that further procrastination would be suicidal and that prices had to be freed straightaway, as the President put it in an interview in mid-October, even before he had met Gaidar.[433]* Yet price liberalization was the kind of decision he had not made before. For the past five years the key to his political triumphs was believing that he knew what most Russians wanted and striving, with maximum visibility, to deliver it: greater openness in the press, the end of privileges and 'social justice', Russian sover-

---

* At their first face-to-face meeting at the end of October, Gaidar found Yeltsin 'fairly well, for a politician, oriented in economic matters'. On 11 December Western experts and advisers gathered in the Kremlin were also pleasantly surprised by Yeltsin's report on the details of the strategy and implementation of 'shock therapy'. Meeting with them immediately after a session on the fate of the Soviet Union and the Commonwealth with top Soviet military commanders, Yeltsin briefed the economists for almost an hour without any notes. (Interview with Anders Åslund.)

eignty, cutting the Party down to size, resisting the putschists. The freeing of prices, which would turn millions of Russians into paupers overnight (no matter how impoverished they had already been made by shortages and by an inflation that had turned their savings into dust), was a break in that pattern: in this case Yeltsin knew Russia needed the reform but he must have been just as certain that most of the people 'could not support' him wholeheartedly, as Gaidar noted.[434] This was Yeltsin's first unpopular decision. (He would confess later that for 'two whole months' he and his advisers had searched for 'more acceptable', 'less onerous' ways to begin the reforms without freeing prices – but could not find one.)[435] For the first time, remarked an astute Russian observer, Yeltsin-the-populist and Yeltsin-the-reformer became adversaries.[436] Such was the drama of the Russian President, and its ending, the commentator continued, would depend not only on his own will and 'unyielding determination' but also on the support he would get from the 'influential public forces' of Russia.[437]

It was to these forces that Yeltsin addressed himself when he unveiled the programme on 28 October at the Congress of People's Deputies of Russia. Broadcast live on radio and television, this was the first ever comprehensive and detailed public elucidation of an impending major reform by a head of the Russian state.

The time of 'small steps' was past, Yeltsin declared. Resorting to deeds, not words, Russians had to begin extricating themselves from the swamp that was pulling them in deeper and deeper. Only a 'large-scale reformist breakthrough' could save Russia's economy from disintegration, its people from poverty, and its state from collapse.[438] Prices would be 'unfrozen'.* This was the hardest measure, but the entire experience of world civilization had shown that fair prices could not be set by the bureaucrat – only by the market.[439]

There would be privatization on a giant scale: in the first three months of 1992 he planned to sell off half of all small and medium enterprises – 10,000 in all, with services and trade privatized first. Subsidies to the enterprises that were to remain the state's property for the time being were to be reduced sharply. The key was quickly to separate enterprises from the state.[440]

The agricultural reforms included privatization of the land and equipment in the possession of loss-making kolkhozes and sovkhozes and the

* First set for mid-November, the price liberalization was twice postponed at the request of Ukraine and Belarus, which begged for time to 'co-ordinate' and 'prepare', and was fixed eventually for 2 January 1992.

right 'at long last' to buy and sell land. The Russian economy would be freed of monopolies, both through the breaking up of large enterprises into competing firms and through further competition with Russian firms yet to emerge and with foreign companies. The state monopoly on currency operations would be abolished and, for the first time in seventy-four years, citizens would be able to buy and sell foreign currencies at points of exchange. Tough fiscal and monetary policies would reduce and, eventually, eliminate the budget deficit and put a stop to the uncontrolled expansion of the money supply.[441]

These were difficult, forced measures, painful in many instances, but necessary. The hardest time, in Yeltsin's estimate, would be the first half-year. He promised 'stabilization' by the autumn of the following year, then a reduction in prices, the saturation of stores with goods and a gradual improvement in people's lives. 'We cannot help everyone,' Yeltsin said, but he promised that there would be soup kitchens and special discount stores for the poor.[442]

'I appeal to you at one of the most critical moments in Russian history,' Yeltsin said. '[I] appeal – determined to conduct deep reforms and seeking support for this determination from all the strata of the population.'[443] He counted on the support and understanding of the people of Russia, something that they had so generously given him in the past.[444] Together the previous August they had defended political freedom; now it was time for economic freedom, freedom for enterprises and entrepreneurs, for people to work as much as they wanted and to earn as much for their labour as they deserved.[445]

If he had their support, if Russians were united in their determination, the situation was 'difficult but not hopeless'. Citing, again, the 'experience of world civilization', Yeltsin declared that there were no incurable economic ailments.[446] A precise diagnosis, strict implementation and co-ordinated, competent actions could overcome any crisis. If only the Russian people worked as hard as they had worked this past August, the reforms would take root. Russia could and would survive the winter!

But he had to have their support in the difficult times ahead. Without the people's trust in the 'new government of reforms' he was about to form, the reforms were doomed.[447] He, the President, was prepared to take full responsibility for the government's policies by becoming his own Prime Minister. Yeltsin concluded:

Today we must all make a decisive choice. To do so requires the will and wisdom of the people, the courage of politicians, the knowledge of experts. Your President has made this choice. This is the most important decision of my life. I have never looked for easy roads in life, but I understand very clearly that the next months will be the most difficult. If I have your support and your trust, I am ready to travel this road to the end with you. The time has come for unity of all civil, ethnic and political forces, the time has come for practical actions in the name and for the benefit of every Russian family, in the name and for the benefit of the Russian state.[448]

While most politicians and economists inside and outside the Congress found much to criticize either in the measures themselves or in the sequence of implementation, for several weeks after the speech they seemed to be awed by the enormity of the political risk that Yeltsin had taken. With his personal plea for trust in his project, 'unprecedented in its weight and consequences', and with his assumption of the Prime Ministership, Yeltsin had 'voluntarily mounted the scaffold', wrote a Russian observer.[449] He had put 'under the axe' not only his reputation as a 'defender of the people', but his 'entire political career'.[450]

In the Congress, too, friends and foes alike were impressed by, as one of the Deputies put it, Yeltsin's having taken on a job that would be 'suicidal' for any other politician.[451] Even his staunchest opponents and shrillest critics – the leader of the Russian Communist Party's faction, Viktor Stepanov, and the leftist nationalist Vladimir Isakov – praised the President's 'courage'.[452] With the Congress's newly elected Chairman (or Speaker), Ruslan Khazbulatov, stressing the need to back Yeltsin,[453] the Russian parliament voted by 876 to 16 to support the Yeltsin–Gaidar programme.[454] The overwhelming majority also supported Yeltsin's candidacy for Prime Minister. At the President's request, all local and national elections were postponed for thirteen months, and he was granted the right to replace local officials.[455] The Congress also gave him the power, for one year, to implement reform by decree, although all decrees could be rescinded within a week by a two-thirds majority of the Supreme Soviet. On 7 November Yeltsin appointed Egor Gaidar First Deputy Prime Minister (as well as Minister of Economy and Finance). Most of the Ministers in the new government, announced four days later, were members of the 'Gaidar team' forged in the all-night debates at Dacha Number 15.

Yeltsin was perfectly aware of the political and personal costs of his October choice. Virtually every one of the explanations and exhortations with which he attempted to win over the public through newspaper and television interviews in the next two months[456] referred to the 'political price' of the reforms. Life would be difficult, he said openly again and again.[457] His major concern was whether the people could understand and withstand the pain[458] – a people who, in the opinion of some prominent Russian economists, were 'ignorant and helpless in economic terms', and had 'little interest, if any, in a market economy'.[459] He had 'ventured to take unpopular measures', Yeltsin said, and could hardly expect 'ardent affection' from the people.[460] He was preparing for 'growing criticism'. If, in the aftermath of the August victory, his portraits were still around 'in some places', he was sure they would be torn down very soon.[461]

Torn portraits were very much in evidence on the day he appointed Gaidar, when 10,000 leftists gathered in Oktyabr'skaya Square at the giant statue of Lenin to commemorate the seventy-fourth anniversary of the October Revolution.[462] Led by the notorious leftist militant and Moscow City Council Deputy Viktor Anpilov of the Communist Initiative Movement, they marched to Red Square holding aloft torn portraits of Gorbachev and posters that read 'What Adolf [Hitler] did not do, Mikhail has done!' and 'You have ruined the country! Be cursed for ever!'[463]

Yeltsin knew that soon, very soon, he would replace Gorbachev as the communist's *bête noire*. He said he was ready for his opponents to exploit popular resentment,[464] but that he did not fear opposition, which was 'a normal thing for a civilized state'.[465] Yet even he could not have imagined how intense, unquenchable and even murderous the hatred of him would become, nor how it would bring him bouts of 'torturing' depression, 'bitter' thoughts at night, insomnia and despair.[466]

On 29 December, four days before price controls were due to be lifted, Yeltsin addressed the nation in a televised speech in which, again, he placed the economic revolution within a grander scheme of the decommunization of Russia. Along with prices set by the state, 'we are abandoning mirages and illusions', Yeltsin said.[467] It was clear that a communist utopia could not be built. It was not Russia that had been defeated; it was communism.[468]

Together with the state-owned economy, Russia was ridding itself of 'the militarization of our life',[469] of the 'anti-human economy' almost entirely devoted to military production. Russia had stopped its 'constant preparation' for war 'with the whole world'.[470] No longer was the entire country working for the defence industry. The Iron Curtain that had separated Russia from 'almost the whole world' was no more.[471]

They had inherited a 'devastated land', 'a gravely ill Russia', Yeltsin continued, but 'we must not despair'.[472] There were no incurable illnesses in the economy. No matter how difficult things were at the time, 'we have a chance to climb out of this pit'.[473] The majority of the Russian people were capable of 'earning their way to a dignified life'.[474] 'Our people are no worse, no lazier than any other. It is necessary only to help people to find themselves in this new life.'[475]

On 2 January Russians would 'see the beginning of what will probably be the most painful – and of course unpopular – measure', Yeltsin said, 'one which for many years the country's leaders were unable to bring themselves to carry out'. That would make 1992:

> a special year. We are faced with creating the foundations of a new life. Of course, this is not easy, but it is still within our strength ... For decades the country has been tormented by a lack of freedom and constant shortages ... Behind us is a good deal of unrest, anxiety, disappointment ... I will not conceal the fact that 1992 – especially the first half of it – is not going to be easy, but we are not going to lose hope. Hope we do have ...

CHAPTER 11

The President vs. the Soviet

THE RUSSIAN PARLIAMENT'S FEATS UNDER Yeltsin's leadership – the determined fight for a greater autonomy from the Union Centre, its brave opposition to the August coup of 1991 and the support for radical economic plans – had obscured that body's decidedly conservative membership. As has already been noted, of roughly 1,500 Deputies, no more than 300 were 'democrats', about the same amount were hard-line leftists and nationalists, and the rest formed a 'swamp' which, as time went by, sided with the 'reds' more and more frequently. The Congress had elected Yeltsin President by only four votes, and virtually every major reform law was passed by very slim majorities.

This record well reflected the legislature's composition. In contrast to the most progressive Gorbachevite members of the Party intelligentsia elected to the prestigious USSR Congress a year before, the bulk of the Russian Congress – a purely symbolic, toy parliament at the time – was picked in 1990 by local Party committees from the bottom of the barrel, or close to it. The industrial and agricultural nomenklatura, the *nachal'nik*s and managers, thus became the majority. Well aware of the legislature's conservative character, Yeltsin could have dissolved the Congress and called for a new election after the August triumph,[1] but he rejected this opportunity of significantly enhancing his power.

The result was not just a diminution of the government's ability to implement reforms. In the vacuum created by the collapse of the totalitarian party-state, there were no rules delineating areas of authority and responsibility between the two branches of power. An intense debate over the pace and scope of the economic revolution quickly deteriorated into a daily battle for power and a constitutional crisis that paralysed the state and threatened to make the country ungovernable.

Propelled by the momentum of the August Revolution and by dread of total economic collapse, the Congress approved Yeltsin's reform programme in October 1991 and granted him emergency powers to implement the economic policy by decree. Yet only a few months later the parliament began to reverse its stance. The majority of its members represented corporate interests that stood to lose a great deal from the key measures of the Yeltsin–Gaidar economic revolution: sharp reduction in government credits and subsidies to industry, prices set by the market, drastic cuts in funding for the military–industrial complex, and privatization that threatened the directors' control over enterprises and their workers.

The price liberalization on 2 January 1992 dramatically broadened the opposition's appeal as the depression deepened, the gap between the new rich and the old poor widened alarmingly and inflation accelerated.

With tens of millions finding themselves suddenly impoverished, their salaries and pensions lagging far behind the daily increases in decontrolled prices and their life-savings* disappearing overnight, the legislature's opposition to the Kremlin derived strength and confidence from the powerful anti-reform backlash in public opinion.

The confrontation began barely two weeks after price liberalization, when Khazbulatov labelled the reform 'anarchic' and called for the resignation of the Gaidar government.[2] In March, under pressure from the legislature, the government abandoned plans for freeing domestic oil prices.[3] The retreat carried enormous economic, political and social costs: in the continuing waste of resources; in the explosion of corruption and economic crime relating to export quotas and resale of oil by industrial enterprises; and in the arbitrage between the domestic and world prices that led to the emergence of instant multi-millionaires and the beginning of what a few years later would be called 'oligarchical capitalism'.

Another long-term consequence of a compromise between the government and the Supreme Soviet† was the way in which the Russian economy was privatized. Originally designed to give most shares to outside investors to ensure greater efficiency and modernization, the policy was changed to satisfy the parliament's demand for majority control by the management and work collectives – in effect, making the directors owners of most of the country's assets.[4] The privatization programme passed by the Supreme Soviet on 11 June 1992 was the last pro-reform law approved by the legislature. After Yeltsin had appointed Egor Gaidar acting Prime Minister four days later,‡ the rejection of reform by the parliament became comprehensive and automatic: it voted down every single reform measure introduced by the government, including privatization of agricultural land, first rejected by the Congress in April 1992.

One of the most intense battles broke out over state credits to industry and agriculture, the money supply and the size of the budget deficit.

---

* Consumer prices increased by 245 per cent in January 1992 and continued to grow by 38 per cent in February, 30 per cent in March and 22 per cent in April. Already, by the second week in January, the price of bread had more than quadrupled.

† Like the 1989 Soviet legislature, on which the Russian parliament was modelled, the Supreme Soviet was a permanent sitting organ of the full Congress of People's Deputies of Russia. The latter convened twice a year for spring and autumn sessions.

‡ While the permanent Prime Minister had to be endorsed by congressional majority, a temporary appointment could be made by the President.

The government considered tight fiscal and monetary policies central to the country's economic revival. The parliament insisted on ever increasing state subsidies, loose credit, and pension and salary increases financed by deficit spending. The Central Bank was under the control of the Supreme Soviet, and the government was powerless to stop the printing of money. Unwilling to bring the inter-bank interest rate below the rate of inflation, as the Supreme Soviet demanded, the Bank's first Chairman resigned in June 1992. His replacement, Viktor Gerashchenko, opened the floodgates of cheap credits and grants. The money supply grew by 28 per cent a month.[5] A monthly inflation rate that had been gradually declining between January and June tripled, and reached over 30 per cent in October.[6] Between June and October 1992, the ruble lost over 40 per cent of its value against the dollar.[7] For the next fourteen months the country would teeter on the verge of hyperinflation. Private investment in industry stopped. An estimated $1 billion was taken out of the country every month.[8]

Understood literally, as it was never intended to be when written by the Central Committee's Propaganda Department in 1978, the Constitution of the Russian Soviet Federated Socialist Republic made the Soviets, then abjectly subordinate to the local Party committees, the foundation of the state. With the demise of the Party in August 1991 and the end of the Union four months later, the constitutional fiction of the 'power of the Soviets' suddenly became a writ of nearly unlimited power. In December 1991, as the members of the highest Soviet of Russia, the Supreme Soviet, the Deputies found themselves masters of the land: not only co-equal to the popularly elected President but, by the letter of the 1978 Constitution, superior to him. A few months after granting Yeltsin the emergency powers to pursue reforms, the Congress wanted much of the authority back. Yeltsin wished to keep it all – and to make the grant permanent.

In this tug of war, the subject of a new constitution grew more urgent by the day. While the need for a new political system was obvious to virtually the entire Russian political class (a Constitutional Commission was set up by the First Congress of People's Deputies of Russia on 9 June 1990), the Congress and the President were at loggerheads over the key arrangements. For the Deputies, the perpetuation of the 'republic of Soviets' meant continuing power and privilege. By contrast, a draft urged by Yeltsin and his pro-reform supporters proposed to abolish the Congress and make Russia a Presidential republic modelled on those of America and France. The change of constitutions would also mean new elections, which for most Deputies, who had neither desire nor talent for democratic politicking, spelled retirement or defeat. Along with authority, they would also lose their large apartments, the provision of chauffeured cars, their trips abroad, their high salaries and their Moscow residence. Their present term ran to 1995 and they were determined to serve until the very last day.

In its duel with the Kremlin, the parliament was managed by Ruslan Khazbulatov. A master of political intrigue, apparat manoeuvres and procedural techniques, he knew the foibles and weaknesses of most of the Deputies and exploited them with consummate skill. It was said at the time in Moscow that no one party, faction or individual had a majority in the Congress – except for Khazbulatov. A moderate democrat and economist, he was picked by Yeltsin as the First Deputy Chairman in 1990: Khazbulatov was an ethnic Chechen and the choice was designed to underscore Yeltsin's solicitude for non-Russian members of the Russian Federation. After Yeltsin was elected President, he supported Khazbulatov's candidacy for the Chairmanship of the Supreme Soviet. Khazbulatov failed to receive the necessary majority of votes but remained acting Chairman until October 1991, when, thanks to Yeltsin's lobbying, he was finally elected.

A professor at the Institute of People's Economy, Khazbulatov wanted to be Prime Minister, and was deeply offended when the President offered the post to Gaidar instead.[9] He claimed that the authors of the '500 Day' programme had stolen his ideas.[10] Relations between the Supreme Soviet and the government were not improved by the fact that, as an economic editor of the prestigious pro-reform journal *Kommunist* in the late 1980s, Gaidar had rejected several articles submitted by Khazbulatov because they were 'banal'.[11]

The first clash between the parliament and the government occurred in April 1992, less than four months after the start of the economic revolution. One after another, the Deputies accused the 'monetarists' in the government of 'impoverishing', 'tormenting' and 'selling out' Russia.[12] The Congress quickly adopted laws mandating lower taxes, increased subsidies and controlled prices. The powers of the executive branch were to be pruned to the point where the Presidency was 'confined to purely representative functions'.[13] Although not yet on the agenda, a change of government was in the air.

After Gaidar had declared that the government would not take responsibility for a radically altered policy and was going to resign, the Congress retreated and adopted a declaration supportive of the 'general line' of the reforms. The parliament also approved, 'in principle',

Yeltsin's proposal to adopt a post-Soviet constitution. In exchange, Yeltsin agreed to dilute the 'monetarist' government with 'red directors' from the military–industrial complex and the gas and oil industries. The new First Deputy Prime Ministers – Vladimir Shumeiko, Viktor Chernomyrdin and Georgiy Khizha – were to be the voice of the Congress in economic matters.

By the autumn of 1992, both sides were resorting to heated and menacing rhetoric. The parliament warned of a 'return to totalitarianism',[14] while the Kremlin regarded any increase in the power of the parliament at the expense of the Presidency as an attack on reform and an attempt, in Yeltsin's words, 'to turn back history' and to resurrect the communist past which Russia had 'done with for ever'.[15] In the second week of November, the Supreme Soviet further limited the government's control over the budget and voted to require every Minister (rather than the Prime Minister only, as Yeltsin requested) to give an annual account to the legislature. The Deputies also wanted greater control over the 'power' services and ministries – Security, Defence and Internal Affairs – as well as over the Ministry of Foreign Affairs.[16] The government complained that these measures violated the principle of the separation of powers, which during the years of glasnost had become accepted by the political class as the cornerstone of democracy, and said it would appeal to the Constitutional Court.[17]

Ruslan Khazbulatov set up a 5,000-strong detachment of armed 'parliamentary guards'. The guards' first campaign was the seizure of the editorial offices of the main national liberal daily, *Izvestia*. Although the newspaper had been independent since 1989, it was, formally, an 'organ of the Supreme Soviet', and now the Supreme Soviet wanted to take possession, change the editorial line and use it in its propaganda war with the Kremlin. Yeltsin ordered the guards disarmed and disbanded. They resisted, precipitating the first armed clash between the Kremlin and the Supreme Soviet – though there were no casualties.

The confrontation came to a head at the Seventh Congress of People's Deputies which opened on 1 December 1992. Several days before, the Constitutional Court had struck down most of the provisions of Yeltsin's 1991 ban on the Communist Party. The Court ruled that, while the Party could not retain the 'ruling structures' (the district, city and *oblast* committees, as well as the Central Committee, Politburo and Secretariat), it was free to organize locally and to set up 'primary cells'.[18] The communist plurality in the Congress was much heartened by the decision.

Compared to the sharp words of the recent past, Yeltsin's opening speech to the Congress was conciliatory and devoid of accusations. He emphasized reform and 'democratic statehood' as the two central goals of his administration. He admitted that structural changes in the economy were proceeding extremely slowly and that, so far, to the majority of Russians the reforms had meant 'more problems and difficulties'.[19]

In some instances, Yeltsin added, the policy could be modified to satisfy the demands of the majority of the legislature. He promised that government credits would continue to flow to state enterprises, which had been suddenly left without state orders. The government would continue to protect home-grown businesses, giving them preference over foreign firms.[20] Yet the mistakes and omissions had been made in the tactics of implementation, not in the 'strategic line' of reform.[21] The objective of the reforms was to create a 'modern economy' in Russia, and Yeltsin was convinced that such an economy would be created.[22] Among the next most urgent tasks were curbing inflation, stabilizing the ruble exchange rate, privatizing large enterprises and introducing private ownership of land, which would 'breathe life into the Russian countryside' and without which 'things would not move along'.[23] He begged for more time. The 'tragedy' of twentieth-century Russia was the inability to implement reforms despite repeated attempts.[24] 'The foundations for Russia's future' had been laid, but the house of reform was still clad in scaffolding and there were 'heaps of debris' around it.[25]

Still, the President averred, there had already been a major breakthrough: for the first time in generations, people were working not for a 'radiant future' but for themselves, their family and kin.[26] For the first time, citizens had been given a chance to 'develop their initiative and entrepreneurial skills', they no longer followed commands but determined their own motivation.[27] There had been nothing like that in Russia before.[28] The people were undergoing a 'moral regeneration'.[29]

Yeltsin pledged to preserve the recently acquired liberties: Russia's future was inseparable from democratic statehood.[30] Freedom of speech and freedom of the press were real achievements.[31] Russia's road was that of liberty and a 'steadfast movement towards a democratic and self-regulating' society:[32]

> The state should serve the individual and not vice versa; this is a fundamental principle of relations between the state and its citizens in the reborn Russia . . .
>
> . . . The fact that we lead the planet in number of missiles is not a fact we want to be proud of; rather, the fact that we have an affluent,

peaceful, dynamic and secure life created by peaceful labour. This is my dream of Russia's future.[33]

He saw the biggest obstacle to both reform and to democratic statehood in the 'savage', 'irreconcilable' and 'painful' battle between the branches of power.[34] The conflict, he said, was assuming an 'increasingly ominous and extreme form'.[35] The Constitution inherited from Soviet times ran counter to the principle of division of powers.[36] The only way out of crisis, and to a post-communist democratic Russian state, was a new constitution adopted by a national referendum.[37] Yeltsin proposed that the Congress adopt a resolution to this effect. (The President had no power to call a referendum; the votes of a quarter of the Congress or one million signatures were required.) Until the referendum, he wanted a truce: a 'stabilization' period, during which the Congress would devote itself to the writing of laws, leaving the management of the economy to the government.[38]

Ruslan Khazbulatov's lengthy oration attacked the government's version of reforms as the 'Americanization' of the Russian economy (which, according to him, 'presupposed a drastic reduction in the state's social functions' and the 'privatization of all and everything'). This strategy had resulted in a collapse of economic policy, a catastrophic decline in production and the impoverishment and abasement of the people. The Chairman of the Supreme Soviet proposed, instead, a 'socially oriented market', improvement in living and working conditions, a 'regulatory price policy', and 'flexibility' in credit and finance. No mention was made of a new constitution or a constitutional referendum.[39]

Only one of the twenty-two Deputies who followed Khazbulatov at the podium had anything positive to say about Egor Gaidar's cabinet. With Russian television and radio broadcasting the speeches live, one speaker after another denounced the 'bankrupt government' to the hearty applause of the Congress.[40] Like Khazbulatov, they passed in silence over the referendum and concentrated instead on multiple amendments to the existing Constitution of the Russian Soviet Federated Socialist Republic of 1978. A two-thirds majority of the Congress was all that was required to amend the Constitution. Often, an amendment adopted one day would be rescinded the next. The changes affected one-fifth of all the Articles and strengthened legislative control over the executive.[41] One such amendment gave the Congress the right to suspend the President's decisions. Soon the Constitution would have over 300 amendments.

After he had nominated Gaidar for Prime Minister, in a *quid pro quo*

Yeltsin agreed to the legislature's long-standing demand for a veto over the appointments of the four key Ministers: Defence, Security, Internal Affairs and Foreign Affairs. The Congress pocketed the concessions and defeated Gaidar's domination. The gathering also voted not to extend the emergency powers of the President in economic matters and rejected Yeltsin's suggestion of a constitutional referendum.

By that time, Yeltsin had sacrificed not only the four key Ministries but also two of his closest friends and confidants: to mollify the Congress, at the end of November he had dismissed the *bête noires* of the opposition, the passionate and caustic anti-communists Information Minister Mikhail Poltoranin and State Secretary Gennadiy Burbulis. In the previous eight days Yeltsin sat impassively while an endless stream of vituperation was directed by Deputies against the policies of his government. He had made no headway whatsoever on the most important issue, that of a constitutional referendum. The Congress rejected virtually all the laws prepared by the government. Now he had lost his Prime Minister.

On the morning following the Gaidar vote, Yeltsin took to the podium immediately after the opening of the session. He accused the Congress of instigating a 'creeping *coup d'état*', blocking the reforms and creating 'unbearable conditions' for the work of the government.[42] Without assuming any responsibility, the leaders of the legislature were becoming the real masters of the country, above the executive. He had counted on an understanding Congress but instead had been faced with a 'wall of silence' or 'aggressive grumbling'.[43] Even the hall, Yeltsin continued, was 'red from the endless insults, from crude personal abuse, from meanness, [and] rudeness'.[44]

The government and the President wanted to continue the reforms to revive the 'very sick' economy. The preferred policies of the Congressional majority, on the other hand, would lead to the restoration of the 'totalitarian, Soviet communist system, deplored by our own people and rejected by the world community'.[45] These positions were irreconcilable. Yeltsin saw no solution other than to speak directly to the citizens of Russia, to whom he 'owed' his Presidency:

There is an authority above the Congress and above the President: the people. I see the only way out of the deepest crisis of power: a national referendum. This would be the most democratic, most law-abiding way to overcome the crisis. I am not calling for the dissolution of the Congress; I am asking the people of Russia to decide who you are with, whose course you support: that of the President, the course of changes, or that of the Congress, the course of curtailing the reforms ... The choice must be made now in order to preserve civil peace and secure stability for Russia. You must make this choice, esteemed voters. In your hands are the fate of the reforms, of the President and of the Congress ... As President I will submit to the will of the people, whatever it might be.

In the meantime, he wanted Russia to know that the Congress had failed to 'demoralize' the cabinet: Ministers would continue decisively to implement the reforms.[46]

The next day, however, Yeltsin agreed to meet with Khazbulatov to work out a compromise. As the negotiations got under way, the parliament quickly passed amendments to the Law on Referendums, annulling the provision for voter initiative in calling a referendum, making referendums an exclusive prerogative of the Congress and prohibiting 'issues pertaining to the highest organs of power' from being put to a referendum.

A day later, on 12 December, in front of the Congress, Yeltsin and Khazbulatov shook hands to cheers and catcalls. The Congress 'suspended' some of the laws and constitutional amendments adopted in the last few days and promised to refrain from passing laws constraining the government's ability to implement economic policies. The 'war of laws' was to stop. The parliament also agreed to put to a referendum, to be held on 11 April of the following year, a constitution drafted by the legislature. Until then, Yeltsin could keep his emergency powers. In exchange, the President rescinded his 'call to the people'. 'There will be no collision, no coup, no other anti-constitutional action,' a joyful Yeltsin announced on national television. 'This is the main thing.'[47]

In addition to seriously damaging his credibility (and thus the success of future attempts to mobilize popular support), the heaviest price that Yeltsin had paid for abandoning his call for an immediate referendum was giving in to the Congress's major demand: the the right to choose the Prime Minister from the President's nominees. Given the vote a few days before, the decision spelled the end of Egor Gaidar's government.

Of all the comrades-in-arms Yeltsin had dismissed in the past few weeks to accommodate the opposition, parting with Gaidar was the most painful sacrifice. A few days before the Congress, the President had told a delegation of Congressional leaders, who had come to 'discuss' a change of government: 'I will not give up Gaidar. Gaidar is the centre, the bull's eye. We will not find anyone better.'[48]

After consultations with the Congress, Yeltsin offered the Security Council Secretary Yuriy Skokov and First Deputy Prime Minister Viktor

Chernomyrdin as candidates for Prime Minister – and stubbornly added Egor Gaidar to the list. 'If Gaidar garners a respectable number of votes, I'll renominate him,' Yeltsin told the leaders of Russia's Autonomous Republics on the eve of the vote. 'If they vote him down, I'll appoint him acting Prime Minister.'[49] In the event, both Skokov and Chernomyrdin surpassed Gaidar by more than 200 votes. Yeltsin then nominated Chernomyrdin, who was approved by a huge majority.

Radical pro-reform 'democrats' thought the compromise was a 'huge mistake' by Yeltsin.[50] To them, Chernomyrdin was 'a symbol of slowing down, of breaking the reforms', as Father Gleb Yakunin, a defrocked Russian Orthodox priest, put it.[51] The Chairman of the parliamentary sub-committee on privatization and a leader of the Democratic Russia faction in the parliament Petr Filippov, who had been one of the government's most effective supporters in the Supreme Soviet, declared that 'the communists have put one of their own at the head of the government'.[52]*

On the evening of Chernomyrdin's election, Gaidar received a call from Naina Yeltsina. You are young, you are intelligent, please, please help Boris Nikolaevich, she begged. He is an older man. Things are very hard for him. And she began to cry.[53]

A few weeks later, in early January 1993, the Supreme Soviet began to retreat from the 12 December compromise. Ruslan Khazbulatov 'doubted' if a constitutional referendum was necessary or even helpful: without any referendums, the Congress had already amended the Constitution to make it 'truly democratic'.[54] In an article published in, of all newspapers, the communist *Pravda*, Khazbulatov extolled the Soviets

---

* These predictions proved at least partly true. The policy of tight budgets and monetary restraint was reversed. Chernomyrdin, who declared state support for industry his major objective, asked the Congress to transfer billions of rubles to the energy industry. In the first two weeks of January 1993, the Central Bank gave out more credits to the government and to enterprises than during almost the whole of the preceding twelve months. The budget deficit rose to 12 per cent of GDP. After relative stabilization in the last few months of 1992, the country was again on the brink of hyperinflation. (Eric Whitlock, 'New Government to Continue Economic Reform?', *RFE/RL Research Report*, 15 January 1993, pp. 25, 26; and Egor Gaidar, *Dni porazhaniy i pobed* ('The days of defeats and victories'), p. 251.)

With Yeltsin locked in a power struggle and preoccupied with a new constitution, there was little progress in the implementation of any major structural reforms, except privatization, which continued apace. Almost the entire second year of the economic revolution was wasted.

as a genuinely Russian, traditional form of representative democracy and proposed a renewed Soviet rule, in which local governments would be subordinated to local Soviets and these, in turn, to the Supreme Soviet.[55]

The extreme left-nationalist wing of the opposition was boosted by the January 1993 decision of the Constitutional Court to overturn Yeltsin's November 1992 ban on the 'national-Bolshevik' National Salvation Front. The Front, which openly called for the overthrow of the regime, supported Khazbulatov.[56]

The Eighth Congress of the People's Deputies, which sat in Moscow from 10 to 13 March, annulled the 12 December agreement. Khazbulatov apologized for having concluded it with Yeltsin ('*Bes poputal*,' he said. 'The devil confused me') and promised that there would be no more compromises with the Kremlin. Adopting the laws and amendments it agreed to 'suspend' on 12 December, the Congress stripped the President of most of the emergency powers. The legislature reaffirmed its control of the key government agencies, including the Central Bank. Invoking Article 104 of the 1978 Constitution of the RSFSR, the Congress declared itself the 'supreme power' in the country. The President was just the 'highest official' and the 'head of executive power'.[57] Observers saw the legislation as a 'sudden and profound loss' of power by Yeltsin.[58]

On 12 March, from the podium of the Congress, Yeltsin appealed to the gathering not to disavow the 12 December compromise and not to enact the laws suspended then. He also urged the legislature not to retreat from its commitment to a constitutional referendum. As he had suggested a week before, the poll was to decide whether Russia should be a Presidential republic; whether the supreme legislature should be a much smaller and permanent bicameral parliament, in place of the Congress; whether the new Russian Constitution should be adopted by a constituent assembly, rather than by the Congress; and whether Russian citizens should have the right to buy and sell land.[59]

Yeltsin also proposed holding a referendum on 25 April. The Congress adopted a resolution stating that it would be 'inexpedient' to hold a referendum in 1993, reaffirmed a constitutional injunction against the President's calling for a referendum, and adjourned.[60]

A week later, on 20 March, in a nationally televised speech, Yeltsin declared that the Congress had 'buried' the referendum on the foundation of a new constitution and on citizens' ownership of land.[61] If the political squabbling were not halted, if the crisis were not resolved and the reforms given powerful momentum, the country would be pushed into anarchy.[62] Therefore, he was calling a referendum for 25 April.

This was to be a vote of confidence in the President and Vice President, a vote that was to determine who was to govern the country: they or the Congress. Until then, to enable the referendum to take place, a 'special rule of governing' would prevail: while neither the Supreme Soviet nor the Congress were to be dissolved, laws that 'suspended' or 'revoked' Presidential decrees were declared null and void.[63]

Almost immediately Yeltsin retreated from this extra-constitutional move. The vague 'special rule' was never implemented. Indeed, when the decree to which Yeltsin referred in his speech was published three days later, it did not mention the 'special rule' at all. On 24 March, Yeltsin invited Khazbulatov and the Chairman of the Constitutional Court, Valeriy Zor'kin, who since the previous December had been acting as mediator, to a meeting in the Kremlin. He again sought to persuade the Congress to drop its opposition to the referendum.[64] By this time, however, the Constitutional Court had already declared Yeltsin's decree unconstitutional. The Congress now had a long-awaited opportunity to finish off the President. Vice President Rutskoy, who stood to become President in the event of Yeltsin's impeachment, openly sided with the parliament. Khazbulatov called an 'extraordinary' Congress, which convened on 26 March.

In a speech to the legislature, Yeltsin urged its members to approve a referendum on the question of confidence in the President and in the Supreme Soviet.[65] 'I have made my choice,' he said. 'I have entrusted my fate to the highest and fairest of arbiters, the people.'[66]

Yeltsin looked exhausted. For the first and last time he appeared in public dishevelled, with his usually perfectly coiffed white mane in disarray. A few days before he had stood, weeping, next to Naina at the grave of his mother. Klavdia Yeltsina had died on 21 March. His bodyguard would write later that Yeltsin 'took very hard' the struggle with Khazbulatov and Rutskoy and was severely depressed, even suicidal, in the spring of 1993.[67]

The Congress rejected the last-minute compromise, tentatively discussed by the Kremlin and the leadership of the Supreme Soviet (one of the proposals called for the cancellation of the referendum in exchange for Presidential and parliamentary elections in November). In the afternoon of 28 March, booths for secret balloting were set up in the ornate St George's Hall of the Kremlin. Two-thirds of the 1,034 Deputies, 689 votes in all, were needed for impeachment, which would mean Yeltsin's instant removal from power.

Egor Gaidar would say three months later that the vote on the evening of 28 March 1993 was 'one of the most dangerous moments in the post-Second World War history of our country, and probably mankind'.[68] Ready to assume the Presidency if Yeltsin was voted out, Rutskoy was prepared to appoint a Prime Minister and Ministers of Defence and of Internal Affairs (police) and the chiefs of the security services.[69] 'At that point,' Gaidar continued, 'it was unclear whose orders the Russian Army, the police and the border guards would follow. Since the August 1991 coup attempt, it was the moment when we came the closest to an outbreak of civil war.'[70]

Over 60,000 pro-Yeltsin demonstrators marched on the streets of Moscow that day. Lasting from morning till late at night, the rally in the Vasilievskiy Spusk (Slope), next to St Basil's Cathedral, was the largest street gathering in Moscow since August 1991. Hundreds of tricolour flags fluttered in a strong and unseasonably warm wind.[71] Among those standing next to Yeltsin on a stage of two flatbed trucks were Sakharov's wife, Elena Bonner, Gaidar and the Mayor of Moscow, Yuriy Luzhkov.[72] On the other side of Red Square, around 10,000 activists of the National Salvation Front and the extreme-left Working Russia and Working Moscow parties demonstrated under red hammer-and-sickle flags in support of the Congress.

'Of course, it is difficult now – everything is so expensive and changing all the time,' said a fifty-nine-year-old woman pensioner, who was close to tears as she watched Yeltsin striding towards the trucks to address the crowd.[73] 'But it is worth it, in the end, we will finally have a normal country, with normal lives . . . That is what Yeltsin is trying to do, and we support him. Those people [the Congress] just want to bring back communism.'[74] The communists had 'gathered new strength', complained a thirty-six-year-old woman in the crowd.[75] The Communist Party was being revived. 'Who can afford not to participate? We'll all go to the barricades [against the communists] if we have to.'[76]

Sustained by coffee and sandwiches provided by the Tverskoy supermarket, the crowd remained on Red Square until late at night, periodically chanting, 'Yeltsin! Yeltsin! Yeltsin!'[77] At 10.20 p.m. the results of the impeachment vote were announced: 617 Deputies had voted yes – seventy-two short of the required two-thirds majority. For the second time, Yeltsin emerged from the Spasskiy Gate of the Kremlin and climbed on to the trucks amid deafening cheers.[78] 'I thank you, my dear Muscovites, for the support,' Yeltsin boomed. 'I will do everything not to violate your trust . . . The communist coup did not happen. They were defeated by the people, by reform, by democracy, by young Russia.'[79]

The next day, the Congress approved a compromise: Yeltsin would rescind the 20 March decree and the legislature would agree to a referendum – provided that the questions were changed. The poll would no longer be a simple choice between Congress and the President or a vote on a Presidential republic, a bicameral parliament or the right to buy and sell land. Instead, as drafted by the Congress, the questions concerned early elections of the legislature and the President, confidence in the President and – this in a country where inflation by now had reached 20 per cent a month! – support for the 'socio-economic policies' of the regime. Furthermore, the parliament insisted that the results of the referendum would be binding only if supported by a majority of all eligible voters, not just of those who came to the polls.* Yeltsin immediately agreed to all the conditions.

The questions thus put in the referendum were: 1. 'Do you trust the President of the Russian Federation, Boris Yeltsin?' 2. 'Do you approve of the socio-economic policies carried out by the President of the Russian Federation and the government of the Russian Federation since 1992?' 3. 'Do you consider it necessary to hold early elections for the Presidency of the Russian Federation?' 4. 'Do you consider it necessary to hold early elections of the People's Deputies of the Russian Federation?'

The short pre-referendum campaign was raucous and intense, with both sides well aware of the stakes involved. Khazbulatov did not conceal his intention, in the event of Yeltsin's defeat, to 'abolish the institution of the Presidency and to create a political system based on the role of the Soviets'.[80] To Yeltsin's champions, the referendum was a choice between two courses: pro-reform democratic and anti-reform 'brezhnevist'.[81] Now, as after the February Revolution of 1917, Russia had a chance to move on to 'the road of democracy and civilization'.[82] A vote for Yeltsin, the 'democrats' insisted, meant a vote for liberty – the most important value, which would, in the end, secure all other benefits: economic progress and dignified existence.[83] A vote for Congress was a vote for communism – a communism 'first allied with and then mutating into fascism and Nazism'.[84]

The day before the referendum, the Kremlin published the 'main principles' of a new constitution. Russia was to become a federated democratic Presidential republic, in which 'there shall be no laws passed that revoke or diminish the rights and liberties of man'.[85] Among those rights and liberties was the right to private property, including land.[86] The three branches of power – the executive, the legislative and the judiciary – were to be independent. The new parliament, or Federal

---

* The Constitutional Court later ruled that only the questions on early elections of the President and the parliament had to be approved by the majority of all registered voters.

Assembly, would consist of a lower house (the Duma) and an upper chamber (the Council of the Federation).[87] Until a new parliament was elected in accordance with a new constitution, the present Supreme Soviet was to remain the country's legislature.

In the Kremlin draft, the President of the Russian Federation would be the head of state and the 'guarantor' of the Constitution. He would nominate the Prime Minister for confirmation by the Federal Assembly and appoint federal Ministers and other high officials. If the Federal Assembly did not approve of the government or if a 'crisis of state power' could not be resolved by other means, the President could, after consultation with the Chairmen of both chambers, dissolve the Assembly. The President would also have the right to call a national referendum.[88]

On 25 April, of 64.5 per cent of eligible Russian adults who turned out to vote, 58.7 per cent (40.5 million) expressed confidence in Yeltsin, 49.5 per cent approved of an early Presidential election (47.1 per cent were against the poll) and 67.2 per cent of a legislative one (30.1 per cent voted 'no'). Yet the result that stunned virtually everyone and was found 'unexpected'[89] and even 'incredible'[90] by the most ardent reformers inside and outside the government was that, after sixteen months of wrenching changes and hardships, 53 per cent of the referendum voters (36.6 million people) approved of the regime's economic and social policies.

Measured against the target (more than 50 per cent) set by the Congress, the vote for an early Presidential election fell 18 per cent short (31.7 per cent of the total electorate), while support for the parliamentary poll was 7 per cent below the mark (43.1 per cent). Thus in formal terms, the referendum had changed nothing in the battle between the legislative and executive branches. Yeltsin, however, seemed unconcerned. He considered the matter resolved unambiguously: the majority of voters had approved of him, early parliamentary elections, the policies of his regime and, by extension, the drafting of a new constitution.[91]

Never petty or malicious in victory and deriving no pleasure from humiliating the vanquished, Yeltsin, as a close adviser put it, usually 'lost interest' in a defeated enemy and 'stepped aside'.[92] On this occasion, too, buoyed by the renewed popular mandate, he let the Congress be.

This loss of tempo hugely disappointed many of his supporters among Moscow's anti-communist intelligentsia.[93] To them, the results of the referendum were a mandate for a 'decisive assault' on the Congress:[94] for dissolving it immediately, for scheduling elections and adopting a post-Soviet constitution. Among the members of Democratic Russia, whose activists had worked round the clock for Yeltsin's victory in the referendum,[95] this view was shared by the entire leadership, including Galina Starovoytova,[96] a State Councillor on National Questions dismissed the previous December, along with Burbulis and Poltoranin, in Yeltsin's pre-emptive concession to the Congress. Democratic activists in the provinces were especially bitter: for almost two years they had had to put up with the continuing dominance of the communist nomenklatura in local Soviets, and the referendum had changed nothing.[97]

On 20 May Yeltsin issued a decree convening a Constitutional Assembly. Each of the republics and regions was to delegate four representatives, two each from the executive and the legislative branches. Also invited to send delegates were fifty of the largest trade unions, fifteen major religious denominations* and ten 'creative unions' (journalists, actors, cinematographers, writers and so on). Parties and political movements invited to participate ranged from pro-Yeltsin 'democratic' (sixteen) to 'centrist' (four) to 'oppositional' (eleven). The latter included such leftist radicals as Viktor Anpilov of Working Russia. Altogether, 700 delegates representing 117 organizations were bidden to attend.[98] The Assembly was to open on 5 June and produce a final draft by the 16th.

Four days before the Assembly was to convene, Khazbulatov told the 2,000 leaders of regional Soviets, who gathered in Moscow for an all-Russian Congress, that giving the Assembly the power to adopt a new constitution was 'tantamount to an attempted coup'.[99] The Supreme Soviet's Chairman called on Soviets to 'intensify' their supervision of local executive bodies.[100] Addressing the same gathering, Vice President Aleksandr Rutskoy said that the government's economic policy was 'a crime against the people' and that the Congress should remove Yeltsin's government within three months.[101] On the day of the Assembly's opening, 10,000 communists and nationalists demonstrated against it on the streets of Moscow. The National Salvation Front issued an appeal to Russian citizens warning of 'the threat of dictatorship'.[102]

On 5 June, Yeltsin greeted 692 delegates.[103] He instructed the Assembly to discuss and combine both the Presidential and the Supreme Soviet's drafts, the latter having 'many good points'.[104] While rejecting the Kremlin's draft out of hand and vehemently opposing a constitutional referendum, the parliament had continued to compose its own

---

* These, in addition to Russian Orthodox, Muslims and Jews, included Catholics, Buddhists, Baptists, Lutherans, Adventists and Old Believers.

version. The Assembly was not to compete with the parliament's Constitutional Commission but to 'revitalize' its work.[105] He suggested that
the Constitution might be placed before the Congress for approval.

Yeltsin insisted, however, that the days of the Soviets were over. In
1918, he said, the Soviets had usurped the power of the Constituent
Assembly disbanded by the Bolsheviks, and today's Soviets were 'direct
heirs' of those illegitimate bodies. 'The soviet type of power cannot be
reformed,' Yeltsin concluded. 'Soviets and democracy are incompatible.'[106]

After the President had finished, Khazbulatov rushed to the podium
to issue a rebuttal. The Chairman of the Assembly, a liberal lawyer
named Sergey Alekseev, was due to speak next. Although Yeltsin gave
the floor to Khazbulatov, the Chairman of the Supreme Soviet was
hooted down, and stormed out of the hall, followed by between fifty
and a hundred delegates.[107] At a press conference after the walkout
and in an 'undelivered speech' published the next day by opposition
newspapers, he declared that Yeltsin's fight against the Soviets was, 'in
fact, a fight against democracy', and that the Presidential draft was
inferior not only to that of the Supreme Soviet but even to the existing
Constitution.[108] If the Assembly managed to work out a text acceptable
to everyone, however, the Congress could pass it the following November, Khazbulatov stated. In the absence of such a text, all constitutional
drafts (of which there were soon to be five, including one by nationalists
and one by communists, published in *Pravda* on 5 June) should be put
to a referendum for the people to choose from.[109]

Yeltsin and the remaining delegates quickly decided to organize a
special session to give Khazbulatov and other critics an opportunity to
speak. Yeltsin dispatched a telegram to those who had left the hall,
imploring them to return. On 7 June most of them did, and the Assembly
began its work. Khazbulatov refused to attend.[110]

By 16 June, when the final draft was to be made public, the Assembly
had agreed only on the Declaration of Main Principles. By these, Russia
was a secular state based on the rule of law. Its 'highest value was
the individual and his inalienable rights'.[111] Most delegates had also
supported the provisions giving the President the right to dissolve the
parliament but had insisted on a detailed description of the conditions
under which he could do so. Yeltsin issued a decree 'asking' the delegates
to complete the final draft by 26 June. When on that day the text
was released, however, many delegates changed their minds and began
registering their objections. Yeltsin concluded that the text could not
be considered final and should be sent to working groups for further

editing. He scheduled another session of the Constitutional Assembly for mid-July.

Among the largest obstacles in the way of consensus was the mechanism of adoption. The delegates proposed five methods – by the Congress of People's Deputies, by the Constitutional Assembly, by a new parliament, elected in accordance with the guidelines of a new constitution, by a joint session of the Congress and the Assembly, or by a national referendum[112] – but failed to settle on any one. Another stumbling block was the division of power and responsibilities between the federal authorities and the twenty-one ethnic 'autonomous' Republics, many of which were insisting on sovereignty and even the right to secession.[113] Yeltsin's concessions to the Republics began to trouble not only left nationalists (who, like the Supreme Soviet Deputy Sergey Baburin, accused Yeltsin of 'destroying the Russian Federation with the slogan of federalism')[114] but also liberals and centrists who worried about the country's turning from federation into a 'loose confederation'.[115]

More than anything else, the question of the balance of power between the President and the parliament continued to separate the Assembly's draft from that of the Supreme Soviet's Constitutional Commission. The latter document stipulated that individual Ministers (and not just the Prime Minister) should be confirmed by the parliament; it gave the parliament exclusive authority over referendums; it did not permit early elections; and, most importantly, it prohibited dissolution of the parliament under any circumstances.[116] 'The two drafts are incompatible,' said the Executive Secretary of the Supreme Soviet's Constitutional Commission. 'I really cannot be optimistic.'[117]

By mid-summer the Supreme Soviet seemed to have recovered fully from the April shock and resumed the 'war of laws' with the Kremlin. The government's decrees aimed at fiscal austerity and lower budget deficits were scuttled by parliamentary revisions that sharply increased spending, particularly on pensions and defence.[118] The Supreme Soviet adopted a state budget with a deficit of 25 per cent of GDP. The Minister of Finance, Boris Fedorov, refused to implement such a budget.[119]

Privatization occasioned the most ferocious political combat. In the first week of May, Yeltsin issued a decree expanding and accelerating the programme. Among the measures was an order to allocate for sale 29 per cent of shares in state-owned enterprises. All small businesses (for instance, cafeterias, barber shops and public baths) were to be privatized by 1 August 1993, while the list of enterprises excluded from privatization (largely in the defence industry) was to be shortened.

Two months later, the Supreme Soviet suspended the decree and asked the Constitutional Court to examine its legality. The parliament also voted to transfer the management of privatization from the radically pro-market State Property Committee, headed by the Deputy Prime Minister Anatoliy Chubais, to the entire cabinet of Ministers.[120] Interrupting a holiday, Yeltsin returned to Moscow to sign a decree that raised to 80 per cent the proportion of shares for sale. The Supreme Soviet cut its summer break to suspend the measure.[121]

By mid-September the parliament was ready to challenge the government directly in the most critical areas. One of Khazbulatov's closest associates, the Chairman of one of the Supreme Soviet's chambers (the Council of the Republic), the communist Veniamin Sokolov, proposed the introduction of price controls, 'state regulation' of the economy, obligatory 'investment' of half of all private banks' assets in the national economy, and the banning of foreign currency from domestic circulation.[122] These measures, as one Russian journalist put it, constituted a 'radical shift in economic policy'.[123] Sokolov proposed convening an extraordinary Congress at the end of October. Khazbulatov was said to approve.[124]

The Supreme Soviet's reach now extended to foreign and defence policy, until then firmly within the President's domain. In July, by a nearly unanimous vote, the legislature asserted Russian sovereignty over the Ukrainian city-port of Sevastopol and overturned an agreement on the division of the Black Sea Fleet concluded by Yeltsin and Ukraine's President Leonid Kravchuk.[125] In an effort to undermine what it perceived to be the pro-Western line of Foreign Minister Andrey Kozyrev, the parliament began debating the expansion of its right to reject international treaties already signed by Russia.[126] The Deputies also passed measures curbing the activities of foreign banks and foreign religious organizations.[127]

Another law subordinated government Ministers simultaneously to the President and to the parliament: they were to follow both Presidential decrees and laws passed by the Supreme Soviet. The Chairman of the Supreme Soviet and its Praesidium could issue their own decrees (*postanovleniya*) and directives (*rasporyazheniya*). In the first six months of 1993 Khazbulatov issued over 630 personal directives, while the number issued by the Praesidium was even greater.[128] At the beginning of August, Khazbulatov urged the parliament to pass a law imposing 'severe' penalties on officials who defied the legislature's edicts.[129] Yeltsin responded by vetoing more laws than ever before (on one day, 13 August, he returned thirteen laws to the parliament), while issuing a record number of decrees that did not require the Supreme Soviet's approval. In the first seven months of 1993, the President signed more than 1,150 decrees.[130]

The provinces were torn by contradictory orders from Moscow. In one of the largest industrial *oblast*s (Chelyabinsk in the south Urals), the local Soviet decided to hold an election for the post of head of the regional administration, until then appointed by the President. Citing procedural violations, a court cancelled the poll. The Soviet held the election anyway. The government refused to recognize the elected official and continued to deal with his predecessor. The Supreme Soviet did the opposite. Some of the *oblast*'s towns and districts followed the government, others sided with the parliament. The local branch of the Central Bank opened its vaults to the elected 'governor', while the Ministry of Finance considered him an impostor.[131]

Each side blamed the other for what observers called a 'cacophony' of laws promulgated within a 'chaotic legal environment',[132] which paralysed implementation and precluded large-scale foreign investment. Yeltsin complained that reforms were being held up by 'political strife and intrigue'.[133] The parliament's leaders accused him of seeking dictatorial powers and leading the country to ruin.[134]

Since May, Khazbulatov had successfully purged the leadership of the Supreme Soviet of dissidents, that is of anyone sympathetic to Yeltsin or even advocating a more flexible policy of limited co-operation with the President. The highly respected heads of the Budget and Foreign Affairs Committees (Aleksandr Pochinok and Evgeniy Ambartsumov) were sternly warned to follow the majority line, while the Chairmen of the critical Committees of Economic Reform and Legislation were dismissed. Their replacements promptly declared that Yeltsin's privatization decree ought to be repealed and that constitutional reform could wait until 1996.*

It was widely assumed in Moscow in July that another attempt to impeach Yeltsin was imminent and would be launched at the end of September or the beginning of October at the latest.[135] When the Supreme Soviet agreed to lower the quorum necessary for major

---

* Ruslan Khazbulatov deployed carrots as well as sticks. Retiring Deputies were entitled to a bonus equal to about two years of average salary (850,000 rubles) and twice as much if they were not able to return to their former 'civilian' jobs. The Supreme Soviet also passed legislation that allowed Deputies the right to 'privatize' their offices and apartments, thus giving the members ownership of prime real estate in the centre of Moscow. (Dominic Gualtieri, 'Russian Parliament Renews Power Struggle with Yeltsin', *RFE/RL Research Report*, 13 August 1993, p. 32.)

decisions from three-quarters to a simple majority,[136] the measure was interpreted as preparation for impeachment.[137]

On 18 September, at a national conference of Soviets, Khazbulatov delivered what the scrupulously centrist *Nezavisimaya Gazeta* called a 'tough anti-President' speech intended to 'sharpen the confrontation'.[138] The most alarming aspect of this address was a personal slight: Khazbulatov joked about 'sobriety' and accompanied his words with 'unambiguous gesticulation'.[139] According to a Supreme Soviet Deputy, the meaning of Khazbulatov's remark was that Yeltsin 'signed edicts under the influence of alcohol'.[140] This was a deliberate and dangerous baiting of Yeltsin, who had never resorted to personal insults in public politics. The timing of Khazbulatov's remarks boded ill for the prospects of reconciliation: shortly before the Chairman spoke, Yeltsin had agreed to the parliament's demand for an early Presidential election.

'Ruslan Khazbulatov is doing everything to make impossible human, and therefore political, contact between himself and the President,' declared a *Nezavisimaya Gazeta* editorial. 'The key issue to worry about now is this: will Boris Yeltsin and Ruslan Khazbulatov become (if they have not already become) mortal enemies? If yes, then it was the Speaker [Khazbulatov] who took the decisive step towards this [confrontation]. And the entire responsibility for the consequences will be his.'[141]

At eight in the evening on 21 September 1993, all Russian television stations began broadcasting Yeltsin's address to the nation. Recorded in the Kremlin several hours earlier, the tape had been delivered to studios and editorial offices by Kremlin couriers, the *feld'yegers*. Yeltsin seemed composed, confident and calm:

> Esteemed fellow citizens. I am speaking to you at one of the most complicated and critical moments, on the eve of extremely important events. In recent months, Russia has been going through a deep crisis of statehood. Literally, all state institutions and political leaders have been drawn into a fruitless and senseless fight to the death.[142]

He had been agonizing over these lines since the beginning of September when he had made the decision: alone and in secret even from his closest aides.[143] Here he was, Yeltsin later recalled, Russia's first elected leader, about to break the law – a 'bad law, a law that had brought the country to the edge of collapse, but the law nevertheless'.[144] To justify ending the crisis this way was difficult and awkward: 'The President violates the Constitution, adopts anti-democratic measures, dissolves the parliament – to strengthen democracy and the rule of law in the country,' Yeltsin wrote later. 'The parliament defends the Constitution – in order to subvert the elected President and establish Soviet power. How entangled we have become in all these contradictions!'[145]

And yet he was convinced that he could wait no longer. Two days before the original date of the announcement (Sunday, 19 September), the Ministers of Internal Affairs, Security and Defence tried to persuade him to postpone the move till the end of the week. Somehow, they said, Khazbulatov and Rutskoy had found out about the plan and had appealed to their followers to come to the White House and remain there. The key objective of the operation – occupying an empty White House and thus avoiding a protracted crisis – had been irretrievably compromised. Yeltsin refused to cancel the operation. He agreed only to postpone the announcement by two days.[146]

On 20 September Egor Gaidar, whom Yeltsin trusted more than almost anyone else and often treated with utterly uncharacteristic, almost fatherly tenderness, asked for an urgent meeting. Brought back into the government and appointed First Deputy Prime Minister and Minister of the Economy only two days before, he too felt that the timing of the move was 'poor'.[147] Yeltsin agreed to meet, then postponed the interview until the following day. On the morning of 21 September, Yeltsin himself called Gaidar to apologize: he would not be able to see him that day either. The President did not want to waste time, 'to discuss something that was already decided', Gaidar concluded.[148] In the interim, Prime Minister Chernomyrdin had also tried and failed, during a 'long and difficult' private session, to change Yeltsin's mind.[149]

Now, in front of the cameras, Yeltsin's task was to persuade the country that the decision, no matter how difficult, had to be made.

You and I hoped that the turning point would come after the April referendum in which the citizens of Russia supported the President and the course pursued by him. Alas, that did not happen. The last few days have finally destroyed the hopes for the resumption of any constructive co-operation . . .

[The Supreme Soviet's] decisions on the budget, privatization and many others compound the crisis and inflict huge damage on the country. All the government's efforts somehow to alleviate the economic situation come up against a blank wall of incomprehension. Hardly a day goes by without the Council of Ministers being harassed, its hands twisted . . .

. . . Esteemed compatriots, the only way of overcoming the paralysis of state power in the Russian Federation is its radical renovation on the basis of the principles of people's power and constitutionality. The existing Constitution does not allow this. Nor does the existing Constitution envisage a procedure of adopting a new Constitution [which would] provide for a dignified exit from the crisis of statehood. Being the guarantor of the security of our state, I am obliged to propose a way out of this deadlock, I am obliged to break this ruinous vicious circle.[150]

The introduction was over. He had finished justifying and defending. The next part was more difficult still: to announce and reconcile the two components of his plan – one repressive, the other democratic – and to convince the country and the world that the former was necessary for and, in the end, counterbalanced by the latter. Yeltsin paused and sipped from a cup of tea on his desk.[151]

Being vested with authority in the 1991 nationwide election – and Russian citizens confirmed their confidence in this authority at the April 1993 referendum – I have approved, by my decree, amendments and addenda to the current Constitution of the Russian Federation ... The Federal Assembly of the Russian Federation becomes the highest body of legislative power. It is a two-chamber parliament, operating on a [full-time] professional basis. The elections are set for 11 and 12 December of this year ... I am in favour, after a certain period, after the sitting of the Federal Assembly, of an early Presidential election being held, and only you, the electors, should decide who will occupy Russia's highest office the next time.[152]

Effective 21 September, the Supreme Soviet and the Congress of People's Deputies were defunct and their powers nullified. The Deputies' privileges, however, were 'guaranteed in full': they were to regain the jobs they had held prior to their election and every Deputy had the right to stand for election to the Federal Assembly. No emergency regime was envisaged and the rights and freedoms of Russian citizens were to be guaranteed.[153]

The measures that I as President of the Russian Federation have to take are the only way to defend democracy and freedom in Russia, to protect the reforms and the Russian market, which is still in its infancy. These measures are essential for protecting Russia and the whole world against the catastrophic consequences of the disintegration of the

Russian state, against anarchy recurring in a country which has an enormous arsenal of nuclear weapons . . .

Esteemed fellow citizens, the time has come when by joining forces together, we can and must put an end to the deep crisis of the Russian state. I rely on your understanding and support. I rely on your common sense and sense of civic duty. We have a chance to help Russia. I believe we will use [this chance] for the sake of peace and calm in our country, for the sake of ridding Russia of this exhausting struggle of which all of us had become tired. Let us preserve Russia for ourselves and our children by joining forces together. Let us preserve it for our children and grandchildren.[154]

*

There were few surprises in the reaction to the President's gambit. Calling the Supreme Soviet 'the guarantor of legality and order in our state' in a front-page appeal in *Pravda*, the Central Committee of the Communist Party of the Russian Federation called on 'soldiers, sailors, militia and state security agencies' to defend the legislature 'against the criminal encroachments of B. N. Yeltsin and his clique'.[155] Everyone to the defence of Soviet power and its supreme organ![156]

The organ of leftist nationalists, *Sovetskaya Rossia*, saw Yeltsin's objectives as organizing a 'semblance of elections in siege conditions', acquiring 'a dictator's powers', dissolving Soviets 'at all levels' and banning 'left-wing and patriotic organizations'.[157] The Supreme Soviet derived its strength from the fact that the law and the 'world's democratic public' were on its side, while 'Yeltsin's lackeys [were] paralysed by fear for their hides.' 'YELTSIN IS AN OUTLAW!' declared the banner headline in the nationalist *Den'*.[158]

To radical democrats and reformers inside and outside the government, Decree No. 1400 had not only prevented the 'dictatorship of the Soviets',[159] it was the beginning of the final attack on the 'system of communist Soviets'.[160] Two years after the collapse of communism, the end of Soviet power was finally in sight.

The Co-ordinating Council of the Democratic Russia movement praised Yeltsin for 'breaking the vicious circle of the power struggle' and called on Russian citizens to prepare for the 11–12 December elections.[161] The Council appealed to the President to act 'with maximum resolution' so that the people might 'calmly express their will' at the elections, which would 'ensure a peaceful democratic way out of the political crisis'.[162]

As for the violation of the Constitution and the dissolution of the legislature, to the President's supporters among the 'democrats' this was an acceptable price to pay to stem the erosion of power, end the spectacle of the government's 'helplessness' and prevent a national catastrophe.[163] 'Decisiveness' was more important now than 'irreproachability' (*bezuprechnost*).[164] 'Yeltsin broke the law,' said Igor Golembiovskiy, editor of the leading liberal daily, *Izvestia*. 'But if you look at the fate of the country, he did the right thing.'[165]

On 21 September, wrote a leading liberal columnist, Russia was confronted with a choice: 'Observe the law "Khazbulatov-style" or break the law once "à la Yeltsin" . . .'[166] The latter was definitely the lesser evil because it led to elections; and there could be nothing more legitimate than to ask the people themselves.[167] As to the charges of dictatorship, they simply did not make sense to Yeltsin's supporters: 'a dictator proposes himself, Yeltsin proposes democratic elections'.[168]

Most of the Moscow intelligentsia, however, brimmed with intense and well-advertised disgust for both the White House and the Kremlin. A plague on both your houses! declared *Nezavisimaya Gazeta* and *Moskovskie Novosti*, through which the Russian capital's political cognoscenti communicated with one another. The parliament and the President were to blame 'in equal measure', wrote Grigoriy Yavlinsky, the leader of a quintessentially urban democratic pro-reform movement.[169] Neither side could absolve itself of responsibility, Yavlinsky continued. While he held no brief for the Supreme Soviet ('It is impossible to support the parliament not only because it was illegitimate but also because it was leading to the establishment of dual power in the country'),[170] Yavlinsky suggested 'mutual renunciation' by both sides of the decisions taken on 21 September, and simultaneous Presidential and parliamentary elections no later than January 1994.[171]

While the supporters of the Supreme Soviet had nothing but scorn for radical reformers (to whom they had long stopped listening and whom they called 'der'mokrats', a play on *der'mo*, 'shit'), the initial response to Decree No. 1400 could not but be disappointing in several other respects. The 'wave of popular indignation', on which the White House had counted so much, failed to materialize. The hearts of the leaders of most local Soviets might have been with their Moscow colleagues, but their minds dictated prudence. Grumbling yet passive, they hedged their bets. In only four of the eighty-nine regions did both the leadership of the *oblast* Soviets and the head of the regional administration, appointed by the President, openly support the Supreme Soviet,*

---

* These *oblast*s were Amur, Belgorod, Bryansk and Novosibirsk. In the elections of 1995–6, the first three elected communist governors.

and only in one case, that of Bryansk, was the President worried enough to dismiss his prefect.

Nothing happened even after the ultimatum of the representatives of sixty-two Soviets, who convened in Moscow and threatened to 'stop the delivery of supplies' to the capital unless the Constitution was restored.[172] The call to block the Trans-Siberian railway produced only a few hundred demonstrators who soon dispersed without violence.[173]

Russia's largest labour organization, the communist-dominated Federation of Independent Trade Unions of Russia,[174] which inherited the enormous resources, facilities and memberships of the official Soviet trade unions, declared its support for the White House on behalf of its fifty million members* and called for protests and strikes. There were no takers. Even the miners of Vorkuta, who seemed always to be on strike, returned to work and issued a statement in support of Yeltsin.[175]

Another unpleasant surprise for the White House was the staunch neutrality of the Russian military. Despite the dramatic diminution of funding and prestige since January 1992, Russian officers and soldiers appeared unmoved by the prospects of restoration of the Soviet Union and its military might, central to the national security agenda of the radical left-nationalist wing of Yeltsin's opponents in the Supreme Soviet. 'The armed forces of the Russian Federation will ... continue to observe strict political neutrality,' the Defence Ministry's spokesman declared hours after Yeltsin's speech.[176] 'The Army will not get involved in any political actions whatsoever,' the Minister of Defence, General Pavel Grachev, confirmed the next day.[177]

The government seemed confident enough to declare repeatedly that it neither wanted to engage the armed forces nor foresaw any need to do so.† Despite daily, often hourly rumours to the contrary, no troops had been moved towards Moscow, much less deployed inside the capital. The

---

* The small 'truly independent' unions declared for Yeltsin (*OMRI Daily*, 28 September 1993).

† First Deputy Prime Minister Sergey Shakhray listed the government's objectives: 'not to impose a state of emergency, not to arrest former People's Deputies, to avert bloodshed in Moscow and the regions, and not to give in to provocations' (interview with the Russian Television Channel (Rossia), 23 September 1993 (FBIS, 24 September 1993, p. 31)). Prime Minister Viktor Chernomyrdin was more emphatic: 'God forbid, no extraordinary measures, nothing extraordinary! ... No use of force or anything like that, this is ruled out, ruled out. This cannot be, and will not be' (interview with the Russian Television Channel (Rossia), 21 September 1993 (FBIS, 22 September 1993, p. 17)).

elite 106th Guards Paratroop (Tul'skaya) division, which Yeltsin visited shortly before 21 September (and which had since featured in every rumour about emergency rule), was busy showing off its skills at combat landing and shooting to the visiting British Secretary of State for Defence, Malcolm Rifkind.[178] Most of the soldiers in regiments around Moscow did what they did every September: almost 23,000 servicemen were picking potatoes in the fields of collective farms.[179]

The White House was also let down by Viktor Chernomyrdin and his government. 'We have counted on him,' said Ruslan Khazbulatov. But 'Chernomyrdin has shown himself a helpless, weak-willed man.'[180] Instead of distancing himself from Yeltsin, the stolid 'Chairman of the Government' – who looked and spoke like a veteran industrial apparatchik and 'red manager' (and, of course, was one), and who had been enthusiastically confirmed by the Congress of People's Deputies less than a year before – chose to justify the President's decision with an energy and conviction few had expected. 'What sort of work is it?' the Prime Minister fulminated in a televised interview. 'What sort of decisions? Look, the government is completely paralysed! How can decisions be made in a situation where your decisions are always followed by counter-decisions [by the Supreme Soviet]? There is an immediate counterweight ... How can we live like this?'[181] The 'cancerous tumour' of dual authority could only have been removed 'surgically', Chernomyrdin concluded.[182] The President's decision was necessary to 'stop the ruinous self-destruction of authority'. It was a decision 'in favour of reform, for the benefit of the economy and the end of instability and uncertainty'.[183]

While indicating that in the past he had had some 'well-grounded' doubts about this course of action, another potential ally of the White House, the young and ambitious First Deputy Prime Minister Sergey Shakhray also sided with Yeltsin. The situation had developed in ways that made the President's choice 'the only possible' one, he said.[184] 'This decision guarantees that society is given a chance to use the only civilized method for resolving the question of power: not on the barricades but through ballot boxes.'[185]

Yet another blow to the power of the Soviets was the uniformity of reaction of the 'civilized world', still defined by the Russian political class as Western Europe, Canada and the United States. Apparently satisfied by Yeltsin's protestations of non-violence and freedom of choice in the next elections, all major democracies supported the regime. Most painful to the White House must have been the attitude of the United States – Russia's perennial model and obsession, whose imprimatur of recognition and respect was precious to Russian leaders across the political spectrum (as it had been to all Soviet leaders since Stalin, no matter what they said in public).*

Even the gentle Vaclav Havel, whom (following their Western friends and colleagues) the Russian intelligentsia considered the paragon of democratic virtue in the post-communist world, professed 'full understanding' of Yeltsin's action. The latter, according to the Czech President, was aimed at solving the constitutional and political crisis in Russia.[186] The Czech Foreign Ministry called the crisis 'not very surprising': the Russian 'superparliament' was inherited from the Soviet past and new elections were thus 'necessary to resolve the situation'.[187]

Yet in the early days of the crisis a few dashed hopes did not seem to matter much. The White House was brimming with feverish exuberance. After the annoying temporizing, after so many inconclusive confrontations and retreats, the battle to the end with the hated President which the 'irreconcilable' opposition had wanted for so long was now joined. In the White House, the leaders of the 'irreconcilables' from the Russian Unity bloc – Sergey Baburin, Ilya Konstantinov and Nikolay Pavlov – were reported to be happy and 'glowing' with contentment.[188] Yeltsin had blundered and now they could finally 'gobble him up'.[189]

In accordance with a constitutional amendment adopted by the Congress a few months before, the President was to be automatically removed from office if he tried to 'violate the Constitution' by dissolving the parliament. After the failed attempt in March, the Supreme Soviet was now able to do what it most wanted. Two hours after Yeltsin's address, a triumphant Ruslan Khazbulatov announced that Yeltsin was no longer President.[190] Three hours later, at an extraordinary session of the Supreme Soviet, Yeltsin was impeached. This time the votes of the 146 members present were enough.[191] At midnight on 21 September, Aleksandr Rutskoy was sworn in as 'acting President of Russia'.

By this time, the Square of Russian Freedom around the White House had been ringed with barricades and between 1,500 and 2,000 'members of pro-communist parties' gathered around bonfires.[192] Rutskoy called on them to 'move from rallies to resolute actions'.[193] The Yeltsin clique, he added, would not 'relinquish power just like that'.[194]

The next morning, 22 September, the Supreme Soviet produced some powerful incentives for the 'clique' to give up. At Sergey Baburin's

---

* 'I support [Yeltsin] fully,' President Clinton stated. 'There is no question that President Yeltsin acted in response to a constitutional crisis that had reached a critical impasse.' (*OMRI Daily*, 22 September 1993.)

suggestion, the Supreme Soviet quickly added two articles to the Criminal Code of the Russian Federation. In the case of government officials, attempts to 'change by force the constitutional system' were to be punished by execution or sentences of ten to fifteen years in prison. For the same offence Yeltsin's supporters outside the government were to be incarcerated for between six and twelve years.[195] Talking to journalists at the White House the next day, Ruslan Khazbulatov confirmed that 'all who supported President Yeltsin [would] be severely punished'.[196] On 30 September, the Supreme Soviet's 'Minister of Internal Affairs' Andrey Dunaev announced that a tribunal set up by the Deputies had sentenced one of the top officials of the Ministry of Internal Affairs to be shot.[197]

The Tenth 'Extraordinary' Congress of People's Deputies, which convened at the White House on the evening of 23 September, opened on the same note of confidence, defiance and indignation. Although only 638* (of 1,041) Deputies had registered, the two-thirds quorum was quickly reached by the expulsion of ninety People's Deputies 'who had supported the *coup d'état* or other moves aimed at using force to change the constitutional structure or who had absented themselves without good reason'.[198]†

In the first two hours, the Congress approved the Supreme Soviet's decree that had stripped Yeltsin of power and appointed Rutskoy acting President. The Congress voted to remove the Ministers of Defence, Security and Internal Affairs and replace them with the candidates nominated by Rutskoy: the retired General Vladislav Achalov; an ex-Minister of Security of Russia, Viktor Barannikov, fired three months before by Yeltsin for corruption; and Andrey Dunaev, former Deputy Minister of

---

* Pro-Yeltsin 'democratic' Deputies claimed later that the actual number of Deputies in attendance was 443 and had been inflated on Khazbulatov's order. (See, for example, Fedor Shelov-Kovedyaev's appeal on the Russian Television Channel (Rossia) on the night of 3–4 October (Washington, DC: Library of Congress, Videotape VBI 2314).)

† Among these were Khazbulatov's deputy, Nikolay Ryabov, and the Chairmen of key committees: Sergey Stepashin (Defence and Security), Aleksandr Pochinok (Budget and Finance) and Evgeniy Ambartsumov (International Affairs and Foreign Economic Relations). All four had resigned.

Ryabov's departure from the Supreme Soviet became inevitable after his relatively moderate reaction to Yeltsin's decree: 'Everyone is aware that early parliamentary elections are necessary, but, on the other hand, it is impossible not to realize that the path towards them is outside the Constitution' (Russian Television Channel (Rossia), 21 September 1993 (FBIS, 22 September 1993, p. 10)).

Internal Affairs of Russia, also recently dismissed by the President.

Freed by the Presidential decree from the last constraints of decorum and no longer forced to contend with the small but vociferous faction of 'democrats' in its midst, the rump Congress let Ruslan Khazbulatov and Aleksandr Rutskoy articulate its positions starkly and without embarrassment. Yeltsin wanted to establish not 'just dictatorial' but 'blatantly tyrannical personal power', Khazbulatov said.[199] Ruling by 'treachery, lies and petty intrigue', the Yeltsin regime had abandoned the people to the whim of the 'savage' market and brought Russia to the 'brink of civil war'.[200] The Belavezhskie Accords proved that the people's interests had always been alien to Yeltsin. And now, thanks to his latest betrayal, Russia risked repeating the fate of the Soviet Union.[201]

The economic reforms were being implemented solely to curry favour with the West and to 'subordinate the country's economy to the raw-material corporations of international financial and industrial groups'.[202] The regime's 'very narrow social base' consisted of those who had amassed 'fabulous riches by robbery', who had built palaces, owned 'several expensive limousines' and holidayed in the Canary Islands – those who wallowed in luxury while 90 per cent of the people suffered unprecedented impoverishment.[203]

The acting President Rutskoy presented an economic agenda. It was time, he said, to carry out the decisions of the Congresses of People's Deputies that had been 'blocked' by the government and 'the former President'.[204] Food prices would be fixed by government decree, brought down by between 50 and 60 per cent and subsidized by the state, which would pay the producers the difference between the set and the market price.[205] Producers who overcharged by as much as one kopeck would be subject to a 1,000 per cent fine.[206] Wages would be quarterly indexed to the rate of inflation, while bank deposits ('illegally made worthless, or, more accurately, confiscated by the anti-people leadership') would be indexed all the way back to 1 January 1992.[207] Many taxes would be cut,[208] while state funding for healthcare, culture, science, education, the armed forces and law enforcement would be revised upwards.[209]

As to the President's offer of early elections, the Congress resolved that simultaneous parliamentary and Presidential elections were necessary in principle but not before the political system was restored to its pre-21 September status.[210] The Congress called for the 'restoration of the system of power envisaged by the Constitution'.[211]

At a press conference the following day, Ruslan Khazbulatov 'firmly declared' that there could be no compromise and no negotiations with the 'fascist regime', the 'junta'.[212] 'What compromise, what are you talking about?' he snapped at a foreign reporter. 'Let's not talk nonsense. There has been a *coup d'état*, it must be suppressed, that's your compromise.'[213] The Speaker urged officers to bring troops to defend the parliament and pledged to 'hold out here for as long as necessary to crush the putsch'.[214]

Indeed, the occupants of the White House appeared to be settling in for a long haul. From the first night, the white-blue-and-red tricolour of post-communist Russia was barely visible in the sea of red banners and black-and-yellow nationalist flags: 'the red flag is the one that dominates', a *Pravda* reporter wrote proudly. 'It is the flag of the great power . . . and the banner of communist parties. It was indeed the communists who were the first to come to this square to oppose dictatorship.'[215] With every passing day, there were more and more hammer-and-sickles until, by the time of the denouement, the official tricolour on top of the building was reported to have been torn down.[216] The façade of the White House was soon covered with leaflets and posters: 'Revive the Communist Party of Russia!', 'All power to the Soviets!', 'Lenin's cause lives and wins!', 'Non-Russians – out of Moscow!', 'Let's reveal the ethnicity of all who work in the mass media!', 'Blacks – out of Moscow!'[217]

At first furtively, then more and more confidently, men with Kalashnikov submachine guns* in paratrooper camouflage began to venture outside the building and stroll about through the crowd on the Square of Russian Freedom.[218] First noticed on the afternoon of 22 September,[219] they and their less conspicuous armed comrades were to become known to the Supreme Soviet's supporters as 'defenders' and to the rest of Moscow as *boeviki*, the latter term having been used in the Russian mass media to describe guerrillas and terrorists. In the 'Defence Department' of the White House, Russian journalists were told that these were the 'Department's officers'.[220]

The man in charge of the 'Department' was one of Yeltsin's rivals in the 1991 Presidential election, the retired General Albert Makashov.

---

* According to a 'defender', the initial inventory of arms in the White House included 500 submachine guns, six machine guns and 200 pistols (Ivan Ivanov, 'Oni srazhalis' za Rodinu' ('They fought for the Motherland'), *Zavtra*, 1, November 1993). According to a government estimate, there were 1,600 submachine guns, over 2,000 pistols, eighteen machine guns and twelve grenade launchers (the press conference of Vyacheslav Ogorodnikov, head of the Department for the Maintenance of Public Order of the Ministry of Interior, 1 October 1993. ITAR-TASS, 1 October 1993 (FBIS, 4 October 1993, p. 33)).

Addressing the crowd from a balcony on 23 September, Makashov promised 'to make life impossible' for those Deputies who disagreed with the leadership of the Supreme Soviet.[221] He added that he would lay hands on the traitors 'and see to it that they wash their faces in their own blood'.[222]

The 'defenders', who at different times numbered between 400 and 800,[223] were a motley crew. The Kremlin believed that the volunteers had come from as far away as the self-proclaimed 'Soviet Socialist Transdniester Republic' (a Russian–Ukrainian enclave in Moldova) and from Riga, whence hailed the veterans of the long-disbanded and banned OMON of January 1991 fame.[224] With sabres on their belts, Cossacks walked around in tall astrakhan hats, black coats and soft leather boots. Among the 'groups of sinister men, heavy bags slung across their shoulders', a foreign correspondent even spotted a detachment of Ruslan Khazbulatov's compatriots, the Chechens.[225]

Two armed groups constituted the majority of the 'defenders' (and with a steady outflow of Deputies from the White House, soon the majority of all those inside). The first consisted of the members of the Officers' Union, led by Lieutenant-Colonel Stanislav Terekhov. A graduate of the Leningrad Higher Air Defence Military–Political School for commissars (Party supervisors of the military), Terekhov had risen to Komsomol leadership of a military district and been sent to the Soviet Union's top school for 'political leadership' of the armed forces: the Lenin Military–Political Academy in Moscow.[226] Students and teachers of the Academy became the first members of the Officers' Union, organized by Terekhov in late 1991 to 'fight without mercy enemies, traitors and mercenary time-servers who are breaking up the state and demoralizing the Army'.[227] Shortly before he moved to the White House, Terekhov told the Officers' Union 'Assembly': 'The Third World War is not far off; we are on the eve of the decisive battle.'[228]

Members of the Officers' Union formed the backbone of the 'Russian Federation Supreme Soviet's special-purpose motorized rifle regiment' that guarded the White House.[229] The regiment's commander, Colonel Markov, was the Union's district organizer and a former commissar. By his own admission, he had been retired from the Army after he had 'openly opposed the Belavezhskie Accords [which] broke up the Soviet Union and the Soviet Army'.[230] When the *boeviki* of the Officers' Union were implicated in the first death to occur during the crisis, the organization's members inside the White House said that 'even if someone's blood [was] shed, the Motherland [was] worth the price'.[231]

The other most numerous and visible group of armed 'defenders' were members of Russian National Unity or RNE, an acronym for Russkoye Natsional'noye Edinstvo. Their leader, Aleksandr Barkashov, had begun his political career in 1985 as a deputy to Dmitriy Vasiliev, the leader of the Russian nationalist movement Pamyat'. An electrician who had served in the elite *spetsnaz* ('special operation') troops of the Soviet Army and had risen to the rank of corporal, Barkashov's responsibilities in Pamyat' were 'physical fitness', 'protection of demonstrations' and 'distribution of publications'.[232] He left Pamyat' in 1990, disappointed by the 'lack of action',[233] and formed RNE the same year.

In January 1991, during the war between the US-led coalition and Iraq, Barkashov had organized meetings and demonstrations in support of Saddam Hussein.[234] In August 1991 he sent Gennadiy Yanaev a telegram of support.[235] Of the estimated 500 fighters of the RNE, between 100 and 200 came to defend the White House.[236] They were designated a 'special military detachment of the Ministry of Security' and served as bodyguards for Rutskoy, Khazbulatov, Achalov[237] and Barannikov. Barkashov was given the rank of lieutenant-colonel. Even inside the White House the *barkashovtsy* were referred to as 'fascists',[238] the term Russians used for German Nazis. The RNE troops did not seem to mind the comparison. They were quite proud of the parallel and had done a great deal to invite it, with their black shirts and a swastika-like cross of missiles on their sleeves.[239]

'I like Adolf Hitler,' Barkashov had told interviewers four months before.

In the hardest circumstances for his people and his state he managed to revive the state and instil the nation with belief in itself . . . After 1917, exploiting the temporary weakness of the [Russian] nation and state, a huge number of people of Jewish nationality seized top and middle levers of power. After that they inflicted mass terror and genocide on the Russian people. But everything proceeds according to the laws of nature and the force of action is equal to the force of counteraction . . . and they [the Jews] should get out of Russia before it's too late. And the West should not be deceived by the fact that at the moment the power in the state belongs to the anti-people clique which kowtows to the United States. Soon the clique's rule will be over – no doubt about that. And nothing will change this course of events![240]

Obsession with Jews, alongside a hatred of Yeltsin and the *der'mo -krats* united most of the 'defenders' and their comrades on the outside.

'You are a yid – I am not talking to you,' a Cossack with a sabre and a Kalashnikov responded to a question from a passer-by.[241] 'And what are you, little Jew-girl [evreechka], doing here with us?' a Russian journalist was asked as she tried to board a bus full of White House supporters.[242] 'It is time to end with the Jews in the mass media, finance and economy,' a demonstrator in front of the White House told a reporter.[243] And when a riot broke out on 2 October, placards reading 'Papa, kill a Jew!' were seen in the crowd at the corner of the Arbat and the Garden Ring next to 'Kill Yeltsin' posters.[244]

To the 'defenders', the most feared enemy were mysterious Jews named beytars. That word, beytar,* 'filled the air [inside the White House] with something otherwordly, something horrible', recalled. a witness. 'The beytars are more terrifying than regular soldiers,' she was told. 'They will come and kill everyone, and rape pregnant women, and drink children's blood . . .' And who are they, these beytars? the same witness asked a 'defender'. 'Bokser's scum.† They are not human . . . If they get inside, we are all finished.'

Because the original plan to occupy an empty White House on a Sunday failed, the only thing left for the Kremlin to do, if it was to avoid violence and casualties, was, in Yeltsin's words, to 'let them be and [to] ignore their sessions and their congresses'.[245] The President ordered the Moscow militia disarmed[246] – especially those patrolling around the White House.

Dispersing the crowd around the White House (let alone disarming the boeviki inside) was something that the Kremlin did not seem even to have considered. 'How long are you going to procrastinate? This crowd in front of the White House, can't you remove them? . . . There will be more and more [people] as time goes by,' a Russian journalist said in private to Yeltsin's Chief of Staff, Sergey Filatov, on 27 September. 'I understand you,' Filatov answered. 'I have been there myself today. I know that the order [to seal the White House] is not being carried out. Only what are we to do with the crowd? . . . We can't disperse it, can we?'[247]

---

* Betar (the acronym of Hebrew words Berit Yoseph Trumpeldor, or 'Yoseph Trumpeldor League'), youth organization of the Zionist Revisionist party with headquarters in Israel, started as a Jewish scout movement in Latvia in 1923. Its Moscow branch was established in the early 1990s. It instructed about a dozen Jewish teens in the rudiments of karate and the history of Israel. By 1994, the Moscow betar went out of existence.
† Dr Vladimir Bokser, a Jew, was a leader of Democratic Russia. He had no connection whatsoever with the Moscow betar. (Interview with Vladimir Bokser.)

The 'special' government telephone lines to the White House had been cut immediately after Yeltsin's address. Two days later, in response to the gathering of the outlawed Congress, the Kremlin blocked all telephone communication with the building, as well as delivery of electricity, heat and water.

On 25 September, Yeltsin announced what amounted to a blanket amnesty for those who had disregarded Decree No. 1400 – Deputies and ordinary citizens alike. Provided 'their actions did not contain the elements of crime for which liability was established by the Criminal Code of the RSFSR', no one could be prosecuted for supporting 'decisions made since 21 September 1993 by a group of former People's Deputies'.[248] The Decree specified that proceedings could not be instituted against those who participated in rallies and demonstrations in support of the dissolved legislature.[249] An earlier decree granted the Deputies of the dissolved Congress a lump sum amounting to a year's salary and allowed them to keep their most treasured possession, their Moscow apartments, originally 'assigned' only for the term of their membership. They and their families could also continue to use 'special' medical facilities and sanatoriums.[250]

Considering the White House thus bypassed and neutralized, the Kremlin busied itself with the forthcoming election. A stream of decrees and laws were to guide the poll's organization. Published on 22 September, Decree No. 1400, which dissolved the parliament, also established the Central Electoral Commission to organize and supervise the election. All state organs and officials were to assist the Commission in ensuring the electoral rights of citizens.[251] A draft of a new constitution was to be prepared by 12 December.

Two days later, Yeltsin signed a decree appointing the Chairman of the Commission and ordering the regional authorities to submit within five days lists of candidates for members of the Commission.[252] In addition to the regional delegates, the Commission was to include one representative from each of the nationwide (federal) parties and blocs that had been registered for participation in the election.[253] Yet another decree established that the voters would cast two ballots: one for a candidate in their electoral districts and the other for a party or bloc. Two-thirds of the 450 members of the Duma (the lower House of the Federal Assembly) were to be elected by a majority of votes in so-called 'single-mandate' electoral districts and one-third by proportional representation from parties and blocs ('party lists') based on their share of the party-preference vote.[254]

After meeting with the leaders of parties and associations of 'democratic orientation', Yeltsin agreed to change the electoral law by allowing half, rather than one-third, of the Deputies to be elected from party lists.[255] The President hoped that an increased party representation would make it easier for all political parties to participate[256] and provide an incentive for the opposition. He 'preferred the communists and national-patriots to stand for election, rather than on the barricades'.[257]

As to the Presidential election, Yeltsin was vehemently opposed to holding it simultaneously with the legislative poll. It was up to the newly elected Federal Assembly to adopt a law on the Presidential election, which would then be held on 12 June of the following year.[258]

In the meantime, demonstrations in support of the Supreme Soviet were held without any interference by the authorities. On one such occasion, according to *Pravda*, the city administration even sent three trolleys 'so that people could keep warm inside them because it was raining and cold on the street'.[259]

While the Supreme Soviet's access to state-owned television was limited to news reports and snippets of press conferences, print and television journalists (Russian and foreign) could walk into the White House at any time and were not restricted in what they transmitted or published. The Supreme Soviet's own radio station (which operated on a 41-metre band) was not jammed.[260]

All the communist and nationalist newspapers (*Pravda*, Sovetskaya Rossia and *Den'* chief among them) continued to print and freely distribute interviews, manifestos and appeals from the White House. Aleksandr Rutskoy's were especially fervent. In one such plea, he implored his fellow generals, commanders of ground forces, airborne troops, Air Force and Navy, 'not to stand aside' and to 'adopt an active stance'.[261] A 'great power – the Soviet Union – was destroyed before our eyes', Rutskoy reminded them. Now Russia was in 'mortal danger'. At a time when the state was being destroyed, the Army could no longer remain outside politics.[262] He could not understand his Soviet Army comrades, Rutskoy told *Pravda*. 'How is it possible to swear allegiance to the Motherland and then . . . watch in silence as, beginning with the Belavezhskaya Pushcha agreements, it has been torn to pieces and our people insulted? . . . No, I cannot believe that the entire Army consists of silent appeasers.'[263] Rutskoy ended with a call for a general political strike as the only means to 'save Russia and the people'.[264]

Invoking the glory of the Soviet Union, bemoaning its demise and using its fate as a warning were consistent themes in Rutskoy's statements. In another appeal (to the employees of the Ministry of Foreign

Affairs), published in *Pravda* on 1 October, he wrote: 'You Russian diplomats, who have received a fundamental political schooling in Soviet diplomacy, are of course not indifferent to what has happened to the USSR. The tragedy of a great state is now being repeated – this time it is happening to Russia. Are we really going to remain silent observers of this act of barbarity again?'[265]

In the first week of the crisis, anyone could pass through sparse rows of unarmed and sullen militiamen, get into the White House and bring with them all manner of supplies and, as later became apparent, weapons and ammunition as well. 'The cordon is there,' a journalist reported on 27 September, 'but people stroll to and from the White House with no problem whatsoever.'[266]

There was far more vigilance on the other side. *Boeviki* kept a wary eye on the visitors. Suspicious guests were interrogated, beaten up and thrown into the basement. One hapless Russian reporter was seized and interrogated twice after he was overheard telephoning reports to his newspaper. On the second occasion he was saved only by the personal intervention of the Supreme Soviet's press secretary, who accompanied the 'deported' journalist and his guards past the barricades. During the entire journey, the barrel of a Kalashnikov was pressed against the journalist's back.[267] A young man in a Red Cross uniform was not so lucky. The 'snake' had been caught 'transmitting something to somebody' on his radio, the Cossacks explained as they beat their prisoner with a rubber truncheon. 'I am an employee of the Red Cross. Here are my papers . . .', the man pleaded, as he held up his arms to protect his head from the blows. 'Screw your papers. I don't like your face,' responded one of his tormentors.[268]

The White House inhabitants breached the militia cordon at will. On 25 September, Aleksandr Rutskoy led a procession of 'defenders' and sympathizers. Under the red flag with hammer and sickle and the black-and-yellow nationalist banner, the demonstrators circled the White House, passed the US embassy a stone's throw away and the City Administration (the Mehria, as everyone called it, the Mayor's office) and returned 'in high spirits'.[269] The next day, Rutskoy led a march down the Novy Arbat Street, next to the White House.[270]

Every now and then, the newly created 'Ministers' of the Supreme Soviet's 'government' came down to the militia cordon to 'agitate'. On one such occasion, Rutskoy, surrounded by 'defenders' and television cameras, appealed to the militiamen to 'stop assisting the criminals'.[271] He gave them time (four hours) to change their minds and promised to exempt those who did so from criminal charges (which, he pointed out, could result in the death penalty).[272] The militiamen listened politely, but no 'fraternization' was noticed.[273]

Several days later, the 'Ministers' of Security and Internal Affairs, Viktor Barannikov and Andrey Dunaev, embarked on a similar expedition.[274] Barannikov's address was interrupted by a commotion behind him. Two of the Minister's RNE bodyguards (there were swastikas on their sleeves) were beating a scrawny, bearded man. As militiamen looked on without interference – that was not their territory – Barannikov ordered the man brought to him. The victim, who looked as if he had 'said goodbye to life', explained in broken Russian that he was an American reporter. 'There, there, boys,' the Minister reasoned with his troops. 'You shouldn't have . . . he is a journalist.' Barannikov turned to the victim. 'Don't be afraid. Stay next to me as long as you want.'[275] The bodyguards retreated a few paces. 'Hey, did we smack the little kike [*zhidyonok*] around, or what? . . .' 'Only not enough . . .' 'Just you wait, there'll be another time . . .'[276]

The first blood was spilled on the evening of Thursday, 23 September. Eight men in camouflaged fatigues killed a militiaman at point-blank range and forced their way into the headquarters of the CIS Unified Armed Forces on Leningradskiy Prospekt. The attackers disarmed two guards, took their weapons and fled. An elderly woman was killed by a stray bullet when she came to her apartment window. Witnesses identified the Chairman of the Officers' Union, Stanislav Terekhov, as one of the intruders.[277] The assault was immediately linked to the Supreme Soviet's supporters because Viktor Anpilov, the leader of the militant leftist Working Moscow (Trudolvaya Moskva), speaking from the balcony of the White House at the time of the assault, told the crowd that the Officers' Union was storming the CIS headquarters and called on the demonstrators to join the attack.[278]

The following day, the Mayor of Moscow, Yuriy Luzhkov, sent an ultimatum to Rutskoy, Khazbulatov, Achalov, Barannikov and Dunaev. Citing the 'tragic . . . loss of life' outside the CIS military headquarters and the 'anxiety and serious concern' which it had caused among Muscovites, Luzhkov demanded that all firearms and ammunition 'illegally distributed and kept' inside the White House be handed over to 'law-enforcement agencies' to prevent more casualties.[279]

It was not until 28 September, however, that the cordon around the building began to tighten. The President's Chief of Staff, Sergey Filatov, announced that a 'tough blockade' had been imposed in order to prevent the 'use of the large quantity of weapons' accumulated in the White

House and to thwart the 'organization of acts of terrorism by the armed irregular groups' in the building.[280] An official estimate of the number of *boeviki* inside the White House had grown to 600.[281]

Although, with luck, the determined and the enterprising could still get into the White House by climbing over walls and fences from adjacent streets, the new rules made access more difficult even for journalists. For the first time, Deputies were prevented from re-entering the building after a weekend. The square around the White House was surrounded by water-spraying trucks and barbed wire. The militiamen in the chain, however, remained unarmed except for rubber truncheons and plastic shields. As before, there were no obstacles to leaving the White House, and many continued to do so. On 28 and 29 September, 430 people, Deputies and personnel, exited from the building.[282]

Round the clock, from a bright yellow armoured personnel carrier, dubbed the 'Yellow Goebbels' by the 'defenders', loudspeakers blared official news summaries, Yeltsin's decrees, songs[283] and appeals to the Deputies to come out because of the 'futility and danger of possible spontaneous events orchestrated by their supporters, who were not always in control of their emotions'.[284]

On 29 September, after another militiaman had died (he was pushed into the Garden Ring traffic by pro-Supreme Soviet demonstrators and killed by a car), the government of Russia served Rutskoy and Khazbulatov with a 'demand'. In order for the authorities to be able to guarantee the personal safety of individuals inside the White House and of people in the adjacent areas, the occupants would have to leave the building by 4 October and give up their weapons and ammunition.[285] In return, the government guaranteed 'personal safety, freedom of political and public activity' to everyone, as well as freedom either to stay in Moscow or leave, if they so wished. No one would be prosecuted for illegal possession of firearms.[286]

Seemingly indifferent to the tightening knot at its centre, the Russian capital went about its daily business. For a great many, as it turned out, that business included attending the free concert given by the National Symphony Orchestra of the United States in Red Square on 25 September.

The political sympathies of the Orchestra's Director and conductor, Mstislav Rostropovich, and his personal friendship with Yeltsin had been well known since his visit to the besieged White House in August 1991. Although the concert had been scheduled long before 21 September, it turned into a show of support for the President as 100,000 people braved a 'bitter chill'[287] to hear an orchestra led by one of Yeltsin's staunchest allies. For almost two hours, Muscovites stood on the cobblestones of Red Square 'without moving and, it seemed to a witness, almost without breathing'.[288] Yeltsin, who appeared in the front row just before the performance began, received a 'tremendous ovation'.[289]

Hardly by accident, Rostropovich chose two of the most rousing patriotic pieces in the Russian musical canon: Prokofiev's 'Aleksandr Nevskiy' Symphony and Tchaikovskiy's '1812' Overture, complete with cannon volleys and the pealing of the bells of St Basil's Cathedral. 'This concert seems more like a political rally than a cultural event,' the NSO's principal trombonist wrote. 'But whether Slava [Rostropovich] is riding on Yeltsin's coattails or Yeltsin is taking advantage of public exposure is only a conjecture.'[290]

After performing in tails without an overcoat, Rostropovich rushed to his hotel to thaw out, and then was driven to a family dinner in Yeltsin's apartment, where the conductor's wife, the diva Galina Vishnevskaya, was already waiting for him. As they parted after a most enjoyable and relaxed evening, this peculiarly Russian duo – a President and a maestro – promised each other that, when they next saw each other, there would be no special occasion, and certainly no coups, no putsches, just enjoyment of each other's company.[291]

After the nine days of stand-off, neither appeals nor demands seemed to have had any effect on the two aspects of the crisis about which the Kremlin was especially anxious: the weapons distributed inside the White House and the *boeviki* gathered there. 'Above all', Prime Minister Chernomyrdin stated, the government was concerned about the large quantity of weapons in the hands of people 'who have nothing to do with the former parliament'. He promised that the cordon around the building would be completely removed as soon as the weapons had been confiscated and the *boeviki* had left the White House. 'We cannot risk the safety of the nine million people living in Moscow by constantly waiting for something to happen.'[292] 'You are free to leave and take up other work,' Yeltsin told the Deputies inside the White House. 'But . . . all talks must start with the surrender of weapons, because weapons are so dangerous in this situation. Any shot, even an accidental one, would be provocation that would lead to bloodshed. This is unacceptable.'[293]

At the 29 September meeting of the Security Council, chaired by Yeltsin, Chernomyrdin was instructed to negotiate with the Supreme Soviet 'in order to prevent developments around the White House from taking a dramatic turn'.[294] The following morning, Yeltsin met in the

Kremlin with Patriarch Aleksey II to discuss the Church's earlier offer of mediation.

The same afternoon, the White House accepted the Kremlin's invitation to negotiate under the Patriarch's auspices and the two sides met that evening at the Svyato-Danilovskiy monastery. Although not the principals, both sides were represented by major players: the Kremlin's team consisted of Sergey Filatov; First Deputy Prime Minister Oleg Soskovets; and Mayor of Moscow Yuriy Luzhkov. Negotiating for the White House were Deputy Chairman of the Supreme Soviet Veniamin Sokolov and Chairman of the Soviet of Nationalities (the lower house of the Supreme Soviet) Ramazan Abulatipov. The Church was represented by Yuvenaliy, the Metropolitan of Krutitsy and Kolomna, and Kirill, the Metropolitan of Smolensk and Kaliningrad.

The negotiators' good faith and mandate proved formidable. By two o'clock on the morning of 1 October, they had an agreement. The White House blockade was to be lifted in three stages. During the first phase, the government was to restore telephone connections and the supply of water, heat and electricity to the White House.[295] The next stage obliged the leadership of the Supreme Soviet to 'gather, stockpile and hand over' all the weapons inside the White House. At that time, order in and around the building was to be maintained by 'joint security pickets' consisting of militiamen and the staff of the Supreme Soviet's 'security department'.[296] After that, the government pledged 'completely to withdraw all security formations from the building and to lift the external guard'.[297]

Early in the morning of 1 October, electricity, heat and water were switched on, and the telephones in the White House were working again. On the following day, the inhabitants took off overcoats, put out candles and 'washed thoroughly' with hot water.[298] Its electric stoves working again, the cafeteria began to serve, free of charge, hot meals to everyone in the building. Journalists' access to the White House, which had been restored on 30 September after two days of quarantine,[299] continued unimpeded, and reporters arrived 'in droves'.[300] The Deputies still in the building – there were no more than 200 of them[301] – were greatly outnumbered by the visitors, the staff and especially the *boeviki*. The latter were ubiquitous: one of the first arrivals at the cafeteria counted 200 young men with Kalashnikovs.[302]

By mid-morning on 1 October, following the decision of the newly created 'Defence Council' (Achalov, Dunaev and Barannikov)[303] and recommendations of the Supreme Soviet's leadership, the Deputies voted to reject the Svyato-Danilovskiy agreement.[304] Without any preconditions and before anything else was agreed on, the Kremlin should fully lift the blockade, give Deputies 'live airtime on television' and allow the Ministers of Defence, Internal Affairs and Security, appointed by the Congress, to take office.[305]

As far as the firearms of the White House 'defenders' were concerned, the very 'issue of surrendering weapons [was] an error' because the arms rightfully belonged to the Supreme Soviet.[306] Contrary to the allegations of Yeltsin's supporters, there were no 'gang-style formations' in the White House, Rutskoy told reporters.[307] Instead, the White House 'defenders', between 400 and 500 men 'in full combat readiness', maintained order and discipline and were not going to 'organize provocations'. Their weapons had been 'inventoried and stored in a sealed room'.[308] 'The problem of weapons is an artificial problem,' Ruslan Khazbulatov told the Deputies. 'We, the Congress, are responsible for all the weapons on the territory of our country, including nuclear weapons. If [the Kremlin] continues this line [that is, insists on the surrender of the weapons], it would show a lack of seriousness in its attitude towards the negotiations.'[309]

Judging by what they said publicly on that day, both Rutskoy and Khazbulatov appeared to be intent on burning all bridges to the Kremlin. 'It is simply an outrage when a drunken President and his entourage have reduced the country to such a state,' the acting President told journalists. 'No compromise is possible with those who created a political concentration camp in the centre of Moscow.'[310] Ruslan Khazbulatov was more emphatic still: 'This regime is dead, its days are numbered, there is no point in continuing relations with it.'[311] Yeltsin's 'junta', he added, would be 'expelled from the Kremlin'.[312] Khazbulatov called on the Russian Army to abandon its neutrality and side with the White House: 'The armed forces have already seen what happens when they don't take sides. It led to the destruction of the Soviet Union. If they do the same today, it will lead to the destruction of Russia.'[313]

To head the Supreme Soviet's delegation at the Svyato-Danilovskiy negotiations Khazbulatov appointed his hard-line deputy, Yuriy Voronin. Though they dragged on for another three days, within twenty-four hours the talks became irrelevant.

The first violent confrontation of the crisis broke out on the morning of 2 October. Viktor Anpilov's Working Moscow occupied Smolenskaya Square in front of the Ministry of Foreign Affairs and erected barricades across the eight lanes of the Garden Ring. For several hours the rioters fought police with Molotov cocktails, rocks and sharpened metal rods.

Billows of black smoke from tyres, piled up and burned by the rioters, were visible blocks away.[314] By the evening, one militiaman had been killed and twenty-four injured.[315]

Several hundred metres away, Yeltsin was walking down Novy Arbat at the head of a festive procession to mark 500 years of Arbat Street. About halfway, at the intersection of Novy Arbat and the Garden Ring, demonstrators broke through the militia chain and started from the other end of Arbat in the direction of the President. Yeltsin was quickly shepherded into his limousine and whisked away.[316]

The next morning, 3 October, Working Russia, Viktor Anpilov's umbrella national organization, and the equally extreme Russian Communist Worker's Party (RKPR) were to hold a meeting at Oktyabr'skaya Square. Fearing a replay of the Smolenskaya riot, the militia closed the Square. The crowd, growing thicker with every block, began to walk along the Garden Ring,[317] past Neskuchniy Garden and the Central Art House. Soon there were at least 4,000 people under red banners.[318] The militiamen, frightened and defenceless, were not so much overpowered as enveloped by the angry crowd and then spewed out: bruised, often bleeding, their uniforms torn off. Seeing the roaring, scarlet-faced mass, many dropped their gear and fled without looking back.

One after another, the militia cordons across the Garden Ring were smashed: first on the Krymskiy Bridge, where 'all was over in half a minute';[319] then at Smolenskaya Square, where the militia cordon was broken 'like an eggshell', as a Russian television reporter put it.[320] The crowd was almost running. 'Fall in! Regroup! Faster, faster!' the militia leaders shouted.[321] After their drivers had been dragged out and beaten, the militia trucks were taken to the White House.[322]

On Novy Arbat the crowd grew to between 10,000 and 15,000, stretching from the Square of Russian Freedom to the Kalininskiy Prospekt.[323] The cordon around the White House crumbled in minutes. Filmed by intrepid Russian cameramen, grinning *boeviki* in camouflaged fatigues were shooting over the heads of the retreating column of unarmed militiamen. In grey coats, half marching, half running, the latter looked like a flock of terrified penguins.[324] In a few minutes not one militiaman remained in front of the White House. The abandoned street-cleaning trucks were flying red flags.

In front of the White House, the jubilant crowd held up portraits of Stalin.[325] Flags of the Soviet Union were 'everywhere'.[326] Megaphone in hand, Rutskoy stepped out on to the balcony. The crowd roared. 'We have won! . . . Women – step to the side! Men, form fighting detachments! Keep the momentum, forward, to the Mehria!'[327] Khazbulatov

was next: 'This is victory! Now we must build on the success!'[328] Sergey
Baburin told the cheering people that the Army was refusing to obey
Yeltsin's orders. But who needed the Army anyway? 'We are perfectly
capable of arresting all the scoundrels ourselves.'[329] 'Russia, only Russia
must restore the Union!' thundered a leader of the National Salvation
Front, fiery communist Sazhi Umalatova. 'So-vet-skiy So-yuz! So-vet-
skiy So-yuz! Soviet Union! Soviet Union!' responded the crowd.[330]
'"No" to the market, which robs people!' shouted a Working Russia
speaker. 'Motherland and socialism are one!'[331]

What to do with Yeltsin, once he had been captured, was the subject
of a lively discussion. 'Hang him publicly – but not on Red Square.
That would be too much honour for him,' someone suggested.[332] 'Yeah,
let's hang him! No, let's first put the viper in a cage and drive him
around a free Russia and scare people with the sight of him.'[333]

The Deputies, who by now numbered no more than 150,[334] were
called inside to continue the Congress session. Many embraced and
kissed one another. Khazbulatov was greeted by a standing ovation.[335]
'It is time to finish off the fascist dictator Yeltsin,' he said. 'This very
minute a seizure of the Kremlin is being planned under the command
of the acting President. The Kremlin will be taken today!'[336]

Nearby, a communist leader Oleg Shenin was giving an interview:
'No more talk about elections or referendums. We need to establish a
tough state power and to fill the seats of those Deputies who sold
themselves to Yeltsin.'[337] This was the same Shenin who, as a Central
Committee Secretary, had arrived at Gorbachev's villa in Foros on 18
August 1991 to demand that the Soviet President declare a state of
emergency and hand power over to the coup's leader, Gennadiy Yanaev.

A few blocks away, on Smolenskaya Square, another wave of demonstrators marched under red flags. 'Run to the Mehria! They are giving
away truncheons and shields there!' excited teenagers called to one
another. 'We are going to beat kikes!'[338] The crowd chanted: 'All power
to the Soviets! Rutskoy President! Kikes out of the Kremlin!'[339]

Two heavy military trucks rammed into the glass wall of the Mehria.
Crouching behind them, *boeviki* shot at the windows. After a few
minutes the militiamen inside surrendered. One of Luzhkov's deputies,
Aleksandr Braginskiy, was dragged out of the building and beaten.
Unarmed militiamen came out next. Some of them were also beaten and
all stripped of their bulletproof vests and helmets.[340] Goose-stepping as
if on parade, victorious *barkashovtsy* emerged from the entrance. A red
flag with a hammer and sickle was planted on top of the building.[341]
General Albert Makashov, sporting a rakish paratrooper beret and Kal-

ashnikov on his back, proclaimed through a megaphone the victory of a 'revolution against the counter-revolution'.[342]

Suddenly, the square in front of the White House was filled with armed men.[343] There were 'weapons everywhere, plain for all to see'.[344] Met by tumultuous cheering, Barkashov was the first to climb on to a truck bound for the Ostankino Television Centre. Grouped in two columns, the *barkashovtsy* followed their Führer.[345] In addition to smart, short-barrelled submachine guns, they carried grenade launchers.[346] One after another, filled with volunteers and flying red flags, the trucks seized from the militia were departing for Ostankino.[347] There were not enough buses for all those who wanted to fight for the Television Centre. *Barkashovtsy* quickly emptied a bus full of unarmed supporters: 'Quick, quick, make room for those with weapons.'[348] The rest of the crowd started for Ostankino on foot and soon began to stop and commandeer commuter buses.[349]

In Ostankino, two military trucks took turns crashing into the glass doors of the lobby at the Television Centre. The crowd cheered. Grenades from launchers hit the lobby. The building was on fire. A squad of commandos (*spetsnaz*) inside responded with volleys from automatic weapons. The attackers retreated, keeping close to the ground. 'Weapons! Give us more weapons!' called out voices in the crowd.[350] 'Fill the bottles with benzine!' someone ordered through a megaphone. Viktor Anpilov demonstrated how to make Molotov cocktails.[351] At eight o'clock, the First (Ostankino) national television channel went off the air.

At the White House a triumphant Khazbulatov summed up the situation: 'Ostankino has been captured. The Mehria has been captured. I think that today we must take the Kremlin. We need to develop a strategy for this night and the next morning – to complete victory.'[352]

Among those who surrounded Khazbulatov was a fearless young woman reporter who had been at the White House from the first hours of the crisis, recording what she saw, and who was determined to stay there to the end. She prided herself on not taking sides. Her job was to be objective and truthful. Her *Notes from the White House* would become the best chronicle of the crisis. Yet, when she heard Khazbulatov, she thought, 'This is the end . . .'[353] She imagined 'all this scum in Ministers' chairs', and 'fascists' saluting each other on the street by raising their arms, Nazi-style. 'People, if they don't hang us right away, where should we go?' she asked Russian reporters around her. They quickly agreed on Australia: 'the furthest place from here'.[354]

On the fifth floor of the former Central Committee building on Staraya Square, which now housed the Russian government, the usually stolid, deliberate, self-important bureaucrats were agitated.[355] One of them ran up to First Deputy Prime Minister Egor Gaidar: 'You do understand that everything is finished, don't you? Within an hour they are going to slaughter us all!'[356]

As he drove to the makeshift studio of the Russian Television Channel around eight o'clock that evening, Gaidar saw an empty city: no militia, no troops, no people. On the car radio, the White House station came through very clear: we are winning! no compromises now! the last hour of the 'Yeltsinoids' has struck![357]

In the early afternoon of Saturday, 2 October, soon after his disrupted walk down Novy Arbat, Yeltsin left for his country residence, as was his wont on Saturdays. Several hours later, the entire Presidential staff followed the boss to their own dachas in the country and let their office cars go back to Moscow until Monday morning. By late afternoon, the Kremlin was empty.[358]

When the aides were urgently summoned back twenty-four hours later, on the evening of 3 October, they found everything dark and quiet behind the Kremlin wall. Technical personnel had not even been called in. The telephones were silent. Only the President's helicopter, parked on the Ivanovskaya Square inside the Kremlin walls, made the scene different from any other Sunday night.[359]

The head of Kremlin security, General Mikhail Barsukov, had called Yeltsin at his dacha in Barvikha in mid-afternoon. The cordon around the White House was no more. The *boeviki* were storming the Mehria. Armed detachments of the Supreme Soviet's supporters were about to fall on the capital, like an avalanche.[360] Before Barsukov had finished, Yeltsin's heart began to pound. Was this *it*? Was this the beginning of something so unspeakably frightening to the Russian ear? Of something he had been afraid to say even to himself? Yet *it* had come to pass. This *was* civil war.[361]

The Minister of Internal Affairs, General Viktor Erin, to whom Yeltsin spoke next, sounded shellshocked: his militiamen had been spat on, beaten, injured, cruelly mocked, stripped of overcoats and uniforms.[362] Yeltsin quickly signed a decree declaring a state of emergency in Moscow, and authorized the use of firearms by the militia. Next, he called his Minister of Defence, Pavel Grachev. The troops, Grachev said, were ready to enter Moscow.[363] Yeltsin ordered his aides back to the office.

Novy Arbat, through which Yeltsin ordinarily returned to the Kremlin, was no longer safe. An alternative route would take too long. Yeltsin ordered a helicopter, and landed on Ivanovskaya Square shortly after seven. Less than an hour later, he, together with the rest of the country, witnessed what he would later call 'a terrifying event': the silencing of Ostankino.[364]

To the President this was a 'catastrophe', a 'knockdown'.[365] He called Grachev again, and was told the troops were entering the city. When would they come to the rescue of the Ostankino? 'Very soon,' Grachev answered.[366] An hour later, Yeltsin held another conversation with Grachev: where are the troops? 'Moving along the major avenues even as we speak,' Grachev said. Yeltsin asked for confirmation from the highway police, the State Automobile Inspection. No, the streets were still empty.[367]

At half-past two in the morning, the President summed up the information that had reached him. In Ostankino, the battle raged inside the building that housed the Television Centre. The militia, demoralized after two weeks of passivity and orders 'not to respond to provocations',* had disappeared, leaving the city defenceless. On the other side, there were no longer just 'screaming and angry citizens' but experienced soldiers, 'who liked to shoot and knew how'.[368] And then there was the Russian Army of two-and-a-half-million men – among whom, so far, he could find not 'a thousand soldiers', 'not a regiment' yet ready to fight.[369] Yeltsin ordered his limousine and rode to the Ministry of Defence.

Yeltsin later explained his public silence during that night by referring to his need to attend to other, 'more pressing' business: 'I tried to shake my Generals loose from the stress and paralysis ... I pushed them, pressured them to thwart self-doubt, weakness, hesitation. We had already paid dearly for several hours of perplexity. Yes, I was rough and, at the time, many must have taken offence. But ceremonies were the last thing on my mind.'[370]

The President's press secretary recalled that Yeltsin very much wanted to address the nation on the television. Yeltsin had even edited the text of the speech. At the last minute he was dissuaded by aides. Pale, puffy

---

* Yeltsin later 'agonized' over this order. 'I understood how psychologically difficult it was for the militiamen with rubber truncheons to carry out their duties not even ten metres away from bandits armed to the teeth ... [Yet] the key to all our plans was to do everything to prevent even accidental casualties ... [Our hope was] that our resolve and our restraint would force the bandits to cease armed resistance. Now, [in the light of the violence that] occurred, it must be admitted that we were probably wrong. If the militia had been armed and the men had been allowed to respond adequately to the armed assault, the animal-like barbarity in Moscow on the night of 3–4 October might not have taken place. On the other hand, if the militia had carried arms, the tragedy could have been even larger. Don't know, even now, don't know.' (Yeltsin, *Zapiski*, p. 376.)

and anxious, he looked too tired and despondent to cheer anyone.[371] The strongest argument against the speech that night, however, was that he had no good news whatsoever to tell the nation. That became apparent after a few minutes with the Collegium (a conference of top commanders) of the Ministry of Defence. After another incoherent report, Yeltsin asked: 'What are we going to do next?'[372] It was clear to everyone in the room that the most urgent task was, as Yeltsin later put it, to 'neutralize that hotbed of war', the White House.[373] 'So how are we going to smoke them out?' the President repeated.[374] There was a 'grave, dark' and 'dead' silence in the room.[375]

In violation of protocol, the head of the President's security and Yeltsin's confidant, Aleksandr Korzhakov, asked if one of his subordinates, a Captain Zakharov, could suggest a course of action. 'Are you ready to listen?' Yeltsin asked the Generals. Sensing a chance of relief from personal responsibility for fratricide, the Generals nodded enthusiastically.[376]

Zakharov outlined his plan: to position tanks in front of the White House; to warn the defenders; to fire a few shots at the upper floors from tank cannons for 'psychological effect'; and to follow up with a quick assault by *spetsnaz* units.[377] Yeltsin turned to the Chief of the General Staff: 'Do you have ten tanks?' Tanks they had, but not the crews: they were picking potatoes on a collective farm outside Moscow. 'What?' Yeltsin growled. 'In the entire Russian Army you cannot find ten crews? Put officers in the tanks! I give you ten minutes to implement the order . . .'[378]

The commander of the Russian land forces made a few calls to division commanders. The tanks could be mustered by 7 a.m. 'Any other suggestions?' Yeltsin asked. 'All right then, we will start at seven when the tanks arrive'.[379] Yeltsin was ready to get up. 'Boris Nikolaevich,' said Minister Grachev almost in a whisper. 'I need your authorization for the deployment of tanks in Moscow.'[380]* For a few moments, Yeltsin looked at his Minister, then made for the door. He stopped at the threshold, turned around and quietly said: 'I will send you a written order.'[381]

Back in the Kremlin, Yeltsin told his personal assistant, Viktor Ilyushin, to write the order. He quickly signed it and sent it to Grachev by

---

* Korzhakov's version of Grachev's remark suggested an even stronger resistance: 'I will participate in the seizure of the White House only if I have a written order from you' (Aleksandr Korzhakov, *Boris El'tsin: ot rassveta do zakata* ('Boris Yeltsin: from dawn to sunset'), p. 170).

a Kremlin courier.[382] A few hours later, Yeltsin had to persuade the Army again. The officers of the Alfa commando unit had refused to participate in the assault and had been brought to the Kremlin. 'Are you going to carry out the President's order?' Yeltsin demanded. As at the Ministry of Defence, the gathering responded with a 'terrifying silence'. Yeltsin talked for a few minutes: 'You must follow the order ... Don't torture yourselves with doubts ... No one is going to be thrown in jail...' Eventually, following Barsukov's lengthy entreaties, Alfa agreed to be driven to the White House.[383]

Guarded by unarmed militiamen, the darkened makeshift studio of the Russian Television Channel on Fifth Street of Yamskoye Pole played host to a steady stream of uninvited but most welcome guests. Writers, actors, journalists, academics, ex-Deputies and trade unionists,[384] they made their way through the shot-up city to speak to their compatriots through the only national medium remaining in the hands of the government.

As the night wore on, the intelligentsia's perception of the conflict shifted dramatically. It was no longer a mudslinging contest between two branches of power which deserved each other. Nor was the fight about a choice between the Constitution of Soviets and that of a 'Presidential republic'. It was not even Yeltsin against Khazbulatov any more. The unfolding drama had suddenly come to be seen as a battle to the end between democracy and Bolshevism, freedom and gulags – a battle, in a phrase many used, for 'the future of Russia'.

This theme first surfaced in Egor Gaidar's appeal to Muscovites at nine o'clock that evening. As he was about to face the camera, Gaidar asked to be left alone for a few moments. He was about to take on the 'monstrous responsibility'[385] of calling on Muscovites to leave their homes and come into dark and murderous streets, of putting tens of thousands of civilians in harm's way. Was this the right thing, indeed the only thing, to do? Gaidar considered the question that had tormented him for so long: how could tens of thousands of decent, intelligent citizens of Petrograd – many of them military officers – have allowed a not particularly large group of Bolshevik extremists to seize power in October 1917?* Was it because they had not relied on themselves, but

---

* At the same hour, the 1917 parallel occurred to the *Washington Post*'s Moscow correspondent: 'Through most of the afternoon [of 3 October] it seemed as though a Bolshevik-style revolution was unfolding. It appeared, that is, that a mere 5,000 to 10,000 people – determined, ruthless, and facing only apathetic opposition – could grab

had waited for someone else to save and protect them: the provisional government, Aleksandr Kerenskiy, General Kornilov? It was this memory, Gaidar recalled, that in the end outweighed all 'doubts and hesitations'[386] and let him say what he did:

> Those who have chosen the path of armed confrontation are ready to cross a river of blood to maintain their power, to restore the old totalitarian regime and to take our freedom away from us again . . . Today we cannot shift responsibility for the future of democracy, for the future of Russia and for the future of our freedom to the Militia, the Ministry of Internal Affairs and the so-called 'power structures' alone. Today the people of Russia must have their say, Muscovites and all those who care for the freedom of our country and its democratic future must have their say.
>
> We call on those who are prepared to support Russian democracy at this difficult moment to come to its rescue, to gather near the Mossovet building, to stand up together to defend our future and the future of our children, and not to allow our country to be turned once again into an enormous concentration camp for decades to come.[387]

After he had taped the appeal, the First Deputy Prime Minister drove directly to the square in front of the Mossovet. He spoke again and mingled with the crowd – the only senior member of the government to be outside the Kremlin that night.

Back at the Russian Channel's studio the guests followed one another. They had seen 'Soviet power in action', said perestroika's most popular economic essayist Vasiliy Selyunin. Its enforcers were communists and 'Russian fascists'.[388] If Yeltsin could be reproached for anything, it was hesitation, lack of resolve, untimely softness. The 'democrats' were winning, Selyunin concluded, but they would have to put their shoulders to the wheel and 'help Russia'.[389] Like Gavriil Popov at the inception of the Inter-Regional Group, the writer Valentin Osotskiy quoted Anna Akhmatova's famous poem 'Courage' ('Muzhestvo'), written in a besieged Leningrad in February 1942, one of the darkest hours in the war with the Nazis: 'We know precisely what lies on the scales . . .' It was Russia's fate, said Osotskiy, that was on the scales.[390]

Grigoriy Yavlinsky, who, until a few days before, had been among

---

control of a nuclear-armed giant with 150 million people' (Fred Hiatt, 'Pessimism Grips Russian Democrats', *Washington Post*, 4 October 1993).

Yeltsin's and Gaidar's most implacable liberal critics, offered the President his wholehearted support and crisp advice:

> Today Boris Nikolaevich Yeltsin must throw everything he has by way of the troops of the Internal Ministry and the Ministry of Security to suppress the fascist, extremist, bandit detachments gathered in the White House. This is the imperative of the situation. This is Yeltsin's key task tonight.
>
> Citizens must lend all moral and political support to the restoration of order . . . I call on all those who have not stained their conscience and lost their mind to join the forces of order and security, the forces of the Ministry of Internal Affairs and to save the future of our country.[391]

Of at least a dozen short speeches that the Russian Channel broadcast that night, contributions by two women – neither of them a politician, writer or journalist – deserve permanent entries in the annals of Russian political oratory.

Professor of Philology Margarita Chudakova spoke around one-thirty in the morning of 4 October:

> . . . Moscow will not surrender its freedom. We did not surrender it two years ago [in August 1991], and we are not going to surrender it now . . .
>
> Today our choice is clear . . . Don't believe those who are trying to persuade you to leave it all to the politicians. If you stay at home tonight, you will be ashamed of yourselves – in a few hours, in a few months, in a few years!
>
> In the past our country embodied the horrible spectre of communism. It was we who spread this plague all over the world. Today, no matter how belatedly, has come the moment when we can finish it off once and for all.
>
> In the past several months we have been dragged back to the bloody Bolshevik swamp. To those who are marching today under blood-red banners, I would like to say: seventy-four years is enough for any social experiment! Your experiment is over. We, the people of Russia, are not going to let you continue with it.[392]

Half an hour later, the popular theatre and film actress Liya Akhedzhakova delivered a soliloquy that was at once a torrent of rage and a plea, a lament and a philippic. Her voice fell from thunder to intimate whisper and then rose again. Her arms were swept to heaven in supplication and folded on her chest in scorn, condemnation and defiance. She blended it all seamlessly, tastefully and naturally, as only a Russian classical actress with decades of training could.

Those who today look at these snarling, bestial mugs [of the rioters] and share their anger, have learned nothing in the past seventy years. It seems to them that everything was fine then: there was sausage (and someone was thrown in jail); everyone worked so hard (and people were shot for being late for work); and everyone lived so well (and millions were in the gulag)!

For the third day in a row, militiamen are being killed in Moscow, innocent people are being killed. Older women in the cloakroom of Ostankino, women who work there for a pittance and who had no place to hide – they are being shot at with a grenade launcher.

And for what? For the Constitution! What kind of Constitution is this – may it rot in hell! It is the same Constitution under which the people were imprisoned. Do you remember General [Petr] Grigorenko? Do you remember [dissident Anatoliy] Marchenko [who died in prison]? They killed, tortured, put normal people into mental hospitals – all in the name of that Constitution!

Where is our Army? Why is it not defending us from this cursed Constitution?[393]

Akhedzhakova looked directly into the camera and lowered her voice to a stage-whisper: 'My friends! Please don't sleep. Please, don't sleep tonight. Wake up! Decided this night is the fate of our poor Russia, our hapless Motherland. Our Russia is in danger. A horrible fate is in store. Communists are coming.'[394]

When Egor Gaidar reached the square in front of the Mossovet around 9.30 that evening, it was already brightly lit by floodlights and filled with hundreds of people. They milled around, warmed themselves by bonfires, or dragged benches and heavy dollies from food stores to build barricades across Tverskaya.[395] Standing on the ledge of the Mossovet building, a young man was waving the Russian tricolour. 'Yeltsin! Yeltsin! Yeltsin!' chanted the crowd below.[396]

Among them was one of Russia's most revered actors and the best Hamlet of the Russian screen, Innokentiy Smoktunovskiy. In his sixties, his neck wrapped in a thick scarf, he was overheard telling a questioner: 'I have come to defend freedom. In moments like this we must be here.'[397]

'And who are you for?' a *Vesti* reporter asked two women carrying a bench. 'For Yeltsin, for Russia!' they answered loudly and cheerfully.[398] The reporter put the question to a group of men busily preparing Molotov cocktails. 'For Yeltsin, of course. What do you think? Communists would not be here now.'[399] Just off Tverskaya, on Ogaryova Street (now Gazetniy Pereulok), a small crowd was breaking apart a high wooden fence surrounding a construction site. What for? they were asked. To use against Kalashnikovs? 'For stakes through the heart of communism!' was the answer.[400]

Two hours later, a wall-to-wall sea of people extended from the Mossovet all the way to the Moskva Hotel and beyond, towards Manezhnaya Square.[401] A Russian news agency counted 20,000 people;[402] according to Democratic Russia activists, there were 30,000.[403] With his bodyguard holding a black bulletproof shield to his chest, Gaidar was seen talking through a megaphone.[404] Seven thousand men had signed up to serve in pro-Yeltsin *druzhin*s (voluntary detachments) and waited to be given weapons.[405] Still unarmed, many stayed on Tverskaya till morning, guarding the Mossovet and the Central Telegraph.

It is impossible, of course, to determine precisely what and how the appeals from Yamskoye Pole (and the gathering at the Mossovet that followed those appeals) contributed to the eventual outcome. As had been increasingly typical of Yeltsin's Kremlin after the April referendum, only a few days before the administration had given every indication of neither wanting nor needing the assistance of the 'democratic public'. Democratic Russia, which had helped Yeltsin at so many critical moments in the past, had not been given even an hour's advance notice of the 21 September decree, nor had it been consulted in the course of the crisis.[406] When over 10,000 Muscovites had gathered in front of the Mossovet on 26 September at a Democratic Russia meeting to express their full support for Decree No. 1400,[407] the Kremlin had not deigned to send a representative.[408]

Now everything had changed. Anxious and still nearly powerless, Yeltsin sat in his office watching the Russian Channel, which, he later wrote, 'was saving Moscow and Russia'.[409] He would remember Liya Akhedzhakova for the rest of his life.[410] '[Gaidar] would later be reproached [for his appeal],' Yeltsin wrote. 'Why, they would say, he led unarmed, defenceless people against *boeviki*. But his appeal played the role for which it was intended.'[411]

Reluctant to acknowledge a blunder, Yeltsin did not decipher that role. But, like everything else that night, the only effect that counted was the effect on the Army. Like any professional military, Russian officers did not like to shoot at civilians and very much wanted to be popular with the people. Most of all, they wished to be on the winning side. For these reasons, the armed forces had hesitated and finally refused to shoot at Yeltsin and his supporters at the White House in August 1991. These same reasons eventually persuaded the Army to act on the night of 4 October.

The troops watched the Russian Channel with everyone else that night. For the first time since April, marching across television screens were thousands of supporters, rather than detractors, of the regime. It hardly escaped the soldiers' notice that, after Gaidar's appeal, more people gathered around the Mossovet in a few hours than had been camping near the White House for the previous two weeks.

In retrospect, that rarest of sights – Russian soldiers soul-searching and hesitating before shooting at their compatriots on the orders of their political leaders – was among the most heartening memories of the crisis.

The 1,300 troops from the elite Second Guards (Tamanskaya) Motor Rifle and Fourth Guards (Kantemirovskaya) Tank Divisions and from the Tul'skaya and Ryazanskaya paratroop divisions[412] entered Moscow in the early hours of 4 October and were in their positions before 7 a.m. after armoured personnel carriers had broken through the barricades surrounding the White House. But the attack did not begin until two-and-a-half hours later. The interval was filled with lackadaisical shooting, appeals to surrender and, while they waited for the defenders' response, with rather pointless manoeuvres designed to intimidate.

Throughout the day, this routine would be repeated over and over again, stretching what, from the military point of view, could have been an hour-long affair into nearly twelve hours of confrontation. Witnesses recalled long lulls during which the troops signalled to the rebels to give up.[413] 'The clear preference of the military was to scare the anti-Yeltsin demonstrators into surrendering to limit casualties,' concluded an American journalist on the scene. 'The only question was the number of lives that would be lost. And that was largely left to the rebels as they were alternately bombarded with shells and appeals to surrender.'[414]

At around 6.30 a.m. Lieutenant-General Aleksandr Kulikov, whom Yeltsin had appointed Commandant of the 'emergency district' of Moscow, urged the defenders to lay down their arms, promising no sanctions against them if they surrendered and threatening 'elimination' if they continued armed resistance.[415] Negotiations began at 6.45 and ended a few minutes later in bitter acrimony.[416] At 7.13 a.m. the Kremlin made another appeal, broadcast by the Russian Channel: 'The Government of the Russian Federation is hereby making its final demand to all those in and around the White House to surrender their weapons immediately and to leave the building and the adjacent territory . . . This is your last chance and the only opportunity to save Russia and its citizens.'[417]

By that time, Yeltsin had recorded his television address, which was broadcast at 9 a.m.

Dear fellow citizens. I appeal to you at a difficult time. In the capital of Russia, shots are ringing out, and blood is being spilt . . .

Those who have acted against a peaceful city and unleashed bloody fighting are criminals . . . Those who are waving red flags have once again stained Russia with blood . . .

I ask you, respected Muscovites, to give your support to the morale of the Russian soldiers and officers. They are our people's Army and militia, and today they have one task: to protect our children, to protect our mothers and fathers, to stop and disarm the people involved in the pogrom, the murderers.

I am appealing to all political forces in Russia, for the sake of those whose lives have already been cut short, for the sake of those whose innocent blood has already been shed. I ask you to forget what only yesterday seemed important: internal disagreements. All who hold dear peace, and tranquillity, the honour and dignity of our country, all who are against the war, should be together . . .

The armed fascist–communist mutiny in Moscow will be crushed within the shortest time limit . . .*

I consider it my duty also to appeal to the people of Moscow. During the past day and night we have become fewer. Innocent civilians have fallen victims to the thugs. We bow our heads in memory of those killed.

Many of you answered the call of your heart and spent the night in the centre of Moscow . . . tens of thousands of people risked their lives. Your will, your civic courage and the power of your spirit have proved to be the most effective weapons.

I bow low before you.[418]

---

* Yeltsin announced the banning of the 'public associations' that had 'taken part in illegal disturbances'. Later on the same day, he signed a decree prohibiting publication of leftist and left–nationalist publications. Other newspapers were to be subjected to censorship. Three week later, he lifted the ban on all newspapers and on all but five groups. The censorship was abolished as well.

Half an hour later, supported by machine-gun fire from the armoured personnel carriers, the troops forced their way into the building and occupied its first two floors. Around 10 a.m., Aleksandr Rutskoy asked for negotiations with Yeltsin. Prime Minister Chernomyrdin responded by promising to halt the assault if the defenders laid down their weapons and came out under white flags. Shortly after ten o'clock a white flag appeared at a window. Chernomyrdin ordered the troops to hold fire and demanded that the defenders emerge from the building without weapons, guaranteeing, in that event, their personal safety. The ceasefire lasted for almost an hour and a half until Ruslan Khazbulatov sent word that the White House was ready to negotiate with Yeltsin, but not to surrender.[419]

A 'steady crackle of small-arms fire' from the White House[420] resumed. The defenders shot indiscriminately at soldiers and civilians alike, killing and injuring onlookers,[421] who stubbornly refused to disperse. Snipers on the roof and the upper floors of the White House pinned down a column of government troops for hours.[422] Shortly after noon, the attackers called out to the White House through a loudspeaker: 'Occupants of the White House. Give yourselves up, while you still have a chance.'[423] The response was a fusillade of small-arms fire.[424]

Minutes later, a dozen heavy T-72 tanks, which had been deployed in front of the building, on the Kalininskiy Bridge across the Moskva river and on the other side of Krasnopresnenskaya Embankment, fired twelve[425] shells at the upper floors of the White House, which were occupied by Achalov's headquarters[426] and snipers. Of the twelve, ten shells were duds (they penetrated the building but did not explode) and two were stuffed with explosives.[427] The top four floors were set on fire.

To Egor Gaidar the sound of the cannonade's heavy thumping brought enormous relief. The thousands of people who had trusted him and whom he had called on to the streets the previous night had been spared.[428] Gaidar's feelings were shared by many close by and afar. Asked, on the same day, if the use of regular troops was justified, 78 per cent of polled Muscovites answered yes.[429]* In a joint statement

---

* Asked, in the same poll, whom they 'trusted the most', 71 per cent named 'President and government' and 4 per cent 'Supreme Soviet, Rutskoy and Khazbulatov' (19 per cent did not trust either side, and the rest gave no answer). As for responsibility for the events of the past two days, 47 per cent blamed Khazbulatov, 45 per cent Rutskoy, 17 per cent Supreme Soviet and 15 per cent Yeltsin (respondents could name more than one culprit). (All-Russian Centre for the Study of Public Opinion, 4 October 1993, 'Situatsiya glazami Moskvichey' ('The situation as seen by Muscovites'), *Moskovskie Novosti*, 10 October 1993, p. 8.)

Presidents Lennart Meri of Estonia, Guntis Ulmanis of Latvia and Algirdas Brazauskas of Lithuania called the struggle in Moscow 'a contest between a democratically elected President and anti-democratic power structures'.[430] Their Moldovan counterpart, Mircea Snegur, called Aleksandr Rutskoy's supporters 'communist, imperialist forces who want to turn Russia into a concentration camp'.[431] Eduard Shevardnadze (chairman of the Georgian parliament) declared that 'Georgians [would] think of Yeltsin's victory as our own.'[432] Vaclav Havel said that the events of the previous twenty-four hours had been 'not the result of a power struggle but, rather, a fight between democracy and totalitarianism'.[433]

After fifteen minutes, the shelling stopped and the loudspeakers announced another ceasefire so that the defenders could 'abandon the building without arms'. There were no takers, and at 12.40 the government troops resumed small-arms barrage.[434] An hour later, the shooting died down to allow into the White House a six-man peace deputation dispatched by the conference of representatives of Russian regions that had convened in Moscow a few days before. The delegation, under a white flag, was led by the President of Kalmykia, Kirsan Ilyumzhinov. Soon, another President, Ruslan Aushev of the Ingush Autonomous Republic, who like Rutskoy was a veteran of the Afghan war, entered the building in an effort to persuade his former comrade to surrender.[435]

At about the same time, several large groups of defenders, unarmed and under white flags, walked out of the White House. One man, in a camouflage uniform, was detained. The rest were escorted by the troops to the crowd of spectators and released.[436]

At 2.30 p.m. three men under a white flag walked from the White House to say that Rutskoy and Khazbulatov were ready to surrender if they received guarantees of personal security. Half an hour later, Defence Minister Pavel Grachev arrived to negotiate.

While Rutskoy and Khazbulatov demanded assurances of personal safety (from, among others, ambassadors of Western nations), two officers of the Alfa commando unit left their weapons at the entrance and walked into the White House.[437]* 'We want to get out unarmed people,' they told the Deputies huddled near the Council of Nationalities

---

* Although they had eventually agreed to be conveyed to the scene, the Alfa commandos had and procrastinated until one of their officers, a young lieutenant, was killed by a White House sniper after he had climbed out of his armoured personnel carrier to help a wounded soldier (Korzhakov, *Boris El'tsin*, pp. 174, 176).

on the third floor. 'We do not want to shoot at civilians ... If you agree [to leave], we promise to make an exit corridor for those without weapons. There will be buses waiting at the entrance. They will take you to the nearest safe Metro entrance.'[438]

At 17.45, with battle still raging on the upper floors, Deputies boarded buses with curtains at the windows.[439] After they had been found standing with a small group of Deputies, Khazbulatov and Rutskoy were ordered to board another bus to be driven to the Lefortovo Prison. There was a delay while Rutskoy's aides ran upstairs to collect his personal effects and clothes. Finally, Rutskoy, too, entered the bus, a huge duffle-bag in hand.[440]

There were few *barkashovtsy* or Officers' Union fighters among the prisoners. Most of the *boeviki* were said to have escaped through the many underground tunnels under the White House.[441] One of them later told a radical, 'national-patriotic' newspaper, *Zavtra* (formerly *Den'*), how he and a comrade, armed with Kalashnikovs, had climbed out of a White House window, lifted the cover of a manhole and then emerged near Hammer Centre (World Trade Centre) on Krasnopresnenskaya Embankment, about half a mile from the White House.[442] Spotted and pursued by a 'special designation' militia patrol, he 'showed them that he could shoot': taking aim 'just under the line of the helmet', he shot one of the soldiers in the face.[443]

In early afternoon the vicinity of the White House was full of men with the same 'concentrated' facial expressions, who appeared to know exactly what they were doing.[444] Soon they began sniping at passers-by and spectators from rooftops, attics, balconies and windows.[445] On one occasion a Russian reporter saw eight rifles pointing in her direction from three balconies on the upper floor of a building on Kalininskiy Prospekt.[446] Later, three men in black uniforms suddenly burst out of a building on the corner of Arbat and Garden Ring and began shooting from submachine guns.[447] In a building near by, an eighteen-year-old girl was killed when she was putting a bouquet of flowers on a window-sill.[448] Like many of the civilians killed around the White House,[449] she was shot in the head. The 'snipers' war' continued all night long. On the brick wall of a bell tower near the White House, one of the snipers scratched, 'I have killed five people and am very content.'[450]

According to the Kremlin, twenty soldiers were killed storming the White House; forty defenders were found dead inside.[451] At least twenty people were said to have been killed in Ostankino.[452] Altogether, on 3 and 4 October, according to different official and unofficial counts, between 146 and 178 people were killed, and over 1,000 injured.[453]

No Deputy was killed or injured. Three – Ruslan Khazbulatov and the Generals Albert Makashov and Vyacheslav Achalov – were arrested.

At a Kremlin dinner that night, Yeltsin was given a sealed envelope, said to contain a present he would dearly like to see. Inside was Ruslan Khazbulatov's clay pipe. Yeltsin took it out and held it in his palm for a few moments. Then, with a flick of the wrist, he flung the pipe against the wall, smashing it into a myriad tiny pieces.[454]

CHAPTER 12

The Nadir

YELTSIN MOVED QUICKLY TO IMPLEMENT the plan laid out in Decree No. 1400: national elections and the adoption of a new constitution. Despite the urging of many of his radical supporters, who advocated a permanent ban on 'all pro-communist and pro-fascist parties',[1] the President refused to extend the two-week-old 'state of emergency'.* He lifted the ban on all but five militantly leftist, anti-Semitic groups, which had participated in the 3–4 October 1993 uprising: the National Salvation Front, the Russian Communist Workers' Party, the Russian Communist Youth Union, the Officers' Union and Aleksandr Barkashov's Russian National Unity. Apart from these organizations, no party or bloc, no matter how hostile to the regime, was barred from campaigning. The Communist Party of the Russian Federation was allowed to participate in the 12 December elections, as was Aleksandr Rutskoy's People's Party of Free Russia. They were among the thirteen parties qualified for a place on the national party list ballot by collecting 100,000 signatures.

'There is, of course, a temptation (and the President is being nudged in that direction by many) to use the opportunity to cut off the communists and related parties from participation in the election,' Yeltsin said.

---

* On 4 October Yeltsin outlawed 'public associations' that had 'taken part in illegal disturbances'. Later on the same day, he signed a decree that prohibited publication of leftist and left-nationalist publications. Press censorship was introduced.

Banned were the Communist Party of the Russian Federation and militant splinter communist groups: Viktor Anpilov's Working Russia and Working Moscow, the Russian Communist Workers' Party, the All-Russian Communist Party of Bolsheviks, the All-Russian Youth Union, the United Labour Front and the National Salvation Front. Among the extreme nationalists prohibited were the Party of the Revival of the Great Power, the Officers' Union, the Russian Party, the Patriotic Youth Front, Russian National Unity, Russian National Council, Russian All-People's Union and the National-Patriotic Front 'Pamyat''.

Forbidden to publish were the 'establishment' communist press (*Pravda*, *Glasnost*, *Sovetskaya Rossia* and *Rabochaya Tribuna* ('Workers' Tribune'); the organ of the 'national-patriotic' opposition *Den'*; and several much smaller leftist and extreme nationalist, anti-Semitic publications: *Russkiy Vestnik* ('Russian Herald'), *Russkoye Voskresenie* ('Russian Resurrection'), *Pul's Tushina* ('Tushino's Pulse', published in Moscow's working district, Tushino), *Nasha Rossia* ('Our Russia'), *Krasnaya Presnya* ('Red Presnya', a Moscow district), *Put'* ('The Way'), *Molniya* ('Lightning') and *Soyuz Ofitzerov* ('Officers' Union'). ('Dosie "MN"', *Moskovskie Novosti*, 10 October 1993, p. 7A.)

I don't think this would be a right thing to do.

If we have indeed decided to create a law-based state, we must act within the framework of law. Openly criminal organizations might be barred from the election campaign. But it is an entirely different matter to prevent parties from nominating candidates and campaigning for them only because they are against the reforms. If we take this route, we will be virtually indistinguishable from the Bolsheviks, who first banned and then repressed oppositional political movements because of their non-acceptance of Soviet power.

Only courts may exclude these forces from the political process. Only an open court hearing which adheres to all legal procedures may decide if this or that party meets the standards of a democratic system . . . If we talk about a free choice for the people, then let us create conditions for making such a choice truly free.[2]

Among the thousands of locations where they collected the signatures needed to qualify for the party slate of candidates, the communists stationed themselves near the Lenin Museum on Red Square, 'amid steady invective against Yeltsin and democrats in general'.[3] A few hundred metres away, near St Basil's Cathedral, Russia's Choice, the party of anti-communist democrats and free marketeers, canvassed passers-by as part of their own campaign to collect signatures.[4]

Along with the lifting of the proscription of political opposition, Yeltsin rescinded censorship and the ban on communist and nationalist newspapers. In order to be allowed to resume publication, the two leading national communist dailies, *Pravda* and *Sovetskaya Rossia*, were required to change their editors, the newspapers' names and their ideology. Apart from the installation of a new editor at *Pravda*, neither paper complied with these conditions (*Sovetskaya Rossia* went to court to fight the order on the ground that it was illegal), and both were soon being published as before. 'WE RETURN' read the banner headline on the 2 November 1993 issue of *Pravda*. 'Let it be clear to everyone, we are not changing our conviction,' declared the front-page editorial. 'We remain faithful to the best traditions of *Pravda*, we remain the tribune of the left forces and the champions of socialist values.'[5] According to its editor, the daily *Pravda* remained 'a radical and pro-communist newspaper'.[6]

The banner of leftist 'national-patriotic' opposition, *Den'* ('Day'), changed its name to *Zavtra* ('Tomorrow') and resumed weekly publication with no interference by the authorities. The front page of its first issue, in November 1993, carried an editorial written by the newspaper's founder and editor, Aleksandr Prokhanov:

[We] are determined to continue resistance . . . The term 'government of occupation' has been filled with terrifying content . . . The murderers who have blown up the Great [Soviet] Empire . . . continue to serve the Prince of Darkness and Mammon . . . In every line and every letter we shall be faithful to the memory of Russian martyrs, our sisters and brothers, shot to death and burned in the terrible days of the coup. Their eyes, their groans, their wounds will breathe in our creations and our thoughts . . . The same two forces will continue to struggle for our future: that of light and that of darkness. Realizing the awful might of darkness, we shall shape the future in accordance with the principles of light . . .[7]

Stretched across the entire front page beneath the editorial was a photograph of Stalin with three dozen top Soviet generals.

On 29 October Yeltsin signed a decree on Informational Guarantees for Participants in the Election Campaign of 1993. The measure laid down the rules that were to be followed in all subsequent national elections: equal amounts of free time for all registered parties and blocs on the state-owned television and radio networks; the drawing of lots to determine the schedule for campaign broadcasts; and oversight by a non-governmental Information Arbitration Tribunal, composed of leading journalists and lawyers. Each of the registered national parties and blocs was entitled to a total of one hour of free time on national television (between 7.25 and 8.25 in the morning or 18.45 to 19.45 in the evening). Every one of 1,567 registered candidates was to be given airtime for a campaign speech on a radio station and a television channel covering his or her district.

The main state-owned national television network, First Channel/ORT (Ostankino), was to devote one hour in the morning and one in the evening to a discussion of party platforms of all nationally registered parties and blocs.[8] In addition to free time, all television and radio stations were to publish their prices and sell airtime at reduced rates to any registered candidate or party that wished to buy it. Candidates' airtime was theirs to dispose of. There was to be no editorial interference. 'Neutrality was so strict', wrote a scholarly observer, 'that television journalists were reduced to traffic police. They were not allowed to provide commentary, analysis or even searching questions.'[9] The left-nationalist candidates used much of their time to attack Yeltsin's 'crimes'.[10]

When, on 12 December, the Russians went to the polls, the general revulsion over the October bloodshed, the novelty and the confusion, as well as the frigid gloom of the Russian winter, resulted in the lowest turnout since the first perestroika elections in March 1989: only 55 per cent of adults came to vote for the Deputies in a new bicameral parliament, the Federal Assembly, and in the constitutional referendum – barely enough to make the poll valid.* The post-Soviet Russian Constitution was adopted by 58 per cent of voters.

Like the Constitution of Charles de Gaulle's 'authoritarian republic' of 1958, on which it was modelled, Yeltsin's Constitution was written in the shadow of a just-thwarted civil war. As in France, the composition, the national debate and the referendum were undertaken in terrible haste: nine weeks, between 5 October and 12 December 1993. (In the French case, it took a few weeks more: from 3 June to 28 September 1958.)

The results of Russia's first multi-party elections on 12 December 1993 confirmed – if only in the breach – the pattern of post-communist politics. By then, the sequence had been fairly well established. A severe economic crisis forces the first post-communist government to employ 'shock therapy': price liberalization, privatization, fiscal austerity and a tight money supply. After the initial breakthrough, which eliminates rationing, shortages and queues, and makes money valuable again, the popular mandate for change is quickly eroded by inflation, by a growing and ostentatious inequality, by unemployment, corruption and crime and by a precipitous decline in formerly subsidized industries – a decline that is most precipitous among the mastodons of the early 'socialist industrializations' (coal mining, metallurgy and shipbuilding), and in the light industries crushed by the opening of the market to foreign competition (food, clothing and cars).

Henceforth, popular support for market reforms was to depend on caveats and safety devices. First in Lithuania and Poland and then in the eastern part of the united Germany and in Hungary, ex-communists won the executive branch or achieved majority coalitions in legislatures. As they turned to the left, the key eligibility criterion used by the voters was the former communists' ability to maintain the newly found and dearly held liberties. Those who promised to impose a human face on primitive capitalism were first required to show such a face – pink, rather than bright red – themselves. Where such demonstrations were

---

* By Yeltsin's decree, a turnout of just half of all eligible voters was necessary to adopt the Constitution. The turnout figure was never fully and satisfactorily documented, and the Central Electoral Commission was accused of inflating the numbers.

persuasive come election time, the left met with success. Where the ex-communists were not found reliable enough to uphold democracy once in power, the protest vote sought other outlets and remained a potential source of instability.

Such was the case in Russia in December 1993. Several reasons, historical and contemporary, explained the failure of the KPRF to recast itself in a social-democratic mould and to repeat the electoral successes of the Polish, Hungarian and Czech left. One was the virtual absence in the Russian political tradition of an effective and lasting non-violent democratic left, which the Gorbachev era (1987–91) had been too brief to change. A few small and hesitant steps towards social democracy (such as the Democratic Platform, a quasi-social-democratic movement within Gorbachev's CPSU) had failed to produce even the beginning of a viable moderate successor to the Party, which until its last hour remained both monopolistic and impervious to evolution.

After the August Revolution this legacy, not surprisingly, proved singularly inauspicious for the development of the moderate left. Most Party members, passive and cynical for decades, simply vanished from the rolls. Others defected to the anti-communist regime,[11] and proceeded, either enthusiastically or opportunistically, to fill new (or to remain in the same) administrative positions. No more than 6 or 7 per cent of communists renewed their membership after August 1991.[12]

Unfortunately for Russian social democracy (and, more importantly, for Russian post-communist transition), the most cohesive and best-organized segment of the former CPSU turned out to be the 'traditionalists', for whom any evolution towards the centre was treason and no appellation more offensive than 'social democrat'. With the 3 October rampages and the red banners over the barricades set up by Working Moscow still fresh in the voters' mind, the first election in Russia did not identify (let alone empower) a moderate left. The Russian anti-communist revolution did not end with a moderate left presiding over market-oriented stabilization and national reconciliation.

In the absence of a trustworthy left opposition, much of the protest vote shifted towards the populist nationalist demagogue Vladimir Zhirinovskiy and his Liberal Democratic Party of Russia (LDPR), which finished first in the party-list poll,* with 23 per cent of the

---

* Half of the 450 Deputies in the Duma, the Federal Assembly's powerful lower chamber, were elected by direct majority vote and the other half through proportional representation from the party-list vote. On the right, the pro-government Russia's Choice received 15 per cent of the party vote and the 'democratic' opposition bloc Yabloko 8 per cent;

vote. Zhirinovskiy undoubtedly profited from his image as an outsider,* untainted by the national shame of the 3–4 October violence. Just as important was his ability to project energy and sincerity in a message articulated simply and with feeling – unlike the rather wooden demeanour of most other leaders.

The deck was further stacked in Zhirinovskiy's favour because of several peculiarly Russian circumstances that did not obtain in any other post-communist nation. None of the latter lost an empire or military superpower status. None had a military–industrial complex which consumed at least a third of its GNP and employed at least one in five adults. The post-imperial trauma, the wound left in the Russian national psyche by the loss of superpower status, the fear of unemployment by the many millions of workers in the formerly best-paid defence jobs, and the dramatic reduction in power and status of the armed forces – all contributed to the LDPR's stunning upset. Not surprisingly, the LDPR's most solid support was in the Army and among workers at state enterprises.

Yet the key to the LDPR's success was a careful and deliberate positioning as a third force, distinct from both the restorationist communists/Agrarians and the 'liberal-radicals' of Russia's Choice. The LDPR was, as the leading Russian observer Igor Klyamkin put it, 'simultaneously against the communists and against the "democrats"':[13] acknowledging, deploring and promising to alleviate the pain of market transition, without going back to the *ancien régime* either in politics or in the economy. Zhirinovskiy's party 'most definitely supported the

---

on the left, the Communist Party received 12 per cent and their rural comrades, the Agrarian Party, 8 per cent. In the political centre, Women of Russia garnered 8 per cent, the Democratic Party of Russia 6 per cent and the Party of Russian Unity and Concord 7 per cent (the numbers are rounded up or down).

The upper House, the Council of the Federation, consisted of 178 Deputies elected from Russia's eighty-nine regions.

* Three years before, in the 1990 Polish Presidential election, Stanislaw Tyminski, a demagogue very much like Zhirinovskiy, received exactly the same percentage of the national vote. He accused the government of 'betraying the nation by selling enterprises to foreigners', called for a 'declaration of economic war on the West', and promised to 'make Poland rich within one month' of his election.

Tyminski's success, like Zhirinovskiy's, occurred in the absence of a viable centre-left alternative. Three years later, such a party, the Democratic Left Alliance, did appear and, with the Polish Peasant Party, won first the legislature and later the Polish Presidency.

market economy' – but in conjunction with 'extreme great-power nationalism'.[14] This was a party of 'national capitalism'.

Despite the LDPR's success in the party-list vote, the party with the largest overall number of Deputies in the Duma was Egor Gaidar's radical pro-reform and pro-regime party Russia's Choice, whose motto was 'Liberty, Property, Law' (*Svoboda, Sobstvennost', Zakonnost'*). Together with the 'democratic' opposition party Yabloko, pro-reform forces had a modest plurality in the Duma: ninety-three seats as compared with eighty-one for communists and their rural comrades, the Agrarians, and sixty-four seats for the LDPR.

The 'democrats' blamed Yeltsin for Zhirinovskiy's success. The President never endorsed Russia's Choice, which, until the very last day of the campaign, secretly hoped for at least a pat on the back. (One of RC's campaign posters featured a colour photograph of Yeltsin and Gaidar shaking hands.) Apparently determined to cultivate an image as the father of the nation (and to protect himself from the risks of party politics in a volatile young democracy), Yeltsin deliberately distanced himself from the perennially squabbling 'democrats'.

On election night the campaign headquarters of Russia's Choice on Gertzen Street bristled with anger and disappointment aroused by Yeltsin's withholding of his endorsement (which the RC's pollsters estimated had cost the party 10 to 15 per cent of the vote). Yet, even as they longed for Yeltsin's nod, the radical 'democrats' were desperately trying to emerge from Yeltsin's giant shadow and announce their arrival to the world. The charismatic era in Russian politics had lasted for too long, they told themselves, and would soon be checked by an era of large, nation-wide and well-organized parties.

One of the Duma's first acts, in late February 1994, was to grant blanket amnesty for the August 1991 putschists and the leaders of the 1993 Red October. Those who had resisted the rebellion were dismayed. On the day when the Duma voted the amnesty, Oleg Poptsov, director of the Russian Television Channel, was giving his employees medals for courage under fire. To Poptsov, the Duma act meant a denial of that courage and of that fire: there had been 'no 147 killed, no assault on Ostankino, no assault on the Mehria, no Rutskoy calling to crush the hated regime . . . And there has been no terrifying inscription on the bell-tower: "I have killed five people and I am very content." There has been none of that.'[15] As soon as he received the text of the legislation, the Procurator General Aleksandr Kazannik, appointed by Yeltsin four months earlier, ordered the release of the prisoners.

Yeltsin was 'shocked'.[16] At the very least he had expected to negotiate the terms of the release with the Duma, and was taken aback by the speed with which the parliament was setting free those who five months before would almost certainly have killed him if they could. To all Yeltsin's angry expostulations, Kazannik, who had given up his Supreme Soviet seat for Yeltsin five years before, retorted: 'the Procurator General cannot interfere with acts of the Duma'. Personally opposed to the amnesty but resenting the Kremlin's pressure on him to obstruct the law, Kazannik resigned on the day the amnesty took effect.[17]

An incensed Yeltsin threatened to rearrest the amnestied prisoners and summoned a new Procurator General and the Minister of Internal Affairs into his office. Yet, after much fulmination, a day passed with no action, then another. 'A braking mechanism of sorts must have been at work,' the President's press secretary later speculated. The government's implementation of the Duma's decision was one of the first instances of compliance with the new Constitution, then barely two months old. To continue challenging the Duma would have risked the barely established constitutional order. The Constitution's 'father' swallowed his anger and his pride because 'a new, sharp confrontation' with the parliament was 'completely contrary to his intentions'.[18]

Shortly after four in the afternoon, on Saturday, 26 February, they emerged from the gates of the Lefortovo Prison: Makashov, Anpilov, Barkashov, Dunaev, Konstantinov – seventy-four in all. Rutskoy, already dressed in a general's uniform,[19] was greeted by a crowd of his supporters chanting 'Rutskoy – president!'[20] He and Khazbulatov were whisked away in 'gorgeous' Mercedes limousines.[21] Asked what he planned to do now, Barkashov answered, 'Exactly what I did before.'[22]

For all its bitterness, the amnesty affair established a precedent and set the tone in the relations between the newly elected legislature and the President. Although the Kremlin's natural urge was to dominate and that of the Duma to obstruct and confront, slowly and painfully both attempted restraint. Often unruly, shrill and completely inexperienced, under the surprisingly skilful and moderating leadership of the Agrarian communist Ivan Rybkin, the Duma soon began to learn to work, despite ideological chasms within the body and between the legislature and the Kremlin. While decrying the Constitution as both illegitimate and unfairly skewed towards the executive, the opposition abided by it. A bad law, the Russian political class seemed to have concluded, was better than no law at all. The machinery of Russian self-government gradually became workable. For the first time in Russian history, a parliament freely elected by universal vote and the executive began to co-operate within a constitutional framework adopted by a national plebiscite, tense and conflict-ridden though their relationship was.

Of the 461 legislative measures passed by the Fifth Duma,* 282 were signed into law by Yeltsin. Among them were constitutional amendments regarding the Constitutional Court, arbitration courts, referendums, and the first part of the Civil Code. The Kremlin and the two Houses of the Russian parliament (the Duma and the Council of the Federation) managed to agree on critical appointments that enabled the state to function: the justices of the Constitutional Court; the Procurator General; the justices of the Supreme Court and of the Higher Arbitration Court; and the Chairman of the Central Bank.

In September 1995, Yeltsin placed another milestone in the development of Russian democratic self-rule by signing a decree that authorized the election of regional governors ('heads of regional administrations') and local legislatures beginning in December 1996.

In a letter to lawmakers of the Fifth Duma, Yeltsin declared that, despite all the 'disagreements' and 'problems', the Deputies had 'succeeded in solving the main task – Russia's transition to civilized parliamentarism . . . You have every reason to consider yourselves standing at the source of Russian democratic statehood.'[23]

That statehood was further strengthened by the second post-communist national legislative elections on 17 December 1995, although the results reflected serious deficiencies in the political institutions and portended damaging discord ahead. The Communist Party of the Russian Federation (KPRF), led by Gennadiy Zyuganov, became by far the largest faction in the parliament and, combined with other left-nationalist Deputies, came close to controlling 200 (out of 450) votes in the Duma. Still, the communists and their allies did not attain a majority in the Duma. Russian voters continued to be wary. The left-of-centre political space, which in post-communist nations would become critical to stability and to the emergence of non-confrontational politics, remained unclaimed in Russia.

Perhaps the most disturbing aspect of the 1995 election was the Russian voters' rejection of most of the choices offered to them by the Russian political class. Of the forty-three parties which fielded candidates, only four (the communists, the LDPR, Our Home Is Russia and Yabloko) managed to garner more than the 5 per cent of the national party-list vote which entitled a party to claim a number of Duma seats

---

* The First Duma was elected in 1906 and the last (Fourth) dissolved following the February 1917 Revolution.

proportionate to its share of the vote. The composition of Russia's second post-communist parliament thus reflected the wishes of less than half of the voters: 49 per cent of the votes were cast for parties and blocs that failed to make it into the Duma.

Major casualties of this self-disfranchisement were pro-reform and pro-government parties, notoriously incapable of forming alliances or even agreeing not to run against each other in single-mandate districts.* While they were only slightly behind the left in the absolute number of votes, the 'democrats' elected far fewer Deputies.

As it had since 1987, Yeltsin's political biography paralleled that of his country with remarkable closeness. The wave of transformation crested between the autumn of 1991 and the spring of 1992 with price liberalization, the ban on the Communist Party and strongly pro-Western 'liberal internationalism' in foreign policy. Then, while still moving forward, the wave gradually began to lose its force, speed, purity and height. It clung more and more closely to the bottom, deriving shape and colour from the rock shelf of the national political tradition, its *modus operandi* and its rhetoric. It swept up sand, rotting weed and an occasional dead fish. Of the latter, the wretched Chechnya war was the largest. Conceived and prosecuted amid near unanimous public opposition, the Chechnya war revealed – just beneath the surface of Russia's first democracy – militarism, incompetence, brutality and appalling disdain for the lives of Russian soldiers and Chechen civilians alike.

As with almost everything else about Yeltsin between January 1994 and January 1996, the military solution to the festering Chechen crisis was part of the inexorable pull of a Russian political custom: the one in which a 'small victorious war' always seemed (although, in fact, almost never had been) the answer to an autocrat's waning fortunes. The strongest impulse, however, came from the endorsement of Zhirinovskiy's heated nationalist rhetoric and his 'shrill great-power patriotism'[24] by one-fifth of the Russian electorate. Reform and democracy no longer united and inspired, Yeltsin appeared to think. What the people wanted in these times of painful and confusing change was a show of Russia's military might. 'This is what is needed!' Yeltsin seemed to have decided.[25] Those who surrounded him at the time (and many in the political class outside the Kremlin as well) agreed.[26]

* Altogether 14 per cent of the votes (9.6 million) went to the pro-reform parties that failed to overcome the 5 per cent barrier.

There was, to be sure, much to recommend some sort of decisive action. Formerly a part of the Chechen-Ingush Autonomous Republic inside Russia, the small mountainous Chechnya (which lay between Russia in the north and west, Georgia in the south and Russian Dagestan in the east and whose population was 1.2 million) declared independence in November 1991. In the spring and summer of 1993, Chechen President Dzhokhar Dudaev, a former major-general in the Soviet Air Force, dissolved the parliament, killed scores of demonstrators and established himself as a brutal, erratic and paranoid dictator, whose enemies, both real and imagined, were swiftly murdered by his small army of bodyguards.

The Chechens' hatred of Russia stemmed from a century of war and suffering. A nation of fearless Muslim warriors, for whom the gun was the most prized personal possession, Chechnya's confrontation with Russia dated back to the nineteenth century, when it had resisted Moscow's conquest of the Caucasus for decades, longer than any other people of the region. After the Second World War, Stalin arrested and exiled the entire Chechen people to Kazakhstan, where tens of thousands of them died of hunger and disease.

Under Dudaev, Chechnya soon developed into a painful thorn in Russia's side. Even those who would soon deplore and passionately oppose the war did not defend the regime which had turned Chechnya into a lawless enclave bristling with weapons. Trains passing through Chechnya were routinely robbed and passengers were advised in advance to barricade themselves inside their compartments. Criminals of all kinds sought refuge there, confident that they would never be extradited to Russia. Kidnapping, money-laundering, gun-running and the printing of counterfeit rubles became vast and lucrative businesses. An oil refinery in the Chechen capital of Grozny filled Dudaev's coffers with money that was used to buy huge quantities of weapons.

Moscow was worried lest the rebellion spread to the entire region and a fundamentalist Muslim Republic of North Caucasus be created on Russia's southern border.[27] Russia also stood to lose millions of dollars if it failed to secure an oil pipeline running through Chechnya and carrying (that, at any rate, was the plan) hundreds of thousands of barrels of oil from the Caspian fields to terminals in the Russian Black Sea port of Novorossiysk. After three years of benign neglect, economic blockade and covert subversion, something needed to be done – both for the sake of the territorial integrity of the Russian state and in response to the Zhirinovskiy challenge. The latter, political imperative proved decisive.

After several failed attempts to dislodge Dudaev by arming and aiding his many Chechen foes (most recently an uprising on 26–27 November 1994), and assured by the Russian Minister of Defence, Pavel Grachev, that Grozny could be taken by 'two paratroop regiments in a few hours',[28] Yeltsin signed a decree on the 'restoration of constitutional order' in Chechnya. On the morning of 11 December 1994, some 40,000 federal troops, led by two tank columns, entered Chechnya from Russian North Ossetia.

Badly outnumbered but skilful, well supplied, tenacious and immensely brave, the Chechens proceeded to inflict enormous damage on the Russian Army from the outset. Raw Russian draftees – untrained, dispirited, hungry and cold – were slaughtered by the hundred. Despite the Russians' overwhelming preponderance, it took them a month and a half of house-to-house firefights, reminiscent of Stalingrad, and daily missile and bombing raids by Russian jets to capture Grozny. Another month passed before the federal troops established effective control of the city after an orderly retreat by the Chechen defenders. By that time 24,000 civilians (and perhaps as many as 30,000) had died, along with at least 1,800 Russian troops.[29] Every evening, the prime-time news programmes of Russian television brought the images of the carnage to the Russian people: dead and bleeding civilians, the bodies of Russian soldiers, torn apart by grenade shrapnel, charred, mutilated.

Contrary to the Kremlin's expectations, the fall of Grozny did not lead to peace talks on Russian terms. The Chechen guerrillas moved to the mountains and continued to ambush and kill Russian troops in brilliantly executed lightning attacks. Soon they made good their often repeated threat of raids on Russian territory.

On 14 June 1995, over two hundred Chechen fighters, armed with grenade launchers and heavy machine guns, rode in two buses and two trucks into Budennovsk, 110 kilometres north of Chechnya in southern Russia, after bribing their way through traffic police checkpoints along the way. They promptly killed twenty police officers and seized a local hospital with over 2,000 patients and medical personnel. Filmed by Russian television crews, Russian troops tried twice without success to dislodge the Chechens, who used patients (many of them pregnant women from the maternity ward) as a shield.

Faced with pleas from the patients to cease the assault and with millions watching the débâcle on television, the authorities agreed to negotiations between the Chechens and Prime Minister Viktor Chernomyrdin. Two days later, a convoy of Chechens and volunteer hostages reached the Chechen border, where the latter were released. The death toll in Budennovsk exceeded 120 police officers, Russian troops, Chechens and hostages.

The next day, the Duma passed a vote of no-confidence in the government. Yeltsin quickly dismissed Minister of Internal Affairs Viktor Yerin, Deputy Prime Minister Nikolay Yegorov and the chief of the Federal Counter-Intelligence Service Sergey Stepashin, the latter for the failure of his agents to learn about the attack before it occurred. The first serious post-1993 political crisis had been temporarily defused.

Even more humiliating for Moscow was the second Chechen raid into neighbouring Dagestan in January 1996. Led by Dudaev's son-in-law, Salman Raduyev, the guerrillas captured the town of Kizlyar and the air force base on the outskirts, seized pilots, policemen and civilians and retreated to the village of Pervomayskoye on the Chechen–Dagestani border. Although completely surrounded by Russian troops and pounded by heavy artillery during several days of futile negotiations, the raiders not only managed to escape into Chechnya during a fierce night battle, but also brought out over 100 hostages, who were subsequently exchanged for Chechen prisoners of war and the bodies of guerrillas. The commander of the operation on the Russian side was Mikhail Barsukov, Yeltsin's confidant and the former head of Kremlin security, who had been made Minister of Security and head of the Federal Security Service six months before.

Although the war was fought with extreme brutality by both sides, civilian deaths were overwhelmingly caused by federal troops. In addition to the indiscriminate shelling during the siege of Grozny, the case most publicized by the Russian mass media and by opponents of the war inside and outside the Duma was a massacre of civilians in Samashki, a village twenty-nine kilometres west of Grozny and the home of the Dudaev clan.

On the night of 7–8 April 1995, federal troops surrounded the village and ordered the inhabitants to surrender weapons within an hour and a half. After the deadline had passed, Russian soldiers entered the village and began killing everyone in sight, throwing grenades into the basements where the villagers were hiding, and burning homes with flame-throwers. At least 100 (and perhaps as many as 250) civilians, mostly women, children and the elderly, were thus murdered.[30]

Russian liberals had no illusions about Dudaev's Chechnya. One of the leading opponents of the war, Oleg Poptsov, whose state-owned network provoked the Kremlin's fury by broadcasting some of the most gruesome images of the carnage, wrote: 'Today Chechnya is, in essence, the centre of the [Russian] criminal world . . . Black market, narcotics, counterfeit money – all adds up to a criminal boom . . . Robbery, banditry, murder – all is true. That is what Dudaev's regime is.'[31] Virtually no one in Russia supported Chechnya's secession, and everyone recognized the need for Moscow to establish control over what was part of Russia. Yet, from the first minutes of the television coverage of the siege of Grozny, the military option – so massive, so inept, so reminiscent of Afghanistan in its indiscriminate cruelty – terrified and angered the Russian public.

Their greatest disappointment, and biggest worry, was Yeltsin himself. His mistakes and weaknesses had been well known to them for five years. Yet, until now, the 'democrats' had believed this about him: he was, as one of them put it, both the 'locomotive' of reform, who pushed it along with almost inhuman energy and persistence, and its 'battleship', whose thick armour enabled a 'weak, tender, shieldless' democracy to survive and flourish.[32] Without this protection, they believed, the reform would long ago have been destroyed either by a consolidated communist nomenklatura or by an 'enraged crowd'.[33] Now both the direction of the locomotive and the reliability of its armour were suddenly in question.

The President for whom so many had worked selflessly and so many more had voted in the 1989, 1990 and 1991 elections and in the April 1993 referendum suddenly looked to 'democrats' like a Soviet *vozhd*': blind in his obstinacy, brutal, incompetent and deaf to public opinion. 'Yeltsin completed the destruction of the communist regime and liquidated the last colonial empire on earth,' wrote a columnist for a leading liberal weekly. 'But the Chechen crisis showed us another Yeltsin – not one destroying the empire but one striving to hold it together by iron clamps, not a fighter against totalitarianism but a "strong arm", whose strength no one would be advised to test.'[34]

The man whom they remembered standing on the tank, amid eager and devoted supporters, now would not even show his face to the Russian people, address them on television or go to the parliament to explain himself. Yeltsin's admission to hospital on 10 December for a 'planned operation on the nasal septum',[35] just as federal troops were pouring into Chechnya, seemed to the 'democrats' to show shameless disregard for public opinion, an act of ultimate political cowardice, and evidence of a sudden degeneration. One of Yeltsin's most devoted champions in the Duma, Sergey Yushenkov of Russia's Choice, threatened to start impeachment proceedings against the President for 'kindling inter-ethnic dissensions, organizing and provoking mass murder of Russian citizens'.[36]

Desperate to minimize the effects of the most serious political error of his life, Yeltsin lied to his former supporters about Chechnya, lied offensively, crudely and brazenly in a Soviet-like manner. He lied about his intentions in Chechnya before the war, lied after the war began and continued to lie about the war's character and about its course. 'In moments of crisis, instead of open and honest explanations, you and the heads of bodies appointed by you feed us such transparent and inept lies that we are left simply dumbfounded,' a leading dissident and human rights activist, Sergey Kovalev, told Yeltsin in his letter of resignation from the Chairmanship of the President's Human Rights Commission. 'The fragile bridge of trust between society and the state, created with such difficulty in the face of century-old tradition, has once again been destroyed.'[37]

On 27 December 1994, when Yeltsin at long last addressed the nation about the Chechen war, he said he had 'given an order to rule out bombing which can result in casualties among Grozny's peaceful inhabitants'.[38] Yet bombing, shelling and missile attacks of horrific ferocity continued for another month. After the Presidential palace was finally taken by federal troops on 19 January 1995, Yeltsin issued a statement, 'informing everybody that the military stage of the restoration of the Russian Constitution is effectively over'.[39] Instead, the war went on for a year and a half. A year later, in January 1996, Egor Gaidar saw Yeltsin on television, defending the bloody fiasco in Pervomayskoye. The President's explanation was so 'completely divorced from reality', and to watch him was so 'unbearably, painfully embarrassing',[40] that, after a year of protests and demonstrations organized by Russia's Choice, Gaidar resigned from the Presidential Council (a voluntary advisory board of prominent liberal intellectuals), severing his last official link to the Kremlin.

For the intelligentsia, the regime's behaviour was a chilling throwback to Soviet days: they were being forced 'not to believe their own eyes', to stop thinking and analysing, to feel neither compassion towards their Chechen compatriots nor shame for the Kremlin's actions.[41] Most offensively, they were being asked to relieve the authorities of public scrutiny and allow them to choose freely 'which Russian citizens they would shoot'.[42] No matter what Yeltsin did afterwards, this deeply personal betrayal would never be forgotten.

Now the very nature of the regime, which 'democrats' had called their own, was gravely suspect. Until Budennovsk, the President's inner circle became synonymous with the 'party of war': the Ministers of Defence and Internal Affairs, Pavel Grachev and Viktor Yerin, the head of the

Federal Counter-Intelligence Service Sergey Stepashin, Yeltsin's chief bodyguard Aleksandr Korzhakov and the head of Kremlin security Mikhail Barsukov.[43] It was they who, 'under the pseudonym "Yeltsin"', seemed to make policies and run the country, not the distant, incoherent and increasingly infirm President.[44]

Russian liberals heard ominous echoes in the explosions of bombs in Grozny and salvoes from tank cannons. In the perennial tug of war between Russia imperial and Russia liberal (or liberalizing), the latter had always been sacrificed to the former: from Alexander II's suppression of the Polish uprising in 1863–4 to Russian tanks crushing the Prague Spring and the remnants of the post-Stalin 'thaw' with it a century later.[45]

Now some leading 'democrats' were predicting the introduction of a state of emergency in Russia, cancellation of the Presidential election, 'suppression of all democratic institutions' and a dictatorship.[46] 'We are sure that if troops enter Chechnya the entire responsibility for the bloodshed there would be yours personally,' democratic Deputies in the Duma warned Yeltsin on 9 December 1994, 'and the current regime will turn from a democratic into a police one.' The continuation of war or, even more so, Russia's victory at the price of devastation and thousands of civilian casualties would mean the 'funeral of glorious democratic reforms in a great nation'.[47]

The Chechen war seemed destined to become post-Soviet Russia's first major childhood illness, from which its democracy could emerge either crippled (perhaps even fatally) or strengthened by a victorious societal opposition to the Kremlin's war. For quite a while, the latter scenario seemed remote, almost fantastic.

Buried in Grozny was Yeltsin's magic ability to read Russia's mind. Never before had he so completely miscalculated the country's mood. Many liberal commentators predicted confidently that, having grown addicted to simple solutions, the regime would not be able to turn back.[48] And Yeltsin, who had begun as a 'democratic leader', seemed destined to end his career 'in an entirely different role'.[49]

In February 1995, in the aftermath of the battle for Grozny, the leading pro-reform magazine which had formerly been among Yeltsin's staunchest supporters put the ruddy, puffy, angry and tired face of the President on its cover with the headline: 'YELTSIN. WHAT IS HAPPENING TO HIM?' In the same issue, one of the editors, an ex-dissident and a prominent human rights activist, wrote: 'From now on, the possibility of Yeltsin's running as a [Presidential] candidate of united democratic forces is completely excluded. Not only because his chances are already slim and will virtually vanish by election time. It is excluded, first and foremost, by moral considerations.'[50]

With the defeat of Red October, revolutionary anti-communism, which until now had been the main source of Yeltsin's popularity, was no longer synonymous with democracy. It was seen now only as a necessary, not a sufficient, condition of a successful democratic transition. Some of the best Russian analysts declared the end of Yeltsin's 'negative anti-communist legitimacy'.[51]

Between the autumn of 1993 and the spring of 1994, Yeltsin's approval rating shrank by a third, from 30 per cent to 20 per cent.[52] The October victory began to look almost Pyrrhic. Yeltsin the charismatic revolutionary hero seemed no more. In a Russia liberated from Soviet totalitarianism, the change that Charles de Gaulle noticed in his own fortune in post-Liberation France was now Yeltsin's lot: 'The current of popular enthusiasm which had been poured so generously on me', the General observed, 'was now channelled in various directions.'[53]

The 1993 Duma elections offered Yeltsin little by way of guidance. The reforms were neither decidedly endorsed nor resoundingly rejected. (While bemoaning the humiliation of a great state and its people, Zhirinovskiy never attacked the market, the reforms or capitalism as such.) And while the radical reformist Russia's Choice became the largest faction in the Duma, the communists and the Agrarians together received almost one-third of the party-list vote. For the first time since 1989 Yeltsin seemed rudderless, incapable of gleaning and interpreting the country's mood. Yesterday's certainties dissolved, and new ones were slow to emerge. He became wary, often appearing immobilized.

He did not abandon the reforms, but he clearly distanced himself from the daily fight for their implementation. In 1994 the pace of change slowed dramatically after the two major anti-inflation measures of the previous autumn: the abolition of 'centralized' subsidized government credits and the raising of the Central Bank's refinancing rate above the rate of inflation.[54] Yeltsin's last direct contribution to the economic revolution was the November 1993 decree that gave former collective farmers legal title to the land and property of the kolkhozes and that revoked a moratorium on land sales by private citizens.[55]

As usual, without the President's daily urging, the government was less than eager to implement risky and often unpopular measures. A breakthrough in market reform was not among the immediate plans of the new cabinet, headed by two former Soviet industrial production managers: Viktor Chernomyrdin and his First Deputy, Oleg Soskovets.

In January 1994 Gaidar resigned from the post of First Deputy Prime Minister, soon followed by Minister of Finance Boris Fedorov.

The enormous expense of the Chechen war made irresistible the option of letting up a bit and printing money to cover the ballooning budget deficit. By January 1995 the monthly inflation rate had jumped to 16 per cent and the ruble had fallen to an all-time low of 4,004 to the dollar. The only way to prevent the catastrophe of hyperinflation was to shrink the budget, depressing the already miserable earnings of those employed by the government: millions of workers in the military–industrial complex, physicians, teachers, scientists, professors and scholars. The regime's anti-inflation tsar, Anatoliy Chubais, now Deputy Prime Minister, fought to cut spending and eventually prevailed. The printing of money stopped, inflation was kept in check and even began to decrease steadily, but the drop in real incomes in the winter of 1994–5 equalled that of January 1992, when prices had been liberated.[56]

In the Russian political firmament, Yeltsin looked more and more like a black hole: a giant star exerting enormous gravitational pull on everything around it, but coming to the end of its life, depleted of fuel and incapable of projecting light. Now, the enemies he could see, feel, understand, outwit and vanquish had gone. Democracy (which to Yeltsin was free elections, freedom for political opposition and absence of government censorship of the press) was no longer in danger from the reds or browns of the GKChP, the National Salvation Front, Working Moscow or Russian National Unity, and the reforms were not directly threatened by Khazbulatov and his Supreme Soviet minions. They were supplanted by menaces no less tenacious or merciless but far less amenable to a frontal political assault: inflation, depression, poverty, cynicism, alienation of the people from power and corruption. Suddenly, Yeltsin's arsenal was rusting and his troops dwindling.

Although the revolution was far from over, these were mostly democratic, rather than revolutionary, politics. The latter kind had required and rewarded 'attacks, confrontation, a publicly conducted struggle for clear and simple goals',[57] noted Gennadiy Burbulis, who had been Yeltsin's chief strategist between 1990 and 1992. In the former, much of the drama was gone and, with it, the intoxication of battle, the éclat and the popular adoration. Even a decent approval rating had to be earned by slow, thankless, often frustrating and exhausting work.

This was, as Yeltsin's press secretary described it, 'an entirely different field and an entirely different game' which, at the age of sixty-three, Yeltsin had to learn to play, a game whose rules were still evolving and for which his previous experience was of 'little use'.[58] After clearing the ground of huge stumps and boulders, he seemed not to know how to till and husband the field. In 1994 the Kremlin press secretary often found the President at a bare desk in 'deep and sad pensiveness'.[59]

Yeltsin 'was used to mammoth exertions of will and mind, which brought quick and visible results,' recalled a close observer.[60] 'When he did not see quick harvest from the seeds he had sown . . . he began to get anxious and fade.'[61]

With the stolid and cautious Viktor Chernomyrdin running the country's day-to-day affairs, Yeltsin, perhaps for the first time in his adult life, found himself with time to kill. He was, suddenly, at the summit, with no peaks to conquer and, most devastatingly, no plan of action which he could say with confidence that Russia wanted or needed.

Periods of passivity, depression and apathy[62] had almost always followed his major victories – most conspicuously after the August Revolution, the April 1993 referendum and Red October.[63] Decisive and focused in a fight, he fell into long periods of melancholic inactivity once 'the mission [was] accomplished and the foe lay smitten'.[64] Yeltsin himself admitted that both in politics and in sport he needed a crisis to be at his best. 'If it was an ordinary game [of volleyball] you would not see me [playing my best] but if the game was close, I could work wonders . . . You need a big needle on hand [to jab me].'[65] Answering his own question – whether he was a strong man or a weak one – Yeltsin answered: 'In an urgent situation, I am, as a rule, strong. In ordinary ones, I can be lackadaisical . . . sometimes not at all like the Yeltsin the people are used to seeing.'[66]

The contrast between the Yeltsin of crisis and the Yeltsin of stasis was reminiscent of the poles in the manic–depressive cycle:

> When things were bad, especially when there was danger, his capacity for work was enormous and his nervous energy contagious. In calmer times, Yeltsin often moped. Sometimes one got the impression that he resented his duties, did not know what to do with himself; he grew morose and unpleasant to deal with. On such days he left the Kremlin early, sometimes right after lunch, and made for the dacha in Barvikha, where he was not supposed to be disturbed. At such moments, one had to avoid troubling him with ideas or papers. The chance of his [attending to] them was minimal.
>
> But when he was on the upswing, he swallowed papers like a computer. Daytime was too short for him and he 'bit off' night hours and, waking up at two o'clock or three o'clock in the morning,

ordered papers brought to him. He easily remembered all the key ideas and phrases.[67]

From early 1994, the withdrawal into self-isolation and introspection grew unprecedentedly protracted. The President was 'almost always in an awful mood',[68] his press secretary remembered, and spent more and more time at the dacha–sanatorium of Barvikha. In February and March of that year he was absent from the office for five weeks.[69] Two years before, his staff had been awed by his 'huge store of energy' and 'inexhaustible appetite for work'.[70] He had rarely left the Kremlin before eight or nine o'clock in the evening, usually worked on Saturdays, and took work home for Sundays.[71] In his weekly schedule, every hour was filled.

Now, gaping white spaces pockmarked the President's schedule. More and more frequently, meetings were cancelled. Drafts of documents and analytical papers were no longer returned with his comments. His staff was happy to find a black-ink tick in the corner – a sign that Yeltsin had at least looked at the paper.[72] The journal of his press secretary was replete with gloomy entries: 'President's in an awful mood ... President left for the Kremlin hunting estate Zavidovo for several days ... A meeting of the Security Council was cancelled ... The President will not be in the office today ... The President looked awful.'[73]

Depression and insomnia, from which he admitted to suffering in the aftermath of his dismissal in 1987,[74] continued to torment Yeltsin. He woke at one, two or three o'clock in the morning, got up and could not go back to sleep.[75] Many blamed October 1993. As Egor Gaidar put it, 'the sin of bloodshed was on his soul'.[76] In the words of another former aide and confidant, Yeltsin 'had blood on his hands and the burden was crushing him'.[77]

The other, perhaps more enduring, anguish was caused by guilt for the distress that the first two years of radical economic reform he had initiated and defended had caused millions of his compatriots:

I have had to live through it all: the debilitating fits of depression, heavy thoughts in the night, insomnia, headache, despair and grief at the sight of dirty, impoverished Moscow and other Russian cities, the barrage of criticism which bursts every day from newspaper pages and the television screen, the hounding at the Congresses [of People's Deputies], the entire weight of decisions made, grudges against those who used to be close but, in time of need, deceived, did not help, did not endure.[78]

*

Yeltsin's drinking became embarrassing: probably a result of the depression, the need to cope with it, to break it, or at least to get some sleep. Whatever the reason, the abuse of alcohol was a new problem. A predilection for strong drink had always been readily indulged but never before allowed to interfere with his work. Helped by his massive physique, Yeltsin could consume a great deal with no sign of damage to his work. He always knew when to stop. Now that ability and that self-control began to crumble.

He was likely to drink not only at dinner, but at lunch as well. 'Do you have the green one?' was his first question to the waiter at a small luncheon in the Kremlin.[79] The 'green one' was Yeltsin's favourite vodka, flavoured with herbs. Often, he drank before receptions and met visitors of 'a high rank' looking merry after 'a nice glass of vodka'.[80]

In the early autumn of 1994, this habit surfaced in a manner that millions of Russians found humiliating. On 31 August in Berlin, at a ceremony marking the departure of the last Russian troops from Germany, a clearly inebriated Yeltsin snatched the baton from the conductor of the Berlin Police Orchestra and began to conduct. He ended the performance by singing a Russian folk song.[81]

Another, somewhat less obvious *faux pas* occurred several weeks later at a US–Russian summit at the Roosevelt Hyde Park museum and estate in New York State. After downing one glass of wine after another at lunch,[82] Yeltsin emerged for a joint press conference much animated, gesticulating expansively and joking loudly and incessantly. 'You said that this meeting was going to fail!' he reprimanded the journalists in a stentorian voice. 'Now you yourselves have failed!' President Clinton's uproarious but visibly laboured laughter helped defuse the situation.

A marked change had also occurred in the ways Kremlin business was conducted. It was as if, after swimming relentlessly from 1989 on against the current of his own habits and his political upbringing, after refashioning himself from a rough Party boss into a democratic leader, Yeltsin had tired and let the previously resisted tide carry him. Much in his character that he had tried to control by daily and hourly effort was on display more and more frequently: impatience, intolerance of his subordinates' weaknesses and mistakes, petulance.[83] The habitual brusqueness now often degenerated into boorishness and rudeness. He could easily humiliate and mock his employees and visitors, treating them like a 'lord treats a grovelling servant'.[84] Kremlin aides inquired from officers on duty in the President's reception room about the boss's state before making an appointment. There were days when they avoided seeing him at all cost.[85]

As if seized by senility, Yeltsin appeared to drift inexorably back to his political youth, running the government like the Kremlin of the Brezhnev era, a Kremlin neglectful of policy-making, rife with intrigues and infighting, obsessed with the paraphernalia of power and rank, cloaked in secrecy and pomp, slack with incompetence and tainted by corruption. Visibly relishing his enormous powers, he delighted in managing the Kremlin court: promoting, demoting, firing and shifting around high officials with the enthusiasm of a Byzantine autocrat.

It was widely assumed by liberal Kremlin aides that their offices were bugged and that anything they said on the telephone or to one another was recorded by the Kremlin's mini-KGB, run by the chief of Yeltsin's bodyguards, Aleksandr Korzhakov, and the head of Kremlin security, Mikhail Barsukov. When they needed to discuss something particularly sensitive or private, top staffers did so by writing each other notes on slips of paper or by speaking as they walked along the Kremlin's long corridors.[86] The practice of secret denunciations was back, and Korzhakov–Barsukov were quite open about collecting dossiers on staffers and investigating informers' reports.[87]

Without exception, none of his most powerful associates – First Deputy Prime Minister Oleg Soskovets, First Deputy Prime Minister and later Speaker of the Council of the Federation Vladimir Shumeiko, Secretary of the Security Council Oleg Lobov and, of course, Viktor Chernomyrdin – had played any role whatsoever in the revolutionary drama of the previous five years. (Although Chernomyrdin, considered by many at the time of his appointment as little more than a communist stooge, had shown great fortitude during the October 1993 confrontation.) They were from the pre-revolutionary milieux, which Yeltsin knew so well, in which he felt comfortable and where, until less than nine years before, he had spent his entire life and made his brilliant Soviet career: communist managers of the Soviet economy (*khozaystvenniki*), energetic and successful 'tough guys' (*krepkie muzhiki*).

More and more, he surrounded himself with loyal or at least obsequious mediocrities, whom Egor Gaidar classified as *podkhalimy* and *nedoumki*: 'toadies' and 'half-brains'.[88] Incompetent (and often spectacularly bungling) in discharging direct responsibilities – be that shoring up the economy, fighting the war in Chechnya or catching terrorists, criminals or hostage takers – they became Yeltsin's hunting, eating, drinking and fishing buddies, as well as sauna companions. Frequent banquets and gargantuan meals liberally lubricated by vodka were an almost daily occurrence. Tennis was abandoned, and Yeltsin began to gain weight at an alarming pace.

His inner circle now consisted of Korzhakov, Barsukov, Minister of Internal Affairs Viktor Yerin, the Head of the President's Administration Pavel Borodin, First Deputy Oleg Soskovets, Pavel Grachev and his personal tennis coach, Shamil Tarpishchev.[89] Anyone outside this clique found it hard to speak to the President.* The man whose key strength and appeal had been his openness,[90] whose accessibility and trust in his subordinates had once been so attractive to those who worked for him,[91] was now less and less available even to his top staff. Press conferences, once Yeltsin's favourite pastime, were becoming difficult to arrange.

The 'gilded screen of Kremlin protocol' suddenly rose between Yeltsin and his former comrades-in-arms,[92] the 'democrats'. Even the liberals inside the Kremlin – Georgiy Satarov, Mikhail Krasnov, Yuriy Baturin and Yeltsin's own Chief of Staff Sergey Filatov – were often unable to reach the President.

He was also very ill. Like a long-distance runner after crossing the finish line, Yeltsin suddenly felt the pain of injuries from all the accidents and traumas of which he had more than his fair share.[93] Of these, the damage done by the crash landing in Spain in May 1990 was especially serious. Although the surgery was successful in restoring movement, every jolt to his back thereafter caused acute pain.[94] His right leg, control over which he temporarily lost after the crash, continued to hurt, and even on his best days Yeltsin dragged it slightly.[95] He also suffered from lower-back radiculitis,[96] inflammation of the roots of the spinal nerves, which could be excruciatingly painful.

But the most troubling of Yeltsin's ailments was cardiac ischaemia, or insufficient supply of blood to the heart because of complete or partial blockage of the coronary arteries. One of the most prevalent heart diseases, ischaemia causes severe chest pain, which often spreads to the back and the arm.[97] As a top Russian cardiac surgeon told a reporter, the pain could no longer be extinguished with nitroglycerine, the most common Russian palliative: one would need 'more effective means'.[98] It was widely rumoured in Moscow at the time that in Yeltsin's case such means were strong painkillers chased with drinks.

---

* The only exception at the time was Aleksandr Solzhenitsyn, who returned to Moscow in July 1994, after twenty years of exile in the United States. Yeltsin worked hard to prepare for the meeting and was anxious to find the right tone in which to speak with the man whose moral authority he recognized. In the end they talked for four hours and even drank a little vodka, which was very unusual for the teetotal Solzhenitsyn. (Vyacheslav Kostikov, *Roman s Prezidentom. Zapiski press-sekretarya* ('A novel with president. Notes of a press secretary'), p. 339.)

Yeltsin's malady became life-threatening after it caused a heart attack (or a myocardial infarct) in July 1995. Three months later, in October, he suffered another heart attack. Both times he had to be hospitalized in Barvikha for over two weeks. In between, he had what seemed to be a mild heart attack during the flight back to Moscow from the Hyde Park summit.[99] Yeltsin's inability to get out of the plane to meet the Irish Prime Minister during a stop-over at Shannon airport on 30 September[100] became the second major international embarrassment, a month after the Berlin antics.

A few weeks after the October 1993 events, Yeltsin was scheduled to meet with the *crème de la crème* of the Russian intelligentsia and thank them for their support. Some of the best Russian writers, poets and literary critics had been invited: Ales' Adamovich, Bulat Okudzhava, Fazil' Iskander, Boris Vasiliev, Daniil Granin, Bella Akhmadulina, Yuriy Nagibin, Robert Rozhdestvenskiy and the dean of Russian literary scholars, Academician Dmitriy Likhachev.

On the morning of the appointed day, Yeltsin's press secretary Vyacheslav Kostikov learned that the President had postponed the session. Ordinarily, Kostikov would have voiced no objection, but because of the calibre of the invited guests and the tactlessness of the abrupt cancellation he decided to urge the President to change his mind.[101] He waited for Yeltsin outside the President's office. Usually Yeltsin liked to talk while walking down the long carpeted corridors, to hear the latest newspaper gossip and jokes. Sometimes he would stop near a window and wistfully look out, like a 'Kremlin prisoner' wishing to be free.[102]

This time he walked more slowly than usual, dragging his leg. Couldn't the meeting just be shortened? Kostikov asked. 'What a cruel man you are, Vyacheslav Vasilievich,' Yeltsin said. 'Have you no sympathy for the President at all?' Thinking that Yeltsin was joking, an encouraged Kostikov pressed on. 'Don't worry about talking. Just thank them and let them speak. That's what they want . . . Can't you just sit with them?'

Suddenly Yeltsin stopped and turned to Kostikov. 'Don't you understand?' he said with what Kostikov described as 'metal in his voice'. 'It's difficult for me even to sit today.'[103]

CHAPTER 13

Campaign '96: 'Choosing Russia's Fate'

J ANUARY 1996 WAS A MONTH of public opinion polls in Russia. Increasingly sophisticated and reliable, national surveys were conducted by a dozen Moscow firms for their clients: newspapers, television, political parties, coalitions in search of 'their' Presidential candidate, and candidates looking for 'their' electorate and for ways to woo it.

Yeltsin's figures were very bleak. No more than 10 per cent of Russians said they would vote for him in the Presidential elections on 16 June.[1] By comparison the KPRF's Chairman Gennadiy Zyuganov was chosen by 20 per cent of those polled, Grigoriy Yavlinskiy by 13 per cent, Vladimir Zhirinovskiy and Aleksandr Lebed by 10 per cent each. Of the major contenders, only Viktor Chernomyrdin (7 per cent) and Egor Gaidar (3 per cent) trailed Yeltsin.[2]

Two strategies emerged in the Kremlin in response to this disaster. Aleksandr Korzhakov and First Deputy Prime Minister Oleg Soskovets (whom Yeltsin in January appointed 'co-ordinator' of his as yet unannounced Presidential campaign) wanted Yeltsin's message, behaviour and programme to appeal to the leftist electorate. After a year of incessant scolding by the liberal media over Chechnya and after the resignation (in January 1996) of the last leading democrats (Kovalev and Gaidar) from the Presidential Council (again over the Chechen war), the two Yeltsin confidants saw little use for the 'democrats' or their agenda. Only by 'playing on the communists' field'[3] could Yeltsin hope for re-election.

Korzhakov believed that the conflict between Yeltsin and the communists had been largely artificial, engineered by the President's advisers: Georgiy Satarov, Anatoliy Chubais (before he was fired by Yeltsin in January 1996) and Yeltsin's Chief Aide Viktor Ilyushin.[4] Korzhakov was prepared to offer the communists posts in the government in exchange for their endorsement of Yeltsin.[5] In mid-April, according to Korzhakov, he and Viktor Chernomyrdin talked about cancelling (or 'postponing') the election and securing the communists' consent by offering them ministerial portfolios.[6] At the beginning of May, Korzhakov would make this plan public.[7]

In charge of collecting the million signatures required for registering a Presidential candidate, Soskovets nearly disqualified Yeltsin from running by failing to collect enough of them in time. In the end, the President's place on the ballot was saved only by several dozen national volunteer 'action groups'.[8] Meanwhile, the Communist Party's 500,000 card-holding members collected the necessary signatures by 23 February – almost two months ahead of the deadline.

In the government rest home of Arkhangelskoye near Moscow, at a dacha next door to the one occupied by the Korzhakov–Soskovets election team, a group of public opinion experts, campaign managers and public relations specialists had been quietly assembled by Georgiy Satarov, Yeltsin's long-time speechwriters Aleksandr Il'yin and Ludmila Pikhoya, and Viktor Ilyushin, who secured their access to the President.[9] At these unofficial headquarters, the cancellation of the election, advocated by Korzhakov & Co., was viewed as a catastrophe – the end of Russia's five-year experiment in democracy.[10] Like Egor Gaidar, they believed that 'the refusal to hold the election is absolutely unacceptable if we want Russia to advance along the democratic path'.[11] Even the communists' victory in a free and fair election would be 'absolutely' preferable to a scenario in which cancellation would 'make heroes out of the communists'.[12] As Satarov put it, he and his comrades felt that they had one task and one task only: to win the election.[13]

Even in that frigid and dark January, such a proposition did not look hopeless to them. Very thin and spotty, the silver lining could nevertheless be discerned through the clouds. First, Yeltsin's main liabilities – pension and wage arrears, and the war in Chechnya – were not beyond redress. Progress in both areas would improve his chances very quickly.[14] Second, the Yeltsin candidacy had some formidable 'situational' reserves, as a leading Russian pollster put it.[15] When paired in a two-horse race with candidates unacceptable to a sizeable segment of the electorate – Zhirinovskiy or Zyuganov – Yeltsin's ratings doubled or even tripled: 23 per cent said they would vote for Yeltsin against Zyuganov[16] and 30 per cent preferred the President in a direct contest with Zhirinovskiy.[17]

Most of all, the Satarov team hoped that the enormity of the stakes, which was already obvious to intellectuals on the left and right, would soon become clear to most of the electorate. 'In June the people will have to choose not politicians but a political course,' *Pravda* stated on 17 January.[18] At the other end of the political spectrum, the liberal *Novoye Vremya* declared that the fate of Russia was 'at stake': the country might not be able to survive another communist experiment, 'even in a weaker version'.[19] The pro-reform, muckraking *Moskovskiy Komsomoletz* was just as emphatic: 'We are all actually selecting not so much one individual or another as a political and economic system.'[20]

The Yeltsin campaign could succeed if it managed to persuade voters that the choice was between continuation of the present course (no matter how flawed and uneven) and a sharp, perhaps 180-degree, turn. The polls seemed to indicate that, once Yeltsin became a 'symbol of resistance to communist restoration', the hardships and disappointments of transition and the blunders of the past two years might recede before the immediate danger.[21]

Critical to the Satarov group's strategy was the presence of a vast and stable pro-reform and anti-communist constituency. While the 'hard-core' anti-Yeltsin and mostly pro-communist electorate ranged between 29 per cent ('My sympathies have never been and are not now with B. N. Yeltsin')[22] and 42 per cent (they would not 'support Yeltsin under any circumstances'),[23] 54 per cent of those surveyed in the autumn of 1995 said they did not 'consider the communist system acceptable for Russia'.[24] Asked in January 1996 if the country should return to the communist system, 39 per cent of a nation-wide sample agreed, while 61 per cent disagreed.[25]

These figures were almost identical to those relating to another polarizing issue: prices set by the market. Asked in January 1996 if it was 'better' to have plenty of expensive goods in the stores or 'few' at low prices controlled by the state, 59 per cent of those surveyed preferred the former situation and 41 per cent the latter.[26] These results, in turn, corresponded closely to respondents' own situation: 36 per cent said that 'our miserable situation can't be tolerated any more', while 57 per cent said that their life was 'hard but we can get by' or that 'everything is not too bad and it is possible to live'.[27] Yeltsin's potential electorate seemed especially solid among younger Russians. In poll after poll, with a uniformity that excluded accident, Russians between twenty and forty-four years old (38 per cent of the population)[28] rejected communism by a very wide margin – no matter how the questions were phrased.

Beyond the polls, the Satarov team's strategy rested on the country's voting record. In the December 1995 national legislative elections, over 31 per cent of the total vote (twenty-one million) was cast for pro-reform parties (either pro-regime or opposition) and another 15 per cent (eleven million) went to anti- or non-communist nationalists: Vladimir Zhirinovskiy's LDPR, and Aleksandr Lebed's Congress of Russian Communities (KRO). There were also centrists (Women of Russia, Union of Labour and two smaller parties) with another 7 per cent (five million) of the party-list vote. In a two-man run-off Yeltsin could count on capturing the lion's share of the first group and a significant proportion of the other two.

In addition, the turnout for the Presidential poll was likely to be considerably greater than that at the legislative election: people were voting for the occupant of the Kremlin, the ruler, not the widely disparaged *govorlin'ya* (a place of talk) of the Duma. Besides, June in Russia was far more conducive to the discharge of civic duty (and to almost anything else) than December. Since the very disciplined communist electorate tended to turn out in force regardless of weather, the candidate of the united left could count on a relatively small addition to the twenty-two million votes that were cast for the four leftist parties in 1995. Most of the increase would thus have to come from the anti-communist and pro-reform electorate, which, being younger and busy with school, business and children, had been notoriously truant before: by some estimates 60 per cent of urban youth had ignored the 1995 election.

Finally, there was the memory of another stark confrontation: the April 1993 referendum.[29] Then, with the monthly inflation rate at 20 per cent, forty million Russians (59 per cent of the vote) had forgiven the regime's errors and 'expressed confidence' in Yeltsin, and thirty-seven million (53 per cent) had voted to continue the reforms by approving of the regime's 'socio-economic policies'. Satarov and his colleagues hoped that fear of the alternative – the scuttling of reforms and a return to the Soviet past – would again save the President.

It is this scenario that a leading political columnist of the liberal *Literaturnaya Gazeta* would outline two months later. Having listed Yeltsin's enormous handicaps – the war in Chechnya; the wage arrears; 'rampant' crime; the 'insolent' and 'swollen' bureaucracy, 'bogged down' in theft and bribery; the 'nouveau riche' who 'wallowed in luxury' and whose 'striking wealth' was in 'disgusting' contrast with the 'poverty of the majority of Russians' – he still insisted that:

> No matter how long a list of Yeltsin's mistakes and miscalculations we come up with ... THIS DOES NOT GIVE US THE RIGHT TO VOTE AGAINST HIM. The reason is simple and well known: the alternatives to him are the communists, whose breakthrough to power will mean, unequivocally, a national catastrophe for Russia ... The voting procedure ... [will] resolve ... whether Russia is to continue forward, in the direction of a free market and democracy, or turn back, to the 'bright' Brezhnev–Chernenko past![30]

For Yeltsin to win, the anti-communist electorate would have to be galvanized by the stark contrast between the 'national-patriotic' vision of Russia and his own. Tens of millions of Russians also had to be persuaded that the sixty-five-year-old President was capable – physically and mentally – of guaranteeing the stability of democracy and reform, that he could be trusted with the job.[31] For the Satarov plan, this last objective – demonstrating the President's fitness for the task – was both central and the least certain. It required nothing less than the return of a pre-1994 Yeltsin. A few photographs and recorded speeches would not do: Yeltsin had a lot to atone for. There had to be an electrifying jolt, a genuine break with the torpor and decay of the past two years, an abrupt and credible end to the drift and complacency, the sloth and the hibernation.

More than a feat of will, such a strategy presupposed a mammoth physical effort. After two years of lassitude and illnesses, the exertion of a vigorous campaign (and only such a campaign would do the trick) could, quite literally, kill him. It was this danger on which Korzhakov incessantly harped as he insisted on a deal with the communists and the postponement of the poll.[32] Only recently back at work after his second heart attack in half a year, Yeltsin was to choose between the two strategies. As always before major decisions, he brooded, and took no one into his confidence.

At the end of January 1996, at the World Economic Forum in Davos, Switzerland, some of Russia's richest men anxiously listened to the communist candidate Gennadiy Zyuganov and the leader of the only democratic faction in the Duma, Yabloko's Grigoriy Yavlinsky. Frightened by the former and utterly unimpressed by the childish petulance, political ineptitude and all-consuming megalomania of the latter, they delegated two of the most powerful tycoons, Vladimir Gusinskiy and Boris Berezovskiy, to talk to another guest, Anatoliy Chubais – right there, in the hotel. 'While you, pardon the expression, democrats, "intensely analyse the situation" and conduct "active negotiations" between yourselves, 16 June is around the corner and, as things are now, the outcome is predetermined,' Chubais said he was told. 'We could not coexist with Zyuganov and shall either fight him with all the means available (and, trust us, we do have them!) – or emigrate from Russia. We are ready to commit everything we have not to let this happen.' In Davos, Chubais agreed to try and help Yeltsin's still unannounced but already near-comatose campaign.

This was a wrenching decision, not only because Yeltsin had just dismissed Chubais, reprimanding the former Deputy Prime Minister on national television and blaming him for the lacklustre performance of Viktor Chernomyrdin's Our Home Is Russia party in the recent election. In volunteering his services, Chubais went against what was then a strong consensus among the pro-reform 'democrats': not to support Yeltsin until he apologized for the blunder of the Chechen war and dismissed those of his advisers and Ministers who were responsible for it.

In the absence of any other distinction or achievement since the '500 Days' programme eight-and-a-half years before, opposition to the Kremlin was Grigoriy Yavlinsky's sole claim to national prominence. His strategy, in pursuit of which his faction in the Duma voted with the communists time and again, had always been that the worse things were for the regime, the better. Now that, with customary disregard of reality, he imagined himself among the front-runners for the Presidency, the vehemence with which he refused to help Yeltsin's candidacy intensified. He announced, on national television, that there was little difference between Yeltsin and the communists, and that even if, by a miracle, Yeltsin reached the second round (if no candidate garnered more than 50 per cent of the vote, there was to be a run-off between the top two contenders), he would lose to a communist candidate in a two-man race.[33] In any case, in the autumn of 1994, in a statement distributed in the Duma, Yavlinsky had declared that 'democracy in Russia can be built without Yeltsin'.[34]

While Yavlinsky's stance was hardly surprising, Chubais's own party, Russia's Choice (recently renamed Russia's Democratic Choice, or DVR), was leaning towards non-cooperation. When the party's ruling council gathered in March, the widely respected former dissident and political prisoner Sergey Kovalev (who, as we have seen, had resigned as Chairman of the President's Commission on Human Rights in January in protest against the Pervomayskoye débâcle) insisted that absolutely no aid or comfort be given to the Kremlin. Russian troops had killed tens of thousands in Chechnya, Kovalev said. Yeltsin had appeared drunk on television. He had lied to the Russian people, lied in public! If Russia's Choice advised its supporters to vote for Yeltsin, Kovalev warned, it would lose much more than its influence. It would lose face.[35]

One could easily, Chubais responded, have extended the list of Yeltsin's transgressions. He himself could contribute quite a few items. And, should they decide not to help Yeltsin in the election, such a position:

> would be morally very satisfying: we would be left unsoiled. But perhaps we ought to think not so much about what's good for the party as what's good for the country. I don't think that anyone sitting here today has illusions on this score: as things stand today, on 16 June Zyuganov will become President of Russia. And we must decide on the basis not of how we would look but of how Russia would look after 16 June.

We have been reminded today of the thousands killed in Chechnya.

But let's ask ourselves: how many thousands, including those in this hall, will be rotting away in [prison] camps? How many will be able to attend the next congress of our party – of other parties allied with us? Oh yes, we can insist on a 'democratic agreement' [with the President], we can form a shadow cabinet of the most talented, young and brilliant minds.

But don't we understand what would be the end result of all these discussions, negotiations, appeals? Isn't it clear that there is one and only one question facing Russia today: will there be a second coming of communism – or not?

I can, for months on end, ask myself dozens of the hardest moral questions, but I accepted the offer [of the top Russian entrepreneurs] and I will make sure that all the resources these people can muster will be used in ways to ensure that Zyuganov never becomes President of Russia.[36]

At the time, a number of pro-reform journalist were beginning to view the coming campaign in the light of the same brutal (but also liberating) choice. Yet most democrats saw no way out of the terrible moral and practical dilemma. Even if they followed Chubais, their votes would be wasted on the Yeltsin they had seen in the past two years. 'It was unbearable to see how he was being manipulated,' Gaidar recalled. 'It was torture to watch him [in January] not understanding at all what was going on. And it is for this Yeltsin that we had to vote? After Pervomayskoye, I was convinced that his chances of winning were zero.'[37]

The despondency was exacerbated by the first glimpses of the Korzhakov–Soskovets operation. Although there were a number of competent and talented people around Yeltsin, wrote a leading Russian public opinion expert, the decisions were being made by 'grey, mediocre men, incapable of effective thinking or effective action'.[38] In desperation, as he later described his state of mind in early 1996, Gaidar half-heartedly attempted to talk Chernomyrdin or Nizhniy Novgorod's Governor Boris Nemtsov into running as a candidate of united pro-reform forces. Yet, even as he did so, Gaidar did not believe for a moment that either of them could provide serious competition for Zyuganov.[39]

The DVR continued to put forward conditions for a 'dialogue' with the Kremlin – peace in Chechnya and the dismissal of Grachev, Barsukov and Chief of Staff Nikolay Yegorov, responsible for Pervomayskoye[40] – but they had little hope of response, much less action. When on 2 March 900 representatives of 240 public organizations that had endorsed Yeltsin gathered in Moscow under the chairmanship of Sergey Filatov, no prominent 'democrat', save the 'godfather of glasnost' Aleksandr Yakovlev, was in the hall.[41]

On 15 February, in a speech in Ekaterinburg, a tired, hoarse and coughing[42] Yeltsin announced his intention to run for re-election. While the decision was expected, the chosen strategy was anxiously awaited by the competing factions in the Kremlin and by the entire political class as they tried to determine which version of the campaign Yeltsin had finally adopted: that of Korzhakov–Soskovets ('playing on the communist field') or the Satarov group's aggressively pro-reform stance. As it turned out, there was no need to read between the lines. The accomplishments he singled out (and the mistakes he acknowledged and promised to correct), the threats he warned of and the agenda he announced – all translated into a coherent, assertive, vigorous and even pugnacious campaign message which he reiterated in the 'State of Russia' address to the Federal Assembly a week later. Its three parts, which would become the key themes of the next four months, were the record of reform and democracy; the danger of communist restoration; and the promise of stability.

Remember the 'huge queues for bread and sugar in 1991?' Yeltsin asked the Ekaterinburg audience. Remember how people stood in queues even at night and warmed themselves beside bonfires?[43] All gone. The stores were full, and their children and grandchildren would never know what shortages and ration coupons were. What had brought about this plenty? Free-market prices introduced in 1992![44] Hyperinflation had been curbed, there were plenty of currency and gold reserves in the state Treasury and the ruble was stable.[45]*

More important still, 'for the first time in Russian history, large-scale transformations [were] taking place without the suppression and destruction of political opponents'.[46] The Russian people now had the most precious right – the right to choose.[47] Free elections were 'the only way for the state to recover', the only way to ensure that, little by little, the time-servers and incompetent and corrupt *nachal'nik*s were got rid of.[48] Free elections, Yeltsin emphasized, were there to stay; their role

---

* Monthly inflation in January was 3 per cent compared with 21 per cent in January 1995. In 1996 annual inflation would be 22 per cent compared with 131 per cent in 1995 – and 2,500 per cent in 1992. In July the ruble would become *de facto* convertible: for the first time since 1913, it could easily be bought and sold for foreign currencies both inside and outside Russia.

was to guarantee that the state served its citizens, not the other way around.[49]

For the first time in its history, Russia had no political prisoners. No one was expelled from the country or deprived of citizenship for reasons of ideology or religion. People could travel abroad freely and freely return home.[50] Information from abroad flowed into Russia unhindered. No one jammed radio broadcasts from the West and the 'strictest censorship' of materials from abroad had been long forgotten.[51] Russia had become an 'open state'.[52]

A state-enforced monopoly on ideology was a thing of the past as well. State coercion in cultural matters had been replaced with pluralism – something about which so many earlier generations of Russians could only dream about.[53] Previously forbidden books, including the Bible and the Koran, were now freely available. The mass media were free to criticize the government, and Russians complained not by whispering in their kitchens, but on television, in newspapers and on the streets and squares of Russian cities![54] In short, the 'country enjoyed full-scale freedom of political, public and trade union activity'.[55] There was freedom of conscience, speech, the press and information; freedom of meetings, demonstrations and rallies.[56]

All of these achievements, Yeltsin continued, were now at risk. In the short time since 1992 Russians might have forgotten that the 'border which separates us from the grey, stifling yesterday' was very fragile.[57] Look at the stock market and foreign investments. They were all frozen. Why? Because the markets were waiting for the results of the election: either the reforms remained and continued to develop, or they would be rolled back: privatization destroyed, joint-stock companies dismantled and privatized housing taken away.[58] The greatest danger of all was to democracy. The opposition leaders were still 'prisoners of dogmas rejected by life'. They believed they could turn history back.[59] As in 1917, they were bent on redistributing power and property. Russia could again perish 'under the red wheel', Yeltsin declared, invoking Aleksandr Solzhenitsyn's famous metaphor.

On 16 June, the voters would not only elect the President; they would choose 'Russia's future life and determine Russia's fate'.[60] That was why the country needed him – to finish what had been started, to 'bring to a successful end' the cause to which he had completely committed himself.[61] He was confident that he could lead Russia 'through disturbances, worries and insecurity'. With the spectre of civil war again on the horizon, he would provide unity and stability to a country which, as in 1917, could be torn between 'the Reds and the Whites'. He would navigate Russia between the extreme right, which wanted reform 'at any cost', and the extreme left, which would destroy 'everything that has been accomplished so far'. He stood for reform – but with a human face. Having learned from the experience, he would adjust the course – but he would not turn back.[62]

Had he made mistakes? 'Of course' he had – many mistakes.[63] They had left 'scars on this heart' and had caused him many a sleepless night.[64] The regime had asked for people's sacrifices but had failed to explain 'what we were doing and why'.[65] The government had done little to protect investors against unscrupulous speculators. The 'effectiveness' of the fight against crime was low. Bribery and abuse of office were widespread.[66] The Chechen war and the disgraceful delays in the payments of pensions and salaries were the worst failures of the regime. He promised to 'undo the Chechen knot' within the next few months and find money for payments by the end of March.

The adjusted course of reform, he explained, meant that, following liberalization and financial stabilization, the next tasks were to secure investment in the economy, stimulate production and overhaul taxation and the management of state properties.[67] Private ownership of land should be 'firmly secured', including citizens' rights to dispose of their land in any way they saw fit, not least mortgaging and leasing it.[68] Now that political liberties had been firmly established, it was time to pay attention to people's social and economic rights. The state would begin compensating pensioners for the savings lost to inflation, first by paying interest and eventually by repaying the pre-1992 principal.[69] Rampant corruption and bribery would be dealt with resolutely and mercilessly: 1,200 people had already been arrested,[70] including a former Procurator General.[71]

Despite the mistakes, the reform policy was the only correct one and 'under no circumstances' would he abandon it.[72] He would continue the tight monetary policy in order to sustain the hard-won victory against inflation, despite the desperate need for money to pay salaries and pensions. Invoking the memory of the late 1980s, he pledged not to allow a single 'wooden (*derevyannyi*) ruble' to circulate.[73]* Most of all, he

---

* Only in one instance did the Ekaterinburg speech appear to echo the Korzhakov–Soskovets strategy of 'playing on the communist field'. Borrowing from the KPRF's slogans of 'social justice', for a minute or so Yeltsin fulminated about the high salaries of the presidents of private companies. Then he just as abruptly changed the tone by reminding the audience that those salaries had been approved by stockholders and boards of directors. He ended by saying that he had nothing against high salaries for the manage-

would defend democracy and freedom. He concluded the 'State of Russia' address with a hymn to both:

> It is important to understand that freedom and democracy are not something that someone has dreamed up, they are not a national feature of a particular people . . . They are the only possibility for ensuring a worthy life, they are the main condition for progress and prosperity. On the basis of Russian and world experience, having made my own choice, I confirm that only a democratic state structure can ensure a worthy future for Russia.
>
> No matter who comes to power in the coming Presidential election, he should remember that it is the destiny of the country's leader to strengthen freedom and democracy in Russia . . . Herein lies the highest responsibility of the state and its duty to future generations of Russians . . .
>
> I believe in Russia's ability to implement the ideals of freedom and democracy. I believe in the people of Russia . . . I believe in our young people, who are free and talented, who will not allow the country to be turned back and who are capable of moving it forward.[74]

Behind the stage curtain the men and women of the Satarov team felt their 'eyes welling up with tears': 'Here was this elderly president with his hoarse voice showing this tremendous determination.'[75] The relief, even jubilation in their camp[76] was not just because the boss had chosen their game plan. Suddenly, after two years of humiliating hibernation, 'Boris arose!' recalled a man who drafted most of the Ekaterinburg speech.[77] After lying unclaimed, rusting and all but forgotten for two years, Yeltsin's 'incredible political instinct' had turned up again, miraculously intact.[78] After this speech, indeed, Moscow wits recalled a Russian proverb: *Mastersvo propit's nel'zya* ('You cannot completely lose your talent, no matter how hard you drink').

Yeltsin's address had comprised a surprisingly energetic defence of his record, a powerful description of what was at stake, and graphic warnings of the 'Red danger'. After repeated drafting and redrafting, Yeltsin had forged a message that, in effect, shifted the entire dynamic of the coming contest: from a referendum on the Russian version of capitalism and on the regime's blunders, which he was almost certain

---

ment, provided the employees were paid decently. (Ekaterinburg speech, 15 February 1996, p. 49.)

to lose, to a vote on the benefits of democracy and the dangers of communism, in which he had a good chance of prevailing.

Now the Satarov group were confident that the election would be held, come hell or high water. As Georgiy Satarov told a foreign interviewer two weeks later: 'When he makes a decision, he is like a tank that makes straight for the target, flattening anything it encounters in its path. If he has decided to run and win, I really do not know what can prevent him.'[79]

What, or rather who, could prevent him from achieving re-election emerged on the same day, 15 February, at the Fourth All-Russian Conference of the Communist Party of the Russian Federation. The Party's Chairman, Gennadiy Zyuganov, was unanimously nominated Presidential candidate.

Four months short of fifty-two, Zyuganov had begun his full-time Party career almost thirty years before in the Propaganda and Agitation Department of the Oryol *oblast* Party Committee and rose, rather slowly, to become the Deputy Chief of the Central Committee's Propaganda Department. In the intra-Party struggle between the pro-perestroika supporters of Gorbachev and Yakovlev on the one side and Ligachev on the other, Zyuganov sided with the conservatives. In 1990 he joined the hardline KPRF and was elected one of seven Secretaries of the new party's Central Committee at its founding Congress. A year later he co-authored *The Word to the People*, a virulent anti-perestroika manifesto, which accused the Gorbachev leadership of betraying communism and destroying the Soviet Union. While *Word* would become the ideological credo of the organizers of the August putsch three weeks later,[80] Zyuganov himself spent the coup in the Party sanatorium in the Crimea. He returned to the capital five days after the coup had unravelled.

After the Constitutional Court overturned Yeltsin's decree prohibiting the KPRF, Zyuganov was elected Chairman of its Central Executive Committee. From the beginning, the Party's leadership included nearly all the prominent veterans of the anti-Gorbachev and anti-Yeltsin resistance: Egor Ligachev; Svetlana Goryacheva, the leader of the Group of Six who had sought to remove Yeltsin from the Chairmanship of the Russian Supreme Soviet in early 1991; the August putschists Anatoliy Lukyanov, Vasiliy Starodubtsev and General Valentin Varennikov; and Generals Albert Makashov and Vladislav Achalov, both of whom would lead the Supreme Soviet's troops in the battle in October 1993.

After cleansing itself of 'Gorbachevite defilers', as Zyuganov put it, by 1995 the KPRF had re-created 20,000 'primary organizations'.[81] Its active, dues-paying membership quickly reached 550,000[82] – many times the size of all other parties, blocs and movements combined. Free to travel abroad, Zyuganov and his comrades recreated the CPSU's links to over 100 communist and leftist parties 'all over the planet'.[83] Of all the communist leaders he met, Zyuganov was most impressed with Fidel Castro, whom he beheld in Havana during the First World Solidarity-with-Cuba Conference. To Zyuganov, Fidel was 'without a doubt one of the largest political figures of the contemporary world'.[84]

Although he deplored the 'Presidential coup' of 21 September 1993, Zyuganov stayed away from the White House and called on Party members not to get involved in the fighting. A month later, while decrying the illegitimacy of the new Constitution and the new parliament, he ran for a Duma seat at the head of the KPRF's national list, was elected and then re-elected in December 1995. The communist faction under Zyuganov's stewardship quickly became a strong 'national-patriotic' plurality in the Duma, comprising 40 per cent of the Deputies.

Quite unlike the 'democrats', the 'popular patriots' found little difficulty in uniting around a single Presidential candidate. As early as 17 March 1996, the Congress of 'popular-patriotic forces' endorsed Zyuganov at its founding session in Moscow. Among the signatories of the 'Accord on co-ordinated actions in support of the single candidate to the Presidency of the Russian Federation G. A. Zyuganov' were veterans of the 'Second October Revolution' of 1993: Aleksandr Rutskoy, Stanislav Terekhov and Viktor Anpilov, all of whom spoke at the Congress. Zyuganov later suggested Anpilov as the head of the state First Channel/ORT (Ostankino) television network,[85] Russia's largest.*

---

* Asked about his plans for Russian television, Anpilov answered that he would fire all the Jews and limit foreign programming to no more than 10 per cent. (See Ellen Mickiewicz, *Changing Channels*, p. 216.) 'We see those Jewish faces [on the screen] and [they] insult us,' Anpilov said. In an interview on Russian television, Anpilov said that he had 'something very witty' to show and reached for a campaign poster of Yeltsin shaking hands with the Mayor of Moscow, Yuriy Luzhkov. The picture was doctored to show both men wearing yarmulkas. 'They are in Jewish caps,' Anpilov said. That, he continued, explained the ruin of Russia under Yeltsin. (Victor Anpilov, interview on the nightly news programme *Itogi*, NTV, 9 June 1996, as quoted in Michael McFaul, *Russia's 1996 Presidential Election*, p. 117 n. 60; Mickiewicz, *Changing Channels*, pp. 216, 180, 182.)

The leader of Working Russia was equally straightforward on the economic policy of the future regime. All banks were to be nationalized, and ex-bankers would 'work for

Among dozens of 'popular-patriotic' parties, movements and blocs that united in support of Zyuganov's candidacy, none could match the influence of the *Zavtra* weekly. Although the paper enjoyed nowhere near the millions of readers daily reached by *Sovetskaya Rossia*, *Sel'skaya Zhizn'* or *Pravda*,* which Zyuganov called the KPRF's 'tried and true friends',[86] it was *Zavtra*'s unmistakable rhetoric that framed Zyuganov's oeuvre. Many a 'national-patriotic' leader claimed the honour of 'educating Zyuganov', but no other claim could be corroborated as solidly as that of *Zavtra*'s editor, Aleksandr Prokhanov, who declared: 'Zyuganov emerged . . . from our laboratory.'[87]

It was with Prokhanov that Zyuganov co-wrote *The Word to the People*. It was to Prokhanov that he turned after the August Revolution. Prokhanov recalled how a 'shocked and depressed' Zyuganov – orphaned by the Party's abrupt demise and suddenly without a chauffeured car and a large office in the Central Committee's building – would come to *Zavtra*'s editorial office bringing with him a traditional Russian peasant lunch: slices of salted suet wrapped in newspaper.[88] 'We received him as a companion in distress,' Prokhanov remembered, 'and he submerged himself into a kind of intellectual laboratory.'[89]

For Prokhanov, this was a most natural union: 'Russian patriots' supported the Communist Party because 'for Russian patriots the very idea of communism is Russian'.[90] Although not a Party member, Prokhanov was later credited by the KPRF's leadership with being the 'essential force' that after August 1991 had nursed the KPRF back to life.[91]

As friends do in Russia, Zyuganov and Prokhanov addressed each other as *ty*, instead of the formal *vy*. Zyuganov called the fifty-eight-year-old editor 'Sasha', a diminutive of Aleksandr.[92] Prokhanov served as the candidate's 'issue adviser' and often travelled with him.[93] In the spring of 1996, he was mentioned as a possible Minister of Information in a Zyuganov government. Writers and philosophers who gathered around Prokhanov were prominent among those who gave the communist campaign 'strategic and ideological advice'.[94] The weekly's deputy

---

the Central Bank'. For those who refused, 'there was enough room at the lathe', that is, at plants and factories. (Michael Gordon, 'Yeltsin's Communist Rival Tries to Moderate his Message', *New York Times*, 21 May 1996, p. A10; and Lee Hockstader, 'Rancor Rears its Head in Communist Ranks', *Washington Post*, 22 May 1996, p. A26.)

* The print-run, which *Zavtra*, like other Russian newspapers, listed on its last page, was 100,000. See also Michael Specter, 'Muse of Anti-Yeltsin Forces Is Feared But Never Ignored', *New York Times*, 2 May 1996, p. A10.

editor, Vladimir Bondarenko, accompanied Zyuganov on many campaign trips and was often seen whispering advice in his ear.[95] 'The newspaper [*Zavtra*] very courageously stood up for the interests of the Fatherland,' Zyuganov wrote in 1995.[96]

The world of *Zavtra* rested on the three pillars of Great Russian nationalism, anti-Semitism and communism. According to a student of *Zavtra*, this explosive mixture proved rather effective in September and October 1993, when the 'incendiary journalism' of *Zavtra*'s predecessor *Den'* had relentlessly inflamed the passions of the Supreme Soviet's supporters and contributed to the conflagration.[97] Like October 1993 ('a second October Revolution'), the winter and spring of 1996 were, to *Zavtra*, a continuation of the Bolshevik struggle with Yeltsin's 'anti-people', 'bourgeois' regime. In early February, the paper called on its readers to reject whatever bribes might issue from Yeltsin's hands, which were 'covered with blood', and instead, 'with babies in your arms and supporting the elderly by the elbow, go this summer to the polling stations: to vote for President Zyuganov!'[98] Invoking a famous Bolshevik Civil War poster, familiar to every Russian from school history lessons ('Have you signed up for the Red Army?'), on *Zavtra*'s front page a wounded young veteran pointed a finger at the reader: 'Have you signed up for the anti-Yeltsin coalition?'[99]

'I am an anti-democrat,' Prokhanov said in May 1996. 'I am a Russian nationalist. And so is Zyuganov. I support him completely.'[100] To *Zavtra*, every communist victory was a triumph of Russian nationalism and, hence, a defeat for Russia's sworn enemies. 'Hanukkah has been spoiled,' thus began the newspaper's report of the communists' success in the December 1995 parliamentary elections.[101] After that victory, *Zavtra* changed its masthead from 'The Newspaper of Spiritual Opposition' to 'Newspaper of the Russian State'. In an editorial under the new slogan, Prokhanov wrote: 'Having taken the Duma, we will take the Kremlin.'[102]

Zavtra's tenets were few and simple. Russia was an occupied country; democracy and the market economy had been imposed on it from abroad; only an authoritarian government with a strong military could save it; Russia's destiny was to save humanity; the borders of the Soviet Union were the borders of Great Russia and should be restored; any patriotic Russian would support Zyuganov.[103]* Between 1992 and 1996

---

* Typical of *Zavtra*'s peculiar habit of seeking divine intercession in bringing back the militantly and ruthlessly atheistic Soviet state was this verse: 'God, who let the Soviet state / Flourish in its miraculous power and glory, / God, who saved the Soviets from

Zavtra had constructed a political philosophy that, in the same observer's view, presented 'a very worrying agenda', in which Jews and Americans were the major 'demons'.[104] As summarized by an astute American essayist and veteran Moscow reporter, *Zavtra*'s pages brimmed with 'racists, militarists, and loons of all varieties' and 'had enough slander, bile and anti-Semitism . . . to fill an issue of [Hitler's] *Der Stürmer*'.[105]

This message was served in a breathless, over-heated, near-hysterical style, full of Biblical archaisms, convoluted syntax and exclamation marks. A thick, steaming brew of eschatology, paranoia and dark prophesying, it was part entreaty, part jeremiad, and teemed with grotesque and gruesome images. In a characteristic editorial *Zavtra* described the Belavezhskie Accords as the work of 'the three butchers [Yeltsin, Kravchuk and Shushkevich, who] attacked the Soviet Union and hacked it to death with axes, grunting and scattering around bloody and twitching limbs. It was not the [communist] party that they were cutting up, not communism, nor yet strategic missiles; they were murdering "Russian civilization" which was ripening in the womb of the USSR. . . [like] a *bogatyr'* ["baby-giant"].'[106]

In February Zyuganov met with the 'people's writers' in *Zavtra*'s editorial office and received their enthusiastic endorsement. 'Zyuganov is a truly Russian candidate for the highest post,' said one of the 'Russian writers' present. 'He is Russian by origin, by his way of thinking, by his language and by his feelings towards the Fatherland. Best of luck to you, Gennadiy Andreevich.'[107]

In April Zyuganov appeared before *Zavtra* readers in an immensely long and loving interview with Vladimir Bondarenko. Zyuganov said that he was 'saddened to watch television where [Jewish] comedians Khazanov and Ivanov are shown all the time. Where are ethnic Russians?'[108] He was 'pained' by seeing Russia's cinemas 'occupied by aggressive, dirty, rude and insolent American mass culture, which glorified violence and debauchery', and which 'destroyed [people's] psyche'.[109] He was greatly disturbed by the 'recoding of the entire national ideology'.[110]

To eliminate any doubts whatsoever on the all-important issue of

---

calamities, / God, who crowned them with the thunder of victory, / God, have mercy on us in these times of trouble, / God, return Soviet rule to us!' (Gennadiy Zyuganov, 'Rossia – strana slova' ('Russia is a country of the word'), interview with Vladimir Bondarenko, *Zavtra*, 17, (April) 1996, p. 3).

his racial purity,* Zyuganov declared in the opening paragraph of his electoral address, 'I am Russian by blood.'[111] Apparently convinced that Zyuganov's veins were free from any, and especially 'Judaic', contamination, a *Zavtra* contributor proclaimed the KPRF's Chairman 'Russian, therefore ours!'[112] A banner headline above Zyuganov's portrait in *Zavtra*'s election issue explicitly linked ethnicity and electoral choice: 'RUSSIAN, VOTE FOR ZYUGANOV!'[113]

Much like *Zavtra*'s editorialists, Gennadiy Zyuganov believed that Russia was a 'unique civilization':[114] embodied first in Kievan Rus, then in the 'tsardom of Muskovy', then in the Russian empire, and finally in the Soviet Union.[115] Of its many majestic features, two were crucial to the Russian–Soviet civilization: the empire and socialism. 'Empire is a historically and geopolitically necessary form for the development of the Russian state,' Zyuganov wrote.[116]

Socialism, too, was not an option for Russia, but an inalienable, natural, organic essence of its civilization. The 'incompatibility of capitalism and the popular mentality of the Russians' was, according to Zyuganov, a 'historic fact'.[117] Capitalism was 'inconsistent with the flesh and blood, with the being, with the habits and with the psychological make-up' of Russia.[118]

Fearful of Russia's destiny, the West, led by the United States, had conspired to destroy Russia, 'to weaken, divide and economically enslave'[119] it in order to forestall the 'coming collapse of the capitalist system'.[120] Who were they, these 'conductors' and 'scriptwriters'[121] of the anti-Russian conspiracy? 'Who is destroying Russia?'[122] Zyuganov asked. His answer was the 'international financial oligarchy', the 'worldwide corporation' which uses the political, military and economic power of the United States to achieve its 'mercenary interests and purposes';[123] 'transnational cosmopolitan forces' which saw the technological advances of the end of the twentieth century as an opportunity to fulfil 'their dream of a world superstate'.[124] The 'real behind-the-scenes orchestrator of Russia's troubles' was 'the cosmopolitan elite of international capital'.[125] For these people, the 'Motherland was where profit

---

* Unblemished ethnicity of the candidate was important to the KPRF's leadership as well. One of the most prominent communists in the Duma, the Chairman of the parliament's National Security Committee, Viktor Ilyukhin, declared in January that the Party's choice must be 'an ethnic Russian with a Russian face and a Russian name . . .' (Alexei Zverev, 'V prezidenty vyzyvali?' ('Has there been a call for the President?'), *Moskovskiy Komsomoletz*, 6 January 1996, p. 2.)

was'.[126] Their object was to remake the Russian people in their own image. Their means were 'money, provocations, molestations, lies'.[127]

To Russian Jews, these dark hints were as clear as they were troubling. The idea of the financial elite's global supremacy seemed copied directly from the 1905 *Protocols of the Elders of Zion*, with its central theme of Jewish conspiracy aimed at world domination. From 1948 on, moreover, several generations of Russians had come to know that 'cosmopolitans' meant 'Jews'. Just as disturbing, especially to the Moscow Jewish intelligentsia, must have been Zyuganov's lamentations about Stalin's untimely death. For it was the tyrant's demise that had stopped the preparation for an all-Union *Kristallnacht* to be followed by the arrest of all Soviet Jews and their deportation to concentration camps in the Far East.

In the end, Zyuganov dispenses with veils and euphemisms:

[Beginning in the nineteenth century] the world view, culture and ideology of the West were increasingly under the impact of the Judaic diaspora, whose influence began to grow not even by the day but by the hour. With the expansion of the [capitalist] market, the Jewish diaspora, which had traditionally controlled the financial life of the [European] continent, was becoming a sort of holder of the 'control packet' of shares of the entire economic system of Western civilization. The Western consciousness was more and more moulded by the notions embedded in Jewish religious beliefs: exclusivity and the 'divine mission' to rule the world ... [With] the Islamic civilization frozen in its development and thus posing no threat to Western domination, and with other world cultures incapable of resisting the military, economic and ideological advance of the West, the Slavic civilization embodied in the Russian empire became the last barrier to Western hegemonism.[128]

Mikhail Gorbachev, too, was a willing participant in an immense, ruthless and skilfully executed anti-Russian plot. Perestroika was deliberate sabotage.[129] Its cardinal sin was the 'de-ideologization' of the Soviet state and its capitulation before 'Western values'.[130] Unlike the Chinese communist reformers, whose 'strong and effective system of controlling political phenomena' Zyuganov admired, Gorbachev gambled the Party's political monopoly away.[131]

Yeltsin had continued and completed the business of national self-annihilation started by Gorbachev. A puppet whose strings were being 'pulled from across the ocean',[132] Yeltsin had seized power 'with the help of the world oligarchy', and had proceeded to follow the directions of 'powerful international forces'.[133] His government was a government of 'national betrayal',[134] his supporters, the 'Yeltsinoids',[135] 'denationalized democrats',[136] fifth columnists and agents of influence.[137] By more radical means, Yeltsin had implemented Gorbachev's policies and ensured 'untold calamities' for the Russian people.[138] The Yeltsin regime had 'lost the Motherland, its honour and conscience, betrayed its own people, its ideals and its sacred treasures, and the glory of its ancestors'.[139] Both Gorbachev and Yeltsin, according to Zyuganov, were 'totally immoral' and 'anti-people'.[140]

Yeltsin's worst malefaction was the destruction of the twentieth-century incarnation of Russian civilization: the Soviet *derzhava*, the mighty proud state and its vast empire. ('That crime', Zyuganov called the Belavezhskie Accords.)[141] Thus the choice that Russia faced in the 1996 election was more than a choice of leaders or even of political regime. Behind the din of multi-party politics, Gennadiy Zyuganov discerned 'the struggle of two forces': those of 'national renaissance', led by the communists, and those of 'national treason', in the Kremlin.[142]

Reprinted in scores of national and local pro-communist newspapers with a combined print-run of well over 10,000,000 and excerpted in millions of leaflets around the country, Zyuganov's election programme began with the question 'Where is the country's wealth?'[143] It was being stolen and taken abroad by 'insatiable carnivores', while the people, especially pensioners and veterans, were being steadily impoverished, cast aside and forgotten.[144]

The reforms had profited only a tiny minority: the 'comprador bourgeoisie'. Privatization was an orgy of pilfering, a giant theft of the state's assets, quickly sold for a song.[145] The regime's only successes were the taming of inflation and the contraction of the budget deficit – but these had only been achieved by means of the barbaric non-payment of salaries and pensions.

If Yeltsin remained in power, the situation would become hopeless: the regime was incapable of changing its pernicious course, which had brought so much decay and suffering. Yeltsin's government was the tool of a corrupt bureaucracy and of the tycoons of the 'comprador bourgeoisie' who did the bidding of their foreign masters.[146] Thus, Zyuganov reiterated, 'the Motherland's fate for many years' would depend on the choice made on 16 June.[147]

Instead of 'monetarism–liberalism', forced on Russia by the IMF and its lackeys,[148] Zyuganov's economic programme envisaged a forceful and unabashed reintroduction of state control and central direction of the economy: 'the leading role of national ownership and state regulation of production'.[149] Zyuganov proposed to restore state ownership of all natural resources. He would keep in the hands of the state 'vitally important' industries, transportation, energy and communication, and reintroduce a state monopoly in natural resources and 'strategic goods' and state control of their export.[150] The buying and selling of land would remain prohibited.[151] Zyuganov promised not to expropriate those private entrepreneurs who wanted to work 'honestly' and be useful to the Motherland.[152]* At the same time, he urged the adoption of a Law on Nationalization that would spell out 'under what conditions and following what legal procedure nationalization could take place'.[153]

The revival of the Russian economy would begin with the state's heavy investment in and 'urgent state support' for the military–industrial complex – 'aviation, space hardware, armaments' – which, in turn, would pull the entire national economy up to a new 'technical economic level'.[154] In every branch of industry, Russian producers would be guaranteed advantages over foreigners. Special efforts would be made to protect with high import tariffs light, textile and food industries, which lay devastated by the flood of better and cheaper goods from abroad.[155]

If elected, Zyuganov would guarantee all citizens the right to employment, rest, housing, free education, free healthcare and dignified old age.[156] Salaries, pensions and stipends would be raised to a subsistence minimum. Not just older people but the entire population would be compensated for the pre-1992 savings annihilated by the so-called reforms.[157] He promised affordable prices for essential food, public transportation, utilities and rent and free housing for the needy.[158] Children would be guaranteed daycare and summer and sports camps, and young people were promised education, job training and jobs. Healthcare, recreation, tourism and sports facilities would be developed, upgraded and made affordable to the 'working people'.[159]

Zyuganov admitted that some political freedoms existed in Russia – because the opposition had forced the regime to uphold them.[160] He promised to preserve 'broad popular dialogue', freedom for political parties, freedom of opinions, freedom of religion and freedom of

---

* The survival of private property after victory was the most contentious issue in the Central Committee. Zyuganov appeared to have prevailed but, as his Deputy Valentin Kuptsov noted 'ruefully' in May 1996, 'the abolition of private property is one of the main tenets of Marxism' and 'still causes the most arguments' (Alessandra Stanley, 'Red Scare', *New York Times Magazine*, 26 May 1996).

information. The platform stipulated, however, that democracy as practised by the Yeltsin regime was confined to 'the right of citizens and
parties to say what they please'. What was needed instead was the
'power of the vast majority of the working people'.[161]

Zyuganov's electoral programme ended with italicized slogans:

power will be returned to the people . . .
   the worker will be guaranteed a job . . .
   the woman will be able to raise children and be confident of her
future . . .
   the veteran, the invalid, the sick will be socially protected, attended
to and cared for . . .
   the cheated bank account holder will regain his savings
   the thief will be put in jail

   FOR PEACE AGAINST CIVIL WAR!
   FOR HONEST LABOUR AGAINST PARASITES!
   FOR LAW AND ORDER AGAINST LAWLESSNESS AND
VIOLENCE!
   FOR FRIENDSHIP AND BROTHERHOOD OF THE
PEOPLES AGAINST HATRED AND MALICE!

   FOR TRUTH AND PURITY AGAINST LIES AND
DEBAUCHERY!
   FOR THE POWER OF THE PEOPLE!
   FOR HONOUR AND DIGNITY OF THE RUSSIAN
GREAT POWER!

'Two leaders, two irreconcilable forces, joined battle,' *Izvestia* wrote
on 16 February.[162] The titles of the candidates' electoral programmes
illustrated the chasm in values and priorities: Zyuganov's *Russia,
Motherland, People*, and Yeltsin's *Russia: individual, family, society,
state*.[163] In the next four months, crisscrossing the country, they would
tirelessly and stubbornly bring their opposing visions of Russia's past,
present and future to tens of millions of voters.

Yeltsin wanted Russians to choose between the past and the future:
the past of Stalin and famines, gulag and radio jamming, the Iron Curtain
and censorship, ration coupons and two-hour queues for milk and eggs,
'the past when there was nothing in the shops but pickled cucumbers
and people travelled by train to Moscow to buy sausages', as he put
it;[164] and the future of a free and prosperous capitalist Russia to which
today's difficulties were only a prelude. His promise was liberty and

reform – free of mistakes, malfeasance, corruption and the worst hardships of the past four-and-a-half years.

Zyuganov wished the country to choose between a different past and the miserable present: the past of the red banner over Berlin, of Sputnik, of nuclear superpowership, of Gagarin and Zhukov – and the present of empty tank plants and abandoned nuclear testgrounds, of the humiliation of poverty, delayed salaries and unemployed scientists and engineers, the sudden impoverishment of millions and the sickening excesses of the few. Zyuganov's was a promise of a revived and mighty *derzhava*, a socialist Motherland,* where there would be jobs and cheap bread for all.

For conveying this message, Zyuganov's campaign relied on the traditional tools of Party propaganda: the newspaper, the leaflet, the poster. Door-to-door agitation and meetings with the *aktiv* of the faithful were preferred to mass rallies (except during the May Day and Victory celebrations on 1 and 9 May) and to the 'bourgeois' novelty of paid advertisements in newspapers, on the radio or on television. 'We have our own information technique,' Zyuganov told *Pravda*. 'It is called "From person to person, from house to house, from heart to heart." We are well organized. Our organization covers the whole of Russia.'[165]

As early as February 1996, the KPRF decided to 'rely primarily' on print in its propaganda,[166]† and Zyuganov's campaign did not attempt to buy airtime on national television until a few hours before the official deadline of the second round on 1 July.‡ Apart from its mistrust of national television networks, whose owners and employees the 'national-patriots' quite rightly deemed hostile to their cause, the KPRF's allegiance to print stemmed from its main advantage over the

---

* Lest he alienate his core supporters, Zyuganov reiterated that 'social democracy had no support and no future in Russia' (Andrey Fedorov, 'Zyuganov nakanune vyborov . . .' ('Zyuganov on the eve of the elections'), *Argumenty i Fakty*, 15–21 April 1996, p. 9).

† According to the Central Electoral Commission audit of the candidates' funds, less than one-fourth of the 1.65 billion rubles (approximately $305,000) that the Zyuganov campaign had spent by 15 May went to 'campaigning in the media' (that is, advertisement). The rest was spent on the 'publication and distribution of leaflets, posters and other campaign products'. (Igor Bel'skiy, 'Russia: Election Bank Funds of Presidential Candidates Cited', ITAR-TASS, 23 May 1996 (FBIS-SOV-96–102 (Article Id: drsov102aa–96014, http://wnc.fedworld.gov/cgi-bin . . .)).)

‡ Claiming that the request came too late, the First Channel/ORT network refused to sell the time.

regime (and over every one of the pro-reform parties and movements): the Party press. The three largest communist dailies alone, distributed throughout the country, had a combined print-run of nine million.[167]* In his December 1994 interview with *Zavtra*, Zyuganov proudly admitted to Prokhanov that the 'Party has managed everywhere to resume publication of newspapers'.[168] By the spring of 1996 Zyuganov had the support of 150 national and local pro-communist newspapers and magazines.[169]

Zyuganov felt that the 1995 parliamentary elections had vindicated the reliance on local press. 'We did not [in 1995] use the central [Moscow] mass media – they are backed by big money,' he told supporters in Barnaul, the capital of the Altai region, in a long question-and-answer session, recorded by *Zavtra*'s deputy editor, who was travelling with the candidate. 'We went to the *oblast* and *rayon* [district] press, which is today read by 90 per cent of the citizens of Russia, and this tactic proved justified.'[170] According to Zyuganov, the Party's refusal to pay astronomical sums to buy television time in 1995 proved the correct decision as well: 'We had no regrets: the people relied more on live speech than on the "box".'[171]

This was a justified gamble. In 1995, an estimated 23 per cent of Russians over fifteen years of age read only local papers.[172] In the countryside, as in Soviet times, a district newspaper was often the sole communication with the world outside one's village. In the end, wrote a leading member of the 'democratic' opposition, the communists solidified 'control over a significant portion of regional and local press and other means of mass communications which covered a far greater area and had much more influence than central [Moscow-based] ones'.[173]

Another unique asset of the Zyuganov campaign was the size of the KPRF's organization: 530,000 members in 20,000 Party cells.[174] No other party or bloc, not even all parties and blocs combined, could compare with this army of volunteer activists. 'The Communist Party cells have been preserved everywhere,' complained the Chairman of Yeltsin's campaign in a Central Russian region. 'We are taking measures to catch up but we cannot do in a few days what they have done in two years.'[175]

The KPRF could mobilize thousands[176] of door-to-door 'agitators'. In Krasnoyarsk, for example, each communist was to cover a certain

---

* The print-run of *Sovetskaya Rossia* was 3.8 million, that of *Sel'skaya Zhizn'* 3.3 million, and *Pravda*'s 1.9 million. The actual readership exceeded the print-run by several factors.

number of apartments or housing blocks, where he would 'talk to their occupants and hand them campaign materials', while the Krasnoyarsk regional Party newspaper, *Tovarishch* ('Comrade'), devoted more than half of each issue to Zyuganov's campaign.[177] In addition, the KPRF fielded more than twice as many poll watchers as the Yeltsin campaign and supplied local electoral commissions with some of their most experienced polling-station personnel. 'We invested all the money in the periphery, in the provinces,' Zyuganov said. 'And there was not a single population centre where our colleagues did not campaign.'[178]

Much of this mammoth effort was co-ordinated from the Duma, whose Speaker was *Pravda*'s former editor Gennadiy Seleznyov, and most of whose committees were chaired by the communists or their allies. The 'popular-patriotic' bloc in the legislature translated its plurality into an aggressive appropriation of the parliament's formidable resources. Long before the campaign officially began, the KPRF started using the legislature's telephones, office space and personnel to promote its candidate.[179] In 1996 the needs of Zyuganov's campaign so dominated the Duma apparatus that even making a photocopy became difficult for non-communist members.[180]

Of course, the Duma communists' assistance to the Zyuganov campaign extended well beyond the control of office equipment. Just before the Congress of 'popular-patriotic' forces endorsed Zyuganov on 17 March, the Duma adopted two resolutions that declared the Belavezhskie Accords illegal, 'brazenly violating the will of the Russian people', and therefore null and void. Zyuganov hailed this denunciation as consistent with the Party's 1993 and 1995 platforms, both of which had called for the cancellation of the Accords.[181] Several days earlier, the Duma had 'disavowed' Yeltsin's decree that permitted the buying and selling of land.[182]*

Another crucial asset of the Zyuganov campaign (in addition to its dominance of the provincial press, its vast membership and organization, and its solid base in the Duma) was the sympathy of local economic and political cadres. One of the KPRF's 'secret directives' after August 1991 was an order to communists to 'work in the power structures at the regional level', Zyuganov proudly told Prokhanov during one of their long, heart-to-heart chats in the pages of *Zavtra*.[183] The alacrity and foresight with which, having quickly recovered first from paralysing fear and then from bewilderment at the absence of repression, the KPRF

---

* The KPRF's faction in the Russian Supreme Soviet, had voted for the Belavezhskie Accords in December 1991 (Fedorov, 'Zyuganov nakanune vyborov').

proceeded to seize opportunities offered to the former communist nomenklatura by the 'velvet revolution' were now paying off handsomely. 'We need not doubt', wrote a liberal Moscow daily, 'that many officials will meet [Zyuganov] with far greater hospitality than will the people.'[184]

Although their commitment to Zyuganov's cause differed considerably from region to region, throughout the country both 'red directors' and 'red *nachal'niks*' provided invaluable logistical and material assistance to the 'popular-patriotic' campaign. Two weeks before election day, only forty-nine of eighty-nine heads of Russian regions had endorsed Yeltsin.[185]

Vitaliy Mukha, Governor of the Novosibirsk region, was typical of the ostensibly neutral local leaders whose hearts were with Zyuganov and in whose regions his campaign was especially energetic and well funded. The First Secretary of the *oblast* Party Committee, Mukha stayed on as the head of the Regional Administration after the August Revolution. In 1993 he sided with the Supreme Soviet, defied Decree No. 1400 and was fired by Yeltsin. In December 1995, backed by the KPRF, he ran for Governor and came first in a field of several candidates.

In the 'red regions' and most of the countryside, the elite did not hide their preference for Zyuganov. Among the executives of the Volgograd *oblast* and districts, for instance, only one among more than thirty publicly supported Yeltsin.[186] In the Lipetsk *oblast*, where the names of Lenin and Engels had been returned to squares and streets, and where 'red directors' controlled enterprises 'almost completely', pro-Zyuganov agitation was conducted in the workplaces themselves.[187] 'We will find out who voted for whom,' the workers were warned.[188]

In the countryside, kolkhoz and sovkhoz chairmen rooted for Zyuganov just as openly. In a typical story told by a Russian scholar, two Moscow teachers who taught summer school in a village in the Arkhangel'sk region in the north-west in 1996, came to a local *nachal'nik* to ask for a blackboard. 'I have been hauled over the coals by my boss: there were two votes for Yeltsin in the entire district, and – guess what? – both in my village,' the man retorted angrily. 'You have spoiled the entire picture for us – and now you come begging for a blackboard!'[189]

Since most of the local newspapers were subsidized or entirely underwritten by provincial administrations, it went without saying, as a liberal journalist put it, that, following the local leadership's line, the district and regional press in many areas campaigned for the communist candidate 'openly and free of charge'.[190] For instance, out of the thirty-five city, regional and district newspapers analysed by Yeltsin's supporters in the typical pro-Zyuganov agricultural region of Volgograd in May 1996, fifteen were found to be 'negative' (anti-Yeltsin), six 'neutral', nine without a well-defined position, and only six 'positive' (pro-regime).[191]

Zyuganov's well-organized campaign had begun much earlier than Yeltsin's. By his own admission, the communist candidate had spent the previous two years visiting seventy-two of Russia's eighty-nine regions.[192] By the end of April 1996 he had campaigned in all the largest areas: Central Russia, Siberia, Volga and the Urals.[193] At the campaign stops, Zyuganov would be welcomed on the platform or the tarmac with bread and salt by local Party functionaries, communist Deputies of local and federal Dumas, and rank-and-file well-wishers. Under police escort he would then ride in a black Volga saloon at the head of a motorcade to the city centre for a wreath-laying ceremony at the ubiquitous Lenin monument or a Second World War memorial, where he would be cheered by crowds of supporters.[194]

He would then meet with local officials and business leaders: mayors, heads of regional administration departments, directors of plants and factories, collective farm chairmen. Accompanied by the managers, he would inspect enterprises, hospitals, collective farms, underground military plants and nuclear power stations. At major plants and factories, he would speak to the workers, sometimes as many as a thousand at a time.[195] From podiums surrounded by bouquets of flowers, with giant portraits of Lenin gently rippling on the curtain behind him,[196] Zyuganov addressed rallies in palaces of culture, sports arenas, or, in the case of Novosibirsk, in the city's largest library, which accommodated 8,000 supporters.[197] The audiences were quiet, even reverent.[198]

Most of the time, encounters between Zyuganov and his notoriously disciplined and loyal followers were crowded affairs. People 'crammed into every seat, every inch of space', filling aisles, balconies, foyers and lobbies, and erupting in 'stormy applause' or even ovations.[199] Those unable to get inside watched the candidate on closed-circuit television or listened – sometimes in their hundreds – to loudspeakers set up on the street.[200] Many held red Soviet flags and portraits of Stalin.[201] In the late spring, as the pace of the campaign quickened, Zyuganov claimed to have attended twelve rallies in two days and to have spoken to 140,000 people in four.[202]

In Krasnoyarsk, Zyuganov's supporters welcomed him with a red placard next to the Lenin monument that read 'KRASNOYARSK RESIDENTS FOR ZYUGANOV'. Just before the candidate arrived with a wreath, several hundred anti-communist demonstrators, waving tricolours, hoisted their own streamer – 'YELTSIN THE PRESIDENT OF ALL RUSSIANS' – and thwarted several attempts by the other side to pull it down. Zyuganov quickly laid his wreath and retreated, leaving both slogans flapping in the breeze side by side.[203]

After Zyuganov's motorcade had driven off, two middle-aged women were overheard arguing on the square. 'My daughter graduated from the university and now she has no job and no money,' said one. 'It didn't used to be like this.'

'My sons don't know what Komsomol is,' answered her opponent. 'They don't know what bloodshed is, and I don't want them to know. These times are much better. It's impossible to solve all our problems right away.'

'But all the state enterprises have been shut down.'

'No, they were just broken up to make them work more efficiently.'

'You are a plant from Yeltsin!'

'No, I'm just a teacher. I was just passing by. By the way, how old are you?'

'I'm fifty-nine.'

'Were you ever in your life able to say anything freely? Could you ever come here to the square in the old days and cry that Yeltsin was a crook?'

'I felt free . . . We fought in two wars and restored the economy. We could study and work and I never had to worry about the future . . . Now the whole country has been sold to the West. I'm for the old times and the past. Sure, there were some hard times, but we were reviving the economy . . .

'You see? Now you can voice your opinion. Before you were afraid even to speak!'

'So what? . . . You think I am full of joy that I was given this freedom? This freedom has no effect.'[204]

'We thank the journalists of *Pravda*, *Sovetskaya Rossia*, *Pravda Rossii*, *Zavtra*, *Glasnost* and all 150 local [pro-communist] publications,' Zyuganov said in early May.[205] This was well-earned gratitude. Almost every issue of these newspapers and magazines was by then devoted to the campaign and carried a lengthy interview with the candidate, his top lieutenant or a prominent supporter, who commented on the platform and attacked the competition.

By mid-April Zyuganov's message had been moderated considerably as he sought to expand his base beyond the traditional one-third of the electorate. At virtually every campaign stop and in every interview, whether in print or on television, he pledged support for a 'mixed economy' and tolerance of 'all forms of ownership'. Even though privatization was nothing but robbery that enriched a few and beggared millions, privatized enterprises that 'operated normally', abided by the trade union laws and paid taxes would not be renationalized.[206] He was equally firm in his support for freedom of religion. 'We discussed the question thoroughly at the [KPRF's] Congress, and were able to convince everyone, even the most thick-headed,' Zyuganov told supporters in Altai and readers of *Zavtra*.[207] 'Not only did we throw everything anti-religious out of the charter and programme, we even wrote that any person may believe in whatever he considers necessary.'[208]

Occasional lapses notwithstanding (as when Zyuganov accused the United States of 'destroying the [Russian] nation' by allegedly forbidding the Russian government to restrict import of alcohol),[209] the most macabre claims about the Western conspiracy against Russia had all but disappeared from the communist candidate's speeches and interviews.

Yet the new-found moderation extended only to the exposition of the candidate's own platform. As regards the other half of the message – the critique of the regime and, most of all, of Yeltsin – the ferocity of the assault continued unabated. It would be hard to find in the history of modern democracies another instance in which freely published and distributed newspapers of the main opposition party daily conducted so crudely vicious a campaign against the elected head of state as did Russia's pro-communist newspapers in the spring of 1996.

In *Pravda*, Zyuganov referred to 'the turncoats, destroyers and traitors of the Fatherland who currently rule in the Kremlin'[210] and to Yeltsin as a defiler of all that was sacred to the Russian people, a man who had allowed Russia to be 'ruined and tormented'.[211] In an article in *Pravda Rossii*, a leader of the communist faction in the Duma, Viktor Ilyukhin, called the President 'a perjurer, a liar, a man of low cultural and educational level and an alcohol abuser'.[212] To vote for him, Ilyukhin continued, would mean voting for the 'continued genocide of the Russian people'.[213]

On its front page, *Zavtra* ran editorials under banner headlines: 'RUSSIA IS RULED BY A CRUEL PUPPET',[214] 'GLORY TO THE SOLDIERS, INFAMY TO THE COMMANDER-IN-CHIEF!',[215] 'YELTSIN'S COAT IS SPLATTERED WITH BLOOD',[216] 'PLEASE, O LORD, RID RUSSIA OF YELTSIN!'[217] To add a 'popular' flavour to its anti-Yeltsin propaganda, *Zavtra* appropriated *chastushki*, a form of folk poetry, in which, usually accompanied by concertina or balalaika, Russians for centuries had praised or mocked themselves, their neighbours or the authorities in tight two- or four-line verses, filled with colloquialisms, obscenities, clipped sentences, elisions, and sometimes faulty grammar. An entire page of campaign *chastushki* that appeared in *Zavtra* two weeks before the election[218] contained a customary shot at Jews:

> On TV the *diktor*'s* burring,†
> And the West he's praising, purring.
> Too bad Comrade Stalin's dead:
> Was a master logoped.‡

This pleasant duty discharged, the newspaper moved to the essence of this exercise in folk poetry:

> Good people, move out of the way: Yeltsin's going to Clinton,
> For cheap handouts he is selling Russia.

> Yeltsin's walking in the Kremlin, his mouth never closes:
> He has robbed the entire country and now he is grinning.

> What's so strange about his drinking?
> That to him is normal.
> The more he drinks, the more he lies –
> And the 'reform' is moving forward.[219]

Interspersed among the verses, in giant bold print, were slogans: 'YELTSIN IS WAR! DOWN WITH THE THIEVING REGIME! ZYUGANOV IS THE HOPE OF RUSSIA! YELTSIN – NO! DOWN WITH THE "REFORMS" THAT ROB PEOPLE!

---

* *Diktor* is an announcer, anchorman or anchorwoman.

† To Russian 'patriots', burring (rolling the *r*) is the distinguishing racial characteristic of Jews. For instance, after Moscow voted overwhelmingly for pro-reform parties in the December 1995 legislative elections, in a front-page article *Zavtra* described the Russian capital as an 'insolent, thieving broad' who 'burred with California [*sic*] accent' ('Pokhishchnie Moskvy' ('The stealing of Moscow'), *Zavtra*, 3, January 1996, p. 1).

‡ A logoped is a practitioner of logopedics, the branch of medicine that deals with speech disabilities; a speech therapist. The *chastushka*'s reference is to Stalin's anti-Semitism, especially the purge of 'cosmopolitans' and the 1953 Doctors' Plot, in which the Kremlin physicians – all but one of them Jews – were accused of a conspiracy to kill the Soviet leadership.

YELTSIN, GET OUT! GLORY TO RUSSIA! VOTE FOR ZYUGANOV!'[220]

In the centre of the page was a most unflattering photograph of Yeltsin: with puffed cheeks, vacant look and a silly smile he resembled a drunken frog. Giant letters under the portrait read: 'INSTEAD OF DRUNKEN BOR'KA, LET'S ELECT ZYUGANOV!' A familiar diminutive of 'Boris', 'Bor'ka' was a calculated insult: it was an extremely rude way to address an adult, let alone a sixty-five-year-old man.

Hundreds of anti-Yeltsin cartoons appeared daily in the 'popular-patriotic' press. Yeltsin the candidate was depicted at once as a brazen liar, wily, brutal and imperious – and as a sickly, drunken idiot, manipulated by his entourage. In one cartoon he was an alcoholic desperately clinging to a bottle-shaped Kremlin and screaming 'I will not give it up!', as a muscular worker's arm – sleeve rolled up – prises him loose. Beneath the arm is Zyuganov's campaign motto: 'Russia! Motherland! People!'[221] Another drawing portrayed him as a butcher who, with Russia hung on a meat hook behind him and the word 'MASTER' on his apron, was selling his country.[222] He was a drunken booby who delivered Russia's nuclear secrets to the sneering Western leaders who came to Moscow for a G-7 summit in April 1996. ('You are not playing games with us, are you?' Clinton demands to know. 'Are you sure you've given us all the secrets?')[223]

'By numerous request from Western investors we shall sing a song about democracy called "Now hand over to us the entire Russian land",' Yeltsin, the master of ceremonies, announced in a *Sovetskaya Rossia* cartoon.[224] Watching from the wings is a hook-nosed, Shylock-like character in a skullcap. At the orgy of Russia's dismemberment, he was not a stagehand but the producer and the director. Insofar as the capitalist West was dominated by the world Jewish conspiracy, in its dealings with Russia the West does the Jews' bidding. To the 'popular-patriotic' cartoonists, the disproportionate presence of Jews among Yeltsin's aides and supporters (as well as in the new economic elite) proved that the regime was much worse than simply pro-Western. It was pro-Jewish: created and manipulated by Jews for profit and for the pleasure of seeing Russia destroyed. Yeltsin's crime of selling the Motherland to the capitalist West (a somewhat long and uneven process) paled before the sin of selling it to Jews – a far more immediate and revolting offence.

The anti-Yeltsin cartoons were filled with grotesquely exaggerated 'Jewish' facial features: long beards, wide lips and hooked noses. In one such drawing, entitled 'Soldier and vermin', a handsome Russian veteran towers over Yeltsin, who is sitting among his Jews: grovelling, smirking, howling.[225] The sign on top of the buildings reads 'BANK'. In a similar juxtaposition of healthy, strong and dignified ethnic Russia and shadowy, clamouring and plotting Jews, a cartoon entitled 'The battle banner of the Motherland' portrayed a pair of muscular proletarian arms wielding a hammer-and-sickle banner like a cross to exorcize the repulsive, hook-nosed, bearded devils.[226]

Of all things Russian that Yeltsin had allegedly surrendered or sold to Jews, the purported Jewish dominance of television caused the 'popular patriots' the greatest consternation. 'Mirror, mirror on the wall, tell me / All the truth I want,' a drunken Yeltsin, slumped in a chair, asks a long-nosed character with bulging eyes on the television screen.

In all of Russia, am I not the most sober,
Most honest and most intelligent?

Mirror thus to him replies:
You, of course, without doubt:
You are the most beloved in Russia,
Most EXPENSIVE and necessary.[227]

Like the Jews, Yeltsin himself was portrayed as non-human: a demon, an alien dispatched from some anti-world to destroy Russia. On the front page of *Sovetskaya Rossia*, he was a psychopathic killer crouching on all fours in a pool of blood with the word 'Chechnya' running along the pool's perimeter.[228] He was also a vulture, picking at a carcass (and crowing 'Elect me! Elect me!')[229] and a three-headed dragon, with a dollar sign on its tail, confronted on the battlefield by brave Russian knights.[230] (The setting evoked fourteenth-century Russia's struggle against the Mongol invasion.)

Like the exorcism of the Jewish heresy, in the hands of 'popular-patriotic' cartoonists the struggle against Yeltsin acquired positively eschatological dimensions. It was not 'a battle of ideologies and parties ... but a clash of two universes, a cosmic battle between Good and Evil, Light and Darkness, God and Satan'.[231] According to a front-page *Zavtra* editorial, 'Fighting Yeltsin in the June election, we fight not his human nature, his angry face, the paltriness of his speeches, the foolishness of his laws, but the metaphysical nature of Evil which is expressed through him.'[232] He was the Devil incarnate, 'tortured by Hellish fire burning him from inside'.[233] And when the time came, all of 'humankind will shudder, all the villains and criminals of the world will arise from their graves and, seizing him with their claws, will pull him underground, where, next to roaring flames, the Underground Stoker will be waiting for him'.[234]

For all the emphasis on print media, Zyuganov was by no means a stranger to Russian television viewers or radio listeners. Like all other candidates, he was entitled to an hour and a half of free airtime on the three national state-owned television networks from 14 May to 14 June and to a total of two hours on the four state-run radio stations.[235] (The networks were prohibited from censoring or altering the candidates' material in any way and from refusing to air them.)[236] In the run-off, between 26 June and 1 July, Zyuganov received an additional two hours of free television time: forty minutes on each of the three networks.[237]

While declining to buy airtime, Zyuganov used every free second to which he was entitled by law. In the opinion of an expert, between 14 May and 1 July the Zyuganov campaign disposed of the three-and-a-half hours of free time on state television with far greater skill than his Party had done in the two parliamentary races.[238] 'Smoothly' edited, his advertisements showcased Zyuganov the leader – rallying vast crowds with vigorous speeches, accompanied by triumphal music and heroic shots against national monuments.[239] Citizen Zyuganov was forceful but not shrill in his discourses. He dwelt on what he 'saw in his travels': the general misery, the erosion of the state's authority and the decline of the Army.[240]

Availing himself of an option specified by an election law,[241] Zyuganov chose an interview format for the thirty minutes of free advertisement on the Fifth (St Petersburg) Channel. If elected, Zyuganov promised among many other things that rents would not exceed 15 per cent of people's income.[242] And, whereas Yeltsin was 'trying to finish the armed forces off' and had cut the military–industrial complex 'by 92 to 94 per cent', to Zyuganov the Army was 'the most sacred part of the nation', 'a second Church', and he pledged to support it.[243] 'Today, our Mother Russia and its whole people stand at the crossroads,' he concluded. 'If you choose the wrong road disaster could come. Either we correct the situation ... calmly, peacefully, democratically ... or we lose our country once and for all.'[244]

Although the owners, managers, anchors and staffers of the television networks were very much on Yeltsin's side, his opponent's campaign was far from passed over in silence. While the coverage of Zyuganov's campaign on the three state-owned networks was often subjected to heavy-handed, anti-communist editorializing, an objective observer found that in 'virtually all' of the dozens of news stories on Independent Television Network (NTV) Zyuganov and his supporters were given 'the opportunity to put [his] platform before the viewers with [their] own words', without a voice-over[245] – even though NTV's Director General, Egor Malashenko, served as adviser to the Yeltsin campaign.

In April, NTV's prime-time evening news programme *Segodnya* ('Today') featured Zyuganov's campaign on eleven nights. The communist candidate was interviewed on the war in Chechnya; he forecast his victory and expatiated on his platform; a supporter explained why he favoured Gennadiy Andreevich over Yeltsin. One night, Zyuganov was shown speaking at rallies and visiting churches in Voronezh and Lipetsk; four days later he was seen in Bashkortostan, visiting factories, then in Chelyabinsk, then in St Petersburg, talking to World War veterans.[246] When Zyuganov campaigned in Southern Russia between 26 and 30 May, the NTV crew followed him from Volgograd to Rostov-on-the-Don, Novocherkassk, Stavropol and Nal'chik, and the network aired their reports nightly.[247]

On 21 April and again on the eve of the election, 11 June, Zyuganov had two long live interviews on the country's highest-rated political talk show, *Itogi* ('Results') and on NTV's *Geroy dnya* ('The Newsmaker of the Day') show. His host was one of the left's most passionately hated *bête noires* and Russia's most popular anchor, Evgeniy Kiselev. (In one of the *Zavtra* cartoons, he was in the very select company that accompanied Yeltsin to hell.)

On 1 June, the Echo of Moscow radio, another staunchly pro-reform media outlet, produced a lengthy interview with Zyuganov, followed by a phone-in show. Zyuganov was questioned with great deference, allowing him to dwell unhurriedly on the key points of his platform. The callers, even those who seemed opposed to the candidate, were polite as well. No follow-up questions were allowed.[248]

A debate between Zyuganov's and Yeltsin's campaigns was hosted ten days before the first round by one of the most popular of Russian television hosts, Yuriy Lyubimov, and broadcast by First Channel/ORT. In the event, Zyuganov's representative, a Yuriy Ivanov, 'forcefully and rudely attacked' Yeltsin (represented by former Minister of Finance Boris Fedorov) 'to the applause of many in the studio audience'.[249] The same network broadcast another debate between the two campaigns' advisers a week before the second round. Another surrogate debate was shown on the Rossia network (formerly the Russian Television Channel).[250]

Between the first and second round, when an exhausted and sick Yeltsin virtually disappeared from television screens after a heart attack (awkwardly and to universal derision described by his campaign team as a 'cold'), *Segodnya* ran several segments which, intentionally or not, underscored the glaring difference between the physical form of the two candidates. A youthful and vigorous Zyuganov was shown playing volleyball (and 'demonstrating his excellent physical condition').[251] In two other segments (broadcast without editorial comment), he cele-brated his fifty-second birthday among adoring friends and met with Orthodox priests, one of whom voiced concern that in Yeltsin's Russia mothers were no longer respected and children no longer protected.[252]

On the evening of 1 July, the last day of the campaign's second round, Zyuganov used his last allotment of free airtime for a five-minute prime-time address to the 'tens of millions'[253] of viewers on the two state-owned national networks, First Channel/ORT and Rossia. He told them that Yeltsin had not kept a single promise, and that the President's 'whole campaign strategy [was] built on fear and lies'. During the five years of Yeltsin's rule, he added, Russia had shrunk in size 'by half'. The choice between him and Yeltsin was a choice between 'a strong Russia' and a 'colonial administration'.[254]

At the end of March, Yeltsin removed Soskovets from the chairmanship of his campaign and took over the 'co-ordinating council' himself.[255] The council was sharply divided. Korzhakov, Barsukov, Soskovets and Chief of Staff Nikolay Yegorov continued to believe that Yeltsin could never win on the 'reformist' ticket, that he needed to make a deal with the communists and cancel the elections. Viktor Ilyushin, Sergey Filatov, Egor Malashenko and, most importantly, the President's daughter Tat'yana D'yachenko felt that a vigorous campaign might turn the situation around. In the middle, wary of choosing sides, were Chernomyr-din, Deputy Prime Minister Yuriy Yarov and Mayor of Moscow Yuriy Luzhkov.

Although the council still included Korzhakov, Soskovets, Barsukov and Yegorov and although their team was still occupying the ninth floor of the campaign headquarters at the President Hotel off Bolshaya Yakiminka Street, both the strategy and the management gradually shifted to the Ilyushin–D'yachenko group, which merged with the origi-nal Satarov crew and retained Anatoliy Chubais as manager. A month later, the influence of the Korzhakov–Soskovets faction in the Kremlin diminished dramatically after Yeltsin vigorously disavowed Korzhakov's statements about the 'postponement' of the election. 'I trust the wisdom of the Russian voters,' Yeltsin said. 'That's why elections will be held at the time determined by the Constitution.'[256]

Yeltsin also chose to ignore an appeal by the country's leading bankers and entrepreneurs, which coincided with Korzhakov's statement. Displaying an abject loss of nerve, Russia's 'oligarchs' declared that the contest for the Presidency could result only in a 'spirit of violence and chaos', which would severely damage the 'already fragile Russian statehood'.[257] Instead of an election, they wanted Yeltsin and the 'popular patriots' to unite their efforts in search of political compromise, make concessions to each other and arrive at 'strategic political agreements'.[258] On 30 April the leaders of the group, widely considered to be the four wealthiest men in Russia, came to Zyuganov's Duma office to plead for political peace: Boris Berezovskiy, Mikhail Fridman, Vladimir Potanin and Aleksandr Smolenskiy. They requested a meeting with Yeltsin immediately afterwards, but he would not see them.[259]

Instead, Yeltsin proceeded to woo the voters with everything in his possession. At once Augeas and Hercules, he attempted, in three months, to cleanse the Kremlin's stables of the thick, corroding sediment accumulated over the previous two years of political and personal sloth. The only chance he had to reassemble and energize his splintered anticommunist constituency was to remind them, credibly, of his nearforgotten credentials as a statesman and a reformer. The President had set himself a difficult task, wrote a Russian journalist: to restore trust in the 'bright future of the reforms' among as many as possible of his former supporters, who had been 'offended and humiliated' by the regime.[260]

A thick stream of decrees dealing with the most urgent problems issued from the Kremlin: backlogged salaries and pensions, compensation for savings wiped out by inflation between 1991 and 1996, military reform and the Chechen war. By the end of March, the federal Treasury had transferred money to the regions to pay pensioners and state workers. Yeltsin renewed the land privatization drive by signing, in the second week of March, a decree on the Realization of Citizens' Constitutional Rights in Land. As in November 1993, he affirmed private ownership of land and the right to sell, lease or mortgage it.[261] ('Land is Motherland,' Zyuganov responded. 'And one cannot sell the Motherland at an auction.')[262]

A month and a half later, by way of restarting military reform, Yeltsin promised millions of Russian mothers and their teenage sons the most heartening gift of all: the abolition of military conscription, after almost three centuries of draft, and the creation of professional armed forces by 2000. 'The boys who are now fourteen years old must know that they will not have to serve in the Army in 2000, that they will serve only if they so wish, under contract,' Yeltsin announced in Krasnoyarsk in mid-May.[263] He ordered the discharge of draftees after a year and a half of service (instead of the obligatory two years) if they had served six months in combat, and decreed that only volunteers be sent to serve in 'battle zones' – that is, in Chechnya. At about the same time, Yeltsin moved to satisfy another long-standing demand of his liberal constituency by signing, on 16 May, a decree on the phasing out of the death penalty.

The distance that separated decrees and promises from real changes was still enormous. For instance, only those older than eighty were to be compensated in full for lost savings. The military brass proceeded brazenly to violate the orders relating to discharge and continued to send raw draftees to Chechnya. Yet the mere sight of the President's attention to what was tormenting Russia, his sudden initiative and furious energy were enough to provide, in the words of a leading Russian political columnist, a 'start-up momentum' and to mobilize the 'seemingly disintegrated Yeltsin electoral base'.[264] Suddenly, the communists were deprived of a major issue: an absentee President.

Another trump-card in his opponent's hands was the war in Chechnya. 'If I do not withdraw [federal troops from Chechnya], I can forget about running in the election,' Yeltsin admitted at the beginning of the campaign.[265] On 31 March, in a nationally televised speech he promised a 'political solution' to the Chechen crisis. Federal troops were to be gradually withdrawn and peace negotiations begun. For the first time, Yeltsin announced that Moscow was ready to talk to Dudaev, albeit through intermediaries. Yeltsin also conceded that the status of Chechnya was the subject of negotiations between Moscow and Grozny.[266]

In the middle of May, to the horror of his security detail, Yeltsin announced his intention of travelling to Chechnya. 'I will go to Chechnya myself to sit everybody around the negotiating table,' he told voters in the city of Astrakhan on the Volga. The Chechen leader Zelimkhan Yandarbiyev, who had replaced Dudaev, killed on 21 April, responded by saying that Yeltsin's security 'could not be guaranteed' and that the right to 'avenge their President's [Dudaev's] murder' was 'a matter of honour for any honest Chechen'.[267]

Two weeks later, on 27 May, in the first face-to-face meeting between the top Russian leadership and Chechen rebels, Yeltsin and Yandarbiyev signed in the Kremlin the Agreement on the Cessation of Combat Operations. The President also offered Chechnya its own Constitution and full control over finances and natural resources – within the Russian Federation. A precise division of power between Moscow and Grozny was to be determined by a future treaty.

The next day Yeltsin flew to Chechnya. He landed in Mozdok, Northern Ossetia, and was taken by helicopter to Grozny and then to the Chechen village of Pravoberezhnoye. In Grozny, surrounded by tanks and armoured personnel carriers[268] (as well as by journalists, photographers and television cameras), a cordless microphone in hand, and with the helicopter gunship as a backdrop, Yeltsin met with Chechen elders and spoke to the soldiers of the 205th Motor Rifle Brigade. 'I am grateful to the armed forces of Russia for heroism and courage . . .' Yeltsin said. 'You have been defending your Motherland. You did not let the Russian state fall apart.'[269] The political responsibility for the war was his own, not the soldiers'. 'You have won,' he told the troops.[270]

Yeltsin laid a wreath at the memorial to Russian soldiers killed in Chechnya and gave out medals. He promised the villagers two giant Don harvesters and equipment for a computer classroom in the local school. Using the armour-plating of a personnel carrier as a desk,[271] he signed the decree discharging the draftees who had spent six months or longer in Chechnya (out of at least eighteen months of total service).

Two days later, campaigning in Ufa, Yeltsin proudly declared: 'Peace in Chechnya has been restored, and that means that peace has set in throughout Russia as well.'[272] He knew that he, too, had made peace with millions of his potential voters.

Among examples of the bracing and galvanizing effect of competitive politics on a candidate for national office, few would be likely to match the extent to which making his case to the voters and trying to persuade them of his worth transformed Boris Yeltsin between March and July.

Even before Yeltsin began campaigning in earnest, Egor Gaidar noticed a startling change. 'This was no longer the Yeltsin who only a month before had muttered something about snipers in Pervomayskoye,' wrote the former acting Prime Minister, who was invited to the Kremlin for a talk with the President. 'Crisp and focused', Yeltsin immediately 'grasped the essence of his interlocutor's thoughts and asked the right questions'.[273] Suddenly, sitting before Gaidar was the Yeltsin of their first meeting in October 1991 when the President had pledged his support for a government of reform.[274] Yeltsin's ratings were still catastrophically low, and the Kremlin courtiers were almost openly discussing the cancellation of the election. Yet, as he was leaving the Kremlin, Gaidar felt a fledgling, distant hope that this Yeltsin could 'restore a link with the voters'.[275] For the first time in months, Gaidar began to doubt a communist victory.[276]

It was a 'Western-style' campaign, a witness noted, complete 'with sound bites, daily photo ops and nervous advance men'.[277] In the first few weeks, Yeltsin lost more than nine kilos[278] (and kept his jacket open to show the 'fresh holes' in his belt).[279] He stopped drinking and was 'thinner and fitter' than at any time in the past three years. He spoke smoothly,[280] and sometimes gave a point-by-point description of his campaign platform without consulting a note.[281]

Every morning for three months, no matter where he was, Yeltsin called his economic adviser, Aleksandr Livshits, whom he had put in charge of one of the most critical tasks: clearing the backlog in pensions and wages. At first, the President called at nine, then at eight-thirty, and eventually at eight 'sharp'.[282]

Yeltsin had regained his 'spark and charisma',[283] reported an American journalist. He was 'beaming' and 'perfectly coiffed'.[284] Reporters found him 'happy, witty and assertive'.[285] In crisp white shirts, Yeltsin looked ten years younger. Suddenly, he was a 'new man conducting a new policy'.[286] His Chief of Staff, Nikolay Yegorov, complained to journalists that Yeltsin had so thoroughly revised campaign schedules and routes that they had become unrecognizable.[287] 'I am not travelling to wear out the seat of my trousers in meetings with local leaders,' Yeltsin told Yegorov at the end of April. 'I am travelling to campaign for President Yeltsin.'[288] Journalists who accompanied the President estimated that the ratio of time spent on the street to 'office' time was ten to one – exactly the reverse of what it had been before March.[289]

At times, it seemed that during the previous two years of sickly isolation he had developed an enormous appetite for street politicking, for the world outside government dachas and hunting lodges. The sight of thousands of ordinary men and women who had come to see him and support him – for the first time in almost five years – seemed to invigorate him. He would stop his limousine and, helped by his security detail, climb out to talk to the 'beckoning' passers-by,[290] walk through puddles to greet people,[291] banter with and wade into crowds.[292] *Bains de foule* were again his element. His bodyguards were ordered to carry a cordless microphone and a loudspeaker so that everyone could hear him.[293] This proved a risky experiment. 'Yeltsin, give us back sausage at two rubles and ten kopecks a kilo!' shouted an elderly Cossack woman as she advanced on the President, looking as if she intended to hit him.[294] Yeltsin did not retreat and attempted to explain that those prices could not be brought back but her pension must be raised.

At another campaign stop he was greeted by chants of 'Yeltsin's gang – on trial!'[295] On the central square of Krasnodar, as an enormous crowd looked on, a Second World War veteran refused to shake his hand and told him to resign. The man calmly gave his name, Aleksey Fedorovich Zhikharev, and said that Yeltsin's hands were smeared with 'tears and blood'.[296] There was 'pain and sadness' in the eyes of a stunned Yeltsin, but the practice of diving into the crowds, which gave so much trouble to his bodyguards, continued until election day.[297] 'I have come to look people in the eyes and speak frankly,' Yeltsin declared.[298] But what did *he* get from his plunges into crowds? a Russian reporter asked Yeltsin. 'Confidence,' the President replied. 'Not everything is lost for Russia or for each of us ... Many are having a difficult time. But they are not despondent, they work, they raise children. We are being reborn ...'[299]

Every minute of every campaign stop was packed with activity. He visited battlefields, laid wreaths on Second World War memorials and met with war veterans – a huge constituency that he stubbornly refused to concede to the communists. (Every Russian veteran received a card bearing Yeltsin's machine-made signature.) He went to shops, factories and kolkhozes and spoke with local businessmen, deputies and officials.[300] He went down a mine in Vorkuta.[301] In Tatarstan, following the local tradition of testing a warrior's strength and agility, he hit a clay pot with a long wooden pole while wearing a blindfold.[302] He danced at rock concerts in Rostov and Ufa. On the latter occasion, a witness reports, it was a 'plucky little twist', complete with 'swaying hips, flapping elbows and upper teeth bared over the lower lip'.[303]

He quipped incessantly, and was even self-deprecating. 'I am here in two capacities, as it were: as the incumbent President and as a Presidential candidate,' he announced upon arriving in the Belgorod region, the communists' agricultural stronghold in the south-west. 'It is impossible to divide my work ... As a President I can solve problems, but as a candidate I can make promises.'[304] 'Don't you have any questions for me?' he asked young women about to perform folk dances for him in Ufa.[305] 'Your President is tall and trim,' he said, self-mockingly, at another campaign stop. 'You see on television how the President speaks – it sends a tingle down your spine.'[306]

Every power of incumbency was on display, especially that of the Treasury. From the day of his first campaign speech in Ekaterinburg, where Yeltsin promised $10 million to a local sweets factory which needed investment to develop a line of baby food ('All they were asking for was ten million dollars,' Yeltsin explained. 'How can I refuse to give them ten million, you see?'), and promised another $1 million to a veterans' hospital,[307] pledges of assistance were dispensed with the largess of a travelling tsar. In Yaroslavl' it was a ten-billion-ruble ($200,000) grant to add a wing to a college;[308] in Stavropol, a combine harvester and farm equipment;[309] in Novosibirsk, forty billion rubles ($800,000) to help pay for new Metro stations. He was not going to meet people 'empty-handed', Yeltsin declared.[310] He had a 'small Presidential reserve' in the budget, he explained, 'not a huge one', about 100 billion rubles ($20 million).[311] 'You give me flowers and I'll give you money,' he quipped in Khimki, near Moscow.[312]

Yet even as he was leaving a trail of gifts and promises in his wake, Yeltsin knew only too well that his generosity (at the Treasury's expense) did little to redress the fundamental liability of his candidacy: his health and fitness for the job. So he set out to prove that he would not let the people down. The medium became the message as he campaigned in the sweltering heat of Kislovodsk and in a snow storm in Vorkuta.[313] He stood in the rain, rejecting proffered umbrellas.[314] He struck 'rest' and 'lunch' off his schedule.[315] Among the Russian journalists travelling on Yeltsin's plane (most of them half the President's age), one ended up in a hospital, two were laid up for a week at home and all were sick from 'colds and other ailments' prompted by exhaustion.[316]

In April, May and June, Yeltsin travelled to twenty-six regions, crossing Russia from the Polar Circle to the Caucasus Mountains, and from the Baltic Sea to the Sea of Okhotsk, with Belgorod, Volgograd, Astrakhan, Krasnoyarsk, Omsk, Rostov-on-the-Don, Arkhangel'sk, Ufa and Perm in between. In the last week of the campaign, he laid the cornerstone of the Christ the Saviour Cathedral in Kaliningrad one day, and on the next called on the voters of Khabarovsk, eight time zones away, 'not to lose the spirit of solidarity, hope and faith'.[317] On the same day, 11 June, he spoke in Khanty-Mansiysk in north-western Siberia, where grass had just sprung up in the tundra, and in the southern city of Novocherkassk, some 2,400 kilometres away,[318] where watermelons and the famous large, dark and juicy cherries were about to appear in the bazaars.

For three months, willpower and vitality, which communing with crowds seemed to generate, compensated for his exhausted and badly damaged heart. His press secretary was right when he wrote that, in deciding to run, 'Yeltsin staked his health and, in essence, his life.'[319] Before both of his celebrated impromptu dances in Rostov and Ufa, Yeltsin was nearly laid up with heart trouble, looking 'mortally tired' and pale. As he danced in Rostov, his entourage prayed that he would not 'fall dead right there, on the stage'.[320] (After the first round of voting on 16 June, Yeltsin would suffer another heart attack, undergo a quintuple heart-bypass operation and not fully recover until March 1997.

Only rarely did he break the tempo. One such occasion was his visit, on 7 May, to the home of a Second World War veteran, a colonel, in Otepsovo, a small *posyolok* ('settlement') near Moscow. This was to be a brief photo opportunity: the shaking of hands, the President's congratulations on the eve of the fifty-first anniversary of the Victory, and the veteran's grateful response. Instead, after they had drunk a toast to the Victory (from a bottle produced by the wily host despite the direst warnings of the advance team), the two moved to the kitchen garden and, to the horror of schedulers and the security detail, nearly disappeared among the tall, leafy potato tops under the brilliantly blue sky of the Russian spring. They stood and talked for a long time. Their faces were serious, their conversation quiet and unhurried.[321] No one would ever learn what they spoke about: planting potatoes, weather, grandchildren or the war.

Amid all the noise and the incessant movement, among the forests of outstretched arms and the never-ending flow of scripts to memorize and jokes to make, Yeltsin never lost sight of the tripartite message at the heart of his campaign: reform, freedom and stability. The major theme of his economic discourses was always the same: the state had to be divested of the ownership of the economy as quickly as possible. This, he explained, was his rationale for privatization. 'From the very beginning it was clear to us that there will be no progress if we retain the state's, that is nobody's, property and if people are denied the right to own the means of production ... Privatization was a matter of vital importance.'[322]

Yes, privatization had been marred by corruption and crime and the reforms should (and would) be corrected. Yet the 'essence' and the 'aim' of reform were right and needed no changes.[323] Both privatization and liberalization of prices were not only necessary and inevitable. They were vital for the survival of Russia. 'Full shelves' in grocery stores spoke for themselves.[324] 'We have been heading in absolutely the right direction.'[325]

Russia had to stay the course. For the first time in its history, it had a chance to complete liberal reforms, to carry them through to their conclusion.[326] This chance ought not to be missed. 'The great cause of reform must produce real results': the successful individual, the well-to-do family, a free society and a flourishing Russia.[327] If the reforms were to be interrupted, five or ten years later 'our children and great-grandchildren' would have to begin 'from scratch' – and all the intervening time would have been wasted and all the sacrifices in vain![328]

He had begun the reforms. His commitment to the policy was firm and well tested: 'No one in Russia can doubt that Yeltsin is for reforms.'[329] If he had not wanted to see the reforms through to the end, he would not have run for anything.[330] But Russia needed him to finish what he had started, to 'lick the reforms into shape',[331] to solidify them and make them irreversible. This was the reason to vote for him.

If the past course and the present state of economic reforms required a great deal of explanation and even an apology for 'mistakes', the second part of his record – democratic liberties – represented an absolute good and needed no caveats. 'Freedom' was the first plank of Yeltsin's platform.[332] 'Freedom is the most valuable common property of mankind,' he declared in the ancient Russian city of Yaroslavl'.[333] The experience of all mankind confirmed that there was no other way to 'prosperity and wealth'.[334] In Russia, too, the saturation of the market, after the queues and food rationing of Soviet times, had been achieved because people had been 'allowed to display their initiative'.[335]

Everywhere he went, he reminded people of the 'right to live and speak freely', and 'to choose freely and without fear'.[336] No people 'could be free without a free press'[337] – and that freedom, too, had 'become a reality'.[338] No longer afraid to criticize the authorities, the Russian press had already done a great deal 'for the triumph of democracy' and deserved enormous credit for helping to establish 'public control over all aspects of our life'.[339] Yes, 'slandering the President' had become 'the normal style' of some publications and it pained him to think that other people were libelled as well.[340] Still, freedom of the press had to be maintained: if 'you want to hear the truth, let everybody speak freely'.[341]

Freedom was his greatest pride and the strongest part of his record, one of the great gains of post-communist Russia.[342] 'The freedom to say what we think and to do what we say, the freedom to choose our future' was as central to the identity of post-Soviet Russia as independence itself, he told the 200,000 cheering Muscovites who gathered on Vasilievskiy Spusk near Red Square on Independence Day (12 June).[343] 'Five years ago we chose freedom,' he said. 'There can be no retreat.'[344]

The third cornerstone of his claim to re-election, stability, meant guarding freedom and the reforms from communist restoration. The communist danger to the nation's liberties was looming, he warned. The reforms had not been completed and the 'threat of turning back' was real.[345] But he had enough left in him to defend Russia from the 'second coming' of totalitarian communism. The communist revanche could not be allowed.[346] His resolve was firm, he kept telling them; his health 'OK'; and he had 'the right character'.[347]

The discipline and ingenuity with which Yeltsin wove the warning of communist restoration into his speeches and his impromptu exchanges with people would have pleased the most rigorous American campaign managers who implore their charges to 'stay on message'. 'But do you want a return to communism?' he asked workers in the Moscow suburb of Khimki after commiserating with them about low wages.[348] If Zyuganov won, would the country remain democratic? he asked journalists from the Ivanovo region. 'Will we respect human rights? Will we have freedom? Will this freedom be guaranteed by the firmness of the Constitution and the inviolability of private property?'[349]

The President could be reprimanded for a lot of things, but nobody could deny that since 1991 he had been the 'guarantor' of freedom of speech, and he would not change.[350] He pledged to do his utmost to protect the free press.[351] Would his opponents (who denounced the 'anti-people regime' even as they had availed themselves of 'all the rights and freedoms' that the government guaranteed) retain those liberties if they came to power?[352]

The loss of freedom was the leitmotif of the 'Vote or you lose!' television commercials aimed at younger voters. Aired throughout the country, the advertisements were brutally graphic: a newborn chicken followed by a grilled one, a flock of dolphins in the open sea and headless fish in a can, a pair of hands and a set of handcuffs. In a song that accompanied the film, a young man asked: 'What will I get out of voting?' 'Don't you know?' answered a voice. 'Freedom, you idiot.'[353]

The price of a communist victory might be 'too high', Yeltsin insisted: a collapse of the government, the isolation of the country, which would again become 'the ogre of the civilized world', and perhaps even civil war.[354] The communists, the President averred, were a 'party of revenge', governed by Marxist–Leninist ideas and therefore capable of extreme, 'unlimited actions'.[355] 'I will ensure you freedom of choice, but the choice is up to you,'[356] he stated four days before the election. Vote for a 'free Russia'![357]

Yeltsin was confident that Russia had acquired a taste for freedom and would not want to relinquish it.[358] Having been to 'most of the circles of Bolshevik hell' – the terror, the hunger, the food rationing, the 'spiritual degradation' – Russians would not 'submit again to the communist yoke and kneel again'.[359]

His advertisements were designed to remind the country of that hell. Aside from the arguments before the Constitutional Court in 1992, when the legality of the Communist Party was being decided, the 1996 campaign was the closest the country ever came to a public trial of Russian communism. The advertisements contained horrifying footage from previously closed archives: the Civil War, executions of 'enemies of the people' in the 1920s, destruction of churches and cheering crowds alongside the piles of burning icons, starving children, the bodies of Polish officers murdered in the Katyn forest by the NKVD in 1940.[360] The commercials ended with a voice-over: 'The communists haven't even changed their name. They won't change their methods. It's not too late to prevent civil war and famine.'[361]

The state-owned networks First Channel/ORT and Rossia showed 'historical dramas' and documentary mini-series about the Bolshevik rule. They were entitled most transparently: *Under the Sign of the Scorpion* and *The Time of Great Lies*.[362] On the eve of the election, on 15 June, First Channel/ORT broadcast *Burned by the Sun*, an Oscar-winning film set during Stalin's purges of the 1930s. The movie's director and star, Nikita Mikhalkov, had campaigned for Yeltsin.[363] 'Pray for me,' Yeltsin told well-wishers in the Muslim cultural centre in Yaroslavl'. 'I will protect you from the communists.'[364]

On 14 June, Yeltsin ended his campaign where he had started it four months before to the day: in his beloved Ekaterinburg. He came with his wife, daughters, sons-in-law and grandchildren. He had two main sources of strength, he told the cheering crowd in the Istoricheskiy Garden: 'my family and you'.[365] 'Five years ago,' he continued, 'we chose freedom, the renewal of Russia, a new, worthy life. We stormed the shore, and went forward, and now it is clear that we will solve our problems. We are worthy of a better life, and we will achieve victory.'[366] As the Yeltsin of 1990 and 1991 used to do, he raised his right fist. 'There can be no retreat! Together we will win!'[367]

Backing Yeltsin's candidacy was, by Russian standards, an expensive campaign masterminded by Anatoliy Chubais. According to a spot-check of campaign accounts in the Central Savings Bank (Sberbank), open for inspection by the Central Electoral Commission, as of 15 May Yeltsin had 7.1 billion rubles ($1,420,000) – more than twice the size of Zyuganov's war chest of 2.99 billion rubles ($598,000).[368]

Yet the actual expenses (mostly for carefully researched and well-produced television advertisements and concerts by rock celebrities) were probably several times that. According to one estimate, reproduced in *Sovetskaya Rossia*, at the peak of media buying in the first week of June the Yeltsin campaign spent 14.5 billion rubles ($2.9 million).[369] In the same week, Zyuganov claimed to have spent 12 billion rubles on advertisements, or $2.4 million.[370] Yeltsin's money had come from leading Russian bankers and entrepreneurs. Having failed to persuade him to make peace with Zyuganov and cancel the election, they reverted to the 'Davos plan'. According to rumours circulating in Moscow at the time, money was also 'borrowed' from the Treasury.

In promoting the President, Chubais found ready and eager allies in the Moscow-based liberal newspapers and in national television. Angered by the prospect of censorship and the re-establishment of the 'ideological line of the Party' and frightened by the unbridled anti-Semitism of Zyuganov's allies in *Sovetskaya Rossia* and *Zavtra*, the elite print and broadcast outlets, many of whose owners and employees were Jewish, did everything they could to get Yeltsin re-elected. The thought of Aleksandr Prokhanov as Minister of Information and Victor Anpilov as television tsar concentrated their minds wonderfully.

From April to June, Moscow's print media and television – which only recently had castigated the Kremlin over Chechnya, corruption and dozens of other transgressions in daily exposés (and would resume their criticism the day after the election) – changed their *modus operandi*. From what might be called the 'American way' of political coverage – almost by definition contrarian, profoundly sceptical of the executive's claims and relentlessly probing regardless of who is in power – the elite press switched to the 'European' mode, where the slant in news selection and presentation automatically and openly reflects (and is expected to reflect) a newspaper's party allegiance. Suddenly pro-Kremlin, the liberal media became nearly as partisan as the leftist publications, although they never approached *Sovetskaya Rossia* or *Zavtra* in vituperative zeal.

Much like their colleagues on the left, the Moscow press and television corps now saw the race not as a contest between candidates in agreement on the core properties of the present system (first and foremost, democracy and capitalism) but as an assault on the system itself. As a leading Western observer of Russia's post-communist television noted, the place that used to be reserved for the 'poet–seer' as the conscience of the country was now filled by the television anchors, who 'believed strongly in their duty to educate viewers about the dangers of a Communist victory'.[371]

Temporarily setting aside their internecine squabbles and the skewering of the Kremlin, Moscow print and electronic journalists attempted to save the regime from the cancer that was besetting it before going back to exposing its warts and lancing its many boils. 'Today we can honestly admit: society has survived a civil war, except in its "cold" version,' the head of the First Channel/ORT network's sociological service would write a few days after the election. 'In this situation television, indeed, was not even-handed. *It was biased in favour of democracy*. . . in favour of the survival of the mass media as a public opinion institution. [We were] guided by . . . an instinct for self-preservation . . . It would have been much more pleasant for us simply to inform society, appealing to intelligence. But this will be possible only when we choose between [candidates'] social and economic programmes, not between bad freedom and good prison.'[372]

After the election, the Rossia Television Channel anchor and host Nikolay Svanidze ('Satanidze' of *Zavtra*'s cartoons) would announce that, having 'fought for democracy against a communist revanche', the Russian media's 'love affair' with the regime had ended on election day. The liberal daily *Segodnya* concurred: it had 'fought for stability' and for the 'victory of common sense over idiocy', but now it would 'return to where it belong[ed]: in opposition to the authorities'.[373]

Both the First Channel/ORT and Rossia networks allocated more airtime to Yeltsin's campaign than to Zyuganov's effort. While much of the difference was undoubtedly due to editorial bias, in Russia, as in every country, the head of government had an inherent advantage as the biggest newsmaker. In Yeltsin's case, the President's spectacular revival further skewed the coverage. 'In part, the President so over-whelmingly dominated [the First Channel's and Rossia's] news broadcasts because he personally took the reins of government in his hands,' wrote a Western analyst. 'Previous election campaigns [in 1993 and 1995] had identified a whole range of newsmakers in the administration and spread the time around; this campaign was about a single human dynamo, the President.'[374]

The anti-Zyuganov coverage in the Moscow liberal press was devoted to exposing what the journalists saw as Bolshevik orthodoxy in the KPRF's agenda and tactics, the anti-reform past of its leadership, and the suspiciously cryptic nature of Zyuganov's plans for the future, rather than *ad hominem* attacks on the communist candidate. The exception to this somewhat more restrained version of partisanship was Moscow's most popular, irreverent tabloid *Moskovskiy Komsomoletz*, which before the campaign had specialized in tormenting the government with endless exposés of its corruption, malfeasance and incompetence. (One of its reporters, Dmitriy Kholodov, had been killed while uncovering corruption in the highest ranks of the armed forces.) The newspaper now unashamedly indulged its anti-communist sarcasm.

It is obvious, in retrospect, that both camps vastly overestimated the advantages that the Moscow elite media conferred on a candidate. In the case of the print media, the pro-Yeltsin effort was hopelessly Moscow-centric: outside the capital these newspapers were greatly out-numbered by the combined readership of the myriad communist and pro-communist national and local publications. As the results of the vote would make plain, Moscow-based television too failed to influence the key target audience: rural, small town and 'rust belt' industrial Russia. Indeed, it was precisely in the countryside, where pro-Yeltsin national television was often the only regular source of news and opinion, that Zyuganov, in the end, would beat Yeltsin easily. With Moscow, St Petersburg and most large cities solidly pro-Yeltsin even before the campaign began, the Moscow-based media, both print and electronic, turned out to have preached to the choir.

Most Russian voters, as most voters everywhere, proved impervious to the allegedly all-powerful television. 'Of course, the [Moscow-based] television could have, and perhaps has, persuaded some voters,' wrote an independent Russian student of public opinion. 'And if the gap is only a few points this may decide the election. But most voters seemed to have developed a strong immunity to television propaganda and quite clearly chose their position absolutely on their own.'[375]

Some time between 20 April and 14 May, in the field of ten candidates, Yeltsin caught up with Zyuganov: both were now endorsed by just under 30 per cent of surveyed voters.[376] The closer to the election, the more polarized the electorate became: the share of the eight other candidates in voter preferences had fallen steadily from 50 per cent of the total in January to 24 per cent at the end of May.[377] The demography of the contest remained unchanged. The polls showed Yeltsin well ahead in large cities, especially Moscow and St Petersburg, pre-ponderant among those with higher education and dominant among younger voters (under forty years old).[378] Zyuganov confidently led in rural areas, in small towns[379] and among older and less educated voters.[380]

The young were for Yeltsin because many of them, whom an Ameri-can reporter correctly labelled 'the freest and most advantaged genera-tion of Russians in history',[381] felt that the communists would limit their freedom to choose: foreign travel, goods, books, hairstyles or music. 'I just have to remember what I didn't have before,' said one twenty-year-old college student from St Petersburg. 'I could not afford good clothes or good food. There is a lot of music now, and it is easier to buy a European television set.'[382] Zyuganov 'could make me get a haircut and make us all look the same', added his friend, running his hand through his long blond hair. 'It's a choice between a free life, or under Communists.'[383]

A female student dreaded a return to her parents' life: a boring job and a salary of 100 rubles a month after graduation, 'until I retire'.[384] Another young woman was afraid that 'if they [communists] come to power, they will shut down the private firms where we work'.[385] A student in the philosophy department of St Petersburg University said: 'They used to teach people to become Communist Party leaders here. Now, we study Plato to Kant, and the professors can publish what they like, and no one tells them what to say.'[386]

Yet this most staunchly pro-Yeltsin constituency was also the one least likely to turn out on election day. In a nation-wide survey conducted in May, only slightly over half of respondents between the ages of eighteen and twenty-four said they would vote (while almost three out four people over fifty-four said they would).[387] The lesson of the December 1995 Duma elections – in which an estimated 60 per cent of urban youth did not bother to vote and which, as a result, produced a leftist plurality in the legislature – haunted the Yeltsin campaign.

Obtaining the 'youth vote' became the most important tactical objective of the Yeltsin campaign. It was to attract these boys and girls that the campaign spent millions of dollars on rock concerts by the most popular groups (Nautilus-Pampilius, Alisa, Tsvety) and the leading singers and composers: Pavel Grebenshchikov of Aquarium and Andrey Makarevich of Time Machine.[388] It was to propel them to the ballot box that this very sick sixty-five-year-old President, proud and obsessed with protocol, grimaced and danced awkwardly on stage. (When he stepped into the limelight at a rock concert in Volgograd and delivered a brief unrehearsed speech, the noise from the cheering crowd of 400,000 'exceeded all possible levels'.)[389]

In Ufa, after Yeltsin said his stock farewell line – 'Make the right choice! Vote or you'll lose!' – waved to the roaring crowd and left, Makarevich came to the microphone. In Soviet times, his band had been harassed and banned from recording or performing on the radio. 'I was under a communist regime once, and I don't want a replay of it,' Makarevich said. 'Come cast your vote on 16 June so Time Machine can keep on playing!'[390]

* * *

On 16 June, 70 per cent of Russian voters (seventy-six million people) came to the polling stations. Yeltsin received 35 per cent of the total, Zyuganov 32 per cent.* General Aleksandr Lebed came in third with 15 per cent of the vote. Grigoriy Yavlinsky polled 7 per cent and Vladimir Zhirinovskiy 6 per cent.

Yeltsin's narrow lead obscured two developments that made his victory in the run-off all but certain. (By a quick agreement with Zyuganov and the Duma, the second round was scheduled for 3 July.) First, the polls proved quite accurate: most of the voters in the 'pro-Yeltsin' demographic groups did, in fact, support him overwhelmingly: the young, the educated, the urban, who had benefited most immediately from political and economic liberties and from the economic revival inspired by the dramatic decrease in the rate of inflation from 135 per cent in the previous year to 22 per cent in 1996. University students preferred Yeltsin 84 per cent to 7 per cent. The results in the typical Russian province of Saratov, 500 miles from Moscow, exemplified the national pattern: the overwhelming majority of women in maternity wards voted for Yeltsin, while Zyuganov was equally strong among hospital patients, most of them older people.[391]

The other favourable portent was that Yeltsin's claim on the Lebed and Yavlinsky vote was far stronger than Zyuganov's. To his national total Yeltsin stood to add at least 7 per cent from Lebed's supporters, 4 per cent from Yavlinsky's. He moved quickly to solidify and expand his base. On 17 June, he offered Lebed the post of President's national security adviser and Secretary of the Security Council. One of Lebed's conditions was the dismissal of Minister of Defence Pavel Grachev. Yeltsin instantly complied.

Three days later, the long-brewing animosity between Korzhakov and Chubais came to a head after Korzhakov's men arrested two top campaign aides. Yeltsin responded by firing Korzhakov, Barsukov and, for good measure, Soskovets. Their departure from the Kremlin marked the rout of the 'party of war', and of those who had wanted reconciliation with the communists and the cancellation of the election. Bemoaned by

* The Yeltsin camp charged pro-communist authorities with pressuring villagers, especially elderly ones, to vote for Zyuganov. The President's supporters pointed to a widespread use of mobile ballot boxes in the countryside. In some rural areas up to 25 per cent of all votes were already under the watchful eye of the kolkhoz chairmen and 90 per cent of these votes went to Zyuganov. (*OMRI Russian Presidential Election Survey*, no. 11, 27 June 1996.) Zyuganov declared that the voting had occurred 'without any violations of the law' (*OMRI*, 20 June 1996).

Zavtra as the last 'patriots' and 'derzhavniks' in the Kremlin,[392] these were the officials whose dismissal the liberal opposition had demanded for a year. Perhaps more than anything else he had done or said in the past three months, these 'personnel changes', to which Yeltsin had been driven by the merciless imperatives of democratic politics,* the firing of his four closest aides, confidants and sauna partners, persuaded the country's pro-reform and anti-communist constituencies that the President was determined to leave behind the past two years of weakness, drift and thuggishness. A more painful, more personal sacrifice could hardly be imagined – and it had been accepted.

In the second round of the Presidential election, on 3 July, 69 per cent of the electorate (seventy-five million people) went to the polls. Yeltsin received 54 per cent of the vote (forty million) and Zyuganov 40 per cent (thirty million). Almost 5 per cent of the voters availed themselves of the third option on the ballot and voted 'against all'; the rest of the ballots were deemed invalid. The 'popular-patriotic' bloc, which boasted of fielding 200,000 observers[393] (at least one at each of the country's 93,000 polling stations), found no violations extensive enough to contest the national results.† Hundreds of foreign observers, similarly, found no serious transgressions in the voting procedure or in the counting of votes. Zyuganov said he would 'respect the will of the citizens of the Russian Federation' and congratulated Yeltsin.[394]

All the favourable trends, predicted by polls and indicated by the 16 June vote, had materialized. Yeltsin's appeal to the supporters of the three main non-communist candidates proved stronger than estimated. He claimed over half of Lebed's voters, almost seven out of ten of Yavlinsky's and over one-third of Zhirinovskiy's. The demography of the final result was even starker than the polls had suggested: the young and the urban flocked, overwhelmingly, to Yeltsin's banner – and the

---

* A poll showed that the dismissals 'improved the attitude towards Boris Yeltsin' of 36 per cent of those surveyed and 'worsened' it in the case of 10 per cent (*Analitica Moscow Political Weekly Press Summary*, vol. 3, no. 24, 22–28 June 1996, p. 3).

† The Zyuganov campaign pointed, rightly, to the unnaturally wide fluctuation of votes between the first round and the run-off in a number of rural non-Russian ethnic areas. Tatarstan, Dagestan, North Ossetia and Kalmykia looked most suspicious. The double-digit upsurge in the pro-Yeltsin vote there could be explained only by the pressure imposed on local authorities by the regions' political leaders eager to please the Kremlin.

younger they were, the wider the President's lead was.[*] Yeltsin took eighty-six out of Russia's hundred largest cities.[395] Even in the agricultural 'red belt' in the South-west and South-east, where Zyuganov led him by at least 15 percentage points, Yeltsin won every regional capital. In a country whose fate for centuries had been decided in Moscow and St Petersburg, both cities gave Yeltsin astronomic leads: 77 per cent to Zyuganov's 18 per cent in Moscow, and 74 per cent to 21 per cent in St Petersburg.

Yeltsin gathered both those who wanted the reforms to continue and those who were frightened of the return of a one-party state and a state-owned economy. In the end he won because the election had, as he intended it to, become a referendum on democracy and communism, rather than on market reforms or the Russian version of capitalism. 'The vote in the second round of the 1996 presidential election was a referendum on the political system,' concluded a prominent American student of the Soviet Union and post-communist Russia. 'Social scientists are never going to be more sure of a finding than about this one.'[396] As a would-be Yeltsin voter put it on the eve of the first round, 'Yeltsin made many mistakes. Nobody idealizes him. There's just one reason to vote for Yeltsin: He is the only one in a position to deliver democracy to Russia.'[397]

The fatefulness of the choice made on 3 July is best illustrated by the polarity of positions taken by Yeltsin's and Zyuganov's supporters on some of the most fundamental issues of their country's economic and political organization. Asked to rank the positive economic and social characteristics of a society, 75 per cent of those who planned to vote for Yeltsin chose equal opportunity for 'realization of everyone's abilities', while 22 per cent thought most important equality of income and of standard of living.[398] Among Zyuganov's supporters the numbers were, respectively, 44 per cent and 53 per cent.[399] Among sampled prospective voters for Yeltsin, 75 per cent opposed dictatorship and 16 were in favour; in the Zyuganov camp, the breakdown was 50 per cent to 33 per cent.[400]

On 3 July, the Russians also proved to be very consistent. Polled a year before, 54 per cent of those surveyed did not 'consider the communist system acceptable for Russia'[401] – precisely the percentage Yeltsin

---

[*] According to exit polls, Yeltsin was three times as popular as Zyuganov among those between the ages of 18 and 29 (71 per cent to 23 per cent) In the 30- to 44-year-old category, the President led 57 per cent to 36 per cent. ('How Russians Voted in the Runoff,' *New York Times*, 4 July 1996, p. A8.)

garnered in the second round. The vote also confirmed that, whenever Yeltsin succeeded in presenting himself as a symbol of change and a bulwark against Soviet restoration, he could count on the firm support of four in ten adult Russians: forty million people expressed 'confidence' in the President in the critical 1993 referendum and the same number voted for him on 3 July.

The communists were dealt a blow from which, given the age of their core electorate, they were not likely to recover. The opposition's contention that only a handful of 'new rich' supported the 'occupying', 'anti-people Yeltsin regime' had been buried once and for all. In the first round, when people freely expressed their preferences (as opposed to choosing a 'lesser evil', as many did on 3 July) the two pro-reform, pro-market candidates (Yeltsin and Yavlinsky) together received 42 per cent of the national vote.

Free to compete, the KPRF failed spectacularly in its claim to represent the majority of the Russian people, who had been said to be irresistibly drawn to the communist agenda and needed only an outlet and a banner to rise against the Yeltsin regime. Zyuganov's 34 million out of the total of 108 million registered voters forever disqualified communists from speaking 'for the nation'.* A week after the Presidential election, one of Moscow's most celebrated wits, the producer and writer for the popular *Kukly* satirical show, Viktor Shenderovich, suggested that the KPRF change its name to 'Communist Party of the Countryside'.[402]

The election revealed the contours of Russia's political geography: the solidly pro-communist rural areas of the West and South-west,† southern Siberia‡ and the Amur Basin of the southern Far East;§ and the just as firmly pro-reform industrialized North and Central Russia,

---

* Over the next twelve months, regional elections corroborated this conclusion: of seventeen regions where 'pure' KPRF candidates (as opposed to those of the National Patriotic Union of Russia, in which the KPRF was a key partner) ran for governor in 1996, they won only in five: the reddest of the 'red belt' regions of Bryansk, Ryazan', Volgograd, Vladimir and Stavropol.

† What became known as the 'red belt' around Moscow included the Bryansk, Belgorod, Voronezh, Kursk, Oryol, Penza, Tabov and Smolensk *oblast*s. In all but the last region, Zyuganov was ahead of Yeltsin by over 20 per cent of the vote in the second round. (He led in the Smolensk *oblast* by 18 per cent.)

‡ Orenburg, Omsk, Altayskiy *krai* and Kemerovo.

§ The Chita and Amur *oblast*s.

Siberia, Far East and Urals, and all of the maritime regions.* Much as in two other giant democracies, the United States and India, Russia now boasted both a politically diverse map and the ability to absorb and contain sharp regional differences.

Russia had shown the ability to choose its way without violence, dictatorship or adherence to a single ideology. Of course, a freely elected government was not synonymous with a perfect or even good government. The latter would require different human material and would take decades to emerge. Few Russians had illusions on that score. Yet the ability to elect a government was a necessary condition of making it good. Now there was hope.

In what was destined to be the last such occasion in his life, Yeltsin's personal political victory was also Russia's. As he addressed the nation on 4 July from his office in the Kremlin – trying to look solemn but unable to suppress a smile – he, also for the last time, spoke for millions:

> The most important outcome is already known: the Presidential election has been conducted properly. It was free and honest. On 3 July we all chose a future for our country. I am proud of the fact that we have passed this test. I am proud of Russia. I am proud of you, the people of Russia. Yesterday you stood up for your right to choose: nobody will now take that away from you. This is your merit, your victory. I thank everyone who turned up at the polling stations to exercise their civic duty . . .
>
> Let us not divide the country into winners and losers. Let us work. After all, we have one Russia . . . We have the same Russia and the same fate and thus the same future. On 3 July you once again proved to yourself and the whole world that Russia is a great country and that we are a great people. Together we will revive Russia. Thank you.[403]

Another splendid precedent was established in June 1996. Ten days before the first round, at the Roland Garros tennis stadium in Paris,

---

* Yeltsin outpolled Zyuganov by at least 20 per cent in the Yaroslavl', Vologda, Novgorod, Arkhangel'sk, Murmansk, Leningrad and Kaliningrad *oblast*s and Kamchatka (Central North and maritime); Perm, Sverdlovsk, Chelyabinsk and Tomsk *oblast*s (the industrial Urals and Siberia). He won by at least 10 per cent in Ivanovo and Tula *oblast*s (industrial Central Russia); Tyumen' and Irkutsk *oblast*s and Krasnoyarsk *krai* (oil-producing and industrial Siberia), Sakhalin *oblast* and Primorskiy *krai* (maritime Far East).

Russia's best tennis player, Evgeniy Kafel'nikov, won the French Open. Who knows what makes tennis one of the most accurate indicators of a country's freedom and prosperity – perhaps a combination of the game's fierce individualism and a rather expensive routine of training and travel, which requires the liberty to live and work abroad. Major international prizes in tennis are almost never won by players from poor countries or from countries with repressive regimes. After Kafel'nikov had captured the first Grand Slam in Russia's history, there could be no return to communism – then or ever.

CHAPTER 14

The Last Struggle

The TWO YEARS THAT FOLLOWED the 3 July 1996 re-election must have been among the most frustrating in a life during which ability, energy and luck had generally subjugated and moulded circumstance. Rarely if ever, since the early months of 1992, had Yeltsin been as closely, even as passionately, engaged in economic policy, had as clear an understanding of what needed to be done or applied himself to the reform with so much agility and eagerness. Yet never before had he been circumscribed so ruthlessly. Arrayed against him were the two most formidable enemies any leader can face: failing health and tasks whose complexity made them impervious to short-term exertion, no matter how intense and heroic. The job required a persistence and an application which his infirmities would deny him.

The 3 July run-off marked the victory of the peaceful anti-communist revolution, but the results of the economic revolution were far more ambiguous. By the lights of mature capitalist democracies, much in the Russian economic arrangements of summer 1996 was glaringly flawed. Quite apart from the enormous damage inflicted by errors, malfeasance and sheer ignorance, which invariably accompany such mammoth undertakings, the transition had been distorted by genetic defects inherited from the *ancien régime* and by the circumstances in which the reform was launched.

The soil in which the seeds of Russian capitalism were planted in 1992 was not just hard or barren. In some key respects, its composition was antithetical to the one from which classic Western European capitalism had risen. The country had no living memory of private economic activity unstigmatized by persecution and unmarred by criminality. Its economy was almost completely militarized. In the countryside, devastated by Stalin's murderous collectivization and by half a century of kolkhoz serfdom, alcoholism, isolation and poverty, three generations had grown up with no memory of family farming on one's own land.

Most damagingly, post-communist Russia inherited four centuries of patrimonialism: a system of rule in which political authority was synonymous with control (at times nearly complete) not only of the nation's economy but of its citizens' property as well. Individual and corporate property rights, which in the West had contributed so greatly to the political autonomy of civil society and, eventually, to the emergence of democracy, had been weak in Russia even before the Bolsheviks established a near-perfect patrimonial state – the sole employer of all Russians and the owner of their livelihoods.

To be sure, privatization had gone a long way to divest the Russian state of economic ownership and to separate, for the first time, political authority and economic control. Between 1992 and 1996, in the most extensive effort in history, managed by Anatoliy Chubais, the regime had privatized 77 per cent of large and mid-sized enterprises and 82 per cent of small shops and retail stores. Russian entrepreneurs had started 900,000 new businesses. Non-existent in 1991, by the end of 1996 the private sector accounted for around 70 per cent of GDP.[1] Between ten and fourteen million new jobs had been created (though many of these were combined, illegally, with nominal employment at the old workplace).

Yet conceived in the depth of national crisis, when famine, civil strife and the country's disintegration seemed imminent, Russian capitalism was born into an institutional and legal void. Desperate to accomplish as much as possible before the window of political opportunity was shut by the Supreme Soviet, Russian privatizers transferred the national economy to private ownership before securing the basic institutional and legal structures that over centuries had developed to minimize the defects of capitalism: the sanctity of contract, enforced by independent and largely incorruptible courts; self-policing professional associations; government agencies that protect investors and consumers; and modern civil, commercial and criminal codes.

In addition, the 'velvet revolution' had left the industrial nomenklatura, soon to be known as 'red directors', in possession of all the economic assets which they had formerly managed on the state's behalf. As the Party's grip relaxed towards the end of Gorbachev's rule, they emerged as the most powerful and coherent interest group in Russian politics, determined to keep and to guard their wealth.

How, under these circumstances, does one go about privatizing and, more importantly, ensuring fair treatment of outside buyers and a subsequent restructuring of the enterprise, which in almost every case would have had to involve massive lay-offs? One could, in Bolshevik fashion, send armed detachments to tens of thousands of state-owned enterprises, forcibly eject old managers from their offices and severely restrict the rights of the employees to buy shares. This, at least in the Russia of 1992, would have been a recipe for civil war.

Or one could, as the Poles did, postpone industrial privatization, relying on retail, services, agriculture and foreign investment to revitalize the economy and provide political stability. (China also chose not to privatize state-owned industry and, by the end of 1990s, spent a third of the state budget to keep the loss-making plants and factories afloat.) Given the size of Soviet industry, the complete interpenetration of Soviet state and economy and the miserable condition of agriculture and services, there seemed to be no other way to deal the omnipotent state a mortal blow, to relieve society of a back-breaking burden and, at the very least, clear some of the largest obstacles to a market economy.

Such, in any case, was the dominant view within the State Committee for State Property, which under Chubais became the chief privatization agency. From the first, 'depoliticization' of the economy was the Committee's paramount objective: to take as much out of the state's control as quickly as possible. As the testimony of those in charge makes quite clear, from the very beginning the aim during the first, massive phase (1992–4) was not so much to get the best price for a particular enterprise as to 'depoliticize' the Russian economy.[2]

In the end, a hectic search for a formula that would satisfy the 'red directors' and the increasingly recalcitrant Supreme Soviet left two-thirds of the stock in the hands of managers and employees. Every Russian man, woman and child received 144 million individual privatization 'vouchers' to be exchanged for shares in any enterprise they chose. Yet the novelty of the procedure; the passivity of the Russian workers and their trade unions; the management's near-complete mastery over them; and the absence of a legal and accounting infrastructure to protect the rights of outside investors combined to produce corporate governance antithetical to transparency and accountability. Worst of all, the first phase of privatization did little to effect the desperately needed radical restructuring of the Russian economy: the new 'insider' owners and the 'work collectives' they controlled had little to gain and a great deal to lose from change.

Still, compared with the perpetuation of state ownership of the economy, this insider 'nomenklatura privatization' was viewed by Russian reformers as a lesser evil. 'Controlling managers is not nearly as important as controlling politicians,' wrote associates of Russia's privatization tsar, Anatoliy Chubais, 'since managers' interests are generally much closer to economic efficiency than those of the politicians.'[3]

That was all well and good, in theory. The reality proved far grimmer. After seventy-five years of a state-owned economy, 'red directors' behaved more like corrupt civil servants than entrepreneurs. They continued to steal from the enterprise and cheat the workers, just as they had done after Gorbachev freed them from the terror of a police state without replacing it with the responsibility and discipline of a free market. Control was pre-eminent, productivity and workers' well-being secondary and tertiary. Surveyed in 1995 and 1996, two-thirds of Russian managers polled said that they 'and their workers' would oppose selling a majority of the shares of their enterprises to outside investors even if an outsider would bring capital necessary to modernize and restructure the firm.[4]

Forced to operate on their own, most managers sought 'rent' from the assets and political connections, not profit from production and innovation. Their response to the gradual reduction of subsidies and cancellation of state orders was not restructuring, developing new products or searching for new markets but diminished production, the stripping and sale of assets, profligate and reckless borrowing, withholding of taxes and the accrual of enormous inter-enterprise debts. The regime's timidity in forcing bankruptcies of failed enterprises further strengthened managers' belief in their political invincibility and the eventual demise of market reforms. All they had to do was to wait – and live well while doing so.

One of the schemes, which was responsible for making near-instant millionaires out of battalions of 'red directors', was popular in the years of rampant inflation between spring 1992 and October 1993. Then under the Supreme Soviet's control,* the Central Bank approved 'loans' to enterprises at annual interest rates of 20 to 30 per cent at a time when the rate of inflation was 2,500 per cent in 1992 and 840 per cent in 1993. Dozens of enterprise managers would come to the Kremlin daily, begging for loans to pay for raw materials and salaries. They described the plight of their workers in terms so brutally vivid and heart-breaking that even Egor Gaidar, known as the 'Iron Winnie-the-Pooh' on account of his deceptively round and supple appearance, would authorize loans for at least some of the supplicants. On their way to relieve long-suffering employees, the 'red directors', a bag of freshly printed rubles in hand, would make a quick stop at any of dozens of currency-exchange booths on Moscow corners and turn the entire 'loan' into dollars. With the monthly inflation rate in double digits, a few weeks later they would use some of the dollars to buy back the original ruble amount, pay the workers and deposit the rest in a Swiss bank. As much as $65 billion was estimated to have left the country between 1992 and 1997.[5]

In the second stage of privatization, 1995–6, the Kremlin moved from giving away state property to the selling off of some of Russia's blue-chip companies. This operation, in which twenty-nine of the country's most

---

* The parliament's control over the Central Bank of Russia ended in October 1993. According to the Constitution, the Bank is independent from 'other organs of state power'.

profitable and largest enterprises were auctioned, became known as the 'loan-for-shares' deal. Desperate to plug huge gaps in the budget and to tame inflation (all the while spending billions on the war in Chechnya) the government borrowed from private banks in exchange for the 'management' of the state's shares in the enterprises offered as a collateral. In reality, this was a sale (or, at best, a long-term lease) of choice assets, for there was little hope that the Russian state would ever repay the loans.

It quickly became apparent that there were very few Russian buyers; even fewer were those whose wealth had been obtained entirely by legal methods and who were not in one way or another connected to organized crime. And there were none who could afford to pay anywhere near the book value for the shares. Frightened by political instability and high inflation, foreign investors stayed away. The shares were 'sold' at insider auctions, at bargain-basement prices and to politically better connected (and more generous) banks, many of which acted as organizers of the very auction in which they bid.

The 1995 deal marked the emergence of secretive, tightly knit, bank-led corporate 'financial–industrial groups' (the FIGs), with intimate political connections, not unlike Japanese *kereitsu*s or South Korean *chaebol*s. Much like them, Russian FIGs owed their wealth to political contacts and the state's regulation and 'guidance' of the economy. They obtained export licences and arbitraged between world market prices of raw materials (especially oil) and controlled domestic prices. The latter, which were sometimes as much as one hundred times lower, the regime could not bring itself to free, persuaded by the 'red directors' and their advocates in the Supreme Soviet that to do so would bring Russian industry to a halt. Another source of income was duty-free imports, especially food, liquor and cigarettes, granted to the government favourites. Finally, most banks at the head of the largest FIGs were designated as 'authorized' holders of government revenues (taxes, custom duties) and dispensers of pensions and salaries. Naturally, they used the deposits in schemes similar to the one described above, albeit on a far grander scale.

The economic system that emerged in Russia could not but be sharply distinct from the classic capitalism of the North European (or Anglo-Saxon) variety, inherited and refined by the United States. Instead, the Russian economy quickly exhibited, in a considerably cruder edition, some of the worst aspects of what might be called the French–Italian–Asian version of capitalism. Its features were incestuously overlapping and interchangeable political, corporate and bureaucratic elites; either direct ownership of the economy by the state, or dirigisme's intervention, control and direction; the corruption that such bureaucratic control inevitably breeds; an economy driven by banks and exports, instead of by stock-market and domestic demand; subsidized credits, informal lending practices and loose (or non-existent) disclosure rules, which result in mountains of bad loans; the absence of a Federal Reserve system and of independent institutions of banking and stock-market oversight; protectionism for select industries and restrictions on foreign participation in the economy, especially in banking; and a giant 'shadow' economy.

All over the world, rapid capitalist expansion and large-scale sell-offs of the state's possessions had been attended by massive swindling, bribery and sweetheart deals: from the purchase of state lands by railway companies during the post-civil war march to the west in the United States to Margaret Thatcher's Britain in the 1980s, to Carlos Menem's Argentina in the 1990s and to every post-communist nation and to China. From Poland and Estonia to post-apartheid South Africa, corruption seemed inseparable from quick de-etatization of the economy, restructuring and growth. Yet just as the scope of Russian privatization was without precedent, so was the wealth that nomenklatura capitalists acquired from political connections and insider deals.

Another common feature was the emergence of 'robber barons', who, within a few years, accumulated very sizeable wealth and political influence. In the Russian case, the most notorious of the 'oligarchs', as they came to be known, was Boris Berezovskiy, who began as a car dealer and built an empire of banks, oil companies, television, newspapers and airlines. He used his closeness to the Yeltsin family and his position as informal adviser to Yeltsin's daughter, Tat'yana D'yachenko, to become Deputy Secretary of the Security Council and Executive Secretary of the Commonwealth of Independent States – positions of little real power, but considerable prestige. (After about a year in each post, he was fired by Yeltsin.)

There is little doubt that the secrecy in which Russian robber barons cloaked their dealings resulted in a vast exaggeration of their wealth and power both by the Moscow rumour mill and by the resident correspondents of Western newspapers and television networks, who dutifully package and ship the endless stream of that mill's products. The truth was further obscured by deep suspicion of personal wealth, after eight decades of banishment and criminalization of private economic activity, and by self-aggrandizing claims and accusations with which the perennially warring moguls puffed up their worth and which they hurled at one another through their media outlets.

One such allegation was that the oligarchs had 'bought' Yeltsin's victory in 1996. To be sure, the millions of dollars (and billions of rubles) that they contributed to the campaign, after finally settling on Yeltsin in the beginning of May, paid for much of the advertising and 'Vote-or-you-lose' rock concerts. Yet the evidence, accumulated by advertising and marketing research, had proved time and again that advertising has a very limited ability to change minds where core beliefs and preferences are concerned. The claim also contradicted the solid evidence of very stable and consistent attitudes among key pro- and anti-Yeltsin demographic groups, identified by Russian and foreign pollsters and discussed in the previous chapter. Where Western scholars and journalists were concerned, the acceptance and dissemination of this fabrication reeks of condescension, if not indeed Russophobia and racism. After all, unfolding at the same time, President Clinton's re-election campaign spent perhaps several hundred times more per voter, yet no one suggests that the American voters were 'bought', while an equally preposterous allegation, which depicts millions of Russian men and women as unthinking cattle, is advanced without a blush of shame. Thus deprived of the legitimacy that comes from 40 million votes, Yeltsin was declared by the same experts a toy of the 'rival cliques' of Russian magnates and, in the same spirit of scholarly objectivity and informed inquiry, likened to the former Congo dictator Mobutu Sese Seko.[6]

Equally bizarre was the 'theory' that explained Yeltsin's 'dependence' on the oligarchs by the gifts with which they showered his family – as if the President of Russia, should he decide to do so, needed intermediaries in raiding the country's Treasury. The two firings of Berezovskiy by Yeltsin and the 1997–8 reforms, many of which were explicitly designed to constrain the robber barons' ability to help themselves to the choicest pieces of the privatized economy, further underscored the limits of the oligarchs' sway over the Kremlin. Finally, their alleged indispensability for the survival of the regime was belied by the fact that, when most oligarchs were ruined by the 1998 financial crisis, the regime neither collapsed into anarchy nor solidified into dictatorship, but was saved by the democratic legitimacy of a freely elected parliament and President.

Yet to point to distortions and the limits of our knowledge about the extent of oligarchs' wealth or power is not to deny their enormous and corrupting presence in the Russian economy and politics between 1994 and 1998. Without reliable evidence, untainted by the political agenda of those who reveal it, and without comparing the actors' accounts (unlike the notoriously garrulous Russian politicians, the oligarchs did not publish memoirs), we can only speculate about the nature of Yeltsin's dealings with Russia's richest men. There could be no prosperous country without wealthy people, Yeltsin had said before. Was it his hope that, unlike the ephemeral 'alliances' of Russian politics, the desire to preserve and increase one's wealth would form a permanent base of his regime? Did he then accept the barons' manipulation of state property or its acquisition at ridiculously low prices as the regrettable but temporary and inevitable price of creating a free market economy out of the human and industrial legacy of Soviet communism? Whatever the reasons (and regardless of whether he or his family profited from it directly), Yeltsin cannot be absolved of responsibility for the corrosion of Russian democracy and the Russian economy during the oligarchs' brief but crippling reign, which became synonymous in the public mind with crooked deals, distorted markets, the incestuous closeness of power and money and, most of all, rampant and ubiquitous corruption.

Russian patrimonialism and Soviet totalitarianism had thwarted the development of that precious interlocking network of institutions, laws and what Montesquieu called the 'habits of heart' which had for centuries buttressed Western capitalism and endowed it with its 'civilized' character. Over four generations, until virtually the day of its sudden collapse, the Soviet regime had relentlessly extirpated, suppressed, subverted, co-opted or corrupted any and all voluntary associations in which the habits of self-governance, personal responsibility and peaceful reconciliation of interests could have been instilled and reproduced: neighbourhoods, religious and professional associations, charitable organizations or clubs. People's compliance with the law had been a product of terror and fear, not of freely assumed obligations.

In the absence of terror, post-Soviet corruption was practised on what an observer aptly called a 'breathtaking' scale.[7] In the words of a leading human rights activist and ex-dissident, 'corruption in Russia has become a universal norm of behaviour: It is no longer a violation of the norm, but a change of the norm itself, even an emergence of an alternative (shadow) norm of public behaviour.'[8] From the government buildings in Moscow to the bureaucracies of sleepy provincial towns, the Russian state's offices hosted a never ending auction at which that state's possessions, the regulations that governed them and the bureaucrats that administered the regulations were up for sale.

Like corruption, an explosive growth in crime accompanied every transition from authoritarianism to democracy and from etatism to free markets – from Spain and Portugal in the 1970s to China in the 1980s and 1990s to post-communist nations and South Africa in the 1990s.

Crime mushrooms in the interregnum when the state's ability to police, control and direct is eroded but the institutions of civil society are still weak. It is hardly surprising that, in the 1990s, the largest increases in the incidence of violent crime were recorded in the countries where authoritarian and totalitarian control had been the harshest and longest lasting: Russia, Albania, China and South Africa.

In addition to the sudden collapse of the police state, several other circumstances made post-communist Russia particularly hospitable to organized crime: large and easily accessible markets (domestic and foreign), relatively cheap illicit goods for sale (alcohol, drugs, weapons) and a depressed 'legitimate' economy that makes criminal activity even more attractive by contrast.

Russia was also a gateway to the West for raw or finished drugs from Central and South-east Asia. The illicit goods it had for export were not just controlled substances but the remnants of the world's largest militarized empire (from conventional arms to sophisticated missile and nuclear technology), complete with tens of thousands of engineers and technicians, whose salaries were often unpaid for months at a time. The Russian gangs' ready recruits were not just the usual destitute, those demoralized and dislocated by an economic upheaval, but thousands of unemployed staffers of the enormous Soviet secret police apparatus: from KGB thugs to masters of international espionage.

Yet nothing underlined more vividly the age-old chasm between Russian state and Russian society than pandemic tax-evasion. As with most other blights, history, policy and politics combined with especially pernicious effect. Personal income tax was something entirely new to the Russians. In the case of the census-based 'poll' tax introduced by Peter the Great in 1718, payment was a seigniorial or corporate, rather than individual, responsibility discharged by the feudal lord, the village commune or the town. The wealthiest Russians – the nobles and the merchants – were exempt. Throughout pre-1917 Russian history, most revenue had to be raised by indirect taxes. Of these, the sale of vodka, which was a government monopoly farmed out to select traders, was by far the most profitable. Strained by the enormous standing Army, imperial expansion and endless wars, the Russian state covered the perennial deficit by producing paper rubles (*assignats*), first printed in 1769. Inflation was a constant fixture of the Russian economy.

After 1917, except for the six years of the New Economic Policy (NEP), which established a limited market between 1922 and 1928, the Soviet state was the sole owner and employer and there was no need for taxes, either corporate or individual. Indeed, the very notion of profit remained buried until the mid-1960s when the mildly reformist Prime Minister Aleksey Kosygin attempted, gingerly, to reintroduce it into the Soviet vocabulary and was swiftly thwarted by the industrial nomenklatura.

Almost a decade of improvisation and political expedience between 1987 and 1996 had produced an arcane system of more than 200 overlapping federal and local taxes and a crushing tax burden often amounting to more than 100 per cent of individual and corporate incomes. The predictable effect of such exorbitant, irrational and unfair taxation was compounded by bitterness, cynicism and a deep mistrust of the state born out of the decades of totalitarian lawlessness and by intense ideological division. In addition, for millions of Russians who wished for the return of the Soviet state and voted for the communists, the present regime was simply not legitimate enough to pay taxes to. In 1997, fewer than 5 per cent of Russians would file income tax returns.

While some of the largest FIGs deployed their enormous political power to avoid paying taxes, those without protectors in high places went underground. Russian and foreign experts estimated that between 25 and 40 per cent of the country's GDP came from the 'shadow' economy, concealed from the tax-collector and statistician alike.[9]

Meanwhile, a potentially huge source of revenue remained blocked by the Duma. For almost three years, since Yeltsin's first land-privatization decree in October 1993, the communist-led majority – fearing the emergence of petit-bourgeois landowners, the Bolsheviks' worst enemy – had blocked laws allowing the selling, buying or mortgaging of land, in the city and countryside alike. One can only imagine the untold billions lost to the Treasury from the sale of millions of hectares of state-owned land and from taxes on transactions carried out by private owners.

A central political problem in the transition from 'traditional' societies to industrial capitalism was the fate of 'surplus' labour, mostly peasants and independent craftsmen, unable to compete with more efficient modes of production. Dispensing with entire occupations and branches of industry was a brutal affair, in which enormous suffering was inflicted on hundreds of thousands of men, women and children. In Britain at the beginning of the industrial revolution between 1780 and 1810, eight out of ten farmers and farmhands were forced off the land and, with their families, turned into impoverished vagabonds. Along with the urban poor, they were starved in poorhouses, branded, hanged or shipped to colonies. Since West European capitalism preceded one-person one-vote democracy by over a hundred years, the dispossessed had no voice in policy-making and, short of periodic riots and revolts, they suffered in silence. *Mutatis mutandis*, the same combination of disfranchisement and suppression was applied on the road to developed capitalism by the 'modernizing authoritarianisms' of South-east Asia, Latin America and China. (In the first decades of the twenty-first century several hundred million dispossessed and impoverished peasants are bound to become the key destabilizing force in China, where the fear of this instability has accounted for the absence of political liberalization.)

Among other innovations, post-communism was unique in extending democratic liberties to its own surplus workforce, concentrated mostly in the obsolescent heavy industries (including steel production, coal mining, machine tools, shipbuilding); in collectivized or primitive semi-private agriculture; and in sectors incapable of competing with cheaper and better imports suddenly made available (textiles, food processing, clothing, car and truck making). The millions of surplus workers and adult members of their families enjoyed full political rights, most importantly the right to vote. The parties that represented them were free to compete and to win.

Over the centuries, the political, ideological and economic trends that swept Europe became especially intractable or extreme upon crossing the Russian border. Post-communism was no exception. In addition to the usual assortment of 'surplus' industries inherited by all post-communist economies, Russia was distinguished by a moribund country-side and by the size of its military–industrial complex, the product of sixty years of a wartime economy. Consuming at least 30 per cent of GDP until 1992, the defence industry supported directly or indirectly every third Russian man, woman and child.*

When in October 1996 one of the top Russian bankers, Mikhail Khodorkovskiy, said that the 'whole country [was] a bunch of bankrupt companies',[10] he was not far from the truth. A few months earlier, First Deputy Prime Minister Oleg Soskovets estimated that 35 per cent of all plants and factories were 'technically bankrupt'. Russian experts believed that 80 per cent of the country's 2.6 million industrial enterprises were 'in serious financial trouble', half owed the government back-taxes and one-third were 'outright tax fugitives'.[11]

Unlike the post-communist nations of Central and Eastern Europe, the millions of surplus workers and their families were represented in

---

* In 1998, after several years of relentless budget cuts and arms-control agreements, the Russian state still employed 1.5 million workers in nuclear research and development alone.

national politics not by reformed, social-democratized communists but by the hard-line KPRF at the head of the 'popular-patriotic' bloc, whose Deputies had secured a solid plurality in the national legislature and whose Presidential candidate had received 40 per cent of the vote. Yet again in its star-crossed history Russia found itself in the worst of all worlds: of all post-communist nations (with the exception of Albania) its economic legacy was the heaviest, its surplus population the largest both in absolute and relative terms, and its left the most radical.

A study commissioned in 1989 by Mikhail Gorbachev had concluded that total privatization would, in the very first year, result in forty million unemployed.[12] Even if, by an optimistic estimate, after four years of steady diminution of the state ownership, the number was half that, the political imperative required continuing state responsibility for hundreds of enterprises and for the economic well-being of millions of workers, whom the regime could neither abandon nor, in the absence of minimally sufficient tax revenue, support adequately.

Stalinist industrialization had created thousands of 'company towns', where enterprises owned and operated kindergartens, hospitals, schools and the apartment buildings of their workers. Entire secret 'closed cities' grew around missile and tank plants and nuclear research centres. If there was a politically (and morally) acceptable way to let these plants and factories go bankrupt without government subsidies, without loans and salaries from the Treasury, such a solution could not be found either by the President in the Kremlin or by the Ministers in the White House (where, after a thorough repair and refurbishing, the government moved in 1994).

In the end, as is always the case in revolutions, the regime's central, most painful dilemma was political rather than economic: how, in a functioning, one-person one-vote democracy, deeply divided on the most fundamental issues of economic and social organization – private property, capitalism, Presidential republic – to implement policies that inflict pain (even if only in the short term) on millions of voters represented by an uncompromisingly hostile opposition, free to disseminate its views, to campaign and to get elected to local and national offices.

The answer, of course, was to follow the ebbs and flows of public opinion and the victories, defeats and pauses of the 'velvet revolution'. The chronology of Russian economic reforms reads like a political diary: the blitzkrieg of January–May 1992; the stalemate and the rearguard action between April 1992 and October 1993; another series of breakthroughs between October and December that year; another retrenchment in 1994 and 1995; and the resurgence of 1996. In this capitalism-by-consensus transition, offensives were followed by months of trench warfare and retreats.

Even as the regime cut defence appropriations by 90 per cent between 1992 and 1996, it continued to spend trillions of rubles on 'soft' loans to enterprises, which repaid only 14 per cent of the money lent.[13] It also continued to provide, free of charge, electricity to enterprises that had not paid for it in years. Even though the federal government owned only three out of ten enterprises in 1997[14] and was responsible for less than 20 per cent of the vast backlog in salaries (with the rest pocketed by enterprise owners, managers or local authorities), the people assumed that, in the end, the salaries were the government's responsibility. This was, as the Minister of the Economy put it, the 'price of social peace'.[15]

The most egregious case was that of the miners. An ossified relic of nineteenth-century industrialization, coal mining is a classic example of a surplus industry, depleting state Treasuries in Britain, Germany and Poland alike. Although virtually all Russian mines had been privatized (with the management getting most of the property), miners went on strike regularly and Moscow just as regularly paid them back-salaries, most of which were stolen by the middlemen and managers, almost everywhere connected to organized crime.[16]

The other half of the 'price of social peace' was the impoverished but vast welfare state. The government paid pensions to all women over fifty-five and all men over sixty, and it provided free medical care and free higher education. Among the largest drains on the budget were housing subsidies. The average urban family in Russia paid no more than 3 per cent of actual service costs. Even in Moscow, the country's most expensive city, where all apartments were nominally privatized, the average tenant paid only 17.6 per cent of the cost of electricity, heating and telephone. Every year, the share of the budget consumed by housing subsidies was higher than expenditure on defence.[17]

In the absence of market competition, the cost of utilities, provided by state-controlled 'natural monopolies' (gas, electricity, water), was almost as high as in Scandinavian countries,[18] while the quality of service was incomparably lower. The electricity monopoly charged the equivalent of 6 US cents for a kilowatt, which cost 2.5 cents in the United States.[19] With the state, rather than the tenants, paying the bill, the waste was predictable. For instance, compared to Western Europe and the United States, Russians used three times more water per person.[20]

Rightly considering low inflation and the stable ruble its major accomplishments and the key conditions of economic recovery, the government had since 1995 stoically refused to print money to cover the growing budget deficit. The two most dangerous consequences of this very risky combination of tight monetary and 'soft' fiscal policies were the chronic and severe shortage of money in the economy and the mushrooming of state debt. As the regime tried to hold down inflation, enterprises were forced to deal with one another in barter, which accounted for more than half of all transactions. Russian banks, short of cash, issued promissory notes (*vekseli*) instead of paying in cash. Barter and *vekseli* effectively shielded most economic activity from the tax collector. The vicious circle was now complete.

Unable to raise revenues in amounts anywhere near those commensurate with its expenditures, the regime financed the deficit largely with short-term, high-yield bonds, the GKOs (Gosudarsvennye Kommercheskie Obligatsii, or State Commercial Bonds). In this pyramid scheme, when payments fell due they were covered by the sale of more debt, the servicing of which consumed a growing share of the budget. As the budget deficit drove up bond interest rates, both foreign and Russian investors could get returns as high as 40 per cent simply by lending money to the Russian government for six months and saw little incentive in direct investment in the economy. Some of the largest Russian banks became little more than trading posts for GKOs. Economic recovery (and, with it, the prospect of adequate tax revenue) was eroded by the prohibitively high cost of credit, which in turn deepened the liquidity shortage and further impeded tax collection.

Until 3 July 1996, the central, most urgent question of the Russian transition was: can a non-authoritarian Russia govern itself? Now it was: can a non-authoritarian Russian state support itself?

On 10 July, when the Central Electoral Commission announced the final vote count, Yeltsin addressed the nation on television. He thanked his 'dear fellow citizens' for their understanding and support.[21] For him the victory was a sign of the 'great trust of a great people', and he understood that a huge responsibility had been placed on him.[22] The choice had been made not by 'the force of weapons or a revolution, nor by a decision of a Central Committee'. The people themselves had determined the country's path. 'Russia proved to the whole world that she was a democratic country ... abiding by [her] choice of freedom and democracy.'[23]

He knew that many had voted against him, Yeltsin continued, and he respected their choice. This vote was a 'serious sign' and an important lesson: all was not well in many regions, many enterprises had 'big problems', and he and his government had made serious mistakes.[24] The voters had spoken, and his task was to 'carry their will into practice'. He would see to it that pensions and salaries were paid on time. Fighting corruption was another urgent task. Most important of all, the reforms would be continued, but the focus of the economic policy would be growth in production. His main task was to make sure that enterprises received orders, that people had work, and that there was an improvement in the standard of living of every Russian family.[25]

The election was over. The Russians were now 'a united people', and Russia had everything it needed to ensure that the transition was brought to a successful conclusion in conditions of peace and order. That chance would not be missed: he had 'no doubt about it now!'[26]

Already very sick, Yeltsin managed only two steps in support of the 3 July mandate before surrendering to illness several weeks later. First, immediately after the election, he appointed Anatoliy Chubais the head of the Presidential Administration (Chief of Staff): a signal that the President intended to get involved in economic policy – and to give it a distinctly radical tilt. Moscow's liberal press interpreted Chubais's elevation as Yeltsin's announcement to 'all sorts of red and pink belts [where Zyuganov had received a majority]: no one should doubt the course of reforms'.[27] Indeed, hopes ran so high that the pro-reform pundits hastened to declare the appointment as portentous as Gaidar's ascent to the acting Prime Ministership in May 1992.[28]

A month later, Yeltsin carried out a central promise of his campaign. After scores of broken promises, agreements and ceasefires, and after a last fierce battle in which Chechen forces retook Grozny on 18 August, the commander of the Russian troops in Chechnya, Lieutenant-General Konstantin Pulikovskiy, and the Chief of Staff of the rebel forces, Aslan Maskhadov, initialled a truce. Two weeks later, in the early hours of 31 August, in the Dagestani village of Khasavyurt, Secretary of the Security Council General Aleksandr Lebed and Maskhadov signed an agreement that ended the war. Chechnya was granted 'political autonomy' and Russia was to begin withdrawing its troops immediately.* The final status of the Republic of Ichkeria (as the Chechen

---

* On 25 November Yeltsin ordered the withdrawal of the last Russian detachments from Chechenya. The opposition in the Duma was 'outraged'. The Chairman of the Security Committee of the Duma, communist Viktor Ilyukhin, denounced the move as the 'beginning of the break-up of Russia', and said he intended to initiate impeachment proceedings against the President. (Thomas de Waal, 'Deputies threaten to impeach Yeltsin', *The Times* (London), 26 November 1997, p. 11.)

separatists called their nation) was to be resolved in five years, by 31 December 2001. In the meantime, the Chechens agreed to suspend their drive for independence.

By late August the gravity of Yeltsin's condition could be concealed no longer. He had been absent from the Kremlin for over a month, returning only a few days before his inauguration on 9 August. Conceived as an occasion to celebrate the birth of a new, democratic Russian state and reclaim the symbols of the pre-Soviet past, the ceremony was to be a grandiose affair, complete with a thirty-gun salute and the tolling of the Kremlin bells. The guns were fired, the bells tolled, and St George speared the dragon on the President's banner raised over the Palace of Congresses, but the chief celebrant was pale and stiff, walked slowly on to the Palace stage and slightly slurred his words. From one hour, the ceremony was scaled down to twenty minutes, of which Yeltsin was in public view for only sixteen. He made no speech, just recited the oath of office for forty-five seconds. With his right hand on a copy of the Constitution Yeltsin promised, 'in exercising my powers as President of the Russian Federation, to respect and uphold the rights and liberties of the individual and the citizen'.

Even in the most private instances, Yeltsin could not help making history. When, in a nationally televised interview on 5 September, he announced that he would undergo heart-bypass surgery, it was the first public advance notice of a Russian leader's medical treatment. 'I want to have a society based on truth,' Yeltsin said. 'That means no longer hiding what we used to hide.'[29] He said he wanted an operation because it could lead to a complete recovery: 'passive' life had 'never worked for me and it won't work for me'.[30] He spoke slowly, his face swollen.

The procedure, known as coronary artery bypass grafting, was used to create a new network of vessels carrying blood and oxygen to the heart in order to restore the flow diminished when the original arteries are narrowed or blocked by fat deposits. A rather common cure in Western Europe and the United States (where half a million such operations were performed in 1995), there were at most 4,000 a year in Russia.[31] From the first, however, Yeltsin insisted on a Russian hospital and a Russian surgeon.[32]

Over the next two months Yeltsin was under constant, intrusive and often 'not terribly pleasant' monitoring necessary to raise his condition to an optimal level and determine the date of the operation.[33] He eagerly followed the directions, and, when this or that parameter showed improvement, proudly told the doctors that he carried out his promises.[34]

Just before the operation, he signed a decree delegating his authority, including the 'black suitcase' with codes for activating nuclear weapons, to Viktor Chernomyrdin.

In the early morning of 5 November, delivered from Barvikha to the Moscow Cardiological Centre in the Presidential limousine, Yeltsin insisted on walking into the pre-operation ward himself. He was perfectly coiffed and wore a suit and a tie.[35] He appeared in good spirits and joked as he was being undressed, injected with medications and attached to all manner of equipment. 'You've got your knife ready?' he asked his personal physician.[36]

Three, or at most, four arteries had been thought to be in need of repair. Instead, it turned out to be a quintuple bypass: five clogged vessels had to be detoured. Yeltsin's heart was stopped for sixty-seven minutes,[37] as a heart–lung machine circulated blood. The operation, performed by a twelve-man team, lasted seven hours.

Yeltsin regained consciousness early the next morning. As soon as the breathing tube was removed from his throat, he called an aide and signed a decree reclaiming the powers of the Presidency.[38]

The recovery was long and uneven. Yeltsin did not return to the Kremlin until 23 December and, two weeks later, was hospitalized again with flu and pneumonia. So when, on 6 March 1997, he mounted the podium in the Kremlin's Marble Hall to deliver an annual 'State of Russia' speech to a joint session of the Duma and the upper chamber, the Council of the Federation, those who wished the President and reforms well were prepared to be disappointed, even embarrassed. Yet the twenty-five-minute speech, which contained the highlights of a sixty-six-page address distributed among the Deputies, was delivered confidently, in a firm voice and a commanding style. The speaker looked much thinner than before, and was said to be 'trim', 'vigorous' and 'poised'.[39]

As would happen more and more often in the next year and a half, the President's physical state was the best predictor of his commitment to the reform effort. The address was the most comprehensive and detailed analysis of the state of reforms, of major obstacles to economic recovery, and of the role of the state in a new Russian economy ever made by Yeltsin. The document was remarkable also for its businesslike tone and for the specificity of the measures outlined and of the time allocated to their implementation. A well-integrated list of policies, this was more than an anti-crisis programme. It was a blueprint of the second phase of the economic revolution, the President's plan for rescuing Russian finance, and his agenda for the next eighteen months.

From the first sentence, Yeltsin sketched an unsparing portrait of his country. More than half of the population suffered from delays in the payment of salaries and pensions; the economy was being paralysed by the non-payment of debt owed by one enterprise to another; corruption was corroding the state apparatus.[40] It was intolerable, Yeltsin declared later in the address, that the majority of pensioners, teachers, doctors and soldiers could not, for months on end, receive what was legally theirs.[41] The mutual debts of enterprises reached hundreds of trillions of rubles and they dealt with one another through barter and all sorts of 'money surrogates'. How, under these circumstances, could 'market mechanisms' function?[42] Corruption and organized crime had in effect issued a brazen challenge to the Russian state.[43] Well-organized criminal groups worked hand in glove with corrupted officials, who often protected criminal businesses.

The Russian state was failing its citizens in its main function: as the keeper and enforcer of order. Yet 'order' – which, echoing the dominant concern of public opinion, Yeltsin made the leitmotif of the address – meant to him something different from the notion established by Russian political tradition:

> Our choice is an order based on law. An order that suppresses an individual, his freedom, his initiative and his dignity cannot become the basis of a modern society. It not only would be immoral and politically dangerous, but would doom the country to a hopeless backwardness . . . To establish order, the essence of which would be not a dictatorship and repression but community of purposes, intellect and accord, the energy of reconciliation and creation – this is a truly historic task for Russia.[44]

He welcomed 'serious shifts occurring in public consciousness'.[45] People were adapting to new opportunities afforded by the 'freedom of private activity and private initiative'.[46] They were also actively exploring the new means of protecting their legal rights granted by the Constitution.[47]

Yet, lagging shamefully far behind this new economic and political reality, the Russian state remained unworthy of the country's emerging civil society and private economy. Entirely novel functions of administration 'based on law, not commands' were performed by what was, in essence, the same old state, albeit 'slightly renovated'.[48]

In Yeltsin's design, a new Russian state ought to be a fair arbiter, an enforcer of rules and a helping hand to the poor and the struggling, not a collection of intrusive *nachal'nik*s. Its main task was to establish the rules ('unified, stable and obligatory for everybody') and to secure their fulfilment.[49] Economic justice did not consist of endless exceptions, privileges and exemptions, set up ('arbitrarily and not entirely selflessly') by bureaucrats; it derived from equality of conditions and clarity of rules – especially in relation to budget allocations and taxes.[50]

The 'separation of property and [political] power', which Egor Gaidar saw as the key to civilized capitalism,[51] was Yeltsin's preoccupation as well. Where possible, state contracts and state property ought to be open to free competition in order to increase efficiency, reduce waste, diminish opportunity for corruption and, of course, lighten the burden on the budget. There was, for instance, an untapped reserve of huge wealth in the state's possession: land. No long-term investment in the Russian economy could be secured until 'property rights' were established and land became part of 'market turnover' (that is, could be sold, bought and mortgaged). At the very least, the land on which newly constructed buildings stood ought to become the property of the buildings' owners.[52]

The key entitlement of the Soviet welfare state – heavily subsidized housing and old-age pensions for every woman over fifty-five and every man over sixty – ought to be sorted out and at least partly and gradually opened to the market in order to lighten the weight on the budget, eliminate waste and channel enhanced assistance to where it was needed most. The government, Yeltsin reiterated, spent eight trillion rubles ($1.4 billion) every month to subsidize rents, maintenance and utilities – almost $17 billion* a year, a quarter of all budget expenditure and 4 per cent of the country's GDP.[53] The system was both unfair and wasteful: those with larger apartments (usually the better off) received more assistance. Furthermore, the state monopoly in the utilities raised costs.[54] Yeltsin proposed a vast reform of the 'communal housing complex' to be designed three months from then and to be complete by the year 2000. The measures included the phasing out of subsidies, with tenants paying an increasing share of rent and services, while the state would secure fair competition between suppliers of water, electricity and heat, which in turn would diminish prices.[55]

There were thirty-seven million pensioners in Russia.[56] After promising to end the 'outrage' of delayed pensions by the middle of the year, Yeltsin proceeded to outline another grandiose reform: a gradual (no

---

* The ruble-to-dollar exchange rate fluctuated in 1997 between R5,650 for $1 in the first three months and R5,900 toward the end of the year. An average of R5,775 per dollar is adopted in these pages for calculating the dollar equivalent in 1997.

shorter than twenty years) transition to pension funds (private but strictly supervised by the state), into which an individual would deposit his or her money. Not only would such a system save trillions of rubles for the Treasury and help economic revival (since the funds would invest in the 'most solid projects'), it would make Russian men and women true masters of their savings, no longer dependent on the state and impervious to the 'blunders and arbitrariness of the bureaucrat'.[57]

Divesting the state of some of its largest obligations did not mean, however, that the government should abdicate its responsibilities to those truly in need of assistance. Along with guaranteeing freedom for the enterprising, the state's responsibility was to 'support the weak in a dignified manner'.[58] Yeltsin proposed reducing the enormous but shallow spread of the state's 'social obligations' (almost 100 million Russians were entitled to various forms of pension, stipend, subsidy or privilege),[59] which bankrupted the Treasury but made little difference to the lives of the millions of recipients. Instead, he proposed means-tested, targeted assistance that would cut millions off the rolls and use the saved funds to assist the truly needy effectively and without delays. Thus gradual privatization of housing was to be accompanied by the development of strictly targeted assistance (in the form of subsidies) to poor families.[60]

As for the economy, Yeltsin advocated a shift from the state's intimate involvement and full responsibility, from the interpenetration of 'property and power', which corrupted and stifled both partners, to a separation of the two combined with the enforcement of rules of fair play and competition. 'The state cannot and must not directly interfere in the affairs of private enterprises, but it must create stimuli for them to self-reform,' the President stated.[61] That self-reform should include the separation of the rights and responsibilities of management and ownership. The latter, usurped by the directors of many enterprises, belonged solely to the shareholders. It was the state's responsibility to enforce their ultimate control, without which the affected enterprises would remain 'unreceptive to innovations and unattractive to investors'.[62] Among the 'mechanisms of corporate governance', the acceptance and maintenance of which required state intervention, Yeltsin listed fulfilment of contractual obligations, the training of a new generation of managers, and the establishment of a new system of accounting, which would bring Russia's standards into line with those prevailing in the world's advanced economies.[63]

The burden of the welfare state, bureaucratic control, corruption and dominance by 'red directors' all contributed to the most urgent threat to reform: the budget deficit. It was far more than an economic problem, though it was a very grave one. A chronically impoverished state, incapable of timely and effective discharging of its responsibilities to society, was not worthy of its citizens' trust.[64] This was, more than anything, a crisis of confidence, which created a vicious circle: seeing little or no return from their taxes, people were reluctant to pay them, further undermining the state's ability to meet its obligations to society.[65]

Reduction of the budget deficit required that spending be brought into line with revenue, that budget allocation be transparent and that government contracts be subject to competitive bidding.[66] Not a single government purchase should be made without public disclosure of prices and conditions and of the list of documents demanded from bidders. From now on, officials who placed government orders through 'closed', secret procedures that bypassed open bidding would be regarded as 'directly encouraging corruption'.[67] A federal law governing the new bidding system would be submitted to the Duma within a month. In the meantime, it would be promulgated by a Presidential decree. To reduce waste and corruption further, the government would no longer guarantee commercial loans to enterprises,[68] and the armed forces would be further cut by 200,000 men.[69]

The state had to reduce its dependence on the sale of Treasury bills, the GKOs. Yeltsin gave the government three months to develop a detailed programme that would, by 1999, eliminate the need for domestic borrowing.[70] By that time, the state ought only to service old domestic debts, not to incur new ones. Whenever expenditure exceeded revenue, the budget should be reduced ('sequestered') accordingly.

Finally, urgent tax reform was a key to attracting investment in the country's economy.[71] The current system, under which there were exemptions from the majority of taxes, was contradictory and unfair,[72] and it encouraged tax evasion.[73] A new Tax Code, which, among other things, would drastically reduce the number of taxes and eliminate most privileges, was badly needed. Such a Code would be submitted by the government to the Duma within the next three weeks. Yeltsin urgently recommended that the legislature adopt the law before the end of the year.

As if admonishing himself as well as the Ministers, Yeltsin declared that 'the most important thing now [was] not to allow oneself to relax'.[74] 'For two years, we have not had the courage to begin a most urgent normalization of the financial and tax systems,' but now the time for procrastination, for 'marching in place and political manoeuvres' was past.[75] Instead of 'mending the holes', the government had to take bold decisions.[76] The successful conclusion of reform was now possible and the chance was not to be missed.[77] 'I want to hand over to my successor a country with a dynamically growing economy, with an effective and fair system of social protection, a country whose citizens are confident of their future,' the President declared.[78]

Yeltsin's top political adviser described the address as a 'postponed start' – and a 'last start'.[79] Moscow commentators agreed. What needed to be done – budget cuts, gradual privatization of housing, the tax, pension and enterprise reforms – was 'painful and unpopular'.[80] Tens of thousands of entrepreneurs, 'red directors', corrupt officials, the richest 'oligarchs' and their mouthpieces in the media would resist furiously, supported by the leftist plurality in the Duma, by millions who had voted for the communists, and, silently, by millions more who had been bitterly disappointed and impoverished by the changes.

This was, by the reckoning of Moscow experts, the last political opportunity before the end of Yeltsin's term in 2000: the 'last chance to civilize the Russian economy', to prove that Russia was capable of following the classic route of those Eastern and Central European nations which were now reaping the benefits of consistent and comprehensive reforms.[81] If the chance was missed, the next large-scale change of government would be conducted by 'other political forces'.[82]

Moscow political gossips correctly deduced that some 'cadre decisions' were imminent. Yeltsin himself had announced that he would like to see 'competent, vigorous people' in the government.[83] No one guessed, however, the extent, the speed and the brazenness of the changes announced two weeks later.

More than just a thorough shake-up, the replacement of almost every Minister and Deputy Prime Minister (except for Minister of Internal Affairs Viktor Kulikov and Foreign Minister Evgeniy Primakov) produced the most reformist cabinet since Gaidar's resignation in December 1992 – and a far more experienced one. Yeltsin elevated to Deputy Prime Minister the leading economic liberals: Alfred Kokh, who had taken Chubais's former post of chief privatizer in the State Committee for State Property, and Yakov Urinson, who also became the Minister of Economy. Another new Deputy Prime Minister was Oleg Sysuev, the reformist Mayor of the Volga city of Samara. Both Kokh and Sysuev were in their mid-thirties.

The ministries representing the military–industrial complex – Industry and Defence Industry – were abolished. The President fired the last two prominent Soviet *nachal'niks* in the cabinet: Deputy Prime Ministers Oleg Lobov (who supervised Russian industry) and Aleksey Zaveryukha, who was responsible for agriculture and had lobbied incessantly for more money to kolkhozes and sovkhozes. Even the perennial Chief Aide Viktor Ilyushin got the axe. With his and Lobov's departure, Yeltsin severed his last links to the Sverdlovsk Obkom. He seemed to have kept Chernomyrdin only because a new Prime Minister would have had to be confirmed by the Duma. The President felt very pressed for time.

While keeping Chernomyrdin, however, Yeltsin surrounded his plodding, verbally dyslexic Prime Minister (whose main asset was his ability to find a 'common language' with the Duma) with First Deputy Prime Ministers of entirely different political pedigree and generation. One was Boris Nemtsov, the thirty-seven-year-old Governor of Nizhniy Novgorod, a major military–industrial region 400 kilometres south-east of Moscow (and the site, as Gorkiy, of Andrey Sakharov's exile). One of the few perestroika 'democrats' to become a successful professional politician, Nemtsov was even a greater rarity: a very popular Governor. Appointed the head of the Regional Administration by Yeltsin in 1991, he was elected with 60 per cent of the vote in December 1995.

During his six years in Nizhniy, Nemtsov (who obtained a PhD in physics when he was twenty-six) turned the region into a free-market laboratory. Registration of private business, which in most of Russia involved months of tortuous, bribe-laden petitioning, became so simple that it could be conducted by mail, and the absence of a response meant approval. Without formally privatizing farmland, he succeeded in enabling kolkhoz members to acquire individual plots. Among his many innovations were regional bonds, 'free enterprise zones', in which struggling enterprises were given tax breaks, and a clean-water programme for schoolchildren. Nemtsov had also begun reducing the ruinous and wasteful responsibility of enterprises for housing and other 'social services' in company towns. Instead, plants and factories were encouraged to give workers a monetary equivalent of subsidies through higher salaries, so that the employees could afford to pay for rent and utilities themselves. One of the most determined opponents of the Chechen war, Nemtsov initiated a drive to collect one million signatures for a petition to end the hostilities.

Despite Yeltsin's repeated entreaties, Nemtsov had been reluctant to leave Nizhniy. The tasks the President was calling on him to perform – an overhaul of the Russian welfare state, housing privatization and reform of the natural monopolies (gas, water, electricity, railways) – were, in Nemtsov's words, politically suicidal.[84] Even the well-publicized hints from the Kremlin that he, a Jew and an intellectual, was the anointed successor for the year 2000, had failed to persuade him.

In the end, he succumbed, as he put it, to the 'only thing that could change my mind: the President's will'.[85] After Yeltsin had dispatched his daughter Tat'yana D'yachenko as his emissary to Nizhniy, Nemtsov came to Moscow. As he welcomed Nemtsov in the Kremlin in the presence of television cameras, Yeltsin told the Nizhniy Governor that he had a challenging offer for him: 'young men will set up a fresh young team from scratch'.[86] Yeltsin promised that all ministerial appointments would be cleared with Nemtsov, now a new First Deputy Prime Minister.

'The President is full of commitment to restore order,' Nemtsov told journalists afterwards. 'We will do it together.'[87] He added: 'I will not lie; I will not take bribes or steal. I will explain to people what I am doing, including the most unpleasant things . . .'[88]

Yet the most unambiguous signal of Yeltsin's determination to carry out a 'second economic revolution', and of the amount of political capital he was willing to expend, was given by his choice of the other First Deputy Prime Minister. He appointed Anatoliy Chubais almost immediately after the 6 March address, before anyone else.

Russia's pre-eminent human rights activist and former political prisoner Sergey Kovalev said of Chubais: 'The proverb says: "Tell me who your friends are, and I will tell you who you are." With respect to Chubais, I would put it differently: "Tell me who your enemies are, and I will tell you who you are." '[89] With the sole exception of Yeltsin, there was no one, but no one, among 150 million Russians, whom the 'popular-patriotic' left and its representatives in the Duma hated with greater intensity or denounced with greater venom and frequency than the tall, red-haired, forty-two-year-old who had privatized the Russian economy, conquered wild inflation and organized Yeltsin's Presidential campaign.

The opposition's reaction was prompt. *Sovetskaya Rossia* responded with a page-one cartoon portraying Anatoliy Chubais as a serpent coiled around Yeltsin as the President signed the decree appointing him First Deputy Prime Minister. The serpent's skin was covered with Stars of David.[90] A week after Chubais's appointment, communists in the Duma announced that they would seek a vote of no confidence in the government.[91] A month later, at the KPRF congress, which began with the singing of the Soviet Union's anthem and ended with a rendering of the 'Internationale', the communists declared a 'change of the ruling regime' their main goal.[92]

A PhD in economics from the Leningrad Institute of Engineering and Economy, Chubais belonged to an elite group of young radical economists who had formed the core of Egor Gaidar's government in November 1991. The thirty-five-year-old Prime Minister decided that he could not find a better 'privatization tsar' than his thirty-six-year-old friend. The 'usually unflappable Tolya sighed heavily' and asked Gaidar if he understood that, by this appointment, he had made him, Chubais, into a man who for the rest of his life would be 'accused of selling Russia . . .'[93] By that time, Chubais was a veteran *perestroishik*: a leader of the Leningrad Perestroika movement and the author of its economic programme; a participant in the Democratic Platform organized by his brother Egor; First Deputy Chairman of the Executive Committee of the Leningrad City Soviet and principal economic adviser to Leningrad's first elected Mayor, the radical democrat Anatoliy Sobchak.

In October 1994, Chubais was given the title of First Deputy Prime Minister and ordered by Yeltsin to save the country from hyperinflation – and the regime from collapse. He did so by bringing down the annual rate of inflation from 200 per cent in 1994 to 22 per cent in 1996. As with privatization, however, the politics exacted an exorbitant price. Chubais was not strong enough to take on powerful tax dodgers among the largest banks, enterprises or natural monopolies (especially Prime Minister Chernomyrdin's *alma mater*, the natural-gas giant Gasprom). Nor was he able to eliminate tax exemptions and import subsidies, which some of his fellow Deputy Prime Ministers were busily selling, or to reduce the state subsidies for housing and the utilities. And, of course, he was powerless to stop the war in Chechnya, which cost billions of rubles every day.

Instead, he tamed inflation by drastically cutting the budget's outlays and by plugging the budget holes with proceeds from the sale of short-term government securities (often yielding a 100 per cent after-inflation hard-currency return), and with heavy borrowing abroad. There followed, inevitably, delays in the payment of pensions and wages and further diminution of productive investment, as Russian banks and foreign investors rushed to lend to the government, rather than to the entrepreneur.

Surrounded by the veterans of Gosplan accustomed to the abacus and the slide-rule, Chubais had two computers: a large one on his desk and a personal laptop, which he took with him to every meeting: the laptop contained 'everything', from the tactics of the day's political battles to long-term economic strategy.[94]

Chubais personified modernity in ways that extended beyond the laptops, the fifteen-hour working days and the button-down collars which he had introduced into the Kremlin. When in the autumn of 1996 he was accused by the muckraking *Moskovskiy Komsomoletz* of earning thousands of dollars in speaking and consulting fees, Chubais was expected by everyone to respond as many other Russian politicians had done when faced with similar accusations: by dismissing the charge as 'malicious falsehoods instigated by enemies', and bombarding the 'enemies' with detailed charges of their far greater alleged malfeasance. Instead, he promptly and quietly paid the Treasury the ruble equivalent of $94,000 and laid the matter to rest. A stupefied Moscow was torn between anger at yet further proof of high living by the political class, admiration for the civilized way Chubais had dealt with the matter, and a desperate hope that others, inside and outside the government, would react to media criticism in the same way.

The prodigious chores of 1991 to 1997 revealed Chubais's distinct and consistent *modus operandi*. Although a member of the Russian intelligentsia in its most self-consciously snobbish Joseph Brodsky–Mihkail Baryshnikov Leningrad version, Chubais was a very unusual *intelligent*. In Russian history this most peculiar tribe has manifested two distinct personalities: first, the unyielding fanatic, convinced of his own infallibility, eager to remake the world, and thus self-absolved of any and all crimes that might have to be committed in the process; second, the hesitant moralist who will not act before undertaking an exhaustive soul-searching, which invariably convinces him that from both an ethical and practical point of view a plan (any plan of action) is unacceptably contaminated and hopelessly compromised and must not therefore be embarked on. In its former incarnation, the Russian intelligentsia has been murderous; in the latter, pitiful.

Chubais was a Russian historical rarity: a tough, pragmatic and practical liberal. From privatization to inflation to Presidential elections, in each of these fields, he invariably chose the largest dragon to slay, and pursued it relentlessly – often at the price of letting dozens of smaller ones escape. Hamstrung by the democratic politics of a deeply divided nation, he did not look for 100 per cent solutions. He would take 70 per cent, 60 per cent or even 51 per cent: flawed, to be sure, but on balance the best that could be done under the circumstances to move him a few inches closer to the paramount goal – the non-violent expurgation of the seventy-five-year-old legacy of Bolshevism from the Russian economy and politics.

'So what do we have after five years of reform?' Chubais was asked at the end of 1996. 'What kind of capitalism has been built, Anatoliy Borisovich: "state", "nomenklatura", "criminal"?' 'It is too early to sum up,' Chubais answered. 'The process is not complete. There are giant holes in the edifice. Many weight-bearing parts of the structure are not strong enough. Several segments are simply wrong and even harmful. Yes, there is a danger of a nomenklatura capitalism. There is a danger that the half-constructed building will be frozen in its current version: with all the holes and rusty armature. No matter where you look, you see how much has been done – and how much more still needs to be accomplished. Still, there is a real chance for us to finish the construction of at least the main areas of both the state and the economy by the year 2000.'[95]*

By the third week of March 1997 the new government had defined and made public the goals of the 'second economic revolution' and the policies that would help to attain them. The overarching objectives were the long-promised economic growth, an increase in direct investment in the economy and the liquidation of the backlog in pensions and salaries.[96] The most urgent priorities announced by Anatoliy Chubais were an increase in budget revenues and a shrinking of the budget deficit.[97] Boris Nemtsov was to open government contracts to competitive bids (including military procurement), to take on the natural monopolies (especially electricity and the railways) and force them to lower their tariffs, to cut the cost of housing utilities by 30 per cent through market competition, and to reform the Pension and Social Insurance Fund, which was financed by contributions from employees and employers and was designed gradually to shift the enormous old-age pensions burden from the state on to individuals.[98] The enterprise reform, managed by the Ministry of Economy under Yakov Urinson, was to take Russian industry from the 'red directors' by separating the manager from the owner, by overhauling corporate governance, upholding and protecting shareholders' rights, and enforcing court decisions.[99] This was, as a Russian commentator put it, an attempt by 'pro-market technocrats' to save the country's economy by 'destroying the foundations of nomenklatura capitalism'.[100]

The next six months, between April and October 1997, were the most

---

* As Yeltsin's 'special envoy to the International Financial Organizations', Chubais negotiated in July 1998 a multi-billion-dollar emergency loan to Russia from the International Monetary Fund and the World Bank. Two months later, in an interview with a Russian newspaper, he said that, in order to secure the desperately needed cash, he had 'conned' his negotiating partners by describing the Russian financial situation as considerably better than it was.

intense reform period since 1992. Five years before, however, Yeltsin had not been anything like as closely engaged in the daily management of the economic revolution as he was now. According to the President's chief economic adviser, Yeltsin worked extremely hard preparing for monthly economic meetings with the Prime Minister.[101] He went over every aspect many times. Relishing his mastery of exotic detail, he sometimes interrupted the economic briefing to phone Chernomyrdin and challenge him over the money supply or interest rates.[102]

Dozens of decrees, some of which had been delayed for years by political considerations, were now signed by Yeltsin with a flourish. The bulk of the executive orders was aimed at divorcing 'power and property', the union that was at the foundation of nomenklatura capitalism. Billions of dollars' worth of revenues (for instance from arms sales and customs duties) were no longer to be deposited in a handful of authorized banks, belonging to the richest oligarchs, but were transferred directly to the Federal Treasury.[103] Starting on 1 January 1998, the servicing and distribution of government funds by private banks would be awarded through open and competitive bidding.[104] Another decree prohibited government guarantees for commercial bank loans to enterprises.

Yeltsin signed a decree on open bidding for government contracts, including military procurement. Drafted by Nemtsov, the order made all government contracts costing more than 900 million rubles (around $156,000) subject to competitive bidding, the rules of which were to be published in national newspapers. The winners were to be nominated 'in the media's presence'.[105] 'We are putting all state procurement on a competitive basis,' Yeltsin told the Council of the Federation. 'We are blocking the opportunities for a distribution of our taxpayers' money behind the scenes.'[106]

Direct foreign participation in privatization auctions was now allowed. In addition, Yeltsin signed the 'product-sharing' law which permitted foreign investment in developing several oil, gas, iron and gold sites in exchange for a share of extracted resources.[107] Another Presidential decree lifted restrictions on foreign ownership of shares in Russian oil companies, which since 1992 had been limited to 15 per cent.[108]

Privatization again became a priority. Almost 2,000 enterprises were sold by September 1997, the sales bringing in almost 14.4 trillion rubles ($2.5 billion) – ten times more than the amount received within the same period the previous year.[109] A new mode of privatization dealt another blow to nomenklatura capitalism. The oligarchs could no longer acquire the choicest pieces of Russian industry at bargain-basement prices at 'insider auctions' or by lending to the government in exchange for company shares. (The law prohibiting loans-for-shares deals was signed by Yeltsin in August.)

In a sale that was intended to epitomize the new rules of the game, the government put on the block a 25 per cent stake in the national telecommunication company Svyazinvest. Several oligarchs immediately flew to France, where Chubais was holidaying, to agree on a winner. Chubais reportedly answered: 'He whose bid is the largest will win.'[110] Sealed tenders were submitted, the largest offer carried the day and the winner* had to pay the market price: $1.875 billion, $700,000 of it in cash right away. The losers immediately unleashed a vitriolic attack on Chubais and his team in dozens of newspapers and television programmes they owned or controlled. The Svyazinvest deal was portrayed as rigged. Yeltsin responded by dismissing a key Chubais ally, the privatization tsar Alfred Kokh. This action reflected a pattern in Yeltsin's relationship with the reformers: he would promote them despite the howls of parliament but then unceremoniously dispose of them once a scandal or misstep raised the political cost above what he was prepared to pay.

To Nemtsov, the importance of the Svyazinvest auction (which he insisted had been 'open and fair' and had been won by the 'company that paid more than the rest') extended well beyond the record remittance to the Treasury.[111] This was an attack on those who did not 'need fair rules and democratic capitalism', those who wanted instead a 'bandit capitalism'.[112] Russia faced a 'stark dilemma', Nemtsov added. 'Either the government serves our ['robber-baron'] capital, or it moves to establish . . . regulations that will make it possible to normalize our national situation.'[113]

Striving to reduce the budget deficit, the government imposed a 'sequester', cutting expenditure by 20 per cent across the board. The suddenly aggressive State Tax Service took on some of the most formidable non-payers: among them, a giant metallurgical plant in Chelyabinsk, the Moscow Oil Refinery and the automobile manufacturers of Ulyanovsk. These enterprises were given a deadline and told to pay in cash – or face the dismissal or even prosecution of their directors.[114] Even the biggest Russian company, Gasprom, was no longer able to 'negotiate' its taxes and paid almost fourteen trillion rubles ($2.4 billion) in back-taxes. By the end of May, the government had cleared the

---

* Led by Vladimir Potanin's Uneximbank, the consortium included Deutsche Bank's Deutsche Morgan Grenfell, Morgan Stanley Asset Management and George Soros's Quantum Fund.

pension backlog. By September the interest rate on government bonds had decreased to 20 per cent, its lowest level ever.

Another Presidential decree drafted by Nemtsov forbade budget funding for the purchase of foreign cars for official use. Government garages were ordered to auction off the pride and joy of post-Soviet *nachal'nik*s: the Mercedes, the Opels, the BMWs. From now on, officials were to travel in Russian vehicles. On 15 May Yeltsin signed a decree mandating the filing of income and property declarations by federal and regional officials. He promised that the media would have access to the declarations. Two weeks later, the 'information on income and property' of the President was released, followed by those of Chernomyrdin, Chubais and Nemtsov.[115]

Decentralization of the Russian state continued apace. On 1 August Yeltsin and the Governor of the Samara *oblast*, Konstantin Titov, signed a power-sharing agreement, delineating the rights and responsibilities of federal and local authorities. In the previous three years, Yeltsin had reached over thirty such accords.

In the summer of 1997 the President issued a decree specifying the previously ill-defined rights and duties of 'plenipotentiary representatives of the President' in the provinces. From a kind of roving busybody, the President's representative in the regions was to become (in the words of the top official of the Presidential Administration responsible for 'work with the regions') 'first of all, a co-ordinator, an intermediary', whose job is 'akin to diplomacy'.[116] Charged with supervision of federal agencies, the representatives were now explicitly forbidden to interfere in the work of the local administrations. Those who thought themselves above the governor would be 'asked to leave'.[117]*

The economic independence of the regions was bolstered by a novel procedure of revenue collection announced by Yeltsin in September 1997. Regional branches of national companies were to pay corporate taxes directly to the regions where they were based rather than to those in which their headquarters was located (that is, in most cases, Moscow).[118] Similarly, enterprises would pay federal and regional taxes through the local branches of the Federal Treasury, instead of sending them to Moscow.[119]

With a more equitable sharing of wealth came a fairer division of

---

* Fresh from elections, some of the more popular governors began to demand further reductions in Moscow's power. After a landslide victory in the previous year's election, the Saratov Governor Dmitriy Ayatskov threatened to 'liquidate' the post of Presidential representative in Saratov because such a post was 'unconstitutional'. (*RFE/RL Newsline*, 27 August 1997.)

responsibilities, which significantly unburdened Moscow. Regions were to pay half of the overdue wages owed to state employees, while the federal authorities would provide the other half.[120] In an apparent effort to decentralize revenue collection still further, in September 1997 Yeltsin signed a law that allowed municipalities below the regional level to keep a larger share of federal and regional taxes collected in their areas. According to the Kremlin, the measure was to provide 'some legal guarantees for the financial independence' of local governments.[121]

On 12 November 1997, the Saratov *oblast* Duma put regional autonomy to a critical test by adopting a law that allowed the purchase and sale of farmland, the first such legislation in the country. The next day, the Federal Duma, whose own Land Code Yeltsin had vetoed because it barred the sale of land, passed a resolution denouncing the Saratov measure as unconstitutional. Yeltsin responded by promptly awarding Governor Dmitriy Ayatskov an order 'For services to the Fatherland'.

Behind these exertions was a Yeltsin not seen since 1991: confident, vigorous, even 'chipper'.[122] He bragged about losing nearly thirty kilos since his operation.[123] He again relished risk and battle. He was daunted neither by the size and intricacy of challenges nor by the number and fury of his opponents. He appeared on television almost every day, signing decrees, welcoming Russian and foreign dignitaries, answering impromptu questions from journalists. He extolled the market and a free economy.[124] When he travelled to Denver, Colorado for the G-7 meeting of the leaders of the largest industrial democracies his fitness, energy and good cheer mirrored the newly found respect for Russian democracy and Russian reforms. Except for one hour-long technical session, he was privy to all deliberations and signed the final communiqué. The summit was renamed the 'Summit of the Eight'. And this group of the most powerful free nations was now known as 'G-8'.

Yeltsin felt politically strong enough to raise one of the most divisive issues in a land riven by ideological schisms: Lenin's mummified body in the Mausoleum on Red Square. The issue was so explosive that Yeltsin had left it alone even after the key victories over the communist hard-liners in 1991, 1993 and 1996. He now proposed holding a national referendum on what to do with Lenin's body. He wanted to bury this symbol of the Soviet past. 'Red Square must not resemble a cemetery,' he said. 'The dead must be buried in the earth.'[125] Of course, he added, the communists would 'fight this, but I am used to fighting them'.[126]

Apparently with energy to spare, he reached beyond economic reform and domestic politics to make 1997 the best year of Russia's painful post-imperial adjustment, a year to be remembered as the Year of Peace. On 12 May, he signed a formal peace treaty with the newly elected Chechen President Aslan Maskhadov. Standing in the Kremlin side by side with the former 'terrorist' and 'bandit', now accorded all the honours of a head of state, Yeltsin referred to the area by its indigenous name, Ichkeria – something he had never done before. Yeltsin saw the 'historic significance' of the treaty in putting an end to 400 years of war between Russia and Chechnya.[127] While the negotiations on the final status of Chechnya were postponed until the year 2001 (to allow, as Yeltsin had said earlier, 'for the wounds to heal and for emotions to be replaced by common sense'),[128] in all but form the settlement established the virtual independence of Chechnya. Maskhadov promised that there 'would be no place for terrorists and kidnappers in Chechnya'.[129] Soon Moscow would commit trillions of rubles to the reconstruction of Chechnya and in compensation to its citizens.

A few days later, also in the Kremlin, Moldova's President Petru Lucinschi and the leader of the five-year-old, self-declared Transdniester Republic (a secessionist enclave of ethnic Russians and Ukrainians on Moldova's border with Ukraine) signed a memorandum that effectively affirmed Moldova's sovereignty over the disputed area. The signing was attended by Yeltsin and Ukrainian President Leonid Kuchma – the 'co-guarantors' of the accord.

In June, at another Kremlin signing, the leaders of the Dushanbe regime and of the Islamic opposition ended the five-year civil war in Tajikistan. That same month, President Vladislav Ardzinba of Abkhazia (which had seceded from Georgia after heavy fighting in 1993–4) spent two weeks in Moscow with top-level mediators, Yeltsin's Chief of Staff Valentin Yumashev among them, discussing an 'interim protocol' for settling the conflict. In August, Ardzinba travelled to the Georgian capital of Tbilisi for his first face-to-face meeting with President Shevardnadze since the war began.

In September, in the presence of Viktor Chernomyrdin, the Presidents of North Ossetia and Ingushetia (Autonomous Republics within the Russian Federation) signed an agreement that ended the dispute over North Ossetia's Prigorodny district, where fighting had broken out in November 1992. Over the next two days, in the Lithuanian capital of Vilnius, Chernomyrdin met with the Presidents of Estonia, Latvia and Lithuania to resolve outstanding issues in the border disputes between the Baltic nations and Russia.

Beyond the former borders of the Soviet Union, the Year of Peace yielded the Russia–NATO Founding Act on Mutual Relations, Co-operation and Security. After years of blistering criticism of NATO's decision to expand eastward and include former Warsaw Pact members, Yeltsin decided to forgo a rare chance to propitiate the 'popular-patriotic' left and reap political benefits from a confrontation with the West. He chose to accommodate rather than risk a reprisal of the Cold War. The Act committed both sides to 'building together a lasting and inclusive peace in the Euro-Atlantic area on the principles of democracy and co-operative security'. Russia and NATO affirmed that they did 'not consider each other as adversaries' and stated that they 'shared the goal of overcoming the vestiges of earlier confrontation and competition' while building mutual trust.

Although he was a quintessential 'domestic president' who tended to delegate much of the formation of foreign policy, Yeltsin, who travelled to Paris on 27 May for the signing of the Act, had made Russia's relationship with the United States and NATO his *domaine reservé*. 'Yeltsin was the key to everything,' a top US official told journalists before the signing. 'At critical moments, it was Yeltsin who provided the decisive leadership by giving indisputable signs of where he wanted to go.'[130]

Three days later, in a radio address to the nation after he had signed the NATO–Russia Founding Act, he explained why he had done so:

NATO's plans to expand eastward . . . became a threat to Russia's security. How were we to react to this? Any split [between Russia and the West] is a threat to everybody, and that is why we opted for talks with NATO. The task was to minimize the negative conse-quences of the North Atlantic alliance's expansion and prevent a new split in Europe.

Dear Russian citizens! There have been a lot of changes in Europe in recent years. The barriers that divided the people on four continents have collapsed. Fear is gone and it must now go away completely. We trust each other more and have begun to get to know each other really well. This is what the building of a larger, peaceful Europe means – a Europe in which every nation feels comfortable.

By signing the Russia–NATO document, the leaders of seventeen countries have confirmed that there will be a new, peaceful Europe [which will] not be divided into blocs. Every one of us needs this, and Russia needs it too.[131]

Yet by far the most momentous event of that busy year was the Treaty of Friendship, Co-operation and Partnership between the Russian Federation and Ukraine, signed by Yeltsin and President Leonid Kuchma in Kiev on 31 May. Under the terms of the treaty, the two nations undertook to 'respect each other's territorial integrity' and the 'inviolability of the existing borders', and pledged 'mutual respect, sovereign equality, peaceful settlement of disputes, non-use of force or its threat'.[132] The accord between Europe's largest nation and its sixth most populous was central to the post-Cold War European order.

Coming after five years of difficult negotiations, the treaty was all the more startling because there had been so many auguries of failure. After Ukraine dealt a mortal blow to the Soviet Union by first declaring its independence on 24 August 1991 and then overwhelmingly ratifying that choice in the national referendum in December of that year, the technical complexity of many unresolved issues between Russia and Ukraine bordered on intractability. On more than a few occasions, Yeltsin had salvaged the negotiations by personal intervention.

One such problem was the fate of the Black Sea Fleet, which both nations could legitimately claim. Another contentious point was sovereignty over the beautiful and fecund Black Sea peninsula of Crimea, where ethnic Russians outnumbered Ukrainians by more than two to one. Wrested by Catherine the Great from the Ottoman Empire at the end of the eighteenth century, Crimea had been for almost two centuries a staple of Russian poetry and the most popular Russian resort, teeming with vineyards, tsars' summer palaces and dachas of the best Russian painters, musicians and writers. The peninsula was 'given' to the Ukrainian Soviet Socialist Republic by Nikita Khrushchev in 1954, when an independent Ukraine had seemed beyond the realm of the possible. Another political and emotional hurricane was unleashed by the possibility of Russia's handing over Sevastopol. Designated a City-Hero, it was a symbol of Russian military valour, displayed in the 1854–5 Crimean war against the British and the French and in the Second World War against the Germans.

Perhaps the greatest obstacle to the acceptance of Ukraine as a separate state was its unique place in Russia's historic memory and national conscience. Kiev was the birthplace of the first Russian state and its first Christian city. No other non-Russian part of the Soviet Union was so pivotal to Russian national identity as Ukraine.

In the end, Russia gave up Crimea and Sevastopol and ceded to Ukraine the entire Black Sea Fleet. Some of Sevastopol's naval bays were to be leased by Russia, and half of the Fleet was leased by Russia from

Ukraine, with payments subtracted from Ukraine's multi-billion-dollar debt to Russia for gas and oil deliveries.[*]

In Moscow, meanwhile, the extirpation of the Soviet imperial military machine proceeded implacably. When, in the third week of May, the government undertook its first across-the-board emergency spending reduction ('sequester'), defence was again the target of choice: funding for the armed forces and the military–industrial complex was reduced by 20 per cent.[133]

The new democratic legitimacy continued to erode the Kremlin's traditional deference for the military brass. In May Yeltsin fired the Defence Minister and the Chief of the General Staff for insufficient zeal in reducing and restructuring the armed forces. Two months later he ordered the retirement of 500 generals from the immensely bloated leadership of the armed forces. For the first time since 1945, the Victory Day military parade on Red Square on 9 May was cancelled so as not to disturb the construction of a giant underground shopping mall in adjacent Manezhnaya Square.

The year 1997 turned out to be the best not just of post-communist Russia's first six years. Although far from spectacular either in absolute terms (especially by the standards of old capitalist democracies), the combination of peace, freedom and prosperity was unprecedented in the whole of Russian history. Never before had so many Russians enjoyed as wide an access to what they called the 'civilized world' and its accessories – quality food, goods, services and pursuits – as in 1997. The Russian stock exchange doubled and redoubled again, becoming the best-performing stock market in the world.

The official statistics, however, were of little help in gauging the true

---

[*] The reaction of the 'national patriots' to the accommodations with NATO and Ukraine was predictable. Zyuganov denounced the Act as an 'act of unconditional surrender' and a 'betrayal' of Russia's interests ('Communists Respond to Attacks on Duma', *RFE/RL Newsline*, 30 May 1997). A drawing in *Sovetskaya Rossia* portrayed NATO generals rejoicing as they watched Yeltsin and Leonid Kuchma sawing the Black Sea Fleet in half (30 March 1996, p. 1). Another front-page cartoon in the same paper on 1 April 1997 shows President Bill Clinton and Secretary of State Madeleine Albright reviewing from a stand the Russian 'fifth column': 'Missis Olbrayt, nam by eshchyo v Kitae zaiemet' takuyu kolonnu!' ('Mrs Albright, how I wish we could have such a [fifth] column in China as well!'). Led by Yeltsin, Chernomyrdin, Chubais and Gaidar (with Gorbachev and Yavlinsky in the second row), the traitors carry a banner reading 'MAKE RUSSIA INTO A COLONY OF THE UNITED STATES!'

state of the economy and people's standard of living: between 50 and 70 per cent of trade was transacted in cash to prevent it 'surfacing' in bank ledgers. As much as 90 per cent of all private sector production, sales and profits might have been concealed from the authorities. Russian families were estimated to under-report their income by 40 per cent on average.[134]

From 1994 to 1997, between 35 and 45 per cent of the Russian economy was 'missing' from annual reports filed by the state statistical agency, the Goskomstat.[135] The private sector, where by now almost two-thirds of all Russians worked, was estimated to have grown by leaps and bounds since 1994 and overall production to have increased by 6 to 7 per cent every year. The country's economy as a whole was between 50 and 100 per cent larger than official statistics indicated.[136]

For millions employed by the state, the unreported income came from a second (or third) job, which often paid several times the official amount, and official wages accounted for only 40 per cent of people's income.[137] In private firms and stores, the salaries were said to be between 2.5 and 3.5 times higher than the figures posted by the owners in tax declarations.[138] Russian authorities estimated off-the-book earnings in 1996 to be 250 trillion rubles ($46 billion), or one-tenth of the country's GDP. With the data on people's expenses far more reliable than their self-reported incomes, experts found that both the per-capita income (officially estimated to be between 600,000 and 650,000 rubles or $103–112 a month) and the standard of living were between one-and-a-half and two times higher than reported to tax authorities.[139] Real income rose 2.5 per cent compared with 1996. Although 22 per cent of the population (thirty-one million people) were below the official poverty line, there were 1.4 million fewer of them in 1997 than a year before, and the poverty rate had declined steadily from 34 per cent in 1994.[140]

In 1997, the incidence of car ownership reached 31 per 100 families: a giant increase for a country where seven years before only 18 in 100 families had owned a car.[141] The number of cars in Moscow had tripled since 1989. Tourism became a national passion. Between sixteen and twenty million people, or every ninth Russian, travelled abroad in 1997, on holiday or on business.[142] Hundreds of automated cash machines appeared throughout the country in 1996 and 1997. There were thirty of them, for instance, in the smokestack Ural city of Chelyabinsk, 1,400 kilometres east of Moscow.[143]

Nineteen-ninety-seven was also the year of Russia's new, post-Soviet middle class. Of course, any direct comparison with European, let alone

American, counterparts was meaningless. As in every developing nation, only the very rich (no more than 3 per cent) could enjoy the living standards of the Western middle class. In Russia, this was the privilege of those whose minimal monthly incomes ranged between $4,000 (in Nizhny Novgorod) and $10,000* (in Moscow).[144] Instead, the most prized possessions of Russia's post-Soviet middle class are comparable to those of the post-Second World War European middle class: an apartment of one's own (in the Russian case, recently renovated to install a dishwasher, a cooker and perhaps a washer and dryer), a small car, a wooden shack of a dacha in the country, and an annual trip abroad.

Such possessions and pursuits were within reach of those making over $300 (or over $1,000 in Moscow) each month. Russian experts estimated the size of this income category to range from one-fifth to one-third of the country's population.[145] These were skilled workers in 'successful industrial and commercial enterprises', small and medium-sized entrepreneurs, middle-level managers, lawyers, accountants, teachers, journalists, programmers, drivers or tailors.[146]

In the madness of Moscow traffic, their used but sturdy Volkswagens and Toyotas held their own in the cavalcades of Jeeps, Mercedes and Cadillacs of the 'new Russians'. In their pleasures, and in the freedom and dignified frugality with which they pursued them, the new Russian middle class was quite similar to its counterparts in the West forty years before:

> They need only just enough [money] to realize that they live in a free country. And that [amount] they manage to earn. Many have already been to Paris and Rome, and spent time with their former colleagues and friends in Israel. In their travels they stayed in cheap hotels or at their friends', and did their own cooking. They have become normal citizens of Europe, who can enjoy themselves without luxury, and get a great deal of pleasure for little money.[147]

Already in August 1994, those bound for Paris on an Aeroflot flight were, according to an American reporter, 'positively middle class . . .

---

* Like citizens of all nations that experienced very high inflation most Russians re-calculated their incomes in dollars. Until 17 August 1998 a dollar's equivalent was close to six 'new' rubles, each worth 1,000 'old' ones. 'New' rubles were introduced by Presidential decree at the end of 1997 to underscore the victory over inflation. The average rate of R6=$1 is used in these pages for calculations from January to August 1998.

not wealthy or well connected but simply comfortable, determined and lucky . . . enough to have saved a few hundred dollars': a policewoman, a high-school chemistry teacher, a physiotherapist.[148]

Most of the growth in personal income was limited to large and middle-sized cities, where about half of the Russian population lived. Prosperity was slow to come to the depressed and depopulated countryside, which had never recovered from Stalinist collectivization and the losses of the Second World War, and to small towns, especially in the 'rust-belt' industrial areas. Regional differences were just as dramatic. Urbanized regions of Central Russia, the North-west, the Urals and the Far East boomed – especially those ruled by progressive Governors. In one such region, the free-market haven of the Novgorod *oblast*, per-capita income grew 70 per cent between 1995 and 1997.[149]

Where it did occur; the urban revival was nothing short of spectacular, as any visitor with memories of Soviet times could testify. The queues were gone, and so were streams of shabbily dressed people shuffling along cracked pavements – heads down, briefcases, sacks or the ubiquitous *avos'ka*s in hand – from one filthy store to another in search of fruit, sausage or cottage cheese. Instead, there were clean and colourful displays of produce and goods in the windows and brightly dressed, relaxed pedestrians, often munching on a cake or sandwich they had bought on the street.

Even in the absence of privatization of land, free commerce, market prices, a stable currency and efficient distribution resulted in a surplus of grain. In 1997, for the first time since the early 1960s, Russia could feed itself without importing grain and even had ten million tonnes to export after the 1997 harvest.[150]

The book industry thrived. Free to publish absolutely anything – from romance novels to Bill Gates, and from the memoirs of Egor Gaidar to books about Brigitte Bardot – Russian publishers were doing brisk business. Several thousand new titles, with a total print-run of five million, went on sale every month in Moscow alone.[151] Between 1994 and 1997, Russia's personal-computer market grew by 115 per cent. Another typical middle-class pursuit, charity, had also taken root: the number of independent charities in Russia grew from zero in 1988 to 60,000.[152] There were over 1,600 private high schools in the country: an almost ten-fold increase since 1991.

Unlike Soviet times, not only did milk become regularly available to Russian children everywhere without queues or rationing, but so did such formerly exotic produce as bananas and oranges. As one of the most knowledgeable and objective veteran Western reporters in Russia put it,

After seven years of painful market reform, Russia has not made much progress in restructuring the industrial behemoths that were the foundation of the Soviet economy. But in the retail and consumer sectors, the transition has been a dazzling success. Once a country in which oranges were a rarity, Russia has become a place where even the most obscure Siberian village has access to the full capitalist cornucopia of goods, ranging from computers to kiwi fruit.[153]

In the words of a popular Russian magazine, capitalism brought to Russia 'sneakers, jeans, modern clothes, television sets that did not explode, automatic washing machines, personal computers, effective medications, and much more . . .'[154]

While the lifting of price controls, waning government subsidies and privatization had hurt or impoverished millions of Russians, by 1997 millions of others, just as undeniably, had seen improvement in their daily lives. In 1995 a leading Russian sociologist estimated that a third of the population was doing 'reasonably well', a third was 'coping' and a third had 'suffered enormously'.[155] Two years later, another prominent observer concluded that 'nearly three-fourths of Russian citizens live better today than they did under the communists'.[156]

In 1997 age was as critical a determinant of people's view of their well-being as it was of their voting preference a year before. Those who overwhelmingly chose Yeltsin were the most content: 73 per cent of respondents aged sixteen to twenty-four and 67 per cent of those between the ages of twenty-five and thirty-five thought their lives had got better in the previous year.[157] Of men and women over sixty-five years old, 67 per cent said their existence had become worse or unbearable.[158] 'Most healthy adults under 35 were winners,' the *Economist* concluded.

In the summer of 1997, Moscow was in the midst of a baby boom. The number of babies born jumped by 35 per cent compared with the previous year – the first increase since 1991. 'People are feeling better about their lives and about life in general,' said a leading Moscow gynaecologist.[159] 'At least in Moscow, they feel that maybe things are going the right way. We are seeing women who have put these decisions off and now . . . they have decided that maybe it's worth taking a chance.' A young woman in a maternity ward added: 'I don't know if it's actually the political situation or the money or what. But I feel the climate is better, the hospitals are better, and maybe the country is getting better too.'[160]

Yet the prosperity was also very fragile. With the budget deficit still well over 5 per cent of GDP, the state could not overcome its GKO addiction. Although at a much lower interest rate, it was still borrowing billions of rubles every month. Domestic debt continued to balloon, while direct investment in the economy was stifled by the lure of Treasury bills.

With the government soon running out of measures that could be promulgated by executive order, structural reform began to slow down. Major policy changes required laws, which the Duma refused to pass. One after another, the implementation of key provisions of the 6 March programme fell victim to the legislature's resistance. Defended in the Duma as 'the crown jewels of the Russian economy', the natural monopolies proved invincible to Nemtsov's assault. The First Deputy Prime Minister had to retreat, solemnly pledging that the monopolies would not be broken up or opened to market competition.

The Duma also refused to adopt the key to welfare reform: the draft laws on 'social benefits'. Dispensed to 200 categories of citizens, various benefits (chief among them free public transport and subsidies for housing and utilities) cost the state forty-five trillion rubles ($7.8 billion), or around one-tenth of the entire budget. The government estimated that the reform would have saved thirty trillion rubles ($5.2 billion)[161] and increased assistance to the needy by introducing a means-tested, targeted benefit by eliminating the entitlement of tens of millions of people (in Nemtsov's words, by cutting 'senseless benefits' in order to pay teachers and doctors).[162] First in June, then again in September, the legislature voted down all fifteen draft laws in the government package.

Just as resolutely, the parliament's lower house rejected the privatization of land, critical to the emergence of a market economy, foreign investment and budget revenue. (Yeltsin called private ownership of land 'a tremendous resource for uplifting our economy, first of all agriculture'.)[163] In July the President vetoed a Land Code adopted by the parliament because it prohibited the buying and selling of farmland. 'The whole world works this way,' Yeltsin said. 'What are we afraid of?'[164] Two months later, the Duma overrode the veto. Citing 'flagrant procedural violations', including absentee voting, Yeltsin refused to promulgate what a government spokesman called 'the most reactionary measure ever passed by the Russian parliament'.[165] The President appealed to the Constitutional Court.

By far the most damaging in the short run were the interminable delays in the adoption of a new Tax Code. Reducing the overall tax burden by seventy-three trillion rubles a year ($12 billion, or over 2 per cent of GDP), cutting the number of federal and local taxes from 200 to 30 and establishing three rates no higher than 35 per cent of income, the Code was to become a giant step towards 'normalizing' the Russian economy. Lower and fairer taxes were to encourage the emergence of a large portion of the economy from the 'shadow' realm of concealed incomes and secret cash deals into the open where it could be recorded – and taxed. A simplified and transparent tax system, which drastically diminished the discretionary power of local authorities, was also important to attracting foreign investment.

To the reformers, a new Tax Code was the Holy Grail – the 'main thing', in Egor Gaidar's words, 'standing between us and serious, dynamic economic growth'.[166] If the Duma wanted 'production growth', Gaidar said in June, it ought to adopt the Code; if it did not, it should honestly say that it did not want a healthy economy.[167]

In September, Yeltsin himself pleaded with the legislators: 'A breakthrough can come only if the tax reform is implemented and a realistic budget for 1998 is adopted . . . It is a key task of the Federal Assembly to consider the Tax Code . . .'[168] To no avail. The communist plurality continued to resist the tax overhaul. As 1997 drew to a close, the Duma still would not pass the following year's budget.

Fully recuperated from the shellshock of Yeltsin's spring and summer blitzkrieg, the 'popular-patriotic' opposition launched its autumn offensive. With portraits of Stalin in hand, a thousand cheering delegates – Second World War veterans, Cossacks, nationalists, military officers – gathered in Moscow at the founding congress of the Movement in Support of the Army organized by the Chairman of the Duma's Defence Committee, General Lev Rokhlin. Attended by Viktor Anpilov, Aleksandr Korzhakov and Gennadiy Zyuganov (who made a speech), the gathering burst into applause when Rokhlin declared that 'as long as Yeltsin is in power, Russia will be dying'.[169] The General promised to instigate mass protests and to 'force' a new Presidential election.[170] Ten days later, leaders of thirty-two opposition parties, among them Zyuganov, Rokhlin, Anpilov and Sergey Baburin, met in Moscow 'to discuss strategy'.[171] At the end, a leader of the Duma communist faction, former Prime Minister Nikolay Ryzhkov, told journalists that such 'consultations' would be held every month.[172]

The other side, meanwhile, was embroiled in internecine bloodletting. Despite Yeltsin's intervention and a plea for peace, the oligarchs who had lost out in the Svyazinvest sale attacked the Chubais team in the newspapers and on the television channels they controlled. The barrage culminated in 'Bookgate': Chubais and a number of his closest associates were accused of accepting an advance for a book on privatization from a company associated with the winner of the Svyazinvest auction, the Uneximbank. By Moscow standards, the sum – $450,000 evenly divided between five people – was a laughably small amount: in the very recent past, a Deputy Prime Minister had been likely to make $90,000 in bribes in an average month. Ninety per cent of the money, moreover, had been designated by the recipients for charities. Yet, publicized in dozens of television programmes and newspaper articles throughout the country, for the ordinary Russian the amount was astronomical, and public opinion was much inflamed. This government had set a far higher standard and was now judged by it.

Chubais's team lost some prominent members, including the new privatization tsar Maxim Boyko. While denying any wrongdoing, Chubais submitted his resignation. Yeltsin kept him on but took the Ministry of Finance from him. The sales of government shares in a number of giant oil companies, which had been expected to bring billions to the Treasury, were cancelled, pending re-examination of the terms, while the Duma continued to delay its approval of the privatization of dozens of other enterprises.

Following the pattern of the past several years, late autumn and winter brought about an onset of illness, withdrawal and isolation. Yeltsin completely disappeared from public view between the second week of December and mid-January 1998. As usual, an 'acute viral infection' was officially to blame. Moscow was rife with rumours of a stroke. Interrupted by the President's absence were all the major constituent reforms of the 'second economic revolution' that was supposed to 'civilize' Russian capitalism and to save the budget: reforms of land, welfare and pension, enterprise and corporate governance, housing, and taxation.

In the execution of the 'second economic revolution' Yeltsin could count on two constants to buy time during the complex and painful restructuring of relations between the Russian state and the Russian economy. These were the revenues from the export of oil and the seemingly insatiable appetite of world investors for 'emergent markets'. While attempting to cut taxes and the budget outlays and, at the same time, to shift the burden of the welfare state from the government to corporate and individual taxpayers, the Kremlin relied on oil and the sale of debt (through GKOs and Eurobonds) to provide the minimum margin of safety and to keep the deficit from exploding and the ruble from faltering and falling.

In the last three months of 1997, both crutches grew much shorter.

The price of oil, the sale of which accounted for 60 per cent ($22 billion) of Russia's annual exports, tumbled from twenty-one dollars a barrel in October to fourteen dollars in January 1998 to eleven dollars in March. Between January and March Russian export revenues diminished by 15 per cent and reduced state revenues by almost one-fifth.[173] Simultaneously, the 'Asian' crisis, which began in the summer and autumn of 1997 and devastated financial markets in Indonesia, Malaysia, Thailand and South Korea (whose investors, along with those of Brazil, had been among the most avid purchasers of GKOs), precipitated the flight of investors from emergent markets all over the world. From its all-time high of 571 points in the first week of October 1997 the Russian Trading System index of 105 top Russian companies dropped to slightly over 300 points in March.

GKO rates skyrocketed but the customers were fewer and fewer. The GKO 'pyramid', in which the interest on the old debt was paid with the sale of more debt, looked more precarious with each day. To protect the ruble, the Central Bank sharply raised refinancing rates after cutting it steadily throughout the year. The government had collected only half of the planned tax revenue, and the International Monetary Fund felt obliged to stop the disbursement of a $10 billion loan. Wage arrears began to mount again.

Yeltsin, no longer in hospital but still recuperating in a country residence, in mid-January summoned Nemtsov to the Presidential retreat in snow-bound Valday in the Novgorod *oblast*. There, during a televised chat about ice-fishing and snowmobile rides, the President announced his determination to revive the previous year's stalled agenda: tax cuts and a new Tax Code to stimulate the economy; 'restructuring' of social benefits to cut the budget deficit; lower interest rates and lower yields on Treasury bills to allow the private sector to borrow and invest.[174]

Several days later, Yeltsin demanded, and received, a list of 'twelve major tasks' of the government for the coming year. Signed into a Presidential decree a week later, the document reiterated the Valday orders, gave them numbers and deadlines, and assigned, by name, individual officials, from Nemtsov and Chubais down, to each of the chores.[175] The plan called for annual inflation of no more than 7 per cent (it had declined to 11 per cent in 1997), the diminution of GKO rates to no higher than 18 per cent and, most of all, economic growth of at least 2 per cent. A Tax Code had to be adopted before the end of the year. Nemtsov was again to try and reduce housing and utility subsidies as well as tariffs set by the natural monopolies.[176]

The Duma, meanwhile, postponed until February the 'third reading' of the budget for 1998. The Tax Code was not even on the agenda. The Finance Minister warned that, if the new law was not adopted by the summer, the tax reforms would be delayed for another two years (because of the legislative and Presidential elections in 1999 and 2000) and the existing system would continue to 'throttle industrial production'.[177]

On 17 February Yeltsin delivered his annual 'State of Russia' address. Sustained economic growth was impossible without sound finance, he told the Federal Assembly, and sound finance required a realistic budget and a new tax system. The budget deficit, enterprises' debts to the state and to one another, and 'mutual debt defaults' made the situation increasingly precarious.[178] A system based on 'neglect of debt obligations' was 'fallacious': it was 'dangerous to try and cheat the economy'.[179] The state had 'to learn to do what any housewife knows how to do – to live according to one's means'.[180]

The tax system had to be simplified, the tax burden reduced and 'tax discipline' strengthened.[181] Tax reform was 'our common duty to enterprises and citizens',[182] and could not be delayed any further.[183] A new Tax Code was the key to stable rules of economic conduct; without such rules, investment would be difficult to attract.[184]

All the measures were urgent, and Yeltsin pleaded with the legislators for help. His address was entitled 'Through Common Effort towards the Revival of Russia'. The path ahead, he said, could only be travelled 'together' by the government and the legislature.[185] 'I ask the Deputies', Yeltsin said, 'to show understanding and support' in adopting a realistic, low-deficit budget.[186] He asked them to accept a 'package' of welfare laws with targeted assistance to the needy: if there was not enough money to pay for all the welfare entitlements, 'we must be honest with the people' and 'change the laws'.[187] As for the government, if it could not cope with the 'strategic tasks', Russia would have to have a new one.[188]

Yeltsin finished to tepid applause. Gennadiy Zyuganov said the address was 'the greyest, emptiest and most uninteresting' so far given.[189] To Grigoriy Yavlinsky Yeltsin's speech proved only that 'there were no changes in the life of the country'.[190] Vladimir Zhirinovskiy called the address 'disgusting'.[191]

Of the three television networks, only the Russian Television Channel (Rossia) carried the speech in full. First Channel/ORT (Ostankino) showed footage of the Olympic Games. NTV broadcast a game show.[192]

Yeltsin's health was at best uncertain. Much of his dwindling political capital had been spent in 1997 on promoting and defending the Chubais–Nemtsov–Chernomyrdin government. There was no time left to waste, yet, as was so clearly apparent to him, the dire immediacy of the situation left the country and the political class cold and sceptical. Yeltsin reached for a method of last resort, a talisman as much as a thought-out policy option: a crisis.

Crisis – which created its own dynamics, swept the deck clear of debris and moved events and people at twice their normal speed – had been good to him. 'On s'engage, et puis on voit!' Let's first get in a fight and then we'll see! Napoleon's adage, so beloved by Lenin, described the technique of some of Yeltsin's major victories. To feel, one last time, the intoxicating rush, the incomparable beat of a quickened pulse, to hear the crackle of electricity and to smell ozone in the air – even if there had been another way to break out of the vicious circle strangling the country, Yeltsin may still have engineered a crisis.

On the morning of 23 March he spoke to the nation on television. He looked calm and spoke firmly and clearly. He said he had dismissed Prime Minister Chernomyrdin and the entire cabinet. He had done this to 'make reforms more energetic and effective'.[193] A 'powerful spurt in the economy' was not possible without 'dynamism, initiative, new viewpoints, fresh approaches and ideas' – which the government had recently been lacking.[194]

Yeltsin's choice as Prime Minister, still to be confirmed by the Duma, was the thirty-five-year-old Minister of Fuel and Energy, Sergey Kirienko. With this appointment, Yeltsin forced a generational change that had been too slow to come on its own. This was the first truly post-Soviet government. The revolutionary cabinet led by another thirty-five-year-old, Egor Gaidar, six years before had consisted of those whose scholarly and advisory careers had been made under the old regime. They were theoreticians of the market, rather than practitioners of capitalism. Kirienko, who had become a Minister only six months before, was a successful businessman: a president of a bank and then of a regional oil refinery which he saved from bankruptcy and made profitable.

Kirienko lacked Chernomyrdin's political weight, accumulated in six years of deals and mutual favours. Unlike the former Prime Minister, he spoke not the argot of the industrial nomenklatura laced with obscenities but a clear, grammatically correct Russian – another mighty drawback in the eyes of the 'national-patriotic' plurality in the Duma. Chernomyrdin, although on the other side of the barricades, had a life history very much like theirs. Kirienko was from another universe – and a half-Jew to boot.*

---

* When Yeltsin was about to announce Kirienko's nomination, a leader of the Council of the Federation reportedly called the President to warn him that Kirienko's father was a Jew.

Despite these serious liabilities, Yeltsin apparently felt that he could get Kirienko confirmed by the Duma* and make a new government effective by putting behind it every ounce of political capital he had left. He began by making a major pre-emptive concession: on the day Yeltsin fired Chernomyrdin, Anatoliy Chubais was dismissed as well. During the next four weeks, the President lobbied incessantly. Before the first vote in the Duma, he invited the leaders of the parliamentary factions to the Kremlin for a meeting – and even gave them tea. He asked for their votes, but firmly refused both the factions' involvement in the drafting of the government's programme and the trade of Ministerial posts for votes.

Two days later, the Duma rejected Kirienko: he received less than a third of the total. A week later, the vote to confirm had diminished further. Before the third and final vote on 24 April, Yeltsin sent a letter to each legislator, met with the Speakers of both Houses (communists Gennadiy Selznyov and Egor Stroyev) and persuaded them to endorse Kirienko. He even 'stepped over himself' and called Zyuganov.

In the end, the President's persistence, the prospect of dissolution and the uncertainty of a new election (which for many Deputies would have meant farewell to Moscow apartments, huge salaries, all-expenses-paid trips abroad and a high-on-the-hog existence with a generally light work schedule) gave Kirienko a comfortable majority on the third vote. Most factions were split. The majority of the communists voted against the nomination, and Grigoriy Yavlinsky's entire faction denied Kirienko support by boycotting the vote. 'The Kirienko government has absolutely no future,' Gennadiy Zyuganov warned.[195]

After the final vote, Kirienko praised the Deputies for the 'great courage' they had shown in confirming him. 'The enormous number of problems in the economy makes us all share responsibility for the fate of Russia,' the new Prime Minister added. 'Let us respond to this challenge by deeds, not words. We have no time to waste.'[196]

As, indeed, they did not. Domestic debt was rapidly getting out of hand, while the Duma refused to pass the central measures that would have reduced the deficit by increasing revenue and attracting new investment (a new Tax Code, land privatization, enterprise reform and the break-up of the natural monopolies) and by cutting budget expenditure (welfare,

---

* According to the Constitution (Article 114.4), the President could submit his nominee to the Duma for a confirmation vote three times. If the candidate failed to win a majority, the President was required to dissolve the parliament and call new elections.

housing and pension reforms). Short-term Treasury bills maturing in 1998 alone were worth $33 billion. In May, one-third of budget spending went on servicing the debt.[197] By the end of the year, this item of expenditure was projected to consume over 45 per cent of the budget.[198]

In July unpaid wages grew by 6.5 per cent and stood at almost sixty-six billion rubles ($11 billion). Although no more than 20 per cent of this amount was owed by the federal authorities in Moscow,[199] the government was universally blamed. In the Russian Far East and Kuzbass, miners went on strike and threatened to block major rail lines. Protesters from all over the country demonstrated on Moscow streets and squares. On 8 July, nearly 3,000 defence industry workers from twenty-six cities and seventeen *oblast*s held a rally on Arbatskaya Square. They chanted 'President and Government – resign!' 'Give us back our money!' 'Trial for the Yeltsin gang!'[200]

'We have not been paid salaries in twenty months,' protesters from Nizhniy Novgorod told Russian journalists. 'During the [Great Patriotic] War our plant made 300,000 cannons. Our warehouses are bursting with cannons. If only we could sell them to the Chinese!'[201]

Outside the high pig-iron fence of the White House, miners set up a tent city. Day and night, without a moment's break, operating in shifts, they banged their helmets on the pavement, demanding their pay. A month later, by one of its last acts, the Kirienko government would allocate $4 billion, or 5 per cent of the entire 1998 budget, to payment of miners' wages.

Although in May the budget was cut by one-quarter,[202] the reduction failed either to restore confidence in the ruble or to bring down the astronomical GKO yields. Foreign investors, who held $20 billion of Russia's $70 billion domestic debt and who, nine months before, had bid up Russia's stock market to record levels, were redeeming their GKOs, selling stocks, converting their rubles into dollars and repatriating the profits. The money market was flooded with billions of rubles, putting still more pressure on the currency. The Central Bank was running out of hard-currency reserves with which to maintain the ruble's exchange value within the mandated band of R6 (plus or minus 15 per cent) to the dollar. Between October 1997 and May 1998, the Bank's reserves shrank by 63 per cent: from $23 billion to $14.5 billion.

In the middle of it all, the Duma overrode Yeltsin's veto and passed a law restricting foreign ownership of the government-controlled energy monopoly, United Energy Systems, to 25 per cent. Foreign investors rushed to sell stock across the board, touching off what was at the time the most precipitous one-day fall in the Russian stock market's brief history.

In the third week of July Anatoliy Chubais (now acting as the President's Special Ambassador to the International Financial Organizations) went to Washington to complete negotiations on an emergency loan from the IMF and the World Bank. By the time he landed, the Duma had rejected most of the key provisions in the government's package of twenty-five anti-crisis measures, in effect disavowing the commitment to fiscal austerity and enhanced revenue collection made by the government to the IMF.

'We will not be able to implement the stabilization programme if you do not approve it,' Yeltsin had told the Duma leaders two days before the vote. 'We are all one team.'[203] His plea was in vain. Anxious to deliver the *coup de grâce* to the hated and wobbling regime and mindful of an election the following year, the Duma majority rejected the unpopular value added and land taxes, which were intended to become the major sources of additional revenue. A version of sales tax, approved by the Duma, exempted virtually every product and service, except for luxury items. Voted down too were measures designed to shift more of the tax burden from the corporate sector to individuals, including an increased employee contribution to the Pension and Social Insurance Fund. Even a diluted version of a Land Code, which would have given farmers some land-ownership rights short of buying and selling land, was opposed by the communists and failed to pass. Immediately after the session, the Duma adjourned for its summer recess.*

Instead of a net gain of 102 billion rubles ($17 billion) in emergency savings and revenues the items passed by the legislature were estimated to bring in only 28 billion rubles. 'The key points which should lead the country out of crisis have not been supported by you,' Finance Minister Mikhail Zadornov, formerly a Yabloko leader in the Duma, told the Deputies after the vote.[204]

Although the IMF approved the $21 billion emergency package, it cut almost a billion dollars off the first tranche of $5.6 billion. The disbursement of the second tranche, of $4.3 billion, in September suddenly became very uncertain. The hopes for stabilization were dashed, and the pressure on the ruble resumed.

From February until the end of July, Yeltsin campaigned ceaselessly and intensively for his government and the reforms. He did not take a

---

* On 17 July, almost a year and a half after it had been proposed by the government, the Duma approved parts of a new Tax Code (a lower corporate tax rate and a flat 20 per cent rate for small businesses), but by then the crisis had rendered the matter almost irrelevant.

summer holiday. He cajoled and harangued legislators, bankers and media leaders.[205] Only an occasional slurring of speech, strange, even grotesque facial grimaces, and lapses of comprehension[206] indicated the battle of the man's mind and will with his multiple maladies.

On 17 July, accompanied by Naina in a black headscarf, Yeltsin attended the burial of the remains of Nicholas II, his wife, Tsarina Alexandra, and their children, murdered in Ekaterinburg eighty years before. To the accompaniment of the soaring voices of a church choir, with priests in gold-embroidered white robes swinging their censers, the President and his wife faced the coffins draped in yellow royal flags and bowed their heads: an admission of guilt, and a plea for forgiveness and reconciliation, without which a new Russia would never be able to recover its history and become whole.

The ceremony in St Petersburg's Cathedral of St Peter and St Paul, where the tsars had been buried since Peter the Great, was boycotted by the Patriarch of the Orthodox Church (which was not convinced of the remains' authenticity), by the communists and, following their example, by many leading politicians. Yeltsin himself had hesitated before announcing that he would come 'to bury the bloody red century', as a Russian magazine put it.[207]

'Today is a historic day for Russia,' Yeltsin said in a brief speech in the Cathedral.

For many years we were silent about this awful crime, but we must tell the truth . . . By burying the remains of the innocent murdered we want to expiate the sins of our ancestors.

We are all guilty . . . Burying the victims of the Ekaterinburg tragedy is an act of human justice, a symbol of unification in Russia and a redemption of common guilt.

In the face of the historic memory of the nation, we are responsible for everything . . . We must end the century which has been an age of blood and violence in Russia with repentance and peace, regardless of political views, ethnic or religious origin . . .

Let us remember those who became innocent victims of envy and violence. Let them rest in peace.[208]

*

As the crisis deepened in the second week of August, wherever he went Yeltsin was asked if the ruble would be devalued. No, he answered firmly, never! On 17 August the government announced the end of its efforts to support the ruble: a *de facto* devaluation. The state also defaulted on domestic debt by freezing the bond market. A three-month moratorium was imposed on the repayment of foreign commercial loans by the nation's private institutions. The state was bankrupt.

The GKO default and currency devaluation devastated most of the country's leading banks, which had invested hundreds of billions of rubles in Treasury bills and recklessly staked billions of dollars in forward contracts with foreign banks on the ruble's appreciation. The banks' owners, yesterday's 'oligarchs', plundered whatever ruble assets they had left, including individual accounts, changed them into dollars, shipped the proceeds out of the country and shut the doors, robbing millions of people of their savings. A week later, Yeltsin dismissed the Kirienko government and recalled Chernomyrdin.

To be seen retreating under fire is near fatal to politicians anywhere. In the brutal, zero-sum game of Russian politics, this was political suicide. For the first time in his life, Yeltsin signed an act of full and unconditional capitulation. He had taken the 'most terrifying', the most disastrous step of his political life.[209]

Only a Yeltsin whose intuition was extirpated by illness could have hoped that Chernomyrdin's reappointment could buy time and save the regime. It was too late for that. The 'popular patriots' did not want even a sympathetic government; they wanted a coalition government. They rejected Chernomyrdin twice and called Yeltsin's bluff by daring him to dissolve the Duma.

Yeltsin retreated again by nominating the Foreign Minister, the smart and stolid Evgeniy Primakov. To secure his confirmation, Primakov consulted the Duma so extensively both on Ministerial appointments and on economic strategy that his government became responsible to the parliament rather than to the President. Suddenly, Russia looked like a parliamentary republic. From now on, it would be extremely difficult for any Russian President to exercise his constitutional right to dissolve the Duma and schedule new elections if the two branches of power were to be deadlocked over the government's policies or a candidate for Prime Minister. It seemed that the President might not be able to dismiss a government without the legislature's consent, and might not even be able to appoint individual Ministers.

Yeltsin's popularity sank so low that the numbers – an approval rate of 5, 4, 3 per cent – became virtually meaningless. He was still alive and occupying the Kremlin, but, for the first time since the revolution began in 1989, Russia seemed to have no use for him. It was still Yeltsin's Presidency, but it was no longer the Yeltsin regime – or the Yeltsin era.

If reflection and memory were still compatible with rapidly advancing illness and bitterness, what solace could they bring? That, even before he was gone, his legacy – a flawed but functioning democracy – had been tested and, so far, had held? That, amid financial collapse, with thousands of angry depositors breaking down the doors of banks that had stolen their money, there were no show trials and scapegoats, as there were in Malaysia at the same time, and no riots and pogroms as in Indonesia? That, despite a deafening build-up of communist propaganda, the Red October of 1998 failed miserably to bring millions on to the streets and precipitate a Bolshevik takeover? The very democracy which had made his reforms so slow and uneven had so far saved the country from collapse into violent anarchy, fascism or communist dictatorship.

What memories did Yeltsin seek to recover to alleviate the despair? His greatest triumphs: the Moscow streets in the spring of 1989, Red Square in May 1990, the tank in August 1991, the winning tallies of July 1996?

Or could it have been the late 1950s, and one of his *Sturm und Drang* construction operations, for which he had become famous in Sverdlovsk? Perhaps he remembered the day a fellow engineer came to the site to check the positioning and reliability of the armature and found herself being hoist to the top of the building by Yeltsin himself, a mischievous grin on his sweaty face as he pulled on the rope.[210] Halfway up, the woman decided to certify Yeltsin's building without further inspection. 'Borya, ya tebe veryu!' she cried out to Yeltsin. 'I trust you, little Boris!'[211]

Thirty years later, as he pulled Russia along into the uncertainty and personal responsibility of democracy and the market economy, time and again millions of Russians echoed this cry with their votes in 1989, 1990, 1991, 1993 and 1996. Now – fatally wounded by his own errors, by the implacable hatred and resistance of his enemies, and, most of all, by his inability to deliver miracles to his enormous country and impoverished state and to make freedom heal the sick, punish the corrupt or feed the poor – the man at the rope was now too weak and too sick to manage the revolution and to justify his people's trust.

In Search of a Historic Yeltsin

HISTORY'S MOST PRECIOUS OFFERINGS ARE rarely delivered in spotlessly clean vessels. Yet rarely, if ever, has the contrast between the value and size of a gift and its wrapping been as great as in the post-communist transition.

> The clowns are demolishing the circus. The elephants have run off
> to India;
> tigers sell, on the sidewalk, their stripes and hoops;
> under a leaky cupola, there is hanging, off the trapeze,
> as in a wardrobe, the limp tuxedo
> of a disillusioned magician;
> the little horses, casting off their embroidered blankets, pose
> for a portrait of a new engine. In the arena,
> knee-deep in sawdust, clowns, wildly wielding
> sledgehammers, demolish the circus.
> The public is either absent or doesn't clap . . .[1]

No one has better captured the melancholy and the bitter disappointments of post-communist chaos than the great Russian poet Joseph Brodsky, a Nobel Prize Laureate and an exile from the Soviet Union.

Having risen to rid themselves of totalitarian tyranny, the peoples of newly liberated nations found themselves delivered to the 'clowns': former communist officials, the political and industrial nomenklatura, who demolished the 'circus' of the one-party state and replaced it with a bleak and dirty bazaar in which everything and everybody appeared to be for sale. Of little consolation to those crushed by new responsibilities and uncertainties is one of Isaiah Berlin's immortal observations: 'Liberty is liberty, not equality or fairness or justice or culture, or human happiness or a quiet conscience.'[2]

National differences aside, from Prague to Alma-Ata, from Tallinn to Yerevan, and from Warsaw to Ulan-Bator, much of post-communist politics and society has been a product of an unprecedented discontinuity between the new order and the communist *ancien régime*. Until now, transitions from 'traditional' authoritarianism to 'modern' capitalist democracy had been preceded by centuries of gradually expanding islands of societal autonomy, self-rule and corporate and individual responsibility wrested from the king first by Church and nobility and later by towns and guilds, corporations and universities. By contrast, in this transition from authoritarianism to democracy, the political *tabula rasa* inherited by post-communist societies is historically unique in its emptiness. The same is true of private property and the institutions spawned by it: commercial law, the sanctity of contract and the impartial court, which adjudicates and enforces.

In all of the liberal democracies of the West, capitalism preceded democracy. When Lord Macaulay described what we call today 'liberal capitalism' as a system in which 'the authority of law and the security of property were found to be compatible with a liberty of discussion and individual action',[3] the implied order in this splendid definition – first, private property protected by law, then personal freedom – corresponded to the historical record of the 'classic' evolution of the West. In post-communism the sequence was reversed: basic human and political rights and liberties came first and commanded an incomparably greater popular allegiance than the free market. Capitalism was a consequence (and not always an intended one) of a revolt against the totalitarian communist state.

After depriving generations not only of political liberty but also of economic and social autonomy, communist regimes delivered to their successors not citizens but wards of state. Decades of contest with unjust and often irrational rules turned entire peoples into nations of law-breakers. Ferociously, even fanatically individualistic, jealously protective of his or her private space, a resourceful and wily fighter for personal amenities, the average post-communist man or woman is at once dependent on the state for everything and deeply resentful, cynical and hostile to it.* In the words of a leading Russian political sociologist, the forced 'communist collectivism' has been replaced by 'non-liberal individualism'.[4]

Everywhere and at all times attended by an assortment of crass inequalities, fraud, indignities and cruelty towards the weak and the vanquished, a vigorous and hungry early capitalism (Marx's 'primary accumulation', which had long, and mercifully, faded from the collective memory of the West)† was made even less attractive by the virtual absence in most post-communist nations of personal restraint inculcated

---

* Even in the compact, homogeneous and relatively prosperous Czech Republic, 78 per cent of the people surveyed in the summer of 1997 said they did not trust the government (Christine Spolar, 'Czechs' Post-Communist Boom Running Dry', *Washington Post*, 29 June 1997).

† 'The bloodstained story of economic individualism and unrestrained capitalist competition does not, I should have thought, today need stressing,' wrote Sir Isaiah Berlin. The seemingly boundless amazement and the intensity of righteous indignation which the sight of embryonic post-communist capitalism causes among the writing classes in liberal capitalist societies makes one believe that such 'stressing' would be worth while indeed. (Introduction to *Four Essays on Liberty*, p. xlv.)

by Church, professional association or corporation, or by the habit of charity or personal responsibility. Not only were the post-communist leaders saddled with the unprecedented – and, for many, politically suicidal – task of 'building' capitalism in infant democracies (the two having been separated by centuries in the West and by decades in the 'modernizing authoritarianisms' of South-east Asia and in most of South and Central America), they had to dig the foundation pit in a soil which was as hard as rock.

The newly liberated and very hungry private entrepreneur met a weakened but still omnipresent post-communist state. The state's possessions – huge but no longer shielded by totalitarian repression – lay helpless, like a beached whale, for the vultures to pick at, while the venal bureaucracy (the 'clowns' of the former nomenklatura) controlled access to the beach with licences, quotas, credits, privatization 'options' and rigged 'auctions'. In the normative void left by decades of totalitarian propaganda and terror, this encounter produced an explosion of corruption and organized crime that, with different degrees of violence, engulfed all the post-communist nations.

The transition from communism to liberal capitalist democracy has been complicated by one of the most celebrated features of the victorious anti-communist revolutions of 1989–91: their much applauded 'velvet' character. Other revolutions killed off, arrested, exiled or at least dismissed the old ruling class; these bought them out. The 'velvet' was the largest political bribe in history: the communist nomenklatura handed over political power without a shot (Rumania was the only exception) in exchange for effective ownership of the state assets they had administered on the Party's behalf. When the music of communism stopped, they kept the chairs.*

In the Russian case, each of these genetic handicaps of post-communism was especially devastating. Nowhere, with the possible exception of Albania, was the *tabula rasa* cleaner, or the normative foundations scorched more deeply and for longer, or the beached whale larger, or the nomenklatura that emerged unscathed from the 'velvet revolution' further removed from rational modern management than in

---

* Of the members of the political and economic elites in Poland, Hungary and Russia in 1988, one-third occupied the same offices in 1993 (John Higley, Judith Kullberg and Jan Pakulski, 'The persistence of post-communist elites', *Journal of Democracy*, 2, 1996, pp. 135–6). The political comeback of the communist nomenklatura was formalized in Polish parliamentary and Presidential elections (1993 and 1995), and in parliamentary elections in Hungary (1994) and in Russia (1995).

the country over which Boris Yeltsin was destined to preside. As if these disabilities were not enough, the monumental economic distortions, the incompetence and the moral void bequeathed by decades of Stalinism were compounded by the legacy of pre-1917 Russian political culture, where authoritarianism, imperialism and militarism were combined with patrimonialism, the essence and effect of which are discussed in the previous chapter.

In Yeltsin's case, as in those of all political leaders, history's verdict will be determined not by the starting point, no matter how low, or the route, no matter how arduous or tortuous, but by the direction eventually taken by a new country, whose institutions he so forcefully and decisively shaped. If Russia drifts back into the historical stereotype of a militarized, xenophobic and imperial authoritarianism and if the years of upheaval settle into nothing more than a corrupt oligarchy ruling over a stagnant, backward economy and a mostly impoverished people, then Yeltsin will be remembered as the one who missed a unique opportunity to change Russia's destiny. In this scenario, he ploughed over the soil of communism, but, instead of the seeds of a free, peaceful and prosperous Russian state, sowed it with the dragon's teeth of authoritarianism, discord and poverty.

Quite a few observers outside Russia will find much contentment in such a verdict. Some of them, quite properly, consider Yeltsin the one person most responsible for Russia's lurch to capitalism, and deeply resent him for that course. Alongside Deng Xiaoping, Yeltsin dealt the most severe – perhaps even a fatal – blow to what might be called an anthropological theory of socialism. It had postulated that capitalism, individualism and entrepreneurship simply did not suit other, inherently 'collectivist' cultures and were not sustainable in Russia or China, Vietnam or Cuba. To the proponents of this view, Yeltsin was the destroyer of the last refuge of that perenially elusive bluebird of one-party state socialism 'with a human face', the dream of which – after so many disappointments – had seemed so close to realization in Gorbachev's Soviet Union.

For others, the fall of the Soviet Union and the end of the Cold War wrought an enormous professional – and emotional – void, the recovery from which has proved difficult and protracted. Having invested the best years of their lives in studying the minutiae of the *ancien régime* – counting its tanks and nuclear warheads; learning the arcana of its public discourse; courting its minions and myrmidons for visas, 'access' and 'sources'; and aiding, often at some personal risk, its dissidents –

these dedicated and energetic men and women were, almost overnight, confronted with the irrelevance of it all. Many (although by no means all) have adjusted by treating the years after 1987 as an aberration, a fatally flawed and tragic experiment that produced nothing more than a slightly brighter version of the old Soviet regime. They, too, will welcome Yeltsin's failure.

Finally, there are those who had been sustained for most of their adult lives by the bracing anxieties of the Cold War. The ennobling battle on the side of the Good gave an inimitable purpose and meaning to their existence. Many in this group had used 'Russian' and 'Soviet' interchangeably and adjusted by substituting Yeltsin's country for the totalitarian Soviet Union. And what better incarnation of this continuity could there be than this big, burly and rough Siberian, a living metaphor for Russian 'authoritarianism' and 'imperialism', with a sly smile and a meaty, ruddy face, which made him look tipsy even when he was absolutely sober, scheming when he was at his most open, and menacing when he was at his friendliest?

Conor Cruise O'Brien wrote of Edmund Burke that he was capable of exciting 'extraordinary malevolence among the people who never knew him'.[5] In addition to his quite real sins and failures, the biases of his observers made Yeltsin a worthy competitor to Burke in both the number of his detractors and the intensity of their rancour.

If, on the other hand, a Russia peaceful, free, open to the world and gradually growing richer begins to take root, one will have to look for Yeltsin's historic provenance not among the 'clowns' of post-communism but in much more elevated company. This club, perhaps history's most exclusive, consists of those who took over great countries on the very brink of a national catastrophe, held them together, repaired and restored them, and, in the process, changed them fundamentally for the better.

Few occasions in modern history qualify: either the country lacks size and prominence, or the scope and severity of the crisis are insufficient, or no one man possessed indispensable centrality. By these criteria two other very tall men come the closest to being Yeltsin's predecessors. Their adversary was not just a sudden erosion of the state's coherence or viability throughout the country's territory but a catastrophic break-down of popular agreement on national ends and means and on the meaning of citizenship. On 1 June 1958 when de Gaulle came to Paris to take over France, the state was wracked by what his pre-eminent biographer called 'institutional debility'.[6] The political system was near collapse, the economy near bankrupt and inflation ridden, the country on the verge of a civil war and about to be taken over by mutinous soldiers. For Abraham Lincoln, the spectre of fratricide and disintegration became a reality after five weeks in office, on 12 April 1861.

Both de Gaulle and Lincoln were shrewd political operators, given to manoeuvring, temporizing and, quite often, demagoguery. They were masters of ambiguity, shifting alliances, retreats and patience (often maddening to zealots in their camps), in search of the best timing and propitious circumstances. Allies and closest advisers were got rid of rudely and ruthlessly once they had outlived their political usefulness.

Yet the longer the perspective and the more the dry factual outlines were filled with true meaning, the clearer it became that the technology of power (whether deployed on the battlefield, in high office or on the floor of Congress or the National Assembly) was less instrumental to Lincoln's and de Gaulle's success than seemed at the time. Power alone was enough to prevail in a few battles, but was not enough to govern in the absence of a dictatorship and, most certainly, not enough to forge a new 're-dedicated' nation (in Lincoln's case) or a new polity (in de Gaulle's) – or (in either case) to reinvigorate, 'unite' and 'lift' (*rassembler* and *élever*) their countries, to use de Gaulle's favourite terms.

Their genius, and the key to their indispensability, was the gift to sense the evolution and direction of national consensus long before it became apparent to most. They felt the ever so slight turn of the wheel in the hands of the nation's fate and gave expression to a national consciousness 'not yet aware of itself', as Jean Lacouture wrote of de Gaulle's 18 June 1940 call to arms from London. Counter-intuitive, even politically suicidal as they seemed at the time, the routes on which they embarked were not only accepted by most of the voters but appeared, in retrospect, the only correct decisions to have taken.

Until that magic moment when they hear the hoofbeat of History's horse, these 'men of crisis' appear only to react to events, not to shape them, like General Kutuzov in Tolstoy's *War and Peace*. Much to the despair of their friends and allies, they were evasive and elusive, furtive, supremely opportunistic and blatantly dissembling. 'My policy is to have no policy,' Lincoln said.[7] 'In politics or strategy, there exists, I believe, no absolute truth. There are only the circumstances,' de Gaulle agreed.[8] The roads to the emancipation of the slaves and to Algerian independence were twisted and lengthened by this *modus operandi*.*

---

* The 'slowness' with which he moved against slavery frustrated not only zealous abolitionists but many of the Republican leaders both in the Senate and in the House of Representatives. Many became opposed to his renomination for President in 1864.

Yet, once they were convinced that the moment had arrived, the 'men of crisis' became rigid in their confidence and pursued their vision against enormous odds, at considerable risks to their own and other people's lives, and with a resolve, single-mindedness and tenacity which were at once majestic and frightening. For their deeply divided nations, both chose one vision of the future over any other and imposed it with what a Lincoln biographer called 'ruthless determination'.[9] Those who disagreed were at best ignored, and often deceived and abandoned, as were one million of the French in Algeria whom de Gaulle first exalted with his 'Je vous ai compris' and 'Vive Algérie Française!' in June 1958. In Lincoln's case, they were declared outside the law and killed on the battlefield of a civil war.

The acquisition, retention and aggregation of personal power were, to them, inseparable from the good of the nation, and, as such, were to be defended to the last. Victory was invariably preferable to peace. De Gaulle's idea of himself seemed to be that of 'a modern Moses' guiding his flock towards a still very misty Promised Land.[10] There is little doubt that, in his heart of hearts, Lincoln would have found this comparison appropriate in his own case.

Neither man hesitated to deploy large-scale and often indiscriminate violence – be that the war of 'terrifying efficiency and brutality' in the spring and summer of 1959 against the Algerian Army of National Liberation,[11] when more than a million Muslims were interned in *regroupement* (concentration) camps, or the Union's campaign in the South. 'Grant has the bear by the hind leg, while Sherman takes off the hind,' Lincoln commented famously as General Sherman's troops continued their devastating advance through Georgia and South Carolina. 'Hold on with a bull-dog grip, and chew & choke, as much as possible,' the President urged General Grant.[12]

When they found themselves constrained by pre-existing laws, the 'men of crisis' overstepped, discarded or radically changed them. De Gaulle wrote a new constitution, tailored to his vision of France and his ambition. 'I changed the Constitution of France when I found that it was not working,' the General explained.[13] Two years later, he decided

---

Calling Lincoln a 'fickle-minded man', who had been 'reluctant to announce emancipation, slow to enroll Negro troops, unwilling to fight for equal pay for blacks who enlisted and publicly silent on Negro voting', influential African Americans, Frederick Douglass among them, initially backed Frémont for the 1864 Republican nomination. (David Herbert Donald, *Lincoln*, pp. 314, 315, 477, 541.)

to amend the French Constitution by arranging the direct national election of the President, which he expected to win easily. The Council of State found his 'interpretation' of the Constitution illegal. De Gaulle ignored the ruling. The National Assembly voted the bill down. De Gaulle dissolved the Assembly, called a constitutional referendum, and won it.

Bound by the Constitution of a slave-holding republic, whose laws he swore to uphold on Inauguration Day, Lincoln readily admitted that the measures to which he resorted to win the war were in violation of the existing laws. He claimed that 'often a limb must be amputated to save a life', and 'measures, otherwise unconstitutional, might become lawful' if necessary to preserve a nation. In what might surely become a motto of the 'men of crisis', Lincoln declared: 'The right of revolution is never a legal right . . . At most, it is but a moral right exercised for a morally justifiable cause.'[14] He proceeded to invoke 'emergency powers', including suspension of the writ of habeas corpus for those 'guilty of any disloyal practice, affording aid and comfort to Rebels against the authority of the United States'.[15]*

In the end, however, neither Lincoln nor de Gaulle crossed the line beyond which fundamental democratic principles were irreparably compromised. 'Dictators' to their critics, they belonged instead to that rare political breed: authoritarian democrats.

Logical in retrospect, such a designation would have seemed an oxymoron to their contemporaries. Furious accusations of authoritarianism were levelled against both men. The vitriol against Lincoln was not confined to the understandably overheated lore of his Confederate enemies, who routinely labelled him a 'despot', 'tyrant' and autocrat who had arrogated more power than 'King, Emperor, Czar, Kaiser, or even despotic Caesar himself'.[16] Even those who agreed with his agenda

---

* At least 15,000 civilians were arrested by Union soldiers, while hundreds of others were tried and convicted by military courts. Those who resisted the conscription were jailed and the suspension of the writ of habeas corpus was used to deny them trial. Chief Justice of the Supreme Court Roger B. Taney ruled that the Chief Executive had acted unlawfully, reminded Lincoln of his oath and warned that, if the violations continued, 'the people of the United States [would] no longer [be] living under government of laws'. Lincoln ignored the ruling, and later threatened to jail and exile judges who 'used the writ of habeas corpus to interfere with the draft'. He was, 'with difficulty', dissuaded by his cabinet. (James M. McPherson, *Abraham Lincoln and the Second American Revolution*, p. 57, and Donald, *Lincoln*, pp. 299, 489.)

felt increasingly uncomfortable with the means by which the President implemented it. Declared a radical Republican Congressman in 1865, 'when I came into Congress ten years ago, this was a Government of law. I have lived to see it a Government of personal will. Congress has dwindled from a power to dictate law and the policy of the Government to a commission to audit accounts and appropriate moneys to enable the Executive to execute his will and not ours.'[17]*

Qualities that produce saviours of nations travel poorly in the less elevated spheres of day-to-day drudgery. Occluded and softened by time and accomplishment, both men's personal flaws were deplored with vehemence by many among the political classes, the intelligent-sia and the elite media of both the United States and France. Again, Lincoln fared much worse. Melancholic and moody, 'unquenchably ambitious',[18] prideful and an obsessively single-minded loner, he handed his critics a strong case. Alternating between 'grandiosity and depression', given to 'outbursts of antic humor',[19] he was, to them, a 'vulgar buffoon'.[20] This slow, calculating and 'plodding'[21] man was, in the opinion of one of his foremost biographers, one of the 'least experi-enced and most poorly prepared men ever elected to high office', rescued only by his 'enormous capacity for growth'.[22]

Thus, in the end, stands confirmed yet another of Isiah Berlin's axioms:

> Greatness is not a specifically moral attribute. It is not one of the private virtues . . . A great man need not be morally good, or upright, or kind, or sensitive, or delightful, or possess artistic or scientific talent. To call someone a great man is to claim that he has intention-ally taken . . . a large step, one far beyond the normal capacities

---

* The critics' fears of authoritarianism were justified in at least one regard: in both cases national integrity and an effective political system were restored at the price of the expansion of the powers of central government over the regions and of the executive branch over the legislature.

De Gaulle created a political system labelled 'an authoritarian republic' and 'a kind of monarchy tempered by plebiscite'. Lincoln's legacy, in addition to federal currency, federal taxes (including an income tax) and national bonds, was formidable centralization of the Republic. Of the first twelve Amendments to the Constitution, eleven limited the power of the federal government in one way or another. By contrast, the six Amendments that followed Lincoln's time in office 'radically expanded the power of the federal govern-ment at the expense of the states'. (Raymond Aron, *Memoirs*, p. 258; Stanley Hoffmann, *Decline or Renewal? France since the 1930s*, p. 267; and McPherson, *Lincoln*, p. 62.)

ВЫБОР РОССИИ—
ЕЛЬЦИН!

The Duma campaign, December 1993: a Russia's Choice poster.

On the election night at Russia's Choice headquarters. From left: Egor Gaidar, Anatoliy Chubais and Gennadiy Burbulis.

After the Chechen war had begun: a new Yeltsin behind the mask.

Campaign – 1996: 'Dmitry Donskoy against Boris Yeltsin'.

Campaign – 1996: Next to Zyuganov's head (on the left) is the slogan 'Peace, Work, Justice'; next to Yeltsin: 'STOP THE HORROR IN RUSSIA. SAY "NO" TO YELTSIN!'

The rhymed caption below reads:
'We know Yeltsin's big ideas:/ Europe, the [United] States, the rich …/ Zyuganov is taking another route:/ Russia, Motherland, People!'

Campaign – 1996: Yeltsin: 'I will not let go!' The caption under the muscular worker's arm reads: 'RUSSIA! MOTHERLAND! PEOPLE!'

Campaign – 1996: A drunken Yeltsin sold Russian television to the Jews.

Campaign – 1996: With Jews directing the show (the figure in the skull cap peering from behind the curtains), Yeltsin is selling Russia to the West. 'Following numerous requests from Western investors we shall sing a song about democracy called "Now hand over to us the entire Russian land."' The 'singer', next to Yeltsin, is Anatoliy Chubais. Behind them are leading pro-reform politicians.

Campaign – 1996:
'The battle banner
of the Motherland' –
exorcising Jewish
demons with a red flag.

Campaign – 1996: 'Soldier and Vermin'.
Yeltsin (top left) and his supporters. The
letters in the background read 'Bank'.

НОВОЕ
ВРЕМЯ
25   июнь 1996
Быка за рога

The liberal media's view
of the presidential
campaign: Yeltsin as
Theseus against Zyuganov
the Minotaur.

Yeltsin on the campaign trail: in Belgorod on 4 April and in Yaroslavl' on 3 May 1996.

In Rostov on 10 June 1996.

15 June 1996, ending the first round of the campaign where he began it, in Ekaterinburg, with Naina, his daughters, sons-in-law and grandchildren behind him.

Before the second round: an election poster on an armoured personnel carrier in Grozny, Chechnya on 1 July 1996, and Yeltsin campaigning in Tatarstan.

Anatoliy Chubais (as a Jewish serpent) and Yeltsin signing a decree appointing Chubais First Deputy Prime Minister.

Signing the Chechnya peace accord with Aslan Maskhadov on 12 May 1997.

Protesters in Moscow, 7 October 1998.

Above: At the opening of a memorial synagogue and Holocaust Museum at Victory Park, Moscow, 2 September 1998: with President of the Russian Jewish Congress Vladimir Gusinskiy (to Yeltsin's right), Mayor of Moscow Yuriy Luzhkov, and Chief Rabbi of Russia and the Commonwealth of Independent States Adolf Shayevich.

of men, in satisfying, or materially affecting, central human interests.[23]

*

In contrast to both Lincoln and de Gaulle, Yeltsin's place in history is still obscured by a lack of distance and by the passions of the day. Much of his record is provisional and open to widely conflicting interpretations.

Much, but not all. Even the short life of Russian post-communism, over which Yeltsin presided, is sufficiently illuminating, provided judgment is not rushed, provided the visible is not automatically equated with the significant, and provided the pens are suspended every now and then in the air to allow the mind to extract meaning, not just transmit the picture.

While it is very tempting and natural – because easy and quick – to judge countries by the standards of other peoples and other countries (usually one's own), the only meaningful (and, of course, fair) measure of progress is a comparison with the country itself, its own history and that of its historical and geographic 'neighbourhood'. Anyone embarking on such an expedition must beware of what a leading US historian of the Civil War calls 'presentism': a tendency to 'read history backwards, measuring change over time from the point of arrival rather than the point of departure'.[24]

Measured in this way – from the point of departure – the distance travelled by Yeltsin's Russia was nowhere greater than in the philosophy and ideology of a new Russian state, its *raison d'être* and its behaviour outside the country's borders.

Russian modernizations, invariably initiated from above, have unfolded in two distinct patterns of very unequal frequency and longevity. In the dominant type, which might be called Petrine after Peter the Great, the country's progress was equated with, and effected by, the expansion and modernization of the state, which was to be made more efficient in carrying out the ruler's agenda.

The other paradigm was inaugurated by Alexander II, who liberated Russian peasants from serfdom, shifted a great deal of power from Moscow to local councils (*zemstvo*s) and introduced trial by jury, among dozens of other reforms. Society was granted a measure of autonomy from and partnership with the state, whose domination was reduced both in scope and in depth. The protagonists here, in addition to Alexander II, were Alexander I and Catherine (both at the beginning of their rule), Khrushchev (with maddening inconsistency) and Gorbachev. In the systemic character of reforms that redefined the fundamentals of the relationship between the Russian state and society to the benefit of the latter, no other Russian leader came closer to Alexander II than Yeltsin, who may have even surpassed the 'Tsar-Liberator'.*

Unprecedented in scope, the transfer of national wealth from state to private owners (no matter how incompetent or corrupt) and the institutionalization of popular sovereignty through free elections broke the back of the Russian patrimonial state. It no longer owned either the people's means of subsistence or national politics. Civil society began to re-emerge from the state's debilitating shadow.

Yeltsin struck at the heart of the Russian state-building tradition, which for four centuries – from Ivan the Terrible to Leonid Brezhnev – rested on the three cornerstones: militarism, imperial expansion and the maintenance of the empire. Faithfully implementing commitments made by Mikhail Gorbachev, Boris Yeltsin completed a historically unprecedented – peaceful and voluntary – contraction of the world's last empire. In September 1995, the withdrawal of Russian troops from the Paldiski submarine training base in Estonia put an end to Russian and Soviet presence in East-Central Europe. In the first four years of Yeltsin's rule, Moscow moved back to Russia 800,000 troops with military hardware and supplies, 400,000 civilian personnel and 500,000 family members.[25] The lands acquired and held during two-and-a-half centuries of imperial conquests, from Peter the Great to Brezhnev, were restored to the occupied nations. Russia returned to its seventeenth-century borders.†

The liberation of foreign lands was paralleled by domestic demilitarization unprecedented in Russian history (and, probably, that of the world

---

* A mere enumeration of the rulers in each category quickly establishes which of the two modes has been more successful, lasted longer and left a deeper imprint in Russian history. All of the longest reigns unfolded within the Petrine paradigm: Peter, Catherine the Great and Stalin. By contrast, Alexander II was assassinated, Khrushchev was ousted and Gorbachev resigned. To the many precedents he has already established, Yeltsin may very well add becoming the first Russian modernizer of the 'Alexandrine' type to serve out his term in office.

† 'Why does Boris Nikolaevich need [the new Russian national coat-of-arms of] a two-headed eagle?' Gennadiy Zyuganov asked sarcastically in a campaign speech in April 1996. 'He has already moved the frontier of the empire to Bryansk and Smolensk. Soon one will be able to see the border from a Kremlin window. Where would this eagle look?' ('Znat' i deystvovat'. Kandidat v prezidenty ot vechayet na voprosy zhiteley Urala' ('To know and to act. The Presidential candidate answers the questions of Ural residents'), *Zavtra*, 15, (April) 1996).

as well). 'Reduction' is a clearly inadequate term to describe the devastation that Yeltsin visited on the institution that for two centuries had been the very heart and highest pride of the Russian authoritarian state. When Yeltsin took over Russia, no less than 30 per cent (and very likely considerably more) of the country's GDP was spent on the military. By 1996, that share had dropped to 5 per cent. In May 1997 Yeltsin promised to diminish the military's share of GDP to 3 per cent by the year 2000.[26] As if determined to illustrate the incompatibility of a fledgling democracy and militarism, Yeltsin persistently and systematically decimated and downgraded Russia's hypertrophied armed forces, their industrial base and their institutional place of honour. Along with the state's ownership of the national economy, Yeltsin's reforms ended the Russian military's unchallenged claim on the choicest resources and the best men. In the space of a few years, from an omnipotent and omnipresent overlord, the military–industrial complex was reduced to a neglected and humiliated beggar.

Along the way, the troop level shrank from around 4 million in January 1992 to 1.7 million by late 1996. At the same time, Yeltsin promised what surely will be the *coup de grâce* of Russian militarism: the end of conscription and the establishment of an all-volunteer armed force of 600,000.

It has been said that the drastic reduction in defence funding was due to the economic crisis inherited from the Soviet Union and that Yeltsin had no choice but to cut back – as if national priorities are determined by accountants and as if, throughout human history, economic rationale has not been invariably and completely overridden by fear, hatred, wounded national honour, messianic fervour or dictator's will.* Russia's unprecedented unilateral disarmament was caused by rearranged national priorities, not by a weak economy. In one of the most dramatic reversals of national tradition, the government, in effect, announced that 'it would spend more on defense when the economy improves enough to [allow it to] do that', as a leading Russian defence analyst put it.[27] In the previous seventy years, the military's needs, not the country's economic performance, had determined what the armed forces received.

Apart from demilitarization, the most momentous event in Russia's

---

* In the twentieth century, was it a 'strong economy' and excess of wealth that fed the military projects in the Soviet Union in the 1930s and immediately after the Second World War; in Vietnam between the 1950s and 1980s; in an Armenia reclaiming and defending Nagorno-Karabach from Azerbaijan in the 1990s; in Pakistan, Iran or Iraq, as they develop nuclear arsenals today?

post-imperial adjustment was accommodation with an independent Ukraine. The 31 May 1997 Treaty of Friendship, Co-operation and Partnership between the Russian Federation and Ukraine was the most important development in European diplomacy since the French–German rapprochement engineered by de Gaulle and Konrad Adenauer in 1958, and just as pivotal to peace and stability on the continent.

The success of the settlement was made more remarkable by the fact that virtually all precedents argued against it. Similar post-imperial divorces – England and Ireland, India and Pakistan, and, of course, Yugoslavia – were attended by horrific bloodshed. This history compelled many experts to predict an equally violent, perhaps even nuclear, conflict between the two states. In no other instance was the tempering of Russia's imperial ambition put to a harsher test than a trial by an independent Ukraine.

The patience and perseverance that Yeltsin displayed in negotiating with a much weaker neighbour was absolutely without precedent for a Russian leader. Apparently having concluded that an independent and friendly Ukraine was essential to an environment in which Russian democracy and the reforms had a chance of succeeding, he never in six years of domestic crisis and upheaval veered from that goal.

In no other arena of Russian foreign policy was Yeltsin's personal contribution as direct, sustained or consistently central to success. In Moscow he overcame the fierce resistance of much of the political class, from 'national patriots' to liberals, evaded dozens of stern resolutions by the Supreme Soviet and Duma and ignored fiery statements by the country's top political leaders. Over and over again, he pretended not to hear the shrill voices declaring Sevastopol a 'Russian city', Crimea 'Russian territory' and the Black Sea Fleet a 'Russian fleet'. As late as December 1996, the upper House of the Russian legislature, the Council of the Federation, called on Yeltsin not to negotiate with Ukraine about the Black Sea Fleet until a special commission had examined the status of Sevastopol.

On the other side of the table, a young nation, eager to establish an identity separate from Russia for the first time in over 300 years, demanded from its leaders an equally rigid negotiating stance. Yeltsin was alternately accommodating and blustering towards both his domestic critics and his Ukrainian negotiating partners, playing one off against the other to enlarge his room for manoeuvre. He temporized and was deliberately ambiguous. At innumerable summits with Ukrainian leaders he agreed on what was politically possible at that time, postponing the rest until a more propitious moment.

Even when negotiated agreements were reached, Yeltsin delayed enforcement, which he knew would lead to a crisis, and he never followed up on some of his own public threats. Thus, having declared time and time again that Russia would stop providing Ukraine with oil and gas if an agreement on the Black Sea fleet were not reached, Yeltsin quietly continued one of the most generous bilateral foreign assistance programmes in the world.* After the Treaty was signed, 'triumphant and relieved' Ukrainian officials told reporters that 'only Yeltsin had the political will and strength to drop Russia's residual claims on Ukraine, and they [had] prayed that Mr Yeltsin would not die before doing so'.[28]

Unlike many a leader in both the 'developing' and the 'developed' world (from China and Malaysia to Great Britain and Argentina), Yeltsin resisted the temptation of making nationalism a central organizing principle of national unity and cohesion at a time of dislocation and disarray.† He never resorted to jingoism to palliate the pain of market reform. A 'Weimar' Russia – defeated in the Cold War, bereft of empire, fallen from global superpowerdom and in the throes of a sharp economic decline – did not become a National Socialist Russia.

Even when a chance to propitiate the left-nationalist opposition and bolster his domestic standing by stoking nationalist paranoia was handed to him on a silver platter, Yeltsin demurred. After much blustering in response to NATO's expansion into Central Europe, the Russian President chose to accommodate rather than reprise the Cold War. 'It has already happened more than once that we, the East and the West, failed to find a chance to reconcile,' Yeltsin said in February 1997, as he prepared for the final negotiations with NATO. 'This chance must not be missed.'[29]

---

* In 1997, Ukraine's debt to Russia was estimated at between $3 billion and 'at least' $3.5 billion (see, for instance, *RFE/RL Newsline*, 30 May 1997, and Michael Gordon, 'Russia and Ukraine Finally Reach Accord on Black Sea Fleet', *New York Times*, 29 May 1997).

† Perhaps the most consistent and effective Russian economic reformer, Prime Minister Petr Stolypin (1906–11), who undertook to create private family farms by breaking up communal ownership of land, sought to gain support for his policies among conservatives in the Third Duma (1907–11) by blisteringly nationalistic rhetoric. In a country recently humiliated by defeat in the war with Japan, he found an eager audience. Great Russian nationalism 'increasingly figured' both in Stolypin's policies and in the decisions of the Third Duma. (Melissa Kirshchke Stockdale, *Paul Miliukov and the Quest for a Liberal Russia, 1880–1918*, pp. 176, 184, 185.)

The cumulative effect of the principal achievements of Yeltsin's foreign and security policy – the withdrawal of Russian troops from East-Central Europe and the Baltic countries; radical demilitarization of the Russian economy; the peaceful divorce with Ukraine; accommodation with NATO; and the first steps towards the effective inclusion of Russia in the West's key military, political and economic structures through the Russia–NATO Founding Act of 1997 and the G-8 summits in Denver and Birmingham – may be summarized quite simply: not since the middle of the sixteenth century, when Russian expansion began, has there been a Russia less aggressive, less belligerent, less threatening to neighbouring countries and to the world than Yeltsin's Russia.

Yeltsin's foreign and security policies represent several fundamental shifts from and even reversals of centuries of national tradition. He abandoned the tradition of the state's unchallenged preponderance (particularly in national security and foreign policy) over domestic economic, political and social progress. 'The first duty of the sovereign is to preserve the internal and external unity of the state,' the great Russian historian Nikolay Karamzin told Tsar Alexander I in a 1818 memorandum. 'Solicitude for the welfare of social classes and individuals must come second.'[30] The Russian patrimonial *état* was its own *raison*.

Completing what Gorbachev's 'new political thinking' had begun, Yeltsin revised the very criteria of national greatness. As he put it in a televised address on the seventh anniversary of the Declaration of State Sovereignty of Russia:

A great power is not mountains of weapons and subjects with no rights. A great power is a self-reliant and talented people with initiative ... In the foundation of our approach to the building of the Russian state ... is the understanding that the country begins with each of us. And the sole measure of the greatness of our Motherland is the extent to which each citizen of Russia is free, healthy, educated and happy ...[31]

As we have seen, in the context of Russian history, the voluntary shedding of empire is far more than 'decolonization'. Unlike the colonial possessions of Western powers, the maintenance of the Russian empire had repeatedly proved incompatible with democratization and the strengthening of civil society. 'Constitutional forms on the model of the West would be the greatest misfortune here,' Russia's greatest liberalizing Tsar, Alexander II, wrote to his son and heir Nicholas in 1865, 'and would have as their first consequence *not the unity of the State but the disintegration of the Empire into pieces.*'[32]

Throughout Russian history, a preoccupation with the integrity of the empire interrupted, set back or altogether stopped domestic political liberalization: from Alexander II, whose reforms were sidetracked by the suppression of the 1863–4 Polish uprising;* to Khrushchev's deStalinization, weakened by the crushing of the 1956 Hungarian revolution; to the mildly decentralizing 'Kosygin' economic reforms of 1965, abandoned after the 1968 invasion of Czechoslovakia; to Gorbachev's temporary retreat from reform in the winter of 1990–1 as he attempted to stop the march of the Baltic nations towards independence.

'At decisive moments it was not only the government but also Russian society which found itself unable to opt clearly for freedom if its price seemed to involve a threat to the country's unity and greatness,' wrote Adam Ulam.[33] Of the many 'cursed' questions that recur in Russian social, political and spiritual development, 'Russia imperial versus Russia free' was among the most persistent and painful. Boris Yeltsin is the first Russian ruler ever to have chosen the latter unequivocally over the former.

'Russia has always surrounded herself with [geographic] space that she dominated, as she expanded ceaselessly,' Yeltsin wrote in his memoirs. 'She strained herself, seizing more and more territories, and brought herself into a direct confrontation with all of Western civilization. As a result, she broke down . . . Such a degree of self-isolation is impossible.'[34] Accordingly, he has forged the new Russian national idea: separated from empire and drained of chauvinism and militant nationalism. 'To "unpack" imperial pretensions from Russian self-definition is not an easy task,' wrote a US observer of Russian post-communist transformation. 'Many Russian nationalists . . . pursue the most bigoted and jingoistic expressions of national identity possible. Boris Yeltsin, even at the height of his "Russian-ness", never pandered to such sentiment.'[35]

Following Gorbachev, Yeltsin woke Russia up from its solemn dreams

---

* Because of the militant chauvinism that swept Russia in the wake of the Polish rebellion, the circulation of the banner of Russian constitutional liberalism, Aleksandr Herzen's underground magazine *Kolokol*, fell precipitously. Neither the magazine nor its publisher would ever regain their intellectual sway over Russian society. It would take almost forty years until Petr Struve and Pavel Milyukov resurrected the movement in their newspaper *Osvobozhdenie* and, later, in the programme of the Kadet (Constitutional Democratic) Party.

and made it speak prose. Gone was Russian messianism ('Third Rome', 'pan-Slavism', 'Marxism–Leninism', 'world socialism'), which for centuries had been a key legitimizing component of Russian statehood. The Russian state and its purpose were finally demystified and desacralized. The end of the domestic and the Central-East European empire signalled the emergence in Russia of the fundamental institution of modernity: a secular nation-state, the foundations of which in the West had been laid by the Reformation four centuries before. This must be what a Russian scholar meant when he noted, brilliantly, that the end of the Soviet empire and the end of the Middle Ages in Russia happened on the same day: 21 August 1991.[36]

August 1991 and July 1996 heralded the arrival of a post-communist Russia – and a Russia whose institutions yielded only a first crude approximation of a democracy prone to spectacular lapses and distortions. Among the dozens of defects, several were especially troubling. With no usable legacy from the *ancien régime*, the institutional base of Russian democracy – an effective separation of powers, an independent and respected judiciary, a responsible and well-regarded parliament – was narrow and vulnerable. The links between polity and society, which had begun to emerge during perestroika, were thin and fragile. At times the entire political edifice seemed to be suspended in air with little by way of political and civic institutions to bear it up.

A great deal of the Russian democratic experiment would be found incongruous and even offensive in a mature liberal democracy. In Yeltsin's Russia, society's control over state was far from assured, much less made routine. Such tried and true instruments of this control as political parties (with the notable exception of the communists) failed to create mass followings. The division of power between the legislative and executive branches was lopsidedly in the latter's favour. The incompetent, rapacious, secretive and haughty bureaucracies continued to lord it over millions of citizens. The legitimacy of the new Russian state was daily undermined by the lack of improvement in the lives of most people, the never-ending delays in the payment of salaries, and the government's inability to curb crime or help the dispossessed.

In the first few years after 1992, economic dislocation, privatization, inflation and the drastic cuts in the budget outlays by a near-bankrupt state combined to produce a dramatic decrease in the standard of living as measured by the officially recorded income from salaries and pensions. In the minds of millions of Russians the galling unfairness of 'nomenklatura privatization' was linked to poverty, which was no longer obscured by secrecy, propaganda and lying statistics. A large majority of Russians were critical of the way their country was governed and had little confidence in the existing political institutions.

Yet Russian democracy survived the turmoil and the disappointments. Between 1993 and 1997, Russians voted in six national elections and referendums. On only one occasion – the Duma elections and the simultaneously held constitutional referendum in December 1993, two months after the bloodshed at the White House – did the turnout fall below 64 per cent of all eligible voters.

Thirteen electoral blocs or parties and 1,567 candidates outside the party lists competed in the 1993 legislative elections. In the 1995 Congressional elections, there were forty-three blocs and 2,688 candidates. There were ten candidates on the 1996 Presidential ballot, and 236 contenders for the fifty governorships at stake in 1996 alone. Opposition candidates were free to campaign and to win. Gennadiy Zyuganov defeated Yeltsin in thirty-two of eighty-nine regions. Candidates supported by the leftist People's Patriotic Union of Russia won a third of the contested governorships. Only half of the incumbent governors, appointed by Yeltsin, were re-elected. By the end of 1996, as a Russian scholar put it, 'the formation of the skeleton of the Russian political system, rooted in the 1993 Constitution, [was] largely accomplished'.[37]

To this process, the 1996 Presidential election was central. Under the most difficult circumstances, Yeltsin made, in the words of a Russian observer, a 'symbolic choice' and 'pledged allegiance to basic democratic values'.[38] Even in a political career notable for extraordinary personal courage, the decision of a very sick Yeltsin to stake everything on a seemingly hopeless electoral race takes a place of honour, next to October 1987 and August 1991.

Yeltsin's decision to run in 1996 created an enormously important precedent of popular legitimation. The regime's 'need to seduce the national electorate [was] in itself a very important fact', wrote a foreign student of Russian politics. 'The wielders of power were afraid of public rejection, but could not, or did not want to, run away from it. In this way, they demonstrated that popular sovereignty has imposed itself as a genuine democratic constraint in a country that otherwise was still far from being a democratic state.'[39]

The 1995–6 electoral cycle also legitimized the democratic system of regional governance and began to extend popular sovereignty where, in the end, it mattered most: to the local, daily, mundane affairs of the Russian people. 'The main result of the elections in the regions of the Russian Federation cannot be described mathematically,' wrote a liberal

Moscow expert. 'Its essence is the fact that the bureaucratic monopoly on local power – a 400-year-old monopoly – became the responsibility, even if only to a limited degree, of the [local] authorities to the voters.'[40]

Unlike the Asian modernizing authoritarian regimes in the 1980s (and unlike China, Indonesia and Malaysia in the 1990s), Russia's very imperfect but functioning grass-roots democracy, with freedom of speech and of the press, a political process open to opposition and regular free elections, supplies a measure of political stability. Eventually, popular sentiment for a less corrupt, more open and more equitable political and economic system is likely to translate itself into an effective force for change.

One momentous precedent has already been established: the end of the war in Chechnya. Never before in Russian history had non-violent political competition and free electoral choice borne so directly and effectively on the Kremlin's major national security policy. As a Russian commentator put it, 'In the Chechen war Russia was defeated, first and foremost, by herself: in Moscow political battles and in public opinion, rather than in military operations or negotiations [with the enemy].'[41]

In its explicitness and anti-government animus, in the audacity and the gruesomeness of aired images, the coverage of the Chechen war by Russian television, including the state-owned channels, was probably without parallel for any country at war – save, perhaps, that of the United States in Vietnam. Night after night, there were endless pictures of Grozny and its inhabitants tormented by the indiscriminate assaults by Russian artillery and bomber, the burned-out skeletons of buildings, the ground littered with dead and wounded.[42] 'One morning, there was a [government] statement that Russian warplanes were not bombing Grozny,' boasted the President of the private NTV network. 'That very evening, we showed our piece from Grozny, with Russian warplanes dropping bombs. It had an enormous effect.'[43]

Several times, after the Kremlin had declared Grozny taken by federal troops, the nightly news broadcasts showed fierce fighting for every building. The difference between Moscow's assertions and battlefield pictures was 'striking',[44] a witness reported. Just as striking was the networks' ability to withstand the pressure to comply with the official line. Yet no matter how much some members of the government would have liked to wring the necks of newspapers and networks, the Rubicon was never crossed. Not a single newspaper or television channel was censored, much less closed down, and not a single public opponent of the war harassed, much less arrested or harmed.

The new liberties and the privatized economy of Yeltsin's Russia had combined to take away from the Kremlin one of its most cherished assets: secrecy and the ability to mould public opinion in matters of national security. Suddenly, society found itself capable of scrutinizing the executive in the most jealously guarded of all undertakings – the prosecution of war. The authorities 'thought this would be like Afghanistan', said the NTV President. 'They didn't take the media into account.'[45] The Kremlin attempted to fight a Soviet war in post-Soviet Russia. This proved a doomed undertaking.

The imperatives of democratic politics left Yeltsin no choice: facing a run-off after barely winning the first round of the Presidential election, he sought to expand his constituency by an alliance with a candidate who had made the ending of the war the centrepiece of his platform: General Aleksandr Lebed. Having promised his voters peace in Chechnya, Lebed, with a lusty eye on the year 2000 Presidential election, was bent on keeping his word.

The wretched Chechen war proved that even a highly imperfect democracy weakens (if it does not eradicate) the imperial urge. It revealed a Russia in which civil society is neither lethargic nor powerless. Although tardy in bestowing on Russia many of its blessings, Russian democracy showed itself mature enough to make unpopular military engagements politically very risky. Just as the circumstances surrounding the war's beginning epitomized the legacy of imperial and authoritarian Russia, so was the exit from Chechnya emblematic of the promise of its democratic future.

Russia's most prominent human rights activist and one of the fiercest liberal critics of Yeltsin and the war, Sergey Kovalev, provided the best summary of the historic significance of Russia's exit from Chechnya:

The war was won by freedom of speech. By the several dozen honest journalists – just a few dozen – who continued to describe the truth about Chechnya to hundreds of thousands of readers and tens of millions of television viewers, despite pressure from the government . . .

In 1996, the more perceptive politicians seeking office understood that the country would not support anyone who would not promise to stop the bloodshed . . . It was at this moment that Yeltsin made several highly public moves toward a peaceful settlement of the conflict. It was exactly then that Lebed . . . beckoned the voters with the promise of immediate peace . . .

This, in fact, is democracy at work: society has mechanisms with which it can force the authorities to do what it demands, and not what the authorities themselves would like to do.

The Chechen crisis was the first serious battle for democracy in Russia. It would be going too far to say that our newborn, weak, sickly, uncertain civil society won this battle. But at least it did not lose.[46]

*

With the sole and tragic exception of Chechnya, Yeltsin managed to avert, without resorting to violence, a widely prophesied disintegration of Russia. He also developed a *modus vivendi* unprecedented in national history between central and local powers and laid the foundation of a genuinely federal, decentralized Russian state.

Never before had Russia managed to remain whole in the absence of armed and rigidly centralized authoritarianism. Every time the autocratic Centre (Moscow) was weakened – most spectacularly in the twenty-nine years between the death of Ivan the Terrible and the ascension of the first Romanov Tsar, Michael, in 1613; and then again between the February Revolution of 1917 and the consolidation of the Soviet state in 1920 – Russia swiftly dissolved into a conglomerate of quasi-independent and belligerent principalities.

From Gorbachev's Soviet Union, Russia inherited a virtual collapse of the key instruments of statehood: a worthless currency, almost wholly supplanted by barter; the near-collapse of inter-regional commerce; and a proliferation of local laws and regulations that effectively abrogated the state's sovereignty.* In the autumn of 1991, the disintegration of Russia was a plausible forecast.

Yeltsin was confronted with the same seemingly indissoluble link between authoritarianism and national integrity. Unlike smaller nations (and like the United States, India or Brazil), Russia was too large and too diverse to be both centralized and democratic. Only rigid and armed centralism had achieved national unity. 'It should now be clear,' a prominent pro-reform economist (and later Minister of Economy), Evgeniy

---

* In December 1990, under pressure from the provinces, the Congress of People's Deputies of Russia amended the Constitution of the Russian Federation and declared all of Russia's twenty-one ethnic 'autonomous Republics' to be 'Republics', making their status equal to that of the constituent Republics of the Soviet Union. Six months later, the Supreme Soviet of Russia adopted decrees that granted the status of 'Republic' to four out of the five ethnic 'autonomous provinces'. By the end of 1992, four of the newly created Republics – Tatarstan, Chechnya, Tuva and Buryatia – had declared various degrees of independence from Russia.

Yasin, predicted in December 1992, 'Russia in the foreseeable future cannot be simultaneously united and democratic.'[47]

Yeltsin, by contrast, believed that Russia could be democratic and whole at the same time. Indeed, he told regional leaders in the spring of 1996, 'Russia will have a truly democratic, prosperous and civilized future only on the basis of the development of federalism.'[48] He wished 'to build a federation, brick by brick, from the bottom up'.[49] The devolution of power to the provinces was to occur gradually – in exchange for their acceptance of Moscow's sovereignty over national security, taxation, and a share in natural resources. In November 1991, he proposed to enshrine in a new Russian constitution the division of Russia into semi-autonomous 'lands' (*zemli*), akin to German *Länder* or American states.[50] Each 'land', Yeltsin explained:

> would have its own legislative and executive organs. I have visited three German *Länder* and found that the division of functions [between the states and Bonn] is very strict. And there Chancellor Kohl does not meddle in the lives [of the states] by telling them what to do. [If he did] he would be told 'Sorry, but this is our business.' I think we will come to this too.[51]

Although this project was never realized because of the increasingly acrimonious disagreement between the President and the Supreme Soviet, in March 1992 Yeltsin masterminded the Federal Treaty – the first attempt at laying down the contours of Russia's post-Soviet statehood. The Treaty negotiations were the first instance of the tactic that Yeltsin would deploy in the settlement with Ukraine: a painstaking and incremental effort in which progress and momentum accrued from agreeing on what was possible at the time and ignoring or obfuscating that which could not be resolved and might lead to a rupture. In the end, the Treaty was signed by all the Republics with the exception of Tatarstan and Chechnya.

What mattered most were not the advantages and concessions that emerged from the Treaty's tug of war but a new (and for Russia revolutionary) principle of contractual equality between the provinces and the Centre in the assignment of rights and responsibilities. By lengthening the leash, rather than tightening (and, almost certainly, breaking) it, Yeltsin 'created a breathing space, allowed tempers to cool, [and] prevented Russia from falling apart'.[52] In the end, he achieved the compromise he sought: the Republics pledged adherence to the principle of the 'territorial unity' of the Russian Federation in exchange for the right to 'decide their internal problems themselves' and to 'expand their economic independence'.[53] 'Inter-regional co-operation', Yeltsin said at the time, was the 'best cure for separatism' and would 'do more for the unity of Russia than any state power'.[54]

A Ural native and descendant of migrants from Central Russia, Yeltsin was likely to be more sympathetic to the urge for autonomy and less protective of Moscow's control. As a former Obkom First Secretary, he knew well the crushing burden of the economic and political responsibilities of local leaderships squeezed in a vice between the needs of their regions and orders from Moscow. 'This is what we have [in the Russian political tradition]: a vertical system of life,' Yeltsin wrote. 'Those who are at the top trample underfoot those who are on the bottom. This is what used to be known as "Russia whole and undivided". Yet towards the end of the millennium even this fundamental feature of ours is bound to change . . . The power of Russia is in . . . her towns, her provinces.'[55]

A year and a half after the signing of the Federal Treaty, Yeltsin laid another cornerstone of a decentralized Russian state. In one of those epiphanies that had punctuated his rise since 1987, he arrived at a seemingly counter-intuitive and doomed arrangement that in retrospect proved to be the only viable solution. On 15 February 1994 after three years of negotiations, Moscow signed a treaty with the most populous of the Republics, Tatarstan: an oil-rich enclave of 3.7 million people (nearly half of them ethnic Russians) roughly the size of Ireland, in the Volga–Urals region 700 kilometres from Moscow.

The Treaty granted Tatarstan most of the rights of a sovereign nation: its own flag, constitution and laws; the right to collect taxes; and ownership of the natural resources in its territory, foremost of them oil. The Republic was to draft its own budget and conduct its own foreign trade. Its youth were exempt from all-Russian military conscription.

'The very idea of signing an agreement with part of itself' was, a commentator correctly noted, quite 'unorthodox'.[56] Moreover, the agreement was imbued with 'constructive ambiguity', especially on the subject of ultimate sovereignty: was it Moscow's or Kazan's? The Treaty committed the signatories only to 'mutual delegation of powers'.[57] Yet it was precisely this deliberate vagueness,* this highly individualized

---

* Four years later, Yeltsin fashioned the exit from Chechnya in a similar way: independence short of the right to its own currency and to diplomatic representation abroad and a five-year 'transitional period', during which the differences between Moscow and Grozny were to be settled.

and differentiated approach to solving the federal crisis one step at a time, and, most importantly, the principle of direct and equal negotiations between Moscow and provinces that endowed the agreement with subtlety and flexibility and so made it a model for rebuilding the Russian state.

The 1994 formula gave each Republic a chance to negotiate on the basis of its own strengths and weaknesses, with richer enclaves gaining greater autonomy for themselves (and relief for Moscow from most of its financial responsibilities), while economically weaker regions traded sovereignty for assistance from the Centre. By November 1995, thirteen Republics had signed bilateral treaties with Moscow. Soon they were joined by ethnic Russian *oblast*s, jealous of the Republics' prerogatives and insisting on equal treatment for all eighty-nine 'subjects of the Federation'. By the summer of 1997, when Yeltsin signed power-sharing treaties with governors of five *oblast*s, the total number of such treaties grew to thirty-one. The dangers of secessionism and of the country's disintegration were now safely behind.

In 1995 Yeltsin authorized direct elections of governors ('heads of administrations'), who had formerly been appointed by the President. In the view of a Russian scholar, elections resulted in the 'further decentralization of political and economic power and the weakening of the Federal centre'.[58] As all newly elected governors were *ex officio* Deputies of the upper House of the Russian parliament, the Council of the Federation, the regional influence on national policies and politics grew even stronger. Thus, in Yeltsin's second term, an entirely new entity was beginning to take shape: a decentralized but nevertheless whole Russian state, consisting of self-governing provinces.

*

We, the multi-ethnic people of the Russian Federation,
united by a common destiny on our land,
asserting human rights and liberties, civil peace and concord,
preserving historically established state unity,
proceeding from the generally recognized principles of the equality
and self-determination of peoples,
revering the memory of our forebears who passed down to us love
and respect for the Fatherland, faith in goodness and justice,
reviving the sovereign statehood of Russia and asserting the permanence of its democratic foundation,
seeking to ensure the well-being and prosperity of Russia,
proceeding from responsibility for our Motherland before present
and future generations,

recognizing ourselves as part of the world community, adopt the
CONSTITUTION OF THE RUSSIAN FEDERATION.

Thus began the 1993 Russian Constitution – a critical piece of
Yeltsin's legacy. 'We the people' was only one of many borrowings
from the Constitution of the United States. Nor was the Declaration of
Independence far from the Russian framers' minds when they proclaimed that 'the main rights and liberties of man are inalienable and
each person is endowed with them at birth'.

Yeltsin's Constitution proclaimed 'diversity' of ideologies, prohibited
the establishment of a state ideology and recognized 'political diversity',
the multiplicity of political parties and separation of Church and state.
'Cruel and humiliating' punishment was banned. No one could be convicted twice 'for the same offence' and no one was 'obliged to testify
against himself, his spouse or close relatives'. The freedom of the mass
media was guaranteed, and censorship forbidden.

Another formative influence was the French Fifth Republic: the political system fashioned by Charles de Gaulle between 1958 and 1962.
That this should be so is hardly surprising. It is difficult to find two
European nations at once as different and as similar as Russia and
France. Europe's two largest countries, they have in common centuries of
war, of grand conquests and invasions by mortal enemies, of battlefield
triumphs and horrific defeats which imperilled the very survival of the
nation. This history has instilled in them an 'eternal vigilance against
the machinations of foreign states'[59] and a self-perceived 'special destiny'
of being 'constantly in danger' (in de Gaulle's words);[60] an intense and
militant patriotism, often bordering on xenophobia, with tanks parading
through the hearts of their capitals on national holidays; and a recurrent
national concern about the 'contamination' of their languages by foreign
words.

Nihilism and cynicism were somehow combined with a reverence for
raison d'état and for the state as the embodiment of national glory. The
supreme leader – the tsar, the *vozhd'*, the *khozyain*, *le roi*, the President
– was at once revered and resented, heroically defended and cruelly
overturned. National unity was a fetish, as was a unique national mission and destiny. Both nations have proved highly susceptible to universal, monistic political doctrines. Theories that explain everything at once
are national passions – as is the adulation of the *écrivain* and the *philo-
sophe* as the giver and enforcer of national purpose and national mores.
In modern times, in both Russia and France, intellectuals were in thrall to
intensely Manichaean ideologies and were fascinated by totalitarianism.

Like no other European capitals, Moscow and Paris utterly dominated their countries' lives through sweeping and rigid intellectual and aesthetic fashions.

Both nations might also be unique in having what de Gaulle called a 'propensity for division and quarrel'.[61] Contentious, fiercely individualistic, truculent and passionately partisan (except when the Fatherland – the *otechestvo* and the *patrie* – are in mortal danger), the French and the Russians appear to have difficulty with the Anglo-Saxon tradition of building and sustaining grand coalitions, based on compromise and consensus. 'The French only make reform in the course of revolution,' de Gaulle said.[62] The two Constitutions were alike too in the circumstances surrounding their adoption: a deep political crisis, verging on a civil war; the text written behind closed doors by the leader's advisers; and a national referendum after less than three months of public debate.

But of course what attracted Yeltsin the most was the central feature of de Gaulle's creation: an exalted Presidency and the asymmetry in the powers of the executive and the legislative branches. The labels affixed to de Gaulle's document by contemporaries were to be repeated by Yeltsin's critics for years to come: an 'elective monarchy',[63] a 'monarchy tempered by plebiscite',[64] an 'authoritarian republic',[65] a 'monarchie républicaine',[66] 'dictatorship' and 'le coup d'état permanent'.[67] (In a letter to his son de Gaulle himself called his creation a 'popular monarchy'.)[68]

The only elected representative of the entire people, the President was the living embodiment of state and nation, their self-appointed guardian, and protector of the Constitution – 'arbiter', to use one of de Gaulle's favourite terms. The inequality of the executive and legislative branches in both republics was epitomized by the right of the Russian and French Presidents to dissolve parliament. The 1993 Russian Constitution limited this right to two specific occasions: if the parliament passed a vote of no-confidence in the government twice within three months (the alternative was to dismiss the government), and if the Duma thrice rejected the President's choice for the 'Chairman of the government' (the Prime Minister).* Yeltsin never dissolved the Duma but used the

---

* The Russian parliament cannot be dissolved before a year has elapsed following an election, nor within the six months preceding it.

The French President may dissolve the National Assembly and schedule new elections for any reason and at any time (except twice within twelve months). De Gaulle dissolved the parliament in 1962 because of the Assembly's censure of the government. Mitterrand

threat of dissolution to sustain the reformist agenda and reformist governments in 1997 and 1998.

The Kremlin must have the Duma's consent to the appointment of the Prime Minister and it can neither appoint nor dismiss the Chairman of the Central Bank and the Procurator General without the approval of the Duma. The Russian parliament (the Federal Assembly) may override a Presidential veto by a two-thirds majority in both Houses, and then the President has to sign the measure into law. The Duma's difficulty in challenging the executive branch more effectively stemmed not so much from an insurmountable constitutional limitation but, rather, from the deep ideological divisions between factions and the monstrous egos of their leaders. For them, advancing a political agenda was, most of the time, secondary to ensuring complete control of their followers. Indeed, on those rare occasions when it managed to forge a working majority, the Duma showed itself capable of blocking – for years – government-sponsored legislation (for instance, land privatization, a new Tax Code). In matters relating to the Duma's constitutional prerogatives, the legislature could bypass the Kremlin altogether, as when it voted the 1994 amnesty for the instigators of the events of August 1991 and October 1993.

In the spring and summer of 1997 the Federal Assembly created a landmark precedent by mustering a two-thirds majority in both Houses and overriding the President's veto of three measures: the so-called Trophy Art bill, which prohibited the return of art and museum objects seized by the Soviet Union in the Second World War; the Law on the Government, which strengthened parliamentary oversight of the Kremlin and required that the entire cabinet resign if a Prime Minister were dismissed by the President; and the Freedom of Conscience and Religious Associations bill, which hindered some denominations, 'cults' and 'sects' in acquiring legal status in Russia. After rancorous and protracted battles, in which both sides appealed to the Constitutional Court, and the establishment of 'conciliatory commissions', Yeltsin signed all three measures into law.

The flaws in the political system Yeltsin has bequeathed Russia are great and many. The 'perils of presidentialism', of which the leading 'transitologist' Juan Linz warned post-authoritarian countries,[69] were,

---

followed suit in 1981 and 1988. In what might be the single largest political blunder in the history of the Fifth Republic, Jacques Chirac in 1997 resorted to dissolution and new elections, in which the ruling coalition was routed by the socialist bloc.

in the Russian case, exacerbated by centuries of rigidly centralized authoritarian rule and further magnified by seven decades of Soviet totalitarianism.

There was always the danger of the incumbent's refusal to leave office
and of his attempts to reinterpret (or even rewrite) the Constitution to
allow extensions of his term and to turn an 'authoritarian republic' into
a dictatorship. There was more than a little doubt that the Presidents
of Belarus, Kazakhstan, Turkmenistan, Uzbekistan and Kyrgyzstan, who
had modelled their constitutions on that of Russia, would ever voluntarily vacate their office.

As in the case of France, the Russian 'authoritarian republic' is both
sustained by and perpetuates the ephemeral nature of national political
parties. Only the Russian left, the KPRF, could field a truly national
party and cobble together a lasting coalition (as did the French communists and socialists, united by Mitterrand in 1971). Again as in France,
the representation of the rest of Russia's political spectrum is weak
and incoherent by Western European standards. With the parliament's
policy-making role severely limited, the major (if not, indeed, main)
function of Russian 'parties', much like that of their French counterparts,
is to serve as stepping stones in their leaders' quest for the Presidency
or for a permanent political presence.

A paradoxical result is a strange depoliticization of the powerful
Presidency. Without firm and lasting links to a truly national party,
insulated from such a party's commitments and agenda and beholden
ultimately only to his perception of the nation's mood, the 'President
of the people' is likely to exhibit an ideological flexibility bordering on
rank opportunism, to disregard electoral promises and to change positions with the ease of a weathervane. Much to the chagrin of radical
reformers, Yeltsin's policies and personnel decisions in the aftermath of
the nationalist and communist successes in the 1993 and 1995 parliamentary elections fit this pattern very comfortably.*

One may not, of course, equate one of the oldest democracies, blessed
with centuries of a vibrant and refined civil society, with a newly emergent quasi-democratic polity, preceded by decades of totalitarian communism and centuries of autocratic despotism. And yet, *mutatis mutandis*,

---

* For this, too, there is a French precedent. De Gaulle's political and economic agendas
were always nebulous beyond the restoration and protection of France's *grandeur*. Mitterrand was more protean still, beginning with 'a clean break with capitalism' (which
included zealous nationalization, protectionism, wage and price freezes and a tax on
'large fortunes') and ending with privatization and monetarism.

the similarities between France in 1958 and Russia in 1993 were undeniable: deep and intense ideological divisions ('ideological abysses', Stanley Hoffmann called them);[70] an absence of truly national parties; a
parliament where a working majority is a rarity and where factions
behaved, to recall de Gaulle again, like 'delinquent peer groups'.[71] De
Gaulle's 'elective and democratic monarchy'[72] made the Fifth Republic
France's longest-lived regime (after the Third Republic) and by far the
most stable one since 1789. De Gaulle's Constitution produced a republic whose institutions were both 'legitimate and capable of action'.[73]
The Yeltsin Constitution might do the same for Russia.

As some of the key symptoms of the illness were the same, so, per-
chance, might be the cure. Of all the available models of Western democracy, the Fifth Republic was not just the political regime closest to
Russian tradition – a version of it may very well have been the only one
capable of procuring a modicum of political stability during the decades
of transition. In Raymond Aron's words: 'when the nation is so profoundly divided, you get no common will. With the Constitution of the
Fifth Republic, perhaps, there will not be a common will, but there will
be a will.'[74]

To an observer brought up in the Anglo-Saxon parliamentary tradition or accustomed to America's inveterate suspicion of the executive,
the 'authoritarian republic' is a strange and menacing political animal.
And yet the Fifth Republic did combine 'complete liberty with absolute
monarchy'.[75] Both human and political rights were exercised freely and
not infringed. Critics were not silenced, opposition was allowed complete liberty, independent media were many and diverse.

'An all-powerful Assembly is satisfactory when the Assembly knows
what it wants,' Aron wrote in 1960. 'But when there is no majority in
an all-powerful Assembly, nothing results but chaos.'[76] No one who has
ever watched the kaleidoscope of Russian parliamentary politics, in
which blocs and coalitions, solemnly proclaimed one day, splintered
and changed colour a week later; who heard Vladimir Zhirinovskiy's
speeches and watched his vicious clowning; who read the almost
monthly calls for the dismissal of the government; who witnessed a
Duma fractured and paralysed by ideological schism, factionalism and
the system of political spoils,* could wish for an all-powerful Russian
parliament just yet. A parliamentary republic in today's Russia is likely

---

* As no party held a majority in the Duma, the Chairmanships of the committees in the
legislature were distributed proportionate to factional strength. The communist faction
appointed nine Chairmen; Our Home Is Russia, the Liberal Democratic Party of Russia

to vindicate another of Raymond Aron dictums: 'If the French Assembly gets 200 Communists and the rest are divided, things will be the same as before . . .'[77]

In time, a devolution of power from the President to parliament would be both inevitable and beneficial – when the divisions in the Duma are no longer about the change of the political and economic system but about a range of choices within it; when a succession of parliamentary elections produces a breed of legislators who feel bound by their word and honour both to their constituencies and to Russia's national interest and who are driven by responsibility as much as by Presidential ambition.

In France, a redistribution of power between the executive and parliament did occur in an unexpected way through *cohabitation*, in which the leader of the parliament's majority (or even plurality) became the Prime Minister. Such an arrangement seems quite conceivable in Russia as well. The 'round table' consultations between Yeltsin and the Speakers of both Houses, introduced in 1997, were the first step in that direction. The Russian version of *cohabitation* became reality when Yeltsin was forced by the Duma to appoint Evgeniy Primakov in September 1998.

'In present-day France, General de Gaulle is the best possible monarch in the least bad of possible governments,' Aron wrote on the first anniversary of de Gaulle's regime. 'He manipulated the 1958 revolution in order to produce an authoritarian republic, not fascism nor a military despotism.'[78] History's verdict on the Russian 'authoritarian republic' that Yeltsin forged in 1993 is likely to be the same.

In political history, that which proves most important in the long run is usually most difficult to define, categorize and measure. Some of the most critical components of Yeltsin's legacy fall into this category. When nations attempt to change their destiny, much is decided outside the framework of laws and institutions, and in the daily interactions of polity and society where the spirit of a new social contract between the state and the people is born.

A great deal in Yeltsin's legacy impedes the emergence of such a contract. While bridging a politically polarized society, supplying a

---

and Yabloko were given four Chairmanships each, and the Agrarians and Russian Regions two. Composed in such a way, committees operated on the basis of consensus, rather than majoritarian principles. Sluggishness and legislative incoherence were the inevitable results.

measure of governability and preserving basic political and civil rights and liberties, the Russian authoritarian Presidency encroached on the prerogatives of the legislative branch and weakened the checks and balances of democracy. The dominance of the executive slowed a critically important transition from an electoral to a liberal democracy: in the former, society is periodically called on to arbitrate an open competition within the political class for the ownership of the state; in the latter, the state is owned, scrutinized and policed by society. Yeltsin planted in Russia the irreducible tripartite core of a modern democracy – mass media free from government censorship, freedom of political opposition, and the ability of voters to choose freely among political alternatives through honest elections. However, these are necessary but not yet sufficient conditions for genuine societal self-rule.

Yet, just as it stifled the nascent civil society in some instances, the political order fashioned by Yeltsin was benign, even nurturing, in others. The first of these was the tolerance of public criticism. Although subject to manipulation, bribery and intimidation by business moguls and local authorities (which subsidized the rent, plant and utilities of most national and local newspapers), the Russian mass media were free from government censorship.

By 1995, criticism of the President was no longer limited to newspapers. Television, including state-owned channels, eagerly joined the game. The wholly state-owned Russian Television Channel covered both Yeltsin's 'conducting' of a German band in August and the President's 'oversleeping' when he missed his appointment with the Prime Minister of Ireland at Shannon airport a month later. The privately owned NTV was at the forefront. Every Saturday night the President and his government were skewered on the popular *Kukly* ('Puppets') show, a brilliant and outrageous satire.* After one of the most sarcastic shows in June 1995, in which the President, his entourage and the

---

* In one of the skits Yeltsin was a conceited Robinson Crusoe, enjoying his mastery over an island (which the Russian viewer immediately recognized as the Kremlin) but wondering if he could ever get back to civilization alive. 'I am here quite alone,' Crusoe–Yeltsin narrates as he writes in his journal. 'I have no idea what happened to my mates.' 'What do you mean, you don't know?' exclaims his faithful companion, the parrot. 'You have drowned them all yourself!' 'Now, you hold your tongue, stupid bird,' Yeltsin replies. 'They were not "drowned" but swept away by a revolutionary wave.' For a Russian, especially a Moscow, audience, accustomed to brutal Kremlin intrigues and the President's thirst for power, this exchange rang unmistakably and hilariously true. (Videotape in the author's archive.)

leaders of the opposition were portrayed as down-and-out alcoholic beggars (and Yeltsin, dressed as a woman, begged on a train holding a baby with the face of his then chief bodyguard and confidant, Aleksandr Korzhakov), the President's office filed a libel suit, but dropped it a month later.

In the autumn of 1996 Russian television broke the most sacred of traditional Russian taboos and made public details of the Chief Executive's medical condition. When heart-bypass surgery was performed on Yeltsin several weeks later, it became, as previously noted, the first such instance of which the country had been notified beforehand. After that, the President's health became the staple of Russian television. During Yeltsin's next 'disappearance' in January 1997, his health was the subject of all prime-time television news and talk shows.

In the autumn of 1997 Aleksandr Korzhakov published memoirs full of the most embarrassing details of Yeltsin's personal life and health. During the pre-publication publicity campaign Korzhakov told Western journalists that Yeltsin was a 'helpless, quivering old man'.[79]* Yeltsin's spokesman responded by saying that, while the President was, of course, upset by some of the things in Korzhakov's book, he intended to do nothing to halt or delay publication.[80] Half a year later, Aleksandr Korzhakov was elected to the Duma from the Tula region.

Yeltsin considered freedom of press and its independence from 'orders of political *nachal'nik*s' one of the new Russia's main 'achievements':

This freedom has resulted in an intensive proliferation of publications and television channels, in a multiplicity of opinions and views. This is how it should be. A truly democratic society is impossible without freedom of speech and of the press.

Of course, not everyone likes it this way. Every now and then we hear loud reprimands: 'You are not writing correctly, you are not showing in a right way, what you produce ought to be softer, nobler, prettier.' In short, we are being pushed towards an imposition of certain prohibitions on the mass media. And this, no matter how you

* Previewing excerpts from the book which it published in August 1997, London's *Times* (13 August) wrote: 'Yesterday [Mr Korzhakov] described his relationship with Mr Yeltsin as "a divorce, final and irrevocable". After Mr Yeltsin reads the 500-page book, divorce may be putting it mildly. In page after page Mr Korzhakov describes his former employer as mentally unstable, and at times suicidal, an alcoholic who allowed Russia's key reform period to be hijacked by a corrupt bureaucracy and a criminal business class.'

slice it, is already censorship. First, of course, this would be a 'limited' censorship, and then, you understand, more and more. This we have already seen. We know where this leads. That is why we shall not allow political and ideological censorship.

We can see how much society needs freedom of speech, how much it has already got used to it. Therefore, it is impossible to go back to the era of humiliating lies and a false unity of thought.[81]

Building on Gorbachev's legacy of tolerance, the first Russian President institutionalized and vastly expanded it beyond tolerating just tiny and amorphous organizations of 'loyal' opposition, like the Inter-Regional Group. This freedom of action for organized and radical opposition, unremittingly hostile to the regime and the Chief Executive personally, makes Yeltsin's the most tolerant regime in Russian history outside the ten months between February and October 1917.

In 1992, the Constitutional Court declared invalid Yeltsin's August 1991 ban on the Communist Party's local organizations. The President complied. Although the Court upheld the prohibition of a nation-wide communist organization, a few months later the CPSU (reconstituted as the Communist Party of the Russian Federation, the KPRF) was again by far the largest political organization in Russia. In 1993, the Constitutional Court struck down another Presidential ban: on the National Salvation Front, a radical leftist-nationalist organization which openly called for the overthrow of the Yeltsin government. Again, the authorities obeyed the Court's order.

Twice in the first two years of his rule, Yeltsin had opportunities (indeed, was expected by most of the political class) to silence implacable opponents: in August 1991 and October 1993. He chose, instead, to allow them to continue their activities. After defeating a violent opposition and succeeding in the adoption of a new constitution that gave the executive branch 'significantly greater power' than before, the regime, wrote two Russian scholars,

did not use its new power for the *de facto* elimination of the legislative branch (as did the Italian and German fascists, and as the Russian fascists dream of doing in the future). On the contrary, parliamentary elections were held [and] the legislative branch was formed, which, although unequal in its power to the executive, preserved its independence and an opportunity of significant influence on how society is governed.[82]

In vain would one search through Russia's blood-stained history for words akin to those uttered by Yeltsin on 5 October 1993 – a call to national mourning and reconciliation from the leader who the previous day had suppressed an armed rebellion:

One should not say that someone has won and someone has lost. Today these words are misplaced, they are blasphemous. We have all been burned by the deadly breath of fratricide. People, our compatriots, were killed. One cannot bring them back. Pain and suffering have entered many families. However different their beliefs, they were all children of Russia. This is our common tragedy, our common sorrow – the great sorrow. Let us remember this madness, so that it will never be allowed to repeat itself.[83]*

Yeltsin's lenience towards unrepentant and violent enemies would be remarkable in any revolution. In the Russian political tradition, it was truly amazing. Those who in August 1991 sent the tanks to the White House in preparation for a deadly assault were never even brought to trial.† Every legal excuse was made: from disqualifying the prosecutors because of their public statements to the defendants' poor health to insufficient time for preparing a defence. While in prison awaiting trial for their role in the coup, Vasiliy Starodubtsev and Anatoliy Lukyanov were elected to the Duma. In 1997 Starodubtsev ran on the communist ticket for Governor of the Tula *oblast* and won.

With the exception of Ruslan Khazbulatov, and Generals Achalov and Makashov, who commanded the rebel forces, not one of the 1,041 Deputies of the rebellious Congress of People's Deputies was arrested or banned from politics. Many became Duma Deputies again in December

---

* Yeltsin's first public statement after the 1996 victory in the Presidential election also called for national reconciliation: 'Let us not divide the country into winners and losers. Let us work. After all, we have one Russia. We have the same Russia and the same fate, hence the same future.' (Boris Yeltsin, Address of the President on national television, 4 July 1996 (FBIS, 5 July 1996, p. 1).)

† The only exception was General Valentin Varennikov, who insisted on being tried and was acquitted. In Kiev during the coup General Varennikov, who was at the time Commander of Ground Troops of the Soviet Union, sent to Moscow coded telegrams urging his fellow plotters 'immediately to take measures to liquidate the adventurist Yeltsin and his gang'. (Yeltsin, *Zapiski*, p. 115.) In 1995 he campaigned for a Duma seat and was elected.

1993.* The February 1994 amnesty, legislated by the Duma and, after initial protest, signed by Yeltsin, was the first time in Russian history that the executive was forced by the legislative branch to grant pardon and complete freedom of political activity to a regime's violent and unrepentant foes. Two years later, General Albert Makashov was elected to the Duma on the communist ticket.† In the same 1995 election, Viktor Anpilov narrowly missed becoming a Deputy at the head of Working Russia's party list.

In October 1996, Aleksandr Rutskoy was elected governor of the Kursk *oblast*. Representing the Kremlin at Rutskoy's pompous inauguration, rife with heavy nationalist and Russian Orthodox themes, was one of the most market-oriented and anti-communist Governors of Russia (soon to become First Deputy Prime Minister), Boris Nemtzov of Nizhniy Novgorod. Rutskoy's first official trip outside Kursk was to Moscow, where he met with the President's Chief of Staff Anatoliy Chubais. Commenting on Rutskoy's reconciliation with the Kremlin, a leading Russian political weekly noted with some melancholy that 'no one seems to have been surprised' by it. 'Yet such behaviour by former enemies', the editorial continued, 'should have been considered a major political sensation of our time.'[84]‡

And so it was. The return to politics of the losers of August 1991 and October 1993 established a critical precedent: a defeat in the struggle for power (even after a violent confrontation) no longer meant the end of one's political life. Boris Yeltsin's 1988 debt to Gorbachev, who allowed the ostracized Party boss his political rebirth, had been repaid with interest.

* * *

* Among them was the leftist nationalist Sergey Baburin, who two months earlier had introduced in the Supreme Soviet the bill mandating execution for some of the opponents of the Rutskoy–Khazbulatov 'government'. Baburin was re-elected in December 1995.

† On 6 October 1998 at a meeting of communists and 'popular patriots' Makashov, looking directly at a television camera, said, 'Vsekh zhidov – v mogilu!' ('All yids – into the grave!'). Convalescing in the Crimea, an 'indignant' Yeltsin immediately denounced the remarks as 'aggressive' and demanded an investigation by the Procuracy. In the Duma, only 107 of 450 members voted for a mildly worded resolution that 'expressed concern' about Makashov's remarks.

‡ The other leader of the 1993 rebellion, Ruslan Khazbulatov, continued to live in one of the poshest Moscow neighbourhoods (Granatniy Pereulok) in a huge apartment intended for Leonid Brezhnev. As the Chairman of the Supreme Soviet, Khazbulatov, in retirement since February 1994, had 'appropriated' the flat free of charge.

Over the past two centuries, few indicators of the nature of Russian political regimes were as sensitive and precise as their approach to the 'Jewish question': freedom for Jews to practise their religion, to follow tradition, to engage in specifically Jewish cultural projects, and to enjoy a general freedom from stigma and freedom from discrimination in jobs and education. Greater acceptance of Jews invariably coincided with periods of political tolerance; increased discrimination always heralded a turn towards reaction and repression for the country as a whole.

Taking over the country which added the word *pogrom* to the world's vocabulary, a country where only a few years before a difference in the percentage of one's Jewish blood determined admission to a prestigious college (it was an axiom in Moscow in the 1970s that even half-Jews could not be admitted to Moscow University, while quarter-Jews had a chance) and prospects of employment, and where systematic purges had made politics and government pristinely *judenfrei*, Yeltsin unabashedly promoted Jews to positions of the highest responsibility.

During Yeltsin's two terms in office, Jews in the top echelons of the government included First Deputy Prime Minister Boris Nemtsov; Deputy Prime Minister and Minister of Economy Yakov Urinson; Deputy Secretary of the Security Council Boris Berezovskiy; the President's Deputy Chief of Staff and chief economic adviser Alexander Livshits (who at one time also served as Minister of Finance); Deputy Chief of Staff Mikhail Komissar; the long-time Adviser to the President on Inter-Ethnic and Regional Problems, Dr Emil Pain; Chairman of the State Committee for Housing and Civil Engineering Ephim Basin; Deputy Minister of the Economy Zinovy Pak; and Minister Without Portfolio for Co-ordination and Analysis of Economic Programmes Evgeniy Yasin.*

Russia's new internal passports, which began to be issued in October 1997, did not contain the bane of the Russian Jews: the infamous 'fifth point', the line for 'nationality'. The object of innumerable sardonic jokes told by Jews in Soviet times, the 'nationality' line in the passports was an often insurmountable barrier to better education and better jobs for hundreds of thousands of men and women. In the words of a leading

---

* In opening the government to Jews, Yeltsin was probably moved not by some extraordinary judophilia but by the Ural–Siberian tradition of diversity, acceptance and meritocracy, touched on in the first chapters of this book. Anyone who travelled beyond the Urals even in Soviet times could not fail to notice a strange insouciance, a blessed unawareness of the 'Jewish question', which figured so prominently in Central and especially Southern Russia.

Russian ethnographer, the line 'targeted [a Jew] for discrimination . . . provoked the state to grossly violate his or her rights'.[85] Without the 'fifth point', in the opinion of a prominent Jewish human rights activist, 'a bureaucrat won't have grounds to practice his xenophobia'.[86]

Along with the liberties and opportunities that democracy and a privatized economy brought to millions of Russians, the end of state anti-Semitism suddenly created a world most Russian Jews had thought utterly impossible only a few years before. 'Life for [Russian] Jews has never been better,' observed the *New York Times*'s Moscow correspondent in the spring of 1997. 'The state-sponsored discrimination of the Soviet era has been abolished, opening doors to the highest branches of academia, business and government.'[87] Suddenly, it was 'no longer shameful to be Jewish in Russia', noted a prominent Moscow Jew. 'Nobody is hiding the fact that they are Jewish anymore . . .'[88]

After peaking in 1990 and 1991, when a total of 255,000 Jews, mostly from Russia, left the Soviet Union, Jewish emigration from formerly Soviet territory declined steadily. By 1993 the numbers decreased to around 60,000 a year, with the majority of emigrants, for the first time, coming from non-Russian parts of the former USSR.[89] By the end of 1995, with the number of departures from Russia dropping sharply, for the first time since the early 1970s there were more Jews leaving from Ukraine than from Russia, where at least 1.7 million Jews lived at the time.[90]

Even young Moscow Jews – traditionally the segment of the Russian Jewish community that was the most Zionist, pugnacious, vociferous and sensitive to anti-Semitism – appeared to be swayed by what a resident American reporter called 'the blossoming and institutionalization of Jewish life in a more democratic Russia', where the 'state ideology of atheism and organized anti-Semitism has all but disappeared'.[91] A pioneering study of Moscow Jewish youth organizations found in 1997 that an overwhelming majority of the activists interviewed (79 per cent) did not consider anti-Semitism a problem.[92] 'I can calmly come to work at a Jewish organization and can talk about my Jewish life at my work place,' a young Jewish activist told an American researcher. Another added: 'As a group we don't have the fear as before. In the Metro I can loudly say Israel or Jewish.' Said a third: 'The generation older than me might say it's not possible to have not met with [state] anti-Semitism. However, I could walk around Moscow waving an Israeli flag, and no one would say anything.'[93]

By the mid-1990s the wish to leave (or to stay provisionally and warily) was slowly being replaced by an attempt to make Russia home while freely asserting a new-found confidence and pride in Jewishness. The revival of Jewish religious, cultural and communal life in Russia after near-total extinction was astonishing. 'Russian Jews . . . have re-established Judaism as a religion and a culture,' an American journalist reported in the spring of 1997. 'Religious schools and synagogues are flourishing . . . All over Russia there are Hebrew schools and universities, ultra-Orthodox Lubavitch communities, soup kitchens and kosher shops.'[94]

On 3 April 1996, the first day of Passover, hundreds of Moscow Jews jammed the short street before Moscow's main synagogue to taste Russian-made matzohs. 'Khleb [bread] Filippova, Moscow Guild of Bakers, Kosher for Passover', read a small white label in Russian. At the time, the Chief Rabbi proudly explained that Filippov's was the first kosher bakery in Russia in 'at least 50 years'.[95] A year and a half later, along with the Orthodox Patriarch and the Supreme Mufti of Russia's Muslims, that same Rabbi, Pinchas Goldschmidt, addressed the nation as one of its 'spiritual leaders' on the state-owned, commercial-free, public television channel Kul'tura ('Culture'), launched the day before.

In January 1998, the fiftieth anniversary of the murder by Stalin's secret police of Russia's greatest Yiddish actor and director Solomon Mikhoels was marked with a festival of Jewish art in Moscow. Begun with a star-studded concert at the Bolshoi and a candlelit midnight vigil at the enormous Rossia concert hall, it lasted for a week and included myriad concerts (including one by an Israeli dance company), readings, documentary film screenings, and, for the first time since Khrushchev's brief 'thaw' in the early 1960s, a staging of *The Diary of Anne Frank*. The festival was organized by some of Russia's most prominent actors and writers (Jewish and non-Jewish) and was sponsored by banks and businesses.[96]

Freedom to publish began to bind Russian Jews into a community again. By 1993 there were three Russian-language Jewish newspapers in Moscow, the largest of which, the *Jewish Gazette*, had a circulation of 42,000. (There were about 180,000 Jews in Moscow at the time.)[97] A monthly magazine, *Lekhaim* (from the Hebrew *l'chiam*, 'to life'), started in December 1991 as an eight-page, black-and-white newsletter. Four years later, it was a state-of-the-art publication, its eighty pages in full colour, with dozens of advertisements for Jewish businesses and banks, and a circulation of 50,000.[98]

The thoroughly assimilated community began to recover the nearly forgotten faculty of bringing up its young as Jews. Moscow's first Jewish summer camp opened in the summer of 1993 and took in 600 children.

Between 1990 and 1996, sixteen Jewish educational institutions sprang up in Moscow alone: kindergartens, colleges, rabbinical schools.[99] Among them was a private school run by the Lubavitch sect. In September 1993, when it enrolled 200 boys and girls (with some 100 more on the waiting list), the Moscow city administration gave the school a city-owned building – the first time the Russian capital had given a public facility to a Jewish group.[100]*

The communal entry of Russian Jews into an emerging Russian civil society was heralded by the 11 January 1996 establishment of the Russian Jewish Congress, whose founding members were 400 leading Russian Jews, including some of the country's wealthiest bankers and businessmen. The organizer and chief sponsor of the event, Vladimir Gusinskiy, the owner of NTV and one of the 'Big Seven' Russian tycoons, was unanimously elected the RJC's first President. Moscow's ubiquitous Mayor Yuriy Luzhkov delivered his trademark ebullient speech, urging Jewish émigrés to return to Russia.

But for the presence of some leading Russian writers, playwrights, scholars and rabbis, this was a quintessentially 'new Russian' scene: cavalcades of giant bullet-proof black Mercedes limousines (for the masters) and Toyota Land Cruisers (for the retinue) sweeping up to the entrance of the Slavyanskaya Radisson Hotel; burly bodyguards, in shiny double-breasted suits with enormously wide lapels, talking non-stop on their cellular phones; and a Swiss kosher catering company serving salmon, meat dishes and vegetables flown in from 'all over' Europe and the United States.[101] Russian Jews and the new Russia seemed to mesh quite seamlessly.

Yeltsin's greeting to the Congress was delivered by his personal representative:

---

* When a former leader of Moscow's 'refuseniks', Natan (formerly Anatoliy) Shcharanskiy, returned to Moscow in 1997 as the Israeli Minister of Industry and Trade, he confessed that of all the transmogrifications in the life of Russia since he was arrested in 1977 and expelled from the Soviet Union in 1986, 'the most dramatic sense of change' was at a meeting with teachers from Jewish schools. 'There were people from a thousand different Jewish schools,' an astonished Shcharanskiy told a reporter. 'They were complaining about tight budgets, they were squabbling over different systems of education. It was like a New York school board. To think that 20 years ago the big thing was an underground class of 40 students. And here we are debating different systems of education.' (Serge Schmemann, ' "Closing the Circle", Sharansky Visits Russia', *New York Times*, 28 January 1997.)

In spite of the fact that Russian Jews made a weighty contribution to the history of the Russian state, it has become possible only now, thanks to the political and economic reforms carried out in our country, to implement the idea of uniting the secular and religious communities into the Russian Jewish Congress. [The RJC] will undoubtedly show the international community that Russia is advancing further towards the creation of a democratic and law-governed society . . . [102]

At the time the polls placed Yeltsin behind almost all other announced Presidential candidates. This message to a Jewish gathering further alienated him from the 'popular-patriotic' voters, while promising little by way of additional support. 'You have to understand the mood in Russia, the complicated political situation,' one of Russia's most celebrated comedians, Gennadiy Khazanov, who attended the Congress (and who entertained the crowd in front of the White House on 20 August 1991), told a reporter. 'No one in the U.S. or Israel can vote for Yeltsin. Under the circumstances, he was brave to even send a message.'[103]

Yeltsin was even more vulnerable politically when, in the middle of the harshest political crisis of his Presidency, two weeks after the financial collapse of 17 August 1998, he attended the opening of a memorial synagogue and Holocaust Museum at Victory Park in Moscow. 'It is a temple of remembrance of those Jews who died at the fronts in the Great Patriotic War,' Yeltsin declared. 'Those destroyed by the Nazi regime, those who died of hunger and disease in those terrible years . . . It is terrible to see the appearance of home-grown [Russian] fascists, racial and national intolerance . . . It is inadmissible.'[104] Vladimir Gusinskiy said it was the first time in Russian history that the head of state had attended the opening of a synagogue.[105]

When Moscow Jewish youth activists voted for Yeltsin in 1996, in addition to the reasons that compelled most of the Russian middle class (and most of Moscow) to make the same choice, they were moved by other considerations. They felt 'protected by Yeltsin'.[106] 'Jewish life' would continue to grow, some of them said, 'as long as Yeltsin won'.[107] Had he lost to Zyuganov, most of them would have left Russia for good.[108]

A critical part of Yeltsin's legacy was the emergence of a Russian middle class independent of the state. After nearly five generations in the state's employ (and centuries of near-complete dependence on it), service to the state was no longer the sole option for an engineer or physician, writer or scholar, economist or film director. Startlingly, it was not even the most attractive one. The Russian intelligentsia was making a home for itself outside the Kremlin's court. The umbilical cord, which for centuries had both nourished and strangled, had been severed.*

Suddenly it was possible for many Russian professionals to live dignified and, for younger and luckier ones, increasingly comfortable lives without the state's support. '[Russia's] rising middle class is beginning to find its place in a new order,' noted an American reporter, 'where hard work and professionalism – rather than simply connections and brute force – bring some reward.'[109]

Within a few years, the 'privatization' of the nation's intellect and creativity,[110] this de-etatization of the backbone of a modern democracy, the middle class, resulted in the reversal of some of the most fundamental relationships between Russian society and the Russian state. Suddenly, politics (in the most literal sense of sharing in the power of the state) lost much of its allure. The thrall in which the Tsar and the General Secretary had held the intelligentsia for centuries, the fascination which stemmed from the mystery, envy and fear of absolute power – all of this was dissipated.

To be what a leading Russian writer and playwright, Aleksandr Gelman, called *nenachal'nik*[111] (literally, a 'non-boss', someone without the power of political office) became prestigious, even honourable – something not to bemoan but to celebrate:

> Really, how much better it is to be a rank-and-file citizen, with all the inconveniences inherent in this state, than to be a big *nachal'nik*. You are a free man! You are the owner of your own body, brain, time ... We love life, not power. We are patriots of life. And for that life likes us ... And those who, forgetting everything, rushed into national politics ... have lost freedom in a free country.[112]

Despite frequent setbacks and daily slights at the hands of the incompetent, corrupt and still formidable bureaucracy, the emerging Russian middle class readily exercised and staunchly defended its newly granted rights and liberties: freedom of professional and political association;

---

* The demise of the totalitarian state brought with it the end of the intelligentsia as a coherent and powerful political actor. No longer feared and bribed, lionized and punished by the state, its place was no longer behind the throne. Beneficial in the long run for the Russian arts, this depoliticization was painful, even tragic, for many a Russian writer, artist, actor.

uncensored information from Russia and abroad; the possession and exchange of foreign currencies; and freedom to travel.

The latter liberty was seized on with special avidity. The first, tentative signs of economic stabilization (in the summer of 1994) coincided with a veritable explosion of foreign travel. At the time, the British embassy issued 53,604 tourist visas, or a 63 per cent increase over the summer of 1993.[113] Italy, Spain, Germany and Greece also saw a record number of Russian tourists. The French embassy was receiving 700 applications a day – compared to a total of 2,700 Soviet tourists who had visited France in all of 1988.[114]

As in all other post-authoritarian societies, the Russian middle class spearheaded the daily effort of guarding and expanding society's autonomy. It staked out areas where the state should not intrude and guarded them jealously. Thus established, the principle of societal rights and immunities gradually spread to the rest of society. The instruments of societal defence against the state were weak and rudimentary, but their emergence and proliferation were quite real.

In 1997 Yeltsin signed a decree on confidentiality, guaranteeing the protection not only of the state's secrets, but also professional and commercial ones. 'Doctors, lawyers, notaries – all now have secrets,' commented a Russian magazine. 'Anyone can now go to court, if his personal confidentiality has been violated.'[115] In a country where, as the magazine put it, 'traditionally the state [has been] above the individual', the decree was an attempt to protect the rights of the latter.[116]

The enforcers of such protection, the Russian courts, were woefully underfunded because of the chronic shortfall of tax revenue, were often staffed by incompetent judges and were still far from independent, especially in the provinces. Yet Russian judges were rapidly becoming a self-governing corporation, independent of the state. The all-Russian Congress of Judges and the Council of Judges maintained chapters and qualification commissions in every region.[117] A 1992 law established appointments for life. Although judges had to serve a lengthy probationary term, already by the end of 1996 one in five of them were irremovable. Even during probation, the judges could not be removed by government officials: the power of removal was now an exclusive right of the qualification commissions, elected by the Congress of Judges.[118]

The two key elements of Alexander II's Judicial Reform of 1864 were revived: trials by jury, and the introduction of elected justices of the peace. Most important of all, a 1992 law allowed judicial review of the actions of government officials, who could no longer count on favourable rulings or ignore unfavourable ones. The number of suits against officials rose from under 10,000 in 1992 to 34,000 in 1995. The rate of successful challenges reached 70 per cent.[119]

In February 1998, the Constitutional Court struck down as unconstitutional the 1995 government regulations that tied residence rights to registration with local authorities. Registration, ruled the Court, was only a routine matter of notifying authorities. It had no bearing on whether a citizen could or could not reside in a particular area. Only citizens themselves had the right to choose where they wanted to live.[120]

In another decision issued on a suit brought by a Moscow resident, the Court ruled that the authorities could not require citizens to produce residence permits as a precondition to the issue of passports for foreign travel.[121] In an article entitled 'The first victory', the man who had brought the action wrote:

> The very fact that the Court has agreed to rule on the case, a fact unprecedented because of our mentality and traditions, attests to an enormous positive shift among the judges. Even though this shift has touched only the members of the Constitutional Court, it is still a significant victory, since overcoming one's prejudices and stereotypes is truly a very important human achievement.[122]

Not even the Kremlin was assured of a favourable ruling. Dismissed by Presidential decree in December 1994 following a row with the head of the regional administration, the elected Mayor of Vladivostok, Viktor Cherepkov, sued the President in a Moscow district court. In April 1996 the court found his dismissal unlawful. Twelve days later, Yeltsin signed a decree restoring Cherepkov to office.

At about the same time, the Constitutional Court overturned a federal law that imposed additional levies on the provinces, among them a tax on electricity supplied to industrial enterprises. The Krasnoyarsk *krai* legislature, which brought the suit, argued that federal taxes could be introduced only by legislation, not by decrees. The Court ruled in Krasnoyarsk's favour, and the tax was abolished.

After the federal Supreme Court had informed judges of regular courts in 1995 that it was their 'right and duty to apply the Constitution directly, whenever they saw its clear violation',[123] constitutional matters were no longer confined to the Constitutional Court. Among the more conspicuous results of this ruling were instances in which judges threw out criminal charges of desertion against recruits who claimed a constitutional right to perform alternative non-military service.[124] The coercive power of the Russian state was further undermined by Yeltsin's 29 July 1998 decree that transferred Russian prisons and labour camps from the police (Ministry of Internal Affairs) to the civilian authority of the Ministry of Justice.

Perhaps the most spectacular affirmation of the authority of the newly empowered courts occurred on 2 November 1998, when a St Petersburg judge suspended proceedings brought by the successor to the KGB, the Federal Security Service, against a former naval captain accused of espionage. Three years before, the defendant, Aleksandr Nikitin, had contributed to a report published by a Norwegian environmental group on the dumping of nuclear waste by submarines of the Russian Northern Fleet. Nikitin was arrested in February 1996 and held without trial for ten months. After the defence had protested against the detention, he was released on bail – itself an occurrence without precedent in espionage cases. 'This is a major victory,' said Nikitin's lawyer. 'There are no easy victories to be won against the FSB.* The judge has made a courageous decision . . .'[125] He added that there had been no other case in Russian history when treason charges had been 'sent back for further investigation'.[126]

A revolution that fails to live up to the fullness of its promise is not a revolution that has not happened.

With the exception of the three Baltic countries, as regards both democratization and market reform Yeltsin's Russia was far ahead of all post-Soviet states from west to east: Belarus, Moldova, Ukraine, Georgia, Armenia, Azerbaijan, Turkmenistan, Tajikistan, Kyrgyzstan, Uzbekistan and Kazakhstan. And, while lagging behind the three smaller, far less militarized nations of Central Europe with living memories of a pre-communist economic and political order (Poland, Hungary, the Czech Republic), Russia's record of democratization, political stabilization and human rights was considerably more impressive than in the rest of its geographic neighbourhood, the northern half of the Eurasian continent to the east of Poland and Slovenia: Rumania, Yugoslavia, Turkey, Iran, Iraq, Pakistan, Afghanistan and China.

As he looked back over the decade of revolutionary change begun by Gorbachev and consolidated by Yeltsin, a leading member of the liberal opposition party Yabloko saw:

---

* FSB stood for Federal'naya Sluzhba Bezopasnosty, or Federal Security Service, the main domestic security agency.

the collapse of the imperial–communist monster, a fundamental shift in the consciousness of an impressively large segment of citizens towards the values of the civilized world, the rudiments of democratic institutions and parties and the emergence of free mass media – not much for a European nation at the end of the 20th century, but not too little, either.[127]

In the aftermath of the 1995–6 electoral cycle, Russians recognized one another's right to differ and endeavoured to coexist. 'Pluralism of political loyalties', as a Russian observer put it, began to grow roots in the Russian soil, giving rise to 'civil peace'.[128]

Perhaps the best news in this record (and the best hope for the future) was the Russian people's stubborn adherence to the democratic ideal. Allegiance to democracy was alive and well in Yeltsin's Russia. Despite the dizzying swiftness and chaos of transition, despite all manner of distortions and flaws, despite bitter disappointment at how short of the democratic ideal their country fell, stable majorities of Russians kept faith with the ideal itself. What might be called the democratic constituency, which extended well beyond parties and ideologies, persevered and grew.

In 1991, slightly over half of those polled agreed that 'people should be free to say whatever they want, even if what they say increases tensions in society'.[129] By 1996, more than three in four Russians supported the proposition.[130] After two national referendums, two national parliamentary elections and the Presidential campaign, six out of ten Russians agreed that 'voting gives people like me some say about (or some influence on) how the government runs things'[131] and felt it was their duty to vote.[132] A huge majority (88 per cent) recognized that they could choose from several parties and candidates while voting, and a majority felt that they were free to criticize the government.[133]

Having tasted liberties, Russians were increasingly reluctant to abandon them. While, in general, the need for 'a strong leader who would impose strict order' was recognized by seven in ten respondents,[134] the authoritarian temptation was studiously resisted, and neither crime nor economic distress seemed to increase its appeal. If in 1994 one-third of those surveyed opposed a dictatorship to 'restore order in Russia',[135] three years later the opposition to a dictatorship grew to 55 per cent.[136] 'The rejection of non-freedom [*nesvoboda*] is characteristic of the majority of Russians regardless of their political orientation,' concluded Russia's two leading pollsters.[137] 'This is one of the most important results of the past few years.'[138]

*　　*　　*

Like the country he led, the first Russian President was a study in contradiction and evolvement: at once sadly, hopelessly and gruesomely in the past – and daringly and inspiringly in the future. He personified and condensed the clashes that daily and hourly were joined in the new Russia. It is this duality, this quality of work-in-progress, that makes Yeltsin such a fascinating subject for a biographer – and such a difficult one.

He was the man who ordered troops into Chechnya and for a year and a half prosecuted a war there – incompetently, with appalling brutality and in complete disregard of his country's public opinion; who eroded the newly created constitutional order and cheapened free political discourse by playing cynical palace games and ignoring the freely elected parliament; and who was responsible for a great deal of the alienation of the people from power in the new Russia. He was also a man who allowed untrammelled freedom for his most outrageous and crudest critics, and risked everything by seeking popular mandates for his policies and his office in free elections open to those same critics.

In the grip of authoritarian habits and urges, he was bound by self-imposed and self-enforced constraints. He thirsted for power and was zealous to acquire and hold it. Yet both the mode of acquiring that power (through two honest elections) and the uses to which he put it – greatly weakening the power of the state over society and the power of Moscow over Russia – were utterly novel for that country.

In the case of Yeltsin, the difficulty of arriving at a coherent and final judgment is not unlike the predicament that bedevilled Samuel Johnson as he tried to pass a verdict on the subject of his first biography: his mysterious friend and one-time mentor, the poet Richard Savage. Savage was a raffish, deceitful, manipulative, violent and, on one occasion, murderous man. Boswell averred that Savage's 'character was marked by profligacy, insolence and ingratitude'.[139] Johnson himself acknowledged that the man's weaknesses were 'indeed very numerous' and described them in great detail.[140]

Yet, unmatched both in the mercilessness of his insight into the human heart and in his compassion for its frailties, Johnson also recorded that Savage 'knew very well the necessity of goodness'.[141] He was a man 'of whom ... it must be confessed that ... virtue ... could not find a warmer advocate'.[142] To Johnson, his subject's advocacy of 'virtue' was not mere hypocrisy. His Savage was a man who knew the right thing to do and did it on occasion and quite spectacularly – even as he failed to do it consistently (or, indeed, most of the time). Johnson concluded that:

this at least must be allowed him, that he always preserved a strong sense of the dignity, the beauty and the necessity of virtue ... His actions, which were generally precipitate, were often blameable; but his writings, being the productions of study, uniformly tended to the exaltation of the mind, and the propagation of morality and piety. These writings may improve mankind when his failings shall be forgotten; and therefore he must be considered, upon the whole, as a benefactor to the world.[143]

In one of the most powerful and subtle judgments in a work that is dazzlingly replete with profound and elegant insights, Johnson pronounced Savage 'not so much a good man, as the friend of goodness', who 'mistook the love' of virtue for its 'practice'.[144]

Was not Savage to virtue what Yeltsin was to democracy? Was not Yeltsin, although not a democrat, a 'friend' of democracy – in the same way that the slave-owning Thomas Jefferson, who declared that all men were created equal, was a 'friend' of equality?*

As befits a 'friend' of democracy, Yeltsin left behind a hybrid: a polity still semi-authoritarian, corrupt and mistrusted by society, but also one that was governable, one in which the elite's competition for power was arbitrated by popular vote, and in which most of the tools of authoritarian mobilization and coercion appear to have been significantly dulled. The political organism that he cultivated had many severe defects, genetic as well as acquired – yet it was capable of development and of peacefully thwarting communist restoration without succumbing to authoritarianism.

Wherein does Yeltsin's greatness lie? asked one of the best observers of Russian politics (herself, it must be added, an entirely new Russian species: a female political columnist). He was neither a great thinker nor a master administrator.[145] But he had, Marina Shakina declared, in answer to her own question, courage to make choices ('personal choices to which the historic choice of Russia [was] so tightly welded') – and he had the enormous shoulders on which to bear the responsibility for their consequences, a weight which 'would have flattened all Russian politicians known to us at the time'.[146]

---

* The paradox did not escape Dr Johnson, who addressed it with customary directness: 'How is it that we hear the loudest yelps for liberty among the drivers of negroes?' (Samuel Johnson, 'Taxation No Tyranny', in Donald L. Green, ed., *Samuel Johnson's Political Writings*, p. 454).

Indeed, Yeltsin's entire public life had been full of choices which were, in retrospect, fateful for Russia. In 1987 he chose to urge a faster pace for perestroika. In 1990 he divorced the Russian national idea from communism and empire, left the Communist Party and committed himself to the radical free-market reforms spelled out in the '500 Days' programme. In 1991 he chose to resist the communist reaction in the winter and the spring, and, again, on 19 August. He chose to put an end to the Soviet Union in Belavezhskaya Pushcha. In 1992 he launched an economic revolution. He chose decentralization over a Russia ruled from the Centre and laid the foundation of a federated Russian state.

In 1993 he chose to cut the Gordian knot of a political crisis by dissolving the Congress of People's Deputies – and then chose a Presidential republic over a dictatorship. In December 1994 he chose to restore Russia's sovereignty over Chechnya and then chose to end that war by surrender twenty-one months later. In 1996 he chose to run for the Presidency, instead of cancelling the election for fear of losing it, and authorized governorship elections in the Russian regions (many of which, he knew only too well, the opposition was going to win).

Some of these choices surprised even those closest to him. More often than not, critical decisions were not preceded by a hint, much less by a sequence of steps from which the choices could be divined. They were arrived at by lonely and imperceptibly slow accretion, absorption and digestion of information and events. After 1991, Yeltsin made his choices with increasing slowness, painfully, often after much hesitation, backtracking and weaving, and lost momentum. Behind him stretched a road full of detours, occasional dead ends (of which the war in Chechnya was the epitome) and potholes.

And yet, in the end, at almost every critical juncture, despite the mistakes that preceded the decision, he moved in the direction of greater political liberty over authoritarian constraints; market over state control of the economy; society over state; and integration into the world, peace and accommodation over autarky, militarism and revanchism. 'He either consciously or unconsciously tried to avoid decisions pregnant with the restoration of the [Soviet] past,' wrote a Russian scholar.[147]

After Yeltsin's victory in 1996, a leader of the Russian liberal reformers Egor Gaidar (who had led the democratic opposition to the Chechen war and publicly broke with Yeltsin over it) told an interviewer: 'Yeltsin's administration is not our administration. Chernomyrdin's government is not our government. But the victory is ours . . . For me Yeltsin is a tool of history, and, overall, he performs his role quite adequately . . . He will not extinguish private property. He will not gag

a free press. He is not a threat to the institutions of civil society ...
This is the key. The rest is secondary.'[148]*

When much of the story told in these pages fades and notoriously parsimonious history reduces Yeltsin's life's work to one sentence, it is likely to read: 'He made irreversible the collapse of Soviet totalitarian communism, dissolved the Russian empire, ended state ownership of the economy – and held together and rebuilt his country while it coped with new reality and losses.'

Russia's first President both cast away stones and gathered them – a role that only a handful of leaders in history were lucky enough to be given and even fewer proved capable of performing. He managed, somehow, to resolve the key dilemma of modernity, which had evaded many a ruler since at least Louis XVI: he secured a modicum of legitimacy, acceptance and stability for a regime that undertook one of history's most extensive and most rapid economic modernizations. He engineered a transition to the market without resorting to terror and dictatorship, and he married capitalism and democracy in a country that had known little of the former and none of the latter.

Lincoln relied on a democratic political system and his country's allegiance to liberty and equality to forge a new nation. De Gaulle used the equally strong bonds of patriotism to reconstruct democracy in a proud and old nation. Yeltsin had neither democracy to bind the nation nor national solidarity to help invent and sustain democratic politics. The country, its political system and its economy had to be reinvented simultaneously. Against impossible odds, he succeeded.

The cursed pendulum of Russian history – between deadly anarchy (what Pushkin famously called 'Russian *bunt* [revolt], senseless and merciless') and mortifying authoritarianism – had been stopped. Yeltsin created and sustained a political space in which for the first time Russia could determine its way, without the violence, death and repression that had attended this choice in the past. He gave Russia the opportunity to catch its breath, what the Russians call *peredyshka*.

In that sudden breach with the pattern of Russian history, all sorts of wonders became possible. Russia was no longer 'doomed to roll downhill to some hellish bottom', the 'godfather of glasnost', Aleksandr

---

* One is reminded of Raymond Aron, who, after many years and scores of articles critical of de Gaulle, acknowledged the soundness of a friend's response to Aron's public censure of the General: 'I see no one other than de Gaulle who can preserve the basic freedoms that you have spent your lifetime defending' (Aron, *Memoirs*, p. 259).

Yakovlev, wrote in 1993. 'From now on Russian soil can give rise not only to thistles and witches' weeds but to fruit and flowers useful and bountiful.'[149]

There is a poem by the great Russian poet Osip Mandel'shtam. The poem's hero is a Decembrist, a *dekabrist*, a participant in Russia's first anti-authoritarian mass political action: the failed December 1825 uprising of progressive military officers who sought to establish a Russian republic. Many years later, we find this brilliant officer, the best that the Russian nobility and intelligentsia had to offer, exiled in a god-forsaken Siberian hamlet. Everything the man had he sacrificed to the 'sweet liberty of citizenship'. But, alas, the 'blind' Russian gods would not accept the offering. (The poem was written in 1917, the year when the Russian democratic experiment was ended by the Bolsheviks.)

Our Decembrist is still unrepentant. He believes the uprising would have succeeded but for the treachery and timidity of the 'pagan Senate'. But the poet does not share this rebellious optimism, and concludes with a stanza, unmatched in Russian poetry for the grace of resignation and for its haunting, melancholy beauty:

> Everything's in disarray, and no one's there
> To say, as cold sets in, that disarray
> Is everywhere, and how sweet becomes the prayer:
> Rossia, Lethe, Lorelei.[150]

There is no better description of Russia's century-old tragedy. Oblivious to its own history (hence 'Lethe'), doomed to reject the daily effort at incremented betterment and instead to succumb again and again to the vision of a paradise conveyed by the angelic singing of murderous sirens ('Lorelei'), Russia had seemed destined to travel, in the words of another great poet of the twentieth century, 'the never altered circuit of its fate'.[151]

From Mikhail Speranskiy, who advised Alexander I at the beginning of the nineteenth century, to Evsey Liberman, who for a while had the ear of the Communist Party leadership in the 1960s, there was no shortage of purveyors of political and economic reform. Yet, with the exception of Alexander II, the rulers lacked the will to take enormous risks over the long run; to defend reform with cunning and, if necessary, force; and to surround it with political cover thick and sinuous enough for reform to take root outside the salons of Moscow and St Petersburg and to mature. In the end, after exhaustive attempts at achieving the 'sweet liberty of citizenship', the 'cold' and the 'disarray' would set in, enveloping Russia in yet another period of authoritarianism, impoverishment and dissipation of its immense natural riches and talent.

The attributes of the traditional Russian state – authoritarianism, imperialism, militarism, xenophobia – are far from extinguished. Yet more and higher hedges have been erected against their recurrence under Yeltsin's *peredyshka* than at any other time in Russian history.

In the first century AD, a writer and philosopher recorded a scene that he claimed to be typical of any 'great city of Greece or Italy' at the time:

> One may see in all the crowd and cram and crush everyone calmly doing his own business; the piper piping and teaching to pipe ... while the crowd passes by and does not interfere with him; the trainer producing his dancers for a stage play without noticing a few fights going on, and buying and selling and so forth, harping and painting pictures ... I myself saw all people doing all sorts of things ... piping, dancing, one giving a show, one reciting a poem, one singing, one reading a story or a fable, and not one of them preventing anyone else from his own particular business.[151]

There is something so quintessentially 'Western' in this vignette that it would strike anyone familiar with Russia both before and, especially, after the Bolsheviks as forever alien and unattainable there. More than a simple absence of secret police, censorship, the Party or the KGB, it was the ability of everyone to go their own way without supreme arbiters and enforcers of order and propriety in the business of living. Nine years of Yeltsin's rule made such scenes commonplace in Russian cities and towns.

Brutalized for centuries – rulers and ruled alike – by terror and lies, gnarled by fear and poverty, paralysed by total dependence on the state, the Russian people's journey from subjects to free individuals is not going to be easy or fast. Yet, like a convalescing invalid, Russia is beginning to hobble away from the prison hospital that tsars and commissars built – with its awful food, stern nurses, short visiting hours and ugly uniforms. It is not out of the hospital yard yet, but it can no longer be stopped.

The sublime pleasures and terrifying responsibilities of Unsupervised Life are Russia's at last.

BORIS YELTSIN:
A BRIEF CHRONOLOGY

1931 *February 1*, Born in the village of Butka, Talitsk district, Sverdlovsk (now Ekaterinburg) region

1934 Family moved to Kazan

1936 Family moved to Berezniki, Perm region

1949 Admitted to the Ural Polytechnic Institute (UPI) in Sverdlovsk

1955 Graduated from UPI with a diploma in civil engineering

1955–1960 Appointed a construction supervisor (*prorab*), senior construction supervisor, Regional Construction Administration (Trest) Yuzhgorstroy

1960 Promoted to Senior Engineer of the Civil Construction Administration (SU) Number 13

1961 Joined the Communist Party of the Soviet Union

1962 Promoted to manager (*nachal'nik*) of SU-13

1965 Promoted to *nachal'nik* of the Sverdlovsk Homebuilding Administration (Kombinat)

1968 Appointed Head of the Construction Department of the Sverdlovsk Regional Party Committee (Obkom)

1975 Appointed a Secretary of the Sverdlovsk Obkom

1976–1985 First Secretary of the Sverdlovsk Obkom

1981
January Awarded the Order of Lenin, the Soviet Union's highest medal, for 'the service to the Communist Party and the Soviet state and in connection with the 50th birthday'
March 'Elected' Full Member of the Central Committee

1985
April Appointed Head of the Construction Department of the Party's Central Committee
July Appointed Secretary for Construction of the Central Committee
December Appointed First Secretary of the Moscow City Party Committee (Gorkom)

1986
February 'Elected' Candidate (non-voting) member of the Politburo

1987
October 21 In a speech at the meeting of the Central Committee criticized conservatives in the Party leadership, bemoaned the slow pace of political and economic reform and the incipient 'cult of personality' of the General Secretary Mikhail Gorbachev
November 12 Dismissed from the post of the First Secretary of the Moscow Gorkom
November 19 Appointed First Deputy Chairman of the USSR State Construction Committee

1989
March 26 Elected to the Congress of People's Deputies of the USSR from Moscow with 92 per cent of the vote
May 29 Elected to the Supreme Soviet of the USSR
July 19 Announced the formation of the radical pro-reform faction in the Congress of People's Deputies: the Inter-Regional Group of Deputies
July 29 Elected one of the five co-Chairmen of the Inter-Regional Group
September 9–17 Travelled in the United States, visited and spoke in nine cities

1990
March 4 Elected to the Congress of People's Deputies of the Russian Soviet Federated Socialist Republic

(RSFSR) from Sverdlovsk with 72 per cent of the vote

May 29 Elected Chairman of the Supreme Soviet of the RSFSR

June 12 Presided over the adoption by the Congress of People's Deputies of the RSFSR of the Declaration of 'national sovereignty of the Russian Soviet Federated Socialist Republic'. Russia was declared a 'democratic, law-abiding state within a renewed Soviet Union'. All citizens of Russia were guaranteed the 'inalienable right' to a 'dignified life' and 'free development'. All citizens, political parties and public organizations that operated within law were guaranteed participation in the management of state and public affairs

July 13 Announced his resignation from the Communist Party of the Soviet Union at the Twenty-Ninth Party Congress

August 3 In a speech to the Supreme Soviet of Latvia declared solidarity with Estonia, Latvia and Lithuania in their struggle for independence

August 12 In Ufa, the capital of the Bashkir Autonomous Soviet Socialist Republic, declared Russia's willingness to delegate to non-Russian ethnic regions 'as much power as you yourselves can swallow'

September 11 Urged by Yeltsin, the Supreme Soviet of the Russian Federation voted to adopt the radical market reform programme '500 Days'

1991

January 13 Following the attack by troops of the Ministry of Internal Affairs of the USSR on the television centre in Vilnius (Lithuania) flew to Tallinn (Estonia) and signed with the Presidents of Estonia, Latvia and Lithuania the joint statement denouncing 'the acts of armed violence against the independence of . the Baltic states'

January 20 Issued 'Appeal to the Peoples of Russia' denouncing 'the slide of the Union leadership toward lawlessness and violence', and calling on the citizens of Russia to 'reaffirm opposition to the old order'

February 19 In a nationally televised interview 'dissociated' himself from 'the positions and policies' of Mikhail Gorbachev and called for his 'immediate resignation'

June 12 Elected President of Russia in the field of six candidates with 57 per cent of the vote

July 20 Ended the communist party-state in Russia by signing a decree that banned political parties from 'state bodies and organizations', including armed forces and police

August 19–21 Led a nation-wide resistance to a communist *coup d'état*

August 23 Suspended the 'activity of organs and organizations' of the Communist Party of the Russian Federation pending investigation of the Party's 'anti-constitutional activity' during the coup

August 24 Signed decrees recognizing the Republic of Estonia and the Republic of Latvia, which declared their independence from the Soviet Union on August 20

September 10 Rescinded the ban on communist newspapers

October 28 Presented a programme of radical market reform in a speech to the Congress of People's Deputies of the Russian Federation

November 6 Signed the decree 'stopping the activities' of the Communist Party of the Soviet Union (on the territory of Russia) and of the Communist Party of the Russian Federation and transferring their property to the Russian state

November 7 Appointed Egor Gaidar Deputy Prime Minister in charge of economic reform

December 3 Recognized independence of Ukraine

December 8 In Belavezhskaya Pushcha near Minsk, co-signed with President of Ukraine and Chairman of the

Supreme Soviet of Belarus agreements to dissolve the Soviet Union. The Commonwealth of Independent States was formed

December 26 The Russian Soviet Federated Socialist Republic changed its name to the Russian Federation (Russia)

1992

January 2 The implementation of the Yeltsin–Gaidar market reform began with the elimination of state control over most prices

March Unveiled a draft of the Federal Treaty codifying relations between federal and regional authorities

June 15 Appointed Egor Gaidar Acting Chairman of the Government (Prime Minister)

December 15 Following the vote in the Congress of People's Deputies, replaced Gaidar with Viktor Chernomyrdin. As part of a broad political compromise, the Congress acceded to Yeltsin's demand for a constitutional referendum to be held in April 1993

1993

April 25 Following a failed impeachment attempt in the Congress of People's Deputies, Yeltsin received a majority in a national referendum on the questions about the 'trust in the President' (59 per cent) and the regime's 'socio-economic policies' (53 per cent)

June 5 Opened and chaired the inaugural session of the Constitutional Assembly

September 21 Issued a decree dissolving the Congress of People's Deputies of the Russian Federation and calling for parliamentary elections on December 12, 1993

October 4 Following armed attacks by leftist nationalists on the government offices and the Ostankino television centre, ordered tank bombardment of the Supreme Soviet's building. Under the 'state of emergency' law, banned communist

and nationalist organizations and publications

October 18 Ended the 'state of emergency' and rescinded the ban on opposition parties and newspapers.

October 29 Signed a decree guaranteeing each of the registered national parties and blocs, including the Communist Party of the Russian Federation, equal access to free air-time on state-owned radio and television networks

1994

February 15 Signed a Treaty with Tatarstan, the most populous of the ethnic Republics inside Russia

December 11 Ordered Russian troops into the breakaway Republic of Ichkeria (formerly the Chechen–Ingush Autonomous Republic)

1996

February 15 In a speech in Ekaterinburg announced his decision to run for re-election and outlined an electoral platform of 'adjusted' economic reforms, civil and political liberties, and 'stability'

May 27 Met in the Kremlin with the leader of the Chechen rebels, Zelimkhan Yandarbiyev, and signed the 'Agreement of the Cessation of Combat Operations' in Chechnya; granted Chechnya broad autonomy, including a separate constitution and full control over finances and natural resources

June 16 Finished first in the field of 10 candidates with 35 per cent of the vote

July 3 In a run-off defeated the Chairman of the Communist Party of the Russian Federation Gennadiy Zyuganov, 54 per cent to 40 per cent

August 31 In the Dagestani village of Khasavyurt, Yeltsin's personal representative, Secretary of the Security Council General Aleksandr Lebed, signed an agreement with the Chechen commander Aslan Maskhadov. Chechnya was granted

'political autonomy.' Federal troops began to withdraw from Chechnya.
November 5 Underwent quintuple coronary artery bypass surgery
1997
March 6 In a 'State of Russia' address to the joint session of the Federal Assembly outlined resumption of radical economic reforms and sharp reduction of the budget deficit
March 17 Overhauled the Cabinet of Ministers, appointed radical reformers to top positions in the government, creating the most reformist government since December 1992
May 12 Signed a peace treaty with President of Chechnya Aslan Maskhadov
May 27 At a NATO summit in Paris signed the NATO–Russia 'Founding Act on Mutual Relations, Co-operation and Security between NATO and the Russian Federation' with the leaders of the NATO member countries
May 31 With Ukrainian President Leonid Kuchma signed in Kiev a 'Treaty of Friendship, Co-operation and Partnership' between Russia and Ukraine. The treaty affirmed the 'inviolability of existing borders', and ceded to Ukraine the Crimean peninsula, including the city and naval base of Sevastopol, as well as the former Soviet Black Sea Fleet
July–September Vetoed a Land Code adopted by the parliament because it prohibited the buying and selling of farm land. Calling 'private ownership' of land 'a tremendous resource for

uplifting our economy, first of all, agriculture', Yeltsin refused to promulgate this 'most reactionary' law after parliament overrode the veto
November 4 Signed a decree lifting restrictions on foreign ownership of shares in Russian oil companies
1998
March 23 In a televised address to the nation, announced the dismissal of Prime Minister Viktor Chernomyrdin and the entire cabinet of Ministers; cited the need to 'make reforms more energetic and effective' as the reason for the overhaul. Nominated 35-year-old Sergey Kirienko for confirmation by the Duma as Prime Minister
July 17 Attended the burial of Nicholas II, Tsarina Alexandra and their children in St Petersburg's Cathedral of St Peter and St Paul. In a brief speech called the interment 'an act of human justice, a symbol of unification in Russia and redemption of common guilt' and called for ending 'the century which has been an age of blood and violence in Russia with repentance and peace, regardless of political views, ethnic or religious origin . . .'
July 29 Signed a decree transferring the country's prisons and labour camps from the police (the Ministry of Internal Affairs) to the civilian administration by the Ministry of Justice
August 23 Following the devaluation of the ruble and Russia's default on domestic and foreign debts, dismissed the government of Sergey Kirienko

GLOSSARY

[of Russian words which recur in the text after their original definition]

aktiv – a list or gathering which included, in addition to the members of the Regional Party Committee, other leading members of the Obkom nomenklatura: managers of more important plants, chairmen of kolkhozes, local journalists and writers, military officers and so on. In essence, the political, economic, military and cultural leadership of the province

apparat – staff, usually of a government or Party organization

avos'ka – shopping bag

barak – communal wooden hut

baytushka – local priest

bazy – vegetable depots

blat – use of connections to obtain quality goods and services

BMP (boevaya mashina pekhoty) – fighting infantry vehicle, or armoured personnel carrier

boeviki – guerrillas or terrorists; White House defenders during the 1993 Red October

brigada – crew

brigadir – crew leader

Buro – the highest executive body of a Party committee, usually with only a few members; also shorthand for a meeting of the members of the Buro

chastushka – a four-line folk verse, usually sung

defitsit – goods in short supply

derzhava – great power

GKChP (Gosudarstvennyi Komitet po Chrezvychaynomu Polozheniyu) – State Committee for the State of Emergency, the leaders of the August 1991 putsch

GKO (Gosudarsvennye Kommercheskie Obligatsii) – State Commercial Bonds

glasnost – openness

Glavk – a union or regional economic administration in the Soviet Union

Gorkom – acronym for Gorodskoy Komitet, the City Committee; the highest Party organ in a city

gospriemka – state produce acceptance, or quality control

Gosstroy – the Soviet Union's chief building administration

instruktor – a full-time staffer in a Party organization from the District Committee to the Central Committee

Ispolkom – executive council

kolkhoz – a collective farm

kombinat – large factory or plant, or construction organization

krai – territory or region

kulak – rich peasant

limitchiki – guest workers

master – construction foreman

mat – foul language

Mehria – mayor's office

mikrorayony – suburbs

muzhik – peasant

nachal'nik – boss; also the official title of the head of many organizations, including construction ones

nakaz – request from nominating organizations for candidates to elective offices

naryady – work-pay sheets

nomenklatura – collective name for the posts and their occupants whose appointment was approved by Party organization on the corresponding level; the Soviet nobility

ob'ekt – construction site

Obkom – acronym for Oblastnoy Komitet, the Regional Committee; the highest Party organ in a region

oblast – province

operativka – short staff meeting

otdel – department

peredyshka – an opportunity to catch one's breath, to take stock

Pervyi – first: nomenklatura slang for the Obkom First Secretary

pochin – initiative: a political or economic propaganda campaign ostensibly 'from below'

postanovlenie – resolution; decision by official bodies

povest' – novella

propiska – residence permit

prorab – construction site supervisor

pyatiletka – five-year plan

Raikom – acronym for Raionniy Komitet, the District Party Committee; the highest Party organ in an urban or rural district

rayon – district

samizdat – underground manuscript publication and dissemination network

samogon – moonshine

SNG (Sodruzhestvo Nezavisimykh Gosudarstv) – the Commonwealth of Independent States, or CIS

sovkhoz – a state-owned collective farm

spetsnaz – special forces

spravka – memorandum

trest – the largest of construction organizations, usually consisting of several *upravlenie*s

uchastok – construction site

upravlenie – intermediate construction organization

vekseli – promissory notes

vozhd' – the supreme leader

vstrecha – question-and-answer session

yarmarka – fair

zakaz – food parcel for a member of the nomenklatura

zaveduyushchiy, or **zav** – head of a department

zapiska – a written note

NOTES

Chapter 1: To Survive, to Dare, to Succeed!

1. Izabella Verbova, 'Za tysyachi kilometrov ot Belogo doma' (Thousands of kilometres away from the White House), interview with Yeltsin's mother, Klavdia Vasilievna, *Vecherniaa Moskva*, 2 October 1991. Unless an English-language source is referenced, all translations from Russian are by me.
2. Andrey Goryun, *Boris Yeltsin – svet i teni* (Boris Yeltsin – light and shadows), Sverdlovsk: Voenniy Zheleznodorozhnik Publishers, 1991, Part I, p. 5.
3. Boris Yeltsin, *Ispoved' na zadannuyu temu* (A confession on the required topic), Riga: Rukitis Publishers, 1990, p. 15.
4. *Ibid.*, p. 16.
5. Goryun, *op. cit.*, Part I, p. 5.
6. *Ibid.*
7. Boris Yeltsin, *The Struggle for Russia*, New York: Times Books, 1994, pp. 94–8
8. Goryun, *op. cit.*, Part I, p. 5.
9. *Ibid.*
10. Yeltsin, *Ispoved'*, p. 17.
11. *Ibid.*
12. *Ibid.*, p. 18.
13. *Ibid.*, p. 16.
14. *Ibid.*, p. 18.
15. *Ibid.*
16. Goryun, *op. cit.*, Part I, p. 8.
17. *Ibid.*
18. Yeltsin, *Ispoved'*, p. 18.
19. Goryun, *op. cit.*, Part I, p. 8.
20. Yeltsin, *Ispoved'*, p. 22.
21. *Ibid.*, p. 20.
22. *Ibid.*, p. 19.
23. *Ibid.*
24. *Ibid.*, p. 17.
25. *Ibid.*

26. *Ibid.*, p. 20.
27. *Ibid.*, p. 21.
28. *Ibid.*
29. *Ibid.*
30. *Ibid.*
31. *Ibid.*, pp. 22, 23.
32. *Ibid.*, p. 24.
33. Boris Yeltsin, interview for the video archive of the Museum of Youth Movements, Ekaterinburg, July 1990.
34. V. P. Bukin and V. A. Piskunov, *Sverdlovsk. Perspektivy razvitiya do 2000 goda* (Sverdlovsk. Plans for development to the year 2000), Sverdlovsk: Sredne-Uralskoye Publishers, 1982, p. 173.
35. A. Kozlov, *Vekhi istorii* (The milestones of history), Sverdlovsk: Sredne-Uralskoye Publishers, 1973, p. 46.
36. L. Kozinetz, *Kamennaya letopis' goroda. Arkhitektura Ekaterinburga–Sverdlovska XVIII–nachala XX veka* (The stone record of the city. The architecture of Ekaterinburg–Sverdlovsk from the eighteenth to the twentieth centuries), Sverdlovsk: Sredne-Uralskoye Publishers, 1989, p. 22.
37. Bukin and Piskunov, *op. cit.*, p. 34.
38. Kozinetz, p. 23.
39. V. Tsundani, 'Naselenie Urala i Zapadnoy Sibiri vo vtoroy polovine XVIII – pervoy polovine XIX veka' (The population of the Urals and West Siberia from the second half of the eighteenth to the first half of the nineteenth century). *Istoricheskaya demografii: novye podkhody, metody, istochniki. Tezisy VIII Vserossiyskoy konferentsii po istoricheskoy demografii* (Historical demography:

new approaches, methods, sources. Theses for the Eighth All-Russian Conference on Historical Demography), Moscow: Russian Academy of Sciences, 1992, p. 46.

40. *Manifest Uralskogo Politicheskogo Dvizhenia* (The Manifesto of the Ural Political Movement), Ekaterinburg: 1992, p. 3.

41. Anton Chekhov, *Polnoe sobranie sochineniy* (Collected works), Moscow: Khudozhestvennaya Literatura, 1960, vol. XI, p. 420.

42. *Ibid.*

43. *Ibid.*

44. V. G. Ayrapetov, A. V. Bakunin and L. S. Boyarskikh, *Sverdlvoskaya oblast' za 50 let* (The Sverdlovsk province in the last fifty years), Sverdlovsk: Sredne-Uralskoye Publishers, 1984, p. 17.

45. V. Motrevich, 'Bezhentsy' (The refugees), *Ural'skiy Rabochiy*, 22 June 1991.

46. Antoinette May, *A Biography of Marguerite Higgins*, New York: Beaufort Books, 1983.

47. Archive of the Ural Polytechnic Institute.

48. Museum of Youth Movements, Ekaterinburg.

49. Goryun, *op. cit.*, Part I, p. 8.

50. Michael Dobbs, 'Yeltsin: Russian Rebel without a Pause', *Washington Post*, 31 March 1991, p. A23.

51. *Ibid.*

52. Yeltsin, *Ispoved'*, p. 75.

53. *Ibid.*, p. 25.

54. *Ibid.*, p. 26.

55. *Ibid.*, p. 27.

56. *Ibid.*

57. *Ibid.*, p. 26.

58. Goryun, *op. cit.*, Part I, p. 9.

59. Yeltsin, *Ispoved'*, p. 25.

60. *Ibid.*

61. Goryun, *op. cit.*, Part I, p. 9.

62. Archive of the Ural Polytechnic Institute, student record book no. 494087.

63. Yeltsin, *Ispoved'*, p. 28.

64. *Ibid.*

65. *Ibid.*, p. 29.

66. Archive of the Ural Polytechnic Institute.

67. *Ibid.*

68. *Ibid.*

69. *Ibid.*, student record book no. 494087.

70. Yeltsin, *Ispoved'*, p. 29.

71. Goryun, *op. cit.*, Part I, p. 9.

72. *Ibid.*, p. 10.

73. *Ibid.*

74. Yeltsin, *Ispoved'*, p. 70.

75. *Ibid.*, p. 73.

76. *Ibid.*, p. 72.

77. *Ibid.*

Chapter 2: The Builder

Biographical details of those interviewed by the author can be found at the end of the Bibliography.

1. Yeltsin, *Ispoved'*, p. 33.

2. *Ibid.*

3. *Ibid.*

4. *Ibid.*, p. 34.

5. *Ibid.*

6. *Ibid.*, p. 35.

7. Interview with Sergey Ivanovich Peretrutov.

8. Interview with Ivan Mikhaylovich Dyagilev.

9. Interview with Sergey Peretrutov.

10. Goryun, *op. cit.*, Part I, p. 9.

11. *Ibid.*, Part I, p. 11.

12. Interview with Ivan Dyagilev.

13. Yeltsin, *Ispoved'*, p. 35.

14. Interview with Sergey Peretrutov.

15. Goryun, *op. cit.*, Part I, p. 9.

16. Interview with Ivan Dyagilev.

17. Yeltsin, *Ispoved'*, p. 36.

18. Interview with Sergey Peretrutov.

19. Interview with Ivan Dyagilev.

20. Interview with Lidiya Aleksandrovna Khudyakova.

21. Yeltsin, *Ispoved'*, p. 42.

22. *Ibid.*

23. *Ibid.*, p. 72.

24. *Ibid.*

25. *Ibid.*, p. 73.

26. *Ibid.*, p. 74.

27. *Ibid.*

28. Interview with Lidiya Khudyakova.
29. Interview with Sergey Peretrutov.
30. Yeltskin, *Ispoved'*, p. 36.
31. Interview with Sergey Peretrutov.
32. *Ibid.*
33. Yeltsin, *Ispoved'*, p. 36.
34. Interview with Sergey Peretrutov.
35. *Ibid.*
36. *Ibid.*
37. *Ibid.*
38. Yeltsin, *Ispoved'*, p. 37.
39. *Ibid.*
40. Yeltsin, *Ispoved'*, p. 42.
41. *Ibid.*, p. 43.
42. *Ibid.*
43. Interview with Sergey Peretrutov.
44. *Ibid.*
45. *Ibid.*
46. *Ibid.*
47. *Ibid.*
48. Goryun, *op. cit.*, Part I, p. 11.
49. Interview with Sergey Peretrutov.
50. *Ibid.*
51. *Ibid.*
52. Yeltsin, *Ispoved'*, pp. 37–8.
53. Interview with Mira Shvartz.
54. Interview with Sergey Peretrutov.
55. Yeltsin, *Ispoved'*, p. 38.
56. 'Lichnoye Delo, El'tsin Boris Nikolaevich' (The personal file of Yeltsin Boris Nikolaevich), 17 February 1960. The Party Archive of the Sverdlovsk Region, holding 2992, registry 6, log 527.
57. Yeltsin, *Ispoved'*, p. 39.
58. 'Lichnoye Delo . . .', 14 March 1960. The Party Archive of the Sverdlovsk Region, holding 2992, registry 6, log 527.
59. *Ibid.*, 22 January 1960.
60. Yeltsin, *Ispoved'*, p. 39.
61. 'Lichnoye Delo . . .', 17 March 1961. The Party Archive of the Sverdlovsk Region, holding 2992, registry 9, log 408.
62. *Ibid.*
63. *Ibid.*
64. Interview with Sergey Peretrutov.
65. Interview with Vasiliy Vasilievich Gudkov.
66. *Ibid.*

67. Interview with Sergey Peretrutov.
68. *Ibid.*
69. Yeltsin, *Ispoved'*, p. 42.
70. Interview with Ivan Dyagilev.
71. *Ibid.*
72. Interview with Sergey Peretrutov.
73. Interview with Ivan Dyagilev.
74. Interview with Sergey Peretrutov.
75. *Ibid.*
76. Interview with Ivan Dyagilev.
77. Interview with Sergey Peretrutov.
78. Yeltsin, *Ispoved'*, p. 74.
79. *Ibid.*
80. Goryun, *op. cit.*, Part I, p. 10.
81. *Ibid.*
82. *Ibid.*
83. Interview with Ivan Dyagilev.
84. Yeltsin, *Ispoved'*, p. 74.
85. *Ibid.*, p. 75.
86. *Ibid.*
87. Interview with Ivan Dyagilev.
88. *Ibid.*
89. Yeltsin, *Ispoved'*, p. 74.
90. Naina Yeltsina, 'Rossiya zhivyot i stroitsya' (Russia lives and builds), interview with *Argumenty i Fakty*, No. 11, March 1996, p. 3.
91. Yeltsin, *Ispoved'*, p. 75.
92. *Ibid.*
93. *Ibid.*
94. *Ibid.*
95. Goryun, *op. cit.*, Part I, p. 9.
96. *Ibid.*
97. *Ibid.*
98. Yeltsin, *Ispoved'*, p. 29.
99. Interview with Ivan Dyagilev.
100. Interview with Sergey Peretrutov.
101. Interview with Ivan Dyagilev.
102. Staff research by the Museum of Youth Movements, Ekaterinburg.
103. Interview with Sergey Peretrutov.
104. *Ibid.*
105. *Ibid.*
106. *Ibid.*
107. Interview with Ivan Dyagilev.
108. Goryun, *op. cit.*, Part I, p. 11.
109. Interview with Ivan Dyagilev.
110. Interview with Sergey Peretrutov.
111. *Ibid.*
112. Interview with Klavdia Ivanovna Bersenyova.

113. *Ibid.*
114. *Ibid.*
115. *Ibid.*
116. Interview with Artur Klavdievich Ezhov.
117. Interview with Ivan Dyagilev.
118. *Ibid.*
119. Interview with Vasiliy Gudkov.
120. Interview with Artur Ezhov.
121. *Ibid.*
122. Interview with Ivan Dyagilev.
123. Goryun, *op. cit.*, Part I, p. 11.
124. Interview with Klavdia Bersenyova.
125. Goryun, *op. cit.*, Part I, p. 11.
126. Interview with Lidiya Khudyakova.
127. *Ibid.*
128. Interview with Klavdia Bersenyova.
129. Interview with Sergey Peretrutov.
130. Interview with Klavdia Bersenyova.
131. Interview with Artur Ezhov.
132. Interview with Sergey Peretrutov.
133. *Ibid.*
134. Yeltsin, *Ispoved'*, p. 41.
135. Interview with Artur Ezhov.
136. Interview with Vasiliy Gudkov.
137. Interview with Artur Ezhov.
138. Interview with Yakov Petrovich Ryabov.
139. Interview with Sergey Peretrutov.
140. *Ibid.*
141. Interview with Yakov Ryabov.
142. *Ibid.*
143. *Ibid.*
144. Yeltsin, *Ispoved'*, p. 70.
145. Goryun, *op. cit.*, Part I, p. 11.
146. *Ibid.*
147. Interview with Viktor Vasilievich Popov.
148. *Ibid.*
149. *Ibid.*
150. *Ibid.*
151. *Ibid.*
152. *Ibid.*
153. *Ibid.*
154. Interview with Artur Ezhov.
155. *Ibid.*
156. Interview with Viktor Popov.
157. *Ibid.*
158. *Ibid.*
159. Interview with Lidiya Khudyakova.
160. Interview with Viktor Popov.
161. Interview with Artur Ezhov.
162. Interview with Vasiliy Gudkov.
163. Interview with Artur Ezhov.
164. Interview with Viktor Popov.
165. *Ibid.*
166. *Ibid.*
167. *Ibid.*
168. *Ibid.*
169. *Ibid.*
170. Interview with Ivan Dyagilev.
171. *Ibid.*
172. Interview with Sergey Peretrutov.
173. Interview with Ivan Dyagilev.
174. *Ibid.*
175. *Ibid.*
176. Interview with Mira Shvartz.
177. 'Lichnoye Delo . . .' The Party Archive of the Sverdlovsk Region. A copy in the author's archive.
178. Interview with Lidiya Khudyakova.

Chapter 3: The Pervyi

1. *The New Shorter Oxford English Dictionary*, Oxford: Clarendon Press, 1993, p. 1874.
2. Yeltsin, *Ispoved'*, p. 46.
3. Interview with Sergey Borisovich Vozdvizhenskiy.
4. Interview with Vasiliy Gudkov.
5. Interview with Yakov Ryabov.
6. *Ibid.*
7. *Ibid.*
8. *Ibid.*
9. Yeltsin, *Ispoved'*, p. 46.
10. Mikhail Voslenskiy, *Nomenklatura* (The nomenklatura), London: Overseas Publication Interchange, 1990, pp. 123–4.
11. Yeltsin, *Ispoved'*, p. 46.
12. *Ibid.*
13. *Ibid.*
14. *Ibid.*
15. *Ibid.*, p. 47.
16. *Ibid.*
17. *Ibid.*

18. *Ural'skiy Rabochiy*, 3 November 1976.

19. Jerry Hough, *The Soviet Prefects: The Local Party Organs in Industrial Decision-Making*, Cambridge, MA: Harvard University Press, 1969.

20. Yeltsin, *Ispoved'*, pp. 53–4.

21. Ayrapetov, Bakunin and Boyarskikh, *op. cit.*, p. 17: 4,557,000 in January 1983.

22. *Ibid.*

23. *Ibid.*

24. *Ibid.*

25. Boris Yeltsin, Introduction to *ibid.*, p. 6.

26. Bukin and Piskunov, *op. cit.*, p. 10.

27. Boris Yeltsin, 'Sotsialisticheskoye sorevnovanie i uskorenie nauchino-tekhnicheskogo progressa' (Socialist competition and acceleration of scientific–technological progress), *Partiynaya Zhizn'*, 21, (November) 1979, p. 31.

28. 'Otvety na voprosy, zadannye studentami vuzov goroda Pervomu Sekretariu OK KPSS, chlenu TsK KPSS, Deputatu Verkhovnogo Soveta, tov. Yeltsinu B.N.' Fond 4, opis 10, delo 90. Partiynii Arkhiv Sverdlovskoy Oblasti (Answers to questions posed by students of the institutes of higher education of the City to the First Secretary of the Regional Committee of the CPSU, Member of the Central Committee of the CPSU, Deputy of the Supreme Soviet of the USSR, Comrade B. N. Yeltsin. Holding 4, register 10, log 90, p. 122. The Party Archive of the Sverdlovsk Region). Where the questions were numbered, the number is given after a colon following the page reference.

29. 'Rodonachalnik Uralskoy Nauki' (Forefather of Ural science), *Ural'skiy Rabochiy*, 3 March 1984.

30. Boris Yeltsin, *Sredniy Ural: rubezhi sozidania* (Middle Ural: the stages of creation), Sredne-Uralskoye Publishers, 1981, p. 5.

31. 'Dlya blaga truzhennikov poley i ferm' (For the good of workers of fields and farms), Yeltsin speech at the All-Russian Conference on the Integrated Construction of and the Provision of Amenities to Agricultural Settlements in Russia, *Ural'skiy Rabochiy*, 20 July 1983.

32. *Ibid.*

33. Yeltsin, *Ispoved'*, p. 48.

34. Boris Yeltsin, 'Chem silyon rukovoditel' (What are a leader's strengths?), *Pravda*, 26 October 1980.

35. *Ibid.*

36. 'Organizatsionnyi plenum oblastnogo komiteta KPSS' (The organizational Plenum of the Oblast Committee of the CPSU), *Ural'skiy Rabochiy*, 22 January 1984.

37. Yeltsin, *Ispoved'*, p. 60. Emphasis added.

38. *Ibid.*

39. Yeltsin, 'Chem silyon rukovoditel'.

40. *Ibid.*

41. *Ibid.*

42. Vadim Danilov, 'Pryamo ili posredstvom?' (Directly or indirectly?), *Pravda*, 3 April 1980.

43. Yeltsin, *Ispoved'*, p. 54.

44. Danilov, 'Pryamo ili posredstvom?'

45. Interview with Artur Ezhov.

46. Boris Yeltsin, 'Otchyot oblastnogo komiteta KPSS' (Report of the Oblast Committee of the CPSU), *Ural'skiy Rabochiy*, 23 January 1981.

47. Boris Yeltsin, 'Podskazyvayut pis'ma' (The letters suggest what needs to be done), *Pravda*, 21 April 1983.

48. 'Otveti na voprosy', p. 81.

49. 'Povyshat' effectivnost' zhivotnovodstva' (To improve the effectiveness of cattle-raising), Yeltsin's speech to a conference of livestock experts, *Ural'skiy Rabochiy*, 12 November 1981.

50. 'Vsyo, chto nametila Partiya – vypolnim!' (Everything the Party outlined – we will fulfil!), Yeltsin's speech before the *aktiv* of the

provincial and city Party organizations, *Ural'skiy Rabochiy*, 13 November 1976.

51. *Ibid.*

52. *Ural'skiy Rabochiy*, 15 January 1977.

53. *Ibid.*

54. *Ibid.*

55. *Ibid.*

56. Boris Yeltsin, 'Vo slavu Rodiny' (For the glory of the Motherland), speech at a celebratory meeting to mark Leonid I. Brezhnev's greetings to the agricultural workers of Sverdlovsk and the fulfilment by the province of the annual plan for agricultural production, *Ural'skiy Rabochiy*, 26 October 1977.

57. *Ibid.*

58. Boris Yeltsin, 'Leninskie printsipy' (Leninist principles), *Izvestia*, 19 July 1977.

59. *Ibid.*

60. Boris Yeltsin, 'Kollektiv – glavnyi nastavnik' (The collective is the main teacher), *Izvestia*, 3 January 1978.

61. 'Vsyo, chto nametila Partia'.

62. *Ibid.*

63. Boris Yeltsin, 'General'nomu, Sekretary TsK KPSS to varishu, Leonidu Il'ichu Brezhnevu' (To the General Secretary of the Central Committee of the CPSU Comrade Brezhnev, Leonid Il'ich) in *Pozdravleniya i Privetstviya v Svyazi s Semidesyatiletiem Generalnogo Sekretarya TsK KPSS tov. Brezhneva L. I.* (Congratulations and greetings in connection with the seventieth birthday to the General Secretary of the Central Committee of the Communist Party of the Soviet Union Comrade Brezhnev), Moscow: Pravda Publishers, 1977, pp. 73–4.

64. *Ibid.*

65. Yeltsin, 'Leninskie printsypy'.

66. Boris Yeltsin, 'Lichnyi primer delegatov partiynogo s'ezda i konferentsiy na proizvodstve i v obshestvennoy zhizni' (Personal example set by the delegates to the

Party conferences in their work and public life), *Partiynaya Zhizn'*, 9, (May) 1977.

67. 'Pretvorim v zhizn' agrarnuyu politiku partii' (The Party's agricultural policy must be implemented), Yeltsin's speech at a Plenum of the Sverdlovsk Obkom, *Ural'skiy Rabochiy*, 15 July 1978.

68. Boris Yeltsin, 'Ne chislom – umeniem' (Not by the numbers but by the skill), *Pravda*, 28 January 1978.

69. *Ibid.*

70. *Ibid.*

71. 'Znat', chtoby umet'' (To know, in order to be able to do), Yeltsin's interview with *Pravda*, 4 November 1979.

72. *Ibid.*

73. Danilov, 'Pryamo ili posredstvom?'

74. Letter to *Pravda*, in response to the article 'Pryamo ili posredstvom?'

75. *Ibid.*

76. 'Vsyo, chto nametila Partiya'.

77. *Ibid.*

78. *Ibid.*

79. 'Rabotat' luchshe, povyshat' effektivnost' i kachestvo!' (To work better, to improve effectiveness and quality!), Yeltsin's speech before the Party-managerial *aktiv* of the province, *Ural'skiy Rabochiy*, 14 January 1977.

80. *Ibid.*

81. *Ibid.*

82. 'Reshenia XXVI s'ezda KPSS vypolnim!' (We will fulfil the resolutions of the Twenty-Sixth Congress of the CPSU!), Yeltsin's speech to the *aktiv*, *Ural'skiy Rabochiy*, 18 March 1981.

83. *Ibid.*

84. 'Rabotat' luchshe'.

85. Yeltsin, 'Otchyot oblastnogo komiteta KPSS'; and 'Reshenia XXVI s'ezda KPSS vypolnim!'

86. 'Rabotat' luchshe'.

87. 'Reshenia XXVI s'ezda KPSS vypolnim!'

88. 'Rabotat' luchshe'.

89. Boris Yeltsin, 'Videt' i predvidet'' (To see and to foresee), *Pravda*, 13 August 1981.

90. Yeltsin, 'Otchyot oblastnogo komiteta KPSS'.

91. *Ibid*.

92. Interview with Mira Shvartz.

93. Boris Yeltsin, 'Pretvorim v zhizn agrarnuyu politiku partii'.

94. *Ibid*.

95. *Ibid*.

96. *Ibid*.

97. *Ibid*.

98. *Ibid*.

99. Boris Yeltsin, 'Intensivnye faktory rosta' (The factors of growth based on efficiency), *Sovetskaya Rossia*, 13 March 1979.

100. Yeltsin, *Sredniy Ural*, p. 46.

101. *Ibid*.

102. *Ibid*.

103. 'Reshenia XXVI s'ezda KPSS vypolnim!'

104. Yeltsin, 'Videt' i predvidet''.

105. Vadim Danilov, 'V besede uchastvuyut vse' (Everyone participates in the discussion), Yeltsin press conference for the editors of local radio, television and newspapers. *Zhurnalist*, 3, (March) 1984.

106. Yeltsin, 'Chem silyon rukoviditel'.

107. Yeltsin, 'Videt' i predvidet''.

108. *Ibid*.

109. *Ibid*.

110. Yeltsin, *Sredniy Ural*, p. 41.

111. Yeltsin, 'Chem silyon rukoviditel'.

112. *Ibid*.

113. *Ibid*.

114. *Ibid*.

115. *Ural'skiy Rabochiy*, 23 January 1981.

116. Boris Yeltsin, 'Novizna sil'na podderzhkoy' (Support is innovation's strength), *Izvestia*, 6 July 1984.

117. 'Rabotat' luchshe . . .'

118. 'Podskazyvayut pis'ma'; Boris Yeltsin, 'Sovershenstvuya stil' raboty' (Perfecting the style of work), *Kommunist*, 11, (July) 1983, p. 63.

119. 'Podskazyvaut pis'ma'.

120. Yeltsin, 'Novizna sil'na podderzhkoy'.

121. 'Rabotat' luchshe . . .'

122. Yeltsin, 'Lichnyi primer . . .'

123. Yeltsin, 'Kollektiv . . .'

124. See, for example, Yeltsin, 'Ne chislom – umeniem'.

125. 'Znat', chtoby umet''.

126. *Ibid*.

127. Boris Yeltsin, 'Kompleksnye programmy Urala' (The integrated programme for the Urals), *Izvestia*, 29 January 1981.

128. Yeltsin, 'Intensivnye faktory rosta'.

129. 'Tovaram dlya naroda – partiynoye vnimanie' (Consumer goods must have the Party's attention), Yeltsin speech to a Plenum of Sverdlovsk Obkom, *Ural'skiy Rabochiy*, 15 July 1981.

130. *Ibid*.

131. Boris Yeltsin, 'Initsiativa, rozhdennaya vremenem' (An initiative whose time has come), *Izvestia*, 30 July 1981.

132. 'Tovaram dlya naroda'.

133. *Ibid*.

134. Yeltsin, 'Initsiativa'.

135. *Programma Kommunisticheskoy Partii Sovietskogo Soyuza* (Programme of The Communist Party of The Soviet Union), Moscow: Politizdat, 1974, p. 65.

136. *Ibid*.

137. Allan Kroncher, 'Does New Decree on Saving Raw Materials Portend More Central Control?', *Radio Liberty Research* (RL 275/81), 13 July 1981, p. 1.

138. Abram Bergson, 'Soviet Economic Slowdown and the 1981–1985 Plan', *Problems of Communism*, May–June 1981, p. 27, table 2.

139. Allan Kroncher, 'Deputy Minister Dismissed in Soviet Oil Scandal', *Radio Liberty Research* (RL 412/81), 16 October 1981, p. 1.

140. David Dyker, 'The Soviet Energy Balance and the Conundrum of Oil',

Radio Liberty Research (RL 43/81), 27 January 1981.

141. R. W. Apple Jr, 'Russians Urged to Work More, Waste Less', *New York Times*, 28 February 1981.

142. *Ibid.*

143. *Ibid.*

144. Andrey Aleksandrov-Agentov, 'Brezhnev i Khrushchev' (Brezhnev and Khrushchev), *Novoye Vremya*, 22, 1993, p. 36.

145. *Ibid.*

146. *Ibid.*

147. *Ibid.*

148. Goryun, *op. cit.*, Part I, p. 14.

149. Yeltsin, *Ispoved'*, p. 53.

150. Yeltsin, 'Sotsialisticheskoye sorevnovanie'.

151. Interview with Stanislav Dmitrievich Alekseev.

152. 'Rech tovarisha B. N. Yeltsina' (The speech of Comrade B. N. Yeltsin), *Pravda*, 26 February 1981.

153. *Ibid.*

154. *Ibid.*

155. *Izvestia*, 25 February 1981.

156. *Pravda*, 25 February 1981.

157. *Pravda*, 1 March 1981.

158. *Pravda*, 26 February 1981.

159. *Ibid.*

160. *Ibid.*

161. *Ibid.*

162. *Ibid.*

163. *Ibid.*

164. Leonid Brezhnev, 'Otchyot Tsentral'nogo Komiteta Kommunisticheskoy Partii Sovetskogo Soyuza i Ocherdnye Zadachi Partii v Oblasti Vneshney i Vnutrenney Politiki' (Report of the Central Committee of the Communist Party of the Soviet Union and the Party's main tasks in foreign and domestic policies. *Pravda*, 23 February 1981.

165. *Ibid.*

166. *Ibid.*

167. *Ibid.*

168. *Ibid.*

169. *Ibid.*

170. *Ibid.*

171. *Ibid.*

172. *Ibid.*

173. Fedor Tyutchev, 'Tsitseron' (Cicero), in *Stikhotvoreniya. Pis'ma* (Poems. Letters), Moscow: Sovremennik, 1978, p. 55.

174. Robert Conquest, 'Today the Soviet Party Congress Opens', *Washington Post*, 23 February 1981.

175. *Ibid.*

176. See, for example, Jean Lacouture, *De Gaulle*, vol. II: *The Ruler: 1945–1970*, New York: Norton, 1992, p. 239.

177. Vladimir Vysotskiy, 'Tovarishchi uchyonye' (Comrades scholars), in Vladimir Vysotskiy, *Sochineniya v dvukh tomakh* (Collected works in two volumes), Moscow: Khudozhestvennaya Literatura, 1993, volume I, p. 412.

178. *Ibid.*

179. Goryun, *op. cit.*, Part I, p. 16.

180. Yeltsin, *Sredniy Ural* p. 101.

181. *Ibid.*

182. *Ibid.*

183. *Ibid.*, pp. 101–2.

184. Ayrapetov, Bakunin and Boyarskikh, *op. cit.*, p. 191.

185. *Ibid.*

186. Yeltsin, 'Sovershenstvuya stil' raboty', p. 64.

187. Interview with Leonid Borisovich Kogan.

188. 'Podskazyvayut pis'ma'.

189. *Ibid.*

190. *Ibid.*

191. *Ibid.*

192. *Ibid.*

193. *Ibid.* See also Yeltsin, 'Sovershenstvuya stil' raboty', p. 63.

194. *Ibid.*

195. *Ibid.*

196. Interview with Lidiya Khudyakova.

197. Interview with Sergey Vozdvizhenskiy.

198. Interview with Valentin Petrovich Lukyanin.

199. Goryun, *op. cit.*, Part I, p. 4.

200. *Ibid.*
201. Interview with Andrey Andreevich Goryun.
202. *Ibid.*
203. 'V besede . . .'
204. *Ibid.*
205. Ludmila Pertzevaya, 'Do Not Worship Blindly', *Moscow News*, 15–22 March 1992.
206. *Ibid.*
207. *Ibid.*
208. *Ibid.*
209. Yeltsin, 'Sovershenstvuya stil' raboty', p. 63.
210. Interview with Leonid Kogan.
211. *Ibid.*
212. *Komsomol'skaya Pravda*, 7 August 1981.
213. 'Zhit' dlya ludey – dolg kommunista' (To live for the people is the duty of the communist), *Komsomol'skaya Pravda*, 25 September 1981.
214. V. Khiltunen and V. Khlystun, 'Net voprosov bez otvetov' (There are no questions without answers). Report on Yeltsin's session with the students of Sverdlovsk, *Komsomol'skaya Pravda*, 7 August 1981.
215. *Ibid.*
216. *Ibid.*; interview with Valentin Lukyanin.
217. *Ibid.*
218. Interview with Leonid Kogan.
219. Khiltunen and Khlystun, *op. cit.*
220. Yeltsin, 'Sovershenstvuya stil' raboty', p. 63.
221. Khiltunen and Khlystun, *op. cit.*
222. Interview with Leonid Kogan.
223. Khiltunen and Khlystun, *op. cit.*
224. 'Otvety na voprosy', p. 53.
225. *Ibid.*, p. 133.
226. *Ibid.*, p. 138.
227. *Ibid.*, p. 141.
228. *Ibid.*, p. 144.
229. *Ibid.*, p. 145.
230. *Ibid.*, p. 15:6.
231. Interview with Leonid Kogan.
232. *Ibid.*
233. Khiltunen and Khlystun, *op. cit.*
234. Interview with Leonid Kogan.
235. Interview with Boris Mikhailovich Balantsev.
236. *Ibid.*
237. *Ibid.*
238. Interview with Valentin Lukyanin.
239. *Ibid.*
240. *Ibid.*
241. *Ibid.*
242. Khiltunen and Khlystun, *op. cit.*
243. Goryun, *op. cit.*, Part I, p. 16.
244. Khiltunen and Khlystun, *op. cit.*; Yeltsin, 'Sovershenstvuya stil' raboty', p. 63.
245. Goryun, *op. cit.*, Part I, p. 16.
246. Interview with Valentin Lukyanin.
247. Interview with Stanislav Alekseev.
248. Interview with Andrey Goryun.
249. *Ibid.*
250. Interview with Valentin Lukyanin.
251. *Ibid.*
252. *Ibid.*
253. *Ibid.*
254. *Ibid.*
255. *Ibid.*
256. Interview with Boris Balantsev.
257. *Ibid.*
258. *Ibid.*
259. 'Otvety na voprosy', pp. 3:22, 23; 7:41, 42; 8:51.
260. *Ibid.*, p. 7:50.
261. *Ibid.*, p. 2:9.
262. *Ibid.*, p. 3:16.
263. *Ibid.*, p. 2:13.
264. *Ibid.*, p. 3:21, 23.
265. *Ibid.*, p. 17:14.
266. *Ibid.*, p. 16:8.
267. *Ibid.*, p. 5:36.
268. *Ibid.*, p. 5:37.
269. *Ibid.*, p. 5:38.
270. *Ibid.*, p. 139.
271. *Ibid.*, p. 140.
272. *Ibid.*, p. 144:9.
273. *Ibid.*, p. 142:3.
274. *Ibid.*, p. 4:26.
275. *Ibid.*, p. 14:44.
276. *Ibid.*, p. 10:13, 14.
277. *Ibid.*, p. 95.

278. *Ibid.*, p. 55.
279. *Ibid.*, pp. 119–20.
280. *Ibid.*, p. 91.
281. *Ibid.*, p. 36.
282. *Ibid.*
283. *Ibid.*, p. 78.
284. *Ibid.*, p. 76.
285. *Ibid.*, p. 74.
286. *Ibid.*, p. 89.
287. *Ibid.*, pp. 89, 91.
288. 'Zhit' dlya ludey . . .'
289. 'Otvety na voprosy', p. 101.
290. *Ibid.*, pp. 5:31, 13:40, 41.
291. *Ibid.*, p. 73.
292. Interview with Boris Balantsev.
293. Interview with Sergey
Khrushchev.
294. Yeltsin, *Ispoved'*, p. 64.
295. *Ibid.*, p. 49.
296. Goryun, *op. cit.*, Part I, p. 15.
297. Yeltsin, *Ispoved'*, p. 59.
298. Interview with Aleksandr
Rifatovich Urmanov.
299. Interview with Lidiya
Khudyakova.
300. Yeltsin, *Ispoved'*, p. 49.
301. *Ibid.*, p. 48.
302. Interview with Lidiya
Khudyakova.
303. *Ibid.*
304. 'Lubit Eltsin ingrat' na lozhkakh'
(Yeltsin loves to play the spoons),
Komsomol'skaya Pravda, 1 February
1992.
305. Yeltsin, *Ispoved'*, p. 50.
306. *Ibid.*
307. 'Lubit Eltsin ingrat' na
lozhkakh'.
308. Interview with Vasiliy Gudkov.
309. Interview with Gennadiy
Ivanovich Belyankin.
310. *Ibid.*
311. *Ibid.*
312. *Ibid.*
313. 'Dlya blaga truzhennikov poley i
ferm'.
314. *Ibid.*
315. *Ibid.*
316. 'Stroit' na sele bol'she, luchshe,
deshevle' (To build more, better and
cheaper in the countryside), report
from the All-Russian Conference on
the Complex Construction of and
Provision of Amenities to Agricultural
Settlements in Russia, *Ural'skiy
Rabochiy*, 20 July 1983.
317. *Ibid.*
318. Interview with Vasiliy Gudkov.
319. *Ibid.*
320. Interview with Sergey
Vozdvizhenskiy.
321. Yeltsin, *Ispoved'*, pp. 62–3.
322. Interview with Vladimir
Dmitrievich Kadochnikov.
323. 'Vsyo, chtoo nametila Partia'.
324. *Ibid.*
325. Yeltsin, *Ispoved'*, p. 63; and
interview with Sergey Vozdvizhenskiy.
326. Interview with Sergey
Vozdvizhenskiy.
327. Interview with Vladimir
Kadochnikov.
328. Yeltsin, *Ispoved'*, p. 63.
329. *Ibid.*, p. 60.
330. *Ibid.*
331. Interview with Sergey Peretrutov.
332. Yeltsin, *Ispoved'*, p. 60.
333. *Ibid.*, pp. 61–3.
334. 'O likvidatsii barakov i zhilikh
pomesheniy v podvalakh v 1982
godu'. Tsentr dokumentatsii
obshestvennykh organizatsiy
Sverdlovskoy oblasti, fond 4, opis
101, delo 188, 1982 g. (On the
liquidation of *barak*s and basement
dwellings in 1982. The Centre for
Documentation of the Public
Organizations of the Sverdlovsk
Region, holding 4, registry 101, log
188, 1982), 30 September 1982, p. 1.
335. *Ibid.*, p. 13.
336. *Ibid.*, p. 10.
337. *Ibid.*, p. 11.
338. Yeltsin, *Ispoved'*, p. 61.
339. *Ibid.*
340. *Ibid.*
341. Goryun, *op. cit.*, Part I, pp. 17–
18.
342. 'O likvidatsii barakov', p. 10.
343. Yeltsin, *Ispoved'*, pp. 61, 62.
344. 'O likvidatsii barakov', p. 10.
345. Interview with Viktor Popov.

346. Interview with Lidiya Khudyakova.
347. Yeltsin, *Ispoved'*, p. 62.
348. *Ibid.*
349. *Ibid.*
350. 'O likvidatsii barakov', pp. 13, 11.
351. 'Otvety na voprosy', p. 22.
352. *Ibid.*, p. 72.
353. *Ibid.*, p. 22.
354. Interview with Sergey Peretrutov.
355. Vladimir Bayev as quoted in Goryun, *op. cit.*, Part I, p. 17.
356. Yeltsin, *Ispoved'*, p. 53.
357. *Ibid.*
358. 'Otvety na voprosy', p. 26.
359. 'Prodovol'stvennaya Programma – delo vsenarodnoye' (Food programme is a cause of all the people), Yeltsin speech at a Plenum of the Sverdlovsk Obkom, *Ural'skiy Rabochiy*, 9 June 1982.
360. *Ibid.*
361. Yeltsin speech at the 26 May 1981 Plenum of the Sverdlovsk Obkom, 'Protokol 2-go plenuma Sverdlovskogo obkoma KPSS, 26 maya 1981 goda' (The minutes of the Second Plenum of the Sverdlovsk Regional Committee of the CPSU), Party Archive of the Sverdlovsk Region, holding 4, registry 100, log 11, p. 20.
362. *Ibid.*, p. 4.
363. Goryun, *op. cit.*, Part I, p. 17.
364. *Ibid.*
365. *Ibid.*, Part I, p. 13.
366. 'Otvety na voprosy', p. 91.
367. Yeltsin, *Ispoved'*, p. 55.
368. 'Prodovolstvennaya Programma'.
369. *Ibid.*
370. 'Podskazyvayut pis'ma'.
371. Goryun, *op. cit.*, Part I, p. 17.
372. Interview with Sergey Vozdvizhenskiy.
373. Interview with Stanislav Alekseev.
374. Interview with Lidiya Khudyakova.
375. *Ibid.*
376. *Ibid.*
377. Interview with Stanislav Alekseev.
378. *Ibid.*
379. Interview with Lidiya Khudyakova.
380. *Ibid.*
381. Interview with Sergey Vozdvizhenskiy.
382. Interview with Valentin Lukyanin.
383. Goryun, *op. cit.*, Part I, p. 16.
384. *Ibid.*
385. Interviews with Sergey Vozdvizhenskiy and Vladimir Kadochnikov.
386. Interview with Sergey Vozdvizhenskiy.
387. *Ibid.*
388. Interview with Gennadiy Belyankin.
389. *Ibid.*
390. *Ibid.*
391. *Ibid.*
392. Interview with Stanislav Alekseev.
393. Interview with Valentin Lukyanin.
394. *Ibid.*
395. Interview with Lidiya Khudyakova.
396. Goryun, *op. cit.*, Part I, pp. 15, 16.
397. Interview with Lidya Khudiakova.
398. *Ibid.*
399. Interview with Mira Shvartz.
400. *Ibid.*
401. Interview with Vasiliy Gudkov.
402. Goryun, *op. cit.*, Part I, p. 15.
403. *Ibid.*
404. Interview with Klavdia Bersenyova.
405. *Ibid.*
406. Goryun, *op. cit.*, Part I, p. 16.
407. *Ibid.*
408. Interview with Andrey Goryun.
409. *Ibid.*
410. Interview with Sergey Peretrutov.
411. *Ibid.*
412. *Ibid.*
413. Interview with Lidiya Khudyakova.

414. *Ibid.*

415. *Ibid.*

416. Y. Tubin, L. Zaks, L. Varynkina, L. Senderova and S. Margulis, *Teatralniy Sverdlovsk* (Theatrical Sverdlovsk), Sverdlovsk: Sredne-Uralskoye Publishers, 1989, p. 158.

417. *Ibid.*, p. 155.

418. Ol'ga Ivanova, 'Vernost' zhanru' (Loyalty to the genre). A review of the Moscow tour of the Sverdlovsk Theatre of Musical Comedy, *Izvestia*, 26 August 1983.

419. Tubin *et al.*, *op. cit.*, p. 160.

420. *Ibid.*

421. Interview with Lidiya Khudyakova.

422. 'Orden na znameni teatra' (Order on the banners of the theatre). A report on the award to the Sverdlovsk Theatre of Musical Comedy of the Order of Labour Red Banner, *Ural'skiy Rabochiy*, 29 October 1983.

423. *Ibid.*

424. 'Otvety na voprosy', p. 36.

425. *Ibid.*

426. Yeltsin, 'Zhit' dlya ludey'.

427. 'Otvety na voprosy', p. 36.

428. Tubin *et al.*, *op. cit.*, p. 117.

429. Interview with Lidiya Khudyakova.

430. Yu. Matafonova, 'Belyi lebed' v tsentre Sverdlovska' (White swan in the centre of Sverdlovsk), report on the opening of the renovated Opera and Ballet Theatre, *Ural'skiy Rabochiy*, 28 December 1982.

431. Interview with Lidiya Khudyakova.

432. *Ibid.*

433. *Ibid.*

434. Opera and Ballet Theatre, Sverdlovsk, Accounting Department.

435. Matafonova, *op. cit.*

436. *Ibid.*

437. *Ibid.*

438. *Ibid.*

439. *Ibid.*

440. Interview with Stanislav Alekseev.

441. *Ibid.*

442. Interview with Vladimir Kadochnikov.

443. *Ibid.*

444. *Ibid.*

445. Yeltsin, *Ispoved'*, p. 50.

446. Interview with Vladimir Kadochnikov.

447. *Ibid.*

448. Interview with Stanislav Alekseev.

449. *Ibid.*

450. *Ibid.*

451. *Ibid.*

452. *Ibid.*

453. *Ibid.*

454. Yeltsin, *Ispoved'*, p. 51.

455. Interview with Yakov Ryabov.

456. Yeltsin, *Ispoved'*, p. 58.

457. *Ibid.*

458. *Ibid.*

459. As quoted in Yeltsin, 'Sovershenstvuya stil' raboty', p. 56.

460. *Ibid.*, pp. 58–9.

461. Yuriy Andropov, 'Rech Generalnogo Secretarya Tsentral'nogo Komiteta KPSS tovarishcha Yu. V. Andropova na Plenume Ts K KPSS 15 iunya 1983 goda' (Speech of General Secretary of the Central Committee of the CPSU Yu. V. Andropov at the Plenum of the Central Committee of the CPSU on 15 June 1983), *Pravda*, 16 June 1983.

462. *Ibid.*

463. *Ibid.*

464. Egor Ligachev, *Inside Gorbachev's Kremlin*, New York: Pantheon Books, 1993, pp. 26, 27.

465. *Ibid.*, pp. 23, 24.

466. *Ibid.*, p. 25.

467. Ligachev speech at the Twenty-Third Sverdlovsk Party Conference, *Ural'skiy Rabochiy*, 22 January 1984.

468. *Ibid.*

469. *Ibid.*

470. *Ibid.*

471. *Ibid.*

472. *Ibid.*

473. *Ibid.*

474. Goryun, *op. cit.*, Part I, p. 21.

475. Interview with Gennadiy Belyankin.

476. *Ibid.*

477. *Ibid.*

478. Yeltsin, 'Sovershenstvuya stil' raboty', p. 67.

479. *Ibid.*

480. 'V besede uchastvuyut vse', pp. 13–14.

481. *Ibid.*, p. 14.

482. *Ibid.*

483. 'Vystuplenie na vechere trudovoy slavy Sverdlovskogo DSK po povodu vruchenya perekhodiashehikh znamyon po itogam 1-go i kvartala 1983 goda i 20-ti letiu obrazovanya DSK' (Speech at the celebratory meeting on the occasion of the award of the prize banners for best results in the first quarter and the twentieth anniversary of the DSK), Party Archive of the Sverdlovsk Region (PASO), 6 May 1983.

484. 'Delo vsei Partii, kazhdogo kommunista' (The business of the entire Party, of every communist), Yeltsin speech at a Plenum of the Sverdlovsk Obkom, *Ural'skiy Rabochiy*, 6 July 1983.

485. *Ibid.*

486. Airapetov, Bakunin and Boyarsikh, *op. cit.*, p. 243.

487. Interview with Valentin Lukyanin.

488. *Ibid.*

489. Konstantin Lagunov, 'Bronzoviy dog' (Bronze mastiff), *Ural*, 8, 1982, p. 52.

490. Interview with Valentin Lukyanin.

491. *Ibid.*

492. Lagunov, *op. cit.*, 9, p. 59.

493. *Ibid.*, p. 68.

494. *Ibid.*, p. 58.

495. *Ibid.*, no. 8, p. 52.

496. Interview with Valentin Lukyanin.

497. *Ibid.*

498. *Ibid.*

499. Interview with Nikolay Grigorievich Nikonov.

500. Nikolay Nikonov, *Povesti* (Novellas), Sverdlovsk: Sredne-Uralskoye Publishers, 1990, p. 80.

501. *Ibid.*, pp. 35, 36.

502. *Ibid.*, p. 27.

503. *Ibid.*, p. 75.

504. *Ibid.*, p. 87.

505. *Ibid.*

506. *Ibid.*, p. 49.

507. *Ibid.*

508. *Ibid.*, p. 102.

509. *Ibid.*, p. 111.

510. Interview with Valentin Lukyanin.

511. *Ibid.*

512. *Ibid.*

513. *Ibid.*

514. *Ibid.*

515. *Ibid.*

516. *Ibid.*

517. Protokol No. 46 zasedanya buro Sverdlovskogo Obkoma KPSS ot 24 maya 1983 goda. *O rabote redaktsii po povysheniyu ideino-khudozhestevennogo urovnya zhurnala 'Ural' v svete trebovaniy XXVI s'ezda partii i postanovleniya TsK KPSS. 'O tvorcheskikh svyaziakh literaturno-khudozhestvennikh zhurnalov s praktikoy kommunisticheskogo stroitelstva'.* Fond 4, opis 106, delo 35 (The minutes of the Buro of the Sverdlovsk Obkom of 24 May 1983. On the work of the editorial staff in the area of raising the ideological and creative level of *Ural* magazine in the light of the demands of the Twenty-Sixth Congress of the Party and the decree of the Central Committee of the CPSU. 'On the creative connection between magazines of belle-lettres and the practice of the building of communism'. The Party Archive of the Sverdlovsk Region, holding 4, registry 106, log 35).

518. *Ibid.*, p. 1.

519. *Ibid.*, p. 2.

520. *Ibid.*

521. *Ibid.*

522. *Ibid.*, p. 3.

523. Interview with Valentin Lukyanin.

524. *Ibid.*

525. *Ibid.*

526. Protokol No. 46, p. 3.

527. *Ibid.*, p. 4.

528. *Ibid.*

529. *Ibid.*, pp. 4–5.

530. *Ibid.*, p. 5.

531. *Ibid.*

532. Interview with Nikolay Nikonov.

533. *Ibid.*

534. *Ibid.*

535. Interview with Aleksandr Novikov.

536. Aleksandr Yakovlev, *Muki prochtenia bytiya* (The torments of reading life), Moscow: Novosti, 1991, p. 31.

537. Nikolay Ryzhkov, *Perestroika: istoriya predatel'stv* (Perestroika: the history of betrayals), Moscow: Novosti, 1992, pp. 33, 94.

538. Yakovlev, *op. cit.*, p. 343.

539. Ryzhkov, *op. cit.*, p. 42.

540. *Ibid.*, p. 236.

541. Ligachev, *Inside Gorbachev's Kremlin*, p. 18.

542. *Ibid.* See also Ryzhkov, *op. cit.*, p. 78.

543. Ryzhkov, *op. cit.*, pp. 78, 79.

544. *Ibid.*

545. Ligachev, *Inside Gorbachev's Kremlin*, p. 75.

546. *Ibid.*

Chapter 4: Perestroika, Mark I

1. Yeltsin, *Ispoved'*, p. 67.

2. *Ibid.*, pp. 67, 68.

3. *Ibid.*, p. 69.

4. *Ibid.*, p. 67.

5. *Ibid.*, pp. 70, 71.

6. *Ural'skiy Rabochiy*, 20 April 1995.

7. Yeltsin, *Ispoved'*, p. 70.

8. *Ibid.*

9. *Ibid.*, p. 69.

10. *Pravda*, 15 December 1985.

11. *Ibid.*

12. 25 December 1985.

13. *Pravda*, 24 April 1985.

14. 'Conversation with the working class of Komsomolsk-on-the-Amur', *Moskovskaya Pravda*, 10 July 1986.

15. *Moskovskaya Pravda*, 28 December 1985.

16. *Ibid.*

17. *Ibid.*

18. *Ibid.*

19. *Moskovskaya Pravda*, 18 January 1986.

20. *Ibid.*

21. *Moskovskaya Pravda*, 10 January 1986.

22. *Moskovskaya Pravda*, 18 January 1986.

23. *Moskovskaya Pravda*, 24 January 1986.

24. *Moskovskaya Pravda*, 25 January 1986.

25. Interview with Yuriy Karabasov, 21 July 1991. At the time of the Conference Karabasov was First Secretary of the Gagarin District Committee. Shortly after he became a Secretary of MGK.

26. *Ibid.*

27. *Ibid.*

28. *Moskovskaya Pravda*, 16 February 1986.

29. *Ibid.*

30. *Ibid.*

31. Celestine Bohlen, 'New "Hands-On" Leader Is Shaking Up Moscow', *Washington Post*, 10 February 1986.

32. *Pravda*, 27 February 1986.

33. *Ibid.*

34. *Ibid.*

35. Yeltsin, *Ispoved'*, p. 120.

36. *Ibid.*, p. 123.

37. *Ibid.*, p.119.

38. *Ibid.*, p. 121.

39. Gary Lee, 'Party Members' Perks Make Some See Red in Moscow', *Washington Post*, 3 March 1986.

40. *Pravda*, 27 February 1986.

41. Sir Isaiah Berlin, *Personal Impressions*. New York: Penguin, 1980, p. 15.

42. *Moskovskaya Pravda*, 6 April 1986.

43. *Moskovskaya Pravda*, 30 March 1986.

44. *Ibid.*
45. *Pravda*, 26 February 1986.
46. *Moskovskie Novosti*, 30 March 1986.
47. Yeltsin's speech. *Moskovskaya Pravda*, 5 October 1986.
48. Vyacheslav Baskov, 'Proshchanie s limitchikom' (Farewell to the limitchik), *Sovetskaya Kul'tura*, 24 September 1987, p. 6.
49. Yeltsin, *Ispoved'*, p. 96.
50. Baskov, *op. cit.*
51. Yeltsin's speech, *Moskovskaya Pravda*, 20 July 1986.
52. *Ibid.*
53. *Moskovskaya Pravda*, 5 October 1986.
54. *Moskovskaya Pravda*, 30 March 1986.
55. *Ibid.*
56. *Ibid.*
57. Yeltsin's speech, *Moskovskaya Pravda*, 3 August 1986.
58. *Ibid.*
59. *Ibid.*
60. 'Vypiska iz vystupleniya t. Yeltsina B. N. pered propagandistami g. Moskvy' (Excerpt from the presentation of Comrade B. N. Yeltsin before the propagandists of the city of Moscow), Radio Liberty, Archiv Samizdata No. 5721, 11 April 1986, p. 6.
61. *Ibid.*, p. 1.
62. *Ibid.*
63. V. Batalova and V. Nechyaev, 'Kogda teryaetsiya perspektiva' (When perspective is lost), *Moskovskaya Pravda*, 18 January 1987.
64. N. Shan'gin, 'Pochemu opazdal avtobus' (Why the bus was late), *Vechernyaya Moskva*, 19 December 1986.
65. 'Vypiska', p. 1.
66. From Yeltsin's speech at the Plenum of the Party organization of the Zhdanovskiy district. *Moskovskaya Pravda*, 3 August 1986.
67. Interview with Yeltsin, *Moskovskaya Pravda*, 14 April 1987.

68. *Moskovskaya Pravda*, 12 February 1986.
69. *Ibid.*
70 *Moskovskaya Pravda*, 6 July 1986.
71. *Moskovskaya Pravda*, 30 March 1986.
72. 'Moskva i moskvichi: god 2000' (Moscow and the Muscovites: the year 2000), *Izvestia*, 28 September 1986.
73. 'Vypiska', p. 1. See also 'Na sovete po gradostroitel'stvu' (In the advisory committee on urban planning), *Vechernyaya Moskva*, 2 February 1987.
74. *Moskovskaya Pravda*, 20 July 1986.
75. L. Ambrosimov, 'Vtoraya professia' (A second profession), *Vechernyaya Moskva*, 16 April 1987.
76. *Moskovskaya Pravda*, 30 March 1986.
77. Boris Yeltsin, 'Pribavlyat' oboroty perestroiki' (To hasten the pace of perestroika). Interview with *Moskovskaya Pravda*, 14 April 1987.
78. 'Vypiska', p. 1.
79. *Ibid.*
80. Yeltsin, 'Pribavlyat' . . .'
81. *Izvestia*, 28 September 1986.
82. Boris Yeltsin, 'Net ni potolka dlya kritiki ni predela dlya glasnosti' (There is neither a ceiling to criticism nor a limit to glasnost). Interview with *Moskovskie Novosti*, 24 August 1986.
83. *Ibid.*
84. *Ibid.*
85. *Moskovskaya Pravda*, 20 July, 1986.
86. Yeltsin's interview, 'Net ni potolka . . .'
87. See, for example, 'Budushchee pyatietazhek' (The future of five-storey buildings), *Moskovskaya Pravda*, 6 September 1987.
88. *Moskovskaya Pravda*, 5 October 1986.
89. 'Vypiska', p. 1.
90. *Moskovskaya Pravda*, 30 March 1986.
91. A. Goldov, 'Pro novogodnuu kartoshku' (About the new year's

potato), *Moskovskaya Pravda*, 7 January 1986.
92. *Ibid.*
93. 'Vypiska', p. 4.
94. *Moskovskaya Pravda*, 12 December 1986.
95. *Moskovskaya Pravda*, 12 June 1986.
96. Yeltsin, *Ispoved'*, p. 90, and 'Vypiska', pp. 8–9.
97. Yeltsin, *Ispoved'*, p. 90.
98. *Ibid.*
99. 'Vypiska', p. 9.
100. *Moskovskie Novosti*, 17 December 1986.
101. 'Vypiska', p. 9.
102. *Ibid.*, p. 2.
103. *Ispoved'*, p. 89.
104. 'Vypiska', p. 9.
105. *Ispoved'*, p. 90.
106. *Moskovskaya Pravda*, 25 January 1986.
107. *Moskovskaya Pravda*, 11 December 1986.
108. *Moskovskaya Pravda*, 29 July 1986.
109. *Moskovskaya Pravda*, 24 July 1986.
110. *Ibid.*
111. *Moskovskaya Pravda*, 7 August 1986.
112. *Moskovskaya Pravda*, 11 October 1986.
113. *Moskovskaya Pravda*, 1 April 1986.
114. Interview with Lev Petrovich Belyanskiy.
115. *Ibid.*
116. *Moskovskie Novosti*, 27 July 1986.
117. *Moskovskaya Pravda*, 28 September 1986.
118. *Ibid.*
119. Interview with Lev Belyanskiy.
120. *Ibid.*
121. *Vechernyaya Moskva*, 26 December 1986.
122. Egor Shikhman, 'Komandirovanniy v oppozitsiyu' (On business in the opposition), *Novoye Russkoye Slovo*, 10 October 1989.
123. *Ibid.*
124. *Ibid.*
125. *Moskovskaya Pravda*, 30 March 1986.
126. *Ibid.*
127. *Ibid.*
128. *Ibid.*
129. *Moskovskie Novosti*, 3 March 1987.
130. *Moskovskaya Pravda*, 12 March 1986.
131. *Moskovskaya Pravda*, 12 February 1986.
132. *Moskovskaya Pravda*, 30 March 1986.
133. *Ibid.*
134. Interview with Lev Belyanskiy.
135. 'Vypiska', p. 5.
136. *Ibid.*, p. 7.
137. *Moskovskaya Pravda*, 24 August 1986.
138. *Moskovskaya Pravda*, 1 December 1986.
139. *Moskovskaya Pravda*, 17 April 1987.
140. *Ibid.*
141. *Ibid.*
142. Interview with Yuriy Karabasov.
143. Interview with Lev Belyanskiy.
144. Interview with Yuriy Karabasov.
145. *Ibid.*
146. *Moskovskaya Pravda*, 24 August 1986.
147. *Moskovskaya Pravda*, 30 March 1986.
148. *Ibid.*
149. *Moskovskaya Pravda*, 23 November 1986.
150. Yeltsin, *Ispoved'*, p. 95.
151. *Ibid.*
152. *Moskovskaya Pravda*, 14 April 1987.
153. Shikhman, *op. cit.*
154. *Moskovskaya Pravda*, 12 April 1986.
155. 'Vypiska'.
156. Interview with Vladimir Volkov, historian, who was at the time a member of the Buro of the Kievskiy Raikom.
157. *Ibid.*

158. 'Vypiska', p. 1.
159. 'Net ni potolka . . .'
160. *Moskovskaya Pravda*, 30 March 1986.
161. *Ibid.*
162. 'Net ni potolka . . .'
163. *Moskovskaya Pravda*, 16 August 1986.
164. *Moskovskie Novosti*, 29 August 1986.
165. *Ibid.*
166. *Ibid.*
167. *Ibid.*
168. *Moskovskaya Pravda*, 4 January 1986.
169. *Moskovskaya Pravda*, 22 January 1986.
170. Yeltsin, *Ispoved'*, p. 91.
171. Interview with Vladimir Volkov.
172. *Moskovskaya Pravda*, 26 July 1986.
173. *Ibid.*
174. *Moskovskaya Pravda*, 27 July 1986.
175. *Moskovskaya Pravda*, 28 August 1986.
176. *Moskovskaya Pravda*, 31 August 1986.
177. *Moskovskaya Pravda*, 28 August 1986.
178. *Ibid.*
179. *Ibid.*
180. *Moskovskaya Pravda*, 7 December 1986.
181. *Moskovskaya Pravda*, 21 February 1986.
182. 'Vypiska', pp. 7, 14.
183. *Ibid.*
184. *Moskovskaya Pravda*, 7 December 1986.
185. *Ibid.*
186. 'Vypiska', p. 3.
187. *Ibid.*
188. *Ibid.*
189. *Moskovskie Novosti*, 24 August 1986.
190. *Ibid.*
191. 'Vypiska', p. 3.
192. Yeltsin, *Ispoved'*, pp. 96–7.
193. *Moskovskaya Pravda*, 20 July 1986.
194. *Moskovskaya Pravda*, 23 July 1986.
195. *Moskovskaya Pravda*, 20 July 1986.
196. *Ibid.*
197. *Moskovskaya Pravda*, 3 August 1986.
198. *Moskovskaya Pravda*, 20 July 1986.
199. *Moskovskaya Pravda*, 3 August 1986.
200. *Moskovskaya Pravda*, 20 July 1986.
201. *Ibid.*
202. *Ibid.*
203. *Ibid.*
204. *Ibid.*
205. *Moskovskaya Pravda*, 7 August 1986.
206. *Ibid.*
207. *Moskovskaya Pravda*, 11 December 1986.
208. *Moskovskaya Pravda*, 20 July 1986.
209. *Ibid.*
210. *Ibid.*
211. *Moskovskaya Pravda*, 3 August 1986.
212. *Ibid.*
213. *Moskovskaya Pravda*, 6 December 1986.
214. *Moskovskaya Pravda*, 4 October 1986.
215. *Ibid.*
216. *Ibid.*
217. *Moskovskaya Pravda*, 5 October 1986.
218. *Ibid.*
219. *Ibid.*
220. *Moskovskaya Pravda*, 14 December 1986.
221. *Komsomol'skaya Pravda*, 30 November 1986.
222. *Ibid.*
223. *Moskovskaya Pravda*, 5 October 1986.
224. *Ibid.* Emphasis added.
225. *Moskovskaya Pravda*, 6 December 1986. Emphasis added.
226. *Moskovskaya Pravda*, 4 December 1986. Emphasis added.

227. *Moskovskaya Pravda*, 29 July 1986.
228. *Ibid.*
229. *Moskovskaya Pravda*, 30 July 1986.
230. *Ibid.*
231. *Ibid.*
232. *Ibid.*
233. *Moskovskaya Pravda*, 20 July 1986.
234. *Ibid.*
235. *Ibid.*
236. *Ibid.*
237. 'Zaklyuchitel'noye slovo General'nogo sekretarya TsK KPSS M. S. Gorbacheva na Plenume TsK KPSS yanvarya 1987 goda' (The concluding remarks by the General Secretary of the Central Committee of the CPSU M. S. Gorbachev at the Plenum of the Central Committee of the CPSU on 28 January 1987). *Pravda*, 30 January 1987.
238. Gorbachev, Mikhail. 'O perestroike i Kodrovoy politike partii.' Doklad General'nogo sekretarya TsK KPSS M. S. Gorbacheva na Plenume TsK KPSS 27 yanvarya 1987 goda' (The concluding remarks by the General Secretary of the Central Committee of the CPSU M. S. Gorbachev at the Plenum of the Central Committee of the CPSU on 28 January 1987). *Pravda*, 30 January 1987.
239. *Ibid.*
240. *Ibid.*
241. Gorbachev, 'Zaklyuchitel'noye slovo . . .'
242. *Pravda*, 25 April 1985.
243. Egor Ligachev's speech in Havana, Cuba, *Moskovskaya Pravda*, 7 February 1986.
244. Mikhail Gorbachev's speech at the April (1985) Plenum of the Central Committee (*Pravda*, 24 April 1985).
245. Vladimir Treml, 'Document on Alcoholism in the USSR Put in Perspective', *Radio Liberty Research* (RL 39/85), 6 February 1985, p. 2.
246. Vladimir Treml, 'Gorbachev's Anti-Drinking Campaign: A Noble Experiment or a Costly Exercise in Futility', *RL Supplement* (RL 2/87), 18 March 1987, p. 8.
247. Leonid Ionin, 'Chetyre bedy Rossii' (Russia's four misfortunes), *Novoye Vremya*, 12, 1995, p. 16.
248. Leonid Frizman, 'Kakim on byl . . .' (What he used to be . . .), *Novoye Vremya*, 12, 1995, p. 19.
249. Treml, 'Document . . .', p. 3.
250. Aaron Trehub, 'Is Gorbachev's Anti-Drinking Campaign Losing its Kick?', *Radio Liberty Research* (RL 323/87), 3 August 1987, p. 2.
251. Treml, 'Gorbachev's . . .', p. 16.
252. Ionin, *op. cit.*, pp. 16–17.
253. *Pravda*, 28 January 1987.
254. 'Uskorenie – novoye kachestvo rosta' (Acceleration – the new quality of growth), *Izvestia*, 26 September 1986. Emphasis added.
255. *Ibid.* Emphasis added.
256. Gorbachev's speech at the Twenty-Sixth Congress of the CPSU (*Pravda*, 26 February 1986).
257. *Pravda*, 28 January 1987.
258. *Ibid.*
259. Mikhail Gorbachev's speech at the Twenty-Sixth Party Congress (*Pravda*, 26 February 1986).
260. See, for example, Henry S. Rowen and Charles Wolf Jr, *The Impoverished Superpower*, San Francisco: Institute for Contemporary Studies, 1990, p. 9.
261. Anders Åslund, *How Russia Became a Market Economy*, Washington, DC: The Brookings Institution, 1995, p. 91.
262. Yeltsin's speech at the February (1987) Plenum of the MGK (*Moskovskaya Pravda*, 23 February 1987).
263. From the speech of Oleg Korolev, Secretary of the MGK, at the February (1987) Plenum of the MGK (*Moskovskaya Pravda*, 23 February 1987).
264. *Moskovskaya Pravda*, 19 July 1986.

265. *Moskovskaya Pravda*, 10 October 1987.

266. *Ibid.*

267. Linda J. Cook, 'Brezhnev's "Social Contract" and Gorbachev's Reforms', *Soviet Studies*, 41 (1), 1992, p. 43.

268. Yakovlev, *op. cit.*, p. 10.

269. 'V TsK KPSS' (In the Central Committee of the CPSU), *Pravda*, 1 October 1986.

270. S. Yu. Andreev, 'Nashe proshloye, nasotoyashchee, budushchee: struktura vlasti i zadachi obshchestva' (Our past, present, future: the structure of power and the tasks of society), in F. M. Borodkin, L. Ya. Kosals and R. R. Ryvkina, *Postizhenie*, Moscow: Progress, 1989, pp. 540, 545.

271. *Ibid.*

272. *Ibid.*

273. *Washington Post*, 12 April 1995.

274. Mikhail Gorbachev, speech to the February (1988) Plenum of the Central Committee (*Pravda*, 19 February 1988).

275. Aslund, *op. cit.*, p. 13.

276. Dmitriy Furman, 'Revolutsionnye tsikly Rossii' (Russia's revolutionary cycles), *Svobodnaya Mysl'*, January 1994, p. 10.

277. Yakovlev, *op. cit.*, p. 31.

278. Eduard Shevardnadze, *The Future Belongs to Freedom*, London: Sinclair-Stevenson, 1991, p. 26.

279. Interview with ITAR/Tass, 13 October 1992.

280. Treml, 'Gorbachev's . . .', p. 6.

281. Ryzhkov, *op. cit.*, p. 243.

282. The GNP figure is from Anders Åslund, 'How Small is Soviet National Income?' in Rowen and Wolf, *op. cit.*, p. 37. The figures for the Soviet budget revenues are from Judy Shelton, *The Coming Soviet Crash*, New York: The Free Press, 1989, p. 9, and for healthcare from Treml, 'Gorbachev's . . .', p. 12.

283. Mikhail Gorbachev, 'Krepit' klyuchevoye zveno ekonomiki' (To strengthen the key link of the economy), *Pravda*, 10 December 1990.

284. Ryzhkov, *op. cit.*, p. 95.

285. *Ibid.*

286. Yakovlev, *op. cit.*, p. 30.

287. *Pravda*, 28 January 1987.

288. *Pravda*, 14 February 1987.

289. Andreev, *op. cit.*, p. 579.

290. *Ibid.*

291. At the meeting with Sovietologists at the Library of Congress on 14 May 1992, Mikhail Gorbachev said he had read some of their works when he was the First Secretary of the Stavropol Regional (Krai) Party Committee.

292. 'Pribavlyat' oboroty perestroiki' (To hasten the pace of perestroika), Yeltsin interview with *Moskovskaya Pravda*, 14 April 1987.

293. *Ibid.*

294. *Moskovskaya Pravda*, 9 August 1987.

295. *Ibid.*

296. *Moskovskaya Pravda*, 23 February 1987.

297. *Ibid.*

298. *Ibid.*

299. *Ibid.*

300. *Ibid.*

301. *Moskovskaya Pravda*, 23 February, 1987.

302. *Ibid.*

303. 'Seven Days in May', Moscow: CBS, May 1987.

304. TASS in English, 7 October 1987 (FBIS-SOV, 7 October 1987, p. 10).

305. TASS in English, 6 October 1987.

306. *Ibid.*

307. *Moskovskie Novosti*, 18 October 1987.

308. *Ibid.*

309. Associated Press, 7 October (*Novoye Russkoye Slovo*, 8 October 1987).

310. *Ibid.*

311. *Ibid.*

312. *Ibid.*

313. *Moskovskaya Pravda*, 15 March 1987.

314. *Moskovskaya Pravda*, 9 August 1987.

315. *Ibid.*

316. *Ibid.*

317. *Ibid.*

318. *Ibid.*

319. *Moskovskaya Pravda*, 15 March 1987.

320. *Ibid.*

321. *Ibid.*

322. *Ibid.*

323. *Moskovskaya Pravda*, 9 August 1987.

324. *Ibid.*

325. *Ibid.*

326. *Ibid.*

327. *Moskovskaya Pravda*, 23 February 1987.

328. *Ibid.*

329. *Ibid.*

330. *Moskovskaya Pravda*, 14 April 1987.

331. *Ibid.*

332. *Ibid.*

333. *Ibid.*

334. Yeltsin, *Ispoved'*, p. 6.

335. 'I vyplesnulos' vozmushchenie' (And indignation boiled over), *Moskovskaya Pravda*, 21 August 1987.

336. *Ibid.*

337. *Ibid.*

338. See G. Alimov and R. Lynev, 'Kuda uvodit Pamyat'' (Where Pamyat' steals off to), *Izvestia*, 3 June 1987; and Andrey Kiselev and Aleksandr Mostovshikov, 'Pogovorim na ravnykh' (Let's talk as equals), *Moskovskie Novosti*, 17 May 1987.

339. Yeltsin, *Ispoved'*, p. 93.

340. Alimov and Lynev, *op. cit.*

341. Kiselev and Mostovshikiv, *op. cit.*

342. *Ibid.*

343. Alimov and Lynev, *op. cit.*

344. V. Ponomarev, 'Volny bez peny ne byvyaet' (There is no wave without foam), *Izvestia*, 30 July 1987.

345. Vladimir Yakovlev, 'Proshchanie s Bazarovym' (Farewell to Bazarov), *Ogonyok*, 36, 1987; Gennady Zhavoronkov, 'More scope for the unofficial', *Moscow News*, 13 September 1987, p. 12.

346. Zhavoronkov, *op. cit.*

347. *Moskovskaya Pravda*, 9 August 1987.

348. *Ibid.*

349. *Ibid.*

350. *Ibid.*

351. *Moskovskaya Pravda*, 21 August 1987.

352. *Ibid.*

353. *Vechernyaya Moskva*, 21 August 1987.

354. N. Abikesheva and S. Sevastianov, 'Pokupatel' dayot sovety' (The consumer gives advice), *Vechernyaya Moskva*, 18 November 1987.

355. *Vechernyaya Moskva*, 21 August 1987.

356. *Ibid.*

357. *Ibid.*

358. *Ibid.*

359. A letter from Dr Dmitriy Sviridov to the author.

360. Yeltsin's speech at the 8 August 1987 Plenum of the MGK (*Moskovskaya Pravda*, 9 August 1987).

361. *Ibid.*

362. *Ibid.*

363. *Ibid.*

364. *Ibid.*

365. From Poltoranin's interview with *Corriere della Sera*, 12 May 1988, as quoted in Kevin Devlin, 'Soviet Journalist Describes Eltsin's Struggle against Party Mafia', *Radio Liberty Research* (RL 206/88), 20 May 1988, p. 5.

366. *Ibid.*

367. *Ibid.*, pp. 3–4.

368. *Ibid.*, p. 4.

369. *Ibid.*, p. 5.

370. *XIX Vsesoyuznaya Konferentsiya Kommunistichestoy Partii Sovetskogo Soyuza. Stenographicheskiy Otchet, Tom II* (The Nineteenth All-Union

Conference of the Communist Party of the Soviet Union. Stenographic Record, vol. II), Moscow: Izdatelstvo Politcheskoy Literatury, 1988, p. 182.
371. Devlin, *op. cit.*, p. 4.
372. *Moskovskie Novosti*, 18 October 1987.
373. *Ibid.*
374. Goryun, *op. cit.*, Part I, p. 27.
375. Yeltsin, *Ispoved'*, p. 8.
376. *Ibid.*, p. 6. In his concluding speech at the 21 October 1987 Plenum, Gorbachev confirmed that Yeltsin had asked to be relieved of his duties and that he asked not to be 'forced to go in front of a Plenum with this request' (*Izvestia TsK KPSS*, 1989, no. 2, p. 282).

Another confirmation of the letter's general thrust came at the Nineteenth Party Conference in 1988, where Gorbachev said that he had received 'a letter from Comrade Yeltsin, in which he asked to be relieved of the post of the First Secretary of the [Moscow] Gorkom' (*XIX Vsesoyuznaya Konferentsiya*, p. 183.
377. *Ibid.*
378. *Ibid.*, p. 7.
379. *Ibid.*, p. 8.
380. *Ibid.*, p. 6.
381. *Ibid.*, p. 8.
382. *Ibid.*
383. *XIX Vsesoyuznaya Konferentsiya*, p. 183.
384. Yeltsin, *Ispoved'*, p. 11.
385. *Ibid.* See also *Izvestiya TsK KPSS*, 1989, no. 2, p. 282.
386. Yeltsin, *Ispoved'*, p. 11.
387. Vasiliy Grossman, *Zhizn' i sud'ba* (Life and fate), Moscow: Knizhnaya Palata, 1989, p. 474. My translation.
388. Yeltsin, *Ispoved'*, p. 12.
389. *Ibid.*
390. *Izvestiya TsK KPSS*, 1989, no. 2, p. 239.
391. Goryun, *op. cit.*, Part II, p. 4. Recollections are those of A. Korolev, a Sverdlovsk worker and a member of the Central Committee.

392. *Ibid.*
393. *Izvestiya TsK KPSS*, 1989, no. 2, pp. 239–41. My translation follows the style of the original with minimal editing for clarity.
394. Yeltsin, *Ispoved'*, p. 138.
395. 'Plenum TsK KPSS – October 1987' (Plenum of the Central Committee of the CPSU – October 1987), *Izvestiya TsK KPSS*, 1989, no. 2, p. 241.
396. *Ibid.*
397. *Ibid.*, p. 243.
398. *Ibid.*, pp. 242, 243.
399. *Ibid.*, pp. 243–4.
400. *Ibid.*, p. 245.
401. *Ibid.*, p. 256.
402. *Ibid.*, p. 249.
403. *Ibid.*, p. 251.
404. *Ibid.*, p. 250.
405. *Ibid.*, p. 256.
406. *Ibid.*, p. 261.
407. *Ibid.*, p. 250.
408. *Ibid.*
409. *Ibid.*, p. 262.
410. *Ibid.*, pp. 256–7.
411. *Ibid.*, p. 274.
412. *Ibid.*
413. *Ibid.*, p. 252.
414. *Ibid.*, p. 257.
415. *Ibid.*, p. 259.
416. Raymond Aron, *Memoirs*, New York: Holmes & Meier, 1990, p. 107.
417. *Izvestiya TsK KPSS*, No. 2, p. 262.
418. *Ibid.*, p. 140.
419. *Ibid.*, p. 263.
420. *Ibid.*, p. 266.
421. *Ibid.*
422. Yeltsin, *Ispoved'*, p. 138.
423. *Ibid.*, p. 141.
424. Yeltsin, *Ispoved'*, p. 141.
425. *Izvestiya TsK KPSS*, 1989, no. 2, p. 254.
426. Yeltsin, *Ispoved'*, p. 140.
427. *Ibid.*, p. 141.
428. *Izvestiya TsK KPSS*, 1989, no. 2, p. 279.
429. *Ibid.*
430. *Ibid.*
431. *Ibid.*, p. 280.

432. *Ibid.*
433. *Ibid.*, p. 281.
434. *Ibid.*, p. 282.
435. *Ibid.*, p. 284.
436. *Ibid.*, p. 286.
437. *Ibid.*
438. *Ibid.*
439. *Ibid.*
440. *Moskovskaya Pravda*, 6 November 1987.
441. William J. Eaton, 'Gorbachev Ally Admits Errors, Asks to Resign', *Los Angeles Times*, 1 November 1987.
442. Yeltsin, *Ispoved'*, p. 143.
443. *Ibid.*
444. *Ibid.*
445. *Ibid.*, p. 144.
446. Interview with Mikhail Poltoranin, 'The Yeltsin File', '*The Second Russian Revolution*', episode 3.
447. *Ibid.*
448. Yeltsin, *Ispoved'*, p. 144.
449. *Ibid.*
450. Interview with Yuriy Karabasov.
451. *Pravda*, 13 November 1987, p. 1.
452. *Ibid.*
453. *Ibid.*
454. *Ibid.*, p, 2.
455. *Ibid.*, pp. 2–3.
456. *Ibid.*
457. *Ibid.*
458. Interview with Lev Belyanskiy.
459. V. A. Zatvornitskiy, 'Trudnyi Urok' (A hard lesson), *Sovetskaya Rossia*, 24 November 1987.
460. Interview with Lev Belianskiy.
461. Interview with Poltoranin, 'The Yeltsin File'.
462. Interviews with Poltoranin and Prokofi'ev, 'The Yeltsin File'.
463. *Ibid.*
464. *Ibid.*
465. Interview with Poltoranin, *ibid.*
466. Zatvornitskiy, *op. cit.*
467. *Ibid.*
468. *Pravda*, 13 November 1987, p. 3.
469. *Ibid.*
470. *Ibid.*
471. *Ibid.*
472. *Ibid.*
473. Interview with Poltoranin, 'The Yeltsin File', *op. cit.*

Chapter 5: Antaeus

1. From Gorbachev's address to the 'leaders of the mass media, ideological agencies and creative unions' on 8 January 1988 (*Izvestia*, 9 January 1988).
2. *Ibid.*
3. Philip Taubman, ' "Who Will Now Dare to Express his Opinion?" Moderator Is Asked', *New York Times*, 16 November 1987.
4. *Ibid.*
5. *Ibid.*
6. Francis X. Clines, 'For Muscovites, Pravda Account of the Yeltsin Ouster Is Riveting Reading', *New York Times*, 14 November 1987.
7. *Ibid.*
8. Francis X. Clines, 'Campus Rally for Yeltsin, a Rare Sight', *New York Times*, 20 November 1987.
9. Celestine Bohlen, 'Champion of Glasnost Always Spoke his Mind', *Washington Post*, 12 November 1987.
10. *Izvestia*, 9 January 1988.
11. *Pravda*, 19 November 1987.
12. Lev Sukhanov, *Tri goda s El'tsinym* (Three years with Yeltsin), Riga: Vaga, 1992, p. 27.
13. Yeltsin, *Ispoved'*, p. 146.
14. Gavriil Popov, 'Kakaya perestroika nam nuzhna' (What kind of perestroika we need), *Moskovskie Novosti*, 20 December 1987, p. 7.
15. Goryun, *op. cit.*, Part II, p. 7.
16. *Ibid.*
17. Mikhail Poltoranin, 'Visiting Boris Yeltsin', *Moscow News*, the German edition, May 1988, Cologne, p. 20 (FBIS-SOV-88-083, 29 April 1988, p. 32); and Agence France-Presse, 'Yeltsin Comments on Dismissal, Interview', Moscow, 1 May 1988 (FBIS-SOV-88-084, 2 May 1988, p. 60).

18. 'Presumed Text of Mr Yeltsin's Speech to CPSU Central Committee', *Le Monde*, 2 February 1988 (FBIS-SOV-88-021, 2 February 1988, pp. 52–3). For a very similar version of the 'speech' see Gary Lee, 'Observers Puzzled by Aftermath of Yeltsin's Speech', *Washington Post*, 4 February 1988.

19. Interview with Yakov Ryabov.

20. *Boswell's Life of Johnson*, ed. George Birkbeck Hill, 6 vols, 1887: vol. I, p. 451.

21. G. A. Yagodin (Chairman of the USSR State Committee for Education), Speech at XIX Party Conference. *Pravda*, 2 July 1988, p. 9.

22. *Ibid.*, p. 147.

23. *Ibid.*

24. *Ibid.*

25. *Ibid.*, p. 148.

26. *Ibid.*

27. The meeting with the students of the Highest Komsomol School, 12 November 1988. Yeltsin made this point in a number of other interviews between autumn 1988 and spring 1989.

28. Interview with Poltoranin, 'The Yeltsin Files', *op. cit.*

29. Yeltsin, *Ispoved'*, p. 147.

30. *Ibid.*

31. *Ibid.*, p. 148.

32. *Ibid.*, pp. 147, 148.

33. *Ibid.*, p. 148.

34. *Ibid.*

35. *Ibid.*

36. *Ibid.*, p. 150.

37. *Ibid.*, p. 148.

38. *Ibid.*, p. 149.

39. *Ibid.*

40. *Ibid.*

41. Sukhanov, *op. cit.*, pp. 32–3.

42. *Ibid.*, p. 33.

43. *Ibid.*, p. 35.

44. *Ibid.*

45. *Ibid.*, p. 36.

46. Interview with Poltoranin, 'The Yeltsin File'.

47. Sukhanov, *op. cit.*, p. 38.

48. *Ibid.*

49. *Ibid.*

50. *Ibid.*

51. *Ibid.*

52. *Ibid.*, p. 40.

53. 'Informatsionnoe soobshchenie o plenume Tsentral'nogo Komiteta Kommunisticheskoy Partii Sovetskogo Soyuza' (Report on the Plenum of the Central Committee of the Communist Party of the Soviet Union). *Pravda*, 19 February 1988.

54. Sukhanov, *op. cit.*, p. 40.

55. *Ibid.*, p. 41.

56. *Ibid.*

57. Mikhail Poltoranin, 'Visiting Boris Yeltsin', *Moskovskie Novosti*, German edition, May 1988 (*FBIS*, 29 April 1988, pp. 31–2). See also Radio Liberty's Krasniy Arkhiv, Item F-619.

58. *Ibid.*

59. *Ibid.*

60. *Ibid.*

61. David Remnick, 'Yeltsin Relegated to the Bleachers; Ousted Moscow Party Chief Chats with Public at Parade', *Washington Post*, 2 May 1988.

62. *Ibid.*

63. Agence France-Presse, 1 May 1988.

64. Yeltsin, *Ispoved'*, p. 149.

65. Poltoranin, 'Visiting Boris Yeltsin'.

66. Goryun, *op. cit.*, Part II, p. 8.

67. *Ibid.*

68. Sukhanov, *op. cit.*, p. 43.

69. *Ibid.*

70. *Ibid.*, p. 44.

71. *Ibid.*, p. 43.

72. *Ibid.*

73. *Pravda*, 29 June 1988.

74. *XIX Vsesoyuznaya Konferentsiya*, vol. 2, p. 121.

75. Andreev, *op. cit.*, p. 587.

76. *Pravda*, 2 July 1988.

77. 'Tezisy Tsentral'nogo Komiteta KPSS K Vseosoyuznoy XIX Partiynoy Konferentsii' (Theses of the Central Committee for the Nineteenth All-Union Party Conference), *Pravda*, 27 May 1988.

78. Gorbachev's speech at the

February 1988 Plenum (*Pravda*, 19 February 1988).

79. From Gorbachev's closing speech at the Conference, *XIX Vsesoyuznaya Konferentsiya*, p. 179.

80. 'Tezisy Tsentral'nogo ...'

81. *Ibid.*

82. *XIX Vsesoyuznaya Konferentsiya*, vol. 2, p. 177.

83. *Ibid.*, p. 124.

84. *Ibid.*

85. *Ibid.*, pp. 124, 123.

86. *Ibid.*, p. 134.

87. *Ibid.*, p. 186.

88. *Ibid.*, p. 175.

89. David Remnick, 'Conference Ending Leaves Soviets Stunned – But Not Speechless', *Washington Post*, 3 July 1988.

90. *Ibid.*

91. *Ibid.*

92. Esther Fein, 'For Rank-and-File Party Delegates, Dust of Openness Was Exhilarating', *New York Times*, 3 July 1988.

93. *Pravda*, 29 June 1988.

94. *Ibid.*

95. *Ibid.*

96. *Ibid.*

97. *Ibid.*

98. *Ibid.*

99. Speech by German Zagaynov, XIX Party Conference (*Pravda*, 2 July 1988).

100. Speech by Fedor Morgun (*XIX Vsesoyuznaya Konferentsiya*, vol. 2, p. 14).

101. Speech by Veniamin Yarin (*Pravda*, 1 July 1986).

102. Speech by Vladimir Kabaidze (*Pravda*, 1 July 1988).

103. *Ibid.*

104. 'World Exclusive' interview with Boris Yeltsin, BBC Television, 30 May 1988 (FBIS, 31 May 1988, pp. 40–1).

105. *Ibid.*

106. *Ibid.*

107. *Ibid.*

108. *Ibid.*

109. *Ibid.*

110. *Ibid.*

111. *Ibid.*

112. *Ibid.*

113. From Gorbachev's 1 June 1988 press conference. In M. K. Gorshkov and V. V. Zhuravlyova, eds, *Gorbachev–Yeltsin: 1500 dnei politicheskogo protivostoyania* (Gorbachev–Yeltsin: 1,500 days of political confrontation), Moscow: Terra, 1992, p. 68.

114. Goryun, *op. cit.*, Part II, p. 9.

115. Sukhanov, *op. cit.*, p. 53.

116. *Ibid.*

117. *Ibid.*, p. 54.

118. *XIX Vsesoyuznaya Konferentsiya*, vol. 2, p. 37.

119. *Ibid.*

120. Yeltsin, *Ispoved'*, p. 161.

121. *Ibid.*

122. 'The Yeltsin File', *The Second Russian Revolution*, episode 3.

123. *Boris El'tsin: prevratnosti sud'by* (Boris Yeltsin: the vicissitudes of fate), Sverdlovsk Studio of Documentary Films, March 1989.

124. 'The Yeltsin File'.

125. *Boris El'tsin: prevratnosti sud'by*.

126. *Ibid.*

127. *Ibid.*

128. *XIX Vsesoyuznaya Konferentsiya*, vol. 2, p. 54.

129. Speech by German Zagaynov (*Pravda*, 2 July 1988).

130. *XIX Vsesoyuznaya Konferentsiya*, vol. 2, p. 55.

131. *Ibid.*

132. *Ibid.*, p. 56.

133. *Ibid.* The text that follows is based on *ibid.*, pp. 56–62.

134. *Ibid.*

135. *Ibid.*

136. *Ibid.*

137. *Ibid.*

138. *Ibid.*

139. *Ibid.*

140. *Ibid.*, p. 61.

141. *Ibid.*

142. Yeltsin, *Ispoved'*, p. 172.

143. *Pravda*, 27 May 1988.

144. Speech by German Zagaynov (*Pravda*, 2 July 1988).

145. *Ibid.*

146. Speech by Vadim Nizhelskiy (*Pravda*, 2 July 1988).

147. Speech by Academician Leonid Abalkin (*Pravda*, 30 June 1988).

148. Speech by Alim Chabanov (*XIX Vsesoyuznaya Konferentsiya*, p. 127).

149. Yeltsin's speech at the Conference (*ibid.*, p. 58).

150. Speech by Veniamin Yarin (*Pravda*, 1 July 1988).

151. *Ibid.*

152. *Pravda*, 30 June 1988.

153. *Pravda*, 29 June 1988.

154. Speech by Vadim Nizhelskiy (*Pravda*, 2 July 1988).

155. Speech by German Zagaynov (*Pravda*, 2 July 1988).

156. *Ibid.*

157. *XIX Vsesoyuznaya Konferentsiya*, vol. 2, p. 104.

158. *Ibid.*, p. 105.

159. *Ibid.*, p. 73.

160. *Ibid.*, pp. 180–3.

161. *Ibid.*, p. 102.

162. *Ibid.*

163. *Ibid.*, p. 103.

164. Goryun, *op. cit.*, Part II, p. 13.

165. Yeltsin, *Ispoved'*, p. 173.

166. *Ibid.*

167. *Ibid.*

168. Sukhanov, *op. cit.*, p. 59.

169. Yeltsin, *Ispoved'*, p. 174.

170. Goryun, *op. cit.*, Part II, p. 13.

171. Sukhanov, *op. cit.*, p. 60; Yeltsin, *Ispoved'*, p. 174.

172. Yeltsin, *Ispoved'*, p. 174.

173. *Ibid.*

174. *Ibid.*

175. *Ibid.*, p. 174.

176. Sukhanov, *op. cit.*, p. 61.

177. *Ibid.*

178. Aleksandr Ol'bik, 'Sotsial'naya spravedlivost' – kompas perestroiki' (Social justice is the guiding star of perestroika), *Sovetskaya Molodezh* (Riga), 4 August 1988.

179. *Ibid.*

180. *Ibid.*

181. *Ibid.*

182. *Ibid.*

183. Aleksandr Ol'bik, Introduction to Sukhanov, *op. cit.*, p. 3.

184. Sukhanov, *op. cit.*, p. 65.

185. *Ibid.*, p. 4.

186. *Ibid.*, p. 67.

187. Yeltsin, *Ispoved'*, p. 151.

188. Sukhanov, *op. cit.*, p. 66.

189. *Ibid.*

190. *Ibid.*, pp. 66–7.

191. Goryun, *op. cit.*, Part II, p. 14; Yeltsin, *Ispoved'*, p. 152; 'Politik ili avantyurist?' (Politician or adventurer?), *Molodaya Gvardia* (Perm), 4 December 1988. Answers to questions at a meeting with students of the Highest Komsomol School, 12 November 1988.

192. Sukhanov, *op. cit.*, p. 68.

193. *Ibid.*, p. 69.

194. *Ibid.*

195. *Molodaya Gvardia* (Perm), 4 December 1988.

196. *Ibid.*

197. *Ibid.*

198. *Ibid.*

199. *Ibid.*

200. *Ibid.*

201. *Ibid.*

202. *Ibid.*

203. *Ibid.*

204. *Ibid.*

205. *Ibid.*

206. 'Vera v perestroiku dolzhna byt!' (There must be faith in perestroika!). Answers to questions at the meeting with students of the Highest Komsomol School on 12 November 1988. *Komsomoletz Tajikistana* (Dushanber), 22 January 1989.

207. *Ibid.*

208. *Molodaya Gvardia* (Perm), 4 December 1988.

209. *Komsomoletz Tajikistana*, 22 January 1988.

210. *Ibid.*

211. *Molodaya Gvardia* (Perm), 4 December 1988.

212. *Ibid.*

213. Anatoliy Sobchak, *Khozhdenie vo vlast'* (A journey into power), Moscow: Novosti, 1991, p. 16.

214. 'El'tsin: Nuzhno izbavit'sya ot ravnodushiya i strakha' (Yeltsin: One must get rid of indifference and fear), *Propeller* (the student newspaper of the Moscow Aviation Institute), 21 February 1989.

215. David Aikman, 'One Bear of a Soviet Politician', interview with Boris Yeltsin, *Time*, 20 March 1989.

216. *Boris El'tsin: prevratnosti sud'by.*

217. TASS, 26 March 1989 (FBIS, 28 March 1989, p. 43).

218. *Boris El'tsin: prevratnosti sud'by.*

219. Yeltsin, *Ispoved'*, p. 13.

220. Goryun, *op. cit.*, Part II, p. 14.

221. Jonathan Steele, 'Boris Yeltsin Sails through Constituency Reselection', *Guardian* (London), 17 January 1989.

222. *Ibid.*

223. *Ibid.*

224. *Ibid.*

225. Interview with *Sovetskaya Estonia*, 19 February 1989.

226. 'Where Perestroika went wrong', by Boris Yeltsin. Exclusive interview', *Sunday Telegraph* (London, 26 March 1989. (FBIS-SOV-89-058, 28 March 1989, pp. 42–3.)

227. Anatoliy Shabad, 'Sakharova v deputaty', in Tatyana I. Ivanova, ed., *Andrey Dmitrievich: vospominaniya o Sakharove* (Andrey Dmitrievich: memoirs of Sakharov), Moscow: Terra, 1990, p. 116. Sakharov's decision to withdraw his candidacy from the Oktyabr'skiy district was announced at the district electoral meeting on 17 February 1989 (Moscow Radio, 17 February 1989 (FBIS, 21 February 1989, p. 79)).

228. Shabad, *op. cit.*, pp. 116–17.

229. Yeltsin, *Ispoved'*, p. 31.

230. *Ibid.*

231. *Bereznikovskiy Rabochiy*, 16 February 1989.

232. David Remnick, 'Boris Yeltsin, Adding Punch to Soviet Politics . . .', *Washington Post*, 18 February 1989.

233. *Ibid.*

234. *Ibid.*

235. *Ibid.*

236. *Ibid.*

237. *Ibid.*

238. Yeltsin, *Ispoved'*, p. 32.

239. *Ibid.*

240. *Ibid.*, p. 5.

241. Sergey Task, 'Postoronniy' (The strange), *Novoye Russkoye Slovo*, 20 October 1989.

242. *Ibid.*

243. *Ibid.*

244. Jonathan Steele, 'Yeltsin Wins Crowds on Campaign Trail', *Guardian*, 6 March 1989.

245. *Ibid.*

246. *Ibid.*

247. *Ibid.*

248. *Ibid.*

249. *Ibid.*

250. *Sovetskaya Rossia*, 23 February 1989; and Yeltsin, *Ispoved'*, p. 44.

251. *Sovetskaya Rossia*, 23 February 1989.

252. Agence France-Presse, 22 February 1989 (FBIS, 23 February 1989, p. 68).

253. Yeltsin, *Ispoved'*, p. 45.

254. Agence France-Presse, 22 February 1989.

255. Yeltsin, *Ispoved'*, p. 64.

256. Goryun, *op. cit.*, Part II, p. 15.

257. *Ibid.*

258. *Ibid.*

259. *Moskovskaya Pravda*, 21 March 1989.

260. *Moskovskie Novosti*, 29 January 1989.

261. Here and below Yeltsin's electoral programme is quoted from the text that appeared in *Moskovskaya Pravda*, 21 March 1989.

262. See, for instance, his interview with *La Repubblica*, 24 March 1989 (FBIS, 29 March 1989, p. 38).

263. Interview with the Sverdlovsk documentary film group on 27 March 1989 (the video archive of the Museum of Youth Movements, Ekaterinburg).

264. *Komsomol'skaya Pravda*, 31 December 1988.

265. Interview with the Sverdlovsk documentary film group on 30 January 1989 (the video archive of the Museum of Youth Movements, Ekaterinburg).

266. *Ibid.*

267. Speech in the 'Ural' House of Culture, Sverdlovsk, 26 February (from the documentary film *Boris El'tsin: prevratnosti sud'by*).

268. *Sovetskaya Estonia*, 19 February 1989.

269. *Bereznikovskiy Rabochiy*, 16 February 1989.

270. *Ibid.*

271. *Propeller*, 21 February 1989.

272. *Ibid.*

273. *Sovetskaya Estonia*, 19 February 1989.

274. *Ibid.*

275. *Ibid.*

276. *Ibid.*

277. *Ibid.*

278. From an answer at the session in the Highest Komsomol School, 12 November 1988 (*Molodaya Gvardia* (Perm), 4 December 1988).

279. *Sovetskaya Estonia*, 19 February 1989.

280. *Ibid.*

281. *Ibid.*

282. *Bereznikovskiy Rabochiy*, 16 February 1989.

283. BBC World Service, London, 24 March 1989 (FBIS, 24 March 1989, p. 37).

284. *Propeller*, 21 February 1989.

285. BBC, 24 March 1989 (FBIS, 24 March 1989, p. 37).

286. Aikman, *op. cit.*, p. 44.

287. 'B. N. El'tsin: Lyudyam ochen' vazhna pravda' (B. N. Yeltsin: Truth is very important to people). *Sovetskaya Estonia*, 19 February 1989.

288. Steele, 'Yeltsin Wins Crowds'.

289. Boris Yeltsin, interview with Martin Sixsmith, BBC World Service, 24 March 1989 (FBIS, 24 March 1989, p. 37).

290. Boris Yeltsin, interview with Ezio Mauro, *La Repubblica* (Rome), 24 March 1989 (FBIS, 29 March 1989, pp. 38–9). See also, *Sunday Telegraph* (London), 26 March 1989.

291. Aikman, *op. cit.*, p. 44.

292. From a press conference of Vadim Medvedev, the Soviet Union's newly appointed ideology chief (TASS International Service, 16 March 1989 (FBIS, 17 March 1989, p. 72)).

293. 'Informatsionnoe soobshchenie o plenume Tsentral'nogo Komiteta Kommunisticheskoy Partii Sovetskogo Soyuza' (Report on the Plenum of the Central Committee of the Communist Party of the Soviet Union), *Pravda*, 17 March 1989.

294. *Ibid.*

295. Vladimir Tikhomirov, 'Schitayn svoim partiynym dolgom' (I consider this my Party member duty), *Moskovskaya Pravda*, 19 March 1989.

296. *Ibid.*

297. *Ibid.*

298. *Ibid.*

299. Interview with Sverdlovsk documentary film group on 27 March 1989 (the video archive of the Museum of Youth Movements, Ekaterinburg).

300. Ezio Mauro, 'Interview with Boris Yeltsin', *La Repubblica*, 24 March 1989 (FBIS, 29 March 1989, p. 38).

301. *Ibid.*

302. *Moskovskaya Pravda*, 25 March 1989.

303. *Ibid.*

304. *Ibid.*

305. *Ibid.*

306. Bill Keller, 'Marchers in Moscow Cheer Maverick', *New York Times*, 20 March 1989.

307. *Boris El'tsin: prevratnosti sud'by.*

308. *Ibid.*

309. *Washington Post*, 19 March 1989.

310. *Ibid.*

311. Agence France-Presse, 21 March

1989 (FBIS, 22 March 1989, p. 50).

312. 'Stenogramma mitinga o prinyatii obrascheniya v adres TsK KPSS 20 Marta 1989 g. Mesto: Foye DK UPI' (Protocol of the meeting to adopt a letter to the Central Committee on 20 March 1989. Place: the lobby of the House of Culture of the UPI), a copy in the author's archive, p. 2.

313. *Ibid.*, p. 3.

314. *Ibid.*, p. 4.

315. G. Sapozhnikova, 'Pheonomen El'tsina, ili chto proiskhodit v Moskve?' ('The Yeltsin phenomenon, or what is happening in Moscow?), *Molodezh Estonii*, 25 March 1989.

316. *Ibid.*

317. From a photocopy of a leaflet. The author is given as 'Nestor Pushler', from the collection 'Commentaries'.

318. A photocopy of the original in the author's possession.

319. *Ibid.*

320. Michael Dobbs, 'Thousands March to Support Yeltsin . . .', *Washington Post*, 20 March 1989; Keller, *op. cit.*

321. *Boris El'tsin: prevratnosti sud'by.*

322. *Ibid.*

323. Sapozhnikova, *op. cit.*

324. *Ibid.*

325. *Ibid.*

326. Agence France-Presse, 22 March 1989 (FBIS, 23 March 1989, p. 27).

327. *Moskovskaya Pravda*, 23 March 1989.

328. See, for instance, Pierre Glachant, 'Yeltsin Rally Biggest Since 1917', Agence France-Presse, 25 March 1989 (FBIS, 27 March 1989, p. 46); and David Remnick, '10,000 Stage Rally for Boris Yeltsin on Eve of Soviet Legislative Elections', *Washington Post*, 26 March 1989.

329. Glachant, *op. cit.*

330. *Ibid.*

331. *Boris Yeltsin: prevratnosti sud'by.*

332. 'Nashi narodnye deputaty' (Our

people's Deputies), *Izvestia*, 28 March 1989.

333. *Ibid.*

334. *Ibid.*

335. Remnick, 'Boris Yeltsin, Adding Punch'.

336. 'Moskvichi delayut vybor' (Muscovites are making their choice), *Moskovskaya Pravda*, 27 March 1989.

337. *Ibid.*

338. *Ibid.*

339. *Vechernyaya Moskva*, 27 March 1989.

340. Interview with Dr Aleksandr Urmanov, Yeltsin's campaign adviser.

341. *Ibid.*

Chapter 6: The Year of Truth

1. *Boris El'tsin: prevratnosti sud'by.*

2. *Ibid.*

3. See, for instance, Simon Schama, *Citizens*, New York: Vintage Books, 1989, chs 3, 4.

4. A Chernyak, 'Edoki po statistike i v zhizni' (Food consumers in statistics and in reality), *Pravda*, 1 September 1988.

5. Anatoliy Komin, 'Davay schitat'!' (Let's count!), *Komsomol'skaya Pravda*, 13 August 1986.

6. V. Radaev and O. Shkaratan, 'Vozvrashchenie k istokam' (The return to the sources), *Izvestia*, 16 February 1990.

7. Yu. Rytov, 'Kak zhivut pensionery' (How pensioners fare), *Izvestia*, 20 August 1988.

8. 'Nuzhna pomosh' (Help is needed), *Izvestia*, 21 September 1988.

9. Vasiliy Ignatovich Ostapchuk, 'Ya trudilsya skol'ko mog . . .' (I worked for as long as I could . . .). Letter to *Izvestia*, 3 September 1987.

10. Cherniak, *op. cit.*

11. Evgeniy Chazov, 'Kogda bolezn obgonyaet lekarstva' (When the disease is faster than medicine), interview with *Literaturnaya Gazeta*, 3 February 1988.

12. V. Kurasov, 'Izlechema li

lekarstvennaya problema?' (Can we cure the medicine problem?). *Izvestia*, 21 October 1989.

13. Pavel Sergeev, 'Defitsit lekarstv. Ch'ya vina?' (The deficit of medicine. Whose fault is it?). Interviewed by N. Gogol, *Pravda*, 13 July 1989.

14. *Pravda*, 28 September 1987; and Chazov, *op. cit.*

15. B. Mironov, 'Rebyonok bez prismotra?' (Is anyone minding the child?), interview with Professor V. I. Kulakov, Director of the All-Union Scientific Research Centre for the Protection of the Health of the Mother and Child. *Pravda*, 10 August 1987.

16. *Ibid.*

17. V. Korneev and S. Tutorskaya, 'Lekarstva, kotorykh zhdut' (Medicines that the people are waiting for). *Izvestia*, 28 January 1988.

18. *Ibid.*

19. A letter to the women's magazine *Rabotnitza*. Reprinted in *Novoye Russkoye Slovo*, 2 June 1989.

20. Chazov, *op. cit.*

21. G. A. Yagodin, Speech at XIX Party Conference, *Pravda*, 2 July 1988, p. 9.

22. O. Drunina, 'K chemu privodit bezdushie' (The results of indifference), *Trud*, 19 January 1988.

23. *Ibid.*

24. Interview with the director of the Research Institute of Housing, *Literaturnaya Gazeta*, 31 August 1988.

25. *Ibid.*

26. *Ibid.*

27. I. Voytko, 'Negde zhit' . . .' (No Place to Live . . .), *Pravda*, 2 July 1989.

28. *Ibid.*

29. V. Tolstov, 'Kak obespecheny zhil'yom krupneyshie goroda strany' (How well are the largest cities in the country provided with housing?), *Izvestia*, 4 September 1988.

30. Yu. Shchekochikhin, 'Lev prygnul!' (The lion has jumped!),

Literaturnaya Gazeta, 20 July 1988.

31. See for example, S. Polevoy, 'Nich'i deti' (No one's children), *Pravda*, 8 October 1988.

32. Andranik Migranyan, 'Dolgiy put' k everopeyskomu domu' (A long road to the European home), *Noviy Mir*, July 1989, p. 184.

33. *Ibid.*

34. Maxim Gorkiy, 'Nesvoevremennye mysli' (Untimely thoughts), *Literaturnoye Obozrenie*, 9, 1988, p. 103.

35. *Literaturnoye Obozrenie*, 10, 1988, p. 106.

36. *Literaturnoye Obozrenie*, 12, 1988, p. 87.

37. See, for example, Vladlen Sirotkin, 'Eshchyo raz o "belykh pyatnakh"' (Once again about 'blank spots'), *Nedeliya*, 12 June 1989.

38. Aleksandr Tsipko, 'Istochniki Stalinizma' (The sources of Stalinism), Part IV, *Nauka i Zhizn*, 2, February 1989, p. 53.

39. *Ibid.*

40. *Noviy Mir*, (May) 1988.

41. Vasiliy Grossman, *Vsyo techyot* (Forever flowing), Frankfurt/Main: Possev-Verlag, V. Gorachek KG, 1970, p. 170.

42. *Ibid.*

43. *Ibid.*, p. 111.

44. *Ibid.*, p. 197.

45. *Ibid.*

46. Zakharov was interviewed on Soviet television on 21 April and Karyakin spoke at the First Congress of People's Deputies. FBIS, 1 May 1989, pp. 57–8, and *Pervyi S'ezd Narodnykh Deputatov SSSR. Stenograficheskiy otchyot* (The First Congress of People's Deputies of the USSR, a transcript), 4 volumes. Moscow: Supreme Soviet of the USSR, 1989 (hereafter *Pervyi S'ezd*), vol. II, p. 363.

47. Yuriy Afanasiev, 'Otvety istorika' (A historian's answers), *Pravda*, 26 July 1988.

48. Yuriy Afanasiev, interview with

Sovetskaya Molodezh, 7 July 1989.
49. Migranyan, *op. cit.*, p. 183.
50. Schama, *op. cit.*, p. 438.
51. Lord (Thomas) Macaulay, *The History of England*. New York: Penguin Classics, 1986, p. 273.
52. Boris Yeltsin, polling-station press conference, 26 March, filmed by the documentary film group of the Museum of Youth Movements, Ekaterinburg.
53. Videotape in the Museum of Youth Movements, Ekaterinburg, 27 March 1989.
54. David Remnick, 'Yeltsin: Gorbachev Indecisive . . .', *Washington Post*, 21 May 1989.
55. Boris Yeltsin, interview with Moscow television, 19 May 1989 (FBIS, 22 May 1989, p. 69).
56. Boris Yeltsin, interview with *La Vangardia* (Barcelona), 21 May 1989 (FBIS, 1 June 1989, p. 38).
57. Remnick, 'Yeltsin: Gorbachev Indecisive'.
58. *Ibid.*
59. A. Gamov and S. Karkhanin, 'Krikom doma ne postroish' (A house is not built by shouting), *Sovetskaya Rossia*, 23 May 1989.
60. *Washington Post*, 23 May 1989.
61. Agence France-Presse, 21 May 1989 (FBIS, 22 May 1989, p. 68), and Francis X. Clines, '25,000 Rally for Rebels in New Soviet Congress', *New York Times*, 22 May 1989.
62. Migranian, *op. cit.*
63. Interview with Andranik Migranyan, *Sovetskaya Kul'tura*, 24 June 1989.
64. Migranyan, 'Dolgiy put''.
65. Vitaliy Tretyakov, 'Fenomen Borisa El'tsina' (The Boris Yeltsin phenomenon), *Moskovskie Novosti*, 16 April 1989.
66. *Ibid.*
67. *Ibid.*
68. *Ibid.*
69. *Ibid.*
70. *Ibid.*
71. *Ibid.*
72. *Ibid.*
73. Osip Mandel'shtam, *Sobranie sochineniy v chetyryokh tomakh* (Collected works in four volumes), Moscow: Terra, 1991, vol. I, p. 202.
74. Alexandr Solzhenitsyn, *Gulag Archipelago*, New York: Harper & Row, 1978, vol. III, p. 475.
75. See, for instance, Lewis A. Coser's discussion of George Herbert Mead's social psychology in Coser, *Masters of Sociological Thought*, New York: Harcourt Brace Jovanovich, 1971, pp. 334–5.
76. 'S'ezd: povorot k potrebnostyam cheloveka' (The Congress: turning towards the needs of man), *Sel'skaya Zhizn'*, 13 June 1989.
77. Andrey Sakharov, interview with *Ogonyok*, 31 July 1989.
78. N. Bondaruk 'Den' sed'moy', (Day seven), *Izvestia*, 2 June 1989.
79. *Ibid.*
80. Fedor Burlatskiy, 'Perviy, no vazhniy shag' (The first, important step), *Literaturnaya Gazeta*, 14 June 1989.
81. Vladimir Nadein, 'Den' perviy' (Day one), *Izvestia*, 26 May 1989.
82. 'S'ezd Narodnykh Deputatov. Stenograficheskiy otchyot' (The Congress of People's Deputies. A transcript), *Izvestia*, 26 May 1989.
83. A. Plutnik, 'Den' desyatiy' (Day ten), *Izvestia*, 8 June 1989.
84. Sobchak, *op. cit.*, p. 36.
85. *Pervyi S'ezd*, vol. II, p. 80.
86. Speech by Vasiliy Starodubtsev, *Pervyi S'ezd*, vol. II, p. 3.
87. Speech by A. Chabanov, *Pervyi S'ezd*, vol. II, p. 108.
88. *Ibid.*, and speech by A. Korshunov, *Pervyi S'ezd*, vol. II, p. 213.
89. Speech by Pavel Bunich, *Pervyi S'ezd*, vol. II, p. 93.
90. *Ibid.*
91. Speech by V. Belov, *Pervyi S'ezd*, vol. II, p. 156.
92. Speech by Yu. Chernichenko, *Pervyi S'ezd*, vol. II, p. 172.

93. Speech by Yu. Sharipov, *Pervyi S'ezd*, vol. II, p. 149.

94. *Ibid.*

95. *Ibid.*

96. Speech by A. Likhanov, *Pervyi S'ezd*, vol. II, p. 146.

97. Speech by B. Oleynik, *Pervyi S'ezd*, vol. II, p. 40.

98. Speech by A. Korshunov, *Pervyi S'ezd*, vol. II, p. 213.

99. Speech by Kirill Mazurov, *Pervyi S'ezd*, vol. II, pp. 179–80.

100. Speech by I. Egorova, *Pervyi S'ezd*, vol. II, p. 72.

101. *Ibid.*, p. 73.

102. Speech by A. Yablokov, *Pervyi S'ezd*, vol. II, p. 98.

103. See, for example, speeches by S. Arutunian, First Secretary of the Armenian Communist Party, by A. Mutalibov and by V. Ardzinba in *Pervyi S'ezd*, vol. II, pp. 49–55, 28–34 and 317–24.

104. See, for instance, speeches by A.-M. Brazauskas, First Secretary of the Communist Party of Lithuania, and by I. Kh. Toome, Chairman of the Council of Ministers of Estonia, in *Pervyi S'ezd*, vol. II, pp. 72–7 and 102–7.

105. Speech by B. Oleynik, *Pervyi S'ezd*, vol. II, p. 35.

106. Speeches by D. Kugultdinov and I. Drutze, *Pervyi S'ezd*, vol. II, pp. 440–4 and 124–31.

107. Speech by V. Rasputin, *Pervyi S'ezd*, vol. I, pp. 458–9.

108. *Ibid.*

109. Speech by Yu. Vlasov, *Pervyi S'ezd*, pp. 81–2.

110. *Ibid.*

111. Speech by A. Ridiger, *Pervyi S'ezd*, vol. II, p. 56.

112. Speech by Ch. Aitmatov, *Pervyi S'ezd*, vol. II, pp. 288, 289.

113. *Pervyi S'ezd*, pp. 80, 81.

114. Speech by Yu. Vlasov, *Pervyi S'ezd*, p. 77.

115. A. Plutnik, 'Den' chetvertiy' (Day four), *Izvestia*, 30 May 1989.

116. Burlatskiy, *op. cit.*

117. *Ibid.*

118. *Ibid.*

119. *Ibid.*

120. 'S'ezd: povorot k potrebnostyam cheloveka', *op. cit.*

121. Burlatskiy, *op. cit.*

122. Vladimir Nadein, 'Den' pyatiy' (Day five), *Izvestia*, 31 May 1989.

123. Speech by Yu. Karyakin, *Pervyi S'ezd*, vol. II, p. 361.

124. Speech by A. Emel'yanov, *Pervyi S'ezd*, vol. II, p. 84.

125. Vl. Arsenev, 'S'ezd v televizionnom izmerenii' (The Congress in the television dimension), *Izvestia*, 16 June 1989.

126. *Ibid.*

127. *Ibid.*

128. N. Bondaruk, 'Den' vtoroy', (Day two), *Izvestia*, 27 May 1989.

129. Speech by P. Bunich, *Pervyi S'ezd*, vol. II, p. 89.

130. P. Gutionov, 'Den' dvenadstatiy' (Day twelve), *Izvestia*, 10 June 1989.

131. N. Bondaruk 'Den' sedmoy'.

132. Francis X. Clines, 'It's Moscow Live: New Faces, New Ideas and Impertinence', *New York Times*, 26 May 1989.

133. Francis X. Clines, 'Soviet TV's Biggest Hit: 200 Million Watch Political Drama', *New York Times*, 31 May 1989.

134. Transcript of the Congress, *Izvestia*, 26 May 1989.

135. Bondaruk, 'Den vtoroy'.

136. E. Gonzalies, 'Den odinnadtsatiy' (Day eleven), *Izvestia*, 9 June 1989.

137. Yeltsin, *Ispoved'*, p. 178.

138. 'S'ezd Narodnikh Deputatov. Stenograficheskiy otchyot' (The Congress of People's Deputies. A transcript), *Izvestia*, 27 May 1989.

139. Speech by B. Kruzhkov, in *Izvestia*, 27 May 1989.

140. Speech by A. Kraiko, in *Izvestia*, 27 May 1989.

141. *Izvestia*, 27 May 1989.

142. Nadein, 'Den' perviy'.

143. Interview with Radio Budapest,

27 May 1989 (FBIS, 2 June 1989, p. 33).

144. V. Dymov, 'Slyshat' drug druga' (To listen to one another), *Pravda*, 29 May 1989.

145. Michael Dobbs, 'Makeup of Supreme Soviet Decried; Thousand Protest Exclusion of Yeltsin from Standing Legislature', *Washington Post*, 29 May 1989.

146. As quoted in Dawn Mann, 'El'tsin Rides a Political Roller Coaster', *Report on the USSR*, 9 June 1989, p. 14.

147. Dobbs, 'Makeup of Supreme Soviet'.

148. *Ibid.*

149. *Izvestia*, 31 May 1989.

150. *Ibid.*

151. *Pervyi S'ezd*, vol. II, p. 45.

152. *Ibid.*, pp. 43–4.

153. *Ibid.*, pp. 44, 48.

154. *Ibid.*, pp. 44, 45, 48.

155. *Ibid.*, pp. 46, 47.

156. *Ibid.*, pp. 48, 46.

157. Interview with Milan's *Corriere della Sera*, 16 June 1989 (FBIS, 20 June 1989, p. 7).

158. *Ibid.*

159. Boris Yeltsin, speech to the Supreme Soviet, Moscow television, 24 July 1989 (FBIS, 25 July 1989, p. 33).

160. Interview with *Corriere della Sera*, 16 June 1989 (FBIS, 20 June 1989, p. 8).

161. *Ibid.*

162. Ye. Domnysheva, 'Ya ne storonnik polumer!' (I am not a proponent of half-measures!), *Literaturnaya Gazeta*, 28 June 1989.

163. Answers to questions at the meeting with the students of the Moscow Institute of Aircraft Engineering (MAI), as quoted in *Vestnik Vysshey Shkoly* (Higher Education Herald), 9 September 1989, p. 4.

164. *Ibid.*

165. Boris Yeltsin, 'Bol'she dela' (More real work), interview with *Trud*, 8 August 1989.

166. *Ibid.*

167. Irina Inoveli, 'Narodniy Deputat B. N. El'tsin: "Ya za pravdu, kakoy by ona ni byla"' (People's Deputy B. N. Yeltsin: 'I am for the truth, no matter what it is'), *Zarya Vostoka*, 1 August 1989.

168. Domnysheva, *op. cit.*

169. *Ibid.*

170. *Ibid.*

171. *Ibid.* See also, *Vestnik Vysshei Shkoly*, 9 September 1989, p. 4.

172. *Corriere della Sera*, 16 June 1989 (FBIS, 20 June 1989, p. 8).

173. 'Reshenie sotsialnykh problem neotlozhno' (Resolution of social problems must not be postponed), Boris Yeltsin, interviewed by V. Tolstov, *Izvestia*, 20 July 1989.

174. Yu. Apenchenko, 'Kuzbass. Zharkoye Leto' (Kuzbass. A hot summer), *Znamya*, 10, 1989, p. 166.

175. As quoted by Viktor Medikov in his speech to the Supreme Soviet (FBIS, 18 July 1989, p. 70).

176. A. Solovyov, 'Neozhidanniy povorot ...' (Unexpected turn ...), *Izvestia*, 14 July 1989.

177. Apenchenko, *op. cit.*, p. 177.

178. *Ibid.*, p. 183.

179. *Ibid.*

180. Moscow television, 18 July 1989 (FBIS, 19 July 1989, p. 62).

181. V. Klimov, 'Problemy kopilis' godami' (Problems accumulated over the years), *Trud*, 13 July 1989; and V. Kostyukovskiy, 'Po starym i novym schetam: ostanavleny raboty na ryade shakt Mezhdurechenska' (Old and new bills to pay: work stopped at a number of mines in Mezhdurechensk), *Sovetskaya Rossia*, 13 July 1989.

182. R. Lynev, 'Ob'edinit' direktorskuyu banyu' (Merge the managers' bathhouse), *Izvestia*, 26 July 1989.

183. TASS, 14 July 1989 (FBIS, 14 July 1989, p. 41).

184. Apenchenko, *op. cit.*, p. 171.

185. V. Kostyukovskiy, 'Prizyv k blagorazumiyu' (Appeal to reason), *Sovetskaya Rossiya*, 19 July 1989.

186. P. Voroshilov and A. Soloviev, 'Konstruktivniy dialog s gornyakami' (Constructive dialogue with miners), *Izvestia*, 18 July 1989.

187. Radio Moscow, 18 July 1989 (FBIS, 19 July 1989, p. 66).

188. V. Kostyukovskiy, 'Indikator naprazhyonnosti. S plenuma Kemerovskogo obkoma KPSS . . .' (The indicator of tension. At the Plenum of the Kemerovo Obkom of the CPSU . . .), *Sovetskaya Rossiya*, 10 August 1989.

189. Valeriy Vyzhutovich, 'Raschistka otvalov' (Clearing the waste), *Izvestia*, 23 July 1989.

190. *Ibid.*

191. Kostyukovskiy, 'Indikator . . .'

192. Apenchenko, *op. cit.*, p. 179.

193. David Remnick, 'Soviet Progressives Begin to Shape Legislative Alliance', *Washington Post*, 22 April 1989.

194. N. Zhelnova and L. Novikova, 'Ot imeni naroda' (On behalf of the people), interview with Boris Yeltsin, *Argumenty i Fakty*, 10–16 June 1989.

195. 'S'ezd Narodnykh Deputatov', *Izvestia*, 29 May 1989.

196. Deutschlandfunk Radio Network, Cologne, 13 June 1989 (FBIS, 13 June 1989, p. 32).

197. Radio Moscow, 19 July 1989, recording of the session of the Supreme Soviet (FBIS, 20 July 1989, pp. 45–6).

198. *Ibid.*

199. Macaulay, *op. cit.*, p. 273.

200. Interview with *Corriere della Sera*, 16 June 1989 (FBIS, 20 June 1989, p. 7).

201. 'Bol'she dela'.

202. *Ibid.*

203. See, for instance, Yeltsin's interviews with *Al-Musawwar* (Cairo) on 16 June 1989 (FBIS, 20 June 1989, p. 57), and with *Panorama*, Budapest television, 28 June 1989 (FBIS, 30 June 1989, p. 49).

204. Mezhregionalnoy gruppy narodnykh deputatov (Inter-Regional Group of People's Deputies), *Informatsionnyi Byulleten'* (Information bulletin), Moscow: Mezhregionalnoy gruppy narodnykh deputatov, 15 September 1989, p. 4.

205. *Ibid.*

206. Pankov, *op. cit.*

207. *Informatsionniy Byulleten'*, p. 4.

208. Pankov, *op. cit.*

209. *Sunday Telegraph* (London), 30 July 1989 (FBIS, 31 July 1989, p. 51).

210. *Informatsionniy Byulleten'*, p. 2.

211. *Ibid.*, p. 1.

212. I. Lavrovskiy, L. Telen' and E. Chrnova, 'Raskol? Net, dialog!' (Schism? No, a dialogue), *Sotsialisticheskaya Industria*, 1 August 1989.

213. Melanie Newton, 'USSR This Week', *Report on the USSR*, 11 August 1989, p. 33.

214. *Ibid.*

215. Andrey Romanov and Vladimir Shevelev, 'Men'shinstvo ob'edinilos'' (The minority has consolidated), *Moskovskie Novosti*, 6 August 1989.

216. *Ibid.*

217. TASS, 30 July 1989 (FBIS, 31 July 1989, p. 52).

218. *Newsday*, 31 July 1989.

219. *Informatsionniy Byulleten'*, p. 2.

220. *Ibid.*

221. *Ibid.*, pp. 2, 3.

222. *Izvestia*, 29 May 1989.

223. *Ibid.*

224. *Informatsionniy Byulleten'*, p. 9.

225. *Ibid.*, p. 5.

226. *Ibid.*

227. *Ibid.*

228. *Ibid.*

229. *Ibid.*, p. 6.

230. TASS, 31 July 1989 (FBIS, 31 July 1989, p. 53).

231. Moscow television, 31 July 1989 (FBIS, 1 August 1989, p. 38).

232. R. I. Pimenov, 'Kakim on byl' (What he was like), in Tatyana I. Ivanova, ed., *Andrey Dmitrievich. vospominaniya o Sakharove* (Andrey

Dmitrievich: memoirs of Sakharov), Moscow: Terra, 1990, p. 200.

233. *Det Fri Aktuelt* (Copenhagen), 2–3 December 1989 (FBIS, 8 December 1989, p. 98).

234. Elena Bonner, 'Polupravda ne luchshe lzhi' (Half-truth is not better than lie), *Literaturnaya Gazeta*, 11 November 1992.

235. Yuriy Chernichenko at the MDG's conference on 10 March 1990 (Washington, DC: Library of Congress, Videotape VAC 9402).

236. Gavriil Popov's opening remarks (Washington, DC: Library of Congress, Videotape VAC 9390).

237. 'Soveshchanie Mezhregional'noy deputatskoy gruppy', 29 April 1990 (Washington, DC: Library of Congress, Videotape VAC 9404).

238. A conference of the MDG, 24 September 1989 (Washington, DC: Library of Congress, Videotape VAC 9392).

239. Interview with *Det Fri Aktuelt*, *op. cit.*

240. *Ibid.* See also Yeltsin's remarks at a meeting of the Group's chairmen with Muscovites on 3 November 1989 (Washington, DC: Library of Congress, Videotape VAC 9388).

241. Boris Yeltsin, interview with Radio Liberty, 'Soviet Media News Budget', *Krasnyi Arkhiv*, no. 556, 19 October 1989, p. 5.

242. Interview with *Det Fri Aktuelt*, *op. cit.*

243. See the transcript of the session of the Supreme Soviet in *Izvestia*, 17 October 1989.

244. For Yeltsin's assertions, see for example *Ispoved'*, p. 190, the videotape of his 3 November 1989 remarks at the meeting of the MDG's co-chairmen (Washington, DC: Library of Congress, Videotape VAC 9388) or his interview with *Sovetskaya Molodezh*, part II, 4 January 1990.

245. For this last version, see for instance a leading Russian writer,

Tatyana Tolstaya, in *New Republic*, 16 and 23 September 1991.

246. Agence France-Presse, 5 December 1989 (FBIS, 6 December 1989, p. 104).

247. A conference of the Inter-Regional Group of Deputies, 24 September 1989 (Washington, DC: Library of Congress, Videotape VAC 9392).

248. *Ibid.*

249. Interview with *Det Fri Aktuelt*, *op. cit.*

250. *Ibid.*

251. *Izvestia*, 18 December 1989.

252. *Ibid.*

253. Interview with Yeltsin by INTERFAX (Moscow World Service in English), 27 December 1989 (FBIS, 28 December 1989, p. 78).

254. *Ibid.*

255. Andrey Sakharov, 'Poslednee interv'yu "LG"' (The last interview with *Literaturnaya Gazeta*), interviewed by E. Domnysheva, *Literaturnaya Gazeta*, 20 December 1989.

256. The session of the MDG, 24 September 1989 (Washington, DC: Library of Congress, Videotape VAC 9392).

257. *Ibid.*

258. An interview with Ludmila Pikhoya and Aleksandr Il'yin.

259. Interview with Galina Starovoytova. See also the videotape of the 3 November 1989 meeting of the Group's co-chairmen with Muscovites (Washington, DC: Library of Congress, Videotape VAC 9388).

260. The conference of the MDG, 10 March 1989 (Washington, DC: Library of Congress, Videotape VAC 9402).

261. *Ibid.*

Chapter 7: America, America ...
1. See for example, letter to the author from Dr S. Frederick Starr, 19 April 1994; a videotape of Yeltsin's account of the trip at an Inter-

Regional Group meeting in the House of Cinema (Moscow) on 27 September 1989 (the Museum of Youth Movements, Ekaterinburg); and Natasha Sharymova, 'Okazyvaetsya, kapitalizm ne zagnivaet' (Capitalism, it turns out, is not decaying), a transcript of Yeltsin's press conference in New York on 10 September 1989 (*Novoye Russkoye Slovo*, 12 September 1989).

2. Starr, *op. cit.*

3. Alex Heard, 'Rolfing with Yeltsin', *New Republic*, 9 October 1989, p. 11.

4. Pavel Voshchanov, 'El'tsin v Amerike' (Yeltsin in America), *Komsomol'skaya Pravda*, 27 September 1989.

5. *Ibid.*; Sukhanov, *op. cit.*, p. 88.

6. Jack F. Matlock, *Autopsy on an Empire*, New York: Random House, 1995, p. 248.

7. Interview with Ambassador Jack Matlock.

8. Voshchanov, *op. cit.*

9. Matlock, *op. cit.*, p. 248.

10. Sharymova, *op. cit.*

11. Sukhanov, *op. cit.*, p. 157; and Voshchanov, *op. cit.*

12. Vladimir Kozlovskiy, ' "Eltsingate", ili sputniki Eltsina o ego poezdke v SShA' ('Yeltsingate', or Yeltsin's companions on his trip to the United States), *Novoye Russkoye Slovo*, 25 September 1989.

13. Voshchanov, *op. cit.*; Moscow television, 25 September 1989 (FBIS, 25 September 1989, p. 110).

14. Vladimir Kozlovskiy, 'Ochevidtzy govoryat, chto Eltsin ne greshil' (Witnesses say Yeltsin did not step over the line), *Novoye Russkoye Slovo*, 21 September 1989.

15. Voshchanov, *op. cit.*; Eleanor Randolph, 'Yeltsin's "Spree" Denied', *Washington Post*, 19 September 1989.

16. Valentin Yumashev, 'Poezdka, o kotoroy govoryat' (The much talked-about trip), interview with Boris Yeltsin, *Ogonyok*, 41, 7–14 October 1989, pp. 30–1.

17. Sukhanov, *op. cit.*, pp. 107–8.

18. Kozlovskiy, 'Ochevidtzy govoryat'.

19. *Ibid.*

20. Starr, *op. cit.*

21. Letter to the author from Lotti Ross, Assistant Director of Program Operations, Chicago Council on Foreign Relations, 17 April 1994.

22. Interview with Darren Narayana, an officer at the International Division of Norwest Bank Corp., which co-sponsored Yeltsin's speech in Minneapolis.

23. Don Oberdorfer, 'Yeltsin: Gorbachev Has Year to Prove Self', *Washington Post*, 12 September 1989.

24. *Ibid.*

25. *Ibid.*

26. *Ibid.*

27. Starr *op. cit.*

28. *Ibid.*

29. Marvin Howe, 'Opposition Leader from Soviet Union Begins Visit to U.S.', *New York Times*, 10 September 1989.

30. Celestine Bohlen, 'Yeltsin, the Moscow Populist, Takes Manhattan (in Stride)', *New York Times*, 11 September 1989.

31. Transcript of the *MacNeil/Lehrer Newshour*, 11 September 1989, p. 11.

32. Jo Ellen Meyers Sharp, 'Visiting Soviet Views Indiana Farming Firsthand', *Indianapolis Star*, 15 September 1989.

33. *Ibid.*

34. Bohlen, 'Yeltsin, the Moscow Populist'.

35. Yumashev, *op. cit.*

36. Boris Yeltsin, speech at Johns Hopkins University's Baltimore campus on 12 September 1989, audiotape.

37. 'Boris Yeltsin at Columbia', a transcript of Boris Yeltsin's speech at Columbia University on 11 September 1989.

38. Bohlen, 'Yeltsin, the Moscow Populist'.

39. 'Yeltsin at Columbia', p. 4.

40. Sharymova, *op. cit.*

41. Bohlen, 'Yeltsin, the Moscow Populist'.
42. *Ibid.*
43. *Ibid.*
44. Yeltsin, speech at Johns Hopkins University.
45. Sharymova, *op. cit.*; and Yeltsin, speech at Johns Hopkins University.
46. Yeltsin, speech at Johns Hopkins University. See also Fen Montaigne, 'Yeltsin Dazzles Phila. Audience with Talk of "Abyss"', *Philadelphia Inquirer*, 14 September 1989.
47. Yeltsin, *Ispoved'*, p. 186.
48. Yeltsin, speech at Johns Hopkins University.
49. *Ibid.*
50. Yumashev, *op. cit.*
51. *Ibid.*
52. Interview with Stephen Hayes of the American Center for International Leadership, which helped organize Yeltsin's visits to Indianapolis, Baltimore and Texas.
53. Jon Schwantes, 'For Yeltsin, a Day of Pigs, People, Philosophy', *Indianapolis News*, 15 September 1989.
54. Yumashev, *op. cit.*
55. Sharp, *op. cit.*; and Schwantes, *op. cit.*
56. Schwantes, *op. cit.*
57. Yeltsin, speech in the House of Cinema.
58. 'Yeltsin's Gloomy Glasnost', *San Francisco Chronicle*, 9 September 1989.
59. See photograph in *Minneapolis Star Tribune*, 15 September 1989.
60. Bill McAuliffe, 'Yeltsin Pays Call on Reagan in Rochester', *Minneapolis Star Tribune*, 15 September 1989.
61. 'Yeltsin Displays Bedside Humor', *Los Angeles Times*, 15 September 1989.
62. Sukhanov, *op. cit.*, p. 134.
63. McAuliffe, *op. cit.*
64. Sukhanov, *op. cit.*, p. 135.
65. Howe, *op. cit.*
66. Sharymova, *op. cit.*; and Yeltsin, speech in the House of Cinema.
67. Sharymova, *op. cit.*
68. Yumashev, *op. cit.*
69. *Ibid.*
70. *Ibid.*
71. Sharymova, *op. cit.*
72. Sukhanov, *op. cit.*, p. 144.
73. *Ibid.*
74. *Ibid.*, p. 145.
75. *Ibid.*, p. 146.
76. *Ibid.*, p. 147.
77. *Ibid.*, pp. 143–4.
78. Yumashev, *op. cit.*
79. Yeltsin speech in the House of Cinema.
80. Voshchanov, *op. cit.*
81. Sukhanov, *op. cit.*, p. 149.
82. *Ibid.*
83. Yumashev, *op. cit.*
84. *Ibid.*; and 'Bomba dlya Deputata' (A bomb for a Deputy), *Smena*, 20 September 1989.
85. Sukhanov, *op. cit.*, p. 150.
86. Yumashev, *op. cit.*
87. *Ibid.*
88. Yeltsin, speech in the House of Cinema.
89. See, for instance, a transcript of CBS News, *Face the Nation*, Sunday, 10 September 1989; 'Yeltsin at Columbia', p. 5; Yeltsin, speech at Johns Hopkins University.
90. Martin Sieff, 'Schmoozing and Boozing, Boris Charms America', *Washington Times*, 21 September 1989.
91. *Face the Nation*.
92. Transcript of *MacNeil/Lehrer Newshour*, 11 September 1989, p. 8.
93. Sieff, *op. cit.*
94. See, for instance, *Face the Nation*, p. 2; *MacNeil/Lehrer Newshour*, pp. 7, 9; 'Yeltsin at Columbia', pp. 6–7; Stephen Broening, 'Yeltsin Appeals for Rescue of Perestroika', *Baltimore Sun*, 13 September 1989; Montaigne, *op. cit.*; Patricia M. Szymczak, 'Yeltsin: Let Republics Determine their Fate', *Chicago Tribune*, 13 September 1989; Joe Ellen Meyers Sharp, 'Yeltsin Says U.S. a Key to Success of Perestroika', *Indianapolis*

Star, 15 September 1989; Frank Trejo, 'Yeltsin calls for ousters', *Dallas Morning News*, 16 September 1989.

95. See, for example, Yeltsin, speech at Johns Hopkins University.

96. See, for example, Trejo, *op. cit.*; and 'Yeltsin at Columbia', p. 8.

97. 'Yeltsin at Columbia', p. 9. See also *MacNeil/Lehrer Newshour*, p. 9.

98. 'Yeltsin at Columbia', p. 8.

99. *MacNeil/Lehrer Newshour*, p. 9.

100. Trejo, *op. cit.*

101. Martin Sieff, 'He's Just a Buffoon to Some, But Brash Yeltsin Has a Vision', *Washington Times*, 26 January 1990.

102. See, for example, Eric Black, 'Yeltsin Says his Criticism Actually Aids Gorbachev', *Minneapolis Star Tribune*, 14 September 1989.

103. Sieff, 'He's Just a Buffoon'.

104. Eric Black, 'Yeltsin Looks Like Candidate on U.S. Tour', *Minneapolis Star Tribune*, 15 September 1989.

105. 'Yeltsin at Columbia', p. 8.

106. *Ibid.* See also Szymczak, *op. cit.*

107. Martin Sieff, 'Yeltsin, in Travels across U.S., Baled Plenty of Political Fodder', *Washington Times*, 18 September 1989. See also Black, 'Yeltsin Says his Criticism'.

108. Natasha Sharymova, 'Perestroiku nado spasat'' (Perestroika must be saved), *Novoye Russkoye Slovo*, 13 September 1989.

109. *MacNeil/Lehrer Newshour*, p. 10.

110. *Ibid.*

111. Sieff, 'He's Just a Buffoon'.

112. Black, 'Yeltsin Says his Criticism'. See also Don Oberdorfer and David Hoffman, 'Yeltsin Asks Bush to Aid Soviet Reform Process', *Washington Post*, 13 September 1989.

113. *MacNeil/Lehrer Newshour*, p. 10.

114. See, for example, Montaigne, *op. cit.*

115. Sieff, 'He's Just a Buffoon'. See also Oberdorfer and Hoffman, *op. cit.*

116. Oberdorfer and Hoffman, *op. cit.*

117. *Ibid.*

118. See, for example, Sharp, 'Visiting Soviet'; Trejo, *op. cit.*; Sieff, 'Schmoozing and Boozing'; 'Yeltsin at Columbia', p. 12; and 'Bomba dlia Deputata'.

119. Matlock, *op. cit.*, p. 248.

120. Sukhanov, *op. cit.*, p. 90.

121. Eagleburger's speech in Georgetown University on 13 September 1989 (*Novoye Russkoye Slovo*, 16–17 September 1989).

122. Interview with Dr Rice.

123. Susan Bennett, 'Bush Risks a Controversy by Joining Yeltsin Meeting', *Philadelphia Inquirer*, 13 September 1989.

124. 'Yeltsin Seeks Private U.S. Funds', *Indianapolis Star*, 13 September 1989.

125. Bennett, *op. cit.*

126. Interviews with General Brent Scowcroft and Dr Rice.

127. Interview with Dr Rice.

128. Sukhanov, *op. cit.*, p. 122.

129. *Ibid.*, p. 123.

130. Maureen Dowd, 'Yeltsin's Back – But without the Bluster', *New York Times*, 23 June 1991.

131. Interview with Dr Rice.

132. *Ibid.*

133. Interview with General Scowcroft.

134. Sukhanov, *op. cit.*, p. 125.

135. *Ibid.*

136. Interview with Dr Rice.

137. Sukhanov, *op. cit.*, p. 125.

138. *Ibid.*, p. 126.

139. Interview with Dr Rice.

140. *Ibid.*

141. *Ibid.*

142. Sukhanov, *op. cit.*, p. 126.

143. *Ibid.*, p. 127.

144. Interview with General Scowcroft.

145. Oberdorfer and Hoffman, *op. cit.*

146. Interview with Dr Rice. See also Michael R. Beschloss and Strobe Talbott, *At the Highest Levels: The*

Inside Story of the End of the Cold War, New York: Little Brown & Company, 1994, p. 104; and Matlock, *op. cit.*, p. 251.

147. Matlock, *op. cit.*, p. 251.

148. 'Moscow Hero Flops in D.C.', *U.S. News and World Report*, 25 September 1989, p. 20.

149. Beschloss and Talbott, *op. cit.*, p. 104.

150. 'Moscow Hero Flops in D.C.', p. 20.

151. Oberdorfer and Hoffman, *op. cit.*; and Beschloss and Talbott, *op. cit.*, p. 104.

152. Beschloss and Talbott, *op. cit.*, pp. 104–5.

153. The George Huntingdon Williams Memorial Lecture and the press conference following the speech, Johns Hopkins University, Baltimore, 12 September 1989, audio and video recordings in the author's archive.

154. Interview with Professor Robert Legvold of Columbia University.

155. *Ibid.*

156. *Ibid.*

157. 'Yeltsin at Columbia', p. 4.

158. *Ibid.*, p. 3.

159. Sharymova, 'Okazyvaetsya'.

160. 'Yeltsin at Columbia', p. 12.

161. *Ibid.*, p. 13.

162. *Ibid.*, p. 14.

163. Broening, 'Yeltsin Appeals for Rescue of Perestroika'.

164. Schwantes, *op. cit.*; and 'Coming to America', *Time*, 25 September 1989, p. 36.

165. Yeltsin, speech at Johns Hopkins University.

166. Yeltsin, press conference in Baltimore.

167. See, for instance, Yeltsin, speech at Johns Hopkins University, and *Chicago Tribune*, 18 September 1989.

168. Interview with Stephen Hayes.

169. 'Yeltsin at Columbia', p. 4. See also 'U.S. Slums, Look Good to Yeltsin', *Chicago Sun-Times*, 13 September 1989.

170. Bohlen, 'Yeltsin, the Moscow populist . . .'

171. See, for example, Andi Prior, 'Speaking at Shriver Hall, Boris Yeltsin Calls for Radical Reform of Soviet Economy', *Johns Hopkins Newsletter*, September 1989.

172. Sukhanov, *op. cit.*, p. 104.

173. See, for example, Martin Sieff, 'Yeltsin Pays Reagan Visit in Hospital', *Washington Times*, 15 September 1989; Prior, *op. cit.*; and Sharymova, 'Okazyvaetsya'.

174. Sieff, 'Schmoozing and Boozing'.

175. *Ibid.*

176. Sieff, 'Yeltsin, in Travels across U.S.'.

177. James Boswell, *Life of Johnson* (World's Classic Series), ed. R. W. Chapman. Oxford: Oxford University Press, 1991.

178. Interview with Claudia McBride, Program Director at the World Affairs Council of Philadelphia.

179. Montaigne, *op. cit.*

180. Interview with Darren Narayana.

181. Starr, *op. cit.*

182. Prior, *op. cit.*; Sieff, 'Schmoozing and Boozing'; Szymczak, *op. cit.*; Montaigne, *op. cit.*

183. Schwantes, *op. cit.*

184. Interview with Professor Legvold.

185. Interview with Darren Narayana.

186. 'Coming to America', p. 36; and interview with Lotti Ross.

187. Interviews with Lotti Ross, Anne Garside and Stephen Muller.

188. Interviews with Claudia McBride, Professor Legvold and Stephen Hayes.

189. Sieff, 'Schmoozing and Boozing'.

190. Interview with Stephen Hayes.

191. Interview with Professor Legvold.

192. *Ibid.*

193. Interview with Felicity Barringer, who covered the Johns Hopkins visit for the *New York Times*.

194. Interview with Darren Narayana.

195. Interview with Felicity Barringer.

196. *Ibid.*
197. Interview with Stephen Muller.
198. *Ibid.*
199. Paul Hendrickson, 'Yeltsin's Smashing Day', *Washington Post*, 13 September 1989.
200. Interview with Stephen Muller.
201. *Ibid.*
202. *Ibid.*
203. Sukhanov, op. cit., p. 118.
204. *Ibid.*
205. *Ibid.*
206. Viktor Yaroshenko as quoted in Starr, *op. cit.*
207. Yeltsin's interpreter, Harris Coulter, as quoted in Randolph, *op. cit.*
208. As related next day to Dr Starr by Viktor Yaroshenko (Starr, *op. cit.*).
209. Yeltsin, *Ispoved'*, p. 188.
210. *Ibid.*
211. Yumashev, *op. cit.*, p. 30.
212. Sukhanov, *op. cit.*, p. 120.
213. Broening, *op. cit.*
214. *Ibid.*
215. Interview with Dr Jill McGovern, Executive Assistant to the President of Johns Hopkins University at the time of Yeltsin's visit.
216. Hendrickson, *op. cit.*
217. Interview with Dr McGovern.
218. *Ibid.*
219. *Ibid.*
220. Interview with Stephen Muller.
221. Interview with Dr McGovern.
222. 'Boris Yeltsin's Press Conference' (a videotape) and 'Boris Yeltsin at Johns Hopkins University' (an audiotape) (Office of News and Information, Johns Hopkins University).
223. Broening, *op. cit.*
224. Prior, *op. cit.*
225. Interview with Gerald Martineau.
226. *Ibid.*
227. Kozlovskiy, 'Ochevidtsy govoryat'.
228. Yeltsin, speech at Johns Hopkins University; and his press conference in Baltimore.
229. Sieff, 'He's Just a Buffoon'.
230. Sukhanov, p. 121.
231. Interview with Dr Muller.
232. Boris Yeltsin, The George Huntington Williams Memorial Lecture and the press conference following the speech, Johns Hopkins University, Baltimore, 12 September 1989, audio and video recordings in the author's archive.
233. *Ibid.*
234. Hendrickson, *op. cit.*
235. *Ibid.*
236. Interview with Dr Muller.
237. Hendrickson, *op. cit.*
238. Interview with Paul Hendrickson.
239. Hendrickson, *op. cit.*
240. Interview with Paul Hendrickson.
241. *Ibid.*
242. Randolph, *op. cit.*
243. *Ibid.*
244. Interview with Vittorio Zucconi.
245. *Ibid.*
246. *Ibid.*
247. *Pravda*, 18 September 1989.
248. Interview with Vittorio Zucconi.
249. *Ibid.*
250. 'Writer Admits Yeltsin Source Is Nonexistent', *Washington Post*, 21 September 1989.
251. Michael Dobbs, 'Yeltsin's American Tour Hits Home', *Washington Post*, 19 September 1989.
252. *Ibid.*
253. *Ibid.*
254. Scott Shane, 'Pravda, Caught in a Lie, Apologizes to Yeltsin', *Baltimore Sun*, 22 September 1989.
255. *Literaturnaya Gazeta*, 39, 1989.
256. Julia Wishnevsky, 'Pravda Editor in Trouble?', *Radio Liberty*, 20 October 1989.
257. Shane, *op. cit.*
258. *Ibid.*
259. Interview with Vittorio Zucconi.
260. Dobbs, 'Yeltsin's American Tour'.
261. Sukhanov, *op. cit.*, pp. 168–9.
262. Interview with Vittorio Zucconi.

263. Vitaliy Tretyakov, 'O Eltsine i glasnosti bez granitz' (On Yeltsin and glasnost without boundaries), *Moskovskie Novosti*, 24 September 1989.

264. Dobbs, 'Yeltsin's American Tour'.

265. Yumashev, *op. cit.*

266. Yeltsin, speech in the House of Cinema.

267. V. Dolganov and V. Romanyuk, 'V komitetakh i komissiyakh verkhovnogo Soveta SSR . . .' (In the Joint and Standing Committees of the USSR Supreme Soviet . . .), *Izvestia*, 22 September 1989.

268. *Ibid.*

269. *Pravda*, 21 September 1989.

Chapter 8: The Year of Choice

1. Vasiliy Selyunin, 'Soviet Reformer Fears Collapse of Economic House of (Ration) Cards', *Glasnost*, January–March 1990, p. 57.

2. 'Anatomy of a Soap Crisis', *Soviet/East European Report*, vol. 7, no. 6, 1989, p. 1.

3. Selyunin, *op. cit.*, p. 58.

4. Letter from V. Belyakov, *Kommunist*, 15, (October) 1989, p. 39.

5. A. Zinoviev, 'Khvatit li na zimu kartoshki?' (Are there enough potatoes for the winter?), *Izvestia*, 13 November 1989.

6. L. Trushina, 'Talony na ves' god' (Ration coupons for the entire year), *Izvestia*, 30 January 1990.

7. A. Stepovoy and S. Chugayev, 'Predlozhenie Prezidenta: polozhenie v strane obsudim v pyatnitsu' (The President's suggestion: let us discuss the situation in the country on Friday), *Izvestia*, 15 November 1990.

8. *Ibid.*

9. *Report on the USSR*, 9 March 1990, p. 40.

10. *Ibid.*

11. Selyunin, *op. cit.*, p. 57.

12. John E. Tedstrom, 'The Goskomstat Report for 1989: An Economy out of Control', *Report on the USSR*, 16 February 1990, p. 2.

13. John E. Tedstrom, 'First Quarter Economic Results: Can It Get Any Worse?', *Report on the USSR*, 1 June 1990, p. 5.

14. A. Sizov, 'Sverim tsifry' (Let's compare the numbers), *Kommunist*, (October) 1989, p. 63.

15. Egor Gaidar, 'Trudniy vybor' (A difficult choice), *Kommunist*, 2, (January) 1990, p. 28.

16. Vasiliy Selyunin, 'Posledniy shans' (The last chance), *Literaturnaya Gazeta*, 2 May 1990.

17. Gaidar, *op. cit.*, p. 24.

18. Tedstrom, 'The Goskomstat Report for 1989', p. 2.

19. *Ibid.*

20. Selyunin, 'Posledniy shans'.

21. Ed A. Hewett, 'The New Soviet Plan', *Foreign Affairs*, Winter 1990–1, p. 147.

22. Tedstrom, 'The Goskomstat Report', p. 2.

23. M. Berger, 'Bol'nye den'gi' (The sick money), *Izvestia*, 15 November 1989.

24. Tedstrom, 'The Goskomstat Report', p. 3.

25. Gaidar, *op. cit.*, p. 31.

26. V. V. Zhuravlev, L. N. Dobrokhotov and V. N. Kolodezhnyi, eds, *Istoriya sovremennoy Rossii, 1985–1994* (A history of modern Russia, 1985–1994), Moscow: Terra, 1995, p. 52.

27. *Ibid.*, p. 51.

28. Gennadiy Shipit'ko, 'Vyvoz tovarov zapreshchyon' (The export of goods prohibited), *Izvestia*, 24 February 1990.

29. Gaidar, *op. cit.*, p. 25.

30. Selyunin, 'Soviet Reformer'.

31. Viktor Loshak, ' "Wine Rebellion" in Sverdlovsk', *Moscow News*, 21 January 1990.

32. *Vremya*, First Channel/ORT (Ostankino), 4 January 1990 (FBIS, 8 January 1990, p. 97).

33. Don Van Atta, 'Farms Declare

"Grain Strike"', *Report on the USSR*, 23 February 1990, p. 10.

34. Igor Klyamkin, 'Politicheskiy dnevnik' (A political diary), *Gorizont*, 9, 1990, p. 2.

35. Selyunin, 'Posledniy shans'.

36. *Ibid.*

37. *Ibid.*

38. *Vremya*, First Channel/ORT (Ostankino), 4 January 1990 (FBIS, 8 January 1990, p. 97).

39. Bill Keller, 'Upheaval in the East: Russians; Cry of "Won't Give My Son!" And Soviets End the Call-Up', *New York Times*, 20 January 1990.

40. *Ibid.*

41. Zhuravlev *et al.*, *op. cit.*, p. 59.

42. 'Sozdan izbiratel'nyi blok "Demokraticheskaya Rossia"' (An election bloc 'Democratic Russia' has been created), *Ogonyok*, 6, February 1990, p. 17.

43. *Ibid.*, p. 18.

44. *Ibid.*

45. 'Boris El'tsin: ya ne budu brat' samootvod' (Boris Yeltsin: 'I will not withdraw'), *Sovetskaya Molodezh* (Riga), 1 February 1990; and interview with Aleksandr Urmanov.

46. 'Boris El'tsin: ya ne budu brat' samootvod'.

47. Yuriy Bogomolov, 'B. N. El'tsin: dumayu, chto menya podderzhat' (I think that I will get support), *Literaturnaya Gazeta*, 24 January 1990).

48. Interview with Aleksandr Urmanov.

49. TASS, 29 January 1990 (FBIS, 30 January 1990, p. 52).

50. R. Amos, 'Interv'yu s narodnym deputatom SSSR B. N. El'tsinym' (Interview with the USSR People's Deputy B. N. Yeltsin), *Sovetskaya Estonia*, 20 February 1990; and 'Boris El'tsin: ya ne budu brat' samootvod'. See also, Bogomolov, *op. cit.*; Andrew Neil and Peter Millar, 'Yeltsin: Russians Risk a Civil War', *Sunday Times* (London), 11 February 1990.

51. Amos, *op. cit.*

52. A. T., 'Beloye na krasnom' (White on red), *Russkaya Mysl'*, 16 February 1990.

53. *Ibid.*

54. Barbara Amiel, 'A Cry from the Heart of Russia', *The Times* (London), 6 March 1990.

55. *Ibid.*

56. Neil and Millar, *op. cit.*

57. Francis X. Clines, 'Moscow's Maverick with a Purpose', *New York Times*, 3 March 1990.

58. Interview with Larisa Mishustina, Deputy of the Congress of People's Deputies of Russia (1990–3) and of the Duma (1993–5).

59. *Ibid.*

60. Interview with Aleksandr Urmanov.

61. *Ibid.*

62. *Ibid.*

63. *Ibid.*

64. *Ibid.*

65. Egor Yakovlev, 'V poiskakh soglasiya' (In search of accord), *Moskovskie Novosti*, 14 January 1990.

66. Yuriy Mityunov, 'Pochemy ya golosoval protiv' (Why I voted 'nay'), *Russkaya Mysl'*, 16 February 1990.

67. Rene De Bok and Willem Wasink, 'Interview with USSR Deputy Boris Yeltsin', *La Stampa* (Turin), 24 January 1990 (FBIS, 13 February 1990, p. 2).

68. Yakovlev, *op. cit.*

69. Bogomolov, *op. cit.*

70. *Ibid.*

71. Interview with Yeltsin, *Corriere della Sera* (Milan), 9 March 1990 (FBIS, 21 March 1990, p. 5). See also, Amiel, *op. cit.*

72. 'Pre-Election Programme of Boris Yeltsin', *Sovetskaya Molodezh*, (Riga), 6 February 1990 (FBIS, 7 March 1990, p. 108).

73. *Ibid.*

74. *Ibid.*

75. *Ibid.*

76. *Ibid.*

77. Zhuravlev *et al.*, *op. cit.*, p. 54.

78. *Ibid.*

79. *Ibid.*

80. Moscow World Radio Service, 5 February 1990 (FBIS, 13 February 1990, p. 74); and Bogomolov, *op. cit.*

81. Amiel, *op. cit.*

82. Interview with *Manichi Shimbun*, 18 January 1990 (FBIS, 23 January 1990, p. 9).

83. 'Pre-Election Programme', p. 109.

84. Japanese news service, JIJI (Tokyo), 20 January 1990 (FBIS, 23 January 1990).

85. Radio Madrid, 28 April 1990 (FBIS, 3 May 1990, p. 26). See also Anton La Guardia, 'Yeltsin Urges Action to Avoid Revolution', *Daily Telegraph* (London), 28 April 1990.

86. Interview with *Manichi Shimbun*.

87. Interview with ITV Television Network (London), 29 April 1990 (FBIS, 3 May 1990, p. 27).

88. *Ibid.*

89. Amos, *op. cit.*

90. Neil and Millar, *op. cit.*

91. Amos, *op. cit.*

92. *Ibid.*

93. *Ibid.*

94. Bogomolov, *op. cit.*

95. 'Pre-Election Programme', p. 109.

96. Amos, *op. cit.*; Bogomolov, *op. cit.*

97. 'Pre-Election Programme', p. 108.

98. David Remnick, 'Protesters Throng Moscow Streets to Demand Democracy; Rally Is Biggest in the Capital since Bolshevik Revolution', *Washington Post*, 5 February 1990; Zhuravlev *et al.*, *op. cit.*, p. 61; A. Zhilin, G. Drugoveiko and V. Trusov, 'Politicheskiy fevral': trevogi i nadezhdy' (Political February: alarms and hopes), *Moskovskaya Pravda*, 6 February 1990.

99. Remnick, 'Protesters Throng Moscow Streets'; and Agence France-Presse, 4 February 1990 (FBIS, 5 February 1990, p. 52).

100. *Materialy Plenuma Tsentral'nogo Komiteta KPSS*, 5–7 fevralia 1990 g. (The materials of the Plenum of the Central Committee, 5–7 February 1990), Moscow: Politizdat, 1990, p. 349.

101. *Ibid.*

102. *Ibid.*, pp. 376, 377.

103. 'Rech Prezidenta SSSR M. S. Gorbacheva na vneocherdnom tret'em S'ezde narodnykh deputatov SSSR' (The speech of the President of the USSR at the Third Extraordinary Congress of People's Deputies of the USSR), *Izvestia*, 16 March 1990.

104. Zhuravlev *et al.*, *op. cit.*, p. 66.

105. *Ibid.*, p. 67.

106. 'What's in a Slogan?', *New York Times*, 2 May 1990.

107. Front-page photograph, *New York Times*, 2 May 1990; Zhuravlev *et al.*, *op. cit.*, p. 67; 'What's in a Slogan?'

108. Zhuravlev *et al.*, *op. cit.*, p. 67. See also Bill Keller, 'Soviets Moving to Outlaw Insults to Gorbachev', *New York Times*, 14 May 1990.

109. Selyunin, 'Posledniy shans'.

110. Zhuravlev *et al.*, *op. cit.*, p. 68.

111. Nikolay Travkin interviewed by V. Glotov, 'Kak izbirali predsedatelia' (How they were electing the Chairman), *Ogonyok*, 9–16 June 1990, p. 2.

112. 'Ob obrazovanii Rossiyskogo buro TsK KPSS' (On the creation of the Russian Buro at the Central Committee of the CPSU), Gorbachev's speech at the Plenum of the Central Committee, 9 December 1989, *Pravda*, 10 December 1989.

113. Interviews with Larisa Mishustina, democratic Deputy from Sverdlovsk, and Aleksandr Urmanov, a manager of the Yeltsin 1990 campaign.

114. 'Vzaimoponimanie – opora perestroiki' (Mutual understanding is the basis of perestroika), *Izvestia*, 25 April 1990.

115. *Ibid.*

116. Zhuravlev *et al.*, *op. cit.*, p. 68.

117. Interview with ITV Television Network.

118. Interview with *Manichi Shimbun*.
119. Interview with ITV Television Network.
120. Madrid Domestic Service (Radio), 4 May 1990 (FBIS, 7 May 1990, p. 38).
121. Amos, *op. cit.*
122. 'Pre-Election Programme', p. 109.
123. Mikhail Bocharov as quoted in Dawn Mann, 'The RSFSR Elections: The Congress of People's Deputies', *Report on the USSR*, 13 April 1990, p. 11.
124. Zhuravlev *et al.*, *op. cit.*, p. 68.
125. V. Igrashev, S. Pastukhov and Ye. Sorokin, 'V delovom nastroe' (In a businesslike mood), *Pravda*, 23 May 1990.
126. *Ibid.*
127. *Ibid.*
128. 'S'ezd Narodnykh Deputatov RSFSR. Stenographicheskiy otchyot' (The Congress of People's Deputies of the RSFSR. A transcript), *Sovetskaya Rossia*, 25 May 1990.
129. *Ibid.*
130. *Ibid.*
131. *Ibid.*
132. *Ibid.*
133. *Ibid.*
134. *Ibid.*
135. *Ibid.*
136. 'Rech M. S. Gorbacheva na S'ezde Narodnykh Deputatov Rossii' (The speech of M. S. Gorbachev at the Congress of People's Deputies of Russia), *Izvestia*, 25 May 1990.
137. *Ibid.*
138. *Ibid.*
139. *Ibid.*
140. *Ibid.*
141. *Ibid.*
142. *Ibid.*
143. 'S'ezd Narodnykh Deputatov RSFSR' (The Congress of People's Deputies of the RSFSR), *Sovetskaya Rossia*, 27 May 1990.
144. *Ibid.*
145. *Ibid.*
146. *Ibid.*

147. *Ibid.*
148. *Ibid.*
149. *Ibid.*
150. Sukhanov, *op. cit.*, pp. 264, 265.
151. 'S'ezd Narodnykh Deputatov', *Sovetskaya Rossia*, 27 May 1990.
152. *Ibid.*
153. Sukhanov, *op. cit.*, p. 265.
154. *Ibid.*, p. 266.
155. *Ibid.*
156. A. Davydov and V. Kurasov, 'B. N. El'tsin – Predsedatel' Verkhovnogo Soveta RSFSR' (B. N. Yeltsin is Chairman of the Russian Republic's Supreme Soviet), *Izvestia*, 29 May 1990.
157. Sukhanov, *op. cit.*, p. 268.
158. Davydov and Kurasov, *op. cit.*
159. Moscow television, 28 May 1990 (FBIS, 29 May 1990, p. 117).
160. *Ibid.*
161. *Ibid.* (p. 118).
162. *Ibid.* (p. 121).
163. Travkin, 'Kakizbirali', p. 3.
164. Celestine Bohlen, 'Russian Voters Lobby Parliament for Yeltsin', *New York Times*, 28 May 1990.
165. Travkin, 'Kakizbirali', p. 3.
166. *RFL/RL Daily Report*, 30 May 1990, p. 4. See also Celestine Bohlen, 'Yeltsin Is Elected Russian President in 3d-Round Vote', *New York Times*, 30 May 1990.
167. *RFL/RL Daily Report*, 30 May 1990, p. 4.
168. P. Gutionov, 'Posle vyborov' (After the election), *Izvestia*, 31 May 1990.
169. Travkin, 'Kakizbirali', p. 3.
170. Klyamkin, *op. cit.*, p. 15.
171. *Ibid.*
172. *Ibid.*, p. 16.
173. *Ibid.*, pp. 15–16.
174. *Ibid.*
175. Moscow Radio, 29 May 1990 (FBIS, 20 May 1990, p. 109).
176. *Ibid.*
177. 'Vystuplenie tovarisha El'tsina' (The speech by Comrade Yeltsin), *Sovetskaya Rossia*, 30 May 1990.
178. *Ibid.*

179. *Ibid.*

180. *Ibid.*

181. *Vremya*, First Channel/ORT (Ostankino), 29 August 1990, (Washington, DC: Library of Congress, Videotape VBH 9091).

182. *Ibid.*

183. Klyamkin, *op. cit.*, p. 17.

184. 'Deklaratsia gosudarstvennogo suvereniteta Rossiyskoy Sovetskoy Federativnoy Sotsialisticheskoy Respubliki priniataya pervym s'ezdom Narodnykh Deputatov RSFSR' (The Declaration of State Sovereignty of the Russian Soviet Federated Socialist Republic Adopted by the First Congress of People's Deputies), *Sovetskaya Rossia*, 14 June 1990.

185. Zhuravlev *et al.*, *op. cit.*, p. 71.

186. *Ibid.*

187. Moscow television, 29 May 1990 (FBIS, 30 May 1990, p. 91).

188. Aleksandr Ol'bik, 'Ya veryu v Russkoye chudo' (I believe in the Russian miracle), interview with Boris Yeltsin, *Sovetskaya Molodezh*, 3–4 August 1990.

189. *Ibid.* See also Aleksandra Lugovskaya, 'Boris El'tsin: nikto ne smog menya postavit' na koleni' (Boris Yeltsin: no one has ever made me kneel), *Soyuz*, 38, (September) 1990, as reprinted in *Doverie*, January 1991.

190. Julia Wishnevsky, 'Two RSFSR Congresses: A Diarchy?', *Report on the USSR*, 27 June 1990, p. 3.

191. 'Press-konferentsia po itogam pervogo s'ezda narodnykh deputatov Rossii' (Press conference at the conclusion of the First Congress of People's Deputies of Russia), 22 June 1990, a videotape, Museum of Youth Movements, Ekaterinburg.

192. Lugovskaya, *op. cit.*

193. Moscow Radio, 22 June 1990 (FBIS, 25 June 1990, p. 109).

194. 'The conversation of People's Deputies V. Isakov and V. Skrypchenko with B. N. Yeltsin on 22 June 1990', videotape, Museum of Youth Movements, Ekaterinburg.

195. Boris Yeltsin, press conference, 30 May 1990, Moscow television (FBIS, 1 June 1990, p. 78).

196. Ol'bik, *op. cit.*

197. 'Press-konferentsia B. N. El'tsina' (B. N. Yeltsin's press conference), *Sovetskaya Rossia*, 31 May 1990.

198. Boris Yeltsin, press conference, 26 June 1990, Moscow television (FBIS, 27 June 1990, p. 90).

199. Radio Riga, 27 July 1990 (FBIS, 27 July 1990, p. 67).

200. An audio recording of Yeltsin's speech quoted in M. K. Gorshkov and V. V. Zhuravliova, eds, *Gorbachev–El'tsin: 1500 dnei politicheskogo protivostoyania* (Gorbachev–Yeltsin: 1,500 days of political confrontation), Moscow: Terra, 1992, p. 224.

201. Lugovskaya, *op. cit.*

202. *Vremya*, First Channel/ORT (Ostankino), 13 August 1990 (Washington, DC: Library of Congress, Videotape VBH 9092).

203. M. Lukanin, 'Vstrecha s voeynnymi moryakami' (Meeting with sailors), *Krasnaya Zvezda*, 28 August 1990.

204. Moscow Radio, 10 August 1990 (FBIS, 13 August 1990, p. 81); and *Vremya*, First Channel/ORT (Ostankino), 10 August 1990 (FBIS, 13 August 1990, p. 81).

205. Bill Keller, 'Boris Yeltsin Taking Power' *New York Times Magazine*, 23 September 1990, p. 80.

206. *Vremya*, First Channel/ORT (Ostankino), 12 August 1990 (FBIS, 13 August 1990, p. 83).

207. Keller, 'Boris Yeltsin . . .', pp. 34, 80.

208. V. Fedorov and N. Zhdankin, 'Pochemu bastovali shakhtyory, ili krivoe zerkalo planovo-ubytochnoy ekonomiki' (Why the miners went on strike, or a distorting mirror of the plan-and-loss economy), *Izvestia*, 28 July 1989.

209. Keller, 'Boris Yeltsin . . .', p. 34.

210. As quoted in N. Morozov, 'Neprostoy dalog: poezdka B. El'tsina

po Tatarii' (Difficult dialogue: B. Yeltsin's tour of Tatar ASSR), *Pravda*, 9 August 1990.

211. *Vremya*, First Channel/ORT (Ostankino), 12 August 1990 (FBIS, 13 August 1990, p. 84).

212. Boris Yeltsin, speech at the Twenty-Eighth Party Congress. *Pravda*, 8 July 1990, p. 4.

213. *Ibid.*

214. *Ibid.*

215. *Ibid.*

216. Interview with Aleksandr Urmanov; and *XVIII s'ezd Kommunisticheskoy partii sovetskogo Soyuza: 2–13 iulya, 1990 goda: stenograficheskiy otchyot* (XXVIII Congress of the Communist Party of the Soviet Union: the transcript), Moscow: Politicheskaya Literatura, 1990, vol. II, pp. 500–1.

217. 'Zakluchitelnoye slovo M. S. Gorbacheva na 28 s'ezde KPSS' (The concluding remarks of M. S. Gorbachev at the Twenty-Eighth Congress of the CPSU), *Pravda*, 14 July 1990.

218. 'XVIII s'ezd', vol. II, p. 244.

219. Zhuravlev *et al.*, *op. cit.*, p. 83.

220. 'Obeshchaniyami syt ne budesh' (You cannot feed one with promises), *Ogonyok*, 27 January–3 February 1990, p. 1.

221. *Ibid.*

222. *Ibid.*

223. Gary Lee, 'Soviet Miners Launch Strike, Oust Party Officials', *Washington Post*, 11 July 1990.

224. *USSR Today. Soviet Media News and Features Digest*, Radio Liberty Monitoring Service, 24 August 1990.

225. Zhuravlev *et al.*, *op. cit.*, p. 83.

226. *Vremya*, First Channel/ORT (Ostankino), 29 September 1990 (FBIS, 1 October 1990, p. 40).

227. *Megapolis-Express*, 27 September 1990.

228. Zhuravlev *et al.*, *op. cit.*, p. 84.

229. V. Dolganov, 'Boris El'tsin: sabotazh est'!' (Boris Yeltsin: yes, there is sabotage!), interview with Yeltsin, *Komsomolskoye Znamya*, 30 September 1990.

230. Lugovskaya, *op. cit.*

231. Moscow television, 1 September 1990 (FBIS, 4 September 1990, p. 88).

232. *Ibid.*

233. *Ibid.*, p. 94.

234. *Ibid.*, p. 88.

235. Lugovskaya, *op. cit.*

236. Moscow television, 15 August 1990 (FBIS, 16 August 1990, p. 64).

237. Boris Yeltsin, press conference in the House of Soviets on 1 September 1990. Moscow Television, 1 September 1990 (FBIS, 4 September 1990, p. 89).

238. *Ibid.*, p. 88.

239. *Ibid.*, p. 94.

240. *Ibid.*, pp. 89–92.

241. *Vremya*, First Channel/ORT (Ostankino), 29 August 1990 (Washington, DC: Library of Congress, Videotape VBH 9091).

242. See, for instance, Francis X. Clines, 'A Free-Market Plunge? Gorbachev's Not Ready', *New York Times*, 26 April 1990.

243. As quoted in Bill Keller, 'Gorbachev Is Said to Delay Soviet Economic "Shock Therapy" Plan', *New York Times*, 25 April 1990.

244. '500 dnei. Konspekt Programmy' (500 Days. The gist of the Programme), *Komsomol'skaya Pravda* (special edition), 29 September 1990.

245. S. Shatalin, N. Petrakov, G. Yavlinsky, S. Aleksashenko, A. Vavilov, L. Grigoriev, M. Zadornov, V. Martynov, V. Mashits, A. Mikhailov, B. Fedorov, T. Varygina and E. Yasin [the Programme's authors], 'Chelovek, svoboda, rynok' (Man, liberty, market), *Izvestia*, 4 September 1990.

246. *Ibid.*

247. Shatalin *et al.*, *op. cit.*

248. *Ibid.*

249. '500 dnei'.

250. Hewett, *op. cit.*, pp. 164–5.

251. *Ibid.*, p. 167.

252. M. Berger, ' "Sosenki" bez

"Sosen"' (Little pines without pines), *Izvestia*, 27 August 1990.

253. *Ibid.*

254. Yeltsin's press conference, 1 September 1990, p. 89.

255. Igor Klyamkin, 'Oktyabr'skiy vybor prezidenta' (The October choice of the President), *Ogonyok*, 17–24 November 1990, p. 6.

256. 'Pochemu segodnya neosushchstvima programma "500 dnei"' (Why the '500-Day' programme cannot be implemented today), *Komsomol'skaya Pravda*, 4 November 1990.

257. Leonid Nikitinskiy, 'Skol'ko Rubikonov na puti Gorbacheva?' (How many Rubicons will Gorbachev have to cross?), *Komsomol'skaya Pravda*, 12 April 1991.

258. S. Razin, 'Chya ruka v moyom karmane?' (Whose hand is in my pocket?), *Komsomol'skaya Pravda*, 14 February 1991.

259. Hewett, *op. cit.*, p. 166.

260. 'Pochemu'.

261. Stanislav Shatalin, 'Khochu opravdat'sia pered narodom' (I want to clear myself before the people), *Komsomol'skaya Pravda*, 16 January 1991.

262. Boris Yeltsin, speech at the session of the Supreme Soviet of the RSFSR, *Sovetskaya Rossia*, 16 October 1990.

263. Grigoriy Yavlinsky, 'Yavlinsky's Death Ray', interviewed by Ye. Yakovlev, *Moscow News*, 6 January 1991, p. 9.

Chapter 9: 'Rolling Up the Sleeves, Raising the Fists'

1. 'Trudnyi dialog Presidenta i armii' (Difficult dialogue between the President and the Army), *Izvestia*, 14 November 1990.

2. Radio Moscow, quoted in Alexander Rahr, 'Gorbachev and Yeltsin in a Deadlock', *Report on the USSR*, 15 February 1991, p. 2.

3. 'The Statement of the KGB Chairman on Soviet Television', *Radio Liberty Soviet Media News Budget*, 11 December 1990.

4. Boris Yeltsin, speech at the Fourth Congress of People's Deputies of the USSR on 20 December 1990. In M. K. Gorshkov and V. V. Zhuravlyova, eds. *Gorbachev–El'tsin: 1500 dney politicheskogo protivostoyaniya* (Gorbachev–Yeltsin: 1,500 days of political confrontation), Moscow: Terra, 1992, p. 287.

5. *Ibid.*, pp. 288–9.

6. *Ibid.*, pp. 287–9.

7. Boris Yeltsin, Anatoliy Gorbunovs and Vitaustas Lansbergis, 'Joint Statement', 14 January 1991, read by Yeltsin at the press conference in the Hall of the Council of Nationalities of the Supreme Soviet of Russia. Author's transcript of his own recording. (See also *Rossiyskaya Gazeta*, 15 January 1991.)

8. L. Levitskiy, 'Verkhovnyi Sovet Estonii podtverdil svoy vybor' (The Supreme Soviet of Estonia has confirmed its choice), *Izvestia*, 15 January 1991.

9. Yeltsin, press conference on 14 January 1991.

10. Boris Yeltsin, 'Appeal to the Russian Soldiers in the Baltics', read at the press conference in the Hall of the Council of Nationalities of the Supreme Soviet of Russia, 14 January 1991. Author's archive. See also *Rossiyskaya Gazeta*, 15 January 1991.

11. Press conference on 14 January 1991. For a summary see also I. Demchenko and V. Kurasov, 'Press-konferentsia Borisa El'tsina' (Boris Yeltsin's press conference), *Izvestia*, 15 January 1991; and a report by Evgeniy Kiselev, broadcast on Radio Rossii on 15 January 1991 and reprinted in *Doverie*, January 1991, p. 14.

12. Interview with Igor Klyamkin, 16 January 1991.

13. Press conference on 14 January 1991.

14. 'Otkrytoye pis'mo Predsedatelya Verkhovnogo Soveta RSFSR B. N. El'tsina narodam Pribaltiki' (Open letter from Chairman of the Supreme Soviet of the RSFSR B. N. Yeltsin to the people of the Baltics), *Rossiyskaya Gazeta*, 19 January 1991.

15. Zhuravlev *et al.*, *op. cit.*, p. 98.

16. Original in the author's archive.

17. The author's transcript of the 16 January 1991 meeting at the Institute of the Economy of World Socialist System.

18. Interview with Igor Klyamkin.

19. Francis X. Clines, 'Moscow 1991', *New York Times Magazine*, 3 March 1991, p. 37.

20. M. Reshetnikova, 'Neizvestnyi El'tsin' (Unknown Yeltsin), *Zerkalo*, 3, September 1990 (reprinted in *Doverie*, January 1991).

21. 'Za vashu I nashu svobodu' (For your freedom and ours), *Rossiyskaya Gazeta*, 22 January 1991.

22. Marina Shakina, 'Something Has Happened to Perestroika', *New Times*, 5–11 March 1991, p. 5.

23. Sergey Lamakin and Oleg Poptsov, interview with Boris Yeltsin, First Channel/ORT (Ostankino) of Soviet television, 19 February 1991. In Gorshkov and Zhuravlyova, *Gorbachev–El'tsin*, pp. 313–14. See also *Sovetskaya Rossia*, 23 February 1991.

24. Radio Rossii, 11 March 1991 (FBIS, 12 March 1991, p. 77).

25. 'Konfrontatsia bezrassudna. Ob interv'yu B. N. El'tsina Tsentral'nomu televideniyu' (Confrontation is foolhardy. B. N. Yeltsin's interview on Central Television), *Izvestia*, 20 February 1991.

26. TASS, 20 February 1991 (FBIS, 21 February 1991, p. 29), and *Pravda*, 22 February 1991.

27. Svetlana Goryacheva, *et al.*, 'Politicheskoye zayavlenie Verkhovnomu Sovetu RSFSR, narodnym deputatam RSFSR' (Political statement to the Supreme Soviet of the RSFSR, People's Deputies of the RSFSR), *Sovetskaya Rossia*, 22 February 1991.

28. I. Sichka, '1991, Fevral'. Boris opyat' ne prav?' (February, 1991. Is Boris wrong again?), *Komsomol'skaya Pravda*, 22 February 1991.

29. Gorbachev, speeches at a Minsk plant on 26 February and before the 'scientific and creative intelligentsia of Byelorussia' on 28 February as reported in *Sovetskaya Rossia*, 28 February, and *Pravda*, 1 March, respectively.

30. Boris Yeltsin, speech in the House of Cinema, 9 March 1991, in Gorshkov and Zhuravlyova, *op. cit.*, pp. 322, 323.

31. TASS, Radio Moscow International Service, 7 March 1991 (FBIS, 8 March 1991, p. 71).

32. A. F. Vostrochenko, L. I. Khitrun, G. M. Khodyrev (USSR People's Deputies), V. A. Volodin, Yu. A. Guskov, B. F. Zubkov, G. E. Kondryukov, Ch.-D. B. Ondar, Yu. N. Semenov, V. N. Stepanov, V. N. Tkihomirov, V. I. Chaptynov (RSFSR People's Deputies), N. P. Kiselev, Chairman of Kirov Regional Soviet and M. A. Shestov, Chairman of Tver Regional Soviet, 'Vremya derzhat' otvet. Zayavlenie chlenov Soveta Federatsii RSFSR o sotsial'no-ekonomicheskom i politicheskom polozhenii v respublike' (Time to answer: statement by members of the RSFSR Federation Council on the socio-economic and political situation in the Republic), *Sovetskaya Rossia*, 20 March 1991).

33. Alexander Rahr, 'Yeltsin Intensifies Campaign against Gorbachev', *RFE/RL Daily Report*, 25 March 1991, p. 7.

34. V. Lukashevich, 'Kto i kogo khochet postavit' na koleni' (Who wants to bring whom to his knees), *Krasnaya Zvezda*, 28 March 1991.

35. V. Gerasimov, 'Otdadim v zalog Rossiyu?' (Should we mortgage Russia?), *Pravda*, 25 March 1991.

36. Rahr, 'Yeltsin Intensifies Campaign . . .'

37. Interview with Artur Ezhov.

38. *Ibid.*

39. *Ibid.*

40. Shakina, *op. cit.*

41. Sergey Kozheurov, 'Na samom li dele possorilsya Boris Nikolaevich s Mikhailom Sergeevichem?' (Have Boris Nikolaevich and Mikhail Sergeevich really quarrelled with each other?), *Komsomol'skaya Pravda*, 1 March 1991.

42. David Remnick, 'Yeltsin Is Hailed at Moscow Rally', *Washington Post*, 25 February 1991; Serge Schmemann, 'Huge Rally in Moscow Calls on Gorbachev to Resign', *New York Times*, 11 March 1991; Anthony Robinson, 'Thousands March for Yeltsin', *Financial Times*, 11 March 1991; '400,000 Attend Pro-Yeltsin Rally in Moscow', Radio Moscow, 22 February 1991 (FBIS, 25 February 1991, p. 38).

43. *Pravda*, 12 March 1991, and *RFL/RE Daily Report*, 11 March 1991, p. 6.

44. Radio Rossii, 24 February 1991 (FBIS, 25 February 1991, p. 38); Francis X. Clines, '40,000 Rally to Support Yeltsin against Gorbachev', *New York Times*, 25 February 1991; TASS, 10 March 1991 (FBIS, 11 March 1991, p. 34); Radio Rossii, 10 March 1991 (FBIS, 11 March 1991, p. 75).

45. Remnick, 'Yeltsin Is Hailed at Moscow Rally.

46. Clines, '40,000 Rally to Support Yeltsin against Gorbachev'.

47. Schmemann, *op. cit.*

48. 'Obrashchenie soveta rabochikh komitetov Kuzbassa k grazhdanam oblasti, Rossii, strany' (Appeal of the Council of Workers Committees of Kuzbass to the citizens of the region, Russia, the country), *Russkaya Mysl'* (Paris), 1 February 1991.

49. Moscow television, 5 March 1991 (FBIS, 6 March 1991, p. 39).

50. Francis X. Clines, 'Soviet Opposition Defies Ban on Rally', *New York Times*, 28 March 1991; and Leyla Boulton, 'Violent Clash Feared in Moscow', *Financial Times*, 28/29 March 1991.

51. Vladimir Kozlovskiy, 'Oy, chto-to budet . . .' (My, my, there's going to be trouble . . .), *Novoye Russkoye Slovo*, 28 March 1991.

52. *Ibid.*

53. TASS International Service, 26 March 1991 (FBIS, 27 March 1991, p. 52).

54. Kozlovskiy, 'Oy, chto-to budet'.

55. Francis X. Clines, 'Rally Takes Kremlin Terror and Turns It into Burlesque', *New York Times*, 29 March 1991.

56. Viktor Shirokov, 'Na grani fatal'nogo i neobratimogo raskola okazalis' Rossiiskie parlamentarii na svoem "ocherednom vneucherednom" s'ezde, no v itoge sumeli nayti kompromiss' (At their 'scheduled extraordinary' Congress the Russian parliamentarians found themselves on the brink of a fatal and irreversible split, but in the end managed to find a compromise), *Pravda*, 9 April 1991.

57. Yeltsin's speech at the Third Extraordinary Congress of People's Deputies of the RSFSR, *Rossiyskaya Gazeta*, 31 March 1991.

58. *Ibid.*

59. *Ibid.*

60. *Ibid.*

61. Radio Rossii, 1 April 1991 (FBIS, 2 April 1991, p. 78).

62. TASS, 2 April 1991 (FBIS, 3 April 1991, p. 66).

63. Boris Yeltsin, speech at the Third Congress of People's Deputies of Russia, *Rossiyskaya Gazeta*, 31 March 1991.

64. Dawn Mann, 'Pavlov Meets with Miners', *RFE/RL Report*, 26 March 1991, p. 4.

65. Francis X. Clines, 'Striking Coal Miners Defend Yeltsin', *New York Times*, 31 March 1991.

66. 'Zayavlenie Predsedatelia Verkhovnogo Soveta RSFSR B. N. El'tsina' (Statement of the Chairman of the Supreme Soviet of the RSFSR B. N. Yeltsin), *Rossiyskaya Gazeta*, 5 April 1991.

67. Russian Television Channel (Rossia) report of the Congress, 4 April 1991 (FBIS, 5 April 1991, p. 51).

68. Matlock, *op. cit.*, p. 664.

69. Boris Yeltsin, press conference in Paris, 17 April 1991, *Russkaya Mysl'*, 19 April 1991.

70. Baudouin Bollaert, 'Eltsine ménage Gorbatchev', *Le Figaro*, 16 April 1991.

71. Yeltsin, *Zapiski*, p. 42.

72. Vera Tolz, 'More on Joint Declaration, Yeltsin's Reaction', *RFE/RL Daily Report*, 26 April 1991, p. 4.

73. Yeltsin's interview with the 'Parliamentary herald of Russia', Moscow television, 4 May 1991 (*Kuranty*, 7 May 1991).

74. V. Lynev, 'Tsel' – obnovlenie Rossii. B. N. El'tsin otvechaet na voprosy Izvestiy' (The goal is the renewal of Russia. B. N. Yeltsin answers *Izvestia*'s questions), *Izvestia*, 23 May 1991; and Alexander Rahr, 'Yeltsin Calls Gorbachev an Ally', *RFE/RL Report*, 13 May 1991, p. 7.

75. *Pravda*, 25 April 1991.

76. Sergey Kornilov, 'Shtabisty' (The headquarters staff), *Rossiyskaya Gazeta*, 8 June 1991.

77. Vadim Bakatin, 'Vadim Bakatin: esli u nas kto-to vysovyvalsya, golova letela v luchshem sluchaye v Parizh' (If anyone made any trouble, he was sent, at least, to Paris), *Komsomol'skaya Pravda*, 31 May 1991.

78. Leyla Boulton, 'Russians Promised Cheap Vodka and Reform', *Financial Times*, 7 June 1991.

79. Leyla Boulton, 'Ryzhkov Campaign Plays to the Patriotic Voter', *Financial Times*, 5 June 1991.

80. *Ibid.*

81. *Ibid.*

82. N. Belan, 'Nikolay Ryzhkov: skazhu otkrovenno . . .' (Nikolay Ryzhkov: let me tell you frankly . . .), *Sovetskaya Rossia*, 30 May 1991.

83. Lynev, 'Tsel''.

84. 'Vykhod iz krizisa i obnovlenie Rossia – na puti reform. Tezisy programmy Predsedatelya Verkhovnogo Soveta RSFSR B. N. El'tsina' (Reforms will provide a way out of crisis and renewal of Russia. The main planks of the electoral reform programme of the Chairman of the Supreme Soviet of RSFSR B. N. Yeltsin), a copy in the author's archive.

85. *Ibid.*, pp. 4 and 5.

86. Lynev, 'Tsel''.

87. Boris Yeltsin, speech to the Council of Representatives of Democratic Russia, 1 June 1991, *Rossiyskaya Gazeta*, 4 June 1991.

88. *Ibid.* See also 'Vykhod iz krizisa', p. 4.

89. 'Vykhod iz krizisa', p. 3.

90. Yeltsin, speech to Democratic Russia, 1 June 1991.

91. 'Vykhod iz krizisa', p. 3.

92. Lynev, 'Tsel''.

93. *Ibid.*

94. Michael Dobbs, 'Yeltsin Woos the Military', *Washington Post*, 2 June 1991.

95. Vitaliy Tretyakov, 'Eto fantastichno. Rossia nakonets-to dozhila do togo, chtoby narod sam vybiral glavu gosudarstva' (It is incredible. Russia has finally lived to see the day when the people themselves choose the head of state), *Nezavisimaya Gazeta*, 11 June 1991.

96. Boris Yeltsin, inaugural speech in the Kremlin, 10 July 1991, Moscow television (FBIS, 10 July 1991, pp. 63–4).

97. Boris Yeltsin, press conference in the Kremlin, 25 May 1991, Moscow television (FBIS, 28 May 1991, p. 64).

98. Mikhail Gorbachev, interview with Soviet journalists, 8 July 1991,

as reported by V. Grishchenko, 'Prezident beryot s soboy nashe soglasie' (The President is taking with him our consent), *Izvestia*, 9 July 1991.

99. Boris Yeltsin, interview with Soviet journalists, 9 July 1991, *Izvestia*, 10 July 1991.

100. TASS, 9 July 1991 (FBIS, 10 July 1991, p. 68).

101. Grishchenko, *op. cit.*

102. *Ibid.*

103. Yeltsin, *Zapiski*, p. 54.

104. *Ibid.*

105. John Lloyd, 'Yeltsin to back Gorbachev in poll', *Financial Times*, 10 July 1991.

106. Mikhail Gorbachev, 'O proekte novoy Programmy KPSS. Doklad M. S. Gorbacheva na Plenume TsK KPSS 25 iulya' (About a new programme of the CPSU. The report of M. S. Gorbachev to the Plenum of the Central Committee, 25 July), *Pravda*, 27 July 1991.

107. Yeltsin, *Zapiski*, p. 54.

108. *Ibid.*, p. 73.

Chapter 10: The Revolution

1. TASS, 06.18 (Moscow time), 19 August 1991 (FBIS, 19 August 1991, p. 8).

2. TASS, 05.29 (Moscow time), 19 August 1991 (FBIS, 19 August 1991, p. 9).

3. A. Golovkov and A. Chernov, 'Proryv' (Breakthrough), interview with Anatoliy Sobchak, *Moscow News*, 1 September 1991.

4. *Ibid.*

5. *Ibid.*

6. *Ibid.*

7. *Ibid.*

8. Russian Television Channel (Rossia), 10.05, 19 August 1991 (FBIS, 19 August 1991, p. 12).

9. *Ibid.*

10. First Channel/ORT (Ostankino), 20.40 (Moscow time), 20 August 1991 (FBIS, 21 August 1991, p. 12).

11. *Ibid.*

12. *Ibid.*

13. TASS, 05.29 (Moscow time), 19 August 1991 (FBIS, 19 August 1991, p. 9).

14. The State Committee for the State of Emergency, 'Address to the Soviet People', TASS, 05.38 (Moscow time), 19 August 1991 (FBIS, 19 August 1991, pp. 10–11).

15. *Ibid.*

16. 'Vstrecha Sovetskogo rukovodstva s zhurnalistami' (Soviet leadership meets with journalists), *Pravda*, 20 August 1991, p. 1.

17. 'Address to the Soviet People'.

18. 'Vstrecha . . .'

19. 'Address to the Soviet People'.

20. 'Vstrecha . . .'

21. *Ibid.*

22. Gennadiy Yanaev, 'Address to heads of state and government and the Secretary General of the United Nations', TASS, 06.27 (Moscow time), 19 August 1991 (FBIS, 19 August 1991, p. 8).

23. 'Address to the Soviet People'.

24. 'Decision No. 1 of the State Committee for the State of Emergency', Moscow Central Television, Second Programme Network, 10.05 (Moscow time), 19 August 1991 (FB1S-SOV-91-160, 19 August 1991, p. 13.

25. 'Address to the Soviet People'.

26. *Ibid.*

27. *Ibid.*

28. 'Decision No. 1', p. 12.

29. 'Address to the Soviet People'.

30. *Ibid.*

31. 'Vstrecha . . .'

32. *Ibid.*

33. 'Dogovor o Soyuze Suvernnykh Gosudarstv' (Treaty on the Union of Sovereign States), *Sovetskaya Rossia*, 15 August 1991, p. 3.

34. *Ibid.*

35. *Ibid.*

36. *Ibid.*

37. 'A statement by Anatoliy Lukyanov', TASS, 19 August 1991 (FBIS, 19 August 1991, pp. 19–20).

38. *Vremya*, First Channel/ORT (Ostankino), 20.00 (Moscow time), 19 August 1991 (FBIS, 20 August 1991, p. 21).

39. Aleksandr Korzhakov, *Boris El'tsin: ot rassveta do zakata* (Boris Yeltsin: from dawn to sunset), Moscow: Interbook, 1997, p. 2.

40. *RFE/RL Daily Report*, 19 August 1991, p. 2.

41. *Ibid.*

42. *Ibid.*

43. Michael Dobbs, 'Russian Leader Becomes Focus of Opposition', *Washington Post*, 20 August p. A20.

44. *Vremya*, First Channel/ORT (Ostankino), 20.00 (Moscow time), 19 August 1991 (FBIS, 20 August 1991, p. 21).

45. Boris Yeltsin, Ivan Silaev and Ruslan Khazbulatov, 'K grazhdanam Rossii' (To the citizens of Russia), *Rossia*, 'a newspaper of the Supreme Soviet of the RSFSR. Special edition', copy in the author's archive. See also FBIS, Annexe, 20 August 1991, p. 1 (a transcript of a broadcast by Tokyo NHK No. 1 Television Network).

46. Boris Yeltsin, 'Ukaz Prezidenta Rossiyskoy Sovetskoy Federativnoy Sotsialisticheskoy Respubliki, No. 59, 19 avgusta 1991 goda' (Decree of the President of the Russian Soviet Federated Socialist Republic, No. 59, 19 August 1991), copy in the author's archive. See also *Rossiyskaya Gazeta*, 23 August 1991, p. 2.

47. Boris Yeltsin, 'Ukaz Prezidenta Rossiyskoy Sovetskoy Federativnoy Sotsialisticheskoy Respubliki, No. 61, 19 avgusta 1991 goda' (Decree of the President of the Russian Soviet Federated Socialist Republic, No. 61, 19 August 1991), copy in the author's archive. See also *Rossiyskaya Gazeta*, 23 August 1991, p. 2.

48. 'Ukaz No. 61'.

49. *Vremya*, First Channel/ORT (Ostankino), 20.00 (Moscow time), 19 August 1991 (FBIS, 20 August 1991, p. 21); Oleg Kupriyanov,

'Moskva, 19–21 avgusta' (Moscow, 19–21 August), *Novoye Russkoye Slovo*, 24–25 August 1991, p. 4; 'Make it known', *Washington Post*, 20 August 1991, p. A15.

50. Alexander Lebed, *My Life and my Country*, Washington, DC: Regnery Publishing, 1997, p. 304.

51. 'Make it known'.

52. Jamey Gambrell, 'Seven Days that Shook the World', *New York Review of Books*, 26 September 1991, p. 56.

53. *Ibid.*

54. Leyla Boulton, 'Yeltsin plays on his popularity to turn back the military tide', *Financial Times*, 20 August 1991, p. 2.

55. *RFE/RL Daily Report*, 156 Extra, 19 August 1991, p. 1.

56. TASS, 20.46 (Moscow time), 19 August 1991 (FBIS, 20 August 1998, p. 12).

57. Boris Yeltsin, 'Ukaz Prezidenta Rossiyskoy Sovetskoy Federativnoy Sotsialisticheskoy Respubliki No. 63' (Decree of the President of the Russian Soviet Federated Socialist Republic No. 63), copy in the author's archive. See also *Rossiyskaya Gazeta*, 23 August 1991, p. 3.

58. 'Ukaz No. 63'.

59. Boris Yeltsin, 'Ukaz Prezidenta Rossiyskoy Sovetskoy Federativnoy Sotsialisticheskoy Respubliki, No. 64, 20 avgusta 1991 goda' (Decree of the President of the Russian Soviet Federated Socialist Republic, No. 64, 20 August 1991), *Rossiyskaya Gazeta*, 23 August 1991, p. 2.

60. *Ibid.*

61. Boris Yeltsin, 'Ukaz Prezidenta Rossiyskoy Sovetskoy Federativnoy Sotsialisticheskoy Respubliki, No. 68, 20 avgusta 1991 goda (Decree of the President of the Russian Soviet Federated Socialist Republic, No. 68, 20 August 1991), copy in the author's archive. See also *Rossiyskaya Gazeta*, 23 August 1991, p. 2; Boris Yeltsin, speech to the Supreme Soviet of

Russia on 21 August 1991 (FBIS, 22 August 1991, p. 61).

62. B. N. El'tsin, A. V. Rutskoy, I. S. Silaev and R. I. Khazbulatov, 'Predsedatelyu Verkhovnogo Soveta SSSR tov. Luk'yanovu A. I.' (To the Chairman of the Supreme Soviet of the USSR, Comrade Luk'yanov A. I.), 20 August 1991. A copy in the author's archive. See also 'Rossiyskoe rukovidsvo – Luk'yanovu' (The Russian leaders to Luk'yanov), *Rossiyskaya Gazeta*, 23 August 1991, p. 2; and FB1S, 21 August 1991, p. 58.

63. El'tsin *et al.*, 'Predsedatelyu . . .'.

64. *Ibid.*

65. Press Association (London), 20 August 1991 (FBIS, 21 August 1991, pp. 57–8).

66. Boris Yeltsin, 'K soldatam i ofitseram Vooruzhyonnykh Sil SSR, KGB SSSR, MVD SSSR, 19 avgusta 1991 goda' (To the soldiers and officers of the armed forces of the USSR, of the KGB of the USSR, and of the Ministry of Internal Affairs of the USSR, 19 August 1991), copy in the author's archive. See also FBIS, 20 August 1991, Annexe, p. 57.

67. 'K soldatam'.

68. *Ibid.*

69. Iain Elliot, 'Three Days in August: On-the-Spot Impressions', *Report on the USSR*, 6 September 1991, p. 63.

70. Kupriyanov, *op. cit.*; Gambrell, *op. cit.*, p. 56.

71. Kupriyanov, *op. cit.*

72. Elliot, *op. cit.*, p. 64.

73. *Ibid.*

74. Dobbs, 'Russian leader . . .'.

75. Kupriyanov, *op. cit.*

76. Elliot, *op. cit.*, p. 64.

77. Kupriyanov, *op. cit.*

78. A. Batygin, 'Vchera na utilsakh Moskvy' (Yesterday on the streets of Moscow), *Pravda*, 20 August 1991, p. 2.

79. *Ibid.*

80. Kupriyanov, *op. cit.*

81. Agence France-Presse, 12.49 (Moscow time), 19 August 1991 (FBIS, 19 August 1991, p. 14).

82. *Vremya*, First Channel/ORT (Ostankino), 20.00 (Moscow time), 19 August 1991 (FBIS, 20 August 1991, p. 21).

83. *Ibid.*

84. Elliot, *op. cit.*, p. 64.

85. *Ibid.*

86. Kupriyanov, *op. cit.*

87. Elliot, *op. cit.*, p. 63.

88. I. Abakumov, V. Gavrichkin and V. Nadein, 'V eti trevozhnye dni' (In these troubled days), *Izvestia*, 22 August 1991, p. 2.

89. Agence France-Presse, 16.47 (Moscow time), 19 August 1991 (FBIS, 20 August 1991, pp. 19–20).

90. A. Vasinskiy and G. Shipitko, 'V usloviyakh chrezvychaynogo polozheniya' (Under the state of emergency), *Izvestia*, 21 August 1991, p. 1.

91. Kupriyanov, *op. cit.*; Vasinskiy and Shipitko, *op. cit.*

92. Gambrell, *op. cit.*, p. 57.

93. Elliot, *op. cit.*, p. 63; *Vremya*, Channel One/ORT (Ostankino), 20.00 (Moscow time), 19 August 1991 (FBIS, 20 August 1991, p. 21).

94. Elliot, *op. cit.*, p. 63.

95. Kupriyanov, *op. cit.*

96. Abakumov, Gavrichkin and Nadein, *op. cit.*

97. Gambrell *op. cit.*, p. 56.

98. *Ibid.*; and V. V. Zhuravlev, L. N. Dobrokhotov and V. N. Kolodezhnyi, eds, *Istoriya sovremennoy Rossii, 1985–1994* (History of modern Russia, 1985–1994), Moscow: Terra, 1995, p. 115.

99. Zhuravlev *et al.*, *op. cit.*, p. 115.

100. *Vremya*, First Channel/ORT (Ostankino), 20.00 (Moscow time), 19 August 1991 (FBIS, 20 August 1991, pp. 21–2).

101. Elliott, 'Three Days in August . . .', p. 65; Gambrell, *op. cit.*, p. 56.

102. Elliot, *op. cit.*, p. 65.

103. Agence France-Presse, 02.05

(Moscow time), 20 August 1991 (FBIS, 21 August 1991, p. 59).

104. *Ibid.*, and INTERFAX, 20 August 1991 (FBIS, 21 August 1991, p. 59).

105. Evgeniy Evtushenko, '19 avgusta' (19 August), *Literaturnaya Gazeta*, 21 August 1991, p. 1.

106. Gambrell, *op. cit.*, p. 56.

107. Agence France-Presse, 2.05 (Moscow time), 20 August 1991 (FBIS, 21 August 1991, p. 59).

108. Radio Vilnius, 23.25 (Moscow time), 20 August 1991 (FBIS, 21 August 1991, p. 67).

109. A. Golovenko, 'Mitinguet ploshchad'' (The square holds a rally), *Pravda*, 21 August 1991, p. 1.

110. Abakumov, Gabrichkin and Nadein, *op. cit.*; and Vladimir Nadein, 'Staraya shpana lezet v geroi' (Old dregs clamouring to be heroes), *Izvestia*, 23 August 1991, p. 6.

111. Yeltsin, *Zapiski*, p. 112.

112. *Ibid.*

113. *Ibid.*

114. Korzhakov, *op. cit.*, p. 93.

115. Agence France-Presse, 20.53 (Moscow time), 20 August 1991 (FBIS, 21 August 1991, p. 71).

116. Korzhakov, *op. cit.*, p. 93.

117. Yeltsin, *Zapiski*, pp. 118–19. See also David Remnick, *Lenin's Tomb: The Last Days of the Soviet Empire*, New York: Random House, 1993, p. 483.

118. Boris Yeltsin, 'Ukaz Prezidenta Rossiyskoy Sovetskoy Federativnoy Sotsialisticheskoy Respubliki, No. 62, 19 avgust 1991' (Decree of the President of the Russian Soviet Federated Republic, No. 62, 19 August 1991), copy in the author's archive. See also *Rossiyskaya Gazeta*, 23 August 1991, p. 2.

119. Yeltsin, *Zapiski*, p. 104.

120. Boris Yeltsin, speech to the Supreme Soviet of Russia, 21 August 1991, Moscow Central Television, *Vostok* and *Orbita* broadcasts for Siberia and Far East (FBIS, 22 August 1991, p. 61).

121. Yeltsin, *Zapiski*, p. 104.

122. *Ibid.*, p. 110.

123. Korzhakov, *op. cit.*, p. 89.

124. Yeltsin, *Zapiski*, p. 108. See also Korzhakov, *op. cit.*, p. 95.

125. Yeltsin, *Zapiski*, p. 108.

126. *Ibid.*, p. 109.

127. Gambrell, *op. cit.*, p. 56.

128. Z. Eroshok, 'My zhivy – my ne pogibli v ocherdyakh' (We are alive – we have not perished in queues), *Komsomol'skaya Pravda*, 27 August 1991, p. 2.

129. Gambrell, *op. cit.*, p. 57.

130. *Ibid.*

131. *Ibid.*

132. Alexei Barabashev, 'In the Human Chain at the White House', *Woodrow Wilson Center Report*, vol. 3, no. 3, November 1991, p. 1.

133. Abakumov, Gabrichkin and Nadein, *op. cit.*

134. *Ibid.*

135. Gambrell, *op. cit.*, p. 57.

136. Kupriyanov, *op. cit.*

137. Abakumov, Gavrichkin and Nadein, *op. cit.*

138. Zhuravlev *et al.*, *op. cit.*, p. 115, Barabashev, *op. cit.*, p. 2.

139. Eroshok, *op. cit.*

140. *Ibid.*

141. *Ibid.*

142. INTERFAX, 12.02 (Moscow time), 21 August 1991 (FBIS, 21 August 1991, p. 69).

143. *Ibid.*

144. Radio Vilnius, 23.25 (Moscow time), 20 August 1991 (FBIS, 21 August 1991, p. 67).

145. DPA, Hamburg, 12.10 (Moscow time). 21 August 1991 (FBIS, 21 August 1991, p. 66).

146. Press Association, London, 00.10 (Moscow time), 20 August 1991 (FBIS, 21 August 1991, p. 66).

147. *Ibid.*

148. *Nezavisimaya Gazeta*, 2, September 1991, p. 14.

149. Abakumov, Gabrichkin and Nadein, *op. cit.*; Kupriyanov, *op. cit.*;

'Nochnoye ubiystvo' (Murder in the night), *Doverie* (extra edition), 22 August 1991, p. 3; Yeltsin, *Zapiski*, pp. 125–6.

150. Yeltsin, *Zapiski*, pp. 119, 111.

151. *Ibid.*, p. 120.

152. Korzhakov, *op. cit.*, p. 93; Yeltsin, *Zapiski*, p. 119.

153. Korzhakov, *op. cit.*, p. 94. See also, Yeltsin, *Zapiski*, p. 120.

154. Korzhakov, *op. cit.*, p. 95.

155. *Ibid.*, p. 81.

156. *Ibid.*, p. 113.

157. Radio Triana, 07.54 (Moscow time), 21 August 1991 (FBIS, 21 August 1991, p. 64).

158. Eroshok, *op. cit.*

159. *Ibid.*

160. *Ibid.*

161. Gambrell, *op. cit.*, p. 58.

162. *Ibid.*

163. Eroshok, *op. cit.*

164. See, for example, Nadein, *op. cit.*; and Albert Plutnik, 'Politicheskiy dnevnik. V avguste 91-go' (Political diary. In August 1991), *Izvestia*, 23 August 1991, p. 1.

165. Nadein, *op. cit.*

166. *Ibid.*

167. Mark Teeter, 'An American's Diary', *Woodrow Wilson Center Report*, vol. 3, no. 3, November 1991, p. 3.

168. Eduard Shevardnadze, 'The Tragedy of Gorbachev', *Newsweek*, 9 September 1991, p. 31.

169. 'Ex-Aide Blames Gorbachev for "Team of Traitors"', *New York Times*, 22 August 1991, p. A13.

170. Russian Television Channel (Rossia), 23 August 1991 (FBIS, 26 August 1991, p. 61).

171. Plutnik, 'Politicheskiy dnevnik'.

172. Nadein, *op. cit.*

173. Tatyana Tolstaya, 'When Putsch Comes to Shove', *New Republic*, 16 and 23 September 1991, p. 22.

174. Gambrell, *op. cit.*, p. 59.

175. *Ibid.*

176. Mikhail Gorbachev, press conference, 22 August 1991, First Channel/ORT (Ostankino) (FBIS, 23 August 1991, pp. 23, 28).

177. Mikhail Gorbachev, statement, 24 August 1991. First Channel/ORT (Ostankino) (FBIS, 26 August 1991, p. 15); and Mikhail Gorbachev, decree by the President of the Soviet Union, 24 August 1991 (FBIS, 26 August 1991, p. 15).

178. V. Raskin, 'Moskovskie ulitsy, 19 avgusta' (Moscow streets, 19 August), *Sel'skaya Zhizn'*, 20 August 1991.

179. 'Zayavlenie Sekretariata TsK Kompartii RSFSR' (Statement by the Secretariat of the Central Committee of the Communist Party of the RSFSR), *Sovetskaya Rossia*, 22 August 1991, p. 1.

180. *Ibid.*

181. Tolstaya, *op. cit.*, p. 18.

182. Lebed, *op. cit.*, pp. 316–17; Natalie Gross, 'The Military in Coup and Revolution', *Jane's Intelligence Review*, vol. 3, no. 10, October 1991, pp. 9–11.

183. Carey Schofield, 'Anti-Coup Leaders – The Men of the Future?', *Jane's Intelligence Review*, vol. 3, no. 10, October 1991, pp. 5–8. On Lebed's sojourn at the White House, see Korzhakov, *op. cit.*, pp. 87, 88, 91, 92; and Yeltsin, *Zapiski*, pp. 113–14.

184. V. Filin, 'Pochemu Kryuchkov, skazav "A", ne skazal "B"?' 'Why, having said 'A', did Kryuchkov not say 'B'?), *Komsomol'skaya Pravda*, 28 August 1991, p. 4; and Remnick, *Lenin's Tomb*, pp. 482–3.

185. Yeltsin, *Zapiski*, p. 131.

186. *Doverie* (extra edition), 21 August 1991, p. 2.

187. *Ibid.*

188. Boulton, 'Yeltsin plays on his popularity'.

189. Gambrell, *op. cit.*, p. 56.

190. David Remnick, 'Crisis Jolts Masses out of Passivity and onto Moscow Streets', *Washington Post*, 21 August 1991, p. A1.

191. Barabashev, *op. cit.*, p. 2.
192. *Ibid.*
193. Abakumov, Gavrichkin and Nadein, *op. cit.*
194. Barabashev, *op. cit.*, p. 2.
195. Remnick, 'Crisis Jolts Masses'.
196. T. Alayba, speech at a meeting in Sverdlovsk on 21 August 1991 (*Doverie*, 21 August 1991, p. 2).
197. Evgenii Anisimov, 'A View from Leningrad', *Woodrow Wilson Center Report*, vol. 3, no. 3, November 1991, p. 6.
198. Eroshok, *op. cit.*
199. *Ibid.*
200. Teeter, *op. cit.*, p. 4.
201. Gambrell, *op. cit.*, p. 56.
202. Abakumov, Gavrichkin and Nadein, *op. cit.*
203. Eroshok, *op. cit.*
204. Abakumov, Gavrichkin and Nadein, *op. cit.*
205. Eroshok, *op. cit.*
206. Barabashev, *op. cit.*, p. 2.
207. Kupriyanov, *op. cit.*
208. Korzhakov, *op. cit.*, p. 90; Gambrell, *op. cit.*, p. 57.
209. Abakumov, Gavrichkin and Nadein, *op. cit.*
210. Elliot, *op. cit.*, p. 64.
211. Gambrell, *op. cit.*, p. 56.
212. Barabashev, *op. cit.*, p. 2.
213. Boris Yeltsin, speech at a victory rally, 22 August 1991, Russian Television Channel (Rossia) (FBIS, 22 August 1991, pp. 68–70).
214. 'Boris the Humble?', *Washington Post*, 26 August 1991, p. A10. See also Gambrell, *op. cit.*, p. 60.
215. Yeltsin, speech at the victory rally (p. 68).
216. Gambrell, *op. cit.*, p. 58.
217. *Ibid.*
218. *Ibid.*
219. *Ibid.*, p. 60.
220. *Ibid.*
221. First Channel/ORT (Ostankino), 24 August 1991 (FBIS, 26 August 1991, p. 74).
222. Boris Yeltsin, 'Obrashchenie Prezidenta Rossia k sograzhdanam' (Address of the President of Russia to fellow citizens), *Izvestia*, 20 August 1992, pp. 1, 2.
223. Boris Yeltsin, interview with Russian Television Channel (Rossia), 25 August 1991 (FBIS-SOV-91-165, p. 73).
224. Boris Yeltsin, news conference for Russian and foreign journalists on 7 September 1991, Russian Television Channel (Rossia), 7 September 1991 (FBIS-SOV-91-174, 9 September 1991, p. 66). See also Boris Yeltsin, speech at the CSCE Conference on the Human Dimension on 11 September 1991, Radio Rossii, 11 September 1991 (FBIS-SOV-91-177, 12 September 1991, p. 2).
225. Yeltsin, speech at the CSCE Conference, p. 3.
226. Yeltsin, press conference, 7 September 1991, p. 66.
227. *Ibid.*, p. 69.
228. Yeltsin, speech at the CSCE Conference, p. 2.
229. *Ibid.*
230. *Ibid.*, p. 1.
231. Yeltsin, press conference, 7 September 1991, p. 66.
232. Yeltsin, speech at the CSCE conference, pp. 1, 2.
233. *Ibid.*, p. 1.
234. *Ibid.*
235. *Ibid.*, p. 2.
236. Yeltsin, press conference, 7 September 1991, p. 68.
237. A. Ivanov, 'Lubyanka i strana menyayut oblik' (Lyubyanka and the country are changing their appearance), *Vechernyaya Moskva*, 23 August 1991, p. 1.
238. Dmitriy Barinov, 'Posledniy den' Feliksa' (Feliks's last day), *Kuranty*, 24 August 1991, p. 3.
239. *Ibid.*
240. Photographs in *Kuranty*, 24 August 1991, p. 3.
241. Ivanov, 'Lubyanka'.
242. Yu. Kazarin, 'KGB budet zhit'?' (Will the KGB live?), *Vechernyaya Moskva*, 30 August 1991, p. 1.

243. 'Vandalizm – proyavlenie rabstva' (Vandalism – a manifestation of slavery), *Kuranty*, 27 August 1991, p. 1.

244. Eduard Polyanovskiy, 'Narod sam podnyal svoy flag' (People themselves raised their flag), *Izvestia*, 20 August 1992, p. 1.

245. 'Vandalizm'.

246. Yeltsin, interview, 25 August 1991, p. 73.

247. 'Dorogie Moskvichi!' (Dear Muscovites!), appeal by the Moscow City Council and the Mayor of Moscow, *Vechernyaya Moskva*, 23 August 1991, p. 1.

248. *Ibid.*

249. 'Rano vpadat' v eyphoriyu' (Too early to become euphoric), *Kuranty*, 24 August 1991, p. 2.

250. Sergey Stankevich, 'Ostanovit' inertsiyu revolyutsionnuyu' (To stop revolutionary inertia), *Vechernyaya Moskva*, 26 August 1991, p. 2.

251. Yeltsin, 'Obrashchenie Prezidenta Rossia k sograzhdanam', p. 2.

252. *Ibid.*

253. *Ibid.*

254. Yeltsin, speech at the CSCE conference, p. 2.

255. *Ibid.*

256. Boris Yeltsin, 'Ukaz Prezidenta Rossiyskoy Sovetskoy Federativnoy Sotsialisticheskoy Respubliki No. 79, 23 avgusta, 1991 goda "O priostanovlenii deyatel'nosti Kommunisticheskoy partii RSFSR"' (Decree of the President of the Russian Soviet Federated Socialist Republic no. 79, 23 August 1991, 'On suspension of the activity of the Communist Party of the RSFSR'), copy in the author's archive.

257. *Ibid.*

258. Mikhail Gorbachev, 'Zayavlenie M. S. Gorbacheva' (A statement by M. S. Gorbachev), *Vechernyaya Moskva*, 26 August 1991, p. 1.

259. Mikhail Gorbachev, 'Ukaz Prezidenta Soyuza Sovetskikh Sotsialisticheskikh Respublik "Ob imuschestve Kommunisticheskoy Partii Sovetskogo Soyuza"' (Decree of the President of the Union of Soviet Socialist Republics 'On the property of the Communist Party of the Soviet Union'), *Vechernyaya Moskva*, 26 August 1991, p. 1.

260. See, for instance, B. Yakovlev, 'Pamyatniki i my' (Monuments and us), *Vechernyaya Moskva*, 26 August 1991, p. 3.

261. Vera Tolz, 'What Remains of the CPSU', *OMRI System Search*, 2 October 1991 (http://solar.rtd.utk.edu, 8/28/97), and Vera Tolz, 'Communists Oppose Yeltsin's Decree', *OMRI System Search*, 8 November 1991 (http://solar.rtd.utk.edu, 8/28/97).

262. Boris Yeltsin, decree 'On the Activities of the CPSU and the Communist Party of the Russian Soviet Federated Socialist Republic', TASS, 6 November 1991 (FBIS-SOV-91-216, 7 November 1991, p. 52).

263. *Ibid.*

264. Tolz, 'Communists Oppose Yeltsin's Decree'.

265. Vera Tolz, 'Another Communist Party Created in RSFSR', *OMRI System Search*, 26 November 1991 (http://solar.rtd.utk.edu, 8/28/97).

266. Vera Tolz, 'Union of Communists Holds Press Conference', *OMRI System Search*, 27 November 1991 (http://solar.rtd.utk.edu., 8/28/97).

267. *Ibid.*

268. Yeltsin, press conference, 7 September 1991, p. 71.

269. Sergey Stepashin, 'Chistka v KGB SSSR' (Purge in the KGB of the USSR), *Kuranty*, 30 August 1991, p. 4.

270. Kazarin, *op. cit.*

271. *Ibid.*

272. Stepashin, *op. cit.*

273. Boris Yeltsin, 'Ukaz Prezidenta Rossiyskoy Sovetskoy Federativnoy Sotsialisticheskoy Respubliki 22 avgusta, 1991 goda "O deyatel'nosti TASS, Informatsionnogo agenstva

'Novosti', i ryada gazet po dezinformatsii naseleniya i mirovoy obshchestvennosti o sobytiyakh v strane"' (Decree of the President of the Russian Soviet Federated Socialist Republic 'Regarding actions of TASS, the Novosti information agency and a number of newspapers directed at disinforming the populace and world public about the events in the country', 22 August 1991), copy in the author's archive.

274. 'Gazeta Pravda' (The newspaper *Pravda*), *Vechernyaya Moskva*, 30 August 1991, p. 1.

275. 'I viydut, veroyatno, kak vsegda' (And will be published, most likely, as always), *Komsomol'skaya Pravda*, 28 August 1991, p. 1; and 'Opyat' "Pravda"?' (Again *Pravda?*), *Kuranty*, 30 August 1991, p. 1.

276. Vera Tolz, 'Yeltsin Cancels his Own Decrees', *RFE/FL Daily Report*, 11 September 1991, p. 3.

277. Vera Tolz, 'Most Officials Did Not Support Yeltsin during Coup', *OMRI System Search*, 24 October 1991 (http://solar.rtd.utk.edu., 8/28/97).

278. Boris Yeltsin, 'Ukaz Prezidenta Rossiyskoy Sovetskoy Federativnoy Sotsialisticheskoy Respubliki, No. 70, 21 avgusta, 1991 "Ob otstranenii ot ispoleneniya obyazannostey predsedateley ispolnitel'nykh komitetov kraevogo and ryada oblastnykh Sovetov narodnykh deputatov RSFSR"' (On removal from office of Chairmen of the executive committees of a *krai* Soviet and a number of regional Soviets of People's Deputies), Decree No. 70, 21 August 1991; and Boris Yeltsin, 'Ob otstranenii ot ispoleneniya obyazannostey predsedateley ispolkomov oblastnykh Sovetov narodnykh deputatov' (On removal from office of Chairmen of the executive committees of regional Soviets of People's Deputies', Decree No. 78, 23 August 1991). Copies in

the author's archive. See also *Rossiyskaya Gazeta*, 23 August 1991, p. 3.

279. Boris Yeltsin, 'Zayavlenie' (Statement), 20 August 1991, copy in the author's archive.

280. 'Obrashchenie Mossoveta' (The appeal of Mossovet), *Vechernyaya Moskva*, 30 August 1991, p. 1, copy in the author's archive.

281. See, for example, Leonid Batkin, 'Oshibka El'tsina?' (Yeltsin's mistake?), *Kuranty*, 30 August 1991, p. 4.

282. Yeltsin, *Zapiski*, p. 165.

283. Boris Yeltsin, 'Obrashchenie v Verkhovniy Sovet RSFSR v svyazi s prinyatiem Zakona RSFSR "O vyborakh glavy administratsii"' (Address to the Supreme Soviet of the Russian Soviet Federated Socialist Republic regarding the adoption of the RSFSR law 'On the Election of the Head of Administration'), *Rossiyskaya Gazeta*, 19 October 1991, p. 1.

284. *Ibid.*

285. Boris Yeltsin, report on the draft Constitution delivered to the Congress of People's Deputies of the RSFSR on 2 November 1991, TASS (FBIS-SOV-91-213, 4 November 1991, p. 57).

286. *Ibid.*

287. *Ibid.*

288. *Ibid.*

289. *Ibid.*

290. *Ibid.*

291. *Ibid.*, p. 58.

292. *Ibid.*, p. 57.

293. *Ibid.*, pp. 57, 58.

294. *Ibid.*, p. 58.

295. *Ibid.*

296. *Ibid.*, p. 57.

297. *Ibid.*

298. *Ibid.*, p. 58.

299. *Ibid.*

300. *Ibid.*, p. 57.

301. *Ibid.*

302. 'Postanovlenie s'ezda narodnykh deputatov Rossiyskoy Sovetskoy Federativnoy Sotsialisticheskoy Respubliki o proekte Konstitutsii

Rossiyskoy Federatsii i dal'neishey rabote Konstitutsionnoy komissii' (Resolution of the Congress of People's Deputies of the Russian Soviet Federated Socialist Republic regarding the draft Constitution of the Russian Federation and further work of the Constitutional Commission), *Rossiyskaya Gazeta*, 20 November 1991, p. 2.

303. Batkin, *op. cit.*

304. Celestine Bohlen, 'Yeltsin Supports Moves for Continuing Talks on Revising Treaty', *New York Times*, 28 August 1991, p. 1.

305. Yeltsin, *Zapiski*, p. 143.

306. Ann Sheehy, 'Commonwealth Emerges from a Disintegrating USSR', *RFE/RL Research Report*, 3 January 1992, p. 7.

307. *Ibid.*

308. *RFE/RL Daily Report*, 25 November 1991, p. 1.

309. Boris Yeltsin, decree 'On the recognition of Estonia's independence, 24 August 1991, Radio Rossii (FBIS-SOV-91-165, 26 August 1991, pp. 85–6); and Boris Yeltsin, decree on the recognition of Latvia's independence, 24 August 1991, TASS (FBIS-SOV-91-165, 26 August 1991, p. 86).

310. Paul Goble, 'A Decree that Changed the World', *RFE/RL Daily*, 22 August 1997.

311. *Ibid.*

312. Boris Yeltsin, 'Bystrye reformy – edinstvenniy shans Rossii' (Rapid reform is Russia's only chance), interview with *Izvestia* on 25 November 1991; *Izvestia*, 29 November 1991, p. 3.

313. Ann Sheehy, 'Union Treaty: Appeal to Ukraine, Armenia, Georgia, Moldavia', *OMRI System Search*, 14 October 1991 (http://solar.rtd.utk.edu, 8/28/97).

314. Bohdan Nahaylo, 'Kravchuk Says Definitely No to Joining New Union', *OMRI System Search*, 25 November 1991 (http://solar.rtd.utk.edu, 8/28/97). See also,

315. Boris Yeltsin, press conference, on 30 November 1991 in Moscow, TASS (FBIS-SOV-91-231, 2 December 1991, p. 42).

316. Bohdan Nahaylo, 'Gorbachev Cannot Imagine New "Union" without Ukraine', *OMRI System Search*, 14 October 1991 (http://solar.rtd.utk.edu, 8/28/97).

317. *Ibid.*

318. Alexander Rahr, 'Solzhenitsyn Welcomes Disintegration of USSR', *OMRI System Search*, 9 October 1991 (http://solar.rtd.utk.edu, 8/28/91).

319. Ann Sheehy, 'Gorbachev Pleads for Union Treaty to Be Signed', *OMRI System Search*, 4 December 1991 (http://solar.rtd.utk.edu., 8/28/97).

320. 'O priznanii Rossiey nezavisimosti Ukrainy. Zayavlenie Borisa El'tsina' (On the recognition by Russia of the independence of Ukraine. A statement by Boris Yeltsin), *Izvestia*, 4 December 1991. See also Boris Yeltsin, 'Statement on the recognition of the independence of Ukraine', TASS, 3 December 1991 (FBIS-SOV-91-223, 4 December 1991, p. 57).

321. *Ibid.*

322. *Ibid.*

323. Boris Yeltsin, Gennadiy Burbulis, Stanislav Shushkevich, Vyacheslav Kebich, Leonid Kravchuk and Vitold Fokin, 'Soglashenie o sozdanii Sodruzhestva Nezavisimykh Gosudarstv' (Agreement on the creation of the Commonwealth of Independent States), *Rossiyskaya Gazeta*, 10 December 1991, p. 1.

324. *Ibid.*

325. See Chapter 9, p. 414.

326. Boris Yeltsin, speech to the Supreme Soviet of the Russian Federation, 12 December 1991, Russian Television Channel (Rossia) (FBIS-SOV-91-239, 12 December 1991, p. 39).

327. *Ibid.*

328. *Ibid.*

329. *Ibid.*

330. Vyacheslav Kebich, Gennadiy Burbulis and Vitold Fokin, 'Zayavlenie pravitel'stv Respubliki Belarus, Rossiyskoy Federatsii i Ukrainy o koordinatsii ekonomicheskoy politiki' (Statement of the governments of the Republic of Belarus, the Russian Federation and Ukraine on the co-ordination of economic policy), *Rossiyskaya Gazeta*, 10 December 1991, p. 1.

331. Yeltsin *et al.*, 'Soglashenie o sozdanii'. See also Boris Yeltsin, Stanislav Shushkevich, and Leonid Kravchuk, 'Zyavlenie glav gosudrastv Respubliki Belarus, RSFSR, Ukrainy' (Statement by the heads of state of the Republic of Belarus, the RSFSR, Ukraine), *Rossiyskaya Gazeta*, 10 December 1991, p. 1.

332. *Ibid.*

333. Yeltsin, speech to the Supreme Soviet, 12 December 1991.

334. Boris Yeltsin, speech to the Supreme Soviet of the Russian Federation, 25 December 1991, Radio Rossii (FBIS-SOV-91-248, 26 December 1991, p. 38).

335. *Ibid.*

336. Boris Yeltsin, 'Nam ochen' trudno, no my vystoim' (It is very difficult for us, but we will stand our ground), interview with *Trud*, 14 December 1991, p. 1; Yeltsin, speech to the Supreme Soviet, 12 December 1991, p. 39, 40; and his speech to the Supreme Soviet, 25 December 1991, pp. 38, 39.

337. Boris Yeltsin, address to the nation, 29 December 1991, Moscow Central Television Vostok Programme and Orbita Networks (FBIS-SOV-91-250, 30 December 1991, p. 27).

338. *Facts on File*, vol. 51, no. 2664, 12 December 1991, p. 929.

339. Zhuravlev *et al.*, *op. cit.*, p. 137; and Sheehy, 'Commonwealth Emerges'.

340. XINHUA, 13 December 1991 (FBIS-CHI-91-241, 16 December 1991, p. 5).

341. Yeltsin, *Zapiski*, p. 157.

342. *Ibid.*, p. 150.

343. *Ibid.*, p. 151.

344. *Ibid.*, p. 150.

345. *Ibid.*, p. 152.

346. *Ibid.*

347. *Ibid.*, p 151.

348. Yeltsin, *Zapiski*, p. 159; and Korzhakov, *op. cit.*, p. 123.

349. Yeltsin, *Zapiski*, p. 159.

350. Korzhakov, *op. cit.*, p. 129.

351. Yeltsin, speech to the Supreme Soviet, 25 December 1991, p. 39.

352. Boris Yeltsin, interview with CNN, 25 December 1991, *New York Times*, 26 December 1991, p. A3.

353. Gorbachev, *Memoirs*, pp. 672, 673.

354. Mikhail Gorbachev, 'Gorbachev ukhodit i ostayotsya' (Gorbachev leaves and stays), interview with *Komsomol'skaya Pravda*, 24 December 1991, p. 2.

355. Boris Yeltsin, 'We Are Taking Over', interview with *Newsweek*, 30 December 1991, p. 21.

356. 'Ekonomika SSSR v yanvare–sentyabre 1991 goda' (The USSR economy in January–September 1991), *Ekonomika i Zhizn'*, 43, (October) 1991, p. 7.

357. *Ibid.*

358. *Ibid.*, p. 8.

359. *Ibid.*, p. 7.

360. Margaret Shapiro, 'Soviets Double Aid Request', *Washington Post*, 20 September 1991, p. A16.

361. TASS, 12 December 1991 (FBIS-SOV-91-239, 12 December 1991, p. 24).

362. Åslund, *op. cit.*, pp. 43, 48, 49;

and Michael Ellman, 'Shock Therapy in Russia: Failure or Partial Success?', *RFE/RL Research Report*, 28 August 1992, p. 49.

363. Ellman, *op. cit.*, p. 49; see also Egor Gaidar, *Dni porazheniy i pobed* (The days of defeats and victories), Moscow: Vargius, 1997, p. 135.

364. Åslund, *op. cit.*, p. 50.

365. A. Sizov, 'Sverim tsyfry' (Let's compare the figures), *Kommunist*, 15, (October) 1989, p. 63.

366. V. Konovalov, 'Neob'yavlennaya zabastovka krest'yan vsekh respublic' (The announced strike of the peasants of all the Republics), *Izvestia*, 16 November 1991, p. 2.

367. Gaidar, *Dni porazheniy*, p. 82.

368. Arkadiy Vol'skiy, interview with *Der Spiegel* magazine, ADN, Berlin, 21 October 1991 (FBIS-SOV-91-204, 22 October 1991, p. 36).

369. Konovalov, *op. cit.*

370. 'A tovarov vsyo men'she. Sotsial'no-ekonimicheskoye polozhenie RSFSR v yanvare–sentyabre 1991 g.' (But there are increasingly fewer goods. RSFSR's socioeconomic situation in January–September 1991), *Rossiyskaya Gazeta*, 31 October 1991, p. 1.

371. INTERFAX, 22 November 1991 (FBIS-SOV-91-229, 27 November 1991, p. 28).

372. *Ibid.*

373. Gaidar, *Dni porazheniy*, p. 134.

374. Ellman, *op. cit.*, p. 49.

375. Keith Bradsher, 'Gorbachev Asks a Huge Increase in Food Relief', *Washington Post*, 13 September 1991, pp. A1, A12.

376. Shapiro, 'Soviets Double Aid Request'.

377. Gaidar, *Dni porazheniy*, p. 133.

378. *Ibid.*

379. *Ibid.*

380. *Ibid.*

381. *Ibid.*, p. 134.

382. Mark Rhodes, 'Food Supply in the USSR', *Report on the USSR*, 11 October 1991, p. 11.

383. O. Shapovalov, 'Narodnoye sredstvo ot goloda' (A popular way to fight famine), *Komsomol'skaya Pravda*, 28 December 1991, p. 3.

384. 'Zapasaysya, kto mozhet' (Stock up, if you can), *Trud*, 5 October 1991, p. 1.

385. *Ibid.*

386. Ludmila Butuzova, 'Zhizn' zamechatel'nykh ocheredey' (The life of remarkable queues), *Moskovskie Novosti*, 30 August–6 September 1998, p. 18.

387. *Ibid.*

388. *Vesti*, Russian Television Channel (Rossia), 28 November 1991 (FBIS-SOV-91-233, 4 December 1991, p. 31).

389. Rhodes, 'Food Supply'.

390. Gaidar, *Dni porazheniy*, p. 153.

391. Boris Yeltsin, interview with First Channel/ORT (Ostankino), 20 November 1991 (FBIS-SOV-91-225, 21 November 1991, p. 56).

392. *Ibid.*

393. Yeltsin, *Zapiski*, p. 163.

394. *Ibid.*, p. 245, and Åslund, *op. cit.*, p. 17.

395. Gaidar, *Dni porazheniy*, p. 87; Yeltsin, *Zapiski*, p. 245.

396. Åslund, *op. cit.*, p. 17.

397. Yeltsin, *Zapiski*, p. 245.

398. See, for instance, Egor Gaidar, 'V nachale novoy fazy' (At the beginning of a new phase), *Kommunist*, 2, (January) 1991, pp. 8–19.

399. Andrey Kolesnikov, 'Dzhoker vlasti' (The joker in power), *Novoye Vremya*, 48, 1996, p. 9.

400. *Ibid.*

401. *Ibid.*, pp. 43–4.

402. Yeltsin, *Zapiski*, p. 246.

403. *Ibid.*, p. 165.

404. Vyacheslav Kostikov, *Roman s Prezidentom. Zapiski press-sekretarya* (A novel with president. Notes of a press secretary), Moscow: Vargius, 1997, p. 157, and Gaidar, *Dni porazheniy*, p. 106.

405. Kostikov, 'Roman . . .', p. 157.

406. Gaidar, *Dni porazheniy*, p. 106.

407. Interview with Egor Gaidar.

408. *Ibid.*

409. Yeltsin, *Zapiski*, p. 396.

410. *Ibid.*, p. 164.

411. Kostikov, *op. cit.*, p. 157.

412. *Ibid.*

413. *Ibid.*

414. Yeltsin, *Zapiski*, p. 164.

415. *Ibid.*, p. 235.

416. Egor Gaidar, speech to the Supreme Soviet of the Russian Federation, 28 December 1991, Russian Television Channel (Rossia) (FBIS-SOV-91-250, 30 December 1991, p. 39).

417. *Ibid.*, and Gaidar, *Dni porazheniy*, p. 109.

418. Zhuravlev *et al.*, *op. cit.*, p. 133. See also Keith Bush, 'El'tsin Economic Reform Program', *Report on the USSR*, 15 November 1991, p. 2.

419. Zhuravlev *et al.*, *op. cit.*, p. 133.

420. Gaidar, *Dni porazheniy*, p. 93.

421. *Ibid.*, p. 83.

422. *Ibid.*

423. Gaidar, speech to the Supreme Soviet, 28 December 1991, p. 40.

424. *Ibid.*

425. Åslund, *op. cit.*, p. 187.

426. *Ibid.*

427. *Ibid.*, pp. 235, 236.

428. *Ibid.*, p. 236.

429. Yeltsin, *Zapiski*, p. 157.

430. *Ibid.*, pp. 157, 158.

431. *Ibid.*, p. 158.

432. *Ibid.*

433. Boris Yeltsin, interview with Russian Television Channel (Rossia), 17 October 1991 (FBIS-SOV-91-202, 18 October 1991, p. 58).

434. Interview with Egor Gaidar.

435. Yeltsin, address to the nation, 29 December 1991, p. 29.

436. Valeriy Vyzhutovich, 'My boyalis' shokovoy terapii. I prishli k shokovoy khirurgii' (We were afraid of shock therapy. And now have come to shock surgery), *Izvestia*, 29 October 1991, p. 1.

437. *Ibid.*

438. Boris Yeltsin, speech to the Congress of People's Deputies of the Russian Federation, 28 October 1991, *Sovetskaya Rossia*, 29 October 1991, p. 2.

439. *Ibid.*

440. *Ibid.*

441. *Ibid.*, pp. 2, 3.

442. *Ibid.*, p. 2.

443. *Ibid.*

444. *Ibid.*

445. *Ibid.*

446. *Ibid.*

447. *Ibid.*

448. *Ibid.*

449. Vyzhutovich, 'My boyalis' shokovoy terapii'.

450. *Ibid.*

451. Alexander Rahr, 'Yeltsin Gets Support from All Factions', *RFE/RL Daily Report*, 29 October 1991, p. 1.

452. *Ibid.*

453. Alexander Rahr, 'Khazbulatov Will Support Yeltsin', *OMRI System Search*, 31 October 1991 (http://solar.rtd.utk.edu, 8/28/97).

454. Radio Moscow World Service, 1 November 1991 (FBIS-SOV-91-212, 1 November 1991, p. 42).

455. *Ibid.*

456. See, for instance, Yeltsin, interview with First Channel/ORT (Ostankino), 20 November 1991.

457. Yeltsin, 'Bystrye reformy'.

458. *Ibid.*

459. Pavel Bunich as quoted in Serge Schmemann, 'Russia Acts: Going It Alone', *New York Times*, 25 November 1991, p. A13.

460. Yeltsin, 'Nam ochen' trudno'.

461. *Ibid.*

462. John Lloyd, 'Red Square shows scorn for Gorbachev "the westerner"', *Financial Times*, 8 November 1991, p. 1.

463. *Ibid.*

464. Yeltsin, interview with CNN, 25 December 1991.

465. Yeltsin, interview with First Channel/ORT (Ostankino), 17 October 1991.

466. Yeltsin, *Zapiski*, p. 239.
467. Yeltsin, address to the nation, 29 December 1991, p. 27.
468. *Ibid.*, p. 28.
469. *Ibid.*, p. 27.
470. *Ibid.*
471. *Ibid.*
472. *Ibid.*, p. 28.
473. *Ibid.*
474. *Ibid.*
475. *Ibid.*

Chapter 11: The President vs. the Soviet

1. Yeltsin, *Zapiski*, p. 165.
2. Douglas Stanglin, 'In Russia, Economic Reform Collides with Democracy', *U.S. News and World Report*, 27 January 1992, p. 49; John Lloyd, 'Power Battle "May Destroy Russian Reform Plans"', *Financial Times*, 16 January 1992, p. 1; and Alexander Rahr, 'The Rise and Fall of Ruslan Khazbulatov', *RFE/RL Research Report*, 11 June 1993, p. 13.
3. Gaidar, *Dni porazheniy*, pp. 167–8.
4. Maxim Boycko, Andrei Shleifer and Robert Vishny, *Privatizing Russia*, Cambridge, MA: The MIT Press, 1995, pp. 78–9.
5. Åslund, *op. cit.*, p. 192.
6. *Ibid.*, p. 184, Table 6-1.
7. *Ibid.*, p. 193.
8. *Ibid.*, p. 192.
9. Egor Gaidar, *Dni porazheniy*, p. 171; Rahr, 'Rise and Fall'.
10. Rahr, 'Rise and Fall'.
11. Gaidar, *Dni porazheniy*, p. 171.
12. *Ibid.*, p. 175.
13. Alexander Rahr, 'The Roots of the Power Struggle', *RFE/RL Research Report*, 14 May 1993, p. 10.
14. As quoted in Alexander Rahr, 'Political Struggle on the Eve of the Congress', *RFE/RL Daily Report*, 12 November 1992, p. 1.
15. As quoted in Suzanne Crow, 'Yeltsin: Russia Will Not Retreat from Reform', *RFE/RL Daily Report*, 12 November 1992, p. 1.
16. Alexander Rahr, 'Power Struggle Continues between Yeltsin and Parliament', *RFE/RL Daily Report*, 12 November 1992, p. 1, and Rahr, 'Political Struggle'.
17. Rahr, 'Political Struggle on the Eve ...'
18. Julia Wishnevsky, 'The Constitutional Court', *RFE/RL Report*, 14 May 1993, p. 14.
19. Boris Yeltsin, opening speech at the Seventh Congress of People's Deputies, 1 December 1992, Russian Television Channel (Russia) (FBIS-SOV-92-232-S, p. 6).
20. *Ibid.*, p. 7.
21. *Ibid.*, p. 6.
22. *Ibid.*, p. 7.
23. *Ibid.*, p. 8.
24. *Ibid.*, p. 11.
25. *Ibid.*, p. 4.
26. *Ibid.*, p. 9.
27. *Ibid.*, p. 8.
28. *Ibid.*, p. 9.
29. *Ibid.*
30. *Ibid.*, p. 10.
31. *Ibid.*, p. 9.
32. *Ibid.*, p. 11.
33. *Ibid.*
34. *Ibid.*, p. 4.
35. *Ibid.*
36. *Ibid.*, p. 10.
37. *Ibid.*
38. *Ibid.*
39. Ruslan Khazbulatov, speech at the Seventh Congress of People's Deputies, 1 December 1992, Russian Television Channel (Russia) (FBIS-SOV-92-232-S, pp. 12–15).
40. Julia Wishnevsky, 'Deputies Attack Economic Reform', *RFE/RL Daily Report*, 4 December 1992, p. 2.
41. Alexander Rahr, 'Russian Congress Criticizes Cabinet, Seeks New Powers', *RFE/RL Daily Report*, 4 December 1994.
42. Boris Yeltsin, speech at the Seventh Congress of People's Deputies, 10 December 1992, *Izvestia*, 10 December 1992, p. 1.
43. *Ibid.*

44. *Ibid.*
45. *Ibid.*
46. *Ibid.*
47. As quoted in Serge Schmemann, 'Yeltsin Bargains with Congress, Reducing Pressure at the Meeting', *New York Times*, 13 December 1992, p. A1.
48. Kostikov, *op. cit.*, p. 138.
49. *Ibid.*, pp. 157–8.
50. Margaret Shapiro, 'Yeltsin Forced by Russian Parliament to Abandon Reformist Prime Minister', *Washington Post*, 15 December 1992, p. A18.
51. *Ibid.*
52. *Ibid.*
53. Gaidar, *Dni porazheniy*, p. 238; Yeltsin, *Zapiski*, p. 251.
54. Zhuravlev *et al.*, *op. cit.*, p. 177.
55. Ruslan Khazbulatov, 'Slovo o sovetakh' (A word about the Soviets), *Pravda*, 4 March 1993, p. 1.
56. Rahr, 'Roots of the Power Struggle', p. 12.
57. Julia Wishnevsky, 'Constitutional Crisis Deepens after Russian Congress', *RFE/RL Research Report*, 26 March 1993, p. 1.
58. Erik Whitlock, 'The Russian Government, the Central Bank, and the Resolution on Constitutional Reform', *RFE/RL Research Report*, 26 March 1993, p. 3.
59. Wendy Slater, 'No Victors in the Russian Referendum', *RFE/RL Research Report*, 21 May 1993, p. 11.
60. Wishnevsky, 'Constitutional Crisis', p. 4.
61. Boris Yeltsin, address on First Channel/ORT (Ostankino), 20 March 1993 (FBIS-SOV-93-053, 22 March 1993, p. 13).
62. *Ibid.* (p. 15).
63. *Ibid.* (p. 14).
64. Kostikov, *op. cit.*, p. 172.
65. Boris Yeltsin, speech at the Ninth Congress of People's Deputies of Russia on 27 March 1993, *Izvestia*, 27 March 1993, p. 1.
66. *Ibid.*
67. Korzhakov, *op. cit.*, p. 203.
68. Egor Gaidar, 'After Yeltsin's Victory, What Is Next for Reform?', speech at the Heritage Foundation on 23 June 1993, *The Heritage Lectures*, no. 453, p. 1.
69. *Ibid.*
70. *Ibid.*
71. Kostikov, *op. cit.*, p. 177.
72. *Ibid.*, p. 178.
73. Margaret Shapiro, 'Moscow Has Biggest Demonstrations since '91 Coup Attempt', *Washington Post*, 29 March 1993, p. A14.
74. *Ibid.*
75. *Ibid.*
76. *Ibid.*
77. *Ibid.*
78. Serge Schmemann, 'Russians Fill Streets, Not Barricades', *New York Times*, 29 March 1993, p. A6.
79. *Ibid.*
80. Rahr, 'Rise and Fall', p. 15.
81. Dmitriy Volkogonov, 'Nel'zya strane vtoroy raz proigrat' bol'shevikam' (The country must not lose to the Bolsheviks again), *Izvestia*, 24 April 1993, p. 8.
82. *Ibid.*
83. *Ibid.*
84. Yuriy Karyakin, 'Ne tot nynche moment, choby bezhat' ot politiki' (This is not the time to run away from politics), *Izvestia*, 24 April 1993, p. 8.
85. 'Osnovnye printsipy novoy Konstitutsii Rossii' (The main principles of a new constitution of Russia), *Izvestia*, 24 April 1993, p. 5.
86. *Ibid.*
87. *Ibid.*
88. *Ibid.*
89. Kostikov, *op. cit.*, p. 180.
90. Gaidar, *Dni porazheniy*, p. 266.
91. *Ibid.*, p. 267.
92. Kostikov, *op. cit.*, p. 168.
93. *Ibid.*, p. 180.
94. *Ibid.*
95. Interview with Aleksandr Urmanov.

96. Interview with Galina Starovoytova.

97. *Ibid.*, p. 182.

98. Evgeniy Krasnikov, 'Konstitutsionnoe Soveshchanie: mnogo zvannykh, no malo izbrannykh' (The Constitutional Assembly: many are called but few are chosen), *Nezavisimaya Gazeta*, 25 May 1993, p. 1; Wendy Slater, 'Yeltsin Expands Constitutional Assembly', *RFE/RL Daily Report*, 2 June 1993, p. 1; and Vera Tolz, 'Drafting the New Russian Constitution', *RFE/RL Research Report*, 16 July 1993, p. 8.

99. Wendy Slater, 'Khazbulatov Addresses Deputies' Conference', *RFE/RL Daily Report*, 2 June 1993, p. 1.

100. *Ibid.*

101. Wendy Slater, 'Rutskoy Calls for Government to Be Disbanded', *RFE/ RL Daily Report*, 2 June 1993, p. 1.

102. Wendy Slater, 'NSF Warns of Dictatorship', *RFE/RL Daily Report*, 7 June 1993, p. 1.

103. Wendy Slater, 'Yeltsin Opens Constitutional Assembly', *RFE/RL Daily Report*, 7 June 1993, p. 1.

104. Tolz, 'Drafting', p. 9.

105. *Ibid.*

106. *Ibid.*

107. *Ibid.*, p. 9; and Wendy Slater, 'Khazbulatov Walks Out of Assembly', *RFE/RL Daily Report*, 7 June 1993, p. 1.

108. Tolz, 'Drafting', p. 9.

109. *Ibid.*, pp. 8, 9.

110. *Ibid.*, p. 10.

111. Vera Tolz, 'Assembly Adopts Declaration on the Draft Constitution', *RFE/RL Daily Report*, 17 July 1993, p. 1.

112. *Ibid.*; and Tolz, 'Drafting', p. 10.

113. Tolz, 'Drafting', p. 7.

114. *Ibid.*, p. 6.

115. *Ibid.*, p. 1.

116. 'Visions for Russia', *Washington Post*, 5 June 1993, p. A15.

117. Margaret Shapiro, 'Drafting Constitution in the Kremlin', *Washington Post*, 5 June 1993, p. A15.

118. Dominic Gualtieri, 'Russian Parliament Renews Power Struggle with Yeltsin', *RFE/RL Research Report*, 13 August 1993, p. 31.

119. Åslund, *op. cit.*, p. 198.

120. Dominic Gualtieri, 'Russia's New "War of Laws"', *RFE/RL Research Report*, 3 September 1993, p. 12.

121. *Ibid.*

122. Sergey Chugaev, 'R. Khazbulatov prizyvaet vozrodit' Soyuz, A. Rutskoy preduprezhdayet o podgotovke prezidentom gosudarstvennogo perevorota, V. Sokolov predlagaet sozvat' vneocherdnoy s'ezd' (R. Khazbulatov calls for revival of the [Soviet] Union, A. Rutskoy warns of President's preparation for a coup, V. Sokolov proposes convening an extraordinary Congress), *Izvestia*, 18 September 1993, p. 2.

123. *Ibid.*

124. *Ibid.*

125. Gualtieri, 'Russian Parliament', p. 30.

126. *Ibid.*

127. *Ibid.*

128. Gualtieri, 'Russia's New "War of Laws"', pp. 14, 15.

129. *Ibid.*, p. 13.

130. *Ibid.*, p. 14.

131. Gaidar, *Dni porazheniy*, pp. 259–60.

132. Gualtieri, 'Russia's New "War of Laws"', p. 15.

133. *Ibid.*, p. 10.

134. *Ibid.*

135. The author's fieldnotes from the trip to Moscow in July 1993.

136. Gualtieri, 'Russian Parliament', p. 32.

137. The author's fieldnotes.

138. Ivan Rodin, 'Mirnoe nastuplenie El'tsina natalkivaetsya na "vooruzhennuyu oboronu" Rutskogo i Khazbulatova' (Yeltsin's peace offensive is confronted by the "armed defence" of Rutskoy and

Khazbulatov), *Nezavisimaya Gazeta*, 21 September 1993, p. 1; and Vitaliy Tretyakov, 'El'tsin–Khazbulatov: skhvatka ne na zhizn', a na smert'?' (Yeltsin–Khazbulatov: a battle to the end?), *Nezavisimaya Gazeta*, 21 September 1993, p. 1.

139. Tretyakov, 'El'tsin–Khazbulatov'; Rodin, *op. cit.*

140. *Libération* (Paris), interview with Deputy Evgeniy Koyokin, 24 September 1993, pp. 18–19 (FBIS-SOV-93-186-S, 28 September 1993, p. 19).

141. Tretyakov, 'El'tsin–Khazbulatov'.

142. Boris Yeltsin, address to the nation, First Channel/ORT (Ostankino), 21 September 1993 (FBIS, 22 September 1993, 'Presidential–Parliamentary Crisis in Russia', p. 1).

143. Yeltsin, *Zapiski*, p. 347.

144. *Ibid.*

145. *Ibid.*, p. 361.

146. *Ibid.*, pp. 355, 356.

147. Gaidar, *Dni porazheniy*, p. 277.

148. *Ibid.*

149. *Ibid.*

150. Yeltsin, address to the nation, 21 September 1991, pp. 1–2.

151. Veronika Kutsyllo, *Zapiski iz Belogo doma* (Notes from the White House), Moscow: Kommersant Publishers, 1993, p. 11; John Kohan, 'Now who rules Russia?', *Time*, 4 October 1993, p. 47.

152. Address to the nation, p. 2.

153. *Ibid.*

154. *Ibid.*, pp. 2, 3.

155. 'Iz politicheskikh shtabov' (From the political headquarters), *Pravda*, 23 September 1993, p. 2.

156. *Ibid.*

157. Aleksandr Frolov, 'Eshchyo est' vremya' (There is still time), *Sovetskaya Rossia*, 28 September 1993, p. 5.

158. 'El'tsin vne zakona!' *Den*, 38, September 1993.

159. Oleg Poptsov, *Khronika vremyon*

'tsarya Borisa'. *Rossia, Kreml'* 1991–1995 (A chronicle of the times of Tsar Boris. Russia, the Kremlin 1991–1995), Moscow: Sovershenno Sekretno Publishers, 1996, p. 318.

160. Kostikov, *op. cit*, p. 225.

161. ITAR-TASS, 23 September 1993 (FBIS, 24 September 1993, p. 42).

162. INTERFAX, 1 October 1993 (FBIS, 4 October 1993, p. 65).

163. Poptsov, *op. cit.*, p. 333.

164. *Ibid.*

165. As quoted in Russell Watson, Dorinda Elliott, Andrew Nagorski, Betsy McKay and John Barry, 'Yeltsin's Coup de Grâce', *Newsweek*, 4 October 1993, p. 72.

166. Otto Latsis, 'Ne "nulevoy", a minusovyi' (Not a 'zero' [option] but a minus [one]), *Izvestia*, 28 September 1993, p. 2.

167. *Ibid.*

168. Poptsov, *op. cit.*, p. 318.

169. Grigoriy Yavlinsky, 'Na luchshiy khod sobytiy ya ne nadeyus', nado gotovit'sya k khudshemu' (I do not hope for a better course of events – one should get ready for the worst), *Nezavisimaya Gazeta*, 23 September 1993, p. 2.

170. *Ibid.*

171. *Ibid.*

172. Radio Rossii, 30 September 1993, and ITAR-TASS, 30 September 1993 (FBIS, 1 October 1993, pp. 36, 37).

173. Interview with Nikolay Medvedev, Chief of the Department of Territorial Affairs of the Presidential Administration, ITAR-TASS, 30 September 1993 (FBIS, 1 October 1993, p. 10).

174. *OMRI Daily*, 28 September 1993.

175. *Ibid.*

176. ITAR-TASS, 21 September 1993 (FBIS, 22 September 1993, p. 14).

177. ITAR-TASS, 22 September 1993 (FBIS, 22 September 1993, p. 16).

178. ITAR-TASS, 21 September 1993 (FBIS, 22 September 1993, p. 15).

179. Interview with Colonel-General

Mikhail Kolesnikov, First Deputy Minister of Defence, Mayak Radio Network (Moscow), 2 October 1993 (FBIS, 4 October 1993, p. 35).

180. Lyubov' Tsukanova, 'Dnyom i noch'yu v "Belom dome"' (The 'White House' during the day and at night), *Rossiyskie Vesti*, 28 September 1993, p. 2.

181. Interview with the Russian Television Channel (Russia), 21 September 1993 (FBIS, 22 September 1993, p. 17).

182. ITAR-TASS, 22 September 1993 (FBIS, 22 September 1993, p. 18).

183. *Ibid.*

184. Russian Television Channel (Rossia), 23 September 1993 (FBIS, 24 September 1993, p. 31).

185. *Ibid.*

186. *OMRI Daily*, 22 September 1993.

187. *Ibid.*

188. Kutsyllo, *op. cit.*, p. 23.

189. *Ibid.*

190. Radio Rossii, 21 September 1993 (FBIS, 22 September 1993, p. 10).

191. *Ibid.* (p. 11).

192. 'Khronika sobytiy 21 sentiyabrya' (A chronicle of the events of 21 September), *Kommersant-Daily*, 22 September 1993.

193. Ravil' Zaripov, Ol'ga Gerasimenko, Irina Savvateeva and Aleksandr Orlov, 'Komu nuzhna velikaya Rossia, a komu – "Beliy dom"' (Some need great Russia, and some – the 'White House'), *Komsomol'skaya Pravda*, 23 September 1993, p. 2.

194. *Ibid.*

195. Radio Odin, 22 September 1993 (FBIS, 22 September 1993, p. 12); Kutsyllo, *op. cit.*, p. 22.

196. Radio Rossii, 23 September 1993 (FBIS, 24 September 1993, p. 12).

197. Radio Rossii, 30 September 1993 (FBIS, 30 September 1993, p. 21).

198. Radio Rossii 23 September 1993 (FBIS, 24 September 1993, pp. 9, 10); Tsukanova, *op. cit.*

199. Aleksandr Frolov, 'Drama prozreniya. S desyatogo chrezvychaynogo S'ezda narodnykh deputatov RF' (A drama of seeing the light. From the Tenth Extraordinary Congress of People's Deputies of the Russian Federation), *Sovetskaya Rossia*, 25 September 1993, p. 1.

200. *Ibid.*

201. *Ibid.*

202. Valentina Nikiforova, 'Rossia protiv diktatury' (Russia against dictatorship), *Pravda*, 25 September 1993, pp. 1–2.

203. *Ibid.*

204. *Ibid.*

205. 'Rutskoy kak ekonomist i volshebnik' (Rutskoy as economist and magician), *Moskovskiy Komsomoletz*, 24 September 1993.

206. *Ibid.*

207. Frolov, 'Drama prozrenia'; Nikiforova, *op. cit.*

208. Sergey Chugaev, 'V Belom dome rasschityvayut na massovye besporyadki' (White House counts on mass disturbances), *Izvestia*, 25 September 1993, p. 2.

209. Nikiforova, *op. cit.*

210. Frolov, 'Drama prozrenia'.

211. *Ibid.*

212. Tsukanova, *op. cit.*

213. Kutsyllo, *op. cit.*, p. 57.

214. Tsukanova, *op. cit.*

215. Viktor Trushkov, 'Anafema' (Anathema), *Pravda*, 28 September 1993, p. 2.

216. Russian Television Channel (Rossia), 3 October 1993 (Washington, DC: Library of Congress, Videotape VBI 2311).

217. 'Moskva. Voskresenie, 3 oktyabrya. Khronika smutnogo vremeni (Den' vtoroi)' (Moscow. Sunday, 3 October. A chronicle of the times of troubles. Day two), *Moskovskie Novosti*, 10 October 1993.

218. Kutsyllo, *op. cit.*, p. 56.

219. 'Silovye vedomstva ne khoteli by vmeshivat'sya v konflikt' (Power

ministries would like not to get involved in the conflict), *Kommersant-Daily*, 23 September 1993, p. 3.

220. *Ibid.*

221. Russian Television Channel (Rossia), 23 September 1993 (FBIS, 24 September 1993, p. 17).

222. *Ibid.*

223. Ivan Ivanov, 'Oni srazahlis' za Rodinu' (They fought for the Motherland), *Zavtra*, 1, November 1993; ITAR-TASS, 1 October 1993 (FBIS, 4 October 1993, p. 33).

224. See, for instance, Yeltsin, *Zapiski*, p. 374; and Korzhakov, *op. cit.*, p. 174.

225. B.C., 'Rutskoy still very dangerous to Russia', *Libération* (Paris), 24 September 1993 (FBIS, 28 September 1993, p. 19).

226. Aleksey Chelnokov, 'Kommissar Terekhov predveshchal "tret'yu mirovuyu"' (Commissar Terekhov predicted the Third World War), *Izvestia*, 29 September 1993, p. 2.

227. *Ibid.*

228. *Ibid.*

229. Viktor Trushkov, 'Prisyaga komandira polka' (The oath of the commander of the regiment), *Pravda*, 28 September 1993, p. 1.

230. *Ibid.*

231. Elena Tregubova, 'Narodnye deputaty nazvali Viktora Anpilova i Stanislava Terekhova agentami spetssluzhb El'tsina. Chleny Soyuza ofitserov schitayut, chto Rodina stoit chelovecheskikh zhertv' (People's Deputies call Viktor Anpilov and Stanislav Terekhov agents of Yeltsin's special services. Officers' Union members think Motherland is worth human sacrifices), *Segodnya*, 25 September 1993, p. 2.

232. 'Dos'ie "MN"' ('Moskovskie novosti's' dossier), *Moskovskie Novosti*, 10 October 1993; and Dmitriy Zgerskiy and Vasiliy Dvorykin, 'Ulybka Adol'fa Aloisivicha' (The smile of Adolf, son of Alois), *Novoye Vremya*, 41, 1993, p. 13.

233. Zgerskiy and Dvorykin, *op. cit.*

234. 'Dos'ie "MN"'.

235. *Ibid.*

236. Ivanov, *op. cit.*; Aleksey Chelnokov, 'Pulya prervala podpol'nuyu odisseyu glavnogo Rossiskogo fashista' (A bullet interrupted an underground Odyssey of the chief Russian fascist), *Izvestia*, 4 January 1994; Zgerskiy and Dvorykin, *op. cit.*; and 'Dos'ie "MN"'.

237. Aleksey Chelnokov, 'Ekho sobytiy oktyabrya 93-go goda: chto kroeytsya za taynymi dos'ie Barkasheva?' (Echo of the events of October 1993: what is behind Barkashev's secret dossiers?), *Izvestia*, 6 September 1995.

238. Kutsyllo, *op. cit.*, p. 42.

239. 'Dos'ie "MN"'; and 'Moskva. Voskresenie'.

240. Zgerskiy and Dvorykin, *op. cit.*

241. Douglas Stanglin and Victoria Pope, 'Yeltsin draws the line', *U.S. News and World Report*, 4 October 1993, p. 35.

242. Seda Pumpyanskaya, 'Den' kogda proizoshyol obval' (The day when the avalanche happened), *Novoye Vremya*, 41, 1993, p. 9.

243. Yuriy Furmanov, 'Krasnye v Belom dome' (The reds in the White House), *Novoye Vremya*, 41, 1993, p. 12.

244. Kostikov, *op. cit.*, p. 246.

245. Yeltsin, *Zapiski*, p. 356.

246. Kostikov, *op. cit.*, p. 245.

247. Kutsyllo, *op. cit.*, p. 56.

248. 'Ukaz Prezidenta Rossiyskoy Federatsii "Ob otvetstvennosti lits, protivodeystvyushchikh provedeniyu poetapnoy konstitutsionnoy reformy"' (Decree of the President of the Russian Federation 'On the liability of persons opposing stage-by-stage implementation of constitutional reform'), *Rossiyskie Vesti*, 29 September 1993.

249. *Ibid.*

250. 'Ukaz Prezidenta Rossiyskoy

Federatsii "O sotsial'nykh garantiyakh dlya narodnykh deputatov Rossiyskoy Federatsii sozyva 1990–1995 godov"' (Decree of the President of the Russian Federation 'On social guarantees for People's Deputies of the Russian Federation of the 1990–1995 convocation'), *Rossiyskie Vesti*, 28 September 1993.

251.'Ukaz Prezidenta Rossiyskoy Federatsii "O poetapnoy Konstitutsionnoy reforme v Rossiyskoy Federatsii"' (Decree of the President of the Russian Federation 'On Stage-by-Stage Constitutional Reform in the Russian Federation'), *Trud*, 22 September 1993, pp. 1–2.

252. ITAR-TASS, 24 September 1993 (FBIS, 24 September 1993, p. 3); and 'Polozhenie o vyborakh deputatov Gosudarstvennoy dumy' (The regulation concerning the election of Deputies of the State Duma), *Rossiyskie Vesti*, 28 September 1993, p. 3.

253. ITAR-TASS, 24 September 1993; 'Polozhenie . . .', p. 3.

254. ITAR-TASS, 1 October 1993 (FBIS, 4 October 1993, p. 25).

255. Mayak Radio (Moscow), 30 September 1993 (FBIS, 1 October 1993, p. 7).

256. *Ibid.*

257. *OMRI Daily*, 1 October 1993.

258. First Channel/ORT (Ostankino), 27 September 1993 (FBIS, 28 September 1993, p. 1).

259. Valentina Nikiforova, Nikolay Musienko, Egor Saltykov and Viktor Kharlamov, 'Ostorozhno, dveri zakryvayutsya. Sleduyushchaya ostanovka – politseyskoye gosudarstvo' (Attention: the doors are closing. Next stop is a police state), *Pravda*, 29 September 1993, p. 1.

260. *Ibid.*

261. Aleksandr Rutskoy, 'Ya obrashchayus' k vam kak ofitzer' (I appeal to you as an officer), *Pravda*, 24 September 1993, p. 1.

262. *Ibid.*

263. Valentina Nikoforova, 'Dom Sovetov, s'ezd nachal rabotu' (House of Soviets: Congress has started its work), interview with Aleksandr Rutskoy, *Pravda*, 23 September 1993, p. 1.

264. *Ibid.*

265. *Pravda*, 1 October 1993.

266. Kutsyllo, *op. cit.*, p. 56.

267. *Ibid.*, pp. 118, 121.

268. *Ibid.*, p. 115.

269. Tsukanova, *op. cit.*

270. *Ibid.*

271. *Ibid.*

272. *Ibid.*

273. *Ibid.*

274. Radio Rossii, 30 September 1993 (FBIS, 30 September 1993, pp. 21–2).

275. Kutsyllo, *op. cit.*, p. 85.

276. *Ibid.*

277. First Channel/ORT (Ostankino), 23 September 1993 (FBIS, 24 September 1993, p. 23); ITAR-TASS, 24 September 1993 (FBIS, 24 September 1993, p. 23); Watson, Eliott, Nagorski, McKay and Barry, *op. cit.*, pp. 70–1.

278. Russian Television Channel (Rossia), 23 September 1993 (FBIS, 24 September 1993, p. 17); ITAR-TASS, 24 September 1993 (FBIS, 24 September 1993, p. 24).

279. ITAR-TASS, 24 September 1993 (FBIS, 24 September 1993, p. 49).

280. Press conference of Sergey Filatov and Yuriy Luzhkov, First Channel/ORT (Ostankino), 1 October 1993 (FBIS, 4 October 1993, p. 51).

281. *Ibid.*

282. INTERFAX, 29 September 1993 (FBIS, 30 September 1993, p. 14).

283. D. Khomyakov, '"Zheltyi Gebbels" i pervaya ataka' (The 'Yellow Goebbels' and the first attack), *Zavtra*, 1, November 1993.

284. First Channel/ORT (Ostankino), 29 September 1993 (FBIS, 30 September 1993, p. 14).

285. ITAR-TASS, 29 September 1993 (FBIS, 30 September 1993, p. 5).

286. *Ibid.* (p. 6).

287. Milton Stevens, 'And the Band Played On', *Washington Post*, 17 October 1993, p. G8.

288. Tatyana Ivanova, 'Teper' vsyo budet inache' (Everything will be different now), *Novoye Vremya*, 40, 1993, p. 9.

289. Stevens, *op. cit.*

290. *Ibid.*

291. Yeltsin, *Zapiski*, p. 374.

292. ITAR-TASS, 1 October 1993 (FBIS, 1 October 1993, pp. 2–3).

293. 'Interview with President Boris Yeltsin', First Channel/ORT (Ostankino), 1 October 1993 (FBIS, 1 October 1993, p. 5).

294. ITAR-TASS, 29 September 1993 (FBIS, 30 September 1993, p. 1).

295. Radio Rossii, 1 October 1993 (FBIS, 1 October 1993, p. 1).

296. *Ibid.*

297. Sergey Filatov, interview with ITAR-TASS, 1 October 1993 (FBIS, 1 October 1993, p. 2).

298. INTERFAX, 2 October 1993 (FBIS, 4 October 1993, pp. 45–6).

299. Russian Television Channel (Rossia), 30 September 1993 (FBIS, 1 October 1993, p. 23).

300. Kutsyllo, *op. cit.*, p. 104.

301. Mayak Radio (Moscow), 2 October 1993 (FBIS, 4 October 1993, p. 45).

302. Kutsyllo, *op. cit.*, p. 105.

303. Russian Television Channel (Rossia), 1 October 1993 (FBIS, 1 October 1993, p. 3).

304. Radio Rossii, 1 October 1993 (FBIS, 1 October 1993, p. 3); and Russian Television Channel (Rossia), 1 October 1993 (FBIS, 1 October 1993, p. 3).

305. Russian Television Channel (Rossia), 1 October 1993 (FBIS, 1 October 1993, p. 3).

306. *Ibid.*

307. Andrey Apostolov, 'Aleksandr Rutskoy: nikakikh kompromissov, krome vozvrashcheniya zakonnosti' (Aleksandr Rutskoy: no compromises but restoration of legality), *Segodnya*, 2 October 1993, p. 1.

308. *Ibid.*

309. Kutsyllo, *op. cit.*, p. 104.

310. Apostolov, *op. cit.*

311. Agence France-Presse, 1 October 1993 (FBIS, 1 October 1993, p. 20).

312. *Ibid.* (p. 21).

313. *Ibid.*

314. ITAR-TASS, 2 October 1993 (FBIS, 4 October 1993, p. 12); Kutsyllo, *op. cit.*, p. 107.

315. Pumpyanskaya, *op. cit.*, p. 8.

316. Kostikov, *op. cit.*, p. 246.

317. Videotape VBI 2311, Washington, DC: Library of Congress.

318. *Ibid.*

319. Pumpyanskaya, *op. cit.*, p. 8.

320. Videotape VBI 2311.

321. Pumpyanskaya, *op. cit.*, p. 8.

322. *Ibid.*

323. Kutsyllo, *op. cit.*, p. 114.

324. *Vesti*, Russian Television Channel (Rossia), 23.05, 3 October 1993 (Washington, DC: Library of Congress, Videotape VBI 2311).

325. Lee Hockstader, 'Police Flee in Face of Surging Mob', *Washington Post*, 4 October 1993, p. A14.

326. *Ibid.*

327. Kutsyllo, *op. cit.*, p. 114; Furmanov, *op. cit.*; Russell Watson, Dorinda Elliott, Rod Norland, Betsy McKay and Jane Whitmore, 'Hollow Victory', *U.S. News and World Report*, 18 October 1993, p. 48.

328. Kutsyllo, *op. cit.*, p. 114; Pumpyanskaya, *op. cit.*, p. 9.

329. Furmanov, *op. cit.*

330. Furmanov, *op. cit.*, p. 12; 'Moskva. Voskresenie', p. A4.

331. *Ibid.*

332. *Ibid.*

333. 'Moskva. Voskresenie', p. 3.

334. ITAR-TASS, 3 October 1993 (FBIS, 4 October 1993, p. 54).

335. *Ibid.*

336. *Ibid.*; Watson, Elliott, Norland, McKay and Whitmore, *op. cit.*

337. *Ibid.*

338. Galina Kova'skaya, Stepan

Koval'skiy, Georgiy Osipov, Yuliya Rakhaeva, Marina Shakina and Ol'ga Shakina, 'Oskolki tryokh dney' (Fragments of three days), *Novoye Vremya*, 42, 1993, p. 13.
339. *Ibid.*
340. Kutsyllo, *op. cit.*, p. 115.
341. Videotape VBI 2311, Washington, DC: Library of Congress.
342. *Ibid.*
343. ITAR-TASS, 3 October 1993 (FBIS, 4 October 1993, p. 49).
344. Hockstader, *op. cit.*
345. 'Moskva. Voskresenie', p. 4.
346. *Ibid.*
347. Videotape VBI 2311, Washington, DC: Library of Congress.
348. Pumpyanskaya, *op. cit.*, p. 9.
349. 'Moskva. Voskresenie', p. 4.
350. Pumpyanskaya, *op. cit.*, p. 9.
351. *Ibid.*
352. Kutsyllo, *op. cit.*, p. 117.
353. *Ibid.*, p. 118.
354. *Ibid.*
355. Gaidar, *Dni porazheniy*, p. 289.
356. *Ibid.*
357. *Ibid.*
358. Kostikov, *op. cit.*, pp. 246, 247, 248.
359. *Ibid.*, p. 248.
360. Yeltsin, *Zapiski*, p. 378.
361. *Ibid.*
362. *Ibid.*, p. 379.
363. *Ibid.*
364. *Ibid.*, p. 380.
365. *Ibid.*, p. 383.
366. *Ibid.*, p. 380.
367. *Ibid.*, p. 382.
368. *Ibid.*, p. 381.
369. *Ibid.*, p. 383.
370. *Ibid.*, pp. 383, 386.
371. Kostikov, *op. cit.*, pp. 256–7.
372. Yeltsin, *Zapiski*, p. 384; Korzhakov, *op. cit.*, p. 168.
373. Yeltsin, *Zapiski*, p. 385.
374. Korzhakov, *op. cit.*, p. 168.
375. Yeltsin, *Zapiski*, p. 384; Korzhakov, *op. cit.*, p. 168.
376. Korzhakov, *op. cit.*, p. 169.
377. Yeltsin, *Zapiski*, p. 385; Korzhakov, *op. cit.*, p. 170.

378. Korzhakov, *op. cit.*, p. 169.
379. *Ibid.*, p. 170; Yeltsin, *Zapiski*, p. 386.
380. Yeltsin, *Zapiski*, p. 386.
381. Korzhakov, *op. cit.*, p. 170.
382. Yeltsin, *Zapiski*, p. 386; Korzhakov, *op. cit.*, p. 170.
383. Korzhakov, *op. cit.*, pp. 172, 173.
384. Videotapes VBI 2311–VBI 2314, Washington, DC: Library of Congress; Poptsov, *op. cit.*, p. 345.
385. Gaidar, *Dni porazheniy*, p. 290.
386. *Ibid.*
387. Russian Television Channel (Rossia), 3 October 1993 (FBIS, 4 October 1993, p. 29; Videotape VBI 2310, Washington DC: Library of Congress).
388. Videotape VBI 2313, Washington, DC: Library of Congress.
389. *Ibid.*
390. *Ibid.*
391. Videotape VBI 2314, Washington, DC: Library of Congress.
392. Videotape VBI 2313, Washington, DC: Library of Congress.
393. Videotape VBI 2314, Washington, DC: Library of Congress.
394. *Ibid.*
395. Videotape VBI 2313, Washington, DC: Library of Congress.
396. *Vesti*, Russian Television Channel (Rossia), 00.50, 4 October 1993 (Washington, DC: Library of Congress, Videotape 2313).
397. Poptsov, *op. cit.*, p. 347.
398. *Ibid.*
399. *Ibid.*
400. Koval'skaya *et al.*, *op. cit.*, p. 13.
401. Videotape VBI 2313, Washington, DC: Library of Congress.
402. ITAR-TASS 04.32, 4 October 1993 (FBIS, 4 October 1993, p. 63).
403. Interview with Vladimir Bokser.
404. Videotape VBI 2313, Washington, DC: Library of Congress.
405. Interview with Vladimir Bokser.
406. *Ibid.*
407. Alexander Rahr, 'Democrats Demonstrate for Yeltsin', *OMRI*

System Search, 27 September 1993 (http://sdar.rtd.ukk.edu:81/cgi-bin/friends/omr/select-rec.pl).

408. Interview with Vladimir Bokser.

409. Yeltsin, *Zapiski*, p. 382.

410. *Ibid.*

411. *Ibid.*

412. Aleksandr Peltz, 'Press-konferentsia Ministra oborony Rossii' (Press conference of the Minister of Defence of Russia), *Krasnaya Zvezda*, 6 October 1993.

413. Serge Schmemann, 'Rutskoi and Khasbulatov Seized with Hundreds of their Supporters', *New York Times*, 5 October 1993, p. 16; Michael Gordon, 'Yeltsin Attack Strategy: Bursts Followed by Lulls', *New York Times*, 5 October 1993, p. 17.

414. Gordon, *op. cit.*

415. ITAR-TASS, 06.32, 4 October 1998 (FBIS, 4 October 1993, p. 1.

416. 'The Clock Runs Out for Revolt', *New York Times*, 5 October 1993, p. A16.

417. Russian Television Channel (Rossia), 07.13, 4 October 1993 (FBIS, 4 October 1993, p. 30).

418. Russian Television Channel (Rossia), 09.00, 4 October 1993 (FBIS, 4 October 1993, pp. 20–1).

419. 'The Clock Runs Out; Chronology of the Confrontation', *Washington Post*, 5 October 1993, p. A32; and INTERFAX, 11.07, 4 October 1993 (FBIS, 4 October 1993, p. 2).

420. Schmemann, 'Rutskoi and Khasbulatov'.

421. 'Moskva. 4 oktyabrya . . .', *Moskovskie Novosti*, 10 October 1993, p. 5.

422. Gordon, *op. cit.*

423. *Ibid.*

424. *Ibid.*

425. Lee Hockstader, 'Under Fire, Hard-Liners Watch as Crusade Crumbles', *Washington Post*, 5 October 1993, p. A32; Gaidar, *Dni porazheniy*, p. 294.

426. Ivanov, *op. cit.*; Kutsyllo, *op. cit.*, p. 137.

427. Gaidar, *Dni porazheniy*, p. 294.

428. *Ibid.*, p. 293.

429. All-Russian Centre for the Study of Public Opinion, 4 October 1993, 'Situatziya glazami Moskvichey' (The situation as seen by Muscovites), *Moskovskie Novosti*, 10 October 1993, p. 8.

430. *OMRI Daily*, 5 October 1993.

431. Robert Seely, 'Ex-Soviet Nations Give Support', *Washington Post*, 5 October 1993.

432. *Ibid.*

433. *OMRI Daily*, 5 October 1993.

434. ITAR-TASS, 13.18, and INTERFAX, 13.55, 4 October 1994 (FBIS, 4 October 1993, p. 6).

435. Radio Rossii, 15.00, and ITAR-TASS, 15.54, 4 October 1993 (FBIS, 4 October 1993, pp. 7–8).

436. Radio Rossii, 15.00, 4 October 1993 (FBIS, 4 October 1993, p. 7).

437. 'Moskva. 4 oktyabrya . . .', p. 7.

438. Kutsyllo, *op. cit.*, p. 152.

439. 'Moskva. 4 oktyabrya . . .', p. 7.

440. Korzhakov, *op. cit.*, p. 195.

441. *Ibid.*, p. 175.

442. I.T., 'Tanki bili po Rossii i po nam . . .' (The tanks shot at us and at Russia), *Zavtra*, 1, November 1993.

443. *Ibid.*

444. Pumpyanksaya, *op. cit.*, p. 11.

445. Mayak Radio (Moscow), 13.40, 4 October 1993 (FBIS, 4 October 1993, p. 5).

446. *Ibid.*

447. 'Moskva. 4 oktyabrya . . .', p. 7.

448. Poptsov, *op. cit.*, p. 348.

449. Schmemann, 'Rutskoi and Khasbulatov'.

450. Poptsov, *op. cit.*, p. 348.

451. Kutsyllo, *op. cit.*, p. 120.

452. Hockstader, 'Under Fire'.

453. Kutsyllo, *op. cit.*, p. 120; Watson, Elliott, Norland, McKay and Whitmore, *op. cit.*, p. 48.

454. 'Moskva. 4 oktyabrya . . .', p. 7; Korzhakov, *op. cit.*, p. 198.

Chapter 12: The Nadir

1. A statement by the Public Committee of Russian Democratic Organizations, TASS, 5 October 1993 (FBIS, 6 October 1993, p. 33).

2. 'Boris Yeltsin: kak prezident, ya bol'she drugikh zainteresovan v sotsial'noy stabil'nosti' (Boris Yeltsin: as President, I am more than anyone interested in social stability), *Izvestia*, 16 November 1993, p. 4.

3. Serge Schmemann, 'Russians Scramble to Fill an Unformed Parliament', *New York Times*, 1 November 1993.

4. *Ibid.*

5. 'My vozvrashchaemsya' (We are returning), *Pravda*, 2 November 1993.

6. Lee Hockstader, 'Truth Told, Pravda Lives', *Washington Post*, 15 April 1997.

7. Aleksandr Prokhanov, 'A. Prokhanov. Slovo redaktora' (A. Prokhanov. A word from the editor), *Zavtra*, 1, November 1993, p. 1.

8. Inga Prelovskaya, 'Teleekran ni za kogo golosovat' ne sobiraetsya' (The television screen is not going to vote for anyone), *Izvestia*, 23 October 1993.

9. Ellen Mickiewicz, *Changing Channels: Television and the Struggle for Power in Russia*, New York: Oxford University Press, 1997, p. 150.

10. Celestine Bohlen, 'Candidates Take to Airwaves as Russian Vote Approaches', *New York Times*, 27 November 1993, p. 1.

11. Kiva Maydannik, 'Levye dvizheniya v postavtoritarnom obshchestve' (Left movements in a post-authoritarian society), *Svobodnaya Mysl'*, 9, June 1994, p. 27.

12. *Ibid.*, p. 22.

13. Igor Klyamkin, *Novaya demokratiya ili novaya diktatura* (A new democracy or a new dictatorship). Moscow: Fond Obshestvennoye mnenie, 1994, p. 14.

14. *Ibid.*

15. *Ibid.*

16. Kostikov, *op. cit.*, p. 286.

17. *Ibid.*, pp. 290, 293, 294.

18. *Ibid.*

19. *Ibid.*, p. 290.

20. *Ibid.*, p. 291.

21. Poptsov, *op. cit.*, p. 377.

22. Kostikov, *op. cit.*, p. 287.

23. Boris Yeltsin, 'Letter to the Federation Council', TASS, 9 December 1995 (FBIS, 11 December 1995, p. 36).

24. Leonid Vasiliev, 'Sumeet li prezident realizovat' svoy posledniy shans?' (Will the President be able to make the best of his last opportunity?), *Novoye Vremya*, 8, 1995, p. 14.

25. Interview with Egor Gaidar.

26. *Ibid.*

27. Poptsov, *op. cit.*, p. 413.

28. See, for example, Gaidar, *Dni porazheniy*, p. 331.

29. *Facts on File*, vol. 55, no. 2873, 21 December 1995, pp. 960–1, and vol. 55, no. 2830, 23 February 1995, p. 133.

30. 'Russian Troops Carry Out Massacre in Samashki', *RFE/RL Newsline System Search*, 14 April 1995; *Facts on File*, vol. 55, no. 2841, 11 May 1995, p. 349; and Mickiewicz, *op. cit.*, pp. 260–1.

31. Poptsov, *op. cit.*, pp. 409, 411, 422.

32. Kostikov, *op. cit.*, p. 44.

33. *Ibid.*

34. Kronid Lubarskiy, 'My vse glyadim v napoleony . . .' (We are all dreaming of becoming a Napoleon . . .), *Novoye Vremya*, 7, 1995, p. 16.

35. TASS, 10 December 1994 (FBIS, 10 December 1994, http://wnc.fedworld.gov/cgi-bin/re, Article ID:drsov238 b_94004).

36. Echo of Moscow Radio, 9 December 1994 (FBIS, 9 December

1994, http://wnc.fedworld.gov/cgi-bin/
re, Article ID:drsov238_c_ 94008).

37. Sergey Kovalev, 'Otkrytoe pis'mo
B. El'tsinu' (An open letter to B.
Yeltsin), *Izvestia*, January 24, 1998,
p. 2

38. Embassy of the Russian
Federation, 'Yeltsin Addresses the
Nation on Chechnya', Press Release
No. 40, 27 December 1994, p. 3.

39. *Facts on File*, vol. 55, no. 2828,
p. 26E.

40. Gaidar, *Dni porazheniy*, p. 357.

41. Ludmila Telen', 'Okonchatel'nyi
diagnoz' (The final diagnosis),
Moskovskie Novosti, 4–11 December
1994, p. 5.

42. *Ibid*.

43. Valeriy Vyzhutovich,
'Prezidentskiy konvoy' (The
President's convoy), *Moskovskie
Novosti*, 25 December 1994–1
January 1995, p. 6.

44. *Ibid*.

45. Yuriy Burtin, 'Ne tebya b'yut –
molchi' (They are beating someone
else – so shut up), *Moskovskie
Novosti*, 4–11 December 1994, p. 6.

46. Vladimir Lysenko, 'Lovushka dlya
demokrata' (A trap for a democrat),
Moskovskie Novosti, 4–11 December
1994, p. 7; Len Karpinskiy, 'Boevoy
zalp v chest' Konstitutsii' (A salvo in
the Constitution's honour),
Moskovskie Novosti, 11–18
December 1994, p. 7; Pavel
Voshchanov, ' "Nu vot ya i v
Kremle!" A chto dal'she?' ('At last I
am in the Kremlin!' But what next?),
Komsomol'skaya Pravda, 7 December
1994, p. 2.

47. Karpinskiy, *op. cit*.

48. Butrin, *op. cit*.

49. Lysenko, *op. cit*.

50. Lubarskiy, *op. cit.*, p. 18.

51. I. M. Klyamkin, V. V. Lapkin and
V. I. Pantin, 'Politicheskiy kurs
Yeltsina: predvaritelnye itogi'
(Yeltsin's political course: preliminary
results), *Polis*, 3, 1994, p. 165.

52. *Ibid.*, p. 163.

53. As quoted in Lacouture, *op. cit.*,
p. 113.

54. Åslund, *op. cit.*, p. 199.

55. Don Van Atta, 'Yeltsin Decree
Finally Ends "Second Serfdom" in
Russia', *RFE/RL Research Report*, 19
November 1993, p. 38.

56. *Ibid*.

57. Gennadiy Burbulis, interview with
Novoye Vremya, 7, 1995, p. 20.

58. Kostikov, *op. cit.*, p. 301.

59. *Ibid.*, p. 306.

60. *Ibid.*, p. 301.

61. *Ibid.*, p. 127.

62. Gaidar, *Dni porazheniy*, p. 106.

63. *Ibid.*, and Kostikov, *op. cit.*,
p. 180.

64. Gaidar, *Dni porazheniy*, p. 106.

65. Boris Yeltsin, interviewed by
El'dar Ryazanov, First Channel/ORT
(Ostankino), 16 November 1993
(FBIS, 17 November 1993, p. 27).

66. Yeltsin, *Zapiski*, p. 304.

67. Kostikov, *op. cit.*, p. 65.

68. *Ibid.*, p. 284.

69. Martin Ebon, 'Yeltsin's V.I.P.
Depression', *Psychiatric Times*,
October 1996, p. 35.

70. Kostikov, *op. cit.*, p. 296.

71. *Ibid*.

72. *Ibid.*, p. 297.

73. *Ibid.*, p. 307.

74. Yeltsin, *Ispoved'*, pp. 147–8, and
Zapiski, p. 31.

75. Korzhakov, *op. cit.*, p. 202;
Yeltsin, *Zapiski*, pp. 19, 197.

76. Interview with Egor Gaidar.

77. Interview with Galina
Starovoytova.

78. Yeltsin, *Zapiski*, p. 239.

79. Kostikov, *op. cit.*, p. 25.

80. Korzhakov, *op. cit.*, p. 240.

81. About to surrender the last vestige
of the Soviet Union's victory in the
Second World War, a very 'nervous'
and 'depressed' Yeltsin, to use his
bodyguard's words, began drinking in
the morning (*ibid.*, p. 213).

82. *Ibid.*, p. 205.

83. Gaidar, *Dni porazheniy*, p. 107;
Kostikov, *op. cit.*, pp. 310, 333.

84. Gaidar, *Dni porazheniy*, p. 107.
85. Kostikov, *op. cit.*, p. 35.
86. *Ibid.*, pp. 10, 11, 342; and Poptsov, *op. cit.*, p. 385.
87. Kostikov, *op. cit.*, pp. 15–16.
88. Interview with Egor Gaidar.
89. Korzhakov, *op. cit.*, p. 155; Poptsov, *op. cit.*, p. 392.
90. Egor Gaidar as quoted in Kostikov, *op. cit.*, p. 296.
91. *Ibid.*, p. 322.
92. *Ibid.*, p. 298.
93. Yeltsin, *Zapiski*, pp. 295–6.
94. *Ibid.*, p. 198.
95. Kostikov, *op. cit.*, pp. 17, 307.
96. *Ibid.*, p. 197.
97. Ilya Mil'shteyn, 'Vysokaya bolezn'' (A solemn illness), interview with a leading Russian cardiac surgeon, Mikhail Alshibay, *Novoye Vremya*, 5, 1996, p. 14.
98. *Ibid.*
99. Korzhakov, *op. cit.*, pp. 209–11.
100. *Ibid.*, p. 211.
101. Kostikov, *op. cit.*, pp. 194–5.
102. *Ibid.*
103. *Ibid.*, p. 196.

Chapter 13: Campaign '96: 'Choosing Russia's Fate'

1. Yuriy Levada, 'Poprobyuem podschitat' shansy kandidatov' (Let's try and figure out the candidates' chances), *Novoye Vremya*, 8, 1996, p. 8.
2. *Ibid.*
3. Interview with Aleksandr Urmanov.
4. Korzhakov, *op. cit.*, p. 364.
5. *Ibid.*, p. 368.
6. *Ibid.*
7. See, for instance, Aleksandr Gamov, 'Pochemu Korzhakov voznik iz prezidentskoy teni?' (Why has Korzhakov emerged from Presidential shadow?), *Komsomol'skaya Pravda*, 7 May 1996, pp. 1–2; 'Korzhakov. "Observer". Vybory' (Korzhakov, *The Observer*. Election), *Moskovskiy Komsomoletz*, 7 May 1996, p. 1.
8. Lyubov' Volodina, 'Boris El'tsin oglasit predvybornuyu platformu na s'ezde svoikh storonnikov' (Boris Yeltsin to unveil election platform at Congress of his supporters), *Rossiyskie Vesti*, 28 March 1996, p. 1.
9. Interview with Aleksandr Urmanov.
10. *Ibid.*
11. Egor Gaidar, 'Prezident otvetil mne pis'mom' (The President answered me with a letter), interview with *Moskovskie Novosti*, 11–18 February 1996, p. 10.
12. *Ibid.*
13. Georgiy Satarov, '"My Job? Getting Yeltsin to Win"', interview with *La Stampa* (Turin), 3 March 1996, p. 8.
14. Interview with Aleksandr Urmanov. See also Levada, *op. cit.*, p. 9.
15. Levada, *op. cit.*, p. 9.
16. 'Dognat' i peregnat': shansy na uspekh v rossiyskikh prezidentskikh vyborakh' (To catch up and overtake: chances of success in Russia's Presidential election). The results of public opinion polls conducted by Nugzar Betaneli, Director of the Institute of Parliamentary Sociology, *Moskovskiy Komsomoletz*, 16 April 1996, p. 2.
17. Levada, *op. cit.*, p. 9.
18. Viktor Trushkov, 'Korolevskie mucheniya' (The king's torments), *Pravda*, 17 January 1996, p. 1.
19. Leonid Vasiliev, 'Eshchyo odnogo eksperimenta Rossia ne vyderzhit' (Russia will not survive another experiment), *Novoye Vremya*, 9, 1996, p. 10.
20. 'Dognat' i peregnat''.
21. Levada, *op. cit.*, p. 10.
22. 'Dognat' i peregnat''.
23. Levada, *op. cit.*, p. 9.
24. Igna Mikhaylovskaya, 'Russian Voting Behavior as Mirror of Social–Political Change', *East European Constitutional Review*, Spring/Summer 1996, p. 60.
25. 'The Views of Rank and File Russians', *American Enterprise*, July/

August 1996, p. 57. The polling was conducted by Professor Richard Rose of the University of Strathclyde, Scotland.

26. *Ibid.*

27. *Ibid.*

28. *Rossia v tsifrakh, 1995: kratkiy statisticheskiy sbornik* (Russia in figures, 1995: short statistical compilation), Moscow: Goskomstat, 1995, p. 25.

29. Interview with Aleksandr Urmanov.

30. Oleg Moroz, 'Osobennosti natsional'noy okhoty za golosami izbirateley v vesenne-letniy sezon 1996 goda' (Peculiarities of national vote-hunting in the spring–summer 1996 season), *Literaturnaya Gazeta*, 10 April 1996, pp. 1, 11.

31. Interview with Aleksandr Urmanov.

32. See, for instance, Korzhakov, *op. cit.*, p. 364.

33. Grigoriy Yavlinsky, interview on the *Itogi* programme, NTV, 14 April 1996 (FBIS-SOV-96-073, 16 April 1996, http://wnc.fedworld.gov/cgi-bin, Article Id:drsov073aa_96014).

34. Grigoriy Yavlinsky, 'Zayavlenie frakzii Yabloko' (A statement by the Yabloko faction), 27 October 1994, copy in the author's archive.

35. Sergey Kovalev, speech at the Plenum of the Council of Russia's Democratic Choice, *Novoye Vremya*, 13, 1996, p. 10.

36. Anatoliy Chubais, speech at the Plenum of the Council of Russia's Democratic Choice, *Novoye Vremya*, 13, 1996, pp. 10–11.

37. Egor Gaidar, 'U menya net sindroma belobiletnika' (I don't have a draft-dodger complex), interview with *Novoye Vremya*, 28, 1996, p. 12.

38. Boris Grushin, 'Opyat' na avos'? (Leaving everything to chance again?), *Novoye Vremya*, 8, 1996, p. 10.

39. *Ibid.*

40. Egor Gaidar, press conference, 26 February 1996, NTV (FBIS-SOV-96-039, 29 February 1996, http://wnc.fedworld.gov/cgi-bin/re, article Id:drsovo39_b_96007).

41. Lyubov Tsukanova, 'Izbiratel' progolosyuet za togo, kto dast emu perspektivu' (The voter will vote for the one who offers him a future), *Rossiyskie Vesti*, 5 March 1996, p. 1.

42. *Itogi*, NTV, 18 February 1996 (FBIS, 21 February 1996, http://wnc.fedworld.gov/cgi-bin/re, Article ID drsov34_b_96009).

43. Boris Yeltsin, speech in Ekaterinburg, 15 February 1996, Russian Television Channel (Rossia) (FBIS, 16 February 1996, p. 46).

44. *Ibid.*

45. *Ibid.*

46. Boris Yeltsin, address to the Federal Assembly, 23 February 1996, Russian Television Channel (Rossia), live (FBIS, 26 February 1996, p. 14).

47. Yeltsin, speech in Ekaterinburg, p. 47.

48. *Ibid.*

49. *Ibid.*

50. *Ibid.*

51. Yeltsin, address, 23 February 1996, p. 15.

52. *Ibid.*

53. *Ibid.*

54. *Ibid.*

55. *Ibid.*

56. *Ibid.*

57. Yeltsin, speech in Ekaterinburg, 15 February 1996, p. 47.

58. *Ibid.*, p. 48.

59. *Ibid.*, p. 51.

60. *Ibid.*

61. *Ibid.*

62. *Ibid.*

63. *Ibid.*, pp. 46, 48.

64. *Ibid.*, p. 46.

65. Yeltsin, address, 23 February 1996, p. 14.

66. *Ibid.*, p. 17.

67. Yeltsin, speech in Ekaterinburg, pp. 48, 50.

68. Yeltsin, address, 23 February 1996, p. 16, and speech in Ekaterinburg, p. 50.

69. Boris Yeltsin, responses to questions from the audience after Ekaterinburg speech, Russian Television Channel (Russia) (FBIS, 16 February 1996, p. 52).

70. Yeltsin, speech in Ekaterinburg, p. 49.

71. Aleksandr Pashkov, 'El'tsin reshil ostat'sya, no i Zyuganov khochet porulit'' (Yeltsin has decided to stay, but Zyuganov also wants to rule a bit). *Izvestia*, 16 February 1996, p. 1.

72. Yeltsin, speech in Ekaterinburg, p. 46.

73. *Ibid.*, p. 49.

74. Yeltsin, address, 23 February 1996, pp. 20–1.

75. Lee Hockstader, 'Yeltsin Campaign Rose from Tears to Triumph', *Washington Post*, 7 July 1996, p. 1.

76. Interview with Aleksandr Urmanov.

77. *Ibid.*

78. *Ibid.*

79. Satarov, *op. cit.*

80. Aleksandr Prokhanov and Gennadiy Zyuganov, 'Slovo k narodu' (A word to the people), *Sovetskaya Rossia*, 23 July 1991, p. 1.

81. Gennadiy Zyuganov, *Za gorizontom* (Beyond the horizon), Moscow: Informpechat', 1995, pp. 4, 5.

82. *Ibid.*

83. *Ibid.*, pp. 132, 133.

84. *Ibid.*, p. 147. This interview with Gennadiy Zyuganov on the results of his Cuban trip first appeared in *Sovetskaya Rossia*, 1 December 1994.

85. Michael McFaul, *Russia's 1996 Presidential Election: The End of Polarized Politics*, Stanford: Hoover Institution Press, 1997, p. 44.

86. Zyuganov, *op. cit.*, p. 5.

87. *Ibid.*

88. Alessandra Stanley, 'Red Scare', *New York Times Magazine*, 26 May 1996, p. 45.

89. *Ibid.*

90. Vadim Dubnov and Andrey Kolesnikov, 'Chetyre maski Gennadiya Zyuganova' (The four masks of Gennadiy Zyuganov), *Novoye Vremya*, 22, 1996, p. 9.

91. *Ibid.*

92. Zyuganov, *op. cit.*, pp. 127, 128.

93. Michael Specter, 'Muse of Anti-Yeltsin Forces Is Feared But Never Ignored', *New York Times*, 2 May 1996, p. 1.

94. McFaul, *op. cit.*, p. 46.

95. Lee Hockstader, 'New Russian Communists Put On a Moderate Face', *Washington Post*, 20 May 1996, p. A1.

96. Zyuganov, *op. cit.*, p. 142.

97. Kathleen Parthé, 'What Would "Tomorrow" Bring Russia?', unpublished paper, 1996, p. 3.

98. 'Ne voz'myom vziatku iz krovavykh ruk!' (We shall not take a bribe from hands covered with blood!), *Zavtra*, 8, February 1996, p. 1.

99. *Zavtra*, 6, February 1996, p. 1.

100. Specter, 'Muse of Anti-Yeltsin Forces'.

101. Kathleen Parthé, 'Trust in Zyuganov Is Naïve and Ominous', letter to the editor, *New York Times*, 2 June 1996.

102. Parthé, 'What Would "Tomorrow" Bring Russia?', p. 1.

103. *Ibid.*

104. Kathleen Parthé, 'Zyuganov: Man of Letters', unpublished paper, 1996, p. 3.

105. David Remnick, 'Hammer, Sickle, and Book', *New York Review of Books*, 23 May 1996.

106. Aleksandr Prokhanov, 'My – iz russkoy tsivilizatsii' (We are from the Russian civilization), *Zavtra*, 31, August 1996, p. 1.

107. Nikolay Anisin, 'Za!' (For!), *Zavtra*, 9, February 1996, p. 4.

108. Gennadiy Zyuganov, 'Rossia – strana slova' (Russia is a country of the word), interview with Vladimir Bondarenko, *Zavtra*, 17, April 1996, pp. 1, 3.

109. *Ibid.*, p. 1.
110. *Ibid.*
111. Gennadiy Zyuganov, 'Rossia, Rodina, Narod! Predvybornaya platforma kandidata na post prezidenta Rossiyskoy Federatsii Zyuganova Gennadiya Andreevicha' (Russia, Motherland, People! Electoral platform of Gennadiy Andreevich Zyuganov, a candidate for President of the Russian Federation), *Sovetskaya Rossia*, 19 March 1996, p. 2.
112. Vl. Stroganov, 'V Rossii est' eshcho rezervy . . .' (Russia still has reserves . . .), *Zavtra*, 24, June 1996, p. 8.
113. 'Russkiy, golosuy za Zyuganova!' (Russian, vote for Zyuganov!), *Zavtra*, 26, June 1996, p. 1.
114. Gennadiy Zyuganov, *My Russia*, New York: M. E. Sharpe, 1997, p. 101.
115. Gennadiy Zyuganov, *Rossia i sovremenniy mir* (Russia and today's world), Moscow: Informpechat', 1995, p. 18; *My Russia*, p. 101.
116. Gennadiy Zyuganov, *Derzhava* (The great power), Moscow: Informpechat', 1994, p. 30.
117. Zyuganov, *Rossia*, p. 93.
118. Zyuganov, *My Russia*, p. 137; *Derzhava*, p. 173.
119. Zyuganov, *My Russia*, p. 81.
120. Zyuganov, *Za gorizontom*, p. 74.
121. Zyuganov, *My Russia*, p. 80; *Rossia*, p. 39.
122. Zyuganov, *My Russia*, p. 80.
123. *Ibid.*
124. *Ibid.*, p. 85.
125. *Ibid.*, p. 80.
126. Zyuganov, 'Rossia, Rodina', p. 2.
127. *Ibid.*
128. Zyuganov, *Za gorizontom*, pp. 17–18.
129. *Ibid.*, p. 19.
130. Zyuganov, *Rossia*, p. 8.
131. Zyuganov, *My Russia*, p. 106.
132. *Ibid.*, p. 80.
133. Zyuganov, *Rossia*, p. 21.
134. Zyuganov, *My Russia*, p. 87.
135. *Ibid.*, p. 81.
136. *Ibid.*, p. 113.
137. *Ibid.*, p. 85.
138. Zyuganov, *Za gorizontom*, p. 116.
139. Zyuganov, *Derzhava*, p. 86.
140. *Ibid.*, p. 132.
141. Zyuganov, *Za gorizontom*, p. 35.
142. *Ibid.*, p. 136.
143. Zyuganov, 'Rossia, Rodina'.
144. *Ibid.*
145. Gennadiy Zyuganov, *From Destruction to Construction. Russia's Road to the 21st Century. Main Provisions of the Social and Economic Program of G. A. Zyuganov, Candidate for President from the Popular Patriotic Forces*, Moscow: 25 May 1996. Federal News Service. (A copy in the author's archive.)
146. *Ibid.*, p. 7.
147. Zyuganov, 'Rossia, Rodina'.
148. *Ibid.*
149. Zyuganov, *My Russia*, p. 122.
150. Zyuganov, 'Rossia, Rodina'.
151. *Ibid.*
152. *Ibid.*
153. Zyuganov, *My Russia*, p. 153.
154. *Ibid.*, p. 146; Zyuganov, 'Rossia, Rodina'.
155. Zyuganov, *From Destruction*, p. 12.
156. Zyuganov, 'Rossia, Rodina'.
157. *Ibid.*; and Zyuganov, *From Destruction*, p. 23.
158. Zyuganov, 'Rossia, Rodina'.
159. *Ibid.*
160. *Ibid.*
161. Zyuganov, *My Russia*, p. 122.
162. Pashkov, *op. cit.*
163. Boris Yeltsin, 'Rossiya: Chelovek, Sem'ya, Obshchestvo, Gosudarstvo. Programma deystviy na 1996–2000 gody'. (Russia: Individual, Family, Society, State. Action programme for the years 1996–2000), Moscow, 27 May 1996.
164. Boris Yeltsin, speech at the

Solombala timber and wood-working complex, Arkhangel'sk region, 24 May 1996, ITAR-TASS (FBIS, 29 May 1996, http://.wnc.fedworld.gov/cgi-bin, Article Id:drsov103aa_96005).

165. Gennadiy Zyuganov, 'Eshchyo nemnogo, eshcho chut'-chut' . . .' (Just a little bit more, just a little bit . . .), interviewed by Aleksandr Skrypnik and Leonid Fedorov, *Pravda-5*, 31 May–7 June 1996, pp. 1, 3.

166. Valentin Kuptsov, Deputy Chairman of the KPRF, speech at the Fourth Party Conference, *Informationniy Bulleten'* (KPRF), 35, no. 2 (20 February 1996), p. 22, as cited in McFaul, *op. cit.*, p. 46.

167. Anatole Shub, *Russian Readership Survey Finds Top, Local Papers Strong*, Washington, DC: Office of Research and Media Reaction, US Information Agency, 30 May 1995, p. 2.

168. As quoted in Zyuganov, *Za gorizontom*, p. 132.

169. Gennadiy Zyuganov, 'Patrioticheskaya vlast' vosstanovit spravedlivost'' (A patriotic government will restore justice), interview with *Pravda*, 5 May 1996, p. 2; Gennadiy Zyuganov, interview with Echo of Moscow Radio, 1 June 1996 (FBIS-SOV-96-107, http://wnc.fedworld.gov/cgi-bin . . ., Article Id:drsov107aa_96012, p. 11). The same figure, 'over 150 [pro-communist] print publications', was given by Russia's most popular weekly news-magazine *Argumenty i Fakty*. (Andrey Fedorov, 'Zyuganov nakanune vyborov . . .' (Zyuganov on the eve of the elections . . .), *Argumenty i Fakty*, 15–21, (April) 1996, p. 9).

170. Gennadiy Zyuganov, 'Znat' i deystvovat''. Kandidat v prezidenty otvechayet na voprosy zhiteley Urala' (To know and to act. The Presidential candidate answers the questions of Ural residents), recorded by Vladimir

Bondarenko, *Zavtra*, 15, April 1996, p. 1. See also the 26 March INTERFAX report on Zyuganov's trip to Barnaul, 'Gernady Zyuganov Remarks in Barnaul' (FBIS-SOV-96-060, Article Id:drsov060_d_96003, http://wnc.fedworld.gov/cgi-bin).

171. Zyuganov, 'Eshcho nemnogo'.

172. Shub, *Russian Readership Survey*.

173. Viktor Sheynis, 'Proyden li istoricheskiy rubezh?' (Have we passed a historic watershed?), *Polis*, 1, 1997, p. 88.

174. See, for instance, Zyuganov's interview with Echo of Moscow Radio, 1 June 1996, and his 'Eshcho nemnogo'.

175. Michael Gordon, 'Selling of Yeltsin Hits Obstacles in Heartland', *New York Times*, 14 May 1996, p. A12.

176. Sheinis, *op. cit.*, p. 88.

177. 'Strana nepugannykh izbirateley' (A country of wild voters), *Moskovskiy Komsomoletz*, 28 May 1996, p. 2.

178. Zyuganov, 'Znat' i deystvovat''.

179. McFaul, *op. cit.*, p. 36.

180. *Ibid.*, p. 118, n. 67.

181. Zyuganov, 'Znat' i deystvovat''.

182. Vladimir Isakov, 'Pervaya treshchina' (The first crack), *Sovetskaya Rossia*, 19 March 1996, p. 3.

183. Zyuganov, *Za gorizontom*, p. 138.

184. Aleksandr Budberg, 'Kommunisty proigrayut provintsiyu esli B. N. vyigraet gubernatorov' (The communists will lose the province if B. N. wins the governors), *Moskovskiy Komsomoletz*, 13 April 1996, p. 2.

185. INTERFAX, 31 May 1996 (FBIS-Sov-96-106, 31 May 1996, Article Id:drsov106aa_96010, http://wnc.fedworld.gov/cgi-bin).

186. 'Strana nepugannykh izbirateley'.

187. Anatoliy Boykov, 'Goroda za El'tsina, sela za Zyuganova' (Cities

are pro-Yeltsin and villages are pro-Zyuganov), *Moskovskiy Komsomoletz*, 31 May 1996, p. 2.

188. *Ibid.*

189. N. I. Biryukov, 'Vozmozhno li v sovremennoy Rossii prognozirovat' electoral'noye povedenie?' (Is it possible to forecast the electorate's behaviour in Russia?), *Polis*, 1, 1997, p. 114.

190. Budberg, 'Kommunisty proigrayut'.

191. 'Strana nepugannykh izbirateley'.

192. Zyuganov, 'Znat' i deystvovat'', 'Escho nemnogo' and interview with Echo of Moscow Radio, 1 June 1996.

193. Zyuganov, interview with Echo of Moscow Radio, 1 June 1996.

194. R. Aliev, 'Zyuganov in Novosibirsk', *Sovetskaya Sibir'*, 6 June 1996, p. 1; Yuriy Khotz, ITAR-TASS, 5 June 1996 (FBIS-SOV-96-115, 14 June 1996, Article 1d: drsov 115aa_96016, http:/wnc.fedworld.gov/cgi-bin . . .); Stanley, 'Red Scare', p. 27; Anatoliy Belozertsev, 'Rossia – samaya glavnaya partiya. O poezdke Gennadia Zyuganova v Povolzh'e i na Ural' ('The most important party is Russia'. On Gennadiy Zyuganov's trip to the Volga region and the Urals), *Pravda*, 23 April 1996, p. 2.

195. Stanley, 'Red Scare', p. 26; Aliev, *op. cit.*; Zyuganov, 'Znat' i deystvovat''.

196. Aliev, *op. cit.*

197. *Ibid.*; Sergey Ivanov, 'Doroga zhizni skvoz' blokadu' (The road of life through the blockade), *Sovetskaya Rossia*, 10 April 1996, p. 2.

198. Stanley, 'Red Scare', p. 33.

199. *Ibid.*; Aliev, *op. cit.*; Ivanov, 'Doroga zhizni'.

200. Aliev, *op. cit.*; Ivanov, 'Doroga zhizni'.

201. Stanley 'Red Scare', pp. 27, 33.

202. Zyuganov, 'Eshcho nemnogo', and interview with Echo of Moscow Radio, 1 June 1996, p. 1.

203. Khotz, *op. cit.*

204. Lee Hockstader, 'Russians Face a Stark Choice', *Washington Post*, 15 June 1996, p. A21.

205. Zyuganov, 'Patrioticheskaya vlast''.

206. See, for example, Gennadiy Zyuganov's interviews 'Patriotichskaya vlast'', 'Eshcho nemnogo' and 'Znat' i deystvovat''.

207. Zyuganov, 'Znat' i deystvovat''.

208. *Ibid.*

209. *Ibid.*

210. Gennadiy Zyuganov, 'My vmeste vozrodim Rossiyu' (Together we will revive Russia), *Pravda*, 1 July 1996, p. 1.

211. Gennadiy Zyuganov, 'Veteranam Velikoy Otechestvennoy voyny, truzhennikam tyla, voinam Rossiyskoy Armii i Flota, vsem grazhdanam Rossii' (To the veterans of the Great Patriotic War, the workers of the home front, warriors of the Russian Army and Navy, and all Russian citizens), *Pravda Rossii*, 7 May 1996, p. 1.

212. Viktor Ilyukhin, 'Pochemu ya budu golosovat' protiv B. El'tsina' (Why I will be voting against B. Yeltsin), *Pravda Rossii*, 11 April 1996, p. 1.

213. *Ibid.*

214. 'Rossiey pravit zhestokaya kukla' (Russia is ruled by a cruel puppet), *Zavtra*, 4, January 1994, p. 1.

215. 'Slava soldatu, pozor verkhovnomu!' (Glory to the soldier, shame to the commander-in-chief!), *Zavtra*, 3, January 1996, p. 1.

216. 'Pal'to El'tsina zalyapano krov'yu' (Yeltsin's coat is splattered with blood), *Zavtra*, 17, April 1996, p. 1.

217. 'Gospodi, izbav' Rossiyu ot El'tsina!' (Lord, rid Russia of Yeltsin!), *Zavtra*, 16, April 1996, p. 1.

218. 'Slyshish, diktor kak kartant? . . .' (Here the announcer burring . . .), *Zavtra*, 24, June 1996, p. 8.

219. 'Chastushki', *Zavtra*, 24, June 1996, p. 8.

220. *Ibid.*
221. *Sovetskaya Rossia*, 6 June 1996, the election insert *Izbiratel'*.
222. *Sovetskaya Rossia*, 16 March 1996.
223. 'A tyne temnish? . . . Tochno – usyo vylozhil?!' (You are not playing games with us, are you? . . . Are you sure you have not given us everything?!), *Sovetskaya Rossia*, 25 April 1996. The inscriptions on the files around Yeltsin read: 'Top Secret. New Generation of Nuclear Reactors. Strategic Nuclear Research. Russia's Nuclear Shield'.
224. 'Po magochislennym zayvkam zapadnykh investorov . . .' (Responding to too many requests by western investors . . .), *Sovetskaya Rossia*, 5 May 1996.
225. 'Soldat i mraz" (Soldier and vermin), *Zavtra*, 15, April 1996, p. 1.
226. 'Boevoe znamya Rodiny' (The battle banner of the Motherland), *Zavtra*, 18, May 1996, p. 1.
227. 'Svet moy zerkal'tse . . .' (Mirror, mirror on the wall . . .), *Sovetskaya Rossia*, 29 February 1996, p. 2.
228. 'Podpisat' ukaz o prekrashchenii voennykh deystviy v Chechne ruka, ponimaesh, kak-to ne podnimaetsya' (Somehow, you see, I cannot lift my hand to sign a decree on ending the war in Chechnya), *Sovetskaya Rossia*, 20 February 1996, p. 1.
229. *Zavtra*, 21, May 1996, p. 1.
230. 'I eto Chudo-Yudo pobedim, matushku Rus' vozrodim!' (And we will vanquish this Judo-monster, and will revive Mother Russia!), *Sovetskaya Rossia*, 23 February 1996, p. 3; 'Dmitriy Donskoy protiv Borisa El'tsina' (Dmitriy Donskoy against Boris Yeltsin), *Zavtra*, 7, February 1996, p. 1.
231. *Zavtra*, 7, February 1996, p. 1.
232. 'Boris El'tsin: patologiya vlasti' (Boris Yeltsin: pathology of power), *Zavtra*, 12, March 1996, p. 1.
233. *Ibid.*
234. *Ibid.*
235. 'Instruktsiya o poryadke predostavlenia efirnogo vremeni na kanalakh gosudarstvennykh teleradiokompaniy kandidatam na dolzhnost' Prezidenta Rossiyskoy Federatsii, izbiratel'nym ob'edineniyam, initsiativnym gruppam izbirateley i publikatsii agitatsionnykh predvybornykh materialov v periodicheskikh pechatnykh izdaniyakh' (Instruction on making broadcast time on the channels of the state-owned television and radio networks available to the candidates for the position of the President of the Russian Federation, electoral blocs and grass-roots groups of voters, and on the publication of the campaign materials in the periodic press publications), *Rossiyskaya Gazeta*, 17 April 1996, pp. 5, 6; and 'Grafik raspredeleniya besplatnogo efirnogo vremeni . . .' (Schedule of free airtime . . .), *Rossiyskaya Gazeta*, 12 May 1996, p. 3.
236. Mickiewicz, *op. cit.*, p. 172; and 'Instruktsiya'.
237. '2x2 Televison' (Moscow) (FBIS, 24 June 1996, http://wnc.fedworld.gov/cgi-bin . . . , Article Id:drsov122aa_96009); and *OMRI Daily*, 25 June 1996, p. 2 (http://www.omri.cz1).
238. Mickiewicz, *op. cit.*, p. 172.
239. *Ibid.*
240. *Ibid.*
241. 'Instruktsiya', Article 1.5.
242. Gennadiy Zyuganov, interview on St Petersburg Fifth Channel, 14 June 1996 (FBIS, 18 June 1996, p. 2, http://wnc.fedworld.gov/cgi-bin . . . , Article Id:drsov117aa_96050).
243. *Ibid.*, p. 6.
244. *Ibid.*, p. 12.
245. Mickiewicz, *op. cit.*, pp. 178, 179.
246. *Ibid.*, p. 179.
247. *Segodnya*, NTV, 26, 27, 29, 30 May (FBIS, 29, 31 May and 4 June, http://wnc.fedworld.gov/cgi-bin . . . , Article Id's: drsov103aa_96009 and

96011, 105aa_96004 and
107aa_96010).

248. Zyuganov, interview with Echo
of Moscow Radio, 1 June 1996,
p. 10.

249. Mickiewicz, *op. cit.*, p. 178.

250. *Ibid.*

251. *Ibid.*, p. 185.

252. *Ibid.* See also Gennadiy
Zyuganov, press conference, NTV,
Segodnya, 26 June 1996 (FBIS-SOV-
96-125, 28 June 1996, p. 1, Article
1d: drsov125aa_96009).

253. Interview with Professor Ellen
Mickiewicz.

254. *OMRI Daily*, 2 July 1996.

255. Lyubov Tsukanova, 'Kto budet
vesti izbiratel'nuya kampaniyu Borisa
El'tsina' (Those people who will be
running Boris Yeltsin's election
campaign), *Rossiyskie Vesti*, 27
March 1996.

256. David Hoffman, 'Yeltsin Vows
No Delays in Election; President
Contradicts Adviser's Statement',
Washington Post, 7 May 1996,
p. A11.

257. B. Berezovskiy, V. Gorodilov,
V. Gusinskiy, A. Dundukov,
N. Mikhaylov, S. Muravlenko,
L. Nevzlin, A. Nikolaev, D. Orlov,
V. Potanin, A. Smolenskiy,
M. Fridman and M. Khodorkovskiy,
'Vyiti iz tupika!' (Exit from a dead
end!), *Izvestia*, 27 April 1996, p. 2.

258. *Ibid.*

259. Elena Dikun and Anatoliy
Kostyukov, 'Kuptsy pritsenivayutsya,
tovar prikidyvaetsya' (The buyers are
looking, the wares are pretending),
Obshchaya Gazeta, 5–11 May 1996,
p. 9.

260. Aleksandr Gamov, 'Ulichniy
El'tsin sovsem ne pokhoz na
kabinetnogo' (Yeltsin on the street is
not at all like Yeltsin in the office),
Komsomol'skaya Pravda, 23 April
1996, p. 2.

261. See, for instance, 'Ukaz o zemle,
no ne o mire' (A decree on land, but
not on peace), *Novoye Vremya*, 11,

1996, p. 4; and 'Dosi'e "MN"'
(*Moskovskie Novosti*'s dossier),
Moskovskie Novosti, 17–24 March
1996, p. 5.

262. Gennadiy Zyuganov, 'Den'
soprotivlyayushcheysya pechati' (The
day of the newspapers of resistance),
letter to the participants in the festival
of the newspaper *Pravda*, *Pravda*, 7
May 1996, p. 1.

263. INTERFAX, 18 May 1996
(FBIS-SOV-96-098, 18 May 1996,
p. 1, http://wnc.fedworld.gov/cgi-
bin . . . , Article
Id:drsov098aa_96011). See also NTV,
18 May 1996 (FBIS-SOV-96-098, 18
May 1996, p. 1, http://
wnc.fedworld.gov/cgi-bin . . . , Article
Id:drsov098aa_96002).

264. Ludmila Telen', ' "Pervyi
zvonok"' ('The first call'),
Moskovskie Novosti, 21–8 April
1996, p. 6.

265. Oleg Moroz, 'Dudaev zhelaet,
choby rossiyskim prezidentom stal ego
tovarish po partii' (Dudaev wants his
[Communist] Party comrade to
become Russian President),
Literaturnaya Gazeta, 20 March
1996, p. 10.

266. Boris Yeltsin, address to the
nation on the settling of the war in
Chechnya, 31 March 1996, First
Channel/ORT (Ostankino) (FBIS-
SOV-96-063, 1 April 1996, p. 1).

267. Chrystia Freeland, 'Yeltsin
pledges to face Chechnya death
threat', *Financial Times*, 5 May 1996,
p. 1.

268. Mikhail Gurevich, 'Slovo i delo
prezidenta' (The word and deed of the
President), *Rossiyskie Vesti*, 29 May
1996, p. 1.

269. Pavel Anokhin, 'Tretiy sil'nyi
khod Borisa El'tsina v Chechenskoy
politike' (The third master move of
Boris Yeltsin in the Chechen policy),
Rossiyskie Vesti, 29 May 1996, p. 1.

270. Speech to federal troops in
Grozny, Chechnya, INTERFAX, 28
May (FBIS-SOV-96-103, 29 May

1996, http://www.fedworld.gov/cgi-bin . . . , Article Id:drsov103_d_96012).

271. Vladimir Solov'yov, 'Lightning Excursion to Grozny', *Sel'skaya Zhizn'*, 30 May 1996, p. 1. (FBIS-SOV-96-105, 31 May 1996, Article 1d: drsov105aa_96005, http:/fedworld-gov/cgi-bin . . .); Gurevich, *op. cit.*

272. Lynn Berry, 'Chechen Guerillas Shot Down Copter', *Washington Times*, 31 May 1996, p. 3.

273. Gaidar, *Dni porazheniy*, p. 361, and 'U menia net sindroma', p. 12.

274. Gaida, *Dni porazheniy*, p. 361.

275. *Ibid.*

276. Gaidar, 'U menia net sindroma', p. 12.

277. Lee Hockstader, 'Invigorated Yeltsin Hits Hustings', *Washington Post*, 1 June 1996, p. A17.

278. McFaul, *op. cit.*, p. 23.

279. Gamov, 'Ulichniy El'tsin'.

280. *Ibid.*

281. Boris Yeltsin, remarks in Chelyabinsk, NTV, 16 February 1996. (FBIS-SOV-96-034, 21 February 1996 drsov034_b_96005, http://wnc.fedworld.gov/cgi-bin . . .).

282. Interview with Aleksandr Livshits.

283. Hockstader, 'Invigorated Yeltsin'.

284. *Ibid.*

285. Aleksandr Gamov, 'Kumiry shumnoyu tolpoy kochyut po strane velikoy' (Noisy crowds of idols are roaming the great country), *Komsomol'skaya Pravda*, 13 April 1996, p. 2.

286. Leonid Ionin, 'Tretiy El'tsin' (The third Yeltsin), *Novoye Vremya*, 23, 1996, p. 7.

287. Gamov, 'Ulichniy El'tsin'.

288. *Ibid.*

289. *Ibid.*

290. Tatyana Malkina, 'Prezident El'tsin vzyal probu nastroyeniy v Chernozyom'e' (President Yeltsin tested the mood in the Black Soil region), *Segodnya*, 5 April 1996, p. 1.

291. *Ibid.*

292. Hockstader, 'Invigorated Yeltsin'.

293. *Ibid.*, and Gamov, 'Ulichniy El'tsin'.

294. Gamov, 'Ulichniy El'tsin'.

295. *Ibid.*

296. *Ibid.*

297. *Ibid.*

298. *Ibid.*

299. *Ibid.*

300. See, for example, Malkina, 'Prezident El'tsin'; and NTV's broadcast of Yeltsin's visit to Chelyabinsk, 16 February 1996 (FBIS, http://wnc.fedworld.gov/cgi-bin/re . . . , Article Id:drsov034_b_96005).

301. 'Vtoroye dykhanie' (A second wind), *Moskovskie Novosti*, 9–16 June 1996, p. 8.

302. Boris Vishnevskiy and Aleksandr Gamov, 'Prezident v Tatarii bil gorshki, a v Sibiri agitiroval Mukhu' (President broke pots in Tatarstan and canvassed Mukha in Siberia), *Komsomol'skaya Pravda*, 11 June 1996, p. 2.

303. Hockstader, 'Invigorated Yeltsin'.

304. Malkina, 'Prezident El'tsin'.

305. Hockstader, 'Invigorated Yeltsin'.

306. Gamov, 'Kumiry shumnoyu tolpoy'.

307. Pashkov, *op. cit.*

308. Vladmir Semyonov, 'Stavka – na neposredstvennuyu rabotu s izbiratelyami' (Emphasis on direct work with voters), *Rossiyskie Vesti*, 6 May 1996, p. 1.

309. Gamov, 'Ulichniy El'tsin'.

310. *Ibid.*

311. Yeltsin, speech in Ekaterinburg, 15 February 1996, p. 48.

312. Gamov, 'Kumiry shumnoyu tolpoy'.

313. Aleksandr Gamov, '. . . A zamenit' seychas nekem' (But there is no one to replace him now),

Komsomol'skaya Pravda, 2 July 1996, p. 2.

314. *Ibid.*

315. *Ibid.*

316. *Ibid.*

317. 'Yeltsin Visits Kaliningrad Region', ITAR-TASS, 23 June 1996 (FBIS-SOV-96-122, http://wnc.fedworld.gov/cgi-bin . . . , Article Id:drsov122_b_96002), and 'Address to the citizens of Khabarovsk', Radio Rossii, 23 June 1996 (FBIS-SOV-96-123, 26 June 1996, Article Id:drsov123aa_96001, http://wnc.fedworld.gov/cgi-bin . . .).

318. ITAR-TASS, 11 June 1996 (FBIS-SOV-96-114, 13 June 1996, Article Id:drsov114aa_96002, http://wnc.fedworld.gov/cgi-bin . . .); and ITAR-TASS, 11 June 1996 (FB1S-SOV-96-113, 12 June 1996, Article Id:drsov113aa_96002, http://wnc.fedworld.gov/cgi-bin . . .).

319. Kostikov, *op. cit.*, p. 161.

320. Korzhakov, *op. cit.*, pp. 357, 332.

321. Interview with Aleksandr Livshits.

322. Boris Yeltsin, 'Glavnoye, chtoby Rossiya okonchatel'no sdelala svoy vybor v pol'zu svobody' (The most important thing is for Russia to choose freedom), interview with *Rossiyskaya Gazeta*, 5 June 1996, p. 3.

323. Boris Yeltsin, speech in the Khanty-Mansiyskiy Autonomous District, 11 June 1996. ITAR-TASS (FBIS-SOV-96-114, 13 June 1996, Article Id:drsov114aa_96002, p. 1, http://wnc.fedworld.gov/cgi-bin . . .).

324. Yeltsin, 'Glavnoye, chtoby Rossiya'.

325. *Ibid.*

326. Yeltsin, speech in the Khanty-Mansiyskiy Autonomous District.

327. Yeltsin, interview with *Kaliningradskaya Pravda*, 18 May 1996 (FBIS-SOV-96-109, 6 June, Article 1d: drsov109_d_96001, p. 3, http://wnc.fedword.gov/cgi-bin . . .).

328. *Ibid.*

329. Interview with the Yaroslavl' city television ITAR-TASS, 2 May 1996 (FBIS-SOV-96-087, 6 May 1996, Article Id:drsov087_a_96002, http://wnc.fedwordl.gov/cgi-bin . . .).

330. Boris Yeltsin, remarks in Chelyabinsk, NTV, Moscow, 16 February 1996 (FBIS, Article Id:drsov034_b_96005, http://wnc.fedworld.gov/cgi-bin/re, p. 1).

331. Yeltsin, 'Glavnoye, chtoby Rossiya', p. 3.

332. Yeltsin, 'Rossiya: Chelovek, Sem'ya', p. 1.

333. Boris Yeltsin, speech in Yaroslavl', 3 May 1996, ITAR-TASS (FBIS-SOV-96-088, 7 May p. 2, Article Id:drsov088_b_96005, http://wnc.fedworld.gov/cgi-bin . . .).

334. INTERFAX, 3 May 1996 (FBIS-SOV-96-088, 7 May 1996, Article Id:drsov088aa_96006, http://wnc.fedworld.gov/cgi-bin . . .).

335. Yeltsin, speech in Yaroslavl', ITAR-TASS, 3 May 1996, p. 1.

336. Boris Yeltsin, speech at the Independence Day rally and concert in Moscow, 12 June 1996, Mayak Radio (FBIS-SOV-96-115, 14 June, Article Id:drsov115aa_96001, http://wnc.fedworld.gov/cgi-bin . . .).

337. Boris Yeltsin, speech at the National Congress of Independent Media, 16 May 1996, INTERFAX (FBIS-SOV-96-096, 20 May, Article Id:drsov096aa_96003, http://wnc.fedworld.gov/cgi-bin . . .).

338. Boris Yeltsin, speech at a meeting of journalists from Russian provinces, 6 May 1996, INTERFAX (FBIS-SOV-96-089, p. 2, 8 May, Article Id:drsov089_b_96008, http://wnc.fedworld.gov/cgi-bin . . .).

339. Yeltsin, speech at the National Congress of Independent Media; and speech at the Krasnoyarsk Television and Broadcasting Company, 17 May 1996, ITAR-TASS (FBIS-SOV-96-097, p. 2, http://wnc.fedworld.gov/cgi-bin, Article Id:drsov097aa_96004).

340. Yeltsin, address to regional media workers, 6 May 1996, p. 2.

341. *Ibid.*

342. INTERFAX, 3 May 1996 (FBIS, 6 May 1996, p. 5).

343. Yeltsin, speech at the Independence Day rally and concert in Moscow, p. 1.

344. Boris Yeltsin, speech in Ekaterinburg, 14 June 1996, INTERFAX (FBIS-SOV-96-117, http://wnc.fedworld.gov/cgi-bin . . . , 18 June, Article Id:drsov117aa_96033).

345. Yeltsin, speech in Yaroslavl', 3 May 1996, p. 2.

346. INTERFAX, 3 May 1996 (FBIS, 6 May 1996, p. 5).

347. Yeltsin, remarks in Chelyabinsk, 16 February 1996, NTV Moscow (FBIS-SOV-96-034, 21 February 1996, Article Id:drsov_b_96005, http://wnc.fedworld.gov/cgi-bin . . . , p. 1).

348. Gamov, 'Kumiry shumnoyu tolpoy'.

349. INTERFAX, 26 April 1996 (FBIS-SOV-96-083, 30 April 1996, Article Id:drsov083aa_96002, http://wnc.fedworld.gov/cgi-bin . . . , p. 1).

350. Yeltsin, speech in Yaroslavl', 3 May 1996, p. 2.

351. Yeltsin, address to the National Congress of Independent Media, 16 May 1996.

352. *Ibid.*

353. Anna Paretskaya, 'New Commercials Tell Youth "Vote and You'll Win"'; and Laura Belin, '. . . As Entertainment Programs Keep Up Anti-Communist Drumbeat', *OMRI Daily*, 27 June 1996 and 2 July 1996.

354. Boris Yeltsin, responses to questions submitted by journalists from the Ivanovo Region. INTERFAX, 26 April 1996 (FBIS-SOV-96-083, 30 April 1996. Article Id:drsov083aa_96002, http://wnc.fedworld.gov/cgi-bin).

355. Boris Yeltsin, interview with *Delovye Lyudi* magazine, INTERFAX, 6 May 1996 (FBIS, 7 May 1996,

Article Id:drsov088_b_96003, http://wnc.fedworld.gov/cgi-bin . . .).

356. Yeltsin, speech at the Independence Day rally and concert in Moscow, 12 June 1996.

357. Boris Yeltsin, speech in Novocherkassk, 11 June 1996, ITAR-TASS (FBIS-SOV-96-113, http://wnc.fedworld.gov/cgi-bin . . . , 12 June 1996, Article Id:drsov113aa_96002).

358. Yeltsin, 'Glavnoye, choby Rossiya', pp. 1, 3.

359. INTERFAX, 26 April 1996 (FBIS-SOV-96-083, 30 April 1996, Article Id:drsov083aa_96002, http://wnc.fedworld.gov/cgi-bin . . . , p. 1).

360. *OMRI Daily*, 21 and 27 June, 2 July 1996.

361. Laura Belin, 'Yeltsin Stays Off Screen during Free Air Time', *OMRI Russian Presidential Election Survey*, 12, 2 July 1996, p. 1.

362. *OMRI Daily*, 2 July 1996.

363. Laura Belin, 'Anti-Communist Entertainment on TV', *OMRI Daily*, 21 June 1996.

364. INTERFAX, 3 May 1996, 1230 GMT (FBIS-SOV-96-088, 6 May 1996, p. 5).

365. INTERFAX, 14 June 1996 (FBIS-SOV-96-117, 14 June 1996, http://wnc.fedworld.gov/cgi-bin . . . , Article Id:drsov117aa_96033).

366. *Ibid.*

367. *Ibid.*

368. Igor Bel'skiy, 'Russia: Election Bank Funds of Presidential Candidates Cited', ITAR-TASS, 23 May 1996 (FBIS-SOV-96-102, Article Id:drsov102aa_96014, http://wnc.fedworld.gov/cgi-bin . . .).

369. 'El'tsin deneg ne zhalel!' (Yeltsin did not stint on money!), *Sovetskaya Rossia*, 20 June 1996, p. 4.

370. *Ibid.*

371. Mickiewicz, *op. cit.*, p. 266.

372. Vsevolod Vil'chek, 'Televideniyu pokoy tol'ko snitsya' (Television can only dream of tranquillity), *Moskovskie Novosti*, 7–14 July

1996, p. 5. Emphasis in the original.

373. OMRI *Russian Presidential Election Survey*, 15, 9 July 1996.

374. Mickiewicz, *op. cit.*, p. 171.

375. Biryukov, 'Vozmozhno li v sovremennoy Rossii prognozirovat' electoral'noye povedenie?', p. 113.

376. INTERFAX, 14 May 1996 (FBIS, 14 May 1996, p. 14); and 'Polling Russian Electorate', *Washington Post*, 23 May 1996, p. A31.

377. Public Opinion Foundation, *Novoye Vremya*, 23, 1996, p. 10.

378. Yuriy Levada, Director of the All-Russian Centre for the Study of Public Opinion, 'Vsyo reshitsya vo vtorom ture' (Everything will be decided in the second round), *Izvestia*, 30 April 1996, p. 2.

379. *Ibid.*; and INTERFAX, 23 April 1996 (FBIS-SOV-96-082, 26 April 1996, p. 3).

380. *Analitica Moscow Political Weekly Press Summary*, vol. 3, no. 24, 22–28 June 1996, p. 1.

381. Hockstader, 'Russians Face a Stark Choice', p. A21.

382. David Hoffman, 'Are Young Russians Fearful Enough to Vote?', *Washington Post*, 22 May 1996, p. A1.

383. *Ibid.*

384. *Ibid.*

385. *Ibid.*

386. *Ibid.*

387. Hoffman, 'Are Young Russians Fearful Enough?', p. A26.

388. 'El'tsin deneg ne zhalel!'

389. Hockstader, 'Invigorated Yeltsin', and Tatyana Malkina, 'Boris El'tsin uveren, chto ob'edinilsya s tret'ey siloy' (Boris Yeltsin is confident that he has allied himself with the 'third force'), *Segodnya*, 12 May 1996, p. 1.

390. Hockstader, 'Invigorated Yeltsin', p. 20.

391. Mikhail Klopyzhnikov and Aleksandr Nikolaev, 'Zerkalo postsovetskoy demokratii' (A mirror of post-Soviet democracy), *Svobodnaya Mysl'*, June 1997, p. 50.

392. 'Lebed' "sdal" patriotov El'tsinu' (Lebed 'delivered' the patriots to Yeltsin), *Zavtra*, 26, June 1996, p. 1; 'V shest' chasov vechera posle vyborov' (At six o'clock after the election), *Zavtra*, 29, July 1996, p. 1.

393. ITAR-TASS, 16 June 1996 (FBIS-SOV-96-117, 18 June 1996, Article Id:drsov117aa_9608, http://wnc.fedworld.gov/cgi-bin . . .).

394. Gennady Zyuganov, news conference after the second round of the presidential election, ITAR-TASS, 4 July 1999 (FBIS-SOV-96-130, 8 July 1996, Article Id:drsov130aa_96034, http://wnc.fedworld/gov/cgi-bin . . .)

395. McFaul, *op. cit.*, p. 71.

396. William Zimmerman, 'Foreign Policy, Political System Preference, and the Russian Presidential Election', paper delivered at the annual meeting of the American Association for Advancement of Slavic Studies, 16 November 1996, p. 8, as quoted by McFaul, *op. cit.*, p. 74.

397. 'No Illusion on Democracy, a Student Favors Yeltsin', *Washington Post*, 15 June 1996, p. A20.

398. Sheinis, *op. cit.*, p. 88.

399. *Ibid.*

400. Anatole Shub, *Political Continuities Overshadow Yeltsin Comeback in Russian Election*, Washington, DC: Office of Research and Media Reaction, US Information Agency, 19 July 1996, p. 1.

401. Inga Mikhailovskaya, 'Russian Voting Behavior as a Mirror of Social–Political Change', *East European Constitutional Review*, Spring/Summer 1996, p. 60.

402. Viktor Shenderovich, 'Spisok nadezhd' (A list of hopes), *Moskovskie Novosti*, 7–14 July 1996.

403. First Channel/ORT (Ostankino), 4 July 1996 (FBIS-SOV-96-130, 5 July 1996, p. 1).

Chapter 14: The Last Struggle

1. Joseph R. Blasi, Maya Kroumova and Douglas Kruse, *Kremlin Capitalism*, Ithaca: Cornell University Press, 1997, p. 26; and Stanley Fisher, 'The Russian Economy at the Start of 1998', paper delivered at the US–Russian Investment Symposium, Cambridge, MA: John F. Kennedy School of Government, Harvard University Press, p. 2.

2. Boycko, Shleifer and Vishny, *Privatizing Russia*, p. 11.

3. *Ibid.*, p. 65.

4. Blasi, Kroumova and Kruse, *op. cit.*, p. 179.

5. 'From Marx, maybe to market', *Economist*, 12 July 1997, p. 11.

6. Peter Rutland, 'Yeltsin: the Problem, not the Solution', *The National Interest*, Fall 1997.

7. Daniel Williams, 'High Russian Officials Duck Anti-Corruption Initiative', *Washington Post*, 25 July 1997.

8. Lev Timofeev, 'Novaya teoria sotsializma' (A new theory of socialism), *Moskovskie Novosti*, 8–15 December 1996.

9. See, for instance, Yakov Urinson, 'Krizis v Rossii est', no katastrophy ne budet' (There is a crisis in Russia, but a catastrophe will not happen), *Izvestia*, 10 July 1998, p. 4; and Avi Shama, 'Notes from Underground: Russia's Economy Booms', *Wall Street Journal*, 24 October 1997, p. A10.

10. As quoted in John Varpoli, 'Economic Reform Casts a Long Shadow in Russia', *Transition*, 21 March 1997, p. 8.

11. Blasi, Kroumova and Kruse, *op. cit.*, p. 179.

12. Yakov Urinson, 'Vsyo chto effiktivno dlya ekonomiki, boleznenno dlya obshchestva' (Everything that is positive for the economy is painful for society), *Moskovskie Novosti*, 17–24 May 1998, p. 10.

13. Mikhail Zadornov, 'Vlezayem v dolgi?' (Are we assuming too much debt?), *Moskovskie Novosti*, 7–14 June 1998, p. 6.

14. Yakov Urinson, 'Ya podderzhu vsyo, cho pol'zuetsya sprosom' (I will support everything for which there is demand), *Novoye Vremya*, 15, 1997, p. 18.

15. Urinson, 'Vsyo, chto effektivno'.

16. See, for example, Elena Lyakhova, 'Anatomiya ugol'nogo vorovstva' (The anatomy of the coal thievery), *Izvestia*, 15 July 1998, p. 4.

17. Urinson, 'Krizis v Rossii'.

18. Boris Nemtsov, 'Za obman nalogovykh sluzhb nado sazhat' v tyur'mu' (Lying to the tax services ought to be punished by jail), interview with *Izvestia*, 19 March 1997, p. 2.

19. *Ibid.*

20. *Ibid.*

21. Boris Yeltsin, televised address to the nation, 10 July 1996, ITAR-TASS (FBIS-SOV-96-134, 11 July 1996, p. 14).

22. *Ibid.*, p. 15.

23. *Ibid.*

24. *Ibid.*

25. *Ibid.*

26. *Ibid.*

27. V.L., 'Staryi slukh luch'she novykh dvukh' (An old rumour is better than two new ones), *Moskovskie Novosti*, 14–21 July 1996, p. 3.

28. *Ibid.*

29. Alessandra Stanley, 'Yeltsin Says He Will Have Heart Surgery', *New York Times*, 6 September 1996.

30. Stanley Hoffman, 'Yeltsin to Have Heart Surgery; Rules for Replacement Untested', *New York Times*, 6 September 1996, p. A26.

31. Stanley, 'Yeltsin Says'; Yuriy Belenkov, Chief Cardiologist of the Russian Federation, 'On bystro razdyshalsya . . .' (He quickly began breathing normally . . .), *Moskovskie Novosti*, 10–17 November 1996, p. 4.

32. David Hoffman, 'Yeltsin Heart Operation Called a Success',

Washington Post, 6 November 1996, p. A3; and Belenkov, *op. cit.*

33. Belenkov, *op. cit.*

34. *Ibid.*

35. *Ibid.*

36. Hoffman, 'Yeltsin Heart Operation'.

37. Belenkov, *op. cit.*

38. Hoffman, 'Yeltsin Heart Operation'; and Belenkov, *op. cit.*

39. Andrey Kolesnikov and Dmitriy Orlov, 'Evangelie ot Borisa' (The gospel according to Boris), *Novoye Vremya*, 10, 1997, p. 6; and Vandora Bennett, 'Feisty Yeltsin Vows Reform, Good Rule and New Cabinet', *Los Angeles Times*, 7 March 1997, p. 1 (http://www.latimes.com).

40. Boris Yeltsin, State of Russia address to the Federal Assembly, 6 March 1997 (http://www.maindir.gov.ru, 26 June 1997), p. 3.

41. *Ibid.*, p. 18.

42. *Ibid.*, p. 26.

43. *Ibid.*, p. 27.

44. *Ibid.*, pp. 39, 40.

45. *Ibid.*, p. 6.

46. *Ibid.*

47. *Ibid.*

48. *Ibid.*, p. 10.

49. *Ibid.*, p. 4.

50. *Ibid.*, p. 21.

51. Gaidar, *Dni porazheniy*, p. 365.

52. The 6 March 1997 State of Russia address, p. 3.

53. *Ibid.*, p. 20.

54. *Ibid.*

55. *Ibid.*

56. *Ibid.*, p. 18.

57. *Ibid.*, p. 19.

58. *Ibid.*, p. 7.

59. *Ibid.*, p. 18.

60. *Ibid.*, p. 20.

61. *Ibid.*, p. 22.

62. *Ibid.*

63. *Ibid.*, pp. 22, 23.

64. *Ibid.*, p. 21.

65. *Ibid.*, pp. 15, 21.

66. *Ibid.*, p. 16.

67. *Ibid.*, p. 28.

68. *Ibid.*, p. 16.

69. *Ibid.*, p. 38.

70. *Ibid.*, p. 17.

71. *Ibid.*, p. 24.

72. *Ibid.*

73. *Ibid.*

74. *Ibid.*, p. 40.

75. *Ibid.*, p. 3.

76. *Ibid.*, p. 9.

77. *Ibid.*, p. 5.

78. John Thornhill and Chrystia Freeland, 'Russia: Yeltsin returns with all guns blazing', *Financial Times*, 7 March 1997, p. 1 (http://www.ft.com).

79. Georgiy Satarov, as quoted in Kolesnikov and Orlov, 'Evangelie ot Borisa', p. 7.

80. Andrey Kolesnikov, 'Peresadka mozga' (Brain transplant), *Novoye Vremya*, 10, 1997, p. 8.

81. *Ibid.*

82. *Ibid.*

83. Alessandra Stanley, 'Yeltsin Pledges Housecleaning and Reform', *New York Times*, 7 March 1997, p. 1 (http://www.nytimes.com).

84. 'New Top Minister Promises Honesty, Reform', Reuters, 17 March 1997 (*Russia Today*, http://www.russiatoday.com).

85. *Ibid.*

86. David Hoffman, 'Yeltsin Picks Reformist for Cabinet Post', *Washington Post*, 18 March 1997, p. A12.

87. *Ibid.*

88. Hoffman, 'Yeltsin Picks Reformist'.

89. As quoted in 'Tsitata nedeli' (The quote of the week), *Novoye Vremya*, 47, 1997, p. 7.

90. *Sovetskaya Rossia*, 13 March 1997, p. 1.

91. 'Duma Communists Intend to Initiate Vote of No Confidence in Government', INTERFAX, 18 March 1997, p. 1 (http://www.maximov.com).

92. Dmitriy Kostenko, 'S'ezd KPRF provozglasil glavnoy zadachey

kommunistov "smenu pravyashchego v strane regima"' (The KPRF congress declared 'change of the ruling regime' their main task), Natsional'naya Sluzhba Novostei, 24 April 1997, p. 4 (http://www.nns.ru).

93. Gaidar, *Dni porazheniy*, p. 198.

94. Andrey Kolesnikov, 'Dzhoker vlasti' (The joker in power), *Novoye Vremya*, 48, 1996, p. 10.

95. Anatoliy Chubais, 'Mne nepriyatny razgovory o moyem "vsemogushchestve"' (I dislike the talk of my 'omnipotence'), interview with *Novoye Vremya*, 48, 1996, p. 7.

96. Viktor Chernomyrdin, Anatoliy Chubais and Boris Nemtsov, press conference, 26 March 1997, Natsional'naya Sluzhba Novostei, 27 March 1997, p. 1 (http://www.nns.ru).

97. *Ibid.*, p. 2.

98. *Ibid.*; and Boris Nemtsov, 'Razgovory o podkovyornoy bor'be vitse-prem'erov s prem'erom – vymysel' (Stories about behind-the-scenes struggle between the Deputy Prime Ministers and the Prime Minister are fiction), *Izvestia*, 6 May 1997, p. 1.

99. Urinson, 'Ya podderzhu vyso', p. 18.

100. Andrey Kolesnikov, 'Novaya nomenklatura' (A new nomenklatura), *Novoye Vremya*, 16, 1997, p. 14.

101. Interview with Aleksandr Livshits.

102. *Ibid.*

103. 'Chubais Wants to Bar Commercial Banks from Collecting Custom Duties . . .', *RFE/RL Newsline*, 7 August 1997; and Boris Yeltsin, speech to the Council of Federation, 24 September 1997, transcript by Federal News Service, p, 3 (http://www.fnsg.com, 29 September 1997).

104. *Ibid.*, and 'Presidential Decree Tightens Control over Budget Funds', *RFE/RL Newsline*, 14 May 1997.

105. Nemtsov, 'Razgovory of podkovyornoy', p. 2.

106. Yeltsin, speech to the Council of Federation, 24 September 1997.

107. 'Yeltsin Approves Production-Sharing List', *RFE/RL Newsline*, 23 July 1997.

108. 'Yeltsin Lifts Limits on Foreign Ownership of Shares in Russian Oil Companies', *RFE/RL Newsline*, 5 November 1997.

109. Andrey Kolesnikov, 'Kapitalizm novogo tipa' (Capitalism of a new kind), *Novoye Vremya*, 52, 1997, p. 8.

110. *Ibid.*

111. Boris Nemtsov, 'Nemtsov opposes "robber capitalism"', *Komsomol'skaya Pravda*, 29 July 1997 (RIA-NOVOSTI, 6 August 1997, p. 1, http://www.ria-novosti.com).

112. *Ibid.*

113. *Ibid.*, p. 2.

114. 'Government Commission Targets More Tax Debtors', *RFE/RL Newsline*, 23 July 1997.

115. 'Svedeniya o dokhodakh i imushestve Prezidenta Rossiyskoy Federatsii El'tsina Borisa Nikolaevicha' (Information about the income and property of the President of the Russian Federation, Boris Nikolaevich Yeltsin), Natsional'naya Sluzhba Novostei (http://www.nns.ru), 2 June 1997; 'Svedeniya o dokhodakh pervogo zamestitelya predsedatelya pravitel'stva RF Anatoliya Chubaisa' (Information about income of the First Deputy Chairman of the government of the Russian Federation Anatoliy Chubais), *ibid.*, 13 June 1997; 'Svedeniya of dokhodakh pervogo zamestitelya predsedatelya pravitel'stva RF Borisa Nemtsova' (Information about the income of the First Deputy Chairman of the government of the Russian Federation Boris Nemtsov), *ibid.*

116. Anna Ostapchuk, 'Ne soglyadatay, a posrednik' (Not a spy,

but an intermediary), interview with the Deputy Chief of the Presidential Administration, Aleksandr Kazakov, *Moskovskie Novosti*, 20–27 July 1997.

117. *Ibid.*

118. Yeltsin, speech to the Council of Federation, 24 September 1997, p. 4.

119. *Ibid.*

120. *Ibid.*, p. 5.

121. *RFE/RL Newsline*, 1 October 1997.

122. Barry Renfrew, 'Revitalized Yeltsin Running Hard', Associated Press, 3 July 1997 (*Zhiwriter*, http://www.nd.edu, 8 July 1997, p. 1).

123. Steven Erlanger, 'Russia Sits with "Big 8", Party Crasher No More', *New York Times*, 22 June 1997, p. 6.

124. Yeltsin, speech to the Council of Federation, 24 September 1997, p. 2.

125. David Hoffman, 'Yeltsin Proposes Plebiscite on Whether Lenin's Body Should Be Buried Formally', *Washington Post*, 7 June 1997, p. A19.

126. *Ibid.*

127. INTERFAX, 12 May 1997 (FBIS-SOV-97-132, 13 May 1997, Article Id:drsov05121997000308, http://wnc.fedworld.gov).

128. The 6 March 1997 State of Russia address, p. 3.

129. INTERFAX, 12 May 1997.

130. Michael Dobbs, 'For Clinton, Sticking with Yeltsin Sealed Agreement on NATO', *Washington Post*, 27 May 1997.

131. Boris Yeltsin, radio address on NATO accord, 29 May 1997, Informantsionnoye Agenstvo Ekho Moskvy (FBIS-SOV-97-149, http://wnc.fedworld.gov, 31 May 1997).

132. 'Dogovor o druzhbe, sotrudnichestve and partnerstve mezhdu Rossiyskoy Federatsiey i Ukrainoy' (Treaty of friendship, co-operation and partnership between the Russian Federation and Ukraine), Natsional'naya Sluzhba Novostei (http://www.nns.ru), 2 June 1997.

133. *RFE-RL Newsline*, 7 May 1997. See also Michael R. Gordon, 'Russia's Premier to Slash Budget, Trimming Military and Subsidies', *New York Times*, 22 May 1997.

134. Shama, *op. cit.*

135. *Russia's Real Economy: Estimating the Informal Sector, 1994–1997*, Santa Monica, CA: The Rand Corporation, 1998, as quoted in Harley Balzer, 'Russia's Middle Class', *Post-Soviet Affairs*, vol. 14 (2), 1998, p. 171.

136. Shama, *op. cit.*; and Balzer, *op. cit.*, p. 177.

137. Urinson, 'Krizis v Rossii est''.

138. Igor Birman, 'Na Rusi zhivyotsya luchshe, chem schitayetsya' (People live better in Russia than is commonly assumed), *Izvestia*, 4 December 1997, p. 2.

139. Shama, *op. cit.*; Birman, *op. cit.*; RMRC (Russian Market Research Co.), *Inside Russia*, Executive Summary, vol. I, Moscow, 1997, as quoted in Balzer, *op. cit.*, p. 177.

140. Steve Liesman, 'Surprise: The Economy in Russia Is Clawing Out of Deep Recession', *Wall Street Journal*, 28 January 1998, p. A11; and 'The makings of a Molotov cocktail', *Economist*, 12 July 1997, p. 5.

141. *Ibid.*

142. Reuters, 'Middle Class Is Russia's Big Hope', *Russia Today*, 27 February 1998 (http://www.russiatoday.com); and Birman, *op. cit.*

143. Balzer, *op. cit.*, p. 181.

144. Andrey Savin, 'Bogatymi v Rossii stanovyatsya po blatu' (One needs connections to become rich in Russia), *Izvestia*, 22 April 1998, p. 6.

145. Balzer, *op. cit.*, p. 176, n. 16.

146. *Ibid.*, p. 173.

147. Aleksandr Gel'man, 'Katekhizis nenachal'nika' (The catechism of a non-boss), *Moskovskie Novosti*, 28 September–5 October 1997, p. 3.

148. Lee Hockstader, 'The Russian

Invasion', *Washington Post*, 15 August 1994.

149. Blair A. Ruble and Nancy Popson, 'The Westernization of a Russian Province: The Case of Novgorod', *Post-Soviet Geography and Economics*, 39, no. 8, 1998, pp. 441 and 442, table 3.

150. 'Harvest Up in 1997, But Problems Remain', *RFE/RL Newsline*, 8 January 1998.

151. David Hoffman, 'It Isn't Tolstoy, But Russians Are Reading Up a Storm', *Washington Post*, 5 July 1997, p. A21.

152. 'Russian love in a cold climate', *Economist*, 15 August 1998, p. 37.

153. Chrystia Freeland, 'Moscow: A flash in the pan', 8 September 1998, p. 1 (http://www.ft.com).

154. Erlen Bernshteyn, 'Okna rosta v Pizanskoy bashne' (Windows of growth in the Tower of Piza), *Novoye Vremya*, 7, 1998, p. 25.

155. Tatyana Zaslavskaya quoted in Balzer, *op. cit.*, p. 177.

156. Birman, *op. cit.*

157. 'Some do eat cake', *Economist*, 12 July 1997, p. 8.

158. *Ibid.*

159. Michael Specter, 'In Moscow Baby Boom, a Vote for the Future', *New York Times*, 27 August 1997.

160. *Ibid.*

161. 'Government Seeks Duma Approval for Social Spending Reductions . . .', *RFE/RL Newsline*, 17 June 1997.

162. 'Reaction to Vote on Social Legislation', *RFE/RL Newsline*, 26 September 1997.

163. Yeltsin, speech to the Council of Federation, 24 September 1997, p. 4.

164. 'Yeltsin to Veto Land Code', *RFE/RL Newsline*, 25 July 1997.

165. 'Official Vows Constitutional Court Appeal on Land Code', *RFE/RL Newsline*, 25 September 1997, and 'Yeltsin Criticizes Duma's Stance', *RFE/RL Newsline*, 30 September 1997.

166. 'Gaidar Stresses Importance of Adopting New Tax Code', *RFE/RL Newsline*, 13 June 1997.

167. Egor Gaidar, 'Dyadinogo karmana ne sushchsestvuyet' (There is no such thing as a rich uncle's pocket), *Novoye Vremya*, 22, 1997, p. 18.

168. Yeltsin, speech to the Council of Federation, 24 September 1997, p. 4.

169. Michael R. Gordon, 'Yeltsin Foe Tries to Harness the Military's Discontent', *New York Times*, 21 September 1997.

170. *Ibid.*

171. 'Opposition Leaders Confer on Strategy', *RFE/RL Newsline*, 30 September 1997.

172. *Ibid.*

173. Mikhail Zadornov (Minister of Finance), 'Za polchasa do obvala' (Half an hour before collapse), *Izvestia*, 29 May 1999, p. 2.

174. 'Yeltsin Demands Policies to Stimulate Economic Growth', *RFE/RL Newsline*, 14 January 1998; Stephanie Baker, 'Yeltsin Orders Cabinet to Kickstart Economy', *RFE/RL Newsline*, 15 January 1998.

175. 'Yeltsin Launches 1998 Government Program', *RFE/RL Newsline*, 27 January 1998.

176. 'Chubais, Nemtsov Given Difficult Tasks', and 'Plan Sets Ambitious Economic Targets', *RFE/RL Newsline*, 27 January 1998.

177. 'Zadornov Says Time Running Out for Tax Code', *RFE/RL Newsline*, 11 February 1998.

178. State of Russia address to the Federal Assembly, Federal Information Systems Corporation, Official Kremlin International Broadcast, 17 February 1998, p. 3.

179. *Ibid.*

180. *Ibid.*, p. 2.

181. *Ibid.*, pp. 2, 3.

182. *Ibid.*, p. 2.

183. *Ibid.*

184. *Ibid.*, p. 3.

185. *Ibid.*, p. 2.

186. *Ibid.*

187. *Ibid.*, p. 4.

188. *Ibid.*

189. Carol J. Williams, 'Russia Needs Strategy for Upsurge', *Los Angeles Times*, 18 February 1998, p. 4.

190. *Ibid.*

191. *Ibid.*

192. 'Major Networks Indifferent to Speech', *RFE/RL Newsline*, 17 February 1998.

193. Boris Yeltsin, address to the nation, 23 March 1998, Reuters, 24 March 1998 (http://www.nytimes.com).

194. *Ibid.*

195. Aleksandr Bekker, 'Tekhnokratiya na marshe' (Technocracy on the march), *Moskovskie Novosti*, 17–24 May 1998, p. 5.

196. CNN, 'Yeltsin nominee confirmed as Prime Minister', 24 April 1998, p. 2 (http://www.cnn.com).

197. Urinson, 'Vsyo, chto effektivno'.

198. Evegeniya Pis'mennaya, 'Prezident reshil pokonchit' s byudzhetnym krizisom' (President decided to end the budget crisis), *Financial Izvestia*, 12 May 1998, p. 1.

199. 'Russia suspends debt payment to avoid full default', Associated Press, 20 August 1998, p. 2 (http://www.cnn.com).

200. Egor Zhuravlev, Sergey Krayukhin and Vladimir Borodin, 'Oboronshchiki grozyat igrushechnymi avtomatami' (Workers of defence industry brandish toy machine guns), *Izvestia*, 9 July, p. 1.

201. *Ibid.*

202. Bekker, 'Tekhnokratiya'.

203. Charles Clover, 'Yeltsin urges Duma to pass tax law', *Financial Times*, 15 July 1998 (http://www.ft.com).

204. 'Parliament in Moscow Feels Pressure and Votes Sales Tax', *New York Times*, 17 July 1998, p. A3.

205. Celestine Bohlen, 'Yeltsin, Campaigner for his Country', *New York Times*, 4 June 1998, p. 12.

206. *Ibid.*

207. Aleksandr Pumpyanskiy, 'Lev zashevililsya' (The lion has moved), *Novoye Vremya*, 29, 1998, p. 15.

208. Boris Yeltsin, speech at the burial of Tsar Nicholas II and his family, 17 July 1998, Reuters (http://www.cnn.com).

209. Andrey Kolesnikov, 'Stepanych vtoroy svezhesti' (The not-so-fresh Stepanovich), *Novoye Vremya*, 35, 1998, p. 6.

210. Interview with Mira Shvartz.

211. *Ibid.*

Epilogue: In Search of a Historic Yeltsin

1. Joseph Brodsky, 'MCMXCV', *New York Review of Books*, 8 June 1995, p. 18.

2. As quoted in Michael Ignatieff, 'On Isaiah Berlin (1909–1997)', *New York Review of Books*, 18 December 1997, p. 10.

3. *The History of England*, New York: Penguin Classics, 1986, p. 51.

4. Igor Klyamkin, 'Sovetskoye i zapadnoye: vozmoshen li sintez?' (The Soviet and the Western: is synthesis possible?) *Polis*, 4, 1994, p. 62.

5. Conor Cruise O'Brien, *The Great Melody*, Chicago: University of Chicago Press, 1992, p. xxxvii.

6. Lacouture, *op. cit.*, p. 223.

7. David Herbert Donald, *Lincoln*, New York: Touchstone, 1995, p. 332.

8. Stanley Hoffmann, *Decline or Renewal? France since the 1930s*, New York: Viking Press, 1974, p. 189.

9. Donald, op. cit., p. 489.

10. Hoffmann, *Decline or Renewal?*, p. 88.

11. Charles Williams, *The Last Great Frenchman: A Life of General De Gaulle*, New York: John Wiley & Sons, 1993, p. 400.

12. James M. McPherson, *Abraham Lincoln and the Second American*

Revolution, New York: Oxford University Press, 1990, p. 102.

13. As quoted in Douglas Johnson, 'In Pursuit of Greatness', *Times Literary Supplement*, 22 January 1999, p. 36.

14. McPherson, *op, cit.*, pp. 28, 129.

15. Donald, *op. cit.*, p. 380.

16. McPherson, *op. cit.*, p. 44; Donald, *op. cit.*, p. 547.

17. As quoted in Donald, *op. cit.*, p. 562.

18. *Ibid.*, p. 14.

19. *Ibid.*, pp. 94, 102.

20. *Ibid.*, p. 547.

21. McPherson, *op. cit.*, p. 114.

22. Donald, *op. cit.*, p. 14.

23. Berlin, *Personal Impressions*, p. 32.

24. McPherson, *op. cit.*, p. 16.

25. Vadim Makarevskiy, 'Voeyyat' ne mozhem. I ne budem' (We cannot fight. And we will not), *Novoye Vremya*, 38, 1995, p. 29.

26. Lee Hockstader, 'Yeltsin Fires Defense Chiefs', *Washington Post*, 23 May 1997.

27. Pavel Felgengauer quoted in Michael Specter, 'Yeltsin's Plan to Cut Military Touches a Nerve', *Washington Post*, 28 July 1997.

28. Elizabeth Pond, 'Ukraine: A Concession to post-Cold War Realities', *Sun*, 4 June, 1997.

29. David Hoffman, 'Yeltsin Seeks Compromise on NATO', *Washington Post*, 24 February 1997.

30. As quoted by Adam Ulam in *Russia's Failed Revolutions*, New York: Basic Books, 1981, p. 13.

31. Boris Yeltsin, 'Teleobrashchenie Prezidenta RF Borisa El'tsina' (Televised address by the Russian Federation's President Boris Yeltsin), Natsional'naya Sluzhba Novostei, 12 June 1997, p. 2 (http://www.nns.ru/chronicle/obr1206.html, 13 June 1997).

32. Gosudarstvenny Arkhiv Rossiyskoy Federatsii (The State Archive of the Russian Federation), 665-1-13, 30 January 1865 (Emphasis in the original). I am grateful to Professor Richard Wartman of Columbia University for sharing a copy of this document with me.

33. Ulam, *op. cit.*, p. 128.

34. Yeltsin, *Zapiski*, pp. 383–94.

35. Blair A. Ruble, 'Politics, Economic Growth, and Nationalism in Today's Russia', keynote speech at the WEFA Group Fall International Outlook Conference, Philadelphia, 30 October 1996, *Eurasia Economic Outlook*, November 1996, p. 1.

36. Egor Yakovenko, 'Ot imperii k natsional'nomu gosudarsvu' (From the empire to a nation-state), *Polis*, 6, 1996, p. 126.

37. A. M. Salmin, 'Vybory 1995–1996 i transformatsiya politicheskogo rezhima v Rossiyskoy Federatsii' (The 1995–1996 elections and transformation of the political regime in the Russian Federation), *Polis*, 1, 1997, p. 122.

38. *Ibid.*, p. 121.

39. Marie Mendras, 'Yeltsin and the Great Divide in Russian Society', *East European Constitutional Review*, Spring/Summer 1996, pp. 51–2.

40. Dmitriy Orlov, 'Schitayut vse!' (Everyone is counting!), *Novoye Vremya*, 1–2, 1997, p. 11.

41. Valeriy Tishkov, 'Geopolitika Chechenskoy voyny' (The geopolitics of the Chechen war), *Svobodnaya Mysl'*, April 1997, p. 68.

42. Mickiewicz, *op. cit.*, p. 249.

43. *Ibid.*

44. *Ibid.*, p. 245.

45. As quoted in *ibid.*, p. 244.

46. Sergei Kovalev, 'Russia after Chechnya', *New York Review of Books*, 17 July 1997.

47. *Rossia*, 51 (109), 16 December 1992, p. 14.

48. 'K sisteme sovetov vozvrata nikogda ne budet' (We will never go back to the system of soviets), remarks at the meeting with members of the Russian regional legislatures, *Rossiyskie Vesti*, 17 April 1996, p. 3.

49. Elizabeth Teague, 'Federalization à la carte', *Perspective*, November–December 1994, p. 1.

50. Boris Yeltsin, report on the draft Constitution delivered to the Congress of People's Deputies of Russia on 2 November 1991, TASS (FBIS-SOV-91-213, 4 November 1991, p. 58).

51. 'Boris E'ltsin: bystrye reformy – edinstvenniy shans Rossii' (Boris Yeltsin: rapid reform is Russia's only chance), *Izvestia*, 29 November 1991, p. 3.

52. Teague, *op. cit.*, p. 7.

53. *RFE/RL Daily Report*, 2 December 1992.

54. *Ibid.*

55. Yeltsin, *Zapiski*, p. 395.

56. Teague, *op. cit.*, p. 7.

57. *Ibid.*

58. Lilia Shevtsova, *Politicheskie zigzagi postkommunisticheskoy Rossii* (Political zigzags of post-communist Russia), Moscow: Carnegie Endowment for International Peace, 1997, p. 30.

59. Hoffmann, *Decline or Renewal?*, p. 268.

60. *Ibid.*, p. 259.

61. As quoted in John Laughland, *The Death of Politics: France under Mitterrand*, London: Michael Joseph, 1994, p. 27.

62. Aron, *Memoirs*, p. 170.

63. *Ibid.*, p. 64.

64. Hoffmann, *Decline or Renewal?*, p. 267.

65. Aron, *Memoirs*, p. 258.

66. Maurice Duverger, *La Monarchie Républicaine*, P. Laffont, Paris: 1974, p. 188, as quoted in Jack Hayward, ed., *De Gaulle to Mitterrand: Presidential Power in France*, New York: New York University Press, 1993, p. 72.

67. François Mitterrand, *Le Coup d'état permanent*, Paris: Julliard, 1964.

68. Charles de Gaulle, *Lettres, Notes et Carnets*, IX, Paris, 1986, p. 94 as quoted in Hayward, *op. cit.*, p. 22.

69. Juan J. Linz, 'The Perils of Presidentialism', *Journal of Democracy*, 1 (Winter), 1990.

70. Hoffmann, *Decline or Renewal?*, p. 486.

71. *Ibid.*, p. 80.

72. Aron, *Memoirs*, p. 64.

73. Hoffmann, *Decline or Renewal?*, p. 279.

74. Raymond Aron, *France: The New Republic*, New York: Oceana Publications, 1960, p. 36.

75. Aron, *France*, p. 30.

76. *Ibid.*, p. 47.

77. *Ibid.*, p. 37.

78. Aron, *Memoirs*, p. 258.

79. *RFE/RL Newsline*, 27 June 1997.

80. *The Times* (London), 10 August, 1997.

81. 'Obrashchenie prezidenta RF Borisa El'tsina k zhitelyam Rossia' (An address of President of the Russian Federation Boris Yeltsin to the inhabitants of Russia), 14 March 1997, Natsional'naya Sluzhba Novostei, 17 March 1997, p. 1 (www.nns.ru/chronicle/obr1403.html).

82. Leonid Gordon and Nataliya Pliskevich, 'Razvilki i lovushki perekhodnogo perioda' (The forks and traps of the transitional phase), Part II, *Polis*, 5, 1994, p. 101.

83. First Channel/ORT (Ostankino), 6 October 1993 (FBIS, 7 October 1993, p. 10).

84. *Novoye Vremya*, 46, 1996, p. 4.

85. Valeriy Tishkov, who heads a Moscow institute for ethnology and anthropology, as quoted in David Hoffman, 'Russia's New Internal Passport Drops Nationality, Drawing Praise and Protest', *Washington Post*, 25 October 1997.

86. *Ibid.* The quoted activist is Viktor Kogan-Yasniy.

87. Alessandra Stanley, 'Is Success Good for Russia's Jews?', *New York Times*, 15 April 1997.

88. *Ibid.* The person quoted is Tankred Golenpol'skiy, the head of the Anti-Defamation Committee of

the Russian Jewish Congress and editor of the *International Jewish Newspaper*, published in Moscow.

89. Steven Erlanger, 'In a Less Arid Russia Jewish Life Flowers Again', *New York Times*, 19 September 1993.

90. Steven Erlanger, 'Rebirth of Jewish Life in Russia Cuts Emigration', *New York Times*, 3 December 1995.

91. Erlanger, 'In a Less Arid Russia'.

92. Matthew London, 'The Rise of Moscow Jewish Groups: Civil Society Development in Russia', unpublished master's thesis at the School of Foreign Service, Georgetown University, Washington, DC, 1997, p. 55.

93. *Ibid.*, pp. 55–6.

94. Stanley, 'Is Success Good for Russia's Jews?'

95. 'Why This Matzoh Is Different from All Others: It's Moscow's', *New York Times*, 4 April 1996.

96. Alessandra Stanley, 'A Jew Stalin Killed Now Symbolizes Rebirth', *New York Times*, 14 January, 1998.

97. Erlanger, 'In a Less Arid Russia'.

98. Erlanger, 'Rebirth of Jewish Life'.

99. 'Why This Matzoh Is Different'.

100. Erlanger, 'In a Less Arid Russia'.

101. Alessandra Stanley, 'Russia's Jews Organize, with Swiss Caterer's Help', *New York Times*, 11 January 1996.

102. 'The New Jewish Public Organization in Russia', ITAR-TASS, 10 January 1966.

103. Stanley, 'Russia's Jews Organize'.

104. Reuters, 3 September 1998, (*Russia Today*, p. 1, http://www.russiatoday.com).

105. *Ibid.*

106. London, *op. cit.*, p. 57.

107. *Ibid.*

108. *Ibid.*, p. 58.

109. Fred Hiatt, 'Progress, Russian-Style', *Washington Post*, 28 September 1997.

110. Aleksandr Asmolov, 'Privatizatsiya soznaniya' (Privatization of consciousness), *Moskovskie Novosti*, 11–18 October 1998, p. 5.

111. Gelman, *op. cit.*

112. *Ibid.*

113. Lee Hockstader, 'The Russian Invasion', *Washington Post*, 15 August 1994.

114. *Ibid.*

115. *Novoye vremya*, 11, 1997, p. 5.

116. *Ibid.*

117. Peter H. Solomon Jr, 'The Persistence of Judicial Reform in Contemporary Russia', *East European Constitutional Review*, Fall 1997. p. 55.

118. *Ibid.*, p. 51.

119. *Ibid.*

120. *RFE/RL Newsline*, 3 February, 1998.

121. *RFE/RL Newsline*, 20 January 1998.

122. Aleksandr Avanov, 'Pervaya pobeda' (The first victory), *Moskovskie Novosti*, 22–29 March 1998, p. 3.

123. Solomon, *op. cit.*, p. 55.

124. *Ibid.*

125. Arkady Ostrovsky and John Thornhill, 'Nikitin case: Successor to KGB humbled', *Financial Times*, 30 October 1998, p. 1 (http://www.ft.com), and Reuters, 'Suspension of Nikitin Trial Hailed', 2 November 1998 (*Russia Today*, http://www.russiatoday.com).

126. Reuters, 'Suspension of Nikitin Trial', p. 1.

127. Viktor Sheynis, *op. cit.*, p. 92.

128. E. B. Shestopal, ' Vybory proshli: peyzazh posle bitvy' (The elections are over: a landscape after the battle), *Polis*, 1, 1997, p. 123.

129. Richard B. Dobson, *Is Russia Turning the Corner? Changing Russian Opinion, 1991–1996*, Washington DC: Office of Research and Media Reaction, US Information Agency, September 1996, p. 52, table 22.

130. *Ibid.*

131. *Ibid.*, p. 56, table 26.

132. Whitefield and Evans, p. 224, table 2.

133. Steven A. Grant, *How Unsteady Is Russian Democracy? Poll Confirms a Bumpy Reality*, Washington, DC: Office of Research and Media Reaction, US Information Agency, 1 May 1997, p. 2.

134. Dobson, *op. cit.*, p. 51, table 21.

135. *Ibid.*, p. 55, table 25.

136. Grant, 'How Unsteady Is Russian Democracy?', p. 2.

137. Igor Klyamkin, Vladimir Lapkin and Vladimir Pantin, 'Chto znachit "russkiy poryadok"?' (What does 'Russian order' mean?), *Moskovskie Novosti*, 20–27 April 1997. The article is based on a survey of 1,600 people conducted by the Institute of Sociological Analysis in November 1996.

138. *Ibid.*

139. James Boswell, *Life of Johnson*, World's Classic series, ed. R. W. Chapman, Oxford: Oxford University Press, 1991, p. 118.

140. Samuel Johnson, *The Lives of the English Poets*, London: Everyman's Library, 1983, p. 272.

141. *Ibid.*, p. 313.

142. *Ibid.*, p. 269.

143. *Ibid.*, p. 276.

144. *Ibid.*, pp. 275–6.

145. Marina Shakina, 'El'tsin. Chelovek, kotoriy umeet delat' vybor' (Yeltsin. A man who can make choices), *Novoye Vremya*, 40, 1994, pp. 11, 13.

146. *Ibid.*, p. 13.

147. Yuriy Fedorov, in Shevtsova, *op. cit.*, p. 53.

148. Gaidar, 'U menia net sindroma belobiletnika', p. 13.

149. Aleksandr Yakovlev, 'Ne tol'ko kodovskoy bur'yan . . .' (Not only witches' weeds . . .), *Novoye Vremya*, 27, 1993, p. 31.

150. Osip Mandel'shtam, 'Dekabrist' (Decembrist), in Osip Mandel'shtam, *Sobranie sochineniy v chetyryokh tomakh* (Collected works in four volumes), ed. G. P. Struve and B. A. Filippov, Moscow: Terra, 1991, vol. I, p. 66, translated by Leon Aron.

151. Robert Graves, 'To Juan at the Winter Solstice', in *Robert Graves: Collected Poems, 1975*, New York: Oxford University Press, 1988, p. 137.

152. Dion Chrysostom, Speech 20, as quoted in W. H. D. Rouse's introduction to *Great Dialogues of Plato*, New York: Mentor Books, 1959, p. 7.

BIBLIOGRAPHY

BORIS YELTSIN

BOOKS

Sredniy Ural: Rubezhi Sozidania (Middle Ural: the stages of creation). Sverdlovsk: Sredne-Uralskoye Publishers, 1981.

Ispoved' na zadannuyu temu (A confession on the required topic). Riga: Rukitis Publishers, 1990.

Zapiski Prezidenta (The President's memoirs). Moscow: Ogonyok Publishers, 1994.

The Struggle for Russia. New York: Times Books, 1994.

SPEECHES, STATEMENTS, DECREES AND ARTICLES

'Request for admittance to the Communist Party of the Soviet Union submitted to the Party Cell of the Yuzhgorstroy trest, 17 February 1960.' Personal file of Yeltsin Boris Nikolayevich, the Party Archive of the Sverdlovsk Region, holding 2992, registry 6, log 527. A copy in the author's archive.

'Vsyo, chto nametila Partia, – vypolnim!' (Everything the Party outlined – we will fulfil!). *Ural'skiy Rabochiy*, 13 November 1976.

'Rabotat' luchshe, povyshat' effektivnost' i kachestvo!' (To work better, to improve effectiveness and quality!). *Ural'skiy Rabochiy*, 14 January 1977.

'Lichnyi primer delegatov partiynogo s'ezda i konferentsiy na proizvodstve i v obshestvennoy zhizni' (Personal example set by the delegates to the Party congress and conferences in their work and everyday life). *Parti'naya Zhizn'*, 9, (May) 1977.

'Leninskie printsypy' (the Leninist principles). *Izvestia*, 19 July 1977.

'Vo slavu Rodiny' (For the glory of the Motherland). *Ural'skiy Rabochiy*, 26 October 1977.

'General'nomu' Sekretaryu TsK KPSS tovarishchu Leonidu Il'ichu Brezhnevu' (To the General Secretary of the Committee of the CPSU Comrade Brezhnev, Leonid Il'ich). *Pozdravlenia i Privetstviya v Svyazi s Semidesyatiletiem Generalnogo Sekretarya TsK KPSS tov. Brezhneva L.I.* (Congratulations and greetings in connection with the seventieth birthday of the General Secretary of the Central Committee of the Communist Party of the Soviet Union Comrade Brezhnev). Moscow: Pravda Publishers, 1977, pp. 73–4.

'Kollektiv – glavnyi nastavnik' (The collective is the main teacher). *Izvestia*, 3 January 1978.

'Ne chislom – umeniem' (Not by numbers but by skill). *Pravda*, 28 January 1978.

'Pretvorim v zhizn' agrarnuyu politiku partii' (The Party's agricultural policy must be implemented). *Ural'skiy Rabochiy*, 15 July 1978.

'Intensivnye faktory rosta' (The factors of growth based on efficiency). *Sovetskaya Rossia*, 13 March 1979.

'Sotsialisticheskoye sorevnovanie i uskorenie nauchino-tekhnicheskogo progressa' (Socialist competition and acceleration of scientific–

technological progress). *Partiynaya Zhizn'*, 1, (November) 1979, pp. 27–36.

Letter to *Pravda* in response to the article 'Pyramo ili posredstuom' (Directly or indirectly?) (3 April 1980), *Pravda*, 27 May 1980.

'Chem silyon rukovoditel'' (What are a leader's strengths?). *Pravda*, 26 October 1980.

'Otchyot oblastnogo komiteta KPSS' (Report of the Oblast Committee of the CPSU). *Ural'skiy Rabochiy*, 23 January 1981.

'Kompleksnye programmy Urala' (The integrated programmes for the Urals). *Izvestia*, 29 January 1981.

'Rech tovarisha B. N. El'tsina' (The speech of Comrade B. N. Yeltsin). *Pravda*, 26 February 1981.

'Initsiativa, rozhdennaya vremenem' (An initiative whose time has come). *Izvestia*, 30 July 1981.

'Videt' i predvidet'' (To see and to foresee). *Pravda*, 13 August 1981.

'Povyshat' effectivnost' zhivotnovodstva' (To improve the effectiveness of cattle raising). *Ural'skiy Rabochiy*, 12 November 1981.

'Reshenia XXVI s'ezda KPSS vypolnim!' (We will fulfil the resolutions of the Twenty-Sixth Congress of the CPSU!). *Ural'skiy Rabochiy*, 18 March 1981.

Speech at the 26 May 1981 Plenum of the Sverdlovsk Obkom.

'Protokol 2-go plenuma Sverdlovskogo obkoma KPSS, 26 Maya 1981 goda' (Minutes of the Second Plenum of the Sverdlovsk Regional Committee of the CPSU). Party Archive of the Sverdlovsk region, holding 4, registry 100, log 11.

'Tovaram dlya naroda – partiynoe vnimanie' (Consumer goods must have the Party's attention). *Ural'skiy Rabochiy*, 15 July 1981.

'Prodovol'stvennaya Programma – delo vsenarodnoye' (Food programme – is a cause of all the people). *Ural'skiy Rabochiy*, 9 June 1982.

'Vystuplenie na vechere trudovoy slavy Sverdlovskogo DSK po povodu vrucheniya perekhodyashchikh znamyon po itogam 1-go i kvartala 1983 goda i 20-tiletiyu obrazovanya' DSK (Speech at the celebratory meeting on the occasion of the award of the prize banners for best results in the first quarter and the twentieth anniversary of the DSK). The Party Archive of the Sverdlovsk Region (PASO). 6 May 1983.

'Sovershenstvuya stil' raboty' (Perfecting the style of work). *Kommunist*, 11, (July) 1983.

'Delo vsey Partii, kazhdogo kommunista' (The business of the entire party, of every communist). Speech at the XIII Plenum of the Sverdlovsk regional committee of the CPSU, *Ural'skiy Rabochiy*, 6 July 1983.

'Dlya blaga truzhennikov poley i ferm' (For the good of the workers of fields and farms). Speech at the all-Russian conference on the integrated construction of, and the provision of amenities to, agricultural settlements in Russia, *Ural'skiy Rabochiy*, 20 July 1983.

'Podskazyvayut pis'ma' (The letters suggest what needs to be done). *Pravda*, 21 April 1983.

Introduction to Ayrapetov, V. G., A. V. Bakunin and L. S. Boyarskikh, *Sverdlovskaya oblast' za 50 let* (The Sverdlovsk province in the last fifty years). Sverdlovsk: Sredne-Uralskoye Publishers, 1984, pp. 1–13.

'Novizna sil'na podderzhkoy' (Support is innovation's strength). *Izvestia*, 6 July 1984.

'Vypiska iz vystuplenya t. El'tsina B. N., 11 aprleya s.g. pered progandistami g. Moskvy' (Excerpt from the speech by Comrade B. N. Yeltsin on 11 April of this year to the propagandists of the city of Moscow). *Radio Liberty*, Arkhiv Samizdata, No. 5721.

'Doklad pervogo sekretarya MGK KPSS B. N. El'tsina' (Speech of B. N. Yeltsin, First Secretary of the MGK KPSS). *Moskovskaya Pravda*, 20 July 1986.

'Aktivnee vesti perestroiku' (To conduct perestroika more actively), speech at a Plenum of the Moscow City Party Committee. *Moskovskaya Pravda*, 20 July 1986, pp. 1–2.

'Perestroike – neobratimyy kharakter: iz vystuplenii v preniiakh' (To make perestroika irreversible: excerpts from the speeches). *Moskovskaya Pravda*, 5 October 1986.

Speech at the February (1987) Plenum of the MGK, *Moskovskaya Pravda*, 23 February 1987.

'Energiyu perestroiki – v prakticheskie resul'taty' (Channel the energy of perestroika into practical achievements), speech at a Plenum of Moscow City Party Committee. *Moskovskaya Pravda*, 9 August 1987, pp. 1–3.

Speech at the XIX All-Union Conference of the Communist Party of the Soviet Union, 1 July 1988. In *XIX Vsesoyuznaya Konferentsiya Kommunisticheskoy Partii Sovetskogo Soyuza. Stenograficheskiy Otchet*. Moscow: Izdatelstvo Politicheskoy Literatury, 1988, vol. 2, pp. 55–62.

'Perestroika prineset peremeny' (Perestroika will bring changes). Planks in the election platform. *Moskovskaya Pravda*, 21 March 1989.

'V redaktsiyu gazety "Moskovskaya Pravda"' (To the editorial office of *Moskovskaya Pravda*).

Moskovskaya Pravda, 25 March 1989.

Speech at the First Congress of People's Deputies of the USSR, 31 May 1989. In *Pervyy S'ezd Narodnykh Deputatov SSSR, Stenograficheskii Otchyot*. Moscow: Supreme Soviet of the USSR, 1989, vol. II, pp. 43–9.

Speech to the Supreme Soviet, 24 June 1989, Moscow television (FBIS, 25 July 1989).

'Boris Yeltsin at Columbia'. Transcript of the speech at Columbia University, New York, NY, 11 September 1989.

The George Huntingdon Williams Memorial Lecture, Johns Hopkins University, Baltimore, 12 September 1989, audio and video recordings in the author's archive.

Speech at the meeting of the Inter-Regional Group, House of Cinema, Moscow, Russia, 24 September 1989. Ekaterinburg: Museum of Youth Movements, videotape.

Speech at the Second Congress of People's Deputies of the USSR, Session 5. *Izvestia*, 18 December 1989.

Speech at the First Congress of People's Deputies of Russia, 25 May 1990. *Sovetskaya Rossia*, 27 May 1990.

'Vystuplenie tovarisha El'tsina' (The speech by Comrade Yeltsin). *Sovetskaya Rossia*, 30 May 1990.

Speech at the Twenty-Eighth Party Congress. *Pravda*, 8 July 1990, p. 4.

Speech at the session of the Supreme Soviet of the RSFSR, *Sovetskaya Rossia*, 16 October 1990.

Speech at the Fourth Congress of People's Deputies of the USSR, 20 December 1990.

In M. K. Gorshkov and V. V. Zhuravlyova, eds, *Gorbachev–El'tsin 1500 dney politicheskogo protivostoyaniya* (Gorbachev–Yeltsin: 1,500 days of political confrontation). Moscow: Terra, 1992.

'Otkrytoye pis'mo Predsedatelia Verkhovnogo Soveta RSFSR B. N. El'tsina narodam Pribaltiki' (Open letter from the Chairman of the Supreme Soviet of the RSFSR B. N. Yeltsin to the peoples of the Baltics). *Rossiyskaya Gazeta*, 19 January 1991.

'Appeal to the Russian Soldiers in the Baltics', 13 January 1991. The author's transcript of his own recording. (See also *Rossiyskaya Gazeta*, 5 January 1991.)

Boris Yeltsin, Anatoliy Gorbunovs and Vitaustas Lansbergis, 'Joint Statement', 14 January 1991, read by Yeltsin at the press conference in the Hall of the Council of Nationalities of the Supreme Soviet of Russia. The author's transcript of his own recording.

'Press-konferentsiya Borisa El'tsina' (Boris Yeltsin's press conference). The author's transcript. (See also *Izvestia*, 15 January 1991.)

Speech at a pro-democracy meeting in the House of Cinema, 9 March 1991. In *Rossiyskaya Gazeta*, 12 March 1991.

Speech at the Third Extraordinary Congress of People's Deputies of the RSFSR. *Rossiyskaya Gazeta*, 31 March 1991.

'Zayavlenie Predsedatelya Verkhovnogo Soveta RSFSR B. N. El'tsina' (Statement of the Chairman of the Supreme Soviet of the RSFSR B. N. Yeltsin). *Rossiyskaya Gazeta*, 5 April 1991.

'Vykhod iz krizisa i obnovlenie Rossia – na puti reform. Tezisy programmy Predsedatelia Verkhovnogo Soveta RSFSR B. N. El'tsina' (Reforms will provide a way out of crisis and renewal of Russia. The main planks of the electoral reform programme of the Chairman of the Supreme Soviet of the RSFSR B. N. Yeltsin,

May–June 1991). A mimeographed copy in the author's archive.

Speech to the Council of Representatives of Democratic Russia', 1 June 1991. *Rossiyskaya Gazeta*, 4 June 1991.

Speech at the Presidential Inauguration in the Kremlin, 10 July 1991. Moscow television (FBIS, 10 July 1991, pp. 63–4).

Boris Yeltsin, Ivan Silaev and Ruslan Khazbulatov. 'K grazhdanam Rossii' (To the citizens of Russia), 19 August 1991. *Rossia*, 'a newspaper of the Supreme Soviet of the RSFSR. Special edition'. A copy in the author's archive (see also *Rossiskaya Gazeta*, 23 August 1991, p. 2).

'Ukaz Prezidenta Rossiyskoy Sovetskoy Federativnoy Sotsialisticheskoy Respubliki, No. 59, 19 avgusta 1991 goda' (Decree of the President of the Russian Soviet Federated Socialist Republic, No. 59, 19 August 1991). A copy in the author's archive (see also *Rossiyskaya Gazeta*, 23 August 1991, p. 2).

'Ukaz Prezidenta Rossiyskoy Sovetskoy Federativnoy Sotsialisticheskoy Respubliki, No. 61, 19 avgusta 1991 goda' (Decree of the President of the Russian Soviet Federated Socialist Republic, No. 61, 19 August 1991). A copy in the author's archive (see also *Rossiyskaya Gazeta*, 23 August 1991, p. 2).

'Ukaz Prezidenta Rossiyskoy Sovetskoy Federativnoy Sotsialisticheskoy Respubliki, No. 62, 19 avgusta goda 1991' (Decree of the President of the Russian Soviet Federated Republic, No. 62, 19 August 1991). A copy in the author's archive (see also *Rossiyskaya gazeta*, 23 August 1991, p. 2).

'Ukaz Prezidenta Rossiyskoy Sovetskoy Federativnoy

Sotsialisticheskoy Respubliki, No. 63, 19 avgusta 1991 goda' (Decree No. 63 of the President of the Russian Soviet Federated Socialist Republic, 19 August 1991). A copy in the author's archive (see also *Rossiskaya Gazeta*, 23 August 1991, p. 3).

'Ukaz Prezidenta Rossiyskoy Sovetskoy Federativnoy Sotsialisticheskoy Respubliki, No. 64, 20 avgusta 1991 goda' (Decree of the President of the Russian Soviet Federated Socialist Republic, No. 64, 20 August 1991). *Rossiyskaya Gazeta*, 23 August 1991, p. 3.

'Ukaz Prezidenta Rossiyskoy Sovetskoy Federativnoy Sotsialisticheskoy Respublicki, No. 68, 20 avgusta 1991 goda' (Decree of the President of the Russian Soviet Federated Socialist Republic, No. 68, 20 August 1991). *Rossiyskaya Gazeta*, 23 August 1991, p. 2. A copy in the author's archive (see also *Rossiyskaya Gazeta*, August 1991, p. 3).

'K soldatam i ofitseram Vooruzonnykh Sil SSR, KGB SSSR, MVD SSSR, 19 avgusta 1991 goda' (To the soldiers and officers of the armed forces of the USSR, of the KGB of the USSR, and of the Ministry of Internal Affairs of the USSR, 19 August 1991). A copy in the author's archive (see also *Rossiskaya Gazeta*, 23 August 1991, p. 2, and FBIS, 20 August 1991, Annexe, p. 57).

'Zayavlenie' (Statement), 20 August 1991.

'Ukaz Prezidenta Rossiyskoy Sovetskoy Federativnoy Sotsialisticheskoy Respubliki, No. 70, 21 avgusta 1991 Ob otstranenii ot ispoleneniya obyazannostey predsedateley ispolnitel'nykh komitetov kraevogo i ryada oblastnykh Sovetov narodnykh deputatov RSFSR' (On removal from office of the Chairman of the executive committee of a *krai* Soviet and a number of regional Soviets of People's Deputies, Decree No. 70, 21 August 1991). A copy in the author's archive (see also *Rossiyskaya Gazeta*, 23 August 1991, p. 3).

Agence France-Presse, 02.05 (Moscow time), 20 August 1991 (FBIS, 21 August 1991, p. 59). Speech at a rally outside the White House.

B. N. El'tsin, A. V. Rutskoy, I. S. Silaev and R. I. Khazbulatov. 'Predsedatelyu Verkhovnogo Soveta SSSR tov. Luk'yanovu A. I.' (To the Chairman of the Supreme Soviet of the USSR, Comrade Luk'yanov A. I.), 20 August 1991. A copy in the author's archive.

Speech to the Supreme Soviet of Russia, 21 August 1991, Moscow Central Television, *Vostok* and *Orbita* broadcasts for Siberia and Far East (FBIS, 22 August 1991).

'Ukaz Prezidenta Rossiyskoy Sovetskoy Federativnoy Sotsialisticheskoy Respubliki, No. 76, 22 avgusta 1991 goda "O deyatel'nosti TASS, Informatsionnogo agenstva 'Novosti', i ryada gazet po dezinformatsii naseleniya i mirovoy obshchestvennosti o sobytiyakh v strane"' (Decree of the President of the Russian Soviet Federative Socialist Republic 'Regarding actions of TASS, the Novosti information agency and a number of newspapers directed at disinforming the population and world public about the events in the country', 22 August 1991). A copy in the author's archive.

Speech at a victory rally, 22 August 1991. Russian Television Channel (Rossia), 22 August 1991 (FBIS, 22 August 1991).

'Ukaz Prezidenta Rossiyskoy Sovetskoy Federativnoy

Sotsialisticheskoy Respubliki, No. 79, 23 avgusta 1991 goda "O priostanovlenii deyatel'nosti Kommunistichekoy partii RSFSR"' (Decree of the President of the Russian Soviet Federative Socialist Republic 'On suspension of the activity of the Communist Party of the RSFSR'), Decree No. 79, 23 August 1991). A copy in the author's archive.

'Ukaz Prezidenta Rossiyskoy Sovetskoy Federativnoy Sotsialisticheskoy Respubliki, No. 78, 23 avgusta 1991 "Ob otstranenii ot ispoleneniya obyazannostey predsedateley ispolkomov oblastnykh Sovetov narodnykh deputatov"' (On the removal from office of Chairmen of the executive committees of regional Soviets of People's Deputies), Decree No. 78, 23 August 1991). A copy in the author's archive.

Decree on the recognition of Estonia's independence, 24 August 1991. Radio Rossii (FBIS-SOV-91-165, 26 August 1991, pp. 85–6).

Decree on the recognition of Latvia's independence, 24 August 1991. TASS (FBIS-SOV-91-165, 26 August 1991, p. 86).

Speech at the CSCE Conference 'On the Human Dimension', 11 September 1991. Radio Rossii (FBIS-SOV-91-177, 12 September 1991).

'Obrashchenie v Verkhovniy Sovet RSFSR v svyazi s prinyatiem Zakona RSFSR "O vyborakh glavy administratsii"' (Address to the Supreme Soviet of the Russian Soviet Federative Socialist Republic regarding the adoption of the RSFSR law 'On the Election of the Head of Administration'). *Rossiyskaya Gazeta*, 19 October 1991, p. 1.

Speech at the Congress of People's Deputies of the Russian Federation, 29 October 1991. *Sovetskaya Rossia*, 29 October 1991.

Decree 'On the Activities of the CPSU and the Communist Party of the Russian Soviet Federative Socialist Republic', 6 November 1991. TASS (FBIS-SOV-91-216, 7 November 1991).

'O priznanii Rossiey nezavisimosti Ukrainy. Zayavlenie Borisa El'tsina' (On the recognition by Russia of the independence of Ukraine. A statement by Boris Yeltsin). *Izvestia*, 4 December 1991.

Boris Yeltsin, Gennadiy Burbulis, Stanislav Shushkevich, Vyacheslav Kebich, Leonid Kravchuk and Vitold Fokin. 'Soglashenie o sozdanii Sodruzhestva Nezavisimykh Gosudarstv' (Agreement on the creation of the Commonwealth of Independent States). *Rossiyskaya Gazeta*, 10 December 1991, p. 1.

Boris Yeltsin, Stanislav Shushkevich and Leonid Kravchuk. 'Zyavlenie glav gosudarstv Respubliki Belarus', RSFSR, Ukrainy' (Statement by the heads of state of the Republic of Belarus', RSFSR, Ukraine). *Rossiyskaya Gazeta*, 10 December 1991, p. 1.

Report on the draft Constitution delivered to the Congress of People's Deputies of the RSFSR on 2 November 1991. TASS (FBIS-SOV-91-213, 4 November 1991).

Speech to the Supreme Soviet of the Russian Federation, 12 December 1991. Russian Television Channel (Rossia) (FBIS-SOV-91-239, 12 December 1991).

Speech to the Supreme Soviet of the Russian Federation, 25 December 1991. Radio Rossii (FBIS-SOV-91-248, 26 December 1991).

Address to the nation, 29 December 1991. Moscow Central Television, *Vostok* and *Orbita* broadcasts for Siberia and Far East (FBIS-SOV-91-250, 30 December 1991).

'Obrashchenie Prezidenta Rossii k

sograzhdanam' (Address of the President of Russia to fellow citizens). *Izvestia*, 20 August 1992.

Speech at the Seventh Congress of People's Deputies, 1 December 1992. Russian Television Channel (FBIS-SOV-92-232-S).

Speech at the Seventh Congress of People's Deputies, 10 December 1992. *Izvestia*, 10 December 1992.

Address to the nation, 20 March 1993. First Channel/ORT (Ostankino) (FBIS-SOV-93-053, 22 March 1993).

Speech at the Ninth Congress of People's Deputies of Russia. *Izvestia*, 27 March 1993.

Address to the nation, 21 September 1993. First Channel/ORT (Ostankino) (FBIS, 22 September 1993, 'Presidential–Parliamentary Crisis in Russia', pp. 1–5).

'Ukaz Prezidenta Rossiyskoy Federatsii "O poetapnoy Konstitusionnoy reforme v Rossiyskoy Federatsii"' (Decree of the President of the Russian Federation 'On Stage-by-Stage Constitutional Reform in the Russian Federation'). *Trud*, 22 September 1993, pp. 1–2.

'Ukaz Prezidenta Rossiyskoy Federatsii "O sotsial'nykh garantiyakh dlya narodnykh deputatov Rossiyskoy Federatsii sozyva 1990–1995 godov"' (Decree of the President of the Russian Federation 'On social guarantees for People's Deputies of the Russian Federation of the 1990–1995 convocation'). *Rossiyskie Vesti*, 28 September 1993.

'Ukaz Prezidenta Rossiyskoy Federatsii "Ob otvetstvennosti lits, protivodeystvyushchikh provedeniyu poetapnoy konstitutsionnoy reformy"' (Decree of the President of the Russian Federation 'On the liability

of persons opposing stage-by-stage implementation of the constitutional reform'). *Rossiyskie Vesti*, 29 September 1993.

Address to the nation, Russian Television Channel (Rossia), 09.00, 4 October 1993 (FBIS, 4 October 1993, pp. 20–1).

Address to the nation, First Channel/ ORT (Ostankino), 6 October 1993 (FBIS, 7 October 1993, p. 10).

'Yeltsin Addresses the Nation on Chechnya'. Embassy of the Russian Federation. Press Release No. 40, 27 December 1994.

'Letter to the Federation Council'. TASS, 9 December 1995 (FBIS, 11 December 1995, p. 36).

Address to the nation, 15 December 1995. ITAR-TASS (FBIS-SOV-95-241, 15 December 1995).

Speech in Ekaterinburg and responses to questions from the audience, 15 February 1996, Russian Television Channel (Rossia) (FBIS-SOV-033, 16 February 1996).

Remarks in Chelyabinsk, 16 February 1996. NTV, Moscow (FBIS-SOV-96-034, 21 February 1996, Article Id: drsov034_b_96005, http:// wnc.fedworld.gov/cgi-bin . . .).

The State of Russia address to the Federal Assembly, 23 February 1996. Russian Television Channel (Rossia) (FBIS-SOV-96-038, 26 February 1996).

Address to the nation on the settling of the war in Chechnya, 31 March 1996. First Channel/ORT (Ostankino) (FBIS-SOV-96-063, 1 April 1996).

'K sisteme sovetov vozvrata nikogda ne budet' (We will never go back to the system of Soviets). Remarks at the meeting of members of the Russian regional legislatures. *Rossiyskie Vesti*, 17 April 1996, p. 3.

Responses to questions submitted by journalists from the Ivanovo region INTERFAX, 26 April 1996 (FBIS-

SOV-96-083, 30 April 1996, Article Id: drsov083aa_96002, http://wnc.fedworld.gov/cgi-bin . . .).

Speech in Yaroslavl', 3 May 1996. ITAR-TASS (FBIS-SOV-96-088, 7 May, Article Id: drsov088_b_96005, http://wnc.fedworld.gov/cgi-bin . . .), and INTERFAX, 3 May 1996, (FBIS-SOV-96-088, 7 May 1996, Article Id: drsov088aa_96006, http://wnc.fedworld.gov/cgi-bin . . .).

INTERFAX, 3 May 1996, 1230 GMT (FBIS-SOV-96-088, 6 May 1996, p. 5).

Speech at the meeting of journalists from Russian provinces, 6 May 1996. INTERFAX (FBIS-SOV-96-089, 8 May, Article Id: drsov089_b_96008, http://wnc.fedworld.gov/cgi-bin . . .).

Speech to the National Congress of Independent Media, 16 May 1996. INTERFAX (FBIS-SOV-96-096, 20 May, Article Id: drsov096aa_96003, http://wnc.fedworld.gov/cgi-bin . . .).

Speech at the Krasnoyarsk Television and Broadcasting Company, 17 May 1996. ITAR-TASS (FBIS-SOV-96-097, Article Id: drsov097aa_96004, http://wnc.fedworld.gov/cgi-bin . . .).

Speech at the Solombala timber and wood-working complex, Arkhangel'sk Region, 24 May 1996. ITAR-TASS (FBIS, 29 May 1996, Article Id: drsov103aa_96005, http://wnc.fedworld.gov/cgi-bin . . .).

'Rossiya: Chelovek, Sem'ya, Obshchestvo, Gosudarstvo. Programma deystviy na 1996–2000 gody' (Russia: Individual, Family, Society, State. Action programme for the Years 1996–2000) Boris Yeltsin's electoral platform. Moscow, 27 May 1996, a photocopy in the author's archive.

Speech to Federal troops in Grozny, Chechnya, INTERFAX, 28 May 1996 (FBIS-SOV-96-103, 29 May 1996, Article Id: drsov103_d_96012, http://wnc.fedworld.gov/cgi-bin . . .).

Speech in the Khanty-Mansiyskiy Autonomous District, 11 June 1996. ITAR-TASS (FBIS-SOV-96-114, 13 June 1996, Article Id: drsov114aa_96002, p. 1, http://wnc.fedworld.gov/cgi-bin . . .).

Speech in Novocherkassk, 11 June 1996. ITAR-TASS (FBIS-SOV-96-113, 12 June 1996, Article Id: drsov113aa_96002, http://wnc.fedworld.gov/cgi-bin . . .).

Speech at 1996 Independence Day rally and concert in Moscow, 12 June 1996. Mayak Radio (FBIS-SOV-96-115, 14 June, Article Id: drsov115aa_96001, http://wnc.fedworld.gov/cgi-bin . . .).

'Teleobrashchenie Prezidenta RF Borisa El'tsina' (a televised address by Boris Yeltsin), 12 June 1996. Address to the nation on Independence Day, 12 June 1996. Natsional'naya Sluzhba Novostey.

Speech at Ekaterinburg, 14 June 1996. INTERFAX (FBIS-SOV-96-117, 18 June, Article Id: drsov117aa_96033, http://wnc.fedworld.gov/cgi-bin . . .).

Address to the citizens of Khabarovsk, Radio Rossii, 23 June 1996 (FBIS-SOV-96-123, 26 June 1996, Article Id: drsov123aa_96001, http://wnc.fedworld.gov/cgi-bin . . .).

Address to the nation after the second round of the Presidential election. First Channel/ORT (Ostankino), 4 July 1996 (FBIS-SOV-96-130, 5 July 1996, p. 1).

Address to the nation, 10 July 1996. ITAR-TASS (FBIS-SOV-96-134, 11 July 1996).

State of Russia address to the Federal Assembly, 6 March 1997 (http://www.maindir.gov.ru, 26 June 1997).

'Obrashchenie prezidenta RF Borisa El'tsina k zhitelyam Rossii' (Address of the President of the Russian Federation Boris Yeltsin to the citizens of Russia). 14 March 1997. Natsional'naya Sluzhba Novostei, 17 March 1997, p. 1 (www.nns.ru/chronicle/obr1403.html).

Radio address on Russia–NATO accord, 29 May 1997. Informantsionnoye Agentso Ekho Moskvy (FBIS-SOV-97-149, http://wnc.fedworld.gov, 31 May 1997).

Speech to the Council of Federation, 24 September 1997. Federal News Service (http://www.fnsg.com, 29 September 1997).

State of Russia address to the Federal Assembly, Official Kremlin Federal Information Systems Broadcast, International Broadcast, 17 February 1998.

Address to the nation, 23 March 1998. Reuters, 24 March 1998 (www.nytimes.com).

Speech at the burial of Tsar Nicholas II and his family, 17 July 1998. Reuters (http://www.cnn.com).

INTERVIEWS WITH YELTSIN

V. Danilov and A. Zdin. 'Znat', chtoby umet'' (To know, in order to be able to do). Pravda, 4 November 1979.

Khiltunen, V., and V. Khlystun. 'Net voprosov bez otvetov' (There are no questions without answers). Kosomol'skaya Pravda, 7 August 1981.

'Zhit' dlya ludey – dolg kommunista. Na voprosy studentov 12 Sverdlovsk a otvechayet chlen TsK KPSS, perviy sekretar' Sverdlovskogo obkama partii B. N. El'tsin' (To live for the people is the duty of the Communist. A member of the Central Committee of the CPSU, First Secretary of the Sverdlovsk Obkom, B. N. Yeltsin, answers the questions posed by the students of Sverdlovsk). Komsomol'skaya Pravda 25 September 1981.

'Otvety na voprosy, zadannye studentami vuzov goroda Pervomu Sekretaryu TsK KPSS, chlenu TsK KPSS, Deputatu Verkhovnogo Soveta, tov. Yeltsinu B. N.' Fond 4, opis 10, delo 90. Partiiniy Arkhiv Sverdlovskoy Oblasti (Answers to the questions posed by the students of the Institutions of Higher Education of the city to the First Secretary of the Regional Committee of the CPSU, Deputy of the Supreme Soviet of the USSR, Comrade Yeltsin, B. N.' Holding 4, registry 10, log 90. The Party Archive of the Sverdlovsk region). 19 May 1981.

V. Danilov. 'V besede uchastvuyut vse' (Everyone participates in the discussion). Press conference for the editors of local radio, television and newspapers. Zhurnalist, 3, (March) 1984.

'Veilleicht war nur ein Mensch schuld' (Perhaps only one man was to blame). Interview with Dieter Gütt and Uwe Zimmer, Stern, 7 May 1986, p. 245.

'Net ni potolka dyla kritiki, ni predela dyla glasnosti' (There is neither ceiling for criticism nor limit to glasnost'). Moskoskie Novosti, 24 August 1986, p. 4.

'Pribavlyat' oboroty perestroiki' (To hasten the pace of perestroika). Moskovskaya Pravda, 14 April 1987.

'Visiting Boris Yeltsin'. Interview with Mikhail Poltoranin, Moscow News, the German edition, May 1988, Cologne, p. 20 (FBIS-SOV-88-083, 29 April 1988, pp. 31–2).

'Yeltsin Comments on Dismissal, Interview'. Agence France-Presse, Moscow, 1 May 1988 (FBIS-SOV-88-084, 2 May 1988, pp. 59–60).

'World Exclusive' interview with Boris

Yeltsin, BBC Television, 30 May 1988 (FBIS, 31 May 1988, pp. 40–1).

Aleksandr Ol'bik. ' "Sotsial'naya spravedlivost" – kompas perestroiki' (Social justice is the guiding star of perestroika). *Sovetskaya Molodezh* (Riga), 4 August 1989.

'Vera v perestroiku dolzhna byt'!' (There must be faith in perestroika!) *Komsomoletz Tadzhikistana* (Dunshabe), January 22 1989. Answers to questions at the meeting with students of the Highest Komsomol School, 12 November 1988.

Politik ili avantyurist? (A politician or an adventurer?). *Moldaya Gvardia* (Perm), 4 December 1988. Answers to questions at a meeting with students of the Highest Komsomol School, 12 November 1988.

Pavel Voshchanov. 'Ne zabyt' o cheloveke' (Don't forget about man). *Komsomol'skaya Pravda*, 31 December 1988.

Mikhail Poltoranin. 'Ministr ili deputat?' (Minister or Deputy?). *Moskovskie Novosti*, 29 January 1989.

Sverdlovsk documentary film group on 30 January 1989 (from the video archive of the Museum of Youth Movements, Ekaterinburg).

'El'tsin: Nuzhno iztant'sya ot ravnodushiya i strakha' (Yeltsin: One must get rid of indifference and fear). *Propeller*, student newspaper of the Moscow Institute of Aircraft Engineering, 21 February 1989.

Sverdlovsk documentary film group on 27 March 1989 (from the video archive of the Museum of Youth Movements, Ekaterinburg).

'B. N. El'tsin: Lyudyamochen' vazhna pravda' (B. N. Yeltsin: Truth is very important to people). *Sovetskaya Estonia*, 19 February 1989.

Sovetskaya Rossia, 23 February 1989, first edition (FBIS-SOV-89-035, 23 February 1989, pp. 69–70).

Boris El'tsin: prevratnosti sud'by (Boris Yeltsin: the vicissitudes of fate). Sverdlovsk: Sverdlovsk Studio of Documentary Films, March 1989.

TASS International Service, 16 March 1989 (FBIS, 17 March 1989, p. 72).

'Miting na Sovetskoy ploshchadi' (A rally on the Sovetskaya square). *Pravda*, 23 March 1989, p. 6.

Ezio Mauro. *La Repubblica*, 24 March 1989 (FBIS, 29 March 1989, p. 38).

'Where perestroika went wrong, by Boris Yeltsin. Exclusive interview'. *Sunday Telegraph*, 26 March 1989. (FBIS-SOV-89-058, 28 March 1989, pp. 42–3).

Moscow television, 19 May 1989 (FBIS, 22 May 1989, p. 69).

La Vangardia (Barcelona), 21 May 1989 (FBIS, 1 June 1989, p. 38).

Radio Budapest, 27 May 1989 (FBIS, 2 June 1989, p. 33).

N. Zhelnova and L. Novikova. 'Ot imeni naroda' (On behalf of the people). *Argumenty i Fakty*, 10–16 June 1989, p. 2.

Al-Musawwar (Cairo), 16 June 1989 (FBIS, 20 June 1989, p. 57).

Andrea Bonanni. *Corriere della Sera* (Milan), 16 June 1989 (FBIS-SOV-89-117, 20 June 1989, pp. 7–9).

'Ya ne storonnik polumer!' (I am not a proponent of half-measures!). Interview with *Literaturnaya Gazeta*, 28 June 1989.

Panorama, Hungarian television, 28 June 1989 (FBIS-SOV-89-125, 30 June 1989, p. 49).

V. Tolstov. 'Reshenie sotsialnykh problem neotlozhno' (Resolution of social problems cannot be postponed). *Izvestia*, 20 July 1989.

Irina Inoveli. 'Narodniy Deputat B. N. El'tsina: "Ya za pravdu, kakoy by

ona ni byla"' (People's Deputy
B. N. Yeltsin: I am for the truth,
no matter what it is'). *Zarya
Vostoka*, 1 August 1989.

A. Pankov. 'Bol'she dela' (More real
work). *Trud*, 8 August 1989.

Answers to questions at a meeting
with students of the Moscow
Aviation Institute (MAI). In
Vestnik Vysshey Shkoly (Higher
Education Herald), 9 September
1989.

Natasha Sharymova. 'Okazyvaetsya,
kapitalizm ne zagnivaet'
(Capitalism, it turns out, is not
decaying). Transcript of Yeltsin's
press conference, New York, NY,
10 September 1989. *Novoye
Russkoye Slovo*, 12 September
1989.

Face the Nation, CBS News, 10
September 1989. Transcript in the
author's archive.

MacNeil/Lehrer Newshour, 11
September 1989, transcript.

Press conference following a speech.
Johns Hopkins University,
Baltimore, 12 September 1989.
Audio and video recordings in the
author's archive.

Valentin Yumashev. 'Poezdka, o
kotoroy govoriat' (The much
talked-about trip). *Ogonyok*, no.
41, 7–14 October 1989, pp. 30–1.

Beseda s narodym deputaton SSSR
B. N. El'tsinym (A conversation
with the People's Deputy of the
USSR B. N. Yeltsin), *Radio
Liberty*, 19 October 1989.

Det Fri Aktuelt (Copenhagen), 2–3
December 1989 (FBIS, 8 December
1989, p. 98).

Agence France-Presse, 5 December
1989 (FBIS, 6 December 1989,
p. 104).

INTERFAX (Moscow World Service
in English), 27 December 1989
(FBIS, 28 December 1989, p. 78).

Egor Yakovlev. 'V poiskakh soglasiya'
(In search of accord). *Moskovskie
Novosti*, 14 January 1990.

R. Amos. 'Interv'yu s narodnym
deputatom SSSR B. N. El'tinsym'
(Interview with the USSR People's
Deputy B. N. Yeltsin). *Sovetskaya
Estonia*, 20 February 1990.

Manichi Shimbun, 18 January 1990
(FBIS, 23 January 1990, p. 9).

'Boris El'tsin: ya ne budu brat'
samootvod' (Boris Yeltsin: I will
not withdraw). *Sovetskaya
Molodezh* (Riga), 1 February 1990.

Rene De Bok and Willem Wasink.
'Interview with USSR Deputy Boris
Yeltsin.' *La Stampa* (Turin), 24
January 1990 (FBIS, 13 February
1990, p. 2).

Corriere della Sera (Milan), 9 March
1990 (FBIS, 21 March 1990,
pp. 5, 6).

ITV Television Network (London), 29
April 1990 (FBIS, 3 May 1990).

Madrid Domestic Service (Radio), 4
May 1990 (FBIS, 7 May 1990).

'Chtoby "ne propustit" menia,
vedyotsia kolossal'naya rabota' (A
colossal campaign is being
conducted in order to 'block' me).
Interview with *Sovetskaya
Molodezh* (Riga), 15 May 1990.

Press conference on 30 May 1990,
Moscow television (FBIS, 1 June
1990, p. 78).

'Press-konferentsia B. N. El'tsina
(B. N. Yeltsin's press conference).
Sovetskaya Rossia, 31 May
1990.

Egor Yakovlev. 'I snova v poiskakh
soglasiya' (Again, in search of
accord). *Moskovskie Novosti*, 10
June 1990.

'Press-konferentsia po itogam pervogo
s'ezda narodnykh deputatov Rossii'
(Press conference at the conclusion
of the First Congress of People's
Deputies of Russia), 22 June 1990.
Videotape, Museum of Youth
Movements, Ekaterinburg.

'The conversation of the RSFSR
People's Deputies V. Isakov and
V. Skrypchenko with B. N. Yeltsin
on 22 June 1990'. Videotape,

Museum of Youth Movements, Ekaterinburg.

Press conference on 26 June 1990, Moscow television (FBIS, 27 June 1990, p. 90).

'Boris El'tsin i Sovet rabochikh komitetov Kuzbassa' (Boris Yeltsin and the Council of Workers' Committees of Kuzbass). A transcript. *Nasha Gazeta*, 19, (26 June) 1990, as reprinted in *Russkaya Mysl'*, 29 June 1990.

Interview for the video archive of the Museum of Youth Movements, Ekaterinburg, July 1990.

Aleksandr Ol'bik. 'Ya veryu v russkoe chudo' (I believe in the Russian miracle). *Sovetskaya Molodezh*, 3–4 August 1990.

Aleksandra Lugovskaya. 'Boris El'tsin: nikto ne smog menya postavit' na koleni' (Boris Yeltsin: no one has ever made me kneel). *Soyuz*, 38, September 1990, as reprinted in *Doverie*, January 1991.

Press conference on 1 September 1990, Moscow Television, 1 September 1990 (FBIS, 4 September 1990).

V. Dolganov. 'Boris El'tsin: sabotazh est'!' (Boris Yeltsin: yes, there is sabotage!). *Komsomolskoye Znamya*, 30 September 1990.

Press conference in the Hall of the Soviet of Nationalities, Supreme Soviet of Russia, 14 January 1991. Transcript of an audiotape in the author's archive (see also *Rossiyskaya Gazeta*, 15 January 1991 and *Izvestia*, 15 January 1991).

Interview with Sergey Lomakin and Oleg Poptsov, First Channel/ORT (Ostankino), 19 February 1991. Transcript printed in 'Pered litsom naroda' (In front of the entire people). *Sovetskaya Rossia*, 23 February 1991. (See also Gorshkov and Zhuravlyova, *Gorbachev–El'tsin*, pp. 313–14.)

'Konfrontatsia bezrassudna. Ob interv'yu B. N. El'tsina Tsentral'nomu televideniyu' (Confrontation is reckless. About B. N. Yeltsin's interview on Central Television). *Izvestia*, 20 February 1991.

Press conference in Paris, 17 April 1991. *Russkaya Mysl'*, 19 April 1991.

'Parlamentskiy vestnik Rossii' (Parliamentary herald of Russia). Moscow television, 4 May 1991 (*Kuranty*, 7 May 1991).

V. Lynev. 'Tsel' – obnovlenie Rossii. B. N. El'tsin otvechaet na voprosy Izvestiy' (The goal is the renewal of Russia. B. N. Yeltsin answers *Izvestia*'s questions). *Izvestia*, 23 May 1991.

Press conference in the Kremlin, 25 May 1991. Moscow television (FBIS, 28 May 1991).

Interview with Soviet journalists, 9 July 1991. *Izvestia*, 10 July 1991.

Russian Television Channel (Rossia), 25 August 1991 (FBIS-SOV-91-165, 26 August 1991).

News conference for Russian and foreign journalists, 7 September 1991. Russian Television Channel (Rossia), 7 September 1991 (FBIS-SOV-91-174, 9 September 1991).

Russian Television Channel (Rossia), 17 October 1991 (FBIS-SOV-91-202, 18 October 1991).

First Channel/ORT (Ostankino), 20 November 1991 (FBIS-SOV-91-225, 21 November 1991).

Boris Yeltsin. 'Bystrye reformy – edinstvenniy shans Rossii' (Rapid reform is Russia's only chance). *Izvestia*, 29 November 1991.

Press conference, 30 November 1991 in Moscow. TASS (FBIS-SOV-91-231, 2 December 1991).

'Nam ochen' trudno, no my vystoim' (It is very difficult for us, but we will stand our ground). *Trud*, 14 December 1991, p. 1.

CNN, 25 December 1991. *New York Times*, 26 December 1991, p. A3.

'We Are Taking Over'. Interview with *Newsweek*, 30 December 1991.

First Channel/ORT (Ostankino), 1 October 1993 (FBIS, 1 October 1993, p. 5).

'Boris El'tsin: kak prezident, ya bol'she drugikh zainteresovan v sotsial'noy stabil'nosti' (Boris Yeltsin: as President, I am more than anyone interested in social stability). *Izvestia*, 16 November 1993, pp. 1, 4.

El'dar Ryazanov. First Channel/ORT (Ostankino), 16 November 1993 (FBIS, 17 November 1993, p. 27).

Interview with the Yaroslavl' city television. ITAR-TASS, 2 May 1996 (FBIS-SOV-96-087, 6 May 1996, Article Id: drsov087_a_96002, http://wnc.fedworld.gov/cgi-bin . . .).

Interview with *Delovye Lyudi* magazine, INTERFAX, 6 May 1996 (FBIS, 7 May 1996, Article Id: drsov088_b_96003, http://wnc.fedworld.gov/cgi-bin . . .).

Kaliningradskaya Pravda, 18 May 1996 (FBIS-SOV-96-109, June 6, Article Id: drsov109_d_96001, http://wnc.fedworld.gov/cgi-bin . . .).

'Glavnoye, chtoby Rossiya okonchatel'no sdelala svoy vybor v pol'zu svobody' (The most important thing is for Russia to choose freedom). Interview with *Rossiyskaya Gazeta*, 5 June 1996, p. 3.

DOCUMENTS, STATEMENTS, RADIO AND TELEVISION BROADCASTS, AND ON-LINE ARCHIVES

Gosudarstvenny Arkhiv Rossiyskoy Federatsii 665-1-13, 30 January 1865.

UPI, Student Record Book No. 494087, the archive of the Ural Polytechnic Institute.

Resolution of the meeting of the buro of the Chkalovskiy District Committee of Komsomol (the city of Sverdlovsk), recommending Boris Yeltsin for the membership in the Communist Party of the Soviet Union, 22 January 1960. *Lichnoye Delo, El'tsin Boris Nikolaevich* (Personal File of Yeltsin Boris Nikolayevich), The Party Archive of the Sverdlovsk Region, holding 2992, registry 6, log 527. A copy in the author's archive.

Recommendations for Party membership submitted on Yeltsin's behalf, 14 March 1960. Personal File of Yeltsin Boris Nikolayevich, the Party Archive of the Sverdlovsk Region, holding 2992, registry 6, log 527. A copy in the author's archive.

Minutes of the meeting of the Party cell of Yuzhgorstroy (Protocol No. 7), 17 March 1961. Personal File of Yeltsin Boris Nikolaevich, the Party Archive of the Sverdlovsk Region, holding 2992, registry 9, log 408. A copy in the author's archive.

Programma Kommunisticheskoy Partii Sovetskogo Soyuza (The Programme of the Communist Party of the Soviet Union). Moscow: Politizdat, 1974.

'O likvidatsii barakov i zhilikh pomesheniy v podvalakh v 1982 godu'. Tsentr dokumentatsii obshestvennykh organizatsiy Sverdlovskoy oblasti. Fond 4, opis 101, delo 188, 1982 g. (On the liquidation of baraks and basement dwellings in 1982. The Centre for Documentation of the Public Organizations of the Sverdlovsk Region, holding 4, registry 101, log 188, 1982). 30 September 1982.

Protokol No. 46 zasedanya buro Sverdlovskogo Obkoma KPSS ot 24 maya 1983 goda. *O rabote redaktsii po povysheniyu ideino-khudozhestevennogo urovnya zhurnala 'Ural' v svete trebovaniy XXVI s'ezda partii i postanovleniya TsK KPSSS. 'O tvorcheskikh svyazyakh literaturno-khudozhestvennikh zhurnalov s praktikoy kommunisticheskogo stroitelstva.* Fond 4, opis 106, delo 35. The minutes of the Buro of the Sverdlovsk Obkom of 24 May 1983. (On the work of the editorial staff in the area of raising the ideological and creative level of *Ural* magazine in the light of the demands of the Twenty-Sixth Party Congress and the decree of the CC CPSU 'On the creative connection between magazines of belle-lettres and the practice of the building of communism'.) The Party Archive of the Sverdlovsk Region, holding 4, registry 106, log 35).

'Seven Days in May'. Moscow: CBS, May 1987, 2 hours.

'Presumed Text of Mr Yeltsin's Speech to CPSU Central Committee'. *Le Monde*, 2 February 1988 (FBIS-SOV-88-021, 2 February 1988, pp. 52–3).

'District Electoral Meeting'. Moscow Radio, 17 February 1989 (FBIS, 21 February 1989, p. 79).

Hungarian television, 20 February (FBIS, 21 February 1989, p. 79).

'Stenogramma mitinga o prinyatii obrashcheniya v adres TsK KPSS 20 Marta 1989 g. Mesto: Foye DK UPI' (Protocol of the meeting to adopt a letter to the Central Committee on 20 March 1989. Place: the lobby of the House of Culture of the UPI.) A copy in the author's archive.

Agence France-Presse, 22 February 1989 (FBIS, 23 February 1989).

Agence France-Presse, 21 March 1989 (FBIS, 22 March 1989).

BBC World Service, London, 24 March 1989 (FBIS, 24 March 1989, p. 37).

Mark Zakharov. Interviewed on Soviet television, 21 April 1989 (FBIS, 1 May 1989, pp. 57–8).

Deutschlandfunk Radio, Cologne, 13 June 1989 (FBIS, 13 June 1989, p. 32).

TASS, 14 July 1989 (FBIS, 14 July 1989, p. 41).

Viktor Medikov. Speech at a session of the Supreme Soviet of the USSR, 17 July 1989, Moscow television, 17 July 1989 (FBIS, 18 July 1989, pp. 69–71).

Radio Moscow, 18 July 1989 (FBIS, 19 July 1989, p. 66).

Vremya, First Channel/ORT (Ostankino) 18 July 1989 (FBIS, 19 July 1989, pp. 62–3).

TASS, 30 July 1989 (FBIS, 31 July 1989, pp. 52–3).

Sunday Telegraph (London), 30 July 1989 (FBIS-SOV-89-145, 31 July 1989).

TASS, 31 July 1989 (FBIS, 31 July 1989, p. 53).

Moscow television, 31 July 1989 (FBIS, 1 August 1989, p. 38).

Informatsionnyi Byulleten' Mezhregional'noy gruppy narodnykh deputatov (Information Bulletin of Inter-regional Group of People's Deputies). Moscow: Mezhregionalnoy gruppy narodnykh deputatov, 15 September 1989.

Minneapolis Star Tribune, 15 September 1989, photograph.

Lawrence Eagleburger. Speech at Georgetown University, Washington, DC, 13 September 1989. *Novoye Russkoye Slovo*, 16–17 September 1989.

Conference of the MDG. 24 September 1989. Washington, DC: Library of Congress, Videotape VAC 9392.

Moscow television, 25 September 1989 (FBIS, 25 September 1989, p. 110).

Yeltsin's remarks at the meeting of the Inter-Regional Group of Deputies in the House of Cinema. 27 September 1989. Ekaterinburg: Museum of Youth Movements. Videotape.

Yeltsin's remarks at a meeting of the Inter-Regional Deputy Group, 3 November 1989. Washington, DC: Library of Congress, Videotape VAC 9388.

Vremya, First Channel/ORT (Ostankino), 4 January 1990 (FBIS, 8 January 1990, p. 97).

JIJI, Tokyo 20 January 1990 (FBIS, 23 January 1990).

TASS, 29 January 1990 (FBIS, 30 January 1990, p. 52).

Agence France-Presse, 4 February 1990 (FBIS, 5 February 1990, p. 52).

Moscow World Radio Service, 5 February 1990 (FBIS, 13 February 1990, p. 74).

Meeting of the Inter-Regional Deputy Group (MDG) Conference, 10 March 1990. Washington, DC: Library of Congress, Videotape VAC 9402.

Meeting at the Inter-Regional Group of Deputies, 9 December 1989. Washington, DC: Library of Congress, Videotape VAC 9390.

Radio Madrid, 28 April 1990 (FBIS, 3 May 1990, p. 26).

Soveshchanie Mezhregional'noy deputatskoy gruppy (Meeting of the Inter-Regional Deputy Group), 29 April 1990. Washington, DC: Library of Congress, Videotape VAC 9404.

TASS, 30 April 1990 (FBIS, 1 May 1990, p. 41).

Photograph. *New York Times*, 2 May 1990, p. 1.

Agence France-Presse, 5 May 1990 (FBIS, 7 May 1990, p. 38).

Moscow television, 11 May 1990 (FBIS, 15 May 1990, p. 44).

Moscow television, 28 May 1990 (FBIS, 29 May 1990, p. 117).

Moscow television, 29 May 1990 (FBIS, 30 May 1990, p. 91).

Moscow Radio, 29 May 1990 (FBIS, 29 May 1990, p. 109).

RFE/RL Daily Report, 30 May 1990, p. 4.

Moscow Radio, 22 June 1990 (FBIS, 25 June 1990, p. 109).

Radio Riga, 27 July 1990 (FBIS, 27 July 1990, p. 67).

Moscow Radio, 10 August 1990 (FBIS, 13 August 1990, p. 81).

Vremya, First Channel/ORT (Ostankino), 10 August 1990 (FBIS, 13 August 1990, p. 81).

Vremya, First Channel/ORT (Ostankino), 12 August 1990 (FBIS, 13 August 1990, pp. 83–4).

Vremya, First Channel/ORT (Ostankino), 13 August 1990 (Library of Congress, VBH 9092).

Moscow television, 15 August 1990 (FBIS, 16 August 1990, p. 64).

Vremya, First Channel/ORT (Ostankino), 29 August 1990 (Library of Congress, VBH 9091).

Moscow television, 1 September 1990 (FBIS, 4 September 1990, pp. 87–94).

Vremya, First Channel/ORT (Ostankino), 29 September 1990 (FBIS, 1 October 1990, p. 40).

USSR Today. Soviet Media News and Features Digest, Radio Liberty Monitoring Service, 24 August 1990.

'Statement of the KGB Chairman on Soviet Television'. *Radio Liberty Soviet Media News Budget*, 11 December 1990.

'The Second Russian Revolution. Episode 3: The Yeltsin File'. Episode 3 of *The Second Russian Revolution*, Brian Lapping Associates for BBC Television in association with the *Discovery* channel and NHK, 1991.

Evgeniy Kiselev. Broadcast on Radio Rossii, 15 January 1991. Reprinted in *Doverie*, January 1991, p. 14.

Resolution of staffers at the Economy of the World Socialist System, 16 January 1991.

Transcript of meeting at the Economy of the World Socialist System, 16 January 1991. Copy in the author's archive.

TASS, 20 February 1991 (FBIS, 21 February 1991, p. 29).

'400,000 Attend Pro-Yeltsin Rally in Moscow'. Radio Moscow, 22 February 1991 (FBIS, 25 February 1991, p. 38).

Radio Rossii, 24 February 1991 (FBIS, 25 February 1991, p. 38).

Moscow television, 5 March 1991 (FBIS, 6 March 1991, p. 39).

TASS, Radio Moscow International Service, 7 March 1991 (FBIS, 8 March 1991).

TASS, 10 March 1991 (FBIS, 11 March 1991, p. 34).

Radio Rossii, 10 March 1991 (FBIS, 11 March 1991, p. 75.).

Radio Rossii, 11 March 1991 (FBIS, 12 March 1991, p. 77).

TASS International Service, 26 March 1991 (FBIS, 27 March 1991, p. 52).

Radio Rossii, 1 April 1991 (FBIS, 2 April 1991, p. 78).

TASS, 2 April 1991 (FBIS, 3 April 1991, p. 66).

Russian Television Channel (Rossia) report of the Congress, 4 April 1991 (FBIS, 5 April 1991, p. 51).

TASS, 9 July 1991 (FBIS, 10 July 1991, p. 68).

TASS, 05.29 19 August 1991 (FBIS, 19 August 1991, p. 9).

The State Committee for the State of Emergency. 'Address to the Soviet People'. TASS, 05.29, 19 August 1991 (FBIS, 19 August 1991, p. 11).

The State Committee for the State of Emergency. 'Address to the Soviet People'. TASS, 05.38, 19 August 1991 (FBIS, 19 August 1991, pp. 10–11).

TASS, 06.18, 19 August 1991 (FBIS, 19 August 1991, p. 8).

Gennadiy Yanaev. 'Address to heads of state and government and the Secretary General of the United Nations'. TASS, 06.27, 19 August 1991 (FBIS, 19 August 1991, p. 8).

'Decision No. 1 of the State Committee for the State of Emergency', Moscow Central Television, Second Programme Network, 10.05 (Moscow time), 19 August 1991 (FBIS-SOV-91-160, 19 August 1991, pp. 12–13).

Russian Television Channel (Rossia), 10.05, 19 August 1991 (FBIS, 19 August 1991, p. 12).

Agence France-Presse, 16.47, 19 August 1991 (FBIS, 20 August 1991, pp. 19–20).

Vremya, First Channel/ORT (Ostankino), 20.00, 19 August 1991 (FBIS, 20 August 1991, p. 21).

First Channel/ORT (Ostankino), 20.40, 19 August 1991 (FBIS, 21 August 1991, p. 12).

TASS, 20.46, 19 August 1991 (FBIS, 20 August 1991, p. 12).

'A Statement by Anatoliy Lukyanov'. TASS, 19 August 1991 (FBIS, 19 August 1991, pp. 19–20).

'A Statement by Anatoliy Lukyanov'. TASS, 19 August 1991 (FBIS, 20 August 1991, p. 21).

RFE/RL Daily Report, 19 August 1991, p. 2.

RFE/RL Daily Report, 156 Extra, 19 August 1991.

INTERFAX, 20 August 1991 (FBIS, 21 August 1991, p. 59).

RFE/RL Daily Report, 20 August 1991, p. A20.

Press Association, London, 20 August 1991 (FBIS, 21 August 1991, pp. 57–8).

Press Association, London, 00.10, 20 August 1991 (FBIS, 21 August 1991, p. 66).

First Channel/ORT (Ostankino), 20.40, 20 August 1991 (FBIS, 21 August 1991, p. 12).

Radio Vilnius, 23.25 (Moscow time), 20 August 1991 (FBIS, 21 August 1991, p. 67).

Agence France-Presse, 20.53 (Moscow time), 20 August 1991 (FBIS, 21 August 1991, a copy in the author's archive, p. 71).

INTERFAX, 00.02, 21 August 1991 (FBIS, 21 August 1991, p. 69).

DPA, Hamburg, 00.10, 21 August 1991 (FBIS, 21 August 1991, p. 66).

Radio Triana, 07.54, 21 August 1991 (FBIS, 21 August 1991, p. 64).

Vladivostok Radio, 21 August 1991 (FBIS, 21 August 1991, p. 58).

'Zayavlenie Sekretariata TsK Kompartii RSFSR' (Statement by the Secretariat of the Central Committee of the Communist Party of the RSFSR). *Sovetskaya Rossia*, 22 August 1991, p. 1.

Mikhail Gorbachev. Press conference, 22 August 1991. First Channel/ORT (Ostankino) (FBIS, 23 August 1991, pp. 23, 28).

Russian Television Channel (Rossia), 23 August 1991 (FBIS, 26 August 1991, p. 61).

Mikhail Gorbachev. Statement, 24 August 1991. First Channel/ORT (Ostankino) (FBIS, 26 August 1991, p. 15).

Mikhail Gorbachev. Decree by the President of the Soviet Union, 24 August 1991 (FBIS, 26 August 1991, p. 15).

First Channel/ORT (Ostankino), 24 August 1991 (FBIS, 26 August 1991, p. 74).

Radio Moscow World Service, 1 November 1991 (FBIS-SOV-91-212, 1 November 1991).

INTERFAX, 22 November 1991 (FBIS-SOV-91-229, 27 November 1991).

Vesti, Russian Television Channel (Rossia), 28 November 1991 (FBIS-SOV-91-225, 4 December 1991).

TASS, 12 December 1991 (FBIS-SOV-91-239, 12 December 1991).

XINHUA, 13 December 1991 (FBIS-CHI-91-241, 16 December 1991).

Egor Gaidar. Speech to the Supreme Soviet of the Russian Federation, 28 December 1991. Russian

Television Channel (Rossia) (FBIS-SOV-91-250, 30 December 1991).

Manifest Ural'skogo Politicheskogo Dvizheniya (The Manifesto of the Ural Political Movement). Ekaterinburg: 1992, p. 3.

Radio Rossii, 11 September 1992 (FBIS, 11 September 1992, p. 19).

INTERFAX, 15 October 1992 (FBIS, 16 October 1992, p. 16).

RFE/RL Daily Report, 2 December 1992.

Russian Television Channel (Rossia), 21 September 1993 (FBIS, 22 September 1993, p. 1).

Radio Rossii, 21 September 1993 (FBIS, 22 September 1993, pp. 10, 11).

ITAR-TASS, 21 September 1993 (FBIS, 22 September 1993, pp. 14, 15).

ITAR-TASS, 22 September 1993 (FBIS, 22 September 1993, pp. 16, 18).

Presidential–Parliamentary Crisis in Russia. Moscow First Channel/ORT (Ostankino), 21 September 1993 (FBIS, 22 September 1993, p. 1).

Interview with Prime Minister Viktor Chernomyrdin. Russian Television Channel (Rossia), 21 September 1993 (FBIS, 22 September 1993, p. 17).

Radio Odin, 22 September 1993 (FBIS, 22 September 1993, p. 12).

First Channel/ORT (Ostankino), 23 September 1993 (FBIS, 24 September 1993, p. 23).

Radio Rossii, 23 September 1993 (FBIS, 24 September 1993, p. 12).

ITAR-TASS, 23 September 1993 (FBIS, 24 September 1993, p. 42).

Russian Television Channel (Rossia), 23 September 1993 (FBIS, 24 September 1993, pp. 17, 31).

ITAR-TASS, 24 September 1993 (FBIS, 24 September 1993, pp. 3, 23, 24, 49).

Interview with Deputy Evgeniy

Koyokin. *Libération* (Paris), 24 September 1993, pp. 18–19 (FBIS-SOV-93-186-S, 28 September 1993).

First Channel/ORT (Ostankino), 27 September 1993 (FBIS, 28 September 1993, p. 1).

INTERFAX, 29 September 1993 (FBIS, 30 September 1993, p. 14).

ITAR-TASS, 29 September 1993 (FBIS, 30 September 1993, pp. 1, 5).

First Channel/ORT (Ostankino), 29 September 1993 (FBIS, 30 September 1993, p. 14).

Radio Rossii, 30 September 1993 (FBIS, 30 September 1993, pp. 21–2).

Radio Rossii, 30 September 1993 (FBIS, 1 October 1993, p. 36).

ITAR-TASS, 30 September 1993 (FBIS, 1 October 1993, p. 37).

Interview with Nikolay Medvedev, Chief of the Department of Territorial Affairs of the Presidential Administration. ITAR-TASS, 30 September 1993 (FBIS, 1 October 1993, p. 10).

Mayak Radio (Moscow), 30 September 1993 (FBIS, 1 October 1993, p. 7).

Russian Television Channel (Rossia), 30 September 1993 (FBIS, 1 October 1993, p. 23).

Agence France-Presse, 1 October 1993 (FBIS, 1 October 1993, p. 20).

Press conference of Sergey Filatov and Yuriy Luzhkov, 1 October 1993. First Channel/ORT (Ostankino) (FBIS, 4 October 1993, p. 51).

INTERFAX, 1 October 1993 (FBIS, 4 October 1993, p. 65).

ITAR-TASS, 1 October 1993 (FBIS, 1 October 1993, pp. 2–3).

ITAR-TASS, 1 October 1993 (FBIS, 4 October 1993, pp. 25, 33).

Radio Rossii, 1 October 1993 (FBIS, 1 October 1993, pp. 1, 3).

Interview with Sergey Filatov. ITAR-TASS, 1 October 1993 (FBIS, 1 October 1993, p. 2).

Russian Television Channel (Rossia), 1 October 1993 (FBIS, 1 October 1993, p. 3).

INTERFAX, 2 October 1993 (FBIS, 4 October 1993, pp. 45–6).

ITAR-TASS, 2 October 1993 (FBIS, 4 October 1993, p. 12).

Interview with Colonel-General Mikhail Kolesnikov, First Deputy Minister of Defence. Mayak Radio (Moscow), 2 October 1993 (FBIS, 4 October 1993, p. 35).

Mayak Radio (Moscow), 2 October 1993 (FBIS, 4 October 1993, p. 45).

Russian Television Channel (Rossia), 3 October 1993 (FBIS, 4 October 1993, p. 29).

Russian Television Channel (Rossia), 3 October 1993 (Washington, DC: Library of Congress, Videotape VBI 2311).

ITAR-TASS 3 October 1993 (FBIS, 4 October 1993, pp. 49, 54).

Vesti, Russian Television Channel (Rossia), 3 October 1993, 23.05 (Washington, DC: Library of Congress, Videotape VBI 2311).

Vesti, Russian Television Channel (Rossia), 00.50, 4 October 1993 (Washington, DC: Library of Congress, Videotape VBI 2313).

Videotape VBI 2310, Washington, DC: Library of Congress.

Videotape VBI 2311, Washington, DC: Library of Congress.

Videotape VBI 2312, Washington, DC: Library of Congress.

Videotape VBI 2313, Washington, DC: Library of Congress.

Videotape VBI 2314, Washington, DC: Library of Congress.

Russian Television Channel (Rossia), 02.30, *Vesti*, 4 October 1993 (Videotape VBI 2313, Washington, DC: Library of Congress).

ITAR-TASS, 04.32, 4 October 1993 (FBIS, 4 October 1993, p. 63).

ITAR-TASS, 06.32, 4 October 1993 (FBIS, 4 October 1993, p. 1).

Russian Television Channel (Rossia),

07.13, 4 October 1993 (FBIS, 4 October 1993, p. 30).

INTERFAX, 11.07, 4 October 1993 (FBIS, 4 October 1993, p. 2).

ITAR-TASS, 13.18, 4 October 1993 (FBIS, 4 October 1993, p. 6).

Mayak Radio (Moscow), 13.40, 4 October 1993 (FBIS, 4 October 1993, p. 5).

INTERFAX, 13.55, 4 October 1993 (FBIS, 4 October, 1993, p. 6).

Radio Rossii, 15.00, 4 October 1993 (FBIS, 4 October 1993, pp. 7–8).

ITAR-TASS, 15.54, 4 October 1993 (FBIS, 4 October 1993, pp. 7–8).

Statement by the Public Committee of the Russian Democratic Organizations. TASS, 5 October 1993 (FBIS, 6 October 1993, p. 33).

Lotti Ross. Letter to author, 17 April 1994.

S. Frederick Starr. Letter to author, 19 April 1994.

Grigoriy Yavlinsky. 'Zayavlenie fraktsii Yabloko' (Statement by the Yabloko faction), 27 October 1994. A copy in the author's archive.

Echo of Moscow Radio, 9 December 1994 (FBIS, 9 December 1994), http://wnc.fedworld.gov/cgi-bin/re, Article ID: drsov233_c_94008).

TASS, 10 December 1994 (FBIS, 10 December 1994, http://wnc.fedworld.gov/cgi-bin/re, Article ID: drsov238b_94004).

'Programma Kommunisticheskoy partii Rossiyskoy Federatsii prinyataya na III s'ezde KPRF 22 yanvaarya 1995 goda.s dopolneniyami vnesyonnymi na IV s'ezde' (Programme of the Communist Party of the Russian Federation adopted at the Third Congress of the KPRF on 22 January 1995 and augmented at the Fourth Congress), Russian communists' homepage, http://www.geocities.com/capitolhill/Lobby/3198/indexrus.htm.

Itogi, NTV, 18 February 1996 (FBIS-SOV-96-034, 21 February, Article ID: drsov_b_96009, http://wnc.fedworld.gov/cgi-bin . . .).

Egor Gaidar. Press conference, 26 February 1996. NTV (FBIS-SOV-96-039, 29 February 1996, Article Id: drsove039_b_96007, http://wnc.fedworld.gov/cgi-bin . . .).

'Gennadiy Zyuganov's Remarks in Barnaul'. INTERFAX, 26 March 1996 (FBIS-SOV-96-060, 28 March 1996, Article Id: drsov060_d_96003, http://wnc.fedworld.gov/cgi-bin . . .).

Grigoriy Yavlinsky. Interview on Itogi, NTV, 14 April 1996 (FBIS-SOV-96-073, 16 April 1996, Article Id: drsov073aa_96014, http://wnc.fedworld.gov/cgi-bin . . .).

INTERFAX, 23 April 1996 (FBIS-SOV-96-082, 26 April 1996, p. 3).

INTERFAX, 6 May 1996 (FBIS, 7 May 1996, Article Id: drsov088_b_96003, http://wnc.fedworld.gov/cgi-bin . . .).

INTERFAX, 14 May 1996 (FBIS-SOV-96-094, 14 May 1996, p. 14).

Igor Bel'skiy. 'Russia: Election Bank Funds of Presidential Candidates Cited'. ITAR-TASS, 23 May 1996 (FBIS-SOV-96-102, 28 May, Article Id: drsov102aa_96014, http://wnc.fedworld.gov/cgi-bin . . .).

Gennadiy Zyuganov, campaign visit and speech in Volgograd, Segodnya. NTV, 26 May 1996 (FBIS-SOV-96-103, 29 May 1996, Article Id: drsov103aa_96009, http://wnc.fedworld.gov/cgi-bin . . .).

Gennadiy Zyuganov, campaign visit to the Rostov Region, Segodnya, NTV, 27 May 1996 (FBIS-SOV-96-103, 29 May 1996, Article Id: drsov103aa_96011, http://wnc.fedworld.gov/cgi-bin . . .).

Gennadiy Zyuganov, campaign visit and speech in Stavropol, Segodnya,

NTV, 29 May 1996 (FBIS-SOV-96-105, 31 May 1996, Article Id: drsov105aa_96004, http://wnc.fedworld.gov/cgi-bin . . .).

Gennadiy Zyuganov, campaign visit to Nal'chik, *Segodnya*. NTV, 30 May 1996 (FBIS-SOV-96-107, 4 June 1996, Article Id: drsov107aa_96010, http://wnc.fedworld.gov/cgi-bin . . .).

INTERFAX, 31 May 1996 (FBIS-SOV-96-106, 31 May 1996, Article Id: drsov106aa_96010, http://wnc.fedworld.gov/cgi-bin . . .).

Gennadiy Zyuganov. Interview with Echo of Moscow Radio, 1 June 1996 (FBIS-SOV-96-107, 4 June 1996, Article Id: drsov107aa_96012, http://wnc.fedworld.gov/cgi-bin . . .).

Yuriy Khotz. ITAR-TASS, 5 June 1996 (FBIS-SOV-96-109, 6 June 1996, http://wnc.fedworld.gov/cgi-bin, Article Id: drsov109aa_96005).

Gennadiy Zyuganov. Interview on *Geroy dnya*, NTV, 11 June 1996 (FBIS-SOV-96-107, 13 June 1996, Article Id: drsov114aa_96004, http://wnc.fedworld.gov/cgi-bin . . .).

INTERFAX, 14 June 1996 (FBIS-SOV-96-117, 14 June 1996, http://wnc.fedworld.gov/cgi-bin . . . , Article Id: drsov117aa_96033).

Gennadiy Zyuganov. Interview on Fifth (St Petersburg) Channel, 14 June 1996 (FBIS-SOV-96-117, 18 June 1996, Article Id: drsov117aa_96050, http://wnc.fedworld.gov/cgi-bin . . .).

ITAR-TASS, 16 June 1996 (FBIS-SOV-96-117, 18 June 1996, Article Id: drsov117aa_9608, http://wnc.fedworld.gov.cgi-bin . . .).

'Yeltsin visits Kaliningrad Region', ITAR-TASS, 23 June 1996 (FBIS-SOV-96-122, http://wnc.fedworld.gov/cgi-bin . . . , Article Id: drsov122_b_96002).

2x2 Television. Television channel (Moscow) (FBIS, 24 June 1996, Article Id: drsov122aa_96009, http://wnc.fedworld.gov/cgi-bin . . .).

Gennadiy Zyuganov, press conference, *Segodnya*, NTV, 26 June 1996 (FBIS-SOV-96-125, 28 June 1996, p. 1, Article Id: drsov125aa_96009, http://wnc.fedworld.gov/cgi-bin . . .).

Radio Moscow World Service, 25 June 1996 (FBIS-SOV-96-124, 27 June 1996, Article Id: drsov124aa_96005, http://wnc.fedworld.gov/cgi-bin . . .).

Gennadiy Zyuganov, 'Election broadcast by the Presidential candidate Gennadiy Zyuganov'. Radio Rossii, 27 June 1996 (FBIS-SOV-96-125, 28 June 1996, Article Id: drsov125aa_9606, http://wnc.fedworld.gov/cgi-bin . . .).

Gennadiy Zyuganov, news conference after the second round of the presidential election, ITAR-TASS, 4 July 1996 (FBIS-SOV-96-130, 3 July 1996, Article Id: drsov130aa_96034, http://wnc.fedworld/gov/cgi-bin . . .)

Gennadiy Zyuganov, televised speech before the second round of the presidential election, First Channel/ORT (Ostankino) and the Russian Television Channel (Rossia), 1 July 1996. *OMRI*, 2 July 1996.

RFE/RL Newsline, 5 March 1997.

'Duma Communists Intend to Initiate Vote of No Confidence in Government. INTERFAX, 18 March 1997, p. 2 (http://www.maximov.com).

RFE/RL Newsline, 21 March 1997.

Viktor Chernomyrdin, Anatoliy Chubais and Boris Nemtsov. Press conference, 26 March 1997. Natsional'naya Sluzhba Novostei, 27 March 1997 (http://www.nns.ru).

Kostenko, Dmitriy. 'S'ezd KPRF provozglasil glavnoy zadachey kommunistov "smenu

pravyashchego v strane regima"'
(The KPRF congress declared
'change of the ruling regime' their
main task). Natsional'naya Sluzhba
Novostei, 24 April 1997 (http://
www.nns.ru).

INTERFAX, 12 May 1997 (FBIS-
SOV-97-132, 13 May 1997, Article
Id: drsov05121997000308, http://
wnc.fedworld.gov/cgi-bin . . .).

'Svedeniya o dokhodakh i
imushchestve Prezidenta
Rossiyskoy Federatsii El'tsina
Borisa Nikolaevicha' (Information
about the income and property of
the President of the Russian
Federation, Boris Nikolaevich
Yeltsin). Natsional'naya Sluzhba
Novostei (http://www.nns.ru), 2
June 1997.

'Dogovor o druzhbe, sotrudnichestve
and partnerstve mezhdu
Rossiyskoy Federatsiey i Ukrainoy'
(Treaty of friendship, co-operation
and partnership between the
Russian Federation and Ukraine),
Natsional'naya Sluzhba Novostei,
(http://www.nns.ru), 2 June 1997.

'Svedeniya o dokhodakh pervogo
zamestitelya predsedatelya
pravitel'stva RF Anatoliya
Chubaisa' (Information about the
income of the First Deputy
Chairman of the government of the
Russian Federation Anatoliy
Chubais). Natsional'naya Sluzhba
Novostei (http://www.nns.ru), 13
June 1997.

'Svedeniya o dokhodakh pervogo
zamestitelya predsedatelya
pravitel'stva RF Borisa Nemtsova'
(Information about the income of
the First Deputy Chairman of the
government of the Russian
Federation Boris Nemtsov).
Natsional'naya Sluzhba Novostei
(http://www.nns.ru), 13 June 1997.

'Middle Class Is Russia's Big Hope'.
Reuters. *Russia Today*, 27
February 1998 (http://
www.russiatoday.com).

'Yeltsin Nominee Confirmed as Prime
Minister'. CNN, 24 April 1998
(http://www.cnn.com).

'Russia suspends debt payment to
avoid full default'. Associated
Press, 20 August 1998 (http://
www.cnn.com).

BOOKS AND PAMPHLETS

Andreev, S. Yu, 'Nashe proshloye,
nastoyashchee, budushchee:
struktura vlasti i zadachi
obshchestva' (Our past, present,
future: the structure of power and
the tasks of society). In F. M.
Borodkin, L. Ya. Kosals and R. R.
Ryvkina, eds, *Postizhenie*,
Moscow: Progress, 1989.

Aron, Raymond. *France: The New
Republic*. New York: Oceana
Publications, 1960.

Aron, Raymond. *Memoirs*. New
York: Holmes & Meier, 1990.

Åslund, Anders. *How Russia Became
a Market Economy*. Washington,
DC: The Brookings Institution,
1995.

Ayrapetov, V. G., A. V. Bakunin and
L. S. Boyarskikh. *Sverdlovskaya
oblast' za 50 let* (The Sverdlovsk
province in the last fifty years).
Sverdlovsk: Sredne-Uralskoye
Publishers, 1984.

Berlin, Sir Isaiah. *Four Essays on
Liberty*. New York: Oxford
University Press, 1969.

Berlin, Sir Isaiah. *Personal
Impressions*. New York: Penguin,
1980.

Beschloss, Michael R., and Strobe
Talbott. *At the Highest Levels: The
Inside Story of the End of the Cold
War*. Little, Brown & Company,
1993.

Blasi, Joseph R., Maya Kroumova and
Douglas Kruse. *Kremlin
Capitalism*. Ithaca: Cornell
University Press, 1997.

Bonet, Pilar. *Nevozmozhnaya Rossiya.
Boris El'tsin, provintsial v Kremle*
(The impossible Russia. Boris

Yeltsin, a provincial in the Kremlin), *Ural*, 4, 1994.

Boswell, James. *Life of Johnson* (World's Classic series), ed. R. W. Chapman. Oxford: Oxford University Press, 1991.

Boycko, Maxim, Andrei Shleifer and Robert Vishny. *Privatizing Russia*. Cambridge, MA: The MIT Press, 1995.

Bukin, V. P., and V. A. Piskunov. *Sverdlovsk. Perspektivy razvitiya do 2000 goda*. (Sverdlovsk. Plans for Development to the year 2000). Sverdlovsk: Sredne-Uralskoye Publishers, 1982.

Chekhov, Anton. *Polnoe sobranie sochineniy* (Collected works). Moscow: Khudozhestvennaya Literatura, 1960, vol. XI.

Clark, Dick, ed. *U.S. Relations with Russia and Ukraine*. Washington, DC: Aspen Institute, 1996.

Coser, Lewis A. *Masters of Sociological Thought*. New York: Harcourt Brace Jovanovich, 1971.

Dobson, Richard B. *Is Russia Turning the Corner? Changing Russian opinion, 1991–1996*. Washington, DC: Office of Research and Media Reaction, US Information Agency, September 1996.

Dobson, Richard. *Russians Choose a President. Results of Focus Group Discussions*. Washington, DC: Office of Research and Media Reaction, US Information Agency, June 1996.

Donald, David Herbert. *Lincoln*. New York: Touchstone, 1995.

Duverger, Maurice. *La Monarchie Républicaine*. Paris: R. Lafont, 1974.

Gaidar, Egor. *Dni porazheniy i pobed* (The days of defeats and victories). Moscow: Vargius, 1997.

Gorbachev, Mikhail. *Memoirs*. New York: Doubleday, 1996.

Gorshkov, M. K., and Zhuravlyova, V. V. eds. *Gorbachev–El'tsin: 1500 dney politicheskogo*

protivostoyaniya (Gorbachev–Yeltsin: 1,500 days of political confrontation). Moscow: Terra, 1992.

Goryun, Andrey. *Boris Yeltsin – svet i teni* (Boris Yeltsin – light and shadows). Sverdlovsk: Voenniy Zheleznodorozhnik Publishers, 1991.

Grant, Steven A. *How Unsteady Is Russian Democracy?* Poll Confirms a Bumpy Reality. Washington, DC: Office of Research and Media Reaction, US Information Agency, 1 May 1997.

Grant, Steven A. *Russian Pre-Election Polls: A Fairly Good Job*. Washington, DC: Office of Research and Media Reaction, US Information Agency, 21 June 1996.

Great Dialogues of Plato, with an introduction by W. H. D. Rowe. New York: Mentor Books, 1959.

Green, Donald L., ed. *Samuel Johnson's Political Writings*. New Haven: Yale University Press, 1977.

Grossman, Vasiliy. *Vsyo techyot* (Forever flowing). Frankfurt/Main: Possev-Verlag, V. Gorachek KG, 1970.

Grossman, Vasiliy. *Zhizn' i sud'ba* (Life and fate). Moscow: Knizhnaya Palata, 1989.

Hayward, Jack, ed. *De Gaulle to Mitterrand: Presidential Power in France*. New York: New York University Press, 1993.

Hoffmann, Stanley. *Decline or Renewal? France since the 1930s*. New York: Viking Press, 1974.

Hough, Jerry. *The Soviet Prefects: The Local Party Organs in Industrial Decision-Making*. Cambridge, MA: Harvard University Press, 1969.

Inside Russia. Executive Summary, vol. I. Moscow: Russian Market Research Company, 1997.

Ivanova, Tatyana I., ed. *Andrey Dmitrievich: vospominania o Sakharove* (Andrey Dmitrievich:

memoirs of Sakharov). Moscow: Terra, 1990.

Johnson, Samuel. *The Lives of the English Poets*. London: Everyman's Library, 1983.

Klyamkin, Igor. *Novaya demokratiya ili novaya diktatura* (A new democracy or a new dictatorship). Moscow: Fond Obshestvennoye mnenie, 1994.

Korzhakov, Aleksandr. *Boris El'tsin: ot rassveta do zakata* (Boris Yeltsin: from dawn to sunset). Moscow: Interbook, 1997.

Kostikov, Vyacheslav. *Roman s Prezidentom. Zapiski press-sekretarya* (A novel with president. Notes of a press secretary). Moscow: Vargius, 1997.

Kozinetz, L. *Kamennaya letopis' goroda. Arkhitektura Ekaterinburga–Sverdlovska XVIII–nachala XX veka* (The stone record of the city. The architecture of Ekaterinburg–Sverdlovsk from the eighteenth to the beginning of the twentieth century). Sverdlovsk: Sredne-Uralskoye Publishers, 1989.

Kozlov, A. *Vekhi istorii* (The milestones of history). Sverdlovsk: Sredne-Uralskoye Publishers, 1973.

Kutsyllo, Veronika. *Zapiski iz Belogo doma* (Notes from the White House). Moscow: Kommersant Publishers, 1993.

Lacouture, Jean. *De Gaulle*, vol. II: *The Ruler: 1945–1970*. New York: Norton, 1992.

Lagunov, Konstantin. *Bronzoviy dog* (Bronze mastiff). *Ural*, 8, 9 and 10, 1982.

Laughland, John. *The Death of Politics: France under Mitterrand*. London: Michael Joseph, 1994.

Lebed, Alexander. *My Life and my Country*. Washington, DC: Regnery Publishing, 1997.

Ligachev, Yegor. *Inside Gorbachev's Kremlin*. New York: Pantheon Books, 1993.

Lombardi, Ben. *Russian Troop Withdrawal from the Baltic Region*. Ottawa: Department of National Defence, April 1994.

Macaulay, Lord (Thomas). *The History of England*. New York: Penguin Classics, 1986.

McFaul, Michael. *Russia's 1996 Presidential Election: The End of Polarized Politics*. Stanford: Hoover Institution Press, 1997.

McPherson, James M. *Abraham Lincoln and the Second American Revolution*. New York: Oxford University Press, 1990.

Mandel'shtam, Osip. *Sobranie sochineniy v chetyryokh tomakh* (Collected works in four volumes), ed. G. P. Strure and B. A. Filippov, vol. I. Moscow: Terra, 1991.

Materialy Plenuma Tsentral'nogo Komiteta KPSS, 5–7 fevralia 1990 g. (The materials of the Plenum of the Central Committee, 5–7 February 1990). Moscow: Politizdat, 1990.

Matlock, Jack F. *Autopsy on an Empire*. New York: Random House, 1995.

May, Antoinette. *A Biography of Marguerite Higgins*. New York: Beaufort Books, 1983.

Mickiewicz, Ellen, *Changing Channels: Television and the Struggle for Power in Russia*. New York: Oxford University Press, 1997.

Mitterrand, François. *Le Coup d'état permanent*. Paris: Julliard, 1964.

Morrison, John. *Boris Yeltsin: From Bolshevik to Democrat*. New York: Dutton, 1991.

Nikonov, Nikolay. 'Starikovaa gora' ('The old man's mountain') in Nikolay Nikonov, *Povesti* (Novellas). Sverdlovsk: Sredne-Uralskoye Publishers, 1990.

O'Brien, Conor Cruise. *The Great Melody*. Chicago: University of Chicago Press, 1992.

Pervyi S'ezd Narodnykh Deputatov SSSR. Stenograficheskiy Otchyot

(The First Congress of People's Deputies of the USSR. A transcript), 6 volumes. Moscow: Supreme Soviet of the USSR, 1989.

Pimenov, R. I. 'Kakim on byl' (What he was like). In Tatyana I. Ivanova, ed., *Andrey Dmitrievich: vospominaniya o Sakharove* (Andrey Dmitrievich: memoirs of Sakharov). Moscow: Terra, 1990.

Poptsov, Oleg. *Khronika vremyon 'tsarya Borisa'. Rossia, Kreml 1991–1995* (A chronicle of the times of "Tsar Boris". Russia, the Kremlin 1991–1995). Moscow: Sovershenno Sekretno Publishers, 1996.

Remnick, David. *Lenin's Tomb: The Last Days of the Soviet Empire.* New York: Random House, 1993.

Robert Graves: Collected Poems, 1975. New York: Oxford University Press, 1988.

Rossia v tsifrakh, 1995: kratkiy statisticheskiy sbornik (Russia in figures, 1995: short statistical compilation). Moscow: Goskomstat, 1995.

Rouse, W. H. D. *Great Dialogues of Plato.* New York: Mentor Books, 1959.

Rowen, Henry S., and Charles Wolf Jr. *The Impoverished Superpower.* San Francisco: Institute for Contemporary Studies, 1990.

Russia's Real Economy: Estimating the Informal Sector, 1994–1997. Santa Monica, CA: The Rand Corporation, 1998.

Ryzhkov, Nikolay. *Perestroika: istoriya predatel'stv* (Perestroika: the history of betrayals). Moscow: Novosti, 1992.

Schama, Simon. *Citizens.* New York: Vintage Book, 1989.

Shelton, Judy. *The Coming Soviet Crash.* New York: The Free Press, 1989.

Shevardnadze, Eduard. *The Future Belongs to Freedom.* London: Sinclair-Stevenson, 1991.

Shevtsova, Lilia, *Politicheskie zigzagi postkommunisticheskoy Rossii* (Political zigzags of post-communist Russia). Moscow: Carnegie Endowment for International Peace, 1997.

Shevtsova, Lilia, ed. *Rossia: desyat' voprosov o samom vazhnom* (Russia: ten questions about the most important issues). Moscow: Carnegie Endowment for International Peace, 1997.

Shub, Anatole. *Political Continuities Overshadow Yeltsin Comeback in Russian Elections.* Washington, DC: Office of Research and Media Reaction, US Information Agency, 19 July 1996.

Shub, Anatole. *Russian Readership Survey Finds Top, Local Papers Strong.* Washington, DC: Office of Research and Media Reaction. US Information Agency, 30 May 1995.

Sobchak, Anatoliy. *Khozhdenie vo vlast'* (A journey into power). Moscow: Novosti, 1991.

Sobyanin, A., and D. Yur'ev. *S'ezd narodnykh deputatove RSFSR v zerkale poimennykh golosovaniy* (The Congress of People's Deputies of the RSFSR in the mirror of name voting). Monograph. Moscow: 1991.

Solzhenitsyn, Alexandr. *Gulag Archipelago*, vol. III. New York: Harper & Row, 1978.

Solovyov, Vladimir, and Elena Klepikova. *Boris Yeltsin: A Political Biography.* Trans. David Gurevich. New York: G. P. Putnam's Sons, 1992.

Stockdale, Melissa Kirshchke. *Paul Miliukov and the Quest for a Liberal Russia, 1880–1918.* Ithaca and London: Cornell University Press, 1996.

Sukhanov, Lev. *Tri goda s El'tsinym* (Three years with Yeltsin). Riga: Vaga, 1992.

XXVIII S'ezd Kommunisticheskoy partii sovetskogo Soyuza: 2–13 iulya, 1990 goda: stenograficheskiy otchyot (XXVIII Congress of the Communist Party of the Soviet Union: the transcript). Moscow: Politicheskaya Literatura, 1990, vol. II.

Tsundani, V. 'Naselenie Urala i Zapadnoy Sibiri vo vtoroy polovine XVIII – pervoy polovine XIX veka' (The population of the Urals and West Siberia in the second half of the eighteenth to the first half of the nineteenth century). In *Istoricheskaya demografiya: novye podkhody, metody, istochniki. Tezisy VIII Vserossiyskoy konferentsii po istoricheskoy demografi* (Historical demography: new approaches, methods, sources. An outline for the Eighth All-Russian Conference on Historical Demography). Moscow: Russian Academy of Sciences, 1992.

Tubin, Y., L. Zaks, L. Varynkina, L. Senderova and S. Margulis. *Teatralniy Sverdlovsk* (Theatrical Sverdlovsk). Sverdlovsk: Sredne-Uralskoye Publishers, 1989.

Tyutchev, Fedor. 'Tsitseron' (Cicero). In *Stikhotvoreniya. Pisma* (Poems. Letters). Moscow: Sovremennik, 1978.

Ulam, Adam. *Russia's Failed Revolutions*. New York: Basic Books, 1981.

Voslenskiy, Mikhail. *Nomenklatura* (The nomenklatura). London: Overseas Publications Interchange, 1990.

Williams, Charles. *The Last Great Frenchman: A Life of General de Gaulle*. New York: John Wiley & Sons, 1995.

Williams, Philip M., and Martin Harrison. *Politics and Society in de Gaulle's Republic*. New York: Anchor Books, 1973.

Willis, David K. *Klass*. New York: St Martin, 1985.

XIX Vsesoyuznaya Konferentsiya Kommunisticheskoy Partii Sovetskogo Soyuza. Stenographicheskiy Otchyot, Tom II (The Nineteenth All-Union Conference of the Communist Party of the Soviet Union. Stenographic record, vol. II). Moscow: Izdatelsvto Politicheskoy Literatury, 1988.

Yakovlev, Aleksandr. *Muki prochteniá bytiya* (The torments of reading life). Moscow: Novosti, 1991.

Zhuravlev, V., L. N. Dobrokhotov and V. N. Kolodezhnyi, eds. *Istoriya sovremennoy Rossii, 1985–1994* (A history of modern Russia, 1985–1994). Moscow: Terra, 1995.

Zyuganov, Gennadiy. *Derzhava* (The great power). Moscow: Informpechat', 1994.

Zyuganov, Gennadiy. *From Destruction to Construction. Russia's Road to the 21st Century. Main Provisions of the Social and Economic Reform Programme of G. A. Zyuganov, Candidate for President from the Popular Patriotic Forces*. Moscow: 25 May 1996. Federal News Service. A copy in the author's archive.

Zyuganov, Gennadiy. *Rossia i sovremenniy mir* (Russia and today's world). Moscow: Informpechat', 1995.

Zyuganov, Gennadiy. *Za gorizontom* (Beyond the horizon). Moscow: Informpechat', 1995.

Zyuganov, Gennadiy. *My Russia*. New York: M. E. Sharpe, 1997.

ARTICLES

Abakumov, I., V. Gavrichkin and V. Nadein. 'V eti trevozhnye dni' (In these troubled days). *Izvestia*, 22 August 1991, p. 2.

Abikesheva, N., and S. Sevast'yanov. 'Pokupatel' dayot sovety' (The consumer gives advice). *Vechernyaya Moskva*, 18 November 1987.

Achalov, Vladislav. 'Zyuganov's "Defence Minister" Vladislav Achalov Speaks: "We Generals Versus Tsar Boris."' *Il Messaggero* (Rome), 2 June 1996, p. 15.

Afanasiev, Yuriy. Interviewed in *Sovetskaya Molodezh*, 7 July 1989.

Afanasiev, Yuriy. 'Otvety istorika' (A historian's answers). *Pravda*, 26 July 1988.

A.G. 'V nachale nomera' (Opening with the issue). *Literaturnaya Gazeta*, 7 April 1993.

Agranyanz, Oleg. 'Uroki dela El'tsina' (Lessons of the Yeltsin affair). *Russkaya Mysl'*, 29 January 1988.

Aikman, David. 'One Bear of a Soviet Politician'. *Time*, 20 March 1989.

Alayba, T. Speech at a protest rally in Sverdlovsk, 21 August 1991. *Doverie* extra edition, 21 August 1991, p. 2.

Aleksandrov-Agentov, Andrey. 'Brezhnev i Khrushchev' (Brezhnev and Khrushchev). *Novoye Vremya*, 22, 1993, pp. 36–7.

Aliev, R. 'Zyuganov in Novosibirsk'. *Sovetskaya Sibir'*, 6 June 1996, p. 1. (FBIS-SOV-96-115, 14 June 1996, Article Id: drsov115aa_96016, http://wnc.fedworld.gov/cgi-bin . . .).

Alimov, G., and R. Lynev. 'Kuda uvodit Pamyat'' (Where Pamyat' steals off to). *Izvestia*, 3 June 1987.

All-Russian Center for the Study of Public Opinion, 'Situatsya glazami Moskvichey' (The situation as seen by Muscovites). *Moskovskie Novosti*, 10 October 1993, p. 8.

Ambrosimov, L. 'Vtoraya professiya' (A second profession). *Vechernyaya Moskva*, 16 April 1987.

Amiel, Barbara. 'A Cry from the Heart of Russia'. *The Times* (London), 6 March 1990.

Analitica Moscow Political Weekly Press Summary, vol. 3, no. 24, 22–28 June 1996, pp. 1, 3.

'Anatomy of a Soap Crisis', *Soviet/East European Report*, vol. 7, no. 6, 1989.

Andropov, Yuriy. 'Rech General'nogo Secretarya Tsentral'nogo Komiteta KPSS tovarishcha Yu. V. Andropova na Plenume Ts K KPSS 15 iunya 1983 goda' (Speech of General Secretary of the Central Committee of the CPSU Comrade Yu. V. Andropov at the Plenum of the Central Committee of the CPSU on 15 June 1983). *Pravda*, 16 June 1983.

Anisimov, Evgenii. 'A View from Leningrad'. *Woodrow Wilson Center Report*, vol. 3, no. 3. November 1991, p. 6.

Anisin, Nikolay. 'Za!' (For!). *Zavtra*, 9, (February) 1996.

Anokhin, Pavel. 'Tretiy sil'nyi khod Borisa El'tsina v Chechenskoy politike' (The third master move of Boris Yeltsin in the Chechen policy). *Rossiyskie Vesti*, 29 May 1996, p. 1.

Apenchenko, Yu. 'Kuzbass. Zharkoye Leto' (Kuzbass. A hot summer). *Znamya*, 10, 1989.

Apostolov, Andrey, 'Aleksandr Rutskoy: nikakikh kompromissov, krome vozvrashcheniya zakonnosti' (Aleksandr Rutskoy: no compromises but restoration of legality). *Segodnya*, 2 October 1993, p. 1.

Apple, R. W., Jr. 'Russians Urged to Work More, Waste Less'. *New York Times*, 28 February 1981.

Arsenev, Vl. 'S'ezd v televizionnom izmerenii' (The Congress in the television dimension). *Izvestia*, 16 June 1989.

Åslund, Anders. 'Russia's Sleaze Sector'. *New York Times*, 11 July 1995.

Asmolov, Alexander. 'Privatizatsiya soznaniya' (Privatization of consciousness). *Moskovskie Novosti*, 11–18 October 1998.

Astafiev, Viktor. 'Istoriya i literatura' (History and literature).

Literaturnaya Gazeta, 18 May 1988.

A.T. 'Beloye na krasnom' (White on red). *Russkaya Mysl'*, 16 February 1990.

'A tovarov vsyo men'she. Sotsial'no-ekonimicheskoye polozhenie RSFSR v yanvare–sentyabre 1991 g.' (But there are increasingly fewer goods. RSFSR's socioeconomic position in January–September 1991). *Rossiyskaya Gazeta*. 31 October 1991.

'A ty ne temnish? . . . Tochno – vsyo vylozhil?!' (You are not playing games with us, are you? . . . Are you sure you have given us everything?!), an anti-Yeltsin cartoon. *Sovetskaya Rossia*, 25 April 1996.

Avanov, Aleksandr. 'Pervaya pobeda' (The first victory). *Moskovskie Novosti*, 22–29 March 1998.

Bakatin, Vadim. 'Vadim Bakatin: Esli u nas kto-to vysovyvalsia, golova letela v luchshem sluchae v Parizh' (If anyone made any trouble, he was sent at least to Paris). Interviewed by V. Mamontov. *Komsomol'skaya Pravda*, 31 May 1991.

Baker, Stephanie. 'Yeltsin Orders Cabinet to Kickstart Economy'. *RFE/RL Newsline*, 15 January 1998.

Balzer, Harley. 'Russia's Middle Class'. *Post-Soviet Affairs*, vol. 14 (2), 1998.

Barabashev, Alexei. 'In the Human Chain at the White House'. *Woodrow Wilson Centre Report*, vol. 3, no. 3, November 1991, p. 1.

Barber, Lionel. 'Bush treads carefully in support for Yeltsin'. *Financial Times*, 21 August 1991, p. 5.

Barinov, Dmitriy. 'Posledniy den' Feliksa' (Felix's last day). *Kuranty*, 24 August 1991.

Baskov, Vyacheslav. 'Proshchanie s limitchikom' (Farewell to the limitchik). *Sovetskaya Kul'tura*, 24 September 1987, p. 6.

Batalova, V., and V. Nechyaev. 'Kogda teryaetsya perspektiva' (When perspective is lost). *Moskovskaya Pravda*, 18 January 1987.

Batasheva, Irina. 'Uroki politicheskoy geografii' (The lessons of political geography). *Novoye Vremya*, 28, July 1996.

Batkin, Leonid. 'Oshibka El'tsina?' (Yeltsin's mistake?). *Kuranty*, 30 August 1991, p. 4.

Batygin, A. 'Vchera na ulitsakh Moskvy' (Yesterday on the streets of Moscow). *Pravda*, 20 August 1991.

B.C. 'Rutskoy Still Very Dangerous to Russia'. *Libération* (Paris). 24 September 1993 (FBIS, 28 September 1993, p. 19).

Bekker, Aleksandr. 'Tekhnokratiya na marshe' (Technocracy on the march). *Moskovskie Novosti*, 17–24 March 1998.

Belan, N. 'Nikolay Ryzhkov: skazhu otkrovenno . . .' (Nikolay Ryzhkov: let me tell you frankly . . .). *Sovetskaya Rossia*, 30 May 1991.

Belenkov, Yuriy. 'On bystro razdyshalsya . . .' (He quickly began breathing normally . . .). *Moskovskie Novosti*, 10–17 November 1996.

Belin, Laura. 'Anti-Communist Entertainment on TV'. *OMRI Daily*, 21 June 1996.

Belin, Laura. '. . . As Entertainment Programs Keep Up Anti-Communist Drumbeat'. *OMRI Daily*, 2 July 1996.

Belin, Laura. 'Yeltsin Stays Off Screen During Free Air Time'. *OMRI Russian Presidential Election Survey*, 12, 2 July 1996, p. 1.

Belozertsev, Anatoliy. 'Rossia – samaya glavnaya partiya. O poezdke Gennadia Zyuganova v Povolzh'e i na Ural' (The most important party is Russia. On Gennadiy Zyuganov's trip to the Volga region and the Urals). *Pravda*, 23 April 1996, p. 2.

Belyakov, V. Letter to *Kommunist*, 15, (October) 1989, p. 39.

Bennett, Susan. 'Bush Risks a Controversy by Joining Yeltsin Meeting'. *Philadelphia Inquirer*, 13 September 1989.

Bennett, Vandora. 'Feisty Yeltsin Vows Reform, Good Rule and New Cabinet'. *Los Angeles Times*, 7 March 1997 (http://www.latimes.com).

Berezovskiy, B., V. Gorodilov, V. Gusinskiy, A. Dundukov, N. Mikhailov, S. Muravlenko, L. Nevzlin, A. Nikolaev, D. Orlov, V. Potanin, A. Smolenskiy, M. Fridman and M. Khodorkovskiy. 'Vyiti iz tupika!' (Exit from a dead end!). *Izvestia*, 27 April 1996, p. 2.

Berger, M. 'Bol'nye den'gi' (The sick money). *Izvestia*, 15 November 1989.

Berger, M. ' "Sosenki" bez "Sosen" ' ('Little pines' without 'pines'). *Izvestia*, 27 August 1990.

Bergson, Abram. 'Soviet Economic Slowdown and the 1981–1985 Plan'. *Problems of Communism*. May–June 1981, pp. 24–36.

Bernshteyn, Erlen. 'Okna rosta v Pizanskoy bashne' (Windows of growth in the Tower of Pisa). *Novoye Vremya*, 7, 1998.

Berry, Lynn. 'Chechen Guerillas Shot Down Copter'. *Washington Post*, 31 May 1996, p. 3.

Birman, Igor. 'Na Rusi zhivyotsya luchshe, chem schitayetsya' (People live better in Russia than is commonly assumed). Interview with Anatoliy Druzenko *Izvestia*, 4 December 1997.

Biryukov, N. I. 'Vozmozhno li v sovremennoy Rossii prognozirovat' electoral'noye povedenie?' (Is it possible to forecast the electorate's behaviour in Russia?). *Polis*, 1, 1997, p. 113.

Black, Eric. 'Yeltsin Looks Like Candidate on U.S. Tour'. *Minneapolis Star Tribune*, 15 September 1989.

Black, Eric. 'Yeltsin Says his Criticism Actually Aids Gorbachev'. *Minneapolis Star Tribune*, 14 September 1989.

'Boevoe znamya Rodiny' (The battle banner of the Motherland). *Zavtra*, 18, May 1996, p. 1.

Bogomolov, Yuriy. 'B. N. El'tsin, dumayu, chto menya podderzhat' (B. N. Yeltsin, I think that I will get support). *Literaturnaya Gazeta*, 24 January 1990.

Bohlen, Celestine. 'Candidates Take to Airwaves as Russian Vote Approaches'. *New York Times*, 27 November 1993, p. 1.

Bohlen, Celestine. 'Champion of Glasnost Always Spoke his Mind'. *Washington Post*, 12 November 1987.

Bohlen, Celestine. 'New "Hands-On" Leader Is Shaking Up Moscow'. *Washington Post*, 10 February 1986.

Bohlen, Celestine. 'Russian Voters Lobby Parliament for Yeltsin'. *New York Times*, 28 May 1990.

Bohlen, Celestine. 'Yeltsin, Campaigner for his Country'. *New York Times*, 4 June 1998.

Bohlen, Celestine. 'Yeltsin Is Elected Russian President in Third-Round Vote'. *New York Times*, 30 May 1990.

Bohlen, Celestine. 'Yeltsin, the Moscow Populist, Takes Manhattan (in Stride)'. *New York Times*, 11 September 1989.

Bohlen, Celestine. 'Yeltsin Supports Moves for Continuing Talks on Revising Treaty'. *New York Times*, 28 August 1991, p. 1.

Bollaert, Baudouin. 'Elstine ménage Gorbatchev'. *Le Figaro*, 16 April 1991.

'Bomba dlya Deputata' (A bomb for a deputy). *Smena*, 20 September 1989.

Bondaruk, N. 'Den' sed'moy' (Day seven). *Izvestia*, 2 June 1989.

Bondaruk, N. 'Den' vtoroy' (Day two). *Izvestia*, 27 May 1989.

Bonner, Elena. 'Polupravda ne luchshe lzhi' (Half-truth is not better than lie). *Literaturnaya Gazeta*, 11 November 1992.

'Boris El'tsin: patologiya vlasti' (Boris Yeltsin: pathology of power). *Zavtra*, 12, (March) 1996.

'Boris the Humble?' *Washington Post*, 26 August 1991, p. A10.

Boulton, Leyla. 'Russians Promised Cheap Vodka and Reform'. *Financial Times*, 7 June 1991.

Boulton, Leyla. 'Ryzhkov Campaign Plays to the Patriotic Voter'. *Financial Times*, 5 June 1991.

Boulton, Leyla. 'Violent Clash Feared in Moscow'. *Financial Times*, 28–29 March 1991.

Boulton, Leyla. 'Yeltsin Plays on his Popularity to Turn Back the Military Tide'. *Financial Times*, 20 August 1991, p. 2.

Boykov, Anatoliy. 'Goroda za El'tsina, sela za Zyuganova' (Cities are pro-Yeltsin and villages are pro-Zyuganov). *Moskovskiy Komsomoletz*, 31 May 1996, p. 2.

Boykov, V. 'Chto govoryat v narode' (What the people are saying). *Izvestia*, 2 July 1990.

Bradsher, Keith. 'Gorbachev Asks a Huge Increase in Food Relief'. *Washington Post*, 13 September 1991.

Brezhnev, Leonid. 'Otchet Tsentral'nogo Komiteta Kommunisticheskoy Partii Sovietskogo Soyuza i Ocherdnye Zadachi Partii v Oblasti Vneshney i Vnutrenney Politiki' (Record of the Central Committee of the Communist Party of the Soviet Union and the Party's main tasks in foreign and domestic policy). *Pravda*, 23 February 1981.

Brodsky, Joseph. 'MCMXCV'. *New York Review of Books*, 8 June 1995.

Broening, Stephen. 'Yeltsin Appeals for Rescue of Perestroika'. *Baltimore Sun*, 13 September 1989.

Budberg, Aleksandr. 'Kommunisty proigrayut provintsiyu esli B.N. vyigraet gubernatorov' (The communists will lose the province if B.N. wins the governors). *Moskovskiy Komsomoletz*, 13 April 1996, p. 2.

'Budushchee pyatietazhek' (The future of five-storey buildings). *Moskovskaya Pravda*, 6 September 1987.

Burbulis, Gennadiy. Interview with *Novoye Vremya*, 7, 1995, p. 20.

Burbulis, Gennadiy. 'Minnoe pole vlasti' (The minefield of power). *Izvestia*, 26 October 1991.

Burlatskiy, Fedor. 'Perviy, no vazhniy shag' (The first, important step). *Literaturnaya Gazeta*, 14 June 1989.

Burov, Yuriy. 'Koril i sulil' (Reprimanded and promised). *Sovetskaya Rossia*, 8 June 1996, p. 4.

Burtin, Yuriy. 'Ne tebya b'yut – molchi' (They are beating someone else – so shut up). *Moskovskie Novosti*, 4–11 December 1994, pp. 1, 6.

Bush, Keith 'El'tsin Economic Reform Program'. *Report on the USSR*, 15 November 1991.

Butuzova, Ludmila. 'Zhizn' zamechatel'nykh ocheredey' (The life of remarkable queues). *Moskovskie Novosti*, 30 August–6 September 1998.

Cassileth, Barrie R., Vasily V. Vlasov and Christopher Chapman. 'Health Care, Medical Practice and Medical Ethics in Russia Today'. *JAMA*, 273/20 (24–31 May 1995), p. 1570.

Chazov, Evgeniy I. Interviewed by Zoriy Balayan. 'Kogda bolezn' obgonyaet lekarstva' (When the disease is faster than medicine). *Literaturnaya Gazeta*, 3 February 1988.

Chelnokov, Aleksey. 'Ekho sobytiy oktyabrya 93-go goda: chto kroeytsya za taynymi dos'e Barkashova?' (Echo of the events of October 1993: what is behind Barkashov's secret dossiers?). *Izvestia*, 6 September 1995.

Chelnokov, Aleksey. 'Kommissar Terekhov predveshchal "tret'yu mirovuyu"' (Commissar Terekhov predicted the Third World War). *Izvestia*, 29 September 1993, p. 2.

Chelnokov, Aleksey. 'Pulya prervala podpol'nuyu odisseyu glavnogo Rossiskogo fashista' (A bullet interrupted an underground Odyssey of the chief Russian fascist). *Izvestia*, 4 January 1994.

Chernyak, A. 'Edoki po statistike i v zhizni' (Food consumers in statistics and in reality). *Pravda*, 1 September 1988.

'Chronology of the Confrontation'. *Washington Post*, 5 October 1993, p. A32.

Chubais, Anatoliy. 'Mne nepriyatny razgovory o moyem "vsemogushchestve"' (I dislike the talk of my 'omnipotence'). Interview. *Novoye Vremya*, 48, 1996.

Chubais, Anatoliy. Speech at the Plenum of the Council of Russia's Democratic Choice. *Novoye Vremya*, 13, 1996, pp. 10–11.

'Chubais, Nemtsov Given Difficult Tasks'. *RFE/RL Newsline*, 27 January 1998.

'Chubais Wants to Bar Commercial Banks from Collecting Custom Duties . . .' *RFE/RL Newsline*, 7 August 1997.

Chugaev, Sergey. 'R. Khazbulatov prizyvaet vozrodit' Soyuz, A. Rutskoy preduprezhdayet o podgotovke prezidentom gosudarstvennogo perevorota, V. Sokolov predlagaet sozvat' vneocherdnoy s'ezd' (R. Khasbulatov calls for revival of the [Soviet] Union, A. Rutskoy warns of President's preparation for a coup, and V. Sokolov proposes convening an extraordinary Congress). *Izvestia*, 18 September 1993, p. 2.

Chugaev, Sergey. 'V Belom dome rasschityvayut na massovye besporyadki' (White House counts on mass disturbances). *Izvestia*, 25 September 1993, p. 2.

Clines, Francis X. 'Campus Rally for Yeltsin, a Rare Sight'. *New York Times*, 20 November 1987.

Clines, Francis X. 'For Muscovites, Pravda Account of the Yeltsin Ouster Is Riveting Reading'. *New York Times*, 14 November 1987.

Clines, Francis X. '40,000 Rally to Support Yeltsin against Gorbachev'. *New York Times*, 25 February 1991.

Clines, Francis X. 'A Free Market Plunge? Gorbachev's Not Ready'. *New York Times*, 26 April 1990.

Clines, Francis X. 'It's Moscow Live: New Faces, New Ideas and Impertinence'. *New York Times*, 26 May 1989.

Clines, Francis X. 'Moscow 1991'. *New York Times Magazine*, 3 March 1991.

Clines, Francis X. 'Moscow's Maverick with a Purpose'. *New York Times*, 3 March 1990.

Clines, Francis X. 'Rally Takes Kremlin Terror and Turns It into Burlesque'. *New York Times*, 29 March 1991.

Clines, Francis X. 'Soviet Opposition Defies Ban on Rally'. *New York Times*, 28 March 1991.

Clines, Francis X. 'Soviet TV's Biggest Hit: 200 Million Watch Political Drama'. *New York Times*, 31 May 1989.

Clines, Francis X. 'Striking Coal Miners Defend Yeltsin'. *New York Times*, 31 March 1991.

Clines, Francis X. '25,000 Rally for Rebels in New Soviet Congress'. *New York Times*, 22 May 1989.

Clines, Francis X. 'Yeltsin in U.S.: Pravda's Ugly Profile'. *New York Times*, 19 September 1989.

'The Clock Runs Out for Revolt'. *New York Times*, 5 October 1993, p. A16.

Clover, Charles. 'Yeltsin urges Duma to pass tax law'. *Financial Times*, 15 July 1998.

'Coming to America'. *Time*, 25 September 1989.

'Communists Respond to Attacks on Duma'. *RFE/RL Newsline*, 30 May 1997.

Conquest, Robert. 'Today the Soviet Party Congress Opens'. *Washington Post*, 23 February 1981.

Cook, Linda J. 'Brezhnev's "Social Contract" and Gorbachev's Reforms'. *Soviet Studies*, 44 (1), 1992.

'A coup d'état is being perpetrated . . .' *Russkaya Mysl'* (Paris), 1 February 1991.

Crow, Suzanne. 'Yeltsin: Russia Will Not Retreat from Reform'. *RFE/RL Daily Report*, 12 November 1992.

Danilov, Vadim. 'Pryamo ili posredstvom?' (Directly or indirectly?). *Pravda*, 3 April 1980.

Davydov, A. 'Manifestatsiya i Informatsiya' (Demonstration and information). *Izvestia*, 20 March 1989.

Davydov, A. and K. Kurasov. 'B. N. El'tsin – Predsedatel' Verkhovnogo Soveta RSFSR' (B. N. Yeltsin is Chairman of the Russian Republic's Supreme Soviet). *Izvestia*, 29 May 1990.

Deeva, Ekaterina. 'URNAgennaya zona' (The ballot box zone). *Moskovskiy Komsomoletz*, 4 June 1996, p. 4.

'Deklaratsia gosudarstvennogo suvereniteta Rossiyskoy Sovetskoy Federativnoy Sotsialisticheskoy Respubliki priniataya pervym s'ezdom Narodnykh Deputatov RSFSR' (The Declaration of State Sovereignty of the Russian Soviet Federated Socialist Republic Adopted by the First Congress of People's Deputies). *Sovetskaya Rossia*, 14 June 1990.

Devlin, Kevin. 'Soviet Journalist Describes Eltsin's Struggle against Party Mafia'. *Radio Liberty Research*, RL 206/88.

de Waal, Thomas. 'Deputies threaten to impeach Yeltsin'. *The Times* (London), 26 November 1997, p. 11.

Dikun, Elena, and Kostyukov, Anatoliy. 'Kuptsy pritsenivayutsya, tovar prikidyvaetsya' (The buyers are looking, the wares are pretending). *Obshchaya Gazeta*, 5–1 May 1996, p. 9.

'Dmitriy Donskoy protiv Borisa El'tsina' (Dmitry Donskoy against Boris Yeltsin). *Zavtra*, 7, February 1996.

Dobbs, Michael. 'For Clinton, Sticking with Yeltsin Sealed Agreement on NATO'. *Washington Post*, 27 May 1997.

Dobbs, Michael. 'Makeup of Supreme Soviet Decried; Thousands Protest Exclusion of Yeltsin from Standing Legislature'. *Washington Post*, 29 May 1989.

Dobbs, Michael. 'Russian Leader Becomes Focus of Opposition'. *Washington Post*, 20 August 1991, p. A20.

Dobbs, Michael. 'Thousands March to Support Yeltsin; Moscow Crowd Demands End to Party Attacks on Kremlin Rebel'. *Washington Post*, 20 March 1989.

Dobbs, Michael. 'Yeltsin: Russia's Rebel without a Pause'. *Washington Post*, 31 March 1991, p. A23.

Dobbs, Michael. 'Yeltsin's American Tour Hits Home'. *Washington Post*, 19 September 1989.

Dobbs, Michael. 'Yeltsin Woos the Military'. *Washington Post*, 2 June 1991.

'Dognat' i peregnat': shansy na uspekh v rossiyskikh prezidentskikh vyborakh' (To catch up and overtake: chances of success in Russia's Presidential election). The results of public opinion polls conducted by Nugzar Betaneli, Director of the Institute of Parliamentary Sociology. *Moskovskiy Komsomoletz*, 16 April 1996, p. 2.

'Dogovor o Soyuze Suverrnnykh Gosudarstv' (Treaty on the Union of Sovereign States). *Sovetskaya Rossia*, 15 August 1991, p. 3.

Dolganov, V., and V. Romanyuk. 'V komitetakh i komissiyakh Verkhovnogo Soveta SSSR. Sredstva nuzhny vsem. Gde ikh vzyat?" (In the committees and commissions of the USSR Supreme Soviet. Everyone needs money. Where [do we] get it?). *Izvestia*, 22 September 1989.

'Dorogie Moskvichi!' (Dear Muscovites!). Appeal by the Moscow City Council and the Mayor of Moscow. *Vechernyaya Moskva*, 23 August 1991, p. 1.

'Dos'e "MN"' (*Moskovskie Novosti*'s dossier). *Moskovskie Novosti*, 10 October 1993.

'Dos'e "MN"' (*Moskovskie Novosti*'s dossier). *Moskovskie Novosti*, 17–24 March 1996, p. 5.

Dowd, Maureen. 'Yeltsin's Back – But without the Bluster'. *New York Times*, 23 June 1991.

Drunina, O. 'K chemu privodit bezdushie' (The results of indifference). *Trud*, 19 January 1988, p. 2.

Dubnov, Vadim, and Andrey Kolesnikov. 'Chetyre maski Gennadiya Zyuganova' (The four masks of Gennadiy Zyuganov). *Novoye Vremya*, 22, 1996.

'Dudaev Calls for Islamic Alliance against the West'. *RFE/RL Newsline*, 26 November 1993.

Dyker, David. 'The Soviet Energy Balance and the Conundrum of Oil'. *Radio Liberty Research* (RL 43/81). 27 January 1981.

Dymov, A. 'Slyshat' drug druga' (To listen to one another). *Pravda*, 29 May 1989.

Eaton, William J. 'Gorbachev Ally Admits Errors, Asks to Resign'. *Los Angeles Times*, 1 November 1987.

Ebon, Martin. 'Yeltsin's V.I.P. Depression'. *Psychiatric Times*, October 1996.

'Ekonomika SSSR v yanvare–sentyabre 1991 goda' (The USSR Economy in January–September, 1991). *Ekonomika i Zhizn'*, 43, (October) 1991.

Elliot, Iain. 'Three Days in August: On-the-Spot Impressions'. *Report on the USSR*, 6 September 1991, p. 63.

Ellman, Michael. 'Shock Therapy in Russia: Failure or Partial Success?' *RFE/RL Research Report*, 28 August 1992.

'El'tsin deneg ne zhalel!' (Yeltsin did not stint on money!). *Sovetskaya Russia*, 20 June 1996, p. 4.

'El'tsin, ty proigral. Ukhodi, muzhik' (Yeltsin, you have lost. Quit, man). *Zavtra*, 16, (April) 1996, p. 1.

'El'tsin vne zakona!' (Yeltsin is an outlaw). *Den'*, 38, September 1993.

Erlanger, Steven. 'In a Less Arid Russia Jewish Life Flowers Again'. *New York Times*, 19 September 1993.

Erlanger, Steven. 'Rebirth of Jewish Life in Russia Cuts Emigration'. *New York Times*, 3 December 1995.

Erlanger, Steven. 'Russia Sits with "Big 8", Party Crasher No More'.

New York Times, 22 June 1997.

Erlanger, Steven. 'Russia's New Budget Raises Doubt on a Stable Economy'. *New York Times*, 28 December 1994, p. A6.

Ermakov, Aleksandr. 'Tovar v Rossii est. Ego by eschio prodat' . . .' (There are goods in Russia. If only we could manage to sell them . . .). *Novoye Vremya*, 13, 1994.

Eroshok, Z. 'My zhivy – my ne pogibli v ocherdyakh' (We are alive – we have not perished in queues). *Komsomol'skaya Pravda*, 27 August 1991, p. 2.

The European Institute of Mass Media, *Moskovskie Novosti*, 7–14 July 1996, p. 5.

Evtushenko, Evgeniy. '19 avgusta' (19 August). *Literaturnaya Gazeta*, 21 August 1991, p. 1.

'Ex-Aide Blames Gorbachev for "Team of Traitors"'. *New York Times*, 22 August 1991, p. A13.

Facts on File, vol. 51, no. 2664, 12 December 1991.

Facts on File, vol. 54, no. 2806, 8 September 1994.

Facts on File, vol. 55, no. 2828, 9 February 1995.

Facts on File, vol. 55, no. 2830, 23 February 1995.

Facts on File, vol. 55, no. 2841, 11 May 1995.

Facts on File, vol. 55, no. 2873, 21 December 1995.

Fedorov, Andrey. 'Zyuganov nakanune vyborov . . .' (Zyuganov on the eve of the elections . . .). *Argumenty i Fakty*, 15, 15–21 April 1996, p. 9.

Fedorov, S. 'Voinstvo so strelami' (An army with arrows). *Pravda*, 28 September 1987.

Federov, V., and N. Zhdankin. 'Pochemu bastovali shakhtyory, ili krivoe zerkalo planovo-ubytochnoy ekonomiki' (Why the miners went on strike, or a distorting mirror of the plan-and-loss economy). *Izvestia*, 28 July 1989.

Fein, Esther. 'For Rank-and-File Party Delegates, Dust of Openness Was Exhilarating'. *New York Times*, 3 July 1988.

Filin, V. 'Pochemu Kryuchkov, skazav "A", ne skazal "B"?' (Why, having said 'A', did Kryuchkov not say 'B'?). *Komsomol'skaya Pravda*, 28 August 1991.

Fischer, Stanley. 'The Russian Economy at the Start of 1998', paper delivered at the 1998 US–Russian Investment Symposium, Cambridge, MA: John F. Kennedy School of Government, Harvard University Press, p. 2.

Freeland, Chrystia. 'Moscow: A Flash in the Pan'. *Financial Times*, 8 September 1998 (http://www.ft.com).

Freeland, Chrystia. 'Yeltsin pledges to face Chechnya death threat'. *Financial Times*, 5 May 1996, p. 1.

Frizman, Leonid. 'Kakim on byl . . .' (What he used to be . . .). *Novoye Vremya*, 12, 1995.

Frolov, Aleksandr. 'Drama prozreniya. S desyatogo chrezvychaynogo S'ezda narodnykh deputatov RF' (A drama of seeing the light. From the Tenth Extraordinary Congress of People's Deputies of the Russian Federation). *Sovetskaya Rossia*, 25 September 1993, p. 1.

Frolov, Aleksandr. 'Eshchyo est' vremya' (There is still time). *Sovetskaya Rossia*, 28 September 1993.

'From Marx, maybe to market'. *Economist*, 12 July 1997.

Furman, Dmitriy. 'Revolutsionnye tsikly Rossii' (Russia's revolutionary cycles). *Svobodnaya Mysl'*, January 1994, p. 10.

Furmanov, Yuriy. 'Krasnye v Belom dome' (The reds in the White House). *Novoye Vremya*, 41, 1993, pp. 12–13.

'Gaidar Stresses Importance of Adopting New Tax Code'. *RFE/RL Newsline*, 13 June 1997.

Gaidar, Egor. 'After Yeltsin's Victory, What Is Next for Reform?' Speech at the Heritage Foundation, 23 June 1993. *The Heritage Lectures*, no. 453.

Gaidar, Egor. 'Dyadinogo karmana ne sushchsestvuyet' (There is no such thing as a rich uncle's pocket). *Novoye Vremya*, 22, 1997.

Gaidar, Egor. 'Prezident otvetil mne pis'mom' (The President answered me with a letter). *Moskovskie Novosti*, 11–18 February 1996.

Gaidar, Egor. 'Trudniy vybor' (A difficult choice). *Kommunist*, 2, (January) 1990.

Gaidar, Egor. 'U menya net sindroma belobiletnika' (I don't have a draft-dodger complex). Interview with *Novoye Vremya*, 28, 1996.

Gaidar, Egor. 'V nachale novoy fazy' (At the beginning of a new phase). *Kommunist*, 2, (January) 1991, pp. 8–19.

Gambrell, Jamey. 'Seven Days That Shook the World'. *New York Review of Books*, 26 September 1991, pp. 56–61.

Gamov, Aleksandr. '. . . A zamenit' seychas nekem' (. . . But there is no one to replace him now). *Komsomol'skaya Pravda*, 2 July 1996, p. 2.

Gamov, Aleksandr. 'Kumiry shumnoyu tolpoy kochyut po strane velikoy' (Noisy crowds of idols are roaming the great country). *Komsomol'skaya Pravda*, 13 April 1996, p. 2.

Gamov, Aleksandr. 'Pochemu Korzhakov voznik iz prezidentskoy teni?' (Why has Korzhakov emerged from the President's shadow?). *Komsomol'skaya Pravda*, 7 May 1996, pp. 1–2.

Gamov, Aleksandr. 'Ulichniy El'tsin sovsem ne pokhoz na kabinetnogo' (Yeltsin on the street is not at all like Yeltsin in the office). *Komsomol'skaya Pravda*, 23 April 1996, p. 2.

Gamov, A., and S. Karkhanin. 'Krikom doma ne postroish' (A house is not built by shouting). *Sovetskaya Rossia*, 23 May 1989.

Ganina, Maya. 'Bez obl'sheniy prezhnikh dnei' (Without illusions of the days past). *Literaturnaya Gazeta*, 13 January 1988.

'Gazeta Pravda' (The newspaper *Pravda*). *Vechernyaya Moskva*, 30 August 1991, p. 1.

Gel'man, Aleksandr. 'Katekhizis nenachal'nika' (The catechism of a non-boss). *Moskovskie Novosti*, 28 September–5 October 1997.

Gerasimov, V. 'Otdadim v zalog Rossiyu?' (Should we mortgage Russia?). *Pravda*, 25 March 1991.

Glachant, Pierre. 'Yeltsin Rally Biggest Since 1917'. Agence France-Presse, 25 March 1991 (FBIS, 27 March 1989, p. 46).

Glukhov, Yuriy. 'Igra na proigrysh bitymi kartami' (Playing to lose with beaten cards). *Pravda*, 29 September 1993, p. 6.

Goble, Paul. 'A Decree That Changed the World'. *RFE/RL Daily Report*, 22 August 1997.

Goldov, A. 'Pro novogodnyuu kartoshku' (About the new year's potato). *Moskovskaya Pravda*, 7 January 1986.

Golovenko, A. 'Mitinguet ploshchad' (The square demonstrates). *Pravda*, 21 August 1991, p. 1.

Golovenko, Aleksandr. 'Kovarstvo i lyubov'. Gennadiy Zyuganov kak zerkalo politichekoy prostitutsii' (Treachery and love. Gennadiy Zyuganov as the mirror of political prostitution). *Moskovskiy Komsomoletz*, 12 March 1996.

Golyaev, Aleksandr. 'Egor Klochkov, Predsedatel' Federatsii nezavisimykh profsoyuzov Rossii: stachechnoye dvizhenie narastaet' (Egor Klochkov, Chairman of Independent Trade Unions of Russia: strike movement grows).

Rossiyskaya Gazeta, 23 September 1993.

Gonzalies, E. 'Den' odinnadtsatiy' (Day eleven). *Izvestia*, 9 June 1989.

Gorbachev, Mikhail. Demokratizatsiya – sut' perestroiki, sut' sotsializma' (Democratization is the essence of perestroika, the essence of socialism). Remarks at the meeting with the 'heads of mass media, agencies in charge of ideology and creative unions', 8 January 1988. *Izvestia*, 9 January 1988.

Gorbachev, Mikhail. 'Doklad General'nogo sekretarya TsK KPSS tovarishcha Gorbachev M. S. 25 fevralya 1986 goda' (Address of the General Secretary of the Central Committee of the CPSU, Comrade M. S. Gorbachev, February 25, 1986). Speech at the Twenty-Sixth Congress of the CPSU, *Pravda*, 26 February 1986.

Gorbachev, Mikhail. 'Gorbachev ukhodit i ostayotsya' (Gorbachev leaves and stays). Interview with *Komsomol'skaya Pravda*, 24 December 1991.

Gorbachev, Mikhail. 'Krepit' klyuchevoe zveno ekonomiki' (To strengthen the key link in the economy). *Pravda*, 10 December 1990.

Gorbachev, Mikhail. 'Ob obrazovanii Rossiyskogo buro TsK KPSS' (On the creation of the Russian Buro in the Central Committee of the CPSU). Speech at the Plenum of the Central Committee, 9 December 1989, *Pravda*, 10 December 1989.

Gorbachev, Mikhail. 'O perestroike i kadrovoy politike partii. Doklad General'nogo sekretarya TsK KPSS M. S. Gorbacheva na Plenume TsK KPSS 27 yanvarya 1987 goda' (On perestroika and the Party's cadre policy. Report by the General Secretary of the Central Committee of the CPSU M. S. Gorbachev at the Plenum of the Central Committee of the CPSU on 27 January 1987). *Pravda*, 28 January 1987.

Gorbachev, Mikhail. 'O proekte novoy Programmy KPSS. Doklad M. S. Gorbacheva na Plenume TsK KPSS 25 iulya' (About a new programme of the CPSU. The report of M. S. Gorbachev to the Plenum of the Central Committee, 25 July). *Pravda*, 27 July 1991.

Gorbachev, Mikhail. 'O sozyve ocherednogo XXVII s'ezda KPSS i zadachakh, svyazannykh s ego podgotovkoy i provedeniem. Doklad General'nogo sekretarya TsK KPSS M. S. Gorbacheva' (On the convocation of the Twenty-Seventh Congress of the CPSU and the tasks associated with its preparation and realization. Address of the General Secretary of the Central Committee of the CPSU M. S. Gorbachev). Speech at the April (1985) Plenum of the Central Committee, *Pravda*, 24 April 1985.

Gorbachev, Mikhail. 'Rech M. S. Gorbacheva na S'ezde Narodnykh Deputatov Rossii' (The speech of M. S. Gorbachev at the Congress of People's Deputies of Russia). *Izvestia*, 25 May 1990.

Gorbachev, Mikhail. 'Rech Prezidenta SSSR M. S. Gorbacheva na vneocherdnom tret'em S'ezde narodnykh deputatov SSSR' (The speech of the President of the USSR at the Third Extraordinary Congress of People's Deputies of the USSR). *Izvestia*, 16 March 1990.

Gorbachev, Mikhail. 'Rech tovarishcha Gorbacheva M. S. pri zakrytii XIX vsesoyuznoy konferentsii KPSS' (Speech by Comrade M. S. Gorbachev at the closing of the XIX all-Union conference of the CPSU). *XIX Vsesoyuznaya Konferentsia*

Kommunisticheskoy Partii Sovetskogo Soyuza. Stenograficheskiy otchet, Moscow: Politizdat, 1988, ppp. 175–85.

Gorbachev, Mikhail. 'Revolyutsionnoi perestroike – ideologiyu obnovleniya. Rech' General'nogo sekretarya TsK KPSS M. S. Gorbacheva na Plenume TsK KPSS, 18 fevralya 1988' (Revolutionary perestroika must have ideology of renewal. Speech of the General Secretary of the Central Committee of the CPSU M. S. Gorbachev at the Plenum of the Central Committee of the CPSU, 18 February 1988). *Pravda*, 19 February 1988.

Gorbachev, Mikhail. Speech at a Minsk plant, 26 February 1991. *Sovetskaya Rossia*, 28 February 1991.

Gorbachev, Mikhail. Speech before the scientific and creative intelligentsia of Byelorussia', 28 February 1991. *Pravda*, 1 March 1991.

Gorbachev, Mikhail. 'Ukaz Prezidenta Soyuza Sovetskikh Sotsialisticheskikh Respublik "Ob imushchestve Kommunisticheskoy Partii Sovetskogo Soyuza"' (Decree of the President of the Union of Soviet Socialist Republics 'On the property of the Communist Party of the Soviet Union'). *Vechernyaya Moskva*, 26 August 1991, p. 1.

Gorbachev, Mikhail. 'Zaklyuchitel'noye slovo General'nogo sekretarya TsK KPSS M. S. Gorbacheva na Plenume TsK KPSS 28 yanvarya 1987 goda' (The concluding remarks by the General Secretary of the Central Committee of the CPSU M. S. Gorbachev at the Plenum of the Central Committee of the CPSU on 28 January 1987). *Pravda*, 30 January 1987.

Gorbachev, Mikhail. 'Zaklyuchitel'noye slovo M. S. Gorbacheva na 28 s'ezde KPSS' (The concluding remarks of M. S. Gorbachev at the Twenty-Eighth Congress of the CPSU). *Pravda*, 14 July 1990.

Gorbachev, Mikhail. 'Zayavlenie M. S. Gorbacheva' (A statement by M. S. Gorbachev). *Vechernyaya Moskva*, 26 August 1991.

Gordon, Leonid, and Nataliya Pliskevich. 'Razvilki i lovushki perekhodnogo perioda' (The forks and traps of the transitional phase). *Polis*, 5, 1994.

Gordon, Michael. 'Russia and Ukraine Finally Reach Accord on Black Sea Fleet'. *New York Times*, 29 May 1997.

Gordon, Michael. 'Russia's Premier to Slash Budget, Trimming Military and Subsidies'. *New York Times*, 22 May 1997.

Gordon, Michael. 'Selling of Yeltsin Hits Obstacles in Heartland'. *New York Times*, 14 May 1996, p. A12.

Gordon, Michael. 'Yeltsin Attack Strategy: Bursts Followed by Lulls'. *New York Times*, 5 October 1993, p. 17.

Gordon, Michael. 'Yeltsin Foe Tries to Harness the Military's Discontent'. *New York Times*, 21 September 1997.

Gordon, Michael. 'Yeltsin's Communist Rival Tries to Moderate his Message'. *New York Times*, 21 May 1996, p. A10.

Gorkiy, Maxim. 'Nesvoevremennye mysli' (Untimely thoughts). *Literaturnoye Obozrenie*, 9, 10 and 12, 1988.

Gorshkov, Mikhail. 'V chyom okazalis' pravy sotsiologi' (Where the sociologists turned out to be right). *Nezavisimaya Gazeta*, 20 June 1996, pp. 1, 3.

Goryacheva, Svetlana, *et al.* 'Politicheskoye zayavlenie Verkhovnomu Sovetu RSFSR, narodnym deputatam RSFSR' (Political statement to the Supreme

Soviet of the RSFSR, People's Deputies of the RSFSR). *Sovetskaya Rossia*, 22 February 1991.

'Gospodi, izbav' Rossiyu ot El'tsina!' (Lord, rid Russia of Yeltsin!). *Zavtra*, 16, (April) 1996, p. 1.

'Government Commission Targets More Tax Debtors'. *RFE/RL Newsline*, 23 July 1997.

'Government Seeks Duma Approval for Social Spending Reductions . . .' *RFE/RL Newsline*, 17 June 1997.

Grishchenko, V. 'Prezident beryot s soboy nashe soglasie' (The President is taking with him our consent). *Izvestia*, 9 July 1991.

Gross, Natalie. 'The Military in Coup and Revolution'. *Jane's Intelligence Review*, vol. 3, no. 10, October 1991.

Grushin, Boris. 'Opyat' na avos'?' (Leaving everything to chance again?). *Novoye Vremya*, 8, 1996, p. 10.

Gualtieri, Dominic. 'Russian Parliament Renews Power Struggle with Yeltsin'. *RFE/FL Research Report*, 13 August 1993, p. 31.

Gualtieri, Dominic. 'Russia's New "War of Laws" '. *RFE/RL Research Report*, 3 September 1993, p. 12.

Gudkov, Lev, and Boris Dubinin, 'Konets kharizmaticheskoy epokhi' (The end of the charismatic era). *Svobodnaya Mysl'*, June 1993.

Gurevich, Mikhail. 'Slovo i delo prezidenta' (The word and deed of the President). *Rossiyskie Vesti*, 29 May 1996, p. 1.

Gutionov, P. 'Den' dvenadtsatiy' (Day twelve). *Izvestia*, 10 June 1989.

Gutionov, P. 'Posle vyborov' (After the elections). *Izvestia*, 31 May 1990.

Harrison, Martin. 'The President, Cultural Projects and Broadcasting Policy'. In Jack Hayward, ed., *De Gaulle to Mitterrand: Presidential Power in France*. New York: New York University Press, 1993.

'Harvest Up in 1997, But Problems Remain'. *RFE/RL Newsline*, 8 January 1998.

Heard, Alex. 'Rolfing with Yeltsin'. *New Public*, 9 October 1989.

Helmer, John. 'Russia's Constitutional Court Chairman Displays Legal Resolve'. *RFE/RL Newsline*, 22 April 1998.

Hendrickson, Paul. 'Yeltsin's Smashing Day'. *Washington Post*, 13 September 1989.

Hewett, Ed. A. 'The New Soviet Plan'. *Foreign Affairs*, Winter 1990–1.

Hiatt, Fred. 'From Red to Yellow'. *Washington Post*, 25 July 1994.

Hiatt, Fred. 'Pessimism Grips Russian Democrats'. *Washington Post*, 4 October 1993.

Hiatt, Fred. 'Progress, Russian-Style'. *Washington Post*, 28 September 1997.

Hiatt, Fred. 'Soviet Union Wins Reprieve on Debt'. *Washington Post*, 22 November 1991, p. A1.

Higley, John, Judith Kullberg and Jan Pakulski. 'The persistence of post-communist elites'. *Journal of Democracy*, 2, 1996.

Hilts, Philip J. 'U.S. and Russian Researchers Tie Anthrax Death to Soviets'. *New York Times*, 15 March 1993.

Hoagland, Jim. 'Russia's Campaign Trail to America'. *Washington Post*, 23 January 1997.

Hockstader, Lee. 'Invigorated Yeltsin Hits Hustings'. *Washington Post*, 1 June 1996, p. A17.

Hockstader, Lee. 'New Russian Communists Put On a Moderate Face'. *Washington Post*, 20 May 1996, pp. A1–A16.

Hockstader, Lee. 'Police Flee in Face of Surging Mob'. *Washington Post*, 4 October 1993, p. A14.

Hockstader, Lee. 'Rancor Rears its Head in Communist Ranks'. *Washington Post*, 22 May 1996, p. A26.

Hockstader, Lee. 'The Russian

Invasion'. *Washington Post*, 15 August 1994.

Hockstader, Lee. 'Russians Face a Stark Choice'. *Washington Post*, 15 June 1996, p. A21.

Hockstader, Lee. 'Truth Told, Pravda Lives'. *Washington Post*, 15 April 1997.

Hockstader, Lee. 'Under Fire, Hard-Liners Watch as Crusade Crumbles'. *Washington Post*, 5 October, 1993, pp. A29–A32.

Hockstader, Lee. 'Yeltsin Campaign Rose from Tears to Triumph'. *Washington Post*, 7 July 1996, p. 1.

Hockstader, Lee. 'Yeltsin Fires Defense Chiefs'. *Washington Post*, 23 May 1997.

Hoffman, David. 'It Isn't Tolstoy, But Russians Are Reading Up a Storm'. *Washington Post*, 5 July 1997.

Hoffman, David. 'Moscow Remains a Perk for Permit Holders'. *Washington Post*, 20 January 1997.

Hoffman, David. 'Powerful Few Rule Russian Mass Media'. *Washington Post*, 31 March 1997.

Hoffman, David. 'Russia's New Internal Passport Drops Nationality, Drawing Praise and Protest'. *Washington Post*, 25 October 1997.

Hoffman, David. 'Yeltsin, Communist Foe Launch TV Attack Ads'. *Washington Post*, 27 June 1996, p. A23.

Hoffman, David. 'Yeltsin Heart Operation Called a Success'. *Washington Post*, 6 November 1996, p. A3.

Hoffman, David. 'Yeltsin Picks Reformist for Cabinet Post'. *Washington Post*, 18 March 1997, p. A12.

Hoffman, David. 'Yeltsin Proposes Plebiscite on Whether Lenin's Body Should Be Buried Formally'. *Washington Post*, 7 June 1997, p. A19.

Hoffman, David. 'Yeltsin Seeks Compromise on NATO'. *Washington Post*, 24 February 1997.

Hoffman, David. 'Yeltsin Seeks to Halt Attacks on Reformers'. *Washington Post*, 16 September 1997, pp. A1, A13.

Hoffman, David. 'Yeltsin to Have Heart Surgery: Rules for Replacement Untested'. *Washington Post*, 6 September 1996.

Hoffman, David. 'Yeltsin Vows No Delays in Election; President Contradicts Adviser's Statement'. *Washington Post*, 7 May 1996, p. A11.

Hoffmann, Stanley. 'Look Back in Anger'. *New York Review of Books*, 17 July 1997.

Horvitz, Paul. 'Bush, Returning to Capital, Moves to Suspend Aid'. *International Herald Tribune*, 20 August 1991, p. 1.

Howe, Marvin. 'Opposition Leader from Soviet Union Begins Visit to U.S.'. *New York Times*, 10 September 1989.

'How Russians Voted in the Runoff'. *New York Times*, 4 July 1996, p. A8.

'I eto Chudo-Yudo pobedim, matushku Rus' vozrodim' (And this Judo-Monster we will vanquish, and will revive Mother Russia!), an anti-Yeltsin cartoon. *Sovetskaya Rossia*, 23 February 1996.

Ignatieff, Michael. 'On Isaiah Berlin (1909–1997)'. *New York Review of Books*, 18 December 1997, p. 10.

Igrashev, V., S. Pastukhov and Ye. Sorokin. 'V delovom nastroe' (In a businesslike mood). *Pravda*, 23 May 1990.

Ilyukhin, Viktor. 'Pochemu ya budu golosovat' protiv B. El'tsina' (Why I will be voting against B. Yeltsin). *Pravda Rossii*, 11 April 1996, p. 1.

'Informatsionnoe soobshchenie o plenume Tsentral'nogo Komiteta Kommunisticheskoy Partii Sovetskogo Soyuza' (Report on the Plenum of the Central Committee of the Communist Party of the Soviet Union). *Pravda*, 19 February 1988.

'Informatsionnoe soobshchenie o plenume Tsentral'nogo Komiteta Kommunisticheskoy Partii Sovetskogo Soyuza' (Report on the Plenum of the Central Committee of the Communist Party of the Soviet Union). *Pravda*, 17 March 1989.

'Instruktsiya o poryadke predostavlenia efirnogo vremeni na kanalakh gosudarstvennykh teleradiokompaniy kandidatam na dolzhnost' Prezidenta Rossiyskoy Federatsii, izbiratel'nym ob'edineniyam, initsiativnym gruppam izbirateley i publikatsii agitatsionnykh predvybornykh materialov v periodicheskikh pechatnykh izdaniyakh' (Instruction on making broadcast time on the channels of the state-owned television and radio networks available to the candidates for the post of President of the Russian Federation, electoral blocs and grass-roots groups of voters, and on the publication of the campaign materials in the periodic press publications). *Rossiyskaya Gazeta*, 17 April 1996.

Introduction to and excerpts from Aleksandr Korzhakov's book *Boris El'tsin: ot rassveta to Zakata* (Boris Yeltsin: from dawn to sunset). *The Times* (London), 13 August 1997.

Ionin, Leonid. 'Chetyre bedy Rossii' (Russia's four misfortunes). *Novoye Vremya*, 12, 1995.

Ionin, Leonid. 'Tretiy El'tsin' (The third Yeltsin). *Novoye Vremya*, 23, 1996.

Isakov, Vladimir. 'Pervaya treshchina' (The first crack). *Sovetskaya Rossia*, 19 March 1996, p. 3.

I.T. 'Tanki bili po Rossii i po nam . . .' (The tanks shot at Russia and at us). *Zavtra*, 1, November 1993.

Ivanov, A. 'Lubyanka i strana menyayut oblik' (Lyubyanka and the country are changing their appearance). *Vechernyaya Moskva*, 23 August 1991.

Ivanov, Ivan. 'Oni srazhalis' za Rodinu' (They fought for the Motherland). *Zavtra*, 1, November 1993.

Ivanov, Sergey. 'Doroga zhizni skvoz' blokadu' (The road of life through the blockade). *Sovetskaya Rossia*, 30 April 1996, p. 2.

Ivanova, Ol'ga. 'Vernost' zhanru' (Loyalty to this genre). *Izvestia*, 26 August 1983.

Ivanova, Tatyana. 'Teper' vsyo budet inache' (Everything will be different now). *Novoye Vremya*, 40, 1993, p. 9.

Ivchenko, L. 'Bednye millionery' (The poor millionaires). *Izvestia*, 21 January 1986.

'I viydut, veroyatno, kak vsegda' (And will be published, most likely, as always). *Komsomol'skaya Pravda*, 28 August 1991, p. 1.

'I vyplesnulos' vozmushchenie' (And indignation boiled over). *Moskovskaya Pravda*, 21 August 1987.

'Iz politicheskikh shtabov' (From the political headquarters). *Pravda*, 23 September 1993.

Jane's Intelligence Review, vol. 3, no. 10, October 1991, p. 446.

Johnson, Douglas. 'In Pursuit of Greatness'. *Times Literary Supplement*, 22 January 1999.

Johnson, Samuel. 'Taxation No Tyranny'. In Donald L. Green, ed., *Samuel Johnson's Political Writings*. New Haven: Yale University Press, 1977.

Kabaidze, V. I. Speech at Nineteenth

Party Conference. *Pravda*, 1 July 1988.

'Kampaniya El'tsina: svadebnoye puteshestive ili pokhoronnaya protsessiaya?' (Yeltsin's campaign: a honeymoon trip or a funeral procession?). *Zavtra*, 23, June 1996, p. 1.

'Kandidaty – krupnym planom. Grafik raspredeleniya besplatnogo efirnogo vremeni na kanalakh obshcherossiskikh televizionnykh kampaniy mezhdu kandidatami na dolzhnost' Prezidenta Rossiyskoy Federatzii (po resul'tatam zherebyovki ot 5 maya 1996 goda)' (The candidates close up. The schedule of the distribution of the free airtime on the channels of the national television companies between the candidates to the post of the President of the Russian Federation [as determined by the drawing of lots on 5 May 1996]). *Rossiyskaya Gazeta*, 12 May 1996, p. 3.

Karpinskiy, Len. 'Boevoy zalp v chest' Konstitutsii' (A salvo in the Constitution's honour). *Moskovskie Novosti*, 11–18 December 1994.

Karyakin, Yuriy. 'Ne tot nynche moment, choby bezhat' ot politiki' (This is not the time to run away from politics). *Izvestia*, 24 April 1993, p. 8.

Kasyanenko, Zhanna. 'Edinenie nadezhd' (The coming together of hopes). *Sovetskaya Rossia*, 19 March 1996.

Kazarin, Yu. 'KGB budet zhit'?' (Will the KGB live?). *Vechernyaya Moskva*, 30 August 1991.

Kebich Vyacheslav. Gennadiy Burbulis and Vitold Fokin. 'Zayavlenie pravitel'stv Respubliki Belarus', Rossiyskoy Federatsii i Ukrainy o koordinatsii ekonomicheskoy politiki' (Statement of the governments of the Republic of Belarus', the Russian Federation and Ukraine on the co-ordination of economic policy). *Rossiyskaya Gazeta*, 10 December 1991, p. 1.

Keller, Bill. 'Boris Yeltsin Taking Power'. *New York Times Magazine*, 23 September 1990, pp. 33–5, 80, 81, 84.

Keller, Bill. 'Gorbachev Is Said to Delay Soviet Economic "Shock Therapy" Plan'. *New York Times*, 25 April 1990.

Keller, Bill. 'Marchers in Moscow Cheer Maverick'. *New York Times*, 20 March 1989.

Keller, Bill. 'Soviet Poll Finds Deep Pessimism'. *New York Times*, 5 November 1989, pp. 1, 18.

Keller, Bill. 'Soviets Moving to Outlaw Insults to Gorbachev'. *New York Times*, 14 May 1990.

Keller, Bill. 'Upheaval in the East: Russians Cry of "Won't Give My Son!" And Soviets End the Call-Up'. *New York Times*, 20 January 1990.

Khazbulatov, Ruslan. 'Slovo o sovetakh' (A word about the Soviets). *Pravda*, 4 March 1993.

Khazbulatov, Ruslan. Speech at the Seventh Congress of People's Deputies, 1 December 1992. Russian Television Channel (Rossia) (FBIS-SOV-92-232-S).

Khomyakov, D. '"Zheltyi Gebbels" i pervaya ataka' (The 'Yellow Goebbels' and the first attack). *Zavtra*, 1, November 1993.

'Khozyain' (The owner). An anti-Yeltsin cartoon. *Sovetskaya Rossia*, 16 March 1996.

'Khronika' (News items). *Pravda*, 19 November 1987.

'Khronika sobytiy 21 sentiyabrya' (A chronicle of the events of 21 September). *Kommersant-Daily*, 22 September 1993.

Kiselev, Andrey, and Aleksandr Mostovshikov. 'Pogovorim na ravnykh' (Let's talk as equals). *Moskovskie Novosti*, 17 May 1987.

Kiseleva, E. N. Reprinted letter to editor of *Rabotnitza*. 'Mnogo li my khotim?' (Do we want a lot?). *Novoye Russkoye Slovo*, 2 June 1989.

Kiva, Aleksey. 'Pretendentov v prezidenty mnogo, no Rossii nuzhen tol'ko odin. Za kogo zhe golozovat'?' (There are many contenders but Russia needs only one. Who should one vote for?). *Rossiyskaya Gazeta*, 1 March 1996, p. 5.

Klimov, V. 'Problemy kopilis' godami' (Problems accumulated over the years). *Trud*, 13 July 1989.

Klopyzhnikov, Mikhail, and Aleksandr Nikolaev. 'Zerkalo postsovetskoy demokratii' (A mirror of post-Soviet democracy). *Svobodnaya Mysl'*, June 1997.

Klyamkin, Igor. 'Politicheskiy dnevnik' (A political diary). *Gorizont*, 9, 1990, p. 2.

Klyamkin, Igor. 'Sovetskoye i zapadnoye: vozmoshen li sintez?' (The Soviet and the Western: is synthesis possible?) *Polis*, 4, 1994, p. 62.

Klyamkin, Igor, and Tatyana Kutkovetz. '"Osobyi put' Rossii: myfi i parodoksy' ('Russia's separate way': myths and paradoxes). *Moskovskie Novosti*, 25 August–1 September 1996.

Klyamkin, I., V. Lapkin and V. Pantin. 'Chto znachit "russkiy poryadok"?' (What does 'Russian order' mean?). *Moskovskie Novosti*, 20–27 April 1997.

Klyamkin, I. M., V. V. Lapkin and V. I. Pantin. 'Politicheskiy kurs Yeltsina: predvaritelny itogi' (Yeltsin's political course: preliminary results). *Polis*, 3, 1993.

Klyamkin, Igor. 'Oktiabr'skiy vibor prezidenta' (The October choice of the President). *Ogonyok*, 17–24 November 1990, p. 6.

Kohan, John. 'Now who rules Russia?' *Time*, 4 October 1993.

Kolesnikov, Andrey. 'Dzhoker vlasti' (The joker in power). *Novoye Vremya*, 48, 1996.

Kolesnikov, Andrey. 'Kapitalizm novogo tipa' (Capitalism of a new kind). *Novoye Vremya*, 52, 1997.

Kolesnikov, Andrey. 'Novaya nomenklatura' (A new nomenklatura). *Novoye Vremya*, 16, 1997.

Kolesnikov, Andrey. 'Peresadka mozga' (Brain transplant). *Novoye Vremya*, 10, 1997.

Kolesnikov, Andrey. 'Stepanych vtoroy svezhesti' (The not-so-fresh Stepanovich). *Novoye Vremya*, 35, 1998.

Kolesnikov, Andrey. 'Tol'ko ne govorite potom, chto vy etogo ne znali' (Just don't say later that you did not know about this). *Novoye Vremya*, 26, 1996.

Kolesnikov, Andrey, and Dmitriy Orlov. 'Evangelie ot Borisa' (The gospel according to Boris). *Novoye Vremya*, 10, 1997.

Kolosov, V. A., and R. F. Turovskiy. 'Osenne-zimnie vybory glav ispolnitel'noy vlasti v regionakh: scenarii peremen' (The autumn–winter elections of the chief executives in the regions: scenarios of change). *Polis*, 1, 1997.

Komin, Anatoliy. 'Davay schitat'!' (Let's count!). *Komsomol'skaya Pravda*, 13 August 1986.

'Komu vygodna smena rezhima?' (Who will profit from a change of regime?). *Moskovskie Novosti*, 31 March–7 April 1996.

Konovalov, V. 'Neob'yavlennaya zabasovka krest'yan vsekh respublik' (The unannounced strike of the peasants of all the republics). *Izvestia*, 16 November 1991.

Korneev, V., and S. Tutorskaya. 'Lekarstva, kotorykh zhdut' (Medicines that the people are waiting for). *Izvestia*, 28 January 1988.

Kornilov, Sergey. 'Shtabisty' (The headquarters staff). *Rossiyskaya Gazeta*, 8 June 1991.

Korolev, Oleg. Speech, 'Fevral'skiy (1987) Plenum Moskovskogo Gorodskogo Komiteta KPSS' (February (1987) Plenum of the Moscow City Committee of the CPSU). *Moskovskaya Pravda*, 23 February 1987.

'Korzhakov. "Observer". Vybory. (Korzhakov. *The Observer*. Election). *Moskovskiy Komsomoletz*, 7 May 1996, p. 1.

Kostyukovskiy, V. 'Po starym i novym schetam: ostanavleny raboty na ryade shakht Mezhdurechenska' (Old and new bills to pay: work stopped at a number of mines in Mezhdurechesk). *Sovetskaya Rossia*, 13 July 1989.

Kostyukovskiy, V. 'Prizyv k blagorazumiyu' (Appeal to reason). *Sovetskaya Rossia*, 19 July 1989.

Kostyukovskiy, V. 'Indikator napryazhyonnosti. S plenuma kemerovskogo obkoma KPSS' (The indicator of tension. At the Plenum of the Kemerovo Obkom of the CPSU). *Sovetskaya Rossia*, 10 August 1989.

Kovalev, Sergey. 'Otkrytoe pis'mo B. El'tsinu' (An open letter to B. Yeltsin). *Izvestia*, 24 January 1995, p. 2.

Kovalev, Sergei. 'Russia after Chechnya'. *New York Review of Books*, 17 July 1997.

Kovalev, Sergey. Speech at the Plenum of the Council of Russia's Democratic Choice. *Novoye Vremya*, 13, 1996, p. 10.

Koval'skaya, Galina, Stepan Koval'skiy, Georgiy Osipov, Yuliya Rakhaeva, Marina Shakina and Ol'ga Shakina. 'Oskolki tryokh dney' (Fragments of three days). *Novoye Vremya*, 42, 1993, p. 13.

Kozheurov, Sergey. 'Na samom li dele possorilsya Boris Nikolaevich s Mikhailom Sergeevichem?' (Have Boris Nikolaevich and Mikhail Sergeevich really quarrelled with each other?). *Komsomol'skaya Pravda*, 1 March 1991.

Kozlovskiy, Vladimir. ' "El'tsingate", ili sputniki Eltsina o ego poezdke v SShA ('Yeltsingate', or Yeltsin's companions on his trip to the United States). *Novoye Russkoye Slovo*, 25 September 1989.

Kozlovskiy, Vladimir. 'Ochevidtzy govoryat, chto El'tsin ne greshil' (Witnesses say Yeltsin did not step over the line). *Novoye Russkoye Slovo*, 21 September 1989.

Kozlovskiy, Vladimir. 'Oy, chto-to budet . . .' (My, my, there's going to be trouble . . .). *Novoye Russkoye Slovo*, 28 March 1991.

Krasnikov, Evgeniy. 'Konstitutsionnoe Soveshchanie: mnogo zvannykh, no malo izbrannykh' (The Constitutional Assembly: many are called but few are chosen). *Nezavisimaya Gazeta*, 25 May 1993, p. 1.

Kroncher, Allan. 'Deputy Minister Dismissed in Soviet Oil Scandal'. *Radio Liberty Research* (RL 412/81), 16 October 1981.

Kroncher, Allan. 'Does New Decree on Saving Raw Materials Portend More Central Control?' *Radio Liberty Research* (RL 275/81), 13 July 1981.

Kuchin, Nikolay. 'Slepaya reforma' (The blind reform). *Novoye Vremya*, 22, 1997, p. 12.

Kulakov, V. I. Interviewed by B. Mironov. 'Rebyonok bez prismotra?' (Is anyone minding the child?). *Pravda*, 10 August 1987.

Kupriyanov, Oleg. 'Moskva, 19–21 avgusta' (Moscow, 19–21 August). *Novoye Russkoye Slovo*, 24–25 August, 1991.

Kuptsov, Valentin. Speech at the Fourth Party Congress. *Informatsionniy Byulleten'* (KPRF), 35, no. 2 (20 February 1996).

Kurasov, V. 'Izlechema li

lekarstvennaya problema?' (Can we cure the medicine problem?). *Izvestia*, 21 October, 1989.

Ladin, A. 'Ne vremya dlya ul'timatumov' (Not the right time for ultimatums). *Krasnaya Zvezda*, 21 February 1991.

La Guardia, Anton. 'Yeltsin Urges Action to Avoid Revolution'. *Daily Telegraph* (London), 28 April 1990.

Latsis, Otto. 'Ne "nulevoy", a minusovyi' (Not a zero' [option] but a minus [one]). *Izvestia*, 28 September 1993, p. 2.

Lavrovskiy, I., L. Telen' and E. Chrnova. 'Raskol? Net, dialog!' (Schism? No, a dialogue). *Sotsialisticheskaya Industria*, 1 August 1989.

'Lebed' "sdal" patriotov El'tsinu' (Lebed "delivered" the patriots to Yeltsin). *Zavtra*, 26, June 1996, p. 1.

Lee, Gary. 'Observers Puzzled by Aftermath of Yeltsin's Speech'. *Washington Post*, 4 February 1988.

Lee, Gary. 'Party Members' Perks Make Some See Red in Moscow'. *Washington Post*, 3 March 1986.

Lee, Gary. 'Soviet Miners Launch Strike, Oust Party Officials'. *Washington Post*, 11 July 1990.

Levada, Yuriy 'Poprobyuem podschitat' shansy kandidatov' (Let's try and figure out the candidates' chances). *Novoye Vremya*, 8, 1996, p. 8.

Levada, Yuriy. 'Vsyo reshitsya vo vtorom ture' (Everything will be decided in the second round). *Izvestia*, 30 April 1996, p. 2.

Levitskiy, L. 'Verkhovnyi Sovet Estonii podtverdil svoy vybor' (The Supreme Soviet of Estonia has confirmed its choice). *Izvestia*, 15 January 1991.

Liesman, Steve. 'Surprise: The Economy in Russia Is Clawing Out of Deep Recession'. *Wall Street Journal*, 28 January 1998.

Ligachev, Egor. Speech at the Twenty-Third Sverdlovsk Party Conference. *Ural'skiy Rabochiy*, 22 January 1984.

Ligachev, Egor. Speech in Havana, Cuba, *Moskovskaya Pravda*, 7 February 1986.

Linz, Juan J. 'The Perils of Presidentialism'. *Journal of Democracy*, 1, (Winter), 1990.

Lloyd, John. 'Red Square shows scorn for Gorbachev "the westerner" '. *Financial Times*, 8 November 1991.

Lloyd, John. 'Yeltsin to back Gorbachev in poll'. *Financial Times*, 10 July 1991.

London, Matthew. 'The Rise of Moscow Jewish Groups: Civil Society Development in Russia'. Unpublished master's thesis, School of Foreign Service, Georgetown University, Washington, DC, 1997.

Loshak, Viktor. ' "Wine Rebellion" in Sverdlovsk'. *Moscow News*, 21 January 1990.

Lubarskiy, Kronid. 'My vse glyadim v napoleony . . .' (We are all dreaming of becoming a Napoleon . . .). *Novoye Vremya*, 7, 1995.

'Lubit Eltsin igrat' na lozhkahk' (Yeltsin loves to play the spoons). *Komsomol'skaya Pravda*, 1 February 1991.

Lukanin, M. 'Vstrecha s voeynnymi moryakami' (Meeting with sailors). *Krasnaya Zvezda*, 28 August 1990.

Lukashevich, V. 'Kto i kogo khochet postavit' na koleni' (Who wants to bring whom to his knees). *Krasnaya Zvezda*, 28 March 1991.

Lyakhova, Elena. 'Anatomiya ugol'nogo vorovstva' (The anatomy of the coal thievery). *Izvestia*, 15 July 1998.

Lynev, R. 'Ob'edinit' direktorskuyu banyu' (Merge the managers' bathhouse). *Izvestia*, 26 July 1989.

Lysenko, Vladimir. 'Lovushka dlya

demokrata' (A trap for a democrat). *Moskovskie Novosti*, 4–11 December 1994.

McAuliffe, Bill. 'Yeltsin Pays Call on Reagan in Rochester'. *Minneapolis Star Tribune*, 15 September 1989.

McFaul, Michael. 'Russia's Bumpy Road to Democracy'. In Dick Clark, ed., *U.S. Relations with Russia and Ukraine*. Washington, DC: Aspen Institute, 1996.

'Major Networks Indifferent to Speech'. *RFE/RL Newsline*, 17 February 1998.

Makarevskiy, Vadim. 'Voeyvat' ne mozhem. I ne budem' (We cannot fight. And we will not). *Novoye Vremya*, 38, 1995.

'Make It Known'. *Washington Post*, 20 August 1991.

'The makings of a Molotov cocktail'. *Economist*, 12 July 1997.

Malkina, Tatyana. 'Boris El'tsin uveren, chto ob'edinilsya s tret'ey siloy' (Boris Yeltsin is confident that he has allied himself with the 'third force'). *Segodnya*, 12 May 1996, p. 1.

Malkina, Tatiana. 'President El'tsin vzyal probu nastroyeniy v Chernozyom'e' (President Yeltsin tested the mood in the Black Soil region). *Segodnya*, 5 April 1996, p. 1.

Mann, Dawn. 'An Abortive Constitutional Coup d'Etat?' *Report on the USSR*, 5 July 1991, pp. 1–6.

Mann, Dawn. 'El'tsin Rides a Political Roller Coaster'. *Report on the USSR*, 9 June 1989.

Mann, Dawn. 'Pavlov Meets with Miners'. *RFE/RL Report*, 26 March 1991, p. 4.

Mann, Dawn. 'The RSFSR Elections: The Congress of People's Deputies'. *Report on the USSR*, 13 April 1990, p. 11.

Matafanova, Yu. 'Belyi lebed' v tsentre Sverdlovska' (White swan in the centre of Sverdlovsk).

Ural'skiy Rabochiy, 28 December 1982.

Maydannik, Kiva. 'Levye dvizheniya v postavtoritarnom obshesve' (Left movements in a post-authoritarian society). *Svobodnaya Mysl'*, 9, June 1994, pp. 21–35.

Megapolis-Express, 'Moskva v blokade' (Moscow blockaded). 27 September 1990.

Mendras, Marie. 'Yeltsin and the Great Divide in Russian Society'. *East European Constitutional Review*, Spring/Summer 1996.

Mettke, Joerg R. 'Taming the Monster CPSU'. Interview with Gavriil Popov and Anatoliy Sobchak. *Der Spiegel*, 6 August 1990.

Mezhuev, B. V. 'Poniatie "natsional'nyi interes" v Rossiyskoy obshchestvenno-politicheskoy mysli' (The notion of 'national interest' in Russian social and political thought). *Polis*, 1, 1997.

Migranyan, Andranik. 'Dolgiy put' k evropeyskomu domu' (A long road to the European home). *Noviy Mir*, July 1989.

Migranyan, Andranik. Interviewed by T. Menshikova. 'Populism'. *Sovetskaya Kul'tura*, 24 June 1989 (FBIS-SOV-89-131, 11 July 1989, pp. 67–73).

Mikaladze, Akakiy. 'Shevardnadze ne obidilsya' (Shevardnadze did not take offence). *Moskovskie Novosti*, 10 October 1993, p. A12.

Milhaylovskaya, Inga. 'Russian Voting Behavior as a Mirror of Social–Political Change'. *East European Constitutional Review*, Spring/Summer 1996.

Mil'shteyn, Ilya, 'Vysokaya bolesn'' (A solemn illness). *Novoye Vremya*, 5, 1996, pp. 14–15.

'Missiz Olbrayt, nam by eshchyo v Kitae zaiemet' takuyu kolonnu! (Mrs Albright, how I wish we could have such a [fifth] column in China as well!). An anti-Yeltsin cartoon. *Sovetskaya Rossia*, 1 April 1997.

Mityunov, Yuriy. 'Pochemy ya golosoval protiv' (Why I voted 'nay'). *Russkaya Mysl'*, 16 February 1990.

Montaigne, Fen. 'Yeltsin Dazzles Phila. Audience with Talk of "Abyss" '. *Philadelphia Inquirer*, 14 September 1989.

Moroz, Oleg. 'Dudaev zhelaet, choby rossiyskim prezidentom stal ego tovarish po partii' (Dudaev wants his [Communist] Party comrade to become Russian President. *Literaturnaya Gazeta*, 20 March 1996, p. 10.

Moroz, Oleg. 'Ne oshibayetsia tol'ko tot, kto . . .' (Only he does not make mistakes who . . .). *Literaturnaya Gazeta*, 14 April 1993.

Moroz, Oleg. 'Osobennosti natsional'noy okhoty za golosami izbirateley v vesenne-letniy sezon 1996 goda' (Peculiarities of national vote-hunting in the spring-summer 1996 season). *Literaturnaya Gazeta*, 10 April 1996, pp. 1, 11.

Morozov, N. 'Neprostoy dalog; poezdka B. El'tsina po Tatarii' (Difficult dialogue: B. Yeltsin's tour of Tatar ASSR). *Pravda*, 9 August 1990.

'Moscow Hero Flops in D.C.' *U.S. News and World Report*, 25 September 1989.

'Moskva. 4 oktyabrya. 'Khronika smutnogo vremeni (Den' tretiy) (Moscow. 4 October. A chronicle of the time of trouble. (Day three)). *Moskovskie Novosti*, 10 October 1993, pp. A5–A7.

'Moskva i moskovichi: god 2000' (Moscow and the Muscovites: the year 2000). *Izvestia*, 28 September 1986.

'Moskva. Voskresenie, 3 oktyabrya. Khronika smutnogo vremeni (Den' vtoroi)' (Moscow. Sunday, 3 October. A chronicle of the time of trouble. Day two). *Moskovskie Novosti*, 10 October 1993, pp. A3, A5.

'Moskvich: delayut vybor' (Muscovites are making their choice). *Moskovskaya Pravda*, 27 March 1989.

Motrevich, V. 'Bezhentsy' (The refugees). *Ural'skiy Rabochiy*, 22 June 1991.

'My vozrashchaemsya' (We are returning). *Pravda*, 2 November 1993.

'My znayem El'tsina zatei', an anti-Yeltsin cartoon. *Sovetskaya Rossia*, 7 May 1996.

Nadein, Vladimir. 'Den' pervyi' (Day one). *Izvestia*. 26 May 1989.

Nadein, Vladimir. 'Den' pyatiy' (Day five). *Izvestia*, 31 May 1989.

Nadein, Vladimir. 'Oglushitel'sniy uspekh s neyasnymi intogami' (A deafening success with unclear results). *Izvestia*, 25 October 1995.

Nadein, Vladimir. 'Staraya shpana lezet v geroi' (Old dregs clamouring to be heroes). *Izvestia*, 23 August 1991, p. 6.

Nahaylo, Bohdan. 'Gorbachev Cannot Imagine New "Union" without Ukraine'. *OMRI System Search*, 14 October 1991 (http://solar.rtd.utk.edu).

Nahaylo, Bohdan. 'Kravchuk Also Disavows Soviet Economic Treaty'. *OMRI System Search*, 8 October 1991 (http://solar.rtd.utk.edu).

Nahaylo, Bohdan. 'Kravchuk on Foreign Visits, Independence and New "Unions" '. *OMRI System Search*, 8 October 1991 (http://solar.rtd.utk.edu).

Nahaylo, Bohdan. 'Kravchuk Says Definitely No to Joining New Union'. *OMRI System Search*, 26 November 1991 (http://solar.rtd.utk.edu).

'Nashi narodnye deputaty' (Our people's deputies). *Izvestia*, 28 March 1989.

'Na sovete po gradostroitel'stvu' (In the advisory committee on urban planning). *Vechernyaya Moskva*, 2 February 1987.

Neil, Andrew, and Peter Millar. 'Yeltsin: Russians Risk a Civil War'. *Sunday Times* (London), 11 February 1990.

Nemtsov, Boris. 'Nemtsov opposes "robber capitalism"'. *Komsomol'skaya Pravda*, 29 July 1997. RIA-NOVOSTI, 6 August 1997 (http://www.ria-novosti.com).

Nemtsov, Boris. 'Razgovory o podkovyornoy bor'be vitse-prem'erov s prem'erom – vymysel' (Stories about a behind-the-scenes struggle between the Deputy Prime Ministers and the Prime Minister are fiction). *Izvestia*, 6 May 1997.

Nemtsov, Boris. 'Za obman nalogovykh sluzhb nado sazhat' v tyur'mu' (Lying to the tax services ought to be punished by jail). Interview with *Izvestia*, 19 March 1997.

'Ne voz'myom vzyatku iz krovavykh ruk!' (We shall not take a bribe from hands covered with blood). *Zavtra*, 8, February 1996, p. 1.

'The New Jewish Public Organization in Russia'. ITAR-TASS, 10 January 1996.

Newton, Melanie. 'USSR This Week'. *Report on the USSR*, 11 August 1989.

'New Top Minister Promises Honesty, Reform'. Reuters, 17 March 1997 (http://www.russiatoday.com).

'Ne otdam!' (I will not let go!). An anti-Yeltsin cartoon. *Izbiratel'* (The voter) insert, *Sovetskaya Rossia*, 6 June 1996.

Nikiforova, Valentina. 'Dom Sovetov, s'ezd nachal rabotu' (House of Soviets: Congress has started its work). Interview with Aleksandr Rutskoy. *Pravda*, 23 September 1993, p. 1.

Nikiforova, Valentina. 'Rossia protiv dictatury' (Russia against dictatorship). *Pravda*, 25 September 1993, pp. 1–2.

Nikiforova, Valentina, Nikolay Musienko, Egor Saltykov and Viktor Kharlamov. 'Ostorozhno, dveri zakryvayutsya. Sleduyushchaya ostanovka – politsyeyskoye gosudarstvo' (Attention: the doors are closing. Next stop is a police state). *Pravda*, 29 September 1993, p. 1.

Nikitinskiy, Leonid. 'Skol'ko Rubikonov na puti Gorbacheva?' (How many Rubicons will Gorbachev have to cross?). *Komsomol'skaya Pravda*, 12 April 1991.

Nikolaev, Stanislav. 'Kazhdoy sem'e – "Zdorovuyu kvartiru"' (A sound apartment for every family). Interviewed by L. Velikanova. *Literaturnaya Gazeta*, 31 August 1988.

'Nochnoye ubiystvo' (Murder in the night). *Doverie*, extra edition, 22 August 1991, p. 3.

'No Illusion on Democracy: A Student Favors Yeltsin'. *Washington Post*, 15 June 1996, p. A20.

Novikov, A. 'Na poroge voyny' (On the threshold of war). *Komsomol'skaya Pravda*, 24 August 1988.

'Novyi kurs' (A new course). An anti-Yeltsin cartoon. *Zavtra*, 5, February 1996, p. 1.

'Nuzhna pomochsh' (Help is needed). *Izvestia*, 21 September 1988.

'Nyet polzuchemu perevorotu! Obrashchenie gruppy narodnykh deputatov i predstavitelei demokraticheskoy intelligentsii' ('No' to the creeping coup d'état. An appeal by a group of People's Deputies and representatives of the democratic intelligentsia). *Izvestia*, 26 October 1992.

Oberdorfer, Don. 'Yeltsin: Gorbachev Has Year to Prove Self'. *Washington Post*, 12 September 1989.

Oberdorfer, Don, and David Hoffman. 'Yeltsin Asks Bush to Aid Soviet Reform Process'. *Washington Post*, 13 September 1989.

'Obeshchaniyami syt ne budesh' (You cannot feed one with promises). *Ogonyok*, 27 January–3 February 1990, p. 1.

'Obrashchenie Mossoveta' (The appeal of Mossovet). *Vechernyaya Moskva*, 30 August 1991, p. 1.

'Obrashchenie soveta rabochikh komitetov Kuzbassa k grazhdanan oblasti, Rossii, strany' (Appeal of the council of workers' committees of Kuzbass to the citizens of the region, Russia, the country). *Russkaya Mysl'* (Paris), 1 February 1991.

'Ochishchenie' (Cleansing). *Pravda*, 13 February 1986.

'Official Vows Constitutional Court Appeal on Land Code'. *RFE/RL Newsline*, 25 September 1997.

Omlinskiy, Vladimir. 'Ten'' (The shadow). *Literaturnaya Gazeta*, 7 September 1988.

OMRI Daily, 22 September 1993.

OMRI Daily, 28 September 1993.

OMRI Daily, 29 September 1993.

OMRI Daily, 1 October, 1993.

OMRI Daily, 5 October 1993.

OMRI Daily, 21 December 1995.

OMRI Daily, 14 June 1996.

OMRI Daily, 21 June 1996.

OMRI Daily, 25 June 1996.

OMRI Daily, 27 June 1996.

OMRI Daily, 2 July 1996.

OMRI Daily, 5 July 1996.

OMRI Daily, 6 July 1996.

OMRI Daily, 4 March 1997.

OMRI Russian Presidential Election Survey, 5, 29 May 1996.

OMRI Russian Presidential Election Survey, 11, 27 June 1996.

OMRI Russian Presidential Election Survey, 15, 9 July 1996.

'Opposition Leaders Confer on Strategy'. *RFE/RL Newsline*, 30 September 1997.

'Opyat' "Pravda"?' (Again *Pravda?*). *Kuranty*, 30 August 1991.

'Orden na znameni teatra' (Order on the banner of the theatre). *Ural'skiy Rabochiy*, 29 October 1983.

'Organizatsionnyi Plenum oblastnogo komiteta KPSS' (Organizational Plenum of the Oblast Committee of the CPSU). *Ural'skiy Rabochiy*, 22 January 1984.

Orlov, Dmitriy. 'Schitayut vse!' (Everyone is counting!). *Novoye Vremya*, 1–2, 1997.

Orttung, Robert W. 'Voters Face a Red-and-White Choice'. *Transition*, 31 May 1996.

'Osnovnye printsipy novoy Konstitutsii Rossii' (The main principles of a new constitution of Russia). *Izvestia*, 24 April 1993, p. 5.

Ostapchuk, Anna. 'Ne soglyadatay, a posrednik' (Not a spy, but an intermediary). Interview with the Deputy Chief of the Presidential Administration, Aleksandr Kazakov. *Moskovskie Novosti*, 20–27 July 1997.

Ostapchuk, Vasiliy Ignatovich. 'Ya trudilsya skol'ko mog . . .' (I worked for as long as I could . . .). Letter to the editor. *Izvestia*, 3 September 1987.

Ostrovsky, Arkady, and John Thornhill. 'Nikitin case: Successor to KGB humbled'. *Financial Times*, 30 October 1998 (http://www.ft.com).

Paretskaya, Anna. 'New Commercials Tell Youth "Vote and You'll Win"'. *OMRI Daily*, 27 June 1996.

'Pal'to El'tsina zalyapano krov'yu' (Yeltsin's coat is splattered with blood). *Zavtra* 17 (April), 1996, p. 1.

'Parliament in Moscow Feels Pressure and Votes Sales Tax'. *New York Times*. 17 July 1998.

Parthé, Kathleen. 'Trust in Zyuganov

Is Naïve and Ominous'. Letter to the editor, *New York Times*, 2 June 1996.

Parthé, Kathleen. 'What Would "Tomorrow" Bring Russia?' Unpublished paper, 1996.

Parthé, Kathleen. 'Zyuganov: Man of Letters'. Unpublished paper, 1996.

Pashkov, Aleksandr. 'El'tsin reshil ostat'sya, no i Zyuganov khochet porulit'' (Yeltsin has decided to stay, but Zyuganov also wants to rule a bit). *Izvestia*, 16 February 1996, p. 1.

Peltz, Aleksandr. 'Press-konferentsia Ministra oborony Rossii' (Press conference of the Minister of Defence of Russia). *Krasnaya Zvezda*, 6 October 1993.

Pertzevaya, Ludmila. 'Do Not Worship Blindly'. *Moscow News*, 15–22 March, 1992.

Pis'mennaya, Evgeniya. 'Prezident reshil pokonchit' s byudzhetnym krizisom' (President decided to end the budget crisis). *Financial Izvestia*, 12 May 1998.

'Plan Sets Ambitious Economic Targets'. *RFE/RL Newsline*, 27 January 1998.

'Plenum TsK KPSS–October 1988' (Plenum of the Central Committee of the CPSU – October 1988). *Izvestia TsK KPSS*, 2, 1989.

Plutnik, A. 'Den' chetvertiy' (Day four). *Izvestia*, 30 May 1989.

Plutnik, A. 'Den' desyatiy' (Day ten). *Izvestia*, 8 June 1989.

Plutnik, Albert. 'Politicheskiy dnevik. V avguste 91-go' (Political diary. In August 1991). *Izvestia*, 23 August 1991, p. 1.

'Podpisat' ukas o prekrashchenii voennykh deystviy v Chechne ruka, ponimaesh, kak-to ne podnimaetsya' (Somehow, you see, I cannot lift my hand to sign a decree on ending the war in Chechnya. An anti-Yeltsin cartoon. *Sovetskaya Rossia*, 20 February 1996.

'Pokhishchnie Moskvy' (The stealing of Moscow). *Zavtra*, 3, January 1996, p. 1.

Polevoy, S. 'Nich'i deti' (No one's children). *Pravda*, 8 October 1988.

Polezhaeva, N. 'Otvetit' delom: s plenuma Zhdanovskogo RK KPSS' (To answer with deed[s]: from the Plenum of the Zhdanov RK KPSS). *Moskovskaya Pravda*, 3 August 1986.

'Polling Russian Electorate'. *Washington Post*, 23 May 1996, p. A31.

'Polozhenie o vyborakh deputatov Gosudarstvennoy dumy' (The regulation concerning the election of Deputies of the State Duma). *Rossiyskie Vesti*, 28 September 1993, pp. 1–3.

Poltoranin, Mikhail. 'Visiting Boris Yeltsin'. *Moskovskie Novosti*, German edition, May 1988 (FB1S-SOV-88-084, 29 April 1988, p. 32).

Polyanovskiy, Eduard. 'Narod sam podnyal svoy flag' (People themselves raised their flag). *Izvestia*, 20 August 1992, p. 1.

Pond, Elizabeth. 'Ukraine: A Concession to Post-Cold War Realities'. *Sun*, 4 June 1997.

Ponomarev, V. 'Volny bez peny ne byvyaet' (There is no wave without foam). *Izvestia*, 30 July 1987.

Popov, Gavriil. 'Kakaya perestroika nam nuzhna' (What kind of perestroika we need). *Moskovskie Novosti*, 20 December 1987, p. 7.

'Postanovlenie s'ezda narodnykh deputatov Rossiyskoy Sovetskoy Federativnoy Sotsialisticheskoy Respubliki o proekte Konstitutsii Rossiyskoy Federatsii i dal'neishey rabote Konstitutsonnoy Komissii' (Resolution of the Congress of People's Deputies of the Russian Soviet Federative Socialist Republic regarding the draft Constitution of the Russian Federation and further work of the Constitutional

Commission). *Rossiyskaya Gazeta*, 20 November 1991.

'Po mnogochislennym zayvkam zapadnykh investorov . . .' (Responding to many requests by Western investors . . .), an anti-Yeltsin cartoon. *Izibratel'*. *Sovetskaya Rossia*, 5 May 1996.

'Pre-Election Programme of Boris Yeltsin'. *Sovetskaya Molodezh* (Riga), 6 February 1990 (FBIS, 7 March 1990, p. 108).

Prelovskaya, Inga. 'Teleekran ni za kogo golosovat' ne sobriaetsya' (The television screen is not going to vote for anyone). *Izvestia*, 23 October 1993.

'Presidential Decree Tightens Control over Budget Funds'. *RFE/RL Newsline*, 14 May 1997.

Press conference of President George Bush. *Washington Post*, 20 August 1991.

Prior, Andi. 'Speaking at Shriver Hall, Boris Yeltsin Calls for Radical Reform of Soviet Economy'. *Johns Hopkins Newsletter*, September 1989.

Prokhanov, Aleksandr. 'A. Prokhanov. Slovo redaktora' (A. Prokhanov. A word from the editor). *Zavtra*, 1, November 1993, p. 1.

Prokhanov, Aleksandr. 'My – iz russkoy tsivilizatsii' (We are from the Russian civilization). *Zavtra*, 31, August 1996.

Prokhanov, Aleksandr, and Gennadiy Zyuganov. *Slovo k narodu* (A word to the people). *Sovetskaya Rossia*, 23 July 1991, p. 1.

'Ptitsa schyastya zavtrashnego dnya: 'Vyberi menya! Vyberi menya!' (The bird of tomorrow's happiness. Elect me! Elect me!). An anti-Yeltsin cartoon. *Zavtra*, 21, May 1996.

Public Opinion Foundation, the polling results, January 1996 to May 1996. *Novoye Vremya*, 23, 1996, p. 10.

Pumpyanskaya, Seda. 'Den' kogda proizoshyol obval' (The day when the avalanche happened). *Novoye Vremya*, 41, 1993, p. 12.

Pumpyanskiy, Aleksandr. 'Lev zashevililsya' (The lion has moved). *Novoye Vremya*, 29, 1998.

'A Puppet Boris Gives Bill Advice He Doesn't Really Need'. *New York Times*, 15 February 1998, p. 7.

Radaev, V., and O. Shkaratan. 'Vozvrashchenie k istokam' (The return to the sources). *Izvestia*, 16 February 1990.

Rahr, Alexander. 'Democrats Demonstrate for Yeltsin'. *OMRI System Search*, 27 September 1993 (http://solar.rtd.utk.edu:81/cgi-bin/friends/omri/select-rec.pl).

Rahr, Alexander. 'Gorbachev and Yeltsin in a Deadlock'. *Report on the USSR*, 15 February 1991, p. 2.

Rahr, Alexander. 'Khazbulatov Will Support Yeltsin'. *OMRI System Search*, 31 October 1991 (http://solar.rtd.utk.edu:81/cgi-bin/friends/omri/select-rec.pl).

Rahr, Alexander. 'Political Struggle on the Eve of the Congress'. *RFE/RL Daily Report*, 12 November 1992.

Rahr, Alexander. 'Power Struggle Continues between Yeltsin and Parliament'. *RFE/RL Daily Report*, 12 November 1992.

Rahr, Alexander. 'The Rise and Fall of Ruslan Khazbulatov'. *RFE/RL Research Report*, 11 June 1993.

Rahr, Alexander. 'The Roots of the Power Struggle'. *RFE/RL Research Report*, 14 May 1993.

Rahr, Alexander. 'Russian Congress Criticizes Cabinet, Seeks New Powers'. *RFE/RL Daily Report*, 4 December 1994.

Rahr, Alexander. 'Solzhenitsyn Welcomes Disintegration of USSR'. *OMRI System Search*, 9 October 1991 (http://solar.rtd.utk.edu:81/cgi-bin/friends/omir/select-rec.pl).

Rahr, Alexander. 'Yeltsin Calls Gorbachev an Ally'. *RFE/RL Daily Report*, 13 May 1991, p. 7.

Rahr, Alexander. 'Yeltsin Gets Support from All Factions'. *RFE/ RL Daily Report*, 29 October 1991.

Rahr, Alexander. 'Yeltsin Intensifies Campaign against Gorbachev'. *RFE/RL Daily Report*, 25 March 1991.

Randolph, Eleanor. 'Soviet Medicine in Dire Straits'. *Washington Post*, 18 November 1991, p. A14.

Randolph, Eleanor. 'Yeltsin's "Spree" Denied'. *Washington Post*, 19 September 1989.

'Rano vpadat' v eyphoriyu' (Too early to become euphoric). *Kuranty*, 24 August 1991, p. 2.

Raskin, V. 'Moskovskie ulitsy, 19 avgusta' (Moscow streets, 19 August). *Sel'skaya Zhizn'*, 22 August 1991.

Razin, S. 'Chya ruka v moyom karmane?' (Whose hand is in my pocket?). *Komsomol'skaya Pravda*, 14 February 1991.

Razin, S. 'Sverdlovsk, 20 avgusta: tenevoy kabinet v lesu' (Sverdlovsk, 20 August: a shadow cabinet in the woods). *Komsomol'skaya Pravda*, 27 August 1991, p. 1.

'Reaction to Vote on Social Legislation'. *RFE/RL Newsline*, 26 September 1997.

Remnick, David. 'Boris Yeltsin, Adding Punch to Soviet Politics; Moscow's Ousted Party Chief is Back in Fighting Form in his Populist Camp'. *Washington Post*, 18 February 1989.

Remnick, David. 'Conference Ending Leaves Soviets Stunned – But Not Speechless'. *Washington Post*, 3 July 1988.

Remnick, David. 'Crisis Jolts Masses out of Passivity and onto Moscow Streets'. *Washington Post*, 21 August 1991, p. A1.

Remnick, David. 'Hammer, Sickle, and Book'. *New York Review of Books*, 23 May 1996.

Remnick, David. 'Protesters Throng Moscow Streets to Demand Democracy; Rally is Biggest in the Capital since Bolshevik Revolution'. *Washington Post*, 5 February 1990.

Remnick, David. 'Soviet Progressives Begin to Shape Legislative Alliance'. *Washington Post*, 22 April 1989.

Remnick, David. '10,000 Stage Rally for Boris Yeltsin on Eve of Soviet Legislative Elections'. *Washington Post*, 26 March 1989.

Remnick, David. 'Yeltsin: Gorbachev Indecisive . . .' *Washington Post*, 21 May 1989.

Remnick, David. 'Yeltsin Is Hailed at Moscow Rally'. *Washington Post*, 25 February 1991.

Remnick, David. 'Yeltsin Relegated to the Bleachers; Ousted Moscow Party Chief Chats with Public at Parade'. *Washington Post*, 2 May 1988.

Renfrew, Barry. 'Revitalized Yeltsin Running Hard'. Associated Press, 3 July 1997 (*Zhiwriter*, http:// www.nd.edu, 8 July 1997).

Report on the USSR, 9 March 1990, p. 40.

Reshetnikova, M. 'Neizvestnyi El'tsin' (Unknown Yeltsin). *Zerkalo*, 3, September 1990. (Reprinted in *Doverie*, January 1991.)

'Rezolyutsia sobrania predstavitelei narodno-patrioticheskikh sil strany – uchastnikov vstrechi s kandidatom na dolzhnost' presidenta Rossiyskoy Federatsii G. A. Zyuganovym' (Resolution of the gathering of the representatives of the popular-patriotic movements of the country – participants at the meeting with the candidate to the post of President of the Russian Federation, G. A. Zyuganov). *Sovetskaya Rossia*, 19 March 1996.

RFE/RL Daily Report, 25 November 1991.

RFE/RL Newsline, 7 May 1997.

RFE/RL Newsline, 30 May 1997.

RFE/RL Newsline, 16 June 1997.

RFE/RL Newsline, 27 June 1997.

RFE/RL Newsline, 11 August 1997.

RFE/RL Newsline, 26 August 1997.

RFE/RL Newsline, 27 August 1997.

RFE/RL Newsline, 24 September 1997.

RFE/RL Newsline, 25 September 1997.

RFE/RL Newsline, 1 October 1997.

RFE/RL Newsline, 5 January 1998.

RFE/RL Newsline, 20 January 1998.

RFE/RL Newsline, 3 February 1998.

Rhodes, Mark. 'Food Supply in the USSR'. *Report on the USSR*, 11 October 1991.

Robinson, Anthony. 'Thousands March for Yeltsin'. *Financial Times*, 11 March 1991.

Rodin, Ivan. 'Mirnoe nastuplenie El'tsina natalkivaetsya na "vooruzhennuyu oboronu" Rutskogo i Khazbulatova' (Yeltsin's peace offensive is confronted by the 'armed defence' of Rutskoy and Khazbulatov). *Nezavisimaya Gazeta*, 21 September 1993, p. 1.

'Rodonachalnik Uralskoy Nauki' (Forefather of Ural science). *Ural'skiy Rabochiy*, 3 March 1984.

Romanov, Andrey, and Vladimir Shevelev. 'Men'shinstvo ob'edinilos'' (The minority has consolidated). *Moskovskie Novosti*, 6 August 1989.

'Rossia i Zapad: Perspektivy partnerstva' (Russia and the West: the outlook for partnership). *Svobodnaya Mysl'*, December 1996.

'Rossiey pravit zhestokaya kukla' (Russia is ruled by a cruel puppet). *Zavtra*, 4, January 1996, p. 1.

'Round and Round They Go. And Where They Stop and Shop'. *New York Times Week in Review*, 12 April 1998, p. 5.

Ruble, Blair A. 'Politics, Economic Growth, and Nationalism in Today's Russia'. Keynote speech at the WEFA Group Fall International Outlook Conference (Philadelphia, 30 October 1996). *Eurasia Economic Outlook*, November 1996.

Ruble, Blair A., and Nancy Popson. 'The Westernization of a Russian Province: The Case of Novgorod'. *Post-Soviet Geography and Economics*, vol. 39, no. 8, 1998.

'Russian love in a cold climate'. *Economist*, 15 August 1998.

'Russian Troops Carry Out Massacre in Samashki'. *RFE/RL Newsline System Search*, 14 April 1995.

'Russian Voters Speak Out on Issues'. *New York Times*, 18 June 1996, p. A10.

'Russkiy, golosuy za Zyuganova!' (Russians, vote for Zyuganov). *Zavtra*, 26, June 1996.

Rutland, Peter. 'Yeltsin: the Problem, not the Solution', *The National Interest*, Fall 1997.

Rutskoy, Aleksandr. 'Rabotnikam Ministerstva Inostannykh Del' (To the employees of the Ministry of Foreign Affairs). *Pravda*, 1 October 1993.

Rutskoy, Aleksandr. 'Ya obrashchayus' k vam kak ofitzer' (I appeal to you as an officer). *Pravda*, 24 September 1993, p. 1.

'Rutskoy kak ekonomist i volshebnik' (Rutskoy as an economist and magician). *Moskovskiy Komsomoletz*, 24 September 1993.

Rybkin, Ivan. 'Sluzhenie zakonu ne terpit suety' (Serving law eschews bustle). *Rossiyskaya Gazeta*, 1 November 1995.

Rytov, Yu. 'Kak zhivut pensionery' (How pensioners fare). *Izvestia*, 20 August 1988.

Sabbat-Swidlicka, Anna. 'The Legacy of Poland's "Solidarity" Governments'. *RFE/RL Research Report*, vol. 2, no. 44, 5 November 1993.

Sakharov, Andrey. 'Poslednee

interv'yu "LG"' (The last interview with *Literaturnaya Gazeta*). Interviewed by E. Domnysheva. *Literaturnaya Gazeta*, 20 December 1989.

Sakharov, Andrey. Interview with *Ogonyok*, 31 July 1989.

Salmin, A. M. 'Vobory 1995–1996 i transformatsiya politicheskogo rezhima v Rossiyskoy Federatsii' (The 1995–1996 elections and the transformation of the political regime in the Russian Federation). *Polis*, 1, 1997.

Sapozhnikova, G. 'Fenomen Yeltsina, ili chto proiskhodit v Moskve?' (The Yeltsin phenomenon, or what is happening in Moscow?). *Molodezh Estonii*, 25 March 1989.

Satarov, Georgiy. 'My Job? Getting Yeltsin to Win'. Interview with *La Stampa* (Turin), 3 March 1996, p. 8. (FBIS-SOV-96-044, 6 March 1996, Article Id: drsov044_b_96011, http://wnc.fedworld.gov/cgi-bin . . .).

Savin, Andrey. 'Bogatymi v Rossii stanovyatsya po blatu' (One needs connections to become rich in Russia). *Izvestia*, 22 April 1998, p. 6.

Savvateeva, Irina. 'Novye pravila eksporta otkryvaut novye vozmozhnosti dlia korruptzii' (The new export regulations present new opportunities for corruption). *Izvestia*, 15 February 1995.

Schmemann, Serge. ' "Closing the Circle", Sharansky Visits Russia'. *New York Times*, 28 January 1997.

Schmemann, Serge. 'Huge Rally in Moscow Calls on Gorbachev to Resign'. *New York Times*, 11 March 1991.

Schmemann, Serge. 'Russia Acts: Going It Alone'. *New York Times*, 25 November 1991, p. A13.

Schmemann, Serge. 'Russians Fill Streets, Not Barricades'. *New York Times*, 29 March 1993.

Schmemann, Serge. 'Russians Scramble to Fill an Unformed Parliament'. *New York Times*, 1 November 1993.

Schmemann, Serge. 'Rutskoi and Khasbulatov Seized with Hundreds of their Supporters'. *New York Times*, 5 October 1993, p. 16.

Schmemann, Serge. 'Yeltsin Bargains with Congress, Reducing Pressure at the Meeting'. *New York Times*, 13 December 1992.

Schofield, Carey. 'Anti-Coup Leaders – The Men of the Future?' *Jane's Intelligence Review*, vol. 3, no. 10, October 1991.

Schwantes, Jon. 'For Yeltsin, a Day of Pigs, People, Philosophy'. *Indianapolis News*, 15 September 1989.

Seely, Robert. 'Ex-Soviet Nations Give Support'. *Washington Post*, 5 October 1993.

Selyunin, V. 'Istoki' (The sources). *Noviy Mir*, May 1988.

Selyunin, Vasiliy. 'Posledniy shans' (The last chance). *Literaturnaya Gazeta*, 2 May 1990.

Selyunin, Vasiliy. 'Soviet Reformer Fears Collapse of Economic House of (Ration) Cards'. *Glasnost*, 2, January–March 1990.

Semiryaga, Mikhail. '23 avgusta, 1939' (23 August 1939). *Literaturnaya Gazeta*, 5 October 1988.

Semyonov, Vladimir. 'Stavka – na neposredstvennuyu rabotu s izbiratelyami' (Emphasis on direct work with voters). *Rossiyskie Vesti*, 6 May 1996, p. 1.

Sergeev, V. M. ' "Neobratimost' peremen": real'nost ili metafora?' (The 'irreversibility of the changes': reality or a metaphor?). *Polis*, 1, 1997.

Sergeev, Pavel. 'Defitsit lekarstv. Ch'ya vina?' (The deficit of medicine. Whose fault is it?). Interviewed by N. Gogol'. *Pravda*, 13 July 1989.

'Sergey Stankevich: vinovniki ostayutsia v teni' (Sergey Stankevich: the culprits remain in the shadow). *Megapolis-Express*, 27 September 1990.

'S'ezd narodnykh deputatov RSFSR' (The Congress of People's Deputies of the RSFSR). *Sovetskaya Rossia*, 27 May 1990.

'S'ezd narodnykh deputatov RSFSR. Stenograficheskiy otchet' (The Congress of People's Deputies of the RSFSR. A transcript). *Sovetskaya Rossia*, 25 May 1990.

'S'ezd narodnykh deputatov. Stenograficheskiy otchet' (The Congress of People's Deputies. A transcript). *Izvestia*, 26 May 1989.

'S'ezd narodnykh deputatov. Stenograficheskiy otchet' (The Congress of People's Deputies. A transcript). *Izvestia*, 27 May 1989.

'S'ezd narodnykh deputatov. Stenograficheskiy otchet' (The Congress of People's Deputies. A transcript). *Izvestia*, 29 May 1989.

'S'ezd: povorot k potrebnostyam cheloveka' (The Congress: turning towards the needs of man). *Sel'skaya Zhizn'*, 13 June 1989.

Shakina, Marina. 'El'tsin. Chevolek, kotoriy umeet delat' vybor' (Yeltsin. A man who can make choices). *Novoye Vremya*, 40, 1994, pp. 11, 13.

Shakina, Marina. 'Something Has Happened to Perestroika'. *New Times*, 5–11 March 1991.

Shama, Avi. 'Notes from Underground: Russia's Economy Booms'. *Wall Street Journal*, 24 October 1997, p. A10.

Shane, Scott. 'Pravda, Caught in a Lie, Apologizes to Yeltsin'. *Baltimore Sun*, 22 September 1989.

Shan'gin, N. 'Pochemu opazdal avtobus' (Why the bus was late). *Vechernyaya Moskva*, 19 December 1986.

Shapiro, Margaret. 'Drafting Constitution in the Kremlin'. *Washington Post*, 5 June 1993, p. A15.

Shapiro, Margaret. 'Moscow Has Biggest Demonstrations since '91 Coup Attempt'. *Washington Post*, 29 March 1993.

Shapiro, Margaret. 'Soviets Double Aid Request'. *Washington Post*, 20 September 1991, p. A16.

Shapiro, Margaret. 'Yeltsin Forced by Russian Parliament to Abandon Reformist Prime Minister'. *Washington Post*, 15 December 1992.

Shapiro, Margaret. 'Yeltsin's "Essential Crackdown" Provokes Charges of Expediency'. *Washington Post*, 16 October 1993.

Shapovalov, O. 'Narodnoye sredstvo ot goloda' (A popular way to fight famine). *Komsomol'skaya Pravda*, 28 December 1991.

Sharp, Jo Ellen Meyers. 'Visiting Soviet Views Indiana Farming Firsthand'. *Indianapolis Star*, 15 September 1989.

Sharp, Jo Ellen Meyers. 'Yeltsin Says U.S. a Key to Success of Perestroika'. *Indianapolis Star*, 15 September 1989.

Sharymova, Natasha. 'Perestroiku nado spasat'' (Perestroika must be saved). *Novoye Russkoye Slovo*, 13 September 1989.

Shatalin, Stanislav. 'Khochu opravdat'siya pered narodom' (I want to clear myself before the people). *Komsomol'skaya Pravda*, 16 January 1991.

Shatalin, S., N. Petrakov, G. Yarlinskiy, S. Aleksashenko, A. Varilov, L. Grigoriev, M. Zadornov, V. Martynov, V. Mashits, A. Mikhailov, B. Fedorov, T. Yarygina and E. Yasin. 'Chelovek, svoboda, rynok' (Man, liberty, market). *Izvestia*, 4 September 1990.

Shchekochikhin, Yu. 'Lev prygnul!'

(The lion has jumped!). *Literaturnaya Gazeta*, 20 July 1988.

Sheehy, Ann. 'Commonwealth Emerges from a Disintegrating USSR'. *RFE/RL Research Report*, 3 January 1992.

Sheehy, Ann. 'Gorbachev Pleads for Union Treaty to Be Signed'. *OMRI System Search*, 4 December 1991 (http://solar.rtd.utk.edu).

Sheehy, Ann. 'Union Treaty: Appeal to Ukraine, Armenia, Georgia, Moldavia'. *OMRI System Search*, 14 October 1991 (http://solar.rtd.utk.edu).

Shenderovich, Viktor. 'Spisok nadezhd' (A list of hopes). *Moskovskie Novosti*, 7–14 July 1996.

Shestopal, E. B. 'Vybory proshli: peyzazh posle bitvy' (The elections are over: a landscape after the battle). *Polis*, 1, 1997.

Shevardnadze, Eduard. 'The Tragedy of Gorbachev'. *Newsweek*, 9 September 1991.

Sheynis, Viktor. 'Proyden li istoricheskiy rubezh?' (Have we passed a historic watershed?). *Polis*, 1, 1997.

Shipit'ko, Gennadiy. 'Vyvoz tovarov zapreshchyon' (The export of goods prohibited). *Izvestia*, 24 February 1990.

Shirokov, Viktor. 'Na grani fatal'nogo i neobratimogo raskola okazalis' Rossiiskie parlamentarii na svoem "ocherednom vneocherednom" s'ezde, no v itoge sumeli nayti kompromiss' (At their 'scheduled extraordinary' Congress the Russian parliamentarians found themselves on the brink of a fatal and irreversible split but in the end managed to find a compromise). *Pravda*, 9 April 1991.

Sichka, I. '1991, Fevral'. Boris opyat' ne prav?' (1991, February. Is Boris wrong again?). *Komsomol'skaya Pravda*, 22 February 1991.

Sieff, Martin. 'He's Just a Buffoon to Some, But Brash Yeltsin Has a Vision'. *Washington Times*, 26 January 1990.

Sieff, Martin. 'Schmoozing and Boozing, Boris Charms America'. *Washington Times*, 21 September 1989.

Sieff, Martin. 'Yeltsin, in Travels across U.S., Baled Plenty of Political Fodder'. *Washington Times*, 18 September 1989.

Sieff, Martin. 'Yeltsin Pays Reagan Visit in Hospital'. *Washington Times*, 15 September 1989.

'Silovye vedomstva ne khoteli by vmeshivat'sya v konflikt' (Power ministries would like not to get involved in the conflict). *Kommersant-Daily*, 23 September 1993, p. 3.

Sirotkin, Vladlen. 'Eshchyo raz o "belykh pyatnakh"' (Once again about 'blank spots'). *Nedelya*, 12 June 1989.

Sizov, A. 'Sverim tsifry' (Let's compare the figures). *Kommunist*, 15, (October) 1989, p. 63.

Slater, Wendy. 'Khazbulatov Addresses Deputies' Conference'. *RFE/RL Daily Report*, 2 June 1993.

Slater, Wendy. 'Khazbulatov Walks Out of Assembly'. *RFE/RL Daily Report*, 7 June 1993.

Slater, Wendy. 'No Victors in the Russian Referendum. *RFE/RL Research Report*, 21 May 1993.

Slater, Wendy. 'NSF Warns of Dictatorship'. *RFE/RL Daily Report*, 7 June 1993.

Slater, Wendy. 'Rutskoy Calls for Government to Be Disbanded'. *RFE/RL Daily Report*, 2 June 1993.

Slater, Wendy. 'Yeltsin Expands Constitutional Assembly'. *RFE/RL Daily Report*, 2 June 1993, p. 1.

Slater, Wendy. 'Yeltsin Opens Constitutional Assembly'. *RFE/RL Daily Report*, 7 June 1993.

'Slava soldatu, pozor verkhovnomu!' (Glory to the soldier, shame to the commander-in-chief). *Zavtra*, 3, January 1996.

'Slyshish, diktor kak kartavit? . . .' (Here the announcer burring . . .). *Zavtra*, 24, June 1996, p. 8.

'Snubbing People Power. Gorbachev's Show of Force Backfires as a New Poll Demonstrates his Growing Isolation'. *U.S. News and World Report*, 8 April 1991, pp. 38–40.

Sobchak, Anatoliy. 'Proryv' (The breakthrough). Interview with A. Golovkov and A. Chernov. *Moscow News*, 1 September 1991.

'Soldat i mraz'' (Soldier and vermin). An anti-Yeltsin cartoon. *Zavtra*, 15, April 1996, p. 1.

Solomon, Peter H., Jr. 'The Persistence of Judicial Reform in Contemporary Russia'. *East European Constitutional Review*, Fall 1997.

Solovyov, A. 'Neozhidanniy povorot: zabastovka shakhterov v Mezhdurechenske prodolzhaetsya' (Unexpected turn: miners' strike in Mezhdurechensk continues). *Izvestia*, 14 July 1989.

Solov'yov, Vladimir. 'Lightning Excursion to Grozny'. *Sel'skaya Zhizn'*, 30 May 1996, p. 1 (FBIS-SOV-96-105, 31 May 1996, Article Id: drsov105aa_96005, http://fedworld.gov/cgi-bin . . .).

'Some do eat cake'. *Economist*, 12 July 1997.

Soto, Luis Feldstein. 'Soviet Urges Democracy at Home'. *Miami Herald*, 18 September 1989.

'Sozdan izbiratel'nyi blok "Demokraticheskaya Rossia"' (An election bloc 'Democratic Russia' has been created). *Ogonyok*, 6, February 1990, p. 17.

Specter, Michael. 'In Moscow Baby Boom, a Vote for the Future'. *New York Times*, 27 August 1997.

Specter, Michael. 'Muse of Anti-Yeltsin Forces Is Feared But Never Ignored'. *New York Times*, 2 May 1996, p. A10.

Specter, Michael. 'Yeltsin's Plan to Cut Military Touches a Nerve'. *Washington Post*, 28 July 1997.

Spolar, Christine. 'Czechs' Post-Communist Boom Running Dry'. *Washington Post*, 29 June 1997.

Stanglin, Douglas, and Victoria Pope. 'Yeltsin Draws the Line'. *U.S. News and World Report*, 4 October 1993, p. 35.

Stankevich, Sergey. 'Ostanovit' inertsiyu revolyutsionnuyu' (To stop revolutionary inertia). *Vechernyaya Moskva*, 26 August 1991, p. 2.

Stanley, Alessandra. 'Is Success Good for Russia's Jews?' *New York Times*, 15 April 1997.

Stanley, Alessandra. 'A Jew Stalin Killed Now Symbolizes Rebirth'. *New York Times*, 14 January 1998.

Stanley, Alessandra. 'Red Scare'. *New York Times Magazine*, 26 May 1996.

Stanley, Alessandra. 'Russia's Jews Organize, with Swiss Caterer's Help'. *New York Times*, 11 January 1996.

Stanley, Alessandra. 'Yeltsin Pledges Housecleaning and Reform'. *New York Times*, 7 March 1997, p. 1 (http://www.nytimes.com).

Stanley, Alessandra. 'Yeltsin Says He Will Have Heart Surgery'. *New York Times*, 6 September 1996.

Steele, Jonathan. 'Boris Yeltsin Sails through Constituency Reselection'. *Guardian*, 17 January 1989.

Steele, Jonathan. 'Yeltsin Wins Crowds on Campaign Trail'. *Guardian*, 6 March 1989.

Stent, Angela, and Lilia Shevtsova. 'Russia's Election: Turning Back'. *Foreign Policy*, 103, (Summer) 1996.

Stepashin, Sergey. 'Chistka v KGB SSSR' (Purge in the KGB of the

USSR). *Kuranty*, 30 August 1991, p. 4.

Stepovoy, A., and S. Chugaev. 'Predlozhenie Prezidenta: Polozhenie v strane obsudim v pyatnitsu' (The President's suggestion: let us discuss the situation in the country on Friday). *Izvestia*, 15 November 1990.

Stevens, Milton. 'And the Band Played On'. *Washington Post*, 17 October 1993, p. G8.

'Strana nepugannykh izbirateley' (A country of wild voters). *Moskovskiy Komsomoletz*, 28 May 1996, p. 2.

Stroganov, Vl. 'V Rossii est' eshcho rezervy . . .' (Russia still has reserves . . .). *Zavtra*, 24, June 1996.

'Stroit' na sele bol'she, lusche, deshevle' (To build more better and cheaper in the countryside). *Ural'skiy Rabochiy*, 29 July 1983.

'Suspension of Nikitin Trial Hailed'. 2 November 1998 (*Russia Today*, http://www.russiatoday.com/rtoday/news/10.html).

'Svet moy zerkal'tse! . . .' (Mirror, mirror on the wall . . .), an anti-Yeltsin cartoon. *Sovetskaya Rossia*, 29 February 1996.

Szymczak, Patricia M. 'Yeltsin: Let Republics Determine their Fate'. *Chicago Tribune*, 13 September 1989.

Task, Sergey. 'Postoronniy' (The strange). *Novoye Russkoye Slovo*, 20 October 1989.

Taubman, Philip. '"Who Will Now Dare to Express his Opinion?" Moderator Is Asked'. *New York Times*, 16 November 1987.

Teague, Elizabeth. 'Federalization à la carte'. *Perspective*, November–December, 1994.

Teague, Elizabeth. 'The Twenty-Eighth Party Congress: An Overview'. *Report on the USSR*, 20 July 1990, p. 2.

Tedstrom, John E. 'First Quarter

Economic Results: Can It Get Any Worse?' *Report on the USSR*, 1 June 1990, p. 5.

Tedstrom, John E. 'The Goskomstat Report for 1989: An Economy out of Control'. *Report on the USSR*, 16 February 1990, p. 2.

Teeter, Mark. 'An American's Diary'. *Woodrow Wilson Center Report*, vol. 3, no. 3, November 1991.

Telen', Ludmila. 'Pervyi zvonok' (The first call). *Moskovskie Novosti*, 21–28 April 1996, p. 6.

Telen', Ludmila, 'Okonchatel'nyi diagnoz' (The final diagnosis), *Moskovskie Novosti*, 4–11 December 1994, p. 5.

'Tezisy Tsentral'nogo Komiteta KPSS k vseosoyuznoy XIX partiynoy Konferentsii' (Theses of the Central Committee for the Nineteenth All-Union Party Conference). *Pravda*, 27 May 1988.

Thornhill, John, and Chrystia Freeland. 'Russia: Yeltsin returns with all guns blazing'. *Financial Times*, 7 March 1997 (http://www.ft.com).

Tikhomirov, Vladimir. 'Schitayu svoim partiynym dolgom' (I consider this my Party member duty). *Moskovskaya Pravda*, 19 March 1989.

Timofeev, Lev. 'Novaya teoriya sotsializma' (A new theory of socialism). *Moskovskie Novosti*, 8–15 December 1996.

Tishkov, Valeriy. 'Geopolitika Chechenskoy voyny' (The geopolitics of the Chechen war). *Svobodnaya Mysl'*, April 1997.

Tolstaya, Tatyana. 'When Putsch Comes to Shove'. *New Republic*, 16 and 23 September 1991.

Tolstov, V. 'Kak obespecheny zhil'yom krupneyshie goroda strany' (How well are the largest cities of the country provided with housing?). *Izvestia*, 4 September 1988.

Tolz, Vera. 'Another Communist

Party Created in RSFSR'. *OMRI System Search*, 26 November 1991 (http://solar.rtd.utk.edu).

Tolz, Vera. 'Assembly Adopts Declaration on the Draft Constitution'. *RFE/RL Daily Report*, 17 June 1993, p. 1.

Tolz, Vera. 'Communists Oppose Yeltsin's Decree'. *OMRI System Search*, 8 November 1991 (http://solar.rtd.utk.edu).

Tolz, Vera. 'Drafting the New Russian Constitution'. *RFE/RL Research Report*, 16 July 1993, p. 8.

Tolz, Vera. 'More on Joint Declaration, Yeltsin's Reaction'. *RFE/RL Daily Report*, 26 April 1991, p. 4.

Tolz, Vera. 'Most Officials Did Not Support Yeltsin during Coup'. *OMRI System Search*, 24 October 1991 (http://solar.rtd.utk.edu).

Tolz, Vera. 'Union of Communists Holds Press Conference'. *OMRI System Search*, 27 November 1991 (http://solar.rtd.utk.edu).

Tolz, Vera. 'What Remains of the CPSU'. *OMRI System Search*, 2 October 1991 (http://solar.rtd.utk.edu).

Tolz, Vera. 'Yeltsin Cancels his Own Decrees'. *RFE/RL Daily Report*, 11 September 1991.

Travkin, Nikolay. 'Kak izbirali predsedatelia' (How they were electing the Chairman). Interview by V. Glotov. *Ogonyok*, 9–16 June 1990, pp. 2–3.

Tregubova, Elena. 'Narodnye deputaty nazvali Viktora Anpilova i Stanislava Terekhova agentami spetssluzhb El'tsina. Chleny Soyuza ofitserov schitayut, chto Rodina stoit chelovescheskikh zhertv' (People's Deputies call Viktor Anpilov and Stanislav Terekov agents of Yeltsin's special services. Officers' Union members think Motherland is worth human sacrifices). *Segodnya*, 25 September 1993, p. 2.

Trehub, Aaron. 'Is Gorbachev's Anti-Drinking Campaign Losing its Kick?' *Radio Liberty Research* (RL 323/87), 3 August 1987, p. 2.

Trejo, Frank. 'Yeltsin Calls for Ousters'. *Dallas Morning News*, 16 September 1989.

Treml, Vladimir. 'Document on Alcoholism in the USSR Put in Perspective'. *Radio Liberty Research* (RL 39/85), 6 February 1985.

Treml, Vladimir. 'Gorbachev's Anti-Drinking Campaign: A Noble Experiment or a Costly Exercise in Futility'. *RL Supplement* (RL 2/87), 18 March 1987.

Tretyakov, Vitaliy. 'El'tsin–Khazbulatov: skhvatka ne na zhizn', a na smert'?' (Yeltsin–Khazbulatov: a battle to the end?). *Nezavisimaya Gazeta*, 21 September 1993, p. 1.

Tretyakov, Vitaliy. 'Eto fantastichno. Rossia nakonets-to dozhila do togo, chtoby narod sam vybiral glavu gosudarstva' (It is incredible. Russia has finally lived to see the day when the people themselves choose the head of state). *Nezavisimaya Gazeta*, 11 June 1991.

Tretyakov, Vitaliy. 'Fenomen Borisa El'tsina' (The Boris Yeltsin phenomenon). *Moskovskie Novosti*, 16 April 1989.

Tretyakov, Vitaliy. 'O Eltsine i glasnosti bez granitz' (On Yeltsin and glasnost without boundaries). *Moskovskie Novosti*, 24 September 1989.

Tretyakov, Vitaliy. 'Pervyi god Prezidenta Borisa El'tsina' (The first year of President Boris Yeltsin). *Nezavisimaya Gazeta*, 22–29 August 1992.

'Trudnyi dialog Prezidenta i armii' (Difficult dialogue between the President and the Army). *Izvestia*, 14 November 1990.

Trushina, L. 'Talony na ves' god'

(Ration coupons for the entire year). *Izvestia*, 30 January 1990.

Trushkov, Viktor. 'Anafema' (Anathema). *Pravda*, 28 September 1993, p. 2.

Trushkov, Viktor. 'Korolevskie muchenia' (The king's torments). *Pravda*, 17 January 1996, p. 1.

Trushkov, Viktor. 'Prisyaga komandira polka' (The oath of the commander of the regiment). *Pravda*, 28 September 1993, p. 1.

Tsipko, Aleksandr. 'Istochniki Stalinizma' (The sources of Stalinism), Part IV. *Nauka i Zhizn'*, 2, February 1989.

'Tsitata nedeli' (The quote of the week). *Novoye Vremya*, 47, 1997, p. 7.

Tsukanova, Lyubov'. 'Dnyom i noch'yu v "Belom dome"' (The 'White House' during the day and at night). *Rossiyskie Vesti*, 28 September 1993, p. 2.

Tsukanova, Lyubov'. 'Izbiratel' progolosyuet za togo, kto dast emu perspektivu' (The voter will vote for the one who offers him a future). *Rossiyskie Vesti*, 5 March 1996, p. 1.

Tsukanova, Lyubov'. 'Kto budet vesti izbiratel'nuyu kampaniyu Borisa El'tsina' (Those who will be running Boris Yeltsin's election campaign). *Rossiyskie Vesti*, 27 March 1996.

Uhlig, Mark A. 'Nicaraguans Hope for Decisive Election'. *New York Times*, 25 February 1990, p. 14.

'Ukaz o zemle, no ne o mire' (A decree on land, but not on peace). *Novoye Vremya*, 11, 1996, p. 4.

Urinson, Yakov. 'Krizis v Rossii est', no katastrophy ne budet' (There is a crisis in Russia, but a catastrophe will not happen). *Izvestia*, 10 July 1998, p. 4.

Urinson, Yakov. 'Vsyo chto effiktivno dlya ekonomiki, boleznenno dlya obshchestva' (Everything that is positive for the economy is painful for society). *Moskovskie Novosti*, 17–24 May 1998.

Urinson, Yakov. 'Ya podderzhu vsyo, cho pol'zuetsya sprosom' (I will support everything for which there is demand). *Novoye Vremya*, 15, 1997.

'Uskorenie – novoye kachestvo rosta' (Acceleration – the new quality of growth). *Izvestia*, 26 September 1986.

'U.S. Slums Look Good to Yeltsin'. *Chicago Sun-Times*, 13 September 1989.

Ustinov, Viktor. Interview with *Novoye Vremya*, 7, 1995, p. 20.

Van Atta, Don. 'Farms Declare "Grain Strike"'. *Report on the USSR*, 23 February 1990, p. 10.

Van Atta, Don. 'Yeltsin Decree Finally Ends "Second Serfdom" in Russia'. *RFE/RL Research Report*, 19 November 1993.

'Vandalizm – proyavlenie rabstva' (Vandalism [is] a manifestation of slavery). *Kuranty*, 27 August 1991.

Varpoli, John. 'Economic Reform Casts a Long Shadow in Russia'. *Transition*, 21 March 1997.

Vasiliev, Leonid. 'Eshchyo odnogo eksperimenta Rossia ne vyderzit' (Russia will not survive another experiment). *Novoye Vremya*, 9, 1996, p. 10.

Vasiliev, Leonid. 'Sumeet li prezident realizovat' svoy posledniy shans?' (Will the President be able to make the best of his last opportunity?). *Novoye Vremya*, 8, 1995, p. 14.

Vasinskiy, A., and G. Shipitko. 'V usloviyakh chrezvychaynogo polozheniya' (Under the state of emergency). *Izvestia*, 21 August 1991, p. 1.

Verbova, Izabella. 'Za tysyachi kilometrov ot Belogo doma' (Thousands of kilometres away from the White House). *Vechernyaya Moskva*, 2 October 1991.

'The Views of Rank and File

Russians'. *American Enterprise*, July–August 1996, p. 57.

Vil'chek, Vsevolod. 'Televideniyu pokoy tol'ko snitsya' (Television can only dream of tranquillity). *Moskovskie Novosti*, 7–14 July 1996, p. 5.

Vishnevskiy, Boris, and Aleksandr Gamov. 'Prezident v Tatarii bil gorshki, a v Sibiri agitiroval Mukhu' (President broke pots in Tatarstan and canvassed Mukha in Siberia). *Komsomol'skaya Pravda*, 11 June 1996, p. 2.

'Visions for Russia'. *Washington Post*, 5 June 1993, p. A15.

V.L. 'Staryi slukh luch'she novykh dvukh' (An old rumour is better than two new ones). *Moskovskie Novosti*, 14–21 July 1996, p. 3.

Volkogonov, Dmitriy. 'Nel'zya strane vtoroy raz proigrat' bol'shevikam' (The country must not lose to the Bolsheviks again). *Izvestia*, 24 April 1993.

Volkov, Vladimir, Daniil Granin, Mark Zakharov, Sergei Karaganov, Andranik Migranyan, Emil' Pain, Margarita Chudakova and Alla Yaroshinskaya. 'B. El'tsin ostayotsya oporoy demokratii v Rossii' (Yeltsin remains the cornerstone of democracy in Russia). *Izvestia*, 7 February 1993, p. 1.

Volodina, Lyubov'. 'Boris El'tsin oglasit predvybornuyu platformu na s'ezde svoikh storonnikov' (Boris Yeltsin to unveil election platform at Congress of his supporters). *Rossiyskie Vesti*, 28 March 1996, p. 1.

Vol'skiy, Arkadiy. Interview with *Der Spiegel* magazine, ADN, Berlin, 21 October 1991 (FBIS-SOV-91-204, 22 October 1991).

Voroshilov, P., and A. Soloviev. 'Konstruktivniy dialog s gornyakami' (Constructive dialogue with miners). *Izvestia*, 18 July 1989.

Voshchanov, Pavel. 'El'tsin v Amerike' (Yeltsin in America). *Komsomol'skaya Pravda*, 27 September 1989.

Voshchanov, Pavel. '"Nu vot ya i v Kremle!" A chto dal'she' ('At last I am in the Kremlin!' But what next?). *Komsomol'skaya Pravda*, 7 December 1994.

Voytko, I. 'Negde zhit' (No place to live). *Pravda*, 2 July 1989, p. 3.

'Vremya derzhat' otvet. Zayavlenie chlenov Soveta Federatsii RSFSR o sotsial'no-ekonomicheskom i politicheskom polozhenii v respublike' (Time to answer: statement by members of the RSFSR Federation Council on the socio-economic and political situation in the Republic). *Sovetskaya Rossia*, 20 March 1991.

'Vremya konkretnykh del' (A time of concrete action). *Moskovskaya Pravda*, 28 December 1985.

'V shest' chasov vechera posle vyborov' (At six o'clock after the election). *Zavtra*, 29, July 1996, p. 1.

'Vstrecha Sovetskogo rukovodstva s zhurnalistami' (Soviet leadership meets with journalists). *Pravda*, 20 August 1991, p. 1.

'Vstrechi s rabochim klassom: prebyvanie M. S. Gorbacheva v Khabarovskom krae' (Conversation with the working class: M. S. Gorbachev's visit to Khabarovsk *krai*). *Pravda*, 30 July 1986.

'Vtoroye dykhanie' (A second wind). *Moskovskie Novosti*, 9–16 June 1996, p. 8.

'V TsK KPSS' (In the Central Committee of the CPSU). *Pravda*, 1 October 1986.

'Vyshe otvetstvennost'' (Higher responsibility). *Pravda*, 15 December 1985.

Vysotskiy, Vladimir. 'Tovarishchi uchyonye' (Comrades scholars), in Vladimir Vysotskiy, *Sochineniya v dvukh tomakh* (Collected works in two volumes), Moscow: Khudozhestvennaya Literatura, 1993, volume I, p. 412.

Vyzhutovich, Valeriy. 'My boyalis' shokovoy terapii. I prishli k shokovoy khirurgii' (We were afraid of shock therapy. And now have come to shock surgery). *Izvestia*, 29 October 1991.

Vyzhutovich, Valeriy. 'Prezidentskiy konvoy' (The President's convoy). *Moskovskie Novosti*, 25 December 1994–1 January 1995, p. 6.

Vyzhutovich, Valeriy. 'Raschistka otvalov' (Clearing the waste). *Izvestia*, 23 July 1989.

Vyzhutovich, Valeriy. 'Smotrite, kto idet!' (Look who is coming!). *Izvestia*, 6 April 1996.

'Vzaimoponimanie – opora perestroiki' (Mutual understanding is the basis of perestroika). *Izvestia*, 25 April 1990.

Watson, Russell, Dorinda Elliott, Andrew Nagorski, Betsy McKay and John Barry. 'Yeltsin's Coup de Grâce'. *Newsweek*, 4 October 1993, p. 72.

Watson, Russell, Dorinda Elliott, Rod Norland, Betsy McKay and Jane Whitmore. 'Hollow Victory'. *U.S. News and World Report*, 18 October 1993, p. 48.

'What on Earth?' *Washington Post*, 2 August 1997.

'What's in a Slogan?' *New York Times*, 2 May 1990.

Whitefield, Stephen, and Geoffrey Evans. 'Support for Democracy and Political Opposition in Russia, 1993–1995'. *Post-Soviet Affairs*, 12 (3), July–September 1996.

Whitlock, Eric. 'New Government to Continue Economic Reform?' *RFE/RL Research Report*, 15 January 1993.

Whitlock, Eric. 'The Russian Government, the Central Bank, and the Resolution on Constitutional Reform'. *RFE/RL Research Report*, 26 March 1993.

'Why This Matzoh Is Different from All Others: It's Moscow's'. *New York Times*, 4 April 1996.

Williams, Carol J. 'Russia Needs Strategy for Upsurge'. *Los Angeles Times*, 18 February 1998.

Williams, Daniel. ' "Citizen Kane" on Pushkin Square'. *Washington Post*, 13 July 1997.

Williams, Daniel. 'High Russian Officials Duck Anti-Corruption Initiative'. *Washington Post*, 25 July 1997.

Wishnevsky, Julia. 'The Constitutional Court'. *RFE/RL Report*, 14 May 1993.

Wishnevsky, Julia. 'Constitutional Crisis Deepens after Russian Congress'. *RFE/RL Research Report*, 26 March 1993.

Wishnevsky, Julia. 'Deputies Attack Economic Reform'. *RFE/RL Daily Report*, 4 December 1992.

Wishnevsky, Julia. 'Pravda Editor in Trouble?' *Radio Liberty*, 20 October 1989.

Wishnevsky, Julia. 'Two RSFSR Congresses: A Diarchy?' *Report on the USSR*, 27 June 1990.

'Writer Admits Yeltsin Source Is Nonexistent'. *Washington Post*, 21 September 1989.

Yagodin, G. A., Speech at XIX Party Conference. *Pravda*, 2 July 1988, p. 9.

Yakovenko, Egor. 'Ot imperii k natsional'nomu gosudarsvu' (From the empire to a nation-state). *Polis*, 6, 1996.

Yakovlev, Aleksandr. 'Ne tol'ko koldovskoy bur'yan . . .' (Not only witches' weed . . .). *Novoye Vremya*, 27, 1993.

Yakovlev, B. 'Pamyatniki i my' (Moments and us). *Vechernyaya Moskva*, 26 August 1991, p. 3.

Yakovlev, Vladimir, 'Proshchanie s Bazarovym' (Farewell to Bazarov). *Ogonyok*, 36, 1987.

Yakovlev, Ye. 'Yavlinsky's Death Ray'. *Moscow News*, 6 January 1991, pp. 8–9.

Yavlinsky, Grigoriy. 'Na luchshiy khod sobytiy ya ne nadeyus', nado gotovit'sya k khudshemu' (I do not hope for a better course of events – one should get ready for the worst). *Nezavisimaya Gazeta*, 23 September 1993, p. 2.

Yeltsina, Naina. 'Rossiya zhivyot i stroitsya' (Russia lives and builds). Interview with *Argumenty i Fakty*, No. 11, March 1996, p. 3.

'Yeltsin Approves Production-Sharing List'. *RFE/RL Newsline*, 23 July 1997.

'Yeltsin Criticizes Duma's Stance'. *RFE/RL Newsline*, 30 September 1997.

'Yeltsin Defiant in Moscow Speech'. *Washington Post*, 19 March 1989.

'Yeltsin Demands Policies to Stimulate Economic Growth'. *RFE/RL Newsline*, 14 January 1998.

Yeltsin descends to hell. A cartoon. *Zavtra*, 23, June 1996.

'Yeltsin Displays Bedside Humor'. *Los Angeles Times*, 15 September 1989.

'Yeltsin Launches 1998 Government Program'. *RFE/RL Newsline*, 27 January 1998.

'Yeltsin Lifts Limits on Foreign Ownership of Shares in Russian Oil Companies'. *RFE/RL Newsline*, 5 November 1997.

'Yeltsin Seeks Private U.S. Funds'. *Indianapolis Star*, 13 September 1989.

Yeltsin signs a decree appointing Anatoliy Chubais First Deputy Prime Minister, an anti-Yeltsin cartoon. *Sovetskaya Rossia*, 13 March 1997.

'Yeltsin to Veto Land Code'. *RFE/RL Newsline*, 25 July 1997.

'Yeltsin's Gloomy Glasnost'. *San Francisco Chronicle*, 9 September 1989.

Zadornov, Mikhail. 'Vlezayem v dolgi?' (Are we assuming too much debt?). *Moskovskie Novosti*, 7–14 June 1998.

Zadornov, Mikhail. 'Za polchasa do obvala' (Half an hour before collapse). *Izvestia*, 29 May 1998.

'Zadornov Says Time Running Out for Tax Code'. *RFE/RL Newsline*, 11 February 1998.

Zagaynov, G. Speech at Nineteenth Party Conference. *Pravda*, 2 July 1988.

'Zapasaysya, kto mozhet' (Stock up, if you can). *Trud*, 5 October 1991, p. 1.

'Zapisalsya v antiel'tsinskuyu koalitsiyu?' (Have you joined the anti-Yeltsin coalition?). *Zavtra*, 6, February 1996, p. 1.

Zaripov, Ravil', Ol'ga Gerasimenko, Irina Savveteeva and Aleksandr Orlov. 'Komu nuzhna velikaya Rossia, a komu – "Beliy dom"' (Some need great Russia, and some – the 'White House'). *Komsomol'skaya Pravda*, 23 September 1993, p. 2.

Zatvornitskiy, V. A. 'Trudnyi Urok' (A hard lesson). *Sovetskaya Rossia*, 24 November 1987.

'Zayavlenie Sekretariata TsK Kompartii RSFSR' (Statement by the Secretariat of the Central Committee of the Communist Party of the Russian Soviet Federated Socialist Republic). *Sovetskaya Rossia*, 22 August 1991.

Zaychenko, A. S. 'SShA–SSSR: lichnoye potreblenie' (US–USSR: personal consumption). *SShA*, December 1988.

Zenova, Natal'ya. 'Voyennaya Tayna' (A military secret). *Literaturnaya Gazeta*, 22 August 1990, p. 12.

Zgerskiy, Dmitriy, and Vasiliy Dvorykin. 'Ulybka Adol'fa Aloisivicha' (The smile of Adolf, son of Alois). *Novoye Vremya*, 41, 1993, p. 13.

Zhavoronkov, Gennadiy. 'More scope

for the unofficial'. *Moscow News*, 13 September 1987.

Zhuravlev, Egor, Sergey Krayukhin and Vladimir Borodin. 'Oboronshchiki grozyat igrushechnymi avtomatami' (Workers of defence industry brandish toy machine guns). *Izvestia*, 9 July 1998.

Zimmerman, William. 'Foreign Policy, Political System Preference, and the Russian Presidential Election of 1996'. Paper delivered at the annual meeting of the American Association for Advancement of Slavic Studies, 16 November 1996.

Zinoviev, A. 'Khvatit li na zimu kartoshki?' (Are there enough potatoes for the winter?). *Izvestia*, 13 November 1989.

Zverev, Aleksey. 'V prezidenty vyzyvali?' (Has there been a call for the President?). *Moskovskiy Komsomoletz*, 6 January 1996.

Zyuganov, Gennadiy. 'Den' soprotivlyayushcheysya pechati' (The day of the newspapers of resistance). Letter to the participants in the festival of the newspaper *Pravda*. *Pravda*, 7 May 1996, p. 1.

Zyuganov, Gennadiy. 'Eshchyo nemnogo, eshcho chut'-chut' . . .' (Just a little bit more, just a little bit . . .). Interview with Aleksandr Skrypnik and Leonid Fedorov, *Pravda-5*, 31 May–7 June 1996.

Zyuganov, Gennadiy. 'My vmeste vozrodim Rossiyu' (Together we will revive Russia). *Pravda*, 1 July 1996, p. 1.

Zyuganov, Gennadiy. 'Patrioticheskaya vlast' vosstanovit spravedlivost'' (A patriotic government will restore justice). Interview with *Pravda*, 5 May 1996.

Zyuganov, Gennadiy. 'Rossia, Rodina, Narod! Predvybornaya platforma kandidata na post prezidenta Rossiyskoy Federatsii Zyuganova Gennadiya Andreevicha' (Russia, Motherland, People! Electoral platform of Gennadiy Andreevich Zyuganov, a candidate for President of the Russian Federation). *Sovetskaya Rossia*, 19 March 1996.

Zyuganov, Gennadiy. 'Rossia – strana slova' (Russia is a country of the word). Interview with Vladimir Bondarenko. *Zavtra*, 17, April 1996.

Zyuganov, Gennadiy. 'Veteranam Velikoy Otechestvennoy voyny truzhennikam tyla, voinam Rossiyskoy Armii i Flota, vsem grazhdanam Rossii' (To the veterans of the Great Patriotic War, the workers of the home front, warriors of the Russian Army and Navy, and all Russian citizens). *Pravda Rossii*, 7 May 1996, p. 1.

Zyuganov, Gennadiy. 'Znat' i deystvovat'. Kandidat v prezidenty otvechayet na voprosy zhiteley Urala' (To know and to act. The Presidential candidate answers the questions of Ural residents). Recorded by Vladimir Bondarenko. *Zavtra*, 15, April 1996.

INTERVIEWS WITH AUTHOR

Alekseev, Stanislav Dmitrievich. (See Sources for Sverdlovsk, Chapter 3.)

Andreas, Dwayne. Former Chairman and Chief Executive Officer of Archer Daniels Midland Company (Decatur, Illinois). One of Yeltsin's hosts during the 1989 visit to the United States. (Interviewed by the author's research assistant, Ms Laura Libanati.)

Åslund, Anders. A leading expert on Soviet and post-Soviet Russian economy. Was an adviser to the Russian government, 1991–4.

Bakatin, Vadim. Former Minister of Internal Affairs of the USSR and, briefly, Chairman of the KGB.

Balantsev, Boris. (See Sources for Sverdlovsk, Chapter 3.)

Barringer, Felicity. Covered Yeltsin's visit to Johns Hopkins University in 1989 for the *New York Times*.

Belyankin, Gennadiy Ivanovich. (See Sources for Sverdlovsk, Chapter 3.)

Belyanskiy, Lev Petrovich. Head of the Department of the Administrative Organs of the Moscow City Party Committee, 1985–7.

Bersenyova, Klavdia Ivanovna. (See Sources for Sverdlovsk, Chapter 2.)

Bokser, Vladimir, MD. A Moscow democratic activist, a leader of Democratic Russia and an organizer of the defence of the White House, 19–21 August 1991.

Burbulis, Gennadiy. Yeltsin's top adviser and campaign manager, 1989–91. State Secretary and First Deputy Prime Minister of Russia, 1991–2.

Dyagilev, Ivan Mikhailovich. (See Sources for Sverdlovsk, Chapter 2.)

Ezhov, Artur Klavdievich. (See Sources for Sverdlovsk, Chapter 2.)

Gaidar, Egor. Minister of Economy and Finance, Deputy Prime Minister, First Deputy Prime Minister and Acting Prime Minister, 1991–2. First Deputy Prime Minister, September 1993–January 1994. The leader of Russia's Choice/Russia's Democratic Choice party and the Chairman of the party's faction in the Duma (1993–5).

Garside, Anne. Professor at Peabody Conservatory of Music in Baltimore. Welcomed Yeltsin at Johns Hopkins University, 1989. (Interviewed by Ms Laura Libanati.)

Goryun, Andrey. Historian, journalist and writer in Sverdlovsk/ Erkaterinburg. Author of the first biography of Boris Yeltsin.

Gudkov, Vasiliy Vasilievich. (See Sources for Sverdlovsk, Chapter 2.)

Hayes, Stephen. Worked for the American Center for International Leadership (Baltimore), which helped organize Yeltsin's visits to Indianapolis, Baltimore and Texas. One of Yeltsin's hosts in Indianapolis.

Hendrickson, Paul. Covered Yeltsin's visit to Johns Hopkins University for the *Washington Post*.

Il'yin, Aleksandr. Yeltsin's speechwriter, 1990–97.

Kadochnikov, Vladimir Dmitrievich. (See Sources for Sverdlovsk, Chapter 3.)

Karabasov, Yuriy. Secretary of the Moscow City Party Committee, 1986–8.

Khrushchev, Sergey. Historian in Sverdlovsk/Ekaterinburg. As a college student, was in the audience during Yeltsin's 19 May 1981 meeting with students.

Khudyakova, Lidiya. (See Sources for Sverdlovsk, Chapter 2.)

Klyamkin, Professor Igor Moiseevich. A leading Soviet and Russian political analyst.

Kogan, Leonid Borisovich. (See Sources for Sverdlovsk, Chapter 3.)

Legvold, Professor Robert. Professor at Columbia University. Yeltsin's host at Columbia in 1989.

Livshits, Aleksandr. Yeltsin's economic adviser, Minister of Finance and Deputy Head of the Presidential Administration, 1994–8.

Lukyanin, Valentin Petrovich. (See Sources for Sverdlovsk, Chapter 3.)

McBride, Claudia. Program Director at the World Affairs Council in Philadelphia and Yeltsin's host in 1989.

McGovern, Jill. Executive Assistant to the President of Johns Hopkins University at the time of Yeltsin's 1989 visit.

Martineau, Gerlad. *Washington Post* photographer covering Yeltsin's visit to Johns Hopkins University in 1989.

Matlock, Ambassador Jack. The US ambassador to the Soviet Union, 1987–91.

Mickiewicz, Ellen. Professor at Duke University, an expert on television in post-Soviet Russia.

Mishustina, Larisa. A manager of Yeltsin's 1990 campaign for Congress of People's Deputies of Russia.

Muller, Professor Stephen. President of Johns Hopkins University and Yeltsin's host in 1989.

Nadein, Vladimir. A leading Soviet and Russian journalist and editor.

Narayana, Darren. An officer at the International Division of Norwest Bank Corp, which co-sponsored Yeltsin's visit and speech in Minneapolis in 1989.

Nikonov, Nikolay Grigorievich. (See Sources for Sverdlovsk, Chapter 3.)

Novikov, Aleksandr. An underground composer and singer in Sverdlovsk. Arrested in 1983.

Peretrutov, Sergey Ivanovich. (See Sources for Sverdlovsk, Chapter 2.)

Petrovskiy, Vladimir. One of the most distinguished Soviet and Russian career diplomats; an Acting Minister of Foreign Affairs of the Soviet Union in September 1991.

Pikhoya, Ludmila. Yeltsin's speechwriter 1990–8.

Popov, Viktor Vasilievich. (See Sources for Sverdlovsk, Chapter 2.)

Rice, Professor Condoleezza, Special Assistant to the president for National Security Affairs and Director of Soviet Affairs at the National Security Council, 1989–92.

Ross, Lossi. Assistant Director of Program Operations, Chicago Council on Foreign Relations, which hosted Yeltsin in 1989.

Ryabov, Yakov Petrovich. (See Sources for Sverdlovsk, Chapter 2.)

Scowcroft, General Brent. National Security Adviser to President George Bush, 1988–92.

Shvartz, Mira Leontievna. (See Sources for Sverdlovsk, Chapter 2.)

Starovoytova, Galina. One of Russia's most prominent anti-communist, pro-democracy activists, a leader of Democratic Russia, and Deputy to Congress of People's Deputies of Russia and the Duma (1990–8); State Councillor and adviser to the President of the Russian Federation on ethnic issues, 1991–2.

Urmanov, Aleksandr. A manager of and speechwriter for Yeltsin's 1990, 1991 and 1996 campaigns.

Volkov, Vladimir. Director, Institute of Slavic and Balkan Studies, member of the Presidential Council.

Vozdvizhenskiy, Sergey Borisovich. (See Sources for Sverdlovsk, Chapter 3.)

Zucconi, Vittorio. The Washington correspondent of *La Repubblica*.

NOTE: FBIS is an acronym for the Foreign Broadcast Information Service – a US government agency which translated print and broadcast material from many countries around the world. Distributed free of charge to US research institutes and libraries, articles published by the FBIS were, and continue to be, invaluable for scholars.

SOURCES INTERVIEWED FOR SVERDLOVSK YEARS CHAPTER 2

Bersenyova, Klavdia Ivanovna. Civil engineer. Worked in the technical department of the Homebuilding Kombinat, headed by Yeltsin.

Dyagilev, Ivan Mikhaylovich. Retired construction-site supervisor. Worked with Yeltsin in the Construction Administration SU-13, where Yeltsin spent the first eight years of his building career. Between 1963 and 1971, Dyagilev and his wife, Katerina, shared the landing with the Yeltsins in the apartment building Number 53, Lenina Street.

Ezhov, Artur Klavdievich. Retired construction manager. Between 1965 and 1968 headed one of the construction administrations of the Homebuilding Kombinat. Succeeded Yeltsin as the *nachal'nik* of the Homebuilding Kombinat.

Gudkov, Vasiliy Vasilievich. Chairman of the Executive Committee of the Sverdlovsk City Soviet from 1976 to 1981.

Khudyakova, Lidiya Alexandrovna. Former First Secretary of the Party Committee of the Chkalovskiy district of Sverdlovsk, where Yeltsin managed a number of construction sites. Head of the Culture Department of the Sverdlovsk Obkom during Yeltsin's tenure as First Secretary.

Peretrutov, Sergey Ivanovich. In 1956, worked as a senior *prorab* in the *upravlenie* SU-13, where Yeltsin worked as a *master*. Reported to Yeltsin when the latter became the Chief Engineer and then *nachal'nik* of SU-13.

Popov, Viktor Vasilievich. Civil engineer; recruited by Yeltsin in 1972 to work in the Department of Construction of the Sverdlovsk Obkom, where Yeltsin headed the Department.

Ryabov, Yakov Petrovich. First Secretary, Sverdlovsk Regional Party Committee, 1971–6, and Yeltsin's mentor and sponsor. (Interviewed by Vladimir Bykodorov).

Shvartz, Mira Leontievna. Deputy Director of the Sverdlovsk Textile Factory. Yeltsin's college friend, a graduate of the Department of Civil Engineering of the Ural Polytechnic Institute. In 1957 Mira Shvartz was the 'customer' (*zakazchik*) for a new building of the Factory, Yeltsin's first major construction project.

SOURCES INTERVIEWED FOR SVERDLOVSK YEARS CHAPTER 3

Alekseev, Stanislav Dmitrievich. Lecturer of the Propaganda Department of the Sverdlovsk Obkom, 1972–85. Head of the Sports Committee, and Captain of the volleyball team of the Propaganda Department.

Balantsev, Boris. Professor of 'social sciences' in Sverdlovsk from 1981. He was among the consultants to the Obkom in preparation for Yeltsin's 19 May 1981 meeting with students.

Belyankin, Gennadiy Ivanovich. Chief Architect of Sverdlovsk during Yeltsin's rule.

Goryun, Andrey Andreevich. Political scientist and journalist in Sverdlovsk; the author of *Boris Yeltsin: Svet i Teni*.

Kadochnikov, Vladimir Dmitrievich. First Secretary of the Kirovskiy *raikom* of Sverdlovsk, First Secretary of the Sverdlovsk City Committee of the CPSU (1983–9) and the last Pervyi in the history of the province (1989–91).

Kogan, Leonid Borisovich. Editor-in-chief of 'socio-political' programming for Sverdlovsk TV. He produced Yeltsin's appearances for television.

Lukyanin, Valentin Petrovich. Editor-in-chief of *Ural* magazine (Sverdlovsk/Ekaterinburg) since 1980. Published *Bronzoviy dog* by Konstantin Lagunov and *Starikova Gora* by Nikolay Nikonov.

Nikonov, Nikolay Grigorievich. Author of *Starikova Gora*.

Vozdvizhenskiy, Sergey Borisovich. Head of the Construction Department of the Sverdlovsk Obkom, then Secretary and member of the Buro during Yeltsin's rule.

INDEX